Ethiopia

the Bradt Travel Guide

Philip Briggs

edition
8

www.bradtguides.com

Bradt Travel Guides Ltd, UK
The Globe Pequot Press Inc, USA

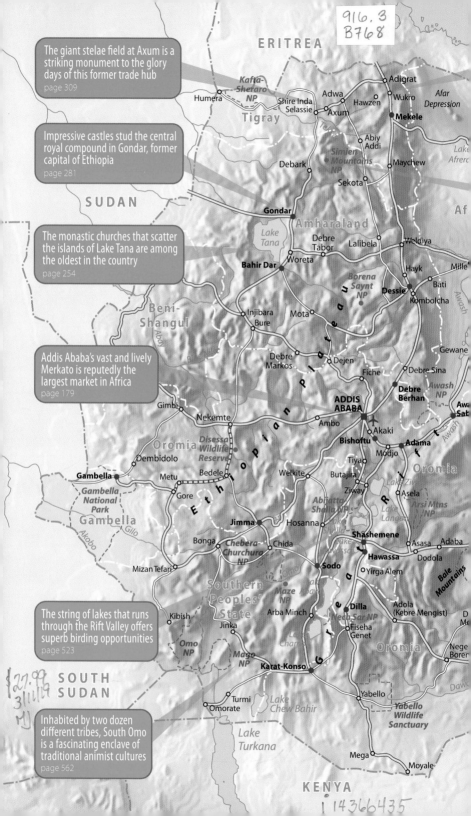

ERITREA

The giant stelae field at Axum is a striking monument to the glory days of this former trade hub
page 309

Impressive castles stud the central royal compound in Gondar, former capital of Ethiopia
page 281

The monastic churches that scatter the islands of Lake Tana are among the oldest in the country
page 254

Addis Ababa's vast and lively Merkato is reputedly the largest market in Africa
page 179

The string of lakes that runs through the Rift Valley offers superb birding opportunities
page 523

Inhabited by two dozen different tribes, South Omo is a fascinating enclave of traditional animist cultures
page 562

Humera

Kafta-Shetaro NP

Shire Inda Selassie
Adwa
Axum
Hawzen

Adigrat
Wukro

Afar Depression

Tigray

Mekele

Abiy Addi

Simien Mountains NP

Maychew

Lake Afrera

Debark

Af

Sekota

SUDAN

Gondar

Amharaland

Lake Tana

Debre Tabor
Lalibela

Weldiya

Bahir Dar
Woreta

Borena Saynt NP

Hayk
Mille

Beni-Shangul

Abay

Injibara
Bure

Mota

Dessie
Bati
Kombolcha

Gewane

Debre Markos

Dejen

Debre Sina

Awash NP

Gimbi

Nekemte

Ambo

Fiche

ADDIS ABABA

Debre Berhan

Awash

Awa
Sab

Oromia

Disessa Wildlife Reserve

Akaki

Bishoftu

Adama

Awa

Dembidolo

Bedele

Welkite

Tiya

Modjo

Oromia

Gambella

Metu

Ethiopian Plateau

Butajira

Lake Ziway

Asela

Arsi Mtns NP

Gore

Ziway

Gambella National Park

Hosanna

Abijatta Shalla NP

Lake Langano

Gambella

Gilo

Akobo

Jimma

Bonga

Chebera-Churchura NP

Chida

Shashemene

Asasa
Adaba

Hawassa
Dodola

Mizan Tefari

Sodo

Yirga Alem

Bale Mountains

Kibish

Southern Peoples' State

Maze NP

Arba Minch

Nech Sar NP

Dilla

Adola (Kebre Mengist)

D
Me

Jinka

Omo NP

Mago NP

Lake Chamo

Fisseha Genet

Oromia

Nege
Borer

Karat-Konso

Great Rift Valley

Yabello

Yabello Wildlife Sanctuary

Daw

SOUTH SUDAN

Turmi
Omorate

Lake Chew Bahir

Mega

Moyale

Lake Turkana

KENYA

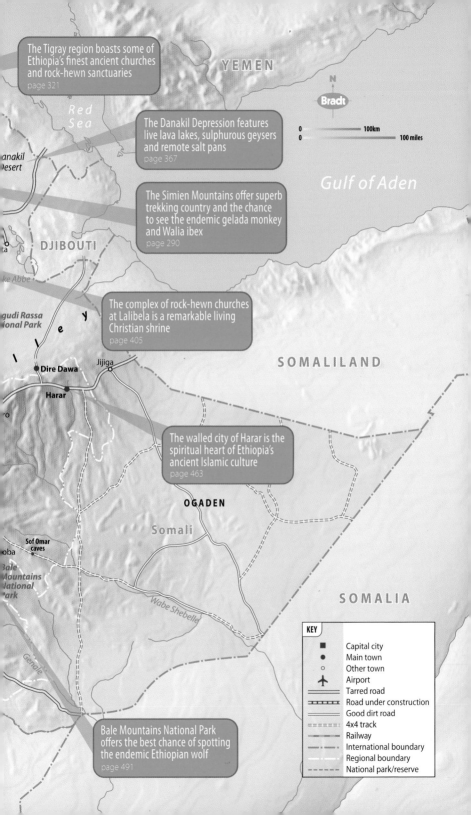

The Tigray region boasts some of Ethiopia's finest ancient churches and rock-hewn sanctuaries
page 321

The Danakil Depression features live lava lakes, sulphurous geysers and remote salt pans
page 367

The Simien Mountains offer superb trekking country and the chance to see the endemic gelada monkey and Walia ibex
page 290

The complex of rock-hewn churches at Lalibela is a remarkable living Christian shrine
page 405

The walled city of Harar is the spiritual heart of Ethiopia's ancient Islamic culture
page 463

Bale Mountains National Park offers the best chance of spotting the endemic Ethiopian wolf
page 491

YEMEN

Red Sea

anakil Desert

DJIBOUTI

Gulf of Aden

0   100km
0   100 miles

SOMALILAND

Dire Dawa
Jijiga
Harar

OGADEN

Somali

Sof Omar caves

Bale Mountains National Park

Wabe Shebelle

SOMALIA

gudi Rassa ional Park

Genale

Bradt

N

KEY

■	Capital city
●	Main town
○	Other town
✈	Airport
	Tarred road
	Road under construction
	Good dirt road
	4x4 track
	Railway
	International boundary
	Regional boundary
	National park/reserve

Ethiopia
Don't miss...

The stelae at Axum
This 23m-high block of granite is accredited to King Ezana
page 309

Rock-hewn churches at Lalibela
Carved in the shape of a symmetrical cruciform tower, Bet Giyorgis is excavated below ground level in a sunken courtyard enclosed by precipitous walls   page 405

Simien Mountains National Park
Ethiopia's premier hiking destination, notable both for its spectacular Afromontane scenery and for its remarkable wildlife
page 290

Tribes of the South Omo Valley
The Karo people are known for their elaborate body painting
page 595

The Danakil Depression
The ellipsoid lava lake of Erta Ale is a spectacular cauldron of seething black magma and glowing molten rock
page 376

Ethiopia in colour

left **A traditional Harari home decorated with baskets and bowls, some of them hundreds of years old**
page 475

below **The Sof Omar Caves, reputedly the largest in Africa, are an important site of pilgrimage for Ethiopian Muslims**
pages 504

<table>
</table>

above   Afar camel caravan crossing salt flats near Dallol page 370

right   Visitors to Mecheke, a traditional Konso town, may be greeted by children playing the *kechaita* page 573

below left   Narga Selassie is one of the most ornately decorated of all the monasteries on Lake Tana page 261

below right   The traditional Ethiopian coffee ceremony is a ritual observed to please and placate spirits known as *zar* page 107

AUTHOR

Philip Briggs (e *philip.briggs@bradtguides.com*) has been exploring the highways, byways and backwaters of Africa since 1986, when he spent several months backpacking on a shoestring from Nairobi to Cape Town. In 1991, he wrote the Bradt guide to South Africa, the first such guidebook to be published internationally after the release of Nelson Mandela. Over the next decade, Philip wrote a series of pioneering Bradt guides to destinations that were then – and in some cases still are – otherwise practically uncharted by the travel  publishing industry. These included the first dedicated guidebooks to Tanzania, Uganda, Ethiopia, Malawi, Mozambique, Ghana and Rwanda, all of which have been updated for several subsequent editions. More recently, Philip wrote the first guidebook to Somaliland, published by Bradt in 2012, as well as new guidebooks to Gambia and Suriname and a revamped guide to Sri Lanka. He still spends at least four months on the road every year, usually accompanied by his wife, travel photographer Ariadne Van Zandbergen, and spends the rest of his time battering away at a keyboard in the sleepy South African village of Wilderness.

CONTRIBUTORS

John Grinling (w *john.c.grinling@gmail.com;* w *ethiopiealacarte.com*), who updated chapters 14–17, as well as parts of chapter 5, for this edition, first worked in Ethiopia with the International Committee of the Red Cross's (ICRC) programme of relief assistance during the 1984–85 famine. Happily married to an Ethiopian lady since, he remained in regular contact with the country before moving to Addis Ababa in 2015. He now organises and accompanies visits to Ethiopia with a special interest in the diversity and the wealth of its traditions, cultures and music.

Frank Rispin, who has helped fact-check and map the Addis Ababa chapter for the past few editions, first went to Ethiopia in 1970, with his wife, Ann, and two small sons, to work at Sandford School. They returned to the UK with an Ethiopian daughter. Returning to Addis in 2002, he soon became involved in tourism. Meanwhile, Ann set about starting new international schools such as BIS Addis, and the Rispins group of schools. He thanks Ms Genet Mengistu for her invaluable help with the new Addis chapter and maps.

Ariadne Van Zandbergen (w *africaimagelibrary.com*), the main photographic contributor to this book, is a Belgian-born freelance photographer and tour guide who first travelled through Africa from Morocco to South Africa in 1994–95. Now married to Philip Briggs and resident in South Africa, she has visited more than 25 African countries and her photographs have appeared in numerous books, maps, periodicals and pamphlets.

PUBLISHER'S FOREWORD *Hilary Bradt*

When people ask me which is my favourite Bradt guide, I answer unhesitatingly: *Ethiopia* by Philip Briggs. Even if they don't ask I tell them, because this is an exceptional book. It receives more fan letters than any other, and one reader who was robbed of the contents of his tent spent two adventurous days retrieving the only possession he couldn't manage without – Philip's guide. In a previous edition I quoted this letter as an example of why readers appreciate this book so much, although I hesitated to repeat it since two stories of robberies could send out the wrong message. So reassure yourselves by reading Philip's *Author's story*, while enjoying the tale as an example of the value an outstanding author can bring to a guidebook.

I left the safety of my overland tour in Kenya to travel Ethiopia independently. I found myself being shot at by bandits with AK47s in northern Kenya about 50km south of the border with Ethiopia. We were treated OK but all I was left with were the clothes I was wearing and my invaluable Bradt guide to Ethiopia. Due to my determination not to let the bandits win I then spent seven weeks travelling around Ethiopia. Your guide is the best I have used as it really does tell you how to get from tiny villages, to ancient sites, to cities, and to meet the ordinary people. Despite such a stressful start to my adventure, and the difficulties with bus travel in Ethiopia, I will never forget what wonderful people Ethiopians are. Without your guide I would have turned back.

Eighth edition published January 2019   First published 1995

Bradt Travel Guides Ltd
IDC House, The Vale, Chalfont St Peter, Bucks SL9 9RZ, England
www.bradtguides.com
Print edition published in the USA by The Globe Pequot Press Inc,
PO Box 480, Guilford, Connecticut 06437-0480

Text copyright © 2019 Philip Briggs
Maps copyright © 2019 Bradt Travel Guides Ltd. Includes map data © OpenStreetMap contributors
Photographs and illustrations copyright © 2019 Individual photographers and artists (see below)
Project Managers: Anne-Marie McLeman and Susannah Lord
Cover research: Pepi Bluck, Perfect Picture

ISBN: 978 1 78477 099 0 (print)
e-ISBN: 978 1 78477 557 5 (e-pub)
e-ISBN: 978 1 78477 458 5 (mobi)

British Library Cataloguing in Publication Data
A catalogue record for this book is available from the British Library

Photographs All photos by Ariadne Van Zandbergen (*www.africaimagelibrary.com*), unless otherwise stated; www.flpa.co.uk: Martin Hale (MH/FLPA), David Hosking (DH/FLPA), Thomas Marent/Minden Pictures (TM/MP/FLPA), Ignacio Yufera (IY/FLPA); Shutterstock: trevorkittelty (tk/S), urosr (u/S); SuperStock (SS)
Front cover Priest outside Asheton Maryam Monastery, Lalibela
Back cover Hamar woman; Church of Debre Berhan Selassie, Gondar
Title page Salt trader, Eastern Tigray; Fasil Gebbi, Gondar; Ethiopian wolf (*Canis simensis*)
Part openers Trinity (Selassie) Cathedral, Addis Ababa (page 131; tk/S), Blue Nile Falls (page 223), Mursi cattle herder, South Omo (page 443; u/S)

Illustrations Carol Vincer
Maps David McCutcheon FBCart.S

Typeset by Ian Spick, Bradt Travel Guides Ltd; and Dataworks
Production managed by Jellyfish Print Solutions; printed in India
Digital conversion by www.dataworks.co.in

Acknowledgements

So many people have contributed towards putting together the eighth edition of this guidebook – not to mention earlier versions – that it is difficult to know where to start! First up, thanks to Kim Wildman and Brian Blatt, respective updaters for the sixth and fifth editions, for holding the fort so competently. On the home front, I'm grateful as ever to my wife, Ariadne Van Zandbergen, for her support, and to the editorial team at Bradt for their support throughout. In Ethiopia, I owe the deepest debt to the two drivers who accompanied me in the north and east – namely Endalkachew Arage and Ephrem Zegeye – for their knowledge, skills and determination to make sure I visited every last new hotel and tourist sight! Hand in hand with their efforts are those of the companies who helped ferry around both me and my co-updater, John Grinling: Mekonnen Mengesha at Galaxy Express, Yared Belete at GETTS, Jane Daniell and Andargachew Girma of Alligan Travel, Nik Puppato of Welcome Ethiopia Tours, Desale Mitiku of Grand Holidays Ethiopia and Dawit Tesfay of Covenant Ethiopia. Frank Rispin, our enthusiastic 'man in Addis Ababa', provided plenty of invaluable input to that chapter, supported by his colleague Genet Mengistu, and wife, Ann Rispin, while music connoisseur John Grinling provided his usual detailed overview of the city's best live venues, as well as tackling the updating for most of southern Ethiopia for this edition. My gratitude for their input to the book also goes to Abdul Ahmed Mohammed, Amakaletch Teferi, Anteneh Asfaw Tafese, Bernard Leeman, Dawit Teferi, Dawit of Mr Martin's Cozy Place, Desta Berhe, Desta Gebreselassi, Dorothea McEwan, Hailu Gashaw, Hans van der Haar, Jan Jackers, Kiros Zeray, Liza Debevec, Louis Guilbaud, Mack at the Addis Regency, Marco Viganó, Mark Chapman, Massey Mekonnen, Mesfin Belay, Shiferaw Asrat, Silvio Rizzotti, Simon at Lodge Du Chateau, Simon Nelson, Sofanit Mulugeta, Temesgen Tadesse, Tewodros Belay Gebru, Tewodros Getnet, Tony Hickey, Willeke Wendrich and Yared Mussie.

John Grinling My wholehearted gratitude goes to the following tour operators, who provided 4x4 vehicles and competent drivers for three 15-day surveys in southeast, southern and western Ethiopia: Jane Daniel of Alligan Travel (**w** *alligan. com*) and driver Zerihun; Desale Mitiku of Grand Holidays Ethiopia Travel & Tours (**w** *grandholidaysethiopia.com*) and driver Fikru; and Nik Puppato of Welcome Ethiopia Tours (**w** *welcomeethiopiatours.com*) and driver Biruk.

Wrapping up the eighth edition of this guidebook, it's strange to think that almost a quarter of a century has passed since I first explored Ethiopia to put together what would become the first modern guidebook to a then practically unknown destination. It was an amazing, revelatory trip, and in many respects one that couldn't be repeated today.

Ethiopia in 1994 could be tough going. Freshly emerged from the oppressive Derg regime, long before the advent of the internet and mobile phones, it felt more isolated and insular than any place I've been before or since. As a rare *faranji*, the non-stop attention of yelling children could be utterly sapping. Ill-advisedly travelling during the rains, the roads (then almost all unsurfaced) were horrendous, and the buses that trundled along them uncomfortable and dangerous. Small-town hotels were crude and often showerless, meals basic and repetitive, rural toilets spectacularly graphic, and sanitation and hygiene so dodgy that I contracted typhoid and Giardia among other less diagnosable illnesses. Yet Ethiopia in 1994 also stands as easily the most absorbing and downright strange trip I've ever undertaken. Every day in this little-known, idiosyncratic land brought fresh moments of discovery and wonder: a chanting priest in a timeworn rock-hewn church, an Ethiopian wolf trotting across the Sanetti Plateau, an *azmari* singing the Amhara blues in a small-town bar, or vice-jawed hyenas being hand-fed on the dusty outskirts of Harar. Truly, I had the time of my life.

Ethiopia in 2018 is a very different prospect. Though hardly a beacon of democracy, the country is less oppressively governed than under the Derg, and more connected to the outside world. It has better roads, more schools, less grinding poverty and greater gender equality; and vast improvements in infrastructure and amenities make it incomparably easier to travel through.

Still, over four recent trips to Ethiopia to research the seventh and eighth editions, I was struck repeatedly – just as I'd been two decades earlier – by what a wonderfully strange and varied country it is. That venerable cast of incanting priests, endemic wolves, grumbling troubadours and suburban hyenas is still present and correct, but a host of newly accessible attractions – the explosive lava lake at Erta Ale, elephant tracking in Chebera-Churchura, bamboo-munching Bale monkeys in Harenna, a funky cabaret in a Gondarine bar – ensured that Ethiopia felt almost as fresh as it did all those years ago. I'm already looking forward to my next visit!

FOLLOW US

Use #ethiopia to share your adventures using this guide with us – we'd love to hear from you.

f BradtTravelGuides & pb.travel.updates
🐦 @BradtGuides & @philipbriggs
📷 @bradtguides
P bradtguides
▶ bradtguides

Contents

KEY TO SYMBOLS

—·—·—	International boundary
✈ ✈	Airport (international/domestic)
⛴	Ferry route (major/small boat)
═══	Paved road (regional maps)
═══	Good dirt road (regional maps)
======	4x4 track
----------	Footpath
━━━	Railway
··········	Hike/trek/footpath featured in the text
‖‖‖‖‖‖	Steps
⛽	Filling station/service garage
🚌	Bus station etc
🚗	Car hire/taxis
ℹ	Tourist information office
⊖	Embassy/consulate
🏛	Museum/art gallery
🎭	Theatre/cinema
🏛	Important/historic building
🏰	Castle/fort/fortification
⬥	Statue/monument
$	Bank/ATM
✉	Post office
✚	Hospital

✚	Clinic/pharmacy
⌂	Hotel/inn etc
▲	Camp site
☆	Nightclub/live music venue
✗	Restaurant etc
♀	Bar
☐	Café
ⓔ	Internet access
♪	Telecommunications
✝	Church/cathedral
☪	Mosque
✿	Garden
✳	Viewpoint
▲	Summit (height in metres)
∴	Archaeological/historic site
♀	Woodland feature
⌇⌇	Waterfall
🏟	Stadium/sporting facility
	Marsh/swamp
	Urban park
	Urban market
	National park/protected area
	National forest park/reserve

LIST OF MAPS

AUTHOR'S FAVOURITES Finding genuinely characterful accommodation or that unmissable off-the-beaten-track café can be difficult, so the author has chosen a few of his favourite places throughout the country to point you in the right direction. These 'author's favourites' are marked with a ✳.

MAPS
Keys and symbols Maps include alphabetical keys covering the locations of those places to stay, eat or drink that are featured in the book. Note that regional maps may not show all hotels and restaurants in the area: other establishments may be located in towns shown on the map.

On occasion, hotels or restaurants that are not listed in the guide (but which might serve as alternative options if required or serve as useful landmarks to aid navigation) are also included on the maps; these are marked with accommodation 🏠 or restaurant ✗ symbols.

Grids and grid references Several maps use grid lines to allow easy location of sites. Map grid references are listed in square brackets after the name of the place or sight of interest in the text, with page number followed by grid number, eg: [154 B2].

WEBSITES Although all third-party websites were working at the time of going to print, some may cease to function during this edition's lifetime. If a website doesn't work, you might want to check back at another time as they often function intermittently. Alternatively, you can let us know of any website issues by emailing e info@bradtguides.com.

Ethiopians use a unique script to transcribe Amharigna and several other languages. This has led to a wide divergence in English transcriptions of Ethiopian place names and other Amharigna words, and also inconsistent use of double characters. Even a straightforward place name like Metu is spelt variously as Matu, Mattuu, etc, while names like Zikwala can become virtually unrecognisable (Zouquela). When consulting different books and maps, it's advisable to keep an eye open for varied spellings and to use your imagination. In this book, we aim to go with the simplest spelling, or the one that we think sounds closest to the local pronunciation. We have also stuck with Ethiopian versions of familiar biblical names: for instance Tewodros (Theodore), Yohannes (John), Maryam (Mary) and Giyorgis (George). The exception is that if hotels or restaurants are signposted in English, then I have normally (but not infallibly) followed the signposted spelling exactly.

Introduction

My first contact with things Ethiopian came by chance, in the early 1990s, when a friend suggested a meal at an oddly named eatery in suburban Nairobi. It turned out to be a memorable evening. The food alone was extraordinary – a delicious fiery orange stew called *kai wat*, splattered on what looked like a piece of foam rubber with the lateral dimensions of a bicycle tyre, and was apparently called *injera* – but even that didn't prepare me for what was to follow.

A troupe of white-robed musicians approached our table and erupted into smirking discord. Then, signalled by an alarming vibrato shriek, all hell burst loose in the form of a solitary Ethiopian dancer. Her mouth was contorted into a psychotically rapturous grimace. Her eyes glowed. Her shoulders jerked and twitched to build up a manic, dislocating rhythm. Beneath her robe – driven, presumably, by her metronomic shoulders – a pair of diminutive breasts somehow contrived to flap up and down with an agitated regularity suggestive of a sparrow trapped behind a closed window. I left that room with one overwhelming impression: Ethiopians are completely bonkers. I knew, too, that I had to visit their country.

A year or two later, I found myself flying to Addis Ababa to research the first edition of this guide. In the months that followed, I discovered Ethiopia to be every bit as fantastic as I had hoped: culturally, historically and scenically, it is the most extraordinary country I have ever visited. Over subsequent years, however, I have also learned that it is difficult to talk about Ethiopia without first saying what it is not.

To the world at large, Ethiopia is practically synonymous with famine and desert. So much so that its national carrier, Ethiopian Airlines, regularly receives tactful enquiries about what, if any, food is served on their flights. This widespread misconception, regarding a country set in a continent plagued by drought and erratic rainfall, says much about the workings of the mass media. It says rather less about Ethiopia.

Contrary to Western myth, the elevated central plateau that covers half of Ethiopia's surface area, and supports the vast majority of its population, is the most extensive contiguous area of fertile land in the eastern side of Africa. The deserts do exist, stretching from the base of the plateau to the Kenyan border and the Red Sea and Somali coast, but they are, as you might expect, thinly populated; they have little impact on the life of most Ethiopians – and they are most unlikely to be visited by tourists. To all intents and purposes, the fertile highland plateau is Ethiopia.

Ethiopia's fledgling tourist industry revolves around the richest historical heritage in sub-Saharan Africa. The town of Axum was for several centuries the centre of an ancient empire that stretched from the Nile River across the Red Sea to Yemen. The medieval capital of Lalibela boasts a cluster of monolithic rock-hewn churches regarded by many as the unofficial eighth wonder of the world. There is also Gondar, the site of five 17th-century castles built by King Fasil and his successors. And all around the country are little-visited monasteries and other rock-hewn churches, many of them more than 1,000 years old and still in active use.

Although historical sites are the focal point of tourism in Ethiopia, they threaten to be swamped by the breathtaking scenery. Every bus trip in the Ethiopian Highlands is a visual treat, whether you are snaking into the 1km-deep Blue Nile Gorge, rolling past the sculpted sandstone cliffs and valleys of Tigray, undulating over the grassy moorland and cultivated fields of the central highlands, winding through the lush forests of the west and south, or belting across the Rift Valley floor, its acacia scrub dotted by extinct volcanoes, crumbling lava flows and beautiful lakes, and hemmed in by the sheer walls of the Rift Escarpment. Mere words cannot do justice to Ethiopia's scenery.

Isolated from similar habitats by the fringing deserts, the Ethiopian Highlands have a remarkably high level of biological endemism. Large mammals such as the Ethiopian wolf, mountain nyala, Walia ibex and gelada monkey are found nowhere but the highlands, as are 30 of the 900-plus species of birds that have been recorded in the country. This makes national parks like Bale and Simien a paradise for natural history enthusiasts, as well as for the hikers and mule trekkers who visit them for their scenery.

Yet over a period of time, Ethiopia's established tourist attractions become incidental to the thrill of just being in this most extraordinary country. The people of the highlands have assimilated a variety of African, Judaic and even Egyptian influences to form one of the most unusual and self-contained cultures on this planet. Dervla Murphy said in 1968 that 'travelling in Ethiopia gives one the Orlando-like illusion of living through different centuries'. This remains the case: the independence of spirit which made Ethiopia the one country to emerge uncolonised from the 19th-century Scramble for Africa is still its most compelling attraction; even today, there is a sense of otherness to Ethiopia that is as intoxicating as it is elusive. Practically every tangible facet of Ethiopian culture is unique. Obscured by the media-refracted glare of the surrounding deserts, Ethiopia feels like the archetypal forgotten land.

Ethiopia confounds every expectation. Many people arrive expecting a vast featureless desert and human degradation, and instead find themselves overwhelmed by the country's majestic landscapes and climatic abundance, and immersed in a culture infectiously besotted with itself and its history. While the rest of the world taps its feet, Ethiopia, I suspect, will always breakdance with its shoulders. And, in case you're wondering, there's really no need to pack sandwiches for the flight.

UPDATES WEBSITE

Administered by author Philip Briggs, Bradt's Ethiopia update website w bradtupdates.com/ethiopia is an online forum where travellers can post and read the latest travel news, trip reports and factual updates from Ethiopia. The website is a free service to readers, or to anybody else who cares to drop by, and travellers to Ethiopia and people in the tourist industry are encouraged to use it share their comments, grumbles, insights, news or other feedback. These can be posted directly on the website, or emailed to Philip (e philip.briggs@bradtguides.com).

It's easy to keep up to date with the latest posts by following Philip on Twitter (🐦 @philipbriggs) and/or liking his Facebook page: 📘 pb.travel.updates.

You can also add a review of the book to w bradtguides.com or Amazon.

Part One

GENERAL INFORMATION

ETHIOPIA AT A GLANCE

Location Horn of Africa bordering Somalia, South Sudan, Sudan, Eritrea, Kenya and Djibouti
Size 1,104,300km²; the tenth-largest country in Africa
Climate Varies by region, from temperate highlands to hot lowland desert
Status Federal republic
Population 108 million (2018 estimate)
Life expectancy 65 years
Capital Addis Ababa, population 4 million
Federal region capitals Dire Dawa (city-state), Adama (Oromia), Mekele (Tigray), Bahir Dar (Amhara), Hawassa (SNNPR), Harar (Harari), Semera (Afar), Jijiga (Somali), Assosa (Benishangul-Gumuz), Gambella (Gambella)
Economy Subsistence agriculture, coffee, *khat*, horticulture, mining, tourism
GDP US$750 per capita (estimate)
Languages Official language Amharigna (Amharic); Oromifa and English are most widely spoken
Religion Main religions are Ethiopian Orthodox Christianity, Islam and Protestant Christianity
Currency Birr
Rate of exchange US$1 = birr 27.7, €1 = birr 32.3 and £1 = birr 36.4 (Sep 2018)
National airline/airport Ethiopian Airlines/Bole International Airport
International telephone code +251
Time GMT +3
Electric voltage 220V current alternating at 50Hz. Plug standards vary; most common are the Type C (European 2-pin) and Type L (Italian 3-pin).
Weights and measures Metric
Flag Horizontal bands of green at the top, yellow in the centre and red at the base. In the middle of this is a symbol representing the sun – a yellow pentagram from which emanate several yellow rays.
National anthem 'March Forward, Dear Mother Ethiopia'
National holiday 28 May, Downfall of the Derg

ETHIOPIA AND ERITREA

The eventful period in Ethiopian politics that preceded the publication of the 8th edition of this guidebook culminated in the progressive new prime minister, Abiy Ahmed Ali, and his Eritrean counterpart, Isaias Afwerki, signing a 'joint declaration of peace and friendship', ending a 20-year border conflict that had claimed tens of thousands of lives. In the wake of this announcement, long-closed phone lines between the two countries reopened, the state-owned carrier Ethiopian Airlines announced the resumption of commercial flights between Addis Ababa and the Eritrean capital Asmara, and long-closed overland borders between the neighbours reopened. Unfortunately, these events occurred too close to publication to be incorporated into relevant parts of the main body of this edition. But, assuming that the new spirit of reconciliation endures, it is to be hoped that overland and air travel between Ethiopia and Eritrea will once again become straightforward, opening up the latter's historic and beautiful Red Sea ports and coastline to trade and travel.

1

Background Information

Ethiopia and neighbouring Eritrea possess a geographic, cultural, historical and linguistic identity utterly distinct from the rest of sub-Saharan Africa. Indeed, one might simplistically label the Ethiopian Highlands as the ecological and cultural meeting point of Africa, Arabia and the Mediterranean. The region's wildlife, for instance, includes not only a plethora of antelopes, monkeys and other creatures typical of Africa, but also some unique variants on a distinctly Eurasian theme, most notable the endemic Ethiopian wolf and Walia ibex. Historically, the ancient Ethiopian kingdoms of D'mt and Axum, both of which centred on the present-day federal region of Tigray, were characterised by an urbanised culture that blended Egyptian, Arabic, Greek and African influences as early as 600BC. Ancient Judaic influences infuse the Ethiopian Orthodox Church, an institution founded in Axum in the 4th century AD, as well as the poorly understood Beta Israel community that inhabited the Gojjam and Wollo regions for many centuries prior to being airlifted to Israel in the 1980s. Completing Ethiopia's Abrahamic hat-trick is Islam, the dominant religion in much of the east, having arrived in the Axumite Empire during the lifetime of the Prophet Muhammad. In contrast to this veritable torrent of ancient Judaic influences, southern Ethiopia is dominated numerically by the Oromo, who followed their own traditional African customs when they first swept up the Rift Valley into Ethiopia in medieval times, and continued to do so until the early 20th century, when the exotic Catholic and Protestant denominations took hold in the region. As a rule, the societies and cultures of southern Ethiopia are more stereotypically African in nature than those of the north, a trend that reaches its apogee in South Omo, a region inhabited by myriad small traditionalist tribes that feel like they strolled straight out of the 19th century.

GEOGRAPHY AND CLIMATE

Far from being the uniform thirstland of Western myth, Ethiopia is a land of dramatic natural contrasts and variety. Altitudes span the second-lowest point on the African continent as well as its fifth-highest mountain, while climatic conditions range from the drenched slopes of the fertile southwest to the scorching arid wastes of the eastern borderlands. Vegetation is diverse. The most extensive indigenous rainforest anywhere in the eastern half of Africa is concentrated in the well-watered highlands of the south and west. The central highlands, though more openly vegetated, are equally fertile, supporting a mosaic of grassland and cultivation throughout the year, and blanketed in wild flowers towards the end of the rains. The drier northeast highlands are generally quite thinly vegetated, except during the rains. The Rift Valley floor south of Addis Ababa has a characteristically African appearance, dominated by grasses and flat-topped acacia trees. Elsewhere, there are the steamy, marshy western lowlands around Gambella, the brittle heath-like Afroalpine moorland of Sanetti Plateau, and the riparian woodland that lines rivers such as the Blue Nile or Omo and freshwater lakes such as Tana, Ziway and Hawassa. Indeed, it is only the vast but seldom visited eastern and southern lowlands that conform to the image of Ethiopia as a featureless desert.

LOCATION The Federal Republic of Ethiopia, formerly known as Abyssinia, is a landlocked republic in northeast Africa, or the Horn of Africa, lying between 3.5 and 15°N and 33 and 48°E. Ethiopia shares its longest border, of more than 1,600km, with Somalia to the east (this border includes part of the as yet unrecognised state of Somaliland). Ethiopia is bounded to the northeast by Eritrea for 910km, and by Djibouti for 340km. It shares a southern border of 830km with Kenya, and a western border of 1,600km with South Sudan and Sudan.

LANDSCAPE The Ethiopian landscape is dominated by the volcanically formed **Ethiopian or Abyssinian Highlands**, a region often but somewhat misleadingly referred to as a plateau, since it is in fact dramatically mountainous. The central plateau, isolated on three sides by low-lying semi-desert or desert, has an average altitude of above 2,000m and includes 20 peaks of 4,000m or higher. The Ethiopian Highlands are bisected by the **Rift Valley**, which starts at the Red Sea, then continues through the Danakil Depression (a desert area that contains one of the lowest points on the earth's surface) and southern Ethiopia to Mozambique in southern Africa. The Rift Valley south of Addis Ababa is notable for its string of eight lakes.

The most extensive ranges on the highlands are the Simien and Bale mountains, both of which are protected in national parks. The Simien Mountains lie in the northern highlands, where they form Africa's fifth-highest massif, rising to a pinnacle of 4,533m at Ras Dejen (also spelt Ras Dashen). The Bale Mountains, which rise to 4,377m, are the centrepiece of the southern highlands east of the Rift Valley.

The Ethiopian Highlands form the source of four major river systems. The best known of these is the **Blue Nile**, or Abay, which rises near Lake Tana in the northwest, and supplies most of the water that flows into Egypt's Nile Valley. The Baro and Tekeze (or Shire) rivers feed the White Nile, the river that flows out of Lake Victoria in Uganda to join the Blue Nile at Khartoum in Sudan. Within Ethiopia, the Blue Nile arcs through the highlands south of Lake Tana to form a vast gorge comparable in size and depth to Namibia's Fish River Canyon and the Grand Canyon in the USA.

Several other **major river systems** run through Ethiopia. The Wabe Shebelle rises in the Bale area and courses through the southeast of the country into Somalia. The Omo River rises in the western highlands around Kaffa to drain into Lake Turkana on the Kenya border. The Awash rises in the highlands near Addis Ababa and then does a southward arc before following the course of the Rift Valley northward and disappearing into a series of desert lakes near the Djibouti border.

CLIMATE Ethiopia shows a wide climatic variation, ranging from the peaks of Bale, which receive periodic snowfall, to regular daytime temperatures of over 50°C in the Danakil Desert (see box, page 6). As a rule, the central highlands have a temperate climate and average daytime temperature of 16°C, belying their proximity to the Equator. The eastern lowlands and the far south are dry and hot. The western lowlands are moist and hot, making them the one part of the country that feels truly tropical. The southern Rift Valley, much of which lies at the relatively high altitude of 1,500m, is temperate to hot and seasonally moist.

The precipitation pattern in the northern and central highlands is that the bulk of the rain falls between mid-June and early October. This pattern changes as you head further south: the rainy season in the Rift Valley generally starts and ends a few weeks earlier than in the highlands, while in South Omo most of the rain falls in March, April and May, and other parts of the south have two rainy seasons, falling either side of the highlands' rainy season of July to September. Contrary to popular perceptions, most highland parts of Ethiopia receive a healthy average annual rainfall figure, with the far west being particularly moist – indeed, much of the southwest receives an average annual rainfall in excess of 2,000mm.

The northeast highlands are much drier, and have a less reliable rainy season, than other highland parts of Ethiopia. Tigray and parts of Amhara are prone to complete rainfall failure; this tends to happen about once every decade. It was such a rainfall failure that, exacerbated by the tactics of the Mengistu government, led to the notorious famine of 1985. In normal years, however, the highlands become something of a mudbath during the rains, with an average of 1,000mm falling over two or three months. Fortunately, from a tourist's point of view, rain tends to fall in dramatic storms that end as suddenly as they start, a situation that is infinitely more conducive to travel than days of protracted drizzle.

ETHIOPIAN CLIMATIC ZONES

Ethiopians traditionally recognise five climatic zones, each of which has distinctive features linked to altitude, rainfall and temperature. These are as follows:

BEREHA Hot and arid desert lowlands that typically lie below 500m and receive significantly less than 500mm of precipitation annually. Not generally cultivatable so mostly inhabited by pastoralists, eg: most of the Somali border area and the Rift Valley north of Addis Ababa.

KOLLA Warm to hot medium-altitude locations that receive sufficient rainfall for cultivation without relying on irrigation, eg: the Rift Valley between Addis Ababa and Awassa, or the Gambella region.

WEYNA DEGA Warm to cool medium- to high-altitude locations typically receiving more than 1,500mm of rainfall annually, often naturally forested, though much of this has been cleared over the centuries. Excellent for cultivation of grains (especially *tef*) and coffee, eg: Addis Ababa, Gondar, Asela, Goba, Jimma, Metu and most other highlands below the 2,600m contour.

DEGA Cool to cold, medium to high rainfall, high-altitude locations that would naturally support grassland or coniferous forest and now are mostly used to cultivate grains such as barley and wheat, eg: Dinsho, Debre Berhan, Mehal Meda, Ankober and other highland areas with an altitude in the 2,600–3,200m range.

WORCH Chilly, medium to low rainfall Afroalpine regions supporting a cover of heath-like vegetation that isn't generally conducive to cultivation, eg: Sanetti Plateau (Bale National Park), the eastern peaks of the Simiens, Guassa Plateau and other plateaux or peaks above 3,200–3,500m.

The local climate charts listed below have been selected partly to highlight conditions in Ethiopia's most popular destinations but also partly to reflect the enormous regional variation in temperature, rainfall and seasons noted in other parts of the country.

	Jan	Feb	Mar	Apr	May	Jun	Jul	Aug	Sep	Oct	Nov	Dec
Addis Ababa (2,400m)												
Max/Min temp (°C)	24/15	24/16	25/17	24/17	25/18	23/17	21/16	21/16	22/16	23/15	23/14	23/15
Rainfall (mm)	20	35	60	85	90	120	230	250	150	30	5	5
Adama (1,130m)												
Max/Min temp (°C)	27/12	28/13	29/14	30/15	30/15	30/15	24/12	26/15	27/14	28/12	27/11	26/11
Rainfall	10	15	60	55	45	60	180	220	100	30	10	20
Axum (2,100m)												
Max/Min temp (°C)	26/8	27/8	29/11	29/13	29/13	27/12	22/12	22/12	25/11	25/10	27/8	26/7
Rainfall (mm)	5	2	10	25	30	65	220	200	65	15	15	2
Bahir Dar (1,850m)												
Max/Min temp (°C)	26/8	27/10	30/13	30/14	29/15	27/15	23/14	24/13	25/13	26/13	27/11	26/9
Rainfall (mm)	4	3	10	25	65	190	415	365	205	75	21	5
Dire Dawa (1,200m)												
Max/Min temp (°C)	28/22	30/23	32/25	32/26	34/27	35/28	33/27	32/26	33/26	32/25	29/23	28/22
Rainfall (mm)	20	35	65	90	45	25	95	130	60	25	10	10
Debark (2,300m)												
Max/Min temp (°C)	20/4	21/4	21/5	22/7	21/7	20/7	17/7	16/7	18/7	19/5	17/4	19/3
Rainfall (mm)	5	5	20	25	90	115	310	270	90	30	15	5
Gambella (530m)												
Max/Min temp (°C)	37/18	38/20	40/22	38/22	35/20	33/20	32/21	32/20	33/20	34/21	33/19	35/19
Rainfall (mm)	5	10	25	50	160	175	220	230	180	100	50	10

Goba (2,800m)

Max/Min temp (°C)	20/4	21/5	21/7	20/8	21/8	21/7	20/7	20/7	19/7	18/7	19/5	20/4
Rainfall (mm)	25	30	75	125	100	50	90	115	120	130	60	15

Gondar (2,120m)

Max/Min temp (°C)	27/10	28/13	29/141	27/14	29/14	25/13	22/13	22/13	25/12	26/12	26/11	27/10
Rainfall (mm)	10	10	25	40	80	160	325	310	125	30	30	15

Harar (1,850m)

Max/Min temp (°C)	25/12	26/13	27/14	27/15	26/14	26/14	24/14	23/14	24/14	26/13	26/12	26/12
Rainfall (mm)	10	20	30	100	50	50	80	150	75	30	10	10

Hawassa (1,780m)

Max/Min temp (°C)	28/10	29/11	29/12	27/13	26/13	25/13	23/14	24/13	25/13	26/11	27/9	27/9
Rainfall (mm)	45	60	80	105	125	100	125	130	125	85	40	30

Jimma (2,300m)

Max/Min temp (°C)	28/9	28/10	29/12	28/13	27/13	26/13	24/13	25/13	25/13	26/11	27/9	27/8
Rainfall (mm)	40	50	85	160	150	210	195	175	160	90	20	30

Lalibela (2,800m)

Max/Min temp (°C)	25/6	24/7	25/8	25/9	26/9	27/9	23/11	22/10	23/9	23/7	23/6	23/6
Rainfall (mm)	10	15	45	40	50	45	235	265	60	25	10	10

Semera (430m)

Max/Min temp (°C)	30/18	10/20	32/21	34/22	37/24	39/26	38/24	36/23	36/24	34/22	32/20	31/19
Rainfall (mm)	3	4	15	10	5	3	20	25	8	3	4	1

Turmi (900m)

Max/Min temp (°C)	33/19	33/20	33/20	30/20	30/20	29/19	28/19	28/19	30/19	30/20	31/19	32/19
Rainfall (mm)	25	35	60	100	80	33	38	25	25	50	75	30

Much of Ethiopia's fascination lies in its historical sites. This is the only country in sub-Saharan Africa with tangible historical remnants that stretch back through the centuries through medieval times to the early Christian era and back further still to when the ancient civilisations of the Mediterranean and Red Sea were in their prime. One might thus reasonably expect there to be a huge body of writing on Ethiopian history and its relationship to other civilisations. But, put simply, there isn't. To quote Philip Marsden-Smedley, author of *A Far Country*:

> Ethiopia crept up on me ... Often, where I'd expected a chapter, in general histories of the Christian Church, books of African art, there was a single reference – or nothing at all. And soon I found the same facts recurring and realised that Ethiopian scholarship was, like its subject, cut off from the mainstream.

In 1994, when the first edition of this book was written, the situation was indeed as Marsden-Smedley describes. No general history of Ethiopia had been published since the 1950s, while general works on African or church history all but ignored the country. Oliver and Fage's landmark *Short History of Africa*, for instance, contained not one reference to Axum, despite its having been the most powerful ancient empire south of the Sahara for around 1,000 years. The one contemporary popular work to deal with Ethiopia was Graham Hancock's 1992 *The Sign and the Seal*, a rather fanciful but still valuable attempt to substantiate the claim that the Ark of the Covenant resides in Axum. Within Ethiopia, a few locally published books of a historical nature were also in print. Even so, there was a clear lack of one central work which a layperson could use as a starting point from which to explore more esoteric, specific or controversial writings. This situation has improved since 1994, with the publication of a few concise general histories (page 644), though these are primarily concerned with modern Ethiopia rather than the ancient civilisations responsible for erecting the Axumite stelae or excavating the churches of Lalibela.

A basic grasp of ancient Ethiopian history is integral to getting the most from the country. Tourism to Ethiopia revolves around historical sites; no less important, Ethiopians identify strongly with their history, and they generally enjoy speaking to visitors who share their enthusiasm. Yet in many respects, Ethiopia is a land with several wholly or partially divergent histories. The traditional history recounted by most Ethiopians – a fabulous landscape populated by such shadowy legends as the Queen of Sheba, King Solomon, the twin emperors Abraha and Atsbeha, the Islamic warrior Ahmed Gragn and an improbable cast of eccentric saints – operates as something of a parallel universe to the more orthodox history acknowledged by Western academics. Furthermore, much widely read writing about Ethiopia is riddled with contradictory dates and ideas, and almost all conventional accounts, including those that inform this guidebook, tend to relate the story from the point of view of the Christian highlanders, and to treat their Islamic and Jewish neighbours/foes as something of a sideshow. Finally, a handful of contemporary Western writers, notably Graham Hancock and Bernard Leeman, have put forward fascinating but unorthodox theories that put a fresh spin on the ancient legends discounted by most proper historians.

Fortunately, it is not the job of this guidebook to resolve these apparent contradictions, nor simply to relate the bland 'facts' of conventional orthodoxies, but rather to help readers engage with the fascination and at times downright

CHANGING DEFINITIONS

In a historical context, Ethiopia generally signifies something very different from the modern country of that name. The term Ethiopic, meaning 'burnt-faced', comes from ancient Greece, and was one of two used to describe the dark-skinned people of sub-Saharan Africa (the other term, Nubian, referred to the almost black-skinned people of the Sudanese Nile). And in a biblical or classical sense, Ethiopia is broadly synonymous with the Axumite Empire, centred on the Ethiopian Highlands north of the Blue Nile. Later, in medieval times and during the Renaissance, when nobody in Europe knew quite where Africa began or ended, Ethiopia was strongly associated with the Christian empire of the highlands which, judging by the distribution of churches from this time, extended south from Tigray to Shewa (around modern-day Addis Ababa). In this context, the term Ethiopia is interchangeable with Abyssinia (the latter deriving from the Arabic word *habbishat*, meaning 'mixed'). And until as recently as the late 19th century, this highland Christian empire was frequently at war with the Islamic empires of the eastern highlands, as well as with the Oromo, neither of which would have regarded themselves as Abyssinian or Ethiopian. It is only in the 20th century, after Emperor Menelik II laid the groundwork for the modern state through his conquest and annexation of vast tracts of Islamic and pagan territory bordering the original Christian empire, that the broadly synonymous terms 'Ethiopia' and 'Abyssinia' relate to the country as we know it today. None of which means for a moment that, in a modern sense, a Muslim from Harar is any less Ethiopian than a Christian from Axum or an Oromo from Adama – just that the term 'Ethiopia' needs to be thought of differently depending on the historical context!

strangeness of Ethiopia's shape-shifting history. Bearing this in mind, what follows, particularly with regard to events prior to around AD1600, often draws equally on the fantastic speculation of folklore and the necessarily conservative speculation of historians, as well as including boxed text detailing a few of the more off-the-wall perspectives. After all, in a sense it matters less that the Queen of Sheba was really Ethiopian or that Haile Selassie was actually descended from the Jewish King Solomon than it does that most Ethiopians believe it to be true, and have done so for centuries. These beliefs have shaped Ethiopian culture so profoundly, and been repeated so often, that even if the events they relate to never actually happened, they have come to attain a kind of vicarious truth.

THE CRADLE OF HUMANKIND? The East African Rift Valley is almost certainly where modern human beings and their hominid ancestors evolved, and Ethiopia has as strong a claim as any African country in this respect. Indeed, based on a wealth of fossil evidence, especially in the Afar region of the northern Ethiopian Rift Valley, it can be assumed that hominins – members of the taxonomic subtribe *Hominina*, which comprises the entire human lineage since its divergence from chimpanzees about six million years ago – have inhabited the Ethiopia region for practically as long as anywhere on earth. Although the specifics of hominin taxonomy are controversial and subject to regular revision, six genera are recognised, five of which went extinct at least a million years ago, the best known being *Australopithecus*. The only extant genus is *Homo*, and this is represented by just one species, *H. sapiens*, the Latin name for modern humans.

The paucity of hominin fossils collected before the 1960s meant that for many years it was assumed the most common australopithecine fossil *A. africanus* was ancestral to the genus *Homo* and thus to modern humans. This linear theory of human evolution blurred when it was discovered that two types of australopithecine had lived at Tanzania's Oldupai Gorge, and that the later species *A. robustus* had less in common with modern man than its more lightly built ancestor *A. africanus*. Then,

THE ARK OF THE COVENANT

In Axum's Maryam Tsion Church lies an artefact that, were it proved to be genuine, would add immense substance to Ethiopian legendeering. Unfortunately, only one person alive has ever seen this artefact. The Ark of the Covenant is, according to Ethiopian Christians, kept under lock and key in Maryam Tsion, and only the official guardian is allowed to enter the place where it is stowed. There is no doubting the importance the legend of the Ark plays in Ethiopian Christianity and few people would question the sincerity of the Ethiopian claim. But, superficially at least, its presence in Axum does seem rather far-fetched.

For those unfamiliar with the Old Testament, the Ark of the Covenant was built by the Children of Israel to hold the Tablets of Law given to Moses by God on Mount Sinai. According to the Bible, God gave Moses precise instructions on its design and embellishments. It was thus vested with a deadly power that was particularly devastating in time of battle. After the Jews settled in Jerusalem, the Ark was enshrined in a temple built by Solomon in the 10th century BC, where it remained until the temple was destroyed by the Babylonians in 586BC. While it resided in Jerusalem, the Ark was the most treasured artefact of the Jewish faith, virtually the personification of God, and in many biblical passages it is referred to simply as Jehovah. After the destruction of Solomon's temple, it disappeared. Despite several attempts over the centuries, the Ark has never been recovered.

Graham Hancock, in his book *The Sign and the Seal*, investigated the Ethiopian claim to the Ark and constructed a plausible sequence of events to support it. Hancock points out, and he is not the first person to have done so, that there is strong reason to believe the Ark vanished from Jerusalem long before 586BC. Nowhere in the Bible is it stated that the Ark was taken by the Babylonians, which seems decidedly strange, considering its religious importance; books written during the reign of Josiah (640BC) hint that it had probably disappeared by then. Hancock suggests the Ark was removed during the reign of Manasseh (687–642BC), a king who horrified religious leaders by desecrating Solomon's temple with an idol they considered to be sacrilegious. He suggests that the Ark was removed from the temple by angry priests and taken out of the kingdom, and that the loss of the Ark, when it was discovered by Josiah, was kept a secret from the laity.

Hancock circumvents the major historical loophole in the Ethiopian Ark theory, namely that the evidence currently available suggests that Axum was founded several centuries after Solomon's time, by dating the Ark's arrival in Axum to King Ezana's well-documented conversion to Christianity in the 4th century. He discovered that the priests at the Lake Tana island monastery of Tana Kirkos claim to have records stating that the Ark was kept on the island for 800 years prior to its removal to Axum. This claim is given some scant support by the presence of several sacrificial stones of probable Jewish origin on Tana Kirkos.

in 1972, the discovery of a two-million-year-old skull of a previously undescribed species, *H. habilis*, at Lake Turkana in Kenya, provided the first conclusive evidence that some *Australopithecus* and *Homo* species had lived alongside each other for at least one million years. As more fossils came to light, including older examples of *H. erectus* (the direct ancestor of modern humans), it became clear that several different hominin species had existed alongside each other in the Rift Valley until

Hancock then discovered that a large Jewish settlement and a temple modelled on Solomon's original had been built on Elephantine Island near Aswan on the Nile River. It is generally accepted this temple was founded in or around the reign of Manasseh, and the fact that the priests at the Elephantine corresponded with priests in Jerusalem is well documented. It appears that the priests here retained sacrificial rites similar to those of the ancient Ethiopian Jewish community known as the Beta Israel, confirming that they too diverged from the Jewish main stream before the rule of Josiah. What's more, the temple was destroyed by the Egyptians around 410BC. The Jewish community on Elephantine is thought to have escaped from the island, but nobody knows where they fled. To all intents and purposes, they vanished. Hancock, naturally enough, suggests they went to Ethiopia. He also claims that this theory accords closely with the legend told to him by an old Beta Israel rabbi he met in Israel, who rejected the Makeda story, but claimed that his ancestors had lived in Egypt for several centuries en route from Israel, and that the Ark that they brought with them resided in the Lake Tana region for even longer before being stolen by the Axumite Christians.

As a non-historian, it is difficult to assess how seriously one should take Hancock's book, but most would cock an eyebrow at any thesis that contrives to incorporate both the Freemasons and the lost city of Atlantis in what eventually expands into a bit of a Theory of Everything. That said, the central thrust of *The Sign and the Seal* (page 642) – the ideas summarised and simplified above – seems soundly plausible, even if, by Hancock's own admission, it is purely circumstantial. Furthermore, if his facts are correct, Hancock has certainly proved it possible that the Ark might be in Axum, having arrived there via Egypt. He has also provided a strong case for the Beta Israel arriving in Ethiopia from the northwest, and he has put a slant on Ethiopian history that makes sense of traditional accounts while explaining many of their more implausible aspects – the reasons why we devote so much space to his ideas here. And if nothing else, *The Sign and the Seal* is a fascinating and most readable book, and a wonderful exercise in 'windmill-tilting'.

Persuasive as Hancock's arguments might be, they are strongly refuted by eminent historian Stuart Munro-Hay, co-author of the more measured 2000 book *The Ark of the Covenant: The True Story of the Greatest Relic of Antiquity*. Munro-Hay points out that the story about the Ark of the Covenant is mentioned in none of the tales about Ezana's conversion, in none of the stories about the Nine Saints or about King Kaleb's conquest of Yemen (against a Jewish king, moreover), or even in the Ethiopian accounts of the end of the monarchy when Queen Gudit attacked the country, or when the Zagwe rose to power. In fact, the first reference to the Ark being in Ethiopia is by Abu Salib, during the reign of Lalibela around 1210, which is 'odd, to say the least, if the Ethiopians then believed that the most powerful symbol of God was in their capital city'. A newer version of this is listed on page 643 – why not read both books and decide for yourself?

perhaps half a million years ago. Increasingly, it looked as if *Australopithecus* and *Homo* belonged to two discrete evolutionary lines with a yet-to-be-discovered common ancestor. The only flaw in this theory was the timescale involved: it didn't seem possible that there had been adequate time for the oldest known hominine species to evolve into *H. habilis*.

In 1974, an almost complete hominid skeleton was discovered by Donald Johanson at Hadar, in Afar Region. The skeleton, named Lucy (the song 'Lucy in the Sky with Diamonds' was playing in camp shortly after the discovery), turned out to be that of a 3.5-million-year-old australopithecine of an entirely new species dubbed *A. afarensis*. This discovery not only demonstrated that bipedal hominins (more accurately, semi-bipedal, since the length of Lucy's arms suggest she would have been as comfortable swinging through the trees as on a morning jog) evolved much earlier than previously assumed, but it also created a likely candidate for the common ancestry of later australopithecine species and the human chain of evolution. As more *A. afarensis* fragments came to light in the Danakil, many palaeontologists argued that the wide divergence in their skull and body sizes indicated that not one but several australopithecine species had lived there at this time, and that any one of them – or none of them, for that matter – might be ancestral to modern humans. This discrepancy was clarified in 1994, when the first complete male *afarensis* skull was uncovered less than 10km from where Lucy had lain. It is now clear that the difference in size is because *afarensis* males were almost twice the weight of females. And if all the Afar australopithecine fossils are of one species, then that species was remarkably successful, as the known specimens span a period of almost one million years.

In 1997, Afar yielded the world's oldest undisputed hominine remains, which were discovered by an Ethiopian graduate student, Yohannes Haile-Selassie, are thought to be around 5.5 million years old, and are ascribed to the species *Ardipithecus kadabba*. In addition, several fossils of *A. ramidus*, a probable descendant of *A. kadabba* that lived at least 4.4 million years ago, have been located in the region. While it remains the case that tracing the line of human ancestry based on the existing fossil evidence is akin to guessing the subject of a 20,000-piece jigsaw based on a random 50 pieces, *Ardipithecus* shows clear affiliations with both chimpanzees and humans, making it a possible candidate for the so-called missing link between hominids and their ape-like ancestors. Interestingly, in the late Miocene and early Pliocene era, when these ancient proto-humans lived, Afar was far moister than it is today, and quite densely forested, which casts some doubt on the accepted notion that the first hominids started to walk upright as an evolutionary adaptation to a savannah environment. New discoveries keep reeling in from Afar. As recently as May 2015, a research team led by Yohannes Haile-Selassie announced the discovery of two 3.3 million–3.5 million-year-old jawbones of what appears to be a previously unknown australopithecine species *A. deyiremeda*. The bones were discovered less than 40km from Hadar, where Lucy was unearthed in 1974, and they lived at around the same time, suggesting the two australopithecine species inhabited the area at the same time.

So, is Ethiopia the cradle of humankind? Well, the specifics of human evolution remain controversial, and are likely to do so for some time, largely because it is impossible to gauge how complete or representative the known fossil record is. The discovery of large numbers of hominid fossils in one area may indicate simply that conditions at the time were suitable for fossilisation, or that current conditions are suitable for recovering those fossils – and, crucially, that palaeontologists are looking there. If a vital link in the evolutionary chain was once distributed in an area not yet explored by palaeontologists, it will remain unknown to science.

What does seem certain is that the entire history of human evolution was enacted in Africa. And the fact that most crucial fossil discoveries have taken place in the Rift Valley of Ethiopia, Kenya and Tanzania makes these three countries the most likely candidates for the cradle of humankind. Ethiopia also stands centre stage with regard to two more recent developments in human evolution. The world's oldest known Stone Age tools, dating back more than 2.5 million years and presumably crafted by australopithecines, have been uncovered in Afar at a site called Gona. Further south, a site alongside the Omo River has yielded the oldest known fossils of anatomically modern humans *H. s. sapiens* in the form of a pair of skulls originally dated to be 130,000 years old upon their discovery in the 1960s, but redated at almost 200,000 years old in 2005.

PREHISTORY The most interesting relics of ancient human activity in the Horn of Africa are a scattering of Neolithic rock art sites at various localities running west from the Somali coastline through Harar to Dilla and the southern Rift Valley. The age of these engravings and paintings remains conjectural, not least because the sensitive pigments cannot be tested without causing some damage, but the most recent panels are at least 3,000 years old and the oldest might be thrice that age. Ethiopian rock art often includes depictions of people and wild animals, but the dominant motif on most panels is stylised representations of domestic cattle. Almost invariably, these are depicted in profile, with only one front and one hind leg, prominent udders, no neck or ears, and prominent arcing horns shown as if seen from above. Among other things, these paintings clearly demonstrate that Ethiopia supported one of the world's earliest pastoral (livestock-herding) societies, dating back some 6,000–9,000 years, several millennia before pastoralism was adopted in Europe or Asia. The art that adorns the rock shelters of Ethiopia also appears to have a strong spiritual dimension, and – bearing in mind that any paintings made on a less durable or protected canvas would have vanished long ago – it probably represents a tiny surviving fragment relic of the region's sophisticated Neolithic artistic tradition.

Along with Afar, the most researched part of Ethiopia in prehistoric terms is the far north: what is now the region of Tigray and the independent country of Eritrea. The nature of the society in this region prior to about 1000BC is uncertain, but conclusive evidence of millet cultivation dating to around 3000BC has been found at Gobo Dura, on the outskirts of Axum, as has indigenous pottery of a similar vintage.

By this time, northern Ethiopia almost certainly had some links with ancient Egypt. Several Greek historians of the 1st millennium BC considered the Egyptians and Ethiopians to be of the same race, and one goes so far as to claim it was Ethiopians, led to the country by the Greek god Osiris in around 3000BC, who founded the Egyptian civilisation. On a far firmer historical footing is the identification of Ethiopia and the neighbouring coastline of Eritrea and Somalia with a mysterious land that the ancient Egyptians knew as Punt or Ta Netjer (Land of God), and believed to be their ancestral home. A number of ancient Egyptian documents refer to a maritime trade with Punt, with the earliest such expedition having taken place in around 2480BC, during the Fifth Dynasty reign of Sahure. Other visits to Punt were recorded during the Sixth, Eleventh and Twelfth dynasties, and while all maritime activity fell victim to the general disarray that gripped Egypt c1775BC following the death of Queen Sobekneferu, it was resumed under Queen Hatshepsut, who dispatched five ships to Punt in around 1525BC. Irregular trade continued for another four centuries, with one final large-scale expedition being dispatched during the reign of Rameses III, whose death in 1167BC initiated a long period of decline in Pharaonic Egypt. Subsequently, the memory of distant Punt was reduced, in the words of Egyptologist Joyce Tyldesley, to 'an unreal and fabulous land of myths and legends'.

The parochial nature of Egyptian trade records means they contain few clues as to the precise location of Punt. What is known for certain is that the Egyptian ships sailed to Punt via the Red Sea, which was then connected to the Nile by a seasonally navigable canal, and that seasonal wind patterns make it unlikely the relatively slow ships of the era sailed further afield than the eastern tip of the Horn of Africa. An African as opposed to Arabian location for Punt is strongly indicated by the types of items it offered for trade, which included frankincense, gold, ivory, ostrich eggs, and skins of wild animals such as giraffe and leopard. Furthermore, a remarkable set of reliefs on the walls of the Hatshepsut funerary temple Deir el-Bahari show the natives of Punt living in stilted beehive huts, set in a grove of date palms and myrrh trees, alongside a long-tailed bird (consistent with the Nile Valley sunbird) and typical African animals such as giraffe, rhinoceros and baboon. All of which

AN AFRICAN QUEEN?

The true identity of the Queen of Sheba – whose encounter with King Solomon is recounted not only in the Bible but also in the Quran, where she is named Bilqis – is an open question. But the notion that she originated in Ethiopia is not quite so far-fetched as some would claim. It seems almost certain that Sheba is a variant spelling of Saba, the name of an ancient kingdom that was centred on Yemen but extended into much of present-day Eritrea and Tigray. In the past, scholars tended to view Saba as an essentially Yemeni polity, and to disregard the Ethiopian legends about Queen Makeda and the associated account in the *Kebra Nagast* as a clever borrowing and reworking of Arabian legends about Queen Bilqis.

But given the close religious, political and linguistic ties between Saba and D'mt, and the fact that the Ethiopian legends claim Makeda ruled over both, many other scenarios are possible. A Sabaean origin for the Queen of Sheba does not, for instance, preclude the possibility that one of her sons went on to form a dynasty in Ethiopia. It could also be argued that the Sabaean monarchy might have had its capital in Ethiopia (at Yeha, for instance, or Adi Akaweh) at the time of Makeda's rule. Indeed, recently discovered inscriptions on the 2,800-year-old Almaqah Temple and other ancient Sabaean tablets uncovered at Adi Akaweh (page 341) indicate that the pre-Axumite rulers of Tigray placed far greater emphasis on the female royal line did than their Yemeni counterparts, which in turn tends to support the notion that the Queen of Sheba/Saba was of African rather than Arabian origin. It is also interesting to note that certain Arabic texts give Bilqis the title Balmaqah, which could be broken down to B'Almaqah, literally 'In honour of Almaqah', the Sabaean moon god to which the massive pre-Axumite temples at Yeha and Adi Akaweh were dedicated.

The truth is anybody's guess. But if you ignore the more obvious mythologising around the Makeda legend (for instance, that her feet turned into the hooves of an ass when she stepped in the blood of a dragon as a child, a disfigurement that only Solomon was able to cure), the notion that the mysterious Queen of Sheba was a monarch of Ethiopia is difficult to discount entirely.

suggests that Punt most likely comprised part of the coastline between present-day Eritrea and northern Somalia, and since many of the items traded there would have been sourced from the interior, that it extended inland into parts of present-day northern and eastern Ethiopia.

Archaeological and written sources leave no room for doubt that northern Ethiopia supported a centralised and partially urbanised civilisation of some magnitude as early as 800BC. Surviving inscriptions indicate that this so-called pre-Axumite society referred to itself as D'mt, and was ruled over by leaders with the title of mukarib. The script and language used on the inscriptions of D'mt is very similar to that used contemporaneously in Saba, a kingdom centred around Sana'a, in what is now the Yemeni interior. The relationship between the two polities is unclear. D'mt is typically portrayed as a vassal of the Sabaean Kingdom, but it would seem this assumption is based on academic convention as much as on hard evidence. The two major pre-Axumite sites in northern Ethiopia are Yeha, the probable capital of D'mt, and the more southerly Adi Akaweh, both of which incorporate the remains of large stone temples dedicated to the Sabaean deity Almaqah, and are estimated to be at least 2,700 years old. Other pre-Axumite relics include stone dwellings, catacomb-like tombs, impressive sculptures (often of regal female figures) and sacrificial altars. In addition to boasting strong religious and cultural links to Saba, D'mt most likely had strong trade links with other ancient civilisations, and much of the indigenous pottery of the era showed Grecian influences. The fate of D'mt is uncertain. In AD280, the affiliated Sabaean Empire, on the opposite side of the Red Sea, finally fell to its centuries-old rival Himyar, which was centred further south, on the port of Aden. D'mt was most likely unaffected by the conquest of Saba, but authorities differ on the question of whether it had already ceased functioning as a civilisation by that time, or was in the process of evolving into the Aksumite Empire, or would continue to function as a separate or vassal state to Axum, centred on Adi Akaweh, until the 10th century AD. Since many pre-Axumite sites in Ethiopia have yet to be excavated, it seems likely that a great deal more detail about D'mt and its demise will emerge in the course of time.

TRADITIONAL HISTORY Ethiopians themselves are in little doubt about their early history. According to oral tradition, Ethiopia was first settled by a great-grandson of Noah named Itiyopis, whose son Aksumai founded the city of Axum and also established a ruling dynasty that endured for between 52 and 97 generations. The last, and many say the greatest, of these monarchs was Queen Makeda, who, in the 11th and 10th centuries BC, owned a fleet of 73 ships and a caravan of 520 camels which traded with places as far afield as Palestine and India. Makeda ruled Ethiopia and Yemen for 31 years from her capital a few kilometres outside modern-day Axum, which, according to Ethiopians, was known as Saba.

Early in her rule, it is claimed, Makeda, the Queen of Saba (better known to Westerners as the Queen of Sheba), travelled to Jerusalem to visit King Solomon. She brought with her gifts of gold, ivory and spices, and in return she was invited to stay in the royal palace. The two monarchs apparently developed a healthy friendship, the result of which was that Makeda returned home not only converted to Judaism but also carrying the foetal Ibn-al-Malik (Son of the King), whose name later became bastardised to Menelik. At the age of 22, Menelik returned to Jerusalem to visit his father. He was greeted by a joyous reception and stayed in Jerusalem for three years, learning the Law of Moses. When he decided to return home, he was, as Solomon's eldest son, offered heirship of the throne, which he declined. Solomon allowed Menelik to return to Ethiopia, but he also ordered all

Ethiopia and Eritrea have many traditions linked to Moses, King Solomon, the Ark of the Covenant, and in particular the Queen of Sheba. Their Orthodox Church has a significant substratum of ancient Israelite religious practices and vocabulary. And until recently the country supported a substantial community known as the Beta Israel, whose religion and traditions linked them to the First Temple built by King Solomon in the 10th century BC and destroyed in 586BC.

Until 1974, the constitution of imperial Ethiopia was based on the *Kebra Nagast*, a document compiled in around 1314. The *Kebra Nagast* claims that Ethiopia and its ruler were divinely ordained as the inheritors and guardians of Solomon's kingdom as well as the true Christian (Monophysite) Church established in AD323 by the Council of Nicaea. The Sheba-Menelik Cycle, which recounts how the Ark of the Covenant was stolen from the First Temple by the high priest of Judah's son, who fled with it to Ethiopia accompanied by Menelik, the son of Solomon and the Queen of Sheba, is also included in the *Kebra Nagast*.

The Christian-era content of the *Kebra Nagast*, which is known as the Kaleb Cycle and concerns the Councils of Nicaea and Chalcedon and the Axumite invasion of Jewish Himyar in Yemen in around AD520, is accepted as historical fact. By contrast, the Old Testament links and traditions of the Beta Israel, although initially received with some enthusiasm, have been discredited mainly because it seemed illogical for the Ethiopians to have had such close ties with ancient Palestine.

The Beta Israel are the most studied people in Africa. Most research was undertaken in the past 60 years, but no recent major works take into account the growing disquiet in Old Testament archaeology over lack of evidence concerning events before the Babylonian conquest of 586BC. Old Testament archaeology is in crisis, with scholars divided into two broad camps, known as biblical 'maximalists' and 'minimalists'. The 'maximalists' believe that Joshua, David and Solomon lived in Ancient Palestine, some claiming that convincing evidence already exists to prove this, others that such evidence will eventually be unearthed. The 'minimalists' range from those who think the pre-586BC account contains some truth but is highly exaggerated, to those who dismiss the entire narrative as a fantasy concocted in Babylon. All the major writers on the Beta Israel are maximalists, although one hints at reservations, and some argue that their Jewish identity was manufactured in the 15th century to emphasise their Agaw identity and to assert their independence from the imperial Christian feudal system and the encroachment of Islam.

The third school of Old Testament thought is known as Arabian Judah. This supports the tradition that the Ark of the Covenant was stolen from Solomon's Temple in the 10th century BC and transported to Ethiopia by Menelik, who there established an Israelite state that appears to have survived at least until the death of Queen Gudit in around AD970. This Cushitic Hebraic-Agaw state, known in antiquity as D'mt, was probably the same as Gudit's realm of Damot, and was absorbed into the Christian Aksumite/Ethiopian state, which commandeered its political and religious legacy. The main Arabian evidence to support this claim comes from the astonishing match of unvocalised Old Testament place names between Medina and Yemen, with the seemingly inexplicable high incidence of high Hebrew vocabulary and Ancient West Arabian grammar in the same area. The Ethiopian evidence is mostly connected with the Beta Israel and the Sheba-

Menelik Cycle of the *Kebra Nagast*, translated into Ge'ez from an Arabic text of about AD520.

The Sheba-Menelik Cycle contains the Law of Moses in a version that omits almost all of the Laws of Deuteronomy, which scholars agree was complied after 641BC. In addition, its Old Testament quotations are not standard and appear to be from an unknown ancient oral or written source. The Ethiopian word for the Ark of the Covenant dates from Solomon's era, while Sabaean inscriptions on two incense burners retrieved at Adi Akaweh near Wukro (one from above Queen Gudit's alleged grave) testify to the rule there in around 750BC of four kings of D'mt and Sabaea (Sheba), three of whom ruled jointly with queens over a mixed population of Semitic ('red') Sabaeans and Cushitic ('black') Hebrews, lending support to the Sheba-Menelik narrative. Also, the Beta Israel traditionally prayed east towards Jerusalem, and the word Falasha, a derogatory term for Ethiopian Jews, is Sabaean in origin, as is *msd-n*, the Beta Israel word for their house of prayer, all of which indicate an Arabian origin. Leslau provides evidence that the Hebrew may have been Cushitic by stating that the Beta Israel retained ancient Hebrew liturgy in their Cushitic Agaw language, although they were unable to understand its meaning. The Hebrew word for Samaritans (denizens of the northern kingdom of Israel) and blacks is the same – *kushi*.

The Sheba-Menelik Cycle does not mention any events after Solomon's reign, so it might well have been written before his death, in around 920BC. And where the Old Testament remains silent on why the high priesthood disappeared from Judah in Solomon's time, during the tenure of the high priest Azariah, the Sheba-Menelik Cycle states that Azariah, whom it identifies as the son of the high priest, stole the Ark and fled to Ethiopia. Furthermore, while the Old Testament has no satisfactory explanation for the Ark of the Covenant's disappearance, nor do any Jewish or Arab traditions, the Sheba-Menelik Cycle has a highly detailed description. Superficially, this account in the *Kebra Nagast* seems like complete lunacy, because its geographical references don't add up. However, the same references match up well against Salibi's hypothetical map of Arabian Judah: for example, the account of Menelik crossing to Ethiopia opposite Mount Sinai makes a great deal more sense if the peak in question was northern Yemen's Jebel al-Nabi Shu'ayb (Mountain of the Prophet Jethro – Moses' father-in-law).

In conclusion, now that archaeology has raised serious doubts that biblical events before 586BC occurred in the area of modern Israel/Palestine, most of what has been written about Ethiopia's biblical links and its Hebraic-Israelite population deserves re-examination. Evidence from Ethiopia suggests that the Old Testament historical account is most probably true, but that it belongs to West Arabia, and to a lesser extent to Ethiopia and Eritrea.

Note: It should be clarified that Dr Leeman's theories are rather unorthodox and that the vast majority of scholars regard the Sheba-Menelik Cycle of the Kebra Nagast *to be little more than a work of medieval fabrication. For those who wish to explore these ideas further, an annotated version of this essay, complete with a full list of references, can be found on our updates website (*w *bradtupdates.com/ethiopia), while several more detailed papers by Dr Leeman can be downloaded from* w *queen-of-sheba-university.academia.edu/BernardLeeman.*

1

his high commissioners to send their eldest sons with Menelik and each of the 12 tribes of Israel to send along 1,000 of their people.

Accompanying Menelik on his journey home was Azariah, the first-born son of the high priest of the temple of Jerusalem. Azariah was told in a dream that he should take with him the holiest of all Judaic artefacts, the Ark of the Covenant. When Menelik was first told about this he was angry, but then he dreamt that it was God's will. King Solomon discovered the Ark's absence and led his soldiers after Menelik's enormous entourage, but he too dreamt that it was right for his son to have the Ark, though he insisted on keeping its disappearance a secret. The Ark has remained in Ethiopia ever since, and is now locked away in the Church of Maryam Tsion in Axum. On Menelik's return, his mother abdicated in his favour. The Solomonic dynasty founded by Menelik ruled Ethiopia almost unbroken until 1974, when the 237th Solomonic monarch, Haile Selassie, was overthrown in the revolution.

Most Ethiopians accept this version of events unquestioningly, but it has never been taken too seriously by Western historians. The oldest written version of the Makeda legend is the so-called Sheba-Menelik Cycle of the *Kebra Nagast*, a highly fanciful 14th-century Ge'ez volume claimed to be a translation of a lost Coptic document dating to the 4th century or earlier. This is an unlikely claim, especially as the *Kebra Nagast* was written at a time when the so-called Solomonic dynasty had reasserted its power after several centuries of Zagwe rule. And much of the book is undoubtedly medieval fabrication and royal myth-making created by weaving patches of Sabaean legend into the relevant biblical passages. Nevertheless, there is probably a significant grain of truth behind the elaboration. To disregard the *Kebra Nagast* entirely is to ignore not just the many biblical references to Ethiopia, but also the considerable Jewish influences that permeate Ethiopian culture.

There are more than 30 references to Ethiopia (or Cush, as it was known to the Hebrews) in the Old Testament. Moses, the most prominent early Hebrew prophet, is known to have married an Ethiopian woman (Numbers 12:1), while Genesis contains a reference to the Ghion River which, it claims, 'compasseth the whole land of Ethiopia'. Even if you take into account the fact that Ethiopia and Cush were once vague geographical terms referring to Africa south of the Sahara, the parts of Africa that are most likely to have been visited by Hebrews are those which were the most accessible. Moreover, the Ghion River is plainly what we now call the Blue Nile, which forms a sweeping arc beneath the part of Ethiopia most influenced by Judaism, and whose source is still referred to as Ghion by Ethiopians. Later, in the Book of Isaiah, we hear of the 'country ... beyond the rivers of Cush, who send ambassadors by sea, in papyrus skiffs over the waters ... a people tall and bronzed', while in the 7th-century BC Book of Zephaniah, the Lord speaks the following words: 'from beyond the rivers of Ethiopia my suppliants, even the daughter of my dispersed, shall bring mine offering', which might well suggest some sort of Jewish dispersal to Ethiopia.

As noted elsewhere, the Ethiopian Orthodox Church is unique in its Jewish influence and the emphasis placed on the Book of Jubilees (Genesis and the first part of Exodus). But the purest Jewish influence in Ethiopia is found among the Beta Israel (literally 'House of Israel'), an ancient Jewish people of mysterious provenance whose tradition relating to Makeda and Solomon is broadly similar to one recounted by Ethiopian Christians. Current academic opinion tends to favour the view that Beta Israel was probably a 4th- or 5th-century Ethiopian offshoot of southern Yemen's Himyarite Empire, whose leaders converted to Judaism in around AD380. But this conventional narrative disregards the archaic nature of the rituals performed by the Beta Israel, which make no acknowledgement of the reforms instituted by King Josiah in 640BC. So, given that the Beta Israel's core territory lay far from the coast, between the Tekeze River and Lake Tana, could it not be that they represent a relic of a much earlier migration from Jerusalem to Ethiopia via the Nile?

Another serious objection to the traditional account is that pre-Axumite civilisations such as D'mt and Saba appear to have been predominantly pagan, worshipping the sun and moon, with later traces of Hellenistic (Greek) influences. Carvings of ibex suggest these animals had a special significance to the people of D'mt and Saba, and the large statues of women found at many such sites suggest a female fertility cult at odds with monotheistic Judaic traditions. But this doesn't preclude the possibility of Jewish and pagan cultures coexisting in northern Ethiopia prior to the arrival of Christianity. Perhaps the Jewish faith spread to Axum long after it had been established around Lake Tana, and went on to influence the unique Ethiopian take on Christianity. Either way, if the traditional account culminating in Menelik's arrival in Ethiopia is actually based on a genuine historical event, could that ancient occurrence have been a Jewish migration that led not to the foundation of Axum but to the establishment of the proto-Beta Israel around Lake Tana?

THE AXUMITE EMPIRE The roots of modern Ethiopia lie in the Axumite Empire, which was centred on the city of Axum, and formed a major force in world trade between the 1st and 7th centuries AD, when it ranked among the world's most important and technologically advanced civilisations. The origins of the Axumite Empire remain obscure, as does its relationship to pre-Axumite civilisations. Older works tend to treat the city of Axum and the empire over which it ruled as a Sabaean implant, established by migrants from Yemen in or around the 1st century BC. But recent research has revealed Axum to be far older than allowed for by this convention – indeed, a large town complete with palaces and megalithic grave-markers stood on a hill above the present-day town centre as early as the 4th century BC – while also indicating that the Sabaean role in its foundation has been overstated. Current thinking is that the founders of Axum were Agaw people who originally spoke a Cushitic tongue but later adopted the Semitic language Ge'ez, which is no longer thought to have derived from Sabaean but rather to be rooted in an Ethiopian Semitic presence dating back to before 2000BC.

Many written sources state that the Axumite Empire became a trade centre of note in the 1st century AD. It would be more accurate to say that the empire is first name-checked and described in a 1st-century Greek document *The Periplus of the Erythraean Sea*, and no concrete evidence exists to date it earlier. However, the Axumite Empire as described in the *Periplus* covered a vast area, and it seems unlikely that it sprang up in a matter of a few years. The main Axumite port back then, 50km from modern-day Massawa (Eritrea), was 'Adulis, a fair-sized village, from which it is a three-day journey to Koloe, an inland town and the first market for ivory'. The writer of the *Periplus* asserts that 'the masses of elephant and rhinoceroses that are slaughtered all inhabit the upland regions' and that from Koloe it was 'another five days' journey to the metropolis itself, which is called Axum, and into which is brought all the ivory from beyond the Nile'. Back on the coast were several 'other Berber market towns, known as the "far-side" ports; lying at intervals one after the other, without harbours but having roadsteads where ships can anchor and lie in good weather'. It also named the Axumite king as 'Zoscales, who is miserly in his ways and always striving for more, but otherwise upright, and acquainted with Greek literature'.

From other written sources, we know that the Axumite Empire traded with India, Arabia, Persia and Rome, and that it expanded to include parts of modern-day Yemen under King Gadarat in the 2nd century AD. Some idea of Axum's contemporary importance is given by the 3rd-century Persian writer, Manni, who listed it as one of the four great kingdoms in the world, along with Persia, China and Rome. The Axumites were a literate people who left behind many inscriptions, some in three languages, with the Ge'ez text being supplemented by Sabaean and Greek translations. They also minted their own gold, silver and bronze coins using locally sourced metals from around AD270 until the early 7th century. That they were skilled masons is apparent from the impressive free-masonry of the subterranean tombs in Axum town. But the most impressive technological achievement of the Axumites was the erection of several solid granite stelae, the largest of which, now collapsed, was 33m high, taller even than the similar granite obelisks of Egypt. Nobody knows how such heavy slabs of rock were erected; the tradition in Axum is that it was with the aid of the Ark of the Covenant.

The most powerful and influential of the Axumite kings was Ezana, who ruled in the early part of the 4th century along with his twin brother Saizana. Ezana was influenced by two Syrian Christians, Frumentius and Aedissius, and in AD337–40 he made Christianity the official religion of his empire. For once, scholars and Ethiopians are in agreement on this point, though some Ethiopians insist on the slightly earlier date of AD320. Ezana's conversion is documented by Roman writer Rufinus, and on Axumite coins minted after AD341, wherein the older sun and moon symbols are replaced by a cross. Ezana was a good military leader who led a campaign to conquer Yemen, and also led an expedition to secure control of the territory as far west as the confluence of the Nile and Atbara rivers, where he left a stele. Many inscribed trilingual stelae listing Ezana's exploits and recording his gratitude to God have been unearthed around Axum.

The most influential of Ezana's actions was undoubtedly his conversion to Christianity. There is a traditional belief that an Ethiopian emissary brought news of the Christian faith to Axum in the time of Queen Candice (around AD50), but there is no suggestion that this led to any changes in Axumite beliefs. Ezana is reliably credited with building Ethiopia's first church, Maryam Tsion, at Axum (wherein the artefact believed by Ethiopians to be the Ark of the Covenant was later placed). His mentor, Frumentius, was consecrated as the first bishop of Axum, Abba Salama. Ezana and his brother, who for many years ruled Ethiopia together, were almost certainly the Abraha and Atsbeha who are, rather optimistically, claimed locally to have initiated the carving of many rock-hewn churches throughout Tigray and as far afield as modern-day Addis Ababa.

Ezana's conversion to Christianity coincided roughly with a similar event on the opposite side of the Red Sea: the adoption of Judaism by the king of the Himyarites in around AD380. It is difficult to say whether there is a meaningful connection between the near-simultaneous conversion from polytheism to different Abrahamic regions of the leaders of what were by then the region's two most important kingdoms. But it did also coincide with a period of heightened military contact between the two powers, epitomised by Ezana's conquest of the Himyar towns of Tihamah and Najran in around AD340, and the subsequent expulsion of the Axumites 38 years later, leading to some speculation among academics that the Himyar adoption of Judaism was either a deliberate snub to the newly converted Axumite emperor, or an attempt by this trade-oriented empire to maintain a neutral standing between the conflicting ideologies of its two most powerful neighbours, Christian Axum and Zoroastrian Persia. Meanwhile, within Ethiopia, the late 4th century appears to be when the term Beta Israel (House of Israel) was first used to distinguish Ethiopian Jews from the newly converted members of the Beta Christian (House of Christ). It remains unclear, however, whether the original Beta Israel, whose version of Judaism excluded any customs that post-dated the reforms of King Josiah 1,000 years earlier, constituted recent migrants from Yemen, or comprised a far more ancient settlement of migrants from Jerusalem.

Christianity made its deepest inroads into the Axumite Empire in the late 5th century, when nine monks from Syria and elsewhere in the Roman Empire fled to Ethiopia and preached widely throughout the region. Known as the Nine Saints or Tsadkan (Righteous Ones), these evangelical refugees are also accredited with building a great many iconic churches within a relatively short distance of Axum, including the one still in use at Debre Damo Monastery. They have been canonised by the Ethiopian Church and each of them has a special holy day dedicated to his memory. Many churches bear one or other of their names – Abba (saint) Aregawi or Mikael, Abba Alef, Abba Tsama, Abba Afse, Abba Garima, Abba Liqanos, Abba Guba, Abba Yemata and Abba Pantalewon. The eponymous monastery founded by Abba Garima south of Adwa is notable for housing the oldest known Ethiopian documents in the form of two illuminated gospels accredited locally to the saint himself. Long dismissed by art historians, who reckoned that the gospels probably dated to around 1100, this outlandish claim was unexpectedly validated in 2010 after carbon-dating tests dated the gospels to AD390–660 – a instructive lesson when it comes to balancing seemingly improbable Ethiopian legends with the more conservative opinions of Western academics.

The last of the great Axumite kings was Kaleb, who took the throne in the early 6th century and whose famous defeat of the Himyarites in AD525 terminated the Judaic empire's three centuries of dominance in Yemen. The retaliatory attack was undertaken following the massacre of up to 20,000 Christian captives who refused to renounce their faith in favour of Judaism following the capitulation of the city of Najran to the Himyar leader Yusuf Dhu Nuwas. Kaleb's reign of more than 30 years coincided with a period of great Axumite prosperity, and his hilltop palace was praised for its beauty by Byzantine traveller Cosmos, who visited it in AD525 and marvelled at the statues of unicorns on its corners, and the tame elephant and giraffe enclosed in the palace grounds. Kaleb's son and successor Gebre Meskel, who ruled from the same palace, is remembered not so much for his military prowess as for being the patron of St Yared, the musician credited with inventing the notation of Ethiopian religious music and with writing many ecclesiastical songs, poems and chants that are still in use today.

ETHIOPIA'S DARK AGE Axum has to this day retained its position as the centre of Ethiopian Christianity. In every other sense, it appears to have fallen into decline soon after Kaleb's rule ended. Many reasons for this have been put forward – local environmental factors such as deforestation and erosion, internal unrest, and the increasing wealth in the east of the empire – but the main factors were almost certainly linked to a growing Islamic influence along the coast of the Horn of Africa. In fact, the Islamic presence in Ethiopia dates back to the lifetime of the Prophet Muhammad, whose wife had fled there in AD615 along with several of his other followers, and was offered protection by the Axumite king and allowed to settle at Negash in present-day eastern Tigray. As a result, Muhammad held Ethiopians in great esteem and warned his followers never to harm them, which is partly why the two religions coexisted peacefully in the region for several centuries afterwards. Nevertheless, by AD750, Islamic traders had almost certainly come to dominate Africa's Red Sea coastline. Soon afterwards, the Islamic port of Zeila, in present-day

Ethiopian traditions relating to the end of the 1st millennium AD are dominated by the memory of a semi-mythical warrior queen called Gudit, Esato (both of which mean 'monster') or Yodit (an Ethiopianisation of Judith), and the destruction she wreaked on the Axumite Empire. Factual information about Gudit is sparse and often contradictory. According to tradition, she was a Jewish princess, born in Lasta to King Gideon IV of the Beta Israel during a time of high religious tension caused by the attempted southward expansion of the Axumite Empire and associated persecution of Jews, who refused to pay taxes to the Axumite monarchy. Gudit inherited the Beta Israel throne from her father after he was killed in battle with the Axumites, and set about protecting her beleaguered kingdom by forming a military alliance with her pagan Agaw neighbours and leading their combined army into Axum in AD852. The Axumite royal family were all slaughtered, save for the ten-year-old prince Anbessa Wedem, who was smuggled away to Shewa, in the vicinity of present-day Addis Ababa. Axum, the holiest city of Ethiopian Christianity, was reduced to rubble, together with its oldest church, Maryam Tsion, but not before the Ark of the Covenant was removed by priests and carried to Lake Ziway. Gudit also laid waste to the monastery of Debre Damo, killing the potential heirs to the Axumite throne housed therein, while dozens of other churches and settlements were burnt to the ground, and Christians were put to death in their thousands. Gudit then claimed the Axumite throne as her own, and ruled for 40 years until her death – swept up by a violent whirlwind near Wukro – in AD892. She was buried at Adi Akaweh, outside Wukro, in a grave marked indecorously with a bare pile of stones.

The Gudit legend almost certainly relates to a genuine historical figure, but much about her remains mysterious. Ethiopian tradition dates her rise to AD852, and also claims that her onslaught precipitated the move of the Axumite

Somaliland, had usurped the old Axumite port of Adulis as the main regional hub of an Indian Ocean trade network that connected the gold-exporting city-states of East Africa's Swahili Coast with Arabia and Asia. Thereafter, the Axumite Empire gradually sank into global obscurity.

The centuries following the collapse of Axumite maritime trade routes are among the most poorly understood in Ethiopia's history. Partly this is because it was a time of global isolation and cultural introspection in Ethiopia; partly because so few contemporary documents and non-ecclesiastic edifices have survived. It was during this time, however, that the Axumite rulers, though diminished in stature, turned their attention southward to extend their political influence over the Beta Israel of Lasta (near Lalibela) and the Lake Tana region, and further south into modern-day Shewa. Indeed, it could be argued that the period between AD750 and 1270 saw the gradual transformation of the Axumite Empire into Abyssinia, a Christian empire that covered most of the Ethiopian Highlands to become the precursor of the country we know today. It is also probably true that this extended period of isolation from other denominations allowed the Ethiopian Orthodox Church to become the cohesive and idiosyncratic institution it is today. Indicative of a renewed religious energy is the fact that most of Ethiopia's hundreds of rock-hewn churches were carved during this period.

Nevertheless, Ethiopia's increasing isolation during this period means that little is known of its domestic politics, a situation paralleling that of, say, Britain monarchy to Shewa. This seems unlikely, however, since various Arab writings suggest that Yemeni and Axumite rulers kept sporadic contact into the 10th century. Furthermore, correspondence between the Nubian and Axumite monarchs in around AD980 states unambiguously that Ethiopia was then plagued by a hostile queen. More likely, then, that Gudit's reign took place in the late 10th century (which, given her legendary destructiveness, might explain why the site of the capital of Kubar – if it ever existed – has never been found). As for Gudit's background, the notion she was a Jewish princess by birth is anything but universal. One popular legend states that she was a beautiful member of the Axumite royal family, exiled in disgrace after being coerced into acts of prostitution by a priest, who went on to marry the King of the Beta Israeli and enjoined him to declare war on Axum as an act of vengeance. Some scholars suggest she was a monarch of Agaw descent, or that she originated from the medieval Kingdom of Damot south of the Nile. A more left-field theory effectively places her as the last Queen of Sheba, or Saba, based partly on the proximity of her alleged grave at Adi Akaweh to a recently discovered Almaqah temple that formed a focal point of pre-Axumite rule during the D'mt/Saba era, and could conceivably have remained the capital of a Jewish rival to Axum into the 10th century. Further confusing matters is the probability that certain folk memories and actions legendarily associated with Gudit are in fact attributable to Ga'ewa, an Islamic queen and ally of Ahmed Gragn who destroyed many Tigrayan churches in the 16th century, and who is also legendarily buried at Adi Akaweh, which is also known as Meqaber Ga'ewa (Grave of Ga'ewa). Whatever the truth, while Gudit is universally reviled by Ethiopian Christians, it should be borne in mind history is written by the victors, and her attack on the Axumite monarchy was almost certainly retaliatory, provoked by its expansionist oppression of Jews and/or other non-Christian cultures.

for several centuries after the withdrawal and collapse of the Roman Empire. It is uncertain, for instance, whether the Axumite kings continued to rule from Axum after AD750, or whether they adopted a series of floating capitals. Arab writings suggest that a permanent capital called Kubar was established to the south of Axum in the 9th century, but this site has never been found, and it was most likely abandoned towards the end of the 10th century. Tradition suggests that this post-Axumite period was the golden age of the Beta Israel, the community of Ethiopian Jews more widely but pejoratively known as Falasha, and who frequently referred to themselves as Esraelawi (Israelites). Also known as the Kingdom of Semien, and centred on the near-eponymous Simien Mountains as well as the Lasta (around Lalibela) and the Dembiya region north of Lake Tana, this little-understood polity was, according to some traditions, established in the 4th century by one King Phineas, a contemporary of the Axumite Ezana, but it probably only gained any real political cohesion in the early 9th century following the rise of the Gideon Dynasty.

THE ZAGWE DYNASTY Shortly after Gudit's death, supposedly in AD892, tradition has it that the Solomonic heir Anbessa Wedem, by then in his early 50s, returned to Axum to defeat Gudit's successor and reclaim his throne. The political climate in Axum remained unstable, however, and in AD922, ten years after the death of Anbessa Wedem, his younger brother and successor Dil Nead was overthrown by Mara Tekle Haymanot, a Christian prince from Lasta. Mara Tekle Haymanot made himself emperor, marrying Dil Nead's daughter Masoba Warq in order to bolster his legitimacy, and adopted the regal name of Zagwe to found the eponymous dynasty. A second contradictory tradition claims that Dil Nead was actually the Axumite emperor overthrown by Gudit, who established a Jewish imperial dynasty that ruled for several generations prior to Mara Tekle Haymanot's ascent to the throne and conversion to Christianity in around 1137.

These conflicting traditions differ by more than 200 years when it comes to the year in which the Zagwe dynasty was established. Paradoxically, while the former tradition is more widespread, possibly because the reclamation of the throne by Anbessa Wedem more closely conforms to the retrospective notion of almost uninterrupted Solomonic rule, the dating implied by the latter tradition is favoured by most credible sources. The second tradition also gains circumstantial support from the probability that both Gudit and Mara Tekle Haymanot hailed from Lasta, which was also the epicentre of Zagwe power. The Zagwe chronology is further confused by the existence of several different lists of kings, with as few as five rulers appearing in some versions, others containing up to 16, and all but the last having reigned, rather improbably, for exactly 40 years.

Despite posthumous uncertainty with regard to dating the Zagwe dynasty, it clearly oversaw an era of renewed stability and unity within its direct sphere of influence. The most renowned Zagwe ruler was King Gebre Meskel Lalibela, who came to power in the early 1180s, and was made a saint by the Ethiopian Orthodox Church after his death. Lalibela ruled from the Zagwe capital Roha (now known as Lalibela in his honour) and is credited with the excavation of a wondrous cluster of rock-hewn churches that represent what is generally regarded to be the pinnacle of Ethiopian Christianity's physical expression of its faith. Despite this, the area over which the Zagwe ruled was small by comparison with the original Axumite Empire or modern-day Ethiopia, comprising the part of the northeastern highlands north of present-day Dessie and south of Mekele. Elsewhere, the Zagwe era witnessed a revival of the Beta Israel in the northwestern highlands, while the Muslim faith, once more or less confined to the coast, gradually spread inland to dominate the formerly pagan Somali interior, Afar and the southeast highlands around Harar and Bale, as well as infiltrating some areas that had traditionally formed part of the Christian empire, including Shewa (near present-day Addis Ababa), which functioned as an independent sultanate from 1180 to 1285.

The introverted Zagwe era ended in 1270, when the throne was seized by Yakuno Amlak, a usurper whose claim to legitimacy was based on his alleged descent from King Solomon via Anbessa Wedem. Some sources claim that the last Zagwe monarch abdicated of his own free will, others that he was killed in battle by the supporters of his supposed Solomonic successor. Either way, the transition appears to have been quite smooth and non-divisive, to such an extent that Yakuno Amlak generously granted certain land and other hereditary concessions to the Zagwe lineage, some of which were upheld into modern times.

THE SOLOMONIC RENAISSANCE In historical terms, the establishment of the Solomonic dynasty in 1270 marks a clear division between the semi-mythical events of the medieval and the ancient eras, and the less speculative Abyssinian era. It was under Yakuno Amlak that the tenuous genealogical link between the post-Zagwe rulers, their pre-Gudit predecessors and King Solomon of Jerusalem became entrenched in the popular Ethiopian imagination. Indeed, the *Kebra Nagast*, which incorporates the earliest known version of the Sheba-Menelik Cycle, was written shortly after the supposed restoration of the Solomonic line, possibly in response to the alleged Zagwe claims of descent from Moses. Artistically, the period after 1270 can be seen as something of a renaissance during which ecclesiastical writing and religious art flourished, most particularly under Zara Yaqob (1434–68), one of Abyssinia's greatest and most influential kings. A conspicuous trend of the post-Zagwe era was the increased wealth and political influence of the Ethiopian Orthodox Church. This trend was initiated almost as soon as Yakuno Amlak took power and transferred one-third of the empire's assets to the monastery of Hayk Istafanos, whose influential abbot Iyasus Moa had been his most important mentor. Hayk Istafanos remained the centre of Abyssinian ecclesiastic power until the 15th century, when it was eclipsed by Debre Libanos further southwest.

The expansionist tendencies of the restored Solomonic dynasty, bolstered by the close ties between church and state, led to a deterioration in relations with the coastal and inland Islamic communities that blocked its access to the burgeoning ports of the Red Sea and the trade routes that served them. The first military blow between the religious rivals was struck in 1290, when Emperor Yagbeu Seyon, son and successor of Yakuno Amlak, led a campaign on Zeila, then capital of the Ifat Sultanate, in response to the latter's annexation of the Sultanate of Shewa five years earlier. This campaign, which met with mixed success, was the first in a series of skirmishes and wars that expanded the smallish inward-looking Abyssinian Empire inherited by Yakuno Amlak into a much vaster entity that incorporated most inland parts of the former Axumite Empire and the Lake Tana hinterland, as well as Shewa and other lands deep in the southern highlands.

In the early 1320s, Sultan Haq ad-Din of Ifat, fed up with the expansionist policies of the Abyssinians, launched a full-scale religious war on his infidel neighbours. This campaign met with considerable success prior to 1328, when Emperor Amda Seyon I defeated Haq ad-Din in battle at Zeila. The vengeful Abyssinian emperor and his army proceeded to pillage Zeila, looting its immense stashes of gold, silver and other treasures, before running amok in several other Islamic regions and razing the towns, killing their inhabitants, and looting their livestock and other possessions. The embittered Muslims of Ifat retreated to lick their wounds, but at the turn of the century they launched a fresh series of attacks on the Christian highlanders under Sultan Sa'ad ad-Din II, who was eventually killed in battle by Emperor Dawit in 1403, on an offshore island near Zeila that still bears his name. The Ifat Sultanate fell into decline following Sa'ad al Din's death, and most of its leaders fled across the Gulf of Aden to take temporary refuge in Yemen.

Solomonic hostility during this period extended not only to Muslims but also to Jews. Amda Seyon I, whose two-decade reign started in 1314, was probably the first Abyssinian emperor to launch a military campaign against the Beta Israel, but it was under Emperor Yeshaq, who took the throne exactly a century later, that full-blown anti-Semitism really asserted itself. Yeshaq annexed the Jewish territories of Semien and Dembiya to Abyssinia, placed them under the rule of Christian governors, and issued a royal decree allowing him to confiscate the land of any Jew who refused to convert. It is probable that Yeshaq first introduced the derogatory term Falasha, meaning 'outsider' or 'landless person', which is still often used to describe Ethiopian Jews. By 1450, the Beta Israel had reclaimed much of its annexed land, and by 1462 its army was sufficiently confident to launch an attack on the Abyssinians. This failed campaign resulted in immense Jewish loss of life both in battle and afterwards, as Emperor Zara Yaqob ordered the massacre of civilian Beta Israel in the aftermath of battle.

In keeping with its new extrovert politics, the Solomonic rulers sent several envoys abroad to strengthen Abyssinian links with Christian communities in the

Sudan, Egypt, Alexandria and Armenia. Internally, the centre of power drifted southwest from Lasta to the Lake Tana hinterland, as the permanent imperial capitals of the past were eschewed in favour of a succession of temporary capitals associated with individual emperors. During the early to mid 15th century, however, it seems probable that a permanent fortified city called Barara was established in Shewa, not far from modern-day Addis Ababa, and that this served as the main residence of several successive emperors for the greater part of the year right through to the early 16th-century reign of Lebna Dengal. Written references to Barara are few and far between, but it is depicted between mounts Zikwala and Menegasha on a map drawn by Italian cartographer Fra Mauro in around 1460, and is also described first-hand in a 1531 document penned by Yemeni writer Arab-Faqih. Some scholars query whether Barara was really a permanent fortified city, as opposed to just another temporary imperial encampment. Either way, its precise location is unknown; Mount Yerer near Bishoftu is a possible contender, as is Mount Borora 30km southwest of Addis Ababa, but both these sites are now eclipsed in the probability stakes by the Entoto Hills, where a vast medieval town and pentagonal fort was recently rediscovered overlooking Addis Ababa.

THE MUSLIM–CHRISTIAN WAR (1528–60) In the early 1420s, Sabr ad-Din, the eldest son of the late Sultan Sa'ad ad-Din II of Ifat, returned to Zeila after two decades of exile in Yemen to found the Adal Sultanate, a powerful and extensive polity that soon came to control a long stretch of coast between Berbera and Assab, running inland to the highlands around Harar. The most celebrated or notorious leader of Adal, depending on your viewpoint, was Ahmad ibn Ibrahim al-Ghazi, a Zeila-born Somali imam better known as Ahmed Gurey or Ahmed Gragn (Somali and Amharic respectively for 'the left-handed'). Still in his teens at the time, Imam Ahmed seized power in Zeila in 1527 following a period of domestic turmoil in Adal, and a year later he relocated his capital to Harar.

In March 1529, Ahmed launched his first attack on the Abyssinians, suffering heavy losses but defeating an army led by Emperor Lebna Dengal (also known as Dawit II) at a site known as Shimbra Kure (Chick-pea Swamp). In 1531, Gragn launched a second and more sustained assault on the Christian highlands. His army laid waste to Barara, the fortified Abyssinian capital, while Lebna Dengal and his troops were trapped on the other side of the Awash River, and went on to loot its churches and palaces for gold, silver, silk and other valuables, as witnessed first-hand by Arab-Faqih, author of a document called *Futuh al-Habasa* (Conquest of Abyssinia). From then on, Gragn led his army of Afar and Somali Muslims on an annual raid into Abyssinia, usually timing it to coincide with Lent, in order to exploit his Christian foes' weakness during this fasting period. By 1535, Gragn held Shewa, Lasta, Amhara and Tigray – in other words, most of Abyssinia – and Lebna Dengal had become a fugitive in his own empire, chased around by Gragn until he was killed in battle near Debre Damo in September 1540. From an Abyssinian perspective, Gragn's was a reign of destructiveness comparable only to that of Gudit several centuries before. Many rock-hewn churches throughout Ethiopia still bear the scars of his campaign. Hundreds of less permanent Christian edifices were destroyed completely, among them Axum's church of Maryam Tsion, which had been rebuilt after Gudit's reign.

Gragn's campaign more or less coincided with the first contact between Europe and Ethiopia, which occurred in 1493, the second-last year of the reign of the youthful Emperor Iskander, with the arrival – via Egypt, India and the Persian Gulf – of Pêro de Covilhã, a 'spy' sent by the Portuguese King John II in search of the legendary land of Prester John. Instead of fulfilling the second part of his mission by returning home, however, Covilhã stayed on in Ethiopia to serve as an adviser to a succession of emperors and regents. He was still there in 1520, when the first full Portuguese expedition to Ethiopia, as documented by the priest Francisco Álvares in the classic book *Prester John of the Indies*, was received at the monastery of Debre Libanos by Emperor Lebna Dengal. Shortly before his death in exile, Lebna Dengal wrote to Portugal asking for help in restoring his kingdom. Were it not for the intervention of the Portuguese, it is quite likely that Ethiopian Christianity would have been buried under the Islamic onslaught.

In 1543, Emperor Galawdewos's army, propped up by the Portuguese, killed Gragn and defeated his army in a battle near Lake Tana. Galawdewos's attempts to rebuild the shattered Christian empire were frequently frustrated by raids led not only by Gragn's wife and nephew, but also by the powerful Queen Ga'ewa, who hailed from the Islamic kingdom of Mazaga in what is now the far northwest of Tigray, and was responsible for the destruction of many churches and monasteries. In 1559, Emperor Galawdewos was killed and his severed head displayed in Harar. But the long years of war had drained the resources of Christians and Muslims alike; the real winners were the pagan Oromo, who expanded out of the Rift Valley into areas laid

THE LAND OF PRESTER JOHN

It was probably during Zagwe rule that the legend of Prester John took root in Europe. The origin of this legend is now rather obscure, but it seems to have taken hold in the 12th century and impressed the European clergy to such an extent that, in 1177, Pope Alexander III sent a message to Prester John (the messenger apparently never returned). The essence of the legend, elaborated on by explorers such as Marco Polo, was that a vast and wealthy Christian kingdom existed somewhere in the 'Indies' (at the time a vague term which covered practically anywhere in the world that was unknown to Europeans) and that it was ruled over by Prester John, who was both king and high priest, and a descendant of the Magi (a group of Persian magicians, three of whom were probably the wise men who attended Jesus shortly after his birth).

As with so many aspects of Ethiopian history, the substance behind the Prester John legend is rather elusive. It is widely thought that the legend originated in Ethiopia, but precisely how knowledge of a Christian kingdom in Africa reached Europe is an open question. One Ethiopian legend is that Lalibela visited Jerusalem prior to becoming the King of Ethiopia. A few modern sources suggest that the Prester John story was founded on a letter sent to Europe by an Ethiopian king called Yohannes, and it was this letter to which the Pope responded. And as far as I am aware, the Ethiopian Church has maintained links with Alexandria throughout its history, so news could have infiltrated Europe through Egypt. Or perhaps the legend of Prester John and the reality of a Christian kingdom in Ethiopia is mere coincidence. Whatever truth lay behind the legend, Prester John was a shadowy fringe presence in medieval lore. References to him are scattered through religious and other mystical writings of the period, and it seems probable that the lure of his wealthy kingdom and desire to communicate with a fellow Christian empire was part of the reason behind the Portuguese explorations of Africa which resulted in their arrival in Ethiopia in 1520.

waste by the fighting. By 1560, the Oromo had virtually surrounded Harar and had overrun much of Shewa, providing not only a buffer zone between the exhausted Christians and Muslims, but also a new threat to both of the established groups.

THE GONDARINE PERIOD (1635–1855) The Christians were faced with a new disaster as Portuguese ex-soldiers settled around the temporary capital on Lake Tana. In 1622, Emperor Susenyos made a full conversion to Catholicism under the influence of his close friend and regular travelling companion, the Spanish-born Jesuit priest Pedro Páez, and he outlawed the Orthodox Church and suspended traditional Church officials. This move was naturally very unpopular with Ethiopian Christians, thousands upon thousands of whom were persecuted to death for pursuing the centuries-old faith they had shared with their oppressor until 1622. Even harsher was the treatment of Jews. Spurred on by the firepower and deeply engrained anti-Semitism of his Jesuit allies, Susenyos totally destroyed the millennium-old kingdom of Beta Israel, slaughtered its leaders, and annexed it to his own empire. Judaism was outlawed, torahs were burned along with all other Jewish writings, and individuals who refused to convert had their land confiscated before being sold into slavery or forcibly baptised.

Increasingly isolated from his subjects, Emperor Susenyos was forced to abdicate in favour of his son Fasil in 1632. The new emperor reinstated the Orthodox Church and also relaxed the Susenyos-era restrictions on Judaism, though by this time the Beta Israel had been utterly destroyed as a political entity, and many other Jewish traditions and artefacts were lost. Tired of Jesuit interference, Fasil also banned all foreigners from Abyssinia, and only one such person, the French doctor Charles Poncet, was permitted to enter the kingdom between the 1640s and the arrival of James Bruce in 1770.

Ethiopia had lacked a permanent capital since 1270. In order to help reunite Church and state, Fasil broke with this tradition by settling at the small town of Gondar, north of Lake Tana. Gondar was named the permanent capital of Ethiopia in c1635, a title it kept for more than 200 years. This move to Gondar signalled an era of relative peace under a succession of strong, popular emperors, most notably Fasil himself and Iyasu I. Then, under Iyasu II (1730–55), the throne was gradually undermined by Ras (Prince) Mikael of Tigray, who assumed an increasing backstage importance, twice assassinating emperors and replacing them with others of his choice. For much of the Gondar period, the war between Christians and Oromo had been a problem, as had priestly fears about contact between the court and exotic Christian denominations. King Ioas (1755–69) lost almost all support by marrying an Oromo woman and insisting on Oromo being spoken in court. By 1779, when Tekle Giyorgis took power, the king's role was little more than ornamental. The period between 1769 and 1855 is generally referred to as the 'era of the princes'; the Gondar-based rulers of this period are remembered as the shadow emperors.

ETHIOPIA UNDER EMPEROR TEWODROS II (1855–69) In 1855, Ethiopia was not so much a unified state as a loose alliance of squabbling fiefdoms run by wealthy local dynasties, which were in turn reigned over by an ineffectual emperor. The empire was threatened not merely by internal power struggles, but also by the external threat posed by Egypt, which wanted to control the Nile from its source in Lake Tana. Were it not for the vision of one Kassa Hailu, Ethiopia could well have collapsed altogether.

Kassa Hailu grew up in the home of Kenfu Hailu, a man who played a major role in campaigns against Egypt and who ruled a minor fief in western Ethiopia.

When Kenfu died in 1839, Kassa was denied the heirdom of the fief he had hoped for, and instead became a *shifta* (bandit), though reportedly not an ignoble one, as he developed a Robin Hood-like obsession with wealth redistribution, and also led several private campaigns against Egyptian intruders. By 1850, he ruled the fiefdom he believed to be his by default. He then led a series of campaigns against other princes. In 1855 he defeated the heir to the throne outside Gondar, and had himself crowned Emperor Tewodros II.

History has cast Tewodros as the instigator of Ethiopian unity, and he is now among the country's most revered historical figures. That he never achieved sustained popularity in his lifetime is due to the brutality and ruthless fanaticism with which he pursued his goals of Ethiopian unity and independence. He attempted, with a fair degree of success, to reunite the fiefdoms under a strong central government, and, less successfully, to modernise the national army. He established an arms factory near his capital of Debre Tabor and gradually accumulated a large arsenal on Makdala Hill near Dessie. Tewodros had strong anti-feudal instincts that led to his abolition of the slave trade and his expropriation of large tracts of fallow Church-owned land for the use of peasant farmers. These socialist efforts won him few friends among the clergy and the nobility and, at any given time during his reign, one or other of the old fiefdoms was in rebellion. The strict discipline he imposed on his army led to a high rate of desertion and the continual internal strife cost many of his soldiers their lives: by 1866, his army had dwindled from 60,000 men to 10,000.

Amid growing unpopularity at home, Tewodros's sense of frustration was cemented by his failure to enlist European, and more specifically British, support for his modernising efforts and quest for absolute Ethiopian sovereignty. In 1867, Tewodros retreated embittered to the top of Makdala Hill. With him, he took several British prisoners in a final desperate bid to lever European support: a fatal misjudgement. In 1869, Britain sent a force of 32,000 men led by Sir Robert Napier to capture Tewodros. Makdala was encircled. Instead of fighting, Tewodros wrote a long letter to Napier listing his failed ambitions and castigating his countrymen for their backwardness. He then put a gun to his head and took his own life.

ETHIOPIA UNDER EMPEROR YOHANNES IV (1872–89) The struggle for succession after Tewodros's suicide took a military form, culminating in the Battle of Assam in 1871, wherein the incumbent emperor Tekle Giyorgis was defeated by his brother-in-law and the ruler of Tigray, Kassa Mercha, whose superior weaponry had been acquired in exchange for supporting Britain in the march to Makdala. Kassa crowned himself Emperor Yohannes IV and ruled from 1872 to 1889. Yohannes was a deeply religious man, a proud nationalist and a skilled military tactician who nevertheless initiated a more diplomatic form of rule than had Tewodros.

Yohannes's ambition of creating national unity through diplomatic rather than military means was thwarted by several factors, including British duplicity and Egypt's ambitions to control the source of the Nile at Lake Tana. Yohannes was also undermined by the actions of Prince Sahle Maryam of Shewa, his main rival for the throne, and eventual successor, who consistently played internal politics while the emperor was occupied by fighting external powers. It was Yohannes who released Sahle Maryam from a ten-year term of imprisonment under Tewodros, and restored him to his regional seat in Shewa. Then, while Yohannes was employed in leading successful campaigns against Egypt at Gundat and Gura in 1875–76, Sahle Maryam repaid the favour by seizing Wollo and inserting his ally Muhammad Ali as its governor. When Yohannes returned from his campaigning, Sahle Maryam was unwilling to risk direct military conflict with Yohannes's superior and more experienced army, so he accepted a diplomatic olive branch in the form of the Leche Agreement of 1878, which formalised the relationship between the emperor and regional leaders.

Yohannes then turned his attention to negotiating with Europe and Egypt for official recognition of Ethiopian sovereignty. His cause was helped greatly when the Mahdist War broke out in Sudan in 1882, and Britain, which that very year had unilaterally occupied Egypt, realised it needed Ethiopia's assistance to rescue its troops from Sudan. The Treaty of Adwa, signed by Yohannes and a British negotiator in 1884, met most of the emperor's demands: most significantly the return of Bogos, a part of Ethiopia occupied by Egypt, and the right to the free import of goods including arms and ammunition. The treaty also allowed Britain dominion over the port of Massawa. While Yohannes faithfully kept his part of the bargain by rescuing British troops from Mahdist Sudan, and eventually gave his life in this cause, Britain broke the spirit of the agreement barely a year after it was signed by handing Massawa to Italy.

Italy was a newcomer to Africa. Nevertheless, with the tacit support of Britain, who had little interest in Ethiopia other than ensuring the source of the Nile was kept out of French hands, Italy proved a major threat to Ethiopian sovereignty. The Italian army occupied several Red Sea ports in 1886. Anticipating a march inland, Yohannes attacked their fort at the port at Saati in January 1887. The Ethiopians were repulsed at Saati, but the next day they attacked and destroyed a force of 500 Italians at Dogali. In March 1888, Yohannes led an army of 80,000 in an attack on Saati, but the Italians refused to leave their fort and fight, and the news of a successful Mahdist attack on Gondar, still the official capital of Ethiopia, and also of Sahle Maryam's plans to rise against the emperor, forced the emperor to deal with these more immediate problems. On 9 March 1889, Yohannes led his troops into battle one last time, attacking the Mahdist stronghold at Metema. The imperial army won the battle, effectively ending the Mahdist threat, but not before their leader was fatally wounded. On 3 November 1889, Sahle Maryam was crowned Emperor of Ethiopia under the throne name of Menelik II.

EMPEROR MENELIK II (1889–1913) Menelik II must properly be regarded as the architect of modern Ethiopia. Prior to his appointment as King of Shewa, Abyssinia was a loosely affiliated cluster of squabbling Christian fiefdoms whose extent more or less coincided with the highland regions of present-day Amhara and Tigray, along with parts of Oromia. It was Menelik II who set about conquering various rebel fiefdoms to incorporate them into a greater Abyssinian polity, as well as expanding his influence over various non-Christian territories – many of which had never formed part of Abyssinia – to mould an empire whose boundaries approximated those of modern-day Ethiopia. Many of these conquests occurred during the reign of Yohannes IV, when the future Menelik II was still Prince Sahle Maryam of Shewa, and were undertaken in a spirit of self-interest and self-promotion rather than nation building, ie: to expand the territory of Shewa, to open up trade routes blocked by hostile fiefdoms, and to demonstrate the prince's considerable leadership skills and military prowess. So it was that the Islamic territories of Harar and Arsi were captured by Sahle Maryam between 1882 and 1888, along with several fiefdoms in the southwestern highlands, and large tracts of Oromo land. It was also while Yohannes IV was in power that Sahle Maryam moved the Shewan capital to the Entoto Hills, a range rich in Solomonic associations, then into a nearby valley to found the modern city of Addis Ababa.

Menelik II came to national power during the most severe famine in Ethiopia's recorded history. The Kefu Qan (Evil Days) of 1888–92 were a direct result of a rinderpest epidemic triggered by the importation of cattle by the Italians, and the crisis was exacerbated by drought and locust plagues. This famine cannot be seen in isolation from the ongoing wars of the 19th century, nor can it be dissociated from the greed of the feuding princes. Peasant resources had been stretched to the limit long before the advent of rinderpest. All of which paved the way for Menelik II to continue his policy of territorial expansion into the early and mid 1890s, which is when the remote likes of Konso, South Omo, Gambella and Benishangul-Gumuz were incorporated into Ethiopia, before the last territorial lines were inked on to the colonial map in the aftermath of the so-called Scramble for Africa.

During Yohannes's time, Menelik had been in friendly contact with the Italians at Massawa, trading promises of peace for weapons to expand his own empire and to challenge the emperor. In May 1889, he signed the Treaty of Wechale, granting Italy the part of Ethiopia that was to become Eritrea in exchange for recognition of Ethiopian sovereignty over the rest of the country. What Menelik didn't realise was that the Italians had inserted a clause in the Italian version of the document, but not in the Amharigna equivalent, which demanded that Ethiopia make all its foreign contacts through Italy, in effect reducing Ethiopia to an Italian protectorate. Italy further undermined the spirit of the treaty when, in 1891, it successfully courted several Tigrayan princes into alliance with Eritrea. When the princes revolted against the prospective colonisers in 1894, Italy was left with one course open to attain its goal of colonising Ethiopia: military confrontation.

In October 1895, Italy occupied Adigrat on the Tigrayan side of the border, and also established a fort at the Tigrayan capital of Mekele. Menelik led a force of 100,000 men to Tigray and, after a couple of inconsequential skirmishes, the two armies met in the hills around Adwa. The memory of the Battle of Adwa, which took place on 1 March 1896, remains one of the proudest moments in Ethiopian history. Through their own faulty map-reading as much as anything, the Italian troops were humiliatingly routed, the first time ever that a European power had been defeated by Africans in a battle of consequence. In Rome, nearly 100,000 people signed a petition demanding Italian withdrawal from Ethiopia and, although Italy retained Eritrea, the borders of which were formalised in 1900, it was to be almost 40 years before they again crossed the Ethiopian border in anger. Ethiopia was the only part of Africa to survive as an independent state following the European scramble.

In many senses, Menelik completed the process of unification and modernisation that had been started by Tewodros and Yohannes. His period of rule saw the introduction of electricity, telephones, schools and hospitals, and also the building of the Addis Ababa–Djibouti railway. It also saw a re-intensification of the slave trade which, although it had been present in Ethiopia since time immemorial, had been curbed if not halted by Tewodros. Slavery was the pretext used by Europe to block Ethiopia's entry to the League of Nations and to sanction against the import of arms and ammunition to Ethiopia. The slave raids, in which many thousands of Ethiopians died, were the major blemish on a reign that oversaw one of the longest periods of sustained peace Ethiopia had known for a long time.

THE RISE OF HAILE SELASSIE (1913–36) Menelik died of old age in 1913. His chosen successor, Iyasu, is remembered as much for his good looks and raffish lifestyle as for anything he achieved. In fact, had he ever been given the chance, Iyasu could well have been the relatively progressive leader that Ethiopia needed to drag it out of feudalism. Iyasu tried to curb the slave trade; he did much to incorporate

Ethiopia's often neglected Islamic population (several of his wives were Muslim and he financed the building of many mosques); and he showed little regard for the ageing and self-serving Shewan government which he inherited from Menelik. Or to put it another way, Iyasu succeeded in annoying the slave-owning nobility, the clergy of the Orthodox Church, and the political status quo. In 1916, while visiting Jijiga in an attempt to improve relations with Ethiopia's Somali population, Iyasu was overthrown. He was eventually captured in 1921 and imprisoned in Fiche in north Shewa.

The two main rivals to succeed Iyasu were Askala Maryam, better known as Zewditu, the sheltered daughter of the dead emperor, and Ras Tefari Mekonnen, the ambitious son of the Harari governor Ras Makonnen and grandson of an earlier Shewan monarch. The Shewan nobility, who had called most of the shots as the ailing Menelik reached the end of his reign, favoured Zewditu for her political naivety and evident potential for ineffectuality. A compromise was reached wherein Zewditu became empress, and Tefari the official heir to the throne. In actuality, the younger, worldlier and better-educated Ras Tefari assumed a regent-like role and the two governed in tandem, a situation that became increasingly tense as Tefari's dominance grew. This ambiguous relationship was resolved in 1930, when the empress's husband was killed in rather murky circumstances in a civil battle. Two days later, Zewditu herself succumbed, apparently to that most Victorian of maladies, heartbreak. Ras Tefari was crowned under the name Haile Selassie (meaning 'Power of the Trinity') in November 1930.

Haile Selassie set to work on drafting a new constitution with the claimed intent of doing away with feudalism and limiting the powers of the regional princes. Consciously or not, the effect of the constitution was further to entrench the regional nobility in a ministerial system based more on heredity than on merit. The first parliament, which assembled in November 1931, consisted of a senate whose members were appointed directly by the emperor, and a chamber of deputies whose members were elected by the landed gentry. The only regional leader to challenge the constitution was Ras Hailu Tekle Haymanot of Gojjam. After attempting to free Iyasu from his confinement in Fiche, Ras Hailu was sentenced to life imprisonment in 1932 and Gojjam was placed under the administration of one of the emperor's allies. Haile Selassie can be credited with creating the first unambiguously unified Ethiopian state. Equally unambiguous was the fact that this state gave no meaningful constitutional protection or power to the overwhelming majority of its citizens.

THE ITALIAN OCCUPATION (1936–41) The first serious challenge to Haile Selassie's rule came not from within the country but from Italy. The immediate effect of the Battle of Adwa had been the abandonment of Italian colonial aspirations south of the Eritrean border, but the humiliation afforded to the Italian army at Adwa still rankled, particularly in the nationalistic fervour that accompanied the rise to power of Mussolini's Fascists in 1922. Mussolini's initial attempts to gain economic control of Ethiopia were disguised behind diplomacy but, by the time Haile Selassie had gained absolute power over Ethiopia, the Italians had more or less abandoned this approach in favour of subterfuge and force. The former tactic was most effective in Tigray, an outlying region of northern Ethiopia with close historical and cultural links to neighbouring Eritrea. Italy charmed the Tigrayan nobility, whose response when war broke out in 1935 varied from lukewarm resistance to taking the Italian side against Ethiopia.

The first harbinger of war was the Walwal Incident of December 1934, wherein a remote Ethiopian military post in the disputed Italian Somaliland border region was attacked by Italian troops. The skirmish was initiated by Italy, and Italy suffered considerably less loss of life than did Ethiopia. Nevertheless, the political climate in Europe was such that countries like Britain and France were more than willing to sacrifice Ethiopian interests to the cause of frustrating an alliance between Mussolini and Hitler. Italy made absurd demands for reparations. Ethiopia took these to the League of Nations (it had become a member state in 1925) for arbitration, but its perfectly valid arguments were ignored; Italy was in effect given a free hand in Ethiopia.

The Italian army crossed from Eritrea to Tigray in October 1935. By 8 November, Italy had occupied Adigrat, Mekele and, to its immense satisfaction, Adwa. The Ethiopian army entered Tigray in January 1936. After a couple of minor Ethiopian victories, most notably at the first Battle of Tembien, Italy's superior air power and its use of prohibited mustard gas proved decisive. The Battle of Maychew, which took place on 31 March 1936, is generally regarded as the last concerted Ethiopian resistance to Italian occupation. Although several minor skirmishes distracted the Italians as they marched from Maychew to Addis Ababa, it was when news of Italy's victory at Maychew reached the capital that the emperor went into exile and the streets erupted into anarchic and unfocused mass violence.

Italy incorporated Ethiopia, Eritrea and Italian Somaliland into one large territory which they named Italian East Africa. Addis Ababa was made the colonial capital, while Jimma, Gondar, Harar, Asmara and Mogadishu became regional administrative centres. The Italian influence on all these cities is still evident today, as it is on several smaller towns. More lasting was the Italian influence on the internal transport infrastructure, particularly in the north, where they cut roads through seemingly impossible territory. This positive legacy must, however, be set against their successful bid to cripple indigenous businesses and replace them with parastatal organisations. This state interventionism proved to be particularly damaging in the agricultural sector: the importation of grain, almost unknown before 1935, became a feature of the Italian and post-Italian eras. Ultimately, though, the high level of internal resistance to the exotic regime, and its eventual collapse in 1941, meant that it was too ineffectual and short-lived to have many lasting effects on Ethiopia.

Throughout the Italian occupation, the Ethiopian nobility combined time-buying diplomacy and well-organised guerrilla warfare to undermine the implanted regime. The Fascists' response was characteristically brutal. When, in 1937, an unsuccessful attempt was made on the life of the Italian viceroy, the Italian Blackshirts ran riot in the capital, burning down houses and decapitating and disembowelling Ethiopians, mostly at random, though the intelligentsia was particularly targeted and few survived the rampage. The Ethiopian resistance won few battles of note, but its role in demoralising the occupiers laid the foundation for the easy British victory over the Italian troops in the Allied liberation campaign of January 1941.

POST-WAR ETHIOPIA UNDER HAILE SELASSIE (1941–74) Haile Selassie was returned to his throne immediately when the Allied troops drove Italy back into Eritrea. Eritrea and Italian Somaliland were placed under the rule of the British Military Administration. When war ended, the UN was left to determine the status of the three countries that had been co-administrated under Italy. Haile Selassie naturally wanted all the territories to be integrated under his imperial government. When it was decided that Italian Somaliland should be governed under a ten-year trusteeship then granted full independence, Ethiopia's demands for Eritrea and the access to the Red Sea it offered became more concerted. To its aid came the

USA and Britain, both of which had a good relationship with Haile Selassie and a vested interest in keeping at least one Red Sea territory in friendly hands. With more than a touch of cynicism on the part of certain of its member states, and after no meaningful consultation with the Eritreans, the UN forced Eritrea into a highly ambiguous federation with Ethiopia.

The US intervention over Eritrea led to a decreasing European role in determining Ethiopian affairs and much stronger links being forged with the other side of the Atlantic. As the oil-rich Middle East came to play an increasingly important role in international affairs, so too did Ethiopia and its Red Sea harbours in US foreign policy. In exchange for using Asmara as its Red Sea base, the USA developed a military training and armoury programme for Ethiopia which, by 1970, absorbed more than half the US budget for military aid to Africa. Little wonder, then, that the world barely noticed when, using the pretext of a minor skirmish the preceding year, Eritrean federation became colonisation. In 1962, Ethiopia formally annexed Eritrea, dissolved the Eritrean Assembly, and placed the federated territory under what was practically military rule. The terms of federation gave Eritrea no recourse to argue its case before the UN. So began a war for self-determination that lasted almost 30 years, cost the lives of more than 100,000 Eritreans, and never once figured on the UN's agenda.

Few modern leaders have become so deeply associated with a country's image for so long a time as did Emperor Haile Selassie. As Ras Tefari, he wielded much of the power behind the throne between 1916 and 1930; as emperor he ruled almost unchallenged, except for the brief Italian interlude, between 1930 and 1974. Despite the mystique that surrounded him, however, Haile Selassie did very little to develop his country. The 1931 constitution created a united empire by entrenching the rights of the nobility; it had done little to improve the lot of ordinary Ethiopians. The revised constitution of 1955 introduced universal suffrage, but the absence of any cohesive political parties and the high salaries offered to parliamentarians attracted self-serving careerists rather than politicians of substance. The low turnouts at elections suggest that political education was non-existent and most Ethiopians saw the constitutional revision for the window dressing it undoubtedly was. In essence, the Ethiopia of 1960 or 1970 was no less feudal than had been the Ethiopia of 1930. The economy remained as subsistence-based as ever, with trade and industry accounting for a mere 10% of GDP. In many respects, and despite its proud independence, Ethiopia lacked an infrastructure comparable even to those of the underdeveloped colonies that surrounded it.

Little wonder, then, that the wave of colonial resistance that swept through Africa after World War II, and which resulted in the independence of most of the former African colonies in the early 1960s, was mirrored by a rising tide of imperial resistance in post-occupation Ethiopia. Underground opposition to the emperor started almost immediately the Italian occupation ended. The most persistent of the dissidents, Takele Woldehawariat, had supported the emperor before the occupation but, like many former resistance leaders, he strongly opposed Haile Selassie's return to power after having sat out the occupation in exile. Takele attempted to install one of Iyasu's sons in place of Haile Selassie and was detained. In 1946 he became involved in another anti-imperial plot, and was detained for another eight years. Takele was killed in a police shoot-out in 1969. By this time, however, a more concerted anti-imperialist movement had emerged, its objections not so much to Haile Selassie himself as to the outmoded feudal system he represented.

The first serious threat to imperial power came in the form of an attempted military coup initiated by the left-wing intellectual Garmame Neway and implemented by his brother, Brigadier-General Mengistu Neway, leader of the Imperial Bodyguard. On 14 December 1960, while Haile Selassie was away in Brazil, the Imperial Bodyguard effectively imprisoned his cabinet at the Imperial Palace, having lured them there by claiming that the empress was terminally ill, then announced that a new government would be formed to combat the country's backwardness and poverty. Haile Selassie flew back to Asmara and from there instructed the military – whose tottering loyalty was secured by the promise of a substantial pay rise – to storm the palace. Garmame Neway was killed in the shoot-out, along with several cabinet members, while his brother Mengistu was captured in the act of fleeing and hanged for treason.

Haile Selassie returned to his palace, but it wasn't quite business as usual from there on, although the last person to recognise this was arguably the emperor himself. Indeed, on the pan-African front, as a spate of former European colonial possessions were transformed into independent self-governing nations during the early 1960s, the figurehead status of Ethiopia's septuagenarian head of state was entrenched by the selection of Addis Ababa as capital of the newly formed Organization of African Unity (OAU) in 1963. On the domestic front, by contrast, the attempted coup sparked a more widespread cry for reform and greater recognition that imperial rule was open to challenge. Between 1963 and 1970, Bale was in a permanent state of revolt, while a successful local coup was staged in Gojjam in 1968. There were also revolts in parts of Sidamo (1960) and Wollo (1970), while Addis Ababa witnessed regular student demonstrations from 1965 onwards, and the military became increasingly divided into imperial loyalist and liberationist factions. From 1967 onwards, the Eritrean Liberation Front (ELF) and Eritrean People's Liberation Front (EPLF) became highly militarised in their bid to achieve full independence for their province.

The ageing Haile Selassie responded to the atmosphere of dissent and loud cries for land reform – most Ethiopian peasants were still subject to the whims of local landlords – with increasingly repressive measures. Matters came to a head over the tragic 1973 famine in Wollo and Tigray. As the BBC aired heartbreaking footage of starving Ethiopians, the imperial government first refused to acknowledge the famine's existence, and then – having retracted its initial denials – failed to respond to the crisis with any action meaningful enough to prevent the estimated 200,000 deaths that ensued. The disgraced cabinet resigned in February 1974 and a new prime minister was appointed shortly thereafter. Too little, too late: at around the same time the armed forces and police had established a co-ordinating committee called the Derg, which – guided by the slogan *Ethiopia Tidkem* (Ethiopia First) – gradually insinuated itself into a position of effective power by arresting officials it regarded to be incompetent and/or self-serving, and replacing the recently installed prime minister with a stooge in July of the same year.

On 12 September 1974, following seven months of ceaseless strikes, demonstrations, local peasant revolts and military mutinies, what little power the octogenarian (and possibly semi-senile) Haile Selassie still wielded was finally curtailed. The military arrested the emperor in his palace, and – in mockery of a grandiose imperial motorcade – drove him to a prison cell in the back of a Volkswagen Beetle, while his embittered subjects yelled out '*Leba!*' ('Thief!'). Details of the imperial imprisonment are unclear and only started to emerge many years later. Certainly, Haile Selassie was still alive when the Derg officially abolished the monarchy in March 1975, and he even made one last (unofficial) public appearance three months later prior to being hospitalised for an operation. It would appear, however, that 3,000 years of supposed Solomonic rule ended in the imperial palace

THE SOLOMONIC DYNASTY

The so-called Solomonic dynasty, referred to both in this chapter and elsewhere in the book, is claimed to have ruled Ethiopia for 3,000 years, a practically unbroken lineage of 237 emperors stretching from Menelik I, son of King Solomon and the Queen of Sheba, to Haile Selassie. Like so much else that passes for Ethiopian history, it is also something of a myth. First of all, even the most imperialist of Ethiopians will accept that the Solomonic chain was broken by several centuries of Zagwe rule prior to the late 13th century, when it was supposedly restored by Emperor Yakuno Amlak. Furthermore, there is no historical base for Yakuno Amlak's claim to Solomonic ancestry. On the contrary, academic opinion is that the legendary foundation of Axum by Menelik was invented (or adapted from a similar Yemeni legend) in the time of Yakuno Amlak to substantiate the new emperor's claim to the throne.

Academic opinion is, of course, only opinion: well founded, but nevertheless an educated guess, based on the lack of any concrete evidence to suggest that the Solomonic legend was in circulation prior to the 13th century. The traditional assertion that Yakuno Amlak was a distant descendant of Solomon has to be regarded as improbable in the extreme, but it is difficult to disprove. Oddly enough, however, one does not need to delve deep into Ethiopia's past to debunk the Solomonic myth. As Harry Atkins correctly points out: 'Even in the 19th century, the last ruler of Gondar was not related to Tewodros II, who was not related to Yohannes IV, who was not related to Menelik II. There is no way that Haile Selassie was the 237th Solomonic Emperor.'

on 27 August 1975, with the ailing and deposed emperor succumbing, probably not to a heart attack, as the official line had it at the time, but to a smothering pillow held in place by his effective successor Colonel Mengistu Haile Maryam. Ethiopia's last emperor was buried next to a latrine outside the palace, only for his remains to be exhumed in the early 1990s and stored for several years in the Menelik Mausoleum in Addis Ababa. Haile Selassie was finally accorded a formal burial at Trinity Cathedral in November 2000.

THE DERG (1974–91) Immediately after the arrest of the emperor, power was handed to the socialist-inspired Military Co-ordinating Committee known as the Derg. Lofty socialist ideals or not, the Derg soon proved to be even more ruthless and duplicitous in achieving its goals than was its predecessor. Despite the ELF and EPLF having helped them get to power, the Derg wanted to retain Eritrea and determined that this should be done through force. In September 1974, they asked the prominent General Aman Andom to lead them and to be their spokesperson; when Aman resigned two months later in protest at the Derg policy on Eritrea, he was placed under house arrest and killed. Fifty-seven important officials were executed without trial, including two previous prime ministers.

A provisional military government was formed by the Derg in November under the leadership of General Tefari Benti. A series of radical policies was implemented, most crucially the Land Reform Bill of March 1975, which outlawed private land ownership and allowed for the formation of collective land use under local *kebele* councils. Disenchantment with US support for the previous government and the persistence of a feudalistic economy into the 1970s made Ethiopia a fertile ground for socialism. Most of the Derg's attempts at collectivisation, villagisation and resettlement were met with neither popular support nor any significant success. Indeed, agricultural productivity grew more slowly than the national population throughout Derg rule.

The number of local and national opposition groups mushroomed in 1975–76. One of the most important was the Tigrayan People's Liberation Front (TPLF), which received training from the EPLF and allied itself to the cause of Eritrean self-determination while demanding a truly democratic Ethiopian government rather than a ruthless military dictatorship. The Derg responded to this outbreak of dissent with mass arrests and executions. The situation was exploited mercilessly by Vice-Chairman Mengistu Haile Maryam, who used it to justify an internal purge of the Derg, a self-serving process that culminated in February 1977 with the execution of seven party leaders including General Tefari. Mengistu thus became the unopposed leader of the provisional government; those who opposed him didn't do so for long.

By 1977, large parts of Eritrea were under rebel rule. There were rumblings from the newly founded Oromo Liberation Front (OLF), the organisation that represented Ethiopia's largest ethnic group. Somali-populated parts of eastern Ethiopia rose against the government army, aided by troops from Somalia, precipitating Russian and Cuban withdrawal from Somalia and support for Ethiopia. The result was a low-scale but occasionally very bloody war (10,000 troops died on each side in 1978) between Somalia and Ethiopia which closed the Djibouti railway line for several years and was only fully resolved in 1988. The unrest spread to the capital, where street conflict resulted in several hundreds of deaths. Furthermore, in early 1979, an estimated one million Ethiopians were affected by a famine in Tigray, Wollo and Eritrea, and at least 10,000 people died.

Mengistu contrived to pull the country back into some sort of order in 1980, as much as anything by arresting and killing opposition leaders, and driving those who survived his purges into exile. Thousands upon thousands of Ethiopians were killed by the army; it is evidence of the cruelty of his regime that when a family wanted to collect a body for burial, it was required to pay the cost of the fatal bullet. Despite the semblance of peace, much of Somali-populated Ethiopia was practically autonomous, and the EPLF and TPLF continued to engage the regime in sporadic conflict.

Ethiopia leapt into the world spotlight in 1985. The latest famine was the worst in living memory. Its roots lay in three successive rainfall failures in Tigray, Wolo, the eastern lowlands and even parts of Gondar and Gojjam, but it was exacerbated by politics: at first a Western refusal to send aid to a socialist country, and then, when aid finally arrived, by Mengistu's unwillingness to help food get to the troublesome province of Tigray. One in five Ethiopians was affected by the famine; one million died, most of them in the northeast. It was a natural phenomenon, but the tragic scale it reached was entirely preventable.

In September 1987, Ethiopia was proclaimed a 'People's Democratic Republic' and technically returned to civilian rule, on the basis of a contrived election in which all candidates were nominated by the Derg. Mengistu was returned to power. In the same year, the Ethiopian People's Revolutionary Democratic Movement (EPRDM), allied to the TPLF and apparently supported by the EPLF, was formed with the major aim of initiating a true national democracy as opposed to regional secession. In May 1988, the government declared a state of emergency in Tigray and Eritrea as an increasing number of major towns, even some as far south as Wollo, fell under rebel rule. Attempted peace talks in April 1989 met with dismal failure. By the turn of the decade, Mengistu remained in control of most of Ethiopia, but his regime's days were numbered.

ETHIOPIA POST-1990 The final nail was driven into the Derg by the collapse of European socialism in 1990. This resulted in a cutback in military aid to Mengistu, and his weakened army was finally driven completely from Tigray and Eritrea. In May 1991, the EPRDM captured Addis Ababa and Mengistu jetted to safety in Zimbabwe. The new transitional government established by the EPRDM and headed by President Meles Zenawi abandoned Mengistu's failed socialist policies, and allowed the EPLF to set up a transitional government in Eritrea. Full independence was granted to Eritrea in April 1993, following a regional referendum that attracted a 98.5% turnout, with 99.8% of votes cast in favour of secession.

Ethiopia may have been the only African country to have avoided long-term colonialism, but equally it was also one of the last to enjoy any semblance of democratic rule. The first move to correct this was taken in December 1994, when the transitional government implemented a federal constitution that divided the country into 11 electoral regions, each of which was guaranteed political autonomy on regional matters and proportional representation in a central government. This move paved the way for the country's first democratic election in May 1995, which saw Meles Zenawi voted in as prime minster alongside President Negasso Gidada (a coupling that was returned to power in the election of 2000) under a democratically elected government that was by far the most egalitarian and least repressive the country had ever known.

Ethiopia's first years of democratic rule were tainted, however, by a gradual deterioration in its relationship with neighbouring Eritrea. The first outward sign of the two countries' growing economic antagonism was the relatively innocuous Eritrean decision, in November 1997, to replace the common currency of the birr with a new currency called the nacfa. The growing estrangement between the two governments – which only ten years earlier had been fighting alongside each other against the Derg – took more concrete expression in May 1998. Up until this point, the EPLF and EPRDM had tacitly agreed that the international boundary between Eritrea and Ethiopia would adhere to the regional border under the Derg. On 6 May, however, Eritrean soldiers approached Badme, the principal town of Ethiopia's 400km^2 Yirga Triangle, provoking a police shoot-out in which both sides suffered fatalities. The joint Ethiopian–Eritrean commission that met in Addis Ababa two days later was unable to defuse the situation, and a second military skirmish followed on 12 May. Ethiopia demanded the immediate withdrawal of Eritrean troops from the Yirga Triangle. Eritrea responded by claiming that the Yirga Triangle historically belonged to Eritrea and had been effectively occupied by Ethiopia prior to the Eritrean attack.

Initially, the abrupt transformation from free border to open hostility – which surprised outside observers and locals alike – seemed unlikely to amount to more than a few border skirmishes over what was, and remains, a relatively insignificant patch of barely arable earth. On 5 June, however, the stakes were raised when Eritrean planes cluster-bombed residential parts of Mekele, including an elementary school, leaving 55 civilians dead and 136 wounded. Ethiopia retaliated swiftly by launching two airstrikes on Eritrean military installations outside Asmara. In the following week, Eritrea launched a second cluster-bomb attack on Ethiopian civilians, targeting the border town of Adigrat, and expelled an estimated 30,000 Ethiopian residents from Eritrea. Despite growing international pressure for a negotiated settlement, both parties set about amassing troops at the border – some estimates place the number as high as 200,000 on each side. Border tension erupted into full-scale military conflict in the first week of February 1999. By the end of that month, it is estimated that at least 20,000 Eritreans had been killed in the conflict, with a similar number of casualties on the Ethiopian side. The total tally of dead and wounded over the ensuing months remains a matter for conjecture; the humanitarian and economic costs of the enforced conscription, mass expulsions of each other's citizens and displacement of thousands of civilians on both sides are impossible to measure.

In part due to Ethiopia's superior diplomacy, and in part because the disputed territory had clearly been under Ethiopian jurisdiction since Eritrean independence, the OAU called for Eritrea to withdraw from all occupied Ethiopian territories on 21 June. Eritrea refused, and another bout of fighting broke out over the next week, leaving thousands more dead on both sides. Eritrea did little to help its increasingly indefensible position when its president refused to attend an OAU peace summit in Libya on 10 July. The pattern of failed attempts at diplomacy, generally initiated by Ethiopia, followed by a fresh outburst of border fighting, persisted for the remainder of 1999. One of the most pointless wars in living memory had by now taken on a significance that extended far beyond the patch of land that had provoked it, and many observers queried whether either side would ever be prepared to back down. By early 2000, a tense virtual ceasefire hung over the border, but the Eritrean government publicly announced that it would not withdraw, and was ready for further conflict. The first diplomatic breakthrough occurred in late February 2000, when the US envoy Anthony Lake and OAU special envoy Ahmed Ouyahia shuttled between Asmara and Addis Ababa in an attempt to secure a negotiated solution. Renewed conflict broke out over May and June, but by this time the Yirga Triangle was firmly back under Ethiopian control, and this final Eritrean attack resulted in an outright victory for Ethiopia, presumably the spur that drove Eritrea to the negotiating table. The ensuing Algiers conference resulted in an immediate ceasefire under the supervision of a UN peacekeeping force. On 12 December 2000 a peace agreement was signed, and the Yirga Triangle was formally restored to Ethiopian territory. Fifteen years after the ceasefire, all land borders between the two neighbouring countries remain closed, while thousands of Ethiopians formerly resident in Eritrea, and vice versa, are still exiled in their nominal home country.

Ethiopia's third general election, held in May 2005, demonstrated a mass retraction of urban support for Meles Zenawi and the Ethiopian People's Revolutionary Democratic Front (EPRDF), probably linked to the loss of economic momentum associated with the Eritrean war. The final poll results, announced almost four months after the main event following repeat elections in 32 controversial constituencies, saw the EPRDF win the third term it sought with 327 of the possible 547 seats as compared with the opposition Coalition for Unity and Democracy's 170. But this represented a dramatic swing from the 2000 election, when all but 12 seats had been held by the EPRDF. Furthermore, the opposition took all 23 seats in Addis Ababa, leaving the government without much credibility in the country's most sophisticated voting bloc. In the wake of the election, Addis Ababa and other cities were rocked by violent clashes between protesters and armed forces that left 193 civilians and six policemen dead, and prompted an EU report questioning how free and fair the election had been.

In 2007, in the midst of increasing tension between its citizenry and government, Ethiopia scaled back its millennium celebration, yet the still-planned festivities went on without major incidents. In 2010, Ethiopia went back to the polls, but the dramatic swing noted five years earlier was reversed as the ruling EPRDF claimed a landslide victory, winning 23 of the 24 parliamentary seats in Addis. While government officials hailed the election as 'free, fair and peaceful', Human Rights Watch and opposition party members reported otherwise, claiming that the ruling party had harassed and intimidated voters. The regime's poor

1

reputation with regard to press freedom and tolerance of opposition was further undermined by two wide-reaching proclamations that ostensibly tackled the threat posed by the Somali terrorist organisation Al Shabaab. Since being passed in 2009, however, the Anti-Terrorism Proclamation (ATP) has routinely been used to target apparently benign political opponents, to stifle anti-government voices, and to detain or gag local editors and journalists, while the Charities and Societies Proclamation (CSP) has restricted the activities of human rights and humanitarian concerns by outlawing any NGO that obtains more than 10% of its funds from sources outside Ethiopia.

The fourth general election, held in May 2010, saw the EPRDF reclaim ground lost in 2005 with interest. Indeed, its dominance was such that it took 499 of the 547 available seats, with the remainder mostly going to parochial regional representatives such as the Somali People's Democratic Party (24 seats), Benishangul-Gumuz People's Democratic Party (nine seats) and Afar National Democratic Party (eight seats). The reasons for this electoral about-face are difficult to ascertain, but include the breakdown of the two powerful multi-party coalitions that had represented such a threat to the status quo five years earlier, a booming economy, and an element of suppression of opposition views. Opposition parties rejected the results, claiming government intimidation of their supporters, while the election, though characterised as peaceful and calm by EU and US observers, also received criticisms from the same quarters for irregularities that fell short of international standards. Still, with 90% of eligible voters turning out on the day, the EPRDF victory evidently represented the popular will irrespective of possible gerrymandering.

Two of Ethiopia's most prominent post-Derg public figures died in 2012. On 16 August, Abune Paulos, Patriarch of the Ethiopian Orthodox Church since 1992, passed away suddenly aged 76 in Addis Ababa. Only four days later, Prime Minister Meles Zenawi died while undergoing medical treatment in Belgium. The death of Meles, aged only 57, after a full 21 years in power, sent shock waves through the country, and his ceremonious funeral at Addis Ababa's Meskel Square was attended by more than 20 African heads of state. Fears of a power vacuum following the death of Meles proved unfounded, as Hailemariam Desalegn, the deputy prime minister of two years' standing, and former President of the Southern Nations, Nationalities and Peoples' Region, stepped into the breach. The EPRDF gained another overwhelming victory in the May 2015 general election under its new leader.

Ethiopia's relationship with several neighbouring states remains uneasy as of early 2018. The Eritrean stand-off still simmers on, with Ethiopia having accused both Eritrea and Somalia of running a proxy war in the region to weaken its government. In the eastern Ogaden region, government troops have engaged in several battles with a Somali separatist organisation called Ogaden National Liberation Front (ONLF). In April 2015, the Ethiopian government declared three days of mourning after 28 Ethiopians were executed by ISIS militants in Libya, and set about repatriating hundreds of other Ethiopian citizens living in Libya with the assistance of Egypt.

Long-simmering ethnic tension erupted more violently than ever on 5 August 2016, when opposition groups called for nationwide protests against human rights abuses by the government and the ongoing political marginalisation of the Oromo, Amhara and other non-Tigrayans. At least 90 protesters were killed by security forces in the space of three days, and by the end of October the death toll had risen to more than 500. The government responded by declaring a six-month State of Emergency, the first in Ethiopia in a quarter of a century, by blocking access to Facebook and other social media sites, and by arresting at least 11,000 alleged opponents, most prominently Dr Merera Gudina, leader of the Oromo Federalist Congress, and his deputy, Bekele Gerba. Some 9,000 political prisoners were released in December, but others remained in detention and the State of Emergency was extended by another three months in March 2017. It was finally lifted in August 2017, but the protests continued, exacerbated by a series of internecine ethnic confrontations along the Oromia–Somali and Oromia–Amhara regional borders. In early 2018, renewed rioting in Oromia led to the release of several hundred high-profile political prisoners, among them Dr Gudina on 16 January and Bekele Gerba on 13 February. Prime Minister Hailemariam Desalegn also annulled the cases against these leaders, or pardoned them, 'in order to improve the national consensus and widen the democratic space'. On 14 February, Hailemariam became the first Ethiopian leader to relinquish power voluntarily when he tendered a shock letter of resignation, stating that stepping down was 'vital in the bid to carry out reforms that would lead to sustainable peace and democracy'. A fresh State of Emergency was declared in the wake of this dramatic announcement, and Desalegn stayed on as caretaker prime minister until 2 April, when a 41-year-old former intelligence officer, Abiy Ahmed Ali, was sworn in as his successor. This represented a significant changing of the guard. Not only is Abiy Ahmed a relatively young Oromo from a mixed Muslim-Christian background, but within the ruling EPRDF alliance, he is a representative of the OPDO (Oromo Peoples' Democratic Organization), the majority party in Oromia, and his appointment is widely seen as a major symbolic step towards redressing past political and economic imbalances.

While the ongoing protests have exposed the EPRDF's manifest failings when it comes to transparency, human rights and placing national unity ahead of ethnic regionalism, it has also presided over the most peaceful, democratic, progressive and egalitarian era in Ethiopia's long and often fractious history. Under its guidance, the economy has expanded beyond recognition, with an average real annual GDP growth of around 10% earning Ethiopia a consistently high ranking among the world's fastest-growing economies in the post-millennial years. Tertiary education has also been a high priority, with state universities and technical schools having been established in most major towns countrywide over the past two decades. The transport infrastructure has also been greatly expanded and improved since the millennium, with new roads being cut, old roads being surfaced, and the recent opening of a metropolitan railway in Addis Ababa together with the first of what should eventually be a vast network of intercity lines. True, much of this growth has been funded by outside investment from China, India, the USA, Europe and elsewhere, but still it is impressive and bodes well for the Ethiopian economy.

Politically, by contrast, the last two years has seen Ethiopia experience its darkest and most fractious period since the fall of the Derg, and it remains to be seen whether the EPRDF will continue with the more ethnically inclusive policy seemingly heralded by the appointment of an Oromo prime minister, or revert to the strong-arm tactics employed since the first State of Emergency was declared in late 2016. The initial signs are promising. More than 8,000 political prisoners were released during the first two months of Abiy Ahmed's tenure; and the new prime minister has also promised to lift the State of Emergency, to reform the country's repressive 'anti-terrorist' bill, to review the ethnic federalism enshrined in the current constitution, to further liberalise the economy, and to negotiate an end to the 20-year stand-off with Eritrea. Sceptics might cite all this as a classic case of a new broom sweeping clean, and an attempted assassination by hand grenade on the new prime minister at a rally in Meskel Square in June 2018 (resulting in the death of two bystanders) clearly demonstrated that not everybody is on board the

In September 2007, Ethiopia began a year-long millennium celebration, which probably had the rest of the world scratching its head. According to the Ethiopian calendar, 11 September marked the start of the year 2000. Why such a difference? For the answer you have to go back some 400 years.

In 1582, the Christian world as a whole dropped the established Julian calendar in favour of the revised Gregorian calendar. Ethiopia did not, and it never has! As a consequence, Ethiopia is seven years and eight months 'behind' the rest of the Christian world. The calendar consists of 13 months (hence the old Ethiopian Tourist Authority slogan '13 months of Sunshine'), of which 12 endure for 30 days each, while the remaining month is just five days in duration (six days in leap years).

Ethiopian New Year falls on 11 September, which means that Ethiopia is seven or eight years behind Western time, depending on whether the date is before or after 11 September. For instance, the year that we consider to be 2020 will be 2012 in Ethiopia from 1 January to 10 September, and 2013 from 11 September to 31 December. It also means that Christian holidays such as Christmas (known locally as Genna) and Easter (Fasika) fall on different dates from their European counterparts. Fortunately, most institutions that are likely to be used by tourists – banks, airline reservation offices, etc – run on the Western calendar, but you can get caught out from time to time.

The 13 Ethiopian months and the corresponding months in the Gregorian calendar are presented below. The dates in brackets are applicable only for the Ethiopian leap year.

Meskerem	September 11 (12)–October 10 (11)
Tikmt	October 11 (12)–November 9 (10)
Hidar	November 10 (11)–December 9 (10)
Tahsas	December 10 (11)–January 8 (9)
Tir	January 9 (10)–February 7 (8)
Yekatit	February 8 (9)–March 9
Megabit	March 10–April 8
Miyazya	April 9–May 8
Ginbot	May 9–June 7
Sene	June 8–July 7
Hamle	July 8–August 6
Nehase	August 7–September 5
Pagume	September 6–September 10 (11)

reformist agenda. Still, there is a strong feeling that the widespread calls for reform first voiced in the post-electoral violence of 2005 are now finally being addressed at the highest level.

GOVERNMENT AND POLITICS

Prior to 1974, Ethiopia was an empire with a feudal system of government, headed from 1930 onwards by His Imperial Majesty Haile Selassie. The emperor was deposed and killed in the 1974 revolution, after which a 'provisional' military dictatorship, known as the Derg (literally 'Committee'), was installed. In 1984,

Mengistu Haile Maryam, leader of the Derg, established the so-called Workers' Party as the sole legal party in Ethiopia. A new constitution, making Ethiopia a one-party republic with a formal president, was enacted in 1987. President Mengistu was ousted in 1991 by two rebel movements, the Ethiopian People's Revolutionary Democratic Front (EPRDF) and Eritrean People's Liberation Front (EPLF).

In 1991, a transitional government was installed by the EPRDF, which was a coalition party comprising the Tigrayan People's Liberation Front (TPLF), the Ethiopian People's Democratic Movement (EPDM) and the Oromo Peoples' Democratic Organization (OPDO). The transitional government, made up of an 87-seat Council of Representatives led by TPLF chairman Meles Zenawi, was charged with drawing up a new constitution to replace the dictatorial systems of the past with a more democratic and federal form of government.

In December 1994, Ethiopia adopted a new federal constitution that decentralised many aspects of government. The country has subsequently been divided into a revised set of nine regions and two city-states, with borders delineated along ethnolinguistic lines. The regions are constitutionally guaranteed political autonomy in most aspects of internal government, although central government remains responsible for national and international affairs and policies.

The new constitution also enforced for the first time in Ethiopian history a democratic parliamentarian government, based around two representative bodies: the Council of the People's Representatives and the Federal Council.

The head of state is the State President, who is elected for a six-year term by a two-thirds majority in a joint session of both councils and can sit for a maximum of two terms. The current president is Mulatu Teshome, whose first term started on 7 October 2013. Executive power is vested in the Prime Minister and Council of Ministers, who are elected from members of the Council of the People's Representatives. Ethiopia's first democratic election was held in May 1995 and won by the EPRDF. On 22 August of that year, the newly elected federal government embarked on its first five-year term under Prime Minister Meles Zenawi, who remained in power until his death in 2012. Meles was succeeded as prime minister by his former deputy Hailemariam Desalegn, who led the EPRDF to its fifth successive electoral victory in May 2015, but resigned dramatically in February 2018, to be replaced by the reformist Abiy Ahmed.

FEDERAL REGIONS Ethiopia has undergone several administrative reshuffles since the early 20th century, the most recent being the implementation of the current federal system in 1995. Prior to 1935 the empire (which then excluded Eritrea) was divided into 34 provinces, many of which had a strong historical or ethnic identity. During the Italian occupation, Ethiopia was jointly administered with the Italian colonies of Eritrea and Italian Somaliland, and divided into six governates. Immediately after the occupation, the imperial government reverted to the old provincial system, but with only 14 divisions, including Eritrea. Under the 1987 constitution drawn up by the Derg, the country was reorganised into 29 regions, many of which closely resembled their pre-occupation counterpart. Although these old provinces no longer possess any administrative relevance, many – such as Lasta, Wag, Shewa and Wollo – describe regions with a strong historical significance, and are still in wide local usage.

In 1995, the federal map of Ethiopia took its present-day shape with the creation of nine ethnically based regional states (*kilil*) and two chartered cities (*astedader akabibi*), all of which have far stronger federal powers than the old provinces. These federal regions are subdivided into a number of second-tier administrative entities, known as zones, many of which are also named and delineated along widely recognised ethnolinguistic lines. Third-tier administrative divisions are called *woreda*, and these are further subdivided into wards. On the whole, *woreda* names are of no interest to tourists, but a few are of historical significance, or are regularly referred to in casual use, or function as 'Special *woredas*' devoted to a particular small ethnic group and with a higher degree of autonomy than normal *woredas*.

The federal regions of Ethiopia are described below in alphabetical order.

Addis Ababa Located more or less at the dead centre of Ethiopia, and surrounded by the state of Oromia, the capital of Ethiopia is governed as a 540km^2 city-state of which less than 5% of the population is rural. According to recent government estimates, the fast-growing population of Addis Ababa now stands at around four million, but in reality it is probably significantly higher. Ethnically, almost half of Addis Ababa's cosmopolitan population is Amhara, with other major groups being Oromo (19.5%), Gurage (16%) and Tigrayan (6%). Around 75% of the city's residents are Orthodox Christians, while 16% are Muslim and 8% belong to other Christian denominations. The capital city is subdivided into ten administrative boroughs or sub-cities and 99 wards. Amharic is the working language, but English is widely spoken.

Afar Although it covers a vast area of 270,000km^2 running up the border with Djibouti and Eritrea, Afar region is arid, thinly populated and almost bereft of large towns. Recent estimates indicate a total population of four million, of which less than 10% live in urban areas. As of 2007, the regional capital is the purpose-built town of Semera, whose population is probably not much larger than 5,000. The Afar comprise roughly 90% of the regional population, while the remainder consists mostly of Amhara, Oromo and other settlers from elsewhere in Ethiopia. Geographically, Afar forms the most northerly part of the Rift Valley, and it is characterised by low-lying plains that receive less than 200mm of rainfall annually and drop to more than 100m below sea level in the Danakil Desert, which is renowned as the site of Erta Ale, a live volcano that hosts the world's oldest lava lake. The Awash River runs through Afar from south to north, draining into a set of desert lakes on the border with Djibouti. Salt and various minerals are mined in the region. Afar is perhaps the world's most palaeontologically productive region, having thrown up the world's oldest Stone Age tools, dating to 2.6 million years back, along with a plethora of hominin fossils up to 5.5 million years old.

Amhara Governed from its large modern capital city of Bahir Dar, on the southern tip of Lake Tana, Amhara covers an area of 170,752km^2 and supports a population estimated at around 23 million. Although the substantial cities of Bahir Dar, Gondar and Dessie all lie within Amhara, roughly 90% of the region's population is rural. The Amhara people for whom the state is named comprise more than 90% of the population. Other major population groups include the Awi (Agaw) and Oromo. Orthodox Christians represent 82.5% of the population, with the remainder being mostly Muslim. Several of Ethiopia's most popular historical sites lie in Amhara, most notably the former imperial capitals of Lalibela and Gondar. Simien Mountains National Park to the north of Gondar rises to the 4,533m Ras Dejen, which is Ethiopia's highest peak, and it also supports the world's greatest concentrations of the endemic gelada monkey and Walia ibex. Lake Tana, Ethiopia's largest body of water and source of the Blue Nile, also falls within Amhara, as does the Blue Nile Falls.

Benishangul-Gumuz The most obscure of Ethiopia's regions, practically never visited by tourists, is Benishangul-Gumuz, which runs for about 2,000km along the border of Sudan and South Sudan to the east of Amhara, but is on average no more than 200km wide. Relatively low-lying but with an annual rainfall in excess of 1,000mm, this remote and poorly developed area is characterised by a hot, humid climate. The regional population of around one million is governed from the small capital town of Assosa in the south.

Dire Dawa Dire Dawa is Ethiopia's second-largest city, with a population of roughly 650,000, but the administrative boundaries of the city-state cover an area of around 130km^2, boosting the total to 1.2 million. Surrounded by the region of Oromia, the dominant ethnic group of this cosmopolitan city is the Oromo (45%), but there are also substantial Amhara, Somali and Gurage populations. Amhara is the official language. The dominant religion, Islam, is adhered to by 71% of the population, while 26% are Ethiopian Orthodox and the remainder follow other Christian denominations.

Gambella The small state, which extends west from the South Sudanese border to cover 25,283km^2, comprises an area of lushly vegetated and humid lowland draining into the Baro River, an important tributary of the Nile. Relatively remote and undeveloped, Gambella region supports a predominantly rural population of fewer than 500,000 ethnically varied people. The main nationalities represented in the vicinity of the regional capital, the small river port of Gambella, are the Nuer and Anuwak, who respectively account for 47% and 21% of the regional population. Minority groups include the Mezhenger, Apana, Komo and various recent migrants from the highlands. Although the state is predominantly Christian, more than half the population subscribes to recently introduced Protestant and evangelical denominations, with the remainder adhering to Orthodox Christianity, Islam or traditional animism. Around 17% of the region is protected in the 5,061km^2 Gambella National Park, which is still home to a fair amount of wildlife.

Harari Consisting of the walled city of Harar and its immediate environs, Harari is essentially a modern revival of the autonomous city-state of Harar, which was one of the most powerful regional political entities from the 16th until the late 19th century, when it was co-opted into Abyssinia by Menelik II. The state covers an area of roughly 335km^2 and supports a population estimated at 250,000, of which more than 150,000 are city dwellers. Around 55% of the population is Oromo, with the Amhara accounting for another 23% and the Harari only 8.5%. Harar's reputation as the spiritual home of Ethiopia's Islamic community is reflected in it being the religion of almost 70% of the regional population, with various Christian denominations making up the remainder. The lush farmland around Harar is known for its *khat* and coffee plantations, but other major crops include sorghum, maize and oranges.

Oromia The vast region of Oromia covers an area of more than 284,540km^2 (almost one-third of the country) and supports a correspondingly large population of at least 35 million people. Ethnically, around 88% of the population is Oromo, and another 7% is Amhara. Aside from the 5% who still practise animist or other traditional religions, the regional split between Christians and Muslims is as good as even. The official language of Oromo, Oromifa, is transcribed with Latin script rather than the Arabic characters used elsewhere in the country. With its mostly fertile soils, Oromia is the bread basket of Ethiopia, producing more than half of the nation's agricultural crop, and it is also home to almost half of its large livestock. Geographically and climatically diverse, Oromia hosts many of Ethiopia's more alluring natural attractions, notably Bale and Awash national parks and the lakes of the Rift Valley and Bishoftu. It is rich in minerals, ranging from gold and platinum to iron ore and limestone. Oromia encircles Addis Ababa (known as Finfine in Oromifa and sometimes signposted as such within the state), and is governed from the national capital. In the year 2000, the federal administration officially relocated to Adama, but 2005 protests by the Oromo Peoples' Democratic Organization succeeded in moving the offices back to Addis Ababa.

Somali Named for the Somali people, this is the second largest of Ethiopia's federal regions, extending across 279,250km^2 east from Oromia and Afar to the border with Somalia. Much of the region is desert or semi-desert, so, despite its vast area, it supports a relatively small population of around nine million. It is an unusually homogenous region, with 96% of the population being ethnically and linguistically Somali, and almost 99% being Muslim. The capital is Jijiga, a smallish town to the east of Harar. Most of the region's residents are pastoralists. The important Wabe Shebelle River runs through the region.

Southern Nations, Nationalities and Peoples' Region Although it smells like the handiwork of a particularly uninspired committee, the name of this 105,900km^2 region does provide an accurate reflection of its incredible cultural diversity. The regional population of roughly 20 million represents some 45 different ethnolinguistic groups, the largest of which are the Sidamo (19%), Wolayta (11%), Hadiya (8%) and Gurage (7%). Religious affiliations are also very varied, with Protestants accounting for 55% of the population, Orthodox Christians 20% and Muslims 14%. As recently as 1994, some 15.5% of the population still practised traditional animist religions, but infiltration of Protestantism in particular has reduced this figure to around 6% today. The regional capital is the modern city of Hawassa, set on the shore of the eponymous lake, and much of the region lies in the relatively low-lying Rift Valley and Kenyan border area. The most important crop is coffee. Aside from the Rift Valley lakes, the most popular tourist attraction is the remote cultural tribes of South Omo Zone.

Tigray Ethiopia's most northerly region is Tigray, which covers 42,000km^2 and is administered from its capital city of Mekele. The population totals around six million, of which 95% are Orthodox Christians and the remainder Muslims. The Tigrayan people, agriculturists who also herd cattle and other livestock, are the dominant ethnic group, accounting for 96% of the regional population. A similar percentage speaks Tigrigna, a Semitic tongue more closely related than any other to the otherwise extinct liturgical language of Ge'ez used by the Ethiopian Orthodox Church. Tigray is drier than other parts of highland Ethiopia, and prone to periodic droughts, but the region is intensively cultivated and in some areas terraced. Tigray has been central to many of the more important events in Ethiopian history, from the adoption of Christianity by the Axumite emperor in the 4th century to the defeat of Italy outside Adwa 1,500 years later. The city of Axum and associated archaeological sites are the main tourist attractions, but the 120 rock-hewn churches scattered throughout the east of the country are also well worth exploring.

ECONOMY

In the early 1990s, Ethiopia was one of the world's poorest nations, with an annual per capita income of US$120, largely as a result of the low level of grass-roots and infrastructural development during the imperial and Derg eras, exacerbated by years of on-off civil unrest and famine. Since the turn of the millennium, by contrast, Ethiopia has consistently experienced one of the world's highest growth rates and, while it remains poor by global standards, the annual per capita income now stands at around US$750, while the nominal GDP of US$50 billion places it among the five largest economies in sub-Saharan Africa. Until recently, this economic boom was largely reflective of increased affluence in the newly emergent middle class, but it does also reflect a more far-reaching improvement in quality of life at all levels. Indicative of this is a sharp recent increase in average life expectancy, from 44 years in 1980 and 52 years in 2000 to 65 years in 2017. Vastly improved education and health facilities have also led to a sharp drop in the birth rate, from around 7.5% in the 1980s to 4.3% today, while the infant mortality rate, though unacceptably high at around 4.5%, is markedly improved from the early 1990s, when it still stood at above 10%.

AGRICULTURE The Ethiopian economy is dominated by agriculture, which is the primary activity of 80% of the labour force, and accounts for 45% of the GDP and 84% of exports. The Ethiopian Highlands are very fertile, and are criss-crossed by large rivers with enormous potential for irrigation projects, but many parts of the country, particularly in the east and northeast, are prone to periodic rain failures and locust plagues, so there is a regular threat of local famine.

Integral to the Ethiopian economy, coffee is the country's main cash and export crop, with 90% of production taking place in medium-altitude parts of Oromia and the Southern Nations, Nationalities and Peoples' Region (SNNPR). Following a large drop in volumes under the Derg, Ethiopia now ranks as the world's fifth-largest coffee exporter, currently producing around 400 million kilograms annually, almost 5% of the global total. Unusually, a full 98% of Ethiopia's coffee is grown by subsistence farmers, whose small but individually cultivated plots tend to produce a higher per acreage yield than the country's scattering of large state farms. All phases of production, from cultivation to drying and packaging, are done by hand in Ethiopia, and it is estimated that at least 25% of the population is directly or indirectly dependent on coffee for the bulk of its livelihood. Endemic to the forests of southwest Ethiopia, the wild coffee plant *Coffea arabica* still grows there in its natural state, while cultivation is mostly in indigenous forests or on mixed smallholdings, so it is a relatively sustainable crop and tends to have a low ecological impact.

The same cannot be said for two other important agricultural sectors, namely cotton and horticulture, both of which are thirsty, while the latter also tends to be heavily reliant on chemical fertilisers. Cotton is grown mostly on irrigated state farms in naturally dry areas such as the Awash Valley, and it is used to weave the traditional cloths for which Ethiopia is famous. Horticulture, a relatively new industry first established in 2004, is also mostly associated with large irrigated farms owned by international investors. Incredibly, within 10 years of this, horticulture generated an export income of almost US$250 million, almost 10% of the national earnings. Ethiopia has an ideal climate for horticulture, and a special government agency called the Ethiopian Horticulture Development Agency has been created to help develop the country as the world industry leader ahead of Kenya and India.

Ethiopia's other major cash crop, generating up to US$270 million annually in export revenue, despite being banned in the EU, is *khat*, which is mostly grown in the highlands around Harar for sale domestically and elsewhere in the Horn of Africa and the Arabian Peninsula. The Ethiopian Highlands are also well suited to the production of various grains, which are generally consumed domestically. Barley, corn, wheat, millet and sorghum are all widely cultivated, but Ethiopia's signature grain is *tef* (*Eragrostis tef*), a domesticated type of grass that might rank as one of the world's oldest cultivars and was until recently practically unknown elsewhere in the world. Mainly used to make *injera* 'pancakes', *tef* is Ethiopia's very own wonder-food, a protein-rich, high-fibre, gluten-free, fast-cooking grain that includes the eight amino acids most essential to humans, and also contains high levels of calcium, iron and other minerals.

Livestock is also very important role to the Ethiopian economy, accounting for about a quarter of the country's agricultural revenue. Indeed, Ethiopia is widely regarded to have the largest livestock population in Africa, amounting to more than 100 million head, with cattle accounting for about half this total, and the remainder being made up of sheep, goats, horses, mules, donkeys and camels. Meat and milk are mainly produced for the domestic market, while oxen, mules and other beasts of burden still play an essential role in transportation, ploughing and the like in the largely unmechanised subsistence agriculture sector. Hides, skins, leather and live animals are exported from Ethiopia. Integral though it is to the economy, Ethiopia's large livestock herd does put some strain on the fragile ecosystems of the Rift Valley and South Omo, whose dry-season landscapes are increasingly moulded by overgrazing. Poultry farming is widely practised but mostly for eggs rather than meat, which is seldom eaten by Ethiopians except on special days.

MINING AND INDUSTRY Ethiopia has a very small mining sector. The most important mineral for the export market is gold, revenue from which increased a hundredfold from US$5 million at the turn of the millennium to more than US$600 million today. Ethiopia is also the world's sixth-largest producer of tantalum, a rare blue-grey hard metal essential to the production of electronic devices such as mobile phones and computers. Important gas reserves are known to exist in the far southeast, but these have yet to be exploited, partly because of the area's instability. In domestic terms, the most important mining industry is the traditional salt extraction practised by the Afar in the vast salt pans that stud the remote Danakil region. Manufacturing, like mining, plays a small role in the Ethiopian economy, contributing only 5% of the GDP.

INFRASTRUCTURE In the mid 1990s, Ethiopia had one of the world's smallest infrastructures as a result of limited development outside the capital during the imperial era, and a general deterioration of facilities under the Derg. The road network, for instance, covered less than 25,000km in 1995, by comparison with more than 300,000km of roads in the UK, which then had a similar population to Ethiopia, but is five times smaller in extent. Furthermore, few asphalt roads existed outside of Addis Ababa back then – the northern circuit through Bahir Dar, Gondar, Axum and Lalibela was all unsurfaced in the mid 1990s – and many trunk routes were painfully slow going at the best of times, and positively treacherous or impassable during the rains. Today, by contrast, Ethiopia boasts a road network of more than 100,000km, and all major arteries out of Addis Ababa are either surfaced or in the process of being upgraded to asphalt. This undeniably represents an impressive overhaul over the past two decades, though Ethiopia's road network still only just scrapes into the global top 100, a low ranking for a country ranked 27th in the world in terms of area and 12th when it comes to population. Still, construction of several new roads is now under way, and the Adama Expressway, a toll road boasting three lanes in either direction, opened in 2015 and is likely to presage the construction of extended multi-lane highways east to Dire Dawa and south to Hawassa. Also on the cards is the expansion of Ethiopia's railway network, which currently comprises a newly constructed line running east from Addis Ababa to Djibouti via Dire Dawa, as well as the metropolitan line in the capital, to extend more than 5,000km along five main lines.

Ethiopia's private sector is rapidly growing but in many respects hampered by government monopolies on several key services. In some cases, for instance the domestic flight network provided by Ethiopian Airlines, these state-owned services are dynamic and well run. Others, notably electricity, most of which is derived from hydro-electric sources, are inadequate to meet the required capacity, though this is likely to change following the pending completion of the Gilgel Gibe III dam, which will add 1,870MW to Ethiopia's production capacity. The state-controlled telecommunications industry, which has a monopoly on the provision of mobile coverage and internet services, as well as landlines, is among the world's clunkiest, with network availability and broadband access lagging far behind most neighbouring countries, let alone Europe or North America.

POPULATION

The population of Ethiopia is estimated at around 108 million people, the second-highest population of any country in Africa, surpassing Egypt and exceeded only by Nigeria, and 12th in the world. The major ethnolinguistic groups are the Oromo (34.5%), Amhara (26.9%), Tigray (6.1%), Sidamo (4%) and Somali (6.2%). More than 40% of the population is aged 14 or under, and the population growth rate stands at roughly 2.5% per annum. As some measure of the effect of this rapid growth, the population was estimated at 24.2 million (excluding Eritrea) as recently as 1968, meaning it has more than quadrupled in 50 years. Back then, only 19 towns outside of Eritrea harboured more than 10,000 people, as opposed to approximately 125 such towns today. The population of Addis Ababa now stands at around four million (though some estimates are significantly higher), up from 1.6 million in 1987 and 2.3 million in 1994. Reliable population figures for other large towns do not exist, and the available estimates are somewhat variable, but other towns whose population exceeds the 200,000 mark include Dire Dawa, Adama, Gondar, Dessie, Mekele, Bahir Dar, Jimma, Bishoftu, Hawassa and Harar.

LANGUAGE

Ethiopia supports a diverse mix of linguistic groups. Some 70 languages are spoken in Ethiopia, most of them belonging to the Semitic or Cushitic branches of the Afro-Asiatic family. The most important Semitic languages are Amharigna (Amharic) and Tigrigna of northern Ethiopia, both of which are related to and possibly descend from Ge'ez, the language of ancient Axum, which is still used by the Ethiopian Orthodox Church. The Gurage and Zay of southern Ethiopia also speak Semitic languages, as do the people of Harar in the east. Amharigna was the official language of Ethiopia under Mengistu and it remains the lingua franca in most parts of the country that are likely to be visited by tourists. These Semitic languages are transcribed in Ge'ez or Ethiopic script, an *abugida* (syllable alphabet) that evolved around the 9th century AD from the ancient *abjad* (consonant-only alphabet) used by the pre-Axumite and Axumite civilisations of ancient Tigray.

Ethiopian churches have probably been decorated with wall paintings ever since the introduction of Christianity in the mid 4th century. The antiquity of this ecclesiastic art tradition is confirmed in an account by 7th-century followers of the Prophet Muhammad who fled to Axum to escape persecution, and describe its original church of Maryam Tsion (which has not survived to our day) as being decorated with paintings.

The oldest Ethiopian churches with extant paintings are probably Debre Selam Mikael in Tigray, which dates from the 11th or 12th century, and the 12th-century Yemrehanna Kristos near Lalibela. The life of Jesus is the dominant theme in these early paintings, which art historians believe to share Byzantine and Coptic connections.

Other early examples can be seen in the rock-hewn churches of Bete Maryam in Lalibela and nearby Geneta Maryam, which date to the 12th and 13th centuries respectively. In these churches, especially Geneta Maryam, the subject matter has expanded so that alongside the usual biblical themes we find influences from other sources, including an abundance of images of animals such as elephant and ostrich.

Of those 14th- and 15th-century Ethiopian churches that weren't destroyed during the Muslim–Christian conflict of the 16th century, most are rock-cut edifices set in the cliffs of Tigray. Paintings from this period include some of the earliest representations of Ethiopian saints, for instance the portrait of Abba Samuel in the 15th-century church of Debre Tsion.

Most Ethiopian churches built during the 16th and 17th centuries comprised a circular outer wall enclosing a quadrangular Holy of Holies, with the four walls of the latter being decorated from top to bottom with paintings. Over this period, the presentation of religious themes became increasingly standardised, so that any two churches built in different parts of Ethiopia from the 18th century onwards tend to have similar themes, layouts, iconographies and styles. Typically,

Known locally as Fidel, the syllable alphabet consists of 33 basic characters, with each of the 26 consonants taking seven different forms depending on which, if any, vowel is to be pronounced after it.

Cushitic languages are dominant in southern and eastern Ethiopia. The most significant of these is Oromifa, the language of the Oromo, Ethiopia's largest ethnic group. The Somali language also belongs to the Cushitic group. Ethiopia's Cushitic speakers transcribe their language using the same Roman alphabet that we do, but with liberal use of double vowels or consonants that theoretically designate variations in pronunciation but in practice seem to be pretty random (in any given town, you might for instance see the Oromo word for hotel transcribed as 'hoteela', 'hooteela', 'hotteella' and other variants thereof). In the Omo river valley, a localised group of languages of Afro-Asiatic origin are spoken. These are known as Omotic languages and are quite closely affiliated to the Cushitic group. Along the western border with Sudan, languages are mostly of the unrelated Nilotic group.

It should be noted that linguistic terms need not imply anything about ethnicity. Many British people with a purely Celtic genealogy, or Afro-Americans for that matter, speak only English, which is a language of the West Germanic branch of the Indo-European group. However, linguistic patterns are the best means available to scientists for tracing the broad sweep of prehistoric population movements, and in some instances – for instance the Oromifa-speaking Oromo – there is a strong association between language and a cohesive ethnic identity. Nevertheless, the

the western and eastern walls relate to the life of Jesus, while equestrian saints dominate the northern wall, and the southern wall is given over to the Virgin Mary.

Post-17th-century church painting also witnessed considerable Ethiopianisation of both subject matter and style. Ethiopian saints such as Tekle Haymanot, Ewstatewos and Abo were regularly depicted during this period, usually near the bottom of the wall, below other non-Ethiopian figures, apparently for theological reasons. By the 17th century, it had also become conventional for bad characters to be portrayed in profile or with one eye.

We also see some Jesuit influences in post-17th-century church art. The Jesuits are known to have brought with them a copy of a well-known European image of the Virgin Mary carrying Jesus on her left hand. This model became the standard iconography in Ethiopia thereafter.

In earlier churches, especially rock-cut ones, paintings used locally sourced pigments applied on a whitewash as fresco. By contrast, the paintings in later churches were made on canvas that was then plastered to the wall, and imported chemical paints were gradually introduced. Although in some cases we know the name of the artist, in most cases the art is anonymous.

Visitors with a strong interest in ecclesiastical art should head to the Lake Tana region, which hosts a wealth of accessible and profusely decorated churches. The oldest, dating to the 1620s, is Gorgora's Debre Sina Maryam. Other superbly painted churches in the Tana region include Ura Kidane Mihret on the Zege Peninsula, Narga Selassie on Dek Island, and Debre Berhan Selassie in Gondar. For older paintings, the rock churches in Lalibela and Tigray need to be visited.

Dawit Teferi is a travel specialist and independent researcher, and can be reached at e dawitunderstanding@yahoo.com.

exclusive use of a Semitic language in Tigray need not mean that all Tigrayan people are of Semitic origin. Just as one would not refer to an English-speaking American as English, it is more accurate to speak of Cushitic or Semitic speakers, rather than Cushites or Semites. It's a semantic point, but one which is often misunderstood, particularly in the African context, where racial characters are frequently but erroneously assigned to people on a purely linguistic basis.

RELIGION

Ethiopia might well be unique among countries outside the Middle East insofar as all three of the major Abrahamic religions – Judaism, Christianity and Islam – have a strong historical presence there. Until recently, a population of indigenous Ethiopian Jews, known as the Beta Israel (or derogatorily as the Falasha), was concentrated in the part of Amhara region formerly administered as Gojjam and Wollo provinces. In medieval times, the Beta Israel were a major force in Ethiopia's internal politics, but several centuries of warfare and persecution had reduced their numbers greatly by the late 20th century, and the 30,000 individuals who survived were airlifted to Israel in the last decade of the Derg's rule. A few isolated Beta Israel communities reputedly inhabit the remote mountains of Lasta district in eastern Amhara.

The main religions in Ethiopia today are Christianity and Islam. Roughly 44% of Ethiopians belong to the Ethiopian Orthodox Church, while another 19% are

Catholic or Protestant, and 34% are Muslim. The remainder mostly adhere to one or other traditional non-Abrahamic belief system. Broadly speaking, but far from rigidly so, the Ethiopian Orthodox Church dominates in the north and west, while Catholicism and Protestantism are bigger in the south, and Islam is the main religion in the east.

The most prominent faith in Ethiopia is undoubtedly the Ethiopian Orthodox Tewahedo Church (EOTC; w *ethiopianorthodox.org*), a decidedly singular institution often but erroneously referred to by outsiders as the Coptic Church, from which it is largely derived. The Coptic Church is an Egyptian Church (*coptic* is an Ancient Greek word meaning 'Egyptian'), which took shape in Alexandria in the 2nd and 3rd centuries AD, and broke away from Rome and Constantinople in AD451 following its adoption of the contentious Monophysitic doctrine, which asserted the single and primarily divine nature of Christ, and was considered heretical by Rome and Constantinople, whose Dualistic philosophy held that Christ had discrete human and divine personalities. The EOTC was founded in Axum in the 4th century AD and its first bishop, Frumentius, was consecrated in Alexandria. Strong ties have always existed between the churches of Ethiopia and Alexandria, and until 1955 the Ethiopian Church *technically* fell under Alexandria's governance. Within Ethiopia, however, it was the Abbot of Debre Libanos and not the archbishop sent from Alexandria who assumed the role of EOTC primate. Since 1955, the EOTC has been self-governing, with its own seat on the World Council of Churches. So, while the EOTC, like the much less numerically significant Coptic Church, practises a Monophysitic form of Christianity, bracketing the two together seems like an all-too-common example of outsiders being reluctant to recognise any institution unique to sub-Saharan Africa.

Even the most casual familiarity with the customs of the EOTC confirms it to be a most singular institution, far further removed from the Coptic Church than most Western denominations are from each other. Apart from the odd emissary from Alexandria, Ethiopian Christianity developed in virtual isolation until the arrival of the Portuguese Jesuits in the 15th century and, although its fundamentals are indisputably Christian, the rituals are infused with all sorts of archaic Judaic influences. Male circumcision is prescribed a few days after birth, for instance, while women are governed by a variety of menstruation taboos. The EOTC also holds regular fasting days, it recognises both the conventional Christian Sabbath of Sunday and the Jewish Sabbath of Saturday, and it indulges in religious dances considered blasphemous by other Christian denominations. Academic consensus tends towards the theory that these customs were acquired through the influence of the Beta Israel and other ancient Jewish sects that lived in pre-Christian Ethiopia. However, it might as easily be the case that the EOTC is simply truer to the very earliest forms of Christianity, which did after all evolve from Judaism, than is any European denomination.

At the heart of Ethiopian mysticism lies an unfathomable, and rather fascinating, relationship between Christianity and the Ark of the Covenant, the very core of Judaism until its apparent disappearance from Jerusalem led to the reforms of Josiah in around 650BC. Ethiopians believe that the original Ark was brought to Axum in the 1st millennium BC and that it rests there to this day. What's more, the most holy item in every Ethiopian church is the *tabot* – a replica of the Ark (or, more accurately, a replica of one of the Tablets of the Law which were placed in the Ark by Moses). The *tabot* is only removed from the Holy of Holies on important religious days, and it is at all times obscured from view by a cover of draped sheets.

EDUCATION

Although Ethiopia has supported literate societies for almost 3,000 years, the provision of education and use of the written word was strongly linked to religious institutions, notably the Ethiopian Orthodox Church, but also Islamic and Protestant/Catholic missionary schools, throughout the imperial era. This shortcoming was nominally addressed towards the end of Haile Selassie's reign but, even as recently as the early 1970s, the national population, which then stood at around 30 million, was serviced by a mere 1,300 primary and secondary schools (one for every 10,000 school-age children). As a result, when the Derg assumed power, the national literacy rate stood below 10%, with females and rural dwellers being particularly poorly served by the limited educational infrastructure. Opportunities for secular tertiary education were more or less restricted to Addis Ababa's Haile Selassie I University, which was established by imperial charter in 1961, and a private university in Asmara (Eritrea). In 1975, the Derg launched a national literacy campaign, sending around 60,000 urban students and teachers to smaller towns and rural areas for two-year terms of service, but this had a limited impact, in part because the implanted teachers were suspected of being government spies. The Derg also adopted a policy theoretically offering free primary education to every citizen, though in practice it lacked the facilities to implement this ideal. Educational curricula were developed with the assistance of various Eastern European governments, in keeping with its slogan 'Education for production, for research and for political consciousness'. All the same, the schooling expectation of a newborn child was still less than three years at the end of the Derg era, while the literacy rate stood at around 25%. The situation has improved greatly under the EPRDF, though the adult literacy rate is still among the lowest in the word, currently standing at around 50% (compared with more than 80% in the likes of Kenya or Tanzania). There also remains a strong gender imbalance, with literacy among males significantly higher than it is for women. However, these figures are distorted somewhat by historical factors, as a huge post-millennial increase in primary school attendance (the net enrolment rate stands at almost 90%, while schooling expectation is eight years) means the literacy rate in the 15–24-year age group is far higher than the national average, and this is likely to keep improving as new generations of scholars mature. Tertiary education has been a high priority under the EPRDF, with some 40 towns countywide now being served by state universities.

MUSIC

Practically unknown to the rest of the world, the music of Ethiopia, in common with so many other aspects of this insular highland country, sounds like nothing you've ever heard before. True enough, on initial contact, many outsiders find the trademark lurching three-four signature, twitchy cross-rhythms, brassy instrumentation, taut pentatonic melodies and nail-on-blackboard vocal affectations somewhat impenetrable, I daresay even a little irritating. But while repeated exposure won't make converts of us all, Ethiopia's diverse blend of the traditional and the contemporary, and of exotic and indigenous styles, must rank as one of Africa's greatest undiscovered musical legacies, reaching its apex with the ceaselessly inventive and hypnotically funky horn-splattered sides of 'Ethiopian swing' recorded for a handful of independent labels in Addis Ababa between 1969 and 1978.

The roots of the music scene that blossomed in Addis Ababa during the dying years of the imperial era are predictably peculiar. It all started in April 1924, when Ras Tefari, then acting as regent for the Empress Zewditu, made a state visit to Jerusalem and was received by a brass band consisting of Armenian orphans. Who knows whether it was the actual music that caught the future emperor's attention, or simply the plight of his fellow Orthodox Christians, who had fled their homeland to escape the genocide perpetrated by their Islamic Turkish neighbours in 1915? Either way, the Arba Lijotch (Forty Children), as they came to be known affectionately by their hosts, arrived in Addis Ababa in September of that year to form the first imperial brass band under the tutelage of long-time Armenian-born Ethiopian-resident music professor Kevork Nalbandian.

The underpaid Arba Lijotch disbanded of its own accord in July 1928. But the foundation stone had been laid for the permanent Imperial Bodyguard Band formed in 1929 under the leadership of Swiss orchestra leader Andre Nicod. Comprising a few dozen arbitrarily chosen slaves from Wollega, the original Imperial Bodyguard Band was by all accounts more notable for its noisiness than its aptitude, but its limited repertoire of stuffy marches nevertheless became something of a fixture at important imperial occasions, and some genuine talent soon started to emerge from the ranks prior to the Italian occupation of 1935. The occupation formed something of a low watermark for the fortunes of Ethiopian musicians, many of whom were imprisoned, in particular the traditional *azmari* minstrels whose subversive lyrics used the time-honoured *sem ena work* (wax and gold) technique of using double entendre or coded language within love songs as a vehicle for stinging political innuendo.

The reinstatement of Haile Selassie after six years in exile was soon followed by the creation of a new Imperial Bodyguard Band under Kevork Nalbandian, who handed over the reins to his equally influential nephew Nerses Nalbandian in 1949. From the mid 1940s to the late 1950s, a succession of foreign music teachers such as Alexander Kontorowicz and Franz Zelwecker were hired to run academies whose graduates went on to play in an ever-growing number of brass-oriented orchestras, all of which – oddly enough – were effectively on the payroll of one or other imperial institution, be it the police, the military or even Addis Ababa municipality. Despite this, the musical vocabulary of these brass bands gradually expanded by exposure to exotic new styles such as jazz, R&B and soul, which were broadcast around the country from the American military radio station in Asmara.

So the scene was set for the explosion of musical fecundity that peaked during the edgy, uncertain, exciting years that separated the failed coup of 1960 from its more consequential 1974 sequel. As was the case elsewhere in the world, the 1960s witnessed immense social changes in Addis Ababa, underlain by the growing sense of the imperial regime as an illiberal, outmoded and ultimately doomed institution. This realisation, initially confined to the educated classes in major urban centres such as Addis Ababa, Asmara and Dire Dawa, though it would spread into rural areas by the early 1970s, stemmed partly from the challenge that the failed coup of 1960 had presented to the notion of imperial immortality. But it was also doubtless associated with the increased exposure to an outside world that was itself changing rapidly, as more and more outsiders became affiliated with broadly left-of-centre institutions such as the Organization of African Unity, Non-Alignment Pact and American Peace Corps, which made Ethiopia their temporary home.

Sadly, the evocative monochrome photographs collected in Francis Falceto's book *Abyssinie Swing* are practically all that remain of the wild R&B-influenced sounds and hedonistic nightclubs that partied until the early morning during the heady early years of the so-called Golden Age of Ethiopian Music. In 1948, the emperor had passed legislation that effectively granted the state-run Hagere Fiker Maheber an exclusive licence to import and produce gramophone records. But this no doubt worthy institution (literally 'The Love of Country Association') concentrated its best efforts on recording dull state events and the like for posterity. As a result, those of us who weren't there can only guess what the music of this era actually sounded like, but mid 1960s photographs of rows of future recording stars such as Mahmoud Ahmed and Tlahoun Gessesse harmonising in finger-clicking unison suggest a greater dependence on vocal harmonies than is evident on the recorded material that would eventually emerge from 'Swinging Addis'.

For the modern audiophile, Ethiopia's musical golden age effectively began in 1969, when Amha Eshete, manager of the country's first non-institutional band, the Soul Echoes, decided to risk imperial wrath and form his own independent label, Amha Records. Despite some initial rumblings from Hagere Fiker Maheber, Amha

Compiled by Ethiopian music expert Francis Falceto, the ever-expanding series of *Ethiopiques* CDs released by French label Buda is of particular significance for making available a vast number of old vinyl recordings that had been out of print since the 1970s. Available in specialist CD shops, the full series, which now numbers 30 volumes, can also be ordered online through the label's website (w *budamusique.com*) or other online retailers such as Amazon. Better still, several volumes can be downloaded from iTunes or more cheaply and no less legally from w emusic.com, a superb site that focuses on non-mainstream recordings.

Highlights of the series – there aren't really any lowlights – include *Ethiopiques 1* and *Ethiopiques 3*, which anthologise some of the most popular tracks released by Amha Records between 1969 and 1975, providing an excellent overall introduction to the era's leading artists such as Mahmoud Ahmed, Girma Beyene, Muluqen Mellesse, Hirut Bekele, Alemayehu Eshete and Tlahoun Gessesse. Either set is a great starting point.

Better still in my opinion, not least for its greater focus on female artists such as the sublime Bizunesh Bekele (the uncrowned 'First Lady' of Swinging Addis) and her unrelated namesake Hirut Bekele, is *Ethiopiques 13: Ethiopian Groove*. This is a re-release of an early 1990s collection of Kaifa's 1976–78 output, also compiled by Francis Falceto, and its present format is marred only by the criminal absence of the trio of early Aster Aweke recordings that ranked as highlights of the original.

Ethiopiques 5 performs a similar round-up of some of the best Tigrigna recordings made by prominent Eritrean artists of the same era, such as Tewelde Redda, Tekli Tesfa-Ezghi and the irresistibly nicknamed Tebereh 'Doris Day' Tesfa-Hunegn. Aside from the linguistic difference, much of this music has a more traditional, drum-based sound than its Amharigna equivalent, and the melodies, based on the same pentatonic scale, are often punctuated by yelps, chants and the wild ululation characteristic of African tribal music from the Cape to the Horn.

was allowed to operate freely and it positively thrived, releasing an average of 20 45rpm singles and two LPs annually, and launching the recording careers of the likes of Mahmoud Ahmed, Muluqen Mellesse, Hirut Bekele, Alemayehu Eshete, Getachew Kassa and Tlahoun Gessesse prior to its closure in 1975. By that time, however, two other labels inspired by Amha were also thriving, Philips Ethiopia and Kaifa Records, the latter formed by the highly influential and long-serving Ali Abdullah Kaifa, better known as Ali Tango. The 500-odd two-track recordings produced by these independent labels collectively form practically the only aural record of the Ethiopian music scene during the last two decades of the imperial era, and it also constitutes the bulk of the music re-released on the *Ethiopiques* CDs since the late 1990s by French label Buda.

So, what did it sound like? Well, on one level, it was strongly derivative of contemporary Western music, as hinted at by the nicknames of popular artists such as the Asmara-based singers Tebereh 'Doris Day' Tesfa-Hunegn and Tukabo 'Mario Lanza' Welde-Maryam. Even the most cursory listen to a few tracks by Alemayehu Eshete, the so-called 'Abyssinian Elvis', suggests a more than passing familiarity with the extended funk workouts of James Brown's backing band, while jazz buffs liken the blazing saxophone work of Getachew Mekurya to Albert Ayler and Ornette Coleman. Elsewhere, you'll hear hints of Stax, Motown, early rock 'n' roll, pop, fusion jazz, hippy-era blues-rock bands such as Santana and Chicken Shack,

The 1970s recordings of Mahmoud Ahmed feature exclusively on *Ethiopiques 6* and *7*. *Ere Mela Mela* is something of a legend as the first Western release by any Ethiopian artist, and it earned rave reviews in the likes of *NME* and the *New York Times*. Other dedicated single-artist releases in the series include *Ethiopiques 9* (funky 'Abyssinian Elvis' Alemayehu Eshete) and *Ethiopiques 14* (revered jazz-influenced saxophonist Getachew Mekurya).

For those with an ear for the more traditional forms, a highly recommended starting point is *Ethiopiques 2*, an anthology of *azmari* and *bolel* singers working the *tej bets* and bars of Addis Ababa. Very different but equally engaging is *Ethiopiques 18: The Lady with the Krar*, a collection of beautiful traditional *azmari* renditions on a lyre-like instrument called a *krar* by former actress Asnaqech Werku – as a bonus, English and French translations of the pithy lyrics are provided with the CD. An excellent new addition to the series, released in 2014, *Ethiopiques 29: Mastawesha* collects 13 lovely 1970s recordings, mostly backed only with a *krar*, by traditional singer Kassa Tessema. Going deeper back still, *Ethiopiques 27: Centennial of the First Ethiopian Music Recordings* is a two-CD collection of the 32 songs recorded by the *azmari* Tessema Eshete in Berlin way back in 1910.

If you're looking to cherry-pick a few *Ethiopiques* tracks to download, here's my selection: 'Ete Endenesh Gedawo' by Muluqen Mellesse (vol 1), 'Yeqer Memekatesh' by Mahmoud Ahmed (vol 1), 'Tezeta' by Seyfu Yohannis (vol 1), 'Bolel' by Zawditu and Yohannis (vol 2), 'Temeles' by Alemayehu Eshete and Hirut Bekele (vol 3), 'Ab Teqay Qerebi' by Tewelde Redda (vol 5), the rocksteady-tinged 'Ewnetegna Feger' by Hirut Bekele (vol 13), the wonderfully haunting 'Ateqegn' by Bizunesh Bekele (vol 13), 'Yegenet Muziqa' by Getachew Mekurya (vol 14) and 'Fegrie Denna Hun' by Asnaqech Werku (vol 17). Or try the two-CD set *The Very Best of Ethiopiques*, which was compiled in 2007 from the first 20 volumes.

and even – in the late 1970s – ska and reggae. But such influences are superficial, as almost every track recorded during this period also displays that distinctively Ethiopic combination of a lopsided rat-a-tat shuffle, uneasy Arabic-sounding pentatonic shifts and strained, quavering, rather nasal vocals. The result, in most instances, is at once edgy and hypnotic, mournful yet danceable, propulsive yet jerky – above all, perhaps, very strange. The recordings of Alemayehu Eshete, for instance, don't really sound like James Brown so much as they evoke the improbable notion of the Godfather of Soul in his funky late 60s pomp being asked to perform an Islamic prayer call!

Over 1974–75, the imperial era came to its final, bloody conclusion, and Swinging Addis collapsed with it, to be replaced by the joyless socialist diktats of the Derg. The live music scene in particular was muted, thanks to an overnight curfew that endured for a full 16 years. The pioneering Amha Records closed in 1975, and its owner left Addis Ababa for the USA. All the same, Ethiopia in the late 1970s wasn't quite the musical wasteland it is sometimes portrayed to have been. Kaifa Records thrived on the demand for fresh recordings to accompany the surreptitious lock-in parties that replaced the nightclub scene of years earlier. Indeed, some of the label's finest vinyl releases date to 1976–78, as anthologised on the out-of-print 16-track CD *Ethiopian Groove: The Golden 70s* (recently reissued with an altered track listing as *Ethiopiques 13*). Furthermore, from 1978 onwards, Kaifa switched its attention

The most consistently popular Ethiopian recording artist since she first appeared on the scene in the late 1970s is Gondar-born, California-based Aster Aweke, who enjoys such a high profile among her compatriots that it would have been remarkable to go a full day in any Ethiopian city on any trip I undertook there from 1994 to 2017 without hearing what *The Rough Guide to World Music* describes as 'a voice that kills'. It is certainly one of the most thrilling vocal instruments ever to have emerged from Africa, pitched somewhere among Aretha Franklin (a stated influence), Kate Bush and Björk, with a fractured but raunchy quality that can be utterly heartbreaking.

The closest thing Ethiopia has produced to a genuine crossover artist, Aster has 20 albums, though her earliest – and some say best – material for Kaifa is available only on hard-to-track-down cassettes in Addis Ababa (and long overdue the attention of *Ethiopiques*). Ten albums are available on CD, of which *Aster* is frequently recommended as the best starting point, for reasons that elude me – aside from the standout acoustic rendition of the chestnut 'Tizita', one of her most compelling recordings ever, it is typified by bland mid-tempo backings and unusually muted vocal performances. My first choice would be the 1993 album *Ebo*, which is distinguished by the propulsive growling opening blast of 'Minu Tenekana', the twitchy, wide-eyed 'Esti Inurbet', and a trio of fine ballads: the wracked 'Yene Konjo', the hauntingly melodic 'Yale Sime' and the pretty but overlong 'Yewah Libane'.

Heir apparent to Aster's long-standing international status as Ethiopia's best-known singer is 34-year-old Ejigayehu Shibabaw, who embarked on a solo career under her more concise nickname of Gigi after stints singing and performing in Kenya, France and South Africa. Gigi is an acknowledged disciple of Aster (in

from vinyl to the cheaper medium of cassettes, resulting in sales of greater than 10,000 copies for a popular release, as opposed to around 3,000 vinyl copies. It was in 1978, too, that a Gondarine teenage prodigy named Aster Aweke (see box above) – destined to become arguably the greatest recorded female vocalist ever produced by Africa – cut a pair of debut 45rpm singles for Kaifa, followed by five full-length cassettes, before relocating to the USA in 1981.

All the same, the dawn of the cassette era does seem to have coincided with a slump in innovative musicianship. Music was recorded prolifically under the Derg, it still sold well, and the likes of Aster Aweke and Mahmoud Ahmed produced some superb vocal performances. But, linked perhaps to the demise of the live music scene and emigration of many of the country's finest musicians, the punch and elasticity that characterised the backing bands captured on Amha and Kaifa's vinyl releases gradually gave way to a more stodgy and synthetic will-that-do? style of backing that detracted from even the most evocative singing. More encouragingly, potential breakthrough artist Gigi (see box above) has reverted to a warmer, more organic live sound on her recent recordings, while several other newcomers attempt to use synthesised backings creatively. Recent years have also seen a resurgence of traditional music in the form of Addis Ababa's *bolel* singers, who mix the pithy sarcasm and grumbling bluesiness of the ancient *azmari* minstrels with more contemporary cultural and political observations.

Today there still exists a little-known trove of what might be termed 'classical' Ethiopian music from the highlands. It is based on a modal system called *qenet*, a 2004 interview with *AfriPOP!*, she states, 'If it wasn't for [Aster] I wouldn't be a singer. I was so much in love with her music and I still love her'), and she possesses a similarly haunting voice, though admittedly it's not quite so strung out or fractured.

Gigi's first album *One Ethiopia* (downloadable from w emusic.com) is likeable enough without being hugely distinguished, but her second eponymous album, which features contributions from the likes of jazz musicians Herbie Hancock, Wayne Shorter, Bill Laswell, Pharaoh Sanders and various traditional Ethiopian musicians, is a stunner. Released in 2001, *Gigi*'s appeal lies in its organic, eclectic sound, which sets typical Amharigna vocal inflections against a rich fusion of jazz, reggae and other African styles – had I heard standout track 'Bale Washintu' blind, for instance, I would have assumed it originated from Mali rather than Ethiopia. The follow-up *Zion Roots*, released in 2004, is also worth a listen, as is the 2010 live recording *Mesgana Ethiopia*.

The release of *Gigi* inspired *AfriPOP!* to proclaim its namesake as 'the most important new African singer on the scene today', while the *New York Times* rated it number one in a year-end round-up of the 'Best Obscure Albums of 2001'. Meanwhile, its bold experimentation across genres and the use of a song traditionally reserved for male singers has drawn criticism from conservative elements in Ethiopian society. But one person who evidently listened favourably is Aster, whose sublime 2004 release *Aster's Ballads* (re-recordings of 12 self-penned classics, many otherwise unavailable except on cassette) has a strikingly fresh and intimate sound, with the tinny keyboard fills that characterise her other CD releases replaced by a warmer, earthier ambience. Her latest two albums, *Checheho (2010)* and *Ewedhalew (2013),* have a similarly contemporary production.

a word that could be translated as scales, or even colourings (like the Hindi word *raga*). There are four main *qenets*: Tizita connotes reminiscence and nostalgia; Ambassel sounds often grandiose and invocatory as it celebrates history; Bati is connected to the central eastern region bearing the same name; Anchihoye is definitely festive.

Nowadays, Tizita is by far the most popular genet, and many contemporary singers, including Mahmoud Ahmet, Kuku Sebsebe or Beza Work, are famous for their interpretations of it. Tradition also requires that the first melody sung on stage should be a Tizita.

Since the new millennium, Ethiopian music has continued to evolve with the emergence of a number of new artists who have garnered attention both locally and internationally, and a cocktail of contemporary international influences – hip hop, R&B, electronic and to a lesser extent reggae or salsa – all becoming more prevalent in the home-grown sounds you hear blasting from speakers in bars, restaurants and shops. Stepping out in 2001, Teddy Afro (real name Tewodros Kassahun) has quickly become one of the most successful, and controversial, singers and songwriters in post-millennial Ethiopia. Born to artistic parents – his mother was a well-known professional dancer and his late father a highly regarded Ethiopian songwriter – Teddy's politically and socially motivated songs from his third album, *Yasteseryal* (2005), became the anthem for anti-government protests in 2005. Afro was accused of hit-and-run manslaughter and imprisoned in April 2008, a charge that some sources claim was politically motivated, convicted of manslaughter in

December 2008, and released from prison eight months later. His fourth album, *Tikur Sew* (2012), once again attracted controversy by championing Emperor Menelik II as a pan-African hero for his victory over Italy at Adwa.

Ethiopia's first home-grown reggae artist, Jonny Ragga (Yohannes Bekele), released his first solo album, *Give Me the Key*, in 2005. The singer, who hails from Addis Ababa, has collaborated with several international artists including American R&B artist K'alyn and South African rapper Zola, and has won several awards, including first place at the Fes'Horn Music Festival in Djibouti in 2006. Another newish arrival is R&B singer Helen Berhe (aka the Ethiopian Beyoncé), who is best known for her cover of Nada Algesa's 'Uzaza Allina' and in 2010 released her album *Tasfelegnaleh* (I Need You). Ethiopian music has increased its global reach in recent years, providing the main inspiration for the inventive fusion of London-based Dub Colossus, whose albums *A Town Called Addis* (2008) and *Addis through the Looking Glass* (2015) infuse classic Ethio-pop and jazz with elements such as reggae and dub. Another modern take on classic Ethiopian sounds can be heard on *Sketches of Ethiopia*, a 2013 release of fresh recordings by jazz multi-instrumentalist Mulatu Astatke, a founding figure of the Swinging Addis era, and perhaps its only active veteran.

In addition to the recordings mentioned in the boxes on pages 56 and 58, a good entry-level compilation of Ethiopian sounds is the *Rough Guide to Ethiopian Music*, which was released in 2004 and includes tracks by artists including Aster Aweke, Mahmoud Ahmed and Alemayehu Eshete. It was followed up by the more contemporary *Rough Guide to Ethiopian Music* (featuring the likes of Dub Colossus and Bole2Harlem alongside more typical golden-era staples) in 2012, and the stylistic focused *Rough Guide to Ethiopian Jazz* in 2016.

It should also be said that Addis Ababa has one of the most stimulating, animated and varied live music scenes of any African capital (see box, page 170).

ETHIOPIAN NAMES

Ethiopians have a different system of naming from most Western countries, one that resembles the Islamic system. As is customary in the West, the first name of any Ethiopian is their given name. The difference is that the second name of any Ethiopian is not an inherited family name, but simply the father's given name. In other words, an Ethiopian man called Belay Tadesse is not Belay of the Tadesse family, but Belay the son of Tadesse, and he would be addressed as Belay. It is polite to address people older than you, or whom you respect, as Ato (Mister) or Waziro (Mrs). Again, you would use the person's own name, not their father's name – Belay Tadesse would be addressed not as Ato Tadesse but as Ato Belay. If Ato Belay has a daughter who is named Genet, she will be known as Genet Belay. If she marries somebody called Bekele Haile, her name won't change to Genet Haile but will stay Genet Belay. She would be addressed as Waziro Genet and her husband as Ato Bekele. If they have a child they name Yohannes, he will be known as Yohannes Bekele.

It is worth noting that Ethiopians will not ask for your surname but for your father's name. When dealing with officials, you should obviously give the parental name on your passport – your surname. You will also find that, even in the most formal of situations, Ethiopians address Westerners according to their custom rather than ours – I am often addressed as Ato or Mister Philip, never by my surname.

ETHIOPIA ONLINE

For additional online content, articles, photos and more on Ethiopia, why not visit **w** bradtguides.com/ethiopia?

2

Wildlife Guide

For wildlife enthusiasts, Ethiopia is a bit of a mixed bag. The once prolific large mammal fauna has been heavily hunted over the centuries, and even those national parks that do protect typical African savannah environments support low volumes of wildlife by comparison with the continent's top safari destinations. Balanced against this, Ethiopia has a unique transitional geographic location that means its fauna, though essentially typical of sub-Saharan Africa, also incorporates elements from the Palaearctic region. This is manifested in the presence of several oddball creatures endemic to Ethiopia, among them the Ethiopian wolf, Walia ibex, gelada monkey, mountain nyala and at least 16 bird species. Indeed, whatever Ethiopia might lack in mammalian abundance, it is one of Africa's key birdwatching destinations, with a national checklist of 920-plus species that incorporates more than 50 Horn of Africa endemics that are logistically difficult or impossible to see anywhere else in the world.

MAMMALS

Ethiopia supports a comparable variety of large mammals to countries such as Kenya and Tanzania, but populations are generally low, with many species being restricted to relict pockets in remote areas. Because game viewing is not a major feature of tourism in Ethiopia, detailed descriptions of appearance and behaviour here are restricted to endemics and other species of special interest. For species seen more readily in other parts of Africa, coverage is limited to details of known or probable distribution and status within Ethiopia. This section should thus be seen as an Ethiopia-specific supplement to any of the continental field guides recommended on page 647.

CARNIVORES Ethiopia's most numerous large carnivore is the **spotted hyena** (*Crocuta crocuta*), which tends to favour thinly populated and lower-lying parts of the country, but also scavenges on the outskirts of some towns. Wild hyenas are most likely to be seen near Aga Edu Cave in Awash National Park and in the Dera-Dilfekar sector of Arsi Mountains National Park. The so-called hyena man of Harar lures a few semi-habituated spotted hyenas to a feeding place outside town every evening. The related **striped hyena** (*Hyaena hyaena*) and **aardwolf** (*Proteles cristata*) also occur in Ethiopia but are very unlikely to be seen.

Africa's three largest felid species are present but scarce. Ethiopia's population of **lion** (*Panthera pardus*) is currently estimated at up to 1,000 individuals, most of which inhibit remote Sudanese cross-border territories such as Gambella and Alatash national parks. The most reliable site

Spotted hyena

63

ETHIOPIAN WOLF

The one predator that every wildlife enthusiast will want to see is the Ethiopian wolf (*Canis simensis*), the rarest of the world's 37 canid species, and listed as Critically Endangered on the 2000 IUCN Red List. The genetic affinities of this unusual predator puzzled scientists for several decades, as reflected in several misleading common names – until recently, outsiders most often called it the Simien fox, while Ethiopians still know it as the red jackal (*kai kebero* in Amharigna). But recent DNA tests have determined that, despite appearances to the contrary, it is neither fox nor jackal, but a closer genetic ally of the European grey wolf than of any other African canid. It probably evolved from an extinct wolf species that colonised the area in the late Pleistocene era. Two distinct races are recognised, distinguished by slight differences in coloration and skull shape, with the Rift Valley forming the natural divide between these populations.

The Ethiopian wolf stands about 60cm high, making it significantly larger than any jackal, and has a long muzzle similar to that of a coyote. It has a predominantly rufous coat, broken up by white throat and flank markings, and a black tail. It is a diurnal hunter of Afroalpine moorland and short grassland, where it feeds mostly on rodents, including the endemic giant mole-rat. Unlike most canids, it is essentially a courser rather than a hunter, though packs have been observed to bring down small antelope, and it will often eat carrion.

As recently as the mid 19th century, the Ethiopian wolf was widespread and common in the Ethiopian Highlands. Its numbers have since dwindled dramatically, for reasons that are not understood precisely but which are probably more related to introduced diseases such as canine distemper and rabies (the culprits, incidentally, for the drastic reduction in continent-wide African hunting dog populations in the last few decades) than to deliberate hunting. The wolf is now practically confined to high-altitude moorland in national parks and on other high mountains.

Today, up to 600 Ethiopian wolves are split between a quintet of viable breeding populations set in five widely scattered locations. The southern race is the more numerous and concentrated. Its main stronghold is Bale National Park, where an estimated 250–300 adults represents a major decline from Chris Hillman's 1976 estimate of 700. Another 50-odd Ethiopian wolves inhabit the recently gazetted Arsi Mountains National Park to the immediate east of Bale. The extent to which the Arsi and Bale populations interbreed, and can thus be treated as one reasonably large gene pool, is unknown.

The northern race of Ethiopian wolf is scarcer and more fragmented. The population in the Simien Mountains never fully recovered from a rabies epidemic several years ago, but it now stands at around 100 individuals, double what it was a few years back. Other minor strongholds for the northern race are the Community Conservation Area at Guassa and Abune Yoseph, each of which supports an adult population of 25–50 individuals. One or two packs probably survive in a few other remote moorland localities, but in such small numbers, and so far from other populations, that their medium-term prospects are bleak. Paradoxically, the Ethiopian wolf is not difficult to see in Bale National Park. On the road through the open Sanetti Plateau, sightings are virtually guaranteed, even from public transport. Hikers, or people who drive up for the day, might encounter wolves a dozen times!

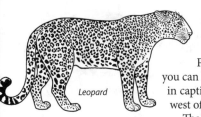
Leopard

for wild lions is Maze National Park, to the south of Sodo Wolayta; but they are also quite often observed at night in Bale National Park's Harenna Forest. The one place where you can be certain of seeing an Abyssinian lion, albeit in captivity, is the Born Free Sanctuary a short drive west of Addis Ababa!

The **leopard** (*Panthera pardus*; often referred to as a tiger, since the Amharigna word *nebir* is used to describe both species) has been recorded in most national parks and also inhabits the forests of the south and west, but it is notoriously secretive and sightings are very unusual. The slighter **cheetah** (*Acinonyx jubatus*) is now very rare in Ethiopia, but an

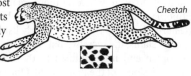
Cheetah

estimated 500 individuals still inhabit the dry plains of the southeast and Rift Valley, representing around one-quarter of the global population of a distinct Sahelian race known as Sudan cheetah (*A. j. soemmeringii*). Smaller nocturnal felids include the **serval** (*Leptailurus serval*), which rather resembles a smaller cheetah, and lynx-like **caracal** (*Caracal caracal*).

Ethiopia's best-known canid is the **Ethiopian wolf** (see box, opposite), but the country also supports all three African jackal species, with **black-backed jackal** (*Canis mesomelas*) commonest in the south and **golden jackal** (*Canis aureus*) in the north. The endangered **African wild dog** (*Lycaon pictus*) was once common in southern Ethiopia but is probably now extinct there. The **bat-eared fox** (*Otocyon megalotis*) is common in parts of South Omo. Widespread but very rarely seen nocturnal predators include the catlike **Abyssinian genet** (*Genetta abyssinica*) and bulkier **African civet** (*Civettictis civetta*).

Black-backed jackal

African wild dog

PRIMATES In addition to the endemic baboon-like gelada monkey (see box, page 66), two species of true baboon species occur in Ethiopia. The **Anubis baboon** (*Papio anubis*) is a large olive-brown primate whose wide habitat tolerance ensures it is common in most national parks, as well as in many other rocky areas and cliffs throughout the south and west of the country. The paler and more lightly built **Hamadryas baboon** (*Papio hamadryas*), which occurs in Awash National Park and the northern Rift Valley, is distinguished by the male's rather splendid mane. The two species frequently hybridise where their ranges overlap.

Anubis baboon

Frequently seen from the roadside in southern and western Ethiopia, the beautiful and acrobatic **guereza monkey** (*Colobus guereza*), also known as the Abyssinian black-and-white colobus, is easily distinguished from other primates by its luxuriant coat of long black hair offset by a white beard and flowing white tail. A dedicated leaf eater, it lives in small family groups in the canopy of forests and riparian woodland, notably on the shore of Lake Hawassa, in the forests of Nech Sar National Park, at Wondo Genet, and on Mount Zikwala.

Guereza monkey

The **grivet monkey** (*Chlorocebus aethiops*) is a semi-terrestrial primate whose light grey-brown coat is offset by a bare black face mask framed with white hair. It occurs in medium to large troops and is typically associated with wooded savannah but likely to occur wherever there are indigenous trees. Present throughout most of Ethiopia, it is replaced in the far south by the similar but duller grey **vervet monkey** (*Chlorocebus pygerythrus*). Formerly listed as a race of grivet but now accorded full species status, the secretive **Bale monkey** (*Chlorocebus djamdjamensis*) is a localised Ethiopian endemic confined to the bamboo belt of the Harenna Forest on the southern slopes of the Bale Massif. Once very seldom seen due to the inaccessibility of its chosen habitat, the Bale monkey can now be located quite easily with a guide in the vicinity of Bale Mountain Lodge. IUCN red-listed as Vulnerable, the Bale monkey is quite common within its limited range, with a total population estimated at several thousand.

The most terrestrial of African primates (and the fastest at up to 50km/h), the **patas monkey** (*Erythrocebus patas*) has a spindly, long-limbed appearance and a russet-tinged coat. In January 2018, it was announced that the Blue Nile

GELADA MONKEYS

The striking and unmistakable gelada monkey (*Thercopithecus gelada*) is the most common of Ethiopia's endemic large mammals, with a total population estimated at 250,000. The male gelada is a spectacularly handsome and distinctive beast, possessed of an imposing golden mane and heart-shaped red chest patch. This patch is thought to serve the same purpose as the colourful buttocks or testicles found on those African monkeys that don't spend most of their lives sitting on their bums!

Unique in that it feeds predominantly on grass, the gelada is something of an evolutionary relict, being the only living representative of a genus of grazing monkeys that once ranged widely across Africa and was ancestral not only to the modern savannah-dwelling baboons, but also to the drills and mangabeys of West Africa, both of which have readapted to rainforest habitats. The gelada is probably the most sociable of African monkeys, with conglomerations up to 1,000 regularly recorded in one field, and its harem-based social structure is probably the most complex of any animal species other than humans. The gelada is confined to the highlands north of Addis Ababa, where it is generally associated with cliffs and ravines. It is very common in the Simien Mountains, its main stronghold, where the population is estimated at 4,500-plus, and many troops are so habituated you can walk up to within a metre of foraging individuals. The gelada is also numerous on the Guassa Plateau, which supports a population of around 3,000 individuals in five troops, some of which are also very well habituated. Other sites where the gelada is regularly observed include the vicinity of Abuna Yoseph, Ankober, Debre Sina and Debre Libanos, and at the Muger River Gorge near Addis Ababa.

patas (*E. p. pyrrhonotus*), a form distinguished by its striking white handlebar moustache, had been identified as a distinct species endemic to western Ethiopia and eastern Sudan.

ANTELOPE A large number of antelope species are present in Ethiopia, many of them with limited distribution, largely because so many different habitats converge around the Ethiopian Highlands.

Bushbuck

The Tragelaphini tribe of medium to large antelope, all characterised by spiralled horns and striking markings, is the best-represented antelope group in Ethiopia, with six species present, including the endemic **mountain nyala** (see box, page 70). The most widespread Tragelaphine is the **bushbuck** (*Tragelaphus scriptus*), a slightly hunchbacked inhabitant of indigenous and exotic forest and riverine woodland. Of particular interest, the handsome **Menelik's bushbuck** (*T. s. meneliki*) is an endemic highland race, commonly seen in Bale National Park and in forests near Addis Ababa, notable for the male being almost black in colour, but with white throat and leg markings, and light spotting on its flanks. The female is reddish-brown with white spotting reminiscent of certain northern hemisphere deer.

Greater and lesser kudu

The **greater kudu** (*T. strepsiceros*) and **lesser kudu** (*T. imberbis*) are both widespread in southern Ethiopia. Both species are dark grey in general colour and have white vertical stripes on their sides (the lesser kudu normally has ten or more stripes, the greater kudu fewer than ten). The greater kudu is the second-tallest of all African antelopes and the male, when fully grown, has magnificent spiralling horns up to 1.5m in length. Both species live in woodland; they are often found alongside each other, though the lesser kudu has a greater tolerance of dry conditions. The easiest place to see both species is the Dera-Dilfekar sector of Arsi Mountains National Park. Both species also occur in Awash National Park, and might be seen outside reserves in the dry acacia woodland of the far south and east. In addition, the greater kudu is very common in Nech Sar National Park and a viable population is present in Abijatta-Shalla. The only African antelope larger than the greater kudu is the **eland** (*Taurotragus oryx*), which has a rather bovine appearance, with twisted horns that seem small for an animal of its size. It is seasonally abundant in more remote parts of South Omo but absent elsewhere.

Eland

Now split across three genera, **gazelles** are medium-sized antelopes with gently curved small to medium-sized horns, a tan coat with white underparts and in some species a black side-stripe. Associated with relatively arid habitats, most gazelles are quite similar to each other in appearance, and half a dozen species occur somewhere in Ethiopia. The long-horned **Grant's gazelle** (*Nanger granti*), which lacks a side-stripe, will be familiar to anybody who has visited East Africa, and reaches the northern extent of its range in Ethiopia's southern Rift Valley, where it is often seen in Nech Sar National Park and along the Moyale road south of Dilla.

The gazelle most likely to be seen by tourists to Ethiopia is **Soemmerring's gazelle** (*Nanger soemmerringii*), which, like Grant's gazelle, has no side-stripe but is easily distinguished by its black face with white cheek-stripes and relatively small, backward-facing horns. Both species have a white rump, but that of Grant's is less extensive and is bordered by black stripes. Soemmerring's gazelle is quite common on the plains around Awash National Park and is often seen along the roads to Harar and Assab. This gazelle, though listed as present in six countries, is now extirpated or very rare in most of them. The nucleus population of a few thousand in the northern Ethiopian Rift Valley is by far the most significant left.

The much paler and very plain **Dorcas gazelle** (*Gazella dorcas*) is a Saharan species that occurs in the Djibouti border area of Ethiopia, where it is quite common. **Heuglin's gazelle** (*Eudorcas tilonura*), red in colour with a thin black side-stripe, occurs locally in the Ethiopia–Sudan border area to the east of the Nile River. Two other gazelle species once present in small numbers in Ethiopia are now both probably extinct there.

An unmistakable gazelle-like antelope with a red-brown coat and a very long neck, the **gerenuk** (*Litocranius waller*) inhabits drier parts of southern Ethiopia and is commonly seen in South Omo, feeding on the higher branches of acacia trees stretched up on its hind legs like a goat. Similar in appearance but with a white eye-ring extending down the nose, the **dibatag** (*Ammodorcas clarkei*) is confined to remote parts of Somali Region unlikely to be visited by tourists and might well be extinct there.

A medium-sized antelope with a plain light tan coat, the **Bohor reedbuck** (*Redunca redunca*) is common in Bale National Park, while the almost indistinguishable **mountain reedbuck** (*Redunca fulvorufula*) is regularly seen at Fentalle volcano in Awash National Park. Related to the reedbuck is the **waterbuck** (*Kobus ellipsiprymnus*), a large antelope with a shaggy brown coat and sizeable lyre-shaped horns; the Defassa race of waterbuck has a pale rump while the common race has an upside-down white 'U' on its rump. Waterbuck are most often seen grazing in relatively open vegetation near water; they are found at a few scattered localities in southern Ethiopia.

Reedbuck

The related **Nile lechwe** (*Kobus megaceros*) is an exceptionally handsome antelope associated with marshy ground and floodplains in the border area of

Sudan and Ethiopia. Its main range is in Sudan, where it is still thought to be present in herds of 1,000 or more. In Ethiopia, it is practically restricted to Gambella National Park, where it is thought to be scarce and vulnerable. Also restricted to the Gambella area, the **white-eared kob** (*Kobus kob leucotis*) is locally common in the swamps of Gambella National Park, which receives a seasonal influx of up to 1.2 million individuals from South Sudan between March and June.

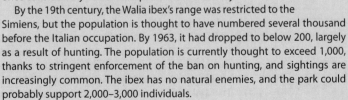

Lechwe

Hartebeest

The **hartebeest** (*Alcelaphus buselaphus*) is a large, tan and rather awkward-looking plains antelope, related to the famous wildebeest or gnu (which doesn't occur in Ethiopia). Three races occur in Ethiopia. The **Lelwel hartebeest** (*A. b. lelwel*) is quite common in parts of South Omo, the **tora hartebeest** (*A. b. tora*) is present in unknown numbers in the northwest lowlands, and the endangered **Swayne's hartebeest** (*A. b. swaynei*), effectively endemic to Ethiopia following extinction in Somalia, is thinly distributed in the southern Rift Valley. The largest populations of Swayne's hartebeest are protected in Senkele Swayne's Hartebeest Sanctuary and Maze National Park. The Senkele population has increased in recent years but, even together with the small population found in Nech Sar National Park, no more than 1,500 individuals remain in the wild. The closely related **tiang** (*Damaliscus lunatus tiang*), a race of the East African topi, is similar in gait and shape to the hartebeest, but the much darker coat precludes confusion. The tiang occurs widely in the Omo Valley and the Gambella region.

The unmistakable **Beisa oryx** (*Oryx beisa*) is a large, handsome, dry-country antelope, easily recognised by its distinctive scimitar-like horns. It occurs in

WALIA IBEX

Ethiopia's rarest endemic is the Walia ibex, formerly widespread in the mountains of the north but now restricted to the Simien Mountains, where it is uncommon but quite often seen by hikers. The Walia ibex is a type of goat that lives on narrow mountain ledges, and can easily be recognised by the large decurved horns of adults of both sexes. The male's horns are larger than those of the female and may measure in excess of 1m. The presence of carved ibex on many pre-Christian religious shrines in Axum indicates that it was once considerably more widespread than it is today.

By the 19th century, the Walia ibex's range was restricted to the Simiens, but the population is thought to have numbered several thousand before the Italian occupation. By 1963, it had dropped to below 200, largely as a result of hunting. The population is currently thought to exceed 1,000, thanks to stringent enforcement of the ban on hunting, and sightings are increasingly common. The ibex has no natural enemies, and the park could probably support 2,000–3,000 individuals.

MOUNTAIN NYALA

Ethiopia's one fully endemic antelope species is the mountain nyala (*Tragelaphus buxtoni*) – not, as its name might suggest, a particularly close relative of the nyala of southern Africa, but more probably evolved from a race of greater kudu. The mountain nyala is similar in size and shape to the greater kudu but it has smaller (though by no means insignificant) horns with only one twist as opposed to the greater kudu's two or three. The shaggy coat of the mountain nyala is brownish rather than plain grey, and the striping is indistinct. Mountain nyala live in herds of five to ten animals in juniper and hagenia forests in the southeast highlands.

The mountain nyala has the distinction of being the last discovered of all African antelopes; the first documented specimen was shot by one Major Buxton in 1908, and described formally two years later. The extent to which mountain nyala numbers declined in the 20th century is undocumented. The antelope probably has always had a somewhat restricted range, but numbers outside of national parks appear to be in decline, and the species is IUCN red-listed as Endangered.

The main protected population is found in the north of Bale National Park, around Dinsho and Mount Gaysay. Numbers here soared from about 1,000 in the 1960s to 4,000 in the late 1980s, but plummeted back to 150 in 1991 as the antelope were shot in revenge for forced removals undertaken by the Mengistu regime. Fortunately, the population quickly recovered to about 1,000, according to transect counts undertaken in 1997. Outside of Bale, a significant mountain nyala population still occurs in the recently created Arsi Mountains National Park and smaller numbers are present in the Kuni Muktar Sanctuary and forests close to Dodola. The global population is estimated at around 2,500 individuals.

dwindling numbers in and around Awash National Park. Large herds also migrate seasonally within the South Omo region.

Dik-diks are small, brown antelopes with tan legs and distinctive extended snouts. Four species are recognised, two of which are found in Ethiopia. All dik-dik species are browsers that live independently of water, and they are generally seen singly or in pairs in dry acacia scrub. **Guenther's dik-dik** (*Madoqua guentheri*) is found throughout the lowlands of southern Ethiopia and is often seen from the roadside, particularly in South Omo and Nech Sar National Park. **Salt's dik-dik** (*Madoqua saltiana*), endemic to the Horn of Africa, is widespread in the dry east, and frequently seen from the Harar road.

The **klipspringer** (*Oreotragus oreotragus*) is a slightly built antelope with a stiff-looking grey-brown coat. It is associated with rocky hills and cliffs and may be seen in suitable habitats anywhere in Ethiopia. It is common in Bale and Simien national parks.

Klipspringer

The **duiker** family is a group of more than 15 small antelope species, most of which live in forest undergrowth.

Until recently, it was assumed that the **common duiker** (*Sylvicapra grimmia*), the only member of the family to inhabit open country, was also the only duiker found in Ethiopia. In 1986, however, a small red duiker (species yet to be designated) was reliably observed in the Harenna Forest within Bale National Park, while in 1996 a similar duiker was observed in Omo National Park. An as-yet-undescribed endemic race or species is not out of the question.

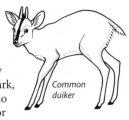

Common duiker

OTHER LARGE MAMMALS

The three non-felid members of the so-called Big Five – **African elephant** (*Loxodonta africana*), **African buffalo** (*Syncerus caffer*) and **black rhinoceros** (*Diceros bicornis*) – were once very common in Ethiopia but are now very localised or, in the last instance, extinct. In the 1980s, the country's elephant population was estimated at around 9,000, most of it concentrated in the southwest; but that number had plummeted to 1,200 in 2007 and probably stands at around 1,000 today. Small elephant populations still occur in Babile Elephant Sanctuary to the south of Harar, as well as in Omo, Mago and Kafta-Sheraro national parks, but the easiest place to see these massive mammals is the recently gazetted Chebera-Churchura National Park near Jimma. The distribution of African buffalo is similarly concentrated in the west, and the population has almost certainly declined since 1998, when it was estimated at 2,000–2,500. It is also likely to be seen in Chebera-Churchura National Park.

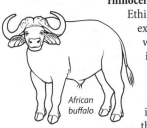

African buffalo

Small numbers of **giraffe** (*Giraffa camelopardalis*) still occur in South Omo, Gambella National Park and elsewhere in the southwestern Kenya and South Sudan border areas. Some uncertainty exists about the taxonomic status of Ethiopia's giraffe, but they probably represent the closest thing in existence to the viable population of Nubian giraffe (*G. c. camelopardalis*), the endangered nominate race that is otherwise restricted to South Sudan, and thought to number fewer than 300 in the wild.

The **common hippopotamus** (*Hippopotamus amphibius*) is widely distributed in the lakes and larger rivers of Ethiopia. It is common in Lake Tana and in most of the Rift Valley lakes, though current details of status are not available. The best places to see hippos are Nech Sar National Park, at the source of the Nile near Bahir Dar on Lake Tana, and at Lake Boye near Jimma.

Three swine species are found in Ethiopia. The **desert warthog** (*Phacochoerus aethiopicus*), a species more or less endemic to the Horn of Africa, occurs in wooded savannah and is frequently seen near water. It is found in most national parks and is especially common around Dinsho in Bale. The **bushpig** (*Potamochoerus larvatus*) is a larger, darker and hairier beast found in forests or dense woodland, and common in all Ethiopian forests, but difficult to see due to its nocturnal habits and chosen habitat. The spectacular **giant forest hog** (*Hylochoerus meinertzhageni*), the world's largest swine, is a hirsute and predominantly West African species represented by a disjunct Ethiopian population that is seen with surprising frequency when walking in Bale National Park's Harenna Forest and Chebera-Churchura National Park.

Warthog

The plains zebra (*Equus quagga*) is the common equine of sub-Saharan Africa. It is found throughout the south of Ethiopia and is the most numerous large mammal in Nech Sar National Park. The larger and more densely striped **Grevy's zebra** (*Equus grevyi*) is restricted to southern Ethiopia and northern Kenya. In Ethiopia, it is thinly distributed in the Kenyan border area east of the Omo Valley, and in the Rift Valley north of Awash National Park.

REPTILES

NILE CROCODILE The order Crocodilia dates back at least 150 million years, and fossil forms that lived contemporaneously with dinosaurs are remarkably unchanged from their modern descendants, of which the Nile crocodile (*Crocodylus niloticus*) is the largest living reptile, regularly growing to lengths of up to 6m. Once common in most large rivers and lakes, it has been exterminated in many areas since the early 20th century, hunted professionally for its skin, as well as by vengeful local villagers. Today, large specimens are mostly confined to protected areas. The gargantuan specimens that lurk around the so-called Crocodile Market in Nech Sar National Park are a truly primeval sight. Other possible sites for croc sightings are the southern Omo River, the Baro River downstream of Gambella, the Awash River near Awash National Park and Nazret, and other large bodies of water at lower to medium altitudes.

SNAKES A wide variety of snakes is found in Ethiopia, though – fortunately, most would agree – they are typically very shy and unlikely to be seen unless actively sought. One of the snakes most likely to be seen on safari is Africa's largest, the **African rock python** (*Python sebae*), which has a gold-on-black mottled skin and regularly grows to lengths exceeding 5m. Non-venomous, pythons kill by strangulation, wrapping their muscular bodies around their prey until it cannot breathe, then swallowing it whole and dozing off for a couple of months while it is digested. Pythons feed mainly on small antelopes, large rodents and similar. They are harmless to adult humans, but could conceivably kill a small child, and might be encountered almost anywhere when slumbering.

Of the venomous snakes, one of the most commonly encountered is the **puff adder** (*Bitis arietans*), a large, thick resident of savannah and rocky habitats. Although it feeds mainly on rodents, the puff adder will strike when threatened, and it is rightly considered the most dangerous of African snakes, not because it is especially venomous or aggressive, but because its notoriously sluggish disposition means it is more often disturbed than other snakes.

Several types of **cobra** (*Naja* spp), including the spitting cobra, are present in Ethiopia, most with characteristic hoods that they raise when about to strike, though they are all very seldom seen. Another widespread family is the **mambas** (*Dendroaspis* spp), of which the black mamba – which will only attack when cornered, despite an unfounded reputation for unprovoked aggression – is the largest venomous snake in Africa, measuring up to 3.5m long. Theoretically, the most toxic of Africa's snakes is said to be the **boomslang** (*Dispholidus typus*), a variably coloured and, as its name (literally 'tree snake') suggests, largely arboreal snake that is reputed not to have accounted for one known human fatality, as it is back-fanged and very non-aggressive.

Most snakes are in fact non-venomous and not even potentially harmful to any other living creature much bigger than a rat. The **mole snake** (*Pseudaspis cana*) is a common and widespread grey-brown savannah resident that grows up to 2m long, and feeds on moles and other rodents. The remarkable **egg-eating snakes** (*Dasypeltis* spp) live exclusively on bird eggs, dislocating their jaws to swallow the egg whole, then eventually regurgitating the crushed shell in a neat little package. Many snakes will take eggs opportunistically, for which reason large-scale agitation among birds in a tree is often a good indication that a snake (or small bird of prey) is around.

LIZARDS All African lizards are harmless to humans, with the arguable exception of the giant **monitor lizards** (*Varanus* spp), which grow up to 2.2m long and could theoretically inflict a nasty bite if cornered. They are sometimes mistaken for a small crocodile, but yellow-dappled skin precludes sustained confusion. Both species present in Ethiopia are predators, feeding on anything from bird eggs to smaller reptiles and mammals.

Visitors to tropical Africa soon become familiar with the **African house gecko** (*Hemidactylus mabouia*), an endearing bug-eyed, translucent white lizard, which as its name suggests reliably inhabits most houses, as well as lodge rooms, scampering up walls and upside down on the ceiling in pursuit of pesky insects attracted to the lights. Also very common in some lodge grounds are various **agama** species, distinguished from other common lizards by their relatively large size of around 20–25cm, basking habits, and almost plastic-looking scaling – depending on the

CHAMELEONS

Common and widespread in parts of Ethiopia, but not easily seen unless they are actively searched for, chameleons are arguably the most intriguing of African reptiles. True chameleons of the family Chamaeleontidae are confined to the Old World, with the most important centre of speciation being Madagascar, to which about half of the world's 120 recognised species are endemic. Aside from two species of chameleon apiece in Asia and Europe, the remainder are distributed across mainland Africa. Several species are present in Ethiopia, including at least two recently described endemics from the Harenna Forest in Bale National Park, and it is highly likely that other endemics await discovery in forests elsewhere in the country.

Chameleons are best known for their capacity to change colour, a trait often exaggerated in popular literature, and one influenced by mood more than environmental background. A more remarkable physiological feature common to all true chameleons is their protuberant round eyes, which offer a potential 180° vision on both sides and swivel independently of each other. Only when one eye isolates a suitably juicy-looking insect will both focus in the same direction. Another unique weapon in the chameleon armoury is a sticky-tipped body-length tongue that is uncoiled in a blink-and-you'll-miss-it lunge to zap a selected item of prey. Many chameleons are adorned with an array of facial casques, flaps, horns and crests that enhance their already somewhat fearsome prehistoric appearance.

In Ethiopia, you're most likely to come across a chameleon by chance when it is crossing a road, in which case it should be easy to take a closer look, since most move slowly and deliberately. The 15cm-long flap-necked chameleon *Chamaeleo delepis* is probably the most regularly observed species of savannah and woodland habitats. The closely related and similarly sized graceful chameleon *Chamaeleo gracilis* is generally yellow-green in colour with a white horizontal stripe along its flanks. Two recently described chameleon species are endemic to the forests of Bale National Park.

species, a combination of blue, purple, orange or red, with the flattened head generally a different colour from the torso. Another common family is the **skinks**: small, long-tailed lizards, most of which are quite dark and have a few thin black stripes running from head to tail.

TORTOISES AND TERRAPINS These peculiar reptiles are unique in being protected by a prototypal suit of armour formed by their heavy exoskeleton. The most common of the terrestrial tortoises in the region is the **leopard tortoise** (*Stigmochelys pardalis*), which is named after its gold-and-black mottled shell, and has been known to live for more than 50 years in captivity. The form present in Ethiopia is the giant leopard tortoise (often designated *S. p. somalica*), which can weigh more than 50kg. Four species of terrapin – essentially the freshwater equivalent of turtles – are resident. The largest is the **African softshell turtle** (*Trionyx triunguis*), which has a wide, flat shell and in rare instances might reach a length of almost 1m.

WEAVERS

Placed by some authorities in the same family as the closely related sparrows, the weavers of the family Ploceidae are a quintessential part of Africa's natural landscape, common and highly visible in virtually every habitat from rainforest to desert. The name of the family derives from the intricate and elaborate nests – typically (but not always) a roughly oval ball of dried grass, reeds and twigs – that are built by the dextrous males of most species.

It can be fascinating to watch a male weaver at work. First, a nest site is chosen, usually at the end of a thin hanging branch or frond, which is immediately stripped of leaves to protect against snakes. The weaver then flies back and forth to the site, carrying the building material blade by blade in its heavy beak, first using a few thick strands to hang a skeletal nest from the end of a branch, then gradually completing the structure by interweaving numerous thinner blades of grass into the main frame. Once completed, the nest is subjected to the attention of his chosen partner, who will tear it apart if the result is less than satisfactory, and so the process starts all over again.

All but 12 of the 113 described weaver species are resident on the African mainland or associated islands, with some 26 represented within Ethiopia alone. About 20 of the Ethiopian species are placed in the genus Ploceus (true weavers), which is surely the most characteristic of all African bird genera. Most of the Ploceus weavers are slightly larger than a sparrow, and display a strong sexual dimorphism. Females are with few exceptions drab buff- or olive-brown birds, with some streaking on the back, and perhaps a hint of yellow on the belly.

Most male Ploceus weavers conform to the basic colour pattern of the 'masked weaver' – predominantly yellow, with streaky back and wings, and a distinct black facial mask, often bordered orange. Eight Ethiopian weaver species fit this masked weaver prototype more or less absolutely, and another five approximate to it rather less exactly, for instance by having a chestnut-brown mask, or a full black head, or a black back, or being more chestnut than yellow on the belly. Identification of the masked weavers can be tricky without experience – useful clues are the exact shape of the mask, the presence and extent of the fringing orange, and the colour of the eye and the back.

The most extensive weaver colonies are often found in reed beds and waterside vegetation, generally with several species present. Most weavers don't

BIRDS

Ethiopia's proximity to the Equator and great habitat diversity mean its avifauna is one of the richest in Africa, with more than 920 species recorded including a high proportion of eagerly sought endemics whose range is restricted to Ethiopia or to the Horn of Africa. It is also very possible that further species await discovery in the little-known forests of the south and west, or elsewhere (the wing of an apparently endemic species of nightjar was discovered as recently as 1992 in Nech Sar National Park, and the live bird was first seen in 2009). Until recently, this rich avifauna was rather poorly covered in non-scientific literature, but that has changed drastically with a glut of superb new publications – including a field guide to the birds of the Horn of Africa, an ornithological atlas to Ethiopia and Eritrea, and two other birding handbooks in the last decade (page 647). This development can only further Ethiopia's burgeoning reputation as a top birding destination, one where a

have a distinctive song, but they compensate with a rowdy jumble of harsh swizzles, rattles and nasal notes that can reach deafening proportions near large colonies. One more cohesive song you will often hear seasonally around weaver colonies is a cyclic 'dee-dee-dee-diederik', often accelerating to a hysterical crescendo when several birds call at once. This is the call of the diederik cuckoo, a handsome green-and-white cuckoo that lays its eggs in weaver nests.

Oddly, while most east African Ploceus weavers are common, even abundant, in suitable habitats, seven species are listed as range-restricted, and three of these are of global conservation concern. The only highly localised weaver whose territory nudges on to Ethiopian soil is the Juba weaver, a Somali-biome species that can be seen in a few specific locations in the southeast. Another species whose range centres on Ethiopia is Rüppell's weaver, which occurs throughout the highlands.

Most of the colonial weavers, perhaps relying on safety in numbers, build relatively plain nests with a roughly oval shape and an unadorned entrance hole. The nests of certain more solitary weavers, by contrast, are far more elaborate. Several weavers, for instance, protect their nests from egg-eating invaders by attaching tubular entrance tunnels to the base – in the case of the spectacled weaver, sometimes twice as long as the nest itself. The grosbeak weaver (a peculiar larger-than-average brown-and-white weaver of reed beds, distinguished by its outsized bill and placed in the monospecific genus Amblyospiza) constructs a large and distinctive domed nest, which is supported by a pair of reeds and woven as precisely as the finest basketwork, with a neat raised entrance hole at the front. By contrast, the scruffiest nests are built by the various species of sparrow- and buffalo-weaver, relatively drab but highly gregarious dry-country birds that are common in the acacia scrub of the Ethiopian Rift Valley.

dedicated visit might easily amass a list of 400 species over a normal-length holiday, and see most of the country's endemics.

It is always difficult to know where to pitch the birding section in a general travel guide. This is because the birds most likely to capture the interest of the casual visitor are not generally those most significant to a serious ornithologist. For a first-time visitor to Africa with a passing interest in birds – an interest that often tends to develop as one travels amid its avian abundance – it will be the most colourful and largest birds that tend to capture the eye: rollers, bee-eaters, cranes, storks, hornbills and such. The truly dedicated, by contrast, will be more than willing to make a two-day side trip to tick a range-restricted endemic lark which, when all's said and done, looks and behaves pretty much like any of a dozen other drab lark species found in Ethiopia. And there will be many visitors who fall between these poles. This section is directed primarily towards reasonably serious birders. The first heading below focuses on endemic and other species that are likely to be of high interest to all visiting birders. The second heading outlines the established itinerary used by most birding tours.

ENDEMICS AND OTHER 'SPECIALS' For any dedicated birdwatcher planning a once-in-a-lifetime trip to Ethiopia, particularly those with experience of birding elsewhere in Africa, a primary goal will be to identify those species whose range is actually – or practically – confined to Ethiopia. Indeed, many ornithological tours are structured almost entirely around this consideration, forsaking time in more generally rewarding and accessible birding areas for trips to remote parts of the country that host one particular endemic.

Ethiopia's 'must-see' birds fall into several categories, the most important of which are the true endemics, species not known to occur outside of Ethiopia. The taxonomic status of some such birds awaits clarification, and new species have been discovered with remarkable regularity in recent decades, making it impossible to say precisely how many birds fall into this category. The most conservative estimate is 16 species, but the spate of recent (and in some cases controversial) splits of what were formerly considered races into full species might boost that figure closer to 25.

A similar number of bird species might be described as former Ethiopian endemics, since their range extends into Eritrea, which became an independent state in 1993. For a variety of reasons – not least the practical consideration that very few visiting birders would be likely to undertake a separate trip to Eritrea at a later stage – these former endemics are treated as full endemics in the main body of this guide.

A third category of birds that any dedicated birder to Ethiopia would hope to encounter constitutes about half a dozen species that are more or less confined to Ethiopia and war-torn Somalia. There are, too, a considerable number of bird species whose range extends throughout the contiguous arid country of northern Kenya, Somalia and southern Ethiopia. In many instances, such birds are easily seen in parts of Ethiopia that are routinely visited by birders for their endemics, whereas their range within Kenya falls into areas infrequently included in birding itineraries.

Finally, there is a miscellaneous group of birds that fit into none of the above categories, but which for one or other reason are likely to be sought eagerly by any visiting birder.

An annotated list covering most of the endemics, near-endemics and other 'key' bird species follows. Names and sequence follow the plates in Redman, Stevenson and Fanshawe's *Birds of the Horn of Africa*, the most useful single-volume field guide for Ethiopia. A single asterisk (*) indicates a species endemic to Ethiopia, a double asterisk (**) one endemic to Ethiopia and Eritrea, and a triple asterisk (***) a near-endemic or a 'Horn of Africa endemic' whose range might extend into Somalia, Sudan, Eritrea and/or the far north of Kenya, but which for all practical purposes is likely to be seen only in Ethiopia. A question mark indicates a controversial or tentative status.

****Wattled ibis** (*Bostrychia carunculata*) Common, widespread and vociferous highland resident. Might be confused with the superficially similar hadeda ibis.

Northern bald ibis (waldrapp) (*Gerontimus eremita*) North African endemic. Formerly bred on cliffs in northern Ethiopian Highlands. Thought to be exterminated until four birds were recorded overwintering in central Ethiopia in 2006. It has been observed several times since, most recently in 2013.

***Blue-winged goose** (*Cyanochen cyanopterus*) Associated with water in the highlands. Reliable sites include Gefersa Reservoir near Addis Ababa, and Sanetti Plateau, Bale Mountains.

Ruddy shelduck (*Tadorna ferruginea*) Only sub-Saharan breeding population on Sanetti Plateau, where commonly observed near water.

Lammergeier (bearded vulture) (*Gypaetus barbatus*) Associated with cliffs and mountains, this magnificent vulture is widespread in suitable Old World habitats, but increasingly rare except in Ethiopian Highlands, which form its major global stronghold.

Golden eagle (*Aquila chrysaetos*) The only population in sub-Saharan Africa was first identified at Bale Mountains in 1988 and confirmed to breed there in 1993. May occur elsewhere in Ethiopia. Requires experience to distinguish from other, more numerous brown *Aquila* eagles.

Vulturine guinea fowl (*Acryllium vulturinum*) Large, distinctive fowl with brilliant cobalt chest. Confined to arid parts of east Africa and the Horn. Very common in suitable habitats in southern Ethiopia.

***Harwood's francolin** (*Pternistis harwoodi*) Range practically restricted to Jemma Valley north of Addis Ababa, where it is quite common. Requires special visit to Jemma Valley.

*****Erckel's francolin** (*Pternistis erckelii*) Large, dark-faced game bird restricted to northern highlands of Ethiopia, but nudging into Eritrea, with another isolated population in eastern Sudan.

*****Chestnut-naped francolin** (*Pternistis castaneicollis*) Near-endemic forest-fringe species common in Bale Mountains and other relatively moist highland areas. The only other confirmed population is in northern Somalia.

*(?)**Black-fronted francolin** (*Pternistis atrifrons*) First described in 1930 but treated as a race of *P. castaneicollis*, this endemic is now thought to be a good species based on field research and molecular studies undertaken in 2013. It is known only from a few hilly sites in the vicinity of Mega in the far south of Ethiopia.

*****Orange River francolin** (*Scleroptila gutturalis*) A strong case exists for splitting Archer's francolin (*S. g. lorti*) as a near-endemic whose main range, centred on Ethiopia's Rift Valley, extends into Somalia and northern Kenya, with a second subpopulation confined to the far northwest of Ethiopia.

Moorland francolin (*Scleroptila psilolaemus*) Highland fowl, very common in Bale and some other Ethiopian moorland habitats, elsewhere occurs only on four less accessible moorland areas in Kenya, where it is relatively uncommon.

White-winged flufftail (*Sarothrura ayresii*) Rare and elusive marsh bird, global population fewer than 1,000, restricted to a few specific localities in South Africa, Zimbabwe and Ethiopia. The main stronghold is Ethiopia's Sultata Plain, 100km north of Addis Ababa. Unlikely to be seen by casual visitors.

****Rouget's rail** (*Rougetius rougetii*) Associated with marshes and vegetation fringing water. Widespread in the highlands, but most easily seen in Bale Mountains, where it is common and confiding.

Wattled crane (*Bugeranus carunculatus*) Endangered and localised resident of grassy or marshy highlands with discontinuous distribution from South Africa to Ethiopia. Sanetti Plateau in Bale Mountains is one of a handful of African sites where it is reliably observed.

*****Heuglin's bustard** (*Neotis heuglinii*) Dry-country species likely to be seen only in Somali border region and South Omo.

Arabian bustard (*Ardeotis arabs*) Localised dry-country bird of North Africa and Arabia; resident in Awash National Park and northern Rift Valley.

***Spot-breasted plover** (*Vanellus melanocephalus*) Locally common in highlands, particularly Bale area, and usually associated with water.

****White-collared pigeon** (*Columba albitorques*) Common to abundant in most highland habitats, including Addis Ababa.

*****African white-winged dove** (*Streptopelia semitorquata*) Restricted-range species of Somalia, Ethiopia and Kenyan border region. Associated with riverine woodland, regularly observed near the Dawa River Bridge between Negele Borena and Yabello.

***Yellow-fronted parrot** (*Poicephalus flavifrons*) Localised forest inhabitant, often seen flying quickly and noisily between tree canopies at Wondo Genet, Menagesha Forest, Dinsho (Bale) and similar habitats.

****Black-winged lovebird** (*Agapornis swinderiana*) Common in most wooded highland habitats. Often observed in the isolated forest patches that tend to surround churches.

*****White-cheeked turaco** (*Tauraco leucolophus*) Striking and vociferous woodland near-endemic often seen in suitable highland habitats, including hotel gardens. Range otherwise extends to a small inaccessible part of Sudan.

Ruspoli's turaco (*Tauraco ruspolii*) Eagerly sought but elusive endemic of southern forests, known from only a handful of localities such as Genale and Arero.

***(Abyssinian) long-eared owl** (*Asio abyssinicus*) Formerly classified as a race of African long-eared owl, this would be regarded as an Ethiopian endemic were it not for a solitary specimen captured on Mount Kenya in 1961. Uncommon, shy and seldom seen unless the location of its daytime roost is known.

*Nechisar nightjar** (*Caprimulgus solala*) Probable endemic known only from one wing found in Nech Sar National Park prior to it being observed on an ornithological expedition led by Ian Sinclair in 2009.

Hemprich's hornbill (*Tockus hemprichii*) Large, striking, cliff-associated hornbill whose range centres on Ethiopia, extending into portions of Somalia and Eritrea, and down the Kenyan Rift as far as Baringo.

****Banded barbet** (*Lybius undatus*) Widespread and quite common resident of woodland. Often seen in southern Rift Valley, but might be seen almost anywhere.

****Abyssinian (golden-backed) woodpecker** (*Dendropicus abyssinicus*) Widespread resident of woodland and forest, but nowhere common.

*(?)**Gillett's lark** (*Mirafra gilletti*) First described in 1975, the Degodi lark (*M. g. degodiensis*), only known from the Bogol Manyo area, was regarded as a rare endemic prior to being lumped with the more common Gillett's lark in 2009.

*(?)**Liben lark** (*Heteromirafra sidamoensis*) First collected in 1968 near Arero junction, 13km from Negele Borena, which remains the best locality. Recent studies indicate it may be conspecific with Archer's lark, an even rarer Somali endemic, and one or other bird was recently recorded in the vicinity of Jijiga.

*(?)**Erlanger's lark** (*Calandrella erlangeri*) A controversial recent split from *C. cinerea*, which it strongly resembles, this is among the more common and conspicuous larks of the Ethiopian Highlands.

*(?)**Brown saw-wing** (*Psalidoprocne antinorii*) Confined to forests in the southern highlands and Rift Valley, where it is the only saw-wing present, and reasonably common. Generally regarded as a race of *P. pristoptera*, but may warrant specific status.

***(?)**Ethiopian saw-wing** (*Psalidoprocne oleagina*) Confined to southwest Ethiopia and southern Sudan, where it is the only saw-wing present and quite likely to be seen around Yabello. Generally regarded as a race of *P. pristoptera*, but may warrant specific status.

*White-tailed swallow** (*Hirundo megaensis*) Endemic to Ethiopia. Restricted to arid acacia woodland around Yabello and Mega. Small parties often seen flying in the vicinity of termite hills. Distinguished from other swallows by conspicuous white tail.

*(?)**Ethiopian cliff swallow** (*Hirundo* spp) Uncollected and undescribed bird recorded by several observers in the vicinity of the Awash River Gorge and Lake

2

Langano. May be more widespread than current knowledge suggests, possibly synonymous with Red Sea cliff swallow, known from one specimen collected near Port Sudan.

***Abyssinian longclaw** (*Macronyx flavicollis*) Widespread resident of high-altitude grassland, particularly common in the Bale area.

*****Somali bulbul** (*Pycnonotus somaliensis*) Recent split from common bulbul ranging between northern Somalia and eastern Ethiopia.

*****Somali wheatear** (*Oenanthe phillipsi*) Rare and localised Somali species with range extended into southeast Ethiopia. Not known from any Ethiopian locality regularly visited by birders. Note that the black-eared wheatear, desert wheatear and red-tailed wheatear all regularly overwinter in Ethiopia but not further south.

*****Sombre rock chat** (*Cercomela dubia*) Excluded from Ethiopian endemic status on the basis of records from one forest in northern Somalia, this is broadly confined to arid, rocky habitats in the northern Rift Valley, for instance Mount Fentalle in Awash National Park.

****Rüppell's (black) chat** (*Myrmecocichla melaena*) Common resident of rocky highlands north of Addis Ababa. Often tame around churches in Tigray and Lalibela.

****White-winged cliff-chat** (*Myrmecocichla semirufa*) Occupies similar habitats to *M. melaena*, and is also most common in the north. It could well be mistaken for the very similar mocking cliff-chat, which often occurs alongside it in similar habitats.

*(?)**Bale parisoma** (*Parisoma griseaventris*) Usually lumped with the practically indistinguishable brown parisoma, but confined to juniper and hagenia woodland and bracken thickets above 3,500m on the northern slopes of Bale Mountains.

*(?)**Ethiopian cisticola** (*Cisticola lugubris*) A nondescript but vocal and conspicuous resident of moist areas and rank grass in the Ethiopian Highlands, this is now widely thought to be a valid split from the winding cisticola (*C. marginatus*).

****Abyssinian slaty flycatcher** (*Melaenornis chocolatina*) Common resident of high woodland and forest both sides of the Rift.

*****White-rumped babbler** (*Turdoides leucopygia*) Common and conspicuous resident of wooded highlands and rivers, with range extending into small portions of Eritrea and Somalia.

***Abyssinian catbird** (*Parophasma galinieri*) Unusual species of undetermined affiliations, notable for its striking, melodic call. Common but elusive resident of juniper and other indigenous highland forest. Often observed at Dinsho (Bale) and in developed hotel grounds in Addis Ababa.

****White-backed (black) tit** (*Parus leuconotus*) Widespread but uncommon resident of forested habitats on both sides of the Rift. Often seen moving restlessly through mid stratum in Dinsho (Bale), Wondo Genet, and developed hotel gardens in Addis Ababa.

*****Shining sunbird** (*Cinnyrus hebessinica*) Brilliantly coloured sunbird common in Ethiopian Rift Valley but with range extending into parts of northern Kenya, Somalia and Eritrea.

*****Ethiopian boubou** (*Laniarius aethiopicus*) Common highland bird with distinctive call, sometimes given as a race of tropical boubou (*L. major*).

****Abyssinian oriole** (*Oriolus monacha*) Similar to black-headed oriole, but inhabits true forest rather than woodland, and has an equally distinct but different call. Fairly common and active in forested habitats.

(Red-billed) chough (*Pyrrhocorax pyrrhocorax*) Eurasian species with isolated Ethiopian population of perhaps 1,200 birds centred on Bale Mountains and northern highlands.

***Stresemann's (Abyssinian/Ethiopian) bush crow** (*Zavattariornis stresemanni*) The proverbial odd bird, loosely affiliated to the crow family, but quite unlike most crows in behaviour and appearance. Confined to a small area of dry thorn bush centred on Yabello, where parties of five or so birds are regularly seen from the roadside.

*****Dwarf raven** (*Corvus edithae*) Recent, controversial split from larger *C. ruficollis*, range more or less confined to Somalia and the eastern half of Ethiopia.

****Thick-billed raven** (*Corvus crassirostris*) Common and widespread throughout the highlands.

*****Somali starling** (*Onychognathus blythii*) Within Ethiopia, formerly thought to be restricted to arid northeast, but has recently been recorded by reliable observers at sites as diverse as Ankober, Bale Mountains and Mount Fentalle. Could be confused with other chestnut-winged starlings, though the long, tapering tail is unique.

****White-billed starling** (*Onychognathus albirostris*) Only chestnut-winged starling with white bill. Associated with cliffs and dwellings. Often seen around churches at Lalibela.

*****Swainson's sparrow** (*Passer swainsonii*) Recent split from grey-headed sparrow, range centred on Ethiopia, where it is common throughout, but extending into Eritrea, Somalia and far northeast of Sudan.

*****Rüppell's weaver** (*Ploceus galbula*) Restricted to the Horn of Africa and Yemen. Common, sociable resident of savannah and light woodland.

*****Juba weaver** (*Ploceus dischrocephalus*) Endemic to Horn of Africa. In Ethiopia, restricted to southeast, regular at Dawa River Bridge between Negele Borena and Yabello.

*****Red-billed pytilia** (*Pytilia lineata*) Pretty but little-known finch, recently split from the extralimital red-winged pytilia, and near-endemic with a small range extension into Sudan. Recorded a few times in the southern Rift Valley, but more common in the western lowlands, for instance around Gambella.

***African citril** (*Crithagra citrinelloides*) Recently split from western and southern specific forms, of which the former nominate race is essentially a bird of the Ethiopian Highlands, with a discrete population confined to southern Sudan.

*****Black-headed siskin** (*Serinus nigriceps*) Common, widespread and distinctive species of high-altitude grassland and heather. Abundant around Bale Highlands.

****White-throated seedeater** (*Serinus xanthopygius*) Confined to the northern highlands, where it is uncommon to rare, and most likely to be seen at Tis Isat or the Ankober area.

*****Yellow-throated serin** (*Crithagra flavigula*) Uncommon and localised dry-country species that went unrecorded for more than a century after three specimens were collected in the 1880s, and formerly regarded by some authorities to be a hybrid rather than a discrete genetic form. Confined to northern Rift, it is now regularly seen on Mount Fentalle and at Aliyu Amba near Ankober.

*****Salvadori's serin** (*Crithagra xantholaemus*) Distinctive and very localised dry-country serin discovered in 1980, and until recently known only from a handful of locations, the best known being Arero and Sof Omar.

***Brown-rumped seedeater (serin)** (*Serinus tristriatis*) Endemic to Horn of Africa. Common and confiding in Addis Ababa and other highland towns, where it seems to occupy a house-sparrow-like niche.

*****Ankober serin** (*Crithagra ankoberensis*) Endemic to Ethiopia. Discovered in 1976 and until recently thought to be confined to a small area of steep escarpment near Ankober, but recent sightings in the Simien Mountains and elsewhere suggest it is actually quite widespread in the highlands.

ORNITHOLOGICAL ITINERARIES
While any ornithological itinerary will depend greatly on available time, level of interest and budget, Ethiopia does boast a defined birding itinerary which, with minor variations, is followed by most organised tours. Unlike the standard 'historical circuit', this itinerary is focused on areas south of Addis Ababa, which is where most of the more localised endemics are to be found, and it can only be covered thoroughly in a private vehicle. Most of the sites mentioned below are covered in detail in the main body of this guide, so what follows are outline itineraries only.

Southern circuit
The main birding circuit through the south requires an absolute minimum of ten days, though two weeks would be more realistic, and the extra four days would effectively double your birding time. With reasonable levels of dedication, luck and skill – or a skilled local bird guide – a total bird list of 350–400 species should be achievable over two weeks on this circuit. About 20 of the Ethiopia–Eritrea endemics are all but certain if you follow this route in its entirety over two weeks, though there are a few (Salvadori's serin, Degodi lark, Abyssinian woodpecker) that are occasionally missed by visiting birders – and you'd be extraordinarily lucky to see a Nechisar nightjar. If possible, there would be much to be said for keeping the day-to-day itinerary reasonably flexible, particularly with regard to sites associated with one specific endemic, so that you can stay on or push ahead depending on how quickly you locate the desired bird. Six Ethiopia–

Eritrea endemics are predominantly found to the north of Addis Ababa, and are thus unlikely to be seen on this southern circuit (for details, see page 84).

Addis Ababa and Rift Valley (*2+ nights*) A typical birding itinerary might start with a night in Addis Ababa, visiting Menagesha Forest (for highland forest endemics) and Gefersa Reservoir (for water-associated and grassland endemics). This can be followed by a night or two in the Rift Valley, where one should stop at as many of the lakes as possible. Ziway is probably the best of the lakes for birds associated with open water and marsh, the Abijatta-Shalla complex for shorebirds, and Hawassa for a mix of good water and acacia woodland species. Another important site in the Rift Valley is Wondo Genet, which is excellent for forest birds, including several endemics. Depending on your time limitations, anything from one night to a week could be spent in the Rift Valley at various lakes and at Wondo Genet.

Bale Highlands (*2–3 nights*) Leaving the Rift Valley, cut up the escarpment from Shashemene towards Bale National Park. The forested park headquarters at Dinsho is the most reliable place in Ethiopia for several localised and endemic forest birds. Allow a full day for the Sanetti Plateau, the best place in Ethiopia to see endemics associated with grassland, as well as a number of other notable species. With reasonable levels of luck, dedication and skill (or at least a skilled guide), a list of well over 200 species, including about half of the birds endemic to Ethiopia (or to Ethiopia and Eritrea), could be expected after two nights each in the Rift Valley and Bale areas. With a third night at Bale, a day trip to the Sof Omar Caves provides a good opportunity to see Salvadori's serin.

Negele Borena and surrounds (*2–3 nights*) From Bale, head south to Negele Borena through the Sanetti Plateau, Harenna Forest and Dolo Mena. This road may be impassable after heavy rain, when the Genale River presents an insurmountable obstacle, so check road conditions first. This is a long drive, so there won't be too much birding time along the way, especially if you want to stop at Genale to look for Ruspoli's turaco. The junction of the Bogol Manyo and Arero roads, 13km from Negele Borena, is the only known site for the endemic Liben lark.

Yabello and surrounds (*1–3 nights*) The road from Negele Borena to Yabello offers good dry-country birding in general, and is home to several species associated with the arid Somali and Kenyan border areas. Three specific sites along this road warrant a stop. The first is the aforementioned junction with the Bogol Manyo road. The next is the Dawa River Bridge, a reliable place to pick up Juba weaver and African white-winged dove. Finally, the forests around Arero are home to Ruspoli's turaco, and the surrounding area is also one of the few known localities for Salvadori's serin. Also at Arero, you should start looking out for Stresemann's bush crow and white-tailed swallow, the two endemics whose restricted range is centred on Yabello. Both of these birds are generally easy to locate and identify, and the odds are you'll have seen them even before you arrive at Yabello. From Yabello, it is possible to drive to Addis Ababa or Awash National Park over a long day, provided you don't stop more often than is necessary. Less frenetic would be to break up the drive with a night at Wondo Genet or at one of the Rift Valley lakes – you could choose where to stay depending on the gaps in your list of birds identified to date. A third option would be to cut through via Konso to Arba Minch and Nech Sar National Park.

Awash National Park (*2–3 nights*) The two most important specials here are sombre rock chat and yellow-throated serin, both regular on Mount Fentalle. Allocate most of a day to seeking out these birds. The undescribed Ethiopian cliff swallow is most easily seen in the Awash Gorge at the southern end of the park. Awash is also one of the best general bird sites in Ethiopia, for which reason a second full day is strongly recommended.

Northern excursions On the whole, northern Ethiopia is of less interest to birders than the south, though any birdwatcher hoping to see all of Ethiopia's endemics would need to undertake two specific trips north, both of which are covered in detail in the regional part of this guide. The first trip is to Ankober, the best place to see the localised Ankober serin and the springboard for a short side trip to Aliyu Amba, a recently discovered site for the yellow-throated serin. This trip could be extended to include the Guassa Plateau near Mehal Meda, a moorland area supporting similar species to the Sanetti Plateau. The second trip leads to the Jemma Valley, the only reliable spot for the endemic Harwood's francolin. On either trip, one would stand a good chance of encountering some of the other four endemics whose range is more or less restricted to the north, ie: white-winged cliff-chat, Rüppell's black chat, white-billed starling and white-throated seedeater. At a serious push, either trip would form a viable day excursion from the capital, though in both cases it would be better to allow for two days and a full night.

Ethiopian wolf (*Canis simensis*) is the rarest
of the world's canid species page 64

above left **Mountain nyala (*Tragelaphus buxtoni*), male**
page 70

above right **Mountain nyala (*Tragelaphus buxtoni*), female**
page 70

left **Greater kudu (*Tragelaphus strepsiceros*)**
page 67

below left **Soemmerring's gazelle (*Nanger soemmerringii*)**
(SS) page 68

below right **Gerenuk (*Litocranius waller*) page 68**

Simien Mountains National Park is the main stronghold of the striking gelada monkey (*Thercopithecus gelada*), the most common of Ethiopia's endemic large mammals page 66

above   **Anubis baboon (*Papio anubis*)** page 65

below left   **Bale monkey (*Chlorocebus djamdjamensis*)** (TM/MP/FLPA) page 66

below right   **Gelada monkey (*Thercopithecus gelada*), male** page 66

above   **Grivet monkey (*Chlorocebus aethiops*)** page 66

below left   **Hamadryas baboon (*Papio hamadryas*)** page 65

below right   **Guereza monkey (*Colobus guereza*)** page 65

above   One of the best places to see common hippopotamus (*Hippopotamus amphibius*) is Nech Sar National Park
page 557

below   Yellow-billed stork (*Mycteria ibis*) page 528

top left	**Blue-winged goose** (*Cyanochen cyanopterus*) page 77
top right	**Spot-breasted plover** (*Vanellus melanocephalus*) page 78
above left	**Rouget's rail** (*Rougetius rougetii*) page 78
above right	**Wattled ibis** (*Bostrychia carunculata*) page 77
left	**Ruddy shelduck** (*Tadorna ferruginea*) page 77
below left	**Moorland francolin** (*Scleroptila psilolaemus*) page 78
below right	**Chestnut-naped francolin** (*Pternistis castaneicollis*) page 77

top left Thick-billed raven (*Corvus crassirostris*) page 81

top right Lammergeier, or bearded vulture (*Gypaetus barbatus*) (SS) page 77

above left Stresemann's bush crow (*Zavattariornis stresemanni*) (MH/FLPA) page 81

above right Abyssinian slaty flycatcher (*Melaenornis chocolatina*) (MH/FLPA) page 80

right Yellow-fronted parrot (*Poicephalus flavifrons*) (IY/FLPA) page 78

below left White-cheeked turaco (*Tauraco leucolophus*) (DH/FLPA) page 78

below right White-rumped babbler (*Turdoides leucopygia*) (SS) page 80

top left	Black-headed weaver (*Ploceus culcullatus*)
top right	Somali ostrich (*Stuthio camelus*)
above left	Rüppell's griffon vulture (*Gyps rueppellii*)
above right	Augur buzzard (*Buteo augur*)
left	Fish eagle (*Haliaeetus vocifer*)
above	Abyssinian scimitar-bill (*Rhinopomastus minor*) (MH/FLPA)

top left Hamerkop (*Scopus umbretta*)

top right African jacana (*Actophilornis africana*)

middle left Wattled crane (*Grus carunculatus*) page 78

middle right Northern carmine bee-eater (*Merops-nubicus*)

above left Malachite kingfisher (*Alcedo cristata*)

above right Abyssinian-roller (*Coracias abyssiniica*)

right Abyssinian ground hornbill (*Bucorvus abyssinicus*)

Compare Ethiopia Tours

Using the Largest Marketplace for African Safaris

⊘ **4,100+** Tours   ⊘ **1,400+** Tour Operators   ⊘ **35,000+** Reviews

Begin your journey at
www.safaribookings.com

— As Featured In —

3

Practical Information

WHEN TO VISIT

Ethiopia can be visited at any time of year. People are sometimes advised against travelling during the rainy season, which peaks over June to August, but there are advantages to travelling at this time, notably that you'll encounter fewer tourists at popular sites such as Lalibela, and that the scenery is so much more impressive when the countryside is green and well watered. A lovely time of year is September through to early October, when the rains subside but the countryside is still a riot of green punctuated by yellow meskel wild flowers. Mid-October to January, when the rains are over but the countryside is still quite green, is the peak tourist season. Many travellers try to schedule their trip to coincide with important festivals such as Ethiopian New Year, Ethiopian Christmas, Timkat or Meskel. The European winter is also the best time for birds, as resident species are supplemented by large numbers of Palaearctic migrants.

SUGGESTED ITINERARIES

Itineraries are subjective things, dependent on how much time you have, your chosen or enforced style of travel, and your interests. So rather than prescribe a few specific itineraries, this section attempts to itemise what is and isn't possible within the confines of a normal vacation period. Perhaps the most important single item of advice when it comes to travel in Ethiopia is to allocate your time realistically. You can, for instance, easily cover the four main attractions of the historical circuit by air in seven or eight days. You could also do it in five or six days at a push, but if you were constrained to that sort of period, it would be more realistic and enjoyable to cut one of the four main sites from your itinerary. Much the same can be said for visitors bussing around the historical circuit. If you really wanted to, you could cover the main attractions in under two weeks, but only if you are prepared for at least half your waking days to be consumed by long bus trips.

THE HISTORICAL CIRCUIT Ethiopia's main tourist focus is the well-defined historical circuit in the north. Covered in chapters 6–12, this route incorporates five of the county's most established tourist centres, namely Bahir Dar (on the shore of Lake Tana close to the Blue Nile Falls), Gondar (famed for its 17th-century castles and also the gateway to Simien Mountains National Park), Axum (with its wealth of ancient stelae and ruins), Lalibela (home to the country's most famous cluster of rock-hewn churches) and Mekele (a popular springboard for visits to the sensational Danakil Desert and the rock-hewn churches of Gheralta), along with a host of other less-publicised attractions.

By road, travelling this loop in its entirety adds up to around 2,500km of driving, and while roads have improved greatly in recent years, many are still in poor repair by international standards and pass through mountainous terrain that isn't conducive to speed. In other words, travelling by bus or private vehicle

TOP PRACTICAL TIPS

As guidebooks become bigger, denser and more detailed, it becomes easier for key advice to get lost in the verbiage. Here are a few important summary points (mostly elaborated upon elsewhere) worth highlighting for first-time visitors:

- **Research domestic flight prices** At the time of writing, people whose international flight to Addis Ababa is with Ethiopian Airlines get a whopping discount of around 60% on all domestic flights, making your choice of international carrier a no-brainer if you are thinking of adding a few domestic flights to your itinerary.

- **Bring a Visa or MasterCard** The most viable way to access cash is to use a credit or debit card to draw local currency at ATMs, which can be found in all larger towns. MasterCard is the most widely accepted option, and Visa is also useful, but other cards are virtually worthless. Debit cards seem to attract fewer fees. See page 97.

- **Don't change or draw more money than you need** It is very difficult to change Ethiopian birr back into hard currency, even at Bole International Airport.

- **Get used to converting US dollar prices in this book to local currency** Most things are best paid for in local currency but, owing to the steady devaluation of the Ethiopian birr in recent years, we have opted to quote prices as a US dollar equivalent, which has proved to be more reliable in the past. See page 97.

- **Couples shouldn't assume they need a double room** Ethiopian hotels typically refer to a room with one double bed as a single room, and to a room with two beds as a double. For this reason, couples should make a habit of looking at a 'single' room before assuming they need to pay extra for a double or twin. (And do note that in this guidebook, we reflect what a room actually is, rather than what the hotel calls it, so if it has a double bed, we call it a double, and if it has two beds, we call it a twin.) See page 103.

- **Travel without timetables** In this book we have made every reasonable effort to give the best transport options and departure points for all routes, but road transport tends to be rather chaotic by Western standards, so it's not an exact science. Most public transport simply leaves when full, rather than operating to a fixed schedule, and departure points are not always centralised. See page 99.

- **They're called mobile phones for a reason** The ubiquity and efficiency of mobile phones has had many positive effects on business in Ethiopia. But is not realistic if you want to rush between sites. Fortunately, Ethiopian Airlines covers all the main towns on the historical circuit. Although internal flights are reasonably efficient, they will not necessarily run at times that allow you to do any significant sightseeing on the day you fly. On this basis, it's best to allow yourself a

when it comes to hotels, restaurants and tourist centres, it means that contact numbers – often those of an individual manager, guide or receptionist – tend to change more regularly than fixed lines. There is nothing we can do about this, but readers are welcome to alert us to any such changes by posting on our updates website (see below).

- **Think offline** Although it has improved greatly in recent years, Ethiopia has a patchy relationship with the internet. Even in Addis Ababa, Wi-Fi and other connections are quite hit-and-miss. Elsewhere, internet access tends to be very slow and erratic. Possibly because of this, Ethiopians tend to phone or text each other rather than email, website and email addresses given by hotels frequently don't work, and emails to working addresses tend not to receive an answer.

- **Maps of Ethiopia are often unreliable** Few reliable road maps exist for Ethiopia, nor is there anything much available for most towns, and even the best maps tend to exclude or misrepresent new or upgraded roads. For this eighth edition, we have made every reasonable effort to make town plans and regional maps as accurate as possible, but they are best used in conjunction with a proper foldout colour map (check out the recommendation on page 649).

- **Plan your loo stops** Public toilets are thin on the ground and, where they do exist, they tend to be quite dirty, and may not have running water or toilet paper. Try to get in the habit of going to the toilet before you go out, and carrying toilet paper with you. Hotels, banks and filling stations are the best places to head for if you need a toilet urgently.

- **Adjust your hotel expectations** Accommodation standards in Ethiopia are generally quite low, and facilities tend to be poorly maintained. Hotels in this book are generally reviewed in this context, and use of words like 'clean', 'smart' or 'stylish' is relative. See page 102.

- **Register your mobile phone on arrival** If you want to use a local SIM card, which allows you not only to make cheap domestic phone calls but also to convert airtime to a data bundle for internet access, the device into which you intend to insert it must have been registered with customs upon your arrival at Bole International Airport.

- **Check for online updates** Our updates website (w bradtupdates.com/ethiopia) is there to publicise important update information sent to us between editions by travellers and people within the industry. Check it out. Better still, contribute!

clear day between flights in every place you visit. This means that to visit all four major centres you need eight nights out of Addis. If you don't have this sort of time, you could think about cutting Bahir Dar or Axum from the itinerary. On the other hand, with more time available, you could easily devote a second day to Axum or Bahir Dar, and any number of days to visiting rock-hewn churches in the Lalibela region (by mule or on foot from town).

The three key multi-day outdoor attractions on the historical loop are the spectacular scenery and wildlife protected in Simien Mountains National Park (SMNP), the multitude of rock-hewn churches scattered around Wukro, Gheralta and elsewhere in northern Tigray, and the volcanic peaks and salt-caked sumps of the searing Danakil Desert. SMNP is easily visited from Gondar, but motorised visitors should ideally allow at least two nights to see it properly, and hikers need to set aside a minimum of four days (including travel to or from Gondar), though six days or longer would be better. The rock-hewn churches of Tigray lie north of the regional capital of Mekele. The possibilities in this area are practically endless, ranging from visiting some of the more accessible churches over a day or two on public transport through to seven-day hikes or driving trips in the Gheralta area. Three- or four-day (two- or three-night) expeditions into the Danakil run out of Mekele and take in the desert's two main highlights: the live lava pool at Erta Ale and the multihued hot springs at Dallol.

Touring the historical circuit by public transport is relatively straightforward. If you have more time than money, it is also much cheaper than flying, at least on a day-by-day basis. But, because it will take much longer, the overall cost will be much the same. The advantages of bus travel are that it allows you to soak up the magnificent scenery and to visit more obscure places of interest. To do a full tour of the historical circuit would use up the best part of eight days on buses alone. Allowing for at least one full day at each of the major tourist attractions, and a few days' rest here and there, anything much less than 18 days – or three to four weeks if you have thoughts of hiking in the Simiens or exploring Tigray in depth – would be heavy going.

If you don't have this sort of time, two compromise options exist. One is to skip Axum and cut across from Gondar to Weldiya via Lalibela, which would still require about five days of pure travel and a very tight minimum of ten days overall. A more sensible compromise might be to go as far as Axum by bus, then to fly back to Addis via Mekele and/or Lalibela.

THE SOUTH There is no single obvious circuit through the south, but there is no desperate need to think through your timing in advance. Shashemene, the transport hub of the south, is less than 5 hours from Addis by bus, and even from more dispersed spots such as Harar, Arba Minch, Negele Borena or Goba, you are now within one day's reach of the capital. In other words, travel in most of this region can be as organised or as whimsical as your temperament dictates.

If you veer towards organised travel, the best way to see a fair amount of the south is to join a tour or hire a vehicle and driver (in Ethiopia, tours and car hire generally amount to the same thing) through an Addis Ababa operator. Tours can be arranged to cater for most tastes, but generally you would be looking at two or three days to see a few Rift Valley lakes, and you could extend this by a day or two by appending either Awash or Nech Sar National Park to your itinerary. To see South Omo properly, eight days is the absolute minimum duration for a round road trip from Addis Ababa.

A more whimsical approach is just that. You could spend weeks exploring the south and east and it would be silly to try to suggest a specific public transport itinerary. The one place in the south that should be singled out here is Bale National Park. Not only is this southern Ethiopia's prime hiking destination, but it is also a good place to see endemic mammals and birds.

OFF-THE-BEATEN-TRACK TRAVEL If you have only a short time in Ethiopia, common sense dictates that you should focus your attention on the places you really want to see. But if you have the luxury of a longer period of time, it is worth exploring some of Ethiopia's less-visited areas. You need not actually head 'off the beaten track' to do this – stopping along the beaten track can amount to the same thing. Ideas of this sort are scattered throughout this guide, but Tigray and its rock-hewn churches offer particularly rich pickings for travellers who want to take things slowly.

A couple of relatively quick off-the-beaten-track trips suggest themselves. One, if you are visiting Bale, is to return to Shashemene via Dola Mena and Negele Borena. A good overnight trip from Addis is to the wonderful but little-visited cluster of historical sites along the Butajira road. And then there is the mother of off-the-beaten-track routes, the loop west through the forested mountains around Nekemte and Jimma to the remote river port at Gambella, for which you should probably allow around ten days.

TOUR OPERATORS

ETHIOPIA
All of Ethiopia's better tour operators are based in Addis Ababa, though many also have satellite operations at the major tourist centres of the north. The following list is selective rather than exhaustive.

Abeba Tours ☎011 557 0801; m 0927 819331; e info@abebatoursethiopia.com; w abebatoursethiopia.com; see ad, page 187. Based in the Ras Hotel, this serves individual, group & business travellers.
Adonay Ethiopia Travel ☎011 896 4342/4; m 0911 514000/40; e adonaytours@yahoo.com; w adonaytour.com. Good selection of hiking, trekking & birdwatching tours plus northern circuit trips, & flexible when it comes to individualised itineraries. Guides speak English, Italian & German.
Alligan Travel ☎+44 (0)208 883 0977 (UK); m 0911 950402 (Ethiopia); e info@alligantravel. com; w alligantravel.com; see ad, page 130. This well-established & competitively priced British–Ethiopian partnership is a responsible travel specialist that offers great support to its clients (which include adventure tour organisers for UK schools). It can plan trips to well-known & more remote parts of Ethiopia for all age groups, & is flexible about making changes at short notice. It has well-trained drivers & guides.
Amazing Ethiopia Tours ☎011 652 2507; m 0911 427728; e info@amazingethiopia.com;

w amazingethiopia.com. Individual, group & business travel. Range of custom & package tours.
Awaze Tours ☎011 663 4439; m 0911 623376; e info@awazetours.com; w awazetours.com; see ad, inside back cover. Operates exclusively in Ethiopia & offers both custom & scheduled tours.
Begoha Tour & Travel m 0929 901860; e begohatourandtravel@gmail.com; w begohatours. com; see ad, 3rd colour section. Car rental, short excursions & full-length tours all over Ethiopia.
Boundless Ethiopia Tours m 0911 056594; e info@boundlessethiopia.com; w boundlessethiopia.com; see ad, 5th colour section. This Dutch owner-managed operator places a strong emphasis on community-based ecotourism.
Celebrity Ethiopia Tour m 0913 555249, 0911 004803; e celebrityethiopiatour@gmail. com; w celebrityethiopiatour.com; see ad, pages 129 & 187. Packages from 7 to 21 days with tours throughout Ethiopia.
Covenant Ethiopia Tours m 0946 473271, 0932 343193; e covenanttoursethiopia@gmail.com, travelcovenant@yahoo.com; w covenantethiopia. com. Specialised in Tigray churches & the Danakil (to which it now offers well-priced daily departures from Mekele), this reliable operator has a comfortable fleet (used, among others, for transfers & tours booked through Gheralta Lodge) & is the only fully licensed agency with satellite offices both in Axum & in Mekele.

Dinknesh Ethiopia Tour 011 156 7837; e dinknesh2012@gmail.com; w dinkneshethiopiatour.com; see ad, inside front cover. Highly rated operator providing a wide range of quality tours with an emphasis on excellent service.

Diversity Tours Ethiopia 011 661 2009; m 0911 615794; e diversitytoursethiopia@gmail. com; w diversitytoursethiopia.com; see ad, page 186. Countrywide operator offering bespoke tours to all sites of interest.

Ethio Travel & Tours m 0929 240110, 0940 373737; e ethiopiatravel@gmail.com; w ethiotravelandtours.com; see ad, page 187. Offering a good range of tours around Ethiopia, Ethio offers daily fixed departure trips to the Danakil that are competitively priced but sometimes accommodate several dozen people in season.

Ethiopia Traditions Travel m 0960 800960, +32 465 722063 (Belgium); e info@ethiopiatraditionstravel.com; w ethiopiatraditionstravel.com; see ad, 3rd colour section. Run by an energetic young Belgian–Ethiopian couple with an office in the grounds of the Itegue Taitu Hotel in Addis Ababa (page 161), this small operator specialises in community stays in villages offering participants deep insights into local cultures & traditions.

Ethiopian Quadrants 011 515 7990, 011 554 4635/6; e ethiopianquadrants@gmail.com; w ethiopianquadrants.com; see ad, 3rd colour section. This small company offers reliable travel advice & bespoke trips based on owner-manager Tony Hickey's 2 decades' experience arranging tours in Ethiopia. In addition to the usual historical circuits, it specialises in the Awash & Afar regions, the rock-hewn churches of Tigray, & trekking, ornithological & adventure tours. Deals regularly with film crews & groups with specialist requirements.

FKLM Tours 011 868 1439; m 0930 110004; e info@fklm-tours.com; w fklm-tours.com; see ad, 3rd colour section. Specialist in tours to Ethiopia & several neighbouring countries.

Galaxy Express Travel 011 551 0355/7646; e galaxyexpressservices1985@gmail.com; w galaxyexpresstourethiopia.com; see ad, 5th colour section. Established in 1985 & still under the same management, this is one of the best-equipped tour operators in Ethiopia, with efficient & responsive staff, a large fleet of well-maintained vehicles, & branch offices in Gondar, Axum & Bahir Dar staffed by articulate, energetic & flexible young guides. Rates are competitive & service is excellent – a recommended 1st contact.

Grand Holidays Ethiopia 011 618 3163; e info@grandholidaysethiopia.com; w grandholidaysethiopia.com; see ad, page 185. Small owner-managed operation with more than 15 years' experience in setting up expertly guided tailor-made itineraries & small-group package departures to all corners of the country, as well as mountain trekking & birding tours.

Grant Express Travel & Tours Services (GETTS) 011 553 4678/4379; m 0911 233289; e gettsethiopia@gmail.com; w gettsethiopia.com; see ad, 5th colour section. Now widely recognised as an industry leader, this dynamic & responsive company benefits from the hands-on attitude of its owner-manager, Yared Belete, a vastly experienced former guide. A good 1st contact for mid-range to upmarket tours almost anywhere in Ethiopia.

Group Tours Ethiopia 011 813 4889; m 0927 819331; w grouptoursethiopia.com; see ad, 4th colour section.

Haile Holidays m 0903 182766; w haileholidays.com; see ad, 4th colour section.

Kibran Tours 011 662 6214/5; e info@ kibrantours.com; w kibrantours.com. Top-end operator with a range of well-planned itineraries across Ethiopia. Professional guides speak fluent English, Italian, German, French & Spanish.

Off-Road Ethiopia Tour m 0911 513264; e info@tourtoethiopia.com; w tourtoethiopia. com. This small but dynamic owner-managed company sets up bespoke tours all over Ethiopia.

Overland Ethiopia Tours m 0911 444601; e info@overlandethiopiatours.com; w overlandethiopiatours.com; see ad, 3rd colour section. Dynamic owner-managed company sets up bespoke tours all over Ethiopia.

Simen Land Tours m 0911 021308; e tesfahundere@yahoo.com; w simenlandtours. com; see ad, 3rd colour section. Especially strong on Simien trekking packages, this small & energetic operator also runs trekking packages to the Bale Mountains & 4x4 excursions into the Danakil & South Omo.

Simien Image Tour & Travel m 0918 776585; e simienimage@gmail.com; w simienimage.com; see ad, 5th colour section. Wide variety of tours for all interests.

Simien Mountain Tours m 0911 904792; e info@simienmountains.com;

w simienmountains.com; see ad, 3rd colour section. Excursions focused on the Danakil Depression & Simien Mountains.

Solomon Berhe Tours m 0911 181051; e sol2rs@ yahoo.com; w solomonberhetours.com. Specialises in birding trips, & also has carefully planned trips to the Danakil Depression, South Omo & elsewhere.

South Expedition Africa m +46 76 096 7856 (Sweden), 0911 663455; e sales@south-expedition-africa.com; w south-expedition-africa.com; see ad, 3rd colour section. Trips to the Omo Valley, Bale Mountains & the Northern historical route.

Sunny Land Tours m 0911 432407/0912 077746; e info@sunnylandethiopia.com; w sunnylandethiopiatours.com; see ad, 4th colour section. Specialist cycling tours throughout Ethiopia.

Tedy Tour & Travel Services \011 371 0824; e info@tedytour.com; w tedytour.com; see ad, 4th colour section. Specialist in Danakil Depression & Erta Ale tours, plus other tour packages in the region.

Travel Ethiopia \011 552 5478; e info@ travelethiopia.com; w https://travelethiopia.com; see ad, 3rd colour section. This reputable & very well-established company offers the usual packages, plus specialist excursions to the remote tribes & Omo National Park on the west of the Omo River.

Village Ethiopia \011 550 8869; m 0911 223003; e villageethiopia@gmail.com; w villageethiopiatour.com. Small but well-established company offering a range of tours to the Historic Route, Simien Mountains & Omo Valley.

Welcome Ethiopia Tours \011 557 8888; m 0929 048988; e info@welcomeethiopiatours. com; w welcomeethiopiatours.com; see ad, page xii. This Swiss owner-managed, Addis Ababa-based company offers expertly guided tours featuring a varied selection of natural & cultural sites throughout Ethiopia, as well as in Djibouti & Somaliland.

Wild Expeditions \011 822 3691; w wildexpeditionsethiopia.com; see ad, 4th colour section. Tailored upmarket tours with a focus on more off-the-beaten-track areas. Also operates an exclusive

private mobile camp that can be set up anywhere in Ethiopia, with prime sites being the Bale Mountains, Chebera-Churchura, Gheralta & the Danakil.

WUB Ethiopia Tours \011 844 9086; m 0929 024029; e info@wubtoursethiopia.com; w wubethiopiatours.com; see ad, page 129. Diverse selection of cultural, historical, trekking, adventure & festival-based tour packages.

Yumo Tours \011 551 8878; m 0911 230203; e info@yumo.net; w yumo.net. Possibly the oldest-functioning tour operator in Addis Ababa, Yumo Tours was founded in 1978 & brings decades of experience to tours around the historical circuit & elsewhere.

UK & INTERNATIONAL

Adventure Associates \+61 2 6355 2022 (Australia); e mail@adventureassociates.com; w adventureassociates.com; see ad, 3rd colour section. Accompanied small-group tours to destinations around the world, including Ethiopia.

Gane & Marshall \01822 600600; e info@ ganeandmarshall.com; w ganeandmarshall.com; see ad, page 84. Tailor-made itineraries; historical & cultural tours.

Imagine Travel \020 3393 5763; e info@ imaginetravel.com; w www.imaginetravel.com. Operator with 25 years' experience.

Journeys by Design \01273 623790; e info@ journeysbydesign.com; w journeysbydesign.com. Tour operator specialising in east & southern Africa.

Rainbow Tours \020 7666 1276; e info@ rainbowtours.co.uk; w rainbowtours.co.uk; see ad, 1st colour section. Tailor-made itineraries for individuals or small groups.

Steppes Travel \01285 601752; e enquiry@ steppestravel.co.uk; w steppestravel.co.uk. Specialists in tailor-made & small-group departures.

TravelLocal w travellocal.com. A reputable UK-based agent whose website allows customers to communicate directly with selected local operators, as well as book their trips.

Wildlife Worldwide \01962 302086; e sales@ wildlifeworldwide.com; w wildlifeworldwide.com. Specialises in tailor-made wildlife holidays.

TOURIST INFORMATION

The Ethiopian Tourist Organisation has an informative website (w *ethiopia.travel*), but no other representation outside the country. The main tourist office on Addis Ababa's Meskel Square sometimes stocks a few informative free booklets but cannot generally offer much current practical advice. There is a regional tourist office in

Ethiopians, like the Swahili of neighbouring Kenya and Tanzania, measure time in 12-hour cycles starting at 06.00 and 18.00. In other words, their seven o'clock is our one o'clock, and vice versa. To ask the time in Amharigna, you say *sa'at sintno*? Times are *and sa'at* (hour 1) through to *asir hulet sa'at* (hour 12). When talking Amharigna, you can be confident all times will be Ethiopian. When talking English, people may or may not give you European time, so check. If they say a.m. or p.m., it will definitely be European time. Otherwise, ask if it is Europe (pronounced like Orop) time or habbishat time; or else convert to Ethiopian time – for instance, if someone says a bus leaves at one, ask if they mean *and sa'at* or *sabat sa'at*. You might also want to change your watch to Ethiopian time. If you have a smartphone with a good time app, you could also set this with dual times, one reflecting a time zone 6 hours earlier (such as Brazil), which would be identical to Ethiopian time.

Here is the full list of times from *and sa'at* to *hulet sa'at*:

13.00	*and*	13.35	*lehulet hamist guda*
13.05	*and kemist*	13.40	*lehulet haya guda*
13.10	*and kesir*	13.45	*lehulet rub guda*
13.15	*and kerub*	13.50	*lehulet asir guda*
13.20	*and kehaya*	13.55	*lehulet amist guda*
13.25	*and kahayamst*	14.00	*hulet*

every regional capital, as well as at some major tourist attractions. The best of these is the Tigray tourist office in Mekele (page 364), which stocks some great booklets about the rock-hewn churches and other regional attractions, and can also give very detailed advice about more obscure churches.

RED TAPE

A valid **passport** is required to enter Ethiopia, and entry may be refused if it is set to expire within six months of your intended departure date. For **security** reasons, it's advisable to detail all your important information in one document and to retain a copy in any phone, laptop or other electronic device you are carrying, as well as sending it to your own email address and a reliable contact at home. The sort of things you want to include on this are travel insurance policy details and 24-hour emergency contact number, passport number, details of relatives or friends to be contacted in an emergency, bank and credit card details, camera and lens serial numbers, etc. Should your passport be lost or stolen while you are on the road, it will be easier to get a replacement if you have a photocopy or scan of the important pages.

If there's any possibility you'll want to drive or hire a vehicle while you're in the country, do organise an **international driving licence** (any AA office in a country in which you're licensed to drive will do this for a nominal fee, as will any IDP-issuing post office in the UK).

VISAS All visitors to Ethiopia require a visa. The most straightforward way to obtain this is to buy an online e-visa, a service that is offered to nationals of all countries as of 1 June 2018, though this could conceivably change during the lifespan of this edition. Single-entry 30-/90-day e-visas cost US$52/72 and can be applied for at the official website (**w** *www.evisa.gov.et*), which accepts Visa, MasterCard and American Express. The website currently only processes applications for single-entry tourist and conference visas for people who intend to enter Ethiopia at Bole International Airport. When you apply online, be sure to type in the correct URL – google 'Ethiopia e-visa' and you might well end up on one of several authentic-looking but bogus websites with names such as www.ethiopiaevisa.com, www.ethiopiaonlinevisa.com or www.evisaforethiopia.com.

We strongly recommend buying an e-visa in advance, but for the time being it is also possible for nationals of so-called tourist-generating countries (ie: Argentina, Australia, Austria, Belgium, Brazil, Canada, China, Czech Republic, Denmark, Finland, France, Germany, Greece, India, Ireland, Israel, Italy, Japan, Kuwait, Luxembourg, Mexico, Netherlands, New Zealand, North Korea, Norway, Poland, Portugal, Russian Federation, Slovakia, South Africa, South Korea, Spain, Sweden, Switzerland, Thailand, the UK and the USA) to buy a 30-/90-day single-entry Visa on Arrival (VoA) at Bole International Airport for US$50/70, or the equivalent in euros or pounds sterling. Visa regulations also technically allow one to buy a six-month multiple-entry VoA for US$100, but this is not yet available in practice, and might never be. Travellers who require a multiple-entry visa, or who will arrive at a land border, or at any airport other than Bole (for instance Dire Dawa) must arrange their visa in advance from an Ethiopian embassy or other mission abroad (as listed in full on the Ministry of Foreign Affairs website **w** *www.mfa.gov.et*).

Anybody who is not from a tourist-generating country and who arrives in Ethiopia without a pre-bought visa is more than likely to be refused entry and put on a plane back home. Note, too, that if you land at Bole with an e-visa or buy a VoA there, and are thinking of exiting Ethiopia overland, there is a risk you will be turned back at the land border on the basis that these services are technically available only to visitors who fly in and out of the country. We heard recently of one person in this situation who had his passport confiscated and was told to go back to Addis Ababa to collect it, then to fly out from there. One way to pre-empt this scenario, especially if you plan to return to Ethiopia anyway, would be to obtain a multiple-entry visa in advance.

Should you need to spend longer in the country than is stamped into your passport, visa extensions can be granted at the Immigration Office off Arat Kilo in Addis Ababa. An initial one-month extension costs US$100 and usually takes 48 hours to process. Further extensions are even costlier. Do not under any circumstance overstay your visa, not even by an hour, or you risk being turned back at immigration when you leave the country, missing your flight, and being forced to spend a costly few days in Addis Ababa regularising your situation before you are allowed to fly out.

Be aware that visa regulations for Ethiopia change with some frequency, and it seems possible that VoAs will eventually be phased out completely once the e-visa system is better established. Any changes of which we are made aware will be posted on our updates website (**w** *bradtupdates.com/ethiopia*).

GETTING THERE AND AWAY

BY AIR All international flights arrive and depart from Bole International Airport in Addis Ababa. Many airlines fly to Ethiopia. Ethiopian Airlines is Africa's oldest airline and has an excellent safety record, but may not be the cheapest option. Bookings can be made online at **w** www.ethiopianairlines.com, or by emailing **e** reservation@ethiopianairlines.com. For a complete list of international and domestic offices and call centres, see **w** www.ethiopianairlines.com.

Other airlines that fly to Addis Ababa include Air China (**w** *airchina.com*), Egyptair (**w** *egyptair.com*), Emirates (**w** *emirates.com*), Fly Dubai (**w** *flydubai. com*), Gulf Air (**w** *gulfair.com*), Kenya Airways (**w** *kenya-airways.com*), Lufthansa (**w** *lufthansa.com*), Saudi Airlines (**w** *saudiairlines.com*), Sudan Airways (**w** *sudanair. com*), Turkish Airlines (**w** *turkishairlines.com*) and Yemenia (**w** *yemenia.com*). In addition, KLM (**w** *klm.com*) operates a code share with Kenya Airways, and South African Airways (**w** *flysaa.com*) code shares with Ethiopian Airlines.

An established specialist UK operator is **Africa Travel** (☎ *020 7387 1211;* **w** *africatravel.co.uk*). Reputable agents specialising in round-the-world tickets rather than Africa specifically are **Trailfinders** (☎ *020 7368 1200;* **w** *trailfinders.com*) and **STA** (☎ *0333 321 0099;* **w** *statravel.co.uk*).

OVERLAND The main overland route south from Europe runs through Egypt and Sudan, entering Ethiopia at Metema west of Gondar. This route was closed for many years due to political instability in Sudan, and it remains potentially volatile, but with Sudanese visa in hand, travellers have been getting through with relative ease since 2003. If you opt to head this way, do keep your ears to the ground, and be prepared to fly over troubled areas, for instance between Cairo and Khartoum or Khartoum and Addis Ababa. Most people cross into Ethiopia at the Metema Yohannes crossing west of Gondar. A regular minibus runs between Gondar and the border, taking about 1 hour. The crossing is straightforward, if rather time-consuming, provided you have the appropriate visa, which must be bought in advance crossing in either direction. In addition, Selam Bus (page 141) now runs a weekly coach service between Addis Ababa and Khartoum. This leaves Addis Ababa on Saturdays at around 05.00 and overnights in Gondar before arriving at Khartoum on Sunday evening. It starts the return trip from Khartoum on Monday morning and also overnights in Gondar en route.

Travellers heading between Ethiopia and more southerly parts of Africa have a more straightforward ride. Several viable routes run between South Africa and Nairobi (the capital of Kenya), the most westerly running through Namibia, Zambia and Tanzania, and the most easterly through Mozambique and Tanzania. The most volatile part of this route, since it is prone to sporadic outbreaks of Somali-related banditry, is the stretch between Nairobi and the Ethiopian border town of Moyale, and this is covered in detail in the box on page 522. It is generally a very relaxed crossing, assuming you have a valid passport and bought an Ethiopian visa in advance.

Following the closure of the historic train service from Addis Ababa to Djibouti via Dire Dawa in 2010, a new electric railway line following the same route started operating in January 2018. Passenger trains run in either direction on alternate days, leaving at 08.00, and the trip takes around 10–13 hours. Djibouti-bound travellers must complete Ethiopian immigration formalities in Addis Ababa. In addition, a surfaced road connects Addis Ababa to Djibouti via Awash and the Afar regional capital Semera.

At the time of writing, overland travel between Ethiopia and Eritrea is impossible. Overland travel between Ethiopia and Somalia is also difficult, the one exception being the self-declared and peaceful independent state of Somaliland, whose capital Hargeisa is only about 3 hours by road from Jijiga in eastern Ethiopia (for further details, see the Bradt guide *Somaliland*).

WHAT TO TAKE

The key to packing for a country like Ethiopia is finding the right balance between bringing everything you might possibly need and carrying as little luggage as possible, something that depends on your own priorities and experience as much as anything. Worth stressing, however, is that almost all genuine necessities are surprisingly easy to get hold of in Addis Ababa and other large or tourist-oriented towns, and that most of the ingenious gadgets sold in camping shops will be dead weight on the road. Indeed, if it came to it, you could easily travel in Addis Ababa with little more than a change of clothes, a few basic toiletries, and a medical kit.

CARRYING LUGGAGE A normal suitcase is ideal for organised tours, or for those who are travelling mostly by air or private transport, though it can be helpful to have one that easily slings across your back or that rolls, or both. Travellers using public transport should either use a backpack or a suitcase that converts into one, depending on whether they intend to do much genuine hiking. For backpackers who don't plan on carrying camping gear, there is much to be said for trying to compress your possessions into a daypack that you can rest on your lap on bus trips, avoiding extra charges for luggage, arguments about where your bag should be stored, and the slight but real risk of theft. A compact bag also makes for greater mobility, whether you're hiking or looking for a hotel in town. Make sure your backpack or suitcase is designed in such a manner that it can easily be padlocked. This won't prevent a determined thief from slashing it open, but it is a real deterrent to casual theft.

CLOTHES Bearing in mind that you can easily and cheaply replace worn items in Ethiopia, or, even better, get them made to measure, take the minimum. A minimum guideline might be one or two pairs of trousers and/or skirts, one pair of shorts, three shirts or T-shirts, a couple of sweaters, a light waterproof windbreaker during the rainy season, enough socks and underwear to last five to seven days, one solid pair of shoes or boots for walking, and one pair of sandals, flip-flops or other light shoes.

Skirts and trousers are best made of a light natural fabric such as cotton. T-shirts are lighter and less bulky than proper shirts, though the top pocket of a shirt (particularly if it buttons up) is a good place to carry spending money in markets and bus stations, since it's easier to keep an eye on than trouser pockets. Despite its equatorial location, much of Ethiopia is decidedly chilly, especially at night, so a couple of sweaters or sweatshirts are essential. There is a massive used clothing industry in Ethiopia, and at most markets you'll find stalls selling jumpers of dubious aesthetic but impeccable functional value for next to nothing – you might consider buying such clothing on the spot and giving it away afterwards. Getting clothes made from local fabrics is also quick and relatively inexpensive.

Ethiopians are modest dressers and the country has a significant Muslim population – you should select your clothing with this in mind. Women should never expose their knees or shoulders in public, so shorts and sleeveless tops are out. It isn't entirely acceptable for women to wear trousers in Muslim areas, but neither will it cause serious offence. Men should always wear a shirt in public places. Trousers are generally more acceptable than shorts, though again this isn't rigid. Sensitivity about dress is more of a factor in the predominantly Muslim eastern regions than it is elsewhere in Ethiopia.

Socks and underwear must be made from natural fabrics, such as cotton. As for footwear, genuine hiking boots are worth considering only if you're a serious off-road hiker, since they are very heavy whether on your feet or in your pack. A good pair of walking shoes, preferably made of leather and with good ankle support, is a good compromise. It's also useful to carry sandals, flip-flops or other light shoes. Flip-flops are useful as protection from the floors of communal showers, and they are very light to carry. Just watch out for irregular pavements!

CAMPING GEAR With cheap rooms being so widely available in Ethiopia, the case for taking camping equipment is less than compelling, unless you plan to hike in remote areas. But if you do, try to look for the lightest available gear. It is now possible to buy a lightweight tent weighing less than 2kg, and you'll also need a sleeping bag and a roll-mat for insulation and padding. If you plan on hiking in the Simiens or Bale, camping gear can be hired on the spot.

OTHER USEFUL ITEMS Most backpackers, even those with no intention of camping, carry a sleep-sheet or a sleeping bag for emergencies, or to use as an alternative to the dirty bedding provided in some budget hotels. Some travellers also like to carry their own padlock: not a bad idea in Ethiopia, particularly if you intend to stay mostly in shoestring hotels or travel to small towns, where not all hotels will supply padlocks.

If you're interested in natural history, it's difficult to imagine anything that will give you such value-for-weight entertainment as a pair of light compact binoculars, which these days needn't be much heavier or bulkier than a pack of cards. Binoculars are essential if you want to get a good look at birds (Africa boasts a remarkably colourful avifauna even if you've no desire to put a name to everything that flaps) or to watch distant mammals in game reserves. For most purposes, 7x21 compact binoculars will be fine, though some might prefer 7x35 traditional binoculars for their larger field of vision. Serious birdwatchers will find a 10x magnification more useful.

All the toilet bag basics (soap, shampoo, conditioner, toothpaste, toothbrush, deodorant, basic razors) are very easy to replace as you go along, so there's no need to bring family-sized packs, but women planning on longer stays might want to stock up on some heavy-duty, leave-in conditioner to minimise sun damage to their hair. Those staying outside Addis Ababa should also carry enough tampons and/or sanitary pads to see them through, since these items may not always be easy to find.

If you wear contact lenses, be aware that the various cleansing and storing fluids are not readily available, and, since many people find the intense sun and dry climate irritates their eyes, you might consider reverting to glasses. Some readers have recommended daily disposable contact lenses to save the hassle and risk of re-using. Most budget hotels provide toilet paper and many also provide towels, but if you are travelling on the cheap, it is worth taking your own with you to make sure you don't get caught short.

A torch will be useful not only during power cuts or when staying in towns without electricity, but also for visiting old churches, which tend to be very gloomy inside. Increasingly important as more and more travellers carry electronic camera equipment is a universal electric socket adaptor for charging your batteries in hotel rooms. Some people wouldn't travel without a good pair of earplugs to help them sleep at night (or through mosque and church calls) and a travel pillow to make long bus journeys that bit easier to endure.

English-language reading material of any description is difficult to locate outside of Addis Ababa, and even there you'll find the range limited. Bring whatever you need with you.

You should carry a small medical kit, the contents of which are discussed on page 120, as are mosquito nets. A pack of facial cleansing wipes or 'wet wipes' can help maintain a semblance of cleanliness on long, dusty journeys, and antibacterial gel is a good way of making sure you don't make yourself sick with your own grime if you're eating on the move.

MONEY

The unit of currency is the Ethiopian birr. Notes are printed in denominations of birr 100, 50, 10, 5 and 1. Smaller denomination centime and birr 1 coins are also minted. The birr has long been one of the strongest currencies in Africa, though in recent years it has devalued significantly. In September 2018 exchange rates were roughly US\$1 = birr 27.7, €1 = birr 32.3 and £1 = birr 36.4.

When it comes to making direct payments, the Ethiopian birr rules. True, MasterCard and Visa can be used to settle room and restaurant bills at some upmarket hotels and to buy Ethiopian Airlines tickets in Addis Ababa, but they are of very limited use for direct payments elsewhere around the country, and a surcharge is often added. Most visitors do, however, obtain all the local currency they require by using their credit or debit card to draw money from the country's vast and ever-growing network of ATMs, which is a very straightforward procedure. Almost all ATMs, including those operated by the Commercial Bank of Ethiopia (CBE), Dashen, Wegagen, NIB and half a dozen other bank chains, now accept international Visa and MasterCards, both in Addis Ababa and in the rest of the country. Most towns of any substance have a dozen or more such ATMs, and they can usually be found outside any bank, as well as in the lobbies or grounds of many tourist-oriented hotels. Note that withdrawals may be limited to birr 4,000 (around US\$150) per transaction and a daily total of around birr 8,000–10,000 (equivalent to US\$300–400). Cards other than Visa or MasterCard are not much use even at ATMs.

Even if you have a card, it's advisable to carry some hard currency cash, just in case the ATM network plays up. During banking hours (⊕ *usually 08.30–16.00 Mon–Sat*), you can change hard currency cash (euros, pounds sterling and US dollars) into Ethiopian birr at almost any bank anywhere in the country. In the case of US dollars, however, you are strongly advised to carry recently issued (post-2006) banknotes, because so many forgeries of older notes are in circulation. Note also that travellers' cheques are no longer accepted. If you are in a real pinch, Western Union and several other services offer money transfers to Ethiopia, but this is a costly and potentially time-consuming option.

It used to be the case that Lalibela lacked foreign exchange facilities, but it is now well equipped with banks and ATMs. These days, the only areas where you might have problems changing or drawing money are inside more-or-less unpopulated national parks such as the Simien or Bale Mountains (though in most such cases, banks and ATMs can be found in nearby towns), throughout the Danakil, and anywhere in South Omo other than Jinka.

PRICES QUOTED IN THIS GUIDE The prices quoted in this book were collected over November 2017 to February 2018. Prices are almost always quoted in Ethiopian birr locally, and are also best paid in local currency, but in order to pre-empt further devaluation in the birr we have opted to convert prices to US dollars, in the likelihood that it will be more meaningful a couple of years down the line.

BUDGETING

Budgeting is a personal thing, dependent on how much time you are spending in the country, what you are doing while you are there and how much money you can afford to spend.

SHORT-STAY BUDGETS Short-stay tourists will find Ethiopia undemanding on their wallets. You can expect to pay an average of around US$50–60 per night for a room in a moderate hotel and, except perhaps in Addis Ababa, you'd struggle to top US$25 per day on food and drink. Most visitors with time restraints will want to fly between some major places of interest, for which they can expect to pay anything from US$50 to US$150 per leg, depending on the exact routing and whether they qualify for the whopping discount on domestic flights offered to those who fly to Ethiopia with the national carrier. Add to that about US$20 per day on guide and entrance fees, and a daily budget of US$160 for one person or US$270 for two looks very generous.

Where Ethiopia does get expensive is when you take organised driving tours and safaris. The low volume of tourists means that arrangements tend to be personalised, and thus a safari to somewhere like South Omo will be far more expensive than a budget safari in Kenya or Tanzania.

There is nothing preventing short-stay visitors from operating on the sort of budget that you would normally associate with long-stay visitors, except that the distances between major attractions make flying virtually essential if you are to see much of the country in a short space of time.

LONG-STAY BUDGETS If you use facilities that are mainly geared to locals, Ethiopia is a very inexpensive country, even by African standards. You can almost always find a basic room in a local hotel for around US$10 or a better room for around US$20–25, while meals at local eateries typically cost US$2–4. Buses are cheap, as are drinks. Rigidly budget-conscious travellers could probably keep costs down to US$20 per day per person, but US$30 would give you considerably more flexibility. At US$60 per day, you could, within reason, do what you like.

If you are on a restricted budget, it is often a useful device to separate your daily budget from one-off expenses. This is less the case in Ethiopia than most African countries, because few travellers will be doing expensive one-off activities such as safaris, gorilla tracking or climbing Kilimanjaro. Nevertheless, there are always going to be days that a variety of factors (historical site and guide fees, air tickets) conspire to make expensive. At current prices, a daily budget of around US$40 with a few hundred dollars spare for one-off expenses would be very comfortable for most travellers.

GETTING AROUND

BY AIR Ethiopian Airlines (w *www.ethiopianairlines.com*) runs a good network of domestic flights connecting Addis Ababa to most major tourist destinations. The best connections are in the north, where at least one flight daily goes in either direction between any combination of Addis Ababa, Bahir Dar, Gondar, Lalibela and Axum (flights to Mekele are slightly less numerous). There are also flights to other parts of the country, such as Arba Minch, Jinka, Kombolcha, Gambella, Jimma, Assosa, Jijiga and Dire Dawa. Internal flights are generally efficient and normally leave to schedule, but you need to check in 2 hours before departure, and last-minute delays still occur from time to time. For this reason, you should ideally allow one non-travel day between flights.

If your time in Ethiopia is limited, flying is far and away the most efficient way to get around. Even travellers who wouldn't normally do so might think about using a couple of domestic flights, especially if they are eligible for the discount offered to anyone whose international flight to Addis Ababa is with Ethiopian Airlines. The full spectacle of Ethiopia's ravine-ravaged landscape is best seen from the air (the leg between Gondar and Lalibela is particularly recommended). You could also save a lot of time by flying out to a far-flung destination – for instance Axum, Arba Minch or Gambella – and working your way back overland, rather than repeating a similar bus trip out and back.

Ethiopian Airlines regularly changes its rulings with regard to domestic flight fares. At the time of writing, the full fare for most legs, booked through the website, is typically around US$200 one-way. For some years now, however, these fares have been vastly reduced (typically to around US$50–60 per leg), but only to passengers whose international flight to Addis Ababa is with Ethiopia Airlines. In order to take advantage of this massive discount, it is best first to book your international flight with Ethiopian Airlines, then to book your domestic flights, answering in the affirmative when a pop-up screen asks in advance whether you hold an Ethiopian Airlines ticket for an international sector. Do be aware, however, that fare rulings might change at any time. We will post any changes of which we are apprised on the updates website (w *bradtupdates.com/ethiopia*).

Ethiopian Airlines offices outside of Ethiopia generally accept credit card payments, as does the website and the main ticketing office in Addis Ababa. Tickets bought at offices elsewhere in the country are cash only. The baggage limit on most domestic flights is 20kg. Luggage, body searches and repeat requests to show your passport are part and parcel of the Ethiopian Airlines domestic flight experience. If you are carrying anything that could possibly be perceived to be an antiquity, it may well be confiscated.

BY BUS, TRUCK OR MINIBUS Ethiopian road transport compares well to that in many other parts of Africa. Buses are rarely crowded, the driving is as sober as it gets in Africa and, because buses rarely indulge in the custom of stopping every 100m to pick up another passenger, you generally get from A to B at a reasonable pace. Also unusual for Africa are organised breakfast and/or lunch stops on longer runs. In fact, the only real problem with bus transport in Ethiopia is the size of the country. The northern historical circuit, for instance, requires more than 2,500km of road travel – at an average progress rate of 60km/h this means that a daunting total of 40–50 hours, or the bulk of five to seven waking days, must be spent on buses.

The best services, closer in style to a Greyhound-type coach than a typical African bus, but still very reasonably priced, are Ethio/Abay (f *ethiobustransportplc.plc*), Selam (w *selambus.wordpress.com*), Limalimo, Falcon (f *FalconCoachET*), Golden (f *goldenBusEthiopia*) and Sky (w *skybusethiopia.com*). Between them, these companies offer daily fixed departures in either direction between Addis Ababa and Bahir Dar, Gondar, Mekele, Axum, Dessie, Hawassa, Jimma, Nekemte and Assosa. Services to Dire Dawa, Harar and Jijiga should hopefully also resume soon. Long-haul fares cost in the ballpark of US$10–20. For fuller details, see page 141.

On other routes, there are government buses and private buses, often divided into three levels, numbered one to three. Where there is a choice, go for a level one bus, which will cost only a little more than lower level buses, but will generally get you where you need to go more quickly and comfortably. As a rule, private buses are preferable for short runs (say up to 150km) and government buses are better for long runs. The reasoning behind this is that government buses are faster and better maintained, which is an advantage over a long distance, but private buses get going more quickly.

On some runs buses leave throughout the morning; on other runs buses leave at a specific time, which will normally be at 05.30 or 06.00. In some cases, you may

3

BICYCLES   *Edited from a letter by Arthur Gerfers*

Bicycle rental is very cheap in Ethiopia, and I personally prefer it to any other form of transport. I rented a bicycle in almost every place where one was available. I found it more pleasant to cover distances on a bicycle, not least because it enabled me to dodge the beggars and manoeuvre through crowds of yelling children with greater ease – though it is amazing how far some of those little chaps will run!

Always TEST DRIVE a bike before renting it. You can't get the feel of a bike if the seat is too high or too low. Often the seat is also too loose. Have the seat adjusted to suit you. Perseverance is the key here. The bike guy doesn't have anything else better to do anyway. Once you have taken the bike for a spin, and it catches your fancy, pay attention to a few other factors:

- Bent handlebars gripped such that the knuckles line up parallel to the legs are going to wear on your wrists more quickly than straight handlebars gripped such that the knuckles line up parallel to the handlebars. If you have a choice (and if you are in no hurry, you probably do), straight handlebars are recommended.
- Proper pedals are a must; without them, your feet will cramp up quickly. If the pedals are broken, missing or do not adjust properly with the turning of the cranks, do not take the bicycle.
- Brakes are important. Make sure they work at least somewhat. Though most Ethiopian cyclists on the road get by without them, and some trips (like flat overland ones) don't require them, brakes are usually necessary in some form.
- Insist on a pump. The bike guy, or his brother or cousin, is bound to have one. And, should you have a flat tyre, you will be glad to have a pump too. Again, perseverance is the key here.

A final note on the day after: it is not unusual to have an especially sore bum on the day after a trying bike ride. The best way to overcome this mild irritation is to ride the bike again as often as possible. The pain will subside in another day or two. These few rules of thumb should ensure a more enjoyable biking holiday!

---

be required to buy a ticket the day before departure; in other cases you just buy it on the spot. So far as possible, local departure patterns are indicated throughout the regional section of this guide, but it is subject to change, so check the current situation the afternoon before you want to travel – and remember that you'll generally, but not always, be quoted departure times in the Ethiopian clock (see box, page 92).

Light vehicles such as pick-up trucks and minibuses are less widely used than in many other African countries. You can, however, rely on there being some form of regular light transport between large towns that are close together (eg: Adwa and Axum, Goba and Bale Robe or Dire Dawa and Harar). It is also possible to use light vehicles to hop between smaller towns on some major routes. Generally, light vehicles are privately owned, and are faster, more crowded and pricier than buses.

Road transport is very cheap. Typically you are looking at up to US$2 per 100km on normal buses and twice that on luxury coaches operated by Ethio, Selam and the like. Road conditions and travel time will also affect the fare on more remote routes. If there is no bus service to where you want to go, then lifts in trucks etc will usually be around double what a bus might cost for that route. On a route where a 4x4 is needed, double it again! Be aware, too, that on some routes you may be expected to pay full price for covering only part of the distance (eg: if you ask a bus going from Shashemene to Ziway to drop you at Langano, you'll probably have to pay the full fare to Ziway).

BY RAIL The historic train service from Addis Ababa to Djibouti via Bishoftu, Adama, Awash Saba and Dire Dawa ceased operations in 2010. A new electric railway line following roughly the same route was inaugurated in late 2016 and started operating in January 2018. Passenger trains run in either direction on alternate days, leaving at 08.00, and are scheduled to take around 5 hours between Addis Ababa and Dire Dawa, and another 5 hours between Dire Dawa to Negad (which involves clearing customs and immigration), though initial reports suggest these timings are slightly optimistic. Fares between Addis Ababa and Dire Dawa are US$16/34/37 for the upper/middle/lower bunk in the standard coach or US$46/49 for the upper/lower bunk in a VIP coach. Note that travellers heading to Djibouti must currently embark at Addis Ababa in order to complete Ethiopian immigration and customs formalities; these cannot be done further east or at the border.

A new line connecting Addis Ababa to Mekele via Awash Saba, Kombolcha and Weldiya is also under construction, and may well become operational during the lifespan of this edition. These lines represent the first two phases in a planned 4,780km network linking Addis Ababa to some 49 regional centres.

BY FERRY Two ferry services run on Lake Tana: a daily service between Bahir Dar and Zege, and a weekly overnight service between Bahir Dar and Delgi or Gorgora. See page 244 for details.

BY TAXI, *GARI* **AND** *BAJAJI* Taxis can be found in many larger towns. Except in Addis and towns with a high tourist turnover (for instance Gondar), they are very cheap but foreigners are frequently asked higher prices and you should expect to bargain. Taxis in Addis are expensive (though still cheap by international standards) and often drivers will refuse to drop their prices for foreigners. In most towns, taxis are now supplemented by cheaper *bajaji* – small three-wheeled *tuk-tuks* imported from India – which typically charge less than US$1 for a short trip and can also be chartered cheaply for out-of-town excursions. In some cooler and more rural areas, horse-drawn carts called *garis* replace *bajaji*.

BY CAR/CAR HIRE It is straightforward enough to hire a vehicle in Addis Ababa, but as a rule a driver will be supplied, so in essence you are really organising a tailored tour or safari. Car hire in Ethiopia is expensive by any standards – the lowest rate you'll get will be about US$150 per day, and US$200 or higher is likely from a reputable tour company. Avis is represented in Ethiopia by Galaxy Express, but most other operators in Addis Ababa can arrange car hire (page 89). If you are thinking of driving yourself, be warned that Ethiopian roads are not what you are used to at home. Many Ethiopian roads are in poor condition, and the pedestrians and livestock share a quality of indifference I've encountered nowhere else in Africa when it comes to dawdling in the middle of the road while a hooting vehicle hurtles towards them at full tilt. See also the box on page 102.

Extracted from an article by John Graham (see w addistribune.com)

The Ethiopian countryside is full of quirky pedestrians. The children have devised a number of games to play with drivers. One of the more charming is 'Let's stand in the road defiantly and see if the car stops before we lose our nerve and run to the side'. This is only slightly more popular than 'Let me see if I can push my friend in front of a car.'

Shepherd boys have a pleasant way of passing their sometimes boring hours – making a line of sharp rocks across the road! Then there is the good old pastime of throwing rocks at cars, something that was not entirely unknown among the urchins where I grew up. One local official, trying to demonstrate to me the gratitude of the people for some good work we were doing, said that our organisation was so good that the children in his *woreda* didn't even throw stones at our cars! As we were driving out, sure enough, one did.

On the adult side, there is the curious criss-cross tradition. This stems from a rural belief that if a person crosses in front of a moving vehicle it will lengthen their life. Of course, if they fail to cross successfully, their life is considerably shortened. On almost every trip, we've had to brake abruptly at least a few times as some pedestrian suddenly hears us from behind and launches him or herself across the road metres in front of us. The loud skidding, honking and occasionally shouting which accompanies this event is usually greeted by the pedestrian with a big smile. I found this galling and irritating, until some kind and patient Ethiopian assured me that the smile was to show embarrassment, not amusement at the chaos they had caused.

The maze of obstacles that one has to negotiate to drive in rural Ethiopia used to leave me breathless in admiration of our drivers. Knowing me too well, my wife pointedly said on our first trip out of town that she felt that local drivers were essential for long trips and I shouldn't consider driving. At the time I sympathised. After a while the psychology of the people and animals at the side of the road, not to mention the manic drivers in the middle, became clearer. Now that I've driven myself all over rural Ethiopia, I recognise a sixth sense that tells me that this donkey is not going to launch itself in front of me, while that other one just might. There is nothing that can protect even the most experienced driver from the full-fledged unexpected dash on to the road by a pedestrian or animal – but the rest becomes relatively straightforward.

ACCOMMODATION

Finding a room in Ethiopia is seldom a problem, and accommodation tends to be inexpensive. It should be understood, however, that hotels aimed at tourists tend, with a few exceptions, to be of poor to middling quality. Most of those exceptions are in the capital, Addis Ababa, though it is increasingly the case that larger towns and other places of interest regularly visited by tourists will have at least one hotel that would be acceptable to all but the most demanding of Westerners. Even so, few hotels outside of Addis Ababa would scrape more than a one-star rating by international standards, and while newer and better-quality hotels seem to open all the time, standards of upkeep are poor, and many two- to three-year-old places contrive to look much older and more timeworn than they actually are. Bearing the above in mind, this book will describe hotels in their Ethiopian context, which means that the use of adjectives such as 'clean', 'smart' or 'stylish' might often seem unduly generous to new arrivals.

The good news for backpackers and budget travellers is that suitable accommodation is plentiful throughout the country. The overwhelming majority of this budget accommodation constitutes unremarkable town hotels geared primarily to the local market, and it is often characterised by some or all of the following flaws: indifferent staff, aesthetically challenged décor, ugly furniture, low standards of cleanliness, an erratic power or water supply, and slack maintenance manifested in the form of broken fittings, leaky plumbing, or advertised facilities that don't work. That said, budget hotels in Ethiopia are generally quite good value, and in most towns you'll find decent en-suite rooms in the US$10–20 range, often cheaper. Even the most basic hotel rooms generally have electric sockets for charging mobile phones, digital cameras and similar devices, though you might first want to confirm they are working.

One quirk to watch out for in Ethiopia is that hotels tend to refer to a room with one bed as a single and to one with two beds as a double. In practice, the overwhelming majority of so-called single rooms in Ethiopia are what we would term a double: they have a bed large enough to sleep two people, and it is perfectly acceptable for a (mixed sex) couple to share the room at the 'single' rate. For this reason, couples whose preference is to share a bed should ask to see a single room before they pay

FARANJI PRICES

It is common practice for Ethiopian hotels to have a two-tiered pricing system, with higher rates being charged to foreigners than to Ethiopians. This is easier to justify in some cases than others. At the more justifiable extreme is the sort of upmarket or mid-range hotel that caters primarily to foreigners and is reasonably priced for what it is, but that effectively offers a discount to locals, who generally earn a lot less than foreigners. At the other extreme is the sort of hotel that caters almost exclusively to a local market, and is priced on that basis, but for some reason feels the need to ask the occasional foreign guest to pay an arbitrarily inflated and non-negotiable 'faranji price', one dictated by greed or discrimination rather than market forces, based on the notion that all foreigners are so rich, or so stupid, that they will pay whatever rate is asked of them. That's the hotel's prerogative, of course, but where faranji prices are significantly higher than the going rate for locals, those hotels that follow a one-price-for-all policy are going to be far better value, and tend to be more favourably reviewed in this book.

Watch out for a more devious approach wherein you take a room after being quoted a normal rate at reception, but are asked to pay a much higher rate by an aggressive hotel owner when you come to check out, on the basis his underling 'forgot' about the faranji price. To avoid being exposed to this sort of contrived misunderstanding, best pay for your room upon arrival. Equally irksome is the practice of charging inflated faranji prices on food and drinks, which has become quite common in the south. A bait and switch method is also often employed, in which the Ethiopian menu lists one set of prices but, when you go to pay, an English menu with higher prices is produced. Food in Ethiopia is pretty cheap, so your wallet doesn't take the same sort of beating it does with hotels. Nevertheless, many travellers prefer to seek out places that charge the same price for all.

extra for a double (which, more often than not, will actually be a twin). Note, too, that the room prices quoted in our listings refer to what a room actually is rather than what the hotel bills it as – if, for instance, a hotel charges US$5 for 'single room' with a double bed that two can share, then we would quote US$5 as the price of a double. Note that most Ethiopian hotels forbid two men to share a room, and many also forbid two women from doing so.

Accommodation entries in this guide are categorised under five main headings: luxury, upmarket, moderate, budget and shoestring. This categorisation is not rigid, since it depends on the feel of any given hotel as much as the price, it is often relative to the other options in that town, and there are many borderline cases. Nevertheless, it should help readers isolate the range of hotels in any given town that best suits their budget and taste. Broadly speaking, **luxury** hotels are truly world-class institutions that meet the highest standards, while **upmarket** hotels are top-drawer for Ethiopia but perhaps not quite so by international standards. **Moderate** hotels are more middling in quality but would still be comfortable enough for tourists used to developing world standards. **Budget** accommodation mostly consists of ungraded hotels that are aimed primarily at the local market but would still be considered reasonably comfortable by hardened backpackers, with facilities such as en-suite hot showers and satellite TV. **Shoestring** accommodation consists of the cheapest rooms around, usually unpretentious local guesthouses. Many shoestring places have shared toilets and showers, and beds may not be clean. If there are no nets, then pitching the inner section of a hiking tent on the mattress will keep bugs at bay. At the most basic off-the-beaten-track places, expect only a mattress on the floor, a rough hole in the ground in a shed as a toilet, and a bucket for washing.

The opportunities for organised camping in Ethiopia are very limited, and the additional weight and hassle involved in carrying camping equipment is difficult to justify. Camping equipment can be hired locally for hikes in Bale Mountains and Simien Mountains national parks, and it will usually be supplied by the operator on organised tours to these locations, the Danakil, or other areas without formal accommodation.

EATING AND DRINKING

To anyone who has travelled elsewhere in Africa, Ethiopian food comes as a welcome revelation. Instead of the bland gristle and starch that is the standard restaurant fare in most African small towns, Ethiopian food is deliciously spicy and you can eat well virtually anywhere in the country. Contrary to many people's expectations, most of Ethiopia is fertile, food is easy to find and portions are generous and very cheap. At local eateries, you'll often find that one plate of food will be adequate to feed two.

ETHIOPIAN DISHES A wide variety of different dishes is available in Ethiopia. Most of them are unique to the country, so it is worth familiarising yourself with their names as soon as you arrive.

The staple source of carbohydrates in Ethiopia is *injera*, a large, pancake-shaped substance made from *tef*, a nutty-tasting grain that is unique to Ethiopia and comes in three varieties: white, brown and red. The *tef* dough is fermented for up to three days before it is cooked, the result of which is a foam rubber texture and a slightly sour taste reminiscent of sherbet. The ritual is to take a piece of *injera* in your hand and use it to scoop up whatever accompaniment it comes with, then stuff the package into your mouth. If you dine with Ethiopians, it is customary for everyone to eat off the same plate.

Ethiopians will often tell you that *injera* is of little nutritional value. This is not the case at all. Gram for gram, *tef* supplies more fibre-rich bran and nutritious germ than any other grain, containing 15% protein, 3% fat and 82% complex carbohydrates. This is partly as a result of it being smaller than any other edible grain and having a proportionately larger husk, which is where most of the nutrients in any grain are stored. *Tef* contains almost 20 times more calcium than wheat or barley, it has two to three times the iron content of other grains, and it is the only grain to contain symbiotic yeast – which means that no yeast needs to be added during the preparation of *injera*.

The most common non-vegetarian accompaniment to *injera* is a dish called *tibs* (or more properly *siga tibs*, literally 'meat fried'), which as its name suggests consists of freshly flash-fried meat, spiced moderately and mixed in with onions and peppers. *Tibs* is often served with a spicy red powder called *mitmita* on the side, or with *awaze*, a sauce made from *beriberi* (powdered chilli) together with lime juice, salt, olive oil and a drop of whisky or wine. Particularly recommended is *shekla tibs*, where the fried meat is served in a clay pot that contains a charcoal burner.

Once ubiquitous on non-fasting days, *siga wot* (meat stew) is now far less popular than it used to be, at least in local restaurants, since, unlike *tibs*, it is not necessarily freshly prepared. Still, you will come across *siga wot* from time to time, especially in more upmarket restaurants. There are two main types of sauce: *kai wot* is red in colour and very hot, flavoured as it is with *beriberi*, onions and garlic, while *alicha wat* has a yellowish colour and is generally quite bland. Other meat dishes, found mainly in large towns, are crumbed meat or fish cutlet (*siga* or *asa kutilet*), roast meat (*siga arosto*), steak (*stek*) and a mildly spicy brown stew (*gulash*). Then there is *kitfo*, a bland form of fried mince, and *kitfo special*, the same dish but uncooked, which should be avoided purely for health reasons, as should *kurt* (pronounced 'court'), which is raw sliced beef.

The most common meat in the highlands is lamb (*bege*), while in drier areas you will most often be served with goat (*figel*). Beef (*bure*) is also eaten, mostly in large towns. In towns near lakes, fish (*asa*) predominates. You might also come across *tripe wat*, which is made with tripe but pronounced *trippy*. The official national dish of Ethiopia, *doro wot* is made with chicken, but is best avoided if you're hungry, as it is traditional to serve only a lonely drumstick or wing in a bowl of sauce. Normally *kai wat* consists of meat boiled in the *kai* sauce, but you may also come across *tibs kai wat*, which means the meat was fried before the sauce was added. If the meat is minced prior to cooking, then the dish is known as *minje tabish*.

Vegans and vegetarians are well catered for, since the Ethiopian Orthodox Church recognises around 200 fasting days, when the consumption of meat or other animal products is forbidden. Every Wednesday and Friday is a fasting day, as are the 40 days of Ethiopian Lent, which generally occupy most of March and April, and various other religious holidays. On fasting days, most places will serve *injera* with a vegan accompaniment. This might be spicy puréed chickpeas served in the form of thick paste-like *shiro tegamino* or the more watery *shiro wot*, or a similar dish made from beans (*kik wot*) or lentils (*misr wot*). Another common dish on fasting days is *atkilt bayinetu*, which more or less translates as 'vegetable buffet', and comprises dollops of one or more of the vegan dishes described above, as well as piles of spinach (*gomon*), beetroot (*kai iser*) and vegetable stew (*atkilt alicha*) heaped discretely in a circle on the *injera*. Meat will still be served in Muslim areas on fasting days, as well as at more tourist-oriented restaurants, but not in more off-the-beaten-track Christian areas.

A popular breakfast dish, and a useful fall-back in the evening if you don't fancy anything else that's on offer, is *inkolala tibs* (literally 'fried eggs', but more like scrambled eggs), cooked on request with slices of onion (*shinkuts*), green pepper (*karia*) and tomato (*tamatim*). Another common breakfast dish is *yinjera firfir*, which consists of pieces of *injera* soaked in *kai wat* sauce and eaten with – you guessed it – *injera*. Note that *firfir* literally means 'torn up': *inkolala firfir* is exactly the same as *inkolala tibs*, but hacked at a bit before it is served. Also popular at breakfast is *ful*, a spicy bean dish made with lots of garlic, a refreshing change from eggs when you can find it.

Menus are normally printed in Amharigna script so you will have to ask what's available ('*Magi min ale?*'). As a rule, you won't understand a word of the rushed reply, so you'll probably have to suggest a few possibilities yourself. The way to phrase this is to start with the type of meat, or vegetable (prefaced with *ye*), then the type of dish. In other words, fried goat is *yefigel tibs*, fish cutlet is *yasa kutilet*, *kai wat* made with lentils is *yemisr kai wat*, and *alicha wat* made with beef is *yebure alicha wat*. If all else fails, ask for *sekondo misto*, which consists of small portions of everything on the menu.

If you feel like a break from *injera* (and most travellers do), you can usually find fresh, crusty bread (*dabo*) as an alternative accompaniment, even in the smallest of villages. In addition, many local restaurants serve pasta skimpily topped with a spicy sauce, as well as pizzas and burgers, neither of which will necessarily conform to the average Westerner's expectations. These days, in all but the most remote of towns you will also find a few restaurants serving proper Western-style food, with the selection being greatest in Addis Ababa, though there is also plenty of choice in the likes of Bahir Dar, Gondar, Lalibela, Mekele, Harar, Dire Dawa, Hawassa and Arba Minch.

An attractive culinary feature of Ethiopia is the numerous pastry shops and cafés that adorn the streets of most medium to large towns. These generally serve a selection of freshly baked iced and plain cakes, wonderful biscuits and good bread, along with coffee, tea and puréed fruit juice. Pastry shops are great for sweet-toothed breakfasts and snacks, and you'll usually walk away with change from US$2. Also on the snack front, look out for *ashet* (roasted maize cobs); the cry of the kids who sell it, which sounds remarkably like *shit*, should attract your attention. *Kolo* is a delicious snack of roasted grains or pulses, sometimes covered in spices, and sold by the handful for a few cents.

KHAT AND MARIJUANA The mildly stimulating leaf known as *khat, qat* or *chat* is grown widely and legally in the southeast highlands of Ethiopia, where it is also consumed enthusiastically by locals (predominantly but by no means only Muslims) and is also transported in copious quantities to Addis Ababa, as well as across the border to Somaliland. The centre of *khat* cultivation and chewing is Harar – at the end of a bus ride in this area it looks as if the vehicle has been overrun by psycho-caterpillars – but you can get the stuff at markets all over the country. It's not expensive, but it's worth taking along an Ethiopian friend to ensure you locate the best-quality stuff – prices do reflect quality and the youngest leaves are the best.

Khat is generally imbibed socially. A few people will gather in a room, grab a few branches each, pick off the greenest leaves, pop them into their mouth one by one, mush it all up into a cud, chew for a few hours and then, with whatever strength is left in their jaw, spit out the remaining pulp. The leaves taste very bitter so a sweet tea or bottle of soft drink helps the medicine go down. Usually the entire afternoon is devoted to group mastication, leaving the assembled company manically talkative and in a mildly heightened state of awareness that the Somali refer to as *mirqaan*. *Khat* has its devotees among travellers, but most find the effort involved in chewing themselves into foul-tasting not-quite-oblivion holds little appeal – especially when all sorts of cheap, pleasant-tasting, no-effort-required alcoholic substances are widely available in the country!

Sticking with leaves green and mind-altering, it should be clarified that the link between Rastafarianism and Ethiopians is by and large a one-way thing. Smoking marijuana is illegal in Ethiopia and less socially acceptable than in most Western countries, so travellers who indulge risk landing themselves in big trouble.

DRINKS Given that the Kaffa province of Ethiopia is thought to be where coffee originated, and the coffee bean accounts for more than half of Ethiopia's exports, it should be no surprise that Ethiopians are coffee mad. The local espresso-style coffee (*buna*), served with two spoons of sugar, is rich, sweet and thoroughly addictive. Coffee with milk is *buna watat*. In small towns, sweet tea (*shai*) is more widely available than coffee.

BACKGROUND TO THE COFFEE CEREMONY   *John Grinling*

The Ethiopian coffee ceremony may also be seen as a ritual to please and placate spirits known as *zar* who, according to beliefs quite common in Ethiopia and surrounding countries, dwell among people and have the capacity to harm, protect or even possess them. Watch a ceremony with minimal attention and you'll notice that fresh grass is strewn over the floor, to make the *zar* spirits – who normally abide in nature – feel at home. Incense is burned, because its perfumed scents are known to please the spirits. The tray on which the coffee is served always has at least one cup more than the number of human participants, again for the *zars*. The lady pouring the coffee holds the *gabana* (coffee pot) high and doesn't mind when the tray gets splashed, because the *zars* like froth, and the more humble among them will drink from the tray. Any popped corn that falls on the ground is meant for the *zars*. In some more extreme and rather secret occurrences, the coffee ceremony is deliberately meant as an opportunity for a *zar* to take possession of one or another of the participants.

The origin of these ritualistic aspects of the coffee ceremony is probably animist, but filtered through the Muslim culture of eastern Ethiopia and Somalia. For this reason, the Ethiopian Orthodox Church once forbade devout Christians to take part in the ceremony, and encouraged its adherents to drink tea and *tella* in preference to coffee. The ceremony was incorporated into the Christian culture in around 1890, probably in the aftermath of Harar and other parts of the east being conquered by Emperor Menelik II and annexed to his empire. So while the Ethiopian coffee ceremony today is essentially a social event, providing an opportunity for family, friends, neighbours and colleagues to spend time together, it can also have a much deeper significance, symbolising that while we must always show respect to our fellow human beings, we should also honour the natural forces that can influence and change our lives.

You'll often be invited to join a traditional coffee ceremony, in which the grains are roasted over charcoal, ground while the water is boiled, then used to make three successive pots of coffee. It is in principle considered rude to leave before the third round has been drunk, but in our modern hurried society, you may explain without creating too much commotion that you are going to drink one cup only, as you have some urgent matter to deal with. Better even is to accept two cups and then go, as it is a widespread belief that you must have two of any food or beverage offered, such as *gursha* (a mouthful put directly in your mouth by your host). It might be perceived that you do not enjoy yourself if you have only one.

The usual soft drinks – Coca-Cola, Pepsi, Fanta – are widely available and very cheap. The generic name for soft drinks is *leslasa*. The Harar Brewery also produces a non-alcoholic malt beverage (apparently aimed at the Muslim population) called Sofi, which tastes similar to cola and is said to be good for an upset stomach.

Tap water is regarded to be unsafe to drink. Locally bottled sparkling mineral water, ubiquitously known as Ambo, the name of the best-known brand, is widely available in recyclable 750ml glass bottles. Still water is also available in eco-unfriendly plastic bottles. The major brand is called Highland, and you will often hear roadside children screaming this word repeatedly in the hope that you will toss them an empty bottle!

Ethiopia's prime soft drink is fruit juice, which is really puréed fruit. What is available depends somewhat on season and location, but the most common juices are banana, avocado, papaya, orange and guava. Highly recommended is the avocado, which sounds odd but is delicious with a squeeze of fresh lime and is sometimes layered with grenadine syrup. If in doubt, ask for *espris*, which consists of layers of all available juices. The result is thick, creamy, healthy and absolutely fantastic. A glass of juice generally costs less than US$1.

The most popular local tipple is *tej*, a meadlike drink made from honey (*mar*) or sugar (*isukalama*). *Tej* varies greatly in alcohol content, with the mildest forms being comparable to beer, and the strongest more like a spirit, so be sure to ask what you are getting. *Mar tej* is a considerable improvement on most African home brews, but not to everybody's taste. *Isukalama tej* is entirely avoidable. *Tej* is not served in normal bars; you will have to go to a *tej bet* to drink it. A 750ml bottle of *tej* costs around US$1. Locally brewed beer, made from millet or maize, is called *tella*. This is similar to the local brew of east and southern Africa, and no less foul in Ethiopia than it is elsewhere in the region.

Acceptable bottled lager is sold throughout Ethiopia. There are several brands, among them Castel, Bati, Bedele, St George, Harar, Walia and Dashen. A 350ml bottle of beer costs less than US$1, with prices varying slightly depending on where you buy it. Draught lager is available in Addis and quite a few other towns around the country, and it is very cheap. Ethiopia has been a wine producer for several decades, but the established Gouder brand is an acquired taste. By contrast, the Acacia and Rift Valley ranges, first produced by the Castel Vineyard outside Ziway in 2014, make for great easy drinking. Imported wines are also available at better restaurants. Imported spirits are served in most bars at very low prices for generous tots.

PUBLIC HOLIDAYS AND FESTIVAL DAYS

In any country you should be aware of public holidays, as many shops will be closed. The most significant practical consequence of public holidays in Ethiopia is that banks close, something you should plan around when you change money, especially if you travel between March and May, when most of the holidays are concentrated. Enkutatash (Ethiopian New Year) and most religious public holidays are generally celebrated with some festivity, so it is worth trying to get to one of the main religious sites – Lalibela, Gondar or Axum – for the occasion.

FIXED DATE HOLIDAYS

7 January	Genna (Ethiopian Christmas)
19 January	Timkat (Ethiopian Epiphany)
2 March	Adwa Day
1 May	International Labour Day
5 May	Patriots' Victory Day
28 May	Downfall of the Derg
11 September	Enkutatash (Ethiopian New Year)
27 September	Meskel (Finding of the True Cross)

MOVEABLE HOLIDAYS Three moveable public holidays are recognised, namely Siklet (Ethiopian Good Friday, which falls two days before the Orthodox Easter Sunday (Fasika) but usually on a different date from its non-Orthodox counterpart), Eid al-Fitr (End of Ramadan) and Eid al-Adha (Feast of Sacrifice). These will be as follows during the probable lifespan of this edition:

	2019	2020	2021
Siklet	26 April	17 April	30 April
Eid al-Fitr	5 June	24 May	13 May
Eid al-Adha	12 August	31 July	20 July

FESTIVAL DAYS Ethiopia has several unique festival days, the best known being Genna (Ethiopian Christmas), Timkat (often referred to as Ethiopian Epiphany), Enkutatash (Ethiopian New Year) and Meskel (the Finding of the True Cross). Enkutatash is celebrated throughout the country, but the other three holidays are associated with the Ethiopian Orthodox Church and tend to be celebrated only in areas where that is the dominant religion. Large numbers of local pilgrims and international tourists descend on the likes of Lalibela, Aksum and Gondar on these religious holidays, causing accommodation to become scarce and prices to skyrocket.

Genna Also known as Leddet, Genna, the Ethiopian equivalent to Christmas, commemorates the birth of Jesus Christ, and its name derives from an Amharic word meaning 'imminent'. It is celebrated on 7 January (a day later in leap years), after 43 days of fasting that culminate in an all-night church vigil on the night before the feast. Like its Western counterpart, Genna is a family-oriented holiday, but there is not a strong tradition of gift-giving, which creates a more devout character. In some areas, the holiday is marked by local festivities such as traditional dancing, as well as a hockey-like game called Yegenna Chewata which was supposedly played by the local shepherds on the night Jesus was born. It is traditional to eat the national dish *doro wot* (spicy chicken stew) over Genna.

Timkat More important to Orthodox Christians than Christmas, this three-day festival commemorating Jesus's baptism in the Jordan River culminates on 19 January (20 January in leap years) with a colourful procession during which the *tabot* (replica Ark of the Covenant) is removed from church altars and

EQUIPMENT Although with some thought and an eye for composition you can take reasonable photographs with a 'point-and-shoot' camera, you need an SLR camera with one or more lenses if you are at all serious about photography. The most important component in a digital SLR is the sensor. There are two types of sensor: DX and FX. The FX is a full-size sensor identical to the old film size (35mm). The DX sensor is half size and produces less quality. Your choice of lenses will be determined by whether you have a DX or FX sensor in your camera as the DX sensor introduces a 1.5x multiplication to the focal length. So a 300mm lens becomes in effect a 450mm lens. FX (full frame) sensors are the future, so I will further refer to focal lengths appropriate to the FX sensor.

Always buy the best lens you can afford. Fixed fast lenses are ideal, but very costly. Zoom lenses are easier to change composition without changing lenses the whole time. If you carry only one lens a 24–70mm or similar zoom should be ideal. For a second lens, a lightweight 80–200mm or 70–300mm or similar will be excellent for candid shots and varying your composition. Wildlife photography will be very frustrating if you don't have at least a 300mm lens. For a small loss of quality, teleconverters are a cheap and compact way to increase magnification: a 300mm lens with a 1.4x converter becomes 420mm, and with a 2x it becomes 600mm. NB: 1.4x and 2x teleconverters reduce the speed of your lens by 1.4 and 2 stops respectively.

The resolution of digital cameras is improving all the time. For ordinary prints an 8-megapixel camera is fine. For better results and the possibility to enlarge images and for professional reproduction, higher resolution is available up to 50 megapixels.

It is important to have enough memory space when photographing on your holiday. The number of pictures you can fit on a card depends on the quality you choose. You should calculate how many pictures you can fit on a card and either take enough cards or take a storage drive on to which you can download the cards' content. You can obviously take a laptop or tablet which gives the advantage that you can see your pictures properly at the end of each day, edit them and delete rejects.

Keep in mind that digital camera batteries, computers and other electronic devices need charging. Make sure you have all the chargers, cables and converters with you. Practically all hotels/lodges have charging points, though power cuts are frequent throughout Ethiopia. When camping you might have to rely on charging from the car battery.

---

swaddled in colourful cloth before being paraded around. Timkat is a big event in Lalibela, but the place to be for the occasion is Gondar, where a magnificent procession climaxes with hundreds of eager participants leaping into Fasilidas's Pool to re-enact the original baptism.

Enkutatash Ethiopia's most important secular holiday, New Year has a double significance as the date when the Queen of Sheba supposedly arrived back in Axum after having visited King Solomon in Jerusalem. It is celebrated vigorously throughout the country on 11 September (12 September in leap years), and has a similar party atmosphere to New Year festivities elsewhere.

Meskel Sharing its name with the yellow flowers that blanket the Ethiopian Highlands at that time of year, Meskel, celebrated on 27 September (28 September in leap years), is associated with a legend, dating to the early 4th century AD, that

DUST AND HEAT Dust and heat are often a problem. Keep your equipment in a sealed bag, and avoid exposing equipment to the sun when possible. Digital cameras are prone to collecting dust particles on the sensor, which results in spots on the image. The dirt mostly enters the camera when changing lenses, so you should be careful when doing this. To some extent photos can be 'cleaned' up afterwards in Photoshop, but this is time-consuming. You can have your camera sensor professionally cleaned, or you can do this yourself with special brushes and swabs made for this purpose, but note that touching the sensor might cause damage and should only be done with the greatest care.

LIGHT The most striking outdoor photographs are often taken during the hour or two of 'golden light' after dawn and before sunset. Shooting in low light may enforce the use of very low shutter speeds, in which case a tripod/beanbag will be required to avoid camera shake. The most advanced digital SLRs have very little loss of quality on higher ISO settings, which allows you to shoot at lower light conditions. It is still recommended not to increase the ISO unless necessary.

With careful handling, side-lighting and back-lighting can produce stunning effects, especially in soft light and at sunrise or sunset. Generally, however, it is best to shoot with the sun behind you. When photographing animals or people in the harsh midday sun, images taken in light but even shade may look nicer than those taken in direct sunlight or patchy shade, which create too much contrast.

PROTOCOL In some countries, it is unacceptable to photograph local people without permission, and many people will refuse to pose or will ask for a donation. In such circumstances, don't try to sneak photographs as you might get yourself into trouble. Even the most willing subject will often pose stiffly when a camera is pointed at them; relax them by making a joke, and take a few shots in quick succession to improve the odds of capturing a natural pose.

Ariadne Van Zandbergen is a professional travel and wildlife photographer specialising in Africa. She runs 'The Africa Image Library' (see ad, page 320). For photo requests, visit the website w africaimagelibrary.com or contact her direct at e info@ africaimagelibrary.com.

claims Emperor Constantine's mother Helen discovered the cross on which Jesus was crucified almost 300 years after the event. According to Ethiopian Christians, a fragment of this holiest of relics given to Emperor Dawit I in the early 15th century is now stowed away in the monastery of Gishen Maryam, to the northwest of Dessie. The colourful festival's showpiece is the burning of a massive pyre at sites such as Meskel Square in Addis Ababa or the park in front of the main stelae field in Axum.

SHOPPING

Ethiopia is not by any stretch of the imagination a shopping destination à la Dubai or London, but urban shops are quite well stocked and you should be able to get hold of most non-specialist requirements, especially in Addis Ababa. Most medium to large towns will have a few stationery shops, pharmacies and small supermarkets, and in smaller towns and villages you'll find a souk (small store) or three selling

Adrian Greenwood

Ethiopia has a long tradition of producing unique and collectable artefacts. In recent years, however, certain outlets have started selling more modern pseudo-ethnic artefacts – often made outside Ethiopia and with no connection to it – designed to attract harassed short-stay visitors wanting to take a present home. These items are best avoided – it is better to support the Ethiopian economy by buying a range of good quality artefacts produced locally. Ideally, you would buy at source (baskets in Harar, *agelgils* in Bahir Dar, Jimma stools in Kaffa, and so on) but, where that isn't possible, a good range of items can be found in Addis Ababa or other tourist centres.

BASKETWORK AND *AGELGILS* For generations, Ethiopians have woven a variety of baskets and containers for daily use. The local technique entails producing a tight coil of straight grass, which is bound in flat grass and sewn on to itself as the coil gets larger. The finer the coil, the better. Coloured grasses are woven into the original to create intricate patterns, complicated work that requires a 3D view at all times.

Harar is said to be the home of the best basket-makers but good examples can be found throughout the north. The people of Harar do have a tradition of 14 different types of basket for dowries, and these naturally coloured old artefacts take pride of place on the walls of their Arabic-style houses. Old baskets are difficult to buy and command premium prices, while more modern pieces, though just as skilfully made, often look quite garish as a result of using chemically produced pigments. A good compromise is to buy modern work in natural tan only.

An *agelgil* is a sort of leather picnic basket used to carry *injera*. Some are made with dark brown leather, others with a dappled animal skin. They come in various sizes and can be bought easily in the Bahir Dar and Lake Tana region.

There is also a pretty long basket made from coarser grasses, woven around 15–40 longer stalks of reeds, usually striped in shades of black, brown and tan. These are decorative and cheap to buy.

SILVER AND CROSSES Crosses are a popular personal adornment with Orthodox Christians. Small crosses are worn as necklaces by individuals, while larger ones are used for ceremonial purposes. Many metals are used and hundreds of designs are available. The best crosses are cut from 1780 silver Maria Theresa thalers, which were once common coinage in Ethiopia, and tend to be very smooth to the touch, particularly older worn pieces. Valuable old pieces are seldom on sale and illegal to export, but cheaper crosses of all types are still produced and can be bought without risking robbing a church of its ancient heritage. Ethiopian cross styles are often described according to their putative town of origin, but it is not clear whether Axum, Lalibela or Gondar crosses really belong to the eponymous town, and they are all freely available everywhere. Decorative silver ornaments produced by Yemeni and Arab craftsmen are popular among the Muslims of Hara and Afar.

TEXTILES AND SHAMAS The locally woven white or off-white cotton cloths typical of highland Ethiopia are easy to buy in any market. The *shama* is the ubiquitous cloth of the male, wrapped around the heads and shoulders on cold mornings, while women often use a more elaborate version with a colourful border to make dresses worn particularly on Sundays and holy days. Decorative wool rugs, usually in shades of brown and tan, with simple designs such as a stylised lion or house, are made in the factory town of Debre Berhan, and make an unusual present.

BETA ISRAEL GOODS Woleka, just outside Gondar, is the place to buy pottery associated with the Beta Israel. These pre-Talmudic Jews specialise in black terracotta figurines of daily life, usually adorned with the Star of David. The better-quality figurines made before Ethiopia's Jews were airlifted to Israel are very collectable, but difficult to find and not very robust. There are also pre-Peace Corps and post-Peace Corps designs, as help was given by US potters to make the figures durable. Both types of design are good. When the original potters were airlifted out, standards dropped enormously but there are now signs of revival. The figurines are sold at a more or less fixed price, and this is very low by Western standards. They are difficult to get home in one piece but can be packed in dirty socks and underwear!

RELIGIOUS PAINTINGS AND MANUSCRIPTS Here one needs to be fairly careful, as many genuinely old manuscripts and church paintings are on the market, probably taken from the plentiful supplies of Orthodox churches. It is both illegal and ethically dubious to export such pieces, and we should develop the same critique of them as we have for items made of ivory or endangered animal skins. Parallel to the genuinely old pieces, however, there is a legitimate movement to recreate modern versions of old designs, with freshly painted icons and copies of manuscripts on parchment. Most cover religious themes, but others cover more quirky Ethiopian themes, in particular the strip cartoon renderings of the story of the birth of Emperor Menelik I to the Queen of Sheba.

WOODWORK Ethiopia has a long tradition of making wooden household items using hardwood trees such as *Cordia africana*, which grows in forests around Jimma. The standard Jimma stool, made out of a single block of wood, is not too expensive, but those with straight or curved backs command a premium. A good purchase is the widely played board game of Gebede or Kalaha, which entails two opponents distributing stones across a wooden board with 12 hollows – a game of skill that contains no element of chance at all, making it excellent preparation for children to learn how to calculate. In South Omo, men often carry headrests to protect their elaborate hairstyles when they lie on the ground. Made out of one piece of wood, these headrests usually have a braided leather handle, and are often decorated with geometrical patterns.

GOURDS, CALABASHES AND CHOICHO Particularly in the south and west, sturdy dry gourds or calabashes, ornamented with leather straps for easier carrying, are used as containers for liquids and dry goods. They are sometimes decorated with basketwork or glass pearls, or incised with geometrical patterns then rubbed with dirt to give a black pattern, or more occasionally engraved with pictures of animals. The choicho is a calabash or terracotta pot, ornately decorated with cowrie shells and leather, used to collect and store milk.

MISCELLANEOUS Jewellery is popular with Ethiopians. Amber is expensive and found mostly around Harar. Elsewhere, cheap coloured glass pearls are easy to find. Lip plates from the Mursi and Suri, or warthog tusks or copper bangles, can often be bought directly from the tribespeople. Stonework is produced near Axum, usually effigies of Solomon and Sheba or icons. Terracotta coffee pots are popular and readily available.

basics and essentials such as batteries, pens, paper, soap, washing powder, dry biscuits, boiled sweets, bottled drinks, incense and toilet rolls (which Ethiopians rather endearingly call *softi*). Shopping for books, maps, travel gear or other more specialist items is best done in Addis Ababa.

MARKETS Although 21st-century mall culture has infiltrated Addis Ababa and a few other large towns in Ethiopia, markets remain an economic and social mainstay of rural and small-town life. Smaller Ethiopian towns and villages typically have one main market day, most commonly but certainly not always Saturday, while others have two. Market day is when farmers and artisans from miles around come to the closest town or large village, to sell their produce, to buy manufactured goods, and to catch up with local news and gossip. Market days are usually the best days to visit off-the-beaten-track areas, as there will be far more transport. In smaller towns, the market is usually rather inactive on other days. In larger towns and cities, things get into full swing on semi-official market days, but there is usually some activity throughout the week. Ethiopia's best urban markets are probably those in Bahir Dar and Axum, while the most spectacular livestock markets are held every Monday at Bati (near Dessie and Kombolcha) and on Monday and Thursday at Babile (near Harar). The many village markets scattered around South Omo are also very worthwhile, though often rather touristy. In many ways, the best way to experience a market is just to stop off at an arbitrary town or village on the right day, and wander around informally. It is worth noting that buying handicrafts and other locally produced goods from markets as opposed to shops actively puts money into the hands of local communities.

HANDICRAFTS AND CURIOS Ethiopia offers a rich variety of locally made products to handicraft enthusiasts. These can be bought at stalls and shops in all major tourist centres, with Addis Ababa, Bahir Dar, Axum and Lalibela being especially well endowed in this respect. A renowned source of traditional hand-woven cloths such as *gabbi* and *shama*, sold in strips of around 90cm wide, is the village of Dorze in the far southwest close to Arba Minch, or the Dorze-dominated market at Shiro Meda in Addis Ababa. Religious artefacts include hand-held crosses, which are made using anything from inexpensive wood and bone to valuable silver and gold, as well as painted icons. Other popular items include goat-hide *agelgil* baskets, traditionally used by local shepherds to carry *injera*, and wooden Jimma stools. When shopping, handicraft stalls or stores generally have fixed prices and offer a more hassle-free experience, but buying at markets is more fun and cheaper, assuming you possess reasonable bargaining skills. See also the box on page 112.

Many of Ethiopia's ancient treasures have been stolen or removed from the country in recent decades, most infamously the 7kg gold Lalibela Cross that was stolen from the Church of Medhane Alem in Lalibela in March 1997 and returned two years later. But many smaller items have gone, mostly never to return, and the authorities have understandably cracked down on what tourists can take out of the country. Indeed, individual tourists should think twice before they buy antiquities – aside from the fact that such behaviour is gradually depleting the country of its cultural resources, many genuine old items will have been stolen from their real owner for resale to tourists.

Adrian Greenwood notes:

> Popular gifts for those back home are *beriberi* spice, incense, tea and coffee. *Beriberi* can be bought in any supermarket in Addis, and it is worth buying the most expensive sort. It comes in rather larger packages than a Westerner might want, but tastes good in goulash, for example. Incense is a little harder to locate but is usually to be found

in a good market. Tea comes in two varieties, Addis tea and Wushwush tea. Both are good and ridiculously cheap. Coffee is of course Ethiopia's number one export. It tastes magnificent in Ethiopia, but some tourists report that it doesn't taste the same back home in Europe. Why not try it for yourself?

NIGHTLIFE

Most Ethiopian towns can be relied upon to have a handful of lively bars, and it's easy enough to follow your nose if you are looking for a sociable drink. The atmosphere in Ethiopian bars is generally easy and inclusive, and locals who speak a bit of English will go out of their way to chat to you. Bars are also often the best place to hear Ethiopia's idiosyncratic traditional and contemporary music, though increasingly the hi-fi is subservient to the television when football is being broadcast live. (For more information about Ethiopian music, see page 53.)

If Ethiopian music is refreshingly odd, the dancing is plain bizarre, particularly the styles that originate in the north but which are now practised in most of the country. In some parts of Ethiopia people traditionally leap up and down like the Maasai, or do the more standard hip wriggling of east Africa. But it is the women of Amhara and Tigray that stick in the mind – fixed grins, hot-coal eyes and madly flapping breasts all held together by shuddering shoulder movements, creating a whirling demonic whole that manages to be robotic and erotic at the same time. Several cultural restaurants and bars in Addis Ababa and elsewhere have resident bands and dancers, and while their shows are inevitably a bit staged, there is no need to be just an observer – audience members frequently join in, and foreigners are always encouraged to provide some amusement by attempting to emulate the moves!

MEDIA AND COMMUNICATIONS

NEWSPAPERS English-language weekly papers published in Addis Ababa include *Fortune* (w *addisfortune.net*) and *Capital* (w *capitalethiopia.com*), both of which come out on Sunday, and the *Reporter* (w *thereporterethiopia.com*). These are widely sold in the streets and supermarkets of the capital, where you might also be able to locate secondhand copies of *Newsweek* and *The Economist* along Churchill Avenue.

TELEVISION The state-owned Ethiopian Broadcasting Corporation (EBC) isn't much to get excited about and the content of its three national channels is mostly in Amharigna. Most hotels in the moderate and higher brackets also subscribe to one of two multichannel satellite services including the South African-based DSTV, which is strong on international news, sport and light entertainment. The increased ubiquity of televisions is something of a mixed blessing – it's great when you want some news from home, or to watch live sport, but there are times when it seems impossible to find a bar or restaurant whose atmosphere isn't dominated by a television shouting at the clientele.

POST Ethiopia has a good internal and international post service, which celebrated its centenary in 1994. Mail between most parts of Europe and Addis Ababa takes around a week, but it can take longer from elsewhere in the world. Post offices can be found in most larger towns and cities, and rates are very cheap.

TELEPHONE Ethiopia has a decent telephone service when compared with most parts of Africa. There are telecommunications centres in most towns, and even functional phone booths. Mobile phones have become extremely popular. The only provider for both land and mobile lines is the government-owned Ethio Telecom (w *ethiotelecom.et*). If you want to buy a local SIM card for your mobile, note that the device must first be registered with customs at Bole International Airport (page 87). Local SIM cards are sold for next to nothing upon presentation of your registered mobile phone and your passport at several shops in Addis Ababa (see the website for a full list), as well as at the Telecom office in most other towns. Airtime can be bought in the form of prepaid scratch cards, which are readily available in most towns. Some international mobile phones work in Ethiopia, but at much higher airtime rates. Mobile coverage is excellent when it works, but the network is often overloaded due to high volume.

Where possible, listings in this book include a landline (indicated by a ℩ symbol and 'nnn nnn nnnn' format), as well as a mobile number (usually starting '09', indicated by a m symbol, and 'nnnn nnnnnn' format). Generally speaking, the mobile network is better than the land network, so it makes sense to try that number first. However, mobile numbers are also more likely to be associated with an individual manager or staff member, which means they are prone to be rendered obsolete by personnel changes. Landlines, by contrast, are usually attached to the listed institution, so are unlikely to change so often. If you dial from outside the country, start with the international telephone code (+251) and drop the leading zero from the individual number.

INTERNET AND EMAIL Ethiopia lags behind the rest of the world when it comes to internet coverage. Indeed, its penetration rate of 15.4% in 2017 is among the lowest in sub-Saharan Africa, in large part due to the state-owned Ethio Telecom's monopoly as the country's sole service provider. This has resulted in internet access being very slow and erratic, with the overloaded network often going down for hours at a time outside of Addis Ababa, though coverage in 2018 is better than it was a few years back. The easiest way to access the internet cheaply and reasonably reliably is to insert a local SIM card in your mobile phone, and convert airtime to a data bundle. If you don't have a local SIM card, almost all hotels in the moderate or higher categories offer free Wi-Fi to guests, as do the majority of budget and shoestring hotels that routinely cater to international visitors, at least when the network is up and running. If your hotel doesn't have Wi-Fi, head to the nearest upmarket hotel, order a coffee or beer there, and you should be allowed to use theirs for free. Some restaurants in the larger centres also now offer free Wi-Fi. In addition, internet cafés, though not as ubiquitous as they used to be, are dotted around Addis Ababa and other large towns. Despite this, we would encourage visitors to Ethiopia to plan on having limited access outside of Addis Ababa, and to warn loved ones or business associates at home that contact may be intermittent. Note also that the government has blocked access to the likes of Facebook and WhatsApp on several occasions since the outbreak of anti-government protests in 2016.

Email and internet are far from being a standard medium of communication in Ethiopia. Except at the very top end of the price scale, very few hotels and other such institutions have websites or email addresses, and even if they do in theory, the URLs and email addresses printed boldly on business cards or signposts are often misspelt or non-existent. We have done our best to validate all URLs and any improbable-looking email addresses before including them in this book, but even this can be problematic, as domains we discover to be expired or suspended might yet be reactivated, and email addresses whose inbox is so full that new emails sent to them bounce back might one day be emptied. Furthermore, even where addresses are valid, a great many Ethiopians are not in the habit of replying to emails, so you are far more likely to get somewhere by phoning instead.

LOCAL INTERACTION

ETIQUETTE Although things are changing, especially in Addis Ababa, Ethiopia remains a very conservative and religious country whose Christian and Muslim inhabitants both tend to dress modestly by international standards. Male travellers are advised to wear long trousers where climatic conditions permit, though shorts may be more practical in hotter areas where people tend to dress more lightly, and a shirt that fully covers their shoulders. Woman should ideally wear a long flowing shirt, and a dress that covers the shoulders and knees, or loose trousers, though the latter might be viewed as quite eccentric attire in more conservative areas.

In Ethiopia, as in many Islamic countries, it is customary to reserve the left hand for ablutions and the right hand for activities that involve direct or indirect contact with other people. For this reason, Ethiopians view it as unhygienic to use the left hand to eat, or to pass money or objects, or to shake hands. This is particularly important when you eat communally, as is customary in Ethiopia. In this situation, you may well find the host or another guest tries to feed you something with their hand. Known as *gursa*, this custom is a sign of respect towards a visitor, and it would be rude to refuse the offering.

When you visit a historic church, be aware that Ethiopian Orthodox Christianity retains several ancient Judaic rituals abandoned by European denominations. Some churches, for instance, retain separate doors for men and women, in which case visitors are expected to use the appropriate entrance. Women are traditionally required to cover their body and hair with a long dress and a scarf before entering a church (a custom no longer imposed rigidly on foreigners, but best adhered to in rural areas where people are unused to tourists) and are forbidden from entering any church at all during menstruation. There are taboos on anybody, male or female, who had sex the previous night or who has already eaten that day entering specific churches on specific days. More mundanely, you can enter a church barefoot or with socks on, but shoes must be removed and left outside.

Ethiopians consider it rude to launch into a conversation of any sort without first exchanging greetings and enquiring after each other's health. Men shake hands elaborately, with both parties bowing and touching shoulders immediately after their hands make contact. Woman tend to greet loudly but without touching, though close friends or relations might lightly kiss cheeks three times.

TIPPING AND GUIDE FEES The qualified guides who work in Ethiopia's main historical centres usually charge a fixed fee of US$15–25 per party per day. They will sometimes be open to negotiation out of season. If you want to arrange informal guides in other areas, it is best to discuss a fee in advance. It is difficult to generalise, but US$1 per hour for a youngster and twice that amount for an adult feels about right, depending on how long you are out, and whether you are in an expensive town or in a rural area where money goes further.

There are some tiresome guides (mostly non-professional) who will routinely go into a sulk after you have paid them in the hope they can manipulate a bit of extra cash out of you, often spoiling what might otherwise have been a good day out in the process. Never give in to this sort of manipulative behaviour! And if any guide happens to pull the old stunt of thrusting your payment back into your hands in feigned disgust at its paltriness, call his bluff – take the money, walk off, and you'll be amazed how quickly he decides that he actually would like the money after all.

Tipping waiters is not quite so customary in Ethiopia as it is in many other countries, but any such tip will be greatly appreciated by a recipient on a pittance of a salary. At upmarket restaurants in Addis Ababa and other tourist centres, the 10% tip customary in many Western countries is a fair-to-generous guideline (in fact, a service charge is levied at many such restaurants, but the odds of this ending up in the hands of the waiters and waitresses is negligible). Elsewhere, it's entirely at your discretion, but it never hurts to leave behind a small note with your bill in a coffee or pastry shop or local restaurant.

OVERCHARGING AND BARGAINING Hotel rates aside, overcharging tourists is relatively uncommon in Ethiopia, but it happens, especially in Addis Ababa and at certain major tourist centres. If you think you are being overcharged, rather than accusing the person of ripping you off, just query the price gently, or simply say it is too expensive for you. This gives the person the opportunity to save face and lower the price in a manner that seems generous.

Bear in mind, however, that bargaining is acceptable to Ethiopians in many situations, and that there *is* a difference between blatant overcharging and asking a flexible price. You will always need to bargain to get a decent price with taxi and *bajaj* drivers, and at curio stalls anywhere in the country. By contrast, overcharging is not a normal practice on buses and on other public transport, whereas it has become institutionalised in the form of non-negotiable '*faranji* prices' at many hotels and restaurants (see box, page 103).

GIFTS AND BEGGING There are beggars everywhere in Ethiopia, especially in Addis Ababa, and most of them make a beeline for foreigners. Ethiopians themselves often give loose change to genuine beggars, and there is no reason why tourists shouldn't follow suit. However, there are also plenty of chancers around – adults and children – who'll try to hit on any passing *faranji* for a handout, and for obvious reasons they are best ignored.

We are often surprised at how many tourists travel around countries like Ethiopia arbitrarily handing out gifts – be it sweets or biscuits, pens or money – to children. It is an understandable response to being in a poor country, and is often tacitly encouraged by tour operators and guides, but we feel strongly that it should be discouraged. For one thing, it reinforces a culture of begging and dependency that is already prevalent in Ethiopia, as epitomised by the common practice of begging for plastic water bottles (the usual refrain being 'Highland, Highland', the brand name of the most common bottled water), as well as more random treats such as biscuits and sweets (both of which can have a detrimental effect on teeth in a country where dental health care is minimal).

In several parts of Ethiopia, children now routinely skip school, preferring to dance and sing for tourists, or simply trail behind them, in the hope of earning some money or begging for treats. Indeed, in parts of the south, we've come across children lining across the road and refusing to move – doing the splits or dancing in the middle of the road as the car approaches – a scenario that seems bound to result in a fatal accident sooner or later. In addition, many young beggars are in fact controlled by adult relatives, who encourage them to abandon their education in order to supplement the family income.

Finally, and more selfishly, encouraging child beggars will only create more hassles for the next group of tourists that passes by. In some Ethiopian towns, independent travellers might be asked for money or sweets or a pen 100 times a day. Equally, there are still places in Ethiopia where children are genuinely friendly and never ask for things. It requires only one naive tourist and a bag of sweets to change that.

RESPONSIBLE TOURISM

Bradt Guides is an advocate of Responsible Tourism, and readers unfamiliar with this concept are pointed to the excellent website of the British organisation Tourism Concern (w *tourismconcern.org.uk*) for further details of what this entails. However, we also think it is important to note that the promotion of Responsible Tourism is not intended to imply that conventional travel is inherently irresponsible or damaging to developing countries. On the contrary, as the world's largest industry, tourism is an immensely powerful economic stimulant, with some 15% of jobs worldwide being tourism-related. All the more so in a poor country such as Ethiopia, where community tourist projects and more straightforward private developments such as hotels and restaurants all create employment and raise foreign revenue. Ultimately, almost any sustainable tourism venture in Africa falls into the category 'trade not aid' and will contribute to the economic development (and/or cultural and environmental preservation) of those countries where it is most needed.

HEALTH   *With Dr Felicity Nicholson*

Ethiopia, like most parts of Africa, is home to several tropical diseases unfamiliar to people living in more temperate and sanitary climates. However, with adequate preparation, and a sensible attitude to malaria prevention, the chances of serious mishap are small. To put this in perspective, your greatest concern after malaria should not be the combined exotica of venomous snakes, stampeding wildlife, gun-happy soldiers or the Ebola virus, but something altogether more mundane: a road accident.

Within Ethiopia, adequate (but well short of world-class) clinics and hospitals can be found in Addis Ababa and a few other major centres, while functional doctor's rooms (known as 'higher clinics'), laboratories and pharmacies are available countrywide. Wherever you go, doctors and pharmacists will generally speak passable English, and consultation and laboratory fees (in particular malaria tests) are inexpensive by international standards – so if in doubt, seek medical help.

PREPARATIONS Sensible preparation will go a long way to ensuring your trip goes smoothly. Particularly for first-time visitors to Africa, this includes a visit to a travel clinic to discuss matters such as vaccinations and malaria prevention. A full list of current travel clinic websites worldwide is available on w istm.org. For other journey preparation information, consult w travelhealthpro.org.uk (UK) or w wwwnc. cdc.gov/travel/ (USA). Information about various medications may be found on w netdoctor.co.uk/travel. All advice found online should be used in conjunction with expert advice received prior to or during travel. The Bradt website now carries a health section online (w *bradtguides.com/africahealth*) to help travellers prepare for their African trip, elaborating on most points raised below, but the following summary points are worth emphasising:

- Don't travel without comprehensive medical **travel insurance** that will fly you home in an emergency.

- Make sure all your **immunisations** are up to date. Parts of Ethiopia are considered a risk for yellow fever – a mosquito-borne disease which is potentially fatal. The vaccine would therefore be recommended unless it is contraindicated, in which case the advice may be to not travel to that area. A yellow fever certificate is required to enter Ethiopia only if you are coming in from another yellow fever endemic zone. Since July 2016, all yellow fever certificates are valid for life regardless of when the vaccine was given, so there is no need to repeat the vaccine if you have proof of the first dose you received. It's also reckless to travel in the tropics without being up to date on tetanus, polio and diphtheria (now given as an all-in-one vaccine, Revaxis) and hepatitis A. Immunisation against meningitis, typhoid, hepatitis B, TB and rabies may also be recommended.
- The biggest health threat at lower altitudes below 2,000 metres is **malaria**. There is no vaccine against this mosquito-borne disease, but a variety of preventative drugs is available, including mefloquine, malarone and the antibiotic doxycycline. The start and stop times of these tablets vary depending on which part of the malarial parasite life cycle they act upon. It is important to be compliant to ensure maximum protection. The most suitable choice of drug varies depending on the individual and the country they are visiting, so visit your GP or a travel clinic for medical advice. If you will be spending a long time in Africa, and expect to visit remote areas, be aware that no preventative drug is 100% effective, so carry a cure too. It is also worth noting that no homeopathic prophylactic for malaria exists, nor can any traveller acquire effective resistance to malaria during short stays. Those who don't make use of preventative drugs risk their life in a manner that is both foolish and unnecessary.
- Though advised for everyone, a **pre-exposure rabies vaccination**, involving three doses taken over a minimum of 21 days, is particularly important if you intend to have contact with animals, or are likely to be 24 hours away from medical help.
- Anybody travelling away from major centres should carry a **personal first aid kit**. Contents might include a good drying antiseptic (eg: iodine or potassium permanganate), Band-Aids, suncream, insect repellent, paracetamol, antifungal cream (eg: Canesten), ciprofloxacin or norfloxacin (for severe diarrhoea), antibiotic eye drops, tweezers, condoms or femidoms, a digital thermometer and a needle-and-syringe kit with accompanying letter from health-care professional. Aspirin should probably be avoided in countries where there is a risk of dengue fever as this can increase the risk of bleeding.
- Bring any **drugs or devices relating to known medical conditions** with you. That applies both to those who are on medication prior to departure, and those who are, for instance, allergic to bee stings, or are prone to attacks of asthma.
- Prolonged immobility on long-haul flights can result in **deep vein thrombosis (DVT)**, which can be dangerous if the clot travels to the lungs to cause pulmonary embolus. The risk increases with age, and is higher in obese or pregnant travellers, heavy smokers, those taller than 6ft/1.8m or shorter than 5ft/1.5m, and anybody with a history of clots, recent major operation or varicose veins surgery, cancer, a stroke or heart disease. If any of these criteria apply, consult a doctor before you travel.

MEDICAL PROBLEMS
Malaria This potentially fatal disease is widespread in tropical Africa, but most prevalent at lower altitudes, with the risk of transmission being highest during and shortly after the rainy season. Within Ethiopia, low-lying areas such as South Omo and Gambella Region should be regarded as high risk for malaria transmission,

while most other places below 2,000m are medium to low risk. Malaria used to be absent from the Ethiopian Highlands, and probably still is at altitudes of greater than 2,300m (for instance Addis Ababa or Lalibela), but it does occur sporadically in the vicinity of Lake Tana and Gondar. So, while the historical circuit of northern Ethiopia is low risk by comparison with many other African destinations, visitors could be exposed to the disease and should take suitable preventative drugs.

Since no malaria prophylactic is 100% effective, it makes sense to take all reasonable precautions against being bitten by the nocturnal *Anopheles* mosquitoes that transmit the disease (see box, page 123). Malaria usually manifests within two weeks of transmission, but it can take months, which means that short-stay visitors are most likely to experience symptoms after they return home. These typically include a rapid rise in temperature (over 38°C), and any combination of a headache, flu-like aches and pains, a general sense of disorientation, and possibly even nausea and diarrhoea. The earlier malaria is detected, the better it usually responds to treatment. So, if you display possible symptoms, *get to a doctor or clinic immediately*. A simple test, available at even the most rural clinic in Africa, is usually adequate to determine whether you have malaria. However, a negative test requires two further negative tests on consecutive days to completely exclude malaria. And while experts differ on the question of self-diagnosis and self-treatment, the reality is that, if you think you have malaria and are not within easy reach of a doctor, it would be wisest to start treatment.

Travellers' diarrhoea Many visitors to unfamiliar destinations suffer a dose of travellers' diarrhoea, usually as a result of imbibing contaminated food or water, and Ethiopia seems to be particularly bad in this respect. Rule one in avoiding diarrhoea and other sanitation-related diseases is arguably to wash your hands regularly, particularly before snacks and meals, and after handling money (birr 1 notes in particular are often engrained with filth). As for what food you can safely eat, a useful maxim is: PEEL IT, BOIL IT, COOK IT OR FORGET IT. This means that fruit you have washed and peeled yourself should be safe, as should hot cooked foods. However, raw foods, cold cooked foods, salads, fruit salads prepared by others, ice cream and ice are all risky. It is rarer to get sick from drinking contaminated water but it happens, so stick to bottled water, which is widely available.

If you suffer a bout of diarrhoea, it is dehydration that makes you feel awful, so drink lots of water and other clear fluids. These can be infused with sachets of oral rehydration salts, though any dilute mixture of sugar and salt in water will do you good, for instance a bottled soft drink with a pinch of salt. If diarrhoea persists beyond a couple of days, it is possible it is a symptom of a more serious sanitation-related illness (typhoid, cholera, hepatitis, dysentery, worms, etc), so get to a doctor. If the diarrhoea is greasy and bulky, and is accompanied by sulphurous (eggy) burps, one likely cause is Giardia, which is best treated with tinidazole (four x 500mg in one dose, repeated seven days later if symptoms persist).

Bilharzia Also known as schistosomiasis, bilharzia is an unpleasant parasitic disease transmitted by freshwater snails most often associated with reedy shores where there is lots of water weed. It cannot be caught in hotel swimming pools, but should be assumed to be present in any freshwater river, pond, lake or similar habitat, even those advertised as 'bilharzia free'. The most risky shores will be within 200m of villages or other places where infected people use water, wash clothes, etc. Ideally, however, you should avoid swimming in any fresh water other than an artificial pool. If you do swim, you'll reduce the risk by applying DEET insect repellent first, staying in the water for less than 10 minutes, and drying off vigorously with a towel. Bilharzia is often asymptomatic in its early stages, but some people experience an intense immune reaction, including fever, cough, abdominal pain and an itching rash, around four to six weeks after infection. Later symptoms vary but often include a general feeling of tiredness and lethargy. Bilharzia is difficult to diagnose, but it can be tested for at specialist travel clinics, ideally at least six weeks after likely exposure. Fortunately, it is easy to treat at present.

Meningitis This nasty disease can kill within hours of the appearance of initial symptoms, typically a combination of a blinding headache (light sensitivity), blotchy rash and high fever. Outbreaks tend to be localised and are usually reported in newspapers. Fortunately, immunisation protects against the most serious bacterial form of meningitis. Nevertheless, other less serious forms exist, and a severe headache and fever – possibly also symptomatic of typhoid or malaria – should be sufficient cause to visit a doctor immediately.

Rabies This deadly disease can be carried by any mammal and is usually transmitted to humans via a bite or deep scratch. Beware village dogs and habituated monkeys, but assume that *any* mammal that bites or scratches you or even licks you without visible skin injury might be rabid even if they don't look unwell. First, scrub the wound with soap under a running tap, or while pouring water from a jug, then pour on a strong iodine or alcohol solution, which will guard against infections and might reduce the risk of the rabies virus entering the body. Whether or not you underwent pre-exposure vaccination, it is vital to obtain post-exposure prophylaxis as soon as possible after the incident. However, having had pre-exposure vaccine makes the post-exposure treatment simpler and more likely to be available in the country. Death from rabies is probably one of the worst ways to go, and once you show symptoms it is too late to do anything – the mortality rate is 100%.

Tetanus Tetanus is caught through deep dirty wounds, including animal bites, so ensure that such wounds are thoroughly cleaned. Immunisation protects for ten years, provided you don't have an overwhelming number of tetanus bacteria on board. If you haven't had a tetanus shot in ten years, or you are unsure, get a booster immediately.

HIV/Aids Rates of HIV/Aids infection are high in most parts of Africa, and other sexually transmitted diseases are rife. Condoms (or femidoms) greatly reduce the risk of transmission.

Tick bites Ticks in Africa are not the rampant disease transmitters that they are in the Americas, but they may spread tickbite fever along with a few dangerous rarities. Ticks should ideally be removed complete, and as soon as possible, to reduce the chance of infection. You can use special tick tweezers, which can be bought in good travel shops, or failing this with your finger nails, grasping the tick as close to your body as possible, and pulling it away steadily and firmly at right angles to your skin without jerking or twisting. If possible douse the wound with alcohol (any spirit will do), soap and water, or iodine. Irritants (eg: Olbas oil) or lit cigarettes are to be discouraged since they can cause the ticks to regurgitate and therefore increase the risk of disease. If you are travelling with small children, remember to check their heads, and particularly behind the ears, for ticks. Spreading redness around the bite and/or fever and/or aching joints after a tick bite imply that you have an infection that requires antibiotic treatment. In this case seek medical advice.

Skin infections Any mosquito bite or small nick is an opportunity for a skin infection in warm humid climates, so clean and cover the slightest wound in a good drying antiseptic such as dilute iodine, potassium permanganate or crystal (or gentian) violet. Prickly heat, most likely to be contracted at the humid coast, is a fine pimply rash that can be alleviated by cool showers, dabbing (not rubbing) dry and talc, and sleeping naked under a fan or in an air-conditioned room. Fungal infections also get a hold easily in hot moist climates, so wear 100% cotton socks and underwear and shower frequently.

Eye problems Bacterial conjunctivitis (pink eye) is a common infection in Africa, particularly for contact-lens wearers. Symptoms are sore, gritty eyelids that often stick closed in the morning. They will need treatment with antibiotic drops or ointment. Lesser eye irritation should settle with bathing in salt water and keeping the eyes shaded. If an insect flies into your eye, extract it with great care, ensuring you do not crush or damage it, otherwise you may get a nastily inflamed eye from toxins secreted by the creature.

Sunstroke and dehydration Overexposure to the sun can lead to short-term sunburn or sunstroke, and increases the long-term risk of skin cancer. Wear a T-shirt and waterproof sunscreen when swimming. When visiting outdoor historical sites or walking in the direct sun, cover up with long, loose clothes, wear a hat, and use sunscreen. The glare and the dust can be hard on the eyes, so bring UV-protecting sunglasses. A less direct effect of the tropical heat is dehydration, so drink more fluids than you would at home.

Snake and other bites Snakes are very secretive and bites are a genuine rarity, but certain spiders and scorpions can also deliver nasty bites. In all cases, the risk

AVOIDING MOSQUITO AND INSECT BITES

The *Anopheles* mosquitoes that spread malaria are active at dusk and after dark. Most bites can thus be avoided by covering up at night. This means donning a long-sleeved shirt, trousers and socks from around 30 minutes before dusk until you retire to bed, and applying a DEET-based insect repellent to any exposed flesh. It is best to sleep under a net, or in an air-conditioned room, though burning a mosquito coil (outside use only) and/or sleeping under a fan will also reduce (though not entirely eliminate) bites. Travel clinics usually sell a good range of nets and repellents, as well as Permethrin treatment kits, which will render even the tattiest net a lot more protective, and helps prevent mosquitoes from biting through a net when you roll against it. These measures will also do much to reduce exposure to other nocturnal biters. Bear in mind, too, that most flying insects are attracted to light: leaving a lamp standing near a tent opening or a light on in a poorly screened hotel room will greatly increase the insect presence in your sleeping quarters.

It is also advisable to think about avoiding bites when walking in the countryside by day, especially in wetland habitats, which often teem with diurnal mosquitoes. Wear a long, loose shirt and trousers, preferably 100% cotton, as well as proper walking or hiking shoes with heavy socks (the ankle is particularly vulnerable to bites), and apply a DEET-based insect repellent to any exposed skin.

is minimised by wearing closed shoes and trousers when walking in the bush, and watching where you put your hands and feet, especially in rocky areas or when gathering firewood. Only a small fraction of snakebites deliver enough venom to be life-threatening, but it is important to keep the victim calm and inactive, and to seek urgent medical attention.

Other insect-borne diseases Although malaria is the insect-borne disease that attracts the most attention in Africa, and rightly so, there are others, most too uncommon to be a significant concern to short-stay travellers. These include dengue fever and other arboviruses (spread by diurnal mosquitoes), sleeping sickness (tsetse flies), and river blindness (blackflies). Bearing this in mind, however, it is clearly sensible, and makes for a more pleasant trip, to avoid insect bites as far as possible; see box, page 123). Two nasty (though ultimately relatively harmless) flesh-eating insects associated with tropical Africa are *tumbu* or *putsi* flies, which lay eggs, often on drying laundry, that hatch and bury themselves under the skin when they come into contact with humans, and jiggers, which latch on to bare feet and set up home, usually at the side of a toenail, where they cause a painful boil-like swelling. Drying laundry indoors and wearing shoes are the best way to deter this pair of flesh-eaters. Symptoms and treatment of all these afflictions are described in greater detail on Bradt's website (w *bradtguides.com*).

SAFETY

Ethiopia is generally a very safe country. Casual theft and pickpocketing are fairly commonplace in parts of the country, most notably Addis Ababa, but this sort of thing is almost never accompanied by violence, and – as in any large city – one should not wander around at night with a large amount of money or important documents.

In other parts of Ethiopia, the risk of encountering pickpockets is mainly confined to bus stations and markets, and even then only in larger towns. At bus stations, this is most likely to be a loner operating in the surge of people getting on to a bus. In the streets, a favoured trick is for one person to distract you by bumping into you or grabbing your arm, while a second person slips his fingers into your pocket from the other side. It's advisable to leave valuables and any money you don't need in a hotel room, to carry the money you do need in a relatively inaccessible place, and to always turn quickly in the other direction if somebody does bump into you or grab you. If you need to go out with important documents or foreign currency, carry it in a concealed moneybelt, and carry some cash separately so that you need not reveal your moneybelt in public.

Thieves often pick up on uncertainty and home in on what they perceive to be an easy victim. In Addis Ababa, where there are plenty of experienced thieves and con artists, always walk quickly and decisively. When you arrive in a new town by bus, stroll out of the bus station quickly and confidently as if you know exactly where you're going (even if you don't). Avoid letting the kids who often hang around bus stations latch on to you. Once through the crowds, you can sit down somewhere and check your map, or ask for directions.

One area of risk that is difficult to quantify is that of armed bandits – *shifta* – holding up a bus. This was quite commonplace a few years ago, but is no longer a serious cause for concern, except perhaps in eastern areas near the Somali border. That said, the sporadic anti-government protests that have broken out in various parts of Oromo and Amhara since 2016 have forced the temporary closure of several roads and have resulted in several attacks on buses and fatal clashes between different ethnic groups or the militia and civilians. Tourists are not likely to be the direct target of any such violence, but there is a risk of being caught in the crossfire, or of having one's travel plans disrupted by road closures, such as occurred between Awash and Harar in December 2017 and between Dessie and Weldiya in February 2018. Keep your ear to the ground.

It is easy enough to let warnings about theft induce an element of paranoia into your thinking. There is no cause for this sort of overreaction. If you are moderately careful and sensible, the chance of hitting anything more serious than pickpocketing is very small. Far more remarkable than the odd bit of theft, especially when you consider how much poverty there is in the country, is the overwhelming honesty that is the norm in Ethiopia.

HASSLES The level of hassle experienced by visitors to Ethiopia is strongly dependent on how they travel. People on organised tours generally experience the country as almost entirely hassle-free, and those who fly or are driven around the country, and who make extensive use of upmarket hotels and professional guides, are also likely to have a smooth trip. By contrast, solitary independent travellers who bus between towns, who seldom explore sites with local guides, and who stay mainly in local hotels, often report the hassle factor to be the highest of any African country.

The most persistent irritant comprises groups of children who follow travellers around yelling '*faranji, faranji*', 'you, you, you', or a variant thereof. This may sound harmless enough, and it is, but the children's persistence can easily exhaust one's reserves of good humour! The best response to this sort of thing is to poke gentle fun at the kids. If a kid shouts 'you', yell 'you' back, or if they shout '*faranji*', respond with '*habbishat*' (Ethiopian). Humour may not always defuse the mob, but it is generally a more successful ploy than showing anger or irritation! (A *very* occasional but more inherently worrying problem is children throwing stones at travellers. Why they do this is anybody's guess, but the best way to deal with it is usually to appeal to an Ethiopian adult to get the children to stop.)

That aside, independent travellers may sometimes find it rather trying to operate in an environment where they have no privacy, and where every move seems to attract comment or attention. This manifests itself in many small ways: beggars will cross the street to catch your attention, arbitrary bores will monopolise your company, aspirant guides will latch on to you for no good reason and later expect to be paid for their imagined service, and even the most straightforward situation such as catching a bus or ordering a meal often entails fuss and complications.

There is no absolute way of dealing with this sort of thing. Generally, however, if you need help or directions on arriving in a town, it is far better to approach somebody yourself than allow yourself to become obliged to a bore, or an aspirant guide, or anybody else who comes across like they have an agenda. Also, when you are travelling rough for a long period, it genuinely helps to take the odd break – an afternoon with a book in the garden of a smart hotel can, for instance, be tremendously therapeutic.

WILD ANIMALS Don't confuse habituation with domestication. Most wildlife in Africa is genuinely wild, and widespread species such as hippo or hyena might attack a person given the right set of circumstances. Such attacks are rare, however, and they almost always stem from a combination of poor judgement and poorer luck. A few rules of thumb: never approach potentially dangerous wildlife on foot except in the company of a trustworthy guide; never swim in lakes or rivers without first seeking local advice about the presence of crocodiles or hippos; never get between a hippo and water; and never leave food (particularly meat or fruit) in the tent where you'll sleep.

CAR ACCIDENTS Dangerous driving is probably the biggest threat to life and limb in most parts of Africa. On a self-drive visit, drive defensively, being especially wary of stray livestock, gaping pot-holes, and imbecilic or bullying overtaking manoeuvres. Many vehicles lack headlights and most local drivers are reluctant headlight-users, so avoid driving at night and pull over in heavy storms. On a chauffeured tour, don't be afraid to tell the driver to slow or calm down if you think he is too fast or reckless.

WOMEN TRAVELLERS

We get very mixed feedback from female visitors to Ethiopia. Broadly speaking, most actual travellers, even those on a tight budget, regard it to be a safe and hassle-free country for women by international standards. These comments by Kim Wildman, the female updater of the sixth edition, are typical:

> From my perspective, Ethiopia has been the easiest, most nonthreatening African country I have travelled in for work. Not once over the three months I conducted my research for this guide was I threatened or harassed in any way. If anything, I was probably shown more respect than a male traveller would be. It's a very easy and friendly country, refreshingly free of amorous male advances that make the likes of Egypt and Turkey such a chore.

Unexpectedly, perhaps, the general feedback from volunteers stationed outside Addis Ababa is far less positive. Former Peace Corps Volunteer Sandra Turay is representative:

> Female volunteers face many gender-specific challenges. They sometimes struggle to be viewed as credible and legitimate contributors in the workplace. Host families may hold them to the same household rules they would their own daughters (ie: early curfews, gender-specific chores). They tend to be scrutinised by the community, whose social norm is that any woman who eats out alone, drinks in public, or shares a soft drink with a member of the opposite gender is at best wanton and at worst a prostitute.

Harassment is commonplace, too. Partly because the media tends to present Western women as easy and loose, this ranges from harmless but annoying non-sexual shouting and cat-calling to unwanted advances and more occasionally sexual assault (in both cases, often based on the assumption that any women who merely has a coffee or tea with a male is open to sleeping with them).

All told, the risk of rape or seriously threatening harassment is probably lower than in many Westernised countries. Teenage boys yelling obscenities at women, though unpleasant, is ultimately a less innocuous variation on the sort of verbal crap that all single travellers have to put up with from time to time in Ethiopia. Even so, it is not an everyday occurrence (unless perhaps you settle in Shashemene), and it is most unlikely to occur in the company of a respected guide or another local person. Women travellers are less likely to hit problems if they refrain from drinking alone, avoid staying in local hotels at the brothel-cum-barroom end of the price scale, and turn down any invitation that could be construed as a potential date.

Dress may also play a role in how you are perceived. In rural areas particularly, both Muslim and Christian, it is good sense to look to what local women wear and follow their lead. To quote a former volunteer: 'If I wear sleeveless clothes then I tend to get a constant stream of comments and stares, even in Addis Ababa, so I wouldn't dress in this manner in smaller towns where *faranjis* are few and far between.' Another reader adds: 'We came prepared with skirts and headscarves, but there was no need to wear them. We wore pants/trousers and that was acceptable. I saw some women travellers wearing shorts, but I'm not sure that I'd feel comfortable with that unless they extended below the knee – even then I'd think twice.'

Our most recent (September 2016) specific feedback from a female traveller is:

As a 27-year-old American woman traveling alone, I experienced quite a bit of harassment, mostly from teenage boys. It was mostly verbal, but a few times I found myself encircled by groups of boys who got a little physical. There were also many cafés/restaurants that I didn't feel comfortable eating in because it would have been very conspicuous that I was the only woman there. A little more disconcertingly, in Harar, I was followed around for 20–30 minutes on two separate occasions by older men. Both times they followed me into shops and one of them even followed me into a restaurant. Appealing to other Ethiopians just got me laughed at. Dressing in long skirts and loose shirts did not make a difference. Taking a guide, and latching on to locals I felt I could trust, seemed to solve the problem.

The same reader added that 'Ethiopia was the trip of a lifetime and the relatively small hassles and frustrations were totally eclipsed by the friendliness of the people and the fascinating history and natural sights.'

A couple of readers have highlighted the problems specifically facing black female travellers in Ethiopia, where women retain a somewhat subservient role by Western standards. European women are not expected to fit the mould, but nobody seems quite certain on which side of the chasm to place black Western women. Black women who travel alone in Ethiopia are in for a strange time, and they will often experience African sexual attitudes at first hand. The obvious area of solution is to dress and carry yourself in a manner that precludes confusion: don't come with a rucksack full of flowing African dresses and bright blouses, but rather wear jeans or preppy clothes, things that would rarely be seen on an Ethiopian woman.

On a practical level female travellers should note that finding sanitary products, in particular tampons, is nigh impossible outside of the capital, so stock up before you depart Addis.

Ethiopia, like neighbouring Kenya, has produced several world-conquering long-distance runners. In 1960, the pioneering Abebe Bikila, a last-minute addition to the team bound for Rome, became an overnight sensation when he won Ethiopia its first Olympic gold medal by winning the men's marathon running barefoot. Abebe repeated the feat in Tokyo in 1964, this time with shoes on, but less than two months after being operated on for appendicitis, setting a new Olympic record in the process. Since then, Ethiopian long-distance runners have claimed another 20 Olympic gold medals. Top male Olympians include two-time 10,000m winner Haile Gebrselassie, who also held the world record for a marathon between September 2007 and September 2011, and three-time gold medallist Kenenisa Bekele. More recently, female Ethiopian athletes have also thrived: Tiki Gelana set a new Olympic record for the woman's marathon at London 2012, while 2016 saw Almaz Ayana Eba, a relative newcomer from Benishangul-Gumuz, win the women's 10,000m at the Rio de Janeiro Olympics, breaking a 23-year-old world record by a full 14 seconds.

Ethiopia's pre-eminence when it comes to long-distance running has often been attributed to the high altitudes at which its athletes train, while others reckon it might be something to do with genetics, diet or body shape. Whatever the reason, running is a popular activity in the highlands, especially around Addis Ababa and the neighbouring Entoto Hills, where altitudes ranging from 2,350m to almost 3,000m are likely to leave even the fittest of European newbies gasping for breath. High altitudes and daunting slopes aside, those planning a few casual jogs in Ethiopia will find it has a wonderful climate for running, particularly the slightly lower Rift Valley.

If you are more serious about testing yourself at altitude, the Great Ethiopian Run, a 10km event held in Addis Ababa every November since 2001, is Africa's busiest road race, attracting more than 40,000 participants; while the 15km Dasani Run was first held in Addis Ababa in June 2015 (for details of both races, see w *ethiopianrun.org*). A newer annual event, first held in Abijatta-Shalla National Park in August 2014, the Ethio Trail (w *ethiotrail. com*) offers the option of a marathon, half-marathon or 12km run at medium altitude. Finally, anyone looking to do some high-altitude training in Ethiopia is pointed to the new Spanish specialist operator Run In Africa (w *runinafrica. com*), which offers bespoke travel packages suited to all running levels. More casual runners might like to partake in the 8.6km guided morning run through suburban Gondar offered by Lodge du Chateau (page 276).

One final point is that you should be aware that, when Ethiopians ask you to play with them, they are not suggesting a quick grope but that you make conversation – the Amharic *techawot* means both to talk and to play.

LGBT TRAVELLERS

Homosexual activity, both male and female, is illegal in Ethiopia, and punishable by up to 15 years' imprisonment. Homosexuality is also regarded as sinful by the Ethiopian Orthodox Church and by Islamic law, for which reason the vast majority of Ethiopians (as many as 97% according to a 2007 Pew Global Attitudes Project) consider it to be unacceptable behaviour. In 2008, a group of prominent religious figures, including the heads of the Orthodox, Protestant and Catholic churches, urged the government to enact a constitutional ban on homosexual activity, likening it to bestiality and blaming it for a perceived rise in sexual attacks on children and young men. None of which necessarily amounts to an obstacle for gay or lesbian travellers wishing to visit Ethiopia, provided they are willing to be discreet about their sexuality. Note, too, that most hotels forbid two men (and in some cases two women) from sharing a room with a double bed.

ALLIGAN TRAVEL

Alligan Travel provides bespoke tours throughout Ethiopia for visitors who want well planned travel. We will ensure that you experience the wealth of Ethiopia's memorable culture, heritage and landscape.

Alligan Travel offers responsible travel which benefits the local people, providing work and income whilst preserving their culture, environment and heritage. We aim to be your "professional friend" in Ethiopia.

"We all enjoyed these 2 weeks very much"
"I don't think that we could have been looked after any better"
"We had a most memorable, refreshing and wonderful holiday"

UK contact: Jane Daniell 020 8883 0977
info@alligantravel.com

Alligan Travel is an Ethiopian registered company.
www.alligantravel.com

Part Two

ADDIS ABABA AND SURROUNDS

Overview of Part Two

The high-altitude capital city of Addis Ababa, located crossroads-like in the very centre of Ethiopia, provides most visitors with their introduction to the country. And while its historic attractions pale by comparison with those of say Axum or Lalibela, Addis Ababa is an enjoyable city, boasting a handful of interesting museums, churches and galleries, along with some truly superb restaurants and a lively music scene. Addis Ababa is also a useful base for day and overnight trips. Nature lovers could choose between the crater lakes of Bishoftu, the forested slopes of Menegasha or the spectacular Muger Gorge, while history buffs won't want to miss out on the rock-hewn church of Adadi Maryam and the nearby field of medieval engraved stelae at Tiya. Though organised day tours are available, Addis Ababa is easily explored independently, and most nearby sites of interest are accessible on public transport.

HIGHLIGHTS

ARAT AND SIDDIST KILO (page 180) The atmospheric mausoleum at Beata Maryam Church, the impressive National Museum and IES Ethnographic Museum, and the low-key Armenian quarter are among the most important landmarks in this pedestrian-friendly university suburb north of the city centre.

RED TERROR MARTYRS' MEMORIAL MUSEUM (page 175) This harrowing installation adjacent to Meskel Square displays relics of and photographs associated with the genocidal Red Terror campaign perpetrated by the Derg.

ADDIS ABABA BY NIGHT (page 170) Half a dozen cultural restaurants provide an excellent introduction to Ethiopia's fiery food and vibrant traditional music and dances, while venues such as V Lounge showcase the contemporary live music scene.

BISHOFTU (page 190) This fast-growing town 50km southeast of Addis Ababa is built around a field of volcanic calderas and pretty lakes, several of which are serviced by top-class resorts, making it an excellent springboard for travels further south or east.

DERA-DILFEKAR (page 203) This outlying block of Arsi Mountains National Park is the best place in Ethiopia to see the magnificent greater kudu and beautiful lesser kudu. It also protects a hyena den where these nocturnal carnivores are frequently seen in daylight.

ADADI MARYAM (page 205) A semi-monolith below ground level, hidden in a deep trench, Adadi Maryam, the country's southernmost active rock-hewn church, resembles a smaller and rougher version of Lalibela's finest churches, and was probably excavated at around the same time.

TIYA STELAE FIELD (page 206) This UNESCO World Heritage Site comprising three dozen engraved megalithic grave-markers was erected about 700 years ago and can easily be visited in conjunction with Adadi Maryam.

MENAGESHA NATIONAL FOREST (page 213) The most important stand of natural forest within easy day-tripping distance of the capital supports a varied selection of endemic birds along with mammals such as guereza monkey and Menelik's bushbuck.

MOUNT WENCHI (page 217) Day walks, guided pony treks and boat trips are all offered by the community-based ecotourism association operating on this massive extinct volcano whose picturesque caldera encloses a crater lake and the 13th-century island monastery of Wenchi Chirkos.

MUGER GORGE (page 219) The dramatic gorge carved by the Muger River 50km north of Addis Ababa is the closest site to the capital for reliable encounters with the endemic gelada monkey.

4

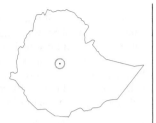

Addis Ababa

The world's fourth-highest capital city, Addis Ababa – which translates, somewhat inaptly, as 'New Flower' – sprawls for 220km² across the southern slopes of central Ethiopia's Entoto Hills, spanning altitudes of 2,350m to more than 2,600m. Climatically, it's a thoroughly encouraging welcome to the country, with comfortable temperatures and cheerful sunny skies alleviated by regular downpours swiftly dispelling any lingering preconceptions about Ethiopia being nothing but parched desert. In certain other respects, Addis, as locals tend to refer to it, can be rather overwhelming on first exposure, with beggars, taxi drivers and hawkers clamouring for the attention of anyone who looks like a tourist, and practised pickpockets doing their utmost to divert it. If that's the case, don't allow first impressions to put you off. Spend a little time in the Ethiopian capital, and you'll soon realise that its less savoury elements carry a lot more bark than bite. Easy to explore on foot, and tolerably safe even at night, districts such as the bustling Piazza, the modern and gleaming Bole Road, and the more down-at-heel Merkato all boast a compelling urban buzz. Addis Ababa also boasts a fantastic dining-out scene, some great nightlife and live music venues, and an engaging spread of museums, galleries and other worthwhile historic landmarks. Furthermore, Addis Ababa possesses a genuine sense of place lacking in those many other African capitals that were designed to be misplaced pockets of Western urbanity in otherwise underdeveloped nations. Indeed, perhaps the highest praise one can direct at chaotic, contradictory and compelling Addis Ababa is this: it *does* feel exactly as the Ethiopian capital *should* feel – emphatically and unmistakably a modern 21st-century city, but also singularly and unequivocally Ethiopian.

HISTORY

The Entoto Hills above Addis Ababa have regularly played an important role in the politics of imperial Ethiopia. An unconfirmed legend states that the heir to the Axumite throne fled there towards the end of the 1st millennium AD to escape the wrath of Queen Gudit, while the presence of the disused rock-hewn church of Washa Mikael on the southern slopes of Entoto indicates strong medieval links with the Zagwe capital of Lalibela. Entoto is also one of a handful of sites put forward as a possible location for a medieval imperial capital known as Barara. This fortified city is depicted standing between mounts Zikwala and Menegasha on a map drawn by the Italian cartographer Fra Mauro in around 1450, and it was razed and plundered by Ahmed Gragn while the imperial army was trapped on the south side of the Awash River in 1529, an event witnessed – and documented two years later – by the Yemeni writer Arab-Faqih. The suggestion that Barara was located on the Entoto Hills is supported by the very recent rediscovery of numerous medieval forts and other significant ruins in the vicinity of the rock-hewn church of Washa Mikael and the more modern Entoto Maryam (page 182).

Addis Ababa itself is a relatively modern entity, founded as the capital of King Sahle Maryam of Shewa in the decade prior to prior his coronation as Emperor Menelik II of Ethiopia in 1889 (see box below). Its expansion to become one of the largest and most important cities in Africa was largely orchestrated by Haile Selassie, who – first as regent to Empress Zewditu, then as Emperor – lived in a palace peripheral to the city centre from 1916 until 1972, interrupted only by the Italian occupation. Factors in the early 20th-century development of Addis Ababa

MENELIK II'S 'NEW FLOWER'

Addis Ababa, officially founded in 1887, and now one of the five largest cities in the sub-Saharan region, is not the only African city of comparable stature to have sprung up from nothing little more than a century ago. However, it is unique in that it owes its existence to the unlikely combination of a grandfather's prophecy, an empress's whim and the timely intervention of an Australian tree.

In the early 1880s, the future Emperor Menelik II – then the King of Shewa – decided to abandon his capital at Ankober in favour of the Entoto Hills. What inspired this move is unclear, but the Entoto area had held great historical significance to the Shewan aristocracy prior to the 16th century, when it was occupied by the Oromo in the wake of the religious upheavals initiated by Ahmed Gragn. The area was reclaimed for Shewa by Menelik's expansionist grandfather Sahle Selassie, who prophesied that his grandson would build a large house in the valley below Entoto, from which would grow a great city.

At the end of the cold rainy season of 1886, Menelik II and his royal entourage moved down from the chilly hilltops of Entoto, to set up camp around the hot springs known as Filwoha. The emperor's wife Taitu fell in love with the natural hot baths and the abundance of mimosa trees there, and suggested that her husband build her a house at the site she christened Addis Ababa – New Flower! Menelik concurred, partly because the site also fitted with his grandfather's prophecy, and the royal party returned to Filwoha semi-permanently at the end of the 1887 rainy season. Posterity has thus settled on 1887 as the year in which Addis Ababa became the capital, if not of Ethiopia then of its future emperor. In reality, the shift to Filwoha was more gradual. Most of Menelik's correspondence prior to 1891 was dispatched from Entoto, and it was only in 1889, months before his formal coronation as emperor, that he set about building a proper palace in the valley.

Outsiders seem to have regarded the move from Entoto to Filwoha as folly. One Frenchman who visited the site in 1887 regarded the notion it might one day house a great city as 'fantasy'. A decade later, European visitors felt the growing lack of firewood – now transported 20km from Menegasha – would force the new flower to die long before it reached full bloom. Indeed, Menelik made tentative plans to relocate his capital some 50km west to a forested site he christened Addis Alem – New World – and have a palace constructed there. Bizarrely, it was a stand of eucalyptus trees planted by a foreign resident in 1894 that would save Addis Ababa. Spurred by his Swiss adviser Alfred Ilg, Menelik II noticed how rapidly these trees grew, and instead of shifting the capital he decided to import vast quantities of eucalyptus seedlings. The residents of the nascent city were initially unimpressed, above all by the smell of the exotic trees, but the eucalyptus's phenomenal growth rate soon swept such delicacies aside.

The Addis Ababa of Menelik's time bore scant resemblance to the modern city, though the imperial palace, at the north end of what is now Menelik II included the arrival of the Djibouti railway in 1917, a contemporaneous influx of Armenian and French traders, who played an important role in the export trade, as well as the introduction of the freehold system that made it the only place in Ethiopia where land ownership was regulated. By 1918, the population of Addis Ababa stood at around 100,000, a figure that decreased drastically during the rainy season, when many peasants evacuated the chilly highland city in favour of family farms in the countryside. The ceremonious coronation of Haile Selassie in

Avenue, remains the seat of government to this day. Even then, the palace was an impressive and well-organised compound: extending over 3km², it enclosed about 50 buildings, employed and housed some 8,000 people, and – courtesy of Ilg's engineering prowess – had piped water by 1894 and electricity by 1905. As early as 1894, Menelik II and Ilg were discussing plans to construct a railway to the French port of Djibouti. By 1897, up to 50,000 people from the surrounding countryside attended the capital's Saturday market, which occupied the site of an older Oromo market near the modern Piazza and below the Church of St George, which had been completed a year earlier. Yet for all that, Menelik's capital was essentially a compacted rural sprawl. Few modern buildings existed outside of the royal compound, and the population stood at a mere 100,000 settled over an area of about 55km²!

The account of Herbert Vivian, who arrived in the Ethiopian capital in 1900, is typical:

I happened to turn around and ask one of my men, 'When on earth are we ever going to reach Addis Ababa?'

'But sah'b, here it is.'

'Where?'

'Here, we have already arrived.'

I looked around incredulously, and saw nothing but a few summer huts and an occasional white tent, all very far from each other, scattered over a rough hilly basin at the foot of steep hills. I would scarcely believe that I was approaching a village. That this could be the capital of a great empire, the residence of the King of Kings, seemed monstrous and out of the question. 'Then, pray, where is Menelik's palace?' I asked with a sneer. The men pointed to the horizon, and I could just make out what seemed to be a fairly large homestead with a number of trees and huts crouching on the top of a hill.

The capital is a camp rather than a town … To appreciate Addis Ababa it is necessary to realise that this strange capital covers some 50 square miles, and contains a very large population, which has never been counted. Streets there are none, and to go from one point of the town to the other you must simply bestride your mule and prepare to ride across country. Three quarters of an hour at least are necessary for a pilgrimage from the British Agency to the Palace, and as much again to the market. On either of these journeys you must cross three or four ravines with stony, precipitous banks and a torrent-bed full of slippery boulders.

Fifteen years after Herbert Vivian's visit, Menelik II was dead, but by then his capital had become, in the words of one contemporary visitor, a 'mushroom city'. Another 15 years on, Haile Selassie was enthroned as emperor, and Addis Ababa entered the modern era as the most populous settlement in Africa between Cairo and Johannesburg – a status it has since relinquished, though it remains sixth on that list today.

1930 signalled a drive for modernisation that included the creation of several new ministries, and the building of several schools, hospitals and roads. It was over this period, and during the Italian occupation of 1935–41, that the present-day city centre and Arada (the Piazza area) took their modern shape. The Italians were also responsible for the relocation of the main market from Arada (on the site of what is now De Gaulle Square) to the Merkato region 2km to its south.

Addis Ababa experienced unprecedented expansion between 1945 and 1974, particularly in the manufacturing sector, which attracted large numbers of rural migrants from all around the country, many of whom struggled to find employment in the fast-growing metropolis. The city also became more outward-looking and cosmopolitan over this period, thanks largely to independent Ethiopia's symbolic significance to the liberation movements that sprung up in most African colonies in the aftermath of World War II. In 1958, Addis Ababa became the base for the UN Economic Commission for Africa (UNECA), and five years later it was chosen as the headquarters of the newly formed Organization of African Unity (OAU). The late 1960s and early 1970s saw Addis Ababa, like so many other world cities, experience a wave of social renewal and liberalisation, one epitomised both by the cosmopolitan funk-influenced live music scene that sprang up in the city, and by the growing trend among young intellectuals to question the legitimacy of the outmoded imperial regime. Things came to a head in 1974 when Emperor Haile Selassie was deposed by the Derg. Instead of experiencing a new dawn under the Derg, however, Addis Ababa stagnated in both economic and social terms, thanks to the new regime's disastrous socialist policies along with a night-time curfew that endured for a full 16 years.

The dark years of the Derg came to an end in 1991, when the EPRDF captured the city. In the federal reshuffle of 1995, Addis Ababa was accorded the status of self-governing city, and was also made temporary capital of Oromia Region, a role it surrendered to Adama in 2000 but regained in 2005 following protests that the shift de-emphasised its central location within Oromia. Divided into ten administrative sub-cities in 2000, post-millennial Addis Ababa has emerged as a cosmopolitan, forward-looking city whose rapid growth has been pivotal to Ethiopia's recent performance as Africa's most consistently expanding economy, with an average annual growth in excess of 10%. The city's population has also mushroomed, from around 1 million in 1974, the year when Emperor Haile Selassie was deposed, to around 4.5 million today. It remains the headquarters of UNECA, while its status as headquarters of the African Union, whose new office complex, inaugurated in 2012, is the city's tallest building at 99.9m, accords Addis Ababa a Brussels-like role as *ipso facto* capital of Africa. Other recent modernisation projects include the ongoing upgrade of Bole Airport to quadruple its passenger capacity, and the recent construction of a new ring road and efficient metropolitan railway line.

GETTING THERE AND AWAY

BY AIR All international flights to Ethiopia and domestic flights to/from Addis Ababa land at **Bole International Airport** [153 G7] (◊ *011 665 0400/99;* e *bole. ap@ethionet.et;* w *addisairport.com*), which lies on the southeast perimeter of the capital, only 5km from the city centre and even closer to the many hotels and other institutions that line busy Bole Road. Most international flights use Terminal Two, while Terminal One is dominated by domestic flights but also handles Ethiopian Airlines flights to/from certain neighbouring countries and most flights to/from the Gulf (and by extension other destinations involving a Gulf-based airline such as FlyDubai and Qatar). Up-to-date details of scheduled arrivals and departures are posted on the airport website along with other useful information.

Bole is way stretched past its optimum capacity, with almost 10 million passengers (85% in transit) passing through annually, which tends to put a strain on baggage handling facilities, particularly during the busiest hours of around 05.30–09.30 and 17.30–21.30. Domestic arrivals need only wait for their baggage to appear on the carousel before they can leave the airport. By contrast, it can take international arrivals anything from 30 minutes to 1 hour (occasionally longer) to clear the airport building, depending on how busy their flight is, and how many other flights landed shortly before it. Upon arrival at Terminal Two, you have three options when you enter the immigration hall. Passengers requiring a **Visa on Arrival (VoA)** must head to the zigzag queue and row of windows on the left of the hall (the near side as you come through the entrance). Those with **e-visas** need to walk through an (often roped-off) 'green carpet' gate that leads to two windows labelled 'e-visa' immediately to the right of the VoA queue. Those with **other pre-bought visas** must head directly to the queues at the right (far) end of the immigration hall, close to the banks.

After clearing immigration, you'll walk into the baggage retrieval hall, where you can collect your luggage from the carousel. Two flights arriving simultaneously can mean rows of cases are lined up next to the carousel, so mark your bags obviously. Either way, hold on to your baggage tags, because you may also be asked to produce them at or after the customs desk.

Once you've collected your luggage, you'll pass through customs, where you may or may not be asked to put your bags through an X-ray machine, and they may also be hand searched. If you intend to buy a local SIM card for a mobile phone or tablet, then you must register the relevant device on arrival, which can be done by turning left into a corridor-like room next to the customs X-ray machine and going to the unsignposted counter on the right. Finally, once all the fun and games are over, you'll find yourself in the rather underwhelming arrivals hall, where there is one ATM, a café and several hotel desks.

Gerry Nicholls notes:

A small percentage of bags don't arrive on the same international flight as the passenger. When this happens, most often they come on the next equivalent flight (whereupon you may have started your domestic trip, a good reason to pack a few essentials in hand luggage). If your bag arrives and you are not there to receive it, it will be placed randomly in the cages beyond the carousels. When you go to retrieve it, take a torch because there are no lights in the cages. Having found your bag, you'll need your baggage tag to get it through customs.

CBE and Dashen Bank maintain foreign exchange desks at the airport, situated not, as might be expected, in the arrivals hall, but rather in the immigration and baggage retrieval halls. This means that if you want to change money at the airport, you must do so either before you join the appropriate queue at immigration, or else after clearing immigration but before passing through customs. We would recommend the latter option, otherwise you risk a new planeload of arrivals piling into the immigration queues ahead of you. There are also ATMs in the baggage retrieval and arrivals hall where you can draw local currency against an eligible credit or debit card. All things considered, however, those who have arranged an airport pick-up might well prefer to deal with this all after they've arrived at their hotel. Note also that, when you leave Ethiopia, changing local currency back into hard currency at the airport is usually impossible in practice.

Most hotels now offer an **airport pick-up**, in many cases for free, so check the situation when you book your room. Establish in advance whether your meet-and-greet will meet you inside the airport building or outside in the car park. As things stand, most non-passengers are forbidden from entering either terminal, so it is most normal to meet outside, at the foot of the trolley ramp to the car park. Should you agree to be met inside, the tourist information office is a useful rendezvous.

If you need a taxi, head outside the terminal to the foot of the trolley ramp and ask the head dispatcher of Yellow Airport Taxis to see the fixed fare list he holds in an A4 file. Fares typically range from US$8 to US$20, depending on how distant your hotel is. Cheaper (or at least more negotiable) blue taxis are available outside the airport, but the saving should be balanced against the added exposure of your luggage to theft (a minimal risk, but perhaps not worth it at this early point in your holiday). A final option is public minibuses, which cost less than US$1, but since the stations around Bole are now quite dispersed, we wouldn't recommend this to anyone who isn't familiar with the system.

Note that a massive terminal expansion increasing Bole's passenger capacity to 22 million was under way in 2018 and is likely to be operational some time in 2019. Look out for updates on our update website (w bradtupdates.com/ethiopia).

Airline offices Ethiopian Airlines (\011 665 6666, 011 517 8231; e reservation@ ethiopianairlines.com; w www.ethiopianairlines.com), which connects Addis Ababa to more than 75 other cities worldwide, has its headquarters on Bole Road close to the airport, but this is not a ticketing office. Tickets can be bought or bookings changed at several branch offices dotted around the city centre. The main ticketing office [159 C7] (\011 551 7000; e addcto@ethiopianairlines.com) is on Gambia Street (Churchill Avenue) opposite the National Theatre but there are also handy offices at the Hilton Hotel [159 F6], on the first floor of the Alem Building on Bole Road [152 D5], on the Piazza [158 C2], and on the first floor of the Radisson Blu Hotel [159 F6] (the latter usually very quiet, so quick).

Other major airlines servicing Addis Ababa are listed below. For charter flights within Ethiopia, try a private company called **Abyssinian Flight Services** (\011 662 0622–4; e bookings@abyssinianflights.com; w abyssinianflights.com).

✈ **Egyptair** [159 B5] 2nd floor, Shashe Bldg, Churchill Av; \011 156 4493/4; m 0912 187655; w egyptair.com

✈ **Emirates** [152 C3] 4th floor, Abyssinia Plaza, Bole Rd; \011 518 1818; w emirates.com

✈ **Fly Dubai** [166 C5] 2nd floor, Blen Bldg, Djibouti St; \011 850 6251/2; w flydubai.com

✈ **Gulf Air** [159 E8] Jomo Kenyatta St; \011 662 3517/22; w gulfair.com

✈ **Kenya Airways** [159 F6] Hilton Hotel, Menelik II Av; \011 551 1548; e addsales@kenya-airways. com; w kenya-airways.com

✈ **KLM** [159 F6] (code share with Kenya Airways) Hilton Hotel, Menelik II Av; \011 552 5541/5495; e klm.com

✈ **Lufthansa** [159 B7] Axum Bldg, Ghana Rd; \011 551 5666; w lufthansa.com

✈ **Qatar** [159 G8] Hayat Tower, Guinea Conakry St; \011 554 4638; w qatarairways.com

✈ **Saudi Airlines** [159 C6] Guinea Conakry St; \011 551 2637/93; w saudiairlines.com

✈ **South African Airways** [159 E8] (code share with Ethiopian Airlines) Bole Rd; \011 553 7880/1; m 0911 510961; w flysaa.com

✈ **Sudan Airways** [159 C6] Ras Desta Damtew St; \011 550 4724; w sudanair.com

✈ **Turkish Airlines** [166 B7] Heritage Plaza; \011 662 7781; w turkishairlines.com

✈ **Yemenia** [159 C6] Ras Desta Damtew St; \011 552 6440; e addisababa@yemenia.com; w yemenia.com

BY BUS Several private companies now operate daily coaches – closer in quality to Greyhound-type service than to a typical African bus – between Addis Ababa and other major centres in Ethiopia. These are, in rough order of preference, Ethio and the affiliated Abay Bus [158 C3] (*booking office in the grounds of the Itegue Taitu Hotel;* m *0947 909090/919191/929292;* f), Selam Bus [159 E7] (*north side of Meskel Sq;* \011 850 0281/2 or 8676 booking hotline; m *0911 403977;* e *salam.bus@ethionet. et;* w *selambus.wordpress.com*), Limalimo [158 C3] (*Itegue Taitu Hotel;* \011 558 2434), Falcon Coach [158 C7] (*1st floor, Yeha Bldg, Ras Makonnen St;* m *0979 404 0404, 0969 404 0404;* f), Golden Bus [158 C7] (*1st floor, Yeha Bldg, Ras Makonnen St;* m *0939 535353;* f) and Sky Bus [158 C7] (*1st floor, Yeha Bldg, Ras Makonnen St;* m *0910 179327;* w *skybusethiopia.com*). Coaches operated by all these companies leave from Meskel Square, almost invariably between 05.00 and 06.30 depending on the exact destination, the main exception being Hawassa, where a second batch of coaches usually leaves at around 13.00. Tickets should be booked in advance, so check timings then.

Destinations currently covered by one or more of these companies are as follows: Debre Markos (*Sky, Abay; US$7; 6hrs*), Bahir Dar (*Abay, Selam, Sky; US$14; 10hrs*), Gondar (*Ethio, Selam, Sky; US$18; 12hrs*), Jimma (*Selam, Falcon; US$9; 6hrs*), Mizan Tefari (*Selam, Golden; US$14; 8hrs*), Assosa via Nekemte (*Selam, Golden, Falcon; US$16; 11hrs*), Hawassa (*Ethio, Selam, Golden; US$8.50; 4hrs*), Arba Minch (*Selam; US$11; 9hrs*), Dessie (*Ethiopia, Selam; US$11; 7hrs*), Mekele via Weldiya (*Ethiopia, Selam, Sky; US$20; 12hrs*) and Shire via Axum (*Selam; US$27; 18hrs with an overnight stop in Mekele*). Most of these companies also used to offer daily services to Dire Dawa (*US$12; 9hrs*), Harar (*US$12; 9hrs*) and Jijiga (*US$15; 11hrs*), but these were suspended after two Selam Buses were burnt by rioters in 2016. The daily Selam Bus to Goba via Dodola and Bale Robe (*US$11; 8hrs*) has also been suspended due to unrest in Oromia. Selam now offers a weekly international coach service to Khartoum (Sudan); this leaves Addis Ababa on Saturdays and takes two days, with an overnight stop in Gondar.

It is usually easiest to buy a ticket at the appropriate booking office a day or two before you travel. There is no online booking service, but with Selam Bus it is now possible to make reservations for any destination by phone (preferably with the help of an Amharic speaker) using the booking hotline number (see above). Once you have made the booking, you'll receive a reference number and be told the price of the fare, which should be paid to the Ambassa Bank. Then you need to communicate the receipt number via the same telephone number, and your seat reservation will be confirmed, allowing you to board your bus, receipt in hand.

Approaching the better private coach companies in quality are the Post Buses connecting Addis Ababa to Bahir Dar and Mekele. These leave from Legahar [159 C8], in front of the old railway station, at 04.30 daily, and tickets can be booked at counter nine of the central post office on Churchill Avenue 08.00–noon and 13.00–17.00 on weekdays. Fares are around US$10 to Bahir Dar and US$14 to Mekele.

Other, cheaper bus services cover these and many other routes, but they are less reliable. Traditionally most buses used to leave from **Merkato bus station** (also known as the **Old Autobus Terra**) [142 B3], which lies along Habte Giyorgis Street about 2km west of the Piazza. This station still services most long-haul destinations to the south and east of Addis Ababa, including Harar, Dire Dawa, Butajira, Arba Minch, Moyale, Goba, Yabello and Jinka, as well as Bahir Dar and Gondar in the northwest. For destinations northeast of Addis Ababa, including Dessie, Weldiya, Mekele and Axum, you need to head to **Lamberet bus station** [143 H4], which lies about 2.5km east of Megenagna (pronounced Megenanya) Circle, and is often

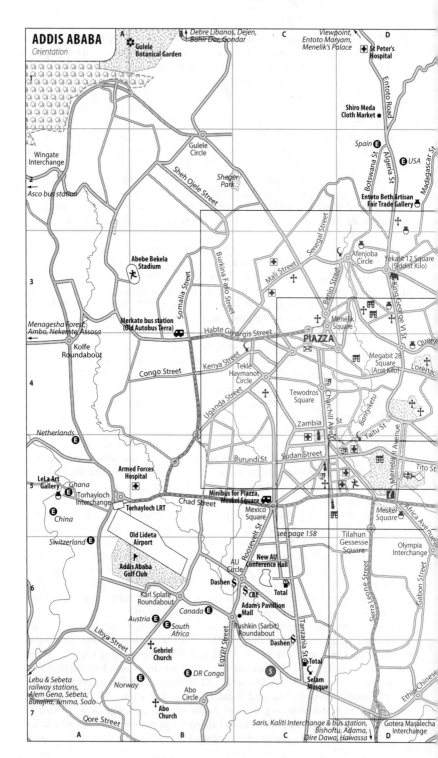

ADDIS ABABA
Orientation

Gulele Botanical Garden

Debre Libanos, Dejen, Bahir Dar, Gondar

Viewpoint, Entoto Maryam, Menelik's Palace

St Peter's Hospital

Shiro Meda Cloth Market ●

Entoto Road

Gulele Circle

Spain **E**

Botswana St

Algeria St

E USA

Madagascar St

Wingate Interchange

Sheh Ojele Street

Sheger Park

Entoto Beth Artisan Fair Trade Gallery

Asco bus station

Senegal Street

Mali Street

Afenjoba Circle

Yekatit 12 Square (Siddist Kilo)

Abebe Bekela Stadium

Somalia Street

Burkina Faso Street

Benin Street

King George VI St

Menelik Square

Merkato bus station (Old Autobus Terra)

Habte Giyorgis Street

PIAZZA

Megabit 28 Square (Arat Kilo)

Queen

Kolfe Roundabout

Congo Street

Kenya Street

Tekle Haymanot Circle

Tewodros Square

Churchill Ave

Bantyiketu

Lorenzo

Menagesha Forest, Ambo, Nekemte, Assosa

Uganda Street

Zambia

Taitu St

Netherlands **E**

Burundi St

Sudan Street

Menelik II Avenue

Tito St

LeLa Art Gallery

Ghana **E**

Torhayloch Interchange

Armed Forces Hospital

Torhayloch LRT

Chad Street

Minibus for Piazza, Meskel Square

Mexico Square

Meskel Square

Africa Avenue

E China

Switzerland **E**

Old Lideta Airport

see page 158

Tilahun Gessesse Square

Olympia Interchange

Addis Ababa Golf Club

AU Circle

New AU Conference Hall

Roosevelt St

Sierra Leone Street

Gabon Street

Karl Splate Roundabout

Canada **E**

Dashen $

$ CBE

Total

Austria **E**

E South Africa

Adam's Pavillion Mall

Pushkin (Sarbit) Roundabout

Dashen $

Tanzania St

Total

Libya Street

Egypt Street

Sefam Mosque

Ethio-Chinese

Lebu & Sebeta railway stations, Alem Gena, Sebeta, Butajira, Jimma, Sodo

Gebriel Church

Norway

E DR Congo

Abo Circle

Abo Church

Qore Street

Saris, Kaliti Interchange & bus station, Bishoftu, Adama, Dire Dawa, Hawassa

Gotera Masalecha Interchange

142

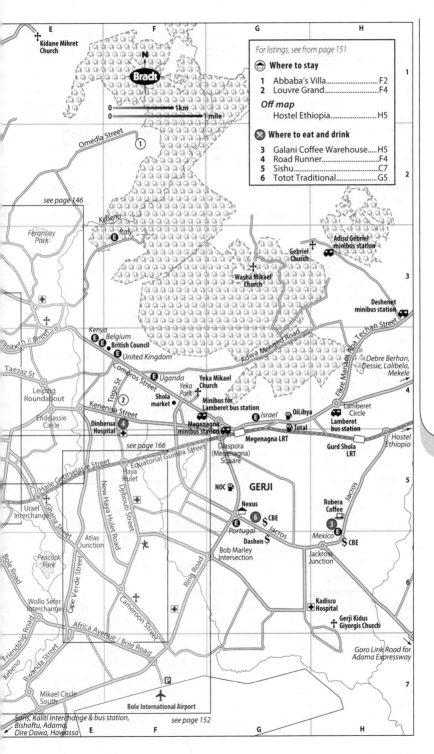

For listings, see from page 151

Where to stay
1 Abbaba's Villa.........................F2
2 Louvre Grand..........................F4

Off map
 Hostel Ethiopia.......................H5

Where to eat and drink
3 Galani Coffee Warehouse.....H5
4 Road Runner............................F4
5 Sishu...C7
6 Totot Traditional....................G5

Kidane Mihret Church

Omedla Street

Bradt

0   1km
0   1mile

see page 146

Feransay Park

Kebena

Italy

Kenya
Belgium
British Council
United Kingdom

Uganda

Comoros Street

Togo St

Yeka Mikael Church

Shola market

Yeka Park

Taezaz St

Leipzig Roundabout

Kenenisa Street

Minibus for Lamberet bus station

Israel

OiLibya

Lamberet Circle

Adisu Gebriel minibus station

Gebriel Church

Washa Mikael Church

Adwa Menged Road

Deshenet minibus station

Fikre Mariam Aba Techan Street

Debre Berhan, Dessie, Lalibela, Mekele

Elizabeth II Street

Endellasie Circle

Dinberua Hospital

Megenagna minibus station

Total

Megenagna LRT

Lamberet bus station

Gurd Shola LRT

Hostel Ethiopia

see page 166

Equatorial Guinea Street

Diaspora (Megenagna) Square

Haya Hulet

NOC

GERJI

Nexus

Portugal

Robera Coffee

Jacros

Ureal Interchange

Haile Gebrselassie Street

Ghana Street

New Haya Hulet Road

Djibouti Street

CBE

Jacros

Dashen

Bob Marley Intersection

Mexico

CBE

Atlas Junction

Peacock Park

Bole Road

Cape Verde Street

Ring Road

Jackross Junction

Wollo Sefer Interchange

Cameroon Street

Kadisco Hospital

Gerji Kidus Giyorgis Church

Friendship Road

Kebena

Rwanda Street

Africa Avenue / Bole Road

Goro Link Road for Adama Expressway

Mikael Circle South

Bole International Airport

Saris, Kaliti Interchange & bus station, Bishoftu, Adama, Dire Dawa, Hawassa

see page 152

143

referred to as Ararat after the nearby hotel of the same name. **Kaliti bus station** [142 D7], 15km south of the city centre on the Bishoftu road, is the place to pick up medium-distance bus and minibus services east and southeast to the likes of Bishoftu, Adama, Modjo, Ziway and Hawassa. Finally, **Asco bus station**, on the old Ambo road 10km northwest of the city centre, is the place to pick up minibuses and buses to Ambo and Nekemte. All these bus stations can be reached easily and inexpensively by passenger minibuses from Stadium, Piazza, Bole Road, Churchill Avenue and other main stops in the city centre, but since long-haul buses tend to leave at or before 06.00, you are best booking these a day in advance and chartering an early morning taxi to your departure point on the morning you leave.

BY RAIL The new railway service to Djibouti via Bishoftu, Adama, Awash Saba and Dire Dawa leaves from a custom-built railway station [142 A7] at Lebu, 12km southwest of the city centre, at 08.00 on alternate days. For further details, see page 101.

ORIENTATION

Addis Ababa is a large city, and many of its main roads and other landmarks have long gone by two or even three names, with the name shown on most maps differing from the one in common use. This confusing situation is further exacerbated by the decision to name 52 of the city's main roads after each of the non-Ethiopian member states of the African Union. All in all, then, Addis Ababa can be a bit confusing – so read through this with map in hand before you start exploring. In its hotel and restaurant listings, this book now tries to use the official names that will be on any map of Addis Ababa you may buy, but elsewhere the everyday name may be used, eg: Arat Kilo or Siddist Kilo.

The **city centre** is more or less rectangular, defined by **Mexico Square** [142 C5] in the southwest, **Meskel Square** [142 D5] (formerly Abiot or Revolution Square, and still referred to as Abiot by minibus drivers) in the southeast, the **Hilton Hotel** [159 F6] in the northeast and **Tewodros Square** [142 C4] in the northwest. The main north–south thoroughfare through the city centre is **Churchill Avenue** [142 C4] (the southern end of which is now officially called Gambia Road). This wide road runs downhill from just below the City Hall to terminate in front of the disused **railway station** [159 C8] (also known as the Legahar). The main thoroughfare from west to east is **Ras Makonnen Street** [159 C7], which runs from Mexico Square to the railway station, where it intersects with Gambia Road. It then continues east past the Addis Ababa Stadium and Meskel Square to become **Haile Gebrselassie Street** [166 A1], which leads east out of the city centre via **Diaspora Square** [143 G4], more usually referred to as **Megenagna** (pronounced Megenanya), towards Debre Berhan, Dessie and Mekele.

Two important roads run south from Ras Makonnen Street. The first is the **Bishoftu road** (officially Sierra Leone Street, but also sometimes referred to as the Debre Zeyit road, after the old name for Bishoftu), which starts west of Meskel Square and leads out of town to most destinations in the south and east. Immediately east of Meskel Square, the road marked on most maps as Africa, OAU or African Union Avenue is almost universally referred to as **Bole Road** [152 B2], since it terminates at Bole International Airport, 5km out of town. Meskel Square and the more westerly Mexico Square are also where the southern and northern limbs of the **Light Rail Transit** respectively meet the central east–west line.

The area known as **Arada** or the **Piazza** [158 C2] lies immediately north of the city centre, from where it can be reached by heading uphill along Churchill Avenue with the City Hall clear in your sights. The Piazza is a loosely defined area, centred on **De Gaulle Square** [158 C2], bounded by Haile Selassie Street and the Taitu Hotel to the east, by Kidus Giyorgis Church to the north, and the City Hall to the west. The Piazza is also a busy shopping area, with a great many budget hotels concentrated in the side streets south of De Gaulle Square. About 1km west of the Piazza, Addis Ketema or **Merkato** [146 A5] is a tight grid of streets centred on what is reputedly

CATCHING MINIBUSES   *Frank Rispin*

Minibuses follow fixed routes along most major roads. They all have a conductor who opens the side door, collects fares and shouts out the name of the destinations. They will stop anywhere to pick you up. If the conductor asks 'Yet?' he wants to know where you are going; reply 'Piazza', etc. If you want to get off before a major destination, say 'Woraj' when you are there. If the conductor asks 'Chaf woraj alla?', it means 'Does anyone want the next stop?' Most locals riding minibuses will have some English, so as soon as you are on, ask your neighbour if it is definitely going to your destination.

After getting on, you know when it is time to pay, as the conductor will politely point his hand in your direction – or if you are in the front seat, tap on your shoulder. Fares are very cheap, seldom more than a few birr, but they tend to increase regularly with fuel prices. Have plenty of birr 1 notes so you don't need change.

Minibuses heading into the city centre will almost always be going to one or more of the four major hubs which stand at the corners of the central Addis area – Arat Kilo in the northeast, the Piazza in the northwest, Mexico Square in the southwest and Stadium/Legahar for the southeast. Most hotels are on or near a main road with minibuses running into one of these points in the city centre. Each of these four hubs has several departure points for outgoing minibuses and you may need to ask for help, or look at the maps here to find the right one. If you are aiming for the National or Ethnographic museums, you must get to Arat Kilo, then change to a northbound Siddist Kilo minibus, or walk! If your hotel is on or near Bole Road you need a 'Bole' minibus on the way back; if on Haile Gebrselassie you need a 'Megenagna' taxi from Stadium/Legahar or from Arat Kilo a 'Kazanchis, Megenagna' minibus. (Note that minibuses are not allowed to stop in Meskel Square, so if you need to go there, hop off at Stadium just to its west, and if you want to be sure a minibus leaving Stadium or elsewhere will head through Meskel Square, ask the conductor or other passengers, using the older name 'Abiot'.)

A handful of the city's 10,000-plus minibus operators are crooks who may try to distract you in order to pick your pocket. To avoid this happening, follow these rules:

1 If a minibus stops to ask where you're heading, ignore it.
2 If you are on your own, only get on a minibus where other people are getting on.
3 Once on a minibus, if you are asked to move from the front to the back row, or from an aisle to a window seat, refuse or get off.
4 If you are asked to open a window, be aware it might be a ruse allowing someone to pick your pocket or bag while you are wrestling with the stuck window.

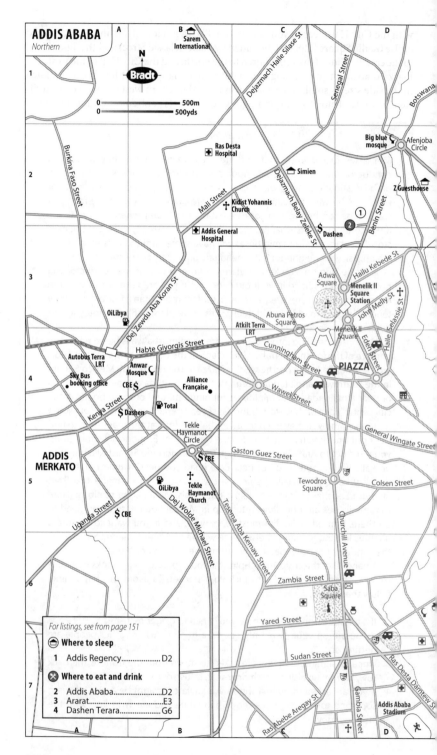

ADDIS ABABA
Northern

N

Bradt

0 ———————— 500m
0 ———————— 500yds

Sarem International

Big blue mosque · Afenjoba Circle

Dejazmach Haile Silase St

Senegal Street

Botswana

Ras Desta Hospital

Simien

Z Guesthouse

Mali Street

Kidist Yohannis Church

Dejazmach Belay Zeleke St

Benin Street

Dashen

① ②

Addis General Hospital

Burkina Faso Street

Hailu Kebede St

Adwa Square

Menelik II Square Station

Abuna Petros Square

John Melly St

Dej Zewdu Aba Koran St

OiLibya

Atkilt Terra LRT

Menelik II Square

Halle Selassie St

Habte Giyorgis Street

Cunningham Street

Eden Street

Autobus Terra LRT

Anwar Mosque

Sky Bus booking office

CBE

Alliance Française

PIAZZA

Wawel Street

Kenya Street

Dashen

Total

General Wingate Street

Tekle Haymanot Circle

Gaston Guez Street

ADDIS MERKATO

CBE

Tewodros Square

Colsen Street

OiLibya

Tekle Haymanot Church

Dej Wolde Michael Street

Tesema Aba Kemaw Street

Churchill Avenue

Uganda Street

CBE

Zambia Street

Saba Square

Yared Street

Ras Desta Damtew St

Sudan Street

Gambia Street

Ras Abebe Aregay St

Addis Ababa Stadium

For listings, see from page 151

🛏 **Where to sleep**
1 Addis Regency.................... D2

✴ **Where to eat and drink**
2 Addis Ababa........................ D2
3 Ararat................................... E3
4 Dashen Terara..................... G6

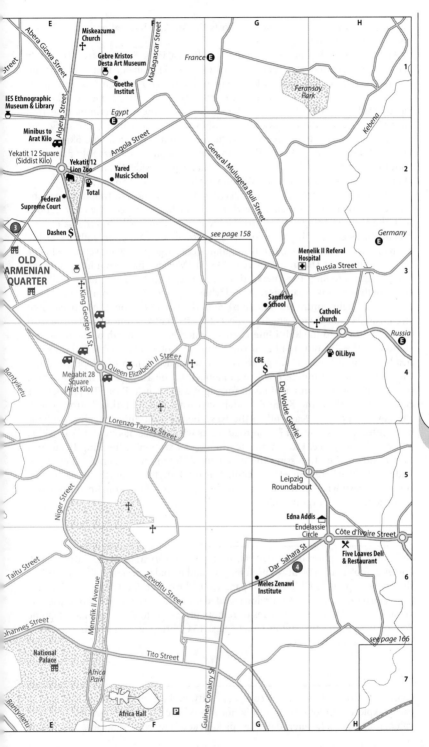

see page 158

see page 166

Miskeazuma Church

Gebre Kristos Desta Art Museum

Goethe Institut

France ⓔ

Feransay Park

Abera Gizwa Street

Madagascar Street

IES Ethnographic Museum & Library

Egypt ⓔ

Algeria Street

Kebena

Minibus to Arat Kilo

Angola Street

Yekatit 12 Square (Siddist Kilo)

Yekatit 12 Lion Zoo

Yared Music School

Total

General Mulugeta Buli Street

Germany ⓔ

Federal Supreme Court

Dashen $

Menelik II Referal Hospital

Russia Street

OLD ARMENIAN QUARTER

King George VI St

Sandford School

Catholic church

Russia ⓔ

CBE $

OiLibya

Bantyiketu

Megabit 28 Square (Arat Kilo)

Queen Elizabeth II Street

Del Wolde Gebriel

Lorenzo Taezaz Street

Niger Street

Leipzig Roundabout

Taitu Street

Edna Addis

Endelassie Circle

Côte d'Ivoire Street

Five Loaves Deli & Restaurant

Menelik II Avenue

Zewditu Street

Dar Sahara St

④

Meles Zenawi Institute

Yohannes Street

National Palace

Tito Street

Guinea Conakry St

Africa Park

Bantyiketu

Africa Hall

P

the largest market in Africa and also hosts the **Merkato bus station** [142 B3] (also known as the Old Autobus Terra).

Arcing north then south to the east of the Piazza, Haile Selassie Street (formerly Adwa Street) emerges at **Megabit 28 Square** [158 E2], a major four-way junction commonly referred to as **Arat Kilo**. The road that runs north from Arat Kilo heads into the Entoto Hills via the National Museum, the university campus at **Yekatit 12 Square (Siddist Kilo)** [147 E2] and the US Embassy. The road running east from Arat Kilo passes the Russian and British embassies before reaching Diaspora Square (more often referred to as Megenagna) then continuing for another 2.5km east to **Lamberet bus station** [143 G4]. The road running south from Arat Kilo passes the Gibe or Old Palace, the Hilton Hotel, the National or Presidential Palace and Africa Hall before it intersects with Ras Makonnen Street at Meskel Square.

A multi-lane ring road around Addis Ababa is now almost fully operational, the only exception being a missing stretch in the northeast between the intersections with the roads running east towards Debre Berhan and north towards Bahir Dar. The northeastern starting point of the Ring Road is the junction with the Debre Berhan road, where six major thoroughfares converge in a two-level interchange formally known as **Diaspora Square** [143 G5] (Megenagna). From here, the road heads south, crossing the intersection known as Bob Marley [143 G6] (after a statue of its namesake that was removed when it was converted from a roundabout to a traffic-light-controlled junction) and then running on a 400m elevated stretch above Bole Road (which connects the city centre to the airport). The road then runs south to the **Kaliti Interchange**, which lies 5km north of the **Kaliti bus station** on the Bishoftu road as it runs south out of Addis Ababa. From here it heads northward, passing huge areas of new condominium developments, and the Makenissa and Jimma Road roundabouts, to the Torhayloch flyover, which is also now the western terminus of the Light Rail Transit. From Torhayloch the road runs north to the Kolfe Roundabout (just west of Merkato), from which the new Ambo road leads off to the west, before continuing northwest of the city centre to cross the old Ambo road on its way to **Asco bus station** [142 A2] at Wingate Interchange. From Wingate, the newest section of the Ring Road runs north and then east, passing the new Gulele Botanical Garden on the left, to Gulele Circle, where it meets the Bahir Dar road on its way north out of the city. It is not known whether the missing northeast section of the Ring Road from here to Megenagna will ever be built.

MAPS

By far the best option is the 1:30,000 *Addis Ababa City Map* (Geo3, 2014) which comes complete with plenty of useful insets, and is sold in several outlets including the book shop in the Ghion Hotel (page 157). The online AddisMap (w *addismap. com*) can be accessed for free, or downloaded for a price in a mobile-phone-friendly version. If you're in need of maps of remote places, go to the Ethiopian Mapping Authority opposite the Hilton Hotel (page 154), bringing along your ID and as much spare time as it takes.

GETTING AROUND

Central Addis Ababa is quite a compact entity, and the city centre and Piazza are easily explored on foot, though it is not a good idea to wander around carrying valuables, especially after dark, as pickpockets are commonplace. Elsewhere, affordable passenger minibuses run every few minutes in almost every direction, as detailed below, and you are unlikely to have much problem using them to get from any given A to any given B within the Ring Road or on major routes outside it. If ever you do get stuck, taxis are prodigious throughout the city, and very cheap by international standards.

PASSENGER MINIBUSES An efficient network of **minibuses** services Addis Ababa's roads from around 05.00 until it peters out at around 20.00–21.00. The minibuses now tend to fill up during the morning and evening commute, when there can be a lot of pushing and shoving for the last minibus of the day, in which case it may be easier to take a taxi. Minibuses are very cheap and overcharging is uncommon, but the crowds can make it easy for pickpockets, so take care (see box, page 145). Overcharging foreigners is not the custom – it might happen once or twice in hundreds of minibus rides. Guideline prices in 2018 range from birr 1.50 for a short journey (up to 2km) to birr 7–10 for a long journey, for instance from the city centre to Asco or Kaliti bus station.

If you spend only a day or two in Addis Ababa, familiarising yourself with this network may not be worth the effort, given that taxis are relatively cheap, but it's easy enough to figure out if you have the time. The **main minibus stops** are dotted around De Gaulle Square on the Piazza [158 B2/C2]; at Arat Kilo [158 E2]; opposite the Autobus Terra near the Merkato [142 B3]; in front of the old railway station [159 C8]; in front of and opposite the stadium on Ras Makonnen Street [159 C7]; and on Churchill Avenue opposite the post office [159 B5]. The minibus station under the Ring Road flyover on Bole Road, a few hundred metres from Bole International Airport, is closed, and the minibuses that used to leave from it now use four or five different small stations depending on their destination (see map, page 152).

One of the most useful **minibus routes** to travellers, described using landmarks favoured by conductors, runs between Bole Airport and the Piazza via Olympia, Abiot (Meskel Square), the Ambassador Theatre and the post office. Other significant routes emanating from the Piazza run to the Merkato and the Autobus Terra, to Mexico Square via the post office and Ras Hotel, and to Arat Kilo (where you can change minibus for Siddist Kilo).

There are also minibuses between Bole Road and Merkato via Olympia, Meskel Square and Mexico Square; Ras Makonnen Street opposite the stadium and Arat Kilo via Meskel Square and the Hilton Hotel; Ras Makonnen Street and Saris (on the Bishoftu road); Ras Makonnen Street and Diaspora Square (Megenagna) via Haile Gebrselassie Street; and Arat Kilo and Siddist Kilo. People hop on and off minibuses the whole time; you'll rarely wait more than 5 minutes for a ride along any of these routes.

BUSES An ever-expanding range of public buses service Addis Ababa: cream and green *higers*, yellow Alliance buses, blue Express buses with destination screens in English, old-fashioned *Isuzu* and the red-and-yellow double-deckers that started operating in December 2017. All are very cheap and safe enough, but they tend to be very, very crowded, especially in rush hours, and pickpocketing can be an issue. Minibuses are probably the preferable option, but if you want to use buses, seek advice at your hotel or from other boarding passengers.

TAXIS Private taxis, usually painted blue, can be found all over the city and you are unlikely to wait long for empty ones to cruise past. Fares are inexpensive by international standards, even the inflated ones generally asked of foreigners, and

THEFT AND SAFETY

Although violent crime of the sort associated with some other large African cities is very unusual in Addis Ababa, pickpockets and con artists are rife, particularly in the city centre, Merkato, Piazza and Bole Road, but also at crowded minibus stands and on buses. A popular strategy is a twin-pronged attack wherein one person (often a cigarette or chewing gum vendor) bumps into you or grabs you on one side, distracting you as their cohort fishes in your opposite pocket. When something like this happens, turn around immediately to see what is happening on your other side. Bag-slashing is also an occasional problem, so if you're carrying anything important (passport or cash) keep it in your moneybelt.

The most common kind of con trick in Addis Ababa involves someone using a ruse to get you conversing, then guilt tripping you into offering them financial assistance of some sort. Typical approaches include a 'How do you like Ethiopia?' line of questioning, or claiming to be the waiter or gardener at your hotel, or asking 'Do you remember me?' Once hooked, you may be in for a straightforward request for money, or something more insidious. Another scam frequently tried on newcomers to Addis involves a friendly 'student' inviting you to a traditional coffee or *tej* ceremony, at the end of which you're presented with a massive bill. We've had more than a dozen letters from readers who fell victim to this ruse, so it seems worth repeating one encounter in full:

After checking into our hotel, we went for a walk around the city. We were approached by a pleasant young student, who said he worked at our hotel and offered to show us around. The next day we took him as an escort to the Merkato. At the end of this trip, he invited us to a coffee ceremony that evening. I should have known better, having done a considerable amount of travelling, but against my better judgement we went to a house where we met 'local' girls in national dress, performing Ethiopian dances and serving Ethiopian food. Unfortunately they were also drinking imported brandy! After a couple of hours we decided to leave and were presented with a bill of US$100 ... Not a good start!

The moral is quite simple. Don't trust any supposed student you meet in Addis Ababa. Assume that anybody who says they work at your hotel, or who claims to remember meeting you yesterday, is a liar. And don't allow a stranger to lure you to a coffee or any other ceremony.

It should be stressed that while the sort of minor hassles mentioned above are commonplace in Addis Ababa, it is a safe city in terms of violent crime, though it would be silly to carry large amounts of money at any time, or to disregard warnings from other sources about any particular trouble spots.

are even cheaper if you are prepared to bargain. Expect to pay around US$5 for a ride within the confines of the Piazza and city centre, up to USS$10 to cross between the centre and outlying areas, and around US$12.50 from the Piazza or city centre to the airport. Always agree the fare before getting in.

Yellow metered taxis are now operated by several different companies. These tend to be more reliable and cheaper than unmetered taxis, provided you book telephonically (four-digit short numbers include 8210, 8294 and 8707), so they are well worth contacting for pre-planned trips, for instance to the airport or to pick up an early morning bus or coach. Be aware that if, for instance, the meter reads birr 100 at the end of the ride, the driver may ask for birr 130 to cover a genuine service fee or tax – ask about this when you book. Be aware that, if you stop a yellow taxi in the street, the driver will most likely claim that the meter is broken and want to negotiate a fare (often very inflated) before you get in. There are two reasons for this: first that the government fixed rates are too low; and, second, that leaving off the meter allows the driver to avoid paying the booking fee to the company.

METROPOLITAN RAIL Inaugurated in 2015, the two-line Light Rail Transit (LRT) – sometimes also called the Addis Light Rail, or ALR – service links Menelik II Square [158 B1] and the Merkato [146 A4] in the north to the Kaliti Interchange (south), Megenagna (east) [143 G5] and Torhayloch (west) [142 A5] via central landmarks such as Mexico Square [159 A8], the south end of Gambia Street [159 C7] and Meskel Square [159 E8]. Trains are regular and speedy, making it an excellent way to travel between relevant parts of the city. For tourists, the most important stops will probably be Menelik II Square (the only underground station, around the corner from St George's Cathedral in Piazza), Autobus Terra (pronounced 'Atobistera'; adjacent to Merkato) and Stadium (the closest station to Meskel Square; serving both lines).

Tickets cost a few birr. To buy one, look for an orange booth with people lined up out the front. There are no signs, and sometimes the booths can be confusingly far away from the station itself, but they are always in its line of sight. You cannot buy a ticket on board or on the platforms. You can purchase single and return tickets, but beyond this they are not reusable. On board a voiceover will remind you not to bring cattle and fowl on to the carriages, while a promotional video for the Chinese company that built the network plays on repeat.

WHERE TO STAY

Addis Ababa has always boasted an astonishing proliferation of accommodation, and that is truer today than ever before. Thanks to an ongoing post-millennial construction boom, the city's handful of world-class international hotels and smattering of more individualistic boutique establishments is supplemented by as many as 100 somewhat formulaic mid-range to upmarket high-rises, and an even greater number of indifferent budget and shoestring lodgings. So the listings that follow, though as exhaustive as space and common sense will allow, are also of necessity highly selective, concentrating on a few dozen places which, for one or other reason, stand out as above average.

Practically all hotels in the international, luxury, boutique and upmarket categories provide a free airport shuttle to overnight guests, but those in the moderate and lower categories tend to charge for the service. Best to check when you book.

INTERNATIONAL HOTELS
The 3 hotels listed below are affiliated to large international chains, & would be regarded as top of the range, or close to it, almost anywhere in the world. They are also very pricey by Ethiopian standards, aimed primarily at a clientele – UN, NGO, government & business travellers – that

isn't footing its own bill. That said, they're the only places that can be recommended to visitors seeking something close to international 5-star facilities.

Addis Ababa Sheraton [159 D5] (294 rooms) Taitu St; 011 517 1717; e reservations. addisethiopia@luxurycollection.com;

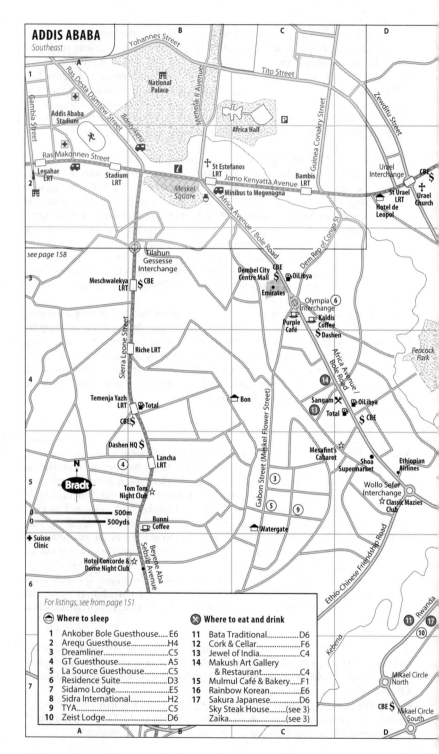

ADDIS ABABA
Southeast

Yohannes Street

National Palace

Tito Street

Ras Desta Damtew Street

Gambia Street

Addis Ababa Stadium

Ras Makonnen Street

Menelik II Avenue

Bantyiketu

Africa Hall

Zewditu Street

Guinea Conakry Street

Legahar LRT

Stadium LRT

Meskel Square

St Estefanos LRT

Jomo Kenyatta Avenue

Bambis LRT

Urael Interchange

CBE

St Urael LRT

Urael Church

Hotel de Leopol

Minibus to Megenagna

Africa Avenue / Bole Road

Dem Rep of Congo St

see page 158

Tilahun Gessesse Interchange

Meschwalekya LRT CBE

Dembel City Centre Mall CBE OiLibya

Emirates

Olympia Interchange 6

Kaldis Coffee

Peacock Park

Sierra Leone Street

Riche LRT

Purple Café

Dashen

Temenja Yazh LRT Total

Bon

Africa Avenue / Bole Road

14

Sangam

OiLibya

CBE

Dashen HQ

Lancha LRT

Gabon Street (Meskel Flower Street)

13 Total

CBE

Mesafint's Cabaret

Shoa Supermarket

Ethiopian Airlines

4

N

Bradt

Tom Tom Night Club

3

5

9

Wollo Sefer Interchange

Classic Mazies Club

0   500m
0   500yds

Bunni Coffee

Watergate

Suisse Clinic

Hotel Concorde & Dome Night Club

Beyene Aba Sebsib Avenue

Ethio-Chinese Friendship Road

Kebena

Rwanda

11 17

10

Mikael Circle North

Mikael Circle South

CBE

For listings, see from page 151

🛏 Where to sleep
1 Ankober Bole Guesthouse..... E6
2 Arequ Guesthouse..................H4
3 Dreamliner..............................C5
4 GT Guesthouse........................A5
5 La Source Guesthouse............C5
6 Residence Suite......................D3
7 Sidamo Lodge..........................E5
8 Sidra International..................H2
9 TYA...C5
10 Zeist Lodge.............................D6

✖ Where to eat and drink
11 Bata Traditional....................D6
12 Cork & Cellar..........................F6
13 Jewel of India........................C4
14 Makush Art Gallery
    & Restaurant........................C4
15 Mulmul Café & Bakery.......F1
16 Rainbow Korean....................E6
17 Sakura Japanese....................D6
   Sky Steak House.........(see 3)
   Zaika..............................(see 3)

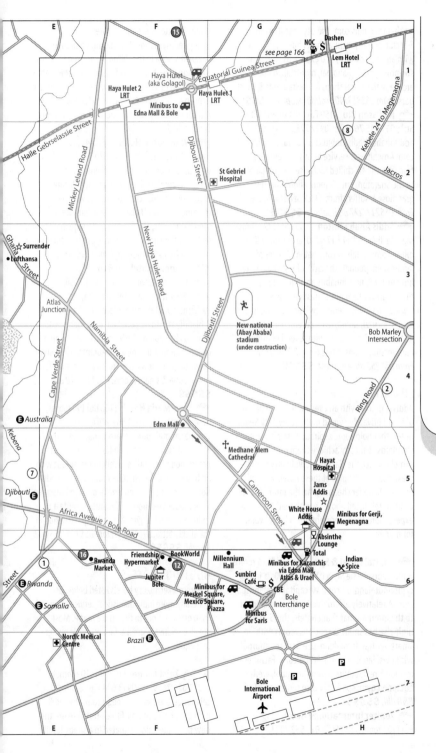

NOC
Dashen
Lem Hotel
LRT

see page 166

Equatorial Guinea Street

Haya Hulet
(aka Golagol)

Haya Hulet 2
LRT

Haya Hulet 1
LRT

Minibus to
Edna Mall & Bole

Haile Gebrselassie Street

Mickey Leland Road

Djibouti Street

St Gebriel
Hospital

Kebele 24 to Megenagna

Jacros

New Haya Hulet Road

Ghana Street
☆ Surrender
● Lufthansa

Atlas
Junction

Namibia Street

Cape Verde Street

Djibouti Street

New national
(Abay Ababa)
stadium
(under construction)

Bob Marley
Intersection

Ring Road

②

Kebena

Ⓔ Australia

Edna Mall ●

Medhane Alem
Cathedral

Hayat
Hospital

Jams
Addis
☆

⑦

Djibouti Ⓔ

Cameroon Street

White House
Addis

Minibus for Gerji,
Megenagna

Absinthe
Lounge

Africa Avenue / Bole Road

Ⓔ Rwanda

Street

①

Ⓔ Somalia

⑯

● Rwanda
Market

Friendship
Hypermarket

Jupiter
Bole

BookWorld

⑫

Millennium
Hall

Sunbird
Café

Minibus for
Meskel Square,
Mexico Square,
Piazza

Total

Indian
✗ Spice

Minibus for Kazanchis
via Edna Mall,
Atlas & Urael

CBE

Bole
Interchange

Minibus for Saris

Nordic Medical
✚ Centre

Brazil Ⓔ

P

P

Bole
International
Airport
✈

w sheratonaddis.com. The city's most luxurious & architecturally inspired hotel has smart suites with all the facilities you'd expect, as well as a swimming pool, piano bar, nightclub, bank/ATM, arcade with several shops & 7 restaurants & snack bars. *From US$353/403 sgl/dbl exc b/fast.* **$$$$$**

🏠 **Radisson Blu** [159 F6] (204 rooms) Tito St; 📞011 515 7600; **m** 0922 728575; **e** info. addisababa@radissonblu.com; **w** radissonblu. com. Amenities & service at this contemporary transatlantic AC-chilled high-rise are comparable to the Sheraton, but it's more affordable, less grandiose & suffers from a lack of outdoor areas. *From US$211/227 B&B sgl/dbl.* **$$$$$**

🏠 **Addis Ababa Hilton** [159 F6] (372 rooms) Menelik II Av; 📞011 517 0000; **e** hilton.addis@ hilton.com; **w** hilton.com. Set in 15 acres of landscaped grounds, the city's oldest chain hotel, built in 1968, now inhabits an architectural time-warp, but amenities include high security (including CCTV), thermal swimming pool, tennis courts, jacuzzi, sauna, gym, several highly rated restaurants, & an arcade with several boutiques, hairdressing salons, a bookshop & bank/ATMs. *From US$250 dbl exc b/fast.* **$$$$$**

LUXURY
Addis is graced with an ever-multiplying brood of bland privately owned multistorey 4- & 5-star hotels that hold some aspirations to transatlantic standards, & mostly achieve them on paper, but somehow lack the class or individuality to quite make the cut. The pick of these hotels is listed below; all are far cheaper than the international chain hotels listed above, & with realistic expectations they represent much better value for money.

🏠 **Capital Hotel & Spa** [166 A2] (114 rooms) Haile Gebrselassie St; 📞011 667 2100; **e** info@ capitalhotelandspa.com; **w** capitalhotelandspa. com. A relatively affordable locally owned rival to the international chain hotels, this 5-star high-rise has smart & spacious rooms with smart neutral décor, king-size bed, soundproof windows, large-screen TV & balcony. Facilities include 5 restaurants, swimming pool, well-equipped gym, spa & day care centre. *US$165 B&B dbl.* **$$$$$**

🏠 **Jupiter International Hotel** [159 F6] (102 rooms) Tito St; 📞011 552 7333;

e info@jupiterinternationalhotel.com; **w** jupiterinternationalhotel.com. Located in Kazanchis close to the Hilton & Radisson Blu, this towering glass high-rise offers rooms comparable in standard to its better-known neighbours, but at a much lower price. Amenities include an elegant restaurant, lobby bar & lounge, business & fitness centres. *US$125/165 B&B sgl/dbl.* **$$$$$**

🏠 **Washington Hotel** [166 A4] (65 rooms) Cape Verde St; 📞011 639 2239; **e** info@ washingtonaddis.com; **w** washingtonaddis. com. This comfortable & conveniently located high-rise has large carpeted rooms with all the amenities you'd expect & spacious granite-tiled bathrooms. The mezzanine lounge, bar & restaurant are unusually stylish, as these things go. *US$95/110/145 B&B sgl/dbl/suite.* **$$$$$**

🏠 **Harmony Hotel** [166 C6] (150 rooms) Off Cameroon St; 📞011 618 3100; **e** info@harmonyhotelethiopia.com; **w** harmonyhotelethiopia.com. This has smart & blandly stylish carpeted en-suite rooms with spacious bathrooms. Facilities include a heated indoor swimming pool, 2 restaurants, a 7th-storey bar with great views over the city, & ground-floor gym, sauna & steam rooms. *US$147 B&B dbl.* **$$$$$**

🏠 **Saro-Maria Hotel** [166 B6] (96 rooms) Off Cameroon St; 📞011 667 2167; **e** stay@ saromariahotel.com; **w** saromariahotel.com. This multistorey 4-star hotel is notable for its accommodating staff & excellent restaurant with an Italian chef. The en-suite rooms have wooden floor & furnishings, king-size bed, large flatscreen TV & modern bathrooms. Facilities include a swimming pool & gym, & a coffee/pastry shop in the slickly attractive lobby. *From US$125/155 b&B sgl/dbl.* **$$$$$**

BOUTIQUE HOTELS
The upmarket/luxury hotels listed below are generally more individualistic & service-oriented than other options in their price range. Most are also relatively small & family-run or owner-managed.

✱ 🏠 **Zeist Lodge** [152 D6] (10 rooms) 📞011 626 2639; **m** 0913 644316; **e** info@ zeistlodge.com; **w** zeistlodge.com. Owned & managed by a dynamic Ethio–Dutch team, this new boutique lodge, situated in a shady family compound 3km from Bole Airport, is notable for its exceptional personalised service & attention to detail. Large, comfortable rooms boast stylish décor dominated by contemporary local artworks, hardwood furniture, king-size beds & traditional cloths, as well as sat TV & sparkling modern bathrooms with imported fittings. *US$85/110 dbl/suite.* **$$$$$**

☀ 🏠 **Abbaba's Villa** [143 F2] (5 rooms) French Embassy area; ☏ 011 114 0035; m 0911 430641; e reservations@abbabasvilla.com; w abbabasvilla.com. This amazing atmospheric 1930s villa, set in a large wooded compound northeast of Siddist Kilo & decorated with antique furniture & artworks, is perfect for a taste of imperial Addis. There is wheelchair access throughout & a lovely tree-shaded rear patio. The owner-manager will provide evening dinner on request. *From US$50/75 B&B sgl/dbl.* **$$$$**

☀ 🏠 **Louvre Grand Hotel** [143 F4] (15 rooms) Off Togo St; ☏ 011 618 7755; m 0911 919382, 0920 558306; e info@louvregrandhotel.com; w louvregrandhotel.com. This owner-managed boutique hotel near the UK embassy recreates something of the feel of Paris between the wars. The beautifully decorated foyer is adorned with Ethiopian & French art & artefacts, while the 1st-floor bistro/bar/restaurant is hung with huge 1920s French-style wall paintings. Spacious en-suite rooms combine a period character with modern amenities. It also has a French menu, wine cellar & wellness centre. *From US$75 bed only.* **$$$$**

🏠 **Sidamo Lodge** [153 E5] (12 rooms) Cape Verde St; ☏ 011 667 2630; e manager@sidamalodge.net; w sidamalodge.net. This stylish boutique hotel 250m north of Bole Road has large self-catering studios, rooms & suites with wooden floors, pastel-coloured walls, minimalist décor, comfortable seating & bedding, well-equipped tiled kitchenette, sat TV & en-suite hot shower. The large reception area is adorned with contemporary Ethiopian artworks & a well-stocked bookshelf. *US$76 studio; US$101/202 1/2-bedroom suite. All rates B&B.* **$$$$$**

🏠 **Sidamo Inn** [166 A4] (28 rooms) Off Ghana St; ☏ 011 667 2630; e manager@sidamalodge.net; w sidamalodge.net. This larger sister hotel to Sidama Lodge is situated off Atlas Junction 1km north of its older namesake & is similar in style & quality. *US$75/90/100 B&B sgl/dbl/twin.* **$$$$$**

UPMARKET

☀ 🏠 **Addis Regency Hotel** [146 D2] (33 rooms) Off Benin St; ☏ 011 155 0000/31; m 0913 141583; e info@addisregency.com; w addisregency.com. Set within walking distance of the Piazza, this family-owned & -managed hotel has established itself as a top choice at its price level due to the excellent value-for-money en-suite rooms & outstanding customer service. A good restaurant with a cosmopolitan menu serves mains in the US$5–8 range, or you can eat at the wonderful Addis Ababa Restaurant around the corner. *From US$79/95 B&B dbl/twin.* **$$$$**

🏠 **Dreamliner Hotel** [152 C5] (96 rooms) Meskel Flower St; ☏ 011 467 4000; e reservation@dreamlinerhotel.com; w dreamlinerhotel.com. Having dropped its rates by 50% since the 7th edition was researched, this slick 9-storey hotel represents a top compromise between price & quality. Large en-suite rooms come with muted décor, TV, coffee/tea, safe, private balcony & hot tub/shower. It is also home to the city's finest Indian & steak restaurants. The 8th-floor gym & bar have superb views. Ask for a rear room. *US$60/70/120 B&B sgl/dbl/twin.* **$$$$**

🏠 **Addissinia Hotel** [166 C4] (40 rooms) Off Djibouti St; ☏ 011 662 3634; m 0911 511569; e info@addissiniahotel.com; w addissiniahotel.com. A popular choice with comfortable en-suite rooms decorated by a top Ethio–American interior designer, efficient & service-oriented owner-manager & staff, above average 1st-floor pizzeria/restaurant & wellness centre. *US$89/99/129 B&B sgl/dbl/suite.* **$$$$$**

🏠 **Residence Suite Hotel** [152 D3] (19 rooms) Off Bole Rd; ☏ 011 557 1075; e info@theresidenceaddis.com; w theresidenceaddis.com. This excellent owner-managed all-suite hotel 2mins' walk from Olympia underpass has very spacious & beautifully designed rooms with sitting area, minibar, free Wi-Fi, free drinking water, hot tub & sat TV. There's a small ground-floor restaurant. *From US$110 B&B dbl.* **$$$$$**

🏠 **Sidra International Hotel** [153 H2] (26 rooms) Off Haile Gebrselassie St; ☏ 011 661 3333/8888; m 0919 191935; e info@sidrahotel.com; w sidrahotel.com. Situated about 10mins' drive from the airport but rather isolated from other restaurants & nightlife, this new 6-storey hotel has a chic rooftop bar with a view over the city to the Entoto Hills & live music Thu–Sat nights, as well as a good spa & restaurant. Modern & well-equipped rooms come with wooden floor & furnishings, wall-mounted sat TV, safe & en-suite hot shower. *US$70/80/150 B&B standard sgl/dbl/suite*. **$$$$**

🏠 **Lion's Den Hotel** [159 G8] (16 rooms) Ketema-Kirkos; 📞 011 554 7734/5; e info@ thelionsdenhotel.com; f. Situated almost opposite the Olympiakos Greek Club, this popular 5-storey place doesn't quite live up to its billing as a boutique hotel, but the unobtrusively decorated suites with lounge, large kitchen, sat TV & hot shower seem like good value. *US$65/75 B&B sgl/dbl*. **$$$$**

MODERATE

✳ 🏠 **Arequ Guesthouse** [153 H4] (9 rooms) Southeast Ring Rd; 📞 011 896 3843; m 0911 744619; e info@arequbandb.com; w arequbandb. com. This quaint & welcoming owner-managed lodge comprises a narrow 6-storey architect-designed building painted pink on the outside & located 100m outside the Ring Rd only 300m south of Bob Marley Intersection & 2km from Bole Airport. The spacious & stylish en-suite rooms with sat TV are all different, each being decorated with individually made furniture & random items recycled from houses demolished elsewhere in Addis, but share an earthy feel dominated by woody textures. There's no lift, so unfit or elderly travellers might want to ask for a 1st-floor room. *US$35/50 B&B dbl/suite*. **$$$**

✳ 🏠 **GT Guesthouse** [152 A5] (13 rooms) Off Bishoftu Rd; m 0930 011199; e gtguesthouse@ yahoo.com; w gtguesthouse.com. This bright pink owner-managed guesthouse has a quiet location a short distance west of the Bishoftu road & some of the most welcoming & obliging staff in the city. Rooms are spread across 3 floors, each of which has 3–4 bedrooms, a well-equipped kitchen & a lounge with French doors leading to a spacious balcony, making it well suited to small groups, as well as individual travellers. *From US$35/55 sgl/dbl*. **$$$$**

✳ 🏠 **Ankober Bole Guesthouse** [153 E6] (16 rooms) Close to Rwanda Embassy; 📞 011 663 4320; e ankober.g.house@gmail.com. Owned & managed by the same friendly English-speaking couple as its older & cheaper namesake on the Piazza, this smart 3-storey guesthouse, its walls decorated with contemporary artworks,

has comfortable en-suite rooms with parquet floor, modern furniture, flatscreen TV & spacious bathroom. It is close to the airport & quite convenient for eating out & nightlife. Very good value. *US$40/60 B&B dbl/twin*. **$$$**

✳ 🏠 **Stay Easy Hotel** [166 B1] (41 rooms) Haile Gebrselassie St; 📞 011 661 6688; m 0938 865555; e info@stayeasyaddis.com; w stayeasyaddis.com. Outstanding value in this range is this well-managed 3-storey hotel, whose smart, compact & spotlessly clean rooms are attractively decorated with a contemporary feel & come with queen-size bed, sat TV, small balcony & en-suite hot shower. A good restaurant is attached & it's convenient for the many eateries on Mickey Leland Rd. *US$45/55 B&B standard/deluxe dbl*. **$$$**

🏠 **AG Palace Hotel** [166 D1] (19 rooms) off Haile Gebrselassie St; 📞 011 662 0456/7; m 0911 405885; e info@agpalacehotel.com; w agpalacehotel.com. This small & well-run semi-boutique hotel stands in a side street near Galagol LRT station & several malls. It has a good reputation & a well-regarded restaurant. *From US$40 dbl*. **$$$**

🏠 **Wudasie Castle Hotel** [166 A3] (24 rooms) Mickey Leland Rd; 📞 011 662 2727; m 0930 195519; e wudasiehotel@wudasiecastle.com; f. This newish 6-storey hotel in the heart of bustling Chechnya has a distinctive castle-like façade & relatively stylish rooms (reachable by lift) with hand-crafted wood furniture, flatscreen TV, fridge & modern hot shower. The staff seem particularly agreeable & there's a bright 1st-floor restaurant with mains in the US$5–6 range. *US$50/55/80 dbl/king-size/twin*. **$$$$**

🏠 **Aclana Lodge** [166 B4] (40 rooms) Off Djibouti St; 📞 011 618 4065; m 0911 375547; e info@aclanalodge.com; w aclanalodge.com. This quiet, friendly & secure guesthouse 3km from Bole Airport has the unpretentious, non-institutional feel of an overgrown family home. The spacious, light & airy en-suite rooms come with king-size beds, sat TV, balcony, mini kitchenette & hot shower/tub. B/fast is taken in a cosy TV lounge & there's a large common kitchen, where self-caterers can prepare meals. Ideal for long-stays & discounts are given for early bookings. Good value. *US$55/65 B&B*. **$$$$**

🏠 **Caravan Hotel** [166 A2] (37 rooms) Off Mickey Leland Rd; 📞 011 661 2297/8; m 0930 109653/4; e caravanhotel@caravanaddis.com;

w caravanaddis.com. This well-managed & obligingly staffed new hotel has comfortable & inoffensively decorated en-suite rooms with sat TV, safe, fridge, coffee-/tea-making facilities, writing desk & hot shower. A good restaurant & bar is attached, & several other good eateries lie within easy walking distance. Good value. *US$50/60 sgl/dbl.* **$$$$**

🏠 Hometown Addis Hotel [166 A4] (23 rooms) Cape Verde St; **m** 0910 446144; **e** info@hometown-addis.com; **w** hometown-addis.com. This unpretentious & well-priced medium-rise close to Atlas has a bright reception area, welcoming staff, ground-floor restaurant open 24/7, & unusually comfortable & attractively decorated rooms with flatscreen TV, fridge & modern bathroom with ceramic tiles & hot shower. *US$50/70/90 B&B sgl/dbl/twin.* **$$$$**

🏠 Hotel Lobelia [166 D7] (31 rooms) Off Cameroon St; **☎** 011 667 3850–3; **m** 0929 922930; **e** info@hotellobeliaaddis.com; **w** hotellobeliaaddis.com. Situated close to the airport & popular Yod Abyssinia Restaurant, this newish medium-rise has spacious modern rooms with wood laminate floor, fridge, flatscreen TV & hot shower. Unexceptional but decent value. *From US$65 dbl B&B.* **$$$$**

🏠 Ghion Hotel [159 E7] (195 rooms) Ras Desta Damtew St; **☎** 011 551 3222; **m** 0911 213129; **e** info@ghionhotel.com; **w** ghionhotel.com. Built in the 1950s & converted to a hotel towards the end of the imperial era, this former palace lies in rambling well-wooded grounds that offer great birdwatching (several endemics present). Facilities include a huge swimming pool, 4 restaurants, a nightclub & casino & on-site ATM. Negatives are the ponderous service & fuddy-duddy décor. Still, en-suite rooms with sat TV, writing desk & hot tub/shower seem fair value & it should appeal to anyone seeking a reasonably affordable green oasis in the city centre. *From US$56/68 sgl/dbl, with 15% discount to walk-ins.* **$$$$**

🏠 Bata Hotel [166 B1] (36 rooms) Haile Gebrselassie St; **m** 0911 204358; **e** info@batahotel.net; **w** batahotel.net. Situated opposite the landmark Debre Damo Hotel, this has very spacious rooms with wooden floor, modern furnishing, sat TV, Wi-Fi, safe, writing desk & en-suite hot shower. *Good value. From US$40/45/59 sgl/dbl/twin.* **$$$$**

BUDGET

✳ 🏠 Toronto Guest House [166 A2] (12 rooms) Mickey Leland Rd; **☎** 011 662 2742; **m** 0911 208568; **e** info@ethioguesthouses.com. Located behind Protection House, this friendly & brightly decorated owner-managed place has clean & comfortable en-suite rooms with wood laminate floor, TV, sitting area & en-suite hot tub/shower. There's also a pleasant ground-floor café & rooftop patio & internet. Top value. *From US$28/32/45 B&B sgl/dbl/suite.* **$$$**

✳ 🏠 Martin's Cozy Place [166 A4] (16 rooms) Atlas Junction; **m** 0910 884585, 0911 465022; **e** coze376@yahoo.com; **w** mmcozyplace.com. Conveniently located 3km from Bole Airport, this friendly & popular owner-managed backpacker hostel has comfortable rooms with hot showers. The communal kitchen, lounge & rooftop terrace are good places to hook up with other travellers & volunteers, & the surrounding area is well equipped with restaurants & bars. Facilities include left luggage, inexpensive airport transfers, sat TV in the lounge, & a book exchange. *US$25/30 B&B dbl with common/en-suite shower.* **$$$**

🏠 Lomi Guesthouse [158 G2] (34 rooms, more under construction) Shewareged Gedle St; **☎** 011 123 3628; **m** 0913 609366; **e** lomiguesthouse@gmail.com; **w** lomiguesthouse.net. Situated near the well-known Sandford School [147 G3] 10mins' walk from Arat Kilo, this quiet owner-managed guesthouse is set in a tranquil manicured garden dotted with seats where you can enjoy a drink or meal (hamburgers, spaghetti or *tibs* can be ordered all day long). En-suite rooms all come with fridge, sat TV & hot water. *US$18/26 standard/deluxe en-suite dbl.* **$$**

🏠 Abyssinia Guesthouse [166 B3] (25 rooms) Off Mickey Leland Rd; **m** 0963 147474, 0911 980098; **e** hotabyssinia711@gmail.com; **f**. This tall & narrow canary yellow hotel is conspicuously located opposite the landmark Yilma Restaurant & offers great access to bustling Chechnya. Small but clean en-suite rooms are built around a covered central courtyard & come with laminate wood floor & hot shower. There are also larger self-catering studios with reasonably well-equipped kitchens. *US$20/35 dbl/studio.* **$$**

🏠 Ras Hotel [159 B7] (96 rooms) Gambia St (Churchill Av); **☎** 011 551 7327; **e** rashotels@gmail.com; **w** rashotel.com. This venerable

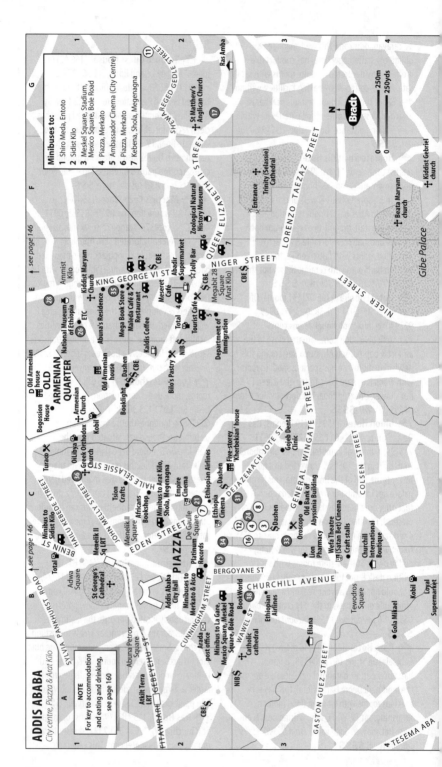

ADDIS ABABA
City centre, Piazza & Arat Kilo

NOTE
For key to accommodation and eating and drinking, see page 160.

Minibuses to:
1 Shiro Meda, Entoto
2 Sidist Kilo
3 Meskel Square, Stadium, Mexico Square, Bole Road
4 Piazza, Merkato
5 Ambassador Cinema (City Centre)
6 Piazza, Merkato
7 Kebena, Shola, Megenagna

250m
250yds

N

Bradt

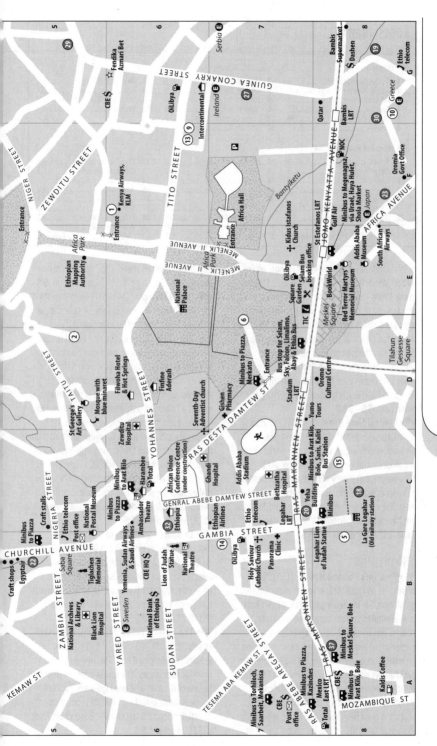

⌂ **Where to stay**

1	Addis Ababa Hilton...........F6	7	Hermon...........................C2	13	Radisson Blu.......................F6
2	Addis Ababa Sheraton.....D5	8	Itegue Taitu.....................C3	14	Ras...................................B7
3	Ankober Guesthouse........C3	9	Jupiter International......F6	15	Wim's Holland House.....C8
4	Baro.................................C3	10	Lion's Den......................G8	16	Wutma.............................C3
5	Buffet de la Gare................B8	11	Lomi Guesthouse..........G2		
6	Ghion..............................E7	12	National..........................C3		

⊗ **Where to eat and drink**

17	Asni Gallery.....................G2	24	KG Corner........................C3	32	The Picnic Basket............C6
18	Café Choché.....................C8	25	Kiyab Café.......................B2	33	Pizza di Napoli.................C3
19	Clay Pot...........................G8	26	Le Montmartre...............E1	34	Ristorante Castelli............C2
20	Cosmos Café....................C7	27	Lime Tree Café...............G7	35	Romina.............................E1
21	Good Times	28	Lucy Lounge	36	Sarem Café......................C1
	Restaurant & Bar.............C2		& Restaurant.................E1	37	Sunrise............................A8
22	Gusto Ristorante.............B5	29	Mamma Mia....................G5	38	Tomoca Coffee..................B3
23	Han.................................F8	30	Olympiakos.....................G8		Wim's Holland
	Itegue Taitu Hotel......(see 8)	31	Oslo Café.........................C3		House....................(see 15)

central landmark – among other things, where Nelson Mandela stayed when he visited Ethiopia in the 1960s – ranks among the city's most characterful hotels with its wood-panelled interiors & shady terrace restaurant. The en-suite rooms don't quite match the location & setting, but you can choose between budget rooms with cold shower on the ground floor, or smarter renovated rooms with hot shower on the upper floors. *US$40/50/70 standard sgl/dbl/twin; US$17 budget dbl.* **$$–$$$**

⌂ **Central Shoa Hotel** [166 D1] (50 rooms) Haile Gebrselassie St; ☎011 661 3354. This pleasant middle-aged medium-rise doesn't have the most central location, on the way out to Megenagna, but plenty of minibuses run past & a cluster of malls & restaurants starts 1km to the west. The en-suite rooms are a little tired-looking but have a balcony, fridge, TV & hot water. Good value. *US$18/22 dbl/twin.* **$$$**

SHOESTRING

✳ ⌂ **Wim's Holland House** [159 C8] (7 rooms) m 0911 887770; e wimshollandhouse@ gmail.com. Set in a leafy garden on a quiet back road around the corner from the old railway station, this friendly & agreeably idiosyncratic owner-managed lodge & campsite is something of an institution in overlanding, but it also caters to backpackers with tents & has a few small rooms, mostly using common hot showers. Amenities include a characterful restaurant with terrace seating, a good book exchange & free luggage storage. A fabulous set-up, but rooms are often

fully booked, so call ahead. *US$7 sgl with common shower, US$12 en-suite dbl, US$4 pp camping.* **$$**

⌂ **Hostel Ethiopia** [143 H5] (9 rooms) m 0968 202772; e stay@safeethiopia.com; w safeethiopia. com. Owned & managed by an energetic US–Ethiopian couple, this attractive new hostel comprises a converted modern house in a secure development in Mehal-Semit (also known as Summit Safari) about 7km east of the city centre. Accommodation is in 4-bed dorms or private rooms with ¾ bed. Amenities include a TV lounge, self-catering kitchen & rooftop balcony. It also offers simple local meals for US$3. Despite the suburban location, regular fast trains run to the city centre from CMC station, only 5mins' walk from the hostel. It is difficult to find, so new arrivals should either arrange an airport transfer when they make a booking, or get their driver to phone Roza at the above number for directions. *US$10 dorm bed or US$20 private room.* **$$$**

⌂ **La Source Guesthouse** [152 C5] (14 rooms) Off Meskel Flower Rd; ☎011 466 5516; m 0973 052932; e lasourceguesthouse@gmail. com; ⓕ lasource.addisababa. Small but clean en-suite rooms at this welcoming new guesthouse come with hot showers & free airport shuttle. *US$18/24 sgl/dbl.* **$$$**

⌂ **TYA Hotel** [152 C5] (15 rooms) Off Meskel Flower Rd; ☎011 470 1530; m 0911 231807; e tyahotel000@gmail.com. This new hotel has a quiet location around the corner from the popular La Source & serves as a good fall-back if it's full. Spotless modern-looking en-suite rooms come with flatscreen TV & hot shower. Good value. *From US$14/16 sgl/dbl.* **$$**

🏠 **Ankober Guesthouse** [158 C3] (15 rooms) Mundy St; 📞011 111 2350; e ankober.g.house@ gmail.com. Comprising a converted former hospital, this welcoming owner-managed guesthouse is the best & priciest of several well-established shoestring options dotted around the Piazza. Quiet & comfortable en-suite rooms come with tiled or wooden floor, TV & hot shower. There's no catering but it's close to many restaurants. *US$20 dbl*. **$$**

🏠 **Wutma Hotel** [158 C3] (15 rooms) Mundy St; m 0923 929698; e wutmahotel@yahoo.com. Boasting a convenient location opposite the Baro Hotel, this clean & well-run hotel has a popular ground-floor restaurant with Wi-Fi & small en-suite rooms with ¾ bed & hot shower. *US$12 sgl or dbl occupancy*. **$$**

🏠 **Baro Hotel** [158 C3] (26 rooms) Mundy St; 📞011 155 1447. A popular backpacker haunt since the 1990s & little changed over all that time, the timeworn Baro provides a safe, affordable & somewhat lassitudinous retreat where new arrivals with realistic expectations can adjust to the tempo of Addis Ababa, look for travel companions, & deal with practicalities such as 4x4 rental, bus bookings & the like. The rundown en-suite rooms with hot shower are no great shakes & variable in quality, so ask to see one first. *US$10/12/18 dbl/queen-size/twin*. **$$**

🏠 **Itegue Taitu Hotel** [158 C3] (70 rooms) Off Dej Jote St, Piazza; 📞011 156 0787; m 0929 308230; e reservations@taituhotel.com; w taituhotel.com. Built for Empress Taitu in 1907, Addis Ababa's oldest hotel was designed by the Armenian architect Minas Kherbekian &, having survived extensive fire damage in 2015, it remains an important backpacker hub. The 1st-floor bedrooms in the main building are rundown but characterful, while those in the annexes are bland & no better than functional. High ceilings, wood-panelled walls, creaky timber floors & time-warped furnishings lend the louche ground-floor Ethiopian restaurant a winning period charm. Within the grounds you'll find several ATMs & tour companies, as well as the Ethio/Abay & Limalimo Bus ticket offices. *US$12 dbl (annex); US$25/33 dbl with common/en-suite shower in the main building*. **$$**

🏠 **Henok Pension** [166 A2] (12 rooms) Off Mickey Leland Rd; 📞011 662 4234; m 0911 214516. Quiet & secure family-run hotel set around a neat concrete courtyard in Chechnya. The clean tiled en-suite rooms are nothing special but do come with TV & hot shower. *US$18/22 with dbl/ king-size bed*. **$$**

🏠 **Hermon Hotel** [158 C2] (15 rooms) 📞011 156 5099; m 0912 372841; e hermon@yahoo. com. Set in a grand old building that must date to the Italian occupation or earlier, this place is rich in period detail, from the curvaceous ceramic-tiled staircase illuminated through stained-glass windows to the ornate etchings in the tall-ceilinged bedrooms. Sadly, it is also quite rundown & poorly maintained, showers have cold water only, & while the location in the heart of the Piazza couldn't be more convenient, it also makes for a lot of traffic noise. Still, decent value at the price. *US$8/12 dbl with common/en-suite shower*. **$$**

🏠 **Buffet de la Gare** [159 B8] (9 rooms) m 0961 045946. This timeworn hotel is tucked away in central green grounds in front of the old railway station. The en-suite rooms with TV are about as good as one could expect at the price. *US$20 dbl*. **$$**

🏠 **National Hotel** [158 C3] (20 rooms) The long-serving pick of the rock-bottom hotels that line the road between the Baro & Itegue Taitu Hotels. Small dark rooms use good common showers. No email or working phone. *US$6 sgl*. **$**

✖ WHERE TO EAT AND DRINK

Addis Ababa has an excellent and ever-expanding dining-out scene. Most international cuisines are represented by at least one quality venue, and a plethora of moderately priced restaurants serving a combination of Italian-influenced dishes, local cuisine and simple meat grills. A speciality of the city is its so-called national and cultural restaurants, both of which are usually housed in a traditional *tukul*-style building and serve a varied selection of meat-based and vegan Ethiopian dishes, supplemented in the case of cultural restaurants by traditional live music and dancing. Note that most mid-range to upmarket restaurants in Addis Ababa add a service charge of 10%, plus 15% VAT, to the listed menu prices.

For snacks, there are literally hundreds of cafés and pastry shops, many of which serve savoury mini-pizzas and spicy hamburgers in addition to cakes, coffee and fruit juices. These include dozens of branches of the Starbucks-like Kaldis, La Parisienne and Yeshi chains, some of which are marked on our maps. The listings below are highly selective (hence the high proportion of author picks), and were whittled down from a far longer shortlist with the aim of providing visitors with a good cross section of cuisine and prices. Given that it is often convenient to eat near your hotel or in a part of town you're visiting for another reason, restaurants are grouped by area rather than by price or cuisine type. Almost all the hotels listed over the previous pages also have adequate to good restaurants.

CITY CENTRE
Restaurants

✳ ✘ **Gusto Ristorante** [159 B5] 3rd floor, Tracon Tower, Churchill Av; m 0934 497861/2; w gustoaddis.com; ⏲ 12.15–14.30 & 19.15–22.30 daily. Formal Italian restaurant whose classic-contemporary décor, quality food, exceptional wine list & professional service would make it a top performer anywhere in the world. The menu changes regularly & is posted on the website. *Mains US$6–16 (pizza & pasta), US$10–22 (meat & fish).*

✳ ✘ **Wim's Holland House** [159 C8] Old railway station; m 0911 608088/887770; ⏲ 08.30–midnight daily. Popular with overlanders, this quirky, brightly decorated & sociable restaurant/bar has a tree-shaded terrace, a good selection of salads & soups, & an interesting menu that combines local dishes (*US$2–4*) with some more unusual Dutch, Surinamese & Hungarian selections (*US$5–6*). *Mains US$3–8.*

✘ **Sunrise Restaurant** [159 A8] ☎ 011 551 6280; ⏲ 11.30–21.00 daily. This family-run stalwart, housed in an old wooden-floored homestead complete with palm-shaded beer garden, serves a good selection of Ethiopian dishes, pasta & roasts. *Mains US$2–3.50.*

Coffee, pastries & snacks

✳ ☕ **Café Choché** [159 C8] Old railway station; m 0913 035486; 🅵; ⏲ 07.20–19.00 daily. This chic but inexpensive café, set in an outhouse of the old railway station & decorated with monochrome imperial-era photos of the Djibouti line, serves some of the city's best coffee, freshly sourced from Jimma. It's a good place to buy coffee beans, too.

☕ **The Picnic Basket** [159 C6] Gambia St (Churchill Av); m 0913 621971; ⏲ 07.00–21.00 daily. Burgers, sandwiches, pasta, salads & other light lunches are the specialities at this popular central bistro, whose country-style interior & terrace seating come across like a transplant from Europe. *Mains US$3–5.*

☕ **Cosmos Café** [159 C7] Ras Makonnen St; m 0911 210215; ⏲ 07.30–19.00 daily. This above-average central café serves good juices, coffee & chocolate cake.

PIAZZA
Restaurants

✳ ✘ **Addis Ababa Restaurant** [146 D2] Off Benin St; ☎ 011 111 3513; ⏲ 08.00–22.00 daily. The city's most characterful & least-contrived national restaurant is housed in a fascinating circular building constructed in the late 1890s for the future Empress Zewditu & her 3rd husband, Wube Atnaf Seged, whose names are still preserved in the original floor ceramics. The traditional décor of Jimma stools & basketry tables, gloriously undermined by a TV wittering away in the background, is complemented by a long menu of Ethiopian cuisine. The *tej* is highly rated too. *Mains US$3–6.*

✘ **Ristorante Castelli** [158 C2] Gandhi Rd; ☎ 011 157 1757; ⏲ noon–14.30 & 19.00–22.00 Mon–Sat. Established in 1948 & still run by the same Italian family, Castelli's is Addis's most famous restaurant, often frequented by visiting celebrities, & booking is advisable. Dining is in various different-sized rooms decorated in post-war Italian style, & seafood is flown in from Djibouti. *Mains US$8–12.*

✘ **Itegue Taitu Hotel** [158 C3] Off Dej Jote St; ☎ 011 156 0787; ⏲ 07.00–22.00 daily. This stalwart hotel serves a good selection of Ethiopian cuisine in traditional décor. The inexpensive lunchtime vegan buffet is recommended. *US$3–5.*

✘ **Pizza di Napoli** [158 C3] General Wingate Rd; m 0913 872222; ⏲ 07.00–21.00 daily. More than 20 types of pizza, along with a good selection of meat & pasta dishes, grace the menu at this affordable pizzeria closer to the popular Baro & Wutma hotels. *Mains US$3–5.*

✗ Good Times Restaurant & Bar [159 C2] Haile Selassie St; ⏰ 08.00–midnight. Set in a handsome old 2-storey building complete with tall inset ceilings, engraved columns, & 1st-floor balcony with an ornate wooden balustrade, this is a grand spot for a raffish beer or coffee in the heart of the Piazza, & it also serves pasta, pizzas & Ethiopian fare. *Mains around US$3.*

✗ KG Corner [158 C3] Off Dej Jote St; m 0911 936395; ⏰ 08.00–22.00 daily. This chilled fast-food joint next to the Itegue Taitu serves tasty burgers, as well as soups, salads, sandwiches, pasta & pizza. Eat indoors or on a terrace from where you can watch one of the city's busiest streets at play. Cheap draught beer & free Wi-Fi are added bonuses. *Mains US$2–4.*

Coffee, pastries & snacks

▭ Kiyab Café [158 B2] Cunningham St; ⏰ 07.30–21.00 daily. Popular with a young, trendy crowd, this excellent 2-storey café has balcony seating & a good selection of cakes, snacks, juices & hot drinks. It also has a full b/fast menu & the food is outstanding.

▭ Oslo Café [158 C3] Dej Jote St; ⏰ 07.00–19.00 daily. One of the best cafés in the Piazza area, this bright, modern place with indoor & terrace seating has great fruit juices, as well as a good range of pastries & coffee.

▭ Sarem Café [158 C1] Haile Selassie St; ⏰ 07.00–21.00 daily. Among the best of the many coffee stops dotted around the Piazza, this funkily decorated café has yummy chocolate cakes, fresh croissants, spicy mini-pizzas & a great choice of juices.

▭ Tomoca Coffee [158 B3] Wawel St; ☎ 011 111 1781/3; w tomocacoffee.com; ⏰ 07.00–20.30 Mon–Sat. Established in 1953, this family-owned coffee shop is a great place to sample one of Ethiopia's most highly rated blends, & if you approve you can buy the beans to take home.

ARAT KILO & SIDDIST KILO
Restaurants

✳ ✗ Ararat Restaurant [147 E3] Welete Yohannes St; ☎ 011 111 3572; ⏰ noon–14.00 & 18.00–22.00 daily. Set in the Old Armenian Club a short walk northeast of the Piazza, this tricky-to-find but well-priced restaurant is the best place to

try a Mediterranean cuisine associated with one of the city's oldest settler communities. Most people share a meze selection, but lentil soup & good kebabs are also on the menu. *US$3–5.*

✳ ✗ Le Montmartre [158 E1] Off King George VI St; m 0969 136374; ⏰ 07.00–22.00 daily. Conveniently located for lunch close to the museums of Arat & Siddist Kilo, this brightly decorated & informal 1st-floor restaurant has hands-on French–Ethiopian management & a menu that reflects both nationalities (specialities include *steak aux frites* & *hachis parmentier*) while also being strong on burgers, pasta & pizza. Food is well prepared & reasonably priced. *Mains US$3–6.*

✗ Asni Gallery [158 G2] Queen Elizabeth II St; m 0911 206697; ☐; ⏰ 10.00–19.00 Mon–Sat. Set in an imperial-era homestead about 1km east of Arat Kilo, this Addis institution is now more bistro than gallery, though occasional exhibitions & events are posted on its Facebook page. The menu is all vegetarian & there's the choice of indoor or garden seating. *Mains US$3–4.*

✗ Lucy Lounge & Restaurant [158 E1] King George VI St; m 0912 476954; w lucyrestaurantaddis.info; ⏰ 08.00–22.00 daily. Situated alongside the National Museum, this lovely semi-outdoor venue has a cosmopolitan menu that includes stir-fries, salads, pasta, sizzler plates & grills, as well as a good selection of Ethiopian dishes. *Mains US$6–8.*

✗ Romina Restaurant [158 E1] King George VI St; m 0911 214335; ⏰ 06.00–23.00 daily. Established in 1973, this bustling & perennially popular pavement restaurant in Arat Kilo provides free Wi-Fi, 3 types of draught beer, & a dauntingly lengthy menu of stir-fries, grills, sandwiches, pizzas & pastas to a mixed crowd of students, local businessmen & travellers. *Mains US$3–6.*

KAZANCHIS & THE NORTHEAST
Restaurants

✳ ✗ Mamma Mia [159 G5] Dar Sahara St; m 0929 002218; ☐; ⏰ 11.30–15.00 Mon–Sun, 18.30–22.00 Mon–Sat. Situated in a beautiful villa next to the Meles Zenawi Foundation, this popular Italian eatery has a very Mediterranean feel, an Italian wine list & a pasta-oriented menu with specialities being gnocchi, liver & Abruzzo sausage. *Mains around US$10.*

✳ ✗ Road Runner [143 F4] Togo St; m 0930 362570; ⏰ 08.00–midnight daily. This popular restaurant, set in an old villa 500m north of Haya Hulet, is especially lively on Fri evenings when it serves a generous barbecue. There's a campfire in the garden every night & a great selection of blues & jazz, as well as music from all over Africa. It serves good pizza, veggie burgers & vegetable quiche, plus a varied selection of meat & chicken grills. If taxi drivers don't know it, ask for Dinberua Hospital. *Mains US$4–7.*

✳ ✘**Dashen Terara Restaurant** [147 G6] Dar Sahara St; 011 554 1437; m 0911 210723; w dashenterararestaurant.com; ⏱ 07.00–22.00 Sun–Wed, 07.00–midnight Thu–Sat. Recently relocated from the city centre to an attractive old suburban homestead with ceramic tile & wood floors & plenty of garden seating, this 40-year-old cultural restaurant serves shiro & other vegetarian fair (*US$3–4*), as well as meat dishes including excellent *tibs* (*US$6–7*). There's traditional live music & dance most nights, starting at 19.30.

Coffee, pastries & snacks

✳ ☕**Lime Tree Café** [159 G7] Nigist Towers, Guinea Conakry St; m 0911 200072; ⏱ 07.00–21.00 daily. Recently relocated to Kazanchis from Bole, this trendy venue is more of a daytime snack location than an evening restaurant, serving a selection of b/fasts, hearty soups, wraps, gourmet burgers, etc, as well as coffee & juices. *Mains & snacks US$2.50–4.50.*

☕**Mulmul Café & Bakery** [153 F1] Togo St; m 0935 986434; ⏱ 06.00–20.45 daily. Widely regarded to be the best bakery in Addis Ababa, with fresh rye & wholewheat loaves daily, plus a wonderful selection of pastries & cakes, most of which can be sampled at the attached café.

☕**Topia Tej Bet** [166 B1] Off Haile Gebrselassie St; m 0911 233647; ⏱ 08.00–22.00 daily. This owner-managed garden bar near the Stay Easy Hotel is set around a leafy courtyard & serves some of the purest & finest *tej* in Ethiopia, as well as excellent raw or cooked *kitfo*. *Tej US$3.50 per litre, kitfo US$4.*

CHECHNYA (MICKEY LELAND RD & ENVIRONS)
Restaurants

✳ ✘**La Mandoline** [166 B2] Off Mickey Leland Rd; 011 662 9482; e lamandoline@hotmail.fr; ⏱ noon–15.00 & 19.00–22.00 Tue–Sun. This top-notch French eatery has indoor or garden seating

& an imaginative menu featuring the likes of fillet steak with blue cheese sauce, lamb shanks & stuffed cabbage. The house speciality is beef fondue for 2. There's a good selection of desserts & wine by the glass. *Mains around US$10.*

✳ ✘**Yilma Restaurant** [166 B3] Off Mickey Leland Rd; m 0911 490909; ⏱ 07.00–22.00 daily exc Wed, Fri & other fasting days. Newly opened in the capital, this branch of Adama's best-known eat-in butchery is the place to head for prime beef, raw or lightly charcoal-seared, & served with bread or *injera*, & spicy *mitmita* dip. Strictly for carnivores. *US$6.25 per 500g (enough to feed 2).*

✘**Bait al Mandi** [166 A3] Mickey Leland Rd; m 0920 242424; ⏱ 10.00–22.00 daily. This attractive courtyard restaurant is attached to a converted house decorated in typical Yemeni style. It serves Yemeni spicy specialities such as half *mandi* or *agda* chicken or lamb in the US$6–10 range. No alcohol.

✘**Eset Restaurant** [166 A4] Mickey Leland Rd; m 0911 643280; ⏱ 09.00–22.00 daily. A very popular spot with locals at lunchtime, this shady courtyard restaurant serves a varied selection of well-prepared local & Western dishes, mostly for around US$3.

✘**Step Up Restaurant** [166 A4] Cape Verde St; ⏱ 07.00–23.00 daily. This pleasant & affordable terrace restaurant near Atlas is very convenient for those staying at Martin's Cozy Place & it serves a varied selection of local & international dishes in the US$3–4 range.

✘**Azmera Shiro** [166 B3] New Haya Hulet Rd; m 0921 791939; ⏱ 07.00–23.00 daily. Boasting one of the city's most extensive vegetarian menus, this traditionally decorated restaurant is most famous for its shiro-based dishes. *Mains US$2–4.*

Coffee, pastries & snacks

✳ ☕**Moyos Café** [166 A4] Mickey Leland Rd; m 0961 616161; ⏱ 07.30–20.30 daily. This 1st-floor bistro has a well-lit boldly coloured interior & healthy menu dominated by pasta, salads, sandwiches, wraps, smoothies, & fruit & vegetable juices. *Mains US$3.50–4, smoothies & juices around US$1.50.*

BOLE MEDHANE ALEM
Restaurants

✳ ✘**Yod Abyssinia** [166 D7] Off Cameroon St; 011 661 2985; ⏱ 11.00–midnight daily. The most popular of Addis Ababa's cultural restaurants, this large traditionally decorated hall also hosts a superb music & dancing show from 19.30 daily. Booking advised. It's handily located for late flights out of Addis! *Mains US$6–10.*

✳ ✗ **ViaVia** [166 A4] Namibia St; m 0927 084046, 0924 116209; �; ⏲ 10.00–midnight (later at w/ends). This trendy Belgian-run 'travellers café' has an aptly globetrotting blackboard menu, indoor & outdoor seating, & a sociable vibe, especially over w/ends, when it often hosts live music or DJ nights (check the Facebook page for these & other events). *Mains US$4–6.*

✳ ✗ **Garden Bräu** [166 C6] Off Cameroon St; ☎011 618 2591/5; w beergardeninn.com; ⏲ 10.00–midnight daily. Bratwurst, schnitzel, roast pork & other German cuisine dominate the menu at the excellent beer house attached to the Beer Garden Inn. It also serves great home-brewed blonde & ebony draught by the tankard. *Mains US$4–6.50, draught US$1.50/500ml.*

✳ ✗ **Kategna** [166 D6] Off Cameroon St; ☎011 829 6214; m 0911 520183; ⏲ 06.00–22.00 daily. A slick modern take on the stereotypical national restaurant, this 2-storey place serves plenty of regional dishes you won't easily find elsewhere in Addis Ababa, including a good vegan selection, while specialities include *tibs firfir* & *doro wot. Mains US$6–10.*

✳ ✗ **Abucci Restaurant** [166 B5] Off Namibia St; ☎011 667 0476; m 0912 501827; ⏲ noon–15.00 & 19.00–22.30 Mon–Sat. This stylish classic-contemporary restaurant, which spans a 2-storey house & wooden garden deck, serves top-quality genuine Italian cuisine, with mains in the US$6–12 range.

✗ **Gebeta** [166 D7] Off Cameroon St; m 0912 020914; ⏲ 08.00–midnight daily. Funky contemporary wine bar with plenty of comfortable seating, an all-Ethiopian menu & an eclectic music selection (with occasional live acts). Attracts a young trendy crowd, especially at w/ends. *Mains US$3–6.*

✗ **Habesha 2000** [166 A5] Off Namibia Rd; ☎011 618 2258; m 0912 838383; ⏲ 08.00–midnight daily. This beautifully decorated cultural restaurant has an excellent music & dance show that starts at 19.30, as well as very good food. Go à la carte if you know your dishes, or try the more expensive buffet if you need a primer. Local & imported wines are well priced. *Mains US$7–9, buffet US$13.*

✗ **Elanos Lounge & Restaurant** [166 D7] Off Namibia Rd; m 0915 740093; �; ⏲ 06.00–late daily. Upmarket wine bar with live Ethiopian jazz starting at 19.00 on Tue & Fri, a stylish interior & deck with cane seating, & varied menu of pizzas, grills, local & Italian dishes in the US$4–8 range.

✗ **Mimi's Addis** [166 B5] Namibia St; m 0911 415645; �; ⏲ 07.00–23.00. Stylish new restaurant with shaded outdoor seating in a leafy courtyard or smart-casual interior. The cosmopolitan menu includes pizzas, grills, stir-fries, pasta & pizza, with most mains at around US$4–6. Barbecue & live music on Tue, starting at 19.00.

✗ **Fusion Bistro** [166 B6] Off Namibia St; m 0910 005151; ⏲ 07.30–21.30. Though it's not really fusion as such, the menu in this attractive 1st-floor restaurant certainly gets around, with North African, Mediterranean, Asian, Mexican & Italian cuisines all represented. *Mains US$5–7.*

Coffee, pastries & snacks

🖵 **Cupcake Delights** [166 B6] Off Namibia St; m 0911 641464; ⏲ 07.00–23.00 daily. Delicious fresh cupcakes, sandwiches, burgers & smoothies, as well as a range of light snacks are on offer at this superior café with free Wi-Fi. *Mains US$4–8, smoothies & cupcakes US$1.50.*

BOLE ROAD & OLYMPIA
Restaurants

✳ ✗ **Bata Traditional Restaurant** [152 D6] Rwanda St; ☎011 663 1096; m 0911 216321; ☑; ⏲ 11.00–midnight daily. This serves delicious Ethiopian fare in a quirky 2-storey building set in an amazing garden that's been cultivated by the family that has owned it for 20 years. *Kitfo* & *chikena tibs* (beef in a clay pot) are specialities on the well-annotated menu, & there's traditional music from all around Ethiopia from 19.30 onwards. *Mains around US$4.*

✳ ✗ **Zaika** [152 C5] Dreamliner Hotel, Meskel Flower Rd; ☎011 467 4000; ⏲ 11.00–16.00 & 17.00–23.00 Mon–Sat. The city's top Indian restaurant stands on the ground floor of the Dreamliner Hotel. The menu will delight spice lovers, with good vegetarian & tandoori selections. *Mains US$3–7.*

✳ ✗ **Sakura Japanese Restaurant** [152 D6] off Rwanda St; m 0984 873551; ⏲ 11.00–14.30 & 17.00–21.00 daily. This brightly decorated &

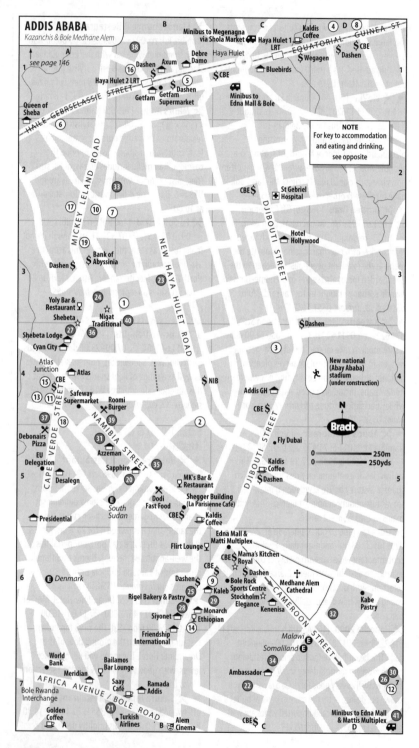

ADDIS ABABA
Kazanchis & Bole Medhane Alem

see page 146

Minibus to Megenagna
via Shola Market

Kaldis Coffee

Haya Hulet 1 LRT

EQUATORIAL GUINEA ST

Haya Hulet

Debre Damo

Wegagen
CBE
Dashen

HAILE GEBRSELASSIE STREET

Haya Hulet 2 LRT
Dashen
Axum

Getfam
Getfam Supermarket
Dashen
CBE

Bluebirds

Minibus to Edna Mall & Bole

Queen of Sheba

MICKEY LELAND ROAD

NEW HAYA HULET ROAD

DJIBOUTI STREET

CBE
St Gebriel Hospital

Hotel Hollywood

Dashen
Bank of Abyssinia

Yoly Bar & Restaurant
Shebeta

Shebeta Lodge
Cyan City

Nigat Traditional

Dashen

NOTE
For key to accommodation
and eating and drinking,
see opposite

Atlas Junction
CBE
Atlas

Safeway Supermarket
Roomi Burger

NIB

Addis GH
CBE

New national
(Abay Ababa)
stadium
(under construction)

N

Bradt

Debonairs Pizza

EU Delegation

NAMIBIA STREET

CAPE VERDE STREET

Azzeman
Sapphire

Desalegn

South Sudan

Dodi Fast Food

Shegger Building
(La Parisienne Café)
CBE
Kaldis Coffee

Fly Dubai

Kaldis Coffee
Dashen

DJIBOUTI STREET

0   250m
0   250yds

Presidential

Denmark

MK's Bar & Restaurant

Edna Mall & Matti Multiplex

Flirt Lounge

CBE
CBE

Mama's Kitchen
Royal
Dashen

Medhane Alem Cathedral

Kabe Pastry

Dashen
Kaleb
Bole Rock Sports Centre
Stockholm
Elegance
Kenenisa

CAMEROON STREET

Rigel Bakery & Pastry

Siyonet
Monarch
Ethiopian

Friendship International

Malawi
Somaliland

World Bank
Bailamos Bar Lounge
Meridian
Saay Café
Ramada Addis

AFRICA AVENUE / BOLE ROAD

Bole Rwanda Interchange

Golden Coffee

Turkish Airlines

Alem Cinema

Ambassador

CBE

Minibus to Edna Mall
& Mattis Multiplex

ADDIS ABABA Kazanchis & Bole Medhane Alem
For listings, see from page 151

🛏 Where to stay

1	Abyssinia Guesthouse....B3	8	Central Shoa...................D1	15	Sidamo Inn.......................A4
2	Aclana Lodge..................B4	9	Harmony...........................C6	16	Stay Easy..........................B1
3	Addissinia.........................C4	10	Henok Pension................A2	17	Toronto Guest House.... A2
4	AG Palace.........................D1	11	Hometown Addis............A4	18	Washington.......................A4
5	Bata...................................B1	12	Hotel Lobelia...................D7	19	Wudasie Castle................A3
6	Capital Hotel & Spa........A2	13	Martin's Cozy Place........A4		
7	Caravan............................A2	14	Saro-Maria.......................B6		

✴ Where to eat and drink

20	Abucci...............................B5	27	Eset...................................A4	35	Mimi's Addis.....................B5
21	Aladdin.............................A7	28	Fusion Bistro....................B6	36	Moyos Café.......................A4
22	Avanti Wine Bar..............C7	29	Garden Bräu.....................C6	37	Step Up.............................A4
23	Azmera Shiro...................B3	30	Gebeta..............................D7	38	Topia Tej Bet....................B1
24	Bait al Mandi...................A3	31	Habesha 2000..................A5	39	ViaVia...............................A4
25	Cupcake Delights............B6	32	Kategna............................D6	40	Yilma................................B3
26	Elanos Lounge &	33	La Mandoline....................B2	41	Yod Abyssinia...................D7
	Restaurant....................D7	34	La Nouvelle.......................C7		

attractively lit restaurant occupies a converted homestead close to Zeist Lodge & serves a long menu of top-notch authentic Japanese cuisine – sushi, chicken teriyaki, soups & Japanese-style meatballs & steaks – in the US$5–8 range.

✳ ✕ **Avanti Wine Bar** [166 C7] Off Bole Rd; m 0911 522660; ⏱ 11.00–15.00 & 18.00–21.00 daily. This classy European restaurant, with its white tablecloths, subdued live piano music & walls decorated with abstract art & posters of musicians, has a superb wine list & a varied selection of salads, soups, grills & Italian specialities such as ravioli & gnocchi. Perfect for a romantic night out. *Mains US$6–8.*

✳ ✕ **Clay Pot** [158 G8] Olympia; m 0931 312199; ⏱ 11.30–22.00 Wed–Sat, 11.30–15.00 Mon & Tue. This friendly & informal eatery is run by 2 well-travelled Ethiopian women whose small & ever-mutating menu includes home-cooked dishes from the likes of Morocco, Jamaica, Korea &, of course, Ethiopia. There's live music on Thu nights. *Mains US$4–6.*

✳ ✕ **La Nouvelle** [166 C7] Bole Ambassador; m 0929 930200; ⏱ 07.00–22.00 Mon–Sat. This smart-casual new restaurant, dominated by wood & wrought-iron fixtures, next to the landmark Ambassador Hotel is already gaining an enviable reputation for its Italian fusion menu. Specialities include Nile perch steak, escalope au vin & homemade lasagne. *Mains US$5–8.*

✳ ✕ **Sishu** [142 C7] Alexander Pushkin St; ☎ 011 869 8535; ⏱ 11.00–18.00 Tue–Thu, 11.00–20.00 Fri–Sun. Though it's a bit out of the way, this revamped warehouse joint with inspired retro décor & an open-air kitchen serves the city's

best & freshest burgers in homemade buns, as well as good steak & other sandwiches. Excellent take-away baguettes. Embwa creamery in the car park serves equally good ice cream. *Mains all around US$5.*

✕ **Aladdin Restaurant** [166 A7] Zimbabwe St; ☎ 011 661 4109; m 0911 613255; e t_kevorkian@ hotmail.com; 📘; ⏱ noon–15.00 & 19.00–22.30 Mon–Sat. Though it's a lot pricier than Ararat, this stalwart of 20 years' standing is the top place in town for Armenian cuisine & is best known for its meze & kebabs. *Meze US$3, mains US$7.*

✕ **Makush Art Gallery & Restaurant** [152 C4] Bole Rd; ☎ 011 552 6848; 📘; ⏱ 11.30–23.30 daily. Situated in the Mega Building, this quality Italian restaurant is reached by walking through its own art gallery, which has some good work for sale. *Mains US$3–6.*

✕ **Cork & Cellar** [153 F6] 4th floor, DH Geda Bldg; m 0921 145252; ⏱ 11.30–14.00 & 19.00–23.30 daily. This hip new venue has live music on Tue & Thu, open mic on Sun, & wine-tasting sessions 17.00–19.00 Mon–Fri. *Tasty & generous portions of Western-style mains are in the US$5–7 range.*

✕ **Olympiakos** [159 G8] Off Dr Congo St; ☎ 011 5530485; 📘; ⏱ 09.00–23.00. Situated in & often referred to as the Greek Club, this relaxed venue with plentiful terrace seating specialises in Greek cuisine but also serves a varied selection of Ethiopian dishes, pizzas & straight grills. *Mains US$6–8.*

✕ **Sky Steak House** [152 C5] Dreamliner Hotel, Meskel Flower Rd; ☎ 011 467 4000; ⏱ 11.00–16.00 & 17.00–23.00 Mon–Sat. Widely regarded to serve the city's best steak, imported directly from South Africa, this 8th-floor restaurant also serves excellent Nile perch & has a good selection of European, Chilean, South African & Ethiopian wine. Portions are less than generous at the price. *Mains US$10–20.*

✗ **Rainbow Korean** [153 E6] Off Zimbabwe St; ⬩011 663 1318; ⊕ 10.00–21.00 daily. Situated next to Rwanda market in Addis Ababa's equivalent to Chinatown, this has an amazing selection of Korean cuisine, with every item on the menu described in detail. Specialities include *galbi* (marinaded meat) & vegetable stir-fry. Good soups too. *Mains US$4–6.*

✗ **Jewel of India** [152 C4] Meskel Flower Rd; ⬩011 557 2510; m 0911 213795; w jeweladdis. com; ⊕ 11.00–15.00 & 18.00–23.00 daily. This popular restaurant just south of Olympia Interchange has an extensive menu of Indian & Chinese meat & vegetarian dishes, including a good tandoor selection. *Most mains US$4–6.*

✗ **Han Restaurant** [159 F8] Bole Rd; m 0933 198888; ⊕ 11.30–13.30 & 17.30–21.00 daily. Beautifully decorated in a rather ostentatious manner, this is widely regarded to be Addis Ababa's

top Asian eatery, but it also seems exceptionally expensive, at least until you recognise that mains are designed to cater to 2 & come with free bottomless green tea. *Mains US$13–18.*

GERJI

✗ **Totot Traditional Restaurant** [143 G5] Next to Nexus Hotel; m 0930 012250; w totottraditionalrestaurant.com; ⊕ 07.00–23.00 daily. This is a cultural restaurant with a difference in the menu & a music & dance show that starts at 18.00 & predominantly reflects the Gurage ethnic group. *Main US$6–10 meat buffet.*

✗ **Galani Coffee Warehouse** [143 H5] Near Jackross Junction; ⬩011 645 5999; m 0911 429491; w galanicafe.com; ⊕ 08.30–19.00 Thu–Sun. This trendy café, art gallery, craft shop & coffee distributor serves superb coffee, *tej* & wine by the glass. A regularly changing menu of filled crêpes, tacos, salads & other yummy light meals, mostly in the US$3–7 range, has plenty of options for vegetarians for US$3–4. Good quality crafts & a selection of contemporary Ethiopian art are also on sale.

NIGHTLIFE

Addis has a lively nightlife. On practically every block of the city centre, you'll find at least one welcoming bar or informal eatery serving inexpensive bottled or draught beer, along with wine and other spirits. There's plenty of live music too, and any of the many cultural restaurants that host traditional music and dancing will make for a safe, entertaining and not-too-late night out for newcomers. Superficially these might come across as quite touristy and cabaret-like, but generally most of the audience comprises middle-class Ethiopians, and the quality of music and dancing is very high. With musical styles that span everything from Afar wailing to meaty contemporary Amharigna pop, and dancing that ranges from the Wolayta hip-shake to the Amhara/Oromo shoulder-shudder, through the more gentle Tigray small steps, and often climaxing in the fantastically energetic Gurage horseriding, this is a great opportunity to get to grips with the extraordinarily diverse thing that is Ethiopian music and dance. In terms of quality of performance, costumes and variety, the pick is probably Yod Abyssinia, but other possibilities include the Dashen Terara, Habesha 2000, Bata, and Totot restaurants (pages 164, 165 and above). If you feel like moving on, check out the box on page 170.

The discotheque and club scene in Addis Ababa is particularly fickle. Three or four steadfast places mentioned in our previous edition have been bumped off the fashionable list as night clubbers rush from one new place to the next without any consideration for their previous favourites.

In early 2018, the hot spots seem to cluster around Edna Mall [166 C6]. The **Surrender** [153 E3] on Ghana Street is crowded at weekends, as is the **A/V Club** in the basement of the Friendship International Hotel [166 B7]. The **Stockholm**

Elegance [166 C6] (on a right turn off Cameron Street just south of Edna Mall and before Kenenisa Hotel) is popular on Sundays, Mondays and Thursdays after the live music concerts. The **Shebeta** [166 A3] (**f**) at the south of Mickey Leland Road features live music on Wednesday's and operates as a discotheque at weekends.

Jolly Bar [158 E2] (**w** *jollyaddis.com*) at Arat Kilo was one of the most sought-after nightclubs in Addis. It closed for renovations for more than a year, but has reopened in 2018 without yet regaining its previous popularity.

As nightlife tends to start after 23.00, a few venues and bars can be recommended for a pleasant warm-up: the **Office Bar** [159 D5] at the Sheraton, especially on Thursdays when the 'beautiful people' show up in numbers. The **Black Rose** [153 F6] (**f**), in the same building as the Cork & Cellar, has a strong following owing to its cosy character and music.

And if you feel like some food late at night/early morning, you can find excellent pizzas and diverse foods at **Mesafint's Cabaret** [152 D5], at the **Dome Night Club** [152 B6] (**f**) in the Hotel Concorde, or at the **Yoly Bar and Restaurant** [166 A3] above the H2O. And a small grocery on the Wollo Sefer Interchange [152 D5] is open day and night all week long, and has sandwiches, drinks and various foods for those late-hour munchies.

CINEMA

For new international films, head to the **Matti Multiplex** [166 C6] (*Edna Mall, Namibia Rd;* ☏ *011 661 6278;* **f** *ednamall*), which has six screenings daily on each of its three screens, and a programme dominated by, but not restricted to, the latest Hollywood blockbusters. Other options include the **Alem Cinema** [166 B7] (*Bole Rd;* ☏ *011 663 6717;* **w** *alemcinema.com*), and the **Empire Cinema** [158 C2] (☏ *011 157 9467*) and **Ethiopia Cinema** [158 C2] (☏ *011 111 6690*) on the Piazza. Also worth checking out is the **Alliance Française** [146 B4] (*Wawel St;* ☏ *011 1569893;* **e** *aef@allianceaddis.org;* **w** *allianceaddis.org*) and **Goethe Institut** [147 F1] (*Algeria St;* ☏ *011 124 2345/6;* **e** *info@addis.goethe.org;* **w** *goethe.de/ addisabeba*), which regularly host plays, art exhibitions, local musical evenings and other cultural activities.

SHOPPING

Shops in Addis are well stocked and they compare favourably to those of most African cities. There are loads of different shops along the lower half of Churchill Avenue, and along Haile Selassie Avenue in the Piazza area. Bole Road is packed with high-rise malls offering a wide range of goods and services.

ART GALLERIES AND INSTALLATIONS

St George's Art Gallery [159 D5] Taitu St; ☏ 011 551 0983; **e** customercare@stgeorgeofethiopia. com; **w** stgeorgeofethiopia.com; ⊕ 09.00–13.00 & 14.30–18.30 Mon–Sat. Situated in an old wooden-floored villa a few doors downhill from the Sheraton, this is probably the best upmarket art & craft gallery in Ethiopia, established in 1991 & still going strong under the same hands-on owner-manager a quarter of a century later. In addition to paintings, it displays & sells everything from hand-crafted furniture & cloths to antique icons & crosses.

LeLa Art Gallery [142 A5] **m** 0911 300756; **e** lelagallery@gmail.com; **w** lela-gallery.com; ⊕ 10.00–18.00 Wed–Sun. Situated in a well-signposted villa near the Chinese Embassy southwest of the city centre, this gallery was founded in 2007 to showcase contemporary Ethiopian art. It holds regular one-off exhibitions featuring established as well as up-&-coming artists.

Addis Ababa has a wonderful, enthusiastic and diverse music scene. The main focus is home-grown Ethiopian music, which, like whisky, might be an acquired taste with its unique rhythms, beat and vibrations aimed to induce trance either by way of distinctive and energetic dance music or through hypnotic wailing melodies with an undeniable Arabic or Oriental clang. Many of the city's talented musicians have also developed an Ethio-jazz style of music thanks to the JazzAmba Music School (w *jazzamba-et.com*), an extension of the famed JazzAmba concert hall which unfortunately burned down along with part of the neighbouring Itegue Taitu Hotel in January 2015.

Marvellous musicians and bands perform in numerous venues on specific evenings. Usually the music starts late, but two of the hotels already listed under *Where to Stay* are notable exceptions for early-to-beds: the **Office Bar** at the Addis Ababa Sheraton [159 D5] hosts live music from 20.30 five nights a week, with the excellent Zagol Band playing a mix of international hits and Ethiopian songs on Thursdays and Saturdays and the Zemen Band on Fridays. Jazz amateurs will enjoy the Tanos Stet Jazzband on Tuesdays. The **Jupiter International Hotel** [159 F6] (w *jupiterinternationalhotel.com/events.html*) also features a good live band every Thursday starting at 19.00.

The steadier venues one should mention are listed below. For a more rootsy Ethiopian ambience in more traditional cabaret-like scenes, try the well-attended **Mesafint's Cabaret** [152 D5] (*off Bole Road*) and **Nigat Traditional Restaurant** [166 A3].

☆ **V Lounge** [158 G7] Same building as Lime Tree Café, Guinea Conakry St; ⧉. Hosts excellent Ethiopian singers & musicians every evening of the week, starting around 21.30, in a 1st-floor pleasant, but sometimes crowded, environment. It is located a few hundred metres south of the Intercontinental Hotel.

☆ **Piano Bar** [166 A7] Same building as Bailamos Bar Lounge, Bole Rd. A personal favourite. A handful of male & female singers chant popular music belonging to the traditional or modern repertoire, or reggae, with a set of musicians who excel in the art of inducing a trance-like mood. Better after 22.00.

☆ **Stokholm Elegance** [166 C6] Near Baritone on a right turn of Cameron St after Edna Mall going towards Bole Airport; ⧉. This venue has a disco nightclub feel but features great live concerts Sun, Mon & Thu, starting around 22.00 but continuing late in the night.

☆ **Dome** [152 B6] Basement of the Concorde Hotel, Bishoftu Rd; ✆ 011 465 4959. Usually crowded with locals, as well as with Chinese & Arabs, the Dome propounds a blend of music, song, quality traditional dances, drinks & azmari performances that generate a blend of happiness, abandon & euphoria experienced nowhere else.

CRAFTS For curio shopping, try the well-stocked stalls and shops that lie near Tewodros Square on Churchill Avenue and on Nigeria Street, just off Churchill Avenue facing the side of the central post office. There are also curio kiosks in most of the smarter tourist-class hotels, and perhaps a dozen dotted around the Piazza. One of the best is **Tsion Crafts** [158 C1] (*Haile Selassie Av;* ⊕ *09.00–18.00 daily*), which stocks a reasonably priced and varied selection of traditional items from all over Ethiopia and several other parts of Africa. An excellent place to buy high-quality hand-woven Ethiopian fabrics, **Shiro Meda Cloth Market** [142 D1], on the Entoto road about 500m north of the US embassy, is the main outlet for the many Dorze weavers who have settled in this part of the city. Prices at stalls and small shops are highly negotiable here, but not at hotel gift shops and more upmarket shops in the city centre.

☆ **Fendika Azmari Bet** [159 G6] Zewditu St; m 0911 547577; w melakubelay.com. Possibly the trendiest nightspot in the country, animated by its owner – world-renowned dancer Melaku Belay – it is also the only one where you are likely to see as many *faranji* as locals. Though it bills itself as an *azmari bet*, the focus is often on contemporary Ethiopian jazz & dancing, as well as DJ evenings when Melaku spins traditional & more poppy 45s evoking Swinging Addis in the 1960s & 70s.

☆ **Classic Mazies Club** [152 D5] To hear the most impressive & moving Tizita, Ambassel, Batti or Anchihoye, the traditional scales, or rather moods, of Ethiopian music, you need to visit this discreet nightspot located a few hundred metres away from Mesafint, on the street leading back to Bole Rd. The programme is interspersed with lighter popular music, but when the singers interpret the traditional repertoire, it is one of the most poignant musical events you'll ever experience.

CULTURAL RESTAURANTS Many tourists also enjoy the music, and the food, at the various cultural restaurants dotted around the city. These include the central **Dashen Terara Restaurant** [147 G6], as well as **Yod Abyssinia** [166 D7], **Habesha 2000** [166 A5], **Bata** [152 D6] and **Totot** [143 G5], all of which present a multi-ethnic floor show of traditional music and dance from all over Ethiopia.

Other restaurants, bars and cafés also offer live music once or twice a week, including:

🍷 **Mama's Kitchen Royal** [166 C6] Tucked away behind Edna Mall; 🅵. Hosts the now famous Monday's Jam Session (*starts 21.30*) attended by a large audience & many talented musicians. On Tue & Thu, the Qariya Groove Band plays a mix of Ethio Jazz & popular music.
🍷 **MK's Bar & Restaurant** [166 B5] Namibia St, opposite Shegger Bldg; m 0912 186001.

Excellent live music on Sun 20.30–22.30 with famed singers Tsedenya, Liya & Armenian born Vahé.
🍷 **Flirt Lounge** [166 B6] Off Cameroon St, near Edna Mall; m 0911 094075. Zagol Band performs on Tue & Hageez Band on Wed, starting at 22.00.

COSTS Most places charge no entrance fee, but will price meals or drinks higher to make up the deficit. Exceptions are **Mama's Kitchen Royal** on Mondays, as well as **Fendika Azmari Bet** with an entry ticket costing US$2.

Warning: Music venues frequently change their programmes. It is therefore recommended to check their Facebook pages, easily found under their names, or to consult the public Facebook group 🅵 *Addis Happening.*

An excellent place to find reasonably priced traditional gifts is the **Entoto Beth Artisan Fair Trade Gallery** (☎ *011 896 5097*; 🅵), a fair-trade organisation that provides employment to HIV/Aids-affected women and families from the Mount Entoto area. It has two gift shops, one on Madagascar Street [142 D2] near Siddist Kilo and a new one on Cape Verde Street next to the Desalegn Hotel [166 A5].

COFFEE Packs of coffee beans can be bought at most tourist craft shops, but there is no guaranteeing their freshness at such sources. Far better to buy the freshly roasted real deal at the likes of the Tomoca Coffee Shop (page 163) on the Piazza or the more central Café Choché (page 162).

MUSIC Inexpensive locally manufactured CDs are sold at several music shops on the Piazza, Haile Gebrselassie Street and Bole Road. In and around the Piazza, you'll find street vendors selling CDs and DVDs of questionable pedigree.

BOOKS For new books, **BookWorld** (**f**) is a chain of nine shops dotted around the city. In addition to a good range of books about various aspects of Ethiopia, it stocks a fair selection of paperbacks and imported magazines. The largest and oldest branch is on Wawel Street below the Piazza [158 B3] (📞 *011 155 9013; ⊕ 09.00–19.00 Mon–Sat*). Other useful branches can be found next to the Red Terror Museum [159 E8] (*Meskel Sq*), in the lobbies of the Addis Ababa Sheraton and Hilton, and at the Friendship Mall near the airport. Another good all-round and well-stocked option is **Booklight** [158 D2] (⊕ *08.00–18.00 Mon–Sat*) on the road between Arat Kilo and the Piazza. For out-of-print non-fiction titles about Ethiopia, try the long-serving **Africans Bookshop** [158 C2] (*Haile Selassie St;* m *0910 444663; ⊕ 09.00–13.00 & 14.30–17.00 Mon–Sat*).

SUPERMARKETS Plenty of supermarkets are dotted around the city, selling a good range of local and imported processed and fresh food. Probably the best overall is the Safeway Supermarket (📞 *011 639 5634;* w *safewaysupermarkets.com*), which has six branches located around the city, the most convenient being on Namibia Road near Atlas Junction [166 A4]. Other good options are the **Friendship Hypermarket** [153 F6] (*Friendship Mall, Bole Rd;* 📞 *011 663 9841*), **Shoa Hypermarket** [152 D5] (*Zefmesh Mall, Megenagna*), **Bambis Supermarket** [159 G8] (*Haile Gebrselassie St;* 📞 *011 552 1105*), **Getfam Supermarket** [166 B1] (*Haile Gebrselassie St*), **Abadir Supermarket** [158 E2] (*King George VI St, near Arat Kilo;* 📞 *011 112 5599*) and the very central **Loyal Supermarket** [159 B5] (*Churchill Av;* 📞 *011 556 5223*). Typical opening hours are 08.00–19.00 Monday–Saturday, but some might open on a Sunday.

OTHER PRACTICALITIES

FOREIGN EXCHANGE AND ATMS Best for changing money are the **Commercial Bank of Ethiopia** (CBE; w *www.combanketh.et*) or **Dashen Bank** (w *dashenbanksc. com*), both of which are represented by several branches dotted around the city including in the Piazza area, or at private foreign exchange bureaux such as those at the Addis Ababa Hilton and Sheraton. You can also draw local currency with either Visa or MasterCard at almost any of the hundreds of ATMs scattered around the city, including ones in the lobby of several tourist-oriented hotels, ranging from the Sheraton to the Itegue Taitu.

EMBASSIES More than 50 embassies, high commissions and other diplomatic missions can be found in Addis Ababa. Those most likely to be of interest to visitors are listed below. For others, or if the contacts below no longer work, visit w embassypages.com/ethiopia for a regularly updated list of embassies.

🄴 Australia [153 E4] Off Cape Verde St; 📞 011 667 2678; m 0967 941377; w ethiopia.embassy. gov.au
🄴 Austria [142 B6] South Africa St; 📞 011 371 0052; w aussenministerium.at/addisabeba
🄴 Belgium [143 E4] Comoros St; m 0911 255583; w ethiopia.diplomatie.belgium.be

🄴 Canada [142 B6] Seychelles St; 📞 011 371 3022; w canadainternational.gc.ca
🄴 Djibouti [153 E5] Off Bole Rd; 📞 011 661 3200; e ibrahim_kamil@hotmail.com
🄴 Egypt [147 F2] 500m northeast of Siddist Kilo; 📞 011 122 6422; **f**

❺ France [147 G1] Angola Rd; ☎011 140 0000; **w** ambafrance.org

❺ Germany [147 H3] Tsehafi Tizaz Afewerk St; ☎011 123 5162; **m** 0911 649107; **w** addis-abeba. diplo.de

❺ Ireland [159 G7] Guinea Conakry St; ☎011 518 0500; **w** dfa.ie/irish-embassy/ethiopia

❺ Israel [143 G4] Asmara Rd; ☎011 646 0999; **w** embassies.gov.il/addis_ababa

❺ Italy [143 F3] Off Eritrea St; ☎011 123 5684; **w** ambaddisabeba.esteri.it

❺ Japan [159 F8] Off Bole Rd; ☎011 667 1166; **w** et.emb-japan.go.jp

❺ Kenya [143 E4] Comoros St; ☎011 661 0135; **w** kenyaembassyaddis.org

❺ Netherlands [142 A5] Ring Rd, Torhayloch; ☎011 317 0360; **w** ethiopia.nlembassy.org

❺ Russia [147 H4] Comoros St; ☎011 661 2060/1828; **w** ethiopia.mid.ru

❺ Serbia [159 G7] Tito St; ☎011 551 7804; **w** addisababa.mfa.gov.rs/cir

❺ Somaliland [166 C7] Off Cameroon St; ☎011 663 5921

❺ South Africa [142 B6] South Africa St; ☎011 371 1002; **w** southafricanembassyethiopia.com

❺ South Sudan [166 A5] Off Namibia St; ☎011 662 0195; **f**

❺ Sweden [159 B6] Yared St; ☎011 518 0000; **w** swedenabroad.se/en/embassies/ethiopia-addis-abeba

❺ Switzerland [142 A6] Ring Rd; ☎011 371 1107; **w** dfae.admin.ch/countries/ethiopia/en/ home/representations/embassy.html

❺ UK [143 F4] Comoros St; ☎011 617 0100; **w** gov.uk/government/world/organisations/ british-embassy-addis-ababa

❺ USA [142 D2] Algeria St (Entoto St); ☎011 130 6000; **w** et.usembassy.gov

MEDICAL FACILITIES The local name for a GP or doctor's surgery is a 'higher clinic'. Most doctors speak passable English and many have in-house laboratories for straightforward blood, stool or urine tests. For other tests or procedures that cannot be performed by an ordinary GP, try the **Suisse Clinic** [152 A6] (*Kera;* ☎*011 416 1649;* **m** *0921 787120;* **w** *suisseclinic.com*) or **Panorama Clinic** [159 B7] (*Gambia St (Churchill Av);* ☎*011 465 1666; or 24hr call-out* **m** *0911 223700*). Possibly the best medical facility in Ethiopia, the Norwegian-run **Nordic Medical Centre** [153 E7] (*Bole Rwanda;* **m** *0929 105653;* **w** *nordicmedicalcentre.com*), staffed by international and Ethiopian doctors and nurses, is open 24/7, operates an ambulance service with trained staff, and can arrange medevac services from many parts of Ethiopia using an air ambulance. Also recommended are the 24-hour **Bethzatha Hospital** [159 C7] (*off Ras Makonnen St;* ☎*011 551 4141;* **w** *bethzatha.com*), or **St Gebriel Hospital** [166 C2] (*off Djibouti St;* ☎*011 661 4400;* **m** *0911 124501/8819;* **w** *stgabrielgeneralhospital. com*). One of the best dentists in town is the **Gojeb Dental Clinic** [158 C3] (*Dej Jote St;* ☎*011 156 6521;* **f**) on the Piazza.

Pharmacists in Addis are generally well stocked and helpful. The **Lion Pharmacy** [158 B3] (*Mahatma Gandhi Rd;* ☎ *011 155 1893*) and 24-hour **Gishen Pharmacy** [159 D7] (*Ras Desta Damtew St;* ☎*011 515 9885*) are recommended.

The US embassy maintains a long, detailed list of recommended general and specialist practitioners and medical facilities at **w** et.usembassy.gov/u-s-citizen-services/doctors.

MEDIA AND COMMUNICATIONS

Internet and email Though not so numerous as they once were, inexpensive internet cafés are still dotted around Addis Ababa. Practically all hotels and many restaurants now offer free Wi-Fi to residents (or indeed anyone who drops by for a coffee or beer), and many also have computers set aside for guests.

Post The central post office is on Churchill Avenue [159 B5], while the original Arada post office is on the Piazza one-way loop. There are several branch post offices dotted around the city, and the queues are rarely daunting. Sending freight out of Addis Ababa is very cheap, but best arranged with your airline.

SWIMMING POOLS Addis Ababa is not often so torrid that a swimming pool is likely to be a high priority. But, should the urge strike, the pool at the Ghion Hotel (with a 10m diving platform; page 157) is a reliable bet, and only costs US$2.50. The pools at the Hilton and Sheraton hotels, fed by natural hot thermal waters, are fabulous, and popular with wealthy Ethiopians and expatriates, but entrance costs around US$10.

TOURIST INFORMATION The **Ethiopian Tourism Organisation** [159 E7] (ETO; \011 551 7470; w ethiopia.travel) has a tourist information office on Meskel Square. It sometimes stocks a few free pamphlets, but isn't much use when it comes to hard travel information. A more useful source of current information about Addis Ababa is the website w addisallaround.com.

TOUR OPERATORS Most of the Addis Ababa-based operators listed on page 89 can arrange city day tours or short excursions further afield. However, the acknowledged leader in this field is **Go Addis Tours** (*formerly Addis Eats;* e *info@ goaddistours.com;* w *goaddistours.com; see ad, page 134*), which specialises in foodie tours that are aimed at short-stay visitors wanting to sample a few representative local eateries in safe company, and take in at least five culinary venues, each with its own speciality. It also runs a range of half- and full-day excursions incorporating markets, restaurants, monuments and other attractions in Addis Ababa

Guide **Genet Mengistu** (e *bamytsega@gmail.com, genetmengistu@yahoo.com*) comes highly recommended from several quarters and can also guide excursions to most sites of interest within day-tripping distance of the city.

For something different, a new company called **Abyssinia Ballooning** (m *0926 845086;* e *info@abyssiniaballooning.com;* w *abyssiniaballooning.com*) runs early-morning hot-air balloon trips immediately outside Addis Ababa, as well as in the Lake Langano area. Flights cost around US$200 per person and scheduled departures are listed on its website.

For the more energetic, **Ethio Cycling Adventures** (m *0929 343987;* e *ethiocyclingadventures@gmail.com;* w *ethiocyclingadventures.com*) runs urban and rural bike rides in and around Addis Ababa. Group sizes are limited to a maximum of ten participants, with experienced guides/leaders at the front and back of each group. Tours include city landmarks, suburban rides, mountain-bike trails, and day and overnight regional rides.

VISA EXTENSION This can be obtained at the **Department of Immigration** [159 E2] (*off Arat Kilo;* ⊕ *08.30–12.30 & 14.00–17.00 Mon–Fri*) This is normally a straightforward procedure, but tedious, and also very expensive following a recent hike in fees to US$100 for the first 30-day extension, then US$150 for any further extension. The procedure normally takes 48 hours, but you can usually pay an additional fee of US$150 for a same-day service, provided you make the application in the morning. Bring your passport, photocopies of the main page of your passport and the one with your existing visa, a passport-sized photograph (there's a photo kiosk outside), the full fee in US dollars (Ethiopian birr are not accepted), and your own pen – as well as a book or some other diversion while you wait!

WHAT TO SEE AND DO

Addis Ababa is also easy to explore independently, using taxis, public transport or your own two feet. An excellent companion to any independent exploration is *Old Tracks in the New Flower: A Historical Guide to Addis Ababa* (Milena Batistoni and

Gian Paolo Chiari, Arada Books, 2004; w *aradabooks.com*), which describes more than 130 historic buildings along a series of different day walks.

CITY CENTRE Central Addis Ababa started to take shape in 1917, following the arrival of the railway at the south end of what is now Churchill Avenue, and its present-day street plan was finalised during the Italian occupation. It is arguably of interest more for its cafés and shops than for any riveting sightseeing, but you could easily spend a day exploring its various museums and other historic landmarks. The institutions described below can all be incorporated into the walking tour described in the box on page 176.

National Postal Museum [159 B5] (*Churchill Av, next to the central post office;* ⊕ *08.00–noon & 13.00–17.00 Mon–Fri; entrance US$0.75*) Established in 1975, this impressive philatelic museum includes a filing cabinet where you can see a copy of every stamp issued in Ethiopia since Emperor Menelik II founded the postal service in 1894. Some of the older issues are blown-up poster-size on the walls, among them series depicting insects, traditional musical instruments and key historical figures. Look out too for a fabulously macabre anti-smoking stamp. For collectors, the museum also sells first-day covers dating back 60 years. Photography is forbidden.

National Archives and Library Agency [159 B5] (*Off Zambia St;* \ *011 551 6247;* w *www.nala.gov.et;* ⊕ *08.30–17.30 Mon–Fri*) The National Archives is home to Ethiopia's largest collection of ancient church manuscripts (355 at the last count), most of which were recovered from old churches and monasteries. The oldest manuscript here is a 15th-century document retrieved from the monastery of Hayk Istafanos. This institution claims to possess a copy of every book ever written about Ethiopia, and it has a good database and helpful staff, but a letter of introduction from a university or government department is required to access it. Assuming you have that in writing, there is no charge to access manuscripts, unless you need photocopies.

Red Terror Martyrs' Memorial Museum [159 E8] (*Cnr Meskel Sq & Bole Rd;* \ *011 515 6197/6206;* w *rtmmm.org;* ⊕ *08.30–18.00 daily; entrance free but donations expected*) Dedicated to the victims of the Red Terror campaign perpetrated by President Mengistu and his Derg regime, this superb installation displays a riveting selection of black-and-white photos dating to the 1975 coup, as well as some more chilling relics (skulls and clothes removed from mass graves) and torture instruments of a genocidal era in modern Ethiopian history.

Addis Ababa Museum [159 E8] (*Off Bole Rd;* \ *011 551 3180;* ⊕ *08.30–17.30 daily; entrance US$2*) This low-key museum 5 minutes' walk south of Meskel Square occupies one of the city's oldest and most distinctive buildings, a turreted two-storey palace built in 1887 for Ras Biru Wolde Gebriel, one of Menelik II's must trusted warlords and advisers. It served as royal residence until the Italian occupation, when it was converted into a clinic, and it was later used as a school, wool factory and hotel prior to being renovated as a museum in 1986, the official centenary of Addis Ababa's foundation. It's a lovely old building with tall ceilings and ceramic tile and dark-wood floors, but it also displays a marvellous and informatively labelled collection of photographs of Addis Ababa from the 1890s through to the 1960s, as well as a collection of old ceremonial and official clothes, and a mini-gallery of 20th century artworks.

A suggested foot itinerary through central Addis Ababa, taking in most of its key landmarks, would start at Tewodros Square, continuing south along Churchill Avenue then Gambia Street, to the junction with Ras Makonnen Street, and following this eastward past the stadium to Meskel Square. From Meskel Square, you could continue northward up shady Menelik II Avenue, then head west along Taitu Street, passing the Sheraton Hotel and possibly the Filwoha Hot Springs en route back to your starting point at Churchill Avenue. Because it is a loop, the tour could be picked up at any point along this circuit. Pickpockets are rife in some areas, so carry no more money than you need for the day, and leave other valuables and important documents behind in your hotel.

Named by Haile Selassie in 1968 to mark the centenary of Emperor Tewodros's suicide, Tewodros Square [158 B4] is a roundabout adorned by a larger-than-life bronze replica of the cannon Sebastopol. On the northeast side of the circle, the rectangular two-storey stone **Wefa Theatre** [158 B4] (formerly Mega Theatre) dates to the 1920s and was originally named the Club de l'Union. A combined cinema, bar, dance hall and casino, the French-owned club acquired a rather seedy reputation that earned it the sobriquet of Satan Bet (Devil's House), a name still in casual use today. Heading downhill along Churchill Avenue, you soon pass the **National Postal Museum** [159 B5] (page 175) to your left. Facing it, the **Tiglachen Memorial** [159 B5], dedicated in 1984, is a tall column topped by a red star commemorating the Ethiopian and Cuban soldiers who died in the Ethiopia–Somalia War of 1978. The **National Archives and Library Agency** [159 B5] (page 175) stands a block to the west and can be reached along Yared or Zambia Street.

Back on Churchill and south of the traffic lights, the **National Theatre** [159 B6] is a well-known landmark of little architectural merit. In a small park next to the theatre is the stylised and rather angular 10m tall **Lion of Judah Statue** [159 B6] commissioned from the French sculptor Maurice Calka in 1955 to commemorate the 25th jubilee of Haile Selassie's coronation. There are several nearby cafés where you can stop for a coffee or snack. A short walk south of this, just past the junction with Ras Makonnen Street, the older **Legahar Lion of Judah Statue** [159 C8] is a more realistic granite statue unveiled by Empress Zewditu and the soon-to-be Emperor Haile Selassie in 1930, months before the former's premature death. Behind this statue, the neocolonial **La Gare Legahar** (railway station) [159 C8] was designed by the Parisian architect Paul Barria, built over 1928–29, and inaugurated by Empress Zewditu in early 1930.

Heading eastward along Ras Makonnen Street, in the shadow of the overhead metropolitan railway, you pass to your left the large **Addis Ababa Stadium** [159 C7], which was built in 1940 and has housed most of the Ethiopian football

Africa Hall [159 F7] (*Menelik II Av;* \011 551 7700; ⊕ *08.00–13.00 & 14.00–17.00 Mon–Fri*) Designed by the Italian architect Arturo Mezzedimi, and built over 18 months prior to its inauguration by Haile Selassie in February 1961, this immense modernist conference centre was, according the emperor, intended to demonstrate 'that it is possible to construct grand buildings here [making] maximum possible use of home-produced materials, in order to stimulate our wealthy middle class … to invest its assets in building to make this "great village" a city and a true great capital'. The hall's best-known feature is the stained-glass *Total Liberation of Africa*, a huge mural created by award-winning Ethiopian artist Afewerk Tekle. Africa team's home internationals ever since (including its fondly remembered 1962 championship victory in the Africa Nations Cup), though it is soon to be usurped by the less central Abay Ababa Stadium on Djibouti Street. A few hundred metres further, you arrive at **Meskel Square** [159 E8], an important landmark and notable among other things for one of the scariest pedestrian road crossings you're ever likely to navigate. The **tourist office** [159 E7] is situated on the northern side of Meskel Square, below the podium used by Mengistu to address the masses in the days when it was known as Revolution Square. The harrowing but worthwhile **Red Terror Martyrs' Memorial Museum** [159 E8] (page 175) stands on the southeast side of Meskel Square, while the **Addis Ababa Museum** [159 E8] (page 175) is a short walk south.

Rising uphill to the northeast of Meskel Square, the shady Menelik II Avenue, bisected by a green traffic island, is lined by a number of historic buildings. On the east of the avenue, the modern **Church of Kidus Istafanos** [159 E7] stands in an attractive green garden overlooking Meskel Square. Built during the Haile Selassie era, this church is notable for the mosaic above the main entrance, depicting the martyrdom of its namesake, St Stephen. On festival days and Sundays, white-robed worshippers congregate in the large grounds, a scene characteristic of rural Ethiopia but transplanted to the big city. Uphill from the church stands the imposing **Africa Hall** [159 F7] (page 176). Further uphill, to the left, a pair of steel gates guard the verdant grounds of the **National Palace** [159 E6], built in 1955 to mark the occasion of Haile Selassie's 25-year jubilee. Since the fall of the Derg, the palace has served as the official residence of the President of Ethiopia and is used mainly in a ceremonial role for official functions. It is closed to the public, and pulling out a camera in the vicinity is emphatically forbidden.

At the junction immediately north of the palace, you have three onward options. The first is to follow the dual Yohannes Street back towards the city centre, passing en route the **Filwoha Hot Springs** [159 D6], which encouraged Menelik to move his capital down from the Entoto Hills. The second option is to continue north up Menelik II Avenue, passing the **Hilton Hotel** [159 F6] to your right and a row of other government buildings to your left. After 200m or so, turn left at the T-junction on to the wide curving Niger Street. Then after another 100m or so turn left into Taitu Street, passing the **Sheraton Hotel** and **St George's Art Gallery** [159 D5] (page 169) en route back to the city centre. The third option, assuming that you want to move on to the museums near the university, or to the Piazza area, is to pick up one of the regular minibuses to Arat Kilo or Siddist Kilo at the T-junction. On your right, on Niger Street the well-guarded **Gibe Palace** [158 E4], built by Emperor Menelik II, is still the seat of the Ethiopian government.

Hall served as the headquarters of the OAU from 1963 onwards, and it is now the permanent headquarters of UNECA. Phone in advance to arrange a visit, and remember that a passport is required to enter.

THE PIAZZA [159 B2] A popular haunt of budget travellers, the area known as the Piazza, or more popularly Arada, lies immediately north of the city centre and west of Arat Kilo. Prior to the 1938 Italian construction of a 'Grand Merkato Indigino' (the present-day Merkato) and simultaneous expansion of the modern city centre, this area was the economic pulse of Addis Ababa and site of the city's most important bank, market, hotel and shops. Arada Market, described by one European visitor as 'picturesque chaos', was held around a sprawling sycamore fig on what is today De Gaulle Square, peaking in activity on Saturdays, which is also when public executions were held right through until the early years of Haile Selassie's rule. In the 1990s, the Piazza ranked as Addis Ababa's glitziest shopping area, and its main thoroughfare was lined with modern boutiques and pastry shops, as well as the British Council. Today, by contrast, it feels rather down-at-heel and provincial in comparison with the neon-and-concrete malls and skyscrapers that characterise the southern suburbs around Bole – though this is not so much a measure of the Piazza's decline but rather of the explosion of post-millennial development elsewhere in the city.

Architecturally, the Piazza is dominated by buildings dating to the Italian occupation and later, but these are interspersed with a scattering of Armenian-influenced relics of the Menelik era. Most of the older buildings are in poor repair, but others have been partially renovated as restaurants or hotels (prime examples being the Hermon Hotel and Good Times Restaurant near De Gaulle Square). One of the few pre-occupation buildings that remains in near-pristine condition – despite some outbuildings having been destroyed by fire in 2015 – is the **Itegue Taitu Hotel** [158 C3], which is practically unchanged in appearance since it was built in 1907, and still worth a look inside for the spacious architecture, period furnishings and excellent national restaurant. Other interesting buildings in the area include the stone **Bank of Abyssinia** [158 C3], which dates to 1905 and lies on the south side of General Wingate Street behind the Taitu. Around the corner, a fabulously sprawling **five-storey house** [158 C2] designed by Minas Kherbekian (the Armenian architect who also designed the Taitu) stood as the tallest in the city prior to the Italian occupation.

Slightly further afield, **Addis Ababa Restaurant** [146 D2] (page 162) is housed in a lovely old building constructed for the future Empress Zewditu in the late 1890s. To get there from the south end of the Piazza, head northwest to Menelik II Square then about 400m north on Benin Street. From the north end of the Piazza it is most easily reached by walking up Sylvia Pankhurst Road then turning right into Benin Street.

ST GEORGE'S CATHEDRAL [158 B1] (⊕ *09.00–noon & 14.00–17.00 daily; combined entrance to cathedral & museum, with guide US$4 inc still photography, video extra*) Commissioned by Emperor Menelik II in 1896 to commemorate his victory over Italy at Adwa, St George's Cathedral was designed by Sebastiano Castagna, built by Italian prisoners of war, and completed in 1911. The coronation site of Empress Zewditu and Emperor Haile Selassie, it was partially destroyed by the Italians, who set fire to it in 1937, but it was restored after the end of World War II, when the renowned artist Afewerk Tekle was commissioned to contribute fresh paintings and tile murals. An interesting museum concerned mainly with the 1930 coronation of Haile Selassie stands in the church grounds, as does the engraved tomb of the popular singer Mary Armide. Despite its central location, St George's Cathedral has a very peaceful atmosphere, tucked away as it is in a grove of trees immediately north of the short road connecting Menelik II and Abuna Petros squares. The former is graced by an impressive equestrian statue of Menelik II, which was sculpted by the German artist Cael Haertel for the Empress Zewditu in 1928, removed and stored in a secret location at the order of Mussolini in 1936, then reinstated in 1941. On the latter, a small plaque commemorates the spot where Abuna Petros, the Patriarch of the Ethiopian Church, was executed by an Italian firing squad in 1936. A statue of Abuna Petros also stands in the church grounds.

ADDIS MERKATO AND SHOLA MARKET [146 A4] Routinely cited as the largest market in Africa, Addis Merkato (literally 'New Market') came into being in the late 1930s, when the Italian administration decided to develop the established market at Arada (the present-day Piazza) as a European-only shopping district and to relocate the 'Merkato Indigino' some 2km further southeast. Today, Addis Merkato, also known as Addis Ketema and most often referred to as plain Merkato, extends over more than 1km² and comprises several thousand small businesses. But from the famed 'open-air' market it used to be, the Merkato has steadily morphed into a soulless jumble of warehouses, wholesalers and obstructed streets which totally lacks charm and can be tedious to explore on foot.

Nevertheless, the true spirit of picturesque marketplaces can still be found in the many tiny markets where woman sell vegetables along footways all around town. Most diverse and enjoyable of all is Shola Market [map, below], located in the vicinity of Megenagna below Yeka Michael Church [143 F4]. With no hassle from the local people, pedestrians can stroll at ease to explore a maze of stalls selling fruits, vegetables, pulses and typical Red Sea salt, or search at length for baskets, pottery, coffee pots or traditional dresses or jewellery to take home as presents. It is a refreshing dive into what constitutes the fundamentals of everyday life in Ethiopia.

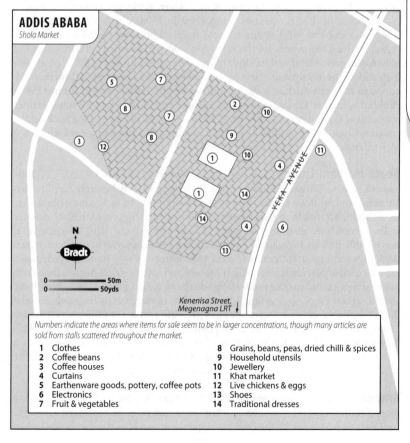

ADDIS ABABA
Shola Market

Kenenisa Street,
Megenagna LRT

Numbers indicate the areas where items for sale seem to be in larger concentrations, though many articles are sold from stalls scattered throughout the market.

1	Clothes	8	Grains, beans, peas, dried chilli & spices
2	Coffee beans	9	Household utensils
3	Coffee houses	10	Jewellery
4	Curtains	11	Khat market
5	Earthenware goods, pottery, coffee pots	12	Live chickens & eggs
6	Electronics	13	Shoes
7	Fruit & vegetables	14	Traditional dresses

ARAT AND SIDDIST KILO Several of Addis Ababa's most interesting historical sites, churches and museums can be found in the vicinity of the roundabouts known colloquially as Arat and Siddist Kilo, which, as their Amharigna names suggest, stand about 4km and 6km northeast of the city centre. Easily reached by minibus from the city centre or the Piazza area, the two roundabouts stand at the southern and northern end of King George VI Street, an area that also forms a major centre of student activity thanks to the presence of several departments of the University of Addis Ababa. Sites of interest are listed from south to north and follow on from the city centre walking tour described in the box on page 176.

Trinity (Selassie) Cathedral [158 F3] (✆*011 123 0093;* ◷ *08.00–13.00 & 14.00–18.00 daily; entrance US$8 inc still photography, US$2 video*) This very large church, whose cornerstone was laid in 1931 by Emperor Haile Selassie, has a rather Arabic façade, while the interior is lavishly decorated by ecclesiastical paintings in both the modern and medieval Ethiopian styles. The cathedral is also the final resting place of Haile Selassie and his wife Menen, whose identical granite crypts have been housed inside it since 5 November 2000, a full 25 years after the emperor's death, following a colourful reburial procession attended by a substantial international Rastafarian contingent including Bob Marley's wife, Rita. In the same compound stands the circular church of Mekane Selassie, which was built by Menelik II in 1890 and has some excellent examples of modern Ethiopian church art, as well as a museum of church treasures inaugurated in 2006. Wander around the leafy compound and you will also come across stone monuments dedicated to the first victims of the Derg regime, to the Ethiopian soldiers who died while resisting the Italian occupation, and to the British officers who died during the Allied campaign that ended the occupation. Several members of the Ethiopian aristocracy are buried in the graveyard, as is famous suffragette and Ethiopian sympathiser Sylvia Pankhurst, former Ethiopian president Meles Zenawi, and Abune Paulos, former patriarch of the Ethiopian Orthodox Church. Look out for squawking flocks of the endemic black-winged lovebird. No photography is permitted in the museum or at Meles Zenawi's grave.

Beata Maryam Church [158 F4] (*Itegue Menen St;* m *0911 482357;* ◷ *07.00–noon & 13.30–17.00 daily; entrance US$2.50*) Built in 1911 by Empress Zewditu, this attractive square stone church, also sometimes referred to as Kidane Mihret after its second *tabot*, has four Axumite-style colonnaded arches on each of its exterior walls, carved lions guarding the entrance, and a roof comprising a large central dome flanked by smaller domes on each corner. Inside, a series of excellent murals depict several important events in Ethiopian history. A low staircase leads down into the eerie subterranean Menelik II Mausoleum, where Addis Ababa's founder is interred in a carved marble tomb alongside the remains of his wife Empress Taitu, their daughter Empress Zewditu, Princess Tsehay (a daughter of Haile Selassie who died at the age of 22) and Abuna Matthias (the Patriarch of the Ethiopian Orthodox Church who presided over the coronation of Menelik II). The remains of Haile Selassie were held here too prior to his formal burial in Selassie Cathedral, and it also houses several centuries-old paintings relocated from the Monastery of Debre Libanos after it was destroyed by the Italians during the occupation.

Arat Kilo [158 E2] The large roundabout colloquially referred to as Arat Kilo is a pivotal minibus hub surrounded by many shops and cafés. The formal name of the roundabout is Megabit 28, the Ethiopian equivalent to 5 May, the date in 1941 when

Haile Selassie returned from exile to a nation liberated from the Italian occupation. A 15m-tall black stone hexagonal pillar, carved in a manner resembling the stelae of Axum, was constructed in the centre of the roundabout in 1942 to commemorate the first anniversary of the emperor's return, and it is still where the main Patriots' Day celebration is held on the morning of 5 May annually.

Zoological Natural History Museum
[158 F2] (*Queen Elizabeth II St;* ☎ *011 123 6770;* ⊕ *09.00–11.45 & 13.30–16.30 Tue–Sun; entrance US$1, camera US$1, video US$2*) This rather uninspired museum 100m east of Arat Kilo contains a collection of stuffed animals that might be of passing interest to first-time visitors to Africa.

Old Armenian quarter
[158 D1] The back roads running west from Arat Kilo and Siddist Kilo host an old residential quarter strongly associated with the Armenian Orthodox community that took refuge in the nascent city at the invitation of Menelik II in response to its persecution by Turkish Muslims in the late 19th century. These Armenian settlers – whose descendants retain a strong presence in the area today – proved to be an important influence on the development of Addis Ababa's music scene, as well as on its pre-Italian occupation architecture. A great many characterful old Armenian buildings are dotted around this quiet suburb, many close to the junction of Tewodros and Welete Yohannes streets. Possibly the oldest extant house in Addis Ababa, dating to around 1886, is the thatched one-storey residence built by **Krikorios Bogossian** on Welete Yohannes Street. It is still owned by the Bogossion family, and interested visitors may be invited to take a look around the period-furnished interior. The Armenian Club, home to the traditional Ararat Restaurant, lies on the same road.

National Museum of Ethiopia
[158 E1] (*King George VI St;* ☎ *011 111 7150;* ⊕ *08.30–17.30 daily; entrance US$0.40*) Ten minutes' walk uphill from Arat Kilo in the direction of Siddist Kilo, the national museum is housed in large green grounds on the left-hand side of the road. Archaeological exhibits include a realistic replica of the 3.5-million-year-old *Australopithecus afarensis* skull known as Lucy (or Dinquinesh – 'thou art wonderful' – to Ethiopians), whose discovery in 1974 forced a complete rethink of human genealogy, proving that our ancestors were walking 2.5 million years earlier than had been previously supposed. It also contains some wonderful artefacts dating to the south Arabian period of the so-called pre-Axumite civilisation of Tigray. These include a number of large stone statues of seated female figures, thought to have been fertility symbols of a pre-Judaic religion. It is interesting that the figures have plaited hair identical to the style worn by modern Ethiopians (it has been suggested that the mythological Medusa of ancient Greece was simply a dreadlocked Ethiopian woman). One almost perfectly preserved statue, thought to be about 2,600 years old and unearthed at a site near Yeha, is seated in a 2m-high stone cask adorned with engravings of ibex. Many of the other statues are headless – probably decapitated by early Christians, who converted many pagan temples to churches. Other items include a sphinx from Yeha, once again emphasising Axumite links with the Classical world, a huge range of artefacts from Axum itself, and a cast of one of the Gragn stones from Tiya. In the gardens stand several monuments, including a replica Olmec head from Mexico Square relocated here in 2013 to make way for the construction of the new railway.

Siddist Kilo
[147 E2] This large roundabout at the north end of King George VI Road is formally known as Yekatit 12 (February 19) Square. It is dominated by the

Yekatit 12 Monument, a towering column topped by a statue of a lion and dedicated to the Ethiopians who died in the retaliatory massacre that followed the attempted assassination of the Italian Viceroy Graziani on 19 February 1937. On the southeast side of Siddist Kilo, the Yekatit 12 Lion Zoo still evidently provides cramped sanctuary to a few bored Abyssinian lions, specimens of the smaller dark-maned race associated with the Ethiopian Highlands, and descendants of the imperial pride that once accompanied Haile Selassie. It is currently closed to visitors while renovations are under way.

IES Ethnographic Museum and Library [147 E1] (*off Algeria St;* ☏*011 123 1068;* ⊕ *08.30–17.00 daily; entrance US$4*) Housing what is widely regarded to be the best museum in Addis Ababa, the Institute of Ethiopian Studies (IES) lies in the main campus of the University of Addis Ababa about 500m north of Siddist Kilo. A former palace of Haile Selassie, the two-storey museum building uses the ground floor to display a varied array of artefacts and daily objects relating to most ethnic groups in Ethiopia, not only the monotheistic highlanders but also, rather refreshingly, the fascinating animist cultural groups of South Omo and the Afar people of the eastern deserts. On the second floor is a superb new exhibition on Ethiopian musical instruments, as well as an impressive collection of visual art – Ethiopian crosses and minutely painted icons – dating back to the Middle Ages. Meanwhile, the IES Library hoards one of the world's most comprehensive collections of books and photocopied articles about Ethiopia – an invaluable resource for researchers. An attached gift shop sells a remarkable range of carefully selected tourist and gift items at reasonable prices, and is a way of supporting the museum.

Gebre Kristos Desta Art Museum [147 F1] (*off Algeria St;* ☏*011 124 2345/6;* w *gebrekristosdestacenter.org;* ⊕ *09.00–17.00 Tue–Sun*) Opened by the Goethe Institut in 2008, this small but excellent gallery showcases several of the most famous works of the Ethiopian artist Gebre Kristos Desta (1932–81), who studied in Germany in the late 1950s and was strongly influenced by Picasso, including his landmark *Golgotha*, a 1963 abstract depicting the crucifixion.

ENTOTO Perched at an altitude of 2,900m only 2km north of suburban Addis Ababa, the church of Entoto Maryam graces the site where Menelik established his original capital after relocating from Ankober to the Entoto Hills in the early 1880s. The most established attraction in the vicinity is the church itself – also the site of a museum and restored palace – but it is also possible to walk or hike from here to a number of other lesser points of interest, notably the abandoned rock-hewn church of Kidus Raguel, the remains of an immense medieval castle, and a hyena den where these sociable scavengers are regularly seen in daylight. Another important point of interest in the eastern Entoto foothills near Yeka is the moderately impressive medieval rock-hewn church of Washa Mikael.

Entoto Maryam and Menelik's Palace [map, page 188] (☏ *011 138 0037/8;* ⊕ *09.00–13.00 & 14.30–17.30 daily, entrance to the church museum & palace US$8*) The octagonal Entoto Maryam stands on the site of the original church where Menelik was crowned emperor of Ethiopia in 1889. Unfortunately, its traditionally painted interior can be seen only during and immediately after services (held every morning until around 09.00), but an attached church museum houses an interesting collection of religious items and ceremonial clothing dating from Menelik's time, as well as a superb 18th-century painting of Jesus being breastfed by Mary. The

museum entrance fee also allows you to poke around Menelik's old palace, a handsome two-storey mud-and-wood construction that was restored in 2010.

To get to Entoto Maryam, follow Algeria Street north of Siddist Kilo for about 7km, passing the US embassy to your right, until you reach the church compound, which is signposted clearly to the right after the last hairpin bend. Using public transport, you can get to within 2km of the church by catching a minibus from Arat Kilo or Siddist Kilo to the Entoto station. Transport is very sporadic past this, though there are occasional buses that continue past Entoto Maryam to Sultata. Alternatively, you could walk the last 2km, a tough uphill slog that can take up to 1 hour. An alternative route back to the city entails following a newly surfaced 5km road past Kidus Raguel, then through some pretty plantation forest, until you reach the intersection with the busy main road from Addis Ababa to Sultata (and on to Bahir Dar and Gondar). If you walk this road, it should be easy to pick up transport back to the city from the junction.

Kidus Raguel and the Pentagonal Fort Not quite 2km west of Entoto Maryam, the less well-known Kidus Raguel (*entrance US$4*) was founded by Menelik II in the 1880s, making it probably the oldest extant church in the immediate vicinity of Addis Ababa. A handsome whitewashed octagonal building with a domed roof and wrap-around wooden balcony adorning the first floor, it has an atmospheric interior decorated with elaborate and well-preserved paintings dating to the late 19th century. Within the same compound, the original Kidus Raguel, thought to date to the 12th or 13th century, is a disused and partially destroyed rock-hewn church with scaffolding outside and a very plain interior. Far more interesting, only 200m from Kidus Raguel, is the substantial remains of a 1ha pentagonal fort (*no entrance fee*) whose 520m stone perimeter wall still stands up to 5m high in parts, and was once topped by a dozen towers. Thought to date to around 1515, this pentagonal fort might possibly have formed part of the mysterious medieval city of Barara, but even if not, it ranks as the most impressive of several recently rediscovered ruins that collectively demonstrate Entoto was an important centre of imperial power in medieval times, and were also presumably what decided Menelik II to establish his capital in the area.

To get to Kidus Raguel, continue north from the Entoto Maryam car park for 500m until you come to a four-way junction, then turn left. The church stands prominently on the left side of the road, and the ruined pentagonal fort is clearly discernible to the left in a thick stand of plantation forest only 200m before it. About halfway between Entoto Maryam and Kidus Raguel, a satellite tower marks a spectacular viewpoint over the city of Addis Ababa. From Kidus Raguel, it is only 3km west to the intersection with the busy Addis Ababa–Sultata road.

Hyena den viewpoint The sheer rugged northern escarpment of Entoto is reputedly home to large numbers of hyena dens who take refuge in its crags and caves by day and head out further afield after dark to scavenge in the city's waste. A good vantage point for seeing some of these heavy-jawed carnivores is the rim of a precipitous eucalyptus-clad clifftop that stands 7.5km northeast of Entoto Maryam, and from where you might see up to a dozen individuals lazing or playing on the slope and plains below. To get there, follow the surfaced road north from Entoto Maryam car park for 500m to a four-way junction where you need to turn right on to a dirt road and continue eastward for another 5.5km, then turn left on to a smaller motorable track that leads to within 100m of the viewing point after 1.5km. Even if you miss out on the hyenas, the view across the Sultata Plains is spectacular.

4

WASHA MIKAEL CHURCH [143 G3] The closest rock-hewn church to Addis Ababa, Washa Mikael (*entrance US$4, photography US$6*) is quite easily visited from the city centre, but draws mixed reactions from the few who make it, since it has long been abandoned and also lost its roof at some point in its rather mysterious history. The rock-hewn edifice now lies in the grounds of the newer church of Tekle Haymanot, whose priests claim that it was excavated in the 4th century by the twin kings Abraha and Atsbeha, and the roof was destroyed by an Italian bomb during the occupation, when it was used as a rebel hideout. Academic opinion, by contrast, is that it was excavated in the 12th or 13th century (certainly it is closer in style to the 12th-century churches at Lalibela than to older churches in Tigray), and that the roof collapsed of its own accord some time before 1897, when the church was desanctified by Emperor Menelik II and its *tabot* sent to the newer Yeka Mikael Church. Whatever the truth, the rather overgrown church is an impressive excavation, a subterranean near-monolith freed from the surrounding rock on three sides and reached via a short tunnel through the rock. Paradoxically, the roofless condition allows you to get a far better idea of the interior's layout than is normally possible. The pillars and walls are still standing, and you can scramble over the rocks into what used to be the Holy of Holies where the *tabot* was stored. There are several windows and candle niches in the walls, and a holy pool is fed by underground springs.

There are several ways to get to the church. In a private vehicle, the most direct route runs north from Comoros Street, which runs between Arat Kilo and Megenagna via the British Embassy and Yeka Park. The road you need is the newly surfaced Adwa Menged Road (so named because it was the route used by Menelik II's army in 1896 on the way to the Battle of Adwa), the junction for which lies about 100m east of the UK embassy. After 2.5km on Adwa Menged Road, much of it passing through eucalyptus plantation forest, turn left almost immediately after you cross a small bridge. From here the road winds uphill for almost 3km to a signposted junction to the left that leads to Washa Mikael after 200m.

Using public transport, catch a minibus from the city centre to Deshenet station [143 H3], which lies just off the Debre Berhan road about 4km past Megenagna. From Deshenet, you can either walk or catch a minibus to Adisu Gebriel station, about 1.5km to the northwest. From Adisu Gebriel, you can either pick up a taxi or walk the last (in parts rather steep) 2km to Washa Mikael, forking left at all unsignposted forks or junctions until you reach the signpost to the church itself, where you need to turn right. If you are thinking of walking, be warned that the footpath to Washa Mikael acquired a reputation as a mugging hot spot a few years back. We have heard nothing one way or the other to indicate whether this is still a problem today, but it might be advisable to take a guide or at least to leave all valuables in your hotel.

Grand Holidays Ethiopia Tours
www.grandholidaysethiopia.com

Grand Holidays Ethiopia Tours, the local travel experts!

For more than 16 years we have fulfilled the dreams and aspirations of many travellers from around the world.

We specialise in small group tours and customised itineraries for various package tours throughout Ethiopia including photography expeditions, cultural tours, and nature and wildlife holidays.

We are also experienced in arranging logistics for film production in Ethiopia.

Trust in us to plan your unforgettable Ethiopian holiday.

Tel: +251911428006
     +251116183163
Lucky Building, Apt 401
Cameron Street, Addis Ababa Ethiopia

info@grandholidaysethiopia
desale@grandholidaysethiopia.com
Skype: delsaegrandholidays
www.grandholidaysethiopia.com

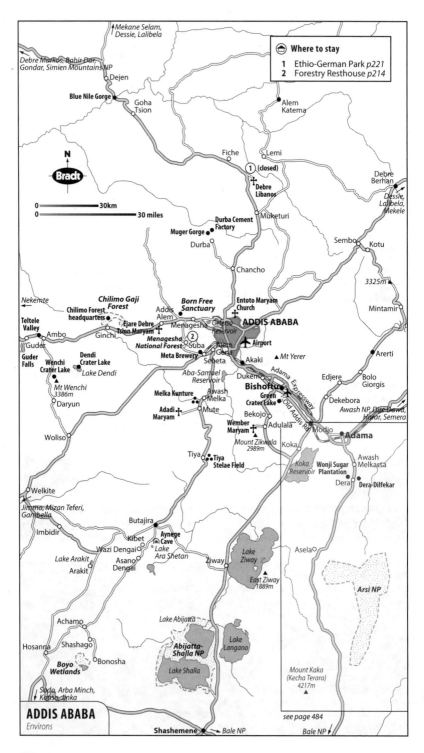

Where to stay
1 Ethio-German Park *p221*
2 Forestry Resthouse *p214*

Mekane Selam, Dessie, Lalibela

Debre Markos, Bahir Dar, Gondar, Simien Mountains NP

Dejen

Blue Nile Gorge

Goha Tsion

Alem Katema

Fiche

Lemi

1 (closed)

Debre Libanos

Debre Berhan

Dessie, Lalibela, Mekele

Muketuri

Durba Cement Factory

Sembo

Kotu

Muger Gorge

Durba

Chancho

3325m

Nekemte

Chilimo Gaji Forest

Chilimo Forest headquarters

Addis Alem

Born Free Sanctuary

Entoto Maryam Church

Mintamir

Teltele Valley

Ejare Debre Tsion Maryam

Menagesha

Gelarsa Reservoir

ADDIS ABABA

Ambo

Ginchi

2

Menagesha National Forest

Suba

Alem Gena

Airport

Guder

Meta Brewery

Sebeta

Akaki

Mt Yerer

Arerti

Guder Falls

Wenchi Crater Lake

Dendi Crater Lake

Lake Dendi

Aba-Samuel Reservoir

Dukem

Adama Expressway

Edjere

Bolo Giorgis

Mt Wenchi 3386m

Daryun

Melka Kunture

Awash Melka

Bishoftu

Green Crater Lake

Dekebora

Awash NP, Dire Dawa, Harar, Semera

Woliso

Adadi Maryam

Mute

Bekojo

Adulala

Old Addis Ra Rd

Modjo

Adama

Wember Maryam

Koka

Welkite

Tiya

Tiya Stelae Field

Mount Zikwala 2989m

Koka Reservoir

Wonji Sugar Plantation

Awash Melkassa

Jimma, Mizan Teferi, Gambella

Imbidir

Butajira

Dera

Dera-Dilfekar

Kibet

Aynege Cave

Lake Ara Shetan

Wazi Dengai

Asano Dengai

Ziway

Lake Ziway

Asela

Arsi NP

Lake Arakit

Arakit

East Ziway 1889m

Achamo

Shashago

Hosanna

Boyo Wetlands

Bonosha

Lake Abijatta

Abijatta-Shalla NP

Lake Langano

Mount Kaka (Kecha Terara) 4217m

Lake Shalla

Sodo, Arba Minch, Konso, Jinka

ADDIS ABABA
Environs

see page 484

Shashemene → Bale NP

Bale NP

N

Bradt

0 ————— 30km
0 ————— 30 miles

5

Around Addis Ababa

Unlike many capital cities in Africa, Addis Ababa is well placed for day and overnight trips to a wide variety of natural and historic attractions. These range from beautiful crater lakes and evergreen forests teeming with birds and monkeys to ancient monasteries, active rock-hewn churches and mysterious engraved stelae. This chapter covers most such attractions within a rough (but not exact) radius of 150km, generally in the form of day or overnight trips out of the city, but arranged in a roughly linear fashion along four main routes that could also be followed sequentially by travellers heading further afield.

The first string of attractions lies between the capital and the modern city of Adama, 100km to its southeast, an area now serviced by the nippy new three-lane Adama Expressway. It includes Bishoftu and its crater lakes, the volcanic Mount Zikwala, and the underrated Dera-Dilfekar sector of Arsi Mountains National Park (which lies closer to Addis Ababa than any other component of the national park network). This Adama Expressway also doubles as a potential springboard for travel further afield, whether it be eastward to Awash National Park and Harar, southeast to the Bale Mountains, or south to the Rift Valley lakes and beyond.

A second string of attractions, highly recommended to those with an interest in history, follows the main asphalt road running south from Addis Ababa to Butajira and Hosanna. Highlights of this region include the prehistoric Stone Age site at Melka Kunture, the ancient rock-hewn church of Adadi Maryam, and the engraved medieval stelae at the Tiya UNESCO World Heritage Site. Butajira and Hosanna also make useful springboards for travel to the Rift Valley lakes and elsewhere in southern Ethiopia.

To the west of Addis Ababa, the hot springs resort at Ambo is of interest mainly to Addis weekenders, but it also provides the best base for visiting the lofty Mount Wenchi and its pretty crater lake. Points of interest between Addis Ababa and Ambo include the Gefersa Reservoir, the new Born Free Sanctuary and the wildlife-rich Menagesha Forest. The road to Ambo and the more southerly parallel road to Woliso both provide access to the little-visited western highlands and the even more remote federal regions of Benishangul-Gumuz and Gambella.

Finally we follow the main road running north of Addis Ababa towards Bahir Dar and Gondar as far north as Dejen on the lip of the magnificent Blue Nile Gorge. The two main sites of interest along this route are the Muger Gorge, the closest place to Addis Ababa to see the endemic gelada monkey, and the historic monastery of Debre Libanos.

EAST TOWARDS BISHOFTU AND ADAMA

The nippy three-lane tolled Adama Expressway now runs 100km southeast of Addis Ababa to the substantial city of Adama (Nazret) via the smaller but more resort-like town of Bishoftu (Debre Zeyit). Both form popular weekend retreats from the capital and might also serve as a first or last stopover for travellers heading east or south. Bishoftu is the more attractive of the two, since it borders several beautiful crater lakes and supports a fantastic variety of birds, but bustling Adama might hold appeal to travellers who prefer urban pursuits. Other minor attractions include the forest-fringed old monastery and crater lake capping volcanic Mount Zikwala, and the opportunity to see greater and lesser kudu on foot or from a car in the Dera-Dilfekar sector of the newly gazetted Arsi Mountains National Park.

BISHOFTU Also known as Debre Zeyit, Bishoftu is a substantial and bustling commercial centre that sprawls for several kilometres along the old main road to Adama some 50km southeast of Addis Ababa. It stands at an altitude of 1,900m on a lush and fertile stretch of the Rift Valley wall pockmarked by numerous ancient volcanic calderas, four of which host beautiful crater lakes that more or less border the town centre. A popular retreat for city dwellers since the imperial era, Bishoftu and its lakes are serviced by numerous resorts catering mainly to the Addis Ababa weekender and conference markets, a selection likely soon to be supplemented by the country's first internationally branded hotel outside Addis Ababa, namely the 152-room Radisson Blu Bishoftu, which is scheduled to open on Lake Babogaya in 2020. For freshly arrived international visitors, this attractively located town forms an agreeable low-key alternative to overnighting in Addis Ababa, and a useful springboard for travels further south or east. It is also an easy goal for a day trip out of the capital.

History The area around Bishoftu is remembered as the site of Ahmed Gragn's victory over Emperor Lebna Dengal in 1529. Several towns were destroyed and churches looted by the Muslim victors, who inadvertently cleared the way for the region to be occupied by the ancestors of its present-day Oromo inhabitants. In 1917, a railway station servicing the track to Djibouti was constructed between lakes Bishoftu and Hora, but contemporary accounts suggest that no further development took place at the site then known as Ada'a (which is still the name of the *woreda* in which Bishoftu lies) prior to 1936. The modern town is essentially a product of the Italian occupation, when the railway station was chosen as the focal point of an important administrative centre and 15,000ha experimental agricultural station. By the end of the occupation in 1941, the nascent town incorporated several dozen Western-style houses, as well as a post and telephone office, a hospital, an airstrip and a large lakeside hotel. Bishoftu has been the site of Ethiopia's main air force base and training centre since 1946, while the country's main veterinary college and agricultural research institute were both founded here in the 1950s. During the late imperial era, Bishoftu was a favoured weekend retreat for Haile Selassie, who imposed on it the 'Christian' name of Debre Zeyit (Mountain of Olives). Bishoftu reverted to its more historically valid Oromo name in the late 1990s, but it is still marked as Debre Zeyit on some maps, and referred to as such by many non-Oromo. Thanks partly to its proximity to Addis Ababa, Bishoftu has experienced rapid population growth in recent decades, from around 27,000 in 1970 to around 200,000 today.

Getting there and away
By rail Bishoftu is potentially an important stop on the new Addis Ababa–Djibouti line. The new railway station lies to the north of the Adama Expressway about 4km east of the town centre as the crow flies, but it is not directly accessible from the

expressway. As things stand, the trains that run between Addis and Djibouti in opposite directions on alternate days don't actually stop here, and it is still unclear whether or when a more regular local service to Addis Ababa and/or Adama will be introduced.

By road In a private vehicle, the quickest route from Addis Ababa is to follow the three-lane Adama Expressway southeast to the Dukem-Bishoftu exit ramp, from where a 4km feeder road connects to a T-junction, where you must turn left on to the Old Addis Ababa Road and follow it for another 4km to central Bishoftu. This trip should take less than 1 hour, depending on traffic conditions between Addis Ababa and Akaki. The toll fee is less than US$0.50.

Heading on to destinations further east, for instance Adama, Awash National Park or Harar, follow the Old Adama Road out of town for 8km, then join the Adama Expressway at the Bishoftu South Toll Plaza. For more southerly destinations such as Ziway, Hawassa or Arba Minch, the best option is a newly surfaced 50km road that runs southwest out of town (past Mikael Church), then south to Adulala, at the eastern base of Mount Zikwala, before veering southeast to connect with the main highway running south through the Rift Valley 1km south of Koka town.

By public transport From Addis Ababa, minibuses to Bishoftu cost around US$1 and leave from Kaliti Bus Station (on the west side of the Adama road about 5km south of the Kaliti Interchange with the Ring Road). You can pick up minibuses to Kaliti from several points in the city centre, including Meskel Square, Merkato Autobus Terra, the Piazza and Saris. Bishoftu's bus station [194 A6] is located about 1km from the town centre along the Addis Ababa road and there is plenty of transport on to Modjo and Adama. A steady stream of local minibuses runs between the town centre and bus station. For those staying at Lake Hora or Babogaya, regular minibuses run north from the town centre to a rank just south of the junction for Salayish Lodge [194 C2], while a contract *bajaj* should cost under US$2.

⌂ Where to stay

Upmarket

✳ ⌂ **Kuriftu Resort & Spa** [194 D2] (92 rooms) ☎ 011 662 3604; m 0924 949494; e bookings@kurifturesorts.com; w kurifturesorts. com. This superb 5-star all-suite resort rivals the top hotels in Addis, but is more attractively located on the northeast shore of Lake Kuriftu. Rooms all feature locally inspired furnishings, flatscreen sat TV, modern bathrooms with 'rain' showers, minibar & private patio with fireplace. Rates include kayaking, mountain biking, table tennis, billiards & access to a cinema, swimming pool & steam room/ sauna/jacuzzi. A good spa & beauty/hair salon is attached. *From US$121/126 standard dbl/twin or US$136/142 at w/ends.* **$$$$$**

✳ ⌂ **Asham Africa** [194 D7] (32 rooms) ☎ 011 437 0710; m 0911 491025; e info@ ashamafrica.com; w ashamafrica.com. Owned by a well-travelled Rwandan–Ethiopian couple, this stylish boutique hotel has a central location overlooking Lake Bishoftu. The individually decorated en-suite rooms, named after different African countries, are adorned with vintage & contemporary artworks, cloth & handicrafts from all over the continent, & come with parquet floor, wrought-iron 4-poster bed with fitted net, sat TV & private balcony with lake view. Other amenities include a spa, gym & lake-facing restaurant serving a good range of Ethiopian fish & continental-style grills in the US$4–6 range. *US$85/101 B&B dbl/ twin or US$95/110 Fri–Sun.* **$$$$$**

⌂ **Pyramid Resort** [194 D7] (41 rooms) ☎ 011 433 1555; m 0930 107550–3; e info@ pyramidresortet.com; w pyramidresortet.com. Situated on the northern rim of Lake Bishoftu, this modern 4-storey hotel is notable for its striking Moroccan-influenced architecture, attractive swimming pool & cosmopolitan restaurant. Warmly decorated en suites come with 4-poster bed, sat TV, private terrace with

The largest and most populous of the federal states defined when the central government redrew the regional map of Ethiopia in 1994, Oromia covers an area of 284,538km² – about 25% of Ethiopia's total area – and its population has doubled from 18 million to 36 million over the subsequent two-and-a-bit decades. The irregular shape of the region has been compared to a lopsided and distended bow tie, with the self-governing city-state of Addis Ababa lying roughly where the knot would be. If you include the self-governing cities of Addis Ababa and Dire Dawa, and the city-sized region of Harari, almost half of the 20 largest urban settlements in Ethiopia lie within Oromia, among them Adama, Jimma, Bishoftu, Shashemene, Nekemte and Asela. In 2000, the Ethiopian government controversially relocated the capital of Oromia from Addis Ababa (known as Finfine in the Oromifa language) to Adama but, following extensive protests, it was returned to Addis Ababa in 2005. More recently, Oromia was the focal point of the widespread anti-government demonstrations that broke out in August 2016; its border areas (in particular with Somali Region) remain volatile at the time of writing.

Divided into 19 administrative zones and around 180 *woredas*, Oromia is a region of vast geographic and climatic diversity. It encompasses not only the highland crags and meadows around Addis Ababa, but also the lush rainforest around Jimma and Nekemte in the west, much of the southern Rift Valley, and the arid acacia scrub towards the Kenyan border. The common factor throughout the region is cultural: Oromia, as its name implies, is the home of the Oromo people, Ethiopia's largest ethnic group. Also referred to as the Galla (a pejorative term no longer used within Ethiopia but frequently encountered in historical writings), the Oromo originally came from the Kenyan border area currently occupied by the Borena, a subgroup of the Oromo. They migrated north from this homeland in the early 16th century, a movement that, whether by chance or design, coincided

lake views & comfortable seating, & en-suite bathroom with combined tub-shower. *Good value at US$87/93 sgl/dbl B&B rising to US$109/115 Fri–Sun.* **$$$$$**

🏠 **Adulala Resort** [194 C2] (47 rooms) m 0911 491050; f. The smart resort has a spectacular location on the north rim of Lake Babogaya. Large landscaped gardens dominated by indigenous trees attract plenty of birds. Open-plan stone-&-thatch suites all come with king-size bed, fireplace, private balcony, sat TV & stylish contemporary furnishing. Amenities & activities include a swimming pool, horseriding, gym, cycling, boating & a spa & restaurant. Be warned that the mossy footpaths can be rather slippery after rain. It feels quite steeply priced in comparison with its competitors in this range. *Standard dbl rooms cost US$139 B&B on w/days & US$164 Fri & Sat.* **$$$$$**

🏠 **Liesak Resort** [194 C2] (38 rooms) m 0933 858584; e reservation@liesakresort.

com; w liesakresort.com. This impressive resort comprises a handsomely curvaceous 3-storey stone-&-thatch building set on the eastern rim of Lake Babogaya. The characterful & spacious split-level rooms have king-size bed, sat TV, minibar, fireplace & private balcony with lake view. A good restaurant is attached. Rates include boat trips on the lake, & use of the gym & swimming pool, but even so it feels a touch overpriced. *US$120/130 B&B for a standard dbl/twin during the week, or US$130/145 over w/ends.* **$$$$$**

Moderate

✳🏠 **Babogaya Lake Viewpoint Lodge** [194 C2] (9 rooms) m 0911 465693; e lakebabogaya@ live.com; w sites.google.com/site/viewpointlodge. This Belgian–Ethiopian owner-managed lodge, which tumbles in 4 sedate terraces down to Lake Babogaya, is consistently praised by travellers & Addis weekenders alike for its relaxed, rustic atmosphere, hands-on management, personalised service, great food &

with Ahmed Gragn's jihad against the Christian empire. It could be argued that the Oromo migration effectively put an end to the war, as both Christian and Muslim Ethiopians found their territory under siege from a third source. Certainly, the Oromo were the main beneficiaries of the holy war, taking advantage of the weakened state of both parties to occupy much of what is now southern Ethiopia, including vast tracts of land that had formerly been part of, or paid tribute to, the Christian empire.

Today, the Oromo are divided into six main groups and hundreds of subgroups, which share a rigid male age-set system, called Geda. At the beginning of every eight-year cycle, marked by a spate of initiations and circumcisions, the age-sets all move up one rung. The dominant age-set consists of 16–24-year-olds, who elect from within their ranks an administrative leader known as the Abagada, who serves until the next eight-year cycle begins. This is an unusually democratic social structure because no hereditary element is involved in political leadership, and because it creates a built-in sell-by date not unlike the limit of two presidential terms written into many modern national constitutions. Once an age-set enters its sixth cycle, its members are regarded as elders, and play an advisory role in governance.

The Oromo believe in one god, known as Waka: traditionalists hold that theirs is the oldest monotheistic religion in the world, and that Moses borrowed his ideas from them. Central to Oromo belief is the sacred staff, or Boku, which symbolises the inviolable Law of God, and is handled only by the incumbent Abagada. The most important traditional festival in the Oromo calendar is the Irrecha, held on 1 October at several sites throughout the region – notably Lake Hora outside Bishoftu. These days, however, traditional Oromo beliefs are increasingly subservient to Christianity and Islam.

plentiful birdlife. The en-suite rooms are basic but comfortable with simple furnishings & hot water; the 2 stilted lakeside rooms have shared bathroom facilities. Well-cooked meals are available in the US$3.50–6.50 range. *US$40/50/65 B&B sgl/dbl/trpl.* **$$$$**

Babogaya Resort [194 C2] (45 rooms) \011 433 7676; m 0920 031933; e info@babogayaresort. com; w babogayaresort.com. This sprawling resort on the north shore of Lake Babogaya, though very comfortable, lacks the ambience of its upmarket competitors & feels quite overpriced. The en-suite rooms & cottages all have hot shower & private balcony. Amenities include 2 dining rooms, minigolf, tennis, sauna & spa, & a boutique art gallery located by reception. *From US$94/109 B&B sgl/dbl inc boat ride.* **$$$$$**

Elame Lodge [194 C2] (9 rooms) m 0911 400420; e info@elamelodge.com; f. If you don't mind the lack of lake views & water access, this is a well-priced & comfortable option, comprising a cluster of beautiful traditional en-suite bungalows,

furnished *tukul*-style & set in lush tropical gardens on the eastern side of Lake Babogaya. All rooms have sat TV & a good restaurant serves Ethiopian & European dishes. *US$22/30 B&B dbl/twin.* **$$$**

Dreamland Hotel & Resort [194 D7] (20 rooms) m 0911 490130/1; e info@ethiodreamland. com; w ethiodreamland.com. Perched on the crater rim above Lake Bishoftu, this well-managed hotel doesn't quite live up to its slogan ('I left my heart in Dreamland'), but the well-appointed & spacious en-suite rooms with sat TV, dark-wood floor & private lake-facing balconies are pretty good value. *From US$36/40 B&B dbl/twin.* **$$$**

Budget
Salayish Lodge [194 C2] (7 rooms) m 0911 403553, 0949 777707; e salayishlodge@ yahoo.com; w salayishlodge.com. Set in a rustic & overgrown garden of fruit (& other) trees that attract plenty of birds, this eco-conscious owner-managed lodge on the northeast rim of Lake

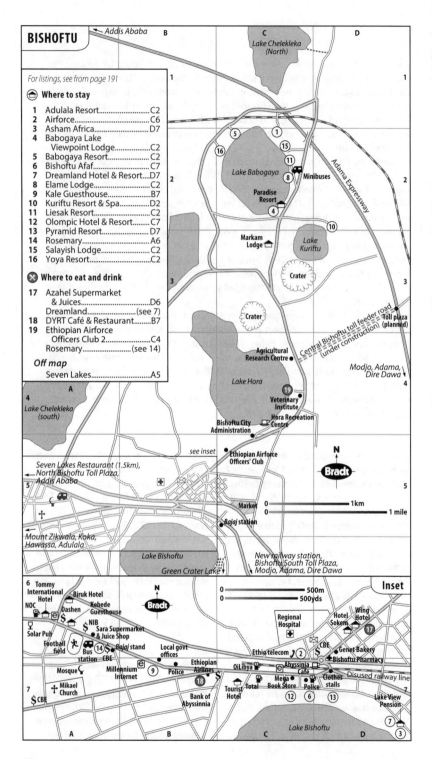

BISHOFTU

← *Addis Ababa*

Lake Chelekleka (North)

For listings, see from page 191

🏠 Where to stay

1 Adulala Resort............................C2
2 Airforce.....................................C6
3 Asham Africa.............................D7
4 Babogaya Lake
    Viewpoint Lodge..................C2
5 Babogaya Resort........................C2
6 Bishoftu Afaf.............................C7
7 Dreamland Hotel & Resort....D7
8 Elame Lodge.............................C2
9 Kale Guesthouse........................B7
10 Kuriftu Resort & Spa...............D2
11 Liesak Resort.............................C2
12 Olompic Hotel & Resort.........C7
13 Pyramid Resort.........................D7
14 Rosemary...................................A6
15 Salayish Lodge..........................C2
16 Yoya Resort...............................C2

✖ Where to eat and drink

17 Azahel Supermarket
    & Juices................................D6
    Dreamland.......................(see 7)
18 DYRT Café & Restaurant........B7
19 Ethiopian Airforce
    Officers Club 2....................C4
    Rosemary.........................(see 14)

Off map
    Seven Lakes............................A5

Lake Babogaya

Paradise Resort

Minibuses

Markam Lodge

Lake Kuriftu

Crater

Crater

Adama Expressway

Central Bishoftu toll feeder road (under construction)

Toll plaza (planned)

Modjo, Adama, Dire Dawa ↘

Agricultural Research Centre

Lake Hora

19 *Veterinary Institute*

Bishoftu City Administration

Hora Recreation Centre

see inset

Ethiopian Airforce Officers' Club

N
Bradt

Lake Chelekleka (south)

*Seven Lakes Restaurant (1.5km),
← North Bishoftu Toll Plaza,
Addis Ababa*

✚

⚓

✝

← *Mount Zikwala, Koka,
Hawassa, Adulala*

Market

Bajaj station

Lake Bishoftu

Green Crater Lake ↓

*New railway station,
Bishoftu South Toll Plaza,
Modjo, Adama, Dire Dawa*

0 — 1km
0 — 1 mile

Inset

6 Tommy International Hotel
Biruk Hotel
NOC
Dashen
Kebede Guesthouse
Solar Pub
NIB
Sara Supermarket & Juice Shop
Football field
14 *Bajaj stand*
Bus station CBE
Local govt offices
Mosque
Millennium Internet
9
Police
Ethiopian Airlines
OiLibya
18
Total
✝ Mikael Church
7
✚ CBE
Bank of Abyssinia
Tourist Hotel
Mega Book Store
Abyssinia Café
12 **6** **13**
Police
Clothes stalls
Disused railway line

Regional Hospital ✚
Ethio telecom
2
CBE
Hotel Sokem
Wing Hotel
17
Genet Bakery
Bishoftu Pharmacy
Lake View Pension
7
3

N
Bradt

0 — 500m
0 — 500yds

Lake Bishoftu

Babogaya offers quirkily charming accommodation in simple but clean bamboo-&-thatch huts with dbl beds, nets & en-suite cold shower. The Sidamo-style restaurant, constructed completely from bamboo thatch, serves inexpensive meals using home-grown veggies & tilapia farmed on the property. *Fair value US$20/25 sgl/dbl B&B, or US$100 for a lakeside cottage sleeping up to 4.* **$$$**

🏠 **Rosemary Hotel** [194 A6] (36 rooms) 📞011 433 9163; m 0911 491052/3; e reservation@rosemaryhotelethio.com; w rosemaryhotelethio.com. Set on the main road close to the bus station, in large green gardens that host one of Bishoftu's best restaurants, this more than serviceable medium-rise has clean & cheerful rooms & larger mini-suites, all with fridge, TV, balcony & en-suite hot shower. Ask for a room facing the garden rather than the road. Great value. *US$20 dbl, US$26 mini-suite.* **$$**

🏠 **Olompic Hotel & Resort** [194 C7] (11 rooms) m 0911 671489. A striking pink-&-grey mock-*tukul* concrete exterior hides comfortable carpeted circular rooms with king-size bed, writing desk, fridge, modern bathroom, sat TV & a tall window to let in the light & highlight the lovely view over Lake Bishoftu. *US$22/24 ground/1st-floor dbl.* **$$$**

🏠 **Kale Guesthouse** [194 B7] (45 rooms) 📞011 848 2986; m 0913 539530. This pleasant new guesthouse near the bus station has clean en-suite dbl & twin rooms with TV, modern décor & hot water. *From US$16 dbl with shower/tub.* **$$**

Shoestring

✳ 🏠 **Yoya Resort** [194 C2] (8 rooms) m 0930 072000/2; e reortyoya@gmail.com. Boasting a lovely leafy location on the northwest shore of Babogaya, this new & exceptionally well-priced resort has spacious clean rooms with TV, fridge & large en-suite bathroom. A shady terrace restaurant is attached. *US$5/6 sgl/dbl.* **$**

✳ 🏠 **Bishoftu Afaf Hotel** [194 C7] (16 rooms) m 0923 982341. This well-run & long-serving hotel has a central location overlooking Lake Bishoftu. The freshly painted rooms are clean & pleasant with en-suite hot showers, but aim to get one as far away from the bar as possible. An inexpensive restaurant with a view serves fish cutlet & other local dishes. *US$9 dbl.* **$$**

🏠 **Airforce Hotel** [194 C6] (18 rooms) 📞011 433 0829. Situated on the opposite side of the railway tracks to the Bekele Molla, this place has functional en-suite rooms with a ¾ bed & cold shower. *From US$6 dbl.* **$**

✖ **Where to eat and drink** All the upmarket hotels listed above have good but relatively pricey restaurants. Other reliable options are as follows:

✖ **Rosemary Restaurant** [194 A6] Set in the large, beautiful garden of the eponymous hotel, this reasonably priced restaurant has a long & varied menu of Ethiopian & Western dishes, from salads & stir-fries to steaks & pasta. Quality & service are both outstanding. *Mains US$3–5.*

✖ **Dreamland Restaurant** [194 D7] ⏲ 07.00–22.00 daily. Situated next to the eponymous hotel & under the same management, this excellent garden restaurant combines a superb lake view with a varied menu embracing salads, soups & pasta dishes for around US$1–2, as well as grills & fish meals in the US$3–5 range. The fish cutlet is a speciality.

✖ **Seven Lakes Restaurant** [194 A5] 📞011 433 7710; m 0927 995974. Situated on the ground floor of the eponymous hotel alongside the Addis Ababa road 2km northwest of the bus station, this restaurant is owned by 2 brothers from India, & the Indian & Chinese cuisine is well

up to Addis Ababa standards. Good vegetarian selection. *Mains work out around US$5 with rice or naan bread.*

✖ **DYRT Café & Restaurant** [194 B7] m 0920 149797; ⏲ 07.00–22.30 daily. Spilling out on to a wide terrace adorned with cane chairs & glass tables, this trendy-looking café serves a variety of Ethiopian dishes, burgers & pizzas in the US$3–4 range. A juice bar is attached & the 1st-floor D Lounge is a wood-dominated bar that opens from 18.00 daily exc Wed.

✖ **Ethiopian Airforce Officers Club 2** [194 C4] ⏲ noon–04.00 daily. Boasting a wonderful location on the relatively undeveloped eastern shore of Lake Hora, this well-priced eatery serves local dishes, grills & fish meals in the US$2–4 range.

✖ **Azahel Supermarket & Juices** [194 D6] Choose from a selection of up to 8 varieties of juice at this low-key supermarket in the old town centre.

What to see and do If you want to chill outside in lakeside luxury, note that the Adulala and Kuriftu resorts both accept day visitors, but charge a day entrance fee equivalent to around US$10–15 per person, inclusive of one main meal and use of sports facilities.

Lake Bishoftu [194 B6] The most central of the lakes dotted around town, alkaline Bishoftu, which extends over around 1km^2 and is up to 90m deep, is nestled within a sheer-sided crater a couple of hundred metres south of the main road. Several hotels and restaurants line the crater rim and offer views across the water to a small waterfall that plunges into the lake from the southern rim. The crater rim can be reached from the town centre by turning uphill at the OiLibya filling station [194 C7] near the Bekele Molla Hotel. Follow the road around the rim for 1km south of the Asham Africa Hotel and you can walk down to the eastern shore along a steep switchbacking road track used by local Oromo pastoralists for watering their cattle. Though the shore is quite sparsely vegetated, the lake supports some interesting waterfowl, including southern pochard, northern shoveler and a wintering population of ferruginous duck, as well as occasional concentrations of lesser flamingo. Rüppell's griffon vultures breed on the cliffs.

Lake Hora [194 C4] The prettiest and least developed of Bishoftu's lakes, Hora is a saline body of water that reaches a depth of almost 40m and extends for about 1.2km^2 across twin craters immediately north of the old town centre. The thickly wooded slopes of the enclosing craters are teeming with woodland birds, and the reed-lined shores are home to various herons, waterfowl and other aquatic species. A short footpath running north from the Bishoftu City Administration [194 C4] leads to the lakeshore, where the Hora Recreation Centre sells drinks and basic meals, and also offers short boat trips for US$2–3. A 6km footpath circumnavigates the crater rim and takes a few hours to walk. We've had reports of theft along this track, so leave your valuables behind or take a local guide.

A colourful and important annual Oromo thanksgiving festival called the Irrecha is held on the shore of Lake Hora on the first day of October. Said to be more than 1,000 years old, Irrecha celebrates the traditional Oromo notion of Waka (One God). Some believers carry a sheaf of leaves or yellow flowers to the water's edge to praise Waka for the bounty of nature, while others dance traditionally in circles, or walk around the lake in small groups. It's a fascinating affair, well worth seeing if you're in the area at the right time – outsiders are made to feel very welcome.

Lakes Kuriftu and Babogaya These two crater lakes lie about 1.5km north of Hora and are the site of most of Bishoftu's top resorts. Both can now be reached on minibuses that run between the town centre and a rank close to the Elame Resort. Tiny Lake Kuriftu [194 C3] is notable less perhaps for any scenic qualities than for its excellent fishing and the popular Kuriftu Resort and Spa on its northern shore. Babogaya [194 C2], also known as Bishoftu Guda, is a larger and very attractive body of water whose lushly vegetated rim was practically unsettled 20 years ago but it is now lined with resorts and half-complete buildings that eyeball each other across the circular lake.

Lake Chelekleka [194 A4 & C1] The most interesting of Bishoftu's lakes in terms of birdlife, Chelekleka doesn't lie in a crater but comprises a large shallow seasonal pan that often dries up entirely towards the end of the dry season. The lake incorporates two separate expanses of flat water, the larger of which lies immediately northwest of the town centre less than 1km from the bus station, while the smaller stands immediately north of the Adama Expressway only 500m from Lake Babogaya. Waterfowl likely to be seen throughout the year include knob-billed duck, pygmy goose and spur-winged goose, and these are supplemented seasonally by migrant garganey, pintail, northern shoveler and ferruginous duck. The lake also sometimes hosts large concentrations of flamingos and pelicans, and the shore is often dense with waders. Several thousand migrant European cranes overnight at the more northerly lake between November and February; it can be quite phenomenal to watch them come in to roost at dusk.

Green Crater Lake [194 C6] Also known as Aranguade Bahir or Hora Hado, the so-called Green Crater Lake is the most beautiful body of water in the vicinity of Bishoftu, set at the base of a very steep crater whose strongly alkaline water supports a high concentration of the algae Spirulina, which creates a green cast in the right light. The algae consumes all the oxygen it produces by day during the night, so that the water becomes anaerobic in the early hours of morning, for which reason fish – and birds that survive mainly by fishing – are entirely absent. The lake does, however, support a good variety of waders, and is notable for the impressive concentrations of 20,000-plus lesser flamingo that regularly aggregate in the shallows. The easiest way to get to the Green Crater Lake from central Bishoftu is to follow the road running east of Bishoftu south past Asham Africa for about 6km, then as you enter a small village, fork right and continue for another 400m to the eastern rim. The road is quite rough and takes about 20 minutes one-way in a 4x4 or *bajaj*. Alternatively, you could make a half-day excursion of it and walk, which takes around 90 minutes in either direction, offering some interesting glimpses into rural Oromo lifestyles en route, as well as passing several impressive acacia and ficus stands alive with birds. Either way, once there, a clear but gravelly footpath leads down through a cleft in the crater rim before switchbacking down to the lakeshore.

Mount Zikwala [194 A5] Of relatively recent geological origin, this 2,989m-high extinct volcano, marked as 'Xiquala' on Fra Mauro's world map of 1459, lies around 30km south of Bishoftu, where it rises more than 600m above the surrounding countryside and dominates the skyline for miles around. The juniper forest on the crater rim, though partially destroyed by fire in 2012, supports a smattering of large mammals, most visibly troops of guereza monkey, but also common duiker and klipspringer. It is also rich in forest birds, including the endemic black-winged lovebird, Abyssinian catbird, Abyssinian woodpecker and a variety of forest starlings. The beautiful lake in the middle of the 2km-wide crater is sacred to Orthodox Ethiopians, who claim that it glows at night. It also often hosts a variety of unusual migrant ducks during the European winter.

Situated on the crater rim, the Church and Monastery of Zikwala Maryam was, according to one local legend, founded by a pair of Egyptian monks as early as the 4th century AD. A more plausible tradition links the monastery's foundation to Gebre Manfus Kidus, also known as Abbo, an Egyptian priest who arrived in Ethiopia in around 1175. The original church was one of several looted and destroyed by Ahmed Gragn in 1529. The older of the two extant churches was constructed by Emperor Menelik II in the 1880s, and its interior is adorned with frescoes of its patron saint, whose St Francis-like reputation for befriending animals extended to living with lions and hyenas. The monks will show you a crack between two rocks, through which it is said only the pure of conscience will squeeze, as well as the sacred stone that is said to mark Abbo's grave. Another tradition has it that the saint's body was taken to Jerusalem by angels and buried next to the tomb of Jesus, while a third claims that he is buried at an ancient monastery near Bui on the road between Tiya and Butajira. The monastery is especially worth visiting on 5 Tekemt and 5 Megabit (15 October and 14 March on non-leap years), when it hosts a large religious festival dedicated to Gebre Manfus Kidus, and is the site of a mass pilgrimage from Addis Ababa and other parts of Shewa.

Zikwala is an easy target for a day trip out of Bishoftu provided you're prepared for a significant uphill hike. To get there, follow the new surfaced road to Koka out of town for about 30km to the village of Adulala at the mountain's eastern base. Plenty of public transport now runs back and forth between Bishoftu and Adulala, usually taking up to 1 hour. Once at Adulala, the steep 10km track to the crater rim is usually motorable in dry conditions, ideally with 4x4 or another high-clearance vehicle, otherwise you will need to walk, which takes around 3 hours in either direction.

MODJO The small town of Modjo (sometimes spelt Mojo), set on the banks of the eponymous river between Bishoftu and Adama, is of some strategic importance as the site of the junction of the main asphalt roads running east from Addis Ababa to Adama, Awash and Dire Dawa and south through the Rift Valley to Shashemene and Hawassa, as well as serving as the main highland 'dry dock' on the new Addis Ababa–Djibouti Railway. Modjo is also the southern terminus of a road running north to Sembo on the main road between Addis Ababa and Debre Berhan, and it may well assume greater importance as and when that road is asphalted in its entirety, which will facilitate direct travel between northern and southern Ethiopia bypassing Addis Ababa (don't hold your breath, however, as progress on this road has been stalled for several years). Should you need to overnight in Modjo, there are plenty of adequate lodgings, notably the popular Daema Hotel (*29 rooms;* \022 116 0022; *US$5/7 sgl/twin with en-suite hot bath, fridge & TV;* **$**).

ADAMA (NAZRET) Ethiopia's third-largest urban centre, with a population now approaching 350,000, is the modern but rather nondescript town of Adama, which stands at an altitude of 1,700m on the fertile plateau that divides the narrowest stretch of the Ethiopian Rift Valley from the central highlands. Situated only 100km southeast of the capital, Adama lacks any notable sightseeing attractions, but it has long served as a popular local weekend retreat thanks mainly to the proximity of a natural spa at Sodere. A more recent hotel construction boom has contributed to the town's emergence as a conference centre. Adama was of some strategic importance to travellers in the late 1990s, prior to the asphalting of the main road through eastern Ethiopia, when it served as the terminus for all long-haul bus services to Dire Dawa and Harar. Today, its claims on international visitors are rather more tenuous, the main point of local interest being the thoroughly worthwhile and readily accessible Dera-Dilfekar sector of Arsi Mountains National Park only 25km to the south. In addition, Adama's vibrant and prosperous feel, combined with its good selection of well-priced hotels, proximity to Addis Ababa and relative lack of hassle, make it an agreeable enough place for fresh arrivals to adjust to contemporary urban Ethiopia.

History Adama started life in the early 20th century as a small railway station on the Djibouti line, and its name alludes to the candelabra tree *Euphorbia candelabrum* (*adami* in Oromo), a cactus-like succulent that grew profusely on the surrounding slopes. It remained a relatively insignificant settlement until 1954, when the Wonji Sugar Plantation (the country's oldest such agricultural concern) was established on the banks of the Awash River about 10km to the south. Other important stimuli to Adama's growth included the construction of three hydro-electric plants downstream of the Koka Dam in the 1960s, and its strategic location as a rail and trucking centre between the capital and the seaports of Eritrea, Djibouti and Somaliland. During the last years of the Imperial era, Adama was renamed Nazret, a corruption of Nazareth, in accordance with a policy to replace secular Oromo place names with something more ecclesiastical. Although the name Adama was officially reinstated in the late 1990s, the town is still referred to as Nazret by most non-Oromo-speaking Ethiopians. In 2000, Adama was earmarked to replace Addis Ababa as the administrative capital of Oromia Region. This ruling by the central government proved to be highly controversial, since many Oromo felt that it was designed to de-emphasise the national capital's central location within Oromia, and it sparked several political rallies, both pro and con. Ultimately, although Adama did serve for a short period as the capital of Oromia, as evidenced by the presence of several ostentatious and all-but-disused administrative buildings on the hillside west of the town centre, the regional government relocated back to Addis Ababa in 2005.

Getting there and away

By rail Adama is an important stop on the new Addis Ababa–Djibouti railway, and the railway station lies to the northwest of the town centre close to the Adama Asela expressway exit. The trains that run between Addis and Djibouti in opposite directions on alternate days stop here, but it is unclear whether a more regular local service to Addis Ababa via Bishoftu will be introduced.

By road Coming from Addis Ababa in a **private vehicle**, hop on to the Adama Expressway and continue to one of the three exits for Adama (the last of which, marked Adama Asela, generally offers the least congested, and thus fastest, access to the town centre). This trip should take no more than 90 minutes (as opposed to up to 3 hours on the old Adama road). The toll fee is US$2. **Minibuses** from Addis Ababa to Adama cost around US$2 and (as with Bishoftu) leave from Kaliti Bus Station 5km south of Kaliti Interchange. Adama's bus station is centrally located about 200m north of the main road and there is plenty of transport to Bishoftu, Modjo (for points further south in the Rift Valley, Asela (for Bale) and Awash Saba (for Harar and Dire Dawa). Minibuses and *bajaji* follow all main roads through Adama and cost a few birr. A contract *bajaj* within town should cost around US$1–2 depending on how far you travel.

 Where to stay *Map, page 200*
Despite its low profile as a tourist centre, Adama boasts the greatest concentration of hotels outside of Addis Ababa, including as many as a dozen broadly similar mid-range high-rises along the main road, and numbers continue to mushroom. The following listing is thus highly selective.

Upmarket
* ⌂ **La Residence Hotel & Spa** (28 rooms) \022 110 0203; m 0930 106845; e info@ laresidence-hotel.com; w laresidence-hotel.com. The most alluring & arguably best-priced boutique hotel within a 100km radius of Addis Ababa, this

palatial 5-storey construction has a prominent location off Peacock Rd on a rise overlooking the town centre. Owned & managed by a dynamic hands-on French–Ethiopian couple, it is built in North African style, with plentiful nooks & arches centred around a covered courtyard & lounge with

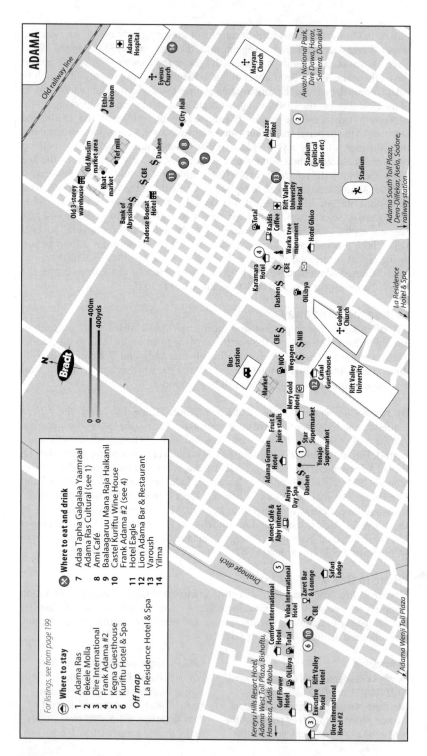

ADAMA

For listings, see from page 199

🛏 Where to stay
1 Adama Ras
2 Bekele Molla
3 Dire International
4 Frank Adama #2
5 Kegna Guesthouse
6 Kuriftu Hotel & Spa

Off map
   La Residence Hotel & Spa

✕ Where to eat and drink
7   Adaa Tapha Galgalaa Yaamraal
8   Adama Ras Cultural (see 1)
9   Ami Café
10 Baalaagaruu Mana Raja Halkanil
    Castel Kuriftu Wine House
    Frank Adama #2 (see 4)
11 Hotel Eagle
12 Lion Adama Bar & Restaurant
13 Varoush
14 Yilma

tall windows that let in plenty of light & offer a splendid view over the town centre. A variety of individually styled high-ceilinged rooms & suites are decorated with imported oriental carpets & antique furnishings, & come with sat TV, hardwood furniture including 4-poster bed with fitted nets, & a spacious bathroom with colourful ceramics & quality imported fittings. An alluring infinity swimming pool, perfectly positioned to catch the sunset, overlooks a large tract of land that's been converted into a wooded park with walking/ running paths. The restaurant serves classy continental cuisine in the US$5–8 range. *Room rate start at US$51 & suites at US$94 dbl, rising by around US$20 on Fri & Sat.* **$$$$**

Moderate

🏠 **Kuriftu Hotel & Spa** (98 rooms) 📞 022 112 4948; m 0949 823939; e kurifturesortadama@ yahoo.com; w kurifturesorts.com. The most appealing of the many hotels lining the main road through Adama feels like a resort rather than a city hotel, thanks largely to its tempting swimming pool area & presence of the affiliated Castel Kuriftu Wine House. Functional rooms in the old wing look ready for refurbishment, but come with sat TV & en-suite hot shower. The newly built stone-&-thatch bungalows behind the swimming pool are a lot larger & classier. *US$24 dbl in the old wing, US$65 dbl for a new bungalow. All rates B&B.* **$$$–$$$$**

🏠 **Dire International Hotel** (77 rooms) 📞 022 110 0384; e direinth@ethionet.et; w direinthotel. com. This multistorey hotel on the Addis side of town is the pick of the dozen or so mid-range hotels lining the main road through the town centre. All rooms are en suite with TV, & the restaurant has a good menu with dishes in the US$2–4 range. Street-side rooms can be noisy. *US$20/28 dbl/mini-suite, US$56 family suite.* **$$–$$$**

Budget

🏠 **Bekele Molla Hotel** (46 rooms) 📞 022 111 2312. This likeable stalwart is set in wooded flowering grounds teeming with birds & dotted with chairs & tables 5mins' walk from the main roundabout along the Awash road. The well-maintained en-suite rooms are all clean with balcony, en-suite shower & sat TV. An outdoor bar serves snacks & drinks near the entrance. *US$9/12 bungalow with cold/hot shower; US$14 dbl in the main building. Rates rise by 15% Fri–Sun.* **$$**

🏠 **Adama Ras Hotel** (67 rooms) m 0920 460882. This former government hotel has rooms centred around a large courtyard swimming pool (don't be put off by the second empty swimming pool you pass outside the main building) & is also home to an excellent traditional restaurant. It is looking a little rundown but it is priced accordingly & offers excellent value in this range. Rooms range from standard sgl with ¾ bed to 1-bedroom suites with king-size bed & 2-bedroom suites with 1 king-size & 1 twin, both with separate lounge with sofa & flatscreen TV. *US$12/16 sgl/dbl, or US$20/24 for 1-/2-bedroom suite.* **$$**

Shoestring

🏠 **Frank Adama #2 Hotel** (5 rooms) 📞 022 112 1644. This time-warped gem 100m north of the main roundabout has slightly rundown but agreeably clean & characterful rooms with period tiled floors, en-suite cold shower & small private balconies. A popular budget restaurant is attached. *US$6/8 dbl/twin.* **$**

🏠 **Kegna Guesthouse** (35 rooms) This very well-priced budget hotel on the west side of the town centre has spotless tiled rooms with dbl bed, en-suite hot shower, wooden furnishings & sat TV. *US$8/10 dbl on ground/1st floor.* **$**

✖ Where to eat and drink *Map, opposite*

Travellers are spoilt for choice when it comes to eating out in Adama, so don't be afraid to venture beyond the highly selective handful of excellent places listed below. For fruit juice, try the row of stalls on the side road connecting the main drag to the bus station.

Moderate to expensive

✖ **Castel Kuriftu Wine House** ⏱ 06.00– 22.00 daily. The top restaurant in central Adama sprawls attractively around the swimming pool at the Kuriftu Resort, with some seating in linen-shaded summer houses suspended over the water. An imaginative menu includes the likes of chicken teriyaki, marinated grilled fish & lamb pot roast in wine, as well as a decent selection of Ethiopian mains & genuine wood-fired oven pizzas. Good wine selection too. *Mains US$4–7.*

✕ Hotel Eagle ⏰ 08.00–late daily. Sprawling over 2 floors around a courtyard dominated by a peculiar statue of a Hiawatha-like figure riding a giant eagle, this popular eatery serves cheap draught beer & a varied selection of tasty curries, steaks, kebabs, pizzas & the usual Ethiopian fare in the US$3–5 range.

✕ Yilma Restaurant ⏰ 09.00–late exc Wed, Fri & other fasting days. This legendary eatery at the north end of the town centre is famed for its lean home-grown beef, which can be served raw or cooked, accompanied by bread or *injera*, with a dish of tangy spice on the side. *US$6–7 for 500g, which should feed 2.*

Cheap to moderate

✕ Baalaagaruu Mana Raja Halkanil ⏰ 19.00–late daily. Superb live music venue also serving inexpensive local staples (*shiro, tibs* & the like), cold beers & good *tej*. The main attraction is the music, performed by a rotating cast of *azmaris* & female singers backed only by a lute-like *masenko* & simple percussion. Few foreigners make it here, so expect your presence to attract plenty of attention from the performers.

✕ Adaa Tapha Galgalaa Yaamraal Restaurant 📱 0911 491541; ⏰ 08.00–late daily. With a laborious name that roughly translates as 'Beautiful Evening Cultural Entertainment', this attractively decorated eatery serves a varied selection of traditional Ethiopian

dishes in the US$2.50–3 range, including local speciality *gomen besiga*, which consists of meat on the bone wrapped in green leaves & *injera*, & baked in a terracotta pot.

✕ Adama Ras Cultural Restaurant 📱 0920 460882; ⏰ 08.00–22.00 daily. Situated outside the eponymous hotel, this newly built replica of the cultural restaurant dotted around Addis Ababa has the choice of indoor & terrace seating & an extensive Ethiopian menu with vegetarian fare at around US$2 & meat dishes in the US$3–4 range.

✕ Varoush Restaurant ⏰ 07.00–22.00 daily. Delicious whole grilled or deep-fried tilapia with bread & salad costs US$4 at this renowned specialist fish restaurant, which lies almost opposite the Bekele Molla.

✕ Frank Adama #2 Hotel 📞 022 112 1644; ⏰ 06.00–20.00 daily. This characterful central eatery is set in an old Italian building with pre-war floor tiles & traditional Ethiopian furnishings. Most items on the extensive Ethiopian menu are in the US$2–3 range.

✕ Lion Adama Bar & Restaurant ⏰ 08.00–late daily. This chilled garden restaurant, complete with a water feature that actually works, is a great spot for a cold draught beer or an inexpensive meal. Pasta & most Ethiopian dishes cost around US$1.50–2.50, but the speciality is *kitfo* at US$4.25.

☕ Ami Café This central café is a great spot for b/fast, fresh juice, bread, pastries & coffee.

What to see and do

Around town A few buildings dating from the Italian occupation or earlier are dotted around the old town centre, among them the Frank Adama #2 and the wooden-balconied Tadesse Boosat Hotel. Also worth a visit while it lasts is the old Muslim market, whose narrow alleys lined with spice and incense shops are almost certainly destined to make way for yet more of the high-rises that now dominate the town centre. Landmarks here include a busy *khat* market, a *tef* mill, and an arched three-storey warehouse that looks like it dates from the early 20th century. So far as we are aware, the only other point of interest in the city centre, situated next to the main roundabout, is a statue of a warka (*Ficus vasta*), a tall fruiting fig tree associated with riverine forest and held sacred by the Oromo people, who often hold rituals underneath its wide canopy.

Sodere [map, page 484] (*186 rooms;* 📞 *022 111 3400;* 📱 *0937868196;* e *info@ sodereresorthotel.net;* w *sodereresorthotel.net; US$35/75 dbl in the old/new wing; day entrance US$2.20*) The hot springs resort of Sodere (often spelt Sodore) stretches for about 1km along the Awash River 20km southeast of Adama. It comprises three spring-fed swimming pools, of which the slightly pricier but far less crowded VIP pool is likely to appeal most to foreign visitors. In addition, quite a lot of wildlife – grivet monkeys, crocodiles, the occasional hippo and plenty of birds – is associated with the Awash River and fringing riparian forest, which can be explored on a network of footpaths. Accommodation at the Sodere is rundown and asks ridiculously inflated *faranji* prices, so better visit as a day trip from Adama. In your own car, follow the Asela road for 13km to Awash Melkassa, where a well-signposted turn-off to the left leads to the resort gates after 7km. Regular minibuses run between Adama and Awash Melkassa, and some continue to the resort gates.

Dera-Dilfekar (Arsi Mountains National Park) [map, page 484] (\022 333 0085; m 0911 055342; e arsimtsnp@gmail.com; w oromiaforest.gov.et; ⊕ 06.00–18.00 daily; entrance US$3.50 pp & US$1 per car, mandatory scout fee US$8 per party)

A thoroughly worthwhile goal for a half-day trip out of Adama or full-day outing from Addis Ababa, the pedestrian-friendly Dera-Dilfekar sector of Arsi Mountains National Park (page 487) offers a rare opportunity for close-up sightings of the magnificent spiral-horned greater kudu and its (elsewhere often elusive) cousin the lesser kudu, as well as supporting a visible population of spotted hyena and more than 180 predominantly acacia-associated bird species. The reserve started life in 1976 as a 0.4km² enclosure created to prevent local wildlife from drowning during a bad flood, but soon after, by agreement between local communities and the zonal administration, it was extended to its present area of 13km². Initially called the Dera-Dilfekar Kudu Sanctuary, it was incorporated into the newly created Arsi Mountains National Park in 2011 to form the smallest, lowest-lying and most northerly and accessible of the park's four discrete blocks (page 486).

Dominated by dry sloping acacia woodland, Dera-Dilfekar protects an estimated 600 greater kudu and 500 lesser kudu, with both species being unusually habituated both to vehicles and walkers, and readily observed from a new 15km track network. Other large mammals include warthog and Anubis baboon (populations estimated at 350 and 450 respectively) and small numbers of bushbuck, klipspringer, common duiker, grivet monkey and possibly leopard. In addition, the Dire Kiltu viewpoint, some 300m on foot from a parking spot 3.5km from the entrance gate, overlooks a gorge and cave where a clan of spotted hyena dens, and individuals are frequently seen in daylight. There are also plans to extend the national park and its road network further northeast to the south bank of the Awash River downstream of Sodere.

Dera-Dilfekar could scarcely be more accessible. The entrance gate and ticket office stand on the east side of the main asphalt road to Asela, some 25km south of Adama, 10km past the junction for Sodere, and a few hundred metres north of the small town of Dera. Plenty of public transport, including direct minibuses between Adama and Dera, runs past the gate. The road network is very rough and requires a 4x4, but it is also permitted to walk, which in many respects is the best way to see this small park and appreciate the close-up encounters with its wildlife. The best time to be there is early morning, when animals (in particular birds) are most active, and temperatures most conducive to walking, but you can be pretty certain of seeing greater kudu at any time of day. Though Dera-Dilfekar is easy enough to visit as a day trip out of Adama, there are a few budget lodges in Dera town, notably the pleasant Wub Miraf Hotel (*8 rooms;* \022 333 0600; m 0911 117772; **$**) which lies less than 1km from the entrance gate and has clean en-suite double rooms with hot water and TV for US$6, as well as a garden restaurant complete with life-size kudu statue. Alternatively, for those self-sufficient in food and water, a very simple campsite (amenities amount to one wooden shelter and a drop toilet; *US$1 pp camping fee*) set in a stand of acacia woodland only 2.5km inside the entrance gate offers a real bush immersion experience complemented by sweeping views to a nearby sugar estate bordering the Awash River. A proper visitor centre is planned, and there is also talk of trying to persuade a private investor to open a private lodge within the reserve.

SOUTH TOWARDS BUTAJIRA AND HOSANNA

Easily explored as a day trip out of Addis Ababa, a trio of fascinating archaeological and historical sites can be accessed from the 135km asphalt road running south from the capital to Butajira. These are the Stone Age palaeontological site and museum at Melka Kunture, the semi-monolithic rock-hewn church of Adadi Maryam and the UNESCO-recognised Tiya Stelae Field. The road to Butajira also forms part of an alternative and relatively traffic-free route to the Rift Valley lakes between Ziway and Hawassa, or to South Omo via Hosanna, Sodo and Arba Minch. With an early start and a private vehicle, you could stop at all three sites and still reach Ziway in one day. Using public transport, you might think about stopping over at Butajira, an agreeable albeit unremarkable Gurage town that forms a good springboard for visiting the lovely Ara Shetan Crater Lake and a few more obscure stelae sites. Another onward option, heading south from Butajira, is the 200km drive via Hosanna to Sodo, at the crossroads of the main road between Shashemene and Arba Minch.

GETTING AROUND To get to any of the places described below from Addis Ababa, follow the Jimma road west for 19km as far as the busy little junction town of Alem Gena, where the 115km road to Butajira branches south. From Alem Gena, it's roughly 30km to Awash Melka, another 5km to the turn-off for Adadi Maryam, then another 35km to Tiya. Leaving from the main Autobus Terra, regular minibuses run from Addis Ababa to Butajira (in some cases continuing on to Hosanna), and there's usually also direct transport to Awash Melka and Tiya before 09.00. Note, however, that once the new rail service from central Addis Ababa to Sebeta opens (possibly in late 2018), it might be better to take a train to Alem Gena and pick up something there. Once on the Butajira road, you may sometimes have to wait a while for transport, as passing buses will often be full, but this is not the problem it was a few years back.

AWASH MELKA AND SURROUNDS Also known as Dilday, Awash Melka is an overgrown village situated 50km south of Addis Ababa on the north bank of the Awash River. It is the closest settlement to Melka Kunture, which lies immediately south of the bridge where the Butajira road crosses the river. Awash Melka also offers access to a trio of waterfalls on the Awash River, and to a mysterious complex of manmade caves known as Dubatu. An important horticultural centre, it is surrounded by large greenhouses where roses are grown for export to Europe. Facilities are limited but there are a few very basic places to stay and eat, of which the Abyssinia Hotel, 1km north of the bridge, is probably the pick.

Getting there and away Awash Melka is 30km from Alem Gena and plenty of transport runs between the two. To get to Melka Kunture from Awash Melka, you need to follow the Butajira road south across the Awash River, then after another 100m turn right on to a signposted 1km motorable track. Any transport heading towards Butajira can drop you at the turn-off for Melka Kunture, and there are also a few minibuses daily to Awash Melka, from where it is a 20-minute walk to the prehistoric site.

What to see and do It's worth stopping at the bridge between Awash Melka and Melka Kunture. Immediately to its east, the river forms a series of three low but powerful waterfalls, the last of which has a wild swirling pool at its base, as it plunges into a deep gorge. You can see the upper waterfall from the bridge, but you get better views of the whole scene by following the footpath running east along the gorge's northern rim. Also on the north of the gorge are some substantial patches of acacia woodland which, together with the raptors and swallows circling above the cliffs, promise rewarding birdwatching.

Melka Kunture Prehistoric Site [map, page 188] (\ *011 157 3102/4;* e *oromiactb@ethionet.et;* w *melkakunture.it;* ⊕ *09.00–12.30 & 13.30–17.00 daily; entrance US$2.50, photography US$3.50, video camera US$4*) One of Ethiopia's most important Stone Age sites, Melka Kunture was discovered in 1963 by Gerard Dekker, who recognised that the exposed layers of rock on the north bank of the flood-prone river represented a fossil record extending back 1.7 million years. Between 1965 and 1995, systematic exploration of the site was undertaken by French palaeontologist Jean Chavaillon. It is now jointly managed by researchers from the University of Rome and the Oromia Culture and Tourism Bureau. Numerous Stone Age artefacts, including basaltic cleavers, hand-axes and other tools, have been unearthed, as have fossils of extinct species of hippo, giraffe, gelada and wildebeest (the last long absent from Ethiopia). In addition, several *Homo erectus* fossils have been found, dating back 1.5 million–1.7 million years, as have more recent cranial fragments of early *Homo sapiens*. An informative site museum spread across four *tukuls* displays a good collection of these artefacts, as well as a collection of prehistoric skull replicas modelled after findings throughout Africa. There is also an open-air excavation site and a prehistoric animal butchering site a short walk away.

Dubatu Downstream of Awash Melka, at a bend in the river known locally as Dubatu, is a complex of artificial caves that corresponds closely with a mysterious site that was visited by Francisco Álvares in 1523 but was not identified again until the early 1970s, when Richard Pankhurst wrote an article about it for the *Ethiopia Observer* (vol 16, no 1). Álvares described a 'very strong' town set in 'a very deep hollow … upon a great river, which made a great chasm' that consisted almost entirely of houses carved into the cliff face with an entrance the size of 'the mouth of a large vat' but 'so large inside that 20 or 30 persons could find room there with their baggage'. Álvares was told that the caves were originally carved by the Gurage, 'a people (as they say) who are very bad, and none of them are slaves, because they say that they let themselves die, or kill themselves, rather than serve Christians'. When he visited, however, the town had been taken over by Christians who had built 'small walled and thatched houses' in the hollow, as well as 'a very good church inside'. In addition, Álvares describes what is evidently a rock-hewn monastery on a cliff further upstream, built on a crag that 'faces the rising sun', and above which were carved 'fifteen cells for monks, all of which have windows over the water'. According to Pankhurst, the vast caves described by Álvares, though long abandoned, can still be entered today, while the disused monastery lies nearby at a place called Wagide.

Adadi Maryam [map, page 188] (⊕ *daily; entrance US$5 inc photography, video camera US$5*) Ethiopia's southernmost functioning rock-hewn church, Adadi Maryam lies to the west of the Butajira road on a small hill 5 minutes' walk from the market in the village of Adadi. Scholars date the church to sometime between the

5

12th and 14th centuries, while local tradition associates it with King Lalibela's visit to nearby Mount Zikwala in 1106. Adadi Maryam is in fact quite similar in style to several churches at Lalibela, albeit smaller, more roughly hewn and undecorated by old paintings or engravings. A semi-monolith hidden below ground level in a deep trench containing a few disused monastic cells, it has a floor area of 300m^2 and is ventilated by 24 windows and ten doors. The tunnel that leads from behind the church to a nearby watercourse was carved later to prevent flooding. More recent Swiss-funded restoration work took place over 1996–98.

Some scholars believe that Adadi Maryam is where Emperor Lebna Dengal first met with Rodrigo de Lima's Portuguese expedition of 1523, as documented by the priest Francisco Álvares. A few years after that, the church was attacked by Ahmed Gragn, who damaged the cross above the entrance and either killed the priests or forced them to flee. It then fell into disuse, to reopen only after it was rediscovered by hunters during the reign of Menelik II. Although Adadi Maryam remains in active use today, its original name is undocumented (Adadi is the Oromifa name for a bush that grows prolifically in the vicinity). It can be visited at any time, but it tends to attract a significant number of worshippers from Addis Ababa on Sundays, and it forms a major site of pilgrimage on 29 January. About 2km northwest of Adadi, Laga Degaga is a complex of rock-hewn caves that most likely housed a monastic community associated with Adadi Maryam prior to the attack by Ahmed Gragn.

Getting there and away The signposted junction for Adadi, a tiny village called Mute, lies on the right-hand side of the Butajira road about 5km south of Melka Awash. It is 12km from Mute to Adadi on a dirt road that can get quite slippery after rain. On non-market days there is no direct public transport from Addis Ababa, but if you catch a minibus from the Autobus Terra to Alem Gena, you might be able to pick up something there. A quicker alternative would be to board a vehicle bound for Butajira, hop off at Awash Melka or Mute, and wait for transport there. This is most prolific on the market days of Thursday and Sunday, when plenty of light transport runs from Melka Awash to Adadi, especially between 07.30 and 09.00, and a bus leaves from the Autobus Terra in Addis Ababa at about 06.00.

TIYA STELAE FIELD [map, page 188] (⊕ 08.00–18.00 daily; entrance US$6 inc photography; optional guide fee US$2.50 per party of up to 4) Situated 85km south of Addis Ababa, Tiya Stelae Field, a UNESCO World Heritage Site since 1980, lies on the west side of the Butajira road in the small Gurage town of Tiya. It comprises 36 stones of up to 2m in height, several of which had collapsed prior to their careful re-erection in their original positions by a team of French archaeologists. The largest stele in the field originally stood 5m high, but while the base remains *in situ*, the main body now stands outside the Institute of Ethiopian Studies in Addis Ababa. Tiya marks the northern limit of a belt of mysterious engraved stelae that stretches across southern Ethiopia through Dilla all the way to Negele Borena (see box, page 511). Little is known about the origin of these monuments, though excavations at Tiya have revealed them to mark the mass graves of males and females who died about 700 years ago aged between 18 and 30, and were laid to rest in a foetal position.

All but four of the stones at Tiya are engraved. Three symbols predominate: stylised swords, plain circles, and what looks like a pair of podgy leaves rising on a stem from a rectangular base. Where all three are present on one stone, the circles are generally near the top, the swords in the middle and the twin leaves close to the base. The meaning of these engraved symbols is open to conjecture. The swords suggest that the people buried were soldiers, and might represent the number of victorious battles they were involved in. The plain circles seem to denote that at least one female is buried underneath that particular stone. The pairs of leaves look like the *enset* (false banana) plantain that is still widely grown in southern Ethiopia. Recent thinking is that they represent a traditional wooden headrest, and are a sort of visual RIP note. On some stones you'll see what looks like a Greek 'E', a symbol for which no plausible interpretation has been thought up. Despite the relative simplicity of the stelae and engravings, they are quite mysterious and haunting, and the repetitive intent that lies behind the symbols is as impressive in its way as the more finely honed and grandiose stelae of Axum.

Tiya invites speculation. Even to the untrained eye, it is clear that these stelae (along with those closer to Butajira) don't fall neatly into the phallic or anthropomorphic schools of decoration found elsewhere in southern Ethiopia, but represent a third, more ornate style of carving. Because of this, it seems likely that they were erected more recently than their more easterly counterparts, probably between the late 12th century and the early 14th. Like the engraved stelae at Axum, these grave-markers predate the local arrival of Christianity, suggesting they could be relics of an otherwise forgotten offshoot of that more northerly pre-Christian stelae-building tradition. Certainly, it would appear that Tiya, situated only 30km south of the roughly contemporaneous Adadi Maryam, marked the medieval boundary between pagan and Christian Ethiopia.

Getting there and away Tiya lies on the Butajira road about 40km south of Awash Melka. In common with other sites along this road, it can be reached by boarding any Butajira-bound transport out of Addis Ababa or Alem Gena. There

GURAGE

Butajira lies at the heart of Gurage country, a mountainous area lying towards the southern end of the central highlands. The Gurage, the fifth-largest ethnolinguistic group in Ethiopia, are historically affiliated to the Amhara of the northern highlands, and have long associations with its Christian traditions, as evidenced by the presence of the rock-hewn church of Adadi Maryam and numerous other abandoned troglodyte dwellings and shrines in their homeland. The Gurage evidently became isolated from Amhara during the time of Ahmed Gragn, and developed independently until they were reintegrated in the 19th century. Today, the area remains a Semitic-speaking enclave surrounded by Oromo and other unrelated peoples, and its people are split between ancient Orthodox Christians and more recent converts to Islam.

The Gurage social structure is unusual in that economic roles are not dictated by caste, class or gender. The Gurage do, however, have a strange relationship with the Watta or Fuga people, who have adopted the Gurage language and customs, and serve the triple role of artisans, hunters and spiritual mediums within Gurage society. It is the Watta who are responsible for erecting the main beams of Gurage houses, which are attractive beehive structures similar to those seen around Sodo and elsewhere in Walaita. A guiding Gurage principle is that 'idleness is a sin, work is the key to success, failure to improve one's land is bad farming and cannot be blamed on the spirits'. Perhaps related to this dictum, or perhaps simply because of Gurage's proximity to Addis, there are many Gurage in the city, and they have a reputation for industry, business acumen and also academic success.

are direct minibuses between Alem Gena and Tiya, but these can take ages to fill up. The stelae field is 400m east of the main road through town, and clearly signposted.

Where to stay, eat and drink Situated in a field behind the NOC filling station, the **Tiya NOC Hotel** (*10 rooms;* m *0911 037885;* **$**) is easily the best place to stay in Tiya. The simple en-suite rooms come with a double bed, cold running water and TV. The filling station has an adequate restaurant and bar.

BUTAJIRA [map, page 188] This pleasantly green and rapidly growing but largely unremarkable town of around 35,000 people sits at an altitude of 2,130m in the fertile hills of Gurage Zone 135km south of Addis Ababa. It is quite a modern town, founded in the late 1920s, and is where prominent resistance leader Ras Desta Damtew, a son-in-law of Haile Selassie, was executed by the Italian military in 1937. Although it is largely bypassed by tourists, Butajira has served as the Peace Corps pre-service training camp since 2013, annually hosting two groups of several dozen volunteers for about ten weeks each. For backpackers, the town forms a convenient overnight stop between Tiya and Ziway – it has an unexpectedly good selection of affordable accommodation – and it is also a good base for visiting the attractive Ara Shetan Crater Lake. The main market day is Friday.

Getting there and away Regular minibuses run directly between Addis Ababa and Butajira, as well as along the 50km asphalt road between Butajira and Ziway in the Rift Valley, and the 200km asphalt road via Hosanna to Sodo (for Arba Minch and South Omo).

Where to stay

Moderate

Rediet Hotel (50 rooms) 046 115 0803; m 0911 994578; e redaethotel@gmail.com. Butajira's top hotel is a 6-storey building with a rather insalubrious location behind the NOC filling station on the right-hand side of the main road as you enter town from the direction of Addis Ababa. The spacious, modern en-suite rooms have tiled floors, sat TV & small balcony, but try for one facing away from the main road. A good restaurant with free Wi-Fi serves international & traditional meals in the US$3–5 range indoors or in the garden out the back. *US$40/60 2nd-/1st-class dbl, US$84 twin.* **$$$$**

Budget

Butajira Bright Hotel (55 rooms) 046 115 0564; m 0923 052554. Butajira's best budget option, situated on the main road opposite the

Dashen Bank, has a large variety of rooms, with those facing away from the road generally being quieter & marginally more expensive. A lively 1st-floor bar & restaurant with free Wi-Fi serves great kebabs, sandwiches & other international dishes in the US$3–5 range. *US$6/8 sgl/dbl using common shower, from US$9/11/12 en-suite sgl/dbl/twin, US$16 family suite.* **$–$$**

Kasetch Fekadu Assore Hotel (52 rooms) 046 115 0443. Set in large greenish grounds about 100m uphill from the Telecommunications Centre on the main road, this slightly rundown but agreeable multistorey block has 6 types of en-suite room, most of which have sat TV, hot water & a balcony. A decent restaurant is attached. *From US$7 for a grotty dbl with cold water to US$10 for a nicer dbl with hot water & US$16 for twin with hot water & TV.* **$–$$**

Where to eat and drink All of the places listed above have decent restaurants. The Rediet probably has the best Western-style food in town, while the Bright is good for affordable light meals, and both have free Wi-Fi. Butajira is a good place to try the highly rated *kitfo* (spicy raw minced beef – if you want it slightly roasted, ask for *kitfo lebleb*) made by the Gurage people and served with the local staple food *kocho*, a thick tasty flatbread made from the *enset*, or false banana, tree. Lamrot Bar and Restaurant (**m** *0916 582623*) is the pick of several restaurants and pastry shops opposite the Kasetch Fekadu Assore Hotel. It has a bright blue terrace serving cheap draught beer, as well as excellent *kitfo*, *tibs* and *shiro wat*. Most dishes are under US$3, but *kitfo* costs US$5.

What to see and do

Lake Ara Shetan [map, page 188] Situated 10km south of Butajira on the east side of the Hosanna road, this pretty emerald-green lake, nestled within the sheer 120m-high walls of an almost perfectly circular explosion crater, is around 400m in diameter and 50m deep. It is the most southerly link in a chain of craters, lava flows and other relicts of geologically recent volcanic activity that runs for 80km northeast along the Rift Valley Escarpment to Bishoftu. Sometimes referred to as Lake Butajira, it is more normally called Ara Shetan (literally 'Lake of Satan') and seems to be viewed as a somewhat malignant presence by locals. Its creation is ascribed to an evil sorcerer who bedevilled the local peasants for years before finally he was mortally wounded at the site of the present-day lake. As the sorcerer drew his dying breath, he drove his spear hard into the ground, and bellowed out a curse, 'Let this be the devil's home', whereupon the earth below him imploded, swallowed him up and filled with water. It is taboo to throw a stone into the lake – legend has it that the devil would hurl it back even harder at the person who threw it, with fatal consequences.

About 15 minutes' walk from the northern rim of Ara Shetan, another very small crater (or possibly sinkhole) called Aynege stands in striking contrast to the surrounding countryside with its thickly wooded cliffs leading down to a small clear pool at the base. A large cave in the side of the crater has been home to a blind Islamic holy man and his extensive family for about 40 years. Visitors are welcome, though a small donation is usually expected, and the holy man has a reputation for getting a little touchy-feely with unaccompanied female travellers. Aynege Crater is said (rather improbably) to connect to the Sof Omar Caves, which lie to the east of the Bale Mountains, on the other side of the Rift Valley. The walk up to the cave offers attractive views back towards a larger, lower-lying, non-volcanic lake called Tinishu Abaya (Little Abaya), which feeds an important irrigation project.

Getting there and away Although Ara Shetan is only 700m east of the main road to Hosanna, it is completely invisible until you actually reach the rim. From the unmarked junction 10km south of Butajira (⊕ *N8 02.449 E38 20.372, or look out for the 145km roadside marker*), you need to follow a motorable track that forks back to the northeast for 500m, bypassing the first prominent fork to your right but taking the second one, from where it is about 300m to the western rim. Any public transport heading between Butajira and Kibet (a village 4km further south) will be able to set you down at the start of this track. You could also charter a *bajaj* for around US$5 one-way for up to five people. A footpath runs around the entire rim, offering wonderful views in all directions, and there is also a quite tricky footpath down the cliffs to the water's edge. From the northernmost point on the rim, a motorable track veers northeast for about 800m to a car park, from where a short but steep footpath leads to Aynege Cave.

Silté Stelae Straddling the Hosanna road only 4km southwest of Lake Ara Shetan, Kibet is the principal town of the Silté people, whose attractive traditional homesteads with tall, domed thatched roofs can be seen dotted around the surrounding countryside. The Silté area is also known for its many medieval stelae,

5

which are similar in shape and decoration to those found around Tiya, though generally more ornately worked. Many have been relocated to Addis Ababa by archaeologists, but those that remain can be visited without paying an entrance fee. Particularly worthwhile and accessible, the decapitated stele known as Asano Dengai [map, page 188] (✪ N7 58.149 E38 17.338) is possibly the most intricately worked individual stone in southern Ethiopia. It stands in isolation below a large fig tree next to a recently built mosque about 400m east of the Hosanna road in the village of Asano, exactly 8km south of Kibet. Rather less compelling are the six stelae, all either decapitated or collapsed, at Wazi Dengai, which lies 800m west of the main asphalt road along an unsignposted dirt road on the southern outskirts of Kibet.

HOSANNA The capital of Hadiya Zone since 1994, Hosanna – often spelt Hosiana or Hoseana – lies at a chilly altitude of 2,400m in a well-watered mountainous region famed as an important centre of *enset* cultivation, though its volcanic soils can grow practically anything. Formerly known as Wachamo, Hosanna is the main town of the Hadiya people, whose culture is affiliated to the Gurage, though they speak a vastly different Cushitic language called Hadinya. Hadiya was annexed to Ethiopia after being conquered by Emperor Menelik II in around 1890, and the town of Hosanna was established as the administrative capital of his appointed governor, Ras Abata Bwayalaw, on Palm Sunday of 1904 (hence the name Hosanna, a phrase strongly associated with that Christian celebration). A minor route focus on the excellent asphalt road connecting Addis Ababa to Arba Minch, Hosanna today is an agreeable enough place with a bustling Saturday market, but it must still be one of the few Ethiopian towns of comparable size (population 75,000) whose hotels are so seldom troubled by the tourist trade.

Getting there and away Hosanna stands at the junction of a 100km road running northeast to Butajira, a 96km road south to Sodo, and a 115km road northwest to Welkite. Plenty of public transport runs to all these towns throughout the day, costing around US$2 and taking about 2 hours in each case. Direct high-speed minibuses to/from Addis Ababa cost US$6, while standard buses cost US$3.75.

 Where to stay, eat and drink *Map, opposite*

Budget

Shambalala Hotel (200 rooms) ☎046 178 0142/3; w shambalalahotelethiopia.com; e shambalalahotel@gmail.com. The Shambalala has a gym & spa, & offers all the modern amenities one can expect from a higher-end establishment. *US$28/33/62 sgl/deluxe/twin.* **$$**

Woze Star Hotel (30 rooms) ☎046 555 1818; m 0911 616727; e contactus@ wozestarhotel.com; w wozestarhotel.com. This brand-new hotel located opposite Ethio Telecom has neat & comfortable rooms. The manager speaks good English. *US$12/20/20 en-suite sgl/dbl/twin.* **$$**

Lemma International Hotel (47 rooms) ☎046 555 4453; m 0911 228623; e cherulmma@

yahoo.com. This smart 1-price-for-all 5-storey hotel has a convenient location backing up the bus station (though rooms facing the back can be quite noisy). The en-suite rooms with TV & Wi-Fi are clean & neat, & the ground-floor restaurant & bar also does a roaring trade. *US$14/16/20 sgl/dbl with king-size bed/twin.* **$$**

Shoestring

Edget Hotel (36 rooms) ☎046 555 2616; m 0911 960234. Located just off the main roundabout above the Bank of Abyssinia, this well-managed hotel has adequate shoestring rooms using common showers on the ground floor, as well as newer en-suite rooms with hot showers in the main 3-storey building. A good restaurant &

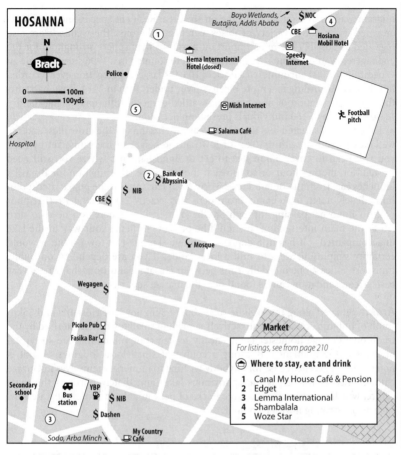

HOSANNA

N

0 ———— 100m
0 ———— 100yds

Police ●

*Boyo Wetlands,
Butajira, Addis Ababa*

$ $ NOC
CBE
Hosiana
Mobil Hotel

Speedy
Internet

Hema International
Hotel (closed)

Hospital

Mish Internet

Salama Café

Football
pitch

Bank of
Abyssinia

NIB

CBE $

Mosque

Wegagen $

Picolo Pub

Fasika Bar

Market

Secondary
school

Bus
station

YBP

$ NIB

$ Dashen

My Country
Café

Sodo, Arba Minch

For listings, see from page 210

Where to stay, eat and drink

1 Canal My House Café & Pension
2 Edget
3 Lemma International
4 Shambalala
5 Woze Star

5

café are attached, & the staff are very helpful. *US$5 dbl using common shower, US$6/8 en-suite dbl without/with TV.* **$**

Canal My House Café & Pension (10 rooms) 046 555 2743; **m** 0911 215452. The

name might be a mouthful, but the clean tiled rooms with TV are great value. There's also a decent ground-floor café. *US$3.50 dbl using common shower, US$5/6 en-suite dbl with cold/hot water.* **$**

What to see and do

Boyo Wetlands [map, page 188] Listed as an Important Bird Area, the Boyo Wetlands, set at an altitude of 1,500m near the small town of Bonosha, consists of an extensive seasonal swamp centred upon a shallow but perennial freshwater lake called Boyo or Bilate (the latter after the river that flows through its eastern tip to eventually empty into Lake Abaya near Arba Minch). There are some interesting thatched Hadiya homesteads in the lake's hinterland, many painted in geometric designs, and you may also notice modern cemeteries marked with engraved stones reminiscent of (and presumably inspired by) their more ancient counterparts around Silté. According to local sources, Boyo's once prolific hippos were hunted to extinction in around 1994, but a couple of refugee pods from Abijatta-Shalla have since recolonised the lake and are quite regularly seen in the open water. For birders, activity peaks during the European winter, when thousands upon thousands of migrant waders and ducks converge on the area. Resident species include black-crowned crane and a variety of ibises, egrets and herons. The wetlands are also regarded as possibly the most important northern hemisphere stronghold for the endangered wattled crane – 62 individuals were counted in a 1996 survey, while an expedition in 2004 encountered a flock of 108, the largest aggregation ever recorded in Ethiopia. According to a more recent survey undertaken in 2014, Boyo harbours the largest population of non-breeding wattled cranes in Ethiopia during the dry season, with up to 160 individuals present on occasion.

Lake Boyo is situated less than 20km east of Hosanna as the crow flies, and the wetlands extend to within 10km of town at the height of the rains. Yet by road you will need to cover 55km just to get to Bonosha, from where you still need to walk for another hour or so to reach the lakeshore. The junction for Bonosha branches east from the Butajira road 31km from Hosanna, at the police checkpoint immediately north of Achamo. From here, it is exactly 24km along a rather poor road to Bonosha, passing through Shashago after 9km, where you need to turn left at the main intersection. It should be possible to make your way to the lake unaccompanied – it lies in a depression about 4km west of town – but it would certainly simplify matters to find a local guide. If you are dependent on public transport, at least one bus daily runs between Hosanna and Bonosha, where very basic accommodation can be found near the market square.

Arakit Situated along the Welkite road about 55km north of Hosanna and 35km south of Imbidir, Arakit is an attractively sprawling small town characterised by the traditional Gurage homesteads and neatly fenced compounds that are so typical of these fertile highlands. Boasting a couple of small local lodgings, Arakit is potentially an excellent base for anybody wishing to immerse themselves in Gurage culture. Also of interest is the eponymous lake immediately north of the town centre, which sometimes hosts large flocks of pelican, ibis and migrant waterfowl such as the striking northern pintail.

WEST TOWARDS AMBO AND MOUNT WENCHI

The highlands immediately west of Addis Ababa offer some of the most worthwhile, and underrated, sightseeing in the vicinity of the capital. For wildlife lovers, birdwatchers and keen walkers, a highlight of the region is the Menagesha National Forest, which can be reached from the main roads to both Ambo and Jimma, while those seeking a more demanding hike or an equestrian adventure are pointed to the scenic Mount Wenchi and its lovely crater lake. Closer to town, the recently opened Born Free Sanctuary is another great birding site which also provides your best opportunity to see black-maned Abyssinian lions in surroundings more edifying than the utterly bleak zoo at Siddist Kilo. The most alluring town in the region is the hot springs resort of Ambo, which lies 125km west of Addis Ababa, and offers good access to Wenchi, as well as to the pretty Guder Falls.

GEFERSA RESERVOIR Dammed in 1938 as a source of water for the expanding capital, the 1.2km² Gefersa Reservoir lies at an altitude of 2,600m in the Akaki catchment area on the western outskirts of Addis Ababa. The lack of fringing vegetation makes it rather bland in scenic terms, but it has long been popular with birdwatchers as a good place to observe several avian endemics not easily seen at the main stops along the northern historical circuit. The ubiquitous wattled ibis and more localised blue-winged goose are virtually guaranteed, while Abyssinian longclaw, Rouget's rail and black-headed siskin are also regular, along with a few interesting non-endemics such as red-breasted sparrow-hawk and (during the European winter) a variety of migrant waterfowl. The reservoir lies about 15km west of central Addis Ababa as the crow flies. The best birding sites are on the northern shore and can be accessed from the old Ambo road. From the city centre, follow the old Ambo road for 2km past the suburb of Gefersa, or take the new Ambo road to the intersection with the old road at Burayu, then turn right on to the old road and follow it back towards Addis Ababa for 3km. Although the entire reservoir is fenced and the entrances are guarded, it no longer seems to be the case that a permit is required to access the shore.

BORN FREE SANCTUARY [map, page 188] (m *0913 119054;* e *bffe@bornfree.org.uk;* w *bornfree.org.uk;* ⏱ *11.00–16.00 daily; entrance free but donations are welcomed, guideline US$15 per party*) Established on a former military training ground in 2009, the Born Free Sanctuary protects 77ha of acacia-dominated woodland at an altitude of 2,600m near the small town of Holeta 20km west of Addis Ababa. The woodland supports a varied selection of naturally occurring mammals, most conspicuously Menelik's bushbuck, warthog, guereza and grivet monkey, but also more secretive nocturnal species such as leopard, spotted hyena and civet. An extensive network of walking trails offers the opportunity to see many forest-associated birds including endemics such as Abyssinian catbird, white-cheeked turaco and white-backed black tit. It also serves as a shelter for rescued and orphaned animals, most of which are released into the wild, though others – notably some impressively maned Abyssinian lions kept in large fenced enclosures – are probably there to stay. Facilities are limited at the time of writing, but a four-storey visitor and education centre, offering great rooftop views into the surrounding canopy, has been under construction for some years now, and there is a picnic area at the base. Tourists are welcome but advance booking is required, and the management advise against visiting on Sunday, when it tends to get busy with day trippers from Addis Ababa. Birdwatchers can request to arrive earlier or stay later than the normal opening times to take advantage of the best birding hours. To get there, simply drive out of Addis Ababa on either the new or old Ambo road until their intersection at Burayu, then continue in the direction of Ambo for another 10km till you see the sanctuary signposted on the right. Using public transport, buses from the Merkato bus station to Holeta, about 6km further west, can drop you at the roadside entrance. Travel time is hugely dependent on traffic as you leave Addis Ababa, so allow up to 90 minutes each way.

MENAGESHA NATIONAL FOREST [map, page 188] (*Entrance US$5, US$1 vehicle, US$6 video camera*) The magnificent Menagesha National Forest incorporates some 25km^2 of indigenous forest along with 13km^2 of exotic plantation, at altitudes ranging from 2,300m to 3,000m on the southern and western slopes of Mount Wechecha. Dominated by tall juniper, hagenia and podocarpus trees, it is the most substantial remaining patch of indigenous forest in the vicinity of Addis Ababa, a dense patch of dark green that can easily be spotted among the surrounding sea of golden brown meadows when flying into the capital from the west. Menagesha Forest has an unusual place in East African history, providing the earliest-known instance anywhere in the region of an official conservation policy being adopted. In the mid 15th century, Emperor Zara Yaqob became concerned at the high level of deforestation on Mount Wechecha, and he arranged for a large tract of juniper forest to be replanted with seedlings from the Ankober area. The forest was protected by imperial decree over the subsequent centuries, until eventually

Emperor Menelik II set it aside as the Menagesha State Forest in the late 1890s. The forest is inhabited by various large mammals and offers birders with limited time in Ethiopia the opportunity to see several key forest species. Above the forest line, the 3,385m-high Mount Wechecha, an extinct volcano, supports a cover of Afroalpine moorland dominated by *Erica* and *Helichrysum* species.

Getting there and away There are two routes to the forest. Coming from the north, it can be accessed along a rough 20km dirt road running south from the Ambo road a few kilometres past the village of Menagesha (just after the junction for the Born Free Sanctuary). This route was closed for several years after a bridge was washed away, and now the bridge is rebuilt it might still require a 4x4 during the rainy season. Just after crossing the bridge, the road passes through a village called Suba, from where it is only 2km further to the park headquarters.

From the south, follow the Jimma road for about 25km out of Addis Ababa to the small town of Sebeta, where you need to turn right on to the dirt access road to the forest just past the Meta Brewery. The approach road from Sebeta is 16km long and is generally in a fair state of repair except after heavy rain. Eventually you will come to a wooden sign marking the entrance to 'Africa's Oldest Park'. After the sign there are still a few kilometres left of double track to get to the park headquarters. There is no public transport to the park headquarters, though you might be able to hire a *bajaj* or *gari* from Sebeta.

Where to stay, eat and drink *Map, page 188*

Forestry Resthouse (3 rooms, 1 dorm) \011 515 4975. This simple but comfortable cottage at the forestry headquarters comprises 1 dbl room, 2 twin rooms, a lounge, a toilet & shower, & a kitchen with a fridge & gas cooker. The bedrooms are rented out individually. There is also an 8-bed dormitory with common shower & kitchen attached. Camping is permitted at the headquarters, as well as at designated spots along the walking trails. Tents are available for rent, but visitors should bring all their own food & drink. Booking is not normally necessary, but you might want to ring in advance to be on the safe side, especially over w/ends. *US$3/6 pp dorm/room. US$2–4 per tent (depending on size).* **$–$$**

What to see and do Menagesha is well organised for day visits and extended stays, and guides are available on weekends by appointment (*contact Ato Haile on* m *0911 389389*). Emanating from the forestry headquarters are five colour-coded walking trails ranging in length from 300m to 9km and variously taking in a lovely waterfall, as well as the 3,385m Damocha Peak. While intended for trekkers, most of these trails are accessible by 4x4 as well, which is great news if you only have one day and want to cover a lot of ground. The most frequently seen large mammals along these trails are guereza monkey and Menelik's bushbuck, but baboon and common duiker are also encountered on occasion, and leopard and serval are both present. The forest birding is superb. The endemic Ethiopian oriole and yellow-fronted parrot are regular around the headquarters. Several other endemics are likely to be encountered – black-winged lovebird, banded barbet, Abyssinian woodpecker and Abyssinian catbird among them – alongside other good forest birds such as crowned eagle, Narina trogon, white-cheeked turaco and Abyssinian ground thrush.

ADDIS ALEM [map, page 188] Situated 55km west of Addis Ababa on the Ambo road, the small town of Addis Alem (New World) was founded and named in 1900 by Menelik II, and it might well have become his capital were it not for the introduction of the fast-growing Australian eucalyptus tree to the Entoto Hills at a time when

Addis Ababa's wood resources were looking decidedly finite. The hilltop palace constructed for Menelik under the supervision of American and Indian engineers prior to 1902, when the planned relocation to Addis Alem was abandoned, became the Church of Ejare Debre Maryam Tsion (*entrance US$2.50*) which today pokes above the forest 1km from the main road to dominate the town's skyline. The circular church, decorated with paintings of lions and cheetahs, is of interest primarily for the Menelik-era treasures it keeps in its adjacent museum (*⊕ 08.30–15.00 Mon–Thu, 09.00–16.00 Sat–Sun; entrance inc with church*). These historical connections aside, Addis Alem is a rather dull little town. If you need to spend the night, the Alemu Gebre Selassie Hotel (*31 rooms; ☎011 283 0024; m 0911 067632*) at the Total filling station has spotlessly clean en-suite rooms for US$10.

CHILIMO GAJI FOREST [map, page 188] (☎*011 646 1150; m 0920 585286; entrance US$2.50*) The 50km² Chilimo Gaji Forest extends northward from the small town of Ginchi, 90km west of Addis Ababa on the Ambo road. An isolated relict of the dry evergreen montane forest that once covered much of this part of Ethiopia, it also incorporates patches of dense closed-canopy forest and offers some stunning views. Monkeys, birds and other forest creatures are abundant. The forest is reached along a dirt road branching north from Ginchi. This road enters the forest 4km out of Ginchi and runs through it for another 6km or so, making access very straightforward with your own transport. Alongside this road, the forest headquarters are housed in a royal lodge built by Haile Selassie for the Empress Menen to celebrate the birth of their son. Community-based management groups in various local villages have been assigned to control adjacent forest patches under signed forest management plans and agreements. These communities can also offer camping space and act as local forest guides. Fees for all services are negotiable.

AMBO This busy small town of around 100,000 inhabitants stands at an altitude of 2,100m on the Huluka River 125km west of Addis Ababa by road. It was temporarily renamed Hagare Hiwot (Healthy Country) by Haile Selassie, who was rather partial to bathing in its therapeutic hot springs, and is referred to as such on some maps. The hot springs still form the centrepiece of a low-key resort connected to the Ambo Ethiopia Hotel, and the town is also home to Ethiopia's most popular brand of mineral water. Other local attractions include the Guder Falls and Teltele Valley. Ambo is a good base for visits to the impressive Mount Wenchi.

Getting there and away Ambo lies 125km west of Addis Ababa, a 2-hour drive along an asphalt road that passes through a pretty but less than dramatic highland area of green cultivated fields set below distant mountains. Regular public transport runs from Addis Ababa to Ambo, leaving from the new Asco Bus Station east of the city centre. Public transport between Ambo and Nekemte runs throughout the day.

🏠 **Where to stay, eat and drink** *Map, page 216*

Budget

🏠 **Abebech Matafaria Hotel** (50 rooms) ☎011 236 2365/6. This popular 5-storey hotel lies in compact but shady grounds close to the bus station. The clean & modern rooms are fair value & the attached restaurant serves a wide range of local & international dishes in the US$3–4.50 range. Standard en-suite rooms all have king-size bed, hot shower, sat TV & balcony, & there are also twin rooms without TV. Tours to local attractions can be arranged at the front desk. *US$12 budget twin, US$16/17 standard sgl/twin, US$20 suite.* **$$**

🏠 **Ambo Ethiopia Hotel** (46 rooms) ☎011 236 2002; e amboethiopiahotel@gmail.com. Built as an elementary school in 1949 & converted to a hotel 6 years later, this former government

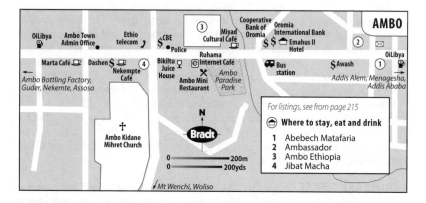

AMBO

For listings, see from page 215

Where to stay, eat and drink

1 Abebech Matafaria
2 Ambassador
3 Ambo Ethiopia
4 Jibat Macha

property, set in a leafy riverfront garden opposite the hot springs resort, was privatised in 2003. An attractive stone building with wooden floors & high ceilings, it remains a tempting & sensibly priced choice, though the rooms don't match the standard set by the (pricier) Abebech Matafaria. The restaurant serves good food indoors or alfresco at US$2–3 for a main course. Entrance into the hot springs is free for guests. Camping is also permitted. *US$5 twin with common shower, US$7/9/13 en-suite sgl/dbl/large suite with sat TV, US$6 per tent.* **$–$$**

Shoestring

Ambassador Hotel (34 rooms) ☏ 011 236 3971. With a good location right across from Abebech Matafaria & rooms with en-suite hot showers, this is worth the slightly higher price it asks by comparison with the other shoestring options. The entrance is hard to find but the name makes sense when you're guided there through a narrow alley next to the Ambassador tailor shop. *US$5 using common shower, US$6 en-suite dbl.* **$**

Jibat Macha Hotel (80 rooms) ☏ 011 236 2253. Located at the intersection of the Woliso & Wenchi roads, this popular shoestring choice has clean, spacious rooms with cold shower. The flowering grounds boast a bar & restaurant, set far enough away from the rooms that noise isn't a discouraging factor. *US$3.50 dbl with common shower, US$5/6 en-suite sgl/dbl.* **$**

What to see and do In addition to the local sites listed below, Ambo is the normal base for day trips to the spectacular Mount Wenchi and associated crater lake to the south.

Ambo Paradise Park [map, above] This hot springs complex and swimming pool (*entrance US$1*) stands in the town centre opposite the Ambo Ethiopia Hotel (guests of which get free entrance). It is worth a visit, whether you want to take a dip in the pool (which is refilled regularly, despite the greenish tint of the mineral-rich water) or just to enjoy the birdlife attracted to the surrounding fig trees.

Ambo Mineral Water Ambo has been the home of Ethiopia's most popular brand of mineral water since a bottling factory was established there in 1930. Rich in calcium, magnesium, potassium and other minerals, the water originates deep underground in a volcanic fissure, then percolates through the rocks to emerge through hot springs that have formed a crossroads on a major trade route for centuries. It is possible to take a guided tour around the bottling factory, 5km along the Guder road, if you call ahead (☏ 011 371 6242; e info@ambowater.com; w ambowater.com).

Teltele Valley [map, page 188] The steep wooded gorge carved by the Teltele and Huluka rivers prior to their confluence 4km west of Ambo contains three waterfalls, the tallest being 25m in height, along with a range of low-key wildlife including Anubis baboon, guereza and a great many birds. The valley is no longer conserved as a park, and a new government hospital now blocks the main access, but it is still visitable. To get there, follow the Guder road for 2km, then turn right on to a rough dirt track (marked by a Renewable Energy Power Station sign) and continue to the top of the hill from where you can hike down around the hospital to the ravine. The guards will allow you to view the falls from a rickety wooden platform for a nominal fee.

Guder Falls [map, page 188] Situated alongside the Nekemte road about 14km from Ambo, the Guder Falls (*entrance US$1.50, US$0.50 for video*) carries an impressive volume of water in the rainy season, and the surrounding riverine forest is rattling with monkeys and birds. To get there from Ambo, catch one of the regular minibuses that cover the 13km road to the small town of Guder, and then walk out along the Nekemte road for 1km, crossing a large bridge, until you reach an unmarked gate to the falls compound to your left. If you want to overnight in Guder, the best choice is the **Guder Falls Hotel** (*21 rooms;* \011 282 0137), which lies above the waterfall in green grounds inhabited by guereza and a variety of birds, charges US$3 for an adequate single room in a chalet, US$2.50 per tent for camping, and serves acceptable meals and drinks. The site would be a delightful retreat for a few days' relaxation if the dwellings and surrounding nature looked less unkempt.

MOUNT WENCHI [map, page 188] This massive extinct volcano rises to an altitude of 3,386m some 20km south of Ambo, and its upper slopes – an extensive plateau covered in Afroalpine heather and moorland – are traversed by a variable dirt road that continues onwards to the town of Woliso on the Jimma road. The volcano's densely cultivated but picturesque caldera supports a population of around 2,500 Oromo farmers, who mostly adhere to Orthodox Christianity. The caldera also encloses a 4km^2 crater lake dotted with small islands, one of which houses the venerable Monastery of Wenchi Chirkos, founded in the 13th century by Tekle Haymanot or in the 15th century by Emperor Zara Yaqob, depending on who you believe. The lake is now the focal point of the community-based Wenchi Eco-Tourism Association (WETA; \ *011 356 0009;* w *wenchi-crater-lake.com*), which can arrange a variety of guided treks, boat trips and pony treks around its shores.

Getting there and away Wenchi is most usually visited as a day trip from Ambo, though it could also be visited out of Woliso, or en route between the two. The gateway village of Wenchi, on the crater rim, lies about 27km from Ambo and 36km from Woliso via Daryun, with either approach taking around 1 hour in a private vehicle (4x4 recommended, especially during the rains). There is no formal public transport to Wenchi. At least one passenger 4x4 usually runs between Ambo and Woliso daily, and this can drop you at Wenchi, but there are no guarantees you will find transport back out the same day. The exception is Sunday, which is the main market day in Wenchi, so there is plenty of traffic in and out. Coming from the south, there is regular transport between Woliso and Daryun, but you would need to hitch or walk the last 13km from there to Wenchi.

Where to stay, eat and drink There is no accommodation at Wenchi. The owners of Ambo's Abebech Matafaria Hotel built a small lodge with eight thatched huts on the crater rim some years back, but it has never properly opened. That aside, the closest place to stay is the basic and inexpensive Hotel Beeteli in Daryun,

13km to the south. It is possible to camp near the lake for US$5 per tent, but you may be expected to pay an additional US$25 for a scout.

What to see and do All activities must be arranged through WETA, which levies a nominal entrance fee of US$2 per person at the signposted park headquarters, as well as an additional US$1.50 for parking. The most popular outing is probably the boat trip to Wenchi Chirkos, which costs US$2 per person. Hiking and guide-assisted pony-trekking options range from the 4km, 1½-hour Fincha Trail, which incorporates a visit to the monastery, to the 16km, 5-hour Bagoba-Abagalalcha trail, which follows the lakeshore before heading to the Dawala hot springs and waterfall. A guide costs US$9–15 per party, depending on your itinerary, while pony rental costs US$6–9 per animal including a local handler.

A more ambitious goal, 10km to the east, is Lake Dendi, which actually consists of two submerged near-circular 2km-wide craters linked by a 100m gap in their shared rim. According to one very excited local, the people who dwell near Lake Dendi live in mortal fear of a solitary but gigantic man-eating crocodile, for which reason they refuse to take boats on to the water. True or not, you could check this out for yourself by hiring a horse in Wenchi – the trip takes about 3 hours in each direction.

WOLISO This small town on the Jimma road 115km southwest of Addis Ababa is sometimes referred to as Ghion in reference to its hot spring, which is holy to Orthodox Christians. The holy water flows into the church of Woliso Maryam, 15 minutes' walk from the main road, which attracts many sick and disabled pilgrims. It is customary for those cured by the water to leave behind artefacts associated with their illness. A collection in the church grounds holds dozens of crutches and walking sticks, as well as chains left behind by the mentally ill, and charms and talismans by those possessed by evil spirits. No fee is charged to visit the church, but a donation is expected.

Getting there and away There is plenty of transport between Addis Ababa and Woliso throughout the day. Self-drivers might want to take a break at the small town of Debre Genet, where a church dedicated to St Gebriel is notable for its large golden dome, excellent paintings, and wooded grounds that have been known to throw up interesting birds such as white-cheeked turaco and Gambaga flycatcher.

Where to stay, eat and drink
Moderate

Negash Lodge (35 rooms) ☎ 011 341 0002/0147; m 0965 181850; e reservations@ negashresort.com; w negashresort.com. Arguably the nicest lodge in western Ethiopia, this recently renovated resort lies in shady green grounds centred on an outdoor pool fed by hot springs. It also contains a gym & one of Ethiopia's only indoor pools, but the far nicer & larger outdoor pool is also genuinely child friendly, since it has a proper shallow end. Both pools are not operational all week long: the outdoor one is emptied & cleaned from Mon to Wed, & the indoor one has employees in attendance at w/ends only. The main building hosts beautifully decorated dbl rooms, while the grounds are also dotted with *tukuls* modelled after various different traditional houses from around Ethiopia. A tree bar constructed under a gracious old ficus tree provides the perfect spot for viewing the garden's prolific birdlife & monkeys. The excellent restaurant serves continental-style chicken, beef & fish mains, as well as wood-fired pizzas, in the US$2.50–5 range. It is a popular w/end retreat from Addis Ababa, but also a good base for visits to Mount Wenchi & horseback excursions, which can be arranged through the in-house tour service. *US$38–45 B&B en-suite dbl or twin, US$65–75 family bungalows.* **$$$–$$$$**

Budget
🏠 **Belay Hotel** (39 rooms) ☎ 011 341 0639. A convenient location near the bus station & good food make this one of the better budget options. Rooms with full-size bed, en-suite hot shower & TV are also exceptionally clean. The large central bar is surrounded by a huge dining room with local & international dishes in the US$2–3 range. *US$6 using common shower, US$11.50/17/23 en-suite sgl/dbl/twin.* **$$**
🏠 **Ebenezer Hotel** (27 rooms) m 0935 525838. Located at the eastern end of town by the Total station, this hotel has well-sized

& comfortably furnished rooms, with TV & hot water, but cleanliness is not their best feature. The attached restaurant/café serves decent meals & has free internet. *Dbl US$6/8 en-suite dbl/queen.* **$–$$**

Shoestring
🏠 **Karazhi Hotel** (28 rooms) ☎ 011 341 1026. En route to the Negash Lodge, this hotel lacks food or a bar, but makes for a quiet place & a good night's sleep. *US$3 using common shower, US$6 en-suite sgl with cold water & TV.* **$**

NORTH TOWARDS DEBRE LIBANOS AND THE BLUE NILE GORGE

The most popular route north out of Addis is the 240km asphalt road to Dejen, a small town set on the northern rim of the Blue Nile Gorge, at the junction of the main road northwest to Bahir Dar and Gondar, and a less widely used route northeast to Dessie and Lalibela. Attractions along the way include the Muger Gorge and Debre Libanos, either of which could make for a straightforward day trip out of the capital, and the more remote Jemma Valley, which is of interest mainly to birdwatchers. You can drive directly between Addis Ababa and Dejen in around 4 hours, but would need to allow another couple of hours apiece for the diversions to Muger Gorge or Debre Libanos. One full day is required to explore the Jemma Valley.

MUGER GORGE The dramatic gorge carved by the Muger River, 70km north of Addis Ababa by road, is the most reliable site close to the capital for encounters with the endemic gelada monkey. The scenery is best in September and October, when the rolling grassland supports a multihued patchwork of wildflowers, and the waterfall that plunges 100m into the gorge below Durba is at its most voluminous. In addition to geladas, birders should look out for Verreaux's eagle, African harrier-hawk, Hemprich's hornbill, the endemic white-billed starling and lammergeier (the latter breeds on the cliffs near the waterfall).

Coming from Addis Ababa, follow the Dejen road for 40km to Chancho, then turn left on to a 30km road running northwest to Durba, from where the rock promontory housing the Durba Cement Factory offers spectacular views over the gorge. Plenty of public transport runs from the Merkato Autobus Terra to Chancho and on to Durba (allow 2 hours for the trip, longer if you need to change vehicles at Chancho). About 2km out of Chancho towards Durba, the Sibale River has a reputation for attracting unusual migrant birds alongside the endemic black-headed siskin, wattled ibis and Abyssinian longclaw.

JEMMA VALLEY Named after the tributary of the Blue Nile that flows through it, the Jemma Valley is of interest to birders as the most accessible site for Harwood's francolin, an Ethiopian endemic restricted to a handful of sites in the Blue Nile watershed. Set at altitudes of 1,300–2,000m, the acacia-covered valley supports several other interesting species including the endemic Rüppell's cliff-chat and white-throated seedeater, and speckle-fronted weaver, black-faced firefinch and stone partridge. Coming from Addis Ababa, follow the Dejen road for 85km to

GRAZIANI'S REVENGE

During the Italian occupation, Debre Libanos was the target of one of the most heinous atrocities committed by the Fascists, who believed some of its monks to have been involved in a failed attempt on Viceroy Graziani's life. On 20 May 1937, the Fascist troops descended on a Tekle Haymanot Day celebration close to the monastery, seized 297 monks, and shot them. A few days later, more than 100 young deacons attached to the Debre Libanos were slaughtered, and Graziani telegraphed Mussolini in Rome to say that: 'Of the monastery nothing remains.' In 1998, an article by Ian Campbell and Degife Gabre-Tsadik revealed that a third related massacre took place about a week later. At least 400 lay people who had attended the Tekle Haymanot Day celebration were detained by the Italians, separated from the monks, tied together, and transported by truck to Engecha on the old Ankober road. According to eyewitnesses interviewed by Campbell, the prisoners were lined up along the edge of two 10m-long trenches, mowed down with machine guns, and buried without ceremony where they fell. For four centuries prior to the 1937 massacre, Debre Libanos had served as the head of the Ethiopian Church, but as John Graham points out:

> Graziani not only killed the priests, he also killed Debre Libanos as the centre of the Church. It never recovered from the loss of the priests and teachers. Although it was resurrected, and a new and wonderful church was built there in the 1950s, it could never become the centre of learning it had previously been.

Muketuri, then turn right on to an unsurfaced 105km road that descends northeast via Lemi to the small town of Alem Katema, via a stretch of the Jemma River where the francolin is very common. Two buses daily run along this road, usually leaving Muketuri at about 05.30 and 08.00 and arriving at Alem Katema 4 hours later. Basic accommodation is available in Muketuri and Alem Katema.

DEBRE LIBANOS Situated 100km north of Addis Ababa, Debre Libanos is one of the oldest monasteries in Shewa and ranks among the most important anywhere in the country. It also boasts a magnificent setting at the base of the 700m-deep Washa Gadel (Dog Canyon), which was carved by a tributary of the Blue Nile in an area that supports plentiful gelada monkeys and birds. The monastery was reputedly founded in 1284 under the name Debre Asbo by Abuna Tekle Haymanot, the most revered of Ethiopian saints, and given its present name by Emperor Zara Yaqob in 1445, about two decades before it usurped Hayk Istafanos as the political centre of the Ethiopian Church under the powerful leadership of Abbot Marha Kristos. It was at Debre Libanos in 1520 that Emperor Lebna Dengal formally received the first Portuguese mission to Ethiopia; here, too, that the priest Francisco Álvares, a member of that mission, made contact with Pêro de Covilhã, the 'spy' sent overland to Ethiopia by King John three decades earlier. For some time afterwards, the chief abbot of Debre Libanos, called the Ichege, was the second most powerful official in the Ethiopian Orthodox Church. The monastery retained its political significance until the Italian occupation, when – as a perceived hotbed of patriotic anti-Italian sentiment – it was destroyed by the Fascist troops (see box above). It remains an important pilgrimage site for Orthodox Christians.

Getting there and away Debre Libanos is usually visited en route to Bahir Dar but it also makes for a perfectly feasible day trip from Addis Ababa. The surfaced 4km feeder road to the monastery runs eastward from the Dejen road exactly 100km north of the capital, a 2-hour drive either way in a private vehicle. At least two buses cover the route daily, leaving Addis Ababa before 07.00 and arriving 2–3 hours later. If you can't find public transport out of the valley, you may need to walk the 4km walk back to the junction, which is very steep but also wonderfully scenic, with a good chance of spotting geladas on the way. Ras Darge's Bridge lies close to the junction for Debre Libanos, and can be reached along a 500m footpath that starts in the grounds of the Ethio-German Park Hotel (which may ask a fee of around US$1.50).

⌂ Where to stay, eat and drink

⌂ **Ethio-German Park Hotel** [map, page 188] (14 rooms) m 0922 383490; w ethiogermanpark.com. Perched on the clifftop above Ras Darge's Bridge about 200m from the junction to Debre Libanos, this hotel offers fantastic views of the gorge, but the bungalows are poorly maintained & seem overpriced for what you get. Shortly before going to print, the hotel closed with no news of when it will reopen. *US$25/40 en-suite dbl/twin.* **$$$**

⌂ **Abdi International Hotel** (41 rooms) 011 135 2247. The pick of several budget hotels in the small town of Fiche, which lies on the Dejen road 15km north of the junction for Debre Libanos, this place has clean rooms & decent food. *Rates in the US$5–20 range.* **$$**

What to see and do

Debre Libanos church [map, page 188] (◔ *daily; entrance US$5 inclusive of photography, video cameras US$2.50*) The modern incarnation of Debre Libanos, built in the 1950s by Haile Selassie to replace the old church destroyed by the Italians, is tucked away in a small wooded gorge that feels intimate and secluded next to the surrounding canyon. The rather ostentatious exterior is typical of latter-day Ethiopian churches, but the attractive marble interior, its domed roof decorated with stained-glass windows of various saints, compensates. A signpost stipulates that entry is forbidden to menstruating women and to anybody who's had sexual intercourse within the previous 48 hours. From the new church, you can follow the footpaths along the adjacent stream – boosted by several waterfalls tumbling over the gorge's edge – to its derelict predecessor.

Tekle Haymanot's Cave About 10 minutes' walk from the main church, on the opposite side of the stream, a medieval cave church full of holy water is still in active use, though you'll need to pay another US$2.50 for a guard to show you the way. This cave was reputedly the personal sanctuary of Tekle Haymanot (literally 'Plant of Faith'), who is the most revered of all Ethiopian saints, having played an instrumental role in the 13th-century reinstatement of the Solomonic dynasty, as well as in the contemporaneous spread of Christianity in North Shewa. Tekle Haymanot is said to have spent seven years in this cave, standing on one leg and praying, while subsisting on one seed a year, fed to him by a bird, until his spare leg withered away and fell off! He also legendarily had six wings, a divine gift granted to him when the devil tried to kill him by cutting a rope he was using to ascend a cliff. Tekle Haymanot died in around 1313 aged 98 and was buried in the cliffside cave, though his body was reinterred in Debre Libanos a few decades later. The priest who keeps the keys to the cave here will gladly bless visitors with holy water, provided that they haven't eaten anything yet that day.

Ras Darge's Bridge Just past the junction for Debre Libanos, Ras Darge's Bridge is a lichen- and moss-stained stone construction that spans the Gur River (an indirect tributary of the Nile) immediately before it plunges hundreds of metres over a cliff into the valley below. Often but misleadingly referred to as the Portuguese Bridge, it has a convincingly timeworn appearance, but was actually built on the cusp of the 19th and 20th centuries by Ras Darge, a close relative of Emperor Menelik II. The bridge was constructed using the traditional sealant of limestone and crushed ostrich shell, and the views from the lip of the gorge above are fantastic. Cross the bridge and follow the cliff edge to your right for a view back to the waterfall and the Washa Gelada – Gelada Cave – where a troop of these striking primates sleeps most nights. Keep an eye open, too, for highland birds such as lammergeier, auger buzzard, Abyssinian ground hornbill and the endemic banded barbet, Abyssinian woodpecker, Rüppell's black chat and white-winged cliff-chat.

BLUE NILE GORGE This truly magnificent gorge, which follows the course of the Blue Nile as it arcs south of Lake Tana towards the Sudanese border, is often claimed to be the largest canyon in Africa, a title also frequently bestowed on Namibia's Fish River Canyon (quite how one measures these things is anybody's guess). Either way, it is a spectacular phenomenon, spanning altitudes of 2,500m to 1,200m, and comparable in scale to America's Grand Canyon. The main 40km road through the gorge connects Goha Tsion and Dejen, which stand on the southern and northern rim respectively, and although it is surfaced, it usually takes at least an hour to drive to due to the steep slopes and multiple curves. The scenery is fabulous, all terraced slopes and euphorbia-studded cliffs, and the modern Japanese bridge across the Nile can be photographed from the older Italian bridge, which now serves pedestrians only.

DEJEN This burgeoning town on the northern rim of the Blue Nile Gorge is the site of an important gypsum factory, as well as an imposing blue-domed church and prominent twin-minareted mosque that leer at each other from opposite sides of the main road. It is a key overnight stop for trucks, but of limited interest to travellers. If you do need to spend a night at Dejen, there is no shortage of accommodation, with the pick being the central Demiss Hotel (m 0911 357666; $), which charges US$6 for a clean double with en-suite cold shower, and also has an above-average restaurant renowned for its fresh *tibs*.

Part Three

NORTHERN ETHIOPIA

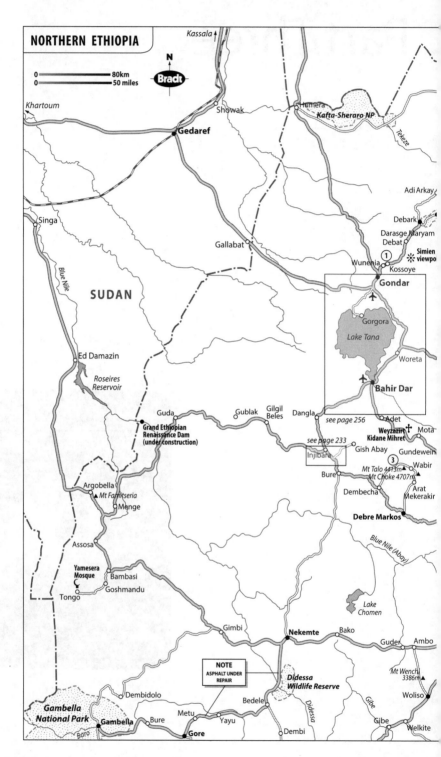

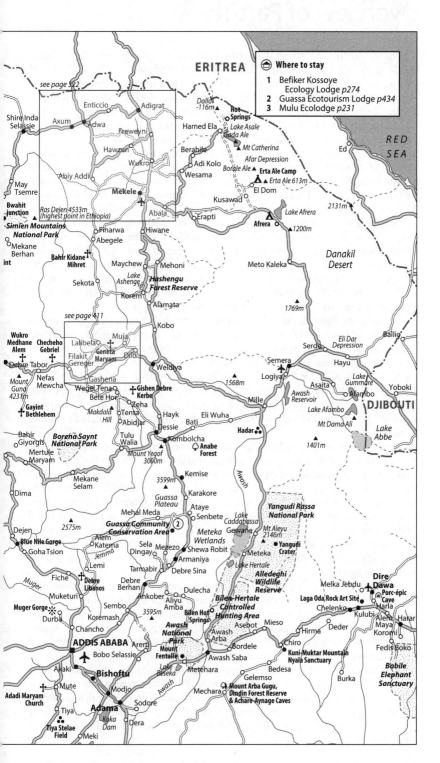

ERITREA

see page 322

Where to stay

1 Befiker Kossoye
  Ecology Lodge *p274*
2 Guassa Ecotourism Lodge *p434*
3 Mulu Ecolodge *p231*

RED
SEA

Shire Inda
Selassie
Axum
Enticcio
Adigrat
Adwa
Freweyni
Dallol
-116m
Hot
Springs
Hamed Ela
Lake Asale
Gada Ale
Hawzen
Berahile
Mt Catherina
Ed
Abiy Addi
Wukro
Adi Kolo
Afar Depression
Wesama
Borale Ale
Erta Ale Camp
May
Tsemre
Erta Ale 613m
Mekele
Kusawad
El Dom
2131m
Bwahit
junction
Ras Dejen 4533m
(highest point in Ethiopia)
Abala
Erapti
Afrera
Lake Afrera
**Simien Mountains
National Park**
1200m
Mekane
Berhan
Finarwa
Hiwane
Danakil
Desert
int
Abegele
Bahir Kidane
Mihret
Maychew
Mehoni
Meto Kaleka
Lake
Ashenge
**Hashengu
Forest Reserve**
Sekota
1769m
Korem
Alamata
Wukro
Medhane
Alem
Checheho
Gebriel
Lalibela
Muja
Kobo
Eli Dar
Depression
Ballig
Serdo
Semera
Hayu
Debre Tabor
Filakit
Gereger
Geneta
Maryam
Dillo
Weldiya
Logiya
Asaita
Lake
Gummare
Yoboki
Mount
Gund
4231m
Nefas
Mewcha
Gashena
1568m
Mille
Awash
Reservoir
Afambo
DJIBOUTI
Gayint
Bethlehem
Wegel Tena
Bete Hor
Gishen Debre
Kerbe
Zeha
Lake Afambo
Bahir
Giyorgis
Makdala
Hill
Tenta
Abidjar
Hayk
Bati
Hadar
Mt Dama Ali
Lake
Abbe
**Borena Saynt
National Park**
Tulu
Walia
Mount Yegof
3000m
Dessie
Kombolcha
1401m
Mertule
Maryam
**Anabe
Forest**
Mekane
Selam
3599m
Kemise
Dima
Karakore
Guassa
Plateau
Ataye
**Yangudi Rassa
National Park**
Dejen
2575m
Mehal Meda
Senbete
Lake
Caddabassa
Gewane
Mt Aleyu
2146m
Blue Nile Gorge
Alem
Katema
Sela
Dingay
Mezezo
Shewa Robit
Meteka
Yangudi
Crater
Goha Tsion
Jemma
Lemi
Armaniya
Meteka
Fiche
Debre
Libanos
Tarmabir
Debre Sina
Lake Hertale
**Alledeghi
Wildlife
Reserve**
Dire
Dawa
Muketuri
Debre
Berhan
Dulecha
Melka Jebdu
Porc-épic
Cave
Muger Gorge
Durba
Sembo
Ankober
Aliyu
Amba
3595m
**Bilen-Hertale
Controlled
Hunting Area**
Laga Oda Rock Art Site
Chelenko
Harla
Muger
Chancho
Koremash
Bilen Hot
Springs
Mieso
Kulubi
Alem
Maya
Harar
Koromi
ADDIS ABABA
Arerti
**Awash
National
Park**
Awash
Arba
Asebot
Hirma
Deder
Fedis Boko
Akaki
Bobo Selassie
Mount
Fentalle
Awash Saba
Bordele
Chiro
**Kuni-Muktar Mountain
Nyala Sanctuary**
**Babile
Elephant
Sanctuary**
Bishoftu
Lake
Beseka
Metehara
Gelemso
Bedesa
Burka
Mute
Modjo
Awash
Mechara
**Mount Arba Gugu,
Dindin Forest Reserve
& Achare-Aynage Caves**
Adadi Maryam
Church
Tiya
Sodore
Adama
Koka
Dam
Dera
**Tiya Stelae
Field**
Meki

225

Overview of Part Three

The historical circuit through the northerly federal regions of Amhara and Tigray has long formed the mainstay of Ethiopia's tourist industry. Traditionally, travel in this scenic highland area has pivoted on four main urban centres: the modern Amhara capital of Bahir Dar on the southern shore of Lake Tana, and a trio of former imperial capitals comprising ancient Axum and its towering engraved stelae, medieval Lalibela and its atmospheric complex of 13 rock-hewn churches, and post-Renaissance Gondar and its magnificent stone castles.

Over recent years, however, striking improvements in the regional road network and standard of tourist amenities have encouraged the emergence of several new tourist hubs, most notably the stunning Simien Mountains National Park north of Gondar, the lovely rock-hewn churches of Gheralta, and the volcano-studded Danakil Desert in the Afar Depression east of the Tigrayan capital, Mekele. And yet the northern circuit remains genuinely rich in off-the-beaten-track possibilities, ranging from the wildlife-rich Afroalpine moorland of the Guassa Plateau and Abune Yoseph to the colourful livestock market at Bati, the 2,800-year-old pre-Axumite temples at Yeha and Ado Akaweh, and any number of beautifully decorated ancient churches. Most travellers take one of three approaches to exploring the region, dependent to some extent on the time available to them, their budget and their need for creature comforts.

The first and least demanding approach is to fly between the main centres such as Bahir Dar, Gondar, Axum, Mekele and Lalibela, exploring their principal tourist attractions and towns, and possibly arranging the odd excursion to nearby places of interest. One could, in theory, get a good feel for the northern circuit over five or six days, since flights generally take only an hour or so, leaving one with plenty of time to explore in between. In practice, however, it would be advisable to dedicate about eight to ten days to a flying excursion around the northern circuit, allowing for a full day between flights to explore at leisure.

A more demanding option is to drive around the historical circuit on an organised tour or with a rented 4x4/driver, or – tougher still – to do the whole circuit using public transport. The advantages of driving over flying are that you get to see far more of the beautiful mountain scenery, and that you have the opportunity of escaping the relatively well-trodden tourist trail to visit more low-key attractions where tourists remain an infrequent sight. The disadvantage is that road travel is time-consuming and often exhausting – recent improvements to several roads notwithstanding, a realistic minimum of 10–12 days is required to cover the circuit by road (excluding a side trip to the Danakil), and closer to three weeks would be realistic using public transport.

Northern Ethiopia is covered in this book as it tends to be on the ground, in a broadly clockwise direction, running northwest from Addis Ababa to Bahir Dar and Gondar, then northeast via the Simiens to Axum and northeast Tigray, then south through Mekele and Lalibela to Dessie, then southwest back to Addis Ababa. Note, however, that as the road network in northern Ethiopia has improved and expanded over recent years, so too are travellers faced with an increasing number of viable alternative route possibilities through the region. Among the most popular for those travelling by road is to drive directly to Lalibela from Gondar or Bahir Dar, bypassing Axum and the rest of Tigray. Meanwhile, for those flying around, the most significant recent development is that Mekele – the main springboard for road travel to the Danakil and Gheralta – now threatens to usurp Axum as the most important air gateway to Tigray.

HIGHLIGHTS

BAHIR DAR (page 241) Set on the southern shore of Lake Tana, the city of Bahir Dar is a bustling commercial centre with a wonderful market and a rewarding live music scene.

LAKE TANA MONASTERIES (page 254) A UNESCO biosphere reserve renowned for its varied and plentiful birdlife, Lake Tana is also home to more than a dozen colourfully painted monasteries set on remote forested peninsulas and islands such as Zege and Dek.

BLUE NILE FALLS (page 251) This sensational waterfall an hour's drive south of Bahir Dar is a must-visit in the rainy season, but it frequently disappoints at other times of year, when most of the river's flow is diverted to drive a neighbouring hydro-electric generator.

GONDAR (page 269) The so-called Camelot of Ethiopia served as the imperial capital for almost 300 years and is noted for its impressive 16th-century castles, as well as the beautifully painted Church of Debre Berhan Selassie.

SIMIEN MOUNTAINS NATIONAL PARK (page 290) This staggeringly scenic massif – the fifth highest in Africa – is home to the country's main concentrations of the endemic gelada monkeys and Walia ibex. Traditionally the preserve of hardened hikers, it now also forms a feasible goal for an overnight trip out of Gondar.

AXUM (page 302) The former capital of the ancient Axumite Empire – legendarily home to both the Queen of Sheba and the Ark of the Covenant – is best known for the engraved obelisks (stelae) that tower over its horizon, but there's plenty else to see here, including ruined palaces, trilingual tablets recounting events that took place 2,000 years ago, and some of the oldest churches in Ethiopia.

MEHELELA PROCESSION (page 313) The easiest religious festival to slot into a casual itinerary, the atmospheric Mehelela takes place before sunrise in Axum almost 100 times annually (on the first seven days of each of the Ethiopian months) and follows the route used by Menelik I when, reputedly, he first brought the Ark of the Covenant to Ethiopia 3,000 years ago.

YEHA TEMPLE (page 318) The enigmatic and half-understood nature of Axum's distant past is amplified by a visit to this extraordinary 2,700-year-old pre-Axumite temple – as tall as a five-storey building – dedicated to the mysterious Sabaean deity known as Almaqah.

GHERALTA ESCARPMENT (page 346) Older than their counterparts at Lalibela, and generally more isolated and remote, the cluster of rock-hewn churches carved into the sandstone cliffs and outcrops of Gheralta are remarkable for their starkly beautiful surrounds, wealth of old paintings and almost biblical atmosphere.

ERTA ALE (page 376) The legendary 'Smoking Mountain' of the Danakil, the utterly spectacular Erta Ale is an active shield volcano that contains the world's oldest semi-permanent lava lake.

DALLOL (page 374) Situated below sea level, the sulphurous geysers of Dallol feed a surreally beautiful field of frost-textured multihued pools, vents and crystalline formations.

ASAITA (page 379) Set on a rise overlooking the Awash River, Asaita may no longer be the capital of Afar, but it is the region's most characterful town, best visited on Tuesday, the main market day.

LALIBELA (page 393) The acknowledged highlight of the northern circuit is the complex of rock-hewn churches in and around Lalibela, an inspirational active shrine to a Christian civilisation that predates its northern European equivalent by centuries.

BATI MARKET (page 429) Held every Monday, Ethiopia's largest market attracts tens of thousands of traditionally attired Oromo, Afar and Amhara villagers to the otherwise undistinguished town of Bati, to buy, sell and barter camels, other livestock, fresh produce and pretty much anything else you can name.

GUASSA COMMUNITY CONSERVATION AREA (page 432) Ethiopian wolves, gelada monkeys and plenty of endemic birds can be found in this accessible highland reserve, which was first set aside by the community 400 years ago and is now the site of a well-organised community project and a great little lodge.

6

Bahir Dar and Lake Tana

A popular first stop on the northern circuit, Bahir Dar has a geographically poignant location on the southern shore of the 3,673km² Lake Tana, adjacent to the outlet where the Blue Nile starts its 4,500km journey to the Mediterranean via Sudan and Egypt. The administrative capital of Amhara Region, Bahir Dar is a bustling modern city with a lively traditional music scene, but it also serves as the springboard for two other major attractions. These are the seasonally sensational Blue Nile Falls, about 30km south of town, and the wealth of atmospheric and beautifully decorated monastic churches that adorn the forested peninsulas and islands of Ethiopia's largest lake.

Bahir Dar is situated around 500km northwest of Addis Ababa and the majority of visitors travel there by air. The two cities are also connected by two asphalt road routes that diverge at Dejen, which stands on the northern rim of the Blue Nile Gorge around 240km north of Addis Ababa (page 222). Heading north from Dejen, you can choose between a 315km westerly road through Debre Markos and Injibara and a 255km easterly road through Mota. With an early start, it is possible to travel between Addis Ababa and Bahir Dar in one day using either road, but you could also break up the trip with an overnight stop, allowing time to explore the likes of Debre Libanos, Debre Markos, Mount Choke, and the crater lakes and waterfalls around Injibara. Alternatively, for devotees of the truly offbeat, a more circuitous and little-used route via Benishangul-Gumuz, the most obscure of Ethiopia's nine federal regions, and its administrative capital Assosa, loops northwest from Addis Ababa via Ambo and Nekemte before reconnecting with the main road to Bahir Dar at Injibara.

DEJEN TO BAHIR DAR VIA DEBRE MARKOS

The western route between Dejen and Bahir Dar via Debre Markos and Injibara has been surfaced in its entirety for some years now and is favoured over its eastern counterpart by almost all long-haul traffic, despite being 60km longer.

DEBRE MARKOS The largest and best-equipped town between Addis Ababa and Bahir Dar, Debre Markos (Mountain of St Mark) is the former capital of the defunct province of Gojjam, and it now supports a population of around 75,000. Set at an altitude of 2,450m in the moist highlands north of the Blue Nile Gorge, it has a chilly highland ambience – indeed, it was formerly known as Mankorar (Cold Place) – and a neatly laid-out centre focused on the parklike Negus Tekle Haymanot Square running south from the main roundabout. Historically, the town's main claim to fame is as the site where some 14,000 Italian troops surrendered to a 300-strong division of the combined Ethiopian–Allied army in April 1941, precipitating the collapse of the Italian occupation. The closest thing to a must-see is the impressively decorated church of Debre Markos, built in 1869 on an attractive juniper-covered hilltop 600m south of the modern town centre. It is also a useful base for day trips to Choke Mountain.

Getting there and away Debre Markos lies 300km (5–6 hours) northwest of Addis Ababa and 250km (4–5 hours) south of Bahir Dar, along a good surfaced road. Public transport is plentiful, but typically takes an hour or two longer. The best option is the direct Abay Bus, which leaves Addis Ababa from Meskel Square at 05.00 daily, arrives at Debre Markos at around 10.30, then starts the return trip at 11.00. The bus leaves Debre Markos from in front of the booking office (m *0931 494949*) below the Gozamen Hotel.

⌂ Where to stay, eat and drink *Map, opposite*

⌂ **Gozamen Hotel** (40 rooms) 058 178 0053; m 0935 983930; e gozamenhotel@gmail. com; . Situated on the main roundabout, this is far & away the top hotel in Debre Markos, despite looking a little less immaculate than when it opened in 2014. An airy ground-floor lobby with leather & dark-wood furnishing incorporates a slick wine bar & superior restaurant with the most reliable Wi-Fi in town & serves a varied selection of local & international dishes in the US$3–4 range. Smart en-suite rooms come with flatscreen TV & hot water. Fair value. *US$31/44/56 sgl/dbl/suite.* **$$$**

⌂ **LBS Hotel** (39 rooms) m 0911 464193; e mmekuriaw@yahoo.com; w lbshoteldebremarkos.com. Opened in 2017, this friendly & enthusiastically staffed hotel has smallish but clean en-suite rooms with TV, hot water & balcony. The 1st-floor restaurant has a varied menu, including a lengthy list of salads, with mains in the US$3–4 range. *From US$20 dbl.* **$$$**

⌂ **FM International Hotel** (30 rooms) 058 771 6670; e fmhotel2000@gmail.com. Also on the main roundabout, this cylindrical multistorey hotel has adequate en-suite rooms with LED TV, hot shower & Wi-Fi. A bright ground-floor café with terrace serves fresh pastries, juice & coffee, & there's a more formal restaurant on the 1st floor. *US$14/24 dbl/twin.* **$$**

⌂ **Fikre Selam Hotel** (21 rooms) 058 771 6902; m 0922 260562. Probably the best of several decent & well-priced shoestring high-rises clustered within a block of the bus station, this has clean dbl rooms with en-suite hot shower & a traditionally decorated bar in the courtyard. The nearby Alazar, Central, National & Ethiopia hotels all look like good fallbacks if it's full. *US$8 sgl.* **$**

✗ **Habesha Cultural House** This traditionally decorated eatery & bar has indoor & terrace seating & serves good shiro, *tibs* & other local dishes for US$2.50 or less.

CHOKE MOUNTAIN Rising to 4,070m some 40km northeast of Debre Markos, this ancient volcanic massif, also known as Choqa Terara, is incised by steep riverine valleys that held glaciers during the last ice age. An important watershed feeding the Nile Basin, Choke is cultivated up to the 3,300m contour, while higher altitudes support an indigenous cover of grassland and moorland studded with giant lobelias. Based out of Debre Markos, an easy goal for a day trip is Arat Mekerakir (Four Arguments), a quartet of basaltic peaks which offer fabulous views as far as Bahir Dar on a clear day, and can be reached by heading out on the unsurfaced Wabir road, passing through the hamlet of Gedamawit after 27km, then continuing northward for another 8km. Another 10km or so north towards Wabir, the indigenous Aba Jime Forest, focal point of the newly created Choke Biosphere Reserve, supports a variety of endemic birds along with guereza monkey, Anubis baboon, bushpig and bushbuck. Closer to Wabir, the spectacularly located 150m-high Molalit Cave has been inhabited by the same family of cattle herders for five generations (reputedly, since 1902) and also contains a small natural lake.

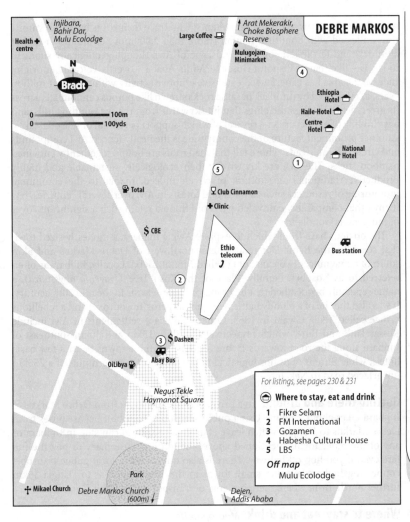

Injibara,
Bahir Dar,
Mulu Ecolodge

Health + centre

Large Coffee

Arat Mekerakir,
Choke Biosphere
Reserve

Mulugojam
Minimarket

N

Bradt

0 ———— 100m
0 ———— 100yds

④

Ethiopia
Hotel

Haile-Hotel

Centre
Hotel

National
Hotel

⑤

Total

Club Cinnamon

+ Clinic

①

$ CBE

Ethio
telecom

Bus station

②

③ $ Dashen

Abay Bus

OiLibya

Negus Tekle
Haymanot Square

For listings, see pages 230 & 231

⊖ **Where to stay, eat and drink**

1 Fikre Selam
2 FM International
3 Gozamen
4 Habesha Cultural House
5 LBS

Off map
Mulu Ecolodge

✝ Mikael Church   Debre Markos Church
(600m)↓

Park

Dejen,
Addis Ababa

For an extended visit to Choke, the recently opened Mulu Ecolodge [map, page 224] (**m** *0932 936599, 0929 116212;* **e** *muluecolodge@gmail.com;* **w** *mululodge.com;* **f** *muluecolodge*) offers a variety of accommodation in the €20–80 range (all full board) and enforces a minimum stay of three nights. The ecolodge works closely with local communities and stands in a substantial patch of indigenous forest that supports guereza monkey, Menelik's bushbuck, common duiker and various endemic birds. It also allows visitors to experience traditional highland farming methods and offers day walks to nearby waterfalls and riverine valleys, horseback excursions, a visit to a nearby village market, and extended treks or 4x4 trips to all the sites described above. To get to Mulu, follow the Bahir Dar road north out of Debre Markos for 50km to Dembecha, then turn right on to the unsurfaced Feres Bet road and continue northeast for another 35km.

INJIBARA AND AWI ZONE Bisected by the main asphalt road to Bahir Dar, the autonomous administrative zone of Awi, to the northwest of Debre Markos, is named after its Agaw-speaking inhabitants, who trace their roots back to Axumite times. Blessed with bountiful rainfall (more than 2,000mm per annum at higher altitudes) and fertile red soil, the landscape of Awi, though geologically subdued today, is – like that of Bishoftu closer to Addis Ababa – overtly volcanic in origin. Indeed, the area has experienced extensive eruptive activity within the last million years, as evidenced by the black basaltic rocks strewn like porous cannonballs across its green fields, the gigantic plugs that jut skywards from the surrounding hills, and a sprinkling of extinct craters, several of which support perennial or seasonal lakes. Another prominent feature of the countryside is the neatly fenced Awi compounds and circular homesteads, whose tall thatched roofs are bound together by entwined bamboo sticks. The Awi are known for their ecologically sustainable and highly productive traditional agricultural practices. Indeed, thanks to the communal monitoring of resources such as water and forests in Awi over several centuries, few if any other comparably cultivated parts of Ethiopia retain such a significant cover of indigenous woodland.

The obvious base from which to explore Awi is Injibara, a modestly sized town that straddles the Bahir Dar road 140km northwest of Debre Markos and 5km south of a magnificent volcanic plug called Mount Zivixi. Locally, Injibara is often referred to as Kosober, literally 'Place of the Koso Tree' (*Hagenia abyssinica*), a name reputedly bequeathed to it by Emperor Haile Selassie in the mid 20th century. It was also the site of a bloody battle between Emperor Tewodros II and a rebellious prince called Tedla Gwalu in 1863. Other significant settlements in Awi include Kessa, Tilili and Bure, which respectively lie 8km, 15km and 30km southeast of Injibara along the road towards Debre Markos. All these towns boast a few basic hotels, while Bure is of minor logistical note as the northern terminus of a 250km unsurfaced road to Nekemte.

Getting there and around In a private vehicle, the drive from Debre Markos to Injibara takes about 2 hours. Using public transport, your best bet are buses from Debre Markos to Dangla, which leave at around 09.00 and can stop in Injibara or any of the other towns mentioned above, though it is customary to pay the full fare even if you hop off halfway. There is also quite a bit of local public transport connecting Injibara to other small towns in the area, as well as to Dangla 35km further north, from where there is plenty of transport on to Bahir Dar.

 Where to stay, eat and drink *Map, opposite*

Arididen Hotel (40 rooms) 058 227 0488; m 0924 359797. Situated opposite the conspicuous & ostensibly smarter (but actually rather scruffy & overpriced) Karned Hotel, this unpretentious medium-rise has clean & spacious en-suite rooms with TV & hot water. *US$5/8 sgl/dbl.* **$**

Adinos Hotel (66 rooms) m 0911 003455. This quiet owner-managed hotel offers the choice of sgls with ¾ bed, & access to powerful common showers in the old wing, or much nicer & brighter en-suite rooms with TV & hot water in a multistorey building that opened in 2016. A fair choice of food & drinks is available. *US$4 sgl in old wing, or US$8/12 sgl/dbl in new wing.* **$$**

What to see and do
Fang Waterfall (*Entrance US$2*) This attractive cascade on the Fetam River south of Tilili is most notable for the striking rock formations it has exposed – a grid of shiny black hexagonal basalt columns whose crystalline shape is associated with lava that cooled unusually quickly. It tumbles about 20m into a tree-lined gorge, and can be very impressive after heavy rain, while in less torrential circumstances

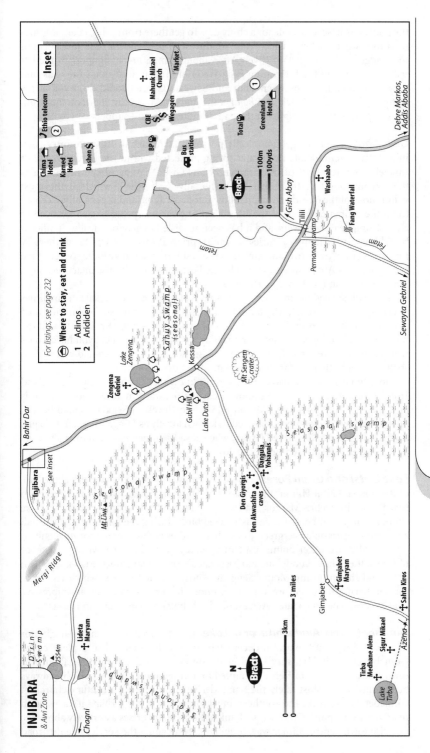

the pool at its base looks safe for a chilly dip. To get there from Tilili, take the gravel road to Sewayta Gebriel, which runs southwest of the Injibara road just north of the bridge across the Fetam River. After about 2km, a green signpost to the left reads 'Welcome to the Interesting Fang Waterfall'. If you don't fancy the walk out, very occasional buses between Tilili and Sewayta Gebriel could drop you at the signpost, or you could pick up a *bajaj* at the junction. It is only 300m on foot from the signpost to the waterfall, but the path is quite steep and slippery.

Gish Abay The most geographically poignant landmark in Agaw country is an inherently unremarkable freshwater spring protected within the grounds of Gish Mikael Monastery east of Injibara. Known as Gish Abay or Abay Minch, this is the starting point of the Gilgil Abay (literally 'Calf Nile'), which is the most voluminous of the 60-odd rivers that flow into Lake Tana, and is generally accepted to be the ultimate source of the Blue Nile. The sacred spring is also believed to have strong healing powers, and it has been regarded as geographically significant by Ethiopians for many centuries – Spanish priest Pedro Páez was taken there by Emperor Susenyos in 1613, making him the first European to visit the source of the Blue Nile. Gish Abay was also visited by the Portuguese Jesuit missionary Jerónimo Lobo in 1629, and by James Bruce in 1770.

Gish Mikael lies 90 minutes' walk south of the town of Sekala (sometimes referred to as Gish Abay), which can be reached along a signposted 40km side road running northeast from the main Bahir Dar at Tilili. It is not permitted to visit the holy spring if you've eaten anything that day, or the priests suspect you have, so it's worth getting there early. There are a few basic hotels in Sekala, should you wish to spend the night there before heading out.

Close to Gish Abay, a trio of holy springs known locally as the Father, Son and Holy Spirit emerge from a hole above a cave into a warm natural pool where it is possible to swim. Further afield, some 15km northwest of Sekala, a small field of obelisks, all but one of them collapsed, is known locally as Dingay Yegragn (Gragn's Rocks) in reference to Ahmed Gragn, who caused so much havoc in the Lake Tana hinterland in the 16th century (page 26).

Lake Dutsi and Gubil Forest The small and seasonal Lake Dutsi lies at the base of the domed Gubil Hill on the western outskirts of Kessa, a small junction town that flanks the Debre Markos road some 2km south of Lake Zengena. The lake supports large numbers of water-associated birds during the rains, while the small and readily accessible evergreen forest that swathes Gubil is noted for its highland forest birds. Two other points of natural interest lie within easy walking distance of Kessa: the Sahuy Floodplain and associated seasonal lake northeast of the main road, and the imposing Mount Sengem, whose wooded slopes, which rise from the southern outskirts of town to an altitude of over 2,500m, hide an impressive 1,000m-deep volcanic crater. At least one basic **hotel** is to be found in Kessa.

Gimjabet, Den Akwashita and Lake Tirba Given the Ethiopian gift for mythologising, you'd expect a decent tall story to be attached to a place called Gimjabet (literally 'Treasury'). But evidently not – local information about this town 10km southeast of Kessa amounted to nothing more than a blank 'It's always been called that.' Most likely the name derives from the 13th-century church of Gimjabet Maryam on the southern outskirts of town, or perhaps it's a waggish reference to the plush Commercial Bank of Ethiopia that rises assertively above the low-rise town centre? Either way, roughly halfway along the serviceable dirt road between Kessa and Gimjabet, immediately outside the compound of Den Giyorgis, the Den Akwashita Caves comprise four overgrown sinkhole-like entrances that open into a large natural tunnel said to run for several kilometres underground. In times of war, the cave system has often served as a refuge (perhaps treasure was stored there too?), and a holy subterranean river passes within 50m of the last entrance, though you need a torch to see it.

The pretty 153m-deep Tirba Crater Lake is nestled in a 1km² caldera 4km southwest of Gimjabet. To get there, follow the road to Azena southwest for 3km until you see Sahta Kiros Church to the left. From here, it's a roughly 30-minute walk to the lakeshore Tirba Medhane Alem, following a footpath that starts opposite Sahta Kiros and passes the Church of Sigur Mikael on the way.

Lake Zengena *(Entrance US$1 pp, plus optional US$4 guide fee)* Foremost among Awi's beauty spots, the spectacular freshwater Zengena Crater Lake makes for an idyllic picnic spot en route between Debre Markos and Bahir Dar. The forested rim of this near-perfect crater is set at an altitude of 2,500m, and the lakeshore lies perhaps 30m below this, but the lake itself is 166m in depth, making it the second deepest in the country. The northern slopes of the crater support an artificial cypress plantation, as well as the recently constructed Church of Zengena Gebriel, but the southern slopes retain a cover of lush indigenous acacia woodland. Grivet monkeys are much in evidence, and there is plenty of birdlife too. The lake is 6km south of Injibara, a couple of hundred metres east of the Debre Markos road, and clearly signposted. A steep 50m footpath leads downhill from the parking area to the shore.

DEJEN TO BAHIR DAR VIA MOTA

Around 60km shorter than the road through Debre Markos, the little-used easterly route connecting Dejen to Bahir Dar via Mota is set to grow in popularity now that it is surfaced as far as Sevatamit (the junction village for the Blue Nile Falls), around 10km before Bahir Dar. It provides access to several interesting historical sites, as well as to the lake Bahir Giyorgis.

DEJEN TO GUNDEWEIN The 100km stretch of road connecting Dejen to Gundewein – the junction for a new surfaced road running to Dessie via Mekane Selam (page 439) – can be covered in around 3 hours without stops. It offers access to two little-visited but interesting churches. The first of these coming from the south is Dima Giyorgis, a medieval monastery set on the rim of the Blue Nile Gorge 14km along a track that branches to the east from the main road at Talema, some 45km north of Dejen and 15km past the small town of Bichena. Back on the main road, the small town of Debre Work (Mountain of Gold), only 7km north of Talema, is home to the hilltop monastery of Debre Work Maryam, which was reputedly founded in Axumite times, has a stone treasury constructed during the 17th-century reign of Yohannes I, and holds several important treasures including an icon said to have belonged to St Luke. Both of these churches are described in some detail in Paul Henze's *Ethiopian Journeys* (page 644).

BAHIR GIYORGIS About 7km northeast of Gundewein as the crow flies, Bahir Giyorgis (literally 'Sea of George') is a lovely 1km² crater lake whose southern shore is hemmed in by steep and lushly forested cliffs pockmarked with three large caves. An unusual feature of the lake are the grass islands that float across its surface,

6

occasionally merging or separating in a manner regarded by locals to be symbolic of the state of the nation (the merging of two islands predicts a period of peace and unity, while a split heralds war or instability). To get to Bahir Giyorgis from Gundewein, follow the new surfaced road towards Dessie east for 5km, then turn northeast on to a track that passes a series of rural homesteads before reaching the forested southern rim after another 5km.

MERTULE MARYAM Boasting a memorable location overlooking the western rim of the Blue Nile Gorge about 30km east of Gundewein, the moderately sized town of Mertule Maryam is named after the venerable monastery that graces a wooded hilltop on its southern outskirts. According to local tradition, Mertule Maryam ('Home of Mary'; *entrance US$3*) is the country's second-oldest church site (after Debre Maryam Tsion in Axum), established during the reign of Abraha and Atsbeha at what was then an important Axumite market town called Agere Selam (Land of Peace). The original church was destroyed by Queen Gudit, after which the site was probably abandoned for several centuries prior to being resurrected as a monastery in the 14th century. Today, the monastery is best known for its disused cruciform stone church, which was constructed in the dying years of the 16th century by Empress Eleni, the long-lived and highly influential wife of Zara Yaqob, and later served as the coronation site of Emperor Susenyos. Built with assistance from the Portuguese settler Pêro de Covilhã, Eleni's palatial church is probably the oldest European-influenced building in Ethiopia, and though much of it is now ruined or obscured by iron sheeting, several ornately engraved apses and arches are still intact. Close by, the circular main church, which probably dates to the 18th or 19th century, has an interior decorated with paintings of a similar vintage. Some fascinating church treasures, including a blue robe confiscated from the body of Ahmed Gragn after his death and a dress once worn by the Empress Eleni, will soon be placed on permanent display in the museum that was under construction in 2014. Providing support to Mertule Maryam's claims to antiquity is a hexagonal column, now topped by a cross, that originally formed part of a sacrificial altar, suggesting that in pre-Christian times a Sabaean temple stood on the same site as the modern-day church. Immediately outside the church compound are several circular two-storey homesteads reminiscent of the traditional houses in Lalibela. Mertule Maryam lies about 40 minutes' drive from Gundewein alongside the new road to Dessie.

MOTA TO BAHIR DAR Situated 30km northwest of Gundewein, Mota is the largest town on the eastern route between Dejen and Bahir Dar, supporting a population estimated at 100,000. It lay at the southern end of an important royal fiefdom during the early Gondarine period, and remained a significant regional market town into the early 20th century. Mota is the closest town to Sebara Dildi, the 17th-century 'Broken Bridge' built across the Nile during the rule of Emperor Fasilidas, and the subject of an aborted search by Thomas Pakenham, described in his book *The Mountains of Rasselas*. All things considered, 4 hours in either direction by mule or foot does seem a long way to go to see a no-longer-functional bridge, but for those in pursuit of the truly esoteric, it might be an alluring option!

Several more compelling but equally little-visited historical sites lie in the vicinity of Mota. The church of **Weyzazirt Kidane Mihret** [map, page 224], situated some 5km east of the Bahir Dar road 15km north of Mota, was constructed for Princess Seble-Wengiel, the daughter of Emperor Fasilidas. It is adorned with some superb 17th-century paintings (including a series on the colonnades depicting the 12 Apostles) and it also houses the mummified remains of its founder and her husband. **Gonji Tewodros**, built on the rim of the Blue Nile Gorge by one of the sons of Emperor Fasiladas, can be reached by continuing along the main Bahir Dar road for 8km past the turn-off to Weyzazirt, then following a side road to the east for 9km. A few inexpensive lodgings can be found in Mota.

About 90km past Mota, you pass through tiny Debre May, the closest town to a trio of minor Gondarine historic sites – Gimb Giyorgis, Gimb Maryam and Yebaba – described on page 253. Around 20km further, only 10km before arriving at Bahir Dar, you arrive at Sevatamit, where a right turn leads to the Blue Nile Falls (page 251).

BENISHANGUL-GUMUZ REGION

The most remote of Ethiopia's nine federal regions, Benishangul-Gumuz is also one the smallest and most thinly inhabited, comprising some 50,700km^2 of dry wooded savannah whose population is estimated at slightly less than one million. Governed from the small town of Assosa, which lies about 270km southwest of Injibara as the crow flies, Benishangul-Gumuz is warmer and lower lying than the highlands to its east, and the terrain is mostly quite hilly, supporting a rather monotonous cover of broadleaved woodland that starts to look very parched towards the end of the dry season. Geographically, the region's dominant feature is the Blue Nile, which flows through it in a broadly northwesterly direction for more than 300km before crossing into Sudan west of Guda. The Grand Ethiopian Renaissance Dam (also known as the Millennium Dam), currently under construction 15km east of the border, will be a 1,800km^2, 63 billion m^3 reservoir powering Africa's largest hydro-electric plant, with an expected output of 6,000MW. Work on the dam started in 2011 and was scheduled for completion in 2017, but as of August of that year it was only 60% ready.

Benishangul-Gumuz is traditionally home to half a dozen ethnolinguistic groups, the most numerically significant of which are the Berta, Gumuz and Shinasha, all of whom retain a largely traditional lifestyle in rural areas. These days, however, around 35% of the regional population is of Oromo or Amhara origin, largely as a result of an extensive resettlement programme undertaken during the drought of 1984. In touristic terms, Benishangul-Gumuz is arguably the least interesting of Ethiopia's federal regions, particularly as most of its limited attractions can only be visited with an official permit from Assosa and a guide. That said, the region retains an offbeat charm that makes it an ideal destination for travel for its own sake, particularly if you enjoy rural markets. The route through Guda and Assosa is also increasingly popular with operators crossing to Bahir Dar and Lake Tana from the Surmi region south of Jimma.

ASSOSA The medium-altitude administrative hub of Benishangul-Gumuz boasts few of the trappings of a regional capital. True, it has grown substantially in recent years, and seen plenty of modernisation, but it remains a somewhat remote and parochial town, with a population estimated at fewer than 25,000, and an innately dusty (or, seasonally, muddy) character that isn't quite contained by the recently asphalted main roads. Tourist attractions amount to little more than the central market (busiest on Wednesday and Saturday), the inauspicious tomb of the town's founder, Sheikh Khojele Al-Hassen (on the road out to the stadium), and a decidedly quirky regional museum (page 239). Still, for those who want to get right off the beaten track, Assosa is quite an agreeable place, served by a couple of adequate hotels and eateries, and it's increasingly accessible from Addis Ababa both by air and coach.

History The discovery of Stone Age tools dating back hundreds of thousands of years in caves close to Assosa confirms that Benishangul has a long history of human habitation. Around 5,000 years ago, pastoralists from Sudan settled in the area, bringing with them domestic livestock, as well as introducing decorated pottery and a culture of schematic rock painting that flourished until around 2,000 years ago. In more recent times, Benishangul has served as a kind of buffer zone between the Christian empires of the Ethiopian Highlands and the animist cultures of the Sudanese Nile Valley.

In 1521, Benishangul was co-opted into the Sudanese sultanate of Sennar (also known as Funj). It was at around this time that Menge, 40km northeast of Assosa, was settled by the Berta, who brought with them the sacred oblong rock known as Bela Shangul (from which derives the name Benishangul). Sennar peaked in importance in the late 16th and early 17th centuries, but it endured until 1821, when it was conquered by Turkish Ottomans and fell under the indirect rule of Egypt. Over the next 60 years, the region thrived as a centre of trade, and was settled by Arab merchants who introduced Islam to the region and whose half-caste descendants came to form a ruling elite known as the watawit. It was one such leader, Sheikh Khojele Al-Hassen, who founded Assosa in the mid to late 19th century. The most important items of export from 19th-century Benishangul would have been gold, which is still mined in the vicinity of Menge, as well as livestock and ivory. The region was also plundered for slaves, who were exported to the bordering Ethiopian Highlands.

In the early 1880s, the Egyptian influence over Benishangul waned as a result of the Mahdist rebellion in Sudan. The rebellion proved to be short-lived, but it did serve to weaken the sheikhdoms established by the watawit earlier in the century, and paved the way for their conquest by Emperor Menelik II in 1896. Following the formal annexation of Benishangul to Ethiopia two years later, Assosa was made provincial capital of the remote region, which the imperial administration neglected to develop, instead exploiting it as a source of slaves and gold until the late 1930s. The thinly populated region around Assosa has since received two major human influxes, the first being a spate of refugees who settled there following Sudanese independence in the 1950s, and the second being the resettlement of 60,000 drought-afflicted Oromo and Amhara highlanders under the Derg regime in the early 1980s. The modern region of Benishangul-Gumuz was created under the 1995 constitution when the northwestern portion of Wollega (Benishangul, southwest of the Blue Nile) was amalgamated with the westernmost portion of Gojjam (Gumuz, northeast of the Blue Nile).

Getting there and away Ethiopian Airlines flies daily between Addis Ababa and Assosa. All **flights** land at the modern Assosa Hidase Airport, which lies about 5km south of town along the surfaced road to Gimbi. If you are staying at the Bamboo Paradise, a free shuttle meets all flights. Otherwise, a string of *bajaji* waits outside the airport to transport passengers to town for US$1–2.

By road Assosa lies about 660km west of Addis Ababa on what is now a good asphalt road running through Ambo, Nekemte and Gimbi. The most comfortable road transport along this route are the Selam Bus, Golden Bus and Falcon Coach to/from Addis Ababa, which leave in either direction at 04.30 and take around 15 hours. The Selam Bus leaves from in front of a clearly signposted office around the corner from the Dashen Hotel.

Most other public transport leaves from the central bus station near the market. This includes a daily bus to Nekemte, leaving in either direction at around 06.00 and taking 5 hours, as well as more local services to the likes of Menge and Bambasi. No direct buses connect Assosa to Bahir Dar, which lie about 600km apart via Gilgil Beles and Injibara, mostly on dirt roads, and the trip cannot realistically be covered in one day; you will need to change buses and most likely stop overnight in Gilgil Beles (page 241).

Where to stay, eat and drink *Map, above*

Budget

Blendana Hotel (47 rooms) m 0911 702759; e blendanahotel@gmail.com; f. Billing itself as the first international hotel in Assosa might be stretching a point, but this modern high-rise is certainly the closest thing to it. The comfortable rooms all come with sat TV, & a choice of tub or shower with hot water. A good restaurant is attached. *$16/22/33 B&B sgl/dbl/twin.* **$$$**

Bamboo Paradise Hotel (48 rooms) m 0911 832357. This well-established 6-storey hotel has adequate en-suite rooms with hot showers, a decent garden bar & restaurant serving Western & Ethiopian dishes, including pizzas, in the US$3–4 range, & a ground-floor café. *US$16 B&B dbl.* **$$**

Tourist information and permits The tourism office (\ *057 875 9107/9;* ⏲ *08.30–12.30 & 14.00–17.00 Mon–Fri*) is in the government building next to the Blendana Hotel. Visitors who intend to restrict their travels in Benishangul-Gumuz to Assosa are not required to report here, but visitors heading to more remote sites are expected to check in, and may also need to buy a permit, which costs US$25 per party per visit, plus another US$5 for every site they intend to visit. A mandatory guide costs another US$10–15 per party per day.

What to see and do

Assosa Regional Museum [map, above] (⏲ *08.00–12.30 & 14.00–17.00 Mon–Fri; entrance US$2*) Housed in the public library, this haphazard museum contains poorly presented displays relating to the culture and traditions of the Berta, Gumuz and other tribes of Benishangul-Gumuz, as well as to Sheikh Khojele Al-Hassen (the founder of Assosa) and the schematic rock art and history of the region. The natural history section amounts to little more than one stuffed leopard that resembles the product of a cheetah copulating with a vacuum cleaner. Still, if you have made it this far, it has to be worth paying the nominal entrance fee to look around.

ARGOBELLA AND FAMITSERIA Situated about 65km north of Assosa along the road to the Sudanese border town of Kumruk, Argobella is a small Berta village situated at the base of sacred twin outcrops known locally as Famitseria. Locals attribute male qualities to the larger of the two rocks, thanks to its distinctly phallic shape, and female qualities to the smaller one, which is said, rather fancifully, to look like a female breast (but actually more closely resembles a clitoris). On the right-hand side of the Kumruk road about 8km past the village, the Argobella gold mine is a quarry-like excavation pitted with deep holes that are still actively mined but far less impressive than the mine outside Menge.

MENGE The small and predominantly Berta town of Menge lies about 50km from Assosa along the road towards Bahir Dar. It is said to be the site of the earliest Berta settlement in Benishangul-Gumuz, and the surrounding hills are where the sacred rock known as Bela Shangul is stowed away. The main point of local interest today is the traditional mine workings on the right-hand side of the Bahir Dar road about 10km past the small town. These are some of the oldest excavations in Ethiopia, and include several narrow deep pits into which a miner is lowered by rope and then fills a bucket with rocks to be raised to the surface by a pulley. The miners aren't the friendliest bunch and, if you want to look around, you will need a permit from Assosa.

BAMBASI AND GOSHMANDU Straddling the Gimbi road 40km south of Assosa, Bambasi served as the capital of a Mahdist sheikhdom established by Ismail bin Muhammad Ali in the late 19th century, when its notorious slave market was also a stopover on the salt trade route between the Ethiopian Highlands and Sudan. Bambasi still hosts an important regional market every Wednesday and Saturday, and there is plenty of minibus transport from Assosa, as well as a couple of basic guesthouses should you want to overnight. Another 20km south of Bambasi along the road towards Yamesera, Goshmandu is worth visiting on Thursdays, when a large general market in the town centre is supplemented by a vibrant livestock market on its southern outskirts. Plenty of minibuses run between Bambasi and Goshmandu on market days, but there is no formal accommodation. You don't need a permit or a guide from Assosa to visit either of these markets.

YAMESERA MOSQUE [map, page 224] Set amid an artificial forest of mango and other fruiting trees, the Yamesera Mosque (⊕ daily; entrance US$5) was built in the 1970s by Sheikh Al-Faqih Ahmed Umar, a Nigerian healer and spiritual leader who was also active in Jimma and Dembidolo and whose body is now entombed at the site. The mosque isn't anything special in architectural terms, but the associated community of around 500 followers is very welcoming and keen to show off the irrigation scheme and small hydro-electric turbine established by Sheikh Al-Faqih on a small river running through the forest. About 200m from the mosque is a large stone outcrop whose indentations are claimed locally to have been made by the sheikh as he prayed, while a short walk uphill from here leads to the traditional village of Belgedez, which hosts a small but very colourful market on Wednesdays. To get to Yamesera, follow the Gimbi road out of Assosa as far as Bambasi, then turn right on to the same southbound road that leads to Goshmandu. About 45km past Bambasi, at the village of Gore, a rough but motorable 7km track to the right runs east to Yamesera. Public transport runs from Assosa to Gore (though it may entail changing vehicles at Bambasi), but those without private transport would need to walk the last 7km. Camping is permitted in the mosque grounds at US$2 per tent, and running water is available, but you would need to be more or less self-sufficient in terms of food and other provisions.

GUDA The closest town to the Grand Ethiopian Renaissance Dam, tiny Guda lies some 200km north of Assosa, at the end of a 10km side road running east from Magentia junction on the main road towards Bahir Dar. A rather stark little place whose Oromo name aptly means 'hot', Guda prides itself on being the site of the fantastically obscure Sheikh Muhammad Bhanjo's Palace, built in 1941 about 1km east of the town centre, and now a substantial ruin. The palace is quite atmospheric, its stone walls overgrown with strangler figs and surrounded by giant baobabs, but it's of limited architectural merit, and few would consider it justifies the hassle and expense of arranging the obligatory US$5 permit in Assosa, then heading to the tourist office in Guda to pick up a guide, who will also expect a fee of some sort. Rather more interesting, at least for birders, is the dusty track to the palace, which runs through a well-wooded (but normally dry) watercourse which supports several colourful species with a limited distribution in Ethiopia, among them Meyer's parrot, little green bee-eater and black-billed barbet. A few small hotels and eateries are dotted along the main road through Guda, none with en-suite rooms. The Blue Nile and Omedela hotels are the pick of the crop, if only because they both possess a generator, but dedicated ironists might prefer to hole up at the more grandiosely named Mankush Sheraton!

GILGIL BELES Situated about 130km west of Guda and 80km east of Injibara, Gilgil Beles (named after the tributary of the Nile that flows through it) is where travellers heading between Assosa and Bahir Dar on public transport must change buses and will most likely need to stay overnight. It's quite a substantial town, certainly by comparison with Guda, though the only point of local interest, so far as we can ascertain, is the **Sunday market** held 35km to the south at Yohannes Barguna. Far and away the best place to stay, the **Tinsae Hotel** (\058 119 0008; m 0911 839847), a high-rise signposted in Amharic only opposite the CBE, charges US$15 for a clean en-suite double with TV, or US$7.50 for a more basic double using a common shower. It has a good restaurant, while fresh juice is available at the **Nahon Juice Bar** opposite.

BAHIR DAR

A pleasant and attractive port characterised by its neatly laid-out palm-shaded avenues, lush vegetation, conspicuous birdlife and sticky tropical ambience, Bahir Dar has little in common with other towns in northern Ethiopia, coming across more like a transplant from the southern Rift Valley. Yet despite its relaxed lakeshore feel and orderly layout, this fast-growing town now ranks as one of the country's largest, one whose population, estimated at around 550,000, has more than trebled since the turn of the millennium. For travellers, the lively market, pretty waterside setting and

6

rewarding live music scene, coupled with some of the country's best tourist amenities, and popular day trips to the Blue Nile Falls and historic lake monasteries such as Ura Kidane Mihret, make Bahir Dar a thoroughly relaxed place to settle into for a few days. That said, the town does unfortunately have a reputation for hassle, and while this seems to have died down greatly in recent years, travellers arriving by bus still tend to be greeted by a reception committee of hotel touts, guides and compulsive yellers. Should you find yourself on the receiving end of this sort of attention, staying at a more expensive hotel, or away from the town centre, will help deflect it.

HISTORY Bahir Dar is essentially a 20th-century entity, but Lake Tana and its hinterland are steeped in history. The presence of an ancient Jewish sacrificial altar 40km northeast of Bahir Dar on Tana Chirkos, the monastic island after which the lake is named, suggests that the region was settled by the Beta Israel more than 2,000 years ago. More recently, between the late 13th and early 17th centuries, the Tana region was the political and spiritual focus of a succession of Ethiopian emperors, who established many temporary capitals on or near the lake. In the 16th century, the Tana region formed the central stage of the war between the Christian empire and Ahmed Gragn, and it is also where the Portuguese force led by Cristóvão da Gama spent most of its time in Ethiopia. Many historic monasteries dotted around Lake Tana date from this pre-Gondarine period, among them Bahir Dar Giyorgis, after which the modern town is named.

Some sources suggest that an important regional market was held close to Bahir Dar Giyorgis in the late 19th century, but when Arthur Hayes visited the site in 1903, urban development amounted to 'two or three huts' inhabited by Weyto villagers who lived on fish and hippopotamus meat. Bahir Dar was still little more than a village when the Italian army arrived there in April 1936 and set about developing the lakeshore site as a modern town centre, dividing it into commercial, residential, military and administrative zones. The Italians also constructed roads connecting Bahir Dar to Dejen and Debre Markos, a port to handle motorboat services to Zege and Gorgora, and an airstrip to receive flights from Addis Ababa and Gondar. By the end of the 1930s, the town supported a population of around 25,000.

After the end of the Italian occupation, the process of urbanisation continued, with the establishment of an imperial administrative office in 1941 and a revenue collection office a year later. In 1945, Bahir Dar was formally made a municipal area, albeit one still overshadowed politically and economically by Gondar and Debre Markos. The primary stimulus for Bahir Dar's rapid subsequent growth as a commercial and industrial centre was the construction of a hydro-electric plant at nearby Tis Abay in 1964. Indeed, it is said that Emperor Haile Selassie, who built a palace outside town in 1967, considered relocating the national capital to Bahir Dar at this time. To the surprise of many, Bahir Dar leapfrogged Gondar, Dessie and Debre Markos – the respective former administrative capitals of the defunct provinces of Gondar, Wollo and Gojjam – when a capital was selected for the redrawn Federal Region of Amhara in 1995. Though the population has more than doubled since then, Bahir Dar received an honourable mention in the 2002 UNESCO Cities for Peace Awards, which cited it having 'managed to address the challenges of rapid urbanisation … develop measures to make it a healthier and more convivial place … [and] shown great determination to tackle difficult issues such as housing shortages, economic stagnation, and lack of electricity'.

GETTING THERE AND AWAY Note that details of local transport – to the likes of the Blue Nile Falls, Zege and other Lake Tana monasteries – are discussed under those sections.

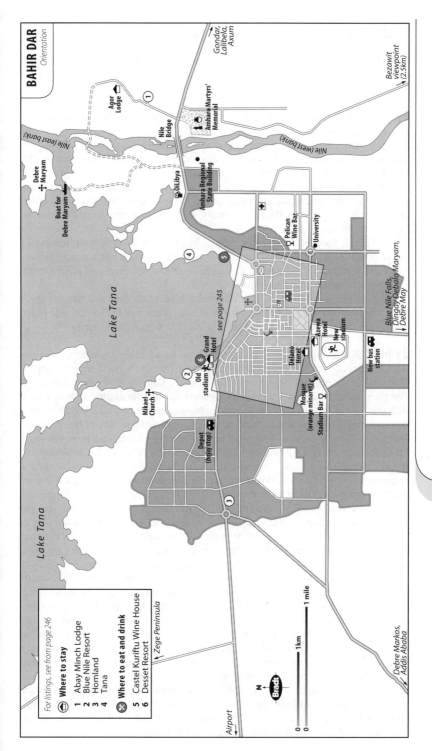

BAHIR DAR *Orientation*

For listings, see from page 246

Where to stay
1 Abay Minch Lodge
2 Blue Nile Resort
3 Homland
4 Tana

Where to eat and drink
5 Castel Kuriftu Wine House
6 Desset Resort

Lake Tana

Zege Peninsula

Airport

Debre Markos, Addis Ababa

Mikael Church

Depot (bajaj stop)

Old stadium

Grand Hotel

Stadium Bar

Mosque (orange minaret)

Dehno Hotel

Azewa Hotel

New stadium

New bus station

Blue Nile Falls, Dinga, Debalo Maryam, Debre May

University

Pelican Wine Bar

Amhara Regional State Building

OiLibya

see page 245

Nile (west bank)

Nile (east bank)

Nile Bridge

Amhara Martyrs' Memorial

Agor Lodge

Gondar, Lalibela, Axum

Bezawit viewpoint (2.5km)

Boat for Debre Maryam

Debre Maryam

Lake Tana

Bradt

N

0   1km
0   1 mile

By air Ethiopian Airlines operates several flights daily between Addis Ababa and Bahir Dar, and at least one daily in either direction to Lalibela and Axum. There are no longer direct flights between Bahir Dar and Gondar. The airport lies about 3km west of the town centre. Most hotels offer a free airport shuttle service, failing which a taxi shouldn't cost more than US$4.

By road Bahir Dar lies 550km from Addis Ababa along the fully surfaced road through Debre Markos, or 485km using a mostly surfaced road through Mota. In a private vehicle, the drive should take around 10 hours whichever route you use. The best bus services from Addis Ababa are Abay, Selam and to a lesser extent Sky (*10–12hrs; daily departures in either direction at 05.30*).

Bahir Dar and Gondar lie 180km apart via a good surfaced road that can be covered in 3 flat hours, though it also offers plenty of scope for diversions (page 261). Minibuses between Bahir Dar and Gondar leave every 30 minutes or so between 06.00 and 16.30.

As of 2017, there is also now one direct bus to/from Lalibela daily, leaving in either direction at 06.00 and taking around 9 hours. If you miss it, catch a minibus to Dessie and hop off at Gashena, from where minibuses leave for Lalibela every 30 minutes or so until mid afternoon.

Long-haul buses to the likes of Addis Ababa, Mekele, Lalibela and Weldiya leave from the new bus station south of the stadium. Transport to Gondar and other more local destinations leaves from the old bus station east of the market.

By boat For several decades, a passenger boat called MV *Tananich* has made a weekly crossing of Lake Tana, connecting Bahir Dar to its northern counterpart Gorgora via the ports of Zege, Gurer (Dek Island), Konzula, Isey Debir and Delgi. The timetable for some years has seen the ferry leaving the marine authority jetty in Bahir Dar at 06.00 every Monday, arriving at Gorgora on Tuesday afternoon, then starting the return trip at 06.00 on Thursday, arriving in Bahir Dar on Friday afternoon. These schedules have never been adhered to strictly, but in recent years the boat's movements have become highly unpredictable. The MV *Tananich* stopped running altogether in late 2016, some say due to engine problems, others as a response to political unrest. When the weekly service resumed in 2017, it followed the same schedule as before, the one significant difference being that it no longer ran as far as Gorgora, but terminated at Delgi. The situation is subject to regular change, so check with the Marine Authority when you arrive in Bahir Dar (and feel free to send us any fresh news for our updates website). Assuming the ferry is still running by the time you get there, the trip is far from luxurious, but it makes for a welcome change of pace if you can slot it into your itinerary. In both directions, an overnight stop is scheduled in Konzula, which has at least one basic hotel. A first-class seat in the salon costs around US$10 for foreigners, a lot more than locals pay to be on the deck, but still a good deal for two days' travel on Ethiopia's largest lake. Apart from seats and tables, the salon's only facilities, if you are lucky, will be lights and running water. There is also a toilet for exclusive use of staff and salon passengers. It would be sensible to bring some food and drinking water with you, though the ferry does stop for an hour or so at a few small villages where you can disembark for local meals, soft drinks and tea. If the ferry terminates in Gorgora (page 266), there are a couple of good places to stay, and it is only 65km further to Gondar on a nippy new asphalt road. If it terminates in Delgi, the Alamenah Hotel is the pick of the local lodgings, and a few buses ply back and forth daily along the 30km dirt road to Chwahit, which lies 50km south of Gondar on the surfaced road to Gorgora.

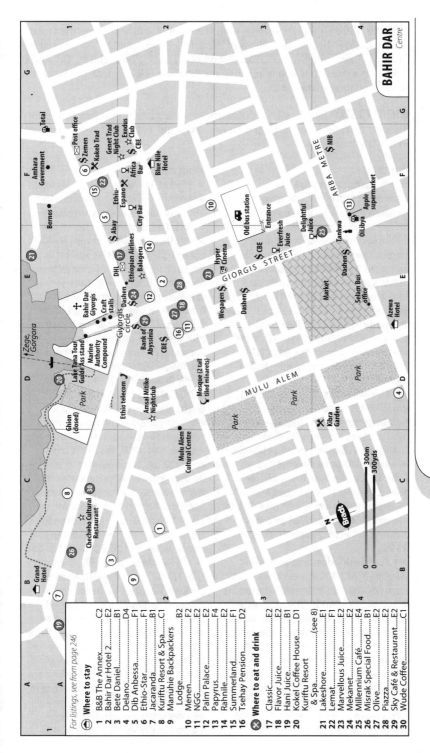

BAHIR DAR Centre

For listings, see from page 246

Where to stay

1	B&B The Annex	C2
2	Bahir Dar Hotel 2	E2
3	Bete Daniel	B1
4	Delano	D4
5	Dib Anbessa	F1
6	Ethio-Star	F1
7	Jacaranda	B1
8	Kuriftu Resort & Spa	C1
9	Manuhie Backpackers Lodge	B2
10	Menen	F2
11	NGG	E2
12	Palm Palace	E2
13	Papyrus	F4
14	Rahnile	E2
15	Summerland	F1
16	Tsehay Pension	D2

Where to eat and drink

17	Classic	E2
18	Flavor Juice	E2
19	Hani Juice	B1
20	Kokel Coffee House	D1
	Kuriftu Resort & Spa	(see 8)
21	Lakeshore	E1
22	Lemat	F1
23	Marvellous Juice	E2
24	Mekanet	E2
25	Millennium Café	E4
26	Misrak Special Food	B1
27	Olive	E2
28	Piazza	E2
29	Sky Café & Restaurant	E2
30	Wude Coffee	C1

Bahir Dar and Lake Tana   BAHIR DAR

6

245

GETTING AROUND Minibuses run from the main roundabout along the Gondar road past Abay Minch Lodge. Plenty of cheap *bajaji* clog Bahir Dar's streets and can easily be chartered for under US$2. Details of organising boat trips to the various Lake Tana monasteries, and of reaching the Blue Nile Falls, are included under the sections on these excursions.

WHERE TO STAY Almost all hotels listed below offer a free airport shuttle to guests. The only exceptions are the central Menen, NGG and Tsehay, which don't typically cater to fly-in tourists.

Upmarket

✱ 🏠 Kuriftu Resort & Spa [245 C1] (28 rooms) m 0920 959797; e booking@ kurifturesorts.com; w kurifturesorts.com. Bahir Dar's one true resort stands in lush gardens verging the lake & city centre. Stylish stone-&-wood bungalows come with king-size 4-poster beds, walk-in nets, flatscreen TV, private patio with daybed, & separate en-suite toilet & shower. A *tukul*-style restaurant serves a great buffet b/fast, & a varied selection of Asian, European & Ethiopian dishes in the US$8–10 range. There's also a stunning guests-only swimming pool & children's pool on a wooden lakeside deck. *From US$57 B&B dbl, but far cheaper through online booking agencies.* **$$$$$**

🏠 Blue Nile Resort [map, page 243] (135 rooms) ✆058 222 2206/7; e reservations@ bluenileresorthotels.com; w bluenileresorthotels. com. This smart 5-storey monolith stands in austerely manicured gardens offering a fabulous view over the lake 1km northwest of the town centre. Idyllic location aside, it feels more like a business hotel than a bona fide resort. Modern en-suite rooms come with AC & flatscreen TV. *Rack rates are US$130/170 sgl/dbl B&B, but drop by as much as 60% though online booking agencies.* **$$$$**

🏠 Abay Minch Lodge [map, page 243] (44 rooms) ✆058 218 1039; e reservation@ abayminchlodge.com; w abayminchlodge.com. Set in shady gardens 500m east of the Nile outlet, this quaint lodge blends contemporary & traditional elements in its stone-&-thatch bungalows, each of which has 2 discrete en-suite bedrooms with king-size or twin bed, TV, private balcony & en-suite showers with control panels from a science-fiction movie. A *tukul*-style restaurant is attached. Rack rates seem steep but are negotiable by up to 50% out of season or for longer stays. *US$95/114/120 B&B sgl/dbl/trpl.* **$$$$$**

Moderate

✱ 🏠 B&B The Annex [245 C2] (4 rooms) e housetheannex@gmail.com; w bbtheannex. com. Set on a quiet road within easy walking distance of the city centre, this charming service-oriented family-run B&B is a welcome alternative to the bland city hotels. Set in a small but lush tropical garden, it consists of a converted house whose 4 dbl & family rooms (the latter sleeping up to 5) are all brightly decorated in local fabrics & come with en-suite showers & net. A freshly cooked b/fast is included in the room rate, & other meals can be arranged by request. There's a communal TV lounge. Bookings by email only. *From US$40/45/60 sgl/dbl/family.* **$$$**

✱ 🏠 Delano Hotel [245 D4] (50 rooms) m 0930 352720; e delanohotelbahirdar@ gmail.com; w delanohotelbahardar.com. This new 7-storey hotel stands out for its efficient management & well-maintained & spacious modern rooms equipped with AC, flatscreen TV, large comfortable beds, bedside lamps, coffee/tea & hot showers. A good albeit rather characterless ground-floor restaurant serves a varied menu of Ethiopian & Western dishes in the US$3–4 range, & there's a sauna & steam bath on the top floor. The only negative is the less-than-central location opposite the new stadium. *From US$30/35 sgl/dbl B&B.* **$$$**

✱ 🏠 Rahnile Hotel [245 E2] (43 rooms) ✆058 220 7575; m 0918 764227; e rahnile@ gmail.com; f. Notable for its unusually high standard of maintenance & on-the-ball staff, this newish hotel is the pick of at least a dozen mid-range multistorey edifices dotted around the city centre. Smart, spacious & well-lit rooms are built around an inner courtyard & come with net, TV, tea/coffee, fridge & bedside lamps. Some also have a lake-facing balcony. Amenities include an elevator & brightly decorated 1st-floor terrace restaurant serving a varied selection of local & international dishes, including pizzas, in the

US$3–5 range. Very good value. *US$26/35/47 sgl/ dbl/twin, suites from US$53; all rates B&B.* **$$$**

🏠 **Tana Hotel** [map, page 243] (60 rooms) 📞058 220 0554. Situated on the lakeshore 1km north of the city centre, this former government hotel stands out for its thickly wooded grounds teeming with colourful birds such as giant kingfisher, double-toothed barbet, Bruce's green pigeon & white-cheeked turaco. Despite the outmoded architecture, the brightly decorated rooms are comfortable enough & have lake views. *US$38/52 sgl/dbl.* **$$$$**

🏠 **Jacaranda Hotel** [245 B1] (47 rooms) 📞058 220 9899; m 0918 353898; f. Modern high-rise, 500m west of the town centre, with spacious, airy & soothingly decorated en-suite rooms with AC, fan, flatscreen TV & small balcony. Good value. *US$30/44/48 B&B sgl/dbl/twin.* **$$**

🏠 **Bete Daniel Hotel** [245 B1] (34 rooms) 📞058 220 1412; m 0918 295266; e betedaniel@ gmail.com. Set on a quiet back road close to the lake, this is a superior high-rise whose innate blandness is offset by good service, sensible prices & bright spacious rooms with terracotta tiles, modern hardwood furniture & king-size bed. Good 1st-floor restaurant with mains around US$3. *US$32 dbl B&B.* **$$$**

🏠 **Summerland Hotel** [245 F1] (24 rooms) m 0918 141268. Pleasant 4-storey hotel on the main waterfront road with friendly staff & clean en-suite rooms with net & private balcony. Rates are negotiable. *US$32/48 dbl B&B.* **$$$$**

🏠 **Homland Hotel** [map, page 243] (69 rooms) 📞058 220 4545; e info@homlandhotelbahirdar.com; w homlandhotelbahirdar.com. This proofreader-baiting medium-rise 2km east of the town centre doesn't score highly on ambience or location, but it has a good reputation with tour operators, & the spacious en-suite rooms are very comfortable & sensibly priced. The new extension has a nice swimming pool. *US$34 dbl with fan; US$52/64 dbl/ twin with AC; all rates B&B.* **$$$**

🏠 **Palm Palace Hotel** [245 E2] (50 rooms) 📞058 220 1923; e reservations@palmpalacehotel. com; w palmpalacehotel.com. Distinguished by its curvaceous bright yellow façade, this well-run 7-storey hotel has clean en-suite rooms with wood laminate floors, large beds, net & TV. There's a ground-floor restaurant & rooftop terrace offering superb views towards the lake. *US$48 dbl.* **$$$$**

Budget

🏠 **Papyrus Hotel** [245 F4] (100 rooms) 📞058 220 5100. Following a recent drop in rates, this indifferently located multistorey hotel (overlooking an OiLibya filling station) with tempting Olympic-size swimming pool seems like pretty good value. The en-suite rooms are on the small side but come with sat TV & net. *US$20/26/30 B&B sgl/dbl/twin.* **$$$**

🏠 **Bahir Dar Hotel 2** [245 E2] (36 rooms) 📞058 220 8888; m 0918 016469; e bahirdar@ gmail.com. This well-priced & newish hotel has small but clean en-suite rooms with net, TV & hot shower. *US$10/16/24 B&B sgl/dbl/twin.* **$$**

🏠 **Dib Anbessa Hotel** [245 F1] (55 rooms) 📞058 220 1436; e dibanbessa_hotel@yahoo.com; w dibanbessa.webs.com. This stalwart hotel has a reasonably attractive location along the main waterfront road, adequate but rather rundown en-suite rooms & an unusually characterful ground-floor bar & restaurant. *US$16/18/22 sgl/dbl/twin B&B.* **$$**

Shoestring

🏠 **Manuhie Backpackers Lodge** [245 B2] (12 rooms, 1 6-bed dorm) m 0918 253484; e manuhielodge@gmail.com; w manuhiebackpackerslodge.com. With a mood reflecting its young, dynamic & articulate owner-manager, Bahir Dar's first backpacker lodge occupies a converted house set on a quiet but reasonably central back road. Already entrenched as a useful source of travel information & a good place to meet travellers, it also operates a budget tour agency, & a restaurant is planned. Services include free airport or bus station pick-up, free parking & bicycle rental. *US$8 dorm bed, US$10 sgl using common shower, US$15 en-suite dbl.* **$$**

🏠 **NGG Hotel** [245 E2] (42 rooms) 📞058 220 6363; m 0918 340460. This friendly 4-storey hotel between the bus station & lakeshore has clean rooms with en-suite hot shower & TV, & a decent traditional restaurant on the ground floor. Avoid getting involved with the touts who often hang out here. *US$10/12/16 sgl/dbl/twin.* **$$**

🏠 **Tsehay Pension** [245 D2] (72 rooms) 📞058 222 1550. Convenient central cheapie where small but clean rooms come with TV & hot shower. *US$6 sgl using common shower or US$9/11 en-suite sgl/ dbl.* **$$**

🏠 **Menen Hotel** [245 F2] (60 rooms) 📞058 220 2800. This prominent medium-rise opposite the old bus station has brightly painted en-suite sgls with TV. *US$8/12 sgl with cold/hot water.* **$**

🏠 **Ethio-Star Hotel** [245 F1] (70 rooms) 📞058 220 2026; **m** 0911 928278; **e** ethiostar2@ yahoo.com. On the main lakeshore road opposite a small forest patch, this medium-rise is good value for money thanks to its one-price-fits-all policy, but the en-suite rooms with nets, hot water & balcony are looking pretty tired. *US$8/12/20 sgl/ dbl/twin.* **$$**

Camping

⚔ **Blue Nile Camping** [map, page 256] (2 huts) **m** +44 7912 609545 (UK), 0905 026236; **e** info@bluenilecamping.com;

w bluenilecamping.com; see ad, page 268. Boasting a superb location in a *khat* & mango farm right above the Blue Nile Falls 30km southeast of Bahir (page 251), this joint British–Ethiopian venture opened in 2017 & offers the choice of camping in your own tent or its pre-pitched tents (equipped with a mattress), or staying in a cosy traditionally styled hut. It also serves homemade *tej*, freshly roasted coffee & Ethiopian food prepared on a wood fire. Activities included exploring the Nile above the falls on a papyrus kayak & guided hikes to Wonkshet Gebriel. To get there from Bahir Dar, drive or bus to Tis Abay (the gateway village to the falls) then take a boat across the Nile, which costs less than US$1 pp one-way. *US$10 pp in a hut or pre-pitched tent, US$4 pp camping in own tent.* **$$**

🍴 **WHERE TO EAT AND DRINK** In addition to the standalone restaurants mentioned below, most of the hostels listed above serve food. For a special night out, the standout in terms of quality and ambience is the waterfront restaurant at the Kuriftu Resort.

Restaurants
Moderate

✴🍴 **Lakeshore Restaurant** [245 E1] **m** 0918 760429; ⏰ 06.30–22.00 daily. Famed for its fish – served grilled, fried, breaded or in a variety of Ethiopian-style stews – this handsome dome-roofed restaurant also has a good wine list & offers a great view over the lake through tall glass windows. *Mains US$3–5.*

✴🍴 **Misrak Special Food** [245 B1] **m** 0989 343655; ⏰ 06.30–22.00 daily. Prone to regular relocation (most recently in Nov 2017), this excellent little restaurant is owned & managed by the former chef from the Kuriftu Resort. Specialities include fish tortilla, meatball sandwiches, beef kebab & chicken curry, but it also serves filled pita bread, burgers, pizzas, pasta dishes & salads. Beer, wine & great smoothies. *Most mains in the US$2–3 range; specialities US$5–6.*

🍴 **Castel Kuriftu Wine House** [map, page 243] 📞058 2263868; ⏰ 08.00–23.00. Set in a large wood-&-thatch building with tall *tukul*-style roof, traditional décor & a superb lakeshore setting, this offshoot of the Kuriftu Resort specialises in quality Ethiopian dishes (notably special *kitfo*) but also does good grills (eg: beef fillet & whole tilapia), accompanied by draught beer or Ethiopian wine. There's a DJ at w/ends 20.00–23.00. *Mains span the US$2–7 range.*

🍴 **Desset Resort** [map, page 243] **m** 0918 340199; ⏰ 06.00–22.00 daily. This beautiful lakeside restaurant, set in landscaped gardens below shady fig trees, offers a lengthy menu of Ethiopian & continental dishes, as well as salads, sandwiches, soups, coffees & beers. *Vegetarian dishes US$2; other mains US$3–4.*

Cheap

🍴 **Classic Restaurant** [245 E2] **m** 0930 111723; ⏰ 07.00–22.00 daily. A popular local lunch spot, this clean little restaurant has indoor & terrace seating & a lengthy menu of Ethiopian dishes, burgers, pasta & pizzas, mostly for around US$2. Good value.

🍴 **Lemat Restaurant** [245 F1] **m** 0918 766475; ⏰ 07.00–22.00 daily. Boasting a breezy terrace & traditionally decorated interior, this popular local eatery has a lengthy Ethiopian menu but is mostly renowned for its *gomen besiga* (sizzling collard leaves & beef). *Mains around US$2.*

🍴 **Olive Restaurant** [245 E2] ⏰ 08.00–21.30. This central 1st-floor eatery has a funky green interior, terrace seating & a varied selection of local dishes in the US$2–3 range.

🍴 **Piazza Restaurant** [245 E2] 📞058 220 0293; ⏰ 07.00–20.00. Unpretentious & central local eatery widely regarded to serve the best vegetarian & vegan fare in Bahir Dar. *Vegetarian dishes under US$2, fish around US$3.*

✗ Sky Café & Restaurant [245 E2] **m** 0918 769789; ⏱ 07.00–22.00. With a 1st-floor balcony facing the domed roof of Bahir Dar Giyorgis, this central eatery is a great place for a burger, local-style meal, juice, coffee or pastry. *Mains US$1.50–3.*

✗ Mekanet Restaurant [245 E2] **m** 0918 221266; ⏱ 11.00–22.00 daily. This shady terrace restaurant, on the 1st floor of Protection House, overlooks Bahir Dar Giyorgis & serves a decent selection of local dishes (*mostly around US$2*) & draught beer.

Coffee, juice & pastry shops

✱ 💻 Hani Juice [245 B1] **m** 0918 207474; ⏱ 08.30–19.00 daily. Recently relocated & extended from a stall to genuine terrace café, Hani quite simply serves the yummiest fresh fruit & vegetable juice this side of Addis Ababa. Most varieties cost less than US$1, but it's worth splashing out on the special mix, which is more like a meal than a drink!

✱ 💻 Wude Coffee [245 C1] **m** 0918 765662; ⏱ 06.30–22.00 daily. This stylish café opposite Kuriftu Resort serves excellent coffee, a good b/fast selection, & what 1 reader claims is the best *shiro tegabino* in the country. Wine & beer available. *Mains under US$2.*

💻 Kokel Coffee House [245 D1] ⏱ 07.00–23.00 daily. This open-air café lapped by the waters of Lake Tana serves inexpensive coffee, beer, sodas & light meals.

💻 Marvellous Juice [245 E2] ⏱ 07.00–18.00 daily. The best of several central juice shops serves a delicious *spris* for under US$1, & inexpensive green & fruit salads.

💻 Flavor Juice [245 E2] ⏱ 07.00–20.00 daily. Good fresh juice, coffee & cakes, as well as a well-stocked supermarket selling Ethiopian wine to take out,

💻 Millennium Café [245 E4] ⏱ 06.30–19.00 daily. Decent selection of pastries & cakes. The special *ful* with avocado is a to-die-for Arabian-influenced b/fast dish.

NIGHTLIFE

✱ ☆ Amsal Mitike Nightclub [245 D2] ☎ 058 220 7700; **w** amsalmitike.com; ⏱ 08.00–late. Owned by the namesake Gondarine singer, this wonderful venue hosts a vibrant Amharic music & dancing revue every night, starting at 20.00. Amsal Mitike herself usually performs a couple of times a week. Popular with locals, it serves traditional dishes in the US$3–5 range. There's no entrance fee, but drinks are 50% more expensive than normal.

☆ Balageru [245 E2] **m** 0918 784844; ⏱ 08.00–01.00. The best-known nightspot in Bahir Dar, but also the most overtly touristy, the recently relocated Balageru hosts traditional Amhara music & dancing every night from 20.00. *Kitfo* is the speciality on the varied Ethiopian menu (*US$2–3*), & it's a good place to sample quality *tej*. There's no cover charge but it's customary to tip the dancers.

☆ Checheho Cultural Restaurant [245 C1] ⏱ 07.00–23.00 daily. Recently rebuilt in the style of a Gondarine castle, this live music venue has *azmari*-style performances nightly at 20.00; the atmosphere is very informal, the clientele predominantly local, & there is no entrance fee, just a mark-up on drinks.

TOUR OPERATORS The following operators and agencies can arrange relatively reliable boat trips to Debre Maryam and the Nile outlet, the Zege Peninsula, and lake monasteries further afield.

BD Backpacker Tours [245 B2] **m** 0984 797574; **e** infosbackpackertours@gmail.com; **w** bdbackpackertours.wordpress.com. Praised by several readers, this newish budget-oriented operator is affiliated to Manuhie Backpackers & has its office in their compound.

Bona Fide Ethiopia Tours [map, page 243] **m** 0918 026386, 0923 439870; **e** info@bona-fideethiopiatours.com; **w** bona-fideethiopiatours.com. Reliable mid-range operator based at the Avanti Blue Nile Resort.

Ephrem Tours [map, page 243] **m** 0911 023242; **e** ephyzn@gmail.com. This very reliable mid-range operator, with an office in the Tana Hotel, is used by several of the better Addis Ababa-based operators to set up boat trips.

Lake Tana Tour Guide Association [245 D1]
m 0918 216698; e bdrguide@gmail.com. Good
budget operator based in the Marine Authority
compound.
Tankwa Tours m 0911 764933; e info@
tankwatours.com; w tankwatours.com.

Countrywide operator based in Bahir Dar & a good
contact for local trips there.
Yetawat Berhan Tours [245 D1] m 0918
457777. A new but well-organised operator with
an office in the Marine Authority compound.

WHAT TO SEE AND DO There's quite a bit to see and do in the immediate vicinity
of Bahir Dar, much of it focused on Lake Tana and the nearby Nile outlet. Almost
all visitors to Bahir Dar make the most popular half-day trip to the Blue Nile Falls,
which lie about 30km southeast of town and are at their best in the rainy season.
Bahir Dar is also a good base for exploring the churches detailed under *Monasteries
of southern Lake Tana* (page 254) and any of the more southerly sites under *Bahir
Dar to Gondar by road* (page 261).

Around town Bahir Dar's most obvious attraction is Lake Tana, whose southern
shore can be explored along a 2km lakeshore footpath running northwest from
the Marine Authority Compound via the Kuriftu Resort to the suburban Blue Nile
Resort. The birdlife along this footpath is exceptional – giant pelicans and herons on
the water, gaudy turacos and barbets in the woodland – and you may also see the
traditional *tankwas* (papyrus canoes) that used to be the main form of lake transport.

Bahir Dar Giyorgis [245 E1] (*Entrance US$2*) The town is named after the
church of Bahir Dar Giyorgis (St George by the Sea), which boasts a prime lakeshore
position on the northeast side of the main roundabout. Originally dedicated to Kiddist
Maryam, the church was probably founded in the early 14th century by Emperor
Amda Tsion, though one tradition credits it to late 13th-century ruler Yakuno Amlak.
The original building, or possibly a 16th-century facsimile dedicated to Giyorgis, was a
thatched circular construction that stood in place until the late 1930s, when the Italians
destroyed it because of its association with the anti-colonial patriotic movement.
Emperor Haile Selassie built an attractive and much larger domed church on the site
in the 1960s. Of greater historical interest, situated at the north end of the church
compound, is a two-storey stone tower which now serves as a museum displaying
artefacts that include some ancient Geez scripts and a cross – reputedly from the 13th
century – that adorned the roof of the original church. Architecturally reminiscent
of the Gondarine palaces, this tower was most likely constructed during the reign of
Susenyos with the assistance of Jesuit priest Pedro Páez, though one improbable local
tradition states it started life as the residence of Laike Maryam, the dignitary who
oversaw the construction of the original church for Emperor Amba Seyon.

Bahir Dar market [245 E4] Bahir Dar's bustling central market, about 500m
south of Giyorgis church, encapsulates the juxtaposition of urban modernity and
rustic traditionalism typical of so many Ethiopian towns. Open daily but busiest on
Saturdays, it is also one of the finest markets in the country, relatively hassle-free and
well worth a couple of hours' exploration. For souvenir hunters not content just to look,
it's a good place to buy an *agelgil* (a type of goatskin 'picnic basket' used by traditional
herders to carry their *injera*), as well as locally produced white *shama* cloths.

Nile Bridge [map, page 243] Inaugurated by Emperor Haile Selassie in 1961,
the 225m-long bridge that crosses the Blue Nile on the Gondar road about 2.5km
northeast of the town centre offers a great view over the river just 3km south of its

outlet from Lake Tana. The bridge is a good spot to look for hippos, which are most often seen partially submerged just to its south in the early morning or late afternoon. A wide variety of water and woodland birds are also likely to be seen, and possibly even the occasional crocodile. It takes about 30 minutes to walk to the bridge from the town centre, and you could also catch a *bajaj* there for next to nothing. Ask the military guard at the bridge before taking any photographs in the vicinity.

Amhara Martyrs' Memorial and Museum [map, page 243] (✎ 058 218 0448; w amharasemaetate.gov.et; ⊕ 08.00–17.30 daily; entrance US$2, photography US$1.50) Inaugurated in 2005, this 40m-high memorial, set in large parklike gardens on the east bank of the Nile immediately south of the Gondar road, commemorates the members of the Ethiopian People's Democratic Movement (EPDM) who lost their lives in the fight to liberate Ethiopia from the murderous Derg regime, and is flanked by several statues and reliefs depicting scenes from the struggle. Below the monument, an absorbing site museum displays hundreds of black-and-white and colour photographs documenting the last years of the imperial era, the formation of the EPDM in Tigray in 1980, and the civil war it waged against the Derg. Period artefacts on display include guns, armaments and documents, along with a collection of musical instruments played by the EPDM band. It's a 30-minute walk from the town centre to the main entrance, which lies 300m past the Nile Bridge, and *bajaji* also cover the route out of town.

Bezawit viewpoint [map, page 243] Rising from the east bank of the Nile some 3km south of the Amhara Martyrs' Memorial as the crow flies, but twice as far by road, Bezawit Hill is dominated by an ostentatious split-level palace built for Haile Selassie in 1967. The palace was only ever used by the emperor on two occasions during the remaining seven years of his rule, but it still serves as an occasional residence for visiting dignitaries, so entrance is forbidden, as is photography. Despite this, the hill is well worth visiting for the views over the river and town to Lake Tana and the Zege Peninsula, especially at dusk. There's a chance of seeing hippos in the river below. To get there, take the first right after the Amhara Martyrs' Memorial, then turn right again after 600m, then left after 200m, and continue south from there, with the river occasionally visible to your right. On foot, it takes about 90 minutes in either direction, being flat most of the way, but quite steep towards the end. A return *bajaj* from the junction to the viewpoint will cost around US$2.50–3.50.

Further afield
Blue Nile Falls [map, page 256] (⊕ 06.00–18.00; entrance US$2 inc still photography, video camera US$2, guide fee US$10/group for up to 5 people) About 35km downstream from Lake Tana, the Blue Nile plunges over a 45m-high rock face to form one of Africa's most spectacular waterfalls, known locally as Tis Isat (Water that Smokes). Eighteenth-century Scottish traveller James Bruce, though not the first European to visit the site (that distinction probably belongs to 16th-century Portuguese priest João Bermudes) famously described the Blue Nile Falls as: 'a magnificent sight, that ages, added to the greatest length of human life, would not efface or eradicate from my memory; it struck me with a kind of stupor, and a total oblivion of where I was, and of every other sublunary concern'.

Bruce's description still rings true at the height of the rains (May or June–October), when the sedate 160m-wide river above the waterfall kicks up a thunderous head of spray before being channelled into a narrow frothing 20m-wide gorge. The phenomenon is less reliable during the dry season, since the river is regularly diverted to feed an adjacent hydro-electric plant, reducing the waterfall to a narrow trickle across a vast expanse of bare rock. Conditions are least predictable over November and December (ironically, peak tourist season), when the flow is high enough to drive all the plant's turbines, but the river is diverted erratically, creating an all-or-nothing situation that can change dramatically from one hour to the next. The waterfall tends to be reliably but moderately impressive over January to April, when only one turbine is used, so less water is diverted. Rumours that the hydro-electric plant will cease operations following the completion of the new Grand Ethiopian Renaissance Dam are difficult to verify. Either way, as Steve Rooke, a regular visitor to Ethiopia, has pointed out: 'Reducing the Blue Nile Falls to a Disneyland-type attraction that is turned on and off at will detracts from the whole experience; more important perhaps is that the lack of water is devastating a spray-soaked ecosystem that has taken thousands of years to evolve.'

Getting there and away The springboard for visits to the Blue Nile Falls is the village of Tis Abay (Smoke of the Nile), which lies 38km southeast of Bahir Dar on an all-weather dirt road that can be quite slippery in the rainy season. Most people visit as a day trip out of Bahir Dar, but it is now possible to camp or take a basic room above the falls at the idyllic Blue Nile Camping (page 248). A half-day tour out of Bahir Dar can be arranged through any hotel or tour operator (page 249), and typically costs around US$15 per person excluding local entrance and guide fees. Alternatively, up to five buses daily run back and forth to Tis Abay, typically leaving Bahir Dar at around 07.00, 10.00, 12.00 and 14.00 (though this is very approximate) and starting the return trip about 1 hour later (so an early start is recommended, in order to be in time to catch the last bus back).

What to see and do The main activity is the lovely walk to the falls. Before embarking on this, you are required to visit the ticket office outside the hydro-electric plant gate to pay the entrance fee. This is also where you can arrange a local guide – technically optional, but more or less mandatory in practice, if only to divert harassment from unofficial guides, curio sellers and the like. From the ticket office, there are two routes to the falls. The longer and more attractive main route entails walking or driving around the hydro-electric plant compound, following a clearly marked 1.2km road that terminates at a large car park. From here, it is about 1km on foot to the first viewpoint, crossing the river below the falls on Alata Bridge, a multi-arched Portuguese stone construction built for Emperor Susenyos in 1626. This stretch of the walk passes some dense riverine woodland that offers good birding, with the likes of white-headed babbler, blue-breasted bee-eater, white-cheeked turaco, white-billed starling, black-winged lovebird and yellow-fronted parrot all present. From the first viewpoint, a 500m footpath runs north along the cliff above the river, offering a series of dramatic views of the falls in season, with a rainbow most likely to be seen in the spray in the morning. From the last and arguably best of these clifftop vantage points, the path descends to cross a Swiss-constructed suspension bridge, arriving after 500m at a final viewpoint situated at the northern end of the falls. In the dry season, it's usually possible to shower in a waist-height pool below a small slipstream here – a breathtaking sensation as the water plunges on you from 40m above – but check with your guide first as this would be suicidal in the rainy season, and be very careful not to go any further towards the main falls, as the currents are deadly. The shorter and flatter alternative route is recommended to late arrivals, or to those with mobility issues. It entails walking through Tis Abay village for 500m to the south bank of the Nile above the falls, then taking a motorboat across the river (*less than US$1 pp one-way*) and walking due east for another 1km to the most northerly viewpoint described above. For reasonably fit travellers with no time restrictions, the ideal option would be to head out along the main route and return via the alternative route. This amounts to about 5km in total, assuming you walk between the ticket office and car park, and it might take anything from 90 minutes to 3 hours, depending on your pace and how often you stop to admire the views and birdlife. A good place to break up the walk with a drink or meal is Blue Nile Camping (page 248), which stands on the north bank of the river, a short distance from the suspension bridge along the shorter alternative route.

Wonkshet Gebriel [map, page 256] (e *wonkshetgedam@gmail.com;* w *wonkshet. com*) Also transcribed as Wenqishet, the monastery of Wonkshet Gabriel was founded in medieval times, destroyed by Ahmed Gragn in the 16th century, and revived a few years ago by priest and healer Abay Yohannes Teklemariam. Set in a forest patch that supports the likes of white-cheeked turaco and yellow-fronted parrot, the complex comprises three monasteries housing a total of 400 monks, and is built around a multitude of natural hot springs whose output has been diverted to create productive vegetable gardens. Abay Yohannes claims to have cured HIV and cancer, and has also performed a variety of more one-off miracles such as extracting razor blades and needles from people's bodies, and delivering the demonic corpse out of a woman who'd been pregnant for 15 years. Photo and video evidence of these works is – rather bizarrely – provided on a Samsung tablet. Accessible on foot only, the monastery lies 2–3 hours from Tis Abay over the mountains (spectacular views) or 90 minutes along the flatter Nile Valley. The best way to visit is as a round hike arranged by Blue Nile Camping (page 248), which charges US$12 per person for the half-day round hike, inclusive of a guide. Healing and exorcism sessions take place in the morning only, so it is recommended you make an early start and take the quicker route out.

Dingay Debalo Maryam [map, page 256] An interesting but demanding side trip from the road to the Blue Nile Falls leads to Dingay Debalo Maryam (literally 'Rock-carved Mary'), the only rock-hewn church in the immediate vicinity of Bahir Dar. Local tradition accredits the excavation of this semi-monolith to King Lalibela, stating that it was executed before he started work on the eponymous complex of churches at his capital, but stylistically it is closer to the churches of northeast Tigray. It is a relatively small church, with three arched doors and an interior split by two rows of square columns, and its treasures include a large drum reputedly donated by Emperor Fasilidas. The church lies 8km south of the main road to Tis Abay, and the junction is signposted (Amharic only) to the right after about 17km coming from Bahir Dar. In dry weather you can drive the first 3km southwest of the junction, but after that you will need to walk the last 5km southeast to the church. As with the Tigrayan churches, unless a service is being held, there is no guarantee the priest with the key will be available to let you in.

Gimb Giyorgis and Gimb Maryam [map, page 256] Also known as Gimb Fasilidas, the enigmatic Gimb Giyorgis, situated some 30km south of Bahir Dar as the crow flies, comprises a 1.7ha compound enclosed by a partially standing 6m-high stone wall, and centred on a large arched subterranean chamber whose purpose is unclear. Its builder is also unknown, but the presence of a substantial but ruinous rectangular Catholic church called Gimb Maryam some 300m to the west suggests it might be synonymous with Sarca, a Jesuit mission established during the reign

Ethiopia's largest lake, Tana has the dimensions of an inland sea, measuring around 85km from north to south, 66km from east to west, and with a surface area of up to 3,673km², depending on seasonal fluctuations. A rather shallow freshwater lake averaging 14m in depth, it is broadly circular in shape, aside from the tear-drop-like southeastern spur upon which lies Bahir Dar, the largest lake port. Tana formed around five million years ago owing to volcanic activity that caused a damlike lava extrusion to block the flow of several rivers. Ecologically, it produces a rich harvest of fish, some 26 species of which have been recorded, more than half of them endemic to the lake. The lake is also renowned for its varied birdlife – flotillas of white pelican are a common sight – while the shallows support small pods of hippos. In June 2015, Lake Tana became the centrepiece of a 5,000km² UNESCO biosphere reserve (w *laketana-biosphere.com*), which could have a significant impact on future tourist developments.

Lake Tana is fed by at least two dozen perennial and seasonal rivers, most significantly the Gilgil Abay, Megech and Gumara, but it has only one outlet, the Abay, or Blue Nile, which exits the southeastern shore on the outskirts of Bahir Dar. Tana's elevated geographic status as the source of the Blue Nile has been cited to explain Ethiopia's many links with the ancient world. The ancient Egyptians were familiar with the lake, which they called Coloe, while the ancient Greeks knew it as it Pseboe, the 'copper-tinted lake ... that is the jewel of Ethiopia'. Links with ancient Egypt are further suggested by the strong resemblance between the papyrus *tankwa* used by local fishermen and similar boats depicted on ancient Egyptian reliefs. The lake's 30-odd islands also support around 20 monasteries, many of which are very ancient and may well be built over pre-Christian religious sites.

of Susenyos. To get there, follow the Mota road south out of Bahir Dar for about 25km to the small junction village of Guberit, then turn right on to the Feres Ewaga road. After 2.5km, you reach Feres Ewaga, where you need to turn left through the marketplace then downhill to a bridge, from where it is another 5.5km to Gimb Giyorgis and Gimb Maryam. Usually you can drive to within 100m of both sites, but if the bridge at Feres Ewaga is broken, as it was in late 2017, you may need to walk.

Yebaba [map, page 256] Situated 3km northeast of Debre May, a small town flanking the Mota road some 32km south of Bahir Dar, this palatial royal residence was built by Yohannes I in the 1670s and used as a retreat by several subsequent Gondarine emperors at least until the 1770s, when James Bruce visited a large market town there. You can drive to within 300m of Yebaba: follow the Mota road south from Bahir Dar for 30km, then as you enter Debre May, directly opposite the telecoms satellite tower, turn left on to a very rough side road that brings you to the site after 3.5km. One of the original circular turrets, standing about 8m tall, is still more or less intact, as are a few other parts of the old stone wall.

MONASTERIES OF SOUTHERN LAKE TANA

Shrouded in mystery and legend, the 20-odd monasteries that stud the islands and peninsulas of Lake Tana have long formed remote, peaceful retreats for their monastic residents, and the more southerly among them also form excellent goals for a day trip out of Bahir Dar. True, none of the churches associated with these monasteries is comparable architecturally to the rock-hewn and Axumite churches of Lalibela and Tigray (indeed, most are relatively modern buildings constructed on the site of a medieval original), but many are beautifully decorated, none more so than the highly accessible Ura Kidane Mihret on the Zege Peninsula and more remote Narga Selassie on Dek Island, whose colourfully painted *maqdas* serve as a virtual visual encyclopedia of Ethiopian ecclesiastical concerns. Many of the lake monasteries also have impressive treasure houses stuffed with a miscellany of bounty reflecting their antiquity. Of particular note to bibliophiles is Kibran Gebriel, with its library of almost 200 old books, while Daga Istafanos hosts the mummified remains of five former Ethiopian emperors, among them Fasilidas, the founder of Gondar. Another feature of several island monasteries is that they practically double as nature sanctuaries, thanks to the conservationist ethos of the Ethiopian Orthodox Church. The Zege Peninsula stands out for supporting what is by far the largest remaining tract of natural forest on Lake Tana, but most of the monastic islands retain a remarkably undisturbed flora. A final attraction of the lake monasteries is the indisputable romance attached to travelling on this beautiful tropical inland sea – not only the largest lake in Ethiopia, but also the source of the Blue Nile, and home to a spectacular selection of waterbirds.

HISTORY The early history of the Lake Tana monasteries is open to conjecture. According to local legend, many date from the early 14th-century rule of Amda Tsion, including a septet whose foundation is associated with a group of monks known as the Seven Stars. These are Daga Istafanos (founded by Hiruta Amlak), Kibran Gebriel (Za Yohannes), Ura Kidane Mihret (Betre Maryam), Bahir Galila Zacharias (Zacharias), Mandaba Medhane Alem (Ras Asai), Gugubie (Afkrene Egzi) and Debre Maryam (Tadewos Tselalesh). At least two churches, including Narga Selassie, date from the more recent Gondarine period. Others are quite possibly a lot older, or may have started life as pre-Christian shrines of some sort. The monastery of Tana Chirkos, for instance, lies alongside a trio of very ancient Judaic sacrificial pillars, and is also legendarily where the Ark of the Covenant was housed prior to the 4th century AD. Many of the monasteries remained unknown to outsiders until the 1930s, when Major Robert Cheesman led a pioneering expedition to visit every last island on Lake Tana, documented in his out-of-print book *Lake Tana and the Blue Nile: An Abyssinian Quest.*

GETTING AROUND As detailed under the descriptions for the individual churches, Debre Maryam lies on an island on the outskirts of Bahir Dar, so you can walk to within a few hundred metres of it, while Ura Kidane Mihret and the other monasteries on the Zege Peninsula can be visited in a private vehicle, or by ferry or bus, or a combination thereof. However, the most usual way to visit these places, and the only way to get to any of the more remote island-bound monasteries, is on an organised boat trip out of Bahir Dar, which can be arranged through your hotel or with any of the local operators listed on page 249. When organising a trip, single travellers and couples will find it pays to put together a group, or to join one, as transport costs are much the same irrespective of group size. Typically, a small group (up to six or eight passengers) will be looking at US$30–40 per party for a 2–3-hour trip to Debre Maryam and the Nile outlet. Further afield, the safest way to travel on the lake is with one of the boats provided by the Marine Authority, which cost US$80 per group (up to five people) for a trip taking in Ura Kidane Mihret, Kibran Gebriel

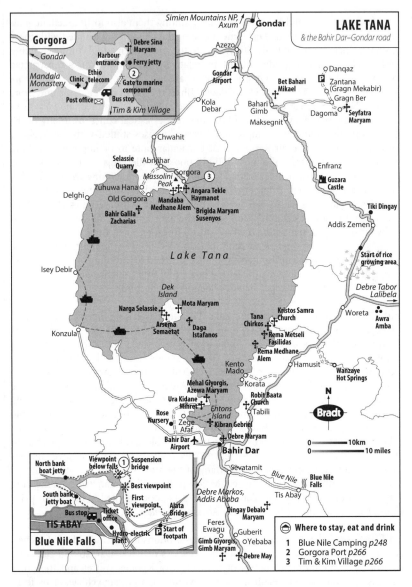

LAKE TANA
& the Bahir Dar–Gondar road

Gorgora

Simien Mountains NP,
Axum
Gondar
Azezo
Gondar
Airport
Danqaz
Zantana
(Gragn Mekabir)
Gragn Ber
Bet Bahari
Mikael
Bahari
Gimb
Dagoma
Seyfatra
Maryam
Kola
Debar
Maksegnit
Chwahit
Selassie
Quarry
Abrijhar
Massolini
Peak
Gorgora
Enfranz
Guzara
Castle
Tuhuwa Hana
Old Gorgora
Angara Tekle
Haymanot
Mandaba
Medhane Alem
Tiki Dingay
Delghi
Bahir Galila
Zacharias
Brigida Maryam
Susenyos
Addis Zemen
Lake Tana
Start of rice
growing area
Isey Debir
*Dek
Island*
Mota Maryam
*Debre Tabor
Lalibela*
Narga Selassie
Arsema
Semaetat
Daga
Istafanos
Tana
Chirkos
Kristos Samra
Church
Woreta
Awra
Amba
Konzula
Rema Metseli
Fasilidas
Rema Medhane
Alem
Kento
Mado
Hamusit
Wanzaye
Hot Springs
Korata
Mehal Giyorgis,
Azewa Maryam
Robit Baata
Church
Ura Kidane
Mihret
*Ehtons
Island*
Tabili
Rose
Nursery
Zege
Afaf
Kibran Gebriel
Bahir Dar
Airport
Debre Maryam
Bahir Dar
Sevatamit
Blue Nile
Blue Nile
Falls
Debre Markos,
Addis Ababa
Tis Abay
Dingay Debalo
Maryam
Feres
Ewagu
Guberit
Yebaba
Gimb Giyorgis,
Gimb Maryam
Debre May

Gorgora (inset)

Gondor
Debre Sina
Maryam
Harbour
entrance
Ferry jetty
Ethio
telecom
Clinic
Gate to marine
compound
Post office
Bus stop
Tim & Kim Village
Mandala
Monastery

Tis Abay / Blue Nile Falls (inset)

North bank
boat jetty
Viewpoint
below falls
Suspension
bridge
Best viewpoint
South bank
jetty boat
First
viewpoint
Alata
Bridge
Bus stop
Ticket
office
Start of
footpath
TIS ABAY
Hydro-electric
plant
Blue Nile Falls

N
0 — 10km
0 — 10 miles

Where to stay, eat and drink

1 Blue Nile Camping *p248*
2 Gorgora Port *p266*
3 Tim & Kim Village *p266*

and the Nile outlet, and double that for a full-day trip to a more remote monastery such as Tana Chirkos or Narga Selassie. The cheaper alternative is to travel with a local boat, which should work out at US$30–40 to visit Ura Kidane Mihret, Kibran Gebriel and the Nile outlet, and US$120 for the more northerly monasteries. There is also an official guide fee of around US$7 for a boat excursion to the monasteries, though many guides will deny this and try to charge more, and it's low enough that a tip will rightly be expected. These rates are for transport and guiding only and exclude the entrance fees charged by individual churches.

Be warned that, while local boats are cheaper than going with a Marine Authority boat, they also tend to have lower safety standards, which can become a genuine issue on this storm-prone lake. We've received regular complaints over the years about unseaworthy vessels, a lack of life jackets, poor captaincy and the like. For this reason, you should avoid booking through the touts who lurk on the streets and hang around many hotels. Instead, book through a respected hotel or an agency that offers some degree of accountability, however small. Even then, you should personally ensure that your boat has enough life jackets for all crew members and passengers, and avoid travelling north of Zege if stormy weather is predicted. Another factor to consider is the horsepower rating on the boat's engine. A cheaper boat with a smaller engine might seem like a better deal, but it could be much slower. Even with a sunshade it can get very hot out on the water. Especially for longer trips, a fast boat is worth the extra expense.

🏠 **WHERE TO STAY, EAT AND DRINK** Almost everybody visits the monasteries as a day trip out of Bahir Dar, but it is possible to overnight in the village of Zege Afaf on the west side of the Zege Peninsula. The pick of the village's two very basic lodges, situated a few hundred metres along the road to Bahir Dar, is the Fikre Selam Guesthouse (*6 rooms;* **m** *0918 783675;* **$**), which charges US$3 for a room using common shower, and has a bar and restaurant attached.

OTHER PRACTICALITIES All the monasteries charge an individual entrance fee, in most cases US$4 per person. This usually includes still photography, but a video camera will be charged extra. Ura Kidane Mihret and Azewa Maryam also both charge a mandatory guide fee of US$10 per party.

All comers are welcome at a handful of monasteries whose monks routinely interact with secular communities, ie: Debre Maryam, Narga Selassie, Ura Kidane Mihret and all other monasteries on the Zege Peninsula. However, women are absolutely forbidden from visiting the other monasteries described below and will be wasting their time (and money) if they try. Some female travellers find this ruling offensive, but it does date back several centuries and, as a well-meaning brochure produced by the monks of Daga Istafanos notes, 'it is not meant to belittle women', but in order that 'young virgin hermits should subdue their body to the service of their God, and the devil should not attack them with the spear of adultery'.

Sunscreen and hats are essential, as are food and plenty of drinking water for full-day boat trips.

THE MONASTERIES This section describes the six most frequently visited monasteries in the southern part of the lake, as far north as Dek Island, and gives passing mention to several less-known monasteries in the same region. It excludes a handful of northern lake monasteries that lie closer to Gorgora (page 265) than to Bahir Dar.

Debre Maryam Situated on the flat 2km-long islet that bisects the outlet where the Nile exits Lake Tana, Debre Maryam is the closest monastery to Bahir Dar, as well as being one of the few to welcome female visitors, and the easiest to visit independently. As with Bahir Dar Giyorgis, it probably dates from the reign of Emperor Amda Tsion, or possibly Yakuno Amlak. Its founder, Abuna Tadewos Tselalesh, was reputedly able to part the lake's water, allowing him to cross to or from the mainland on foot. The circular present-day church was built in the 1970s, though its central *maqdas* dates from the reign of Emperor Tewodros and is decorated with mid-19th-century paintings. Treasures include three ancient Ge'ez goatskin manuscripts, the oldest of which, depicting the four evangelists, dates from the 14th century.

Getting there and away To visit Debre Maryam independently, walk or catch a *bajaj* out of town for 2km until you see the eye-catchingly modern Amhara Regional State Building to your right. Here, just before the road crosses the Nile Bridge, you need to take a left turn on to a rough dirt road that leads north through a marshy area for about 2km before emerging on the south bank of the Nile outlet immediately opposite the island that houses the monastery. It's a 5-minute motorboat or *tankwa* crossing to the island, and you'll probably be asked around US$5 per person for the return trip, though locals pay a lot less. It's advisable to head out early in the day, before the wind starts up, or the water might be too choppy for a *tankwa* to cross.

Kibran Gebriel

The second-closest monastery to Bahir Dar, and visible from the town, Kibran Gebriel lies on a tiny, forested crescent – presumably part of the rim of an extinct volcano – which, somewhat incredibly, provides sanctuary to as many as 40 monks. It was founded in the 13th century by a hermit called Abuna Za Yohannes, who named it after the married couple – Gebriel and Kibran – who rowed him out to the island and later returned there to check on his health. The church, on the highest point of the island, was rebuilt in the 17th century by Emperor Dawit II to a similar design to the better-known Ura Kidane Mihret on Zege. Kibran Gebriel boasts no paintings of note, but it houses the largest library of ancient books in the region – including a beautifully illustrated 15th-century *Life of Christ* and almost 200 other volumes, many donated by emperors who visited the monastery, among them Sarsa Dengal, Fasilidas and Yohannes I. Some of these old manuscripts are on display in a museum close to the main church, while a second museum closer to the jetty houses some lesser treasures.

The island can easily be visited in conjunction with the monasteries on the Zege Peninsula, and is no more than 30 minutes by boat from Bahir Dar, but it is worth trying to be there as early as possible, as the church often closes for the day at around 08.00. Men pay an entrance fee of US$5 to visit the church (assuming it is open) and the two museums, while women must pay US$1.25 but may only visit the museum at the jetty. Women are forbidden from setting foot elsewhere on the island, though a legend that Empress Mentewab once visited it, but declined to enter the church because she was menstruating, would suggest that this has not always been the case. The smaller forested island of Entons immediately south of Kibran used to be a nunnery but was abandoned some years ago.

Ura Kidane Mihret and the Zege Peninsula

Set on the forested Zege Peninsula about 10km northwest of Bahir Dar as the crow flies, Ura Kidane Mihret is arguably the most beautiful church in the Tana region and the most frequently visited, partly because of its proximity to Bahir Dar, and partly because it is open to women as well as men. It was founded in the 14th century by a priest called Betre Maryam (Rod of Mary) who hailed from the Muger River in Shewa and started training as a priest after being visited by two angels at the age of seven. The circular church was built in the 16th century, and its *maqdas* is covered in an incredible jumble of murals, painted between 250 and 100 years ago (the most recent were executed by well-known artist Aleka Engeda during the dying years of Menelik II's reign), many of which have been restored in the last few decades. These paintings are positively Chaucerian in their physicality, ribaldry and gore, and it is no hyperbole to say that they offer a genuinely revealing glimpse into medieval Ethiopia – so do give yourself time to look at them closely. There are also some intriguing line drawings on one of the doors, while a separate museum has a few old crowns of Ethiopian kings, leather-bound Bibles, a massive gold cross and other ancient treasures. Look out for the striking circular cross, 1.5m in diameter, that adorned the church roof from the early 14th-century reign of Amda Tsion until it fell down at some point in the more recent past.

Reachable from Ura Kidane Mihret by boat, or by following a 1.5km footpath southeast through thick forest, **Azewa Maryam** is adorned with several animated 18th-century paintings, and an attached treasury houses several antiquities. More remote, lying about 2km northeast of Ura Kidane Mihret, the disused church of **Mehal Giyorgis** is little more than a shell, but there are some 18th-century murals on the standing walls.

If you are walking, the forest that swathes the peninsula makes an appealing change from the region's characteristic open grassland. Wild coffee dominates the undergrowth, vervet monkeys shake the canopy, parrots screech, hornbills erupt into cacophony, and colourful butterflies flutter above small pools.

Getting there and away The Zege Peninsula is almost 30km from Bahir Dar along a flat and well-maintained dirt road. In a private vehicle or by bicycle, head west out of town along the surfaced airport road then, 2km after passing the Homland Hotel, turn right on to the unsurfaced Konzula road and follow it northwest for 11km, through a rather dry landscape strewn with gigantic volcanic boulders, to a three-way junction where you need to turn right. After 3km, you'll pass a large nursery, from where it's another 10km to Zege Afaf, the gateway village to the peninsula. Using public transport, at least four buses daily run back and forth between Bahir Dar and Zege Afaf (more on Saturday, market day), and the fare is US$0.65. The first bus usually leaves Bahir Dar at 06.00 and the last departs from Zege Afaf at around 16.00. Once at Zege Afaf, a 4x4 can drive along the 3km track to Ura Kidane Mihret in the dry season, but it only takes about 40 minutes to walk, passing through lush forest most of the way. The other churches on the peninsula are accessible on foot only.

In addition to buses, a passenger ferry to the Zege Peninsula leaves Bahir Dar from the Marine Compound at 07.00 daily (be there 30 minutes earlier to buy a ticket, which costs US$2.50). The boat stops at the jetty below Ura Kidane Mihret about an hour later, before continuing on to a second jetty at Zege Afaf, 3km to the west. The ferry returns to Bahir Dar shortly afterwards, so you will most likely need to head back to town by bus.

Tana Chirkos This small monastery, separated from the eastern shore by a marshy corridor, is dominated by a striking spine of rock perhaps 30m high, and fringed by riparian forest supporting several pairs of fish eagle. It acquired something approaching cult status following publication of Graham Hancock's book *The Sign and the Seal*, which attempted to substantiate an ancient tradition that the Ark of the Covenant was stowed on the island for some 800 years before it was transferred to Axum in the 4th century AD by King Ezana.

The age of Tana Chirkos is unknown. One tradition has it that it was founded on the site of an older temple by St Yared and Abuna Aregawi during the 6th-century reign of Gebre Meskel. Another holds that it was founded two centuries earlier by Frumentius, the first Bishop of Axum, who was buried there. Other sources suggest that the island converted to Christianity a mere 540 years ago. Whatever the truth, the architecturally undistinguished church, built about 100 years ago with funding from Ras Gugsa of Debre Tabor, looks timeworn rather than ancient, and none of the paintings that adorn it looks more than a few decades old.

Far more interesting than the monastery itself is a trio of hollowed-out sacrificial pillars that stand alongside it, testifying to the island's importance as an ancient Judaic religious shrine. The local priests say that the pillars date from King Solomon's time and were used to make dyes, which if true would provide some circumstantial support to Hancock's contention that the Ark resided on the island in pre-Christian times. It is also possibly significant that most accounts agree the lake is actually named after Tana Island, suggesting it has been an important landmark or shrine for a very long time. Then again, there is the Ethiopian predilection for far-fetched mythologising – one local tradition has it that the Virgin Mary rested at Tana Island on her (presumably somewhat circuitous) return from Egypt to Israel, while another claims that a 'footprint' on one of the island's rocks was made by no lesser a personage than her immaculately conceived first-born son!

Tana Chirkos lies 3 hours from Bahir Dar by boat; the walk from the jetty to the monastery takes no more than 5 minutes. On the way to the island (or coming back) it is possible to look at two further monasteries, both on small, forested islands about 30 minutes from Tana Chirkos. These are **Rema Medhane Alem**, a recently rebuilt church in which are stored a few interesting old paintings, and **Rema Metseli Fasilidas**, founded during the rule of the eponymous emperor and architecturally undistinguished – though the surrounding forest is rich in birdlife.

Daga Istafanos Home to as many as 200 monks, Daga Istafanos is the largest monastery on the lake, set on a small wedge-shaped islet immediately east of the much larger Dek Island. A reliable and uncontested tradition states that it was founded in the late 13th century by Hiruta Amlak, a nephew of Emperor Yakuno Amlak, who served his apprenticeship under Iyasu Moa at Hayk Istafanos at the same time as the future Archbishop Tekle Haymanot. A less probable tradition has it that Hiruta Amlak was ferried from the mainland to the island on a pair of divine stones that can still be seen in the monastery grounds. Another tradition has it that Daga Istafanos is where the Ark of the Covenant was hidden during Ahmed Gragn's 16th-century occupation of Axum.

The modern church on the island's conical peak, rebuilt after the original burnt to the ground in the 19th century, is relatively unengaging, aside from the unusual monochrome painting of an angel on one of the inner doors. Of far greater interest is a mausoleum holding the mummified remains of at least five Ethiopian emperors: Yakuno Amlak (1268–93), Dawit I (1428–30), Zara Yaqob (1434–68), Susenyos (1607–32) and Fasilidas (1632–76). The glass coffins in which the mummies now lie are recent acquisitions, donated by Haile Selassie after he visited the monastery in 1951. The mummy of Fasilidas is the best preserved of the five, and his facial features are still eerily discernible. A tiny skeleton next to this is said to be the remains of Fasilidas's favourite son, who was crowned as his father's successor but collapsed and died under the weight of the crown.

It is something of a mystery as to when, why and how the mummies ended up on this remote island: some say during the Mahdist invasion of Gondar in the late 19th century, others during the Italian occupation, but there also seems to be good reason to believe that the dead kings were brought here for mummification shortly after they died. Certainly, Daga Istafanos was a popular retreat for several of the above-mentioned kings, and its tranquillity was reputedly also favoured by Tewodros II, who took communion there on several occasions. Several other treasures associated with these kings are stored in the mausoleum: old crowns, a goatskin book with some line drawings dating from the 14th century, and two immaculately preserved

15th-century paintings of the Madonna with uncharacteristically detailed and non-stylised facial features.

Daga Istafanos lies about 3 hours by boat from Bahir Dar, 90 minutes from Tana Chirkos and an hour from Narga Selassie. The walk from the jetty to the church is quite steep, and takes about 15 minutes, with a chance of encountering the odd monkey along the way.

Narga Selassie Situated on the western shore of Dek, the largest island on Lake Tana, Narga Selassie is, with the possible exception of the much older Ura Kidane Mihret, the most ornately decorated of all the lake monasteries. Built in the 18th century for Princess Mentewab (regent for Emperor Iyasu II), the stone walls surrounding the compound, with their domed turrets, are typically Gondarine, and not dissimilar in appearance to the walls surrounding the church next to Mentewab's palace at Kuskuam outside Gondar. The compound, its 'old grey towers, forgotten on this lonely island' looked somewhat neglected when Cheesman visited it in the 1930s, but the church was restored with funding by Haile Selassie in 1951 and the roof underwent further renovations in 2001.

The main church is circular in shape and surrounded by stone pillars (one decorated by an etching of pipe-puffing explorer James Bruce, a close associate of Mentewab). As with Ura Kidane Mihret, the inner walls are covered from top to bottom with a riotous and absorbing collection of paintings, most thought to date from the 18th century. In addition to the usual pictures of saints and their exploits, there is a painting of the church's founder lying prostrate before Mary and the baby Jesus, probably the only contemporaneous portrait of Mentewab to survive. Another interesting painting depicts a church on the back of a fish, the latter about to be speared by an angel – evidently relating to a legend about a town on Lake Tana that was being harassed by a big fish until the angel intervened.

Narga Selassie lies some 3 hours from Bahir Dar by boat, and an hour from Daga Istafanos. The monastery is practically next to the jetty. There are two other monasteries on Dek Island – **Arsema Semaetat** and **Mota Maryam** – but neither is regularly visited by tourists.

BAHIR DAR TO GONDAR BY ROAD

The sites below all lie alongside or close to the 175km main road between Bahir Dar and Gondar, which can be covered in under 3 hours without stops, but also offers plenty to explorative travellers. The more southerly sites could easily be visited as a day trip out of Bahir Dar, and the more northerly ones would make for possible day excursions out of Gondar.

ROBIT BAATA CHURCH Nestled within a magnificent circular forest patch on the west side of the Gondar road, the readily accessible church of Robit Baata was established during the early 15th-century reign of Yeshaq I and is renowned locally for growing holy lemons whose juice is believed to make barren women fertile. The outer walls of the circular church are relatively modern, but the square *maqdas* is reputedly much older, and three sides of it are covered with beautifully executed paintings, some of which are peeling off at the top. Pride of place goes to the depictions of the breastfeeding Virgin Mary and St George on the western wall; these date from around 1920 and are attributed to Aleka Engeda, the artist responsible for the most modern paintings at Ura Kidane Mihret. Entrance costs US$5, though you may be asked for more.

To get to Robit Baata, follow the Gondar road for 15km past the bridge over the Blue Nile until you reach the village of Tabili, which is also serviced by regular minibuses from Bahir Dar. The church lies about 200m west of Tabili and is accessed by circling around to the back of the conspicuous forest patch wherein it lies.

KORATA The most populous and important port on Lake Tana for much of the Gondarine period, Korata (sometime spelt Qorata) was also once the most beautiful city in Ethiopia, according to Guglielmo Lejean, a French explorer who visited there in 1862. Situated on a forested peninsula about 18km northeast of present-day Bahir Dar, the town supported more than 10,000 people in its prime and was renowned for its wonderful stone houses with roofs supported by big pieces of wood. It fell into decline towards the end of the 19th century, and was reduced to little more than a ghost town following a murderous attack by the Italian occupiers in 1936. The last traditional houses were broken down under the Derg, who forced the few remaining inhabitants to resettle elsewhere.

Today, the most significant relic of the old town is a church dedicated to Walatta Petros, a nun of aristocratic birth who suffered immense persecution during the reign of the Catholic convert Emperor Susenyos because of her outspoken refusal to abandon the Ethiopian Orthodox faith, and is now one of the few female saints recognised by that denomination. The original church, by all accounts one of the most handsome in Ethiopia, was destroyed by an Italian hand grenade, but its replacement, built in the 1940s, houses several treasures including an armoured dress reputedly worn by Walatta Petros prior to her death on Rema Island in 1643, and a tapestry donated by Tewodros II. Buried beneath the undergrowth of the 25ha forest that now covers the hill are a few old stone walls and other ruins dating to Korata's 19th-century heyday. There is also a fair bit of wildlife about: baboons and monkeys in the forest, black-crowned cranes in the surrounding swamps, and occasionally hippos on the lake. December is a good time to see the coffee trees full of beans.

Getting there and away The springboard for visits to Korata is the lakeshore hamlet of Kento Mado, which can be reached along a good 11km dirt road that branches west from the Gondar road 27km northeast of Bahir Dar and 2.5km before Hamusit. The forested peninsula upon which lie the church and ruined town is clearly visible on the opposite side of the bay to Kenta Mado, only 800m distant by boat (*around US$20, assuming you can find a willing vessel*) but more like 3km away on foot. You could also travel directly by boat from Bahir Dar (*90mins one-way*), either as a self-contained trip or in combination with a visit to Tana Chirkos.

WANZAYE HOT SPRINGS Bubbling from beneath the earth at temperatures in excess of 42°C to feed a series of pools that empty into a set of rapids on the Gumara River, these hot springs 50km northeast of Bahir Dar are regarded as holy by Ethiopians, and popular for their alleged therapeutic qualities. If you fancy a healing dip in the (frankly, rather off-putting) concrete cubicles fed by the springs, the cramped public bath costs a few birr; or you can take charge of a private bath, taking up to three, for the princely sum of US$4. A more likely reason for a tourist to divert to Wanzaye is the monkeys and colourful birds that inhabit the riparian vegetation along the river. As for **accommodation**, a very rundown former government hotel (*35 rooms;* ✆*058 231 1017;* **$**) charges US$2/3 for a single/double room using common showers. Talk of an upmarket resort being built here seems a touch optimistic. Wanzaye is reached via a 9km dirt road (sometimes impassable after rain) that branches east from the Gondar road at an unsignposted but prominent junction about 10km past Hamusit.

AWRA AMBA (✆ *058 220 2673;* e *amhtour@ethionet.et;* w *visitawraamba.com;* *entrance US$1 pp, guide fee US$2 per party*) Founded in 1972 by Zumra Nuru and a group of like-minded people, the village and weaving co-operative of Awra Amba lies to the east of the Gondar road some 70km from Bahir Dar. It embodies its founder's ideal of living in a community 'where women and men are equal and where all of our children can go to school ... where religion and tradition don't dictate every aspect of our lives and where we work collectively, so we can stand a chance of coming out of poverty'. Probably the closest thing to a non-religious society you'll come across anywhere in Africa (pride of place is given not to a mosque or a church but to a surprisingly well-stocked school library), this isolated community also prides itself on an egalitarian, non-sexist, non-racist work policy (the weaving is shared between men and women), on the formal health care and support it provides to the elderly, and on a preschool aimed primarily at children under the age of seven, but also attended by older people seeking to attain a basic level of literacy.

Better known to Ethiopians than to tourists thanks to a television programme in which the village chairman unveiled his unorthodox religious views to a somewhat startled nation, Awra Amba welcomes foreign visitors, though it's rather quiet on Wednesdays and Saturdays, when most inhabitants are at the market. Ask to be shown the school, the library, the dormitories for elderly members of the community, the innovative *injera* cookers in the adobe houses (whose curvaceous design is reminiscent of similar structures in Mali's Dogon country), and the communal weaving area with its 20 handmade looms. The hand-spun cotton and wool products – *shamas*, scarves, shirts, blankets, etc – are sold on site and cost half what you'd pay for similar goods elsewhere in Ethiopia. Begging is forbidden, but book donations to the communal library are greatly appreciated.

To get to Awra Amba, follow the Gondar road for 60km out of Bahir Dar to Woreta, then after another 3km turn right on to the surfaced 'China Road' that runs east to Debre Tabor and Lalibela. About 8km down the China Road, Awra Amba is clearly signposted to the right. Any bus heading between Bahir Dar and Debre Tabor or points further east can drop you at the junction, from where it's only 2km to the village. Should you wish to stay overnight, simple huts with clean shared showers are available for around US$5.

ADDIS ZEMEN Situated on the Gondar road 20km past the junction with the China Road, the ancient town of Addis Zemen, where Emperor Sarsa Dengal took refuge during an Oromo raid in 1590, is the most substantial settlement between Bahir Dar and Gondar, with a population of around 20,000, and the best place to stop en route for a meal, a cold drink, or a bed for the night. Of some interest to birdwatchers, the seasonal floodplains running north from the junction towards Addis Zemen have recently been developed as rice paddies, and often host a rich variety of aquatic birds including the striking black-crowned crane and various herons, storks and waders. North of Addis Zemen, the road ascends into hillier territory, passing a striking isolated rock formation known as Tikil Dingay or the Devil's Nose.

GUZARA CASTLE Some 65km south of Gondar on the Bahir Dar road, just south of the small village of Emfraz, a rough 1km track to the east leads uphill to this small but rather magnificent and well-preserved hilltop palace, which was probably built for Emperor Sarsa Dengal in 1571. Easily visible from the main road and offering grand views across to Lake Tana, this imposing two-storey building, evidently built with a strong Portuguese input, bears a strong resemblance to the castles built by

Sarsa Dengal's grandson Fasilidas and his successors at Gondar half a century later. Indeed, Guzara's architectural resemblance to the Gondarine castles has led to recent speculation that it was built or substantially rebuilt by Fasilidas after Sarsa Dengal's death. The castle was under scaffolding in 2018, suggesting that further restoration work is planned.

DANQAZ, ZANTANA AND SEYFATRA MARYAM Situated 25km southeast of present-day Gondar, but almost three times as far away by road, **Danqaz** was the semi-permanent capital of Emperor Susenyos from 1619 until his abdication in 1632, and it also served as the capital of his successor Fasilidas for the first three years of his reign. According to Portuguese missionary Manuel de Almeida, who visited Danqaz in 1624, it was a substantial town comprising at least 8,000 houses made of wood, stone and mud, most of them round and roofed with thatch. The town's centrepiece, built with the assistance of skilled Portuguese and Indian artisans, was a 'palace of lime and stone, a structure that was a wonder in that country ... with halls and rooms on the ground floor and upper floor, very well-proportioned, and terraces from which can be seen not only the camp and the whole of Danqaz, but even very distant places in all directions'. Perched at an altitude of 2,800m above a spectacular cliff, the castle built for Susenyos is still there today, a partial two-storey ruin, but very impressive nonetheless, and a clear stylistic precursor to Fasilidas's Castle in Gondar. The only other substantial relic of 17th-century Danqaz, 300m to the southwest, are the walls and arches of a Catholic church that was founded amid much pomp and ceremony in 1628, but abandoned and most likely left uncompleted after Susenyos's abdication and the subsequent expulsion of Jesuits from Ethiopia.

Two other sites can easily be visited in conjunction with Danqaz. **Zantana**, only 6km further south, is reputedly where Ahmed Gragn was buried after he died in battle (some say he was struck by a Portuguese musket ball, others that he was stung to death by one of those bee swarms that habitually go on the rampage at critical junctures in Ethiopian history) on 11 February 1543. Known locally as Gragn Mekabir, the burial site is rather underwhelming – a 20-year-old concrete tomb-marker and nothing else – but many Muslim Ethiopians still make the pilgrimage there on the anniversary of Gragn's death, although, with this being a predominantly Christian area, shrines erected in his memory tend to vanish shortly afterwards.

Rather more impressive is the little-known church of **Seyfatra Maryam**, which lies on the northern outskirts of a substantial village called Dagoma 11km south of Danqaz. Established during the 14th-century reign of Sayfa Arad and reputedly patronised by Emperor Yohannes IV, this circular church has a pastel blue outer wall, but the inner stone wall looks to be very old, and its square *maqdas* is covered from floor to roof with vividly coloured and detailed paintings. Some of these paintings obviously date from the 20th century, depicting as they do Haile Selassie-era officials and aristocrats in contemporary dress, but the priest claims that the church's oldest paintings date from the early 16th-century reign of Lebna Dengal, and have since been touched up, while others are from the 19th century. Refreshingly, no entrance fee is charged to enter this lovely church, but it would be polite to leave something in the donations box.

All three sites lie about 20km east of the main road between Bahir Dar and Gondar. The unsignposted but prominent junction lies 30km south of Gondar, between the 685km and 686km markers, some 5km north of Maksegno Gebeya and 1.5km south of Bahari Gimb. From the junction, a well-maintained dirt road runs east for 21km to Dagoma and Seyfatra Maryam. About 17km along this road, a three-way junction called Gragn Ber (Gragn Door) is reputedly the spot where its namesake was mortally wounded and then rested up against a tree (whose stump still stands there today) before he died. To get to Danqaz, turn left at Gragn Ber, then continue for another 7km to the unofficial car park at the start of the 3km footpath to Danqaz, passing a prominent hilltop satellite tower to the right about 800m before it. Unexpectedly, the car park is actually marked by a signpost reading 'Danqaz', but rather unhelpfully it points in completely the wrong direction – you need to head right (to the northeast) not left. It's a 45-minute walk to the ruined castle and church, which stand above an escarpment at the north end of the tiny village of Gomange, and are easily located, though a guide would be useful if only to prevent the local children's demands for money from spiralling out of control. Zantana lies about 3km from Gragn Ber along the road to Gomange, and the tomb is clearly visible on the opposite side of a small river valley 250m to the east.

BET BAHARI MIKAEL This unusual church, dominated by an 11m-high conical Gondarine-style dome, stands on a low wooded hill on the east side of the main road 500m north of the village of Bahari Gimb and 28km south of Gondar. Local legend states that the church and its dome were constructed during the reign of Emperor Lebna Dengal, with some architectural input from Pêro de Covilhã, and originally served as the castle (*gimb*) of Bahari, a nobleman who died in battle with Ahmed Gragn's army. If this is true, then it is something of an architectural pioneer, being at least a century older than the castles at Gondar. However, some experts think the dome is more likely to be an 18th-century addition. Either way, it's an unusually atmospheric church, though the walls were seriously damaged during a skirmish between government and rebel troops in 1990. A second building immediately west of the old church also has a tall domed roof, constructed in the 1960s by Haile Selassie. The church is visible from the main road and easily reached along a 350m side road close to the 688km marker. The entrance fee of US$5 feels steep given the unadorned nature of the interior, but the priests seem to be open to negotiation.

GORGORA AND NORTHERN LAKE TANA

The most important port on Lake Tana's northern shore, Gorgora is a historic small town whose waterfront is dominated by the leafy Marine Authority compound. Home to the laid-back Tim & Kim Village, Gorgora is a great place to chill out for a few days, highly rewarding for birdwatchers and offering access to several intriguing historical sites, most notably Debre Sina Maryam, a church adorned with some of Ethiopia's oldest surviving wall paintings. More remote attractions include a hilltop lighthouse dating from the Italian occupation, the abandoned castle and church of Maryam Gimb, and several little-visited male-only lake monasteries.

HISTORY Gorgora is essentially a 20th-century creation, but the adjacent monastery of Debre Sina Maryam probably dates to the 14th-century reign of Amda Tsion, and the promontory now known as Old Gorgora, 10km further west, briefly served as the capital of Emperor Susenyos in the early 17th century. The rise of Old Gorgora started in 1607, when Emperor Susenyos granted Pedro Páez a patch of land to establish a Jesuit mission there. Four years later, Susenyos settled on Old Gorgora as the latest of his temporary capitals. Páez, keen to ingratiate himself with the emperor and convert him to Catholicism, constructed a palace for Susenyos in 1614, then shortly afterwards set about building the massive cathedral and castle now known as Maryam Gimb. Páez died in 1622, the same year that Susenyos officially converted, and was buried at Old Gorgora. By that time, Danqaz

6

had more or less replaced Old Gorgora as the imperial capital, but the Jesuit mission continued to thrive until 1632, when Fasilidas expelled the Catholic settlers from his empire. Old Gorgora was abandoned shortly thereafter. The modern town of Gorgora leapt to prominence during the Italian occupation, when a private company called Navigatana installed a car and passenger ferry service connecting it to several other lake ports and islands. The port and ferry were nationalised in the 1970s, since when Gorgora has gradually reverted to backwater status, with a population currently estimated at 5,000.

GETTING THERE AND AWAY

By boat Gorgora was until recently the northern terminus of a weekly ferry service to/from Bahir Dar. At the time this edition was researched, however, the boat travelled only as far as Delgi, which is around 50km from Gorgora via Chwahit. See page 244 for further details.

By road Gorgora lies 65km south of Gondar along an excellent new asphalt road that can be covered in an hour in a private vehicle. Regular buses also run back and forth between Gondar and Gorgora but take longer as they stop to drop and pick up passengers along the way.

WHERE TO STAY, EAT AND DRINK *Map, page 256*

✳ 🏠 Tim & Kim Village (10 rooms) m 0920 336671; e timandkimvillage@gmail. com; w timkimvillage.com. Set in 3ha of natural vegetation running down the lakeshore 1km south of Gorgora, this tranquil & eco-friendly owner-managed lodge offers the choice of smart solar-powered stone-&-thatch en-suite lodges that come with terracotta floor, dbl or twin beds under good netting, private balcony & hot shower, or simple mud houses using common showers & toilets. There is also a campsite. The dinner of the day costs US$6, & is eaten communally in a lovely thatched open-air restaurant with a good book swap & collection of board games. B/fast is available for US$2.50, & sandwiches & snacks for US$2.50–US$4.50. Birding in the ficus-strewn grounds is superb, & the lodge also offers a range of activities including a 4–5hr cultural village tour (*US$15 pp exc entrance to Debre Sina Maryam*), the short but steep hike to Mussolini Peak, & canoe trips to various nearby islands. *US$30/45/50 sgl/dbl/trpl en-suite lodge, US$15/19 sgl/dbl mud house, US$5 pp camping.* **$$–$$$$**

🏠 Gorgora Port Hotel (26 rooms) m 0913 001770. This antiquated government-owned hotel has a wonderful lakeshore position in the well-wooded marine compound, but the en-suite rooms are rather musty & rundown. An adequate restaurant is attached. *From US$8/12 sgl/dbl.* **$$**

WHAT TO SEE AND DO Gorgora, or more specifically Tim & Kim Village, is a great place to relax and enjoy the lovely lake vistas, abundant birdlife and brilliant nocturnal skies. Debre Sina Maryam and the Fascist-built lighthouse on Mussolini Peak lie within easy walking distance of town, while the monastery at Mandaba Medhane Alem is only 5km away by road. Tim & Kim Village also organises 2½-hour canoe trips to birdwatch on the lake, or to visit the most nearby island monasteries (*US$19.50 for the 1st person, US$6 for each additional person, inc a guide, life jackets & waterproof bags*). Motorboat trips to Old Gorgora and the monasteries en route take around 4–5 hours for the round trip, and can be arranged through the ferry ticket office in the Lake Tana Transport Authority compound. The official rate is around US$70 per party, but this is very negotiable.

Debre Sina Maryam A highlight of any visit to Gorgora will be this lovely medieval monastery (*entrance US$4 inc photography*), which lies a few hundred metres from the town centre, and permits women visitors. As is so often the case, the church's history varies with the telling, but it was most likely founded in 1334 or thereabouts by a monk called Hesterus from the town of Debre Sina. The present building, a fine example of a thatched circular church, probably dates from the 16th century, though the carved Axumite windows and frames might well be lifted from an earlier incarnation. The church's most important treasure is a glass-covered painting called *The Egyptian Saint Mary*. A fabulously implausible legend has it that this portrait of the Virgin Mary dates from her period of exile in Egypt, lights up spontaneously from time to time, and has the capacity to revive dead children.

The murals in Debre Sina Maryam rank with the most complex and vivid to be seen in the Tana region, despite having been subjected to some rather clumsy turn-of-the-millennium restoration work. Two particularly striking panels depict the devil rolling about in laughter as Adam and Eve sample the forbidden fruit, and a smug-looking King Herod and his cronies making bloodthirsty work of the newly born children of Israel. Several of the original paintings were executed in the 1620s under the patronage of Melako Tawit, a noblewoman depicted on one mural and usually identified as the elder sister of Emperor Fasilidas. This means they were painted almost 400 years ago, making them significantly older than their counterparts at Ura Kidane Mihret or Narga Selassie, and quite possibly than any other church paintings in the Tana area. The lowest row of paintings is stylistically very different from the row that includes the portrait of Melako Tawit (compare the facial detail of the lower and higher portraits of Mary on the wall as you enter), so it could be they are even older.

Mussolini Peak Known locally by the name given to it during the Italian occupation, this low peak 1.5km west of Gorgora is the site of a conspicuous concrete lighthouse constructed in 1938 to celebrate the Italian victory over Ethiopia two years earlier. Standing about 8m tall, it is decorated with a rather triumphalist engraving of a stabbed and dying lion (symbolising the Lion of Abyssinia) and the Latin phrase 'Usque ad Finem' (meaning 'To the very end'). It's a rather unprepossessing structure, and the light was switched off long ago, but the steep 30-minute walk uphill from town is worthwhile just for the spectacular view over the port and lake.

Mandaba Medhane Alem Set on a narrow forested peninsula 5km southwest of Gorgora, this 14th-century male-only monastery ranks among the most venerated on the northern part of the lake, having been visited by several emperors past, among them Susenyos, Fasilidas, Yohannes I, Bakaffa, Menelik II and Haile Selassie. It was founded by Abuna Yasay, the ascetic son of Emperor Amda Tsion, who reputedly sailed there from Korata on the stone *tankwa* now preserved in a kiosk outside the main church, and its devout and virtuous monks are considered to be angels made flesh. The church underwent major reconstruction in the 1950s, and further renovation in 2012, but parts of the interior, including the painted door-frame and *maqdas*, are very old. An adjacent museum houses a superb collection of manuscripts and painted icons dating back to the 14th to 16th centuries, along with several items donated by various visiting emperors, and more random artefacts such as old grinding stones and a hippo skull. Entrance costs US$4, inclusive of photography. Formerly accessible only by boat or on foot, the monastery is now connected to Gorgora by a good new unsurfaced road.

Brigida Maryam Susenyos and Angara Tekle Haymanot These two venerable island monasteries both lie close to the mainland about 3km south of

Gorgora, and can be visited either by canoe with Tim & Kim Village or else on a boat chartered from the Lake Tana Transport Authority. Women are not permitted. The more interesting of the two is Brigida Maryam Susenyos, which was reputedly built by Amda Tsion in the 14th century, and was later a favoured retreat of Emperor Bakaffa. It is of limited architectural interest, having been reconstructed at least three times owing to fire damage, but its plentiful treasures include a superb 16th-century painting of Mary. Nearby Angara Tekle Haymanot has few treasures and the present-day church dates to the Haile Selassie era. The entrance fee is negotiable.

Old Gorgora The well-wooded promontory of Old Gorgora, situated 10km west of its modern namesake, is the site of a long-since-abandoned Jesuit mission established by Pedro Páez in 1607, and it also served as the capital of Emperor Susenyos for a few brief years in the early 17th century. The peninsula is more or less uninhabited today, but what remains of the cathedral and palace built by Páez – several tall stone walls and towers, their archways engraved with flowers and crosses – is sufficient to hint at its former grandeur. Of some architectural significance as a stylistic precursor to the better-preserved castles at Danqaz and Gondar, Old Gorgora is poorly preserved, remote and rather overgrown, though there is some talk of the ruins being restored by UNESCO. The easiest way to get there is by boat from Gorgora, stopping en route at some of the monasteries described elsewhere in this section. Alternatively, you could drive there with a private 4x4, or even walk, following a signposted 10km track that branches southwest from the Gondar road at Abrijihar, 8km inland of Gorgora, and passes through the village of Tuhuwa Hana about 3km before it reaches Old Gorgora.

Bahir Galila Zacharias Situated 15km southwest of Gorgora, a boat trip of about 1 hour, Bahir Galila Zacharias was founded in the 14th century by a monk called Zacharias, who could reputedly walk on water and gave it an Amharic name meaning 'Sea of Galilee'. The monastery was destroyed and all its monks massacred in the 16th century by Ahmed Gragn, but the present church was built using the original stones. Women are not permitted and the entrance fee is negotiable.

7

Gondar and the Simien Mountains

The largest of the three former capitals that form the backbone of northern Ethiopia's historical circuit, Gondar stands at an altitude of 2,200m in the highlands north of Lake Tana, 730km by road from Addis Ababa, to which it is connected by several flights daily, though many visitors choose to drive there from Bahir Dar, only 175km to the south. Renowned as the site of an impressive cluster of castles dating from its 17th- and 18th-century imperial heydays, Gondar is also graced by one of Ethiopia's most beautifully painted churches in the form of Debre Berhan Selassie. Once known primarily for its historical sightseeing, Gondar is now increasingly perceived to be of interest first and foremost as the springboard for day and overnight excursions to the Simien Mountains National Park, which lies about 100km to its north, and protects the eponymous mountain range, the country's highest at 4,533m. The premier hiking destination in Ethiopia, but also easily explored in a 4x4, this national park is notable both for its spectacularly precipitous Afromontane scenery and for its remarkable wildlife, which includes important populations of Ethiopian wolf, gelada monkey and Walia ibex, along with iconic raptors such as lammergeier, Rüppell's vulture and Verreaux's eagle.

GONDAR

The so-called Camelot of Africa, Gondar is perhaps the most immediately impressive town along the historical circuit, studded as it is with fairy-tale castles, venerable churches and other substantial European-influenced buildings dating from its 17th- and 18th-century heyday. Imposing as they might be, however, Gondar's handsome antiquities are arguably less intriguing and enduringly memorable than their more genuinely ancient and mysterious counterparts at Axum and Lalibela, for which reason we would rank it as the least essential stop of the three for historically minded visitors with insufficient time to visit them all. That said, the well-preserved castles and palaces that grace Gondar's stone-walled Fasil Ghebbi, a UNESCO World Heritage Site, seldom disappoint, while the lavishly painted church of Debre Berhan Selassie and brooding 18th-century palatial complex at Kuskuam both rank highly on Ethiopia's list of must-sees. Historical sightseeing aside, Gondar is a very pleasant city to explore, with a friendly, laid-back, almost countrified mood by comparison with Addis Ababa or even Bahir Dar. It boasts some excellent traditional restaurants and live music venues, and it's also a good place to arrange overnight hikes in the nearby Simien Mountains.

HISTORY

Early years Gondar was established in c1635 as the permanent capital of Emperor Fasilidas (often abbreviated to Fasil). It was founded in the aftermath of a tumultuous century during which the Abyssinian Empire had virtually collapsed under the onslaught of an Islamic army led by Ahmed Gragn, and then experienced a period of intense domestic religious conflict during the reign of Susenyos (Fasilidas's father and immediate predecessor). In 1622, Susenyos, under the influence of Portuguese missionary Pedro Páez, not only had converted to Catholicism, but went one step further by attempting to close down the Ethiopian Orthodox Church and replacing it as state religion with the exotic denomination. The result of this policy was a period of violent instability, during which an estimated 32,000 peasants were killed by the royal army. By 1632, the unpopular Susenyos was left with little choice but to abdicate in favour of Fasilidas, who immediately reinstated the traditional state religion and expelled the Portuguese from the empire.

After a period of several centuries during which Ethiopia was ruled from a succession of temporary capitals, Fasilidas recognised that a more permanent arrangement might encourage greater internal stability. So, after three years based at Danqaz, the last and most elaborate of his father's temporary capitals, Fasilidas relocated 25km northwest to Gondar and set about building the largest and most famous of the castles that grace the Royal Enclosure. One oft-repeated story has it that Fasilidas selected Gondar because it fulfilled an ancient tradition by having the initial letter of 'G'. However, some historians maintain that this 'tradition' was manufactured by the royal myth machine subsequent to the adoption of Gondar as capital. Certainly, Fasilidas's choice of capital would also have been influenced by the site's strategic hilltop location along a well-established trade route in the centre of the empire only 35km north of Lake Tana.

The heyday By the time of Fasilidas's death in 1667, Gondar had become the largest city in the empire, with a population in excess of 60,000. Its founder was succeeded by two popular emperors, his son Yohannes I (1667–82) and grandson Iyasu I or Iyasu the Great (1682–1706). In July 1699, Iyasu's court was visited by the French doctor Charles Jacques Poncet, the first European to enter Ethiopia since Fasilidas had evicted the Portuguese Jesuits 67 years earlier. Poncet was welcomed by Iyasu, who hoped the physician might be able to cure him of a mysterious skin ailment, and he stayed on for nine months at the emperor's invitation. Poncet in turn described the 41-year-old Iyasu as a 'lively and sagacious genius', and penned the only contemporary account of a ceremony typical of Gondar in its late 17th-century pomp. According to the French doctor, the ceremony was attended by 12,000 soldiers in battledress, and the emperor arrived with 'two princes of the blood in splendid dresses … holding a magnificent canopy under which the emperor walked, preceded by his trumpets, kettledrums, fifes, harps and other instruments'.

Despite his medical qualifications, Poncet was a covert agent of King Louis XIV, tasked not only with initiating diplomatic relations between Gondar and Versailles, but also – and more consequentially – with restoring the Jesuit presence in the empire, this time under the auspices of the French rather than the Portuguese. This agenda did not escape the notice of the Orthodox clergy, who were alarmed at the sudden renewal of contact between European Catholics and the emperor only 70 years after the religious strife that took place under Susenyos. Iyasu's 24-year reign came to an abrupt and bloody end in 1706, when he was murdered by his son Tekle Haymanot I, with the support of the clergy. This self-serving act of patricide initiated a renewal of Catholic–Orthodox tension and arguably signalled the beginning of the end of Gondar's heyday. Indeed, Tekle Haymanot became the first of four successive emperors to be crowned and then assassinated in the space of 15 years. A semblance of stability was restored in 1721 with the coronation of Bakaffa, a stern and devout ruler whose attempts to restore unity nevertheless alienated some of his most powerful subjects, and most likely led to his mysterious death in 1730.

Decline and revival
Bakaffa was succeeded by his seven-year-old son Iyasu II under the regency of his mother, Mentewab, who made the fateful decision, on account of her son's extreme youth, to appoint various noblemen and local princes as her regional proxies. Religious tension resurfaced towards the end of Iyasu II's reign, when the emperor became close to Remedius Prutky, a Czech Franciscan who resided in Gondar for the best part of a year prior to being forced out by the Orthodox clergy in 1752. Iyasu II died suddenly in 1755, possibly poisoned by the sister of his mother's second husband, who had been pushed off a cliff with fatal consequences in 1742, and whose family blamed the young emperor for his death.

The factionalism that characterised the Gondarine court under the ineffectual Iyasu II was exacerbated when his infant son Iyoas I was appointed as his successor. Mentewab acted as self-appointed regent to her grandson, a claim heatedly contested by Iyasu's widow, Wubet. A war between the two factions was averted by Mentewab's stepson Ras Mikael Sehul, a powerful Tigrayan prince whose 25,000-strong army took control of Gondar and allowed Mentewab to stay on as regent.

Over the next 15 years, the divisive Ras Mikael (whose nickname Sehul means 'sharp') assumed an increasingly Machiavellian role in Gondarine politics. In May 1769, he had the teenage emperor strangled and installed in his place Yohannes II, an unwilling and disabled 70-year-old son of Iyasu I. Six months later, he poisoned Yohannes II and handed the throne to his 15-year-old son, Tekle Haymanot II. Ras Mikael's reign of terror ended in June 1771, when he was defeated in battle by three rival princes, imprisoned for a year, then forced to retire to Tigray. Meanwhile, the sidelining of his original mentor left the allegiances of the young Tekle Haymanot II torn between a number of powerful princes. His short and fractious reign ended when he renounced the throne to become a monk in 1777.

So began the Zemene Mesafint (Era of the Princes), a period of almost a century during which the former empire split up into a patchwork of fiefdoms ruled by powerful local princes whose families had consolidated their local power bases following Mentewab's move towards decentralisation in the 1730s. Gondar retained its status as capital during this period, but it was presided over by a series of figurehead emperors whose influence outside the city was marginal. Still, in 1855, when the central monarchy was restored by Emperor Tewodros II, Gondar was still probably the largest settlement in Ethiopia, and it also remained the cultural and economic fulcrum of the empire.

Gondar suffered several mighty blows in the second half of the 19th century. In 1864, Tewodros ordered his army to ransack the city, which he believed to be a hotbed of resentment and potential rebellion against his upstart leadership. Two years later, the emperor proclaimed Debre Tabor as his new capital and launched a second and far more destructive attack on its predecessor. According to one French observer, the attack reduced Gondar and several of its churches to 'a heap of blackened ruins', while an Italian explorer who passed through 15 years later was shocked at the 'horrid poverty' that blighted the former capital. Worse was to follow in January 1888, when Abu Angu led the Mahdist army across the border from Sudan to launch a bloody attack on Gondar. Thousands of Gondarine citizens were massacred by the Mahdist army, while the survivors were captured and taken across to Sudan as slaves. And the few central churches spared by Tewodros two decades earlier were almost all razed in the jihad.

Gondar's slump in fortunes continued well into the 20th century. Indeed, photographs of the central Ras Gimb taken c1930 show an isolated building

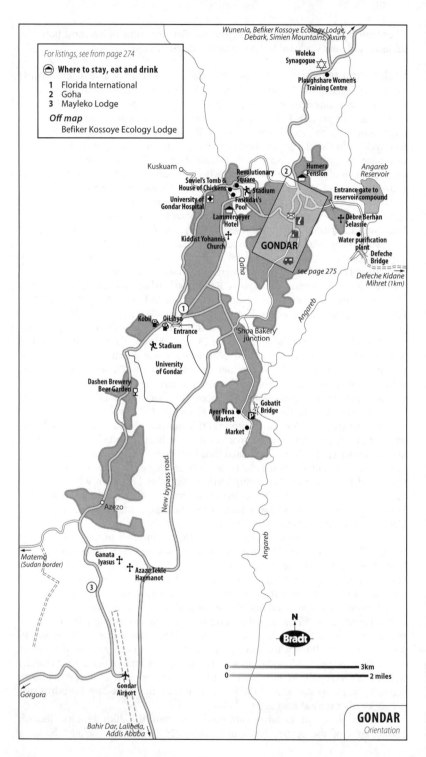

For listings, see from page 274

⌂ **Where to stay, eat and drink**
1 Florida International
2 Goha
3 Mayleko Lodge

Off map
Befiker Kossoye Ecology Lodge

Wunenia, Befiker Kossoye Ecology Lodge,
Debark, Simien Mountains, Axum

Woleka
Synagogue

Ploughshare Women's
Training Centre

Kuskuam

Suviel's Tomb &
House of Chickens
University of
Gondar Hospital
Revolutionary
Square
Stadium
Fasilidas's
Pool
Lammergeyer
Hotel
Kiddist Yohannis
Church

Humera
Pension

Angareb
Reservoir

Entrance gate to
reservoir compound

Debre Berhan
Selassie

Water purification
plant

Defeche
Bridge

Defeche Kidane
Mihret (1km)

GONDAR

Qaha

see page 275

Angareb

Kobil
OiLibya
Entrance

Stadium

'Shoa Bakery'
junction

University
of Gondar

Dashen Brewery
Beer Garden

Ayer Tena
Market
Gobatit
Bridge

Market

New bypass road

Azezo

Matema
(Sudan border)

Ganata
Iyasus
Azazo Tekle
Haymanot

Angareb

Gorgora

N
Bradt

0 ———————————— 3km
0 ———————————— 2 miles

Gondar
Airport

Bahir Dar, Lalibela,
Addis Ababa

GONDAR
Orientation

surrounded by open countryside. The revival of the city is largely creditable to Italy, which established a consulate there in 1929, with the aim of reviving trade between Asmara (Eritrea) and Addis Ababa; then, during the occupation of 1936–41, developed the nascent town as a major administrative centre and military outpost housing up to 40,000 soldiers. Indeed, it was at Gondar that the Italians made their last stand, surrendering to the Allied army on 27 November 1941, following an offensive that claimed the lives of 206 British and Ethiopian soldiers. Much of the modern town centre dates from the Italian period, and hints of Art Deco and other pre-war European styles can still be detected in many of the older buildings that line the central Piazza. Until 1994, Gondar served as the capital and principal town of an eponymous province that was subsequently absorbed into the Federal Region of Amhara. It remains one of the largest cities in Ethiopia, with a population estimated at 600,000.

GETTING THERE AND AWAY
By air Ethiopian Airlines flies daily between Gondar and Addis Ababa, Axum and Lalibela. All flights land at Gondar Atse Tewodros Airport, 15km south of town, and 3km from Azezo off the road to Bahir Dar. Most upmarket hotels offer a free airport shuttle service. Shared taxis between the airport and town centre cost around US$3 per person, and private taxis around US$10.

By boat For details of the Lake Tana ferry service connecting Bahir Dar to the northern port of Gorgora/Delgi, see page 244.

By road Gondar lies 730km from Addis Ababa by road, and most travellers punctuate the trip with a night or two at Bahir Dar. If you want to travel directly, however, you could drive through in one day with a very early start; Ethio, Selam Limalimo and to a lesser extent Sky all operate a reliable daily coach service between Addis Ababa and Gondar, departing in either direction at around 05.30 (*US$18; 12–15hrs*).

Bahir Dar and Gondar lie 175km apart along a good surfaced road that can be covered in 3 hours flat, but also offers scope for diversions to the likes of Bet Bahari Mikael, Danqaz, Guzara Castle and Awra. Minibuses between Bahir Dar and Gondar leave every 30 minutes or so in either direction between 06.00 and 16.30.

To get to Lalibela on **public transport**, catch a minibus to Dessie (*US$11, departing at around 05.00*), and ask to be dropped at Gashena, from where occasional minibuses leave for Lalibela until mid afternoon.

Heading north from Gondar, regular minibuses run back and forth to Debark (for the Simien Mountains) between 06.00 and 15.00 (*around 2hrs*). If you are heading directly to Axum, catch the 05.30 bus to Shire Inda Selassie (*6–8hrs*), where you can easily pick up transport on to Axum.

Almost all buses and minibuses to destinations further afield leave from the main bus station, which lies in Arada about 500m south of Fasil Ghebbi. The main exceptions are the Sky, Selam, Ethio and Limalimo luxury buses, which leave from Meskel Square, bordering Fasil Ghebbi.

ORIENTATION
Gondar lies in a valley run through by two rivers, the Qaha and Angareb, whose confluence lies at the southern end of town. The focal point of the city centre is the historic Fasil Ghebbi. Running north from this, the central business district known as the Piazza still boasts several buildings dating from the Italian occupation. To the south of Fasil Ghebbi, the busier and more down-to-earth district called Arada is the site of the main bus station and market. Although

Gondar is primarily Christian, it also boasts old Islamic and Jewish quarters, which have been segregated since Fasilidas's day, initially at the emperor's insistence, but more recently by custom rather than decree. The old Islamic quarter, about 500m south of Arada, is now known as Addis Alem (New World) and incorporates several old mosques. The former Jewish quarter of Woleka lies 3km north of the city centre alongside the road to Debark.

GETTING AROUND Cheap **minibuses** cover most main roads between central and suburban Gondar. *Bajaji* are readily available – you should pay about US$1–1.50 within the city centre. For suburban destinations such as Fasil's Bath or Debre Berhan Selassie Church you can charter a **taxi** for around US$3 but will invariably be asked a lot more.

GUIDES Avoid hooking up with the aspirant guides who hang around the Piazza. Instead, pick up an official guide at the **Gondar Guides Association**, which has its permanent headquarters just inside the entrance of the Royal Enclosure before the ticket office. The going rate, depending on group size, is US$20–30 for a full day and about half that for a 2–3-hour tour of the Fasil Ghebbi. Most guides can organise day trips to Wunenia and longer trips to the Simien Mountains, but do check prices against those offered by private tour operators before agreeing to anything.

 WHERE TO STAY Note that most hotels in Gondar inflate room prices over the week or so building up to Timkat (19 January) and for a few days after.

Upmarket

✳ 🏠 **Mayleko Lodge** [map, page 272] (30 rooms) **m** 0912 202801; **e** mayleko_lodge@ yahoo.com; **w** maylekolodge.net. The most stylish option in the immediate vicinity of Gondar, this owner-managed boutique lodge lies in large rural gardens near Azezo, 12km south of town & 3km from the airport. Spacious traditional-style bungalow rooms & suites have large en-suite hot showers, private verandas, king-size or twin ¾ beds, stone floors, bamboo ceilings & traditional wooden furniture. There's a row of newer standard rooms with similar facilities but a more minimalist look. An airy restaurant hung with contemporary art serves a regularly changing selection of local & international dishes in the US$5–8 range. There is also a swimming pool, & a spa is under construction. Highly recommended for those seeking individualistic out-of-town lodgings. *US$60/70 standard sgl/dbl, US$80/90 bungalow, US$140/160 suite.* **$$$$–$$$$$**

✳ 🏠 **Befiker Kossoye Ecology Lodge** [map, page 224] (14 rooms) **** 058 111 2324; **m** 0911 250828, 0918 789798; **e** contact@semienkossoye. com; **w** semienkossoye.com. This agreeably quirky lodge, set in 35ha grounds 30km north of Gondar, is neither so slick nor so convenient as Mayleko,

but the views across layers of mountains to the distant horizon are stunning. With gelada, guereza & plentiful highland birds likely to be seen on guided walks, it makes an excellent alternative to Gondar for nature lovers, & it's well placed as a springboard for the Simiens. Semi-detached *tukul*-style stone-&-thatch houses come with 1 dbl & 1 sgl bed, hot shower & plenty of bamboo, wood & local fabrics to emphasise the down-to-earth vibe. Other attractions include horseback trips, a day hike to the remote monastery of Chugie Maryam, & evening bonfires to keep the cold at bay. The restaurant serves a regularly changing menu using mostly home-grown ingredients. *US$65/80/120 B&B sgl/dbl/trpl.* **$$$$**

🏠 **Goha Hotel** [map, page 272] (80 rooms) **** 058 111 0634; **e** info@gohahotel. com; **w** gohahotel.com. This refurbished former government hotel 1.5km north of central Gondar stands out for its wonderful hilltop setting, views over town & swimming pool. The en-suite rooms are decorated with bright colours & traditional fabrics. The restaurant has an imaginative menu with most mains in the US$4–6 range. *US$70/80 B&B sgl/dbl, with a substantial low season discount.* **$$$$**

🏠 **Taye Belay Hotel** [275 C3] (79 rooms) **** 058 111 2252; **m** 0913 820383; **e** reservation@

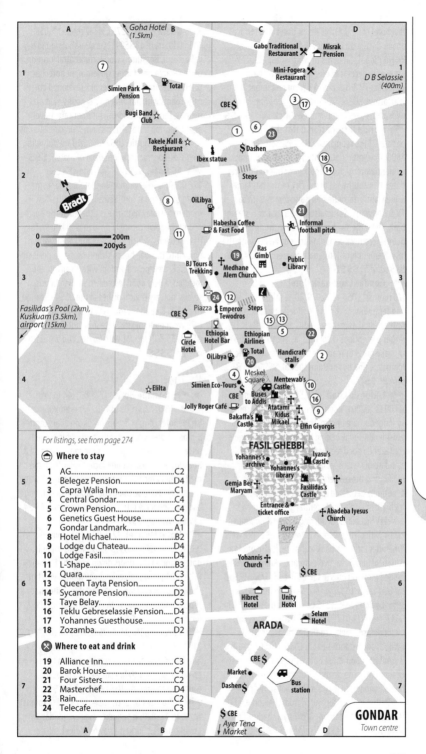

For listings, see from page 274

Where to stay

1	AG	C2
2	Belegez Pension	D4
3	Capra Walia Inn	C1
4	Central Gondar	C4
5	Crown Pension	C4
6	Genetics Guest House	C2
7	Gondar Landmark	A1
8	Hotel Michael	B2
9	Lodge du Chateau	D4
10	Lodge Fasil	D4
11	L-Shape	B3
12	Quara	C3
13	Queen Tayta Pension	C3
14	Sycamore Pension	D2
15	Taye Belay	C3
16	Teklu Gebreselassie Pension	D4
17	Yohannes Guesthouse	C1
18	Zozamba	D2

Where to eat and drink

19	Alliance Inn	C3
20	Barok House	C4
21	Four Sisters	C2
22	Masterchef	D4
23	Rain	C2
24	Telecafe	C3

GONDAR
Town centre

tayehotel.com; **f**. This 4-star hotel on a terrace above the Piazza doesn't fall far short of the international standards to which it aspires. Agreeably decorated en-suite rooms all have hot water, sat TV & balcony. A decent restaurant & bar is attached. *US$60/70/85 B&B sgl/dbl/family room, with a 35–40% discount offered May–Aug.* **$$$$**

🏠 **Florida International Hotel** [map, page 272] (60 rooms) **m** 0918 350860, 0962 880000; **e** info@floridainternationalhotel.com; **w** floridainternationalhotel.com. This multistorey hotel 4km southwest of the city centre has large & pleasantly decorated en-suite rooms with sat TV & hot water. Suites also have a jacuzzi & steam bath. The large swimming pool is a strong selling point. Decent value assuming you can live with the inconvenient location & garish exterior. *US$45/50 B&B sgl/dbl.* **$$$$**

🏠 **Gondar Landmark Hotel** [275 A1] (70 rooms) **** 058 112 2929/30; **e** info@gonderlandmark.com; **w** gonderlandmark.com. Aptly named, this conspicuous monolith feels rather pretentious & soulless, as encapsulated by the fake grass that adorns the terraces. En-suite rooms are fine but nothing special. *US$60/65 B&B sgl/dbl.* **$$$$**

🏠 **Lodge du Chateau** [275 D4] (13 rooms) **m** 0918 152001; **e** lodge@lodgeduchateau.com; **w** lodgeduchateau.com. This small, individualistic, eco-friendly lodge behind the Royal Enclosure gets consistently good reader feedback for the high standard of service set by the engaged owner-manager & the cosy en-suite rooms, which are beautifully decorated using locally made furniture. It's built around a lovely central garden, & there's a breezy upstairs deck offering a large & delicious b/fast with plenty of fresh ingredients & a nice view. Amenities include a book exchange. It also offers a variety of unusual activities from cooking lessons to guided morning runs (page 280). *US$45/55/75 B&B sgl/dbl/trpl, or US$20 pp in a 5-bed dorm.* **$$$$**

🏠 **Lodge Fasil** [275 C4] (13 rooms) **** 058 111 0637; **m** 0911 017991; **e** beffrem@yahoo.com; **w** lodgefasil.weebly.com. This pleasant family-owned lodge stands next to Lodge du Chateau & is similarly good value but slightly cheaper & less characterful. The clean en-suite rooms with tiled floors, wooden ceiling, sat TV & hot shower are in a 2-storey block separated from the popular thatched-roof restaurant & bar by a shady wild olive tree. *US$35/45 B&B sgl/dbl.* **$$$**

🏠 **Quara Hotel** [275 C3] (42 rooms) **** 058 111 0040; **m** 0918 350412; **e** quarahotelgondar@yahoo.com. Boasting a wonderful central location on the Piazza, this former government hotel has brightly decorated but rather old-fashioned en-suite rooms with hot water, TV & dodgy electric fittings. Facilities include an internet café, travel agent, rooftop terrace, hair salon, sauna, restaurant & free airport shuttle. *US$27/31 B&B sgl/dbl, with plenty of room for negotiation out of season.* **$$$**

🏠 **AG Hotel** [275 C2] (44 rooms) **** 058 126 0073; **e** reservations@aghotelgondar.com; **w** aghotelgondar.com; see ad, page 299. This modern 5-storey high-rise is situated at the north end of the town centre in an area well known for its nightclubs, which can make the rooms rather noisy into the wee hours. Otherwise, it's a perfectly decent & well-priced option, with a convenient location, a very good restaurant serving pizzas, steaks, poultry & local dishes in the US$4–5 range, free Wi-Fi & spacious rooms with sat TV, queen-size bed, wooden furniture & en-suite hot shower. *US$45/50 B&B sgl/dbl, with low-season discounts offered.* **$$$$**

Budget

☀ 🏠 **L-Shape Hotel** [275 B3] (44 rooms) **** 058 116 0272; **m** 0918 770272; **e** info@lshapehotel.com; **w** lshapehotel.com. This central 5-storey hotel is consistently praised for its well-priced, spotless & bright en-suite rooms with TV & hot shower. Do ask for one facing away from the road. Other amenities include free luggage storage & a funky (as these things go) ground-floor lounge bar with indoor & terrace seating. *US$9/11/16/24 sgl/dbl/twin/trpl.* **$$**

🏠 **Hotel Michael** [275 B2] (17 rooms) **** 058 111 0020; **m** 0918 350224. This friendly hotel stands a few doors down from the L-Shape & is equally good value. En-suite rooms with hot shower are very clean & comfortable; suites have a separate sitting room with TV. *US$10 dbl or US$12 for a twin or suite.* **$$**

🏠 **Zozamba Hotel** [275 D2] (23 rooms) **** 058 211 0131; **m** 0918 350600. This new 3-storey hotel bordering the city centre has clean tiled en-suite rooms with hot shower & a pleasant courtyard restaurant. *US$12/16 sgl/dbl.* **$$**

🏠 **Yohannes Guesthouse** [275 C1] (8 rooms) **m** 0918 775829; **e** yohannestsegayegondar@gmail.com; **f**. Tucked away on a quiet cul-de-

Tours for the discerning traveller.

 ETHIOPIAN QUADRANTS

To the four corners of the country.

All our tours can be tailored to meet our clients' special interests and are specially planned to make the visitor less of a consumer and more of a participant in Ethiopian life, culture and custom.

E-mail: ethiopianquadrants@gmail.com
        info@ethiopianquadrants.com
Tel: (+251)115157990,11 554 7529, 11 554 6644, 115544635/6
Web: www.ethiopianquadrants.com
P. O. Box 1021, code1250, Addis Ababa, Ethiopia

The Blue Nile Falls is known locally as Tis Abay ('Smoke of the Nile') page 251

The 100-odd rock-hewn churches of Tigray reach their architectural apex along the majestic sandstone cliffs of the Gheralta Escarpment page 346

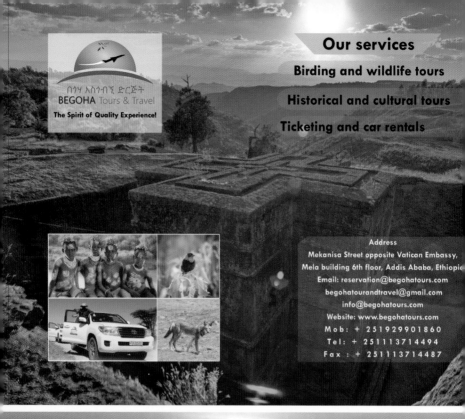

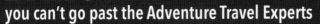

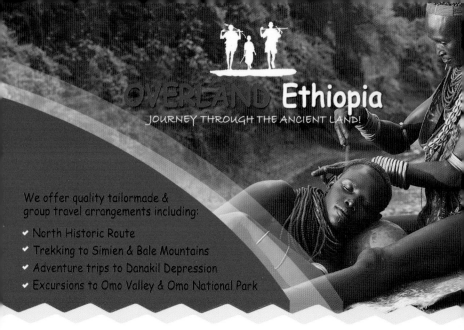

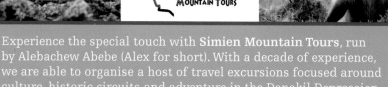

ትራቭል ኢትዮጵያ
TRAVEL ETHIOPIA
... and be seven years younger

More than two decades of experience!

sac at the north end of town, this unsignposted guesthouse feels a bit like a backpackers with its self-catering kitchen, communal TV lounge & large garden where campfires are lit at night. The hands-on owner-manager is a former guide & tourism graduate who runs affordable Simien hikes, leaving every other day. Camping in the garden is permitted. *US$15/25 en-suite sgl/dbl or US$20 dbl using common shower.* **$$**

🏠 **Capra Walia Inn** [275 C1] (17 rooms) ✆058 112 0314/5; e caprawaliainn@yahoo.com; 📘. A solid budget choice for some years now, this 3-storey inn has a quiet but reasonably central location & offers pleasant en-suite rooms with TV, hot water, built-in cupboards, nice wooden furniture & a small private balcony. Twin rooms have 2 ¾ beds & a bathtub. The attached restaurant serves good juice. *US$14/16/24 sgl/dbl/twin.* **$$**

🏠 **Genetics Guest House** [275 C2] (13 rooms) ✆058 112 2332. This central 4-storey hotel has clean, brightly decorated rooms with wooden furniture, king-size bed, telephone, TV & en-suite hot shower. *US$19 dbl.* **$$**

Shoestring

✴ 🏠 **Sycamore Pension** [275 D2] (19 rooms) ✆058 111 0737; m 0918 046535; e sycamorepension@gmail.com; w sycamorepension.com. The standout in this price range has a convenient location on a quiet road bordering the city centre, a friendly & articulate manager, & small but spotless & comfortable tiled rooms with TV & en-suite hot shower. Super value. *US$8/9/11 sgl/dbl/twin.* **$**

🏠 **Central Gondar Hotel** [275 C4] (18 rooms) ✆058 111 7020. A good central choice & very convenient for catching the Addis Ababa-bound coaches that leave from Meskel Square, this unpretentious lodge on the Piazza has comfortable en-suite rooms with tiled floor, writing desk, hot shower & small balcony. *US$12 dbl or twin.* **$$**

🏠 **Crown Pension** [275 C4] (24 rooms) ✆058 111 4788; m 0918 771000. This very reasonable family-run place behind the Taye Belay comes in for frequent praise from readers. The clean tiled rooms are bright & spacious, & come with TV. *US$7/12 dbl using common/en-suite shower.* **$–$$**

🏠 **Queen Tayta Pension** [275 C3] (19 rooms) ✆058 112 2898. Clean & good value, this central hotel has small but well-kept rooms. *US$5 sgl with common shower or US$7/12 en-suite sgl/twin.* **$–$$**

🏠 **Belegez Pension** [275 D4] (14 rooms) ✆058 111 4356; m 0965 330001. This long-serving pension in the back roads behind Fasil Ghebbi is starting to look its age, but it remains very convenient & the rooms are reasonably priced. *US$7 dbl using common shower, US$8/11 en-suite sgl/dbl.* **$–$$**

🏠 **Teklu Gebreselassie Pension** [275 D4] (17 rooms) ✆058 111 1268; m 0918 721507. Unpretentious & usefully located family-run cheapie with unappealing rooms using common shower & much nicer en-suite rooms with ¾ bed, hot shower & small balcony. *US$5/9 sgl/dbl using common shower or US$6 en-suite sgl.* **$**

✗ **WHERE TO EAT AND DRINK** In addition to the standalone restaurants listed below, there are excellent international restaurants at the AG Hotel and out-of-town Mayleko Lodge and Goha Hotel. Other decent places to eat include Lodge Fasil, Taye Belay Hotel and Quara Hotel.

Moderate to upmarket

✗ **Four Sisters Restaurant** [275 C2] ✆058 112 2031; m 0918 736510; e eatgoodatgondar@ yahoo.com; w thefoursistersrestaurant.com; ⏲ 07.00–23.00 daily. Situated next to an informal football pitch 400m north of Fasil Ghebbi, Gondar's most iconic restaurant, owned & managed by 4 friendly sisters, is attractively decorated in traditional style, & also has garden seating. The menu incorporates Ethiopian dishes such as raw or cooked *kitfo* & *shiro tegabino*, a varied selection

of grills, pasta dishes & salads, b/fast, local wines & home-brewed *tej*. There's live after-dinner Amhara music & dancing (from around 20.00). Naysayers will tell you it's a tourist trap, & certainly it caters mainly to a foreign clientele, but the food is delicious & the ambience great. *Mains around US$6, buffet US$9.*

✗ **Masterchef** [275 D4] m 0911 097655; e endeg_belsti@yahoo.com, ⏲ 07.00–22.00 daily. Owned & managed by a hands-on chef trained at the French School in Addis Ababa, this unpretentious bamboo eatery opposite the Belegez Pension is especially strong on homemade pasta & pizzas. Good *tibs* too. *Mains US$4–5.*

Cheap to moderate

✕ **Rain Restaurant** [275 C2] ⏰ 08.00–22.00 daily. Best known for its pizzas (*US$2–4*), this pleasant terrace restaurant also serves a varied selection of Ethiopian meat, fish & vegetarian dishes (*mostly around US$2*).

✕ **Alliance Inn** [275 C3] ⏰ 07.00–21.30 daily. Attached to a small hotel of the same name, this

pleasant 2-tier terrace restaurant has an extensive Ethiopian menu (*US$2–3*) as well good pizzas (*US$4–5*).

✕ **Telecafe** [275 C3] ⏰ 06.00–21.00 daily. Centrally located in front of the post office on the Piazza, this stalwart café serves pizzas, burgers, local meals & a good range of b/fasts (*US$2–4*). There are also cakes, coffee & juice, but no alcohol.

✕ **Barok House** [275 C4] Situated on the Piazza close to Meskel Sq, this informal local eatery serves very fresh meat (try the *shekla tibs*), as well as draught beer around a night-time camp fire.

NIGHTLIFE Gondar has a lively nightlife with plenty of local bars lining the Piazza and the backstreets around the AG Hotel [275 C2]. The town is also well known for its live music scene, and traditional *azmari* singers can be seen and heard in several bars. These places don't charge entrance fees as such, but drinks are marked up to reflect the added entertainment.

✳ ☆ **Inyie Takele Hall & Restaurant** [275 B2] ⏰ 21.30–midnight daily; w inyietakele-mgmt. com. Gondar's hottest live music venue has a varied

nightly revue involving traditional *azmaris*, Aster Awake-influenced Amhara divas & spectacular dance routines set to compelling trance-like rhythms

---

A ROYAL BANQUET AT GONDAR

When James Bruce published the five-volume account of his Ethiopian journey under the title *Travels to Discover the Source of the Nile* in 1790, its contents seemed so outrageous to polite European society that they were widely dismissed as fabrication. Of all the passages in the book, none proved to be as controversial as an account of a banquet held at the Royal Ghebbi in Gondar, from which the following edited extracts are drawn.

A long table is set in the middle of a large room, and benches beside it for the guests. A cow or bull, one or more, is brought close to the door and carved up alive. The prodigious noise the animal makes is the signal for the company to sit down to table.

There are then laid out before every guest – instead of plates – pancakes, and something thicker and tougher. It is unleavened bread of a sourish taste, far from being disagreeable, and very easily digested, made of a grain called *tef*. Three or four of these cakes are put uppermost, for the food of the person opposite to whose seat they are placed. Beneath these are four or five of ordinary bread, which serve the master to wipe his fingers on, and afterwards the servant for bread to his dinner.

Three or four servants then come, each with a square piece of beef in their bare hands, laying it upon the cakes of *tef*, without cloth or anything else beneath them. By this time all the guests have knives in their hands. The company are so ranged that one man sits between two women. The man with his knife cuts a thin piece, which would be thought a good beefsteak in England, while you see the motion of the fibres yet perfectly distinct, and alive in the flesh. No man in Abyssinia, of any fashion whatever, feeds himself or touches his own meat. The women take the steak and cut it lengthwise like strings, about the thickness of your little finger, then crossways into square pieces, something smaller than dice. This they lay upon a piece of *tef* bread, strongly powdered with black pepper and salt; they then wrap it up in the *tef* bread like a cartridge.

that set traditional instruments over synthesised beats. It isn't at all touristy (we were the only non-Ethiopians in attendance on our most recent visit), & audience participation is encouraged. It only really gets going at around 21.00.

☆ **Elilta** [275 B4] ⊕ daily. Situated along a back road 300m northeast of Meskel Square, this is a showier venue with a large stage & vibrant music & dancing representing several different Ethiopian cultural groups, especially Amhara & Gurage.

♀ **Ethiopia Hotel Bar** [275 C3] The fabulously time-warped restaurant/bar at this otherwise rundown & overpriced hotel on the Piazza is something to behold. Presumably a relic of the Italian occupation, it has an imposing kiosk-like doorway, marble tile floor, mirrors & wood panels on the walls, & a tall engraved ceiling

supported by a central wooden column & hung with chandeliers. Definitely worth dropping in for a beer or coffee.

♀ **Dashen Brewery Beer Garden** [map, page 272] ⊕ daily. Situated 8km out of town along the old Azezo road, this garden bar with covered seating serves the best & cheapest draught beer in town, including a delicious unfiltered brew called Cellar. It also does great roast chicken & decent *tibs*, & there's often live music on Sun afternoon. Minibuses to Azezo can drop you there before around 20.00, & it's easy to get a *bajaj* back to town.

✗ **Gondar Landmark Hotel** [275 A1] The terraced outdoor seating here is a great spot for an early evening drink, with good views over the town centre, the sun setting to the right, & large numbers of raptors & egrets circling overhead.

TOURIST INFORMATION The tourist office [275 C3] (⊕ *08.00–16.30 Mon–Fri*) has a good map of Gondar posted on the wall, as well as maps of the Simien Mountains. Nobody was available to provide any meaningful information on our most recent visit.

In the meantime the man, having put up his knife, with each hand resting upon his neighbour's knee, his body stooping, his head low and forward, and mouth open very like an idiot, turns to the one whose cartridge is first ready, who stuffs the whole of it into his mouth, which is so full that he is in constant danger of being choked. This is a mark of grandeur. The greater the man would seem to be, the larger the piece he takes into his mouth; the more noise he makes in chewing it, the more polite he is thought to be. They indeed have a proverb that says: 'Beggars and thieves only eat small pieces, or without making a noise.'

Having dispatched this morsel, which he does very expeditiously, his next female neighbour holds forth another cartridge, which goes the same way, and so forth, until he is satisfied. He never drinks before he has finished eating, and before he begins drinking, in gratitude to the two fair ones that feed him, he rolls up two small cartridges of the same shape and form, and each of his neighbours opens her mouth at the same time, while with each hand he puts the portions into their mouths. He then falls to drinking out of a handsome horn; the ladies eat until they are satisfied, and they all drink together. A great deal of joy and mirth goes around, very seldom with any mixture of acrimony or ill humour.

Those within are very much elevated: love lights all its fires, and everything is permitted with absolute freedom. There is no coyness, no delays, no need of appointments or retirement to gratify their wishes. There are no rooms but one, in which they sacrifice both to Bacchus and to Venus. The two men nearest the vacuum a pair have made on the bench by leaving their seats, hold their upper garments like a screen before the two that have left the bench; and, if we may judge by sound, they seem to think it as great a shame to make love in silence as to eat.

Replaced in their seats again, the company drink the happy couple's health, and their example is followed at different ends of the table, as each couple is disposed. All this passes without remark or scandal, not a licentious word is uttered, nor the most distant joke made upon the transaction.

TOUR OPERATORS Most Gondar-based operators specialise in hikes to the Simien Mountains. The following companies have been recommended:

Ethiopia Simien Tours [275 C3] Ground floor of Taye Belay Hotel; m 0918 350747/770287; e info@simienmountainstours.com; w ethiopiasimientours.com
Ethiopia Trek m 0935 480330; e gismudebark@yahoo.com; w ethiopiatrek.com
Galaxy Express [275 C3] Ground floor of Taye Belay Hotel; ☎058 111 1546; m 0918 770347; e info@galaxyexpresstourethiopia.com; w galaxyexpresstourethiopia.com

Simen Land Tours [275 C2] Ground floor of AG Hotel; m 0911 021308; e tesfahundere@yahoo.com; w simenlandtours.com
Simien Eco-Tours [275 C4] Meskel Sq; ☎058 211 0044; m 0920 732527; e info@simienecotours.com; w simienecotours.com
Simien Mountain Trekking m 0911 904792; e info@simienmountains.com; w simienmountains.com
Simien Trek Tours m 0918 776499; e simientrek@yahoo.com; w simientrek.com

WHAT TO SEE AND DO Gondar's most important tourist attraction is the central Fasil Ghebbi, a walled compound enclosing half a dozen 17th-century castles and palaces, the entrance fee to which also includes access to the suburban Fasilidas's Pool. Other key sites include the church of Debre Berhan Selassie and the acclaimed paintings that cover its interior, and the complex of Kuskuam set on a hill overlooking the city centre. Further afield, Simien Mountains National Park, 100km north of Gondar (page 290), is a popular goal for overnight trips and longer hikes, while a more affordable alternative is the half-day trip to the Wunenia and Kossoye viewpoints 30 minutes' drive north of the town centre.

Those looking to step back from the usual tourist trail might want to look into the bouquet of unusual activities offered both to its own guests and to walk-ins by **Lodge du Chateau**. Most demanding at this lofty altitude is an 8.6km guided morning run through the surrounding suburbs and countryside, undertaken at a gentle pace in a T-shirt with Ethiopia national colours (which you get to take home), with as many stops as you need to catch your breath. It can also arrange cycle hire, and horseback excursions on well-tended animals in the countryside around Gondar. More passive and culturally oriented activities, designed to facilitate unforced interaction with locals in their own home, include hair-braiding and cooking lessons. Email Lodge du Chateau (page 276) or just drop in for more details.

Central Gondar Gondar's best-known attraction is the Royal Enclosure known as Fasil Ghebbi, but the best starting point for a tour is the informative local history museum in Ras Gimb, outside the compound. It is worth making time to take a wander around the cobbled alleys before breakfast, when the historic atmosphere is enhanced by white-robed worshippers making their way to and from morning mass.

Ras Gimb [275 C3] (☎ *058 111 5138*; e *ngzct@yahoo.com*; ⊕ *08.30–18.00 daily; entrance US$4 inc restricted photography*) Situated 200m north of Fasil Ghebbi, the imposing three-storey Ras Gimb (sometimes spelt Ghinb) is the best preserved of all Gondar's castles, and the only one that has stayed in almost continual use since its construction – in its most recent incarnation as a superb local history museum. There is some uncertainty about the castle's provenance, but tradition holds that it was built in the 1650s as the residence of Ras Walda Giyorgis, a military officer who served as first officer and prime minister under Fasilidas, and married the emperor's daughter Eskenderawit (the two were the maternal grandparents of Emperor Bakaffa and great-grandparent of Iyasu II). This legend is substantiated by two quirks. The first is that the castle's location just outside the royal compound mimics the traditional location of the first officer's tent in the temporary capitals and encampments that preceded Gondar. The second is that it was constructed in stone, a building material reserved exclusively for core members of the royal family, such as Eskenderawit.

In the 1730s, Ras Gimb was probably home to Ras Walda Le'ul, the brother of Princess Mentewab (then serving as queen regent), and it doubled as a jail where political opponents were tortured. Today, Ras Gimb is best known as the residence of Ras Mikael Sehul, the Machiavellian prince who dominated Gondarine politics in the 1760s. More recently, the *gimb* was restored as a vice-regal residence during the Italian occupation, after which it served as an imperial holiday home. Indeed, Emperor Haile Selassie stayed there five times between 1946 and 1970, and it also hosted Queen Elizabeth II on a state visit to Ethiopia in February 1965. During the Red Terror campaign of 1977–79, Ras Gimb was used as a torture chamber under the supervision of Major Melaku Tefera, the 'Butcher of Gondar', who was found guilty of 971 charges of murder in 2005, and sentenced to death for the 'inhuman persecution' of dissidents (the sentence was reduced to life imprisonment in 2011). Possibly out of respect for the Derg's victims, Ras Gimb remained closed to the public until October 2017, when it opened as a museum following extensive renovations overseen by the French Centre for Ethiopian Studies and the municipality of Vincennes (twinned with Gondar since 2010).

Surrounded by a shady and well-tended garden, Ras Gimb, with its circular domed turrets and tall castellated stone walls, is a splendid apparition, recalling a smaller (but better preserved) near-replica of the original castle built by Emperor Fasilidas some 600m to its south. The ground floor houses a general history museum focusing on the early days of Gondar, as well as the Derg-era torture chamber, which is preserved as a memorial to the many who were tortured or died there. The first floor is dominated by the bedrooms used by Emperor Haile Selassie and his wife, Menen, both perfectly preserved in period style (the latter complete with a shocking-pink bathroom that lends a surreal 1970s kitschiness to the predominance of sombre clothes, canvasses and dark-wood furnishings). It also houses a collection of traditional artefacts and leads out to the still-intact wooden balcony where Haile Selassie and Elizabeth II greeted a Gondarine crowd in 1965. Just like Fasilidas's Castle, stairs lead up from a fortified rooftop terrace to a small upper study and library that offer fabulous views over the city and surrounding countryside. Displays are well labelled, and the optional (female) guides are knowledgeable and the opposite of jaded.

Fasil Ghebbi and surrounds [275 C5] (\058 111 1536; ⊕ 08.00–12.30 & 13.30–18.00 daily; entrance US$8 pp/day inc still photography, US$3 video camera) Also known as the Royal Enclosure, the Fasil Ghebbi (Fasilidas's Compound), inscribed as a UNESCO World Heritage Site in 1979, lies at the heart of modern Gondar and gives the city much of its character. Surrounded by tall mossy stone walls, the oval 7ha enclosure contains six stone castles and several smaller buildings, and is best explored in the company of one of the knowledgeable guides that can be arranged at the Guides Association office inside the entrance gate.

Fasilidas's Castle [275 C5] The most imposing of all Gondarine constructions is the original three-storey stone, wood and lime-mortar castle built by Fasilidas in around 1640. Displaying a unique combination of Portuguese, Axumite and even Indian influences, the castle was restored between 1999 and 2002 using original construction methods and backed by UNESCO funding. At the time of writing, the only part of the castle open to visitors is the first-floor reception and dining areas, which are reached via a tall flight of stairs and have walls decorated with a symbol similar to the Star of David, the emblem of the Ethiopian royal family after the Solomonic dynasty reclaimed the throne in the 13th century. Above this, the second floor – now closed to the public – housed Fasilidas's prayer room, whose four windows all faced a church, as well as an open roof from where the emperor addressed the townsfolk. Stairs lead from the roof to a small upper room that Fasilidas used as his sleeping quarters, and on to a watchtower-like platform 32m above the ground. As and when it reopens, this platform will offer wonderful views in all directions, stretching as far as Lake Tana to the south on a clear day.

Yohannes's library and archive [275 C5] Respectively situated about 50m and 100m northwest of Fasilidas's Castle are the library and royal archive built by Emperor Yohannes I (1667–82), Fasilidas's bookish son and successor. The library, though small, and closed to the public, is a well-preserved two-storey building whose handsome façade is adorned with cross-shaped windows and arched doors, while the three-storey archive, though partially destroyed when Britain bombed the Italian headquarters situated within the compound in 1941, offers great views back to Fasilidas's Castle from its accessible first-floor balcony.

Iyasu's Castle [275 D5] Situated only 20m north of Fasilidas's Castle, the castle built by Iyasu the Great (1682–1706) is one of the largest in the compound, and the most ornately constructed. In its prime it was reputedly very beautiful, decorated with ivory, gold leaf, precious stones and paintings. Unfortunately, it was partially damaged by an earthquake in 1704, and the ground-floor ceiling collapsed under the British bombardment in 1941, leaving little more than a shell. In rather better condition is the three-room sauna that was constructed by Iyasu alongside his castle. Iyasu is also credited with the construction of the raised walkway that connects his castle to that built by his grandfather.

Other secular buildings Of the four emperors that were assassinated in the 15 years after Iyasu was ousted, only Dawit III (1716–21) left his mark on the Royal Enclosure in the form of a lion cage, which reputedly still held live lions until the last one died in 1992. Dawit III also built a large concert hall, which is still standing today. The two large castles [275 C4] in the far north of the complex were built by Bakaffa I (1721–30) and his wife Mentewab during her term as regent for their son Iyasu II (1730–55). The latter, the most recent construction in the compound, is a small but charming stone building decorated with Gondar crosses, and in such good condition that it was until recently used as a gift shop.

Churches Three historic churches lie within the main walls of the Royal Enclosure, albeit in private compounds that are accessible only through separate entrances (and require foreign visitors to pay a separate negotiable entrance fee). In all cases, however, the original buildings were destroyed during the Mahdist attack of 1888, to be replaced by architecturally undistinguished modern substitutes. The oldest and most interesting of the three is Gemja Ber Maryam [275 C5], which was founded by Emperor Fasilidas in around 1655 and is also reputedly where he is buried. The grave of Walter Plowden, a close associate of Emperor Tewodros I and British Consul who was killed in Gondar, also lies in the church courtyard, while the treasury holds some excellent 19th-century paintings. Atatami Kidus Mikael

[275 C4] is also attributed to Fasilidas while Elfin Giyorgis [275 C4] immediately to its south was built by Dawit III.

Medhane Alem Church [275 C3] Situated 100m west of Ras Gimb, but obscured behind a swathe of tall juniper trees, Medhane Alem is the only one of the seven Gondarine churches whose foundation is attributed to Fasilidas to have survived the Mahdist invasion more or less untouched. Now the seat of the Bishop of Gondar, the restored church is faithful to the original 17th-century design. The extensive paintings on the outer wall of the sanctuary probably date to the late 19th century, but may well replicate much older original paintings.

Suburban Gondar
Debre Berhan Selassie [map, page 272] (⊕ *08.00–18.00 daily; entrance US$4 inc still photography*) Among the most beautiful of Ethiopian churches, Debre Berhan Selassie (Mountain of the Enlightened Trinity) was consecrated with much ceremony by Abuna Markos on Timkat of 1693 after Emperor Iyasu I arrived there on horseback carrying the *tabot* on his head. Iyasu appointed more than 150 people to serve in the church, which was regarded to be Gondar's principal place of worship for at least a century thereafter. Debre Berhan Selassie was the only major Gondarine church to emerge unscathed from the two attacks on the city by Emperor Tewodros in the 1860s, as well as the Mahdist pillaging of 1888 (in the latter case, thanks to the intervention of an angry swarm of bees, or so they'll tell you locally). The original church built for Iyasu I was almost certainly circular, and it probably remained the same shape when it was restored after being struck by lightning in 1707. The rectangular stone church that now stands on the site most likely dates to the late 18th century, but it may well be built around the original *maqdas*. In many respects, it strongly resembles the more imposing Gondarine church built by Fasilidas in Axum, being built to similar dimensions as Solomon's Temple in Jerusalem. The perimeter wall has 12 equidistant round towers representing the 12 Apostles, one of which is larger than the rest and was possibly intended to house relics associated with the Ark of the Covenant. The gateway, built to look like a royal lion couchant, is the '13th tower', and the tail of the lion, which looks like a comma, is carved on the keystone of the arch in the wall to the west of the church, signifying the omnipresence of Christ. Near the top of the south end of the roof, seven niches support a medallion with an ostrich egg on each of its seven prongs, signifying the seven days of creation.

Whatever Debre Berhan Selassie's architectural merit, its greatest point of interest is the beautiful art that graces every corner of the ceiling and walls. The much-photographed ceiling, decorated with 80 cherubic faces painted in neat rows, is probably the most famous single example of ecclesiastical art in Ethiopia. The walls are also painted with dozens of separate scenes: the southern wall concentrates on the Life of Christ, while the northern wall depicts various saints. One of the most striking individual paintings is an unusually fearsome depiction of the devil surrounded by flames, to be found on the wall to the left of the main door, while next to this door is a striking image of a captive Muhammad being led by the devil. The paintings are traditionally held to be the work of the 17th-century artist Haile Meskel, but it is more likely that several artists were involved and that the majority were painted during the rule of Egwala Seyon (1801–17), who is depicted prostrating himself before the Cross on one of the murals.

Debre Berhan Selassie lies 1km from the town centre and can be reached by following the road running east from the staircase next to the administrative offices. It is difficult to miss, situated at the end of a cul-de-sac, and enclosed by a high stone wall and surrounded by juniper trees. Flash photography is forbidden, as it damages the old pigments, so you either need a tripod to photograph the famous ceiling, or to use a table as support. If you visit in the afternoon, wait until about 30 minutes before sunset for the sun's rays to penetrate the interior and enhance the spiritual atmosphere.

Fasilidas's Pool [map, page 272] (*Entrance included in the fee for Fasil Ghebbi; tickets cannot be bought at the pool itself*) Situated about 2km west of the town centre, the 2,800m² sunken bathing pool generally attributed to Emperor Fasilidas is enclosed by a tall stone wall with six turrets, and overlooked by a two-storey building widely said to have been its founder's second residence. Some sources suggest that the pool was in fact the earliest of Fasilidas's constructions, predating his famous castle in the Fasil Ghebbi, while others attribute it to Emperor Iyasu I. Built for ceremonial rather than recreational purposes, the sunken excavation is dry most of the year, but is filled with water for Timkat (page 109), when it forms the centrepiece of a remarkable ceremony wherein thousands of white-robed worshippers converge around the pool to be blessed and sprinkled with holy water by colourfully attired priests carrying *tabots* and crosses. You can walk out to the pool from the town centre, or else take a local minibus from the Piazza to Revolutionary Square, which lies right in front of it.

Suviel's Tomb and the House of Chickens [map, page 272] Easily mistaken for a disused bandstand, the six-pillared domed pavilion standing outside Fasilidas's Pool is said locally to date to the reign of Emperor Iyasu I, who built it as a mausoleum for his father Yohannes I's favourite horse, Suviel. According to this legend, Yohannes I was killed in battle in the Sudan by an unspecified Muslim foe, who then took the injured Suviel captive. Iyasu rescued the horse by dressing as a Muslim, persuading its captors to let him ride it, then fleeing as quickly as he could. The Muslims tried to give chase, but turbo-charged Suviel leapt across a gorge no lesser horse could cross, and he and the future emperor returned safely to Gondar. All of this seems a little far-fetched, given the lack of evidence to support the premise that Yohannes I died in the Sudan. More likely the little pavilion is where the early emperors of Gondar stood during ceremonies held at the pool.

Nearby, a small building known popularly as the House of Chickens is often said to have served as a royal chicken run under Fasilidas, though a pre-Mengistu ETC brochure suggests, more plausibly, that it was once a 'sweating house isolated for the cure of contagious diseases'. The nearby Church of Kidus Yohannes, founded under Iyasu II, was partially destroyed by the Mahdists in 1888, but the original outer walls are still standing, and a well-preserved vestry in one of the turrets now serves as the sanctuary of what is otherwise in effect an open-air church!

Defeche Bridge and Angareb Reservoir [map, page 272] Emperor Fasilidas reputedly constructed seven stone bridges across various roads and dangerous river crossings in and around Gondar. Two survive intact. Defeche Bridge is the more central, spanning the Angareb River a few hundred metres downstream of the eponymous reservoir some 1.5km east of town. To get there, head out towards Debre Berhan Selassie for about 400m, then turn left on to a dirt road leading downhill, and take the fork to the right about 100m after that. About 200m further on, the road passes through the gate to the reservoir compound, where you may have to tip the guard to gain access. It's another 2km from the gate to the bridge, following a scenic road that flanks the reservoir downhill into an unexpectedly rural-feeling valley. About 500m after passing a water purification plant to the right, turn left towards a power substation that stands immediately alongside the river. The bridge itself is almost 30m long and 5m wide, with four arches, and you can walk across it to the ruined guardhouse on the opposite side. It is named for the village to which it leads, and adventurous travellers could continue uphill for 2km past the bridge to the impressive ruins of Defeche Kidane Mihret, which was built by Emperor Bakaffa in the 1720s and comprises a circular outer wall of 27 pillars and arches enclosing a taller *maqdas*.

Gobatit Bridge [map, page 272] The more outlying but more architecturally interesting of the two extant bridges accredited to Emperor Fasilidas, Gobatit Delbi (literally 'Arched Bridge') spans the Angareb River about 4km south of Angareb Bridge and 1km south of its confluence with the Qaha. It is also known locally as the Devil's Bridge, some say due to the number of people that have drowned in flash floods while swimming or washing below it, others due to its central arch being much larger and taller than the others. According to Gondarine architectural expert John Jeremy Hespeler-Boultbee, the most likely explanation for this curious asymmetry, which would have made it impossible for carts to cross it, is that the bridge was constructed in a style popularised by the ancient Romans, with two secondary arches used to support a larger central arch, but the ramps that should have been added to level the deck were never completed. A cross has been erected next to the bridge to make the water holy and protect people from the bridge's satanic associations.

The bridge lies in the suburb of Ayer Tena (formerly Genfo Kuch). Coming from the Piazza, follow the new Azezo road southwest for 4km to 'Shoa Bakery' junction, then turn left and continue for 2.3km until you reach Ayer Tena Market. Parking opposite the market, it's a 5–10-minute walk downhill through huts and fields to the bridge. Using public transport, minibuses from the Piazza can drop you at 'Shoa Bakery' junction, from where you could either walk or catch a *bajaj* to the market.

Kuskuam [map, page 272] (⊕ *08.30–18.00 daily; entrance US$4*) Set at an altitude of 2,250m on Debre Tsehay (Mountain of Sun) 3km west of Fasil Ghebbi, the palatial stone complex of Kuskuam – named after a Coptic convent in Egypt – was constructed as the residence of the Empress Mentewab, who acted as regent to Iyasu II after the death of her husband, Bakaffa, in 1730, and later to their grandson Iyoas I. It is likely that Kuskuam took over from the Fasil Ghebbi as the centre of imperial affairs in the mid 18th century. It was here, for instance, that James Bruce spent several sociable months waiting for permission to visit the source of the Nile at Gish Abay, in the process becoming a close friend and confidant of Mentewab. (It has also been claimed that Bruce had an affair with one of the empress's married daughters, who bore him a child at Kuskuam, though it died before it could be christened.)

Although in a state of partial ruin, Kuskuam makes for a fascinating excursion from central Gondar. The overall shape of the main palace is clearly discernible, with most of the first-floor walls still intact, as is one staircase and part of the first floor. An ornate Gondarine cross is carved over the door to Mentewab's bedroom. Little remains of the queen's personal chapel, which was once adorned with paintings as impressive as those at Debre Berhan Selassie, representing every saint venerated by the Ethiopian Church. A round building ingeniously designed to get around the prohibition on menstruating women entering a church, the chapel has 12 alcoves, which the queen would visit in turn every hour to pray when 'unclean', while a priest stood outside praying and swinging incense. Better preserved is the impressive banquet hall, which must be at least 10m high. Engravings of animals and crosses decorate the outer wall of the banquet hall; there is also an etching of Abuna Yohannes, Patriarch of the Ethiopian Church during Mentewab's regency. The almost cartoon-like style of some of these etchings is similar to those (including one of James Bruce) at the Lake Tana monastery of Narga Selassie, also built by Mentewab.

The church of Kuskuam Maryam, set alongside the royal residence, suffered the same fate as most Gondarine churches during the Mahdist War. Rebuilt during the Italian occupation, it is elaborately decorated, though none of the paintings dates to before 1970. The bones of Mentewab and Iyasu II were retrieved from the ground during the church's reconstruction, and are now housed in a glass coffin in the site museum. There is a big celebration at the church every 15 November.

To get to Kuskuam from the Piazza, drive or catch a shared minibus from the Piazza to the University of Gondar Hospital. Opposite the hospital entrance, a steep 1km cobbled road leads uphill to the church and ruined palace, offering great views behind you over the city centre, and plenty of birdlife in the juniper and olive trees near the ruined palace.

Further afield In addition to the sites listed below, worthwhile goals for a day trip out of Gondar covered in the previous chapter include the Lake Tana port of Gorgora (page 265) and the impressive pre-Gondarine castles built for Emperor Susenyos at Guzara and Danqaz (pages 263 and 264).

THE BEAUTIFUL EMPRESS

Paul Henze has described the Empress Mentewab as 'a subject awaiting a biographer'. And certainly the fondly remembered builder of Kuskuam and Narga Selassie must rank among the most charismatic figures of the Gondarine era – as well, folklore has it, as a queen of great generosity, wit, comeliness and political savvy.

Two contradictory stories relate to Mentewab's union with Bakaffa. One legend has it that Mentewab was raised in humble circumstances in a district called Qara to the west of Lake Tana. In the early 1720s, Bakaffa happened to be travelling through this district when he fell seriously ill. The ailing emperor was taken in by a local farmer, and was nursed back to health by the farmer's beautiful daughter Berhan Mogasa (Splendour of Light). And Bakaffa was so enamoured with his saviour that he married her as soon as he was fit enough to return to Gondar.

The other version, as told by Mentewab's official chronicler, is that she was the daughter of a princess called Yolyana, who dressed her up in the finest cloths and golden jewellery and arranged for her to be introduced to the king. 'When Bakaffa saw her he was very happy because she was so completely beautiful, and he said to her "You have no fault at all!"' recalls the chronicler: 'Then he made her sit beside him and had delicious foods brought, and they ate and drank together. That day he knew her as Adam knew Eve, and she conceived immediately.'

Whichever story is true, there is no doubting Bakaffa's appreciation of the wife who would outlive both him and their eldest son, the Emperor Iyasu – it was he who bestowed upon her the exclamatory throne name Mentewab, which translates as 'How Beautiful Thou Art!'

Azezo This junction town 12km south of Gondar by road actually predated its more illustrious neighbour as a site for imperial castle building. In 1620, Emperor Susenyos, enamoured by his Portuguese visitors' descriptions of the stately gardens of Mediterranean Europe, decided to plant a vast orchard and ornamental garden in the well-watered valley, and a year later, at a ceremony also attended by his then teenage son Fasilidas, he laid the foundation for a church and palace that were completed in 1623 and named Ganata Iyasus (Paradise of Jesus). A few years later, a pool was added to the lovely complex, one believed to be the model on which the more central Fasilidas's Pool was based. A slightly later addition is the hilltop church of Azezo Tekle Haymanot, built by Fasilidas in the 1640s but destroyed during the Mahdist War and rebuilt in rather undistinguished manner in the 1950s. Historically important as this site may be, there isn't much left to capture the imagination of the casual visitor. Now dry and somewhat overgrown, the sunken walls of the pool, which was fed via a subterranean channel leading from the nearby river, are still clearly discernible. There are also a couple of ancient engraved crosses with 16 arms each on the outer wall to the right of the main gate to Azezo Tekle Haymanot, while the small house built into the wall on the other side of the gate was reputedly once lived in by Susenyos. Known locally as Atse Mawegna (Emperor Pool), the site is very accessible, whether by private or public transport, since it lies a mere 250m south of the short (1.6km) stretch of the old Azezo road that connects the junction for the airport to the junction with the new Azezo road.

Woleka and the Ploughshare Women's Training Centre [map, page 272] Situated 3km from Gondar along the main road to Debark, Woleka was for centuries the main residential quarter for the town's Beta Israel, who vacated the site between 1985 and 1992, when the Israeli government airlifted most of Ethiopia's 'Black Jews' to Jerusalem in order to liberate them from the repressive Mengistu regime. In reality, the Beta Israel of Gondar had been discriminated against since ever the city was founded – the name Woleka derives from an Amharic phrase meaning 'stay away', the answer Emperor Fasilidas reputedly gave the Jewish masons who helped build his castle when they asked where they could live. The disused synagogue, whose design mimics a typical circular Ethiopian church, but with a Star of David rather than a cross on its roof, can still be visited for a small fee, and a number of (Christian) craft sellers rather pushily try to hawk the distinctive clay dolls and other artefacts associated with the village's departed Beta Israel. Of less ambiguous merit, the Ploughshare Women's Training Centre (m *0918 778408;* f; ⊕ *08.30–18.00 Mon–Sat*), on the opposite side of the main road to the synagogue, is designed to teach craft-making and other skills to single and HIV-positive women. The gift shop is a good place to pick up traditional black pottery such as coffee ceremony pots and incense burners, along with hand-woven tapestries and other small handicrafts. The curator speaks excellent English and is truly excited to show people around.

Wunenia and Kossoye Often marketed as a half-day trip to the Simiens, which it emphatically isn't, a visit to Wunenia or Kossoye, both perched at breath-draining altitudes of around 2,800m on the Debark road about 25km north of Gondar, does nevertheless form a tantalising alternative for those who don't have the time or money to head further north. Both sites offer splendid sweeping views across layers of mountains to the southern base of the Simien Mountains; indeed, it is said that the area so appealed to Queen Elizabeth II when she was driven between Gondar and Axum in 1965 that she instructed her driver to stop there for tea.

The better option for budget travellers is Wunenia (m *0918 325398; entrance US$2 pp, guide US$8 per party of up to 5*), site of a community project that offers guided 3–4-hour round hikes that come with a good chance of seeing gelada and guereza monkeys, as well as birds of prey such as lammergeier and augur buzzard. The community project can also provide accommodation 1km along the trail at a pair of scenically located but simple stone bungalows (each with two double beds in compartments and common cold showers) that seem steeply priced at around US$24 per person excluding food and drink (which you need to bring from Gondar yourself) and all-inclusive catered overnight hikes at around US$160 for two people. A more popular overnight option, Kossoye is the site of the very agreeable Befiker Kossoye Ecology Lodge (page 274).

Transport to either site can be arranged through private tour operators in Gondar for around US$40 per group. Alternatively several minibuses ply back and forth between Gondar and Kossoye daily, dropping passengers at Wunenia by request. For Wunenia, an early start is recommended, partly because hiking is most pleasant in the morning and skies tend to get hazier as the day progresses, partly because transport usually leaves Kossoye only when full, so it may take a while to find a seat back to Gondar.

DEBARK

The small but well-equipped town of Debark, which straddles the Axum 100km north of Gondar, lies at the junction of the main road into the Simien Mountains and is home to the national park office, where all park fees must be paid and paperwork completed prior to a visit. Situated at a chilly altitude of 2,850m on the historic trade route between Gondar and the Eritrean port of Massawa, it has been an important market town since the early 19th century, possibly earlier, and was also the site of a bloody battle between Emperor Tewodros and a rebellious nephew in 1860. Debark has grown enormously over the past two decades, and its population probably now exceeds 100,000. For those who opt to spend a night there before heading into the mountains, the town is endowed with several good budget hotels, a busy market, a few adequately stocked supermarkets, and an unusually large number of pushy guides and the like. The main market, 100m along the Simien road, is busiest on Saturdays and to a lesser extent Wednesdays.

GETTING THERE AND AWAY The notes below are aimed primarily at those making their own way to or from Debark and organising a Simien hike there. Simien tours arranged through operators in Gondar or further afield are usually inclusive of transport between Gondar and the Simiens.

To/from Gondar Debark lies 103km northeast of Gondar along a newly asphalted road. The drive shouldn't take longer than 2 hours in a private vehicle. Regular minibuses run back and forth between the two towns from around 06.00 to 15.00, take up to 3 hours, and charge a fare of US$2.

To/from Axum The 250km road between Debark and Axum is now almost entirely surfaced, the only exception being the spectacular Italian-built 50km descent from Debark to Zaremo, which is so steep and narrow that it would be impossible to upgrade without closing it. As a result, the driving time between Debark and Axum is now reduced to 5 hours in a private vehicle. Using public transport, the daily bus from Gondar to Shire Inda Selassie can theoretically pick up passengers at Debark, but in practice it is usually full by the time it gets

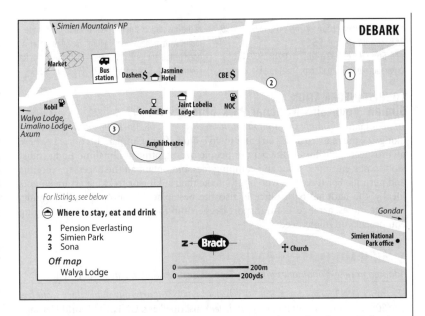

For listings, see below

🏠 **Where to stay, eat and drink**
1 Pension Everlasting
2 Simien Park
3 Sona

Off map
   Walya Lodge

there, so you will need to ask a tour operator or guide in Gondar or Debark to have somebody book you a ticket in Gondar and travel in your seat to Debark to hand it over (a service that usually costs around US$10–15). In the opposite direction, you will need to sleep in Shire Inda Selassie the night before you plan to travel, then catch the early morning bus to Gondar and hop off at Debark. It is also possible, but can be painfully slow, to travel between Debark and Axum using light vehicles that connect various small towns en route.

🏠 **WHERE TO STAY, EAT AND DRINK** *Map, above*

There is a fair selection of accommodation in Debark, but it all comes across as a bit expensive: budget in quality but priced more in line with moderate lodgings in Gondar. About 1km along the Gondar road, a smarter *tukul*-style ecolodge is being constructed by the owner of Pension Everlasting, and should open by 2020. Upmarket accommodation within Simien Mountains National Park is listed on page 294.

🏠 **Walya Lodge** (12 rooms) **m** 0911 613016. Situated 500m along the Axum road, this quiet lodge has spacious tiled rooms with 2 ¾ beds, sofa, attractive ethnic décor, en-suite hot shower & private veranda offering lovely views over the surrounding hills. Inherently, it's far the nicest place to stay in Debark, especially as the location isolates you from the town's sometimes considerable hassle factor, but it lacked sorely for management presence (or English-speaking staff) when we last looked in. A *tukul*-style restaurant is attached. *US$30 twin.* **$$$**

🏠 **Simien Park Hotel** (22 rooms) **m** 0928 955858/9. This long-serving hotel on the main road through Debark has a new wing whose en-suite rooms have hot water & TV, & an old wing where rooms use common hot showers. A decent restaurant serves a varied selection of mains in the US$2–3 range. *US$8/12 sgl/dbl using common shower, US$25/35 en-suite dbl/twin.* **$$–$$$**

🏠 **Pension Everlasting** (8 rooms) **m** 0918 724558. Tucked away on a quiet alley 250m southeast of the main road, this unpretentious new lodge has a friendly owner-manager who speaks excellent English, & smart, brightly painted rooms with hand-crafted wood furniture from Jimma. Full meals in the US$3–4 range are available, & it also sells organic milk, yoghurt, coffee, *tej*, honey & eggs. Other services include guided hikes, 4x4 rental & transfers into the park, & horseback excursions (*around US$8 for 2hrs*). *US$15/23/25/30 B&B sgl/dbl/twin/trpl.* **$$$**

🏠 **Sona Hotel** (32 rooms) m 0918 350935; e sonahotel2006@gmail.com. Situated a block west of the bus station, this has clean & spacious en-suite rooms with modern wooden furniture & hot water. A good restaurant serves local & international dishes for around US$4–5 per main. *US$25/35 sgl/dbl.* **$$$**

TOURIST INFORMATION

Simien Mountains National Park office (📞 *058 117 0407/22;* e *tourism@ simienmountains.org;* w *simienmountains.org;* ⏱ *08.30–17.00 daily*) Situated alongside the main road as you enter town coming from Gondar, this office is where all prospective visitors to the park or people overnighting at Limalimo Lodge must stop to pay entrance, scout and camping fees and obtain all the necessary receipts and permits. For travellers who opt to make their hiking or trekking arrangements locally, the national park office is also the best place to hook up with a guide, arrange mules, arrange 4x4 transport deeper into the park, and rent any camping equipment you might need.

SIMIEN MOUNTAINS NATIONAL PARK

Adapted from text originally written by David Else and Ariadne Van Zandbergen

(*Entrance US$3.50 pp/day, US$1.50/vehicle/day; US$6/party/day mandatory scout fee; US$20/party/day semi-mandatory guide fee*) Inscribed as a UNESCO World Heritage Site in 1979, the awesome Simien Massif, situated about 100km north of Gondar, comprises a high plateau of ancient volcanic rock incised with tall, precipitous cliffs and chasmic river valleys. The range includes at least a dozen peaks that top the 4,000m mark, among them the highest mountain in Ethiopia and fifth-highest in Africa, the 4,533m Ras Dejen (also known as Ras Dashen, and often given incorrectly as 4,620m high). In 1966, the most westerly part of the range was set aside as the 136km² Simien Mountains National Park (SMNP), which has since been expanded eastward to incorporate Ras Dejen and several other comparably high peaks, to cover a total area of 412km². Boasting an altitudinal span of around 2,600m, SMNP incorporates many different habitats, including large tracts of Afromontane forest, a medium-altitude ericaceous belt dominated by heather tussocks, and an Afroalpine habitat of guassa grassland punctuated by giant lobelia shrubs above the 3,500m contour. The park's main attraction is the scenery, which is utterly breathtaking, but it is also an important sanctuary for endemic wildlife, being the only remaining stronghold for the endemic Walia ibex and one of the few protected habitats of the Ethiopian wolf and gelada monkey. SMNP is Ethiopia's most popular trekking and hiking destination, best explored over a three- to ten-day hike or mule trek possibly incorporating an ascent of Ras Dejen and other peaks. However, the recent construction of a good all-weather road running deep into SMNP, as well as the opening of Simien Lodge close to the main entrance gate, has opened it up to overnight visits, and to less strenuous day walks and drives. The name Simien alludes to a near-eponymous Beta Israel kingdom that was centred on the mountains from its medieval heyday until its conquest by Emperor Susenyos in the early 17th century.

Note that, while the park entrance gate is at Buyit Ras, 15km from Debark along the road to Sankaber, all park fees must be paid at the national park office in Debark (see above). Receipts are checked at the entrance gate, and you'll be turned back without them.

MAPS AND FURTHER INFORMATION The excellent 1:100,000 *Simen* [sic] *Mountains Trekking Map* (University of Bern, revised edition 2010) is usually available for around US$15 at the park office in Debark or can be bought online at w stanfords.co.uk. Also worth getting hold of is the 44-page *Simien Mountains National Park Traveller's Handbook* (Frankfurt Zoological Society, 2013), much of which is reproduced online at w simienmountains.org.

CLIMATIC AND ALTITUDINAL CONSIDERATIONS You can visit the Simiens at any time of year, but hikers in particular should try to avoid the main rainy season, which runs from May to September, with around half the annual precipitation falling over July and August. The scenery is most spectacular in the early dry season (October to December), when the countryside still looks quite green and fresh. Hiking conditions are perfect from January to April, but the countryside starts to look browner and skies can be hazier. Whenever you visit, the upper Simiens are usually quite cool by day, and night-time temperatures frequently drop to freezing point. Warm clothing is absolutely essential. A couple of sweatshirts and a thick windbreaker will be ideal. Waterproof gear is necessary over May to September.

Hikers, especially those who have flown in from low-lying areas and had little time to acclimatise, should not underestimate the effects of the high altitude, particularly towards the summit of Ras Dejen. Although severe altitude-related illnesses are unlikely, it is common enough to experience headaches, shortness of breath, loss of appetite and general lethargy at higher altitudes. The best way to avoid these symptoms is to make a steady ascent, spending an extra night at one of the high camps (such as Chennek or Gich) and taking a rest day before you try to conquer Ras Dejen.

GEOLOGY The Simien Mountains were formed about 75 million years ago when an immense dome of basaltic rock was forcibly uplifted by volcanic activity to create a sheer escarpment that towered more than 1,000m above the plains to its north and east. Since then, the original basaltic rock has been incised by massive river canyons and parts have been weathered away by ice and water to form the immense pinnacles and buttresses described so eloquently by Rosita Forbes, the formidable traveller who first reached this region in the 1920s, in her 1925 book *From Red Sea to Blue Nile – A Thousand Miles of Ethiopia*:

The most marvellous of all Abyssinian landscapes opened before us, as we looked across a gorge of clouded amethyst … A thousand years ago, when the old gods reigned in Ethiopia, they must have played chess with these stupendous crags, for we saw bishops' mitres cut in lapis lazuli, castles with the ruby of approaching sunset on their turrets, an emerald knight where the forest crept up on the rock, and far away a king, crowned with sapphire, and guarded by a row of pawns. When the gods exchanged their games for shield and bucklers to fight the new men clamouring at their gates, they turned the pieces of their chessboard into mountains. In Simien they stand enchanted, till once again the world is pagan and the titans and the earth gods lean down from the monstrous cloud banks to wager a star or two on their sport.

WILDLIFE Three large mammals endemic to Ethiopia are resident in the Simiens. Most common is the gelada monkey, with an estimated population of at least 5,000 (some recent sources place it at 20,000). Habituated herds of several hundred gelada are often seen in the vicinity of Sankaber Camp and Simien Lodge, and it is quite something to walk among them as they graze, groom, squabble and make their characteristic whimpering calls – probably Africa's most thrilling primate encounter after gorilla- or chimpanzee-tracking. The Walia ibex, whose range is now restricted to the Simiens, was poached close to extinction in the late 1960s, when just 150 animals survived. The population had increased to 400 by 1989, but it declined to 250 in the early 1990s following the collapse of the Derg. Recent counts suggest the ibex population now stands at more than 1,000 individuals, the highest it has been in at least 50 years. Hikers quite often see ibex from the trail running along the ridge between Gich and Chennek via Imet Gogo. By contrast, the Ethiopian wolf is now very rare, with an estimated population of around 50–100 individuals concentrated mostly on the upper slopes of tall peaks such as Ras Dejen, Bwahit and Kidus Yared. The road between Chennek and Bwahit offers the most reliable endemic viewing, with a near certainty of encountering ibex and gelada, and a fair chance of the wolf, especially in the early to mid morning.

Of the non-endemic mammals, klipspringer and bushbuck are present, but seldom seen. Nor are you likely to see spotted hyena, even though their droppings are often scattered around the camps. More visible is the common jackal, which also haunts the camps.

The number of birds recorded in the Simiens is not high – 180 species to date, many restricted to the lower slopes – but it does include five Ethiopian endemics and another dozen only otherwise found in Eritrea. The mountains are noted for cliff-nesting birds of prey, not only the iconic lammergeier, which can often be seen soaring above the escarpments on the north side of the national park, and at Sankaber and Gich camps, but also Verreaux's eagle, Rüppell's vulture, auger buzzard and various smaller falcons and kestrels.

GETTING THERE AND AWAY
Organised hikes and tours Most travellers explore the Simiens on an all-inclusive hike with one of several specialist operators based in Gondar (page 280), and this will normally include transport from Gondar to Debark and on to the trail head or first overnight camp. Another option for more sedentary visitors is a day (or better overnight) 4x4 tour from Gondar, exploring the park along the all-weather road that runs east from Debark via Sankaber, Chennek and the Bwahit Pass towards Mekane Berhan, and ideally overnighting at Simien Lodge or in Debark. Both options are discussed further on page 295.

Independent visits Travellers making their own arrangements in Debark have four options. The first is to arrange a 4x4 transfer from Gondar to Sankaber (or one of the other campsites), which should cost around US$110–140 per vehicle, though you'll need to make sure the driver is prepared to stop at the park office long enough to allow you to make hiking arrangements. Alternatively, having bussed to Debark, you can arrange a 4x4 transfer to the trail head or camp of your choice at the national park office, an option that costs anything from US$55 to US$120 per vehicle one-way, depending on whether you only go as far as Buyit Ras, head all the way to Chennek, or stop somewhere in between. A much cheaper but less comfortable option is to use the occasional public transport – one bus daily and more regular Isuzu trucks – that bump along the road from Debark (leaving from in front of the market) to Mekane Berhan via Buyit Ras, Sankaber and Chennek, or try for a lift with other tourists. Finally, you could do as everybody had to do prior to the opening of the road through the park, and treat the trip from Debark to Sankaber as the first leg of your hike, following the route outlined on page 296.

HIKING PREPARATIONS AND COSTS The most hassle-free and popular option is to make advance arrangements through an operator in Gondar (page 280). Costs depend on the duration of the hike and group size, but to give some idea, a four-day, three-night hike will typically work out at US$400–550 per head for two people, inclusive of park fees, scout, guide, mules, mule drivers, simple meals and transport between Gondar and the trail heads. The more time-consuming and potentially frustrating alternative is to make direct arrangements at the national park office in Debark, which should cut costs by around 50%, especially if the semi-mandatory requirement to take a guide, as well as a scout, is waived. If you intend to set up your own hike, do leave enough time to complete all the formalities on the afternoon you arrive in Debark before setting off into the mountains the following morning. Be aware, too, that a small tip to the scout, guide and mule driver is appropriate (as a benchmark, around one to two days' extra wages per five to seven days' work). For details of trekking routes, see box, page 296.

Guides and scouts An armed scout must accompany all visitors, whether they explore the park on foot or by vehicle. This costs US$6 per party/day. Most scouts know their way around the park very well, but speak little or no English, which makes communication difficult. For this reason, the national park office recommends that all visitors are accompanied by a guide, a service that costs US$20 a day for up to five people, slightly more for larger groups. The guides are not park employees, but most speak good English, and they are organised into a nasty cartel-like co-operative that operates out of a small building next to the national park office, and whose members are allocated to visitors on a rotational basis. In theory, taking a guide is optional. In practice, the association insists that all visitors must pay in full for one of their members' services on all days or part-days they spend in the park. An exception is sometimes made for 'self-organising' travellers – ie: independent travellers who arrive at Debark on public transport, make arrangements on the spot, and manage to argue their case successfully. Otherwise, anyone who doesn't want a guide (or who queries why they must pay for one on a day when, for instance, they will drive between Limalimo Lodge and Gondar or Axum without even setting foot in the park proper) should be ready to absorb some verbal and possibly physical aggression – all of which will be in vain if, as seems to be the case, the staff at the national park office now simply refuse to acknowledge the existence of, or issue entrance permits to, anybody who doesn't acquiesce to the guides' demands.

Mules Porters are not available, so it is conventional to take mules as pack animals. Carrying all your own gear and food is not recommended, as distances are long and routes undulating. The scout and guide will expect you to hire at least one mule to carry their food and blankets. Each mule costs US$5 per day, and requires a human driver, who costs US$6. Before hiring a mule, check that it's in good condition. If there's a hint of a limp, or cuts or sores under the saddle, don't hire it. And insist that a blanket is placed under the saddle for padding.

Cooks and eating Most organised groups take along a cook, who must be organised through the national park office and costs US$14 per day for up to three people or US$20 for larger groups. For DIY travellers, it will most probably be cheaper and more straightforward to sort out food as you go along. At Sankaber, Gich and Chennek campsites, decent local meals – *shiro* or *tibs* – can usually be had for around US$2 per plate. Elsewhere, basics like *injera* and eggs can be bought at villages en route. If you travel without a cook, you can stock up with biscuits, bread, tinned fish and fruit, and other provisions that don't require any preparation, at a supermarket in Debark, though the choice will be far greater in Gondar or Addis Ababa.

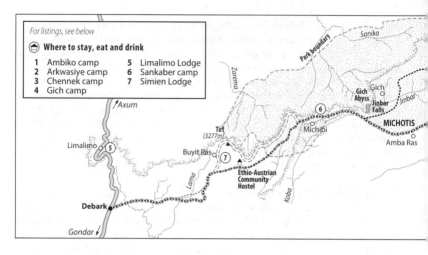

For listings, see below

Where to stay, eat and drink

1	Ambiko camp	5	Limalimo Lodge
2	Arkwasiye camp	6	Sankaber camp
3	Chennek camp	7	Simien Lodge
4	Gich camp		

Travellers occasionally become ill through drinking untreated water. To avoid this, ensure that all drinking water is brought properly to the boil, and carry some purifying tablets as a fall-back.

Equipment and supplies If you don't have all the equipment you need, most obvious items of trekking gear can be rented inexpensively from the park headquarters or at the Simien Park Hotel (page 289) in Debark. This includes two-person tents, sleeping bags, roll mattresses, tables, chairs and simple cooking kits including a kerosene stove and aluminium pots. None of this is strictly necessary for those staying at campsites where hutted accommodation and food is available.

WHERE TO STAY, EAT AND DRINK *Map, above*
Note that the lodges and camps listed below all technically lie in the national park, which means that the full bouquet of entrance, vehicle, scout and guide fees must be paid at the office in Debark for every day or part thereof you spend at any of them, including the morning of departure, and whether or not you have any use for the guide or scout on that day.

* **Limalimo Lodge** (12 rooms) m 0909 063466; e info@limalimolodge.com; w limalimolodge.com. One of the most spectacularly sited, eco-conscious & luxurious lodges anywhere in Ethiopia, Limalimo stands on a 10ha site above a sheer peninsula-like escarpment a few minutes' drive east of the Axum road about 6km north of Debark. The dining area & terrace offer sensational views across a low valley to a long, jagged stretch of escarpment, with all manner of raptors & crows soaring above. Both common area & chalets have a modern minimalist feel, yet also feel very earthy thanks to the innovative use of green technology, with all buildings being constructed with a combination of rammed earth, wood & thatch. Stylish individual chalets are scattered around the

hillside to ensure privacy, & all have lovely views & modern en-suite bathrooms. Activities include a short sundowner walk to the end of the peninsula on which the lodge stands, a ½-day hike along the escarpment to Sankaber, & drives & hikes deeper into the national park. *US$220/320 sgl/dbl inc all meals, most drinks & a community levy, with significant low-season discounts.* $$$$$

* **Simien Lodge** (26 rooms) \ 058 231 0741, 011 552 4758; e lodge@simiens.com; w simiens.com. Attractively located within the park at Buyit Ras, 22km from Debark, this eco-friendly lodge stands at an elevation of 3,260m, making it the highest hotel in Africa. Spacious & stylish *tukul*-style twin or dbl rooms & family suites (sleeping 4) have stone walls, thatched roofs with fibreglass

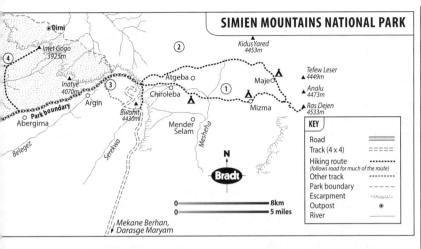

SIMIEN MOUNTAINS NATIONAL PARK

KEY

Road	
Track (4 x 4)	
Hiking route *(follows road for much of the route)*	
Other track	
Park boundary	
Escarpment	
Outpost	◉
River	

insulation, warm duvets, extra blankets & en-suite showers, but be aware that solar-powered features such as hot water & underfloor heating depend on clearish skies, which cannot be guaranteed at this altitude. Good quality buffet or 3-course set menus cost US$15 & a well-stocked bar serves some of the priciest drinks in Ethiopia. The surrounding area is populated by habituated geladas, & the lodge can organise foot & horse treks. High-quality mountain bikes can also be rented. Details of the daily shuttle to Gondar & its airport are included on the website & seats can be reserved when you book accommodation. *US$220/230 sgl/dbl B&B, with 50% off-season discount.* **$$$$$**

National Park campsites and huts The most popular campsites, running from west to east, are Sankaber, Gich, Chennek, Arkwasiye and Ambiko. Of these, the best equipped, offering very basic **hutted accommodation** with beds and bedding, as well as toilets (often filthy), cold showers and running water, are Sankaber (14 rooms), Gich (10 rooms) and Chennek (3 rooms). Adequate local meals are available at these three hutted camps for around US$2 per plate, and beers and soft drinks are sold at Chennek. Facilities at the more easterly campsites are very limited (Ambiko has no water source, and Arkwasiye has neither water nor a toilet), but you can ask to lodge with local people in the village instead, most likely sleeping on the floor or maybe on a wooden platform with goats or cows underneath to provide warmth. If you want to camp anywhere, you will need to be completely self-sufficient with tent and camping equipment, all of which is usually provided by the operator on an organised tour (but do check this) and can also be hired at the park office in Debark. All overnight visitors pay a camping fee of US$0.50 and the huts cost an additional US$4 per person. Lodging with locals is negotiable but shouldn't cost more than US$2 per person per night.

EXPLORING THE PARK

On foot The Simiens are best explored on foot, and there are several route options, depending on the time you have, the distance you want to cover, and whether or not you drive part way into the park. Some people are happy to visit the park for just two days, doing a short walk and staying one night at Simien Lodge or one of the campsites with huts. Others spend ten days or longer in the mountains, trekking all the way from Debark to Ras Dejen, and diverting to several of the smaller peaks. There are several intermediate options. A popular four-day, three-night trek entails sleeping at Sankaber and Gich, then either returning to Sankaber, or going on to

Chennek, depending on whether you can arrange a vehicle to meet you at the latter. An extra day would allow you to summit Bwahit or visit the viewpoint on the way to Ras Dejen. With six to seven days (five to six nights), you could sleep at Sankaber, Chennek, Ambiko (for two nights, going up Ras Dejen in between), then head back to Chennek or Sankaber. For further details, see box, below.

By car A single dirt road runs through the park, branching eastward from Debark, and then passing through Sankaber and Chennek camps en route to the Bwahit Pass, where it branches southward to terminate outside the park boundary

SIMIEN ROUTE STAGES

This box breaks the various trekking routes in the Simiens into day-long stages. You can combine all of the stages to create a major trek, or pick a few to do a shorter one, bearing in mind that distances between camps are quite long, and the altitude can leave you breathless. Times are for walking only; allow extra time for lunch stops, photographs, rests or simply looking at the view.

STAGE ONE: DEBARK TO SANKABER (*5–7hrs*) Prior to the construction of the road into the park, this was how all treks started, but these days most people skip it and travel by vehicle to Sankaber. The route leaves Debark (2,800m) from the market and then heads out of town across the Lama River to climb steeply on to the western plateau. You reach the northern escarpment near Chinkwanit and follow this via the village of Michibi to Sankaber Camp (3,250m). You may cross or follow the road during this stage, but don't let your guide follow it all the way as you'll miss the views between Chinkwanit and Michibi.

STAGE TWO: SANKABER TO GICH (*5–7hrs*) Follow the track east along a narrow ridge, with the escarpment to the north and Koba River to the south. Drop into the Koba Valley, then climb steeply up through an area called Michotis. To your left is the Gich Abyss, as well as the spectacular Jinbar Falls (page 298). About 3–4 hours from Sankaber, the paths divide. Keep left and drop into the valley, across the Jinbar River, then steeply up to Gich Camp (3,600m). From Gich Camp, it's 1–2 hours northeast to the summit of Imet Gogo (3,925m), which offers spectacular views north and east across the foothills and plains.

STAGE THREE: GICH TO CHENNEK (*5–7hrs*) Assuming that you use the track running south along the western escarpment via Imet Gogo, this is possibly the most spectacular stage, offering superb views to the valleys below. Other major peaks you pass on the way are Shayno Sefer (3,962m) and Inatye (4,070m). It's also a good area to look for gelada, Walia ibex and lammergeier. Alternatively, you can miss Gich and go direct from Sankaber to Chennek (3,620m), as described in Stage Four.

STAGE FOUR: SANKABER TO CHENNEK (*6–8hrs*) Follow the directions in Stage Two to where the paths divide. Keep right and uphill here, following the track along the crest of a broad ridge to an area called Abergirna. About 4–6 hours from Sankaber the track descends into the huge Belegez river valley. The track zigzags steeply down, crossing several streams, then climbs up again slightly, passing on the left a U-shaped gap in the escarpment wall (through which you get splendid views), to reach Chennek Camp. Chennek is one of the most spectacular spots in the Simiens, at the small town of Mekane Berhan. This road is open to tourist vehicles, and it provides the opportunity for more sedentary travellers, or those with limited time, to see most of the key habitats in a short space of time, with the near certainty of encountering wildlife such as geladas and lammergeier, and a good chance of the endemic ibex and wolf if you head through to Bwahit. With an early start, it would actually be possible to drive all the way to Bwahit as a day trip out of Gondar, but this would make for a long day and it's hardly the most satisfactory approach. A far preferable option would be to overnight at Simien or Limalimo Lodge, or at one of the camps within the park, and to return to Gondar the next day. With a one-

and the surrounding slopes are thick with giant lobelias and other Afroalpine scrub. It offers stunning views from the escarpment edge, across the foothills, of the surrounding peaks of Imet Gogo and Bwahit (4,430m), and down the Belegez Valley. The surrounding cliffs are a favoured haunt of lammergeier and gelada.

If you stay two nights at Chennek and then return towards Debark, a good destination for a day walk is the viewpoint over the Mesheha River described in Stage Five.

STAGE FIVE: CHENNEK TO AMBIKO (*6–8hrs*) Heading east from Chennek, the track climbs up a valley to the left (north) of Bwahit Peak, which overlooks the camp. About 1½ hours from Chennek, after crossing the Bwahit Pass (4,200m), you reach a viewpoint that overlooks the vast Mesheha river valley and offers a first sighting of the 4,533m Ras Dejen, which is the highest point in a wall of cliffs and peaks on the opposite skyline. From the viewpoint the path drops steeply down, passing through the village of Chiroleba (3,300m), and continues down through tributary valleys to reach the Mesheha River (2,800m; 5–7 hours from Chennek). The path goes steeply up again to reach the village of Ambiko (3,200m) after another hour.

STAGE SIX: AMBIKO TO RAS DEJEN SUMMIT AND RETURN (*7–9hrs*) It's usual to stay two nights at Ambiko, summiting Ras Dejen with a dawn start on the day between. From Ambiko, continue up the valley to reach the small village of Mizma (3,500m), where the path swings left and climbs steeply to reach a ridge crest overlooking a larger valley. Keeping this larger valley down to your left, follow the path eastward, and head towards Ras Dejen's rocky west face, visible at the head of the valley. About 3–4 hours from Ambiko you pass through a gap in an old stone wall, then swing left up a broad ridge to enter a wide semicircular corrie, surrounded by three major buttresses with steep sides of exposed rock. From this point it's impossible to see which buttress is the highest. The summit of Ras Dejen is on the top of the buttress on the left. To reach it, scramble up a gully through the cliffs to reach the cairn (pile of rocks) marking the summit (about 4–6 hours from Ambiko). Once at the summit, you may find yourself questioning whether you are at the right place, as a trick of perspective can make nearby Analu and Tefew Leser peaks, which rise to within 60m of Ras Dejen, look slightly taller. Return to Ambiko by the same route (allow 3–4 hours).

STAGES SEVEN TO NINE From Ambiko, you can return to Debark by the same route over three days. If you want to cut out the last two days, odds are you'll be able to catch a lift with a truck from Chennek to Debark.

or two-night stop in Debark, the park could also be explored by vehicle en route between Gondar and Axum.

Jinbar Falls One of the tallest waterfalls in Africa is formed by the Jinbar River as it plunges more than 500m into a gorge about 3km east of Sankaber. An easy 10-minute footpath starting on the left side of the road to Chennek leads through a lovely lichen-draped forest to a viewpoint facing the waterfall, which is quite narrow but throws up plenty of spray. The viewpoint is also good for raptor watching.

Argin Village Tours The village of Argin, 2km west of Chennek Campsite, is the focal point of a new Community Tourism Management Co-operative that offers two different packages, a 2–3-hour *injera*-baking tour starting at 09.00 and a 4-hour local gastronomy tour that includes *injera*-baking, as well as local beer-making and a coffee ceremony. Both packages include a village walk accompanied by a local guide, and they cost US$10 and US$15 respectively per person for two to five people, with all proceeds being distributed between the local guide, the host family and the co-operative. Full details are available at the national park office in Debark (page 290).

Darasge Maryam Situated on the Janamora Plains south of the national park, Darasge is where Dejazmach Wube of Tigray built a church compound and a church with the architectural assistance of German botanist Wilhelm Schimper and artist Eduard Zander. He made Darasge his headquarters and planned on it being the venue of his coronation as Emperor of Ethiopia. Wube, however, lost the battle of Darasge of 9 February 1855 to the young Ras Kassa Hailu, who was crowned Emperor Tewodros II two days later by the Metropolitan Salama. Wube was imprisoned for the rest of his life, while Tewodros, following the death of his first wife Tewabech in 1858, married Wube's daughter Teru Warq in 1860.

Today, the church of Darasge Maryam is still standing, beautifully set on a podocarpus-covered hill about 2km north of the town of Mekane Berhan. The church compound, surrounded by two stone ring-walls, also features an impressive and mostly intact stone building topped by an 11m-high belfry, sometimes erroneously called a 'bell tower' since it houses three bells imported by Dejazmach Wube, one from a foundry in Rome, one from Strasbourg and one from London. Wube, who died in prison in 1867, is buried in the grave chapel inside the church. The *maqdas* (Holy of Holies) in the centre of the church is covered on all four walls by paintings that most likely date to the 1850s, shortly after the church was consecrated. A more detailed description of the church and its fascinating history is included in Dorothea McEwan's book *The Story of Darasge Maryam* (Lit Verlag, 2013), which is sold at Simien Lodge and through online booksellers such as Amazon.

To get there, use the gravel road through the national park crossing the Bwahit Pass, and then follow it south for another 30km to the town of Mekane Berhan. Some 2km before the town, you have to turn off at an unsignposted track to Darasge. From there, a 10-minute stroll up the green hill to the right brings you to the church. Before heading out this way, be aware that the poor condition of the road through the national park means that the drive from Buyit Ras or Simien Lodge takes around 4 hours in either direction. There is no guarantee a priest will be there to let you in when you arrive.

Janamora Trekking The latest addition to the portfolio of community trekking programmes operated by Tesfa Tours (\ *011 124 5178*; m *0921 602236*; e *info@ tesfatours.com*; w *tesfatours.com*) runs through Janamora *woreda*, an extension of the Simien Massif whose scenic rolling highlands are incised with several gorges to the south, as well as the much larger gorge dividing it from the more easterly summit of Ras Dejen. Tesfa operates three guesthouses in the area, and recommends a stay of at least four nights to make the most if it. The area can be accessed from SMNP via Mekane Berhan (site of Darasge Maryam, page 298), from where the nearest community guesthouse is 2–3 hours on foot. Alternatively, you can come directly from Gondar, following a new but not-yet-complete road to Mekane Berhan to Weyne, from where it is a tough 23-hour walk up on to the plateau (with a mule to carry your bags) and 3–4 hours across the plateau (via Darasge Maryam) to the nearest community guesthouse. Coming from the south, the trail out leads north into the park and you can be picked up and transferred to camp at Chennek Camp, allowing you to explore Janamora in conjunction with SMNP and possibly a stay at one of its upmarket lodges to finish the trip. Rates are around US$70 day inclusive of food, accommodation, guide and pack animals, but exclusive of bottled drinks and transport to the trail head.

8

Axum and Surrounds

Inscribed as a UNESCO World Heritage Site in 1980, the ancient city of Axum is adorned with the tallest stelae (obelisks) ever erected in the ancient world, along with a miscellany of other antiquities, ranging from ruined palaces, dingy catacombs and centuries-old churches to inscribed tablets detailing ancient military campaigns into Yemen and Sudan. As the most important tourist hub in the northerly federal region of Tigray, the ancient city is readily accessible by air from Addis Ababa and several other points along the northern historic circuit, or a long half-day's drive from Gondar and the Simien Mountains to the southeast, and Mekele (the capital of Tigray) in the southeast. When it comes to tourism, Axum tends to attract lower volumes than the likes of Lalibela and Gondar, partly because its attractions are less immediately impressive, but also because it has a relatively poor selection of hotels and other tourist amenities, and is just that much further from Addis Ababa by road. Still, the ancient city – legendarily home to the Queen of Sheba and final resting place of the enigmatic Ark of the Covenant – is a fascinating place, especially if you're able to tie in your visit in with the haunting Mehelela Procession held on the first seven days of each of the Ethiopian months, and make a side trip to the ancient moon temple at Yeha.

SHIRE INDA SELASSIE

The gateway to Tigray coming from the direction of the Simien Mountains, Shire Inda Selassie is a booming town of 70,000, situated 290km north of Gondar and 65km west of Axum. It is one of three surviving charters associated with Emperor Dawit I, who ruled in the late 14th century, and its name derives from that of a nearby monastery established in 1346 (Shire is reputedly a bastardisation of Syria, in reference to refugees from that country who settled there, while Inda Selassie means 'House of the Trinity'). The surrounding area boasts a wealth of intriguing but largely unexcavated Axumite sites, most notably May Adrasha, which lies about 2km out of town alongside the road to Axum. In 2015–16, preliminary excavations undertaken here by the UCLA Shire Archaeological Project uncovered a stone platform and large storage pots dating to 1200BC, indicating that May Adrasha is comparable in antiquity to Axum, and possibly older. Further excavations are scheduled, and medium-term plans include the development of a state-of-the-art information centre. Until this happens, the town lacks for specific sites of interest, though travellers who intend to bus from Axum on to Gondar or Debark will probably need to spend a night there. Shire Inda Selassie also doubles as the springboard for visits to the remote Kafta-Sheraro National Park on the Eritrean border.

GETTING THERE AND AWAY

To/from Mekele Ethiopian Airlines flies once daily in either direction between Mekele and Shire Inda Selassie, a flight you would be likely to use only if those between Mekele and Axum were full. The airport is 1km from the town centre towards Gondar.

To/from Axum A good 65km road connects Shire Inda Selassie to Axum. Minibuses nip back and forth between the two towns throughout the day. The fare is US$1.20 and the trip takes about 1 hour.

To/from Debark and Gondar The 290km road between Shire Inda Selassie and Gondar is among the most dramatic anywhere in Africa, with the jaggedly evocative spines of the Simiens dominating the northeastern skyline as you switchback between Adi Arkay and Debark, a climb or descent of almost 2,000m. The road is now surfaced for all but 50km of its length, a 5–6-hour drive in a private vehicle. One bus runs daily between Shire Inda Selassie and Gondar, leaving in either direction at around 05.30–06.00. Coming from Gondar, it usually arrives in Shire Inda Selassie at midday, leaving you plenty of time to bus on to Axum. Coming from Shire Inda Selassie, it can drop you in Debark (the springboard for Simien treks) though you may need to pay the full fare to Gondar. For southbound travellers, the early departure time means you will need to spend the night before you travel in Shire Inda Selassie rather than Axum. For details of bussing from Debark to Shire Inda Selassie, see page 288.

WHERE TO STAY, EAT AND DRINK

Bahre Negash International Resort (30 rooms) m 0913 271123. By far the best hotel in town, though not very central, this army-run place stands on a hill offering a great view over the city centre & new airport. En-suite rooms have good amenities & there's a decent restaurant & engaged management. *From US$26 dbl.* **$$$**

Gebar Shire Hotel (55 rooms) \ 034 444 3427; e gebshire@ethionet.et; w gebarshirehotel. com. Offering a level of comfort that surpasses the many other lodges dotted around the town centre, this prominent 4-storey landmark on the main roundabout has small budget rooms using common shower & large en-suite rooms with sat TV. The restaurant's vast menu includes chicken, fish, veal, steak, lamb, pasta & rice dishes, as well as a full page of soups & salads. *US$9/11 sgl/dbl using common shower; US$20/22 sgl/dbl en suite.* **$$$**

WHAT TO SEE AND DO

Kafta-Sheraro National Park Gazetted in 2007, this 2,173km^2 national park near Humera, a border town situated 260km west of Shire Inda Selassie by road, forms a southern extension of Eritrea's Gash-Setit Wildlife Reserve. The two parks protect a migratory population of around 100–150 elephants that can usually be found on the Ethiopian side during the rainy season of May to October. Of 25 other mammal species recorded, Anubis baboon, grivet money and warthog are most conspicuous, but the park also protects nine types of antelope including common eland, greater kudu, roan antelope and red-fronted gazelle, and relict populations of leopard and possibly cheetah. Flowed through by the Tekeze River, Kafta-Sheraro supports at least 160 bird species and in 2009 it was discovered to be an important overwintering site for migrant demoiselle cranes, with aggregations of more than 2,000 individuals sometimes recorded, representing around 10% of the global population. Any visit should be treated as a full-on expedition. No entrance fee is levied, but you need to obtain a permit at the park headquarters in Adebay, 7km from Humera, and also to take a scout and road guide (free, but a tip will be expected). From Adebay, you can drive into the park with a 4x4, but you must be prepared to walk in order to see much wildlife.

8

The oldest continuously inhabited town south of the Sahara, Axum (also spelt Aksum) sits at an elevation of 2,130m on the central Tigrayan Plateau, 1,000km north of Addis Ababa and 30km south of the Eritrean border. Historically and archaeologically, it is the most important city in Ethiopia; it also hosts the country's first church, and forms the spiritual home of its unique brand of Christianity. Yet, despite this estimable pedigree, previous editions of this book described Axum as being unexpectedly unkempt and modestly proportioned, and noted that many visitors find its scattered antiquities lack a 'wow factor' comparable to the castles of Gondar or churches of Lalibela. The first of these quibbles, at least, is no longer fair. Axum has grown both upwards and outwards over recent years, and the dusty and pot-holed roads of yore have been transformed into an attractive network of cobbled backstreets bisected by a palm-shaded main drag and dotted with neat parks and open squares. Furthermore, when approached with realistic expectations, this most ancient of Ethiopian capitals does boast a quite astonishing wealth of archaeological relicts: from skyscraping stelae and dank subterranean catacombs to mysterious ruined palaces and illuminating multilingual tablets – not to mention an ancient swimming pool traditionally associated with the legendary Queen of Sheba, and a 4th-century church claimed to house nothing less than the original Ark of the Covenant. Further afield, a handful of characterful old monasteries lie within walking distance of the town centre, while more remote attractions include the pre-Axumite temple at Yeha. At least two days are required to visit most places of interest in the immediate vicinity of Axum, ideally in the company of a knowledgeable local guide; and once you're hooked, the questions that arise during the course of exploring this ancient and enigmatic city will linger on for months.

HISTORY The earliest known settlement at Axum, established during or before the 7th century BC, was a village located on the plateau of Beta Giyorgis, the flat-topped hill that rises to the immediate northwest of the present-day town. By the 4th century BC, this village had expanded to become an important pre-Axumite residential area complete with palaces, other monumental buildings and rock-hewn pit graves marked with small megaliths. Although some settlement appears to have existed at the base of the hill throughout this period, it was probably only in the 2nd century AD that the royal cemetery now referred to as the Stelae Park was established there and the present-day town centre became the focus of imperial and trade activity. It was at around this time that Axum emerged as the capital of the Axumite Empire, and as the most important political and market centre in the Horn of Africa.

Axum's influence peaked over the 3rd to 6th centuries AD, when it ruled over an empire that extended over some 2.5 million km^2 all the way west to the Sudanese Nile and east across the Red Sea to southern Arabia, and controlled a vast trade network whose tendrils reached Mediterranean Africa and Europe, as well as parts of Asia. One product of this exposure is that the empire's rulers adopted Christianity as the state religion in the 4th century AD and Axum became the birthplace of the Ethiopian Orthodox Church, which remains the country's most numerically significant religion to this day. The Church of Maryam Tsion was founded opposite the Stelae Park at around this time.

Axum's influence started to decline after its vassal state in southern Arabia was captured by Persians in the 6th century. By the end of the 8th century, Axum had become completely isolated from its former trade routes to Egypt and the

Mediterranean as a result of the rising Islamic influence in Arabia and North Africa. The city's influence dwindled further towards the end of the millennium, when it was captured by the enigmatic Gudit, a Jewish queen who razed many of the city's and the empire's most important Christian shrines. For a more detailed overview of Axum's history up until the end of the 1st millennium, see page 8.

Not much is known about events in Axum between the 10th and the 15th centuries. Evidently it retained its role as Ethiopia's holiest Christian city, but settlement was largely confined to the small area between Maryam Tsion and the eastern slopes of Beta Giyorgis. The Portuguese missionary Francisco Álvares, who visited Axum in the early 16th century, described it as 'a large town of very good

EXCAVATING AXUM

The earliest archaeological explorations of Axum were undertaken in 1905 by a Tigrayan nobleman, Dejazmach Gebre Selassie, and a year later by Dr Enno Littmann's Deutsche-Aksum Expedition (DAE). The massively detailed report of the later expedition, which includes extensive notes on the two main stelae fields, Kaleb's Palace and several churches, was published in German in 1913. An English translation, edited and annotated by Dr David Phillipson, and lavishly illustrated with line drawings and photographs taken in 1906, was published as *The Monuments of Aksum* in 1997.

Between 1906 and 1992, only two significant excavations took place at Axum, both terminated after the assassination of Haile Selassie in 1974. The French excavations at Dongar Palace and several other sites, initiated in 1952 and supervised by Francis Anfrey, resulted in several sketchy preliminary accounts but no detailed report. Stuart Munro-Hay published a full account of the excavations at the Stelae Park undertaken by Neville Chittick for the British Institute in East Africa in the early 1970s. After Chittick's death, in 1991, Munro-Hay published the most detailed and readable existing account of Axumite society, a book entitled *Aksum: An African Civilisation of Late Antiquity*.

In this book, Munro-Hay writes:

Of all the important ancient civilisations of the past, that of the ancient Ethiopian kingdom of Aksum still remains perhaps the least known … Its history and civilisation have been largely ignored, or at most accorded only brief mention, in the majority of recent books purporting to deal at large with ancient African civilisations, or with the world of late antiquity … When this book was in preparation, I wrote to the archaeology editor of one of Britain's most prominent history and archaeology publishers about its prospects. He replied that, although he had a degree in archaeology, he had never heard of Aksum.

The subsequent decades have seen a number of important new excavations undertaken in and around Axum, the results of which generally remain unpublished. Only a tiny fraction of the known sites around Axum have been excavated, and new sites are being discovered at a faster pace than the established ones are being investigated. It is thus safe to say that almost anything written about Axum today is based on relatively sketchy archaeological foundations. One can only guess at what further excavation of this mysterious city might yet reveal.

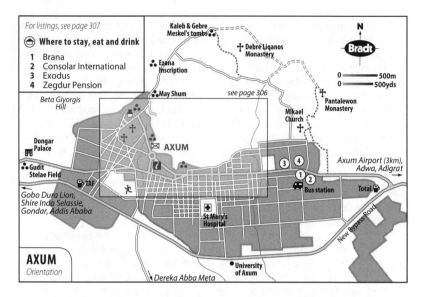

For listings, see page 307

Where to stay, eat and drink
1 Brana
2 Consolar International
3 Exodus
4 Zegdur Pension

Beta Giyorgis Hill

Dongar Palace

Gudit Stelae Field

TAF

Gobo Dura Lion,
Shire Inda Selassie,
Gondar, Addis Ababa

Kaleb & Gebre Meskel's tombs

Debre Liqanos Monastery

Ezana Inscription

May Shum

AXUM

see page 306

Mikael Church

Pantalewon Monastery

Axum Airport (3km),
Adwa, Adigrat

Bus station

Total

New Bypass Road

St Mary's Hospital

University of Axum

Dereka Abba Meta

N

0 ——— 500m
0 ——— 500yds

AXUM
Orientation

houses, such that there are none like them in the whole of Ethiopia, and very good wells of water, and worked masonry, and also in most of the houses ancient figures of lions, dogs and birds, all well made in stone'. About ten years after this, Axum was attacked by the army of Ahmed Gragn, who razed much of the old town and destroyed its premier church. A century later, according to Manuel de Almeida, Axum had been reduced to 'a place of about a hundred inhabitants [where] everywhere there are ruins'.

Axum has grown vastly since Almeida's day. Panoramic photographs taken by the Deutsche-Aksum Expedition suggest it harboured a population of a few thousand in 1909, though – somewhat disorientating at first glance – it appears that the town was then concentrated to the west of Maryam Tsion, while what is now the city centre, east of the watercourse called May Hejja, was more sparsely settled. The town continues to expand in that direction to this day – indeed, much of the urban development east of the Dashen Bank took place since the first edition of this book was researched in 1994. The population today is estimated at around 60,000.

GETTING THERE AND AWAY
By air Ethiopian Airlines flies daily between Axum and Gondar, Lalibela, Mekele and Addis Ababa. The airport is located on the Adwa road almost 5km east of the town centre. Most hotels listed on page 305 offer a free transfer to town, failing which a taxi shouldn't cost more than US$5.

By road A regular stream of minibuses connects Axum to Adwa (*30mins*), Adigrat (*3hrs*) and Shire Inda Selassie (*1hr*). All public transport now leaves from the new bus station at the east end of the town centre.

To/from Gondar or Debark The partly unsurfaced 355km road between Axum and Gondar via Debark takes 6–7 hours to cover in a private vehicle. There is no direct public transport, but at least one bus runs between Shire Inda Selassie and Gondar daily, leaving at around 05.30–06.00 in either direction, and stopping at Debark en route. See page 301 for further details.

To/from Mekele Heading directly between Mekele and Axum, the two towns lie 250km apart along a good surfaced road through Adigrat and Wukro. The drive shouldn't take longer than 4 hours in a private vehicle. At least one local bus runs this way daily, leaving at around 06.00, but it would also be easy to do the trip in stages, changing vehicles at Adigrat and possibly Wukro. Another option is the daily Selam Bus that travels from Addis Ababa to Shire Inda Selassie, a two-day trip that entails an overnight stay in Mekele before stopping at Axum the next day.

To/from Hawzen As things stand, the best route between Axum and Hawzen entails following the road to Mekele via Adigrat, then branching west at Freweyni, a total distance of 185km, all on asphalt. Using public transport, you may need to change vehicles at Adigrat and Freweyni. An alternative 128km route via Adwa and Nebelet (near Maryam Wukro; page 354) is pretty rough going at the time of writing, but should be surfaced in its entirety during the lifespan of this edition.

To/from Lalibela Although most people fly between Axum and Lalibela, you can also drive between the two towns using the 400km route through Adwa, Abiy Addi and Sekota. With an early start and a private vehicle, it may be possible to cover this road in one long, dusty day, but don't count on it. Better perhaps to plan on an overnight stop at Abiy Addi or Sekota, both of which offer access to little-visited but very worthwhile rock-hewn churches.

GETTING AROUND Most sites in the city limits are within walking distance of each other, but plenty of *bajaji* ply the streets, costing up to US$1 for a short charter trip within the city centre. You could also hire them to take you to sites slightly further afield, for instance Kaleb's Tomb or Dongar Palace.

WHERE TO STAY Budget travellers are well catered for in Axum, but the city's ostensibly more upmarket hotels evidently adhere to an 'anything you can do, we can do more disastrously' philosophy. Indeed, there isn't one hotel in Axum we would regard to be genuinely upmarket (at least not on any criterion other than price) and it's debatable whether any of those places we list in the moderate category would have made the cut were it located in the likes of Lalibela or Bahir Dar.

Moderate

Yeha Hotel [306 C1] (63 rooms) \034 775 2377–9; e yehaxum@yahoo.com. This former government hotel used to be Axum's finest & it retains immense potential thanks to an outstanding location on a hilltop swathed in ficus trees rattling with birds & monkeys, & the fine view over the Stelae Park. The carpeted en-suite rooms with TV & erratic hot water are no better than tolerably functional, & in desperate need of refurbishment. The restaurant has a similarly timeworn feel, though the food is better than appearances might predict. Even if you stay & eat elsewhere, it's worth walking out in the evening to enjoy sundowners on the terrace. It's overpriced as things stand, but that might

change if promised renovations in 2018 actually go ahead. *US$60/81/106 sgl/dbl/suite.* **$$$$**

Sabean International Hotel [306 F4] (44 rooms) \034 775 1224; e sabeanreservation@gmail.com; w sabeanhotel.com. Arguably the pick of the more upmarket hotels in central Axum but a poor 2nd to the Yeha in terms of location, this has small but comfortable & well-equipped dbl or twin rooms with en-suite hot shower, TV & modern furnishings. *From US$50/66 B&B sgl/dbl.* **$$$$**

Yared Zema Hotel [306 G3] (60 rooms) \034 775 4817; m 0914 301311; e info@yaredzemainternationalhotelaxum.com; w yaredzemainternationalhotelaxum.com. This 5-storey hotel is the newest & one of the better

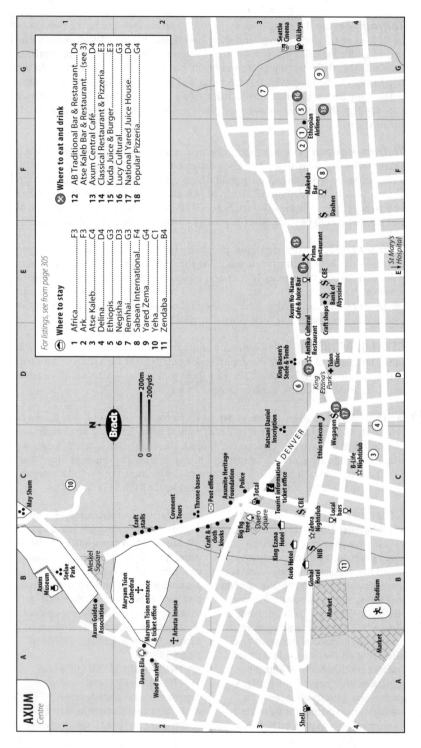

AXUM
Centre

Where to stay
For listings, see from page 305

1	Africa	F3
2	Ark	F3
3	Atse Kaleb	C4
4	Delina	D4
5	Ethiopis	G3
6	Negisha	D3
7	Remhai	G3
8	Sabean International	F4
9	Yared Zema	G4
10	Yeha	C1
11	Zendaba	B4

Where to eat and drink

12	AB Traditional Bar & Restaurant	D4
	Atse Kaleb Bar & Restaurant	(see 3)
13	Axum Central Café	D4
14	Classical Restaurant & Pizzeria	E3
15	Kuda Juice & Burger	E3
16	Lucy Cultural	G3
17	National Yared Juice House	D4
18	Popular Pizzeria	G4

options in its range, though the en-suite rooms – with wood-effect linoleum floor, writing desk, fridge, TV, hot water & small balcony – lack for any pizzazz & are already starting to look quite frayed. *US$55/65/95 B&B sgl/dbl/suite.* **$$$$**

🏠 **Consolar International Hotel** [map, page 304] (41 rooms) 📞 034 775 0210; e info@consolarhotelaxum.com; w consolarhotelaxum.com. This multistorey hotel has spacious but rather cluttered rooms with TV, writing desk, fridge & hot shower. Adequate, as these things go. *US$45/50/55 B&B sgl/dbl/twin.* **$$$$**

Budget

🏠 **Delina Hotel** [306 E4] (25 rooms) m 0911 575042, 0914 744183. This new 4-storey hotel has a quiet but usefully central location, & bright, clean, spacious & well-maintained tiled rooms with flatscreen TV, writing desk & hot shower. Good value. *US$20 dbl.* **$$**

🏠 **Ethiopis Hotel** [306 G3] (25 rooms) m 0910 097644. A new central medium-rise whose decent-sized & well-maintained rooms come with TV & en-suite shower. Ask for one facing away from the main road. Fair value. *US$20/24/30 sgl/dbl/twin.* **$$$**

🏠 **Exodus Hotel** [map, page 304] (26 rooms) 📞 034 775 2498. This old-fashioned hotel near the bus station has an attractively quaint ground-floor restaurant & bar, but the en-suite rooms with hot water are looking a little frayed. Still, fair value. *US$12/16 sgl/dbl.* **$$**

🏠 **Brana Hotel** [map, page 304] (35 rooms) 📞 034 775 2349; m 0913 768442. This multistorey hotel is a bit of an eyesore from the outside, & the interior is just as soulless, but the spacious en-suite rooms with hot water, sat TV, fridge & Wi-Fi are fair value at the price. Rates are very negotiable when it's quiet. *US$30/40 B&B sgl/dbl.* **$$$**

🏠 **Negisha Hotel** [306 D3] (26 rooms) 📞 034 775 4905; m 0912 691933; e negishaksumhotel@gmail.com; w negishahotels.com. An unusual 2-storey hotel with a castle-like stone façade complete with Axumite arches & roof terraces which doesn't quite live up to its potential, thanks partly to the unkempt appearance of the central

courtyard; but it couldn't be more central & the no-frills en-suite rooms with hot shower & TV are relatively reasonably priced. *US$30/35/40 B&B sgl/dbl/twin.* **$$$**

🏠 **Remhai Hotel** [306 G3] (85 rooms) 📞 034 775 3210; e remhhot@hotmail.com; f. Briefly the top spot in Axum, the moribund Remhai has slid downhill of late & its once-popular swimming pool is looking uninvitingly murky. Spacious but shabby en-suite rooms have wooden floor, TV, fridge & hot tub. *US$22/38 B&B dbl/suite.* **$$$**

Shoestring

✱ 🏠 **Atse Kaleb Hotel** [306 D2] (16 rooms) m 0910 217996; e atsekaleb@yahoo.com. Owned by the same family for 30-plus years, this friendly hotel has responsive management & encloses an excellent green courtyard restaurant. There's the choice of simple rooms with common shower or larger & better-maintained en-suite rooms with hot shower. *US$6/12 dbl with common/en-suite shower.* **$–$$**

🏠 **Africa Hotel** [306 F3] (28 rooms) 📞 034 775 3700; m 0911 532526. Consistently popular with backpackers since the mid 1990s, this reasonably priced & relatively central hotel has a good ground-floor restaurant & small but bright rooms with sat TV & hot shower. *US$8/10/12/14 en-suite sgl/dbl/twin/trpl.* **$**

🏠 **Ark Hotel** [306 F3] (18 rooms) m 0914 521574; e daniark.2003@yahoo.com. Situated next to the Africa Hotel & similar in price & standard, this friendly place has adequately clean rooms with balcony, TV & en-suite hot shower. *US$8/10 sgl/dbl.* **$**

🏠 **Zegdur Pension** [map, page 304] (12 rooms) 📞 034 775 1341. The pick of several rock-bottom cheapies close to the bus station, this place has bright clean rooms with ¾ bed & hot shower – especially good value if you get one facing away from the main road. *US$4 sgl.* **$**

🏠 **Zendaba Hotel** [306 B4] (14 rooms) m 0914 301315. This lodge opposite the stadium has clean en-suite rooms with TV & hot shower, & a fair ground-floor restaurant. *US$12 dbl.* **$$**

✕ WHERE TO EAT AND DRINK
Restaurants

✱ ✕ **Kuda Juice & Burger** [306 E3] m 0911 117746; ⏱ 08.00–22.00. Axum's most contemporary-feeling restaurant has open-air

seating in a courtyard shaded by colourful awnings. The speciality is burgers, but it also serves pasta, salads & sandwiches (*mains US$2–3*) as well as a varied selection of juices (*US$1*), & has free Wi-Fi.

✖ **Lucy Cultural Restaurant** [306 G3] m 0914 768399; ⏱ 08.00–22.00. Not as elaborately decorated as the Antika, & lacking the live music, this well-established restaurant next to the Remhai Hotel serves good-value traditional Ethiopian fare. *Mains US$2–4.*

✖ **Atse Kaleb Bar & Restaurant** [306 C4] ☏ 034 775 2222; ⏱ 11.00–22.00 daily. The shady green courtyard restaurant at this stalwart budget hotel has an open kitchen serving some of the best Western-style food in town. Pizzas & burgers are the speciality, but salads, fish & sandwiches are also on the menu. Free Wi-Fi. *Mains US$2–4.*

✖ **Classical Restaurant & Pizzeria** [306 E3] m 0914 769785; ⏱ 10.00–22.00. This central 1st-floor restaurant has a rather gloomy interior but very pleasant terrace seating. The menu is strong on pizzas, burgers, salads, steak & Ethiopian cuisine ranging from roast lamb to *tibs. Most mains US$3–5.*

✖ **AB Traditional Bar & Restaurant** [306 D4] m 0914 193354; ⏱ 07.00–22.00 daily. Though it's starting to look a little gloomy & timeworn, this cultural restaurant has beautiful traditional décor & an excellent Ethiopian menu featuring many unusual & traditional Tigrayan dishes. *Mains US$2–4.*

✖ **Popular Pizzeria** [306 G4] m 0914 010019; ⏱ 06.00–22.00 daily. This clean & modern restaurant has pavement seating & serves a good selection of pizzas, burgers & pasta dishes. *Mains US$2–4.*

Cafés & juice bars

🍵 **Axum Central Café** [306 D4] m 0911 030468; ⏱ 06.00–22.30 daily. On the 1st floor above the Wegagen Bank, this breezy café with a terrace overlooking King Ezana's Park has a good b/fast selection, including yoghurt & *ful*, plus excellent juices, coffee & pastries. *Typical Ethiopian dishes in the US$2–3 range.*

🍵 **National Yared Juice House** [306 D4] ⏱ 06.00–22.30 daily. A good selection of inexpensive & wholesome juices can be drunk in the stuffy interior or at a table out on the pavement.

NIGHTLIFE

✳ ☆ **Antika Cultural Restaurant** [306 D4] m 0923 412415; ⏱ 08.00–late daily. Home to the Antika Dance Group, Axum's top nightspot stands out for the energetic traditional live music & dance performances it hosts at 19.00 daily. It also has a varied menu of Western & Ethiopian dishes in the US$2–4 range. No cover charge for the music but drink prices are marked up.

SHOPPING Axum is particularly well endowed with shops selling Ethiopian handicrafts, ranging from religious icons and other old artefacts to modern carvings and cotton *shama* cloth. The two main clusters are along the south side of the road between Daero Square and the Stelae Park, and along the main road between **King Ezana's Park** and the Africa Hotel.

TOURIST INFORMATION The spanking new Axum Tourist Office [306 C3] (*Daero Sq;* ☏ *034 775 3924;* e *aksumtoutistoffice@ethionet.et;* ⏱ *07.00–18.00*) incorporates a moderately interesting interpretation centre, but is mainly of interest as the place to buy an entrance ticket to Axum's archaeological sites (*US$4 for 3 days*).

Gian Paulo Chiari's 270-page *Guide to Aksum and Yeha* (Arada Books, 2009) covers all sites in and around town in considerable depth, reflecting the most recent available research. Not widely available in Axum, it can be bought at bookshops in Addis Ababa or through the publisher (w *aradabooks.com*).

Situated in a restored palace alongside Daero Square, the **Axumite Heritage Foundation** [306 C3] (☏ *034 775 2871;* w *axumiteheritagefoundation.org;* ⏱ *08.30–22.00 Mon–Sat*) library includes several hundred titles about Ethiopia, many rare or out of print. Casual visitors are welcome to browse.

TOUR OPERATORS AND GUIDES The **Axum Guides Association** [306 B1] next to the entrance to the Stelae Park is the best place to pick up a registered guide, who will ask around US$15 per day per group. Unofficial guides are best avoided. The only nationally registered operator in Axum, **Covenant Tours** [306 C2] (✆ *034 775 2642*; m *0911 185279*; e *travelcovenant@yahoo.com*; w *covenantethiopia.com*), located on the main road to the Stelae Park, can organise excursions to Yeha and the rock-hewn churches of northeast Tigray, as well as car rental and guided city tours of Axum. For budget excursions, another option is **Dallol Tours**, which is based in the Atse Kaleb Hotel (page 363) and has the same contact details.

WHAT TO SEE AND DO Axum's most important cluster of antiquities, including the Stelae Park, Axum Museum and Cathedral of Maryam Tsion, stands at the verge of the town centre about 1km northwest of King Ezana's Park. It is the obvious place to start any exploration of Axum, though you need first to head to the Axum Tourist Office on Daero Square to pay the US$4 entrance fee, valid for three days, which allows access to all secular sites in and around Axum (but not church-related sites such as Maryam Tsion and out-of-town monasteries). The Axum Guides Association outside the Stelae Park is the best place to arrange a guide. Don't forget a torch.

Central sites
Stelae Park [306 B1] Axum's most iconic monument is the field of 120-odd stelae, ranging from small, roughly hewn stones to finely engraved obelisks the height of a ten-storey building, concentrated within an area of 1,000m² opposite the Cathedral of Maryam Tsion. The site incorporates what are probably the three tallest stelae ever erected in ancient times, neatly engraved blocks of solid granite that stand (or, in one case, stood) between 23m and 33m high. The stelae were excavated at the quarry at Gobo Dura, more than 4km to the southwest, and were most probably dragged to their present location by domesticated elephants. There's no entirely satisfactory explanation for how the Axumite engineers erected these massive blocks of stone – tradition has it that the supernatural powers of the Ark of the Covenant were put into play, but a more rational explanation would involve pulleys and elephants.

It is not entirely certain when the stelae were erected. Local traditions link certain of the larger stelae to specific 3rd- and 4th-century Axumite kings, as referred to in the text that follows, but little scholarly evidence exists to support or refute these associations beyond the fact they broadly concur with archaeological findings that the same area served as an imperial burial ground from the 2nd to the 4th centuries AD. The stelae of Axum are not thought to have had any religious significance, but to have demonstrated the power and importance of the ruler who built them, though the storeys and windows in the larger stelae clearly correspond to the number of vaults in the tomb they mark, suggesting that they were perceived to be symbolic portals to the afterlife. Nevertheless, the practice of erecting funerary stelae seems to have died out following the adoption of Christianity as the state religion. Indeed, tradition has it that the last of the accredited stelae was erected by King Ezana, the conqueror of Yemen and parts of modern-day Sudan, who converted during his reign to become Axum's first Christian ruler.

The **Remhai Stele**, credited by tradition to the eponymous 3rd-century king but now shattered into several pieces, was the largest ever erected in Axum, and would weigh 523 tonnes and stand almost 33m high were it still erect. Its collapse is linked by tradition to Queen Gudit, who destroyed many of Axum's finest buildings in the late 10th century, but scholarly opinion is that it toppled over either while it was being erected or soon afterwards, probably because the podium was too small to support it. It is engraved with 13 storeys, the lowest containing a door while the upper 12 each contain a carved window, and like all the other giant stele it has a semicircular head whose symbolic meaning is open to speculation. Today, Remhai's stele lies where it fell all those centuries ago, close to an associated subterranean tomb comprising 12 underground vaults tall enough to walk through. The most striking thing about this tomb is the precision of its masonry, which consists of large blocks of granite held together by metal pins. In the back vault, Remhai's sealed stone coffin lies where it was abandoned after Neville Chittick's excavations were aborted following the 1974 revolution.

The so-called **Roman Stele**, Axum's second largest, is engraved with ten storeys and originally stood about 25m high. Its builder is unknown, and it collapsed and shattered into five main pieces after an unknown perpetrator destabilised it by digging a trench underneath the base, probably in the 8th century. In 1937, during the Italian occupation, it was purloined at the command of Mussolini, shipped to Rome, and reassembled there. Following protracted negotiations between the Ethiopian and Italian governments, the looted stele was eventually returned to its rightful home almost 70 years later. The first block arrived in Axum to scenes of public jubilation on 19 April 2005, and the other two blocks followed shortly afterwards. It was re-erected in 2008, surrounded by an elaborate jungle of scaffolding that has subsequently been removed, leaving it the tallest standing stele in Axum.

For many centuries following the collapses of the Remhai and Roman stelae, Axum's tallest erection was the **Ezana Stele**, which is credited to the king of that name. Standing some 23m high, this stele is carved with a door and nine windows, which are thought to symbolise the door and nine chambers of Ezana's tomb, and the nine palaces built by the king. Ezana's stele is slightly tilted, and at one point there were fears it might eventually topple over, but recent measurements compared with those taken 100 years ago suggest it was erected at this angle. However, the erection of the Roman stele had an adverse effort on Ezana's stele, which now has to be stabilised with a sling attached to a metal pole to prevent it from shifting or tipping over. The nearby Tomb of the Arches is no longer open to the public owing to worries about instability, but you can still look down to see the first archway.

The many smaller monuments scattered around the site include two fallen stelae that would have stood about 19.5m and 14m high, and the tallest non-engraved standing stele measuring around 9m high. Most of the subterranean tombs are unexcavated, but don't miss the so-called Tomb of the Mausoleum, which opened to the public for the 2007 millennium celebration. This tomb has two entrances connected by a corridor, with rock-hewn doors featuring a design commonly seen on similar doors in the churches of Tigray. The west entrance door was damaged (along with many lintel beams) at the time the big stele collapsed, but the east door remains intact. Three 'shaft tombs' serve as skylights that illuminate the stack-stone constructed passage, and five burial chambers line each side.

Axum Museum [306 B1] Exploring the Stelae Park conveys something of the majesty of ancient Axum, but it is the tour through the exemplary site museum that illustrates just how cosmopolitan and technologically advanced the city was. Displays include a collection of rock tablets inscribed in several languages including ancient Sabaean, which consisted of consonants only, but it is similar enough to the Amharigna script that the letters (though not the meaning of the words) are intelligible to modern Ethiopians. An array of Axumite household artefacts ranges from a set of drinking glasses imported from Egypt to a collection of Axumite coins minted between the 3rd and 6th centuries AD. A more recent artefact is a 700-year-old leather Bible, written in Geʿez and decorated with illuminations. Explanatory posters, funded by an American–Italian archaeological research project, provide an overview of the history of Axum and its major archaeological sites in a context that contrasts with the more outlandish myths and legends often recounted by guides as if accepted fact. Now located directly behind the Stelae Park, the museum seems likely to move again in the medium term, as important tombs have been located beneath it. Entrance is included in the ticket price for the Stelae Park, but photography is expressly forbidden.

May Shum (Queen of Sheba's Pool) [306 C1] This small rock-hewn reservoir situated at the northern end of the Stelae Park close to the junction for the Yeha Hotel is the subject of several divergent creation legends. At one end of the timescale is the popular tradition stating it was created 3,000 years ago as a bathing place for the Queen of Sheba. At the other is the more credible story that it was dug by Abuna Samuel, Bishop of Axum, during the early 15th-century reign of Emperor Yeshaq. The notion that the Queen of Sheba ever unrobed and took a dip in May Shum has to be classified as fanciful, but the pool could well have been excavated in Axumite times, along with the stone steps leading down to it, and cleared and possibly enlarged at a later date. Suggestively, the name Axum is thought to derive from the phrase 'Ak Shum', which consists of a Cushitic word meaning 'water' and a Semitic word for 'chief', while 'Mai' is the Tigrigna equivalent to 'Ak' – so that both Mai Shum and Axum translate as 'Water of the Chief', leaving open the possibility that the town derives its name from that of the pool, which would then have to date to pre-Axumite times. Some believe the water to have curative properties, and the pool is still the setting for the climatic baptismal ceremony at Timkat in Axum.

Cathedral of Maryam Tsion [306 B2] (*Entrance US$8*) Ethiopia's first church, the Cathedral of Maryam Tsion (St Mary Zion) was established in the 4th century by King Ezana, on the site of a former pagan shrine. The original church, which consisted of 12 temples, has been destroyed, most probably by the 16th-century Islamic leader Ahmed Gragn, though one version of events is that it was a victim of the rampages of Queen Gudit, and that Gragn destroyed a later replacement church. The foundations of one of these 12 temples have been left undisturbed as a mark of respect, and there is some talk of archaeological excavation taking place below it in the near future. The main entrance to the church compound is situated in front of the sacred fig tree known as Daero Ella, a shrine associated with 6th-century composer Saint Yared, some 200m southwest of the Stelae Park.

Francisco Álvares, who visited Axum in 1520, penned what is, so far as I'm aware, the most detailed surviving description of the church destroyed by Gragn. It was, the Portuguese priest wrote:

a very noble church, the first there was in Ethiopia ... named Saint Mary of Zion ... because the apostles sent [its altar stone] from Mount Zion. This church is very large. It has five aisles of good width and of great length, vaulted above, and all the vaults closed; the ceilings and sides are painted. Below, the body of the church is well worked with handsome cut stones; it has seven chapels, all with their backs to the east, and their altars well ornamented. This church has a large enclosure, and it is also surrounded by another larger enclosure, like the enclosing wall of a large town or city. Within the enclosure are handsome groups of one-storey buildings, and all spout out water by strong figures of lions and dogs of stone. Inside this large enclosure there are two mansions ... which belong to two rectors of the church; and the other houses are of canons and monks. In the large enclosure, at the gate nearest the church, there is a large ruin, built in a square, which in other time was a house, and it has at each corner a big stone pillar, squared and worked. This house is called Ambacabete, which means house of lions. They say that in this house were the captive lions, and there are still some always travelling, and there go before the Prester John four captive lions.

The oldest-functioning church in the compound today was built in the 17th century by Emperor Fasilidas and strongly resembles the castles of Gondar. Some good paintings and musical instruments can be seen inside, but entrance has been denied to all women since Queen Gudit attacked its predecessor in the 10th century. The largest church, its ugly spire competing with the ancient stelae nearby for horizon space, is an overblown hunk of 20th-century architecture built in the 1960s under Haile Selassie. The museum next to the old church is worth visiting for its collection of ancient crowns, crosses and other church relics. Behind the old church stands the so-called Throne of David, where the Axumite emperors were crowned, as well as the Thrones of Judges, a row of a dozen old throne bases damaged by Gragn's army.

Axum's most famous religious artefact, the Tabot or supposed Ark of the Covenant, is currently kept in a sanctified outbuilding within the compound. There's not much chance of being allowed to see it – indeed, only two Westerners claim ever to have had the privilege! Yohannes Tomacean, who viewed it in 1764, described it as 'a piece of stone with a few incomplete letters on it'. A century later, R P Dimotheos, was shown 'a tablet of pinkish marble of the type one normally finds in Egypt … quadrangular, 24cm long by 22cm wide [on which] the Ten Commandments, five on one side, five on the other [were] written obliquely in Turkish fashion'. Dimotheos thought the 'nearly intact' tablet to be perhaps 600 years old, and quite clearly he was shown a different artefact from that seen by Tomacean – almost certainly, both men were allowed to view a *tabot*, but not *the* Tabot.

The entrance fee to the church compound seems steep by comparison with the bulk fee for the city's secular sites, especially for female visitors, who are banned from entering its most interesting church. This does, however, include entrance to the church museum, as well as to the nearby Church of Arbuta Insesa, a circular church constructed in the 17th century by Iyasu I and rebuilt in its present rectangular style in 1962, when several ancient tombs were found underneath it. Refreshingly low-key by comparison with the contemporaneous eyesore built by Haile Selassie next door, Arbuta Insesa is worth visiting for the interesting modern paintings that adorn its walls.

King Ezana's Park and King Basen's Tomb [306 D4 & D3] Two major historical sites lie within the modern town centre. In King Ezana's Park, a tablet inscribed in Sabaean, Ge'ez and Greek stands where it was originally placed in the 4th century AD. Other relics in the park include standing pillars, part of what was presumably Ezana's palace, a stele, a tomb, and an innocuous-looking stone slab that could be mistaken for a park bench but was in fact used for cleaning corpses. Like several other sites that are fenced off around town, it has never been excavated.

Nearby, the customary stele marks the subterranean tomb of King Basen, who ruled over Axum at the time of Christ's birth. Entered via a man-high tunnel, it differs from the tombs in the Stelae Park in that it is hewn out of rock as opposed to having been built from stone blocks. The graves chiselled into the side of the entry tunnel are probably where Basen's family were laid to rest. At the end of the tunnel are two much larger vaults in which the king and his wife are thought to have been entombed. Discrete from the king's tomb, a series of smaller rock-hewn graves is reminiscent of similar but considerably more recent graves carved into the church courtyards of Lalibela.

Mehelela Procession Held before sunrise on the first seven days of each of the Ethiopian months (for the start dates, see box, page 42), this ancient Christian procession is an absolute must if you are in town at the right time. It reputedly dates to pre-Christian times, and follows the route used by Menelik I when he first brought the Ark of the Covenant to Axum some 3,000 years ago, starting at the main entrance of Maryam Tsion Cathedral, in front of Daero Ella, then looping past Arbuta Insesa to Daero Square and returning past the Stelae Park. It starts at about 05.00 (best be there 10–15 minutes early) and attracts thousands of white-robed worshippers, mostly women but also men, who march slowly behind the priests carrying the *tabot*, holding candles and chanting and singing all the way – an utterly magical experience that feels a bit like a low-key version of Timkat or Meskel, but with the advantage that it is held dozens of times annually, not just once, so it is easier to plan around and not at all overrun by tourists. The procession ends with a sermon at Daero Ella, but it is pretty much all over by sunrise, just in time to visit the morning wood market held just to the south.

Further afield Several important sites lie within easy day-tripping distance of Axum. Indeed, most of the sites below could be reached on foot in under an hour from the city centre, the exception being the rock-hewn church of Dereka Abba Meta. A *bajaj* to any of the sites along or close to the main Gondar road would only cost a few dollars. A more remote but very worthwhile goal for a day trip out of Axum are the ruins at Yeha (page 318). Entrance to all the secular sites discussed below is included in the three-day Department of Antiquities ticket issued at the Stelae Park. Entrance to any church-related site is determined by the individual church, but it will usually cost US$4.

Dongar Palace [map, page 304] Discovered as recently as 1950, the ruins known as Dongar, or the Queen of Sheba's Palace, stand about 1km west of the modern town centre close to the southern base of Beta Giyorgis Hill. The popular association with the Queen of Sheba is improbable, given that Francis Anfrey, the French archaeologist who excavated the site in 1952, concluded that it was most probably built in the 7th century AD, though other sources reckon it may date to the 4th century, or even to the pre-Christian era. Still, whenever it was built, the intact floor plan and entrance stairs suggest that it was the most impressive palace ever constructed in Axum, comprising 50-plus rooms and boasting an elaborate drainage system. It stands on the north side of the old Gondar road about 1km west of the Shell filling station, a 20–30-minute walk from the Stelae Park.

Gudit Stelae Field [map, page 304] Situated directly opposite Dongar Palace, this intriguing site contains more than 500 stelae, most of which are half-buried, relatively small and unadorned, though one large stele stood around 21m high before it fell to the ground and smashed into three pieces, while the largest intact stele, also fallen, has a length of 7.5m. Local traditions not only associate the site with Gudit, the Jewish queen who razed much of ancient Axum in the late 10th century, but also maintain that the largest stele marks the Queen of Sheba's grave. Limited archaeological exploration in 1974 and 1994–96 confirmed that this was a burial ground, and unearthed several entombed household artefacts now displayed in the Axum Museum. Many of these artefacts date from the 3rd century AD, suggesting that this cemetery was active at the same time as the Stelae Park, but may have been where lesser dignitaries were buried.

Gobo Dura [map, page 304] Gobo Dura (literally 'Forested Hill'), often mistranscribed as Gobedra, is a 200m-high rocky outcrop rising to the north of the Gondar road less than 3km west of Dongar. Evidence of human habitation dating back more than 6,000 years has been uncovered on the hill, whose southern slopes host two specific sites of interest. The first of these, perhaps 300m from the main road, is the hillside quarry from where came many of the sandstone stelae dotted around Axum. Among the broken rock that litters the hill can clearly be seen rocks from which some of the larger stelae were cut, and there is also one partially carved stele that lies *in situ*.

Another 600m uphill, etched into a flat rock face with a southwest orientation, is the 3.27m-long outline figure of a muscular and maneless big cat known as the Gobo Dura Lion. The story behind this isolated and singular carving has long been a source of speculation. Tradition asserts that the Archangel Mikael was attacked by a lioness here, but repelled it with such force it left an outline in the rock. The presence of a carved cross alongside the carving was for some time thought to indicate a post-Christian date but, given the evidence of ancient habitation on the hill, it seems just as likely that the main figure was carved in pre-Christian times and the cross is a later addition, probably dating from the reign of Gebre Meskel. A controversial French paper published in the *Annales d'Éthiopie* in 2011 stoked further controversy by suggesting the cat depicted is not a female lion but a leopard – an assertion with which it is difficult to disagree once you look at it that way.

Ezana Inscription [map, page 304] Standing some 800m north of the Stelae Park, along the rough road running uphill from May Shum to Kaleb and Gebre Meskel's tombs, this remarkable trilingual tablet, discovered by chance when a farmer chipped it with his plough in the 1980s, underlines how many treasures might still lie buried beneath the soil around Axum. Inscribed in Sabaean, Ge'ez and Greek, the tablet was written at the instruction of King Ezana, and praises God for his help in the conquest of Yemen, itemising the booty of livestock with which his soldiers returned home, before going on to curse an untimely death on anybody who dares damage it. Perhaps for this reason, the tablet still stands exactly where it was originally found, in a hut on the left-hand side of the road coming from town.

Kaleb and Gebre Meskel's tombs [map, page 304] These 'two houses under the ground, into which men do not enter without a lamp', as described by Francisco Álvares in the 16th century, stand on a hilltop about 800m northeast of the Ezana Inscription. Local tradition has it that these tombs, whose entrances lie just 23m apart, were excavated below the palaces of the powerful 6th-century Emperor Kaleb and his son and successor, Gebre Meskel, and the two emperors were buried within them. These assertions are difficult to verify, but there is no strong reason to doubt them either (except perhaps the contradictory legends claiming that Kaleb was buried at Pantalewon and Gebre Meskel at Debre Damo), and the set of raised stone crosses on one tomb, together with the absence of any stelae, implies that they date from the Christian era.

Dr Littmann excavated the site in 1898, at which time the whole construction was buried. Little remains of the palace itself, but the burial vaults underneath it are in excellent condition, though grave robbers have cleared out their contents – all that remain are the stone sarcophagi referred to by Álvares as 'the treasure chests of the Queen of Sheba'! The subterranean architecture is similar to that of Remhai's tomb, which was constructed below the Stelae Park some 300 years earlier. The most obvious difference lies in the masonry: whereas Remhai's tomb was constructed by riveting together cubed stone blocks, this one is made of freely interlocking blocks of irregular shape. Legend has it that a secret tunnel goes all the way from the tombs to Eritrea and/or Yemen.

The uphill walk from the Stelae Park to the tombs might take 30 minutes, passing May Shum and the Ezana Inscription en route. You can also drive to a car park right outside the tombs.

Debre Liqanos Monastery [map, page 304] (*Entrance US$4*) Situated about 500m east of Kaleb and Gebre Meskel's tombs as the crow flies, this hilltop monastery was founded by Abba Liqanos, a Constantinople-born member of the Nine Saints who evangelised in the vicinity of present-day Adwa in the 6th century. The original Axumite church, thought to have been converted by Abba Liqanos and his followers from an older non-Christian temple, was replaced several centuries ago, but fragments such as the pillar next to the baptismal font can still be seen. Women may enter the monastery compound and look at the various holy crosses and books, but not the church. You can easily walk to the monastery in 15–20 minutes following a rough road that runs around the north side of Kaleb and Gebre Meskel's tombs.

Pantalewon Monastery [map, page 304] One of the country's oldest and most historically important churches, Pantalewon is situated little more than 1km north of the bus station on Debre Katin, a sensational euphorbia-clad tooth-like pinnacle that towers more than 40m above the surrounding slopes. It was founded in the early 6th century by Abba Pantalewon, a son of a Byzantine nobleman who entered the monastic life as a child and later became one of the Nine Saints who fled to Ethiopia when the Monophysite doctrine was proclaimed to be heretical. Local tradition has it that Pantalewon spent the last 45 years of his life praying and healing the sick from the confines of a tall, narrow monastic cell in which he was forced to spend 24 hours a day in a standing position. He was also an adviser to King Kaleb, who joined the monastery after he abdicated in favour of his son Gebre Meskel in around AD550. Another plausible local tradition claims that Abba Yared, the contemporary of Gebre Meskel who invented the notation of Ethiopian ecclesiastical music and compiled the *Mazgaba Degwa* (Treasury of Hymns), spent much of his life at Pantalewon.

The church at Pantalewon, set on a tiny platform at the top of the pinnacle, is thought to have been built on the site of an older Sabaean temple, as evidenced by the presence of several pre-Christian carved window stones incorporated into the outer wall. The pinnacle offers stunning views over Axum and surrounds, while the church interior is adorned with an unusually varied and rather random collection of cloth paintings, including what are obviously very old and faded depictions of Mary and Tekle Haymanot. The cherubs on the roof, similar in style to those at Debre Berhan Selassie outside Gondar, are just as clearly quite modern. According to the priests, the sanctuary, which is off-limits to the laity, stands atop a stone staircase leading to a subterranean rock-hewn pit that formed part of the original temple.

Women are not permitted to enter the old hilltop church, but they can explore the rest of the monastery compound, including the brightly painted modern church that stands below the original. Sites of interest here include the stone pit where Abba Pantalewon endured his hermitage, and the nearby rock where King Kaleb sat when he sought the priest's blessing or counsel. Both men are said to have been buried in the stone cemetery in the church compound. Items in the treasury, which the priest will pull out for you to look at one by one, include a beautiful illuminated book of the four gospels, claimed (rather improbably) to be 1,500 years old, and a gold cross that belonged to Emperor Zara Yaqob. There are several possible routes to Pantalewon. From the town centre, follow the main road east, past the junction for the bus station, then turn left (50m before the Consolar International Hotel) on to a side road leading uphill to a large church dedicated to Mikael. From here it is a straightforward 1km, 15–20-minute walk uphill to the monastery, which is visible in front of you all the way. Alternatively, coming from Kaleb and Gebre Meskel's tombs, walk back downhill towards town for about 600m on to a good dirt road that skirts south of Debre Liqanos, then after about 1.8km leave the road and follow a footpath to the left for 600m to the monastery entrance.

Dereka Abba Meta [map, page 304] Rather surprisingly, given Axum's elevated ecclesiastical status, its ancient tomb-carving tradition and the local abundance of suitable sandstone outcrops, the only rock-hewn church in the immediate vicinity is the little-known Dereka Abba Meta, carved into the eastern wall of a wooded gorge almost 10km south of the town centre. The church is named after its Roman-born excavator Abba Meta, a rather shadowy 6th-century figure who (like the church itself) is also sometimes referred to as Abba Libanos (not to be confused with Abba Liqanos) and whose name replaces that of Abba Aregawi in some lists of the Nine Saints. Tradition has it that Abba Meta was exiled to Dereka after he accused the Patriarch of the Ethiopian Church of corrupt practices, and spent several years there secluded in a monastic cell – quite possibly one of the artificial caves carved into the cliff above the church that today bears his name. Eventually, the patriarch received a divine message instructing him to accept Abba Meta's criticisms, and the pardoned priest left Dereka for Gunda Gundo, where he founded a monastery with the support of Emperor Gebre Meskel.

As with many other Tigrayan rock churches, visiting Dereka Abba Meta is not as straightforward as it might be, since the priest with the key lives some distance away, is normally absent on Saturdays (market day in Axum), and is a reliable presence only before 09.00 on Sundays and special mass days. Even when he is available, entry is forbidden to women. We have yet to gain access to the interior, but it reputedly comprises a single chamber large enough to seat 100 people, and two engraved rock columns but no paintings. The artificial caves in the nearby cliff reputedly represent failed early attempts to excavate a church into unyielding rock, but could as easily be disused monastic cells. Even if you fail to enter the church, the surrounding euphorbia-studded rockscapes are quite magnificent, and the lush forest in the gorge – fed by a holy spring – supports plenty of monkeys and birds.

Dereka Abba Meta can be approached to within a few hundred metres by 4x4. From the new southern bypass, take a rough dirt track heading south about 900m east of the TAF filling station. Follow this track for 7km, keeping to the right at any forks. Here, there's a marshy patch in the road, where you could easily get bogged down after rain, so consider walking. After another 1km, there is a spot where you can park your car before walking the last stretch to the top of the gorge, from where a short but steep path runs to the prominent blue-and-white church door.

ADWA AND SURROUNDS

The small town of Adwa, only 20km east of Axum, is of limited interest to tourists but of tremendous significance to Ethiopians, since it was in the surrounding hills that Emperor Menelik II defeated the Italian army on 1 March 1896, thereby ensuring that his empire would be the only African state to enter the 20th century as a fully independent entity. The only real point of interest is Adwa Inda Selassie, a church built in 1868 by Emperor Yohannes IV, and decorated with some superb contemporaneous murals. Otherwise, the most likely reason an independent traveller might want to overnight in Adwa is to get a head start for Yeha the next day, or to pick up early-morning transport southward to Abiy Addi. If you do, it's an attractive enough town, set amid stark granite hills typical of Tigray, and remarkably unaffected by tourism considering its proximity to Axum.

GETTING THERE AND AWAY Adwa lies 20km east of Axum and about 100km west of Adigrat along a good asphalt road. Regular minibuses nip back and forth in both directions throughout the day. There is also at least one bus daily to Abiy Addi, leaving at 08.30, and usually one direct bus to Mekele.

WHERE TO STAY, EAT AND DRINK *Map, below*

Setit Humera Hotel (28 rooms) \034 771 1313; m 0914 788379. Adwa's smartest hotel has pleasant tiled rooms with en-suite hot shower & TV, but note that all rooms are sgl or twin with a ¾ bed, which makes it cramped or costly for couples. A 1st-floor restaurant serves grills, pasta dishes & Ethiopian fare in the US$2–4 range. *US$15/26 sgl/twin.* **$$$**

Senay Selam Hotel (11 rooms) m 0912 389066. Clean & affordable en-suite rooms with queen-size bed, TV & writing desk. *US$7/10 sgl/dbl.* **$**

Maay Assa Hotel (30 rooms) \034 771 3161. Well-priced hotel near the bus station. All rooms en suite. No restaurant. *US$7 sgl or US$11/13 dbl with cold/hot shower.* **$$**

Tefari Pension (10 rooms) \034 771 1221; m 0914 314587. Situated above a clinic next to the bus station, this hotel is as clean & comfortable as you could hope for at the price. *US$5 dbl with en-suite hot shower.* **$**

WHAT TO SEE AND DO The two sites discussed below could easily be visited as a day trip from Axum in a private vehicle.

Madera Abba Garima [322 D2] The monastery of Abba Garima at Madera, 5km east of Adwa as the crow flies, was founded in around AD494 by the eponymous member of the Nine Saints. According to legend, Abba Garima was of royal

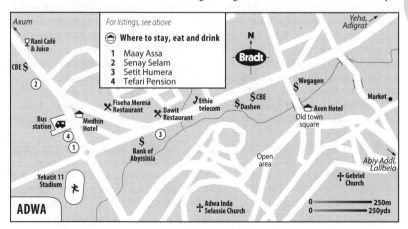

ADWA

Byzantine birth, and he served as the reluctant king of his homeland for seven years before Abba Pantalewon summoned him to evangelise in Axum. There he arrived 3 hours later, on the back of the Archangel Gabriel. The Monastery of Abba Garima was reputedly built by Emperor Gebre Meskel, and its namesake lived there for about 20 years, performing miracles and healing the sick, until one day he ascended to the sky and was never seen again. A holy spring on the hill above the monastery is said to have started life when Abba Garima spat on the spot from where it emerges.

More recently, it was from Abba Garima that Menelik II observed the Italian troops as they approached Adwa prior to Ethiopia's decisive victory over the aspirant colonists in 1896. A year later, Ras Alula, the governor of Hamasien and accomplished military tactician who famously defeated a contingent of 500 Italian troops at Dogali in present-day Eritrea in January 1887, died at Abba Garima of wounds sustained at the Battle of Adwa. Ras Alula's modest tomb still stands outside the rear entrance of the church, and several of his possessions are now held in the treasury.

The church at Abba Garima is said to be 1,500 years old. It looks far newer than that, but the twin stelae and bowl-like rocks that stand in front of its main door might well date to Axumite times. Abba Garima is today best known for its treasury, which contains a fantastic collection of ancient crowns, crosses and other artefacts donated by various emperors and nobles over the centuries, including a silver cross with gold inlays that once belonged to Gebre Meskel, and the crown of Zara Yaqob. The extensive library includes the two illuminated 'Garima Gospels', which were supposedly written and illustrated by Abba Garima himself and have been stowed away in the church ever since. These ancient tomes were first documented for the outside world when they were shown to Beatrice Payne in 1950, since when expert opinion was they that were unlikely to be any more than 1,000 years old. However, recent carbon-dating tests conducted at Oxford University have vindicated the local tradition by dating the Garima Gospels to some time between AD390 and AD660, making them the oldest known illustrated Christian manuscripts anywhere in the world. Stored somewhat perversely in the midst of these ancient treasures is a modern wall clock of the sort you'd find in any suburban Western kitchen – the priests will tell you deadpan it is yet another precious item the church received as a gift!

Abba Garima lies about 10km from Adwa by road. To get there, follow the Abiy Addi road southeast from Adwa for 7km, and then take the rough 3km track signposted to your left. Women are not permitted to enter the church or the treasury, but the priests will sometimes take the most important treasures outside to show female visitors. Equally, sometimes they won't. Male visitors are sometimes welcome to look around the church and treasury, but on other occasions they may be refused entry to one or the other – or to both – unless they can produce a letter of authority. It could well be that your willingness to pay more than the official church entry fee of US$5 plus an additional US$3 for a local guide is the determining factor. And you may well be asked for more to see the Gospel of Abba Garima, which is stored in a glass container to protect it from further wear and tear!

Yeha [322 D1] The village of Yeha, 50km northeast of Axum, might today amount to little more than a small cluster of rustic stone houses dotted among the characteristically rocky slopes of northern Tigray, but it was once the setting for the region's most important city and it still hosts Ethiopia's most impressive pre-Axumite archaeological site. Founded more than 2,800 years ago, Yeha served as the capital of D'mt from around 800BC to 150BC, after which it was most probably usurped by Axum. The relationship between these two ancient capitals is little understood. Rock-hewn tombs similar to those of King Basen in Axum demonstrate that Yeha had its own dignitaries and rulers. It is a matter for conjecture whether Yeha and Axum were always independent political entities, or whether one town ruled over the other. What is clear is that by the time the Axumite Empire entered its most influential period, Yeha was a town of little political significance.

Yeha's single most remarkable antiquity is a well-preserved 12m-high Almaqah Temple comprising at least 52 layers of masonry. Though it's never been carbon dated, this sacrificial temple dedicated to the Sabaean deity Almaqah is at least 2,700 years old, based on stylistic similarities to related ruins in south Arabia, and is thus probably the oldest standing structure in sub-Saharan Africa. Abundant engravings of ibex suggest this animal was of some religious significance to the worshippers who gathered there, while statues of plump, dreadlocked women now housed in the National Museum in Addis Ababa suggest it was associated with a fertility cult. A persistent local tradition, related to Álvares in 1520 and to Henry Salt almost three centuries later, is that the Ark of the Covenant was kept here for a period prior to being taken to Axum.

One of the reasons why the temple at Yeha is in such good condition is that it became the centre of a monastic Christian community in the early 6th century. This church was founded by Abba Afse, one of the Nine Saints, who was guided there by an angel after having spent 12 years living at the monastery of Abba Garima. It seems entirely credible that the high stone monastery surrounding the ancient temple dates to this era; certainly it boasts one of the most remarkable treasure houses of any Ethiopian church, containing many ancient illuminated manuscripts and crowns. Look closely at the church exterior, and you will also see it is inset with stylistically incongruous engravings (notably a stylised row of ibexes) lifted from the older temple.

There is no restriction on women visiting the church, and the entrance fee of US$8 covers the Almaqah Temple as well. At the time of writing, the site is a little disappointing, because the temple is obscured within a monkey puzzle of scaffolding while reconstruction is under way. However, a site museum displaying relics currently housed in the National Museum in Addis Ababa seems likely to open within the church compound during the lifespan of this edition.

A second building called Grat Beal Gabri, though less impressive than the Almaqah Temple in its current incarnation, is claimed to be the largest building erected on the Horn of Africa during the 1st millennium BC. Originally three storeys high, it stood on a 6m-high podium and had a magnificent entrance supported by half a dozen 10m-tall pillars. Thought to have been a palace or administrative centre, the site is currently closed off for excavation and restoration work, but you can see quite a bit of the building from outside the perimeter fence, just behind the Cafeteria Saba.

A striking feature of Yeha, looming high on the northern horizon, is a massive hilltop rock formation that bears an uncanny resemblance to a lion's head in profile, complete with a shadow exactly where the left eye would be. Guides at Yeha will cite a local tradition claiming that it was this eye-catching sphinxian formation that led the rulers of D'mt to select Yeha as the site of a royal capital and temple, and that the Lion of Judah still keeps watch over the church and temple. In fact, no such tradition exists, but all the same, given the enduring symbolic significance of lions to the Ethiopian monarchy (indeed, a bronze of a roaring lion is one of the artefacts uncovered at the ancient tombs of Yeha), it is difficult to dismiss the proximity of the lion rock to the ancient palace and temple as mere coincidence.

Yeha lies 5km north of the main road to Adigrat and the junction is clearly signposted 23km out of Adwa. You can drive there in an hour or so from Axum. There is also now limited public transport between Adwa and Yeha in the form of a few minibuses that run back and forth daily between around 08.30 and 16.00, charging less than US$1 in either direction. The Cafeteria Saba next to the church car park serves basic meals and cold drinks – and should be able to help if you get stuck and are desperate for somewhere to crash.

9

Northeast Tigray and Its Rock-Hewn Churches

The epithet of best-kept secret has been applied to so many modern mediocrities that it feels wholly inadequate when talking about the 100-plus ancient rock-hewn churches carved into the sandstone cliffs of northeast Tigray. Described by British academic Ivy Pearce as 'the greatest of the historical-cultural heritages of the Ethiopian people', this scattered collection of architectural gems, their interiors adorned with medieval paintings and Axumite curves, their stone walls imbued with an aura of spirituality reflecting centuries of continuous use, still serve as active shrines today. More widely scattered than their counterparts at Lalibela, and in most cases relatively difficult to access, the churches of northeast Tigray were almost totally neglected by the tourist industry prior to around 2005. That has changed, thanks largely to the opening of several upmarket lodges and the construction of new surfaced road connections to Axum and Mekele, but even so the churches are best suited to reasonably fit and unhurried travellers. The most impressive and popular cluster of churches is associated with the Gheralta Escarpment, whose sandstone cliffs support the legendary likes of Abuna Yemata Guh, Debre Maryam Korkor and Abuna Abraham Debre Tsion. For budget-conscious backpackers, recommendations include the highly accessible Teka Tesfai cluster, while those wanting to avoid challenging ascents are pointed to suburban Wukro Chirkos and the superlative Abraha we Atsbeha. And for those with a penchant for getting off the beaten track, there are the more remote churches around Atsbi and Abiy Addi or in the Agame Mountains, some of which might still go weeks without being visited by an outsider. And while rock-hewn churches are the region's speciality, other worthwhile sites include the built-up Axumite church of Debre Damo, the magnificent 2,800-year-old sacrificial altar unearthed at Adi Akaweh in 2007, and the Amba Fekada rock art site north of Adigrat, the region's largest town.

ADIGRAT

Straddling the junction of the roads to Axum, Mekele and the Eritrean capital Asmara, Adigrat is a bustling, friendly and cosmopolitan market town set at an altitude of 2,450m at the base of the rugged Agame Mountains. It possesses a distinctively Tigrayan character, boasts strong historical and cultural links to neighbouring Eritrea, and is far less affected by tourism than the likes of Axum or Mekele. While the town itself offers little in the way of compelling sightseeing, Adigrat is a good base from which to explore a number of outlying sites, including the beautiful clifftop monastery of Debre Damo, the trekking routes and rock-hewn churches of the Agame Mountains, and an unusual rock art site at Amba Fekada.

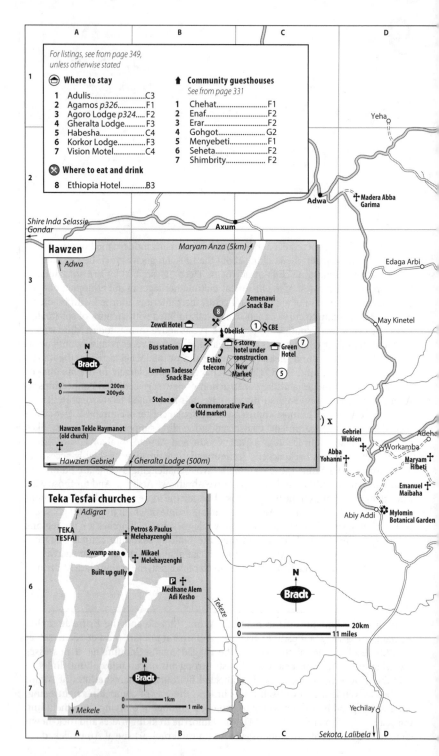

For listings, see from page 349,
unless otherwise stated

Where to stay

1	Adulis	C3
2	Agamos *p326*	F1
3	Agoro Lodge *p324*	F2
4	Gheralta Lodge	F3
5	Habesha	C4
6	Korkor Lodge	F3
7	Vision Motel	C4

Where to eat and drink

| 8 | Ethiopia Hotel | B3 |

Community guesthouses
See from page 331

1	Chehat	F1
2	Enaf	F2
3	Erar	F2
4	Gohgot	G2
5	Menyebeti	F1
6	Seheta	F2
7	Shimbrity	F2

Yeha

Madera Abba Garima

Adwa

Shire Inda Selassie, Gondar

Axum

Hawzen

Maryam Anza (5km)

Adwa

Edaga Arbi

May Kinetel

Zemenawi Snack Bar

Zewdi Hotel

Obelisk

CBE

Bus station

6-storey hotel under construction

Green Hotel

Ethio telecom

Lemlem Tadesse Snack Bar

New Market

Stelae

Commemorative Park (Old market)

Hawzen Tekle Haymanot (old church)

Gebriel Wukien

Adeha

Abba Yohanni

Workamba

Maryam Hibeti

Hawzien Gebriel

Gheralta Lodge (500m)

Emanuel Maibaha

Abiy Addi

Mylomin Botanical Garden

0 — 200m
0 — 200yds

Teka Tesfai churches

Adigrat

TEKA TESFAI

Petros & Paulus Melehayzenghi

Swamp area

Mikael Melehayzenghi

Built up gully

Medhane Alem Adi Kesho

Teleze

0 — 20km
0 — 11 miles

0 — 1km
0 — 1 mile

Mekele

Yechilay

Sekota, Lalibela

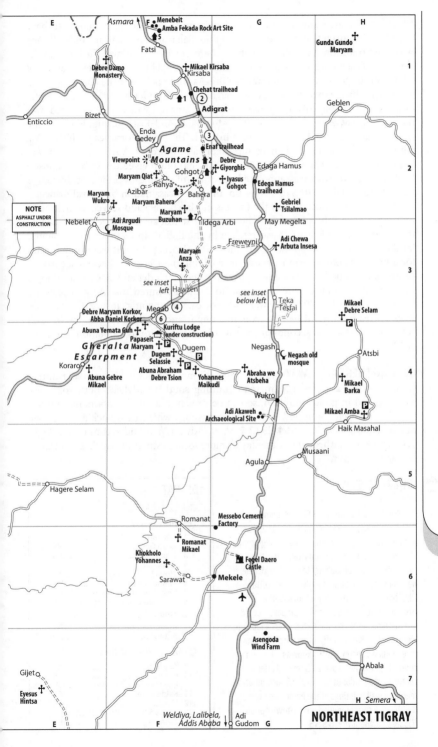

E   F   *Asmara* ↓   G   H

Menebeit
Amba Fekada Rock Art Site
5
Fatsi

Gunda Gundo
Maryam

Debre Damo
Monastery

Mikael Kirsaba
Kirsaba

1

Bizet

Enticcio

Chehat trailhead
2
Adigrat

Geblen

Enda
Gedey

Agame   Enaf trailhead
3
Mountains   Debre
Giyorghis

Viewpoint   2   Edaga Hamus

Maryam Qiat   Gohgot   6   Iyasus
Rahya   Gohgot   Edega Hamus
trailhead

2

Azibar   Bahera   4

Maryam
Wukro   Maryam Bahera   Gebriel
Tsilalmao

Nebelet   Adi Argudi   Maryam
Mosque   Buzuhan   Idega Arbi   May Megelta

NOTE
ASPHALT UNDER
CONSTRUCTION

Freweyni   Adi Chewa
Arbuta Insesa

Maryam
Anza

3

*see inset
left*   Hawzen   *see inset
below left*   Teka
Tesfai

Megab
4

Mikael
Debre Selam

Debre Maryam Korkor,
Abba Daniel Korkor   Kuriftu Lodge
(under construction)

Abuna Yemata Guh   Papaseit   Dugem   Negash   Negash old
mosque

Gheralta   Maryam
Escarpment   Dugem
Selassie   P
Koraro   Mikael
Abuna Abraham   Barka
Abuna Gebre   Debre Tsion   Yohannes
Mikael   Maikudi   Abraha we
Atsbeha   Mikael Amba
Wukro   P

4

Adi Akaweh
Archaeological Site   Haik Masahal

Musaani

Hagere Selam   Agula

5

Romanat   Messebo Cement
Factory

Romanat
Mikael

Khokholo
Yohannes   Fegel Daero
Castle

Sarawat   Mekele

6

Asengoda
Wind Farm

Gijet   Abala

7

Eyesus
Hintsa

Weldiya, Lalibela,   Adi   H *Semera* ↓
Addis Ababa ↓   Gudom

NORTHEAST TIGRAY

E   F   G

HISTORY The area around and immediately north of Adigrat is known to have been an important centre of early Ethio–Sabaean civilisation. Indeed, one persistent tradition states that Menebeit, 20km north of town, was the home of the legendary Queen of Sheba – a claim broadly supported by the recent excavations of what appears to be a vast subterranean pre-Axumite palace at the site (page 331). Adigrat itself is rather more modern, having been founded in 1818 as the capital of Dejazmach Sabagadis of Agame, a powerful warlord whose rule extended over most of Tigray, as well as the Simien Mountains and Eritrean highlands by the time of his execution by a rival prince in 1831. The town's fortunes declined for a while thereafter (indeed, when Johann Krapf passed through Adigrat in 1842, it was largely in ruins and smaller than nearby Kirsaba) but revived under his grandson Sebhat Aregawi, who was appointed governor of Agame by Emperor Tewodros in 1859 and retained that role right up until his assassination by a rival prince in 1914. Adigrat was occupied by the Italians in March 1895 and served as their main military base in Ethiopia prior to their decisive defeat at Adwa a year later. Owing to its proximity to Eritrea, it was retaken by the Italians in October 1935, the first foothold in the campaign that led to the 1936–41 occupation. It was an important focal point of anti-government resistance during the Derg and became a thriving centre of cross-border trade after Eritrea regained its independence from Ethiopia in 1993. Its location on the main road to Asmara ensured that Adigrat played a frontline role in the 1998–2000 war with Eritrea. The ongoing closure of the border with Eritrea has diminished its economic importance in the 21st century, but still Adigrat stands as the second-largest town in Tigray, with a population estimated at 100,000.

GETTING THERE AND AWAY Adigrat lies at the junction of the 130km road running west to Axum and the 120km road running south to Mekele. Both roads are surfaced and in good condition, so can be driven in around 2 hours in a private vehicle. It is well connected with public transport, which runs back and forth all day to Wukro (*90mins*), Mekele (*2.5–3hrs*), Adwa (*2hrs*) and Axum (*3hrs*). Light vehicles also run throughout the day to more local destinations such as Freweyni, Kirsaba and Bizet.

WHERE TO STAY
Moderate

 Agoro Lodge [323 F2] (18 rooms)
\ 034 845 0202; m 0935 406360, 0930 073698;
e agorolodge@hotmail.com; w agorolodge.com.
This commendable community-run ridge-top lodge, 4km south of town off the road to Mekele, has stone en-suite bungalows with terracotta tiles, bamboo furniture & hot showers. The *tukul*-like restaurant serves well-prepared local & international dishes for US$6–8 & offers a fabulous view over the plains. Staff can arrange a 90min hike to Abba Simeon, a little-known rock-hewn church that was rediscovered & revived after centuries of abandonment in 1912 & incorporates medieval wall paintings of the namesake saint & St Mary. A recommended out-of-town option. *US$38/47 B&B sgl/dbl.* $$$$

ADIGRAT
For listings, see from page 324

Where to stay
1	Canaan International	C2
2	Geza Gerelase	B5
3	Hahu	C5
4	Hohoma	B5
5	Hotel Mulu Tesfaye	A3
6	Omna Pension	B5
7	Tesfat Dini Guesthouse	C2
8	Welwalo Centre Bedrooms	C5

Off map
	Agamos Hotel	D1
	Agoro Lodge	D7

Where to eat and drink
9	Abyssinian	A6
10	Genet	C5
	Geza Gerelase Cultural	(see 2)
11	Kaldis Café	C5
12	Lidi	C5
13	Seni & Silvana juice bars	B5
14	Taemi Agami	B4

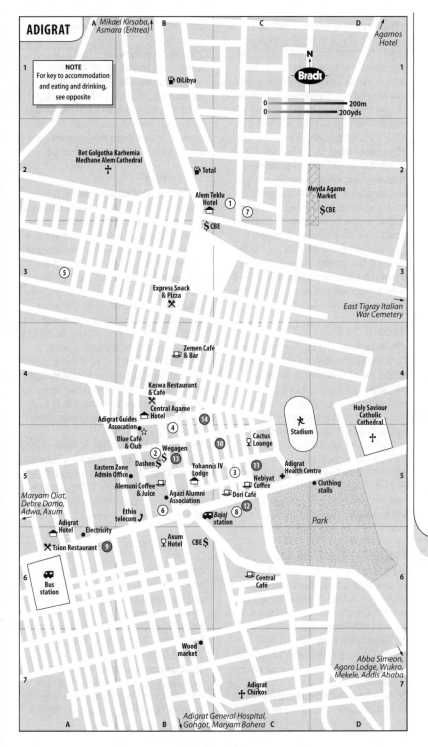

ADIGRAT

A Mikael Kirsaba,
Asmara (Eritrea)

Agamos Hotel

NOTE
For key to accommodation
and eating and drinking,
see opposite

OiLibya

N

Bradt

0   200m
0   200yds

Bet Golgotha Karhemia
Medhane Alem Cathedral

Total

Meyda Agame
Market

Alem Teklu
Hotel (1) (7)

$ CBE

$ CBE

(5)

Express Snack
& Pizza

East Tigray Italian
War Cemetery

Zemen Café
& Bar

Kaswa Restaurant
& Café

Central Agame
Hotel (14)

Holy Saviour
Catholic
Cathedral

Adigrat Guides
Assocation
(4)

Blue Café
& Club

Cactus
Lounge

(10)

Stadium

(2) **Wegagen**
Dashen $ (13)

Eastern Zone
Admin Office

Yohannis IV
Lodge (3)

(11)
Nebiyat
Coffee

Adigrat
Health Centre

Alemuni Coffee
& Juice

Agazi Alumni
Association

Dori Café

• Clothing
stalls

(6)

Ethio
telecom ♪

(12)
(8)

Bajaj
station

Park

Maryam Qiat,
Debre Damo,
Adwa, Axum

Adigrat
Hotel • **Electricity**

Axum
Hotel CBE $

✕ **Tsion Restaurant** (9)

Central
Café

Bus
station

Wood
market

Abba Simeon,
Agoro Lodge, Wukro,
Mekele, Addis Ababa

Adigrat
✝ **Chirkos**

Adigrat General Hospital,
Gohgot, Maryam Bahera

9

🏠 **Canaan International Hotel** [325 C2] (27 rooms) ☎034 445 2821; e info@canaanadigrathotel.com; w canaanadigrathotel.com. The top hotel in the city centre, this new medium-rise has large comfortable en-suite rooms with wood laminate floor, writing desk, flatscreen TV & hot shower. There's a bright café-style restaurant on the ground floor. Very good value. *US$22/30/32 sgl/dbl/twin.* **$$$**

🏠 **Agamos Hotel** [323 F1] (31 rooms) ☎034 245 0262; m 0910 654803; e agamoshotel@gmail.com; w agamoshotel.com. Something of a work in progress, this aspirational new hotel, set on a hillside northeast of the town centre, has spacious en-suite rooms with muted & minimalist wood & fabric décor, writing desk, flatscreen TV, private terrace & hot shower & tub. A bright modern restaurant offers fine views over town & serves Ethiopian dishes & pizza in the US$4–5 range. Grounds look quite barren, but a swimming pool is planned. *US$46–57 B&B dbl.* **$$$$**

Budget

🏠 **Hahu Hotel** [325 C5] (22 rooms) m 0914 732909; e hahuhotel2@gmail.com. This medium-rise near the main roundabout is the pick of a few budget central options thanks partly to its enthusiastic English-speaking owner-manager. Bright modern en-suite rooms come with TV, hot water & balcony. The ground-floor restaurant serves affordable meals in the US$2–3 range. *US$18/26 B&B dbl/twin.* **$$**

🏠 **Hotel Mulu Tesfaye** [325 A3] (35 rooms) m 0930 073702. Not as central as it might be, this new owner-managed medium-rise has smart & well-maintained rooms with flatscreen TV & hot shower. The front rooms are nicest, thanks to their bay windows. *US$8/12 dbl with common/en-suite shower.* **$$**

🏠 **Geza Gerelase Hotel** [325 B5] (29 rooms) ☎034 445 2500; m 0914 403592; e gezagerelasiehotel@yahoo.com. This once-popular multistorey hotel is starting to look genuinely rundown & it can also be noisy at night. The compact carpeted en-suite rooms with hot shower & TV are no better than acceptable at the asking price. *US$12/14/24 sgl/dbl/twin.* **$$**

Shoestring

✳🏠 **Welwalo Centre Bedrooms** [325 C5] (20 rooms) ☎034 445 0443. Situated a block east of the main roundabout, this unpretentious new hotel has represented the best value in Adigrat for some years now. Clean en-suite rooms come with TV, balcony & hot shower. *US$6/8 dbl/trpl.* **$**

🏠 **Tesfat Dini Guesthouse** [325 C2] (10 rooms) ☎034 445 1397; m 0939 958662. Another superior cheapie, this 3-storey hotel opposite the Canaan International offers the choice of smaller rooms with ¾ bed or much larger rooms with king-size bed. All rooms are en suite & clean. *US$6/8 sgl/dbl.* **$**

🏠 **Omna Pension** [325 B5] (9 rooms) ☎034 245 2923. Set in a tall, narrow green building just off the main roundabout, this new pension has very pleasant en-suite tiled rooms with TV & hot shower. Another great shoestring option. *US$8 dbl.* **$**

🏠 **Hohoma Hotel** [325 B5] (7 rooms) m 0914 311138. This enduringly popular family-managed hotel isn't quite the gem it used to be, but the en-suite rooms with TV, separate sitting room & en-suite hot shower remain decent value, as does the popular ground-floor restaurant. *US$10 dbl.* **$$**

✖ WHERE TO EAT AND DRINK

✳✖ **Genet Restaurant** [325 C5] This small but beautifully decorated backstreet restaurant specialises in traditional Tigrayan fare such as *tholoh* (barley balls dipped in a spicy sauce). *Mains in the US$1.50–3 range.*

✖ **Taemi Agami Restaurant** [325 B4] Regarded by many locals to serve the best *tibs* in town, at half the price of the better-known Geza Gerelase. *Mains US$2–3.*

✖ **Geza Gerelase Cultural Restaurant** [325 B5] ☎034 445 2500; ⊕ 06.00–22.00 daily. Affiliated to the eponymous hotel, this beautifully decorated *tukul* restaurant is renowned for its shish kebab & special *tibs* (served in a coal-heated clay pot), but also has a good vegetarian selection. It would be the obvious standout but for a discriminatory price policy that makes it overpriced for foreigners. *Vegetarian mains around US$4; meat dishes US$6.*

✖ **Abyssinian Restaurant** [325 A6] ⊕ 07.00–22.00 daily. Very popular with locals, this bustling eatery near the bus station serves the usual selection of Ethiopian dishes, plus Tigrayan specialities. *Mains around US$2.*

Lidi Restaurant [325 C5] Situated on the ground floor of Welwalo Centre Bedrooms, this diner-like set-up has a large TV that attracts crowds of football fans over w/ends & serves good local food in the US$2–3 range. An eponymous café stands a door down.

Cafés & juice bars
Kaldis Café [325 C5] This trendy coffee shop has outdoor seating & Wi-Fi.
Seni & Silvana juice bars [325 B5] Situated right next to each other on the main road, these 2 juice shops usually have 4 or 5 varieties of fruit available between them.

NIGHTLIFE
Cactus Lounge [325 C5] ⏱ 10.00–late daily. Adigrat's funkiest bar has bright modern décor, pool tables & comfortable indoor & courtyard seating. Popular with a younger crowd. Though first a bar, it also serves burgers, *tibs* & pasta from US$2.

☆ **Blue Café & Club** [325 B5] ⏱ 18.00–late daily. Enjoy blaring Ethiopian pop indoors or chill out on the balcony at central Adigrat's hottest nightspot.
Axum Hotel [325 B6] Cosy bar with sofa seating & brightly decorated walls.

TOURIST INFORMATION AND GUIDES The Adigrat Guides Association [325 B5] (**m** *0913 550959, 0914 761306;* **e** *tesfatigray@gmail.com*), whose guides are affiliated to Tesfa Tours, recently opened an information office in the same building as the Blue Club, opposite the Central Agame Hotel. It arranges trekking and day visits to rock-hewn churches in the Agame Mountains, as well as excursions to the likes of Menebeit and Amba Fekada. Guide fees are around US$20–25 per day.

WHAT TO SEE AND DO
Around town The oldest and most interesting building in town is **Adigrat Chirkos** [325 C7], a church built in the late 19th century by Ras Dasta (the son of Sebhat Aregawi) and notable for the fine paintings depicting angels on the inside walls, and a balcony offering a great view over the town. The town's once legendary central market used to be held in front of the church, but it recently relocated about 1km north to **Meyda Agame Market** [325 D2], which operates on Monday only and, should you happen to be in town then, is a good place to buy Tigrayan coffee pots, the superb pale honey that originates in Ali Tena, and prickly pears (called *beles* locally). Exactly 500m west of the market, the Orthodox Cathedral of **Bet Golgotha Karhemia Medhane Alem** [325 A2] is an impressive rectangular sandstone building that more closely resembles a fort than a typical Ethiopian church. Also rather unusual and striking is the domed Italian-designed **Holy Saviour Catholic Cathedral** [325 D5], which was consecrated in 1969, and comes across like a transplant from Florence, though it also incorporates paintings by renowned Ethiopian artist Afewerk Tekle. At Gola'a, about 3km east of the town centre, the **East Tigray Italian War Cemetery** [325 D3] is the final resting place for 765 Italian soldiers killed in action over 1935–38. Future plans include the construction of a modern archaeological museum, close to the city's only mosque, dedicated to artefacts unearthed at Menebeit and other pre-Axumite sites in and around Adigrat.

Debre Damo Monastery [323 E1] (*Entrance US$10*) The isolated 6th-century monastery of Debre Damo, 20km northwest of Adigrat as the crow flies, is renowned for its ancient Axumite architecture and impregnable clifftop location atop a 3,000m-high *amba*. It was founded in the 6th century by the Syrian monk Abuna Za-Mikael Aregawi, one of the so-called Nine Saints, at the commission of Emperor Gebre Meskel. It is something of a mystery how Aregawi reached the plateau on which the monastery stands. One tradition has it that a flying serpent carried him

The remote and isolated nature of the Tigrayan churches has allowed them to retain an aura of mystery that Lalibela has arguably sacrificed on the altar of tourism. Incredibly, the existence of most of these churches remained unknown to other Ethiopians, let alone to the outside world, prior to the late 1960s. True, since the Tigrayan churches are almost invariably carved unobtrusively into a natural cliff face, they tend to lack the architectural impact of the more grandiose subterranean monoliths in and around Lalibela. Balanced against this, however, are their almost invariably magnificent settings, and the moody interiors decorated with wonderful centuries-old paintings.

Certainly, it is in these Tigrayan backwaters, more than anywhere else, that one is confronted by the radical nature of Ethiopian Christianity. During mass, or at festivals, these remarkable rock edifices witness scenes straight out of the Bible: white-robed worshippers chanting and swaying in prayer, prostrating themselves before the altar, or standing outside the church sharing thick, rough *injera* and beakers of alcoholic *t'ella*. This, one senses, is Christianity much as it would have been practised before the Vatican was built, before Martin Luther or Henry VIII, before Billy Graham – an almost surreal reminder that the religion we associate with American televangelism and quaint European country churches is at root every bit as Middle Eastern as Islam or Judaism.

As to why the rock-hewn churches of Tigray were so often carved into relatively inaccessible cliff faces, it's anybody's guess. For security perhaps, or to foster spiritual isolation, or simply because cliff faces are inherently good places to carve churches, and cliff faces are inherently inaccessible? Certainly, if keeping away outsiders *was* the objective, then the excavators of these churches did an admirable job, judging by the obscurity in which many of these churches languished throughout the first century of regular European presence in Ethiopia. Remarkably, several 19th-century visitors to Tigray – among them Henry Salt, Nathaniel Pierce and Frances Harrison Smith – would have passed within a kilometre of some of these churches without ever suspecting that they existed.

The first outsider to document one of Tigray's rock-hewn churches, probably Wukro Chirkos (page 341), was Francisco Álvares, who stopped in the area in 1521. The same church was visited in 1868 by the British military expedition led by Sir Robert Napier when it passed through the small Tigrayan village then known as Dongolo. For six full decades after this, the outside world assumed that Wukro

there. It is also said that Abba Aregawi's disciple, Tekle Haymanot, sprouted wings to escape when the devil cut the rope up which he was climbing – after which he was able to make regular flying trips to Jerusalem! The monastery has been one of the holiest in Ethiopia since Emperor Gebre Meskel was buried there. Like Gishen Maryam after it, it served for some centuries as a place of imprisonment for princes with a claim to the imperial throne – indeed, it is said that when Queen Gudit overthrew Axum, she massacred up to 400 captive princes there. In 1540, almost a millennium after Debre Damo was founded, Emperor Lebna Dengal, in exile after his defeat by Ahmed Gragn, died there.

Debre Damo's most important architectural feature is its beautiful old two-storey church, which is named after Abba Aregawi, and was also, legend has it, built by him. In reality, much of the building probably dates to the 10th and 11th centuries, which would still make it probably the oldest built-up church in Ethiopia.

Chirkos was the only rock-hewn church in Tigray. In 1928, Dr Enza Parona visited the monastery of Abba Yohanni (page 355) in the Tembien, and four further churches were 'discovered' and described by Antonio Mordini during the Italian occupation, among them Maryam Wukro (page 354) and Wukro Giyorgis (page 354) to the southeast of Adwa. In 1948 Beatrice Playne visited several rock-hewn churches in Tigray, including the formerly undescribed Mikael Amba (page 345) and Hawzen Tekle Haymanot (page 350). Nevertheless, in 1963, when Roger Sauter published the first exhaustive list of all known rock-hewn churches in Ethiopia, fewer than ten were listed for Tigray.

All of which provides context to the buzz that followed the 1966 Conference of Ethiopian Studies, during which Dr Abba Tewelde Medhin Josief, a Catholic priest from Adigrat, announced the existence of at least 123 rock-hewn churches in Tigray, more than three-quarters of which were still in active use. Dr Josief died soon afterwards, but his findings were pursued by Swiss photographer Georg Gerster, who travelled to eight churches (including Petros and Paulus Melehayzenghi, which was apparently overlooked by Josief) to produce a fantastic photographic essay entitled 'Rocks of Faith' for the British *Sunday Times*. Over the next three years, British academics David Buxton, Ivy Pearce and Ruth Plant collectively visited 75 Tigrayan rock-hewn churches and published several papers based on their formative research. The most useful of these first appeared in a 1971 issue of the *Ethiopian Observer* (vol 13, no 3), which was devoted exclusively to the Tigrayan churches and described more than 70 individual churches in full. By 1973, when Ivy Pearce published a supplementary list describing another 17 churches in the *Ethiopian Observer* (vol 16, no 1), the full list of confirmed rock-hewn churches in Tigray had been extended to 153, of which all but 26 were still in active use, and several other churches were known of by word of mouth only. The 1974 revolution put paid to any further research in the region. Surprisingly little of consequence has been published about the Tigrayan churches since the overthrow of the Derg, one notable exception being Claude Lepage and Jacques Mercier's 2005 Anglo–French book *Ethiopian Art: The Ancient Churches of Tigrai*, which includes detailed descriptions and lovely photographs of 30 key churches, and also attempts to place them in rough chronological order. These publications, most long out of print, have been used extensively in compiling this chapter.

The architecture shows strong Axumite influences, built up with layers of thick wood and whitewashed stone, and the wooden ceiling is decorated with animal engravings. It was refurbished in the 1950s under the direction of David Buxton, a leading expert on Axumite architecture. Today, only the portal and narthex are open to the public. Other ancient buildings on the 50ha plateau include a secondary church, built on the very spot where Abuna Aregawi reputedly vanished into thin air at the end of his mortal existence. Near this church are a number of rock-hewn tombs. On the main cliff there are several cramped hermit caves, the inhabitants of which subsist on bread and water lowered from the monastery by rope.

There are two routes to Debre Damo coming from Adigrat. The better-known option involves following the asphalted Axum road west out of town for 42km (or, should you be coming from the direction of Axum, 64km east of Adwa and 23km past Enticcio), then turning north on to a signposted 15km dirt road to the parking area at the base of the cliff. The other route, shorter but rougher and slower, requires you to follow the Asmara road for 7km to Kirsaba, then turn left on to a dirt road that reaches the parking area after 36km. In a private vehicle, the monastery can easily be visited as a day trip out of Axum or Adigrat, or en route between Axum and Adigrat. If you are renting a vehicle for the express purpose of visiting Debre Damo, Adigrat is likely to be the cheapest option – expect to pay around US$30–40 for a 4x4 or minibus compared with up to US$95 from Axum or Adwa.

There is no formal public transport along the road to Debre Damo, so most backpackers catch a bus between Adigrat and Adwa, ask to be dropped at the turn-off, and improvise from there. Once at the junction, hitching or otherwise finding a lift isn't out of the question, but nor can it be guaranteed. So be prepared for a long hot 15km walk in either direction, and take plenty of water, sunblock and a hat, and also maybe some food. If you need to, you can sleep at the monastery, but no food is available, the drinking water is dubious and the insects are prolific.

Women are forbidden from visiting the monastery and male visitors may be interrogated about their faith before being allowed up. The monastery is also off-limits to those without a head for heights and reasonable level of agility, since the only way to reach it (unless you happen to have a helicopter or flying serpent to hand) is by climbing a steep flight of stairs then ascending the final 15m-high cliff with the aid of two leather ropes: one for you to climb with, and the other tied around your waist and pulled by the priest at the top. In addition to the fixed entrance fee, the priest who pulls the strings will expect a tip (around US$2.50 per climber is the acceptable minimum).

Mikael Kirsaba

[323 F1] Situated 7km from Adigrat along the Asmara road, Mikael Kirsaba is a four-chambered rock-hewn church reputedly excavated in the 5th century by the horns of an agitated bull. The original church was doused with petrol by the Italians on their way to Adwa in 1895, but before it could be set aflame, the petrol miraculously turned to holy water. Instead of draining the original rock-hewn edifice, Menelik II ordered a new church to be built above it. Plenty of transport runs from Adigrat to Kirsaba, but women are forbidden from entering the church, and the priest with the key can be difficult to locate. Even if you surmount this obstacle, there is little to see other than a waterlogged pit and some attractive 20th-century paintings.

Amba Fekada Rock Art Site

[323 F1] Probably the most worthwhile rock art site in northern Ethiopia, Amba Fekada lies about 20km north of Adigrat at the northern base of the *amba* (flat-topped hill) for which it is named. Known locally as Dahana, the rock art is thought to be 2,800–3,000 years old, which would make it roughly contemporaneous with the nearby archaeological site at Menebeit. It comprises one well-preserved panel of overlapping monochrome, red paintings depicting farmers ploughing with humpless oxen (the only such paintings in the Horn of Africa), and several mysterious elongated small-headed clawed felids (sometimes claimed to be leopards, but the mane-like spinal extension is more like a male lion) and what appears to be a hunter with bow and arrow performing a ritual killing. Amba Fekada is easily reached by following the Asmara road for about 20km out of Adigrat, passing through the small town of Fatsi, then after another 3km turning right at a clearly signposted junction for Menebeit Archaeological Site. About 1.5km east of the junction, you can park at the military base, then continue on foot to the panel, which is situated in an overhang offering fine views over the cultivated valley below. The site is unprotected at the moment, so we have not given directions, but would suggest you arrange a guide out of Adigrat (page 327). Another possibility is Tesfa Tours, which plans to open a community guesthouse called Menyebeti on Amba Fekada, and can incorporate the rock art site in a longer hike or arrange a standalone day or overnight trip out of Adigrat.

Menebeit [323 F1] A Ge'ez name meaning 'House of the Prophet', Menebeit (sometimes spelt Menyebeti), situated in the valley below Amba Fekada, is also known as Gulo Makeda (Queen of Sheba's Enclosure) in reference to a tradition that it was not only the site of one of the Queen of Sheba's palaces, but also one of the places where the Ark of the Covenant rested on its way to Axum. The focal point of the archaeological site, which has recently been excavated by the Eastern Tigray Archeological Project, led by Professor Catherine D'Andrea, is the church of Enda Tekle Haymanot, whose stone compound is home to several pillars and large stone slabs of pre-Axumite origin. Thought by archaeologists to be part of an abandoned 10ha walled town called Ona Adi, the excavations have uncovered the remains of a palatial stone building that extends almost 10m underground and might well date to the time of the Queen of Sheba, as well as pre-Axumite, Axumite and intermediate pottery spanning a period from the 13th to the 1st centuries BC. There isn't much to see at the site at the moment, but it lies no more than 500m from the military base mentioned in the directions for Amba Fekada, and the church compound is easily visited as part of a 3–4km walking loop in conjunction with the rock art. Further excavations are planned, as is the construction of an archaeological museum focused on Menebeit in Adigrat, and an on-site interpretation centre.

Gunda Gundo Maryam [323 H1] One of Ethiopia's most remote and famous monasteries, Gunda Gundo has a mountainous setting close to the Eritrean border some 40km northeast of Edaga Hamus, a small town that straddles the main road between Adigrat and Mekele, and whose name literally means 'Thursday market'. Set at the base of a valley, the monastery's centrepiece is the 14th-century church of Gunda Gundo Maryam, a massive stone and mud construction with four cruciform pillars and 12 arches. Once an important scriptorium, it also boasts a remarkable library comprising around 800 old manuscripts and books illuminated in the distinct Gunda Gundo style associated with its founder, Abba Estifanos. The treasury also houses several items that belonged to Adigrat's founder, Dejazmach Sabagadis, who is most likely buried at the monastery.

The overnight trip to Gunda Gundo is not for the faint-hearted, as it requires a long high-altitude trek of 5–10 hours in either direction, but the scenery, passing tall cliffs characterised by near-vertical strata, is magnificent. Also of interest are the traditional stone architecture and complex irrigation system used by the local Irob people. To get there, follow the Mekele road south out of Adigrat for about 22km to Edaga Hamus, where you'll see Gunda Gundo Maryam signposted blithely to the left as you enter town. From here, it is another 24km along a flat 4x4-only road to the village of Geblen. From here, you will need to walk, ideally in the company of a local guide, and with plenty of food and water as you can't be certain you'll find any along the way. Using public transport, you may be able to bus to Geblen on Thursday (market day in Edaga Hamus), but on other days you'll most likely have to walk, which takes 4–5 hours. From Geblen, the steep footpath down to Mekarabur takes another 4 hours, pausing about halfway down at Nayloweyti, where there is a small stream. It's then another flattish hour on foot from Mekarabur to the monastery.

Gunda Gundo is a male-only monastery and women are forbidden entry. Independent male travellers will be asked to pay an entrance fee of US$20 per person, but this is evidently negotiable, especially if you have a letter of permission from the TTC in Mekele, and we have heard of people bargaining it down to US$4–8. You can sleep under the stars and eat at the monastery – the monks will supply you with a mattress, sheet and simple food. If you want to overnight in Edaga Hamus the night before, try the **Behre Negash Hotel** (*15 rooms;* \ *034 773 0210;* **$**) on the main roundabout. Gheralta Lodge (page 349) in Hawzen now organises three-day, two-night guided treks to Gunda Gundo (**w** *gheraltalodgetigrai.com/activities/3_eng.html*).

Agame Mountains [323 F2] Rising to a peak of 3,333m a few kilometres west of Adigrat, this spectacular range of red sandstone ridges is notable for its superb hiking opportunities, rugged montane scenery, ancient rock-hewn churches and rural Tigrayan communities that still practise traditional farming methods. There is some wildlife around, too, most conspicuously gelada monkey, hyrax and a wonderful selection of birds, including the mighty lammergeier and bateleur eagle. The Agame Massif is less well known than the more southerly Gheralta Escarpment, and its rock-hewn churches see relatively few foreign visitors, but the area can easily be explored on guided multi-day hikes with Tesfa Treks (see opposite), which has overseen the construction of several community guesthouses connected by ancient rural footpaths. In addition, several of Agame's rock-hewn churches can be visited by 4x4, ideally in the company of a local guide. The most accessible of these are Maryam Qiat, which makes for a straightforward half-day excursion out of Adigrat, and Maryam Bahera, which could be visited out of Adigrat or over the course of a fullish day's drive south to Hawzen, possibly in conjunction with Iyasus Gohgot and/or Maryam Buzuhan. Entrance to any given rock-hewn church is US$6.

Maryam Qiat [323 F2] Possibly the finest rock-hewn church in Agame, Maryam Qiat (also spelt Ki'at) has a pretty cliff-base location in a lush forest patch fed by a quartet of natural springs and inhabited by hyraxes and plentiful woodland birds. The local priest claims that the church dates to the BC era, which sounds like a contradiction in terms, but the Holy of Holies does, in fact, incorporate a Sabaean roof inscription indicating that it started life as a pre-Christian shrine. Hidden behind a built-up extension added in 2014, the ancient and intricately carved olive-wood door leads into a large spherical interior that incorporates six column-like pillars, several tall oval arches and indented ceiling cupolas. Columns and ceiling are covered in very faded paintings of saints, most notably one of Abuna Samuel with a rather pussycat-like lion. The oldest paintings might date to the 14th century but most are probably 18th century.

To get to Maryam Qiat, follow the Axum road out of Adigrat for about 18km to Enda Gedey, then turn left on to a dirt road signposted for the secondary school and continue for 11km to the village of Rahya, passing some splendid views west towards a distinctive outcrop called Amba Nebelet. If using public transport, there are four or five buses that travel daily between Adigrat and Rahya (*about 1hr*), and continue for another 5km to the village of Azibar at the escarpment base. The last bus back to Adigrat generally passes through Rahya at around 15.00, but if you get stuck, you should be able to arrange an inexpensive room in the village. From Rahya, it is a scenic 1.5km walk to Maryam Qiat. The most interesting route starts at a eucalyptus patch at the south of the village, then descends for a few hundred metres though a steep gap in the escarpment, before turning right on to a flat and clear contour path. You can also use a flatter alternative route that starts at the escarpment base about 1.5km out of Rahya on the road towards Azibar, and connects with the first route after about 500m. The priest lives close to the church and local children should usually be able to summon him quite quickly but, if not, you could have a Tigrigna-speaker call him in advance (**m** *0927 773168*).

Iyasus Gohgot, Maryam Bahera and Maryam Buzuhan This trio of churches lies about 10km apart some 20km south of Adigrat, and can be accessed from a (mostly good) 45km dirt road that terminates at Hawzen. The most atmospheric of the churches, and also the most accessible, is Maryam Bahera, which makes a good goal for a half-day driving excursion out of Adigrat or a full-day trip to Hawzen also taking in Iyasus Gohgot and Maryam Buzuhan. The closest of the churches to Adigrat, little-visited Iyasus Gohgot, is carved into a massive rock outcrop in a well-wooded valley, and it has a trapezoid shape, a cylindrical ceiling incised with swastikas, and sacred spring-fed water in the Holy of Holies. Entirely rock-hewn and well lit thanks to its large skylight, Maryam Bahera has a beautiful interior adorned with many well-preserved paintings of the Apostles and the Madonna, while church treasures include an ancient Ge'ez scripture. A tunnel in the left wall of Maryam Bahera reputedly leads all the way to Maryam Buzuhan, which stands 6km to the south and is notable for its engraved ceiling cupolas and cruciform pillars.

The scenic dirt road to these churches runs south out of Adigrat past the general hospital. After about 17km, it crosses a relatively wide river, then 500m further, a left turn leads on to a short side road that returns you to the river and the village of Gohgot. It's about 90 minutes on foot from the village to Iyasus Gohgot, with a rather steep climb at the end. For Maryam Bahera, instead of turning left into Gohgot village, you need to continue south for 3km to the village of Bahera, then turn right on to a rough 2km track that takes you to within 50m of the church entrance. If, from Bahera village, you want to continue to Hawzen, a confusing maze of piste-like tracks runs south to Edaga Arbi (literally 'Friday market', and also known as Dagamba), which lies 6km further south, and is the site of a very colourful traditional Friday market set below gorgeous sandstone cliffs, as well as being the springboard for the 1.5km walk west to the rock-hewn church of Maryam Buzuhan. A very good 18km dirt road connects Edaga Arbi to Hawzen, and plenty of public transport runs back and forth on market days.

Debre Giyorgis Constructed in the ancient Axumite tradition of Debre Damo and Yemrehanna Christos, Debre Giyorgis is a remote and very attractive built-up church with an irregular shape and wooden roof. The church is perched on a ledge three-quarters up a southeast-facing escarpment, and the ascent – not for the faint-hearted or unfit – involves climbing a massive ladder made with lashed-together eucalyptus poles, as well as some recently added concrete steps and a natural pathway. The church is rather irregular in shape but very attractive and well worth the climb. Unlike Debre Damo, women are allowed to visit. It lies 1.5km east of Gohgot village as the crow flies, but a lot further for the wingless, and is most easily visited on the Tesfa hike between the community guesthouses at Gohgot and Enaf.

Tesfa Treks (*011 810 0920/124 5178*; **m** *0923 490495*; **e** *tesfatigray@gmail.com*; **w** *tesfatours.com*) Tesfa's network of spectacular trekking routes through Agame offers an opportunity to visit some or all of the rock-hewn churches described on page 334, but it also exposes the hikers to traditional Tigrayan farming practices and other community activities, as well as the amazing sandstone scenery. Hikers are accommodated in no-frills community-owned and -managed guesthouses, which each sleep six people across three rooms, have a rooftop terrace, eco-toilet and washing facilities, and offer simple but tasty food, coffee and tea, and bottled drinks for purchase. Trekking runs throughout the year, and every season has its own attractions, but mid-August through to October is most attractive scenically. Bookings should be made in advance as communities need to prepare for guests, but last-minute treks are sometimes possible. Depending on group size and exact itinerary, expect to pay around US$70 per person daily, inclusive of food, accommodation, trained guide from Adigrat, and pack animals to carry luggage. It excludes bottled drinks, transport to the trail head and church entrance fees.

For those with sufficient time and energy, the ideal trekking route comprises a diamond-shaped five-day, four-night circuit stopping at the villages of Erar, Shimbrity, Gohgot and Enaf, but several shorter variations are available as the guesthouses are mostly accessible from various trail heads. The ideal starting point for the four-night circuit, about an hour by car from Adigrat, then 90 minutes on foot from the trail head at Rahya, is Erar, the most westerly guesthouse, perched on a sheer escarpment that offers wonderful views to the Adwa Mountains and Nebulet Pillar, and stands within walking distance of Maryam Qiat. From Enaf, it's a 5-hour walk south via Buzuhan Maryam to Shimbrity, where the most southerly guesthouse stands on the western ridge of Agame near Edaga Arbi. About 3 hours' walk northeast of Shimbrity, Gohgot lies 90 minutes on foot from Gohgot Iyasus. A 6–7-hour walk from Gohgot leads to Enaf, which hosts the area's highest guesthouse, perched at 3,000m on a ridge offering stunning views across the hills and valleys of Agame. The track between Gohgot and Enaf has some steep sections, so you need to be fit, but it also passes some lovely churches, most notably Debre Giyorgis. From Enaf it's a 4-hour walk down the mountain to the Agoro Lodge on the edge of Adigrat.

ROCK-HEWN CHURCHES BETWEEN ADIGRAT AND WUKRO

The 75km stretch of asphalt running south from Adigrat to Wukro passes close to at least six rock-hewn churches, all of which are readily accessible either in a private 4x4 or using a combination of public transport and walking. The four most southerly of these churches lie within 2km of each other at Teka Tesfai, a cluster that includes Medhane Alem Adi Kesho, one of Tigray's oldest and finest rock-hewn edifices, which can usually be visited without too much fuss on the priest-locating front. The more northerly and isolated Gebriel Tsilalmao and Adi Chewa Arbuta Insesa are both fine churches, and less than 30 minutes' walk from the main road, but the priest at both tends to be quite elusive. All these churches charge the standard entrance fee of US$6.

GEBRIEL TSILALMAO [323 G2] Carved into the side of a gorge 3km northeast of May Megelta, Gebriel Tsilalmao is a reasonably large church of unknown antiquity supported by unusually thick cruciform columns with double-bracket capitals covered in recent-looking paintings which, according to the priest, have always been there. Other notable features include the neatly cut arches, the engraved roofs of the six bays, two windows cut in Axumite style, an entrance with a built-up porch, and a large room in the back bisected by a column. A pair of evidently disused hermit cells is carved into the outer wall. The church is signposted on the east side of the Wukro road about 30km south of Adigrat and 1km north of May Megelta, and any public transport can drop you there. From the junction, a clear track runs eastward for 2.3km, crossing a seasonal marsh, before it terminates in a narrow gorge from where a 5-minute walk up a staircase leads to the church entrance. The priest now lives at the last house you pass to the right before entering the church, so you might want to stop there to establish whether he is around. If you need to wait, the riparian woodland around the church harbours grivet monkeys and numerous birds (look out for the gorgeous white-cheeked turaco), while Rouget's rail appears to be resident in the marshy patch on the opposite side of the gorge.

ADI CHEWA ARBUTA INSESA [323 G3] This large church dedicated to Arbuta Insesa (Four Animals) has several unusual features, most notably the deepest domed ceiling, almost 5m in height, of any Tigrayan church, and the strange red-and-yellow figures painted stencil-like on the thick columns. It lies about 2km east of Freweyni (formerly Sinkata), a quietly attractive village of stone houses that lies about 40km south of Adigrat at the junction with the newly surfaced northern feeder road to Hawzen and the Gheralta region. Plenty of public transport runs between Adigrat or Wukro and Freweyni. To get to Adi Chewa Arbuta Insesa, follow the Wukro road for about 1.2km southeast of the junction for Hawzen, then turn left about 100m before the NOC filling station, take a right after another 700m, and you'll see the cliffside church's whitewashed façade about 1km in front of you. The church lies about 20m up the cliff face, a walk of less than 5 minutes along a moderately steep footpath. The priest with the key lives about 15 minutes' walk from the church. If he is not around, the local children will fetch him, or you can walk to his house. You could also call him in advance (m 0933 048779). There are half a dozen basic lodgings in Freweyni, of which the pick are the Freweyni Hotel at the junction for Hawzen and the Sunshine Hotel about 1km closer to Adigrat.

TEKA TESFAI [323 G3] The most accessible cluster of churches in Tigray lies between 1.5km and 3km east of Teka Tesfai, a tiny hamlet straddling the Wukro road some 50km south of the Adigrat–Mekele road. The cluster is easily visited as a day trip from either Adigrat or Wukro on public transport, and could be covered as a day trip from Mekele in a private vehicle. It consists of three old churches, Medhane Alem Adi Kesho, Mikael Melehayzenghi, and Petros and Paulus Melehayzenghi, each very different and all within 2km of each other, as well as the new church of Petros and Paulus below its older namesake. The total fees for these churches add up to US$22.50 per person (the two churches of Petros and Paulus share a *tabot* so only one entrance fee is charged), and if your budget stretches to only one, it should undoubtedly be Medhane Alem Adi Kesho. No guide is necessary, but it may be advisable for unaccompanied visitors to arrange one in Wukro – we've had reports of independent travellers being harassed by local children and aspirant guides.

Petros and Paulus Melehayzenghi [322 A5] Visible from the main road 1.5km to its west, the disused cliff church of Petros and Paulus Melehayzenghi has a rock-hewn sanctuary but the main building is up on a high narrow ledge. Its most noteworthy feature is some primitive but fascinating paintings of angels and saints, which can be seen very clearly because the damaged roof lets in a fair amount of light, but are fading dramatically as a result of the added exposure. The church was evidently still in use in the late 1960s, when Ivy Pearce met the priests and was shown 'a large number of very interesting books and manuscripts', as it was a few years later when Paul Henze visited. Sometime in the 1980s, however, the *tabot* was relocated to a new rock-hewn church, cut into the cliff base below its predecessor by Halefom Retta, who claimed to have received instruction from the Archangel Gabriel, and who passed away in 2005. The signposted junction is on the east side

9

of the Wukro road about 500m south of Teka Tesfai (also known as Dinglet). It's about 1.8km from the junction to the car park at the base of the cliff, from where the short but vertiginous foothold-pocked ascent to the disused church should be taken very slowly and carefully. Once up, the view from the ledge, deep into the heart of Gheralta, is superb. Only one entrance fee is charged to see the old and new churches, and the priest lives at the base of the cliff.

CHURCH PRACTICALITIES

The rock-hewn churches of Tigray are not primarily tourist sites but active Christian shrines, and the remote and often parochial character that forms an integral part of their attraction can also be a potential source of frustration to visitors. True, visiting the more popular sites in Gheralta has become very straightforward in recent years, thanks partly to the creation of an organised guide association in Megab (page 347), and you can also almost always visit the suburban Wukro Chirkos and roadside Abraha we Atsbeha without complication. Elsewhere, however, a visit to any rock-hewn church should be approached with some sensitivity towards the older and slower way of life associated with rural Tigray, and a healthy dollop of patience and humour.

The biggest potential obstacle to visiting any church relatively unused to tourists is locating the priest with the key. If the person responsible for locking the church lives some distance away, he may be around to let you in only before or after services. And even if he lives close by, he might be out on his farm, or attending to parish duties, or off shopping at the local market (held on Saturday in Atsbi and the Tembien, and on Wednesday in Gheralta). Furthermore, on any holiday associated with a specific saint, it is customary for priests to head off to the nearest church dedicated to that saint. And even if the priest is around, he may be reluctant to allow tourists into the church during or after any special mass (which generally run from about 10.00 to 15.00). As a result of all this, when it comes to visiting more obscure churches, the odds of getting in probably stand at about 50%. They improve slightly when you are accompanied by a Tigrigna-speaking guide, but even then a degree of flexibility and forbearance is a prerequisite.

Costs can mount quickly. The official receiptable entrance fee for visiting any individual Tigrayan rock-hewn church is US$6, but some churches ask slightly more. None of this money goes to the priest who holds the key and shows visitors around, so he will expect a tip (US$2–8 depending on how many photographs he has been asked to pose for, and how far he has had to walk). In the Gheralta region, you also need to budget for your mandatory guide (page 350), while elsewhere you will be expected to slip a note or two to the person who locates the priest, and in the direction of anybody you photograph in or around the churches. Local kids who offer to carry your daypack or luggage will also expect a tip. So, too, might anybody else who accompanies you to the church, whether or not they actually contributed to the expedition. It's best to carry a stash of change for this purpose.

In order to see the interior of any of these churches properly, you need a torch or a candle. Photographers should not use flash on old paintings, as repeated exposure can damage the pigment (in any event, the combination of ambient light and a tripod will generally produce far richer colours and more atmospheric results).

Mikael Melehayzenghi [322 B6] This unusual church is very different in execution from most other Ethiopian rock-hewn churches, carved as it is into a large domed outcrop about 600m south of Petros and Paulus Melehayzenghi. It is entered via a low doorway, which gives way to a surprisingly large interior with a finely carved dome almost 3m in height. This church is said locally to date to the 8th century, though the southern third was added in the 19th century. A notable decoration is a vivid painting of unknown antiquity that depicts Jesus Christ saving Adam and Eve from (or possibly abandoning them to) a pair of ferocious dragon-like creatures at the Last Judgement. Mikael Melehayzenghi can be reached from the signposted track between the main road and Melehayzenghi by following a much rougher track that branches south about 400m before the car park for Petros and Paulus. The church stands in the prominent outcrop to your left about 800m along this track. The priest lives next to it.

Medhane Alem Adi Kesho [322 B6] Described by Ruth Plant as 'one of the truly great churches of the Tigray', Medhane Alem Adi Kesho is a large excavation whose imposing façade, cut free from the rock behind, incorporates four columns, two large doors, and some quite recent but very attractive paintings. The interior has a cathedral-like atmosphere, and the magnificent roof is dense with patterned etchings. Although Medhane Alem is regarded to be less perfectly executed than Wukro Chirkos and Abraha we Atsbeha, it is one of the most atmospheric Tigrayan churches east of Gheralta, and the airy front cloister offers excellent possibilities for moody interior photographs. Medhane Alem is quite possibly the oldest rock-hewn church in Tigray, described by David Buxton as 'the only church I know that can be placed with confidence in the earliest category of rock-churches [displaying] all the features to be expected in a very early Ethiopian church and not a single one that could point to a later date'. Unsurprisingly, one local tradition links the excavation of the church to the time of Abraha and Atsbeha. Rather less expected is the legend claiming it to be the work of Jesus Christ himself – indeed, it is said that the holes in the rock path leading to the church were made by Christ's horse, echoing (or pre-empting) a similar tradition associated with Beta Giyorgis at Lalibela. By contrast, Buxton estimated that Medhane Alem dated to the late 10th or early 11th century, and represented the Zagwe dynasty's 'earliest-known attempt to copy a Debra-Damo-type church in solid rock'.

Coming from Mikael Melehayzenghi, it's a 2km walk or drive (4x4 only) to Medhane Alem Adi Kesho. Continue southward on the same track that skirts Mikael Melehayzenghi, then turn left after 500m, right after another 700m, then left after another 200m, and you'll reach the parking area below a grove of trees after another 600m. Coming directly from the main road by car, you would be better taking the signposted turn-off about 4km south of Teka Tesfai and 6km north of Negash. It is about 5km from this junction to Medhane Alem Adi Kesho, slightly further on foot than the route via Mikael Melehayzenghi, but far less rough on a vehicle.

WUKRO AND SURROUNDS

Sprawling ever further southward from the banks of Geba River some 75km south of Adigrat and 50km north of Mekele, rapidly expanding Wukro has over the last 20 years morphed almost unrecognisably from a dour and scruffy backwater marked by some of the worst facilities in Ethiopia to an energetic and agreeable small town with plenty to offer tourists. It has also evolved into a town of three distinct parts, which might be called Old Wukro (north of the main roundabout, with a relatively subdued and lived-in feel), New Wukro (brasher, busier, centred on the bus station south of the main roundabout) and Hypothetical Wukro (a more southerly concrete jungle comprising about 100 incomplete medium-rises that epitomise the post-millennial Ethiopian tenet that somebody with half the money required to construct a building should construct half a building). Several sites of interest are dotted around town, most notably the rock-hewn church of Wukro Chirkos, an excellent new museum housing a recently excavated pre-Axumite sacrificial temple, and the out-of-town Mekabir Ga'ewa Archaeological Site at Adi Akaweh, where the temple in question was unearthed. Further afield, Wukro forms a convenient base from which to explore a number of rock-hewn churches, situated as it is at the junction of the main Adigrat–Mekele road, a branch road east to Atsbi, and one west to Hawzen, via Abraha we Atsbeha and Gheralta. It also lies only 20km by road from the fine cluster of churches at Teka Tesfai (page 335).

HISTORY The area around Wukro is steeped in history. The recent discovery of a 2,800-year-old Almaqah temple at Adi Akaweh, only 4km southwest of the modern town, confirms that it formed part of the same pre-Axumite Sabaean culture associated with the temple at Yeha. The town itself is the site of the ancient church of Wukro Chirkos, legendarily excavated during the 4th-century reign of Abraha and Atsbeha, along with a great many other rock-hewn churches in the immediate vicinity. In the early 7th century, Ethiopia's first Islamic community was established with imperial blessings at Negash, only 10km north of Wukro. According to one legend, Adi Akaweh, south of Wukro, is also where the destructive Queen Gudit was swept to her death by a divine gale in the late 10th century. Ado Akaweh is also known as Mekabir Ga'ewa (Grave of Ga'ewa), reflecting a more credible legend that it is the burial place of the eponymous Muslim queen who allied with Ahmed Gragn during the 16th-century campaign against Emperor Galawdewos, and is credited with burning many churches including Wukro Chirkos. In 1521, the Portuguese priest Francisco Álvares overnighted at a place he called Anguguim, which some authorities identify as Wukro and others as Agula about 10km to its south, though his description of a church 'made in a rock, hewn and wrought with the pickaxe, with three aisles and their supports made of the rock itself' would point to the former. In the mid 19th century, when the Napier expedition visited Wukro Chirkos, the small secular settlement outside was still known by its old Ge'ez name, Dongolo, but it seems the name of the church had been adopted by the town by the time of the Italian occupation. The area around Wukro was among the worst-hit parts of Ethiopia during the 1985 drought, and three years later an estimated 175 people were killed when the town was subjected to repeated bombardments by Derg aircraft. Today, Wukro is visibly one of the fastest-growing towns in Ethiopia: officially the population almost doubled from 16,000 to 30,000 between the 1994 and 2007 censuses, and local sources reckon it stands at well over 50,000 today.

GETTING THERE AND AWAY Wukro is an important junction town, connected by regular transport to Adigrat, Mekele and intermediate points. Heading east, a few vehicles daily ply up and down the road between Wukro and Atsbi. Public transport between Wukro and Hawzen (via Abraha we Atsbeha, Megab and Dugem) is rather less frequent, but at least one bus daily passes through at around 09.00 en route from Mekele to Hawzen. Alternatively, catch a minibus north along the Adigrat road as far as Freweyni, and pick up transport to Hawzen from there.

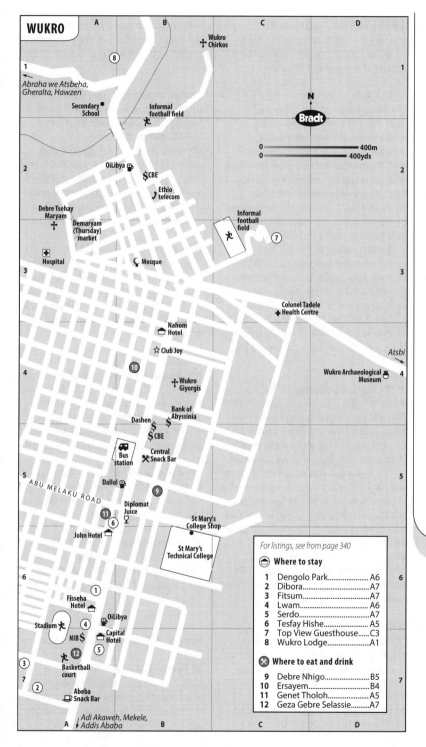

WUKRO

Wukro Chirkos

Abraha we Atsbeha, Gheralta, Hawzen

Secondary School

Informal football field

OiLibya

CBE

Ethio telecom

Informal football field

Debre Tsehay Maryam

Demaryam (Thursday) market

Hospital

Mosque

BradT

N

| 0 | 400m |
| 0 | 400yds |

Nahom Hotel

Club Joy

Wukro Giyorgis

Bank of Abyssinia

Dashen

CBE

Central Snack Bar

Bus station

Dallol

Diplomat Juice

John Hotel

St Mary's College Shop

St Mary's Technical College

Colonel Tadele Health Centre

Atsbi

Wukro Archaeological Museum

ABU MELAKU ROAD

Fisseha Hotel

OiLibya

Stadium

NIB

Capital Hotel

Basketball court

Abeba Snack Bar

Adi Akaweh, Mekele, Addis Ababa

For listings, see from page 340

🛏 **Where to stay**

1	Dengolo Park	A6
2	Dibora	A7
3	Fitsum	A7
4	Lwam	A6
5	Serdo	A7
6	Tesfay Hishe	A5
7	Top View Guesthouse	C3
8	Wukro Lodge	A1

✕ **Where to eat and drink**

9	Debre Nhigo	B5
10	Ersayem	B4
11	Genet Tholoh	A5
12	Geza Gebre Selassie	A7

🏠 WHERE TO STAY

Accommodation options have improved greatly over recent years and there is now one good moderate lodge in Wukro, as well as several more-than-adequate budget hotels. Some superb upmarket accommodation is available at nearby Hawzen and Gheralta.

Upmarket

🏠 **Wukro Lodge** [339 A1] (25 rooms) 🔊 034 440 9360; e info@wukrolodge.com; w wukrolodge.com. Still looking slightly unfinished having opened towards the end of 2017, this potentially stunning out-of-town lodge occupies a eucalyptus-swathed hill overlooking the junction of the back road to Hawzen via Abraha we Atsbeha. The castle-like reception area is complemented by accommodation in circular stone bungalows built in the traditional Tigrayan way but with adobe-style interiors. Rooms are tastefully decorated & come with nets, flatscreen TV, private terrace, coffee/tea & large bathroom with hot water. A swimming pool & restaurant are under construction. Too early to pass definitive judgement, but it looks to be good value, though not quite up to the standard of its (pricier) rivals in Gheralta. *US$42/62/67 B&B sgl/dbl/twin.* **$$$$**

Budget

☀️ 🏠 **Top View Guesthouse** [339 C3] (8 rooms) 🔊 034 443 1167; e khagos1@gmail.com. This converted house overlooking a football field 500m east of the main roundabout is hands-down the nicest place to stay & good value for money. Clean, bright & airy rooms in the main house are not en suite, but each floor has a private bathroom with tub. There is also a row of smaller rooms using common showers at the back. No food or drink is available, but there is a self-catering kitchen if you fancy cooking for yourself. It also has a nice garden with a view & safe parking. *US$10/12 sgl/dbl in main building, or US$6 dbl at the back.* **$–$$**

🏠 **Dibora Hotel** [339 A7] (25 rooms) 🔊 034 443 0788; m 0914 123981. This attractively priced family-run hotel has the advantage of being set back from the noisy main road. Clean & cheerful en-suite rooms have hot showers, marble-tiled floors & TV. There's a pleasant ground-floor café. *US$14/18 dbl/twin.* **$**

🏠 **Serdo Hotel** [339 A7] (20 rooms, more under construction) m 0914 314006. Half-finished for so long that it's difficult to believe it will ever be completed, this 7-storey hotel at the southern end of town has large, clean en-suite rooms with sat TV & hot shower/tub. A bit overpriced at US$16/24 dbl. **$$**

🏠 **Lwam Hotel** [339 A6] (65 rooms) m 0914 757814. An established choice with tour operators, this multistorey hotel is possibly coasting on its reputation, but it is still one of the better choices in this range. En-suite rooms have hot showers. *US$6 dbl with common shower or US$15/19 en-suite sgl/dbl.* **$–$$**

Shoestring

🏠 **Dengolo Park Hotel** [339 A6] (16 rooms) 🔊 034 443 1149; m 0914 783608. Set in a 2-storey building separated from the main road by a pleasant small garden, the clean en-suite rooms with hot water & TV here are a little scruffy but good value at the price. *US$5/6 dbl with common/en-suite shower.* **$**

🏠 **Fitsum Hotel** [339 A7] (12 rooms) m 0914 311092. Situated opposite the stadium at the south end of town, this above-average cheapie has clean, tiled en-suite rooms with ¾ or dbl bed, TV & hot shower. *US$4/6 sgl/dbl.* **$**

🏠 **Tesfay Hishe Hotel** [339 A5] (16 rooms) m 0914 211324. New hotel whose spacious & attractively decorated en-suite rooms all come with hot shower. *US$6/8 sgl/dbl.* **$**

✕ WHERE TO EAT AND DRINK

✕ **Geza Gebre Selassie** [339 A7] m 0914 313745. Still partially under construction, this new outdoor eatery has the only working swimming pool in Wukro & serves good local food in the US$3–4 range.

✕ **Debre Nhigo Restaurant** [339 B5] Good traditional food (especially *shekla tibs*) in an airy courtyard a block east of the main road. *Mains US$2–3.*

✕ **Ersayem Restaurant** [339 B4] m 0914 730420. This popular traditionally decorated eatery, tucked away a block west of the main road, serves good *tibs* but the speciality is *shiro kesiga* (meat in a spicy *shiro* sauce). *Mains US$1.50–2.*

✗ Genet Tholoh [339 A5] m 0914 178589. Tucked away on a side road 200m south of the bus station, this owner-managed hole-in-the-wall is a great place to try the local speciality *tholoh* (barley balls dipped in a sauce). *Mains US$1–1.50.*

SHOPPING The main market [339 A3], held in front of Debre Tsehay Maryam 600m west of the main roundabout, is well worth a visit on the primary market day of Thursday. A smaller market takes place behind the stadium [339 A6] at the south end of town on Monday. There are also several supermarkets on the main road where hikers heading to Gheralta can stock up on packaged foods. For crafts, the shop at the admirable St Mary's Technical College [339 B6] (◷ *08.00–18.00 Mon–Fri*) sells locally made jewellery, as well as great homemade cheese.

TOURIST INFORMATION AND GUIDES The Wukro Archaeological Museum (see below) effectively doubles as a tourist information and guides association office. Recommended guides based in Wukro include Mearg Abay (m *0910 292927*; e *mearg.abay@yahoo.com*) and Gebru Tarekegn (m *0983 115666*).

WHAT TO SEE AND DO
Wukro Chirkos [339 B1] The single most accessible rock-hewn church in Tigray, Wukro Chirkos is a semi-monolith that juts out from a low cliff about 500m northeast of the town centre. Cruciform in plan, the large rough-hewn interior incorporates a reception area with a cupola inset in the ceiling, and three tall naves. Locals claim that Wukro Chirkos was excavated by Abraha and Atsbeha in the 4th century, but David Buxton and other authorities date it to the 10th–12th centuries. The lovely line drawings on the ceiling must be from the 16th century or earlier, since they were partially destroyed when the church was burnt, either by Ahmed Gragn or possibly by Ga'ewa. The external roof and raised porch were added in 1958 due to seepage. The standard entrance fee of US$6 is charged without fuss. Because the church is attached to a large town, it is nearly always open and travellers are likely to be made welcome even during services, which can be quite a spectacle.

Wukro Archaeological Museum [339 D4] (◷ *08.30–17.30 Mon–Sat; entrance US$2*) Situated on the south side of the Atsbi road 1km east of Wukro's main roundabout, this excellent new museum, which opened in October 2015, has displays relating to several important sites in northeast Tigray. Pride of place undoubtedly goes to the incredibly well-preserved 2,800-year-old Adi Akaweh sacrificial altar (page 342), which was discovered as recently as 2007 and surely ranks among the ten most significant ancient artefacts known from Ethiopia. Almost as remarkable is a collection of items discovered in and around the 2nd-century AD tomb of a young noblewoman first unearthed at Maryam Anza (page 351) in 2015. These include several items of Roman origin, among them a bronze mirror, a limestone container used to store kohl eyeliner, and an exquisite mould-blown glass perfume flask, adorned with two very African-looking faces framed by curly hair. Other displays relate to lesser-known Sabaean sites in the vicinity of Edaga Hamus and Adigrat, the monochrome photographs taken by the German archaeological team who excavated Axum in 1906, and Wukro's first electric generator, which still stands exactly where it did when it was first installed in 1985.

Adi Akaweh [323 G4] Also known as Meqaber Ga'ewa (Grave of Ga'ewa), this unique archaeological site 4km southwest of Wukro comprises a temple dedicated to the Sabaean moon god Almaqah, the discovery of which – as recently as 2007

– confirmed that the pre-Axumite Sabaean empire of D'mt stretched much further south than had been previously assumed. The stone walls of the original temple have crumbled, but many well-preserved artefacts remained *in situ* at the time of excavation, including a decapitated statue of a seated female figure, several stones with Sabaean inscriptions, and a miscellany of pots and votive objects. Most extraordinary of all is a perfectly preserved metre-high sacrificial altar which comprises six precision-carved stone parts and has four steps at the base, four false windows engraved on each of its four sides, and an inscribed dedication running around the rim. Both the altar and the surrounding temple date to the 8th century BC, and would have remained in use for about 500 years thereafter. The site itself is evidently even more ancient, as the shrine stands on the ruins of an as-yet-unexcavated temple that must be at least a century older.

Part of the altar dedication at Adi Akaweh reads: 'Wa'ran ... the son of Radi'um and his companion Shakkatum, rebuilt it for Almaqah when he was appointed lord of the Almaqah Temple at Yeha'. This is illuminating in several respects. For one, it provided the first written evidence that Yeha (page 318) has been known by that name since ancient times, and it also confirms its former importance as a political and religious centre. The inscription is also remarkable insofar as it mentions a female member of the royal family, something unheard of among similar Sabaean inscriptions in Yemen. This suggests that Ethio–Sabaean D'mt, possibly influenced by the matrilineal tradition of the Kushitic empires of what is now Sudan, placed a far greater emphasis on the female line and the role of the queen mother than its counterparts in Yemen. It also provides circumstantial evidence to support the theory that the biblical Queen of Sheba, if she did originate from Saba (as is generally agreed), would have been Ethiopian not Yemeni.

Less than 1km south of the archaeological site, the modest stone church of Adi Akaweh Abuna Garima is built on an unexcavated Sabaean site that incorporates possibly the largest pre-Axumite temple anywhere in Tigray. Housed in the modern church are two inscribed stone incense burners that date from the 8th century BC, and namecheck four kings of D'mt, three of whom evidently co-governed with queens, further supporting the view that female monarchs played a far larger role in Ethio–Sabaean than Yemeni–Sabaean culture. Rather bizarrely, this possible connection between Adi Akaweh and the Queen of Sheba, unsuspected until a few years ago, is echoed by two older traditions linking the site to a pair of shadowy warrior-queens that loom large in Ethiopian history and folklore. As suggested by the alternative name Meqaber Ga'ewa, it is said that Queen Ga'ewa, an ally of Ahmed Gragn who reputedly destroyed many Tigrayan churches in the 16th century, was laid to rest at the exact spot where the Almaqah temple was unearthed in 2007. And a variation on this tradition has it that Queen Gudit was buried some 20m below the ground at Adi Akaweh, having been swept to her death by a wind that carried her airborne from Abraha we Atsbeha. Mere coincidence, or evidence of a more complicated relationship between a trio of legendary non-Christian queens whose reigns were separated by two-and-a-half millennia? Who knows!

Shortly after their discovery, the original sacrificial temple and statue were removed to Wukro for safekeeping, to be replaced by life-size replicas, which still stand at Adi Akaweh today. The originals are now on display in Wukro Archaeological Museum, but it is also possible to visit Adi Akaweh (*entrance US$1*) to see the replicas *in situ*. Follow the Mekele road south out of Wukro for 2.5km, then turn right on to a road that leads to a large leather factory after 2.5km. Just before you reach the factory gates, turn left on to a side road that brings you to the archaeological site after another 1.5km. Entrance to the temple site costs US$1. If you want to continue to Adi Akaweh Abuna Garima, it stands on a hilltop less than 1km south of the archaeological site, and you can drive to within 100m of it. Assuming you can locate the priest, expect to pay the usual US$6 to see inside the church.

Abraha we Atsbeha [323 G4] Situated 10km northwest of Wukro as the crow flies, this large rock-hewn church dedicated to the 4th-century twin emperors Abraha and Atsbeha is regarded by many to be the finest in Tigray and as such charges a higher-than-normal entrance fee of US$8. The cruciform interior is 16m wide, 13m deep and 6m high, with a beautifully carved roof supported by 13 large pillars and several decorated arches. There are three sanctuaries, with *tabots* respectively dedicated to Gebriel, Mikael and Maryam. The well-preserved and beautifully executed murals are relatively recent, many dating from the reign of Yohannes IV, and recreate the complete history of the Ethiopian Church. The traditional links with Abraha and Atsbeha mean that this is one of the few Tigrayan rock-hewn churches that has long been known beyond its parish, and it is still the target of a major pilgrimage on 4 Tekemt (normally 14 October), the festival day for these two kings.

Local tradition has it that this church was excavated in AD335–40 by Abraha and Atsbeha, whose mother came from the area. Buxton believed it was carved in the 10th century, but it could be that the church in its present incarnation is an extension of an earlier, smaller rock-hewn edifice. These claims to antiquity are emphasised by its many treasures, among them a prayer cross that legendarily belonged to Abba Salama, the first Bishop of Ethiopia. The mummified bodies of Abraha and Atsbeha are reputedly preserved in a box kept in the Holy of Holies. The last priest who tried to open this box, some years back, was severely burnt on his hands, and nobody has given it a go since!

Probably in the late 10th century, Queen Gudit attacked Abraha we Atsbeha, burnt part of it and destroyed a pillar. The queen became ill while she was inside the church, and ran off with some sacred rocks that gave off a supernatural light. She was killed hours later by a heavenly gale that swept her to a spot outside Wukro, where she is buried beneath a plain stone cairn. The imposing front of the church, reached via a flight of stone stairs and partially free-cut from the cliff, was probably added after Gudit's attack, and lies behind a more recently added Italian portico.

Abraha we Atsbeha is 45 minutes' drive from Wukro along a well-maintained and scenic 17km dirt road that continues westward to the Gheralta. The junction is signposted to the west of the main Adigrat road about 250m north of the bridge across the Geba River. There is very little public transport along this road, and your best chance of getting something is on a Saturday (market day in Megab). In a private vehicle, Abraha we Atsbeha can be visited en route between Wukro and Hawzen, assuming you take the southern route via Megab and Dugem. Vehicles can be parked at a car park only 3 minutes' walk from the church via a short but steep staircase.

Negash [323 G4] Something of an anomaly set in the heart of Ethiopia's main concentration of rock-hewn churches, the small hilltop village of Negash, which straddles the main Adigrat road about 10km north of Wukro, is thought to have been the site of the first Islamic settlement in Ethiopia. The story goes that Emperor Asihima of Axum allowed more than 100 early Islamic refugees, including Muhammad's daughter Rukiya and two of his future wives, to settle at the site in AD615. The name of the town is an Arabic corruption of the Ethiopian *negus* (emperor or king), and may have been chosen as a token of thanks by the refugees.

A more improbable explanation is the obscure but persistent Islamic tradition that Asihima converted to Islam under the direct influence of Muhammad, and was buried at Negash after his death in AD630.

Ancient Negash may be, and sacred too – some Ethiopian Muslims regard it as the most holy Islamic town after Mecca – but the town has little to show for it today. The large modern mosque, often said to be built on the site of the 7th-century original, is the target of an annual pilgrimage and festival, but it's nothing to look at. More interesting, some 200m south of the main mosque is a recently discovered Islamic graveyard (*entrance US$5*), claimed locally to house the remains of the 15 original 7th-century settlers closest to the prophet, among them his daughter Rukiya. You can ask the caretaker to pull back the outer coverings of the tombs of the 'companions of the prophet' to reveal the rich inner coverings. According to locals, the mosque above the tomb, currently being renovated, is about 100 years old and the bodies were relocated there very recently. The same anecdotal sources indicated that neither of the two extant mosques in Negash is built on the site of the original 7th-century mosque, which stood on a ridge about 1.5km further west, should you be interested in following it up.

Churches around Atsbi Situated at an altitude of 2,500m on a plateau 25km east of Wukro, the small town of Atsbi comprises a characteristically attractive Tigrayan assemblage of traditional stone houses along the ancient (and now all but disused) salt caravan route from the Danakil. It also lies at the centre of a trio of important rock-hewn and Axumite churches which tend to see relatively little tourist traffic compared with their counterparts at Gheralta. With a private vehicle, all three churches could be visited over the course of a long half-day out of Wukro. Travellers without a vehicle will need to be prepared for some serious hiking or trekking to see the two most interesting churches in the area. Atsbi is at its most colourful on market day, which is Saturday, and this is also when transport from Wukro is most regular. Unfortunately, however, Saturday is a bad day to visit the churches, as the priests will in all probability be at the market.

Mikael Barka [323 H4] The most accessible of the Atsbi churches, Mikael Barka is visible on the east side of the main road from Wukro, thanks to a brightly painted built-up portico erected in the 1960s. Fortunately the garish façade is not at all representative of this gloomy but very atmospheric rock-hewn cruciform's interior, with its numerous murals on the domed roof and a large cross etched on to one of the 12 columns. One oral tradition associates Mikael Barka with the 6th-century saint Abuna Abraham, another states that the church was founded during the 9th century, and both link the scorched roof to a 10th-century attack by Queen Gudit. By contrast, David Buxton believed Mikael Barka to post-date the Lalibela churches. The church is carved into an isolated small hill 18km from Wukro and 6km from Atsbi, and can be reached along a fairly steep but not arduous footpath in less than 15 minutes. Any vehicle heading between Wukro and Atsbi can drop you there. The family that lives in a stone house at the base of the footpath should know whether the priest is around.

Mikael Debre Selam [323 H3] Photographed in 1966 by Georg Gerster, the first *faranji* to visit it, Mikael Debre Selam, described by Ivy Pearce as an 'extraordinary … church within a church', comprises a striking built-up church and a small rock-hewn church set within an overhang protected by a whitewashed modern portico. The built-up church, reminiscent of Yemrehanna Kristos near Lalibela, is made with alternating layers of whitewashed stone and wood, the latter decorated with geometric patterns. One of the wooden window shutters is decorated with a very old cloth painting of the Virgin Mary and Child. The rock-hewn part of the church, which includes the sanctuary, is small and rather gloomy, but notable for the precise execution of the carved arches and pillars. A sealed cave in the cliff above the church is said to be the tomb of the 6th-century Emperor Gebre Meskel, during whose reign the church was reputedly constructed. While certain archaic features superficially support this local tradition, academic opinion is that Debre Selam post-dates the Lalibela churches.

Mikael Debre Selam is situated at an altitude of 2,670m about 7km north of Atsbi. To get there, follow the main road north out of town for 6km, then turn left and continue for another 1.6km to a car park above the Hidar River, with the church's white portico clearly visible on the cliff above. It is about 2km from here to the church, crossing the river on foot, then following a steepish footpath that offers great views over the valley below. The priest here tends to be quite elusive and you will need to get a local kid to find him. In addition to the usual entrance fee, bank on tipping both the priest and the person who locates him.

An intriguing church that could theoretically be visited in conjunction with Mikael Debre Selam is Zarema Giyorgis, which lies about 6km further along a motorable track that crosses the Hidar River some 2km south of the car park referred to above. This is the only free-standing Axumite-style church in the region, and reminiscent of Debre Damo in construction, but with several carved wooden internal features that date it to the 12th century or earlier. The original building is now housed within a larger stone church built in c2000, and the priests are reluctant to let tourists inside.

Mikael Amba [323 H4] This superb three-quarter monolith, first reported to the outside world by Beatrice Payne in 1948, boasts the most impressive exterior of any rock-hewn church in Tigray – indeed, the façade could be a transplant from Lalibela, and photographs well in the afternoon when it catches the sun. The monks here predictably claim that Mikael Amba dates from the rule of Abraha and Atsbeha, while David Buxton regarded it to be an 11th- or 12th-century excavation. Either way, at the time it was excavated, it must have been the nearest thing to a true rock-hewn monolith in all of Ethiopia, which suggests it was prototypal to the style of church now associated with Lalibela and surrounds. The magnificent interior, its 6m-high ceiling supported by a total of 25 pillars, is unusually well lit owing to the large frontal windows. The interior is modestly decorated by comparison with the Gheralta churches, but the workmanship is so precise it could have been excavated yesterday. Notable features include a large Greek cross hewn into the ceiling, decorated wooden doors, a treasure house containing an ancient metal cross and several old manuscripts, and two outside pools containing holy water.

Mikael Amba stands at an altitude of 2,330m on a flat-topped hill 15km south of Atsbi along a fair dirt road. If you do not plan to visit the other Atsbi churches, it can also be reached more directly from Agula (on the Mekele road about 10km south of Wukro) by following a 27km road running east via Haik Masahal (asphalt and good dirt for the first 18km, then 4x4 only). From the base of the hill, the short but steep ascent now takes less than 5 minutes using a new metal staircase. Once at the top, there are fantastic views over the surrounding landscape of glowing sandstone cliffs, patches of juniper and euphorbia trees, and layered mountains receding to the horizon. This is the one church in Atsbi where the priest with the key is usually present.

It can be said with confidence that the majority of Tigray's rock-hewn churches were excavated prior to the 16th century, since many have turned out to be described in the writings of Manuel Barradas, who lived in Ethiopia in 1624–40. Beyond this, however, the dating of the churches is open to speculation. True, every church has an oral tradition regarding its excavation, but these are often riddled with inconsistencies, and also seem to have acquired something of a competitive edge over the centuries (several churches claim, for instance, to have been the first one excavated in the 4th century by Abraha and Atsbeha, but scornfully discount similar claims made by other churches).

David Buxton, a leading authority on Axumite architecture, produced the most coherent chronological framework for the churches in the form of a 70-page essay published in *Archologia* in 1971. Here, Buxton divided the churches into five broad chronological styles. The earliest, which he ascribes to the 10th and 11th centuries, consists of relatively crude attempts to reproduce the classic built-up Axumite church style in rock. The only church that Buxton placed unambiguously in this prototypal category, based on such archaic features as its colonnaded portico, is Adi Kesho Medhane Alem. Other superficially similar churches, such as Maryam Hibeti, display anachronistic features, suggesting that they are later imitations.

The next chronological architectural style is the Inscribed Cross Church, which peaked in the 11th and 12th centuries. These churches are laid out on a cruciform plan within a larger square, a distinctive Tigrayan style that has no obvious precursor in built-up churches. Buxton places several well-known churches into this category, including Wukro Chirkos, Mikael Imba and Abraha we Atsbeha, and cites the last as 'the most perfect example of the cross-in-square layout'. Buxton reckons these churches predate the excavations at Lalibela, and raises the intriguing possibility that Bet Giyorgis, with its uniquely cruciform exterior, was a conscious attempt to externalise the Inscribed Cross plan.

Buxton describes three further styles. These are Archaic Ethiopian Basilica, then Classic Ethiopian Basilica, the latter probably roughly contemporaneous with the churches at Lalibela. Post-dating the Lalibela churches, the Tigrayan Basilica style includes several of the Gheralta churches, which probably date to the 13th and 14th centuries, and thus post-date Lalibela. A later series of Tigrayan Basilica includes several churches in the Tembien, the one area where oral tradition and academic opinion are in broad agreement, dating most of the excavations to the 14th- and 15th-century reigns of emperors Dawit and Zara Yaqob.

An interesting pattern in Buxton's relative chronology is a broad westward movement in the excavation of Tigrayan churches. Those to the east of what is now the main Adigrat–Mekele road generally predate the Gheralta churches, which in turn predate those in the Tembien. If that is the case, might not the

HAWZEN AND THE GHERALTA ESCARPMENT

A fantastic spaghetti-Western landscape of flat dry plains and towering rock outcrops, the scenically spectacular region known as Gheralta, some 25km west of Wukro, is home to some 30-odd rock-hewn churches, the largest concentration in Ethiopia. Once the preserve of adventurous backpackers but now well established as a tourist destination, Gheralta does not boast the oldest churches in Ethiopia, nor even the most architecturally impressive, but the magnificent settings, atmospheric absolute dating of these churches be linked to the as yet poorly understood shifts of imperial power bases between the collapse of Axum and the rise of Lalibela four centuries later? For that matter, could it not be that some apparent chronological differences are also a reflection of regional variations in style? Buxton himself notes that 'both the monolithic church and the elaborated exterior were specialities of Lalibela, and neither the one nor the other was ever adopted as an ideal by the Tigrayan rock-hewers'. Much the same might be said for the cross-in-square style, which seems to have its epicentre in Wukro, and the various basilica styles that predominate farther west.

Another potential stumbling block in dating the churches is that many would have been extended or redecorated over the centuries, possibly resulting in a variety of anachronistic architectural features. It is clearly the case that many church paintings, though very old, are far more modern than the edifices that house them, while the southern third of Mikael Melehayzenghi is accepted to be a relatively recent addition to a much older church. It is possible, too, that some churches might have started life as partially hewn cave temples in pre-Christian times – a tradition of this sort is attributed locally to the church of Tekle Haymanot in Hawzen, and there are unquestionably rock-hewn tombs in Axum dating from pre-Christian times. It seems reasonable to suppose that some sort of architectural continuum links Ethiopia's various rock-hewn edifices.

The dates of excavation suggested by Buxton, like those ascribed to the churches by oral tradition, are often quoted as immutable fact. It should be noted, therefore, that Buxton himself takes great pains to emphasise that his chronological scheme is no better than provisional, and he frequently phrases his opinions in the guise of educated guesses. His work is also contradicted by an alternative chronology put forward by the Ethiopian art experts Lepage and Mercier in 2006. This has the earliest Tigrayan churches, among them Mikael Amba and Abraha we Atsbeha, being excavated in the post-Axumite, pre-Lalibela period, ie: the 7th to 11th centuries, and dates a greater number, including Maryam Korkor, Maryam Qiat and Abuna Yemata Guh, to the 13th–16th century monastic renaissance associated with the restoration of the Solomonic line under Yakuno Amlak. It is also interesting to note that while no serious suggestion has ever been made that any Ethiopian rock-hewn church dates to the post-Gragn era, at least four such churches (the 'new' Petros and Paulus in Tigray and a trio of churches at Checheho south of Lalibela) have been excavated since the 1990s. The work of latter-day glory hunters, or evidence that the rock-hewing tradition is not as frozen in the past as people tend to think: who knows? As Ruth Plant wrote in the introduction to the most exhaustive inventory of Tigrayan rock-hewn churches yet published, 'it is vital to keep an open mind as to dates'.

interiors and wealth of old paintings and church treasures make it a highly captivating area to explore. The main base for doing this is the small but historic town of Hawzen (aka Hawzien), which is easily reached in a private car or on public transport, and equipped with a good selection of accommodation. Precisely 8km southwest of Hawzen, the tiny village of Megab lies at the base of the northern tip of the Gheralta Mountains, within walking distance of several important churches, and it's also home to the Gheralta Guides Association. The other logistically important village in the region is Dugem, about 10km southeast of Megab.

Gheralta is not for everyone. The region's finest churches are situated in high isolation on the outcrops of the escarpment, and the foot ascents are relatively strenuous and time-consuming. A reasonable level of fitness and agility is required to reach any of these churches, and visiting more than one or two in the course of a day would be challenging indeed. For budget-conscious backpackers, a greater concern might be the relatively limited public transport beyond Hawzen, and the necessity of hiring a member of the Guides Association to visit any of the churches, both of which can make it quite costly and time-consuming to explore. On the plus side, the increased popularity of this region with tourists has encouraged the better-known churches to ensure the key is permanently available, which greatly reduces the risk of hiking all the way to a church only to find you are locked out.

HISTORY In common with nearby Wukro, Hawzen – which appears on the oldest known maps of Tigray – is steeped in history, though our knowledge of it is patchy to say the least. Hawzen's proximity to Adi Akaweh, coupled with the phonetic similarity of its name to the ancient south Arabian place name HWZN, and the recent discovery of inscribed tablets at nearby Maryam Anza, all point to it having been an integral part of the Sabaean trade empire of D'mt in the first millennium BC. The area's significance during the Axumite era is evidenced by the presence of several tall stelae, whose appearance suggests they are of similar vintage to the so-called Gudit stelae outside Axum. In the late 5th or early 6th centuries, Hawzen was reputedly settled by the Sadqan (literally 'Righteous Ones'), a mysterious cult of Christian zealots who fled from somewhere in the Roman Empire to northern Ethiopia, where they were accorded protection by King Kaleb and reputedly lived in rock shelters, subsisted gelada-like on grass only, and tried to convert the locals to their ascetic ways. The eventual fate of the Sadqan is unclear – it seems that many of them were killed by non-Christians because of their extreme religious beliefs, while others reputedly starved themselves to death – but their heaped bones are preserved at several sites associated with them.

Opinion differs as to the dating of the region's rock-hewn churches, but Hawzen Tekle Haymanot and Dugem Selassie, both of which lie on the plains rather than the cliffs, share certain Axumite architectural features that suggest they were originally excavated as tombs between the 6th and 9th centuries AD. The famous cliff churches of Gheralta are clearly much more modern, and might even post-date their counterparts at Lalibela, though most were probably excavated before the end of the 16th century.

More recently, on 22 June 1988, Hawzen was the target of one of the most vicious public excesses of the Mengistu regime when the Ethiopian air force launched a tragic and apparently unprovoked aerial bombardment on its market, killing an estimated 2,500 civilians.

GETTING THERE AND AWAY Several operators in Mekele (page 364) offer organised overnight trips to the Gheralta churches.

By air The closest airport receiving scheduled flights is at Mekele, 100km by road to the south of Hawzen. An airstrip currently under construction on the outskirts of Megab will receive charter flights from Addis Ababa and forms part of a long-term plan to develop Gheralta as a core destination for upmarket tours to Tigray and the Danakil.

By road Once accessible only by dirt road from Wukro, and something of a cul-de-sac in travel terms, Hawzen is gradually emerging as potentially the most important route focus in Tigray. Coming from the east, it is most easily reached along a nippy 23km asphalt road that branches from the main Adigrat–Mekele road at Freweyni (formerly Sinkata), 35km north of Wukro. Alternatively, a good 50km dirt road – likely to be surfaced by 2019 – connects Wukro directly to Hawzen via Abraha we Atsbeha, Dugem and Megab. Southwest of Hawzen, the recent surfacing of the 70km road between Megab to Abiy Addi means that Gheralta now forms a realistic base for day trips to the relatively little-visited churches of the Tembien. A more significant future development is the planned surfacing of the 110km road running northwest to Adwa via Nebelet and Edaga Arbi, which should make it possible to travel directly between Axum and Gheralta on asphalt in under 2 hours. In addition, the rough 4x4-only road running north through the Agame Mountains to Adigrat via Enda Gedey is likely to be upgraded and possibly asphalted in the near future.

For travellers dependent on public transport, regular minibuses now run along the surfaced road between Freweyni and Abiy Addi via Hawzen and Megab. Traffic along the back route between Wukro and Hawzen via Megab is rather scarce, but Dugem and Megab do become something of a focal point for public transport on Saturdays (market day in both villages). Once in Hawzen or Megab, *bajaji* are available to take you to the trail heads for the various churches.

WHERE TO STAY
Upmarket

In addition to the 2 lodges listed below, **Kuriftu Resorts** (w *kurifturesorts.com*), which already operates high-quality resorts in Bishoftu & Bahir Dar, is currently constructing a new lodge at the base of the escarpment 4km south of Megab. Both lodges listed below can arrange transfers from Mekele, Axum or Lalibela, & minibus/4x4 rental for local excursions.

✳ 🏠 **Korkor Lodge** [323 F3] (8 rooms) m 0912 912305; e info@korkorlodge.com; w korkorlodge.com. Situated in 6.5ha grounds about 1km east of Megab, this fabulous new lodge, aimed at visitors spending a few days exploring the nearby churches, now ranks as the most upmarket option in the area. Accommodation is in spacious & stylish en-suite bungalows with wooden furniture, bright décor, tall glass windows & private garden & terrace offering a sensational view to the escarpment. *US$150/200 sgl/dbl FB.* **$$$$$**

✳ 🏠 **Gheralta Lodge** [323 F3] (16 rooms) ☎ 034 667 0344; m 0988 270623; e bookingforprivates@gheraltalodgetigrai. com; w gheraltalodgetigrai.com. This lovely owner-managed resort 1km south of Hawzen is set in immaculate gardens featuring panoramic views of the rock formation after which it is named. The traditional stacked-rock buildings

blend effortlessly with the environment, the spacious en-suite rooms are tastefully decorated, & the freshly prepared Italian meals (*US$9–12 pp*) are simple but delicious. *US$70/100/110 sgl/dbl/trpl, with substantial low-season discounts. US$25/35 budget sgl room/bungalow.* **$$$$$**

Budget & shoestring

🏠 **Vision Motel** [322 C4] (14 rooms) m 0924 293314, 0914 728813. The pick of a few adequate cheapies in Hawzen, this owner-managed hotel is set around a green courtyard & has clean, neat, tiled en-suite rooms with hot showers. A restaurant/bar is attached. *US$16/20/24/32 sgl/dbl/twin/trpl.* **$$**

🏠 **Habesha Hotel** [322 C4] (20 rooms) m 0925 050734. This friendly new hotel, a short distance south of the main road, has clean tiled rooms with hot shower set around a neat concrete courtyard. *US$7/10 dbl with common/en-suite shower.* **$**

🏠 **Adulis Hotel** [322 C3] (24 rooms) m 0914 701093. This long-serving hotel next to the CBE offers the choice of newer & more spacious 1st-floor rooms with tiled floors & en-suite hot shower, or scruffier ground-floor rooms using a common shower. *US$4 sgl with common shower, US$7/12 en-suite sgl/dbl.* **$$**

✗ WHERE TO EAT AND DRINK The best traditional eatery in Hawzen is the **Ethiopia Hotel** [322 B3], which serves good fasting food, *tibs*, *key wot* and *shekla tibs* in the US$2–3 range. It also has draught beer, a pool table, and sat TV for football matches.

TOURIST INFORMATION AND GUIDES It is mandatory to be accompanied by a member of the **Gheralta Guides Association** (m *0914 041123/025315*; ⊕ *07.00–18.00 daily*) when you visit any of the churches in Gheralta, even if you are already travelling with a guide from elsewhere in Ethiopia. These guides can be arranged and collected at the association office in Megab [323 F3], opposite the junction to Abuna Yemata Guh. Fixed fees are US$18 per day for up to five people, or US$23 for six to ten people, or US$27 for larger groups. The guide will also expect a tip of around US$2–4.

WHAT TO SEE AND DO In addition to the sites listed below, Hawzen is a possible base from which to explore the rock-hewn churches in the Agame Mountains (page 332) – an option that should be more straightforward once the new road to Adigrat via Enda Gedey is completed – as well as the churches in the Tembien. The entrance fee to all churches is set at US$6. The recent growth of tourism to Gheralta means that its most popular churches – Abuna Yemata Guh, Debre Maryam Korkor and Papaseit Maryam – now tend to be quite busy, so there is something to be said for heading to a few of the lesser-known churches instead.

Hawzen [323 F3] Hawzen is a bustling little town with several points of interest. About 150m southeast of the main crossroads stands the new marketplace, which hosts a large weekly market every Wednesday. On the east side of the Megab road 200m further south, the old marketplace, where 2,500 people were killed in an aerial bombardment in 1988, has now been restored as a commemorative park. On the opposite side of the road you'll find the four ancient stelae toppled in the same bombardment. Two of them have been re-erected, including one that stands about 4m tall, but they have also, rather bizarrely, been painted yellow and green, which rather undermines their gravitas. About 1km south of the main crossroads, set in a wooded grove next to a river on the west side of the Megab road, Hawzen Tekle Haymanot comprises an undistinguished built-up church whose sanctuary started life as a small rock-hewn funerary church. The rock-hewn part of the church is thought to be one of the oldest in Tigray, based on the finely carved capital and columns, which bear a strong resemblance to the original throne in Axum according to Ruth Plant. Indeed, certain local traditions indicate it might well have started life as a partially rock-hewn temple in pre-Christian times. Unfortunately, the rock-hewn section is off-limits to lay visitors. You may be allowed to peek inside, but even this feels like a relatively underwhelming return for the entrance fee.

Maryam Anza [323 F3] (w *tigraytrust.com; entrance US$1*) The modern church of Maryam Anza, 5km north of Hawzen, is surrounded by a recently discovered archaeological site dominated by Sabaean (pre-Christian Axumite) remains dating back almost 2,000 years. The most noteworthy relict *in situ* is a fallen 4.5 x 1.5m stele topped by the characteristic Sabaean motif of a disc and crescent moon, and engraved with a Ge'ez inscription commemorating the victory of an otherwise undocumented king named Bazat of Agabo in a battle that took place in the late 2nd or early 3rd century AD. Long before this text was translated, the site was known locally as Hawnehaw, literally 'Brother against Brother', presumably in reference to this ancient battle. The stele is now protected within a small fenced enclosure, and although it lies face down, agile visitors could wriggle underneath to see the inscription. Ongoing excavations undertaken at Maryam Anza by Louise Schofield and the Tigray Trust have also revealed several graves thought to be roughly contemporaneous with the inscribed stele. These include a beautifully executed rock-hewn shaft tomb, as well as the grave of a young woman who was buried curled up on her side, her chin cupped in her hand, and her face tilted towards a bronze mirror of Roman origin (now displayed, along with several other treasures held in the tomb, at the Archaeological Museum in Wukro). The present-day hilltop church of Maryam Anza, probably built in the 1980s, stands atop a much older shrine said locally to have been a church that miraculously sunk underground in the 10th century to evade an attack by Queen Gudit, though archaeological evidence points towards it having been (or at least having started life as) a pre-Christian temple similar to those at Adi Akaweh and Yeha. A collection of around a dozen partly damaged Axumite tablets, pillars and other dressed stones associated with the ancient temple are lined up in the churchyard.

Maryam Anza and Hawnehaw Stelae Site are both signposted from Hawzen but with incorrect distances given (2.3km and 6km). To get there, follow the Edaga Arbi road north out of town for about 500m then turn left on to a rough dirt road that leads to the church after 4.5km.

Abuna Yemata Guh
[323 F4] The most spectacularly situated rock-hewn church anywhere in Ethiopia, the small but very beautiful Abuna Yemata Guh is carved into the top of one of the tall perpendicular rock pillars that dominate the southwestern horizon of Megab. The interior, reached via a small crack in the rock, is notable for its extensive and perfectly preserved wall and roof murals, thought to date from the 15th century and regarded by Ruth Plant as 'the most sophisticated paintings found so far in Tigray'. Nine of the Apostles are depicted in a circle in one of the roof domes, while the nine Syrian monks are depicted in the other. The wall paintings include one of the remaining three Apostles, as well as a large frieze of the church's namesake, Abuna Yemata, on horseback. There are stunning views from the narrow ledge that leads to the church, looking over a sheer drop of roughly 200m.

To get to Abuna Yemata Guh, follow the signposted road that forks southwest from opposite the Guides Association in Megab for about 3.5km. From there, the hike takes up to 1 hour, climbing roughly 500m in altitude. The last stretch of the ascent entails a giddying unsupported clamber up a sheer cliff face using handgrips and footholds. It's probably not too dangerous provided that you are reasonably fit and agile, and have a good head for heights, but it should not be attempted if you have any doubts about your agility, or the mildest tendency towards vertigo – panic or freeze on this face, and you would be in serious trouble indeed!

Abuna Gebre Mikael
[323 E4] Situated high on the escarpment 15km southwest of Guh, the little-visited church of Abuna Gebre Mikael, legendarily carved by its namesake in the 4th century, but more likely to date to the 14th, is regarded to be one of the finest in the Gheralta. Set in the base of a 20m-high cliff, the church has an imposing wooden doorway, an unusually ornate carved exterior, and a large cruciform interior supported by eight columns. Both the columns and the neatly hewn ceiling cupolas are decorated with brightly coloured blue-and-yellow paintings that reputedly date to the 15th century and are illuminated through four windows. The footpath to Abuna Gebre Mikael starts at the village of Koraro on the new road to Abiy Addi some 22km southwest of Megab. The steep walk to the church takes 45–90 minutes and involves some clambering and jumping between rocks, though nothing as daunting as the ascent of Abuna Yemata Guh.

Debre Maryam Korkor [323 F4] This monastic church is set on a small plateau atop a sheer-sided 2,480m-high mountain a short distance northeast of Guh. The built-up façade, recently painted bright green, is rather off-putting, but the interior is very atmospheric and large, almost 10m wide, 17m deep and 6m high. Architectural features include 12 cruciform pillars with bracket capitals, and seven arches stylistically reminiscent of those at Abraha we Atsbeha. Predictably, local tradition links the excavation of Debre Maryam Korkor with the twin emperors Abraha and Atsbeha, while Buxton placed it in the early series of Tigrayan Basilica churches, carved after those at Lalibela. The fine artwork on the walls and columns is said locally to date from the 13th century. Ivy Pearce and Ruth Plant both felt that it was probably painted in the 17th century, citing a painting of the Virgin Mary with a circle around her abdomen (indicating the development of the foetal Jesus Christ) as typical of that era.

The track to Debre Maryam Korkor is clearly signposted on the southwest side of the Dugem road about 2km east of Megab. The first 1km of the track is motorable, after which the foot ascent takes around an hour, via a natural rock passage (watch out for loose rocks underfoot) that emerges at an abandoned partially rock-hewn nunnery that was active up until the reign of Zara Yaqob, when the monastery attached to Debre Maryam Korkor was founded. From here, you can use the shorter 'men's route', which involves scrambling up footholds and handgrips on a 60° rock face, or the slightly longer but less vertiginous 'women's route'. From Debre Maryam Korkor a 2- or 3-minute walk takes you to another disused rock-hewn church called Abba Daniel Korkor, set above a sheer precipice with stunning views over the surrounding plains. The entrance fee of US$7.50 covers both the extant church and the two disused ones.

Papaseit Maryam [323 F4] Less spectacular than its counterparts on the high escarpment, this extended cave church is nevertheless recommended to unfit or unadventurous travellers as the trek there is flat and relatively undemanding. The church has an exquisite setting in an oasis-like stand of palms and other lush tropical vegetation at the base of the escarpment, and the walk there passes through patches of acacia woodland studded with some impressively proportioned fig trees, making it an excellent outing for birders. The most important feature of the church is its vivid cloth paintings, which depict various Old and New Testament stories, including Adam and Eve being tempted by the snake, and the 4th-century priest Arius explaining the so-called arian heresy (which asserts that Jesus was the physical son of God and thus subordinate to him) to King Constantine. Most of the church's art was commissioned in the early 19th century by the local governor Bashai Dengeze and his wife Emebet Hirut (both of whom are depicted on the wall), but the paintings of the Nine Saints above the door look older. To get there, follow the Dugem road out of Megab for 3.5km, turn right then after another 1km turn left, and you will reach the car park after another 3km. The flat and gentle 3km walk from there takes about 45 minutes.

Dugem Selassie [323 F4] The village of Dugem boasts a scenic location at the escarpment base 10km southeast of Megab and 14km northwest of Abraha we Atsbeha. It is the site of an unusual rock-hewn church set in a granite outcrop within the compound of the eponymous modern church. The small size of this church, together with features that Ruth Plant found reminiscent of King Kaleb's tomb in Axum, has led some experts to think it was originally carved as a tomb in Axumite times. It is possible to camp within the church compound.

Abuna Abraham Debre Tsion

[323 F4] Few who visit this monastic cliff church, carved into a rusty sandstone face high above the village of Dugem, will disagree with Ruth Plant's estimation that it is 'one of the great churches of the Tigray, both from the architectural and devotional aspect'. Debre Tsion has an impressive and unusually ornate exterior, as well as the largest ground plan of any rock-hewn church in the region. The main body of the church is itself fairly large, and consists of four bays with decorated domed roofs, supported by pillars and walls covered in murals of various Old Testament figures. Arcing behind this is a tall, deep rock-hewn passage, which leads to a decorated cell said to have been the personal prayer room of Abuna Abraham, the monk who reputedly excavated the church in the time of Abraha and Atsbeha and is said to be buried below it. Experts believe the church to date from the 14th century or thereabouts. Among its treasures is a beautiful 15th-century ceremonial fan comprising 34 individual panels, each painted with a figure of a saint. Although the priests will open the fan for a small additional payment, it is starting to fray and tear, and seems unlikely to survive much longer if this happens too regularly.

A motorable track to Debre Tsion is signposted to the southwest of the Wukro road 3.5km southeast of Dugem. You can drive the first 1km or so. From there you need to walk for about 20 minutes across flat fields to the back of the mountain. A steep but otherwise quite easy 30–40-minute hike brings you to the summit and the church – pausing, as is the convention, at the spot where Abuna Abraham is said to have stopped to pray whenever he climbed up. On the way up, the priest can also show you a smaller disused excavation said to have been Abuna Abraham's first attempt at carving a church. Close to the old church lies a natural bed of jagged rocks on which the saint would writhe around while he prayed, demonstrating his faith through self-abuse. There is a festival here on 21 Hidar (normally 30 November).

Yohannes Maikudi

[323 F4] Situated 2km southeast of Debre Tsion as the crow flies, Yohannes Maikudi has been described by David Buxton as 'the most interesting [church dedicated to Yohannes] I have seen, and memorable, too, for its means of access, which is a narrow cleft between bulging walls of bare, glaring sandstone'. Ivy Pearce felt that Yohannes Maikudi had a more 'reverent and holy atmosphere' than any other church she visited in Tigray. The 130m² rectangular excavation is notable architecturally for its Axumite doors, one of which is reserved for male worshippers, the other for females, and a Holy of Holies built into the right side of the main church rather than at the back. The walls and roof are densely covered in well-preserved and evocative paintings very different from any others found in Gheralta (or, for that matter, any others we've seen elsewhere in Ethiopia) and thought by Dale Otto, a member of Ivy Pearce's expedition to Tigray, to display a combination of Byzantine and Nubian influences. Dating to the 18th century, the paintings were executed over 16 days by Abba Gebre Iyasus, according to the Ge'ez script below a self-portrait of the artist flanked by Abuna Yohannes and Abuna Gebre Meskel. The most interesting tableau depicts King Fasilidas on horseback protected by a metre-high row of spike-haired and unusually dark-skinned woman guards that might be mistaken for dancers were they not armed with spears and shields. Other paintings depict King Herod, Abuna Samuel and a lion, and two devils torturing a thief.

Yohannes Maikudi can be visited in isolation, starting at the end of the same motorable track used to reach Debre Tsion, or in conjunction with Debre Tsion. Either way, the steep ascent takes about 1 hour.

9

Maryam Wukro [323 F2] The most remote rock-hewn church described in this section, Maryam Wukro was also, oddly enough, one of the first such edifices in Tigray to be visited by a foreigner, namely Professor Mordini in 1939. Subsequently, Ruth Plant described it as 'a great example of Tigrayan architecture' and David Buxton called it 'the most elaborate and even fantastic cliff church I know'. As with Mikael Debre Selam near Atsbi, Maryam Wukro combines elements of rock-hewn and built-up Axumite architecture, though the rock-hewn part of the church is much larger and airier, with a 10m-high interior comprising three aisles and bays. Notable features include an unsupported double arch, several thick pillars, ancient rock etchings and more modern paintings. The church is said to have been excavated by angels during the reign of Abraha and Atsbeha, who were regular visitors, and there is also a niche in the back where Maryam herself sometimes comes to pray and weep. Reached via a wooden ladder, a more crudely hewn chapel, **Wukro Giyorgis**, is carved into the cliff face above Maryam and has a few floor-level openings looking into the larger church. David Buxton indicated that this church might have been modelled on the Axumite church at Debre Damo, and it also might have had some influence on the architecture of the cliff churches in Lalibela.

Maryam Wukro can be reached by following the good dirt road (reputedly soon to be asphalted) from Hawzen to Adwa for 30km as far as Nebelet, an overgrown village of neat sandstone houses, set in spectacular isolation below the so-called Nebelet Pillars, a tall rock outcrop reminiscent of Gheralta. From Nebelet, a rough 4x4-only track leads to the church. After 4.5km, the track crosses a river that may be impassable by car in the rainy season. It's another 1.5km to the church. Be warned that it may take a while to locate the priest with the key. Once you do, you'll be asked to pay an unusually high entrance fee of US$8, and to cough up a tip before he unlocks the door. If you are continuing on towards Axum, it's 33km by road from Nebelet to Edaga Arbi, a small town set below the ancient hilltop monastery of Abuna Tsama, then another 15km to the intersection with the Abiy Addi road 32km south of Adwa.

ABIY ADDI AND THE TEMBIEN

The gateway town to the most remote of Tigray's major rock-hewn church clusters, Abiy Addi (aka Abi Aday) is also a route focus of sorts, situated at the junction of the little-used direct road between Axum and Lalibela via Sekota, a well-established trunk road running east to Mekele, and a new surfaced road to Hawzen and the Gheralta. In 1843, explorer Charles Beke described Abiy Addi as 'the principal place of the Tembien, and a large market town', and it remains both these things today, though some might feel that its name (literally 'Big Town') rather overstates the case. Historically, the Tembien is remembered as the birthplace of Emperor Yohannes IV and Ras Alula Engida (the general who played a critical role in securing the Ethiopian victory at Adwa), while other Tigrayans know it for its delicious honey and the hyperactive local dancing style known as Awris. Sprawling northward from the fertile banks of the Tankwa River, the town has a population of around 20,000 and an attractive setting below tall sandstone cliffs. It is generally divided into three parts. Kebele One, the oldest and most southerly sector, is where you'll find the old market, and several *tej bets* (where spontaneous Awris dances might break out on any evening). Kebele Two, effectively the town centre, contains the bus station, the large new market, the banks and many restaurants, bars and cheap pensions. Kebele Three, also known as Adigdi, is a rapidly expanding suburb north of the town centre. Local attractions are limited to the Mylomin Botanical Garden immediately south of town, and the nearby church of Tankwa Mikael.

However, the surrounding region is studded with worthwhile rock-hewn churches that still retain a genuinely off-the-beaten-track feel.

GETTING THERE AND AWAY Abiy Addi is now accessible on good surfaced or partially surfaced roads from three directions. In a private vehicle, allow 2 hours to cover the 115km road from Axum via Adwa and May Kinetel, 2 hours for the partially surfaced 95km road from Mekele via Hagere Selam, and one-and-a-bit hours for the surfaced 70km road from Hawzen via Megab. The unsurfaced 150km road south to Sekota (for Lalibela) usually takes around 4 hours in a private vehicle. Public transport to Mekele runs throughout the morning, and a few minibuses run back and forth daily from Freweyni (on the main road between Adigrat and Wukro) via Hawzen and Megab. The only reliable transport to/from Adwa is a daily bus leaving at 08.30 in either direction. Most of the surrounding rock-hewn churches are accessible only to travellers with private transport.

WHERE TO STAY

Mylomin Botanical Garden Lodge (6 rooms) 011 552 8900; m 0911 653534; e mylominlodge@gmail.com; w mylominlodge.com. This pleasant owner-managed lodge, set in spacious green grounds about 2km northwest of the bus station near the hospital, provides accommodation in well-equipped en-suite domed bamboo bungalows modelled rather incongruously on the traditional Gurage. The attached restaurant, also done in traditional Gurage style, serves a fair variety of local dishes in the US$3–4 range. *From US$30 dbl.* **$$$**

Ras Alula Hotel (20 rooms) 034 446 0621. Situated on the outskirts of town opposite the hospital about 1km along the Adwa road, this unexpectedly comfortable 3-storey hotel is the next best option offering decent rooms with en-suite hot shower & a ¾ bed. *US$8.* **$**

Gidey Abaya Pension Centrally located opposite the more prominently signposted Millennium Café, this small owner-managed hotel has clean en suites with a hot shower. *US$5 dbl.* **$**

WHERE TO EAT AND DRINK
A few good and uniformly inexpensive local eateries are dotted around the town centre. Try **Birhan's Café** opposite the CBE for egg sandwiches and salads, **Azeb's** opposite the bus station for *tibs* or fasting food, or the **Aklil Restaurant** 2km west of the main road for delicious *shiro tagatino*.

WHAT TO SEE AND DO
Mylomin Botanical Garden [322 D5] Affiliated with the lodge of the same name, but rather confusingly situated at the opposite end of town, this small private botanical garden lies in the lush riparian forest fed by a natural spring on the north bank of the Tankwa River about 1.5km east of the bus station. Its Tigrigna name literally translates as 'Lemon Water' and it refers to a yellow-spotted snakelike deity once believed to live in the spring water. The garden is a pleasant spot for a beer or coffee, and you can take an outdoor shower in the spring water. More adventurously, you can cross the river and climb up an impressive rocky gorge on the opposite side to visit Sekarta Maryam, a nunnery with rock-hewn cells situated next to the more modern church of Sekarta Mikael. A rather convoluted local legend has it that Sekarta stands on the site of an old pagan shrine dedicated to the aforementioned snakelike deity, which was born to the same mother as the Queen of Sheba 3,000 years ago, and could communicate with nobody else.

Abba Yohanni [322 D5] (*Entrance US$6*) The remote rock-hewn monastery of Abba Yohanni has a fantastic setting midway up a tall golden sandstone cliff on the southwestern face of Debre Ansa Mountain 15km north of Abiy Addi. The façade, partially built after the original rock collapsed during excavation, is visible for miles and very photogenic in afternoon light. The main church is reached via an atmospheric labyrinth of tunnels and nooks, incorporating the desanctified rock-hewn church of Kidane Mihret and opening on to a series of ledges offering great views to the plains below. The rock-hewn church itself is very large, consisting of four domed bays standing up to 9m high and 14 carved columns, and is named after its founder, Abba Yohanni, who is believed to have excavated it in the 14th century. Women are forbidden from entering the main church but may wander through the tunnel complex that leads up to it. To reach Abba Yohanni from Abiy Addi, follow the Adwa road north for 8km, then turn left at the signpost for the Merere Renewable Power Project. After roughly 7km, you should park at the village of Menji, from where it's an easy 10–15-minute walk from the road to the monastery. There is no public transport.

Gebriel Wukien [322 D5] (*Entrance US$6*) The most accessible of the Tembien churches, Gebriel Wukien lies within easy walking distance of the main road between Abiy Addi and Adwa. It appears to be a subterranean monolith, sunk within an excavated trench in a manner similar to several churches at Lalibela, although it is difficult to be sure because of the 20th-century stone roofing and mortar walls that cover and enclose the trench. Ruth Plant regarded Gebriel Wukien to be 'undoubtedly the most remarkable church' of the 15 she visited in the Tembien, and thought the quality of the carving of the four bays and several arches to be comparable to Adi Kesho Medhane Alem. Carved into a cliff behind the church are several monastic cells, as well as a kitchen and eating room. David Buxton placed Gebriel Wukien in the later series of Tigrayan Basilica churches, which ties in with a tradition that it was excavated during the 15th-century reign of Emperor Zara Yaqob. Undermining this rare instance of apparent academic and traditional concord, the local priests reckon that the church was actually excavated by Abba Daniel during the 6th-century reign of Emperor Gebre Meskel, and the only link with Zara Yaqob is the altar cloth he gifted it. Purported relics of the church's earliest days include the tomb of Abba Daniel, a magnificent gold-plated diamond cross that once belonged to him, and the cloth paintings on the main door.

To reach Gebriel Wukien from Abiy Addi, follow the main Adwa road north for 16km. About 2.5km before you reach Workamba, turn left along a side road signposted for the church, then left again after 1.5km. Another 1km further, you will reach a stand of fig trees and a water pump, where you can park your car in the shade. From the water pump, a footpath leads to the church which, despite its proximity to the road, is very well hidden in a thicket of euphorbia and other scrubs. The walk takes no more than 10 minutes, and the gradient is among the gentlest of any approach to a rock-hewn church in Tigray.

Maryam Hibeti [322 D5] (*Entrance US$6*) David Buxton regarded the little-visited and indisputably lovely church of Maryam Hibeti (Hidden Mary) to be a 15th-century replica of Adi Kesho Medhane Alem. The interior, though large, is gloomy and unadorned, dominated by six arched columns, and a natural pool of therapeutic holy water immediately inside the main door. The well-lit and partially sunken cloister, by contrast, is atmospherically earthy because of the lack of adornment, and very photogenic. The church is aptly named, as it lies in a wooded enclave on the side of a gorge, and is invisible until you come within metres of the imposing façade. To get to Maryam Hibeti from Abiy Addi, follow the Adwa road north for roughly 18km to the small town of Workamba (literally 'Gold Mountain'). Turn right at Workamba for 4km until you reach another small village dominated by a war memorial. Turn left at the fork immediately past this village, following an occasionally unclear 4x4 track along a fertile plain for about 10km to the sizeable village of Adeha, where you can park your car and look for the priest. It takes about an hour to walk out there, following a rough footpath that doesn't involve any serious clambering except along the short final ascent to the actual church. The area is relatively low-lying and hot, so take some water.

Emanuel Maibaha [322 D5] (*Entrance US$6*) Situated on the slopes of Mount Zala, the rock-hewn church of Emanuel Maibaha, where the Emperor Yohannes IV was reputedly baptised, is hidden within a prominent whitewashed built-up exterior alongside the old road between Abiy Addi and Hagere Selam. It has a 9m-wide and 10m-deep interior with four large supporting pillars, and a cross on the domed ceiling. To get there, follow the old Hagere Selam road out of Abiy Addi for 22km and look out for the bold white exterior. It is not accessible from the new road from Abiy Addi to Mekele via Hagere Selam.

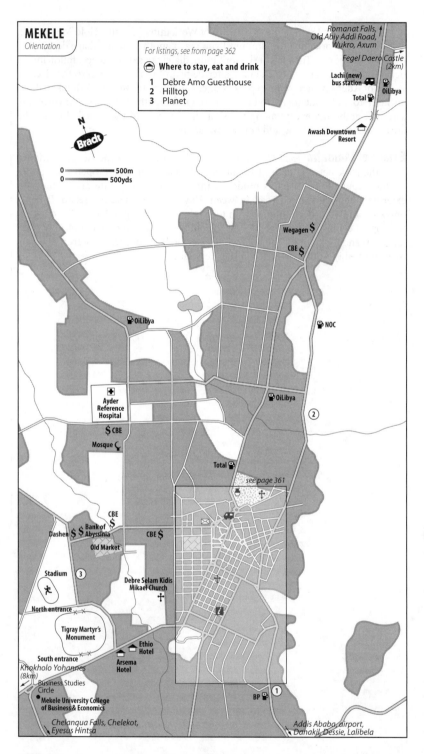

MEKELE
Orientation

For listings, see from page 362

🛏 **Where to stay, eat and drink**
1 Debre Amo Guesthouse
2 Hilltop
3 Planet

Romanat Falls,
Old Abiy Addi Road,
Wukro, Axum

Fegel Daero Castle
(2km)

Lachi (new)
bus station

OiLibya

Total

Awash Downtown
Resort

N
Bradt

0 ——— 500m
0 ——— 500yds

Wegagen $

CBE $

OiLibya

NOC

OiLibya

②

Ayder
Reference
Hospital

$ CBE

Mosque

Total

see page 361

✝

CBE

Dashen $ Bank of
Abyssinia

$ CBE $

Old Market

Stadium

③

Debre Selam Kidis
Mikael Church ✝

✝

North entrance

Tigray Martyr's
Monument

ℹ

South entrance

Khokholo Yohannes
(8km)

Business Studies
Circle

Mekele University College
of Business & Economics

Ethio
Hotel

Arsema
Hotel

BP ①

Chelanqua Falls, Chelekot,
Eyesus Hintsa

Addis Ababa, airport,
Danakil, Dessie, Lalibela

10

Mekele and the Danakil

The Danakil Desert, set in the remote far north of the vast and thinly populated Afar Federal Region, is rapidly emerging from past obscurity to be one of the most popular tourist attractions anywhere in Ethiopia. A searingly hot and forbidding volcanic landscape that dips to more than 100m below sea level, it is renowned as the home of the world's oldest lava lake, nestled within the caldera of Erta Ale, while other attractions include the otherworldly hot springs at Dallol, and salt-caked Lake Asale. The most popular base for trips into the Danakil is Mekele, a large and well-equipped town that serves as capital of Tigray and the main gateway to the northeast of the region (and the rock-hewn churches covered in the previous chapter), but holds little of compelling interest to travellers. The other lesser-used gateway to Danakil is southern Afar, whose main settlements include the characterful former regional capital Asaita, set on a rise overlooking the Awash River, and its somewhat more soulless modern counterpart Semera.

MEKELE

Sprawling across a hill-ringed basin at an altitude of roughly 2,200m, Mekele (also spelt Maqale), the former imperial seat of Yohannes IV and modern regional capital of Tigray, is a large energetic city whose contradictions seem to encapsulate 21st-century Ethiopia. In the city centre, modern high-rises tower flashily above rows of humble stone homesteads, while neatly suited, cell-phone-clasping businessmen hurry past rural Tigrayans ambling easily towards the market. Yet, paradoxically, Mekele is also possessed of a sense of cohesion unusual for urban Ethiopia: clean, orderly, vibrant, neatly laid out, overwhelmingly Tigrayan, largely unaffected by tourism, and refreshingly free of chanting children and self-appointed guides. True, the city boasts few compelling tourist attractions, but it has a great selection of affordable accommodation, while the plethora of restaurants, bars and cafés that line the cobbled roads of Kebele 16 (page 363) make it an attractive place to rest up between bus trips. The town still contains several buildings dating to the time of Emperor Yohannes IV, most notably his stone palace, which is now a museum, and the churches of Tekle Haymanot, Medhane Alem and Kidane Mihret, all built in the 1870s. Lost to modernisation, however, is Mekele's legendary open market, which once served as the urban terminus of an age-old salt caravan route from the Danakil, but now feels more like a low-rent mall comprising four soulless medium-rise blocks on the western verge of the city centre.

HISTORY Mekele is of limited historical importance by comparison with many smaller Tigrayan towns. Unlike Adwa, or even Wukro and Hawzen, it doesn't appear on early maps of the area, nor is it referred to in any document written before the 1830s. The modern city owes its pre-eminence to Emperor Yohannes IV (reigned 1871–89), who believed he had been conceived in the area, and treated it as his de facto capital. During the early years of his reign, when he was based at Tewodros's former capital Debre Tabor, Yohannes IV founded a number of churches in Mekele. He relocated to Mekele in 1881, and the palace he constructed there over 1882–84, now a museum, served as the main imperial residence during the latter part of his reign. Mekele has served as the capital of Tigray ever since, but even as recently as 1970 it was a rustic small town with a population of fewer than 20,000, described by Paul Henze as 'a scattered town which, in spite of its solid stone houses, has a chronically unfinished look' and 'small, even in comparison to most Ethiopian provincial capitals' but also 'lively and developing rapidly'. Today, those last four words seem positively prophetic. Indeed, while Mekele didn't feature among Ethiopia's ten largest towns in the 1984 census, it is now one of the country's three largest cities, thanks largely to its favoured status with the (predominantly Tigrayan) EPRDF government. Estimates of Mekele's population vary wildly, but most probably it stands at around 600,000.

GETTING THERE AND AWAY
By air Ethiopian Airlines flies several times daily between Mekele and Addis Ababa. It also operates a few flights weekly connecting Mekele directly to Axum and Lalibela. It is usually possible to fly between Mekele and Bahir Dar or Gondar in one day routing through Addis Ababa. The recently upgraded airport lies about 5km from the city centre. Taxis are available. The Ethiopian Airlines office [361 C1] is on the main roundabout opposite the museum.

By rail A 567km railway line connecting Awash (on the recently opened line between Addis Ababa and Dire Dawa) to Mekele via Kombolcha and Weldiya was under construction in 2018. When it will start operation is anybody's guess.

By road There are two bus stations. The older and more central station [361 D2], on Iyasu Berhe Road about 500m south of Lucy Park, services most longer-haul destinations to the south, including Addis Ababa, Dessie and Weldiya. The newer Lachi station [map, page 358], 5km north of the city centre and connected to it by regular minibuses, services most of the more local destinations in Tigray. The Selam Bus to Addis Ababa leaves from Lucy Park outside the Seti Hotel.

To/from Addis Ababa and the south Mekele lies 775km from Addis Ababa along an asphalt road through Debre Berhan, Dessie and Weldiya. It is feasible, with a very early start, to drive between the two cities in one day, but preferable perhaps to break things up with an overnight stop en route. Using public transport, Selam Bus [361 B1] (\ 034 441 8853), Abay Bus [361 B2] (m 0904 747474) and Falcon Coach [361 B1] (m 0969 404040) all operate comfortable daily coach services between Mekele and Addis Ababa (around US$20; 14–15hrs), leaving from in front of their various booking offices close to Yohannes Circle [361 C1] at 05.00. Standard buses to Weldiya (5–6hrs), Dessie (8–10hrs) and Addis Ababa (at least 15hrs with a possible overnight stop) leave daily from the old bus station, usually before 06.30.

To/from Lalibela There are five possible routes, as detailed on page 396. It can easily be done in a day in a private 4x4, but there is a risk of having to break it up over two if using public transport via Weldiya.

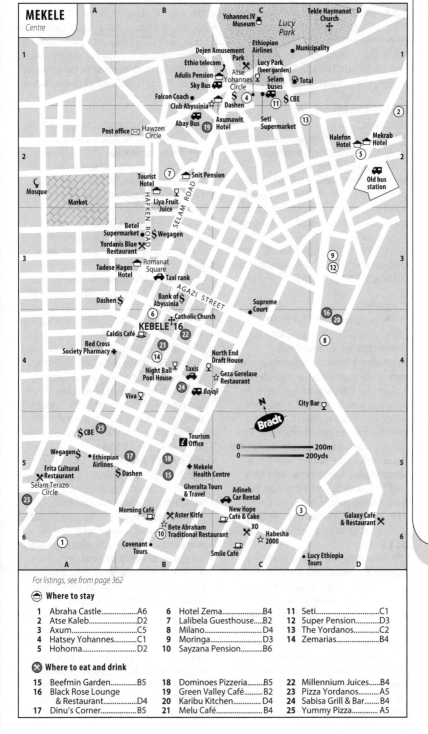

For listings, see from page 362

⌂ Where to stay

1	Abraha Castle	A6	6	Hotel Zema	B4
2	Atse Kaleb	D2	7	Lalibela Guesthouse	B2
3	Axum	C5	8	Milano	D4
4	Hatsey Yohannes	C1	9	Moringa	D3
5	Hohoma	D2	10	Sayzana Pension	B6

11	Seti	C1
12	Super Pension	D3
13	The Yordanos	C2
14	Zemarias	B4

✖ Where to eat and drink

15	Beefmin Garden	B5
16	Black Rose Lounge & Restaurant	D4
17	Dinu's Corner	B5

18	Dominoes Pizzeria	B5
19	Green Valley Café	B2
20	Karibu Kitchen	D4
21	Melu Café	B4

22	Millennium Juices	B4
23	Pizza Yordanos	A5
24	Sabisa Grill & Bar	B4
25	Yummy Pizza	A5

Elsewhere in Tigray Buses and minibuses to Wukro, Hawzen, Abiy Addi, Adigrat and many other destinations in northeast Tigray leave from Lachi bus station throughout the day. All these routes take under 2½ hours. A few buses daily cover the 250km road to Axum (*US$5; 4–6hrs*) usually leaving in the morning. You could also use the Selam Bus from Addis Ababa to Shire Inda Selassie, which overnights in Mekele and passes through Wukro, Adigrat and Axum the next day.

WHERE TO STAY

Upmarket

Planet Hotel [map, page 358] (80 rooms) 034 440 5660; e reservation@ planetinternationalhotel.com; w planetinternationalhotel.com. Situated 1km west of the city centre, Mekele's smartest hotel is a 9-storey, 4-star monolith offering blandly comfortable motel-style rooms with flatscreen TV, safe, minibar & an array of toiletries. Amenities include a large swimming pool, business centre, spa & restaurant. *US$80/120 dbl/twin, US$140– 200 suite. All rates B&B.* $$$$

Moderate

✳ **Zemarias Hotel** [361 B4] (36 rooms) 034 240 6000; m 0930 469091/2; e reservations@zemariashotel.com; w zemariashotel.com. Currently the best value moderate-to-upmarket option in Mekele, this 7-storey hotel in the heart of lively Kebele 16 has large & attractive rooms with wooden floor, writing desk, large flatscreen TV, sitting area, coffee/tea & small but modern bathroom. King-size rooms have a jacuzzi/tub. All water is treated (ask to check out the elaborate ground-floor treatment plant) & amenities include a lift, a good 1st-floor restaurant serving varied local & international mains in the US$5–6 range, & a 7th-floor lounge offering views over the city. *US$50/55/90 dbl/dbl/king-size. Suites from US$105.* $$$$

Debre Amo Guesthouse [map, page 358] (13 rooms) 034 440 0251; m 0914 300881; e debreamo6@gmail.com; w debreamoguesthouse.com. Sometimes confused with the grungier Debre Damo Hotel on the opposite side of town, this friendly owner-managed guesthouse, set alongside the airport road within walking distance of the city centre, has spotless & brightly decorated rooms with private bathrooms (not all en suite). Every floor has a communal lounge. Rates include an excellent freshly cooked b/fast. Recommended. *US$40 sgl,*

US$60/80 sgl/dbl occupancy of a king-size, US$150 family with 2 bedrooms & lounge. $$$$

The Yordanos Hotel [361 C2] (27 rooms) 034 441 3722; e yordares@yahoo.com. This small hotel situated a block south of Lucy Park has stylish & spacious rooms with wooden floor, dark-wood furniture, modern art on the walls, phone, flatscreen TV & fridge. Service could be snappier & some rooms are due some maintenance. The restaurant, however, serving pasta dishes & grills in the US$3–4 range, rates very highly, & has a cosmopolitan wine list. Rates include airport shuttle. *US$40/45/50 sgl/twin/dbl B&B.* $$$$

Axum Hotel [361 C5] (120 rooms) 034 440 5155/7; e axum.d@ethionet.com; w axum-hotels.com. This central landmark offers the choice of large carpeted rooms with a stale 1970s feel in the older building, or plush suites with separate sitting room & bathtub in a newer annex. All rooms have phone, TV & en-suite hot shower. Some are wheelchair accessible. Rates include free airport shuttle & gym use. *US$58/70 dbl/twin; suites from US$76. All rates B&B.* $$$$

Hatsey Yohannes Hotel [361 C1] (32 rooms) 034 440 6760/2; m 0914 310937; e info@hatseyyohanneshotel.com; w hatseyyohanneshotel.com. Formerly a perennial budget favourite, this recently renovated medium-rise opposite Lucy Park has clean en-suite rooms with flatscreen TV, private balcony & hot shower. The lively patio bar on the 1st floor is a great place to socialise over beers & snacks. Overpriced at the current inflated *faranji* prices. *US$40/53/58 B&B sgl/dbl/trpl.* $$$$

Budget

✳ **Hotel Zema** [361 B4] (16 rooms) 034 241 8485; m 0930 371270. This excellent new medium-rise stands in the heart of bustling Kebele 16 & the spacious clean en-suite rooms come with flatscreen TV, wardrobe, hot shower & in some cases balcony. A pleasant ground-floor café with terrace seating is attached. Excellent value. *US$12/14 sgl/dbl.* **$$**

🏠 **Lalibela Guesthouse** [361 B2] (12 rooms) 📞034 440 1522; **m** 0914 707105. This smart & affordable 4-storey hotel, set in central backstreets lined with gold/silversmiths, has clean en-suite rooms with hot water, sat TV, fridge & modern furnishing. *US$12 dbl.* **$$**

🏠 **Hilltop Hotel** [map, page 358] (32 rooms) 📞034 440 5684. Perched on a suburban rise about 1km northeast of the town centre, this rustic hotel stands in charming gardens whose potentially attractive view is ruined by the factories that loom in the foreground. The semi-detached en-suite rooms are comfortable & clean, albeit a touch frayed at the seams, & come with fridge, sat TV & hot bath. Rooms vary in standard, so look before you take one. The restaurant serves decent meals & has a pleasant terrace. *From US$10/16 sgl/dbl.* **$$**

🏠 **Moringa Hotel** [361 D3] (12 rooms) **m** 0914 684980. This modern hotel close to the old bus station has comfortable en-suite rooms with sat TV & hot shower. *US$15 dbl.* **$$**

🏠 **Milano Hotel** [361 D4] (100 rooms) **m** 0914 704997. Home to the most prominent operator of tours to the Danakil & possessed of a genuinely imposing façade & quaintly attractive reception area, this hotel is a deceptively tempting prospect until you see the down-at-heel en-suite rooms, which evoke the torpor of a gone-to-seed Ethiopian government hotel back in the mid 1990s. Overpriced. *US$16/18/24 sgl/dbl/twin.* **$$**

🏠 **Abraha Castle Hotel** [361 A6] (30 rooms) 📞034 440 6555–7. Set in a 19th-century castle built by a local nobleman, this prominent local landmark was converted into a hotel by a grandson of Yohannes IV in the 1960s. It scores highly on character & has an attractive garden setting overlooking the town centre, but the en-suite

rooms are musty & rundown. Abject value at the elevated *faranji* price. *US$30 dbl.* **$$$**

Shoestring

🏠 **Sayzana Pension** [361 B6] (20 rooms) 📞034 441 9670; **m** 0914 314169. Home to Covenant Tours' Mekele office, this outstanding cheapie has spotless & comfortable rooms with TV & hot shower set around a quiet courtyard, & is ideally located for exploring the eateries & bars of Kebele 16. *US$10 dbl.* **$**

🏠 **Hohoma Hotel** [361 D2] (20 rooms) 📞034 2409138. Arguably the pick of several cheapies dotted around the old bus station (if only because it's far enough from the main road to be relatively quiet), this has adequately clean but slightly tired-looking rooms with TV & hot shower. *US$4/10 dbl with common/en-suite shower.* **$**

🏠 **Super Pension** [361 D3] (16 rooms) **m** 0914 762200. Small but comfortable en-suite rooms at a relatively quiet location near the bus station. Decent value. *US$8/10 dbl with cold/hot shower.* **$–$$**

🏠 **Atse Kaleb Hotel** [361 D2] (57 rooms) 📞034 441 5255. This popular cheapie close to the old bus station has clean unpretentious rooms with the choice of en-suite hot or common cold shower. The ground-floor restaurant serves pasta & local dishes for under US$2. *US$4 dbl with common shower, US$8/10 en-suite sgl/dbl.* **$–$$**

🏠 **Seti Hotel** [361 C1] (50 rooms) 📞034 441 0909; **m** 0930 001680. This long-standing hotel has a useful location next to the Selam Bus departure point, but the cavernous rooms are seriously rundown (& have cold water only), while the dimly lit ground-floor restaurant looks no less seedy once your eyes adjust to the dark. Still, decent value at the asking price. *US$4 dbl using common shower, US$6/9/12 en-suite sgl/dbl/twin.* **$**

✕ WHERE TO EAT AND DRINK

Mekele's lively culinary and nightlife scene is centred on the prosaically named Kebele 16, a grid of cobbled alleys running southeast from Alula and southwest from Agazi Street. The area is home to perhaps 100 small bars, cafés, coffee shops, garden bars selling draught beer, and pool houses, as well as some of the city's best restaurants, so you won't have to follow your nose for long to find somewhere that suits your requirements.

Restaurants

✳ ✕ **Karibu Kitchen** [361 D4] 📞034 440 2788; **m** 0914 198387; ⏱ 07.00–midnight daily.

Recently relocated to a well-tended & thickly wooded garden behind the Milano Hotel, this relaxed venue is rated highly for pizza (made in a proper wood oven), but also has a varied selection of pasta dishes, grills & burgers. *Mains around US$5.*

✳ ✖ **Black Rose Lounge & Restaurant** [361 D4] m 0911 513894; e blackrosehiwet@gmail.com; ⊕ 15.00–midnight Mon–Sat. Stylish traditionally decorated Ethiopian restaurant set in large gardens & offering indoor or terrace seating. Good cocktail menu. Tasty Ethiopian dishes (supplemented by burgers, pizza & pasta) in the US$3–4 range.

✳ ✖ **Pizza Yordanos** [361 A5] m 0939 664193; ⊕ 11.00–23.00 daily. Classier than its name suggests, this long-serving Italian & continental restaurant at the southern end of Alula Road has a great atmosphere, with pleasant courtyard seating & a stylish interior whose terracotta tiles & red-&-white tablecloths create a slightly Mediterranean feel. Ice cream & fruit salad are available. Tue & Thu are classical music & candlelight nights. *Mains around US$4.*

✖ **Sabisa Grill & Bar** [361 B4] m 0914 000004; ⊕ 08.00–22.00 daily. The open kitchen at this relaxed semi-outdoor venue concocts a varied selection of pizzas, grills, burgers, pasta & local dishes. Whole roast chicken, feeding 2–3 people for US$14, is the speciality. *Other mains US$3–5.*

✖ **Beefmin Garden** [361 B5] m 0913 211320; ⊕ 08.00–22.00 daily. Smart, modern outdoor restaurant close to the Axum Hotel & particularly strong on grills, curries, pizza, pasta & Ethiopian fare. *Mains US$3–5.*

✖ **Yummy Pizza** [361 A5] m 0917 722155; ⊕ 08.00–22.00 daily. Boasting modern warehouse-like décor, this place specialises in pizza (*US$3–5*), but also has a long list of sandwiches, grills, pasta & local dishes (*US$2–4*).

✖ **Dominoes Pizzeria** [361 B5] This pleasant garden bar in Kebele 16 has pool tables, cheap draught beer, Wi-Fi & tasty pizzas. *Mains around US$3.*

Cafés & juice bars

🍵 **Dinu's Corner** [361 B5] ⊕ 08.00–21.00 daily. Popular for its fast free Wi-Fi as much as the excellent coffee & good cake selection, this attractive café with terrace seating also serves pizzas & a varied selection of other mains in the US$3–5 range.

🍵 **Millennium Juices** [361 B4] Indoor & terrace seating, & a great selection of juices (including a bumper *spris*) for less than US$1.

🍵 **Green Valley Café** [361 B2] ⊕ 09.00–21.00 daily. Popular with a youngish crowd, this deli a block south of Lucy Park has a good b/fast selection, burgers & pizzas, as well as inexpensive coffee, juices, milkshakes & cakes. No alcohol. Terrace seating available. *Mains mostly US$2–4.*

🍵 **Melu Café** [361 B4] Modern café serving a full range of coffees & delicious cakes in the heart of Kebele 16.

NIGHTLIFE

☆ **Geza Gerelase Restaurant** [361 C4] ⊕ 10.30–midnight daily. This cavernous *tukul* restaurant is the most reliable venue in Mekele for live Ethiopian music & dancing, which starts at 19.00 daily.

☆ **Habesha 2000** [361 C6] m 0914 745964; ⊕ noon–23.00 daily. Excellent live Ethiopian

music, with performances starting at 19.00 daily, opposite the Axum Hotel. Also serves excellent *tibs* for around US$3.50 per plate.

♀ **Viva** [361 B4] This bright & comfortable sports bar is a good place to watch international football over a chilled draught beer.

SHOPPING Those stocking up for a visit to Gheralta or the Danakil will find the Betel Supermarket [361 B3] on Hakfen Street and Seti Supermarket [361 C1] opposite Lucy Park to be well stocked with biscuits, tinned foods, wine and other imported goods. Mekele is also a great place to buy traditional dresses, and an unusually high number of dressmakers line the streets around the Alula/Selam roundabout.

TOURIST INFORMATION The organised and helpful Tigray Tourism Office [361 B5] (✆ 034 440 0131; ⊕ 08.00–noon & 14.00–18.00 daily) recently relocated to a building opposite the Mekele Health Centre.

TOUR OPERATORS Mekele is now entrenched as the main start and end point for tours to the Danakil, which can be arranged through the companies listed below, as well as a number of small operators based close to the Axum Hotel. All operators recommended below also offer organised tours to the Gheralta churches and other sites in Tigray.

Covenant Tours [361 B6] Sayzana Pension; m 0913 709926, 0932 343193; e covenanttoursethiopia@gmail.com; w covenantethiopia.com. This owner-managed nationally licensed operator arranges all-inclusive 3-day/2-night private tours to Dallol & Erta Ale for US$2,100/party of 1–5 people (with 2 4x4s) or US$2,400 for 6–10 (with 3 cars). It now offers daily departures to the Danakil on group tours at US$400 pp, with a max group size of 10. Also a good contact for exploring the rock-hewn churches of northeast Tigray, where it works closely with Gheralta Lodge.

Ethio Travel and Tours [361 D4] Milano Hotel; m 0914 027893; e ethiopiatravel@gmail.com;

w ethiotravelandtours.com. The pioneer of daily departures to Danakil, ETT runs 2 all-inclusive itineraries: a 3-day/2-night package to Dallol & Erta Ale & a 4-day/3-night package that also takes in Lake Afrera. These work out US$150–175 pp/day. There are no limits on numbers, so in peak season you might find yourself travelling with up to 50 other people, some of whom might actually be clients of other Mekele-based operators trying to cut costs.

Lucy Ethiopia Tours [361 C6] Opposite Axum Hotel; m 0913 550959; e info@lucyethiopiatours.com; w lucyethiopiatours.com. Among the more reliable of a few small budget operators scattered opposite the Axum Hotel.

WHAT TO SEE AND DO

Yohannes IV Museum [361 C1] (⊕ 08.00–11.30 & 13.30–17.00 daily exc Mon & Fri; entrance US$4) Recently reopened in the wake of a major rehabilitation, the Italian-designed stone palace built for Emperor Yohannes IV in the 1870s now serves as a museum dedicated to its founder. It was described by the British envoy Francis Harrison Smith, who visited Mekele in 1886, as 'like an old-fashioned English church', and it remains an architecturally impressive building. The interior is cluttered with some rather esoteric displays of royal paraphernalia, while the roof offers a great view over town (one that Yohannes IV, phobic about climbing stairs, may never have enjoyed personally). Photography forbidden.

Tigray Martyr's Monument [map, page 358] (⊕ 08.00–17.30 daily; entrance US$2) A prominent hilltop landmark about 1km west of the city centre, the Tigray Martyr's Monument was built on the tenth anniversary of the 1991 overthrow of the Derg in commemoration of the many members of the Tigrayan People's Liberation Front (TPLF) who sacrificed their lives in the civil war. The main monument comprises a massive tower with four supporting prongs at its base and a large globe balanced on top, as well as several statues and reliefs depicting scenes from the war. A short walk away is a superb museum that displays hundreds of (mostly black-and-white) photographs taken from the early 1970s to the early 1990s, many captioned in English, as well as an assortment of paraphernalia including original TPLF battle plans, weapons and radio equipment. Particularly poignant is a wall hung with sepia or monochrome photographs of many of the individual martyrs, male and female, who were killed by the Derg.

Fegel Daero Castle [323 G6] Situated about 7km northeast of the city centre, this disused stone castle was built in the late 19th or early 20th century by Dejach Abraha, the same nobleman responsible for constructing what is now the Abraha Castle Hotel. A two-storey building with stairs leading up to the roof, it is still in good condition, despite having been abandoned for as long as anybody can remember, but the unlocked interior has a rather feral smell, as if livestock dens there, and locals believe

10

it is inhabited by bad spirits. The castle lies about 2km east of the northbound feeder road to the main Adigrat road, and can be reached by turning right into an industrial area some 300m north of Lachi bus station, passing a nursery to your right after about 500m, then continuing along a flat dirt road through cultivated fields towards the village of Fegel Daero. Using public transport, plenty of minibuses run from the city centre to Lachi bus station, from where you could walk in about 30 minutes.

Chelekot [map, page 358]

For much of the 19th century, Chelekot (aka Celicut), set on a green hill 17km south of Mekele, was a far more important settlement than the modern regional capital. Starting in the 1790s, it served as the court of Ras Wolde Selassie, a Tigrayan prince who asserted himself as probably the most powerful regional ruler in Ethiopia at a time when the imperial court at Gondar had little influence beyond its immediate vicinity. A staunch supporter of Solomonic rule, Wolde Selassie was notable among other things for having been served as aide by Nathaniel Pearce, a young Englishman who found his way to the Tigrayan court in 1810, married an Ethiopian woman, and stayed on there for three years after the Ras's death. Henry Salt, the first European to write about the Ethiopian interior since James Bruce's day, visited the court of Wolde Selassie in 1805 and 1810. Even after the death of Ras Wolde Selassie in 1816, Chelekot remained a large and important settlement, with a population estimated at 3,000 living in well-constructed houses when Ferret and Galiner passed through in the 1840s and described it as 'one of the principal towns' of Ethiopia.

The main point of interest in what is now a tiny village is Chelekot Selassie (*entrance US$6*), an architecturally impressive example of the circular *tukul* style of churches built between Salt's visits. The church interior is adorned with beautiful 19th-century paintings, and it houses several treasures dating to the rule of Wolde Selassie. Public transport to Chelekot is limited to one or two minibuses daily, leaving Mekele from the livestock market, but it's a recommended excursion if you have your own vehicle, ideally with high clearance.

Chelanqua Falls [map, page 358]

This tall, narrow waterfall on the Chelanqua (aka Chele Anka) River tumbles for around 60m into a gorge 8km southwest of Mekele, and is particularly dramatic during the rainy season. The waterfall is located about 1.5km from Debir, itself a rather interesting and picturesque village of traditional Tigrayan stone houses. To get there, follow the main road west of Mekele, past the Martyr's Memorial and the College of Business and Economics, and as you reach the outskirts of town follow the tracks south asking for Debir. Once at the village, anybody will lead you to a viewpoint over the gorge and waterfall next to the attractive old church of Debir Maryam. A steep footpath leads from the lip of the gorge to the base of the waterfall, where there is a pool said by locals to be safe for swimming. There is no public transport to Debir, nor would the track be passable in an ordinary saloon car, so the best way to get there is in a private 4x4 or by horse-drawn *gari*.

Romanat Falls [323 F5]

This attractive waterfall on the Katima River, 10km northwest of Mekele as the crow flies, is not as spectacular as its counterpart at Chelanqua, but it is quite a bit more accessible. The river falls in two stages, with the tallest being around 15m high, and there is a pretty pool at the base where you can swim in the startlingly clear water. A deeper pool lies at the base of the second smaller waterfall, which can be reached by walking across some striking rock formations. The easiest way to get there at the time of writing is to follow the feeder road to Adigrat north out of town for 3km past the Lachi bus station, then turn left on to the Abiy Addi road and follow it west for about 12km, past the Messebo cement factory, to the village of Romanat. Just past Romanat, turn left on to a rougher track that brings you to the church of Romanat Mikael after 1.8km. From here, a steep path leads downhill through tangled vegetation, bringing you out at the waterfall after 15 minutes. There are minibuses from Mekele to Romanat. A new road connects the Ayder Hospital northwest of the city centre directly to the Abiy Addi road less than 5km from Romanat.

Khokholo Yohannes [323 F6] Situated about 8km west of Mekele, Khokholo Yohannes is a partially excavated cliff church that incorporates a grotto reputedly hewn into the pumice in the 6th century by a monk called Abune Abraham. The church contains holy water fed by four springs and some lovely paintings that must be at least 200 years old. To get there, head out to the College of Business and Economics and continue west across the roundabout, forking to the right after 500m, then left after 1.5km, then right after about 200m, until you reach the village of Sarawat after another 1.3km. This traditional Tigrayan village flanks the road for about 1km. About 1.5km after exiting Sarawat, you need to fork right, and you will reach the parking spot after another 1.1km. From here, it's only about 500m on foot to the church and grotto, but it is very steep in parts, and some serious clambering is required. Try to visit early in the morning, when the priest with the key is most likely to be around.

Eyesus Hintsa [323 E7] This recently rediscovered rock-hewn church 60km southwest of Mekele has been refurbished with the assistance of the UK-based Eyesus Hintsa Trust. Carved out of sandstone, most likely during the 14th century, Eyesus Hintsa is impressive for both its size and its unique design. The façade features five large round windows reminiscent of the portholes of a modern ship. The interior is elaborately carved in the style of Axumite architecture, with six massive stone pillars topped by arches and a large domed ceiling. Much of the interior was originally covered in frescoes, but tradition holds that these were destroyed by Ahmed Gragn. Recent improvements include solar-powered lighting. A nearby museum houses church antiquities, and a second rock-hewn church, dedicated to Mikael, is built into a nearby limestone cave. The entire site is situated in a scenic river valley teeming with birds and wildlife.

Eyesus Hintsa makes for an excellent day trip out of Mekele. Camping is permitted should you want to stay longer, and a few simple huts are available too. To get there, first head southwest from Mekele to the remote village of Gijet, a 2-hour drive on reasonably good dirt roads. From Gijet, it is another 4km to the church, but the road is poor, so either you need a 4x4 or you could walk. The best time to visit unannounced is right after the morning service, usually 06.00–08.00, or after the evening service at 17.00. At other times you will probably need to locate the priest with the key while you are in Gijet. Better yet, contact the Tigray Tourist Commission a day in advance and they will call ahead so that the priest can be made available. A US$4 entrance fee is charged, and the priest will certainly want a tip. The booklet *Eyesus Hintsa: An Ethiopian Journey through Landscape and Time* by Louise Schofield is available at the on-site museum.

DANAKIL

Straddling the Eritrean border to the east of the Tigrayan highlands, the Danakil, or Dallol, is an area of true desert that extends across the most northerly and volcanically active portion of the Afar Depression. It ranks among the lowest-lying

THE AFAR TRIANGLE

A vast depression that lies at the juncture of the African, Arabian and Somali tectonic plates, the Afar Triangle lies primarily within Ethiopia but also extends across much of Eritrea and Djibouti. Stretching for 600km along its north–south axis, and up to 300km wide, this arid, low-lying region is bounded by the northern Ethiopian Highlands to the west, by the eastern highlands around Harar to the south, and by the Red Sea and Gulf of Aden to the northeast. In tectonic terms, it can be viewed both as a southerly terrestrial extension of the rifting process that formed the Red Sea, and as the northernmost terrestrial section of the Great Rift Valley, with its focal point being the so-called Afar Triple Junction, the point where all three plates meet, at Lake Abbe on the border of Ethiopia and Djibouti.

Although the entire Afar Depression is hot, arid and low-lying by comparison with the highlands to its west and south, conditions are least extreme in the southwest, between Awash National Park and Gewane, where it has a base elevation of around 1,000m (with three isolated volcanic peaks rising to above 2,000m) and receives around 600mm of rainfall annually. The central part of the depression, in the vicinity of Semera, Asaita and the Djibouti border, is much lower lying, with altitudes below 500m, and correspondingly hotter and drier. Further north, the depression reaches its frazzled nadir in the practically unpopulated Danakil Depression, most of which lies below sea level, dipping to an Ethiopian low of –116m at Dallol (outdone in Africa only by Djibouti's Lake Assal, at –155m). The potash mine at Dallol is also ranked as the hottest inhabited place on earth, with an average daily maximum of 41.1°C and an annual rainfall of less than 150mm making it a true desert.

Afar's dominant aquatic feature is the 1,200km Awash River, which rises at Fugnan Bote (The Nostrils) in the Ethiopian Highlands about 50km west of Addis Ababa, then arcs southward past Melka Kunture and Mount Zikwala before changing course to flow in a broad northeasterly direction through the artificial Lake Koka. East of Adama, the river flows along the southern border of Awash National Park, then runs northeast via the recently built Awash Dam near Semera, then on to Asaita, where it feeds an extensive irrigation system. Southeast of Asaita, the Awash finally concedes defeat to the desert, flowing through a series of shallow natural lakes before finally being soaked up by Lake Abbe, a vast and bitterly saline sump set at the meeting point of the three plates that form the Afar Triangle. Awash reputedly translates from Oromifa as 'the beast that consumes everything in its path', a rather harsh assessment of a river that can truly be described as life-sustaining for most of its considerable length.

places anywhere in the planet, dropping to 116m below sea level, while temperatures on the shadeless plains frequently soar above 50°C, and are exacerbated by a fierce gale known as the Gara (Fire Wind). This climatic inhospitality is mirrored by the reputation of the region's nomadic Afar inhabitants (see box, page 370), who traditionally eked out an income as salt miners and traders, transporting their wares by camelback to the Tigrayan highlands. As recently as the 1930s, the Afar of the Danakil were known to greet male strangers by lopping off their testicles. Today, while scrotal intactness is no longer a cause for concern, the desert-hardened Afar are unmatched when it comes to making life difficult for travellers and guides who don't bow to their frequent and inventive demands for fees and tips. This, in short, is a challenging travel destination.

The Afar Triangle is among the planet's most tectonically active areas. More than 30 active or dormant volcanoes – roughly one-quarter of the African total – are shared between the Ethiopian and Eritrean components of the Danakil, following a series of fault-lines running in a north to northwesterly direction. These volcanoes are all geological infants, having formed over the past million years, and a great many took their present shape within the last 10,000 years. The most substantial volcanic range in the Afar Triangle is the so-called Danakil Alps, whose highest peak is Eritrea's 2,219m-high Mount Nabro, 8km northeast of the Ethiopian border. On 13 June 2011, Nabro erupted unexpectedly and violently, killing 31 people and ejecting a 15km-high ash plume that caused major disruption to air traffic. Back in Ethiopia, Erta Ale is one of Africa's most active volcanoes, having hosted a permanent lava flow at least since the late 19th century. Other notable volcanoes include Borale (812m) and Afrera (1,295m), both of which rise in magnificent isolation from the sunken shoreline of Lake Afrera, and the more westerly Alayita, a vast massif that rises to 1,501m and last erupted in 1901 and 1915.

The Afar Triangle has experienced many climatic changes over the past few millennia. On several occasions, most recently about 30,000 years ago, large tracts of low-lying land have been flooded by the Red Sea, whose waters left behind the thick salt deposits that characterise the region after they evaporated – a process pre-empting the probable submersion of the entire region when the three plates drift far enough apart, probably around 10 million years from now. In the meantime, lakes Asale and Afrera, and various other relicts of this periodic flooding, lie at the centre of an ancient salt-extraction industry linking the somewhat restricted economy of Afar to the more naturally bountiful Tigrayan highlands to its west.

By contrast, around five million years ago, much of western Afar stood at altitudes of greater than 1,000m, supporting a moist climate and relatively lush cover of grassland and forest in which our early hominids thrived. Several of the world's most significant hominid fossils have been unearthed in Afar. The best known of these is 'Lucy', which was discovered and nicknamed by Donald Johanson at Hadar in 1974 (page 382). More recently, an Ethiopian graduate student, Yohannes Haile-Selassie, found the 5.5-million-year-old fossils of a bipedal creature whose combination of ape-like and hominid features suggests it might well represent the so-called 'missing link' in the divergent evolutionary paths of modern chimpanzees and humans.

For all that, the Danakil is an area of singular geological fascination: a strange and at times beguilingly beautiful desert landscape studded with austere volcanic calderas, explosive cauldrons of bubbling red lava, malodorous sulphur-caked hot springs, recently solidified black lava flows, and vast, blinding salt flats that stretch for up to a kilometre below the surface. Until ten years ago, the Danakil was also firmly off the beaten track, attracting a couple of hundred visitors annually, but it has started to take off in recent years, not least due to the publicity it was afforded by the 2009 BBC documentary *The Hottest Place on Earth*, and up to 100 travellers might now overnight on Erta Ale on any given night in the high season. This growing popularity, coupled by a vast improvement in roads servicing the region, has made the Danakil far more accessible than it was a few years back. At the same time, the net worth of the ever-mutating plethora of fees charged by the local Afar has increased exponentially, making it near impossible to visit without an experienced Ethiopian guide who knows the area well and has a good relationship with the local authorities, pathfinders and militia.

WHEN TO VISIT The best time to visit is the relatively cool three-month period running from December to February, when average maximum daytime temperatures peak at 36°C and nights drop to around 25°C. November and March are also relatively temperate, at least by Danakil standards. Avoid May to August, when average maximum daytime temperatures top 45°C and nights seldom dip below 30°C. April, September and October are also hotter than average.

SECURITY The Danakil is a volatile region due to its inherent lawlessness coupled with its proximity to the disputed Eritrean border. The most recent incident involving a foreigner occurred in December 2017 when a German tourist was shot dead, and an Ethiopian guide travelling with him fatally injured, on the slopes of

---

THE AFAR

The Afar (or Danakil) regard themselves as the oldest of Ethiopia's ethnic groups, having occupied their inhospitably arid homeland to the east of the Ethiopian Highlands for at least 2,000 years. The Afar have a history of trade with the highlanders that stretches back to the early Axumite period, and possibly before that. Until modern times, Afar country effectively served as Ethiopia's mint, producing the *amoles* (salt bars) that served as currency in the highlands – the Portuguese priest Francisco Álvares recorded that in the early 16th century three or four *amoles* was enough to buy a good slave! Extracted from a number of salt pans scattered around the Afar Depression, the salt bars still form a major item of trade for the Afar people, who transport them on camelback to Tigray along the ancient caravan routes.

Traditionally, the Afar are nomadic pastoralists, living in light, flimsy houses made of palm fronds and matting, which they transport from one location to the next on camelback. Recent decades have seen a trend towards urbanisation, as well as an increased dependence on agriculture in the fertile and well-watered area around Asaita. Nevertheless, the nomadic lifestyle is still widely practised away from the towns, and visitors to the region will often see Afar men driving their precious camel herds along the roadside. The Afar men have a reputation for ferocity and xenophobia – as recently as the 1930s, it was still customary to kill male intruders to the area, and lop off their testicles as a trophy.

By comparison with the highlanders, Afar people tend to be very tall and dark. The women have intricate frizzed and braided hairstyles, and wear long brown skirts, brightly coloured bead necklaces, heavy earrings and brass anklets. The men often wear their hair in a thick Afro style similar to that described in an account by a 14th-century visitor from the highlands. They dress in a light cotton toga, which is draped over one shoulder. Traditionally, Afar men rarely venture far without the curved 40cm dagger they sling around their waist in a long, thin leather pouch. These days, the traditional knife may be supplemented or replaced by a rifle slung casually over the shoulder. Both weapons are frequently put to fatal use in disputes between rival clans.

Arabic sources indicate that, despite Afar's ancient trade links with the Christian highlands, Islam was widely practised in the region as early as the 13th century. In

Erta Ale. Other incidents occurred in 2012, when gunmen attacked a tour group at Erta Ale, killing five tourists on the spot (two more were injured and two more kidnapped along with a local driver and police escort), in 2007, when a group including British Embassy staff from Addis Ababa was taken hostage and released a week later, and in 2004, when a French tourist disappeared without trace. Despite this chequered history, the Danakil was attracting more tourist traffic in 2017 than ever before, and a step up in security following the 2017 incident ensured tours were travelling as normal in early 2018. Nevertheless, the British Foreign and Commonwealth Office (FCO) has advised against all travel to the region for a number of years, as has the US State Department, and it would be irresponsible to pretend that exploring Danakil, and Erta Ale in particular, isn't somewhat riskier than visiting more stable parts of Ethiopia.

PREPARATIONS As things stand, the minimum time needed to see Dallol and Erta Ale is three days and two nights, but an extra day will allow for greater flexibility. This is one part of Ethiopia where independent travel is a pretty unrealistic option,

1577, the Sultan of Harar relocated his capital to a town called Aussa (more or less where Asaita stands today). This move initially sparked some resistance among the surrounding Afar nomads, but it did much to consolidate the Islamic influence in the area, especially as the sultan's army and the Afar were frequently united in battle against the invading Oromo. In 1734, the Sultanate of Aussa fell under the rule of an Afar leader called Kedafu, founder of the Mudaito Dynasty, which has survived into the 21st century.

The tenth and longest-serving Mudaito Sultan of Aussa, Ras Alimirah Hanfare, took the reins in 1944 after bloodlessly ousting his uncle and predecessor Muhammad Yayyo, whom he regarded to be an Italian collaborator. A committed imperialist and ally of Haile Selassie, Alimirah went into exile in Saudi Arabia in 1975, after the Derg confiscated his land in the aftermath of a bloody battle in which the military killed an estimated 1,000 of his subjects. In 1991, following the overthrow of the Derg, Alimirah returned to Ethiopia, and worked closely with the EPRDF towards the creation of a new federal model of government. Unfortunately, relations between the two soured in 1993 over the question of whether Afar territory within the provincial borders of Eritrea should be handed over to the newly independent country or, as the sultan insisted, be integrated into the Afar Federal Region of Ethiopia. Tensions racked up higher after the federal election of May 1995, wherein the EPRDF-affiliated Afar People's Democratic Organisation and Alimirah's Afar Liberation Front each won three of the region's eight seats. The impasse was effectively resolved six months later, when government troops attacked Alimirah's residence in Asaita, overpowered his guards, and confiscated all his weapons and many other items. Alimirah went back into exile for several years, but returned to Asaita in 2001 following negotiations with the EPRDF. By this time, the octogenarian sultan had become rather marginalised in political terms, but he remained a highly respected figure among the Afar, and with many other Ethiopians, due to his patriotic resistance to the Derg and support for Ethiopian unity. The tenth sultan's eventful reign, which spanned two-thirds of a century, ended in April 2011, when he died at his residence in Asaita, aged 95, to be succeeded by his similarly named son Hanfare Alimirah.

and even those with their own 4x4 transport should think in terms of hiring a knowledgeable guide and taking a back-up vehicle and driver, if only to carry the required local guides and scouts you'll need to pick up along the way. However you visit, your party should also be self-sufficient in food and water (bank on a minimum of five litres of drinking water each per day, and carry enough excess in jerrycans to last a few days extra) and will need to take some camping and cooking gear, since accommodation is limited to basic shelters and no firewood is available. Be aware that guides and scouts should theoretically bring all their own food and water, but in practice they seldom do, preferring to scavenge from friends along the way – or, failing that, from their clients!

Maps and further information A must for anybody thinking about a self-drive trip into the Danakil is Luca Lupi's superb map *Afar Region Dancalia*, which can be ordered through his website, w dancalia.it. This website is also an excellent source of information about the region, but most of it is in Italian only.

ACCESS AND ORIENTATION There are two springboards for expeditions to the Danakil. The first and more southerly is Semera, the capital of Afar Region, which lies along the surfaced road between Awash and Djibouti, and also houses the Culture and Tourism Bureau that issues permits for the Danakil. Far more popular these days, however, is Mekele, which has better amenities than Semera, including several specialist tour companies. Both Semera and Mekele are connected to Addis Ababa by good asphalt roads, as well as by daily Ethiopian Airlines flights, so all else being equal, the ideal option would be to use one as a starting point and the other as the end point. Logistically, however, the more convenient option for many travellers is to visit the Danakil as a round trip from Mekele, treating it as an add-on to more extended time on the northern highlands' well-travelled historical circuit.

Mekele and Semera are now connected by a surfaced 350km road through Abala, Erapti, Afrera and Serdo. In a private vehicle, this can easily be covered in one day. Selam Bus also now runs a daily coach service between Mekele and Semera, leaving at 05.30 in either direction, and there are usually a couple of other buses too. No permit is required simply to travel along this main road, and it offers easy access to Lake Afrera, one of the three main highlights of the Danakil. Hamed Ela, the springboard village for Dallol, is also now accessible from Mekele on asphalt, and work has also started on a new surfaced road to the base of Erta Ale. For the meantime, however, both Dallol and Erta Ale are accessible by 4x4 only, and the most direct route between them, nicknamed 'The Crossing', is a rough and confusing piste that requires not only a 4x4 but also a driver who knows the region well.

Organised tours Budget group trips out of Mekele start at US$150–200 per person per day, depending on duration and group size, and can be arranged through several operators, including Ethio Travel and Tours (ETT) (page 365), whose three-day/two-night and four-day/three-night group tours to Danakil now leave daily, and Covenant Tours, which focuses more on bespoke departures. For tours out of Addis Ababa, driving or flying via Semera and/or Mekele, you could approach almost any of the operators listed on page 364, but GETTS is highly recommended for its experienced guides and good cooks, and for offering extras such as a portable toilet and showers, while Ethiopian Quadrants is a good bet for film crews, for visits to more remote sites, or for anything else out of the ordinary. No reputable tour companies are based in Semera.

Permits All visitors to the Danakil, including those travelling from Mekele, require a written permit from the Afar National Regional State's Culture and Tourism Bureau in Semera (page 381). This can be processed in advance by faxing an application through, then following up by phone. The permit fee (inclusive of visits to Dallol, Erta Ale and Afrera) is US$15 per person. If you go on an organised tour, your operator should deal with this bureaucracy on your behalf.

Other fees A variety of official, semi-official and all-but-fabricated fees are levied from visitors to the Danakil. Below, we have listed those fees of which we are aware (all payable in Ethiopian birr), but the Afar are notorious for increasing prices at whim, as well as for inventing new fees, so this may change at any time. The fees listed below are usually included in the cost of an organised tour, but do check this up front. Travellers who try to settle fees themselves, or who take a guide without some experience of Afar negotiation, are in for an expensive and/ or argumentative time!

- Entrance fee/co-ordinator fee at Berahile: US$12 per party
- Local guide fee from Berahile: US$12 per day per vehicle, plus US$30 per trip return transportation
- Policemen fee from Berahile: US$10–12 per day per vehicle, plus US$30 per trip return transportation (at least two policemen are required)
- Dallol local guide fee: US$12 per day per vehicle
- Dallol militia fee: US$10 per militia (minimum four required)
- Dallol co-ordinator fee: US$12
- Erta Ale 'elder' fee (paid to the local chief at Kusawad): US$55 per party
- Erta Ale militia fee: US$40 per party
- Erta Ale camel fee (for transporting camping gear to the top): US$25 per camel
- Erta Ale local/road guide: US$23
- Camping at Ahmed Ela or Erta Ale: US$10 per person per night

WHAT TO SEE AND DO The three main highlights of the Danakil, running from north to south, are the multihued hot springs field at Dallol, the lava lake in Erta Ale volcano, and the salt-encrusted Lake Afrera. Also covered below is Berahile, a relatively large settlement where Dallol-bound travellers coming from Mekele are required to pick up a local guide and two policemen before continuing further north, and the seldom visited Gada Ale and Catherina volcanoes south of Lake Asale.

Berahile The gateway to Danakil coming from Mekele, the small but ancient town of Berahile, set part way down the escarpment at an altitude of 730m, used to be a major stop along the salt caravan route to the highlands, with an estimated one million camels passing through annually. Now serviced by a good road from Mekele, it is more of a terminus than a waypoint, since most caravans coming from the Asale region unload their wares for storage here, before it is taken by truck to the highlands. Still, with its combination of typically Tigrayan stone houses and more austere Afar huts, it is an agreeable point of transition between the highlands and the desert, and all tour groups coming from Mekele need to stop here to show their permit to the relevant authority, and pick up a mandatory local guide and police escort.

Getting there and away Berahile lies about 125km from Mekele, a 2-hour drive on a good surfaced road. From Mekele, follow the southern feeder road past the university to the main road for Addis Ababa, then continue south along it for 8km before turning east on to the surfaced Semera road at the conspicuous Ashengoda wind farm. About 25km along the Semera road, you reach Abala, where you need to branch left and then just keep straight on for about 85km. Note that if you are coming directly from the Gheralta region, it is far quicker to cut east at Agula, some 10km south of Wukro, from where it is only about 80km to Berahile. At least one bus daily runs in either direction between Mekele and Berahile, but your only option for heading deeper into the Danakil from there would be to join a salt caravan bound for Asale.

🏠 **Where to stay, eat and drink** There is no formal accommodation in Berahile, but you should be able to make a plan to camp or to sleep in a local family compound. A few restaurants serve basic local food and cold soft drinks, and there is one bar that serves beer.

Dallol and surrounds Situated in the far north of the Danakil only 15km from the Eritrean border, Dallol is a broad flat-sloped maar that rises inconspicuously no more than 60m above the surrounding salt flats, which are dotted with the world's lowest-lying volcanic vents, standing at around 50m below sea level. The maar formed in 1926 as a result of phreatomagmatic activity, which occurs when emergent magma comes into contact with standing water, causing it to evaporate almost instantaneously in an explosive plume of steam and rock. The area remains geologically volatile: a fresh magma intrusion occurred in 2004 when the shallow magma chamber beneath Dallol deflated, while some local Afar reported seeing an ash plume flare above over the crater in January 2015.

The main attraction of Dallol, indeed a highlight of any expedition to the Danakil, is the surreal multihued fairyland of sulphurous geysers that stands in the centre of the explosion crater, overlooked by a basaltic volcanic outcrop known as the Black Mountain. Here, transparent pools of steaming briny water are studded with conical vents and other crystalline formations, whose frosty shades of green, yellow, orange, red and white – the product of ionised sulphur and potash deposits – make it look as though the whole place has been scattered with dyed icing sugar. It's a strange but exceptionally beautiful phenomenon, especially in the early morning and late afternoon when the light is fantastic and the temperature not too unbearable.

Dallol volcano protrudes from the eastern side of a 1,200km² area of windswept salt-encrusted flats whose cracked surface is supposedly haunted at night by a *jinn* (evil spirit) called Abo Lalu. Known as Asale, these salt flats were once a bay in the Red Sea, and today they dip to an altitudinal low of −116m along the shore of Lake Asale (also known as Lake Karum), the hyper-saline 50km² water body at their southern extreme. The salt of Asale, said to be more than 1km thick in parts, has been mined by the local Afar for millennia, and still is today, though the activity tends to move location from one season to the next. If you can locate the current salt-extraction site, you'll most likely come across hundreds of Afar cameleers chipping at the crust to extract neat rectangular bars. Each 30x40cm tablet weighs about 6.5kg, and the camels that transport them out to Berahile can carry up to 30 bars. The value of a bar increases tenfold between its source in Asale and arriving in the Tigrayan highlands.

Getting there and away The springboard for visits to Dallol and Asale is Hamed Ela (or Ahmed Ela), a very small and equally scruffy village situated at around 30m below sea level 20km to the south of the maar. Hamed Ela is connected to Berahile by a good surfaced 45km road that can be covered in less than 1 hour (so you're talking around 3 hours in total from Mekele). By contrast, the 70km drive south to Kusawad (for Erta Ale) is still very rough and sandy, takes at least 3 hours, and should be attempted only with a local pathfinder. Before leaving Hamed Ela for Asale and Dallol, you'll need to pick up a local guide and two militia at the police station. Allow 3 hours for the round trip from Hamed Ela to Dallol, stopping en route to watch salt caravans cross on the cracked white salt flats of Asale, to look for the shifting shore of the eponymous lake, and to marvel at the spectacular field of hot springs and associated natural rock sculptures about 3km from Dallol. To reach the multicoloured springs in Dallol, you need to park at the base of the volcano then walk for 15 minutes across its outer slope, a moderate ascent across some rough but geologically fascinating terrain.

Where to stay, eat and drink You'll almost certainly spend one night, possibly two, at Hamed Ela. It's a hot, dirty place with no proper hotels or restaurants, but most tour companies rent out one of several local compounds set up for the purpose, and make camp there, sleeping under the stars on simple matting. A few shops sell lukewarm soft drinks and a few other basics, and you can wander 500m out of town to the bar at the military camp for a cold beer or two. There are no proper toilet facilities; some tour companies bring a portable loo, failing which you'll just have to wander a few hundred metres out of town to do your ablutions.

Volcanoes between Dallol and Erta Ale
The rough and sometimes indistinguishable piste track running between Hamed Ela and Kusawad runs roughly parallel to a string of little-known volcanic peaks. About 15km south of Hamed Ela, 287m-high Gada Ale is a prominent and rather active stratovolcano,

POTASH IN DALLOL

Dallol contains one of the world's few surface deposits of potash (potassium salt), which is carried up from its subterranean source by hot springs in the vicinity of Black Mountain at an annual rate of several thousand tonnes. Commercial mining of this resource, used in the making of fertilisers, dates back to World War I, when the Italian colonisers of neighbouring Eritrea constructed a light gauge railway to within 30km of Dallol, and used it to transport around 50,000 tonnes of potash annually from the base of the Black Mountain to their Red Sea ports. Extraction ceased at the end of the war, but resumed intermittently in the late 1920s, and only stopped completely when the British dismantled the railway towards the end of World War II. In the 1950s, a US company called Parsons was granted a potash concession at the site, and established a temporary base made entirely of salt block whose ruins can still be seen below the Black Mountain today. More than 300 exploratory holes were drilled, leading to the discovery of several new potash sites, including the 80-million-tonne Musley deposit only 5km from Dallol, but operations were suspended indefinitely in 1967 after several workers drowned in a flooded shaft. Since the overthrow of the Derg, concessions have been awarded to a Norwegian company and an Indian company, but neither ever mined the area actively, partly due to its political instability. This seems set to change in the near future, however, following the signing of a fresh 20-year mining lease with the Norwegian fertiliser company Yara International in 2017.

whose caldera hosts a boiling hot sulphur and mud lake. About 7km further south, Mount Catherina, whose eastern rim overlooks the remote Lake Bakili, is an astonishing 120m-high tuff ring, composed entirely of volcanic ash, enclosing a 500m-wide crater wherein a small saline lake is fed by thermal springs. Another 15km to the south are three peaks that form the northerly part of the Erta Ale range: the 429m Allu (a relatively active volcano that last erupted in 2008), 613m Dalafilla and 668m Borale Ale.

Erta Ale One of Ethiopia's most singular and physically challenging natural attractions, the 613m-high Erta Ale (literally 'Smoking Mountain') is an active shield volcano whose basaltic caldera holds the oldest of the world's six semi-permanent lava lakes, along with a second pit crater that contained a temporary lava lake in 1968 and 1973. Most spectacular (and photogenic) at dusk and at dawn, the 750m^2 ellipsoid lava lake, enclosed by a crumbling black rim, is an utterly spectacular, once-in-a-lifetime sight, a bubbling cauldron of black magma porridge whose shifting crust repeatedly cracks open to reveal contours of glowing red molten rock. It is also a rather terrifying Hadean phenomenon, regularly belching out nostril-peeling waves of ammoniac gas, while violent fountains of molten rock plume upwards, occasionally reaching above the side of the crater to splatter emphatically on the crusty rim. Anywhere else, this primal and treacherous hellhole, boiling at temperatures in excess of 1,100°C, would be enclosed by a 10m-deep perimeter fence, and tourist visits would be regulated by a litany of safety rules. Here, in the remote wastes of the Danakil, Erta Ale just stands as it is – the proverbial accident waiting to happen.

Scientists think Erta Ale must have a continuous link to a shallow magma chamber, which is fed on a regular basis by magma associated with the formation of the Rift. The lava is usually soft, and easily flows more than 20km from its source, which is why the Erta Ale Massif is far less steep-sided than most active volcanoes. Significant changes in activity were noted at Erta Ale over 2004–05, including high levels of degassing, fissure eruptions on the northern flank, and a fresh breach on the southern crater that caused the lava to overflow its terrace and rise up to within 20m of the main crater rim. In early 2017, a new fissure appeared on the volcano's far flank, together with half a dozen small lava lakes, draining the main lake, which dried up completely for a few months. The main lake had partially refilled by the end of 2017, and though it is not as close to the rim as it had been a year earlier, it remains a phenomenal apparition as of early 2018, throwing up a far larger head of steam than it has in the past.

Getting there and away The first mandatory port of call en route to Erta Ale is the village of Kusawad, where you need to obtain permission from and pay a fee to the local chief, pick up a local pathfinder and military escort, and arrange however many camels you require. Kusawad lies about 2 hours' drive from Afrera, following the surfaced road to Mekele for 30km then taking a rough piste track north, or 3 hours south on the piste from Hamed Ela. A local guide is mandatory. Once you've completed your business at Kusawad, it's only 25km to El Dom, the village at the base of both Erta Ale and the 1,031m Mount Alebagu (the tallest point in the range), but the drive usually takes at least 2 hours due to the rocky terrain (though this will change once the access road is asphalted).

From El Dom, it's a 9km hike or camelback trip to the crater rim, one that takes 2–4 hours depending on your fitness and whether you travel by day or by torchlight. No actual climbing is involved, and the slopes are generally quite gentle, but it's a tough hike all the same, due to the hard underfoot conditions, blistering heat and lack of shade. Many tour operators encourage their clients to climb in the dark to avoid the worst of the heat, which might be a good idea in the hottest months, but also slows down the ascent and increases the risk of stumbling. At other times of year, we would recommend starting the hike at around 14.30–15.00, allowing fitter travellers to visit the lava lake just before dusk, and those less fit to do most of the hiking in natural night. Either way, you need solid shoes, sunblock and a hat, a torch and at least 2–3 litres of water for the ascent.

Where to stay, eat and drink The local Afar people have constructed a couple of dozen stone shelters on the caldera rim. You'll have to bring everything else with you, though, including bedding, food and water. Most people hire camels from the chief at Kusawad to carry all supplies up. Similar shelters are available at El Dom for those who opt to hike up as a day trip, or to spend a second night in the vicinity of the volcano.

Lake Afrera
The 115km² Lake Afrera (sometimes spelt Afreda) is a highly saline water body fed by the abundant thermal springs that rise on its northeast and southeast shores. It is also known as Lake Egogi or Giulietti, the latter in honour of Italian explorer Giuseppe Maria Giulietti, whose pioneering 1881 expedition to the Danakil was curtailed when his entire party was slaughtered by Afar tribesmen in present-day Eritrea. A pair of dormant volcanoes, the 812m Borale and 1,295m Afrera, rise above the eastern and southern shores of the lake, whose emerald-green surface lies at 103m below sea level, making its solitary island, rather aptly named Deset, the world's lowest-lying such landmass.

Lake Afrera is a stunning apparition, or would be were it not compromised by the untidy necklace of salt-extraction pools that clutter its shore. Unlike Lake Asale, where salt is extracted from a thick crust, most of the salt at Afrera is obtained by filling these shallow rectangular pools with the saline water, then waiting for it to evaporate. The largest cluster of these pools emanates from the small town of Afrera, a rather ramshackle settlement of makeshift corrugated iron, plastic, wood and matting buildings set on the lake's eastern shore alongside the main road between Semera and Mekele. The small town provides the easiest access to the lake, along a 2km road running east to a group of freshwater hot springs where you can swim for US$2 per person.

Getting there and away Afrera lies alongside the new surfaced road between Mekele and Semera around 125km from the former and 225km from Semera. Coming from Erta Ale, you need to return to the chief's village at Kusawad, then follow a rough piste track south for around 30km until you connect with the asphalt road from Mekele, then drive for another 30km in the direction of Semera. Afrera is the only one of Danakil's highlights that can be accessed on public transport since any bus between Mekele and Semera can drop you there. Indeed, it is possible to travel by local minibuses all the way between Semera and Mekele, changing vehicles at Afrera, Erapti and Abala, all three of which have shoestring accommodation (sleeping outside, which is quite pleasant in this hot dry climate) were you to get stuck overnight.

Where to stay, eat and drink Most organised tours visiting the lake set up camp at the lakeshore hot springs 2km from Afrera town. Several restaurants and bars line the main road through Afrera, serving basic Ethiopian food and lukewarm beers and soft drinks. A couple of shoestring lodges offer outdoor beds.

Seldom traversed by tourists, the excellent asphalt road that connects the ports of Djibouti (in the country of the same name) and Assab (Eritrea) to Awash (on the main road between Addis Ababa and Dire Dawa) is part of an important trucking route between the Red Sea and Addis Ababa. From the borders with Djibouti and Eritrea (the former bustling with activity, the latter closed since the late 1990s), the road runs southwest for about 500km, mimicking the course of the Awash River, but only occasionally coming within sight of it, until eventually it connects with the Dire Dawa road about 6km east of Awash National Park (page 450). The road passes through the heart of the harsh territory inhabited by the Afar (see box, page 370) who are frequently seen herding their camels along the road, or watering them at occasional isolated pools. Wildlife is more conspicuous than might be expected, most commonly Soemmerring's gazelle and Hamadryas baboon, as well as dry-country birds ranging from Egyptian vulture and various bulky bustards to a variety of nondescript larks and chats.

The largest town in the area is Asaita, which overlooks the Awash River 50km south of the Djibouti road, and has a population of around 30,000. Asaita served as federal capital of Afar Region until 2007, when it was superseded by Semera, which straddles the Djibouti road 8km from the junction for Asaita. Other relatively sizeable towns along the Assab road include Logiya, Mille and Gewane, none of which supports significantly more than 10,000 souls. The Djibouti road is of interest to tourists primarily as the main southern access route to the Danakil Depression, but it also provides access to the remote Yangudi Rassa National Park (and, further south, to Bilen-Hertale Controlled Hunting Area and Alledeghi Wildlife Reserve, both most easily visited in conjunction with Awash National Park; page 449).

Although the Djibouti road is an important trucking route, passenger transport is thin on the ground, and more or less confined to the main road, the side road to Asaita, and the road between Mille and Kombolcha (near Dessie). To see the region properly, you really need a private vehicle, and – if you plan on heading off-road – a back-up vehicle and knowledgeable guide or GPS. Coverage below runs from northeast to southwest, starting at Hayu and the Eli Dar Depression near the border with Djibouti and Eritrea, then running past Asaita through Serdo (the junction for the Danakil), Semera, Mille (the junction for Bati, Kombolcha and Dessie) and Gewane to Yangudi Rassa.

HAYU AND THE ELI DAR DEPRESSION Tiny Hayu (also known as Dichioto), the closest Ethiopian town to the Djibouti border, is a popular stopover with truck drivers. As a consequence, its main road, lined with brightly painted corrugated-iron buildings, has an unexpectedly shiftless and seedy atmosphere and an abundance of crappy hotels, all charging US$2–3 per bed irrespective of whether you take a small sweaty room or (more sensibly) follow the local custom of kipping outdoors. Past Hayu, the Djibouti road descends into the Eli Dar Depression, the only one of Afar's many salt lakes to be bisected by an asphalt road. The descent is rather spectacular, passing over evocatively barren rocky slopes with the lake shimmering off-white below. You may also see salt caravans travelling up the pass. At the base of the depression, Dobi amounts to little more than a tiny collection of rickety shacks that provide shelter from the searing heat and sell lukewarm soft drinks and beers. In a private vehicle, Eli Dar makes for an easy and worthwhile diversion coming to or from Asaita. For backpackers, any bus or truck heading to Djibouti can drop you at Dobi. An early start is recommended – it shouldn't be too difficult to find a lift back out, but there is no formal accommodation should you get stuck in Dobi overnight.

SERDO The 30km road from Hayu to Serdo traverses a bleakly scenic landscape dominated by ancient lava flows and bizarre volcanic outcrops. Soemmerring's gazelle, Hamadryas baboon and ostrich might all be seen, and the road also passes a few small lakes where Afar pastoralists bring their camels to water. Serdo, 40km northeast of Semera, was all but destroyed by a magnitude six earthquake in 1969, but it is of some logistical significance as it lies at the junction with the new asphalt road running north to Mekele via Lake Afrera and the Danakil.

ASAITA The most characterful town in Afar, Asaita (also spelt Aysaiyta) is set on a small rise above the palm-lined east bank of the Awash River some 50km southeast of the Djibouti road. Originally known as Aussa, Asaita has been settled at least since 1577, when Imam Muhammad Jasa of Harar relocated his capital there to found a polity that eventually morphed into the powerful Sultanate of Aussa. The seat of the Mudaito Dynasty from 1734 to the present day, Asaita also served as capital of the Afar Federal Region from 1995 until 2007, when it was replaced by the custom-built town of Semera, partly due to the latter's more convenient location but also, one suspects, to create a physical distance between the traditional seat of the sultan and the modern mechanisms of federal government. Supporting a population of around 25,000, Asaita today has a genuine end-of-the-road feel, and its isolation is underscored by the oppressive dusty heat so typical of Afar. It is also a very friendly and agreeable place, defiantly rustic and overwhelmingly Islamic in character, and a great place to get to meet the local Afar. Ideally, try to be there on Tuesday, when the main market is held. Further afield, Asaita is the gateway to a sequence of little-visited lakes fed by the Awash River as it flows towards the Djiboutian border.

Getting there and away The unsignposted but prominent junction for Asaita lies on the Djibouti road 10km east of Semera. From there it is 55km to Asaita along a well-maintained but narrow asphalt road, stretches of which follow an elevated causeway flanked by the seasonal floodplains of the Awash River and a few permanent pools that host plenty of birds and attract occasional troops of Hamadryas baboon. The drive takes about 1 hour. Several buses run back and forth between Logiya and Asaita daily, stopping at Semera and charging a fare of US$1.35.

Where to stay, eat and drink

Basha Amare Hotel (10 rooms) 033 555 0119; m 0933 805493. Situated about 200m south of the bus station, this long-serving budget hotel has a wonderful location overlooking the Awash River, as well as the best food in town (don't miss the local speciality called *hagabi*, a firm spicy *wat* made from powdered peas). There are a few rooms with a ¾ bed, fan & common shower, but

a far more pleasant option is to sleep outdoors on one of the mattresses & nets set up on the breezy balcony. *US$7.50 pp whether you sleep under a roof or indoors.* **$$**

Lem Hotel 033 555 0050. Situated on the main road coming into the town centre, this is a similar set-up to the above, but it lacks the view & is thus a clear second choice. **$$**

What to see and do

Around town Asaita is a friendly and pleasant town to wander around, its narrow roads lined with pastel-shaded shops and houses, many built in a distinctive local style with roofs extending forward from the front door to create a shaded patio supported by Y-shaped poles. Just south of the bus station, there's a striking mosque whose bulbous whitewashed minaret, adorned with two wooden balconies, recalls a traditional style associated more with Somaliland than Ethiopia. Only 100m west of the town centre, and connected to it by several footpaths, the palm-lined Awash River is flanked by cultivated fields fed by an extensive network of irrigation channels. Several traditional Afar villages lie within walking distance of town, but a visit to one of these is best undertaken with a local guide, which can be arranged through one of the hotels for US$10–15 per group.

Lakes south of Asaita Unusually, the Awash River doesn't empty into the ocean, but instead drains into a chain of six shallow lakes that lie along a tectonic fault-line running southeast towards the border with Djibouti. The most northerly of these lakes are 65km^2 Gummare and 35km^2 Afambo, beautiful freshwater bodies that support a lush fringing vegetation of woodland and reeds, as well as large numbers of crocodiles, hippos and water-associated birds. South of Afambo, the Awash flows between a trio of very small lakes before winding around the west flank of Mount Dama Ali, a dormant volcano whose stark and steep-sided caldera rises to 1,069m. Finally, the river disappears into the hyper-saline Lake Abbe, set in a harsh and otherworldly landscape of wide, barren salt pans and ragged chimney-like rock sculptures. Straddling the border with Djibouti and most easily visited from that side, the Abbe ranks among the most important waterbird sites in Ethiopia, attracting large numbers of Palaearctic migrants during the European winter, though a series of dams further upriver have caused the area of open water to shrink from around 340km^2 to 250km^2 in recent decades.

The only one of these lakes that can be visited with reasonable ease is Gummare, which lies at the base of the Rift Escarpment about 25km from Asaita. To get there in a private vehicle, drive 18km east out of Asaita to the village of Afambo, which comprises around 50 mud-and-thatch Afar homesteads, as well as a police station, where you will need to shell out around US$30 per party on a pathfinder and two armed escorts before proceeding any further. It's a 7km drive from Afambo village to the point where the Awash River flows out of Lake Gummare towards Lake Afambo, another 4km to the south, and accessible on foot only. Using public transport, a twice-daily bus service connects Asaita to Afambo village on weekdays only, leaving Asaita at 08.00 and 15.00 and returning at 11.00 and 17.00, which would give you plenty of time to arrange pathfinders and scouts in Afambo, walk out to Gummare, and still be back in time to pick up the last bus to Asaita.

Very few westerners have visited this area and fewer still have explored it as far as Lake Abbe from the Ethiopian side. Indeed, in 2001, when Peile Thompson undertook a hiking expedition through the region, supported by six camels to carry supplies and water, he followed several routes that hadn't been walked by a *faranji* since Wilfred Thesiger in the 1930s. The routes followed by Peile would be suitable only to experienced and well-prepared adventurers carrying sufficient water to last several days, but he kindly passed on details of a relatively straightforward round hike between Asaita and lakes Gummare and Afambo which could be undertaken over two (or better three) days without inordinate preparation. These are posted online at **w** bradtupdates.com/ethiopia/lakes.

LOGIYA AND SEMERA Situated 8km apart on the Djibouti road 50km northwest of Mille, the twin towns of Logiya and Semera provide something of a study in contrasts. Logiya, the older, larger and more organic of the two, has a bustling aura lacking from most other towns on the Djibouti road, which it sprawls along for perhaps 2km, close to one of the few points where the road skirts the Awash River. The newer, quieter and more contrived Semera, which took over as administrative capital of Afar Region in 2007, comprises a scattering of modern concrete blocks that seem bizarrely misplaced in their isolated desert setting, and though it has fleshed out slightly in recent years, it still feels like the brainchild of a malevolent town planner with a serious grudge against regional government officials and their families. About 5km southeast of Logiya, the earth-filled Awash Dam, built by the Indian government between 2010 and 2014 at a cost of US$600 million, has created a 60km² reservoir that will be used to irrigate the massive Tendaho sugar plantation, as well as a range of other crops, including onions and cotton, grown along the Awash River. The two towns make a convenient stopover between Addis Ababa and the Danakil, and if choose between them you must, you'll find Logiya to be better equipped when it comes to public transport and shoestring accommodation, while Semera has a few smarter hotels and a tourism bureau where you can arrange permits to visit more remote sites in Afar.

Tourist information The Afar National Regional State's Bureau of Culture and Tourism (℡ *033 666 0488;* f *033 666 0209/647;* ☉ *08.30–16.30 Mon–Fri*) stands opposite the CBE in Semera. All travellers heading into the Danakil must obtain a permit from this office, which is best arranged in advance (page 373).

Getting there and away
By air Ethiopian Airlines flies in both directions between Addis Ababa and Semera daily except for Tuesdays. This has made the town an increasingly popular alternative to Mekele as the springboard or end point of an expedition into the Danakil.

By road Semera lies about 600km from Addis Ababa along a surfaced road that could be covered in one day at a push, though a more agreeable option might be to overnight in the vicinity of Awash National Park or Bilen. Logiya is the main regional public transport hub, with several buses daily running back and forth to Dessie via Mille and Weldiya (*US$7; 8–10hrs*), as well as minibuses to/from Gewane. Inexpensive minibuses run back and forth between Logiya and Semera throughout the day, and there are also a few buses daily to Asaita.

Where to stay, eat and drink
Semera has the better accommodation options but they are uniformly overpriced, so budget-conscious travellers would be better off overnighting in Logiya.

Moderate
🏠 **Agda Hotel** (28 rooms) ℡033 666 0839. Set in huge wooded gardens along the Logiya road, this new hotel is comfortably the nicest in Semera, offering such amenities as a swimming pool, Wi-Fi & a bright restaurant/bar serving local & Western meals in the US$2–4 range, as well as cold beers (a scarcity in this Islamic town). The spacious en-suite rooms all come with AC, sat TV & hot water. *US$57.50/79/98.50 B&B 3rd/2nd/1st-class dbl.* **$$$$**

Budget
🏠 **Erta Ale Hotel** (21 rooms) ℡033 666 0323; m 0912 213532. This unsignposted multistorey hotel behind the OiLibya filling station has comfortable en-suite rooms, some with AC. The rooms seem quite basic at the inflated *faranji* price, but are better value if you can persuade them to offer you the local rate, which is about 40% cheaper. The restaurant serves inexpensive *ful* at b/fast time, & excellent roast goat for US$3, but the choice is otherwise more limited than the menu suggests, & no alcohol is served. *US$33/39/44 sgl/twin/dbl.* **$$$**

Lucy Hotel & Pension (20 rooms) m 0910 523394. Set around a large green courtyard 250m along the airport road, this pleasant little local lodging is the cheapest option in Semera although, like everything else in town, it feels overpriced for what you get. The clean rooms are all en suite & come with a fan, & there are also larger rooms with AC. There's no food, but it's only 5mins' walk from the restaurant at the Erta Ale Hotel, & the beers are cold. *US$10/21 dbl without/with AC.* **$$–$$$**

Shoestring

Nazareth Hotel (30 rooms) m 0911 965445. The best of a few cheapies in Logiya, this hotel above the CBE has a range of rooms, from a basic en-suite sgl with cold shower to a relatively smart dbl with hot water, TV & AC. You can also sleep outdoors under a net at its sister hotel (generally referred to as the Nazareth 2) about 1km further towards Addis Ababa. *US$4.25–12.50, or US$1.50 pp for a mattress & net.* **$–$$**

Other practicalities Both Logiya and Semera have a CBE, the last place where you can draw or change money before heading into the Danakil. The most reliable place to get online is the Agda Hotel, which has Wi-Fi. It also has a highly alluring swimming pool, which is open to day visitors for US$3 per person.

MILLE Set on the banks of the eponymous river roughly 150km north of Gewane, the small town of Mille is an important route focus, situated as it is on the junction of the Djibouti road and a new 175km asphalt road running northwest to Weldiya, and only about 1km north of the junction for the older and partially surfaced road running west to Bati, Kombolcha and Dessie. At least one **bus** daily connects Mille to Dessie and another to Weldiya, and there is also plenty of transport to Semera and Asaita. In a **private vehicle**, you're unlikely to spend longer in Mille than is required to refuel the car and grab a cold drink. Using public transport, you may well have to spend a night there between bus trips. At least half a dozen local **guesthouses**, charging US$3–4 for a basic room, are dotted around town – 'recommend' would be too strong a word, but the Central Hotel looks about the best of the bunch.

HADAR About 70km southwest of Mille by road, the formerly obscure and otherwise unremarkable patch of Ethiopian soil known as Hadar leapt to prominence in 1974 when Donald Johanson unearthed what was then the oldest hominid fossil ever discovered: the 3.4-million-year-old remains of a female, nicknamed Lucy, and assigned to a new species, *Australopithecus afarensis*. Hadar is the most famous of several similarly significant palaeontological sites in this part of Ethiopia, but – while the regional council does appear to have vague plans for future development – there is nothing much to see there and it isn't really geared up for tourists. To get there, follow the Bati road out of Mille for 40km to the village of Eli Wuha (literally 'Tortoise Water'), which hosts a busy traditional Afar daily market and has a few bars selling chilled drinks. Ask around, and you should have no difficulty locating a guide to take you to Hadar, which lies about 30km to the southeast. It is not clear whether a permit is still required to visit Hadar – either way, it's unlikely that there would be anybody present at the site to check.

GEWANE This somewhat unremarkable urban sprawl, situated around 150km north of Awash Saba, is distinguished only by the imposing presence of Mount Ayelu, an isolated volcanic peak that rises above the plains immediately east of the town to an altitude of 2,145m. Facilities include three filling stations, a couple of bars with chilled drinks (welcome in this climate) and a few basic hotels. If you need to spend a night, the hotel behind the Shell filling station looks about the best bet, charging US$4 for a clean room with a common shower. Should you be thinking of exploring Yangudi Rassa National Park beyond the main road, the park office is in Gewane. At least one bus daily runs between Awash Saba and Gewane, taking about 4 hours in either direction.

YANGUDI RASSA NATIONAL PARK Proposed in 1977 but never officially gazetted, this 5,400km² national park is named after Mount Yangudi, a dormant 1,383m-high volcano whose impressive caldera, extending over some 6km², lies about 20km east of Gewane, along with the surrounding Rassa Plains. It was originally set aside to protect what was thought to be the world's last population of the African wild ass, a critically endangered species ancestral to the domestic donkey, but this is reputedly now extinct within the park, though small numbers may survive in the adjacent Mille-Serdo Wild Ass Reserve, which extends over 8,766km² to the north. Either way, though the main road passes through both these areas, the odds of actually seeing a wild ass in transit are extremely slim, especially as feral populations of domestic donkeys are also found in the area and the two are difficult to tell apart. You'll improve your chances slightly – but not greatly – if you pick up a guide at the park office in Gewane, and leave the main road. Other wildlife includes beisa oryx, Soemmerring's and dorcas gazelle, gerenuk and possibly Grevy's zebra. A good selection of dry-country birds is resident – the Arabian bustard is a 'special' and ostriches are frequently observed – and the park lies along an important migration passage.

UPDATES WEBSITE

Go to w bradtupdates.com/ethiopia for the latest on-the-ground travel news, trip reports and factual updates. Keep up to date with the latest posts by following Philip on Twitter (🐦 @philipbriggs) and via Facebook (f pb.travel. updates). And, if you have any comments, queries, grumbles, insights, news or other feedback, you're invited to post them directly on the website, or to email them to Philip (e philip.briggs@bradtguides.com) for inclusion.

11

Lalibela and Surrounds

The most important tourist focus on the northern historic circuit, the small town of Lalibela stands high in the mountains of eastern Amhara, remote from the main asphalt road circuit that loops through Bahir Dar, Gondar, Axum, Mekele and Dessie. The town is best known for the atmospheric medieval complex of 13 rock-hewn churches and chapels carved into its physical and spiritual heart, but it also forms a great base for exploring a magnificent highland landscape studded with more isolated but equally ancient rock-hewn and built-up Axumite churches, while trekking options range from community hikes organised by Tesfa to the ascent of Ethiopia's third-highest peak, the 4,284m Abune Yoseph, which is home to the endemic gelada monkey and Ethiopian wolf. Owing to its remoteness, Lalibela is treated as a fly-in destination by the majority of tourists, and its out-of-town airport is serviced by daily flights from Addis Ababa and most other main centres in northern Ethiopia. That said, though it requires at least two days to get there overland from Addis Ababa, Lalibela can be accessed from elsewhere on the northern circuit along several different roads, the most important being the routes from Tigray via Wediya or Sekota, and the more southerly 'China Road' from the Lake Tana region of Western Amhara.

THROUGH ROUTES TO LALIBELA FROM TIGRAY AND WESTERN AMHARA

FROM BAHIR DAR/GONDAR VIA THE 'CHINA ROAD' So nicknamed because it was originally constructed by the Chinese in the 1970s, the 295km 'China Road', running eastward from Woreta to Weldiya, was for many years the best gravel road in Ethiopia and it is now asphalted in its entirety. The road is of some logistical significance as the main southern gateway to Lalibela, with the routes from Bahir Dar/Gondar in the west and Weldiya in the east converging at the junction town of Gashena, 65km south of Lalibela. Most Lalibela-bound travellers race along the China Road in a day, but it traverses some magnificent high-altitude terrain and provides access to several low-key points of interest, as detailed below starting in the west. Note that the fascinating weaving community at Awra Amba (page 263), though most often visited en route between Bahir Dar and Gondar, lies along a 2km dirt side road running south from the China Road only 8km east of Woreta.

Debre Tabor Set at an altitude of 2,600m in a well-watered valley framed by a hilly amphitheatre, Debre Tabor is a substantial town named after the peak immediately to its south, which is said to resemble the eponymous Galilean mountain associated with the transfiguration of Jesus. The town has an impressive historical pedigree that includes two short 19th-century stints as the imperial capital of Ethiopia. Although few travellers stop over there, Debre Tabor is a pleasant enough town, and there are a few sightseeing opportunities in the vicinity. These include the hilltop church of Debre Tabor Iyasus, which overlooks the town centre, a ruined former palace of Yohannes IV, the impressive but little-known rock-hewn church of Wukro Medhane Alem and the Afroalpine highlands of Mount Guna.

History Debre Tabor was founded in 1803 by Ras Gugsa Mursa, the Oromo ruler of Begemder, who reputedly chose the site after he discovered and killed a sleeping leopard there, fulfilling a prophecy made to him by a monk with regard to his future capital. At this time, Ras Gugsa was perhaps the most powerful man in the empire, and Debre Tabor soon vied with Gondar as Ethiopia's *ipso facto* capital. Ras Gugsa died of natural causes in 1825, but the town he founded continued to thrive under his nephew Ras Ali II, who became the ruler of Begemder in 1831 under the regency of his mother, Menen. Ras Ali was an early mentor of Kassa Hailu (the future emperor Tewodros II), who married his only daughter, Tewabech, in 1848 but defeated him in battle five years later, capturing both Debre Tabor and the rest of Begemder. Shortly after his 1855 coronation, Tewodros II relocated the imperial capital from Gondar to Debre Tabor, which grew to become one of the largest towns in Ethiopia, supporting up to 30,000 people during his reign.

In 1860, Tewodros II allowed Henry Stern of the London Society for Promoting Christianity Amongst the Jews to establish a Protestant mission at Gafat, 5km east of Debre Tabor. The mission's ostensible aim was to proselytise among the Beta Israel, but Tewodros II coerced Stern into allowing it to become a virtual munitions factory, manned by newly baptised Muslims and Jews captured during the emperor's various military campaigns. Gafat became associated with the most critical and bizarre episode in Tewodros II's reign, the hostage-taking of Stern and several other missionaries in an attempt to blackmail Queen Victoria into providing military support to his weakened regime. The captives were forced to manufacture a gigantic 6.8-tonne cannon, which the emperor dubbed Sebastopol (after a battle site in the Crimean War). In October 1867, when Tewodros II decided to abandon Debre Tabor for Makdala, taking with him all his hostages and the cumbersome Sebastopol, he burned most of the town centre to the ground. Nevertheless, Debre Tabor, or more accurately Gafat, would go on to serve as the *ipso facto* capital of Emperor Yohannes IV for ten years after his coronation in 1871, and it remained his primary residence even after he formally relocated his capital to Mekele in 1881.

More recently, between December 1989 and February 1990, the EPRDF thrice captured Debre Tabor, and twice surrendered it, over the course of several bloody battles in which many thousands of government troops died. In February 1991, Debre Tabor was the springboard from which the EPRDF launched Operation Tewodros, a two-week offensive that succeeded in driving the government out of the Gondar and Lake Tana regions, and that led to the overthrow of Mengistu within three months. The population stood at only 22,500 in the 1994 census, but it is now estimated at 200,000.

Getting there and away Debre Tabor lies along the China Road 42km east of Woreta, the junction with the main road between Bahir Dar and Gondar. Minibuses to and from Bahir Dar, Gondar and Gashena (for Lalibela) run throughout the day, and the fare to all these places is around US$3–3.50.

Where to stay, eat and drink

Hibret Hotel (28 rooms) 058 441 2017/1195; m 0942 331770; e hthotell@gmail. com, hibertshare@yahoo.com; f. The smartest option in Debre Tabor, this bright pink 3-storey hotel is located directly opposite the bus station & has comfortable but rather cluttered en-suite rooms with hot water, TV & Wi-Fi, as well as a good restaurant on the 1st floor. *US$14/18/20 sgl/twin/dbl.* **$$$**

Gafat Hotel (25 rooms) m 0918 350478; e gafatdebretabor@yahoo.com; w ethiopiahotelgafat.weebly.com. This pleasant & friendly hotel next to the bus station has compact, clean en-suite rooms with hot shower, free Wi-Fi & a great little restaurant & bar on the ground floor. *Very good value at US$6/9.50 sgl/dbl.* **$$**

What to see and do

Debre Tabor Medhane Alem This central church built by Emperor Tewodros II is the only substantial relic of his time in Debre Tabor, perhaps because he razed the rest of the town prior to abandoning it in 1867. It is of limited architectural interest, but the courtyard does contain a massive bell whose existence was first documented by visiting priests in 1879. The bell presumably dates from Tewodros's reign, but its origin is a mystery. Locals relate that it arrived in Ethiopia in 1844 as a gift from Pope Gregory XVI to Dejazmach Wube, only to be commandeered by Tewodros II after he defeated Wube at Darasge Maryam in 1855 and had himself crowned emperor. This cannot, however, be the case if, as seems likely, the purported papal gift to Dejazmach Wube is in fact the Roman bell that still hangs at Darasge Maryam today. Whatever the truth of the matter, the weighty bell has probably never actually hung at Debre Tabor (a tower built for that purpose during the Italian occupation was struck by lightning before it could be completed).

Debre Tabor Iyasus This hilltop church, set at an altitude of 2,850m overlooking the town centre, was reputedly established in the 13th century by monks from Jerusalem and is known to have existed during the early 16th-century reign of Lebna Dengal. The present building dates from the first decade of the 19th century and was built by Ras Gugsa, who is buried in the compound along with four of his successors. A magnificent circular construction, the church is enclosed by a large stone wall, and has a beautiful interior adorned with intricately carved pillars and 19th-century paintings. Treasures include Ras Gugsa's ceremonial robe, and a throne-bed that belonged to Empress Taitu. In the church compound stands a small monument to Ras Gugsa, topped by a Gondarine cupola, and the rock seat used by Ras Alula Ali when he acted as judge. Debre Tabor Iyasus lies about 3km along a steep winding road that runs south from the main road next to Nile Petrol, immediately east of the town's largest roundabout. The ascent road passes through patches of forest rattling with birdlife and also offers some great views back to the town centre. Before visiting this historic church, however, you need to stop in at the Selassie Church, about 500m along the ascent road, to obtain written permission.

Gafat Two relics of Emperor Yohannes IV's reign can be seen in the farmlands around Gafat, 5km east of Debre Tabor. The church of Heruy Giyorgis (*entrance US$1*), set on a small hill swathed in indigenous forest and encircled by a stone wall, houses what is reputedly the oldest Ethiopian flag, dating from Yohannes's reign. About 1.5km north of this stand the foundations and ruined walls of Samarneha Palace, built by Yohannes in the 1870s. To get there, follow the China Road southeast out of Debre Tabor for 2.5km until you see a signpost for Gafat to your left. From here, it's about 2km north on a fair unsurfaced road to Heruy Giyorgis, which lies 150m west of the road, and another 1.5km north to Samarneha, which stands atop a forested hill 5 minutes' walk to the east of the road

Mount Guna Peaking at 4,231m some 30km southeast of Debre Tabor, this little-known mountain is an important watershed for the Nile Basin. It supports more than 40km^2 of Afroalpine moorland above the 3,800m contour, and it used to be home to an isolated population of around 20 Ethiopian wolves, though recent information suggests this is no longer the case. The subalpine zone, rich in wild flowers and home to shepherds draped in blankets, can be explored by 4x4 along a beautiful road that runs south from the China Road at Gassay, 17km east of Debre Tabor, and climbs to an altitude of 3,650m. The higher slopes are accessible on foot only, and we've not heard of any traveller visiting them. In 2015, a 46km^2 community reserve was created to help prevent further erosion and land degradation on the upper slopes of Guna – see w ordaethiopia.org for further details.

Wukro Medhane Alem This spectacular and little-known rock-hewn church, set in an unusual landscape of eroded rocks 15 minutes' drive north of the China Road, is sometimes referred to as Wukro Lalibela and was reputedly excavated by the young prince before he became king. A full monolith, shaded by a UNESCO-donated shelter as of 2013, it is set in a narrow trench excavated some 6m below the ground, and reached via a steep mossy stone tunnel. The interior is divided into four different parts, each with its own *tabot*, and shows some excellent workmanship, including several fine carvings on the ceiling and walls. It also houses a treasury of old crosses, manuscripts and other relics. No formal entrance fee is charged but a donation will be expected, and access can be problematic after around 10.00, as the priest lives some distance away. The signposted junction is at Kimer Dingay, about 28km east of Debre Tabor. From here, proceed north for 300m, then turn left, continue northeast for another 6km, then turn left again on to a rough 4x4-only stretch of piste that leads to the church after about 700m.

Gayint Bethlehem The most singular and perhaps the finest church that can be reached from the China Road west of Gashena, the seminary of Gayint Bethlehem specialises in advanced studies on St Yared, who wrote most of the praise songs used by the Orthodox Church. Enclosed within an unflattering circular thatched *tukul*, Bethlehem is built up in the ancient Axumite style with a rectangular 200m^2 floor plan. Notable features include three old juniper doorways, fantastic carvings on the wooden beams holding up the roof, two basilica domes with ornate designs, plenty of old Ge'ez Bibles, and several wonderful old paintings on deteriorating cloth depicting scenes from the life of Jesus. Outside the church lies a 7m-long fallen Axumite pillar. Not unpredictably, oral tradition dates Bethlehem to the rule of Abraha we Atsbeha, but Thomas Pakenham, the first outsider to see this church, felt that the combination of Axum and Constantinople styles indicated a construction date between the 9th and 11th centuries, while other sources date its construction to the late 14th century. Pakenham's wonderful book *The Mountains of Rasselas* (page 644) contains a full chapter about the church, as well as some great photographs.

Getting there and away Getting to Gayint Bethlehem today is less of a mission than it was for Pakenham in the 1950s, but it's still a considerable side trip. It is reached along a rough road that heads southward from the China Road 70km east

11

of Debre Tabor, at the western edge of Nefas Mewcha, a town of around 20,000 people also sometimes referred to as Lay (Upper) Gayint, the name of the *woreda* of which it is administrative centre. From the junction it is about 23km to Arb Gebeya, the administrative centre of Tach (Lower) Gayint *woreda*, which is also connected to Nefas Mewcha by a solitary bus that runs back and forth three times daily, taking up to 90 minutes in either direction. From Arb Gebeya, it's another 20km or so drive towards Gayint Bethlehem, following a rough track that's usually impassable during the rainy season when the Bashilo River is in flood, then another hour on foot. An early start is recommended and there are a few basic guesthouses in Nefas Mewcha if you opt to spend the night there.

Checheho Gebriel, Arsema and Bal-Egziabher Situated 15km east of Nefas Mewcha, 3km past the village of Checheho, this trio of churches was excavated in the late 1990s by Abba Defar, who started work on them after receiving a holy vision, and who is now in his 80s. The largest church measures about 10m deep by 5m wide, and has several large central pillars. The rock in all three is unusually soft and chalky, giving the interior an attractive white appearance. Two holy pools filled with natural water stand outside the churches. To get there, park outside the prominent church of Checheho Medhane Alem, on the north side of the road, walk east along the asphalt for 300m, then take a steep 200m footpath heading uphill to the left. Also worth stopping at is the Debre Zebit viewpoint about 7km further east along the China Road.

Filakit Gereger Straddling the China Road about 55km east of Nefas Mewcha and 27km west of Gashena, this town of 5,000 historically comprises two settlements, Filakit and Gereger, that once stood about 1km apart but are now more or less contiguous. Gereger, a town of some antiquity, is mentioned in the early 17th-century chronicle of Emperor Susenyos, and it was also visited by Emperor Yohannes I in 1677. Filakit Gereger was the capital of Begemder in the late 18th century, prior to being replaced by Debre Tabor, and it is now the administrative centre of Meket. It is of interest to travellers mainly as the most accessible springboard for community hikes through west Meket operated by Tesfa (page 405).

Gashena An important junction town but otherwise wholly undistinguished, tiny Gashena (mistakenly marked as Bete Hor on some maps) lies 60km south of Lalibela at a chilly altitude of 3,000m. At the time of writing, the first 50km of the road from Gashena to Lalibela is well-maintained dirt, but it is likely to be surfaced in its entirety during the lifespan of this edition. The last 15km, between the town and the airport, is already asphalt. If you need to change vehicles at Gashena, a slow but steady flow of minibuses connects it to Lalibela from early morning to early afternoon, but be warned that drastic overcharging (more than four times the going fare of US$2) is commonplace. Should you get stuck overnight, as late arrivals sometimes do, Gashena has half a dozen basic accommodation options, the most appealing at present being the downmarket **Tesfaye Guade Hotel** (**m** *0913 745258; US$4 dbl using common shower;* **$**). Rather more promising, assuming they have opened, are two hotels currently under construction: the four-storey Kassa Bekele Hotel 100m along the road to Wegel Tena, and the nameless place on the main road behind the Dashen Bank.

FROM TIGRAY VIA WELDIYA Weldiya, the main junction town for Lalibela, lies about 255km south of Mekele along a good asphalt road that takes about 4 hours to cover in a private vehicle. If you are self-driving, note that you will need to make a route choice at Hiwane 55km south of Mekele – keep going straight for the more scenic but slower road to Alamata via Maychew and Lake Ashenge, or fork left for the nippier new road via Mehoni and Hujira. The road between Mekele and Weldiya is serviced by a few direct buses, usually leaving at around 06.00 in either direction. Coming from the south, however, be warned that most buses to Mekele originate in Dessie so may be full by the time they reach Weldiya. If you can't find direct transport, it is possible to do the run between Weldiya and Mekele in stages, and you should get through in a day with a reasonably early start. Major towns and points of interest are as follows.

Maychew This amorphous small town 125km south of Mekele has an ignominious place as the setting of the Battle of Maychew, a 13-hour confrontation that took place on 31 March 1936 and is now remembered as the start of the Italian occupation, the one period in Ethiopia's 3,000-year history when it was ruled by outsiders. Maychew is completely bypassed by the new road through Hujira and there's little to see in town, but there are plenty of hotels should you need to overnight.

Lake Ashenge and Hashengu Forest Situated on the west side of the old Alamata road about 30km south of Maychew, the 14km² Lake Ashenge is a beautiful mountain-ringed body of slightly saline water fed by several small streams but with no known outlet. Ashenge has been the site of two terrible massacres, separated by almost four centuries. On 28 August 1542, it witnessed the Battle of Wofla, which culminated in the capture and eventual grisly execution of Portuguese commander Cristóvão da Gama by Ahmed Gragn. On 3 April 1936, in the wake of their defeat at Maychew, thousands of Ethiopian soldiers were poisoned by mustard gas sprayed around the lake by Italian planes.

Ashenge's old Tigrigna name, Tsada Bahri (White Sea), alludes to the multitudes of waterbirds that congregate there seasonally. Endemics such as wattled ibis, Rouget's rail and black-headed siskin are present throughout the year, supplemented by flocks of ferruginous and maccoa duck, northern shoveler, southern pochard and great-crested grebe during the European winter. The lake lies less than 1km from the main road and several footpaths lead to the lakeshore.

Also of interest to birdwatchers, practically bordering Lake Ashenge, Hashengu Forest Reserve protects part of the indigenous coniferous forest that flourishes at altitudes of 1,600–2,600m on the Alamata Escarpment. It is notable among other things for harbouring the rare endemic plant *Delosperma abyssinica* along with more than a dozen forest birds not normally associated with Tigray, for instance Abyssinian catbird. An all-weather road runs through part of the forest – ask for the turn-off about 2km north of the lake – and camping may be permitted at the guard's encampment.

Alamata Set at the base of a wildly majestic escarpment 80km north of Weldiya, this medium-altitude junction town of 30,000 has something of a frontier atmosphere. It lies at the southern crossroads of the scenic old road to Maychew, or the faster and safer new road through Mehoni. It boasts nothing in the way of tourist attractions other than its spectacular location, though it would be a useful base for exploring Lake Ashenge, only 30 minutes' drive further north. Accommodation-wise, the unquestionable pick is the multistorey **Meaza Hotel** (*48 rooms;* \ *034 774 1232; sgl/dbl US$8/12;* **$$**), which has en-suite rooms with hot water, nets and television, and a good mango-shaded restaurant serving a varied

11

selection of mains (including excellent roast chicken) in the US$3–5 range. Lesser and cheaper options include the veteran **Tewodros Belay Hotel** (*50 rooms;* \034 774 0321; **$**) and new **Ethiopia Hotel** (\034 774 0304; **$**).

Weldiya Situated 120km north of Dessie, Weldiya (often spelt Woldia) is a medium-sized town, set amid pretty rolling hills sloping down to the Tekowuha (Black Water) River, at the junction of the main road north to Tigray and the China Road west to the Lake Tana region and Lalibela. Much smaller than Dessie, but also far older, Weldiya was visited by missionary Johann Krapf in 1842, at which time it was the capital of an important local ruler called Dejazmach Faris Aligas. Krapf described Weldiya as a 'considerably large town [of] a few thousand inhabitants' and was impressed by its weekly market, which attracted 'many hundreds of donkeys and mules loaded with salt-pieces, barley, cloths, etc'. The town is less impressive today, but it can still be lively on the main market days of Tuesday and Saturday. It is also renowned as the birthplace of Sheikh Muhammad Hussein Ali Al Amoudi, owner of the Addis Ababa Sheraton, and the world's richest African according to *Forbes* magazine. Until a few years ago, strategically located Weldiya was an almost obligatory overnight stop on the main road route to Lalibela. It has diminished in significance following the surfacing of the China Road, and the introduction of direct buses between Dessie and Lalibela, but you might still end up overnighting here, especially if you are bussing between Mekele and Lalibela.

Getting there and away Weldiya straddles the asphalt Adigrat road 510km north of Addis Ababa, 120km past Dessie and 260km south of Mekele. The bus station lies about 1km west of the main roundabout at the junction of the Mekele and Lalibela roads. Buses connecting Weldiya to Dessie or Mekele leave at around 06.00, but you should also be able to pick up a seat on a passing vehicle until noon or thereabouts. Heading south from Weldiya to Addis Ababa, plan on changing buses at Dessie. There is usually at least one bus daily to Lalibela, leaving at 06.00 and routing through Dilb or Gashena. The daily bus between Dessie and Lalibela stops in Weldiya, but it is often too full to take additional passengers. Alternatively, catch a minibus from Weldiya to Gashena, and change vehicles there.

Where to stay, eat and drink *Map, opposite*

Lal Hotel (75 rooms) \033 331 0367; m 0930 034708. Established back when tour groups regularly stopped overnight in Weldiya en route to Lalibela, this down-at-heel country cousin to its smarter Lalibela namesake stands in attractive green grounds & has a decent restaurant with a varied menu, terrace seating & the most reliable Wi-Fi in town. The timeworn rooms in the main building are in dire need of renovation; the garden bungalows are newer & more comfortable & come with sat TV, solar-powered hot (a synonym for cold) water & more than a few mosquitoes. It remains the most comfortable option in Weldiya, essentially through lack of competition, but the unrealistic & non-negotiable 2-tier rates (foreigners pay 4–5 times over the odds) earn it the all-Ethiopia-silly-

faranji-price award for this edition. *US$30/40 sgl/dbl in main building, US$45 dbl bungalow; all rates B&B.* **$$$**

Yordanos Hotel (50 rooms) \033 331 1357. The pick of half a dozen rather similar places lining the road between the main junction & the Lal, this agreeable multistorey hotel behind the Total filling station has friendly staff, a restaurant serving excellent *shekla tibs* & reasonably priced rooms with hot water & TV. *US$4 sgl with common shower, US$6/10 dbl/twin.* **$**

Michare Hotel (48 rooms) \033 336 0233. Similar in feel & standard to the Yordanos, this hotel opposite the main junction has the advantage of some of the en-suite rooms being set well back from the main road. The attached restaurant serves a basic menu. *US$6 dbl.* **$**

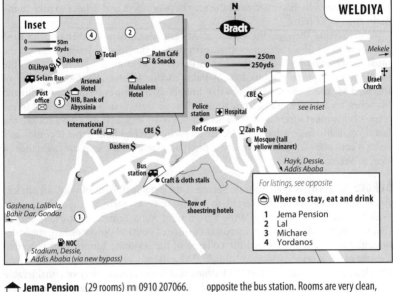

Inset

0 ——— 50m
0 ——— 50yds

④ ②

🍴Total   Palm Café
              🍴& Snacks

OiLibya⛽$ 🏨Dashen

🚌 Selam Bus
          Arsenal
          Hotel   Mulualem
Post   Hotel
office ③ $
📮   NIB, Bank of
        Abyssinia

International
Café 🖵   CBE $

Dashen $

              Bus
              station 🚌 ● Craft & cloth stalls
Gashena, Lalibela,
Bahir Dar, Gondar ①

              Row of
              shoestring hotels
Ç

🚌NOC
Stadium, Dessie,
Addis Ababa (via new bypass)

N

Bradt

0 ——— 250m
0 ——— 250yds

Mekele →

Urael
Church

CBE $

see inset

Police
station ➕ Hospital
  ●

Red Cross ➕   🍷Zan Pub
                Ç Mosque (tall
                  yellow minaret)

              Hayk, Dessie,
              Addis Ababa

For listings, see opposite

🏨 **Where to stay, eat and drink**
1 Jema Pension
2 Lal
3 Michare
4 Yordanos

🏠**Jema Pension** (29 rooms) m 0910 207066. This basic 3-storey hotel on the Gashena road is several notches above most the row of cheapies opposite the bus station. Rooms are very clean, but have only a ¾ bed & use a common shower. *US$4 sgl.* $

FROM TIGRAY VIA SEKOTA The most direct route from Axum to Lalibela is the 390km road running south through Adwa, Abiy Addi (page 355) and Sekota. Mostly unsurfaced, it can be covered in one very long day without stops in a private 4x4, but you could also think about breaking up the trip with a night at Abiy Addi or Sekota, both of which lie close to some worthwhile churches. Using public transport, you'll find it plentiful between Axum, Adwa and Abiy Addi, and also that a few buses run daily between Abiy Addi and Sekota, but Sekota to Lalibela might be tricky (though things should improve once ongoing roadworks are complete). Heading directly from Gheralta to Lalibela, a slightly shorter (360km) variation on this route entails using the new surfaced road from Hawzen to Abiy Addi via Megab, then driving south through Sekota. Coming directly from Mekele, two shorter variations are possible: the 290km road through Samare and Sekota, and a 340km route that veers west from the Weldiya road at Korem to connect with the road to Lalibela 15km south of Sekota.

Abiy Addi to Sekota Heading southward from Abiy Addi, turn right after 15km, at the junction with the road to Mekele via Hagere Selam. Another 19km and an altitudinal plunge to around 1,500m brings you to **Yechilay**, set in an otherwise unexpectedly austere landscape of spindly acacia scrubland populated by the odd herdsman and his coterie of skinny goats and long-horned cattle. Between Yechilay and **Finarwa**, 25km further south, the road bisects an isolated enclave of relatively low-lying Sahelian savannah whose parched appearance – thick red sand, foreboding black rock, dry riverbeds, scraggly trees – comes as a real contrast even to the relatively dry highlands of northern Tigray. It's no surprise to learn that this searing semi-desert, so visually reminiscent of the arid badlands of the Ethiopia–Kenya border region, lay at the epicentre of the dreadful famine of 1985 – indeed, the television footage that first drew global attention to this tragedy

11

was of victims who had evacuated the area between here and Sekota to hike to the main road at Korem.

After passing through the village of **Abegele** about 8km further on, the road crosses a series of watercourses that form part of the Tekeze drainage basin, the most impressive of which is the Tserari River, set at around 1,200m close to the isolated and venerable monastery of **Bahir Kidane Mihret**. A striking feature of this area are the immense baobabs that line the rocky slopes. With bare contorted branches reaching skyward from squat, bulbous trunks, these ancient and obese trees – some must surely be thousands of years old – look as if they have sucked the last drop of life from what was already a cruelly parched landscape. It comes as a relief when, after another 50km or so, the road ascends back into the highlands of Wag to Sekota.

Sekota Sometimes spelt Soqota, Sekota is the principal town of Wag, an ancient Agaw principality that converted to Christianity as early as the 6th century, possibly under the influence of the Syrian saint Abba Yemata. Historians believe that this highland area was an important centre of political power during the little-documented era that followed the collapse of the Axumite Empire and preceded the rise of the Zagwe dynasty at Lalibela. The antiquity of Sekota itself is unknown. Charles Beke, who visited it in 1843, noted that it was then a 'place of considerable size' and 'the grand centre of the salt trade, the Tigrayan merchants coming thus far only, and then returning'. Augustus Wylde, who passed through in the 1890s, was shown a three-storey palace said locally to date to the 1650s, a claim that tallied with its Gondarine appearance. More recently, Wag lay at the heart of the area affected by the terrible famine of 1985.

Getting there and away Sekota lies 155km south of Abiy Addi and 130km north of Lalibela by road. Buses cover the road from Abiy Addi to Sekota, but they are very slow. Using public transport, one bus daily runs between Weldiya and Sekota via Lalibela, usually leaving at around 06.00 in either direction and passing through Lalibela in the mid to late morning. There is also an 85km road connecting Sekota to Korem (on the main road between Mekele and Weldiya). The junction for the Korem road lies about 20km south of Sekota, where you need to fork left for Korem and right if you are heading for Lalibela. It is then a straight 110km drive to Lalibela, with the possibility of diverting to the churches around Bilbilla on the way.

Where to stay, eat and drink The smartest option is **D&G Pension** (m *0948 880111, 0912 791481;* **$$$**), which charges US$15/22 for a comfortable en-suite single/double with hot shower and TV, and also has a restaurant serving Ethiopian and international fare, and the most reliable Wi-Fi in town. Cheaper alternatives are **Alachew Pension** (m *0928 957336;* **$$**), which asks US$10/13 for an en-suite single/double with hot shower, and **Sefiw Semegne Pension** (m *0911 277373;* **$**) where en-suite rooms with cold shower cost US$7/10 single/double.

What to see and do Sekota is quite an attractive town. Indeed, studded with traditional two-storey circular stone dwellings, it is rather reminiscent of Lalibela as it used to look 20 years ago, before tourism initiated a modern construction boom. The town's most noteworthy individual landmark, situated on the main roundabout, is Webila Maryam, a centuries-old church that reputedly contains several interesting paintings, if you can find the priest with the key.

Wukro Meskel Kristos This near-monolithic rock-hewn church lies about 6km from Sekota, 10 minutes' walk east of the road south to Korem/Lalibela. Tradition holds that Wukro Meskel Kristos predates the Lalibela churches (some say it was excavated during the medieval reign of Yemrehanna Kristos, others that it dates to the 6th-century rule of Kaleb), and was the inspiration for many of them, which – if it is true – could mean it is the oldest near-monolith in Ethiopia. Rock-hewn church expert David Buxton, who visited Wukro Meskel Kristos in the 1960s, was of the opinion that the church is more recent, probably excavated in the 14th century. Either way, it's an atmospheric little church, and the ornate façade and decorated interior make it well worth the small effort required to reach it from the main road. Entrance costs US$5, women are forbidden and the church has been covered in scaffolding since 1998.

Six ancient coffins are stowed in the main church, and a second stash of perhaps 50 coffins containing ancient mummies lies in an adjacent cave mausoleum. How the mummies got there is a matter for conjecture. The caretaker priest reckons that the coffins in the church house the bodies of former governors of Wag, while the mummies in the cave were Kaleb-era administrators carried to the church by angels after their death. When David Buxton visited the church in the 1950s, he was told that the mummies were former Wagsuns – kings of Wag – who were customarily exhumed from their original graves about 20 years after their death and reburied in smaller caskets. Another legend has it that these are the bodies of priests who committed an unspecified sin and were struck down violently by God – certainly the few mummies that have spilled out of their coffins don't look like they died a peaceful death!

LALIBELA

Arguably the one place in Ethiopia that no visitor should omit from their itinerary, the singular town of Lalibela is perched at an altitude of 2,630m in a highland landscape of wild craggy peaks and vast rocky escarpments whose stark grandeur recalls the Drakensberg Mountains of South Africa. The traditional houses of Lalibela are of a design unlike anywhere else in Ethiopia, two-storey circular stone constructs that huddle on the steep slopes on which the town is built. But the small town's centrepiece, often cited as an unofficial eighth wonder of the world, is a stunning cluster of 13 medieval rock-hewn churches and chapels that today functions as a kind of living shrine to King Lalibela, the saint accredited with excavating them in the 12th century. Inscribed as a UNESCO World Heritage Site in 1978, the meticulously sculpted churches of Lalibela are the undisputed pinnacle of an architectural tradition dating back to Axumite times. The churches here are *big* – several are in excess of 10m high – and, because they are carved below ground level, they are ringed by trenches and courtyards, the sides of which are cut into with stone graves and hermit cells, and connected to each other by a tangled maze of tunnels and passages.

In size and scope, the church complex at Lalibela feels like a subterranean village. Yet each individual church is unique in shape and size, precisely carved and minutely decorated. Furthermore, while Lalibela has become a lot more touristy than it was a few years back, its rock-hewn churches are not primarily tourist attractions, being prodded and poked away from their original context, nor are they the crumbling monuments of a dead civilisation. What they are, and what they have been for at least 800 years, is an active Christian shrine, the spiritual centre of a town's religious life. Wander between the churches in the thin light of morning, when white-robed hermits emerge, Bible in hand, from their cells to bask on the rocks, and the chill highland air is warmed by Eucharistic drumbeats and gentle swaying chants, and you can't help but feel that you are witnessing a scene that is fundamentally little different from the one that has been enacted here every morning for century upon century. The joy of Lalibela, the thing that makes this curiously medieval town so special, is that it is not just the rock-hewn churches that have survived into the modern era, but also something more alive and organic.

HISTORY When it comes to the early history of Lalibela, little is known for certain. Originally called Adefa (or Arafa), it may have been established as early as the 7th or 8th century AD, probably as the capital of one of the local fiefdoms that rose to prominence when the Axumite Empire disintegrated. In the mid 12th century, a time of great religious conflict in the Mediterranean, Adefa became the coronation site and capital of the upstart Zagwe dynasty. Under the Zagwe, the town was evidently renamed Roha, in tribute to the Mesopotamian city of al-Ruha (Edessa), whose King Abgar V legendarily became an early Christian convert after being cured of leprosy by Jesus, and which had more recently housed a short-lived Crusader state that fell to a bloody Islamic siege in 1144. The most venerated ruler associated with Adefa/Roha is Gebre Meskel Lalibela, the fifth Zagwe emperor, who most likely came to power in the early 1180s and reigned for 40 years, during which time, according to tradition, he was responsible for the excavation of the complex of rock-hewn churches for which the town is famed.

The life of King Lalibela is shrouded in legend. Though he was almost certainly of royal birth, some say he took the throne in place of a rival elder brother called Harbay. One tradition has it that he was covered by a swarm of bees as a young child, an event that his mother took as a sign he would one day be king (indeed, one translation of Lalibela is 'the bees recognise his sovereignty', which covers a lot of ground in four syllables). According to this version of events, Harbay's response to the unwelcome premonition was to poison his younger brother. The assassination attempt failed, but Lalibela was cast into a deep three-day sleep, transported to heaven by an angel and shown a city of rock-hewn churches, which he was ordered to replicate on earth. Another more intriguing legend holds that prior to taking the throne, Lalibela spent 25 years exiled in the original Jerusalem – then a Christian stronghold, having been taken by the Crusaders in 1099 – and it was the capture of this city by Salah ad-Din Yusuf ibn Ayyub (better known to Westerners as Saladin) in 1187 that inspired his vision of carving a 'New Jerusalem' into the rocks of Roha.

Several extant land grants confirm that Lalibela was a genuine historical figure, as does a namecheck in the report written by a Coptic delegation from Alexandria in 1210. But details about the excavation of the churches attributed to him are scant. Some legends state that Lalibela carved the entire complex himself overnight, assisted only by angels; others that the king gathered together craftsmen and artisans from as far afield as Asia and Europe to tackle the project, which took around 23 years to complete, with the standalone Bet Giyorgis being the last to be finished. Another contradictory tradition states that Bet Abba Libanos was excavated as a posthumous memorial to Lalibela by his wife, Meskel Kibre.

Aside from one contemporary document suggesting that Bet Medhane Alem was excavated or substantially modified during Lalibela's reign, no compelling evidence exists to indicate exactly when the churches were carved, or by whom. Logistically, it is conceivable that the entire complex was excavated over 20-odd years, since the tufa into which they are carved is a relatively soft and easily worked rock. Architecturally, however, the churches display a stylistic variety consistent with a much longer time frame, for which reason most modern historians regard it to be perfectly possible, even probable, that Lalibela's role in their creation was more limited than tradition holds. As long ago as 1958, Imgard Bidder proposed that the oldest excavations might predate King Lalibela by many centuries, having started life in pre-Christian times as pagan shrines. More recently, David Phillipson theorised that the original excavations were forts or palaces associated with the fragmentation of the Axumite Empire in the 7th or 8th century. So could it be that King Lalibela was responsible for modifying the original secular excavations to form a cohesive 'New Jerusalem'? Or did he perhaps add one or two churches to a pre-existing religious complex? Or was his role in the excavations even more limited? Based on the scant evidence available, any of these possibilities seems plausible.

Lalibela fell from political prominence in around 1270, when Yakuno Amlak, founder of the Solomonic Dynasty, overthrew the last Zagwe ruler. Little more is heard of the town until the 15th century, when it was evidently revived as a pilgrimage site in line with the Ethiopian Orthodox Church's rehabilitation of the Zagwe legacy. It is unclear why the church reversed its position on a dynasty branded as usurpers during the first two centuries of Solomonic rule, but the earliest known inclusion of King Lalibela in the Ethiopian Book of Saints dates from this period, as does the first written account of his role in excavating the churches at Roha, and the first known paintings depicting him. The historian Michael Gervers recently published a paper that goes one step further by proposing that the Bet Golgotha-Mikael-Selassie complex of churches was excavated in the 15th century as a shrine to the newly sanctified king. By contrast, Claude Lepage and Jacques Mercier's 2012 book on Lalibela cites documentary evidence suggesting that Bet Maryam and Bet Meskel were excavated under the patronage of the Monastery of Debre Libanos in the early 12th century, and goes on to conclude that all the churches accredited to Lalibela most likely date to his reign.

In 1521, Portuguese priest Francisco Álvares visited Lalibela and penned a detailed description of the site in his narrative *Prester John of the Indies*. Álvares recounted the local tradition that King Lalibela was buried at Bet Golgotha, and he also stated that monks believed the churches to have been excavated in 24 hours by pale men, or possibly angels. Poignantly, Álvares concluded his account of Lalibela's wondrous churches as follows:

> It wearied me to write more of these works, because it seemed to me that they will accuse me of untruth ... there is much more than I have already written, and I have left it that they may not tax me with it being falsehood.

WHEN TO VISIT As with most tourist sites in Ethiopia, Lalibela can be visited at any time of year. The most exciting time to be there, however, is during Genna and to a lesser extent Timkat and Meskel, when you get to see the magnitude of its importance as a religious and pilgrimage site during public ceremonies and processions characterised by priests swaying and chanting mournfully. On the downside, hotel rates increase up to fivefold over Genna and Timkat, and things are so hectic that it is not so easy to appreciate the churches on an architectural level.

Conversely, the growing popularity of Lalibela, combined with the inherently confined nature of its main attraction, means that it can start to feel uncomfortably touristy when it gets too busy. For that reason, there's a lot to be said for visiting during the rainy season, June to early October, when tourist volumes are lowest.

GETTING THERE AND AWAY When Thomas Pakenham visited Lalibela in 1955, it was legendarily inaccessible. There was no proper road to the village, which typically received about five parties of foreign visitors annually, following a four-day mule-back excursion from Dessie. Even as recently as the mid 1990s, air and road access to Lalibela was strictly restricted to the dry season. Today, Lalibela is still not connected to any other town by a completed asphalt road, but flights do now run throughout the year, while the construction of good all-weather gravel roads south to Gashena and north to Sekota allows a road approach from any of several directions.

By air Daily flights connect Lalibela to Addis Ababa, Gondar, Bahir Dar and Axum, and there are also a few flights every week to Mekele. The airport [map, page 411] lies about 25km from the town centre along a surfaced 5km side road branching west from the main road to Gashena. All flights are met by most private operators who charge US$3.50 per person for a one-way transfer to/from town. The Ethiopian Airlines [398 G2] office is situated on the main square close to the Bluelal Hotel.

By road Lalibela lies on something of a limb in terms of the rest of the northern circuit and there are several possible approaches, depending on where it slots into the rest of your itinerary. The brief notes below are elaborated upon on page 384. The bus station for all destinations south, east or west of Lalibela lies 1.5km south of the main square alongside the road to Gashena. Transport to Bilbilla and other destinations north of Lalibela leaves from in front of the BP filling station 300m north of the main square. Private or shared vehicles to Mekele, Bahir Dar and Gondar can be arranged through Treasure Transport or Lalibela Eco Trekking (page 404). The latter will also book bus tickets out of Lalibela, but with a 25% service charge.

To/from Gondar or Bahir Dar The only route from the Lake Tana region follows the China Road east from Woreta to Gashena, 60km south of Lalibela (page 384). In a private vehicle, it should take 6–7 hours to cover the 310/365km from Bahir Dar/Gondar to Lalibela. One direct bus connects Bahir Dar to Lalibela daily, leaving at 06.00 in either direction, and taking up to 9 hours. Alternatively, any bus or minibus from Bahir Dar/Gondar to Weldiya (which mostly leave at 05.30) can drop you at Gashena, from where you should get to Lalibela the same day (but be prepared to bed down in Gashena). In the opposite direction, the first minibus to Gashena leaves Lalibela at 05.30–06.00, leaving plenty of time to connect with public transport headed from Weldiya (or Dessie) to Bahir Dar/Gondar.

To/from Weldiya or Dessie The most established option entails following the asphalt China Road west out of Weldiya for 105km as it ascends to Gashena, then taking the 60km road north to Lalibela, a 4-hour drive in a private 4x4. A shorter but rougher alternative is to follow the China Road for 40km as far as Dilb, then turn right on to a 60km dirt road through Muja and Geneta Maryam. One bus daily runs back and forth between Dessie and Lalibela, leaving at 06.00, taking up to 8 hours and stopping in Weldiya (where it may or may not have space for additional passengers). There is also usually at least one direct bus daily between Weldiya and Lalibela sometimes travelling via Muja, other times through Gashena, depending on the state of the roads. If there's no direct bus, catch the earliest possible bus or minibus from Weldiya to Gashena (page 390) and change vehicles there, bearing in mind that transport on to Lalibela tends to thin out or cease altogether in the afternoon.

To/from Addis Ababa If you plan on travelling directly to Lalibela from Addis Ababa, the most direct option is via Weldiya and the China Road, a 675km trip that will require an overnight stay in either Dessie or Weldiya. On public transport, the best approach to this trip is probably to take the Selam bus to Dessie, overnight there, then pick up the next morning's direct bus to Lalibela. An alternative route, shorter on paper but not yet on the ground (though that might change as more stretches of roads are asphalted), runs from Addis Ababa to Dejen, Mekane Selam, Tenta and Gashena, and is described in full on page 384. Leaving Lalibela directly for Addis Ababa, it is worth asking at your hotel or any of the operators listed on page 404 whether any tourist vehicles are heading back empty. If they are, expect to pay around US$15–20 for a lift.

To/from Axum The most direct option is the scenic 390km road via Adwa, Abiy Addi and Sekota (page 391). In a private 4x4, you could just cover this route in one day, but two would be more relaxed – and the minimum duration on public transport.

To/from Gheralta The most direct option is the scenic 360km road from Hawzen via Abiy Addi and Sekota, which is essentially a slightly shorter variation on the route from Axum described on page 391.

To/from Mekele Using public transport, the most reliable option is the 420km route via Weldiya, which is now surfaced almost in its entirely, and can usually but not always be covered in one long day, changing vehicles at Weldiya (and possibly again at Gashena). In a private vehicle, there are four possibilities. Most operators also plumb for the established and well-beaten route through Weldiya, while others prefer the 290km road through Samare and Sekota, which is shorter and more scenic but mostly unsurfaced and relatively isolated. Other options are the 320km route through Waja and Muja, and a 340km route through Korem (which connects with the Lalibela road 20km south of Sekota). All these routes are easily covered in a day by private 4x4.

GETTING AROUND Lalibela is small enough that you can walk between most places of interest on foot, though the combination of altitude and steep slopes can leave even the fittest of visitors feeling quite breathless. Minibuses and *bajaji* run back and forth between the main square [398 G2] and the bus station [398 F6] 1.5km to the south. The fare is US$0.20 or you can splash out on a private hire for around US$2.

WHERE TO STAY Hotel prices in Lalibela are subject to some seasonal whimsicality, reflecting its status as perhaps the one place in Ethiopia where tourists constitute the bulk of the clientele. Prices listed below are official high-season rates as quoted by the hotel itself, but you might be asked for significantly more when large numbers of tourists are in town, and should be able to negotiate a discount when things are quiet. Be warned, however, that it's a no-holds-barred scenario over Timkat or Genna, when many hotels increase their rates fivefold to exploit the demand for rooms. At such times camping may be permitted in the grounds of most hotels; the cost to pitch a tent then often exceeds the standard room rates.

A growing number of rustic accommodation options designed primarily as overnight stops for trekkers can be found in the **mountains around Lalibela** [map, page 411]. These include several community guesthouses operated by Tesfa (page 405), as well as the guesthouse at Agaw Beret in the Abune Yoseph Community Conservation Area. The only options aimed at people looking to spend longer in one place are **Hudad Eco-Retreat** and **Degosach Ecolodge** (page 403).

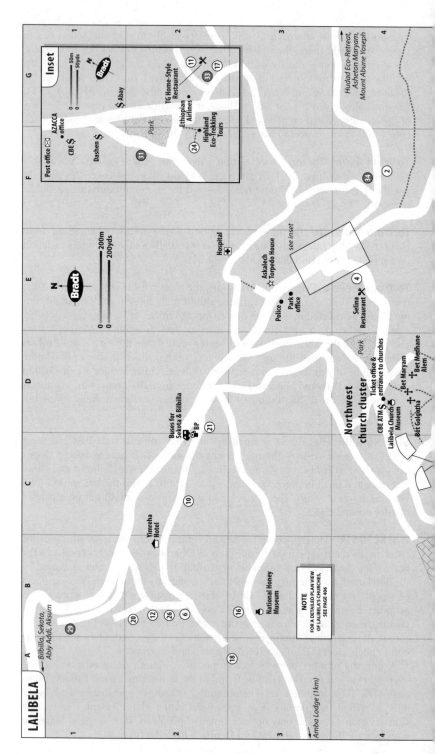

LALIBELA

← Bilbilla, Sekota,
Abiy Addi, Aksum

Amba Lodge (1km) →

Inset

Post office ☒

AZACCA
● office

CBE $

Dashen $

$ Abay

Park

TG Home-Style
Restaurant

Ethiopian ●
Airlines

Highland
Eco-Trekking
Tours

Hudad Eco-Retreat,
Asheton Maryam,
Mount Abune Yoseph →

Hospital ✚

Askalech
☆ Torpedo House

see inset

Police ●

Park ●
office

Selina ✕
Restaurant

Buses for
Sekota & Bilbilla

BP

Yimreha
Hotel

**Northwest
church cluster**

Ticket office &
entrance to churches

CBE ATM $

Lalibela Church
Museum

✝ Bet Maryam

✝ Bet Medhane
Alem

Bet Golgotha ✝

Park

National Honey
Museum

NOTE
FOR A DETAILED PLAN VIEW
OF LALIBELA'S CHURCHES,
SEE PAGE 406

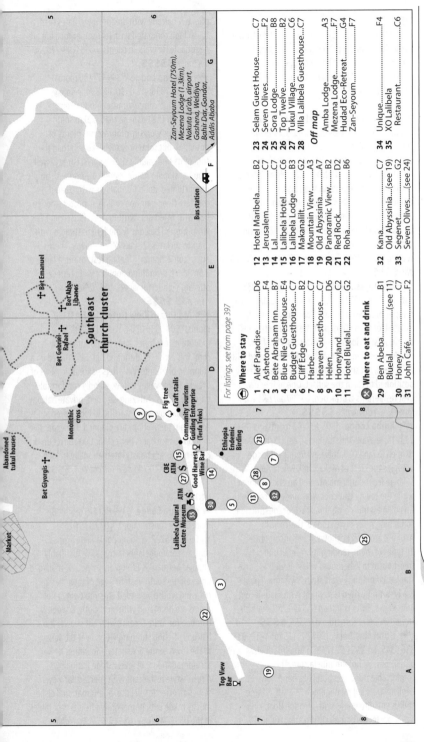

For listings, see from page 397

Where to stay

1	Alef Paradise	D6
2	Asheton	F4
3	Bete Abraham Inn	B7
4	Blue Nile Guesthouse	E4
5	Budget Guesthouse	C7
6	Cliff Edge	B2
7	Harbe	C7
8	Heaven Guesthouse	D6
9	Helen	D6
10	Honeyland	C2
11	Hotel Bluelal	G2
12	Hotel Maribela	B2
13	Jerusalem	C7
14	Lal	C7
15	Lalibela Hotel	C6
16	Lalibela Lodge	B3
17	Makanalit	G2
18	Mountain View	A3
19	Old Abyssinia	A7
20	Panoramic View	B2
21	Red Rock	D2
22	Roha	B6
23	Selam Guest House	C7
24	Seven Olives	F2
25	Sora Lodge	B8
26	Top Twelve	B2
27	Tukul Village	C6
28	Villa Lalibela Guesthouse	C7

Off map

	Amba Lodge	A3
	Mezena Lodge	F7
	Hudad Eco-Retreat	G4
	Zan-Seyoum	F7

Where to eat and drink

29	Ben Abeba	B1
30	Honey	C7
31	John Café	F2
32	Kana	C7
33	Segenet	G2
34	Unique	F4
35	XO Lalibela	C6

	Bluelal	(see 11)
	Old Abyssinia	(see 19)
	Seven Olives	(see 24)
	Restaurant	

Lalibela and Surrounds LALIBELA

11

Upmarket

In addition to the hotels listed below, **Ben Abeba** (page 403) is in the process of constructing hillside accommodation that should be operational some time in 2018/19. Expect it to be the best, & costliest, in town.

✳ 🏠 **Tukul Village Hotel** [399 C6] (24 rooms) ☏ 033 336 0564/5; m 0911 104944; e messay_2005@yahoo.co.uk; w tukulvillage. com. This owner-managed lodge combines traditional stone-&-thatch *tukul*-style architecture with modern amenities in spotless twin & dbl rooms that each takes up an entire floor of a 2-storey *tukul* & features floor-to-ceiling windows, balconies with views over Bet Giyorgis & spacious bathrooms. A good restaurant with courtyard seating is attached. Good value. *US$49/67 B&B sgl/ dbl*. **$$$$**

🏠 **Old Abyssinia** [399 A7] (3 rooms) ☏ 033 836 2758; m 0912 027992; e info@oldabyssinia. com; w oldabyssinia.com. Boasting a scenic & isolated location 500m past the Roha Hotel, this boutique-style lodge comprises 3 stylish family *tukuls*, all built in traditional style & equipped with 2 dbl beds, hot shower & private terrace perfectly positioned to catch the sunset. One of the town's best restaurants is attached. *US$90 dbl B&B with low-season discounts*. **$$$$$**

🏠 **Amba Lodge** [398 A3] (42 rooms) m 0911 223914; e ayalewlidetu@gmail.com. Scheduled to open in Jan 2019, this new upmarket lodge occupies the crest of Mekalt Hill, where King Lalibela legendarily maintained an encampment while the town's churches were under excavation. An architecturally ambitious circular construction combining *tukul*-style stone & thatch with Axumite arches & keyholes, it will incorporate 10 types of room, ranging from small budget tree-houses to 2-bedroom villas, as well as horse stables, community craft stalls, swimming pool & a beautifully sited restaurant with magnificent 360° views. *Rates will span US$15–150, but expect standard dbls to cost around US$55*. **$$$$**

🏠 **Hotel Maribela** [398 B2] (15 rooms) ☏ 033 336 0345; m 0911 971718; e hotelmaribela@ gmail.com; w hotelmaribela.com. This comfortable ridge-top hotel has hands-on English-speaking management & staff, & large stylish en-suite rooms with wooden floor, king-size 4-poster bed, small sitting area, fridge, TV,

phone & balcony with dream views. Rates seem a touch high compared with its competitors, but are negotiable for walk-in clients. *US$65/99/110 sgl/ dbl/suite*. **$$$$$**

🏠 **Mezena Lodge** [399 F7] (30 rooms) ☏ 033 336 1336; m 0930 111354; e info@ mezenalodge.com; w mezenalodge.com. Situated off the Gashena road 2.5km south of town, this work-in-progress has plenty of potential, but somehow feels like less than the sum of its undeniably stylish parts. Large & well-wooded sloping gardens are scattered with amply proportioned stone bungalows with treated concrete floor, bamboo ceiling, 4-poster wooden bed with fitted net, writing desk, flatscreen TV, wrap-around balcony & modern bathroom with granite surfaces, 2 sinks & hot shower. There's also a contemporary-feeling restaurant, a large 2.5m-deep swimming pool & a wide terrace offering wonderful views. *US$70/80/85 sgl/dbl/ twin B&B*. **$$$$**

🏠 **Mountain View Hotel** [398 A3] (30 rooms) ☏ 033 336 0804; m 0911 983396; e info@ mountainview-hotel.com; w mountainview-hotel. com. This architect-designed hotel is situated on a stunning promontory & offers panoramic views of the expansive valley below. Blandly comfortable en-suite rooms with king-size bed, private balcony & hot tub/shower are starting to look frayed at the edges, but renovations are planned. The expansive rooftop terrace bar is perfect for that sunset drink & the restaurant boasts internationally trained cooks. *US$64/77/100 B&B sgl/dbl/trpl*. **$$$$**

Moderate

✳ 🏠 **Sora Lodge** [399 B8] (15 rooms, 8 more under construction) ☏ 033 336 0255; m 0912 035222; e soralodgelalibela@gmail. com; w soralodgelalibela.com. This justifiably popular German- & Ethiopian-owned & -managed hotel on the southwestern edge of town has an old wing whose neat tiled en-suite twin or dbl rooms are decorated with local cloth, & wood & bamboo furniture & come with hot shower & a balcony offering stunning views over the valley to the town centre & Asheton Mountain. Newer accommodation is in lovely stone bungalows. A *tukul*-style restaurant with spectacular views serves an eclectic selection of international dishes mostly made with home-grown fruit & vegetables, in the US$2–4 range. *US$45/55/60 sgl/dbl/*

twin (old wing) or US$55/65/90 sgl/dbl/suite (bungalow); all rates B&B. **$$$$**

🏠 **Harbe Hotel** [399 C7] (16 rooms) 📞033 336 0090; e reservation@harbehotel.com; w harbehotel.com. Opened in 2016, this bright modern owner-managed 3-storey hotel has on-the-ball staff, a cheerful ground-floor restaurant/bar with a very varied international menu (*mains US$5 or 3-course menu US$8*) & a fabulous rooftop barbecue area offering 360° views. Accessed by the only lift in Lalibela, the spacious & uncluttered rooms come with twin or king-size bed, flatscreen TV, wood furniture, private terrace & modern bathroom with hot shower. Good value. *US$55/65/85 sgl/dbl/trpl.* **$$$$**

🏠 **Top Twelve Hotel** [398 B2] (12 rooms) 📞033 336 0110; m 0911 930217; e top12hotel@gmail.com; w toptwelvehotel.com. This attentively managed family-run hotel on the hillside behind the Mountain View has spacious & clean en-suite rooms with attractive traditional décor dominated by bright fabrics & goatskins, hand-crafted wood furniture, sat TV, private balcony & modern bathroom with hot shower. *US$45/55 B&B sgl/dbl.* **$$$$**

🏠 **Cliff Edge Hotel** [398 B2] (18 rooms) 📞033 336 0606; m 0911 729322, 0920 688821; e info@cliffedgehotel-lalibela.com; w cliffedgehotel-lalibela.com. This aptly named 3-storey hotel has a great location overlooking the valley below. The simply furnished dbl & twin rooms all have en-suite hot shower & stunning views from private balconies. There's a good restaurant serving both European & Ethiopian dishes, & free Wi-Fi. *US$45/55/85 B&B sgl/dbl/trpl.* **$$$$**

🏠 **Panoramic View Hotel** [398 B2] (35 rooms) 📞033 336 0270; m 0937 454545; e info@panoramicviewhotel.com; w panoramicviewhotel.com. This comfortable & aptly named hotel has quite large rooms with wood laminate floor, attractive traditional fabrics & private terrace with seating & superb views. The staff are pleasant & enthusiastic, & a good restaurant is attached. *US$55/69/85 sgl/dbl/trpl B&B.* **$$$$**

🏠 **Lalibela Lodge** [398 B3] (16 rooms) m 0911 534900; e info@lalibelalodge.com; w lalibelalodge.com. This attractive lodge has well-priced en-suite cottages with king-size bed, hand-crafted wood furnishings, private balcony & hot shower in the old wing. Much larger & pricier

rooms & suites in the new wing also come with large flatscreen TV & tub. A good restaurant is attached. *US$40/50 sgl/dbl old wing; US$70/130 dbl/suite new wing. All rates B&B.* **$$$$**

🏠 **Jerusalem Hotel** [399 C7] (25 rooms) 📞033 336 0047; m 0911 435432/099443; e lastajerusalem@gmail.com. Once the top place to stay in Lalibela, this 3-storey cliffside hotel is slightly past its prime, though there's no arguing with the stirring views or the friendly & helpful vibe created by an owner-manager of 15 years' standing. The large, clean, tiled rooms come complete with king-size bed & en-suite hot shower. The restaurant serves good traditional & Western dishes. *US$40/50 B&B sgl/dbl.* **$$$$**

🏠 **Roha Hotel** [399 B6] (64 rooms) 📞033 336 0009; m 0911 004229; e mollafentawt@gmail.com. This former government hotel stands in well-wooded grounds offering a decent view over the hills, especially from the new rooftop terrace bar. The en-suite rooms with TV, fan & hot tub/shower are unexciting but comfortable enough. There's an adequate but overpriced restaurant & well-stocked gift & bookshop. *US$44/52 B&B sgl/dbl.* **$$$$**

🏠 **Bete Abraham Inn** [399 B7] (49 rooms) 📞033 336 1065. This multistorey church-owned hotel with colourful exterior frescoes has adequate en-suite rooms with wood laminate floor, sat TV & private balcony which have benefited from recent refurbishment. *US$40/50/70 sgl/dbl/suite.* **$$$$**

Budget

☀️🏠 **Honeyland Hotel** [398 C2] (10 rooms) 📞033 336 0191; m 0911 735041; e besfat2015@gmail.com; w honeylandlalibelahotel.com. As good value for money as you'll find in Lalibela, this central owner-managed gem has clean & spacious rooms with hand-crafted wood furniture, flatscreen TV & hot shower. Some are larger & have a balcony with view, so ask to look at a couple. A cheerful ground-floor restaurant serves a varied menu with most dishes in the US$3–5 range. *US$35/40 sgl/dbl B&B.* **$$$**

☀️🏠 **Lalibela Hotel** [399 C6] (13 rooms) 📞033 336 0027; m 0911 095004; e info@lalibelahotels.com; w lalibelahotels.com. Sensibly priced small hotel whose clean & spacious en-suite rooms boast attractive ethnic décor, sat TV & hot shower. There's a *tukul*-style restaurant, a well-stocked supermarket that carries supplies for trekking, & a good view from the flowering gardens. *US$25/30/42 B&B sgl/dbl/trpl*. **$$$**

☀ 🏠 **Lal Hotel** [399 C7] (100 rooms) 📞 033 336 0008; **m** 0930 034708; ⓕ. Lalibela's largest hotel, set in sprawling green gardens southwest of the town centre, has good amenities including a swimming pool, gym & 3 restaurants. The en-suite bungalow rooms with hot shower & larger & better-equipped *tukul* rooms with flatscreen TV are great value following a recent cut in rates. *US$32/38 sgl/dbl (bungalow) or US$40/45 sgl/dbl (tukul); all rates B&B*. **$$$**

🏠 **Red Rock** [398 D2] (15 rooms) 📞 033 336 1030; **m** 0911 068344; **e** info@ redrocklalibelahotel.com; **w** redrocklalibelahotel. com. Popular central budget hotel with a good downstairs restaurant, & a dynamic English-speaking management. The en-suite rooms with hot water & balcony are very comfortable & 107/8 & 111/12 have fantastic views. *US$25/28/32 sgl/ dbl/twin*. **$$$**

🏠 **Zan-Seyoum Hotel** [399 F7] (30 rooms) 📞 033 336 0893; **m** 0911 048279; **e** info@ hotelzanseyoum.com; **w** hotelzanseyoum.com. This owner-managed hotel has an inconvenient & charmless location 2km along the Gashena road but the en-suite rooms with wood laminate floor, queen-size bed, terrace & modern bathroom are well priced; & the lovely traditional restaurant serves Ethiopian fare in the US$3–4 range & arranges traditional music performances by request. *US$25/35/50 sgl/dbl/trpl B&B*. **$$$**

🏠 **Alef Paradise Hotel** [399 D6] (22 rooms) 📞 033 336 0323; **m** 0911 556211; **e** alparahotel@ yahoo.com; **w** alefparadisehotel.com. This friendly, brightly painted & reasonably convenient 3-storey hotel offers good-value en-suite rooms with attractive traditional furnishing, hot water & spacious balcony. A good restaurant is attached. The location is potentially noisy. *US$20/25/30 sgl/dbl/trpl*. **$$$**

🏠 **Selam Guest House** [399 C7] (11 rooms) 📞 033 336 0074; **m** 0913 840116; **e** selamguesthouselalibela@gmail.com. Tucked away in a quiet backstreet, this unpretentious, welcoming & newly renovated owner-managed guesthouse offers accommodation in en-suite rooms with reflective glass fronts to let in the light, hand-crafted wood furniture & hot shower. *US$35 B&B dbl or twin*. **$$$**

🏠 **Villa Lalibela Guesthouse** [399 C7] (9 rooms) 📞 033 336 0246; **m** 0911 343113.

Comprising a converted family house on a quiet back road, this friendly set-up has large, clean but rather tired-looking en-suite rooms with hot shower & small terrace. A touch overpriced. *US$30/35 sgl/dbl*. **$$$**

Shoestring

☀ 🏠 **Budget Guesthouse** [399 C7] (6 rooms) **m** 0911 456470, 0972 424241; **e** budgetguesthouse@yahoo.com. Owned & managed by a charming couple that speaks good English, this welcoming cheapie has a quiet location & simple but clean & bright rooms with tiled floor & hot shower set around a neat courtyard with seating. *US$20/30 dbl/twin*. **$$**

🏠 **Asheton Hotel** [398 F4] (14 rooms) 📞 033 336 0030; **m** 0911 002623; **e** danielbaboon@ gmail.com; **w** ashetonhotel.com. Lalibela's longest-serving shoestring hotel has reasonably clean & brightly decorated rooms with wooden floor & en-suite hot shower set around a green courtyard. The restaurant serves decent if unexceptional food. Management can be pushy about arranging guides & tours. *US$14/16/20 sgl/ dbl/twin*. **$$**

🏠 **Makanalilt Hotel** [398 G2] (42 rooms) **m** 0942 601145. New & super-central 3-storey hotel with spacious & tolerably clean en-suite rooms with hot shower. *US$16/24 sgl/dbl*. **$$**

🏠 **Hotel Bluelal** [398 G2] (13 rooms) **m** 0921 524295; **e** tebebe2007@yahoo.com. Attached to one of Lalibela's longer-serving traditional restaurants, this has a quiet but conveniently central location & clean no-frill rooms that deliver all you could expect at the price. *US$8 sgl using common shower; US$12/16 en-suite dbl/twin*. **$$**

🏠 **Blue Nile Guesthouse** [398 E4] (4 rooms) **m** 0963 577930. This narrow 2-storey hotel couldn't be more central for exploring the churches, & the clean en-suite rooms with TV & hot shower seem like pretty good value. *US$16/24 dbl/ twin*. **$$**

🏠 **Heaven Guesthouse** [399 C7] (8 rooms) 📞 033 336 0075; **m** 0911 567614. The scruffy en-suite rooms in this rustic compound are indifferent value. *US$20 dbl*. **$$**

🏠 **Seven Olives Hotel** [398 F2] (18 rooms) 📞 033 336 0020. The oldest hotel in Lalibela is centrally located in well-wooded flowering grounds, but the en-suite rooms with hot showers really looked their age on last inspection. Poor value. *US$24 dbl*. **$$$**

🏠 **Helen Hotel** [399 D6] (6 rooms) 📞033 336 0053; **m** 0911 075219, 0912 439118. Probably the scruffiest & dingiest rooms in Lalibela have the twin virtues of en-suite showers & realistic prices. Expect standard rates to rise when the new 4-storey extension at the back is complete. *US$16 twin*. **$$**

Out of town

🏠 **Hudad Eco-Retreat** [map, page 411] (5 rooms) **m** 0937 949356; **e** bookings@lalibelahudad.com; **w** lalibelahudad.com. Set in a 10ha stand close to Asheton Maryam (page 413), this remote owner-managed ecolodge is aimed at keen walkers who really want to get away from it all or hope to connect with local communities. It stands on a 3,300m-high plateau offering stunning views all around, as well as an opportunity to see wildlife such as gelada monkey & lammergeier. There are 4 *tukuls* sleeping up to 4 persons each & 1 family house sleeping 6, & a cafeteria serves decent food. Day hikes run from the lodge to the likes of Asheton Maryam, Mount Abune Yoseph & Yemrehanna Kristos. Only accessible on foot, it's a 2–3hr hike from Lalibela or 60–90mins from the new road to Asheton Maryam. Mules are available to take luggage, but it is easier to leave most of it in Lalibela. Closed Jul & Aug. *US$70/87/99/110 B&B for 1/2/3/4 persons sharing*. **$$$$$**

🏠 **Degosach Ecolodge** [map, page 411] (4 rooms) 📞033 836 3131; **m** 0911 052659; **e** booking@degosachecolodge.com; **w** degosachecolodge.com. Set at an elevation of 3,800m about 10km north of Lalibela as the crow flies, this simple but comfortable *tukul*-style lodge has a spectacular & peaceful rural setting & serves authentic highland cuisine. Activities include horseback excursions, local cultural tours & hikes to the likes of Abune Yoseph (3½hrs), Yemrehanna Kristos (3hrs) & Kenkenit Mikael (1½hrs). The lodge can arrange a 40min road transfer to a car park only 30mins away by foot, or a guided hike or mule-back trip from Lalibela via Kenkenit Mikael (4hrs) or Wedebye Plateau (7hrs). *US$58/72 B&B sgl/dbl, plus US$4 pp lunch or dinner*. **$$$$**

✕ **WHERE TO EAT AND DRINK** If you are staying at one of the hotels listed in the upmarket and moderate category (page 400), most of them have a decent restaurant serving a varied selection of Ethiopian and Western dishes for around US$5–8.

Moderate to expensive

✳✕ **Ben Abeba** [398 B1] 📞033 336 0215; **m** 0922 345122; **w** benabeba.com; 🕐 06.00–22.00 daily. Set atop a cone-shaped hill at the northern end of town, this magical restaurant is a joint Scottish–Ethiopian venture notable for its surreal multi-decked architecture (reminiscent of a witch's hat), the incredible views over the surrounding valleys & hills, & a garden full of attractive nooks where you can chill out after eating. The imaginative menu, which sets various Ethiopian dishes alongside home-style European cooking (shepherd's pie & Scotch egg are popular with homesick Brits) prepared with organic vegetables & fruit grown on site, is not to be missed! It also has great cocktail & dessert menus. Booking for dinner advisable Nov–Feb. Staff can arrange tuk-tuks back to town for up to US$2/party. *Mains US$3–5*.

✕ **Kana Restaurant** [399 C7] **m** 0911 019830; 🕐 08.00–22.00 daily. Attractive rectangular traditionally decorated restaurant serving a variety of local staples in the US$2–5 range, pasta for around US$2.50, & pizzas & grills in the US$5–6 range. Strong on character & quality.

✕ **Old Abyssinia** [399 A7] 🕐 11.00–23.00 daily. Situated in an authentic mud-wall *tukul* offering spectacular views of the hill, this characterful restaurant serves a selection of soups, salads & local & Western dishes in the US$2–4 range. It also offers cookery lessons for US$25–30 pp depending on group size.

✕ **Seven Olives** [398 F2] 🕐 07.00–23.00 daily. With its attractive *tukul*-style restaurant, varied menu & lushly wooded grounds teeming with birds, this time-warped hotel is an appealing spot for a central lunch & dinner. *Mains US$3–5*.

✕ **XO Lalibela Restaurant** [399 C6] 📞034 840 2236; **e** xo-lalibela@gmail.com; 🕐 06.00–22.00 daily. Tucked away unsignposted in the Lalibela Cultural Museum, this smart but under-patronised bistro has a contemporary feel, quiet terrace seating, & an interesting menu incorporating b/fasts, salads, fajitas, pizzas, pasta & grills. *Mains US$3–5.*

Cheap to moderate

✖ **John Café** [398 F2] ⊕ 06.30–19.00 daily. This backpacker favourite has an extensive menu of budget-friendly local & international dishes, & can put together lunchboxes for hikers. Coffee & juices are stocked; alcohol is by special order only. A handicraft shop is attached. *Most mains around US$2; pizza US$3–4.*

✖ **Unique Restaurant** [398 F4] ☎ 033 336 0125; ⊕ 07.00–21.00 daily. This unpretentious little place, distinguished by its 'Recommended by Faranji' signpost, serves tasty pizzas, Ethiopian specialities & roast meat, as well as pancakes for b/fast. Great value. *Around US$2 for a main.*

✖ **Segenet Restaurant** [398 G2] m 0985 157260; ⊕ 07.00–22.00 daily. Bamboo-shaded rooftop restaurant overlooking the main square & serving pizzas, salads, pasta & local dishes in the US$2–3 range.

✖ **Honey Restaurant** [399 C6] m 0911 041006; ⊕ 07.00–22.00 daily. Pleasant new traditional-style restaurant popular with locals & well geared to budget travellers. Specialises in Ethiopian fare, mostly at around US$2.

✖ **Bluelal Restaurant** [398 G2] m 0921 524295; ⊕ 06.00–22.00 daily. This long-serving budget eatery, also known as Chez Sophie, has traditional décor & well-priced food, ranging from local vegetarian fare (*around US$2*) to pizzas & grills (*US$3–4*).

NIGHTLIFE

☆ **Askalech Torpedo House** [398 E3] ☎ 033 376 0087; m 0911 631232; ⊕ 09.00–late daily. Renowned for serving the best & most potent *tej* (honey wine) in town, as well as chilled beers & a limited selection of tasty local dishes, Torpedo is of most interest for the nightly *azmari* performances (accompanied by dancing Amhara waitresses) aimed mostly at a local audience.

♀ **Top View Bar** [399 A7] Situated out towards Old Abyssinia, this unpretentious sundowner spot emphatically delivers the promised views & also serves sensibly priced beer, wine & *tej.*

♀ **Good Harvest Wine Bar** [399 C6] m 0967 521650; ⊕ 08.00–23.30 daily. Traditionally decorated *tukul*-style bar stocking the full range of Ethiopia's better wines. *Around US$2/glass, US$12/750ml bottle, or US$30/2.5-litre box.*

SHOPPING Lalibela is as good a place as any in Ethiopia to buy handicrafts. The two main clusters of craft stalls are on the main square and along the road between the Lal and Roha hotels. To stock up on dried food before trekking to one of the monasteries, Just Supermarket south of Seven Olives Hotel has a fair range of imported goods such as processed cheese, biscuits and chocolate. A few small supermarkets can be found around the Lal Hotel.

TOUR OPERATORS An increasingly popular activity out of Lalibela is overnight treks to Mount Abune Yoseph and the circuit of community guesthouses operated by Tesfa Tours. Treks with Tesfa Tours should ideally be arranged in advance through its Addis Ababa office, but the other operators listed below can put together trips at short notice. Most of these operators will also arrange day trips to outlying rock-hewn churches and monasteries.

Happy Day Ethiopian Tours [398 B2] Top Twelve Hotel; m 0911 711967; e desale_lal@ yahoo.com; w happydaytours.joomla.com. Highly rated for cultural tours in & around Lalibela & also offers trekking packages.

Highland Eco-Trekking Tours [398 F2] Next to Seven Olives Hotel; m 0912 130831; e info@ highlandtrekking.com; w highlandtrekking.com;

see ad, page 187. Reliable operator offering a similar range of treks to Lalibela Eco Trekking.

Lalibela Eco Trekking Tours [398 F2] Seven Olives Hotel; ☎ 033 836 7636; m 0911 052659; e info@lalibela-eco-trekking.com; w lalibela-eco-trekking.com. Notable for its hands-on, responsive management, this trekking specialist arranges hikes to various outlying rock-hewn churches, Abune

right   Harar Gate, the main entrance to Harar's walled city page 468

below   Trinity Cathedral in Addis Ababa is the final resting place of Haile Selassie page 180

bottom   Bati has long been an important trade and cultural crossroads, and hosts Ethiopia's biggest weekly market page 428

above   The Tutu Fela stelae field is the site of about 300 stelae marking ancient graves   page 514

below left   The Amhara Martyrs' Memorial commemorates the members of the Ethiopian People's Democratic
Movement who lost their lives in the fight to liberate Ethiopia from the Derg regime   page 251

below right   Konso villages are dotted with totem-like _waka_ grave-markers, like these displayed in the Konso Museum
page 569

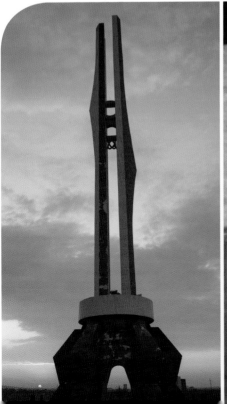 

above Officially the hottest place on Earth, the Danakil Depression features stunning landscapes, including live lava lakes, sulphurous multihued geysers and remote salt pans page 367

left Tikil Dingay, a striking planted rock formation near Addis Zemen page 263

below The area around Dodola offers some of the best trekking in the country, with lush *tef* farming land, forest and moorland page 487

above The Sanetti Plateau supports heath-like vegetation which is typical of the Afroalpine habitat on Africa's highest mountains page 499

right Sightings of Swayne's hartebeest (*Alcelaphus buselaphus swaynei*) are practically guaranteed in Senkele Swayne's Hartebeest Sanctuary page 540

below Chitu Crater Lake in Abijatta-Shalla National Park harbours a semi-resident flock of up to 10,000 flamingoes page 534

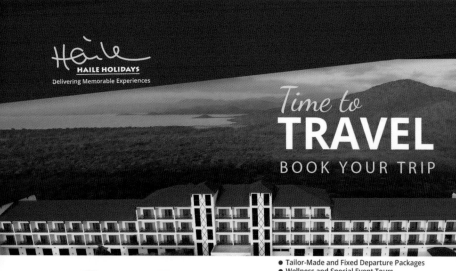

Yoseph & Abuhay Gariya Community Conservation Areas (CCAs), as well as its own Degosach Ecolodge. **Tesfa Tours** ☏011 124 5178; m 0921 602236; e info@tesfatours.com; w tesfatours.com. The pioneer of community-based trekking near Lalibela back in 2003 now operates a circuit of 7 community guesthouses on the Meket Escarpment south of town & 4 on the slopes of Mount Abune

Yoseph. For further details, see box, page 415 or check its excellent website.
Treasure Transport [398 B1] Ben Abeba Restaurant; ☏033 336 0038; m 0911 028953; e b_h2007@yahoo.com; w benabeba.com. Affordable 4x4 or car hire to outlying monasteries, group trips for budget travellers & transfers to Gondar & Bahir Dar.

GUIDES Official guides can be arranged through your hotel or are located outside the ticket office for the rock-hewn churches. Generally, they are very knowledgeable, speak good English, and will greatly enhance your understanding and appreciation of what you see. Typical guiding fees are US$20 per day for one to five people, US$34 for five to ten or US$40 for larger groups. These can sometimes be negotiated down out of season and may escalate when the place is busy. Tips are appreciated but not regarded as obligatory. Unofficial guides ask less than official guides, but they tend to have limited knowledge, to be less respected by the priests, and to be tiresome when it comes to angling for tips. Except when it comes to the subject of money, most guides (official or not) are genuinely helpful, and they'll sort out anything you want from a good local meal or a better hotel to helping you bargain for curios. They can also arrange trips further afield to the likes of Asheton Maryam and Yemrehanna Kristos.

WHAT TO SEE AND DO Lalibela's main attraction is its central complex of 13 rock-hewn churches and chapels. At a push, the churches can all be visited in one rushed afternoon, but it is advisable to split your sightseeing into two half-day sessions, especially as the rather costly entrance ticket covering all 13 churches and chapels, as well as the church museum, is valid for up to five days. Also worth visiting, ideally before you visit the churches, is the insightful Lalibela Cultural Centre Museum opposite the Lal Hotel. The town itself is most lively on Saturdays, when the main market is held in a clearing close to the churches, and hundreds of villagers flock in 'Saturday best' traditional attire, evoking Ethiopia as it was a few decades back.

Rock-hewn churches of Lalibela [map, page 406] (☏ 033 336 0021; ⊕ 06.00–12.30 & 14.00–18.00 daily; US$50 pp entrance fee for up to 5 days, covering all 13 churches & inc still photography, US$50 video camera) Arguably the most impressive historical site anywhere in sub-Saharan Africa, the rock-hewn churches of Lalibela all lie within a roughly triangular 15ha area at the southern end of the town centre. There are two main clusters of churches, separated by a non-perennial rock-cut stream known rather grandiosely as the Jordan River (one of many place names that support the notion King Lalibela conceived of the church as a kind of 'New Jerusalem'). The main entrance and ticket office is on the town side of the northern cluster, which comprises seven churches and chapels whose sense of cohesion does rather support the notion that it was planned as a whole, quite possibly by King Lalibela as the legends suggest. The southern cluster, comprising five churches, lies about 250m further southeast, and comes across as more hotchpotch in design (indeed, several of its individual churches are thought to have been secular in origin and some might predate the reign of Lalibela by five centuries). The triangle's western apex is formed by the iconic Bet Giyorgis, which stands in majestic isolation some 300m from the other churches, on the east side of the main road between the town centre and the Roha Hotel.

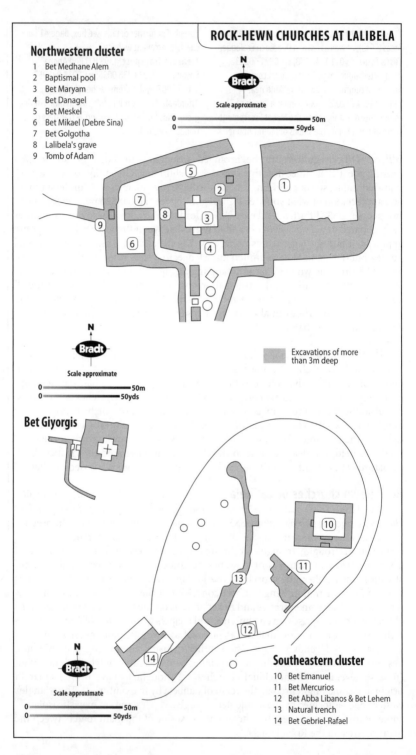

ROCK-HEWN CHURCHES AT LALIBELA

Northwestern cluster

1   Bet Medhane Alem
2   Baptismal pool
3   Bet Maryam
4   Bet Danagel
5   Bet Meskel
6   Bet Mikael (Debre Sina)
7   Bet Golgotha
8   Lalibela's grave
9   Tomb of Adam

N

Bradt

Scale approximate

0 ———————— 50m
0 ———————— 50yds

N

Bradt

Scale approximate

0 ———————— 50m
0 ———————— 50yds

Excavations of more
than 3m deep

Bet Giyorgis

N

Bradt

Scale approximate

0 ———————— 50m
0 ———————— 50yds

Southeastern cluster

10   Bet Emanuel
11   Bet Mercurios
12   Bet Abba Libanos & Bet Lehem
13   Natural trench
14   Bet Gebriel-Rafael

Two main types of church are found at Lalibela. Bet Giyorgis and most of the churches in the northern cluster are subterranean monoliths or three-quarter monoliths, an architectural style unique to Ethiopia. These excavations mimic normal buildings insofar as they are free from the surrounding rock on three or four sides, nestled within artificial courtyards and trenches that were incised deep into the bedrock to leave the free-standing block of rock into which the actual church was carved. The remaining churches, like their counterparts in Tigray, were generally cut into a vertical rock face, often by exploiting existing caves or cracks in the rock. Now at least 800 years old, the churches are threatened by seepage, for which reason a quartet of translucent white shelters has been erected above two of the more vulnerable churches in each of the two clusters. Eye-catching though these shelters most certainly are, they do rather clash with the ancient architecture beneath, so it is to be hoped they will be replaced as and when a more suitable design is approved.

Lalibela is usually at its most compelling and spiritually rewarding in the early morning (ideally around 05.30), when masses are held at many of the churches and most tourists are still in bed or having breakfast. Most reliable for a large turnout at morning mass is Saturday, or any feast days associated with a particular saint, and any guide or hotel receptionist should be able to tell you which of the churches is likely to be your best bet on any given day. Once morning mass is over, tourists increasingly start to outnumber bona fide worshippers, and the churches start to feel like they are maintained less as active shrines of worship than as tourist attractions. Before visiting any of the churches, you need to pop into the official ticket office (500m west and downhill from the main square along the road to the Roha Hotel) and pay your entrance fee, which is valid for up to five days. Be sure to get a receipt, as you will be asked to produce it at every church you visit. The ticket office is also the best place to organise a guide, assuming that you want one and don't have one already. Having paid your fee, you're free to walk where you like and photograph what you like anywhere in the complex (with the obvious exception of the Holy of Holies at the back of each church). It is, however, customary to slip a few birr to any person you put centre frame. Also, note that there are toilet facilities at the ticket office as you enter the northern cluster, but there are no toilets near the southern cluster or Bet Giyorgis.

Northern cluster

Bet Medhane Alem The most easterly church in this cluster, Bet Medhane Alem (House of the Saviour of the World) is also the first church you'll see coming from the ticket office. The most architecturally impressive of the churches at Lalibela (though less impactful perhaps than Bet Giyorgis), it is reputedly the world's largest rock-hewn monolith, standing up to 11m high and covering an area of almost 800m^2. A plain building, supported by 36 pillars on the inside and another 36 around the outside, Bet Medhane Alem has a classical nobility reminiscent of an ancient Greek temple, a similarity that has led some experts to think it was modelled on Ezana's original church of Maryam Tsion at Axum (and thus indirectly on King Solomon's Temple in Jerusalem). The interior of the church is also plain, with several abandoned graves carved into the rock floor, and its vast size creates a cathedral-like austerity. It stands in its own wide courtyard, whose walls are pockmarked with niches originally carved as graves or hermit cells.

Bet Maryam, Bet Meskel and Bet Danagel From Bet Medhane Alem, a short, low tunnel leads west into a larger trapezoid courtyard enclosing a trio of churches. Tradition has it that the largest of these three churches, dedicated to the Virgin Mary, was the first church excavated at Lalibela, and it still remains a particularly popular shrine with local pilgrims. Smaller, more intimate and less imposing than Medhane Alem, Bet Maryam stands about 10m high, with a floor area of around 250m², and an upper floor divided into seven rooms stacked with church treasures. Highlights of the elaborately decorated interior include carvings of the original Lalibela Cross and Star of David, dense paintings on parts of the roof, and a relief of two riders fighting a dragon above the entrance. A veiled internal pillar is reputedly inscribed with the Ten Commandments in Greek and Geëz, as well a description of how the churches of Lalibela were excavated, and the story of the beginning and end of the world. The local priests say that this pillar glowed brightly until the 16th century and claim it would be too dangerous to lift the veil and show it to researchers.

Carved into the northern wall of Bet Maryam's courtyard, the tiny chapel of Bet Meskel (House of the Cross) is barely 35m² in area. In the southern wall, and even smaller, the atmospheric chapel of Bet Danagel (House of the Virgins) was reputedly constructed in honour of 50 Christian maiden nuns murdered by the Roman ruler Julian the Apostate in the 4th century, a legend recorded in the Ethiopian *Book of Martyrs*. Also in the courtyard is a pool believed to cure any infertile woman who is dipped into the water three times at Genna – the water is certainly green and slimy enough to suggest a favourable effect on procreativity. The water level is about 2m below the courtyard, so the women have to be lowered down on a harnessed rope, a rather comic sight!

Bet Mikael, Bet Golgotha and Selassie Chapel The most westerly courtyard in the northern cluster contains the twin churches of **Bet Mikael** (House of Michael, also known as Bet Debre Sina) and **Bet Golgotha** (named after the hill outside Jerusalem where, according to the Gospels, Jesus Christ was crucified), which share a common entrance and together form a semi-monolith. Possibly the most atmospheric of Lalibela's churches, Mikael and Golgotha possess the dank still feel of a dungeon, and are imbued with a pervasive air of sanctity. The historical relationship between the twin churches is confused by the presence of several *tabots*, but the structure suggests they have always functioned separately. The interior of Bet Golgotha (the one church in Lalibela that women are prohibited from entering) is remarkable in that it has seven life-size reliefs of saints carved around its walls, a feature more typical of churches built or excavated during or after the 15th century.

Situated within Bet Golgotha, the tiny **Selassie Chapel**, where King Lalibela was reputedly buried, is the holiest place in Lalibela, and traditionally closed to non-ecclesiastic visitors, though an Italian expedition forced its way in at gunpoint during the occupation. Local tradition holds that the Mikael-Golgotha-Selassie complex, like the other churches in the area, was carved by King Lalibela. However, art historian Michael Gervers argues convincingly that the absence of Axumite features common to the other churches at Lalibela and presence of anachronistic carvings points to Mikael-Golgotha-Selassie having been excavated in the 15th century, presumably as a symbolic tomb for the then-recently sanctified King Lalibela.

The western exit from the courtyard lies at the base of the **Tomb of Adam**, a cruciform hermit's cell decorated by mutilated paintings of the Zagwe kings of Lalibela. Some of the rock-hewn caves near this were recently converted into a church.

Southern cluster
Bet Gebriel-Rafael The strangest church at Lalibela, this fortress-like excavation is surrounded by a deep trench that sometimes fills up like a moat in the rainy season, and it must be crossed on a solid concrete bridge. This appearance and the unusual alignment of the church has long led experts to think it was originally carved not

as a church but as the residence of King Lalibela. More recent architectural studies by David Phillipson indicate that both it and the nearby Bet Mercurios could have been excavated as the core of a fortified palatial complex during the politically unstable 7th and 8th centuries, when the Axumite Empire was in the process of disintegrating. From the outside, Bet Gebriel-Rafael is a very imposing and memorable sight. The northern façade, its height greatly exaggerated by the trench below, is distinguished by a row of arched niches which, although they show strong Axumite influences, give the building a somewhat Islamic appearance. Inside, the church is surprisingly small and plain, decorated only by three carved Latin crosses. The priests reckon that a second set of rooms underneath the church (presumably on a level with the floor of the surrounding trench) can be reached by a tunnel so secret that nobody remembers exactly where it is!

Bet Abba Libanos and Bet Lehem Legend has it that Bet Abba Libanos was built overnight by Lalibela's wife, Meskel Kibre, assisted by a group of angels, possibly after the king's death. It has been built around a cave in a vertical face, and, although the roof is still connected to the original rock, the sides and back are separated by narrow tunnels. The pink-tinged façade, which shows strong Axumite influences in its arched and cruciform windows, lies under an overhang in a manner reminiscent of certain churches in Tigray. The interior of the church is most notable for a small light in the altar wall which, according to the priests, shines of its own accord 24 hours a day. A tunnel of about 50m in length leads from the right aisle of this church to Bet Lehem (House of Bread), a small and simple chapel that might well have been a monastic cell used for private prayers by King Lalibela.

Bet Emanuel Art historians regard this 12m-high church, the only full monolith in the southern cluster, to be the finest and most precisely worked church in Lalibela. This is possibly because it was the private church of the royal family. Set in a deep courtyard, it has an exterior that mimics with remarkable precision the classical Axumite layered wood-and-stone built-up church typified by Yemrehanna Kristos outside Lalibela. An ornamental frieze of blind windows dominates the church's interior.

Bet Mercurios This cave church is dedicated to Saint Mercurios, a 3rd-century Coptic saint who was tortured for his Christian beliefs, and eventually beheaded, by the pagan Emperor Decius, but is perhaps most famous for his heavenly orchestration of the death in battle of the apostatic Emperor Julian a century later. Another church that may have started life as a secular excavation (most probably a jail or courtroom, judging by the iron shackles embedded in the surrounding trench), Bet Mercurios could be as many as 1,400 years old, and has suffered badly from the ravages. Today, the interior is partially collapsed while the rather functional entrance had to be rebuilt from scratch in the late 1980s. Still, there's a beautiful, albeit rather faded, 15th-century wall frieze of what looks like the three wise men or a group of saints, and the church also houses a recently restored painting of a beatific Mercurios, his sword trailing through the guts of the evil emperor Julian, while a trio of what appear to be dog-headed men look on from the right.

Bet Giyorgis This isolated church dedicated to St George is the only monolith in Lalibela left uncovered by a protective shelter, presumably because the view from above is perhaps the town's most iconic sight (and photo opportunity). It must measure close to 15m in height and, like the churches of the northwestern group, it is excavated below ground level in a sunken courtyard enclosed by precipitous walls. Its most remarkable feature, however, is that it is carved in the shape of a symmetrical cruciform tower. The story is that Giyorgis – St George as he is known to us – was so offended that none of Lalibela's churches was dedicated to him that he personally visited the king to set things straight. Lalibela responded by promising he would build the finest of all his churches for Giyorgis. So enthusiastic was the saint to see the result of Lalibela's promise that he rode his horse right over the wall into the entrance tunnel. The holes in the stone tunnel walls are the hoof prints of St George's horse – or so they tell you in Lalibela. Impressive as the church is on the outside, the interior is surprisingly small and unadorned, but very atmospheric.

Lalibela Cultural Centre Museum [399 C6] (⌚ *08.00–17.00 daily; entrance US$1.50*) This first-floor municipal museum, which opened opposite the Lal Hotel in 2013, is far better organised than the chaotic array of exhibits displayed in the church museum next to the ticket office. A series of wall displays outlines the development and aspects of the church complex, and it also has a terrific exhibition of sacred and ethnographic material, ranging from 500-year-old Ge'ez Bibles to typical household objects, all of it well exhibited, though a little short on explanatory material.

National Honey Museum [398 B3] Situated opposite Lalibela Lodge, this new museum, part of a government-built 850-seat conference centre and dedicated to all things honey-related, is scheduled to open in 2019.

AROUND LALIBELA

The mountains around Lalibela are studded with medieval monasteries and churches, many of which are very different from their Lalibela counterparts, and are also less frequently visited by tourists. Two of these monasteries, Nakuta La'ab and Asheton Maryam, can be visited as affordable and relatively straightforward day walks from Lalibela. For those who want to see a good selection of churches and monasteries in one go, a better option would be to rent a 4x4 and explore the Bilbilla area, which hosts three impressive rock-hewn churches, as well as the most accessible of the country's few surviving built-up Axumite churches in the form of Yemrehanna Kristos. Altogether different is the overnight hike to Mount Abune Yoseph, whose upper slopes support a substantial number of gelada monkeys along with one of the few remaining populations of the endangered Ethiopian wolf. Note that entrance fees to these outlying churches are *not* included in the price of the ticket for the churches within Lalibela.

NAKUTA LA'AB [map, opposite] (*Entrance US$8*) The easiest outlying church to reach, Nakuta La'ab is a medieval monastery whose eponymous constructor was both the nephew of and successor to King Lalibela. It consists of a relatively simple church built around a shallow cave in which several holy pools are fed by natural springs. Treasures, some of which are claimed to have belonged to Nakuta La'ab himself, include paintings, crosses and an illuminated leather Bible, which can be brought out into the open and examined in decent light. Aside from Lalibela, Nakuta La'ab is the only Zagwe ruler to be included under a recognisable name in all the available lists of Ethiopian kings, but several contradictory traditions surround his reign and the church that bears his name. One version has it that Nakuta La'ab ruled from this church, which he called Qoqhena, during an 18-month break in Lalibela's monarchy. Another is that he took refuge at the church only after he was

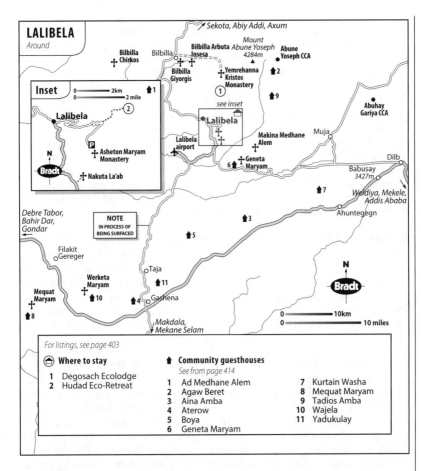

LALIBELA
Around

Sekota, Abiy Addi, Axum

Bilbilla
Chirkos

Bilbilla

Bilbilla Arbuta
Insesa

Mount
Abune Yoseph
4284m

Abune
Yoseph CCA

Bilbilla
Giyorgis

Yemrehanna
Kristos
Monastery

1

2

9

see inset

Lalibela

Abuhay
Gariya CCA

Inset

0   2km
0   2 mile

1

Lalibela

2

Makina Medhane
Alem

Muja

Dilb

N

Asheton Maryam
Monastery

Lalibela
airport

Geneta
Maryam

6

Babusay
3427m

7

Weldiya, Mekele,
Addis Ababa

Bradt

Nakuta La'ab

Ahuntegegn

Debre Tabor,
Bahir Dar,
Gondar

NOTE
IN PROCESS OF
BEING SURFACED

3

5

Filakit
Gereger

Taja

11

N

Werketa
Maryam

Bradt

Mequat
Maryam

10

4

Gashena

8

Makdala,
Mekane Selam

0   10km
0   10 miles

For listings, see page 403

⌂ **Where to stay**

1 Degosach Ecolodge
2 Hudad Eco-Retreat

🏠 **Community guesthouses**
See from page 414

1 Ad Medhane Alem
2 Agaw Beret
3 Aina Amba
4 Aterow
5 Boya
6 Geneta Maryam

7   Kurtain Washa
8   Mequat Maryam
9   Tadios Amba
10 Wajela
11 Yadukulay

deposed. Yet another legend has it that he ascended to the throne only upon the death of Lalibela, and ruled for anything from a few years to half a century before he was deposed by Lalibela's son Yetbarak.

Nakuta La'ab lies about 6km south of Lalibela. It can be reached on foot by following the surfaced airport road out of town, a straightforward walk that takes up to 90 minutes, then turning left on to a clearly signposted 500m track that leads to the monastery. About halfway out, the road passes a small gorge where birders should look out for the likes of white-winged cliff-chat, Rüppell's black chat, paradise flycatcher, northern wryneck and various raptors. If you don't feel like the walk, you can arrange to see the monastery en route to or from the airport.

BILBILLA CHURCH CIRCUIT [map, above] Some 30km north of Lalibela on the road to Sekota, Bilbilla is the focal point of a cluster of four medieval churches, all set within a 10km radius of the small town. The Axumite cave church of Yemrehanna Kristos is the most remarkable of the churches close to Bilbilla, but the rock-hewn trio of Bilbilla Arbuta Insesa, Bilbilla Chirkos and Bilbilla Giyorgis are also well worth a visit, especially as they tend to be far less overrun with tourists than their counterparts in Lalibela. In a rented 4x4, which should cost around US$65–80 per day, the full circuit can be explored over 8 hours or so, including walking times of up to 20 minutes in either direction to each of the churches. Yemrehanna Kristos could also be visited in isolation, either in a 4x4 or on a mule. Using public transport, a few minibuses run to Bilbilla daily from outside the filling station in Lalibela, but only Bilbilla Giyorgis lies within easy walking distance of the village.

Bilbilla Giyorgis (*Entrance US$8*) Carved into a rock face some 500m east of Bilbilla, this three-quarter monolith dedicated to St George has an imposing façade decorated with a frieze said to represent the 12 vaults of heaven, though it is less impressive than it was before protective scaffolding was erected a few years back. The church, said locally to date to the 5th-century rule of Kaleb, is surrounded by a tunnel in a manner that recalls Lalibela's Bet Mercurios and contains several beehives whose 'holy honey' is used to cure abdominal infections. The church is signposted from the village, and you can drive to within 100m of it by 4x4, or walk there from the marketplace in 10–15 minutes.

Bilbilla Chirkos (*Entrance US$8*) A tall semi-monolith encircled by deep trenches, the impressive Bilbilla Chirkos has an intricately worked pink-tinged façade reminiscent of Lalibela's Bet Gebriel-Rafael. Notable features of the interior include the 12 thick pillars, some very old paintings of Maryam and Giyorgis (with dragon) and various other saints, and the cross that is carved into the hemispheric dome in front of the sanctuary. As with Bilbilla Giyorgis, there are several holy beehives. Treasures include several goatskin books including an illustrated 800-year-old Ge'ez history of Kidus Chirkos. The age of Bilbilla Chirkos is unknown. One tradition holds that it is the oldest rock-hewn church in Lasta, excavated during the 6th-century rule of Emperor Kaleb. Other sources suggest it is roughly contemporaneous with the Lalibela churches. The turn-off to Bilbilla Chirkos branches left from the Sekota road 27km past the main square in Lalibela and about 2km before the village of Bilbilla. The church, 6km from the main road, is covered in scaffolding which is clearly visible to the right before you reach the parking area, from where a gentle 500m footpath through a small forest patch and across a stream leads to the church. For adventurous travellers, **Kiddist Arbuta Washa**, the cave in which Lalibela was reputedly born, can be reached by driving 15km past Bilbilla Chirkos then hiking for another 2 hours into the hills.

Bilbilla Arbuta Insesa (*Entrance US$5*) A small sunken semi-monolith set around a small spring that produces holy water, this appears to be a very old excavation, with pillars and doors mimicking the Axumite design of some built-up churches, and it is dedicated to the four beasts, symbols of the four evangelists who followed St John. Less beautiful and imposing than similar churches in Lalibela town, Arbuta Insesa used to be popular with photographers due to the absence of scaffolding, but this has now been erected. To get there, continue driving eastward past Bilbilla Giyorgis for about 5km, then it's a 5-minute walk uphill along a gently sloping path through a patch of euphorbia and other trees.

Yemrehanna Kristos (*Entrance US$16*) The monastery of Yemrehanna Kristos is the undisputed gem among the churches around Bilbilla, not least because it is so fundamentally different from anything in town. Set at an altitude of 2,700m and protected by an unflattering modern outer wall, the main built-up church is a particularly fine example of late Axumite architecture, constructed using alternating layers of wood and granite faced with white gypsum that give it the appearance of a gigantic layered chocolate cream cake. Among many interesting architectural features are the cruciform carved windows, an etched wood-panel roof, a coffered ceiling with inlaid hexagons and a large dome over the sanctuary. Behind the main building, adding an eerie quality to the already dingy cavern, lie the bones of some of the 10,740 Christian pilgrims who, it is claimed, travelled from as far afield as Egypt, Syria and Jerusalem to die at this monastery. In front of the church, a small opening reveals muddy soil, said to be part of a subterranean freshwater lake below the cave. A reliable tradition has Yemrehanna Kristos built in the late 11th or early 12th century by the eponymous third Zagwe emperor, a predecessor of King Lalibela credited with restoring links between the Ethiopian and Coptic churches. An unverified legend states that Yemrehanna Kristos visited Alexandria during his reign, and built the church using wood imported from Egypt and gypsum from Jerusalem. The church and its curative holy water formed an important site of pilgrimage in medieval times.

By road, Yemrehanna Kristos can be reached by continuing 9km east from Arbuta Insesa to a parking area on the right-hand side of the road. From here, it takes about 15 minutes to ascend the steep but fully paved footpath that leads uphill to the monastery through a lovely patch of juniper forest. Reasonably fit travellers unable or unwilling to hire a vehicle might think seriously about visiting this monastery on mule-back – a 10–12-hour round trip from Lalibela.

ASHETON MARYAM [map, page 411] (*Entrance US$8*) Situated at an altitude of 3,200m on the western slopes of Mount Abune Yoseph (page 414), the monastery of Asheton Maryam was probably founded by King Nakuta La'ab, who may also be buried in the chapel. The church is carved out of a cleft in the cliff face, and the execution is rougher than at most other churches in and around Lalibela, but there are some interesting wall paintings and it also houses several ancient crosses, manuscripts and other treasures. The excursion is just as remarkable for the incredible highland setting and the wonderful views on the way up. Though the monastery is less than 5km from Lalibela as the crow flies, you gain around 600m in altitude, following a steep path strewn in parts with loose stones, all in all quite a breathless prospect for visitors coming from low-lying areas. Bank on a 5–6-hour round trip from Lalibela on foot or by mule, or using a combination of the two. There is also a new road, drivable in a minibus, that gets you to within 10 minutes' walk of Asheton Maryam.

GENETA MARYAM [map, page 411] (*Entrance US$8*) A large monolithic church carved into a pink-tinged outcrop near the source of the Tekeze River, Geneta Maryam lies on the western slopes of Mount Abune Yoseph, where it rather resembles a scaled-down version of Bet Medhane Alem. Although it is carved on a rocky hilltop, it lies within a deep trench-like courtyard entered via a large rock-hewn doorway with a cross carved into the side. According to tradition, Geneta Maryam was excavated during the early 13th-century reign of Yakuno Amlak. The outside and interior are supported by pillars, and it contains some elaborate but rather faded paintings credibly said to be more than 700 years old.

Geneta Maryam is about 45 minutes' drive from Lalibela. To get there, follow the Gashena road south of town for 9km, then left turn on to the old Weldiya road and follow it for 17km to the small village also known as Geneta Maryam, and only 700m from the church. You can drive to within 50m of the church, which is reached by a short but steep footpath. Expect to pay around US$50 to rent a 4x4 to take you there and back. It is also possible to hike to the church from Lalibela, or to travel by mule, which takes 4 hours in either direction. Any public transport heading between Lalibela and Weldiya via Muja will pass through the village of Geneta Maryam. The church is a popular trail head for hiking up Abune Yoseph.

MAKINA MEDHANE ALEM [map, page 411] (*Entrance US$8*) This magnificent monastic church, set in a massive cave on a spur of Mount Abune Yoseph, is similar in style to Yemrehanna Kristos in its characteristically Axumite use of layered wood and stone. Although there is little historical evidence to back it up, tradition holds that the church dates to the 6th century AD. More likely it was constructed in the 13th century under Yakuno Amlak, quite possibly in partial imitation of Yemrehanna Kristos. The roof has an elevated dome at one end and an elevated saddleback at the other. The lavishly decorated interior combines intricate geometric patterns with many old paintings, notably one above the door depicting roosters fighting next to the sun and moon. These were probably the work of the same artist who painted the interior of Geneta Maryam and are thus likely to be at least 700 years old. Inaccessible by road, the church lies about 3 hours from Geneta Maryam by foot or mule.

ABUNE YOSEPH, ZIGITE AND ABUHAY GARIYA COMMUNITY CONSERVATION AREA [map, page 411] (*AZACCA;* ✆ *033 361 1095;* m *0920 140020;* e *info@ abuneyosephtourism.org;* w *abuneyosephtourism.org; entrance US$12 pp*) Now administered by the federal government of Amhara, this formal amalgamation of two formerly unofficial Community Conservation Areas (CCAs) protects two disjunct tracts of Afroalpine vegetation in the highlands above Lalibela. The larger of these and the closer to Lalibela, the 53km² Abune Yoseph CCA protects the upper slopes of Ethiopia's third-highest massif, which towers to an altitude of 4,284m some 15km northeast of Lalibela as the lammergeier soars. Smaller and less well known is the 27km² Abuhay Gariya CCA, which is separated from Abune Yoseph by 8km of highland cultivation. Offering fine trekking and wildlife-viewing opportunities, both CCAs support a cover of giant lobelia, giant heather and guassa grass, and form an important stronghold for rare and endemic wildlife. This includes a significant population of Ethiopian wolf (around 180 individuals according to reserve officials, though 25–50 sounds more realistic), along with several thousand gelada monkeys, a few furtive leopards, an isolated troop of Hamadryas baboon in the *Erica* woodland on the northern flank near Ad Medhane Alem, and more than 220 highland bird species.

Abune Yoseph CCA can easily be visited as a 4x4 day excursion following a rough but motorable track that terminates at Agaw Beret Guesthouse and takes around 2 hours to drive in either direction. This track takes you through some pristine stands of lobelias and other Afroalpine vegetation where you are almost certain to see troops of gelada and might possibly encounter a stray Ethiopian wolf. The road also takes you to within 10 minutes' walking distance of the tallest peak Rim Gedele, and within 30 minutes of a striking pair of rocky outcrops known as Big Zigite and Little Zigite.

A more satisfying way to explore Abune Yoseph CCA is by foot or mule-back, though the combination of steep paths, rocky terrain, high altitude and seriously chilly weather (take plenty of warm clothing) mean that this isn't for the faint-hearted. The best overnight base for exploring the CCA is Agaw Beret Guesthouse, which was built by the Frankfurt Zoological Society and provides the highest accommodation in Ethiopia, just below the main peak of Rim Gedele, making it ideal for searching for the elusive wolf. The guesthouse consists of three basic *tukuls*, each with two ¾ mattresses on the floor, and a shared long-drop toilet. If wildlife-viewing or birdwatching in the Afroalpine moorland are your main interest, you could arrange to be driven to Agaw Beret and spend a night or two there. If you are keener on the challenging hike up from Lalibela, Tesfa and the other trekking companies based in Lalibela (page 404) offer standalone treks up Abune Yoseph (minimum two, but better four, nights), or it could be climbed as an extension of a longer Tesfa hike on the Meket Plateau. A good springboard for Abune Yoseph treks with Tesfa is the community guesthouse perched on a spur of the mountain behind Geneta Maryam, and this could be followed by nights at Tadios Amba, Agaw Beret and Ad Medhane Alem. Another possible springboard is Degosach Ecolodge (page 403).

The Abuhay Gariya CCA is currently undeveloped for trekking but plans are in place to build an ecolodge or guesthouse where trekkers could overnight after hiking across from Abune Yoseph. For now, it is possible to drive there from Lalibela in a couple of hours, following the Dilb road for 60km as far as Muja, then turning left at the main three-way junction to arrive at Wandach after 17km. From here, a right turn leads 8km uphill through some spectacular lobelia-studded highland scenery, distinguished by a succession of dyke-like rock formations that look oddly like ancient stone walls, to a weather station perched at an altitude of 3,750m. You would need to arrange a guide to explore on foot from here. For further details about developments at Abuhay Gariya, visit the unsignposted AZACCA office tucked away between the post office and CBE in central Lalibela, or contact Lalibela Eco Trekking Tours (page 404).

TESFA TREKKING: COMMUNITY TOURISM AROUND LALIBELA

Tesfa Tours (page 405), in collaboration with 11 local communities, operates a well-run and highly regarded trekking programme aimed at those who wish to explore the breathtaking scenery and authentic rural culture of the highlands around Lalibela. Each of the associated communities has built and manages a simple but comfortable guesthouse comprising several traditional *tukuls*, proceeds from which go towards economic and social development. Routes range from two nights to longer than a week in duration, and can focus on any or all of three interlinking circuits: West Meket, East Meket and Abune Yoseph. Of these, the original West Meket circuit is the lowest in altitude (2,700–3,000m) and the least physically demanding, following an escarpment that offers fantastic views across the rural landscape, excellent birding and access to the church of Werketa Maryam, with its intriguing cave complex, as well as a dramatic gorge with a waterfall which is home to a large troop of gelada monkeys. The East Meket circuit is even more scenic but higher in altitude (2,700–3,600m) and more physically taxing. Most demanding of all – but especially rewarding for wildlife and peak-baggers – is the circuit on 4,284m Abune Yoseph (page 414) starting at a hut near the rock-hewn church of Geneta Maryam (page 413). Treks between community guesthouses generally take about 6 hours and donkeys are used for all baggage, so you need only carry a small daypack. Rates are around US$70 per day inclusive of food, accommodation, guide and pack animals, but exclusive of bottled drinks, transport and church entry. Tesfa can also arrange transport to the trail head and back from Lalibela, Bahir Dar, Gondar or Mekele. Most treks around Lalibela close during the rains (mid-July to September) but some guesthouses remain open all year. Advance booking is mandatory. Visit the informative and well-organised website w tesfatours.com for further details of route variations and individual guesthouses.

12

Dessie and Southeast Amhara

The southeast of Amhara is a predominately highland region that sees little tourism by comparison with other parts of the northern historic circuit. It is generally traversed only by those heading overland in one or other direction between Lalibela and Addis Ababa via Weldiya, and most visitors aim to get through as quickly as possible. The region's largest town is Dessie, which straddles the main road 390km northeast of Addis Ababa and 290km southeast of Lalibela, and forms a convenient overnight stop for those driving between the two. Dessie wouldn't win any urban beauty contests, but it is well known for its traditional *azmari* singers, and is a good base for visiting the lovely Lake Hayk and associated monastery of Hayk Istafanos. Other substantial towns include Kombolcha, an important industrial centre and transport hub that straddles the Addis Ababa road only 20km south of Dessie, and chilly Debre Berhan, which lies 230km closer to the capital. Eastern Amhara is well suited to travellers seeking off-the-beaten-track experiences, be it the oft-overlooked community reserve that protects the Guassa Plateau and its resident populations of Ethiopian wolf and gelada monkey, little-known but stunning churches such as the plateau-top Gishen Debre Kerbe or modified cave Adkanu Maryam, the fabulous weekly livestock markets at Bati and Ziya, or obscure historic sites such as Makdala Hill and Ankober.

HAYK

One of the most underrated stops along the northern circuit, the sumptuous 23km² Lake Hayk stands at an altitude of 2,030m among rolling green hills 90km south of Weldiya and 25km north of Dessie. Of interest both for its abundant birdlife and the historical monastery of Hayk Istafanos on its western shore, the 85m-deep lake stands within easy walking distance of the otherwise unremarkable small town of Hayk, which straddles the main road between Weldiya and Dessie and is thus readily accessible on public transport. Hayk, incidentally, is simply the Amharigna word for 'lake', but it seems to be the only name in common use. The most likely explanation for this is that its original name was forgotten centuries ago and its modern name derives from that of Hayk Istafanos, which simply means 'Istafanos on the lake'.

GETTING THERE AND AWAY Minibuses between Hayk and Dessie (*30–45mins*) run throughout the day, and any bus between Weldiya and Dessie could drop you or pick you up at Hayk town. To get to the lake from the town's main roundabout, follow the side road that leads northward out of town, almost parallel to the Weldiya road, for about 1km until it forks. The right fork leads downhill to the closest point on the lakeshore and Lago Hayk Lodge after 1km. The left fork runs uphill and parallel to the western shore for about 3km before descending to Hayk Istafanos.

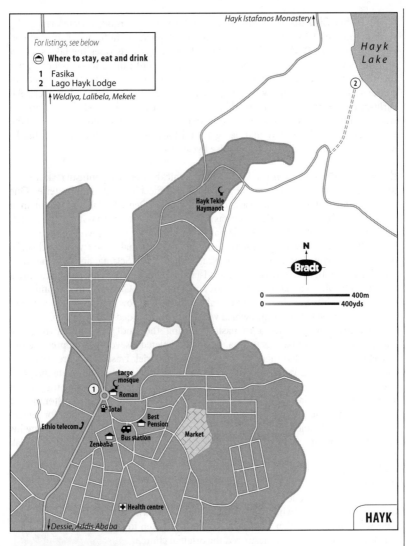

For listings, see below

Where to stay, eat and drink

1 Fasika
2 Lago Hayk Lodge

Weldiya, Lalibela, Mekele

Hayk Istafanos Monastery

Hayk Lake

Hayk Tekle Haymanot

N

Bradt

0 ———————— 400m
0 ———————— 400yds

Large mosque
Roman
Total
Ethio telecom
Best Pension
Market
Bus station
Zenbaba
Health centre

Dessie, Addis Ababa

HAYK

WHERE TO STAY, EAT AND DRINK *Map, above*

Lago Hayk Lodge (4 rooms) m 0943 232000. This recently upgraded lodge has a lovely location in neat stone-walled gardens set back from a stretch of lakeshore teeming with birds. Spacious stone-&-thatch bungalows have slate tile floors, hand-carved wood furniture draped with traditional cloths, private terrace & en-suite bathroom with combined tub/ shower. The associated bar/restaurant, 200m further along the shore & popular with locals at w/ends, serves inexpensive fish dishes fresh from the lake. Other amenities include a roped-off swimming area & dock with several boats. It rather lacks management presence, but otherwise seems like decent value. *US$40/52 sgl/dbl B&B.* **$$$$**

Fasika Hotel (38 rooms) ☎ 033 222 0390. The pick of a few rundown hotels in Hayk town, this friendly high-rise has small & gloomy rooms with ¾ bed, a ground-floor restaurant serving good fresh fish & a rooftop *tukul* bar with a good view. *US$4/6 sgl with common/en-suite shower.* **$**

417

WHAT TO SEE AND DO Hayk is a lovely spot. The deep turquoise water, ringed by verdant hills and fringed by lush reed beds, is still plied by traditional fishermen on papyrus *tankwas*. Birders will be in their element: not only does the lake support a profusion of waterbirds (including large numbers of pink-backed pelican), but the shore and the surrounding fields and forest patches host a rich variety of colourful barbets, woodpeckers, kingfishers, bee-eaters, sunbirds and weavers. An early-morning stroll along the road between the lake and the wooded peninsula on which stands Hayk Istafanos could easily yield between 50 and 100 species, with the monastery grounds in particular being a good spot for flocks of the endemic black-headed lovebird and the lovely paradise flycatcher.

Hayk Istafanos (*Entrance US$4*) Set on a thickly wooded peninsula 4km from town, Hayk Istafanos is one of Ethiopia's oldest and most influential monasteries. One local tradition states that a monastic community called Debre Egziabher (Mountain of God) was established on the lakeshore as early as AD627. Another has it that the church was founded in AD862 by Kala'e Selama, a monk from Jerusalem who converted the local python-worshipping pagans by using his cross to make their venerated snake disappear. Shortly after, Emperor D'il Nead visited Kala'e Selama, and together they founded a church, which was dedicated to Istafanos after a giant flying beast descended from the sky with one *tabot* for Istafanos and another for Giyorgis. The second *tabot* was stored within the church for several centuries but now resides in the adjacent nunnery of Margebeta Giyorgis, which was reputedly founded 800 years ago.

Hayk Istafanos became a monastery during the mid-13th-century reign of Nakuta La'ab, after Abba Iyasus Moa, having completed a seven-year apprenticeship at Debre Damo, was led there by the Archangel Gabriel. Iyasus Moa presided over the monastery for 52 years, sleeping in a sitting position throughout his tenure, and spending his waking hours lugging around a heavy stone cross and kissing the ground 10,000 times every day. Iyasus Moa played a pivotal role in the so-called restoration of the Solomonic line, serving as the mentor of Yakuno Amlak, who trained for several years at Hayk Istafanos prior to becoming emperor in 1270, and also supporting his claim to Solomonic ancestry. After he became emperor, the grateful Yekuno Amlak transferred a third of the realm's property to Hayk Istafanos, which became the most powerful monastery in the country and would remain so for 200 years. Iyasus Moa died in 1293, aged 89, and is buried within the church. During the 15th century, Hayk Istafanos was superseded by Debre Libanos, a monastery founded in western Shewa by Tekle Haymanot (who trained under Iyasus Moa). Nevertheless, it remained sufficiently important that Francisco Álvares was taken to see it in the 1520s, a few years before Ahmed Gragn destroyed the original church.

In Álvares's day, Hayk Istafanos was set 'on a small island' which the monks went 'to and from ... with a boat of reeds'. In 1841, the German missionary Johann Krapf was told the island was called Debra Nayodquad (Mountain of Thunder) and paddled there across a deep 200m-wide channel. Today, the monastery lies on a peninsula and can be reached on foot, though it's not clear whether this is because the water level has retreated, or the channel has been filled. Either way, it's a fascinating and peaceful spot, set in lovely wooded grounds teeming with birds, though the church itself is quite modern. A superb museum (photography forbidden) houses several unusual artefacts, including the heavy stone cross borne by Iyasus Moa, hollowed-out sacrificial stones once used by the pagans he converted, and an illustrated biography of Iyasus Moa reputedly written during his lifetime (making it one of the oldest books in Ethiopia). Women are banned from the monastery grounds but may visit the adjacent nunnery of Margebeta Giyorgis.

DESSIE

One of the largest towns in northern Ethiopia, Dessie (sometimes spelt Dese) boasts an attractive setting at an altitude of 2,600m near the base of Mount Tossa. A rather utilitarian character and limited sightseeing opportunities make it among the least compelling of Ethiopia's major cities, but it's a pleasant enough place, particularly if you enjoy live music, and a convenient stopover between Addis Ababa and more northerly destinations such as Lalibela and Mekele. Sprawling for about 5km along the main northbound road, it now has two main centres. In the south, the historic quarter of Ayiteyef, centred on the roundabout referred to as the Piazza, has a rather hectic feel and scruffy appearance, but it also houses several turn-of-the-20th-century buildings of minor architectural interest. About 4km to its north is a more modern and sedate centre known as Buanbwa Wuha (Place of Water). For reasons we cannot quite fathom, the main road connecting Ayiteyef and Buanbwa Wuha is lined by a row of half a dozen hospitals and what must surely be the world's largest concentration of pharmacies (at least 50 at the last count).

HISTORY Dessie was founded by Emperor Yohannes IV after he saw 'a star with fringes of light' while encamped nearby in 1882. That an impressive comet was visible from the eastern highlands of Ethiopia in late 1882 is well documented, but the emperor, whether consciously or unconsciously echoing the actions of a distant predecessor at Debre Berhan centuries before, perceived the apparition to be a miracle. He immediately set about building a church on the site, which he christened Dessie ('My Joy' – a name whose misplaced ebullience has instigated a skyward arch in the eyebrows of more than one subsequent visitor!).

In 1888, Dessie became the capital of Negus Mikael of Wollo, an Oromo chief who had converted to Christianity under Yohannes IV ten years earlier. Negus Mikael was one of the major political players in late-19th-century Ethiopia, even before he integrated himself into the Shewan imperial family by marrying Emperor Menelik II's daughter in 1893. The son of this union, Iyasu V, was selected by Menelik II as his successor, and became Emperor of Ethiopia in 1913, only to be toppled three years later in an imperial coup masterminded by Ras Tefari (later Haile Selassie). Negus Mikael responded to this insult by leading 120,000 troops against the Shewan monarchy in the Battle of Segale, probably the largest battle fought on Ethiopian soil, between Adwa and Maychew. Mikael was defeated and taken captive. He died two years later.

Negus Mikael oversaw Dessie's emergence as a trading centre of note. With its strategic location on the trade routes between Ankober and Tigray, Mikael's young capital served a crucial role in the war with Italy in 1896. By the outbreak of World War I, the town had become the largest market centre in Wollo. Twenty years later, it was also one of the cities most affected by the Italian invasion, having been subjected to several bombing raids between December 1935 (when the hospital was damaged) and its eventual capture on 15 April 1936. As with Gondar to its west, Dessie became an important administrative centre under the Italian occupation due to its pleasant climate, fertile surrounds and convenient location.

Much of the modern town centre dates to the occupation and subsequent decades, the period over which Dessie outgrew its rustic roots to become the capital of the Wollo region and one of the largest cities in Ethiopia. In 1970, a population of 80,000 made it the third-largest city in the empire after Addis Ababa and Asmara, the latter now part of Eritrea. Dessie lost out to Bahir Dar when the regional capital of Amhara was chosen in 1994 but, owing to a recent spurt of redevelopment, it now supports an estimated 300,000 residents.

GETTING THERE AND AWAY The bus station [421 C3] lies on the east side of the main road 200m north of the Piazza roundabout, hidden behind a row of buildings. Regular minibuses leave there for Kombolcha, taking around 30–45 minutes, as well as to Hayk, a trip of similar duration. More locally, a steady stream of minibuses and *bajaji* also runs along the main road between the Piazza and Buanbwa Wuha throughout the day.

To/from Addis Ababa and the south Dessie lies 390km northeast of Addis Ababa along an asphalt road through Debre Berhan and Kombolcha. It takes about 6 hours in a private vehicle, maintaining a speed that allows you to manoeuvre around the prodigious livestock. The best public transport is the daily Ethio Bus, which leaves in either direction at 05.00. Selam, Falcon and Sky buses between Addis Ababa and Mekele also stop in Dessie. Perhaps a dozen ordinary buses cover the same route daily, mostly leaving in the morning, but they are usually 2–3 hours slower. Direct buses also connect Dessie and Debre Berhan.

To/from Weldiya, Lalibela and the north Weldiya, at the junction of the main road to Mekele and China Road for Lalibela, lies 120km north of Dessie, a drive of up to 2 hours. Plenty of minibuses run between Dessie and Weldiya all day, with traffic being heaviest in the morning. There is also at least one direct daily bus to Mekele (*departs 06.30; 7–8hrs*), and one to Lalibela (*departs 06.00; 8–9hrs*). If you miss these buses, you could head to Weldiya and look for onward transport there. For those with private transport, an adventurous and scenic alternative route to Lalibela runs northeast via Wegel Tena to Gashena, offering access en route to the ancient monastery of Gishen Debre Kerbe (page 423) and historic Makdala Hill (page 425).

To/from Afar At least one bus runs daily in either direction between Dessie and Mille (on the Asaita road) via Kombolcha and Bati.

WHERE TO STAY
Moderate
Golden Gate Hotel [421 C2] (46 rooms) ☎033 312 2929; m 0930 377626; e goldeng2009@gmail.com; w goldengatehoteldessie.com. Dessie's smartest hotel (the only one with a lift) is this new central 6-storey construction whose canvas-shaded raised terrace flanks the west side of the main road. Large modern rooms are tastefully furnished & come with large flatscreen TV, writing desk & modern bathroom with hot shower. The airy pastel-shaded 2nd-floor restaurant serves a varied selection of Ethiopian & international dishes in the US$3–6 range. Very good value. *US$32/48/72 B&B sgl/dbl/ suite.* **$$$**

Time Hotel [421 C1] (27 rooms) ☎033 811 9056; e hoteltimeinfo@gmail.com. This well-run high-rise in Buanbwa Wuha has large, clean & agreeably furnished en-suite rooms with wall-mounted TV, writing desk & hot shower. The

ground-floor restaurant has an extensive menu of well-prepared dishes. Good value. *US$24/28/32/38 B&B sgl/dbl/king-size/twin.* **$$$**

Melbourne Hotel [421 B1] (21 rooms) ☎033 112 4949; m 0949 902279; e info@ melbournehoteleth.com; w melbournehoteleth. com. Situated diagonally opposite the Time Hotel & similar in standard, this new place has clean & pleasant rooms with flatscreen TV, private balcony & writing desk. The 1st-floor restaurant has a varied menu, but service could be snappier. *From US$28/44 B&B dbl/twin.* **$$$**

Budget
Segenet Guesthouse [421 C1] (32 rooms) ☎033 311 0473; m 0939 030303. Bridging the quality & price gap between the moderate hotels listed above & pretty much everything else in Dessie, this modern guesthouse in Buanbwa Wuha has clean & well-furnished en-suite dbl rooms with

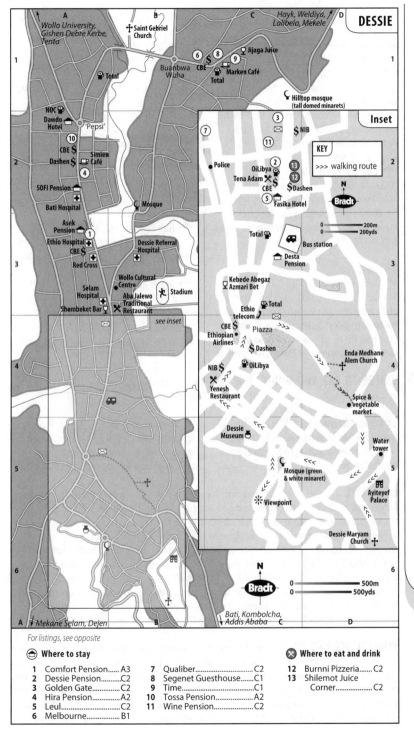

For listings, see opposite

large flatscreen TV & hot shower. A well-priced ground-floor restaurant serves pizzas, burgers & local staples. *US$20/24/30 dbl/king-size/twin.* **$$**

🏠 **Leul Hotel** [421 C2] (26 rooms) ✆033 312 4988. This reasonably smart 5-storey hotel has a useful central location near the bus station & large clean en-suite rooms with flatscreen TV, hot shower & in some cases balcony. The well-stocked ground-floor bar looks like a good place for a dedicated evening's boozing. *US$12/15 with dbl/king-size bed.* **$$**

🏠 **Qualiber Hotel** [421 C2] (20 rooms) ✆033 111 1548. Situated on the University road 600m from the bus station, this 2-storey hotel, set around a small courtyard, has clean, cosy & brightly decorated rooms with en-suite hot shower & TV. *US$13/18 sgl/twin.* **$$**

Shoestring

🏠 **Tossa Pension** [421 A2] (17 rooms) ✆033 111 9225. Located close to 'Pepsi' Circle 2km north of the bus station, this modern family-run pension has been the pick of Dessie's cheapies for some years now. The en-suite rooms are clean & neat with ¾ bed, hot water & TV. Expect prices to shoot up as & when it transforms into the slick-looking 8-storey Tossa Hotel depicted on a billboard outside. *US$8 sgl.* **$$**

🏠 **Comfort Pension** [421 A3] (20 rooms) ✆033 381 1248; m 0914 710436. This very agreeable pension has bright little en-suite rooms with TV & hot shower. Rooms facing the street have a private balcony, but look to be noisier. *US$9/11 dbl/twin.* **$$**

🏠 **Wine Pension** [421 C2] (28 rooms) m 0985 157584. Quiet, clean & well-priced rooms; those using common showers give separate male & female facilities. The 1st-floor restaurant looks good too. *US$7/9 sgl/dbl using common shower, or US$11 en-suite dbl.* **$**

🏠 **Hira Pension** [421 A2] (20 rooms) ✆033 111 6374. This well-priced hotel near 'Pepsi' Circle has bright & spacious tiled rooms with en-suite cold showers. *US$9/14 dbl/twin.* **$**

🏠 **Dessie Pension** [421 C2] (30 rooms) If cheap & central are your main requirements, this venerable hotel opposite the Amba Ras does the job perfectly. The no-frills rooms come with a ¾ bed & sink. The common toilets & showers could, in a cup-half-fullish way, be worse. *US$4 sgl.* **$**

✕ **WHERE TO EAT AND DRINK** The moderate hotels listed above all have decent restaurants, as does the cheaper Segenet Guesthouse.

✕ **Burnni Pizzeria** [421 C2] The pick of Dessie's limited selection of central eateries has terrace seating & serves pizzas, burgers & pasta dishes in the US$2–4 range.

✕ **Shilemot Juice Corner** [421 C3] This busy little café serves the best juice in town, as well as vegetarian platters strong on fresh greens – a rarity in Ethiopia. Nothing costs more than US$2.

NIGHTLIFE Dessie is renowned for its *azmari* bars, where traditional Amhara singers, armed with their one-stringed instruments and perhaps a bit of percussive backing, create spontaneous lyrics about the fine character, intelligence and sexual appetite (or whatever other compliments they come up with) of anybody who offers them a generous tip. Our favourite is the traditionally decorated **Shembeket Bar** [421 A3] (✆033 111 8242; ⊕ *live music from 21.00 daily*), which lies just off the main road close to the Selam Hospital, and has an inclusive feel, with half a dozen male and female singers and musicians often taking part over the course of an evening. Also worth a try are the **Kebede Abegaz Azmari Bet** [421 C3] opposite the Lalibela Hotel and the **Aba Jalewo Traditional Restaurant** [421 B3] almost opposite the Shembeket.

WHAT TO SEE AND DO The only prescribed tourist attraction in town is the hilltop museum, a visit to which could be combined with the historical walk outlined on page 423 to fill a spare afternoon or morning. Otherwise, there are a few fading occupation-era buildings around the Piazza, most notably **Bahil Amba**, a once-grand cinema built entirely with materials imported from Italy. More ambitiously, you could hike to the peak of Mount Tossa, which offers views in all four directions almost as far as the Afar Depression. To get there, head to the west end of the town, drive part of the way up, and you can walk the remainder in about an hour. The main out-of-town attraction is Lake Hayk and the adjacent monastery of Hayk Istafanos (page 418) and you could also use Dessie as base to visit Bati market (page 429) or the attractions listed under Kombolcha (page 428). Further afield, the remote monastery of Gishen Debre Kerbe and battle site at Makdala Hill can be visited individually or together as a round trip from Dessie or along a back route to Lalibela.

Dessie Museum [421 C5] (⊕ 08.30–12.30 & 13.30–17.30 Mon–Sat; 07.30–11.30 Sun; entrance US$1.50) This moderately diverting museum is located in a 22-room house built by nobleman Dejazmach Josef in 1917. It features some interesting ethnographic displays, traditional musical instruments, and religious tracts and other parchments dating back up to 600 years. Other highlights include a cannon gifted to Menelik II by France in 1890 and used at the Battle of Adwa, and a natural history hall featuring some comically inept taxidermal work. Nothing is labelled in English, but the guide is quite knowledgeable. It stands on a hill above the junction for the old Kombolcha road, and offers a good view over the old town centre.

A historical walk This 5km tour, starting and ending at the Piazza roundabout [421 C4], passes through the historic quarter of Ayiteyef and takes in several early 20th-century buildings associated with Negus Mikael, as well as the Dessie Museum and a small market. It follows some steep slopes, so allow around 90 minutes' walking time depending on your fitness, plus a couple of hours to enjoy the sights, all of which can also be reached by car.

Starting at the Piazza roundabout, take the road running east, with the post office to your left, and follow it uphill for about 600m until you see the **Church of Enda Medhane Alem** [421 D4] in a juniper-shaded hilltop compound to your left. This large, circular church, possibly the oldest in town, was built by Negus Mikael on the site of a church reputedly destroyed centuries earlier by Ahmed Gragn, and the interior contains early 20th-century paintings of the prince and his son Iyasu V.

From Enda Medhane Alem, a rutted 300m footpath runs southeast and downhill to a small spice and vegetable market on the north side of the Kombolcha road. Cross the main road, walk uphill for another 300m then, when you reach a T-junction, turn left on to a road that winds uphill for another 500m or so, passing a water tower to the right, to the hilltop **Ayiteyef Palace** [421 D5] and **Dessie Maryam Church** [421 D6]. The so-called palace, actually a massive banquet hall constructed by Negus Mikael in 1915, was partly renovated in 2014 in anticipation of its centenary. Dessie Maryam is a circular *tukul*-style church built by Negus Mikael in 1912 and situated in lovely wooded grounds. The view over the city centre to Mount Tossa is spectacular, especially in the early morning.

Head back downhill, continuing straight past the water tower for 300m, then turn right and continue for another 500m to the roundabout with the old Kombolcha road, which is overlooked by a mosque with a prominent green-and-white minaret. It's worth walking down the **old Kombolcha road** for a couple of hundred metres, as the views over the old town are spectacular. Then climb uphill to the **Dessie Museum** (see above), from where it is an 800m walk back to the Piazza.

GISHEN DEBRE KERBE

Situated 75km northeast of Dessie off a little-used back route to Gashena via Wegel Tena, the monastery of Gishen Debre Kerbe – often called Gishen Maryam after the oldest of its four churches – stands at an altitude of 3,000m atop a magnificently scenic cross-shaped *amba* (flat-topped mountain) whose main axis measures almost 1.5km long. One of Ethiopia's oldest monasteries, Gishen was reputedly founded in the 5th century by King Kaleb, but its main significance to Orthodox Christians is its claim to house the right wing of the cross on which Jesus was crucified (often referred to as the True Cross). Legend has it that this sacred artefact was brought to Ethiopia in the late 14th century, during the reign of Emperor Dawit, and stashed away at Gishen around 50 years later at the instruction of Dawit's son Emperor Zara Yaqob, who regarded the cruciform monastery as the most appropriate place to hoard the holy treasure. In common with the Ark of the Covenant at Axum, the relic of the True Cross is off limits to all but a select few – indeed, it is reputedly stashed Russian-doll-style within four boxes (one made from each of iron, bronze, silver and gold) and suspended by chains within a closed chamber at the end of a tunnel 20m below the ground.

Gishen Amba has a second, more verifiable claim to fame, as the source of Dr Johnson's morality tale of Rasselas, the prince who was imprisoned in a valley encircled by mountains by the King of Abyssinia. During several periods in Ethiopian history, it has been customary for the emperor to protect his throne by imprisoning his potential successors – sons, brothers, uncles and other princes – on a near-impregnable mountaintop. The Portuguese priest Álvares described this practice in his account of his lengthy sojourn in Ethiopia, providing the inspiration for Johnson's tale, as well as – somewhat bizarrely – the vision of an earthly paradise described in Milton's *Paradise Lost*. The tale of Rasselas in turn formed the driving obsession behind Thomas Pakenham's travels in Ethiopia in 1955, documented in his compulsively readable book *The Mountains of Rasselas* (page 644). According to Pakenham, Gishen Amba is one of three mountains that have been used to imprison princes at different points in Ethiopia's history; it was preceded in this role by the monastery at Debre Damo, and succeeded by Mount Wehni near Gondar. Gishen first served as a royal prison in 1295, when Emperor Yakuno Amlak sent his five sons there, and it held a solid stream of similar captives until it was virtually razed by Ahmed Gragn in the 16th century.

Whether or not there's any truth to the True Cross legend, the cruciform plateau and its four churches are very beautiful and sacred, and the drive there is utterly stupendous, offering wonderful views over a succession of hills and river valleys. Gishen is also quite unusual for Ethiopia in that the plateau is inhabited not only by the 400 monks and nuns associated with the monastery, but also by a few thousand secular villagers who live in traditional stone two-storey houses without water or electricity. Time-warped and remote it may be, but Gishen routinely attracts hundreds of thousands of pilgrims at Meskel (the Festival of the True Cross), as well as smaller numbers on the 21st day of every Ethiopian month, a date traditionally associated with St Mary. Another feature of the plateau are the plentiful raptors – including lammergeier and augur buzzard – that nest on the surrounding cliffs and regularly soar overhead.

Gishen was accessible only by foot or by mule-back in Pakenham's day. Today, the monastery is easily reached by 4x4, either as a day trip from Dessie (75km in either direction; allow 8 hours in total) or en route from Dessie to Lalibela via Wegel Tena and Gashena (260km in total; usually doable in a long day). Coming from Dessie, head northwest past the university along a good dirt road that follows a spectacular riverine valley, passing through the small town of Kutaber after 19km, then the tiny riverside village of Ziya (whose marvellous Tuesday livestock market is well worth a diversion) after another 36km, before arriving at the junction for Gishen (signposted in Amharigna only) some 5km further. From this junction, a rough dirt road runs north for 15km, gaining around 1,500m in elevation in the process, before arriving at the car park below Gishen. The final short but steep ascent to the top of the mountain must be done on foot and takes about 15 minutes. If you are continuing to Lalibela, follow the 15km road back to the junction, then turn right and continue for another 35km to Wegel Tena (passing the junction south to Tenta and Makdala Hill after 10km). From Wegel Tena, it is another 75km north to Gashena (page 388) then about 60km to Lalibela. There are a couple of very basic hotels in Wegel Tena should you need to spend the night.

MAKDALA HILL

It was to the 2,800m-high Makdala Hill that the embattled and embittered Emperor Tewodros retreated in 1867, after his dream of a unified Ethiopia had crumbled under the strain of various internal and external pressures, most significantly his own growing unpopularity among his subjects. His once all-conquering army reduced through desertion and rebellion to a tenth of its former size, and his pleas for British alliance unanswered, the emperor was forced to abandon his capital at Debre Tabor and to barricade himself in the hilltop castle at Makdala. In a final desperate attempt to lever Britain into giving him military support, Tewodros took with him a group of European prisoners captured at Gafat, close to Debre Tabor. In 1868, after Britain's attempt to negotiate for the release of the prisoners ended in the negotiator himself being jailed, a force of 32,000 troops was sent to Makdala, under the command of Lord Napier and with the support of the future emperor Yohannes IV. Tewodros took his own life rather than face capture, and was buried in the church at Makdala at the request of his wife. Some of the hilltop fortifications erected by Tewodros at Makdala are still in place, as is Sebastopol, the unmarked bronze cannon built by the missionaries he took hostage at Gafat, and the scenery is magnificent even by Ethiopian standards.

Makdala is situated about 110km northwest of Dessie via the small town of Tenta. Until as recently as 2013, it was accessible only by foot or mule-back, but with a private 4x4 it can now be reached by road. There are two routes from Dessie to Tenta. The shorter and more northerly option entails following directions for Gishen Debre Kerbe, except that instead of turning right at the junction 60km out of Dessie, you need to continue northwest towards Wegel Tena for 10km, then turn left on to a dirt road that arrives in Tenta after about 25km. The longer but possibly quicker alternative follows the surfaced road running west towards Mekane Selam for 80km as far as Tulu Walia, then turns right on to the Gashena road and follows it north for 50km to Tenta. The 17km dirt road to Makdala runs northwest from the more northerly of Tenta's two roundabouts and takes about 1 hour to drive. Using public transport, two buses run daily between Dessie and Tenta via Tulu Walia, leaving at around 05.00 in either direction, but you would need to walk the last 17km to Makdala. Once there, the caretaker will ask a negotiable entrance fee (*up to US$5*).

Set at a chilly altitude of 2,900m in an area whose spectacular scenery is dominated by the mighty gorge carved by the Tikur Abay (Black Nile), Tenta has a pedigree belying its remote location and small size (population 4,000). In addition to being the closest town to Makdala, it served as the turn-of-the-century base of Ras Mikael of Wollo, a close associate of Emperor Menelik II and the father of the uncrowned Emperor Iyasu V, who was born in the village in around 1895. Standing alongside the Gashena road only 4km north of Tenta, the three-tiered circular stone church of Tash Tenta Mikael, which was built by Ras Mikael and houses his domed tomb, is also worth a look. The only other landmarks in Tenta are the pair of statues – one depicting Ras Mikael, the other a suicidal Emperor Tewodros taking aim – that adorn its two main roundabouts. If you need to spend the night, Tenta has one very basic unsignposted hotel, on the same roundabout as the statue of Ras Mikael, but you would be better heading 10km straight to Abidjar where the **Roman Hotel** (*12 rooms;* \033 441 0254; **$**), set in a green central compound 100m east of the main road, charges US$4 for a clean double using common showers, and also serves decent local food and cold beers.

KOMBOLCHA

Divided from larger and more westerly Dessie by 20km of scenic asphalt road, Kombolcha is a substantial manufacturing centre that already houses a major brewery, a metal works and a textile factory, and is soon to be the site of a new Chinese-funded industrial park. It is also home to a newly built airport connected by daily flights to Addis Ababa, and this will shortly be followed by a railway station on the pending line between Awash and Mekele. A rapidly growing university town whose population now stands at around 200,000, Kombolcha has undergone a dramatic post-millennial shape-shift, with the construction of a bypass road and development of a new town centre alongside the Borkana River leaving the old hillside town centre 1km to the southeast looking rather peripheral to the real action. Logistically, Kombolcha undoubtedly comes second to Dessie in terms of agreeable, good-value accommodation, but the lower altitude (around 1,850m) makes it noticeably warmer during the chilly rainy season, and it is better placed for transport to Bati. It is also a good base for day trips to the mysterious Geta Lion and bird-rich Yegof Forest.

GETTING THERE AND AWAY

By air Ethiopian Airlines now operates twice-daily return flights between Addis Ababa and Kombolcha. The poorly signposted new Kombolcha Airport (whose IATA code DSE underscores its proximity to Dessie) is 3km north of the new town centre close to the proposed industrial park.

By rail Kombolcha lies along the railway line under construction between Awash and Mekele. The railway station will be on the Dessie side of town, about 1km past the Sunnyside Hotel.

By road The bus station recently relocated 200m west to a site above the Borkana River and 50m south of the main road through the new town centre. Minibuses ply back and forth between here and Dessie throughout the day, taking 30–45 minutes. There is also quite a bit of transport to Bati on market days, and at least one bus daily runs through to Mille and Asaita via Bati. Coming from the south, any bus bound for Dessie can drop you at Kombolcha. A couple of buses run from Kombolcha to Addis Ababa daily, leaving before 06.00, but most other long-haul buses leave from Dessie.

WHERE TO STAY *Map, opposite*
Two new multistorey hotels currently under construction are likely to vie with each other as the best in town when they eventually open. One stands behind the Total filling station south of the Hikma Hotel, while the other is opposite the Sunnyside Hotel.

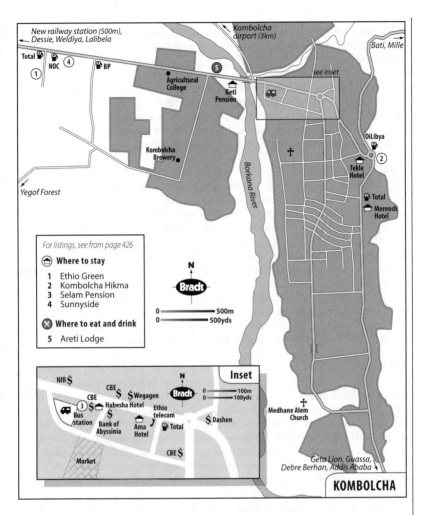

For listings, see from page 426

🏠 **Where to stay**

1   Ethio Green
2   Kombolcha Hikma
3   Selam Pension
4   Sunnyside

❌ **Where to eat and drink**

5   Areti Lodge

Inset

KOMBOLCHA

12

Budget

🏠 **Sunnyside Hotel** (71 rooms) \033 551 3016; e sunnysidehotel.kombolcha@yahoo.com. This multistorey landmark might be the smartest hotel in Kombolcha, but it feels rundown & poor value compared with similarly priced rivals in Dessie. The tired-looking en-suite rooms come with TV & hot shower & rates include use of a gym & rather murky pool. A decent restaurant is attached. *US$39/40/44/52 B&B sgl/dbl/suite/twin.* **$$$$**

Shoestring

🏠 **Ethio Green Hotel** (18 rooms) m 0920 781567. Set in large green gardens with plenty of outdoor seating close to the Sunnyside, this

suburban hotel has en-suite rooms, some with hot shower & others cold only, which could be smarter but are probably more appealing than anything in the town centre. *US$10 dbl.* **$$**

🏠 **Kombolcha Hikma Hotel** (17 rooms) m 0913 318378. Situated on the main roundabout in the old town centre, this former backpackers' hub has been somewhat marginalised by the recent construction of the bypass. Still, the en-suite rooms with nets, TV & hot water in the new upstairs annex are both comfortable & pretty good value (but not so the grotty downstairs rooms). The restaurant & pastry shop with its large open-air veranda is also very agreeable. *US$12/18 dbl/twin.* **$$**

🏠 **Selam Pension** (25 rooms) \033 551 2873. Situated on the main road around the corner from the bus station, this multistorey block stands out for its friendly management & high standards of cleanliness. En-suite rooms come with hot water, TV, small balcony & views towards Mount Yegof on the non-street side. *From US$12 dbl.* **$$**

 WHERE TO EAT AND DRINK *Map, page 427*

✘ **Areti Lodge** ⊕ 08.00–22.00 daily. Set in leaf-shaded manicured gardens a few hundred metres west of the town centre, this attractive, traditionally decorated restaurant ranks several notches above anything else in Kombolcha. Most items on the Amharigna-only menu are in the US$2–4 range, & it also has a pool table & fridge stocked with beer.

WHAT TO SEE AND DO

Yegof Forest Dominating the southern skyline of Kombolcha, the 3,000m-high Mount Yegof is an isolated massif whose forested upper slopes are protected in the 21km² Yegof-Erike National Forest Priority Area. Dominated by juniper trees but interspersed with areas of plantation, the forest gives way to heather and *Hypericum* shrubs at higher altitudes. It is listed as an Important Bird Area following a short 1996 study that recorded 62 species, including national and regional endemics such as Erckel's francolin, Abyssinian woodpecker, white-cheeked turaco and Abyssinian catbird. Relict populations of Menelik's bushbuck, vervet monkey and possibly leopard are also present. To get there, follow the Dessie road out of the town centre across the bridge, take the first left, then turn right after about 800m and left after another 700m (passing the airport to your west), and follow the road south for about 2km until it terminates below the mountain's northern spur.

Geta Lion One of the more intriguing of Ethiopia's lesser-known monuments, this unique monolithic sculpture is suspended from the edge of a small euphorbia-studded hill called Tchika Beret about 10km southeast of Kombolcha. It portrays the front part of a male lion, with bulging oriental-looking eyes, lines representing the mane, ferociously bared teeth, and feet stretched forwards, in a manner so stylised that when Théophile Lefebvre became the first European to see it in 1843, he thought it depicted a hippopotamus or sphinx. When the lion was sculpted, and by whom, is a matter of pure conjecture, but it most likely dates to Axumite times. A Maltese cross carved into the basal rock might indicate that the lion was sculpted after Christianity was introduced to Ethiopia, but the cross could have been carved centuries after the original lion was sculpted. The enigmatic origin of the Geta Lion is compounded by the sculpture's apparent isolation – no similar monument is known within a radius of hundreds of kilometres!

The Geta Lion can be reached by following the Addis Ababa road south of Kombolcha for 9.6km past the junction of the old road and new bypass. From here, it is only 4km to the sculpture, following a rough 4x4 track, signposted in Amharic, that climbs steeply uphill for 2.4km to a T-junction where you need to turn left. From here, it's another 1km to the start of the 500m footpath running north from the road to the sculpture. If in doubt, locals all know the site, so just ask for Anbessa Dingay (Lion Rock). The nearby Geta Mosque, founded in the mid 19th century by renowned Islamic scholar Haji Bushra Muhammad, is a well-known pilgrimage site.

BATI

Situated 40km east of Kombolcha along the old Italian road to Mille, the small town of Bati, set at a medium altitude of 1,500m on the slopes that divide the eastern highlands from the low-lying plains of Afar, has long formed an important trade and cultural crossroads. For more than two centuries, it has also hosted Ethiopia's largest weekly market, now held every Monday, when the resident population of 25,000 more than doubles as Amhara and Oromo villagers and Afar nomads drift in from far and wide to buy and sell livestock, fresh produce and other goods. Indeed, Bati's market has expanded so much in recent years that it is now split across three separate sites: a daily general market a block north of the main road, a weekly livestock market dominated by camels and cattle about 500m to its north, and a vast weekly general market running south from the bus station. If you're in the area on Monday, it is emphatically worth the relatively minor diversion to Bati, not only for the sheer scale of the phenomenon, but also for the glimpse into a facet of Ethiopia very different from anything you'll encounter in the highlands. Coming from the highlands, the Afar seem to belong to another Africa altogether: the women with their wild plaited hairstyles and elaborate ornate jewellery, the

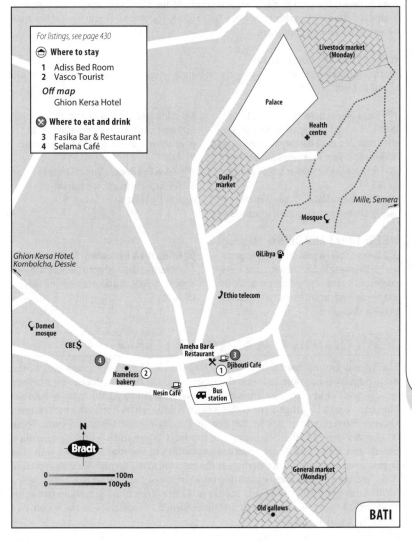

For listings, see page 430

Where to stay
1 Adiss Bed Room
2 Vasco Tourist
Off map
   Ghion Kersa Hotel

Where to eat and drink
3 Fasika Bar & Restaurant
4 Selama Café

Livestock market (Monday)

Palace

Health centre

Daily market

Mille, Semera

Mosque

Ghion Kersa Hotel, Kombolcha, Dessie

OiLibya

Ethio telecom

Domed mosque

CBE

Ameha Bar & Restaurant

Djibouti Café

Nameless bakery

Nesin Café

Bus station

General market (Monday)

N

Bradt

0 ——— 100m
0 ——— 100yds

Old gallows

BATI

tall, proud men strutting around with a Kalashnikov slung over their shoulder, and lethal traditional dagger tucked away in a prominent hide sheath. On other days of the week, Bati is a pretty ordinary place, its sole point of historic interest being the disused gallows – a relic of the Haile Selassie era – that stand in the middle of the general weekly market. Note that you can no longer visit the weekly markets unaccompanied: the local guides association insists that all tourists are escorted by a local guide and pay the fee of US$10 per party.

GETTING THERE AND AWAY A fair surfaced road connects Bati to Kombolcha, and several buses run between the two towns daily, with traffic being heaviest on Monday. The trip takes about 60 minutes in a private vehicle and 90 minutes by bus, and the markets start at 08.00, peaking in activity between 10.00 and 13.00, so it is easy enough to visit as a day trip out of Kombolcha or Dessie. Note that the road from Kombolcha to Bati continues on to Mille, a junction town on the asphalt highway between Awash and Semera (page 382). The Anabe Forest lies off the road between Kombolcha and Bati.

🏠 **WHERE TO STAY** *Map, page 429*
Bati's few hotels tend to fill up quickly on Sunday night, prior to the market, so call ahead to book your room early.

🏠 **Vasco Tourist Hotel** (8 rooms) ☎ 033 553 0548/34. Bati's top offering, set on the south side of the main road above the Abay Bank, this friendly small hotel has large clean rooms with dbl beds. *US$5 dbl using common shower or US$8 en-suite dbl.* **$$**

🏠 **Ghion Kersa Hotel** (7 rooms) m 0913 082619. Situated in scenic grounds adjacent to the Kombolcha road 2.5km out of town, this has small rundown rooms using a common shower, & an acceptable restaurant & bar with a wide balcony. *US$4 dbl.* **$**

🏠 **Adiss Bed Room** (8 rooms) m 0945 111720. Basic rooms with common shower, opposite the bus station. *US$3 sgl.* **$**

✖ **WHERE TO EAT AND DRINK** *Map, page 429*
🍴 **Selama Café** A good b/fast or lunch spot, this has the only fresh juice in town, coffee, excellent *ful* & a few other inexpensive dishes. It's also friendly & efficient, with courtyard seating & unusually clean toilets.

✖ **Fasika Bar & Restaurant** The pick of a few decent eateries clustered along the main road east of the Vasco Hotel, this place serves lean & tastily spiced *tibs*.

DESSIE TO ADDIS ABABA VIA DEBRE BERHAN

The 390km asphalt road that connects Dessie to Addis Ababa forms part of the most popular land route between the capital and Lalibela or Mekele. In a private vehicle, you could drive directly between Dessie and Addis Ababa in up to 8 hours, but buses take a bit longer. The region's main wildlife attraction is the little-known Guassa Plateau, which lies to the east of the main road towards Dessie, some 90 minutes' drive north of Tarmabir, and supports large numbers of gelada monkey, as well as a stable and easily observed population of the rare Ethiopian wolf. The largest town en route, Debre Berhan, is the gateway to the former Shewan capital of Ankober, which has a fantastic setting on a stretch of the eastern Rift Valley noted for its endemic birds and gelada monkeys. Other attractions accessible from this road include several atmospheric but little-visited monasteries in the vicinity of Debre Sina and Tarmabir.

SOUTH TO TARMABIR A few small towns and minor sites of interest run along the road between Kombolcha and Debre Sina, which lies 19km north of Tarmabir, the junction town for the underrated Guassa Plateau.

Kemise This busy little Oromo town 52km south of Kombolcha is a popular truck stop, so it has plenty of inexpensive hotels and restaurants, of which the relatively smart multistorey **Chefa Valley Hotel** is the standout. There is some good birding in the area. About 12km south of town, the main road from Ataye skirts the western fringe of the Borkana Wetlands, a mosaic of open water, mudflats, river, marsh and reed beds, seasonally affected by the river's input but perennially wet due to several hot springs which bubble out in the area. At the end of the rainy season, the ample birdlife at Borkana may disperse to a smaller seasonal swamp about 3km north of Kemise. Either way, without leaving the road you stand a good chance of seeing marabou and saddle-billed stork, the endemic blue-winged goose, pelicans, ibises and much more.

Ataye Marked as Efeson on some maps, this relatively large town 58km south of Kemise is the junction for the only viable road to Arbugabeya, about 30 minutes' drive to the west. Arbugabeya literally means 'Friday Market', and it is indeed the site of an important and colourful traditional Friday market where highlanders from Menz exchange wool, barley and the like with coffee, fruit, salt and other lowland produce brought in from Ataye. Plenty of local transport runs between Ataye and Arbugabeya on Friday. From Arbugabeya, it is theoretically only 25km by road to the Guassa Community Conservation Area (via Sefidmeda junction, about 5km from the community lodge), but this road has been impassable for some years following a landslide (though plenty of locals cover it by foot, especially on Fridays). If you need to overnight in Ataye, the Waliya Hotel near the Commercial Bank of Ethiopia is a superior cheapie.

Senbete This small town 8km south of Ataye is famed for its multi-cultural weekly market, held every Sunday, and the second best in the area (after Bati's Monday market). The market attracts traditional villagers from miles around, predominantly Oromo, but also Afar, Amhara and Argobba. Should you want to spend the night, there are a couple of indifferent small hotels.

Shewa Robit Situated on the banks of the wide but normally dry Robit River 40km south of Senbete, this substantial town is worth a stop on Wednesdays, when it hosts a colourful market. The bright green four-storey Kalid Hotel, on the north side of town opposite the bus station, looks to be the pick of several cheapies.

Mercurios Monastery About 20km south of Shewa Robit and 10km north of Debre Sina, the small town of Armaniya is the base from which one can visit this monastery dedicated to St Mercurios, renowned for housing a very old painting of its namesake on horseback. The reason for this painting's fame, according to two local eyewitnesses, is that the horse miraculously starts to move on procession days, which are normally held on 5 August and 4 December. It all sounds rather improbable, but should you happen to be in the area at the right time, it might be interesting to check it out. The monastery is supposedly 1–2-hours' walk from Armaniya. There are a couple of small lodges in Armaniya should you need a room.

Debre Sina Straddling the main road to Addis Ababa 185km south of Kombolcha, Debre Sina (Amharigna for 'Mount Sinai') stands at an altitude of 2,750m at the base of the monumental Mezezo Escarpment. The scenic location and a bustling Monday and Thursday market aside, this significant – and significantly chilly – town holds little of inherent interest to travellers, but it has good public transport connections in all directions. If need be, it also boasts a fair selection of lodges and restaurants, the pick being the **Tinsae Hotel** (*38 rooms;* m *0921 128540;* **$**), which also has a ground-floor restaurant serving reasonable Ethiopian food and draught beer.

Tarmabir Coming from Debre Sina, the blink-and-you'll-miss-it village of Tarmabir is reached by one of the most spectacular roads in Ethiopia, a 10km ascent that switchbacks through the immense Mezezo Escarpment before passing through the impressive 587m-long Mussolini Tunnel, a relict of the Italian occupation. Tarmabir stands at the junction of the road to the Guassa Plateau, but it also lies close to two other noteworthy minor attractions. The more accessible of these, 5km south of Tarmabir along the main road to Debre Berhan, is the spectacular viewpoint known as **Menelik II's Window** or Germasa. Situated on the east side of the road, the viewpoint comprises a large cleft in the rocks overlooking the Awash Valley and it is also a reliable location for the endemic gelada monkey and Ankober serin.

More offbeat is the attractive and atmospheric monastery of **Adkanu Maryam**, which incorporates a partly hewn cave church excavated on a juniper-covered cliff face during the 15th-century rule of Zara Yaqob. Several hermit cells are carved into the rocks alongside the main courtyard, and a few nuns live in and around the outbuildings. During Lent, large numbers of pilgrims from Addis Ababa and elsewhere congregate around the church to be cured by its holy water. Church treasures include a large silver cross of unspecified date. The monastery can be visited as a side trip from Tarmabir, by following a 20km side road that leads west (right opposite the junction for the Guassa Plateau) to the village of Sela Dingay, which is also connected to Tarmabir by one daily bus and the odd light vehicle. Once in Sela Dingay, the walk to Adkanu Maryam takes 20–30 minutes, offering some great views across the Kaskasa River Gorge on the way. When you ask directions, be aware that an unremarkable modern church also called Adkanu Maryam lies on the road between Tarmabir and Sela Dingay.

Guassa Plateau Situated to the northwest of the main road between Dessie and Addis Ababa, the chilly highland region known as Menz is the ancestral home of the Shewan monarchy and was one of the few parts of the kingdom to escape the Islamic and Oromo incursions of the 16th and 17th centuries. Its central geographical feature is the 110km^2 Guassa Plateau, which spans altitudes of 3,200–3,700m, making it one of the most extensive Afroalpine ecosystems in Ethiopia (or indeed anywhere in Africa) and an important stronghold for endemic wildlife including Ethiopian wolf, gelada monkey and many species of bird. In 2003, the plateau was formally set aside as the **Guassa Community Conservation Area** (GCCA; \011 685 1326; m 0918 143336; e info@guassaarea.org; w guassaarea.org; entrance US$5 pp/24hrs), but it had in fact been protected by a well-defined traditional property resource management system known as Qero for 400 years prior to this, making it one of Africa's oldest conservancies. It is now the site of a well-organised ecotourism project offering comfortable self-catering accommodation in the heart of the plateau and a variety of guided activities focusing on the endemic wildlife and local cultures.

Ecology and wildlife The highest plateau in the Shewan Highlands, Guassa is an important catchment area, feeding 26 streams that eventually flow into the Blue Nile or Awash. It is named after the 'guassa' grass, *Festuca abyssinica*, that grows

Although the Guassa Plateau has long been conserved by local communities for its valuable grass, some ambivalence to this chilly tract of uncultivable highland is implicit in a Menz legend concerning its creation. It is said that many centuries ago, a pregnant woman accused a highly respected monk called Atche Yohannes of having broken his vow of celibacy to father her soon-to-be-born child. The local people asked the woman to repeat this shocking claim in front of the disgraced Atche Yohannes, and so she did, stating: 'Let me turn into stone if I tell a lie.' As she spoke, the woman was transformed into stone, and the betrayed monk abandoned the area with a curse: 'Let this land turn cold and bleak for evermore, and the rich agricultural land become scrub.' As the monk spoke, the plateau, formerly known for its fine *tef*, was transformed into a bleak and uncultivable landscape of windswept heather tussocks and grassy swamps. Many years after the curse had reduced the area to poverty, the elders decided to beg for mercy and forgiveness. They searched far and wide for the monk, but heard that he had long since died. It was then decided to search for his body and rebury it locally, in the hope that his spirit would take pity on them. Atche Yohannes's bones were reburied near the church of Firkuta Kidane Mihret, and a commemorative day for him has been observed throughout Menz on 26 January ever since – but the monk's spirit has evidently yet to relent, and the land remains under the ancient curse.

here in abundance, and which has long been harvested by local communities as grazing fodder, thatch and bedding material, and to make rope, raincoats and brooms. Indeed, it is primarily due to the importance of this grass that sustainable management policies were implemented by local communities at Guassa several centuries ago. Today, the plateau provides sanctuary to seven of Ethiopia's endemic mammals, including what is probably the world's third-largest population of Ethiopian wolf, estimated at around 35 adults, as well as some 3,000 gelada monkeys split across five groups. Other large mammal species recorded in the GCCA include leopard, common jackal, spotted hyena, rock hyrax, klipspringer and grey duiker. In addition, a total of 114 bird species have been recorded, including 14 endemics, among them spot-breasted plover, wattled ibis, thick-billed raven, blue-winged goose, Rouget's rail and Ankober serin. Commonly seen raptors include augur buzzard, mountain buzzard, golden eagle, tawny eagle and lammergeier.

Getting there and away Guassa lies about 265km from Addis Ababa by road, a drive of around 5 hours in a private vehicle. Coming from the main road between Dessie and Addis Ababa, the junction village for Guassa is Tarmabir, which lies about 10km southwest of Debre Sina and 40km northeast of Debre Berhan. From Tarmabir, a reasonably maintained dirt road runs northwest to Mehal Meda, the capital of Menz, via Guassa (a potentially confusing quirk being that, contrary to expectations, the road initially branches *eastward* at Tarmabir, only to cut back in a northwesterly direction above the Mussolini Tunnel). After about 8km, the road offers some amazing views over the escarpment to the Sharobe River, and another 20km further it bisects a eucalyptus forest whose dense undergrowth is frequented by Bohor reedbuck, Menelik's bushbuck and the very localised Erckel's francolin. About 33km out of Tarmabir, it passes through Kosso, where the Two Valleys

Viewpoint offers a spectacular view over the Blue Nile Valley to the west and the Awash Valley to the east. Some 55km out of Tarmabir, turn right at Melaya. The community lodge is signposted to the left after another 22km.

Using public transport, one bus daily runs to Mehal Meda from Addis Ababa, leaving from Lamberet station at around 06.30 and arriving at around 14.00. In addition, up to three buses run from Debre Berhan to Mehal Meda daily, usually leaving at 05.30 and arriving at around 10.00. All buses to Mehal Meda go past the community lodge and can drop passengers there. When you are ready to depart, buses leave Mehal Meda at around 05.30 and run past the lodge before 06.30. They may be full by then, but the staff at the lodge can call through to book you a seat.

🏠 **Where to stay, eat and drink** By far the nicest place to stay is the community lodge listed below, but a few basic hotels in Mehal Meda (**$**) provide a viable alternative for those on a tight budget.

🏠 **Guassa Community Lodge** [map, page 225] (6 rooms) 📞011 685 1326; **m** 0914 462616; **e** info@guassaarea.org; **w** guassaarea.org. The 2nd-highest lodge in Africa lies at an altitude of 3,300m at the southern end of the plateau, only 300m from the road between Tarmabir & Mehal Meda. Built in the traditional stone-&-thatch style, it accommodates up to 12 people in simple twin rooms using common showers & toilets, & a campsite is attached. There's a self-catering kitchen & lounge with log fire, & most visitors bring all their own food, but it is also possible to hire a local cook for US$10/day, & to get limited supplies locally. Booking is highly recommended, as the lodge occasionally fills up, but you can just pitch up & try your luck if you prefer. *Rooms US$16 pp/ day, camping US$5 pp, kitchen hire US$5 per party.* **$$–$$$**

What to see and do

Walks and hikes For wildlife viewing, the area immediately around the lodge is often good for spotting Ethiopian wolves, which come past in the morning or evening, while the cliffs and meadows at Sefidmeda, 4.5km past the lodge in the direction of Mehal Meda, are a favoured grazing ground for geladas. Endemic birds are also often seen in these areas. A number of day and overnight activities can be arranged through the community lodge, ranging from afternoon walks to three-day treks (as detailed on their website). A great goal for a half-day organised walk, about 1 hour in either direction from the community lodge, is Yegura, a spectacularly located village where you can visit a traditional stone-and-thatch compound, and try the traditional Menz bread (like a super-crusty pizza base) and drink *tella* (millet beer). More ambitiously, Firkuta Kidane Mihret, the 16th-century monastery where the legendary Atche Yohannes (see box, page 433) is buried, houses several ancient manuscripts, icons and crosses, hosts an annual pilgrimage and festival on 26 January – and the 2-hour hike from the community lodge is truly spectacular. Provided you've paid your entrance fee, it is permitted to walk unguided along the main road though the GCCA, as well as in the immediate vicinity of the lodge. Hikes further afield must be accompanied by a guide, which costs US$10 per party per day. It is also possible to arrange mules at US$11 per animal per day, ideally with a few days' notice.

Arba Hara Medhane Alem Also known as Arbara Medhane Alem, this spooky monastic cave church has a magnificent cliff setting at an altitude of around 3,200m near Yegam, a village situated 15km south of the community lodge along the road back towards Tarmabir. The church can be reached in 10–15 minutes along a very steep footpath leading downhill from Yegam into a grove of eucalyptus trees. Initially, it might seem anticlimactic – the modern building is less than 50 years old – but for a small donation the priests will lead you downhill into the patch of indigenous bush that hides the old church. Here, an ancient mausoleum is piled high with mummified corpses, some of whose limbs stick out of the wrapping in macabre contortions. Oddly, nobody in Yegam seems to have a coherent theory about how old the mummies are, or how they got there – one local informant reckoned they belonged to a tribe of angel-like beings who descended from the sky at least 100 years ago, while another suggested the bones were brought to the cave by Egyptian vultures!

Mehal Meda The informal capital of Menz, situated some 22km past the community lodge, is an odd little place, far removed from the recognised tourist circuit, very friendly, and equipped with a few budget hotels and eateries. The best day to visit is Saturday, when it hosts the region's largest weekly market, a good place to buy the thick brown or cream hand-spun wool *burnous* and *zietett* cloths for which Menz is famed. An indication of the town's remoteness is that a lot of locals still adhere to the old-style bartering system of exchanging goods of similar value, rather than buying supplies with money.

DEBRE BERHAN Founded by Emperor Zara Yaqob in 1456, this sprawling highland town of 165,000 souls, set at an altitude of 2,800m some 130km northeast of Addis Ababa, has surprisingly little to show for its long and interesting history. Indeed, its oldest extant building is the Church of Debre Berhan Selassie, built in 1906 by Emperor Menelik II on the site of the 15th-century original. Fortunately, it is one of the country's most beautiful and spiritually affecting modern churches, its inner walls decorated with marvellous paintings that include a portrait of Emperor Zara Yaqob looking at a celestial body (the latter reportedly modelled on Halley's Comet when it passed over at the beginning of the 20th century).

History Legend has it that Emperor Zara Yaqob established his capital at Debre Berhan (Mountain of Light) after he saw a miraculous nocturnal light there in 1456 (quite probably Halley's Comet, which passed overhead that year) and took it as a signal of divine approval for his having ordered the stoning to death of a group of heretics a week earlier. The emperor built the original church of Debre Berhan Selassie there, as well as the palace that formed his primary residence until his death in 1468. The adolescent town was later abandoned by Zara Yaqob's son and successor Baeda Maryam, quite probably because two decades of supporting the imperial court and army had depleted the area of natural resources such as firewood. It rose to prominence again 50 years later, when the imperial troops based at Debre Berhan were routed by the Islamic army of Ahmed Gragn, who thereupon declared that 'Abyssinia is conquered'! The area around Debre Berhan was occupied by the Oromo from then until the 1780s, when it was captured by King Asfaw Wossen of Shewa. Long abandoned but never forgotten, Debre Berhan was soon rebuilt by Asfaw Wossen, after which it served as a kind of secondary capital for him and his 19th-century successors through to the reign of King Haile Melakot, who set fire to his palace (and the rest of the town) in 1855 rather than letting it be captured by Emperor Tewodros. The town was revived under King Sahle Maryam (later to become Emperor Menelik II) and served as the short-lived capital of Shewa from 1878 until the early 1880s, when the future emperor relocated his administration to the Entoto Hills. Debre Berhan was the site of an important livestock market in the 1880s and today is renowned for the high-quality blankets produced by the wool factory on the outskirts of town.

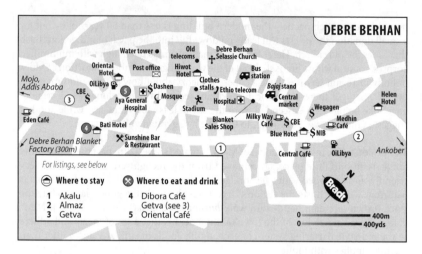

DEBRE BERHAN

For listings, see below

🛏 **Where to stay**   ✖ **Where to eat and drink**

1 Akalu   4 Dibora Café
2 Almaz   Getva (see 3)
3 Getva   5 Oriental Café

Getting there and away Buses between Addis Ababa and Debre Berhan run throughout the morning, taking up to 3 hours in either direction. There is also a fair amount of local transport to the likes of Ankober, Tarmabir, Robit and Efeson. Direct buses from Addis Ababa to Dessie usually pass through Debre Berhan mid morning.

🏠 **Where to stay** *Map, above*

🏠 **Getva Hotel** (71 rooms) \011 637 5040; m 0921 233947; e toget@getvahotel.com; w getvahotel.com. Co-owned by Olympic gold medallist Gete Wami & her running partner/ husband Getaneh Tessema, this high-rise on the south side of town comprises a newish wing where carpeted rooms come with flatscreen TV, fridge & en-suite hot shower, as well as an older wing (the former Eva Hotel) where smaller rooms come with similar facilities. A highly regarded *tukul*-style cultural restaurant serves good Ethiopian & international food in the US$2–3 range. *US$25/35/60 sgl/dbl/twin in new wing; US$12/18 dbl/twin in old wing.* **$$–$$$**

🏠 **Akalu Hotel** (8 rooms) \011 681 1115; m 0922 465265. This long-serving hotel, set on a quiet back road 300m southeast of the town centre, used to be a favourite with tour operators prior to the opening of the slicker Eva. Despite looking a little faded these days, it is still a friendly set-up, & good value, with a restaurant serving decent local food for up to US$2 per portion. *US$5 for an en-suite room with ¾ bed & hot shower.* **$**

🏠 **Almaz Hotel** (20 rooms) m 0911 338260. Among the better of a dozen budget hotels lining the main road at the north end of town, this has basic rooms with ¾ or dbl bed using a common shower. *US$6 dbl.* **$**

✖ **Where to eat and drink** *Map, above*

Aside from the popular cultural restaurant at the **Getva Hotel**, the most happening place in Debre Berhan is the **Dibora Café** opposite, which doubles as a pastry shop and restaurant, and has indoor seating as well as a lively rooftop balcony. Good coffee, fresh juice, pastries and a selection of local meals are served indoors or on the terrace of the agreeable **Oriental Café**.

Shopping Debre Berhan is the site of Ethiopia's oldest wool factory, founded in 1965 on the southern outskirts of town, and the blankets produced there – widely regarded to be the snuggest in the land – can be bought at the **Blanket Sales Shop** (e *dbbf@ethionet.et;* ⏰ *05.00–17.00 Mon–Sat*) for around US$12–18 apiece, depending on size, at an outlet located on the main road between the market and the hospital.

ANKOBER The historic village of Ankober, situated at an altitude of 2,800m on the eastern edge of the escarpment above the Afar Depression, forms an excellent goal for a day or overnight trip out of Debre Berhan. Both the town and the road there are fantastically scenic, passing through rolling green meadows with views over the escarpment and lush Wof Washa Forest that clings to its sheer slopes. The area is also good for endemic birds such as wattled ibis, blue-winged goose and Ankober serin, while gelada monkeys are regularly seen along the road close to the escarpment. Several buildings of minor historical interest can be visited in the sprawling small centre, which today supports a population of fewer than 2,500, and the hilltop site of Menelik II's old palace now houses a characterful mid-range lodge built in period style.

History Ankober, like nearby Debre Berhan, is a settlement of some antiquity, having served as a kind of tollgate along the trade route between the Afar Depression and the highlands since medieval times. It has been suggested, rather improbably, and based largely on phonetic similarities, that it is synonymous with Kubar, a mysterious 10th-century Ethiopian capital mentioned in certain Arab writings. In fact the name Ankober literally means 'Gate of Anko' – Anko, according to local tradition, being the wife of a local Oromo ruler from the 17th century. Ankober was captured in the early 18th century by King Abiye Qedami Qal of Shewa, whose son and successor Amha Iyasus established his capital there in the 1750s, and is regarded as the founder of the modern town. Ankober served as the capital or joint capital of Shewa for more than a century after that, throughout the full reign of four more kings (Asfaw Wossen, Wossen Sagad, Sahle Selassie and Haile Melakot), as well as for two decades under Menelik II prior to his relocating his capital to the Entoto Hills in 1878.

Getting there and away Ankober stands 40km from Debre Berhan along an unsurfaced but reasonably well-maintained road that branches east from the main Dessie road on the northern outskirts of Debre Berhan, a drive of about 1 hour. A few buses cover the road daily, but most of them leave in the morning so an early start is advised, especially if you plan to return the same day.

A new 160km asphalt road should soon connect Modjo, at the intersection of the main roads east to Dire Dawa and south to Hawassa, with the small town of Sembo, which lies about 40km south of Debre Berhan along the road from Addis Ababa. Running via Edjere, Arerti, the Kassem Valley and Koto, this will be the first asphalt road to run directly between southern and northern Ethiopia but bypassing Addis Ababa, and it also passes through some amazing highland scenery, reaching a maximum altitude of around 3,325m between the Kassem Valley and Kotu. All but 30km of the road was complete in early 2018, but the unfinished section was still very rough and passable only with a 4x4. No public transport covers the road at the time of writing, but this is likely to change as and when it is complete.

Where to stay, eat and drink

🏠 **Ankober Palace Lodge** (10 rooms) 📞011 623 0010/2; m 0929 900606; e ankoberlodge@ gmail.com, ankoberlodge@yahoo.com; w ankoberpalacelodge.com. Boasting a commanding location 2km south of town on top of the hill that once housed Menelik II's palace, this attractively rustic lodge is centred on a gigantic 2-storey banquet hall rebuilt in the traditional imperial style, & decorated with traditional artefacts. Comfortable traditionally styled en-suite dbl or twin rooms with hot showers are dotted around the hillside immediately below. European & national dishes are served in the US$4–5 range, & the usual range of drinks is supplemented by excellent home-brewed *tej*. A variety of cultural activities & excursions can be arranged, & guides are available for local sightseeing. The rooms are a steep 470-step hike uphill from the car park, & it can get very chilly at night. *Rates range from US$75/95/125 B&B sgl/dbl/family room with low season discounts.* **$$$$–$$$$$**

🔺 **Bizunesh Bekele Hotel** (5 rooms) m 0912 027644. The pick of 2 very basic lodges in Ankober, this stands on the left-hand side of the road as you enter the village from Debre Berhan. *US$3 sgl using common shower.* **$**

What to see and do

Historical sites A steep road from the village leads 2km downhill to the small but steep juniper-covered hillock once adorned by Menelik II's palace, and now the site of the Ankober Palace Hotel (*entrance US$1 for day visitors*). Locals claim that the hill also once housed the palace of Menelik's grandfather Sahle Selassie, who ruled over Shewa from 1813 to 1847, and whose regular military campaigns co-opted modern-day Addis Ababa into the kingdom and laid the political and economic foundations for Menelik's eventual domination over Ethiopia. All that's left of the original palace is one long stone-and-mortar wall measuring some 1.5m high; it's difficult to say why this one wall should have survived virtually intact when the rest of the palace crumbled to virtual oblivion. Far more impressive is the banquet hall reconstructed as part of the lodge, a fabulous two-storey oval wooden building with a wide balcony and a collection of artefacts (including a massive drum) that reputedly belonged to the emperor.

Three old churches are scattered around the base of the hill. The oldest is Ankober Giyorgis, which was built by Amha Iyasus in 1745 and also offers splendid views all the way to Aliyu Amba. Ankober Maryam was built by Asfaw Wossen in 1775, close to the site where the coffee caravan route to the Red Sea used to leave the village. Ankober Mikael is a beautiful whitewashed church, built in 1825 by Sahle Selassie, and set in a copse of hardwood trees inhabited by gureza monkeys. All three churches now house the tombs of their founders, while the treasury at Ankober Maryam also holds several ancient manuscripts and other ecclesiastic treasures. A fourth church, Ankober Medhane Alem, built in 1840 by Haile Melakot, is where Menelik was crowned King of Shewa and married to Itegue Taitu, but it burned down during the Italian occupation.

Wof Washa Forest Accessible on foot from the main road between Debre Berhan and Ankober, the ancient Wof Washa Forest straddles the Rift Valley slopes ranging from around 2,700m to 3,400m in altitude. Supporting a lush Afroalpine vegetation dominated by African olive, juniper and podocarpus trees, it is home to plenty of gelada and gureza monkey, while Ethiopian wolf sightings and leopard spoor have been reported, and a rich forest birdlife includes the stunning white-cheeked turaco. It is the site of a new community trekking circuit operated by Tesfa Tours (☏ *011 124 5178;* m *0921 602236;* e *info@tesfatours.com;* w tesfatours. com) and comprising four local guesthouses: two on top of the ridges and two in the valley. Trekkers need to be reasonably fit as it involves a descent and ascent of at least 500m at high altitude. Rates are around US$70 per day inclusive of food, accommodation, guide and pack animals, but exclusive of bottled drinks and transport to the trail head.

Birdwatching Ankober is renowned by ornithologists as the type locality of the Ankober serin (*Crithagra ankoberensis*), a rather nondescript seedeater first described in 1979 and initially thought to be restricted to a 20km stretch of escarpment running north from Ankober. The bird has since been recorded at several other localities, but the escarpment running immediately north of the road between Debre Berhan and Ankober remains a good site for this localised species, which is most easily distinguished from other seedeaters found in the area by its streaked crown and what appears to be a pale chin in flight. Other interesting birds to look out for along this road include the endemic blue-winged goose and Abyssinian longclaw, as well as lammergeier, moorland and Erckel's francolin, blue rock thrush and the rare Somali chestnut-winged starling.

Dedicated birders are certain to want to follow the steep road (currently dirt but in the process of being surfaced) that descends from Ankober for 15km to the small town of Aliyu Amba near the base of the escarpment. Although Aliyu Amba is in itself remarkable only for boasting a venerable mosque, the vestigial acacia woodland lining the Melka Jebdu River, 3km out of town along the Dulecha road, is a reliable site for the distinctively marked yellow-throated serin, an Ethiopian endemic otherwise recorded with any regularity only on Fentalle volcano. Those with a private vehicle (preferably 4x4) should expect to take 45 minutes to cover the steep road from Ankober east to Aliyu Amba, from where it is possible to continue southeast along a rough road to Dulecha (23km) and then to the main road near Awash National Park (90km). There is no public transport to Aliyu Amba, but you should have no trouble finding a lift on Thursday, the main market day.

KOREMASH This small clifftop Amhara village offers fantastic views over the Afar lowlands and the valley carved by the Kassem River, a tributary of the Awash. It is also of some historic note, having been chosen as the site of a stronghold and ammunition dump by Haile Melakot, the Negus of Shewa from 1847 to 1855, and father of Menelik II, who continued to use it as an armoury until the turn of the 20th century. Relics of Haile Melakot's reign include a dozen well-maintained stone buildings, each about 15m long, 5m wide and 3m high, some of which have impressive juniper ceilings, on top of which the ammunition was reputedly stored. An active government centre today, the compound was used by the Italians as an administrative and military centre. In one building there is an Italian stone plaque inscribed 'Forttino Botteco', the name they gave Koremash, with the details of the Italian military brigade. To get there, follow the Dessie road out of Addis Ababa to Hamus Gebeya, which lies 70km past Megenagna Circle, then turn right on to a seasonal 4x4 track that reaches the village after about 12km. An entrance fee of around US$1.50 is levied.

THE DESSIE–GUNDEWEIN ROAD

The recent construction of a 310km surfaced road between Dessie and Gundewein via Tulu Walia, Mekane Selam and Mertule Maryam opens up some interesting possibilities for off-the-beaten-track travel in southern Amhara. Gundewein lies on the more easterly of the two main roads connecting Addis Ababa and the Lake Tana region, roughly 100km north of Dejen and 150km south of Bahir Dar (via Mota), and the new road can thus be used to cross between Dessie/Lalibela and Addis Ababa/Bahir Dar. The main attractions accessible from the Dessie–Gundewein road are the little-known Borena Saynt National Park, the new suspension bridge across the Blue Nile, and – shortly before you reach Gundewein – the historic monastery of Mertule Maryam (page 236) and lovely Lake Bahir Giyorgis (page 235). Coming from Lalibela, it would also be possible to connect with the Dessie–Gundewein road using the 130km dirt road between Gashena and Tulu Walia, with possible detours to Gishen Debre Kerbe (page 423) and Makdala Hill (page 425).

In a private vehicle you could comfortably drive from Dessie to Dejen or Bahir Dar in a day, but as things stand you probably need two days to cover the longer (and in parts rougher) route from Lalibela to Gashena. Using public transport, there are plenty of minibuses from Dessie to Tulu Walia, and some continue to Mekane Selam. In addition, a few daily buses or minibuses connect Mekane Selam to Bahir Dar and Dejen via Gundewein and Mertule Maryam (where you may need to change vehicles). Coming from Lalibela, you can use local minibuses to hop from Gashena to Wegel Tena to Tenta to Tulu Walia to Mekane Selam

TULU WALIA Also known as Gimba, the once insignificant town of Tulu Walia (literally 'Mountain of Ibex'), set at an altitude of 3,200m along the Gundewein road 80km west of Dessie, seems to be relishing its new-found role as the unexpectedly bustling transport hub at the three-way junction with the dirt road running north to Gashena via Tenta. Travellers using public transport may well need to change vehicles there, in which case you're unlikely to spend long waiting for onward transport to Mekane Selam or Dessie, but could be in for a serious wait heading north towards Gashena. Fortunately, there's no shortage of decent eateries catering to passing traffic, while the Astu Hotel (m *0914 612142;* **$**) has adequate rooms for US$4.

MEKANE SELAM Capital of Debre Sina *woreda*, Mekane Selam (Place of Peace), 100km west of Tulu Walia, is the largest settlement on the Dessie–Gundewein road, with a population estimated at 10,000. It houses the headquarters for the recently proclaimed Borena Saynt National Park, and is the springboard for visits there. Other tourist amenities are limited to a bank, a bus station, a few no-frills local eateries and a handful of basic lodgings, the pick being the new and relatively smart **Hadese Hotel** (*US$13 en-suite dbl;* **$$**), which is conveniently located in front of the bus station. Cheaper but correspondingly grittier, the **Borena Saynt Hotel** (*8 rooms;* \033 220 0288; m *0914 063407;* **$**) charges US$3 for a clean double using common showers and can be reached by walking along the main road uphill from the bus station for 100m, and taking the second turn to the right.

BORENA SAYNT NATIONAL PARK Designated in 2009 and named after the two *woredas* across which it is split, Borena Saynt protects an area of undulating highlands on the eastern escarpment of the Blue Nile Gorge some 20km northwest of Mekane Selam. The park currently extends over 44km^2, rising from around 1,900m to the 3,727m peak of Mount Yelas, but it is hoped that its area will soon be boosted by an additional 108km^2 of contiguous community-protected land incorporating the 4,280m high Mount Golati. This immense altitudinal span is reflected in the park's varied habitats. These include the extensive Afromontane forest of Denkoro Chaka, which has been protected since the 14th century (and whose name literally means 'deaf', an allusion to the difficulty of communication in the dense interior), as well as Afroalpine moorlands, complete with thickets of giant heather (*Erica arboreal*), on the chilly upper slopes. At least 23 large mammal species are present, including estimated populations of 50 Ethiopian wolf, 1,750 gelada monkey, 640 guereza monkey and 580 Menelik's bushbuck according to a census undertaken in 2013. A bird checklist of 80 species also includes several endemics and near-endemics, among them the very localised Harwood's francolin, as well as white-cheeked turaco, Abyssinian catbird, Abyssinian woodpecker, Abyssinian ground thrush, African hill-babbler and black-headed siskin.

Although tourist development is in its infancy, five trekking routes have been cut through **Borena Saynt** and adjacent community land, and camping is permitted at several designated sites, making the park ideal for adventurous hikers and wildlife lovers who want to get right off the beaten track. A visit of at least three days is recommended, and should be arranged at the helpful park headquarters (♦*033 119 1344*; m *0914 329815*) which lie in Mekane Selam, a few hundred metres along a small gravel road running northwest from the main road 500m west of the bus station. In addition to the one-off entrance fee of US$2 per person plus US$1 per car, a mandatory guide fee of US$5 per day must be paid, and it is also possible to hire mules or donkeys for US$6 per animal per day, and muleteers at the same price. The park entrance lies about 20km drive northwest of town along the same road as the park headquarters, and the forest starts about 5km past that. There is no public transport, so hikers who arrive in Mekane Selam without their own vehicle will need to arrange a road transfer through the headquarters. You will also need to bring all your camping gear, bearing in mind that it gets very cold at night at these high elevations.

SEND US YOUR SNAPS!

We'd love to follow your adventures using our *Ethiopia* guide – why not send us your photos and stories via Twitter (🐦 @BradtGuides) and Instagram (📷 @bradtguides) using the hashtag #Ethiopia? Alternatively, you can upload your photos directly to the gallery on the Ethiopia destination page via our website (w bradtguides.com/ethiopia).

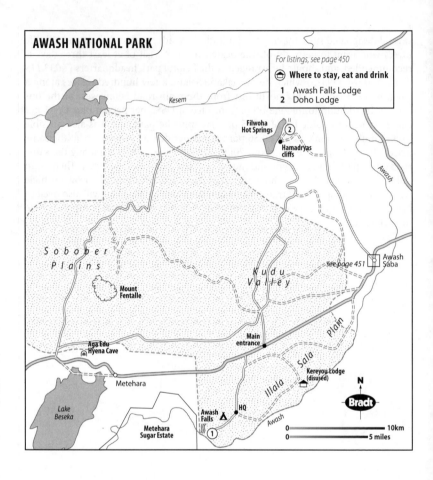

AWASH NATIONAL PARK

For listings, see page 450

🏠 **Where to stay, eat and drink**
1 Awash Falls Lodge
2 Doho Lodge

Kesem

Filwoha Hot Springs

②

Hamadryas cliffs

Awash

S o b o b e r P l a i n s

Mount Fentalle

K u d u V a l l e y

see page 451

Awash Saba

Aga Edu Hyena Cave

Main entrance

Sala Plain

Illala

Metehara

Kereyou Lodge (disused)

N

Bradt

Lake Beseka

Metehara Sugar Estate

Awash Falls

△

HQ

①

Awash

0 — 10km
0 — 5 miles

Part Four

SOUTHERN ETHIOPIA

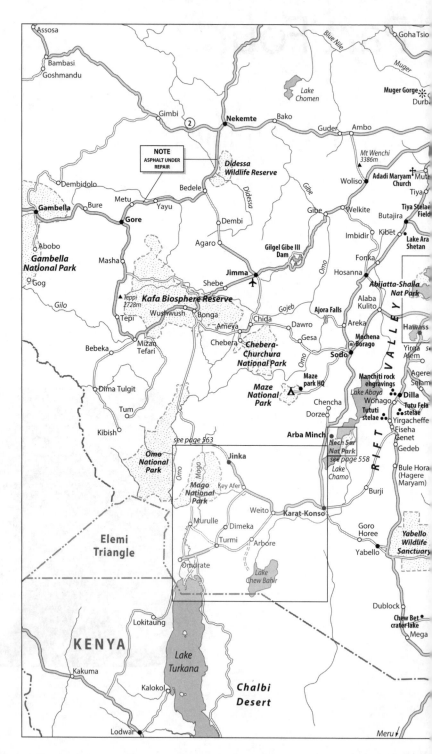

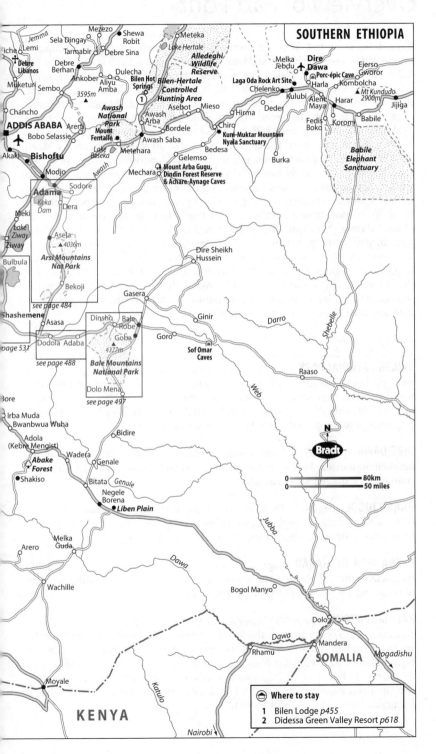

Jemma
Mezezo
Meteka
iche
Lemi
Sela Dingay
Shewa Robit
Lake Hertale
Alledeghi Wildlife Reserve
Melka Jebdu
Dire Dawa
Ejerso
Gwroror
Tarmabir
Debre Sina
Porc-épic Cave
Harla
Kombolcha
Mt Kundudo 2900m
Jijiga
Debre Libanos
Debre Berhan
Ankober
Dulecha
Aliyu Amba
Bilen Hot Springs
Bilen-Hertale Controlled Hunting Area
Laga Oda Rock Art Site
Chelenko
Kulubi
Alem Maya
Harar
Muketuri
Sembo
3595m
Awash National Park
Asebot
Mieso
Hirma
Deder
Fedis
Boko
Korromi
Babile
Chancho
Arerti
Awash Arba
Mount Fentalle
Bordele
Chiro
Kuni-Muktar Mountain Nyala Sanctuary
Babile Elephant Sanctuary
ADDIS ABABA
Bobo Selassie
Awash Saba
Bedesa
Akaki
Bishoftu
Lake Beseka
Metehara
Gelemso
Burka
Modjo
Mechara
Mount Arba Gugu, Dindin Forest Reserve & Achare-Aynage Caves
Adama
Sodore
Koka Dam
Dera
Meki
Asela
4036m
Dire Sheikh Hussein
Lake Ziway
Ziway
Arsi Mountains Nat Park
Bulbula
Bekoji
see page 484
Gasera
Ginir
Darro
Shashemene
Asasa
Dinsho
Bale Robe
Goba
4377m
page 531
Dodola
Adaba
Goro
Sof Omar Caves
see page 488
Bale Mountains National Park
Raaso
Dolo Mena
see page 497
Bore
Irba Muda
Bwanbwua Wuha
Bidire
Adola (Kebre Mengist)
Wadera
Genale
Abake Forest
Shakiso
Bitata
Genale
Negele Borena
Liben Plain
Arero
Melka Guda
Dawa
Wachille
Bogol Manyo
Dolo
Dawa
Mandera
Rhamu
SOMALIA
Mogadishu
Moyale
KENYA
Nairobi
Katulo
Jubba
Web
Shebelle

N

Bradt

0   80km
0   50 miles

Where to stay
1 Bilen Lodge p455
2 Didessa Green Valley Resort p618

Overview of Part Four

Very different in feel from the northern historic circuit, southern Ethiopia is dominated by green highlands and semi-arid plains bisected by a stretch of the Rift Valley studded with pretty lakes. The main attractions of the region are not historical sites but the lovely scenery, plentiful birds and wildlife, and immense cultural diversity. For wildlife lovers, the regional focal point is Bale Mountains National Park, which supports the largest extant populations of Ethiopian wolf, mountain nyala and Bale monkey, along with half those bird species whose range is restricted to Ethiopia and/or Eritrea. The cultural diversity of the south embraces the Mursi and their bizarre lip plates, the ancient fortress-like stone-walled villages of Konso, the tall beak-nosed conical huts built by the Dorze, and the semi-nomadic Borena with their precious cattle herds and singing wells. Tangled into this rich cultural mosaic is Ethiopia's largest ethnolinguistic group, the Oromo, whose one foot is set firmly in the modern world, while the other hoists them up on to the saddle to ride blanketed through the frosty Bale Highlands. The main roads through the south are plied by public transport, while Bale National Park is as easily explored on foot as from a vehicle. More remote areas such as South Omo and Sof Omar are best visited as part of an organised tour or by private 4x4. Altogether different in character is the old walled city of Harar, a UNESCO World Heritage Site that doubles as the spiritual heart of Ethiopia's Muslim community and home to the renowned 'hyena men' and their crepuscular carnivorous allies.

HIGHLIGHTS

AWASH NATIONAL PARK (page 449) Beisa oryx, Hamadryas baboon, spotted hyena and a plethora of colourful birds rank among the more easily spotted wildlife in this scenic national park set in a volcanic landscape on the Rift Valley floor 3 hours' drive east of Addis Ababa. The near-contiguous Alledeghi Wildlife Reserve protects Ethiopia's largest population of the endangered Grevy's zebra.

DIRE DAWA (page 457) Ethiopia's second-largest city is notable for the contrast between the bustling Muslim markets of Megaala and the gracious French-designed colonial-style quarter known as Kezira.

HARAR JUGOL (page 472) The walled inner city of Harar, also known as Gey Ada (City of Saints), can be explored along a maze of narrow alleys that lead past its 83 mosques, 102 shrines and various other historical buildings.

HYENA MEN OF HARAR (page 476) One of Ethiopia's most thrilling wildlife spectacles is provided by the semi-habituated spotted hyenas lured to the outskirts of Harar Jugol by the town's legendary 'hyena men'.

BALE MOUNTAINS (page 491) Majestic scenery, varied vegetation and a wealth of endemics – Ethiopian wolf on the Sanetti Plateau, Bale monkey in the Harenna Forest, mountain nyala in the junipers around Dinsho – combine to make the high-altitude Bale Mountains National Park the top wildlife-viewing and birding destination in Ethiopia, with the added possibility of hiking and trekking between five equipped mountain huts and a tented camp in the adjacent Adaba-Dodola Integrated Forest Management Project.

SOF OMAR CAVES (page 504) Reputedly the largest network of limestone caverns in Africa, Sof Omar was carved by a subterranean stretch of the Web River, which enters the main cave via a magnificent cathedral-like natural hall supported by 20m-high pillars.

SHAPPE ROCK ENGRAVINGS (page 514) Thought to be around 5,000 years old, this beautiful rock art site near Dilla depicts a herd of 70 cattle moving along a vertical face in a steep river gully.

LAKES LANGANO, ABIJATTA AND SHALLA (page 529) A popular weekend retreat from Addis Ababa, rusty-watered Lake Langano is lined by half a dozen resort hotels, while nearby Abijatta-Shalla National Park is home to a profusion of waterbirds, notably large aggregations of flamingos.

HAWASSA (page 540) The most enjoyable city in south Ethiopia, Hawassa doubles as the bustling capital of the Southern Nations, Nationalities and Peoples' Region and as a pretty and well-equipped lakeshore resort town rattling with monkeys and birds.

ARBA MINCH (page 552) This beautifully located town overlooks Nech Sar National Park, home to outsized crocodiles, grunting hippos and graceful zebras, and also provides easy access to the homeland of the Dorze people, who are renowned for their towering beehive-shaped homesteads and cotton-weaving skills.

KONSO (page 566) Listed as a UNESCO World Heritage Site in 2011, the fascinating fortified stone-walled villages of Konso date back hundreds of years and are studded with totem-like *waka* grave-markers, towering generation poles and thatched *mora* community houses.

SOUTH OMO (page 562) Tucked up against the Kenyan border, this remote region, run through by the Omo River, is home to perhaps a dozen different traditionalist ethnic groups – among them the Mursi, Hamar and Kara – whose colourful adornments evoke pre-20th-century Africa.

CHEBERA-CHURCHURA NATIONAL PARK (page 604) Track elephants, buffalo and hippos on foot in this recently created pedestrian-friendly national park, which also hosts an exceptional diversity of forest and woodland birds.

KAFA BIOSPHERE RESERVE (page 607) Centred on Bonga in the lush and little-visited southwestern highlands, this UNESCO-sanctioned reserve is an important biodiversity hot spot renowned as the original home of coffee, which still grows naturally in the forest undergrowth.

GAMBELLA (page 621) Perhaps the most atypical of Ethiopian towns, this languidly characterful tropical African river port lies in the sweaty lowlands close to the South Sudanese border. It is the closest town to the difficult-to-reach Gambella National Park, which hosts a seasonal migration of more than one million antelope.

13

Awash National Park, Harar and Eastern Highlands

Flanked by the arid plains of Afar and the Ogaden, the far east of Ethiopia is bisected by a narrow extension of the southern highlands that points like a crooked finger towards the borders with Djibouti and Somaliland. Comprising the Arba Gugu and Chercher mountains, these eastern highlands – split between the federal regions of Oromia and Somali – are very moist, fertile and scenic, and form an important centre of *khat* and coffee production. The region is best known to travellers for its two largest cities, both of which are effectively governed as autonomous federal regions. Historically, the more significant of these is the ancient walled city of Harar, spiritual home of Ethiopia's Islamic community, and also renowned for the 'hyena men' who earn their keep by feeding wild hyenas nightly on the town outskirts. In economic terms, however, Harar is overshadowed by Dire Dawa, which is the country's second-largest city, despite its rather bleak setting on the hot dry plains 50km further northwest. Other points of interest include the Babile Elephant Sanctuary, the Valley of Marvels, several ancient rock art sites, and the fast-growing town of Jijiga, which serves as capital of Somali Region.

Both Harar and Dire Dawa lie about 510km east of Addis Ababa along a good asphalt road that diverges a mere 25km before it reaches either town. In a private vehicle, one can drive or bus from Addis Ababa to either city in one long day, but you could also break up the journey with a stop at Awash National Park, whose scenic volcanic landscapes provide something of a taster for the Danakil, or at the

TENSIONS IN THE EASTERN HIGHLANDS

Warning The eastern highlands around Harar and Dire Dawa were one of the focal points of Oromo anti-government protests in 2016 and they also emerged as a hotbed of Somali–Oromo tensions and occasional violent clashes in late 2017. One such incident, the burning of two buses by protesters in 2016, caused Selam, Ethio and Sky Buses to suspend all services between Addis Ababa and the far east ever since. The situation is volatile but, at the time of writing, it seems like travel within the city limits of Dire Dawa, Harar or Jijiga is perfectly safe, and there is no significant risk attached to bussing or driving along trunk roads. However, travel along dirt roads and to outlying areas of the eastern highlands – where local children are in the habit of setting up roadblocks to ask for money and stoning the vehicles of drivers who refuse them – cannot be recommended for the time being.

somewhat more obscure Kuni Muktar Mountain Nyala Sanctuary. There are also regular flights from Addis Ababa to Dire Dawa and Jijiga, but not to Harar, and a fast electric train connecting Addis Ababa to Djibouti via Adama and Dire Dawa launched in 2018.

AWASH NATIONAL PARK

Straddling the border of Oromia and Afar a 190km drive east of Addis Ababa, the 756km² Awash National Park [map, page 442] (*entrance US$4 pp/day, US$1/2 per car/minibus, optional scout US$5/day*) protects a starkly magnificent volcanic landscape set in a tract of the Rift Valley floor dominated by semi-arid grassland and acacia scrub, but also incorporating palm forests fed by hot springs, and the riparian woodland that follows the Awash River along its southern boundary. One of Ethiopia's oldest national parks, it was established in 1966 and gazetted three years later, with the primary aim of protecting a varied dry-country fauna that includes Beisa oryx, greater kudu and Soemmerring's gazelle, along with vulnerable populations of several large predators. Unfortunately, poaching has accounted for much of the park's once prolific mammals, but patient visitors can still expect to see a fair amount of wildlife, and the birding is quite outstanding. Scenic highlights include the spectacular Fentalle volcano and its gaping crater, the pretty Lake Beseka, and the powerful Awash Falls at the western head of the 150m-deep Awash Gorge. Access to the park is straightforward, since the main road between Addis Ababa and Harar runs through it for 30km, bookended by the small towns of Metehara and Awash Saba, and there's accommodation to suit all budgets, but it is difficult to explore further without a private 4x4.

GEOLOGY AND WILDLIFE The volcanic landscape is dominated by two geographic features: the dormant Mount Fentalle to the north of the main road, and the deep gorge carved by the Awash River along the park's southern boundary. Evidence of Fentalle's most recent eruption, which probably occurred in the early 19th century, can be seen along the park's western border, around Metehara and Lake Beseka. Here, the plains are strewn with rubble-like old flows of bare black pitchstone, and studded with blister cones (hollow rock domes formed when massive gas bubbles are trapped below the solidifying lava), some of which have broken open to form shelter-like caves. Tectonic activity is also responsible for the hot springs that bubble to the surface northeast of Fentalle. By contrast, the spectacular Awash Gorge has formed over tens of thousands of years as a result of erosion.

Around 80 mammal species have been recorded in Awash, the majority of which comprise inconspicuous bats and rodents and elusive small predators. The ranges of Hamadryas and Anubis baboons overlap in this part of the Rift Valley, and both species, as well as hybrids, are frequently observed alongside the surfaced main road that bisects the park. Other quite conspicuous large mammals are Beisa oryx, Soemmerring's gazelle and Salt's dik-dik, all of which are regularly seen from the main road. Elsewhere, the thick scrub along the Awash River harbours lesser and greater kudu, Defassa waterbuck and warthog, while more developed riverine forest may shelter parties of vervet monkeys and, less commonly, guereza. Swayne's hartebeest was introduced to the park in 1974, while the localised Grevy's zebra used to be resident, but both are now thought to be locally extinct. As is the case in many parts of Ethiopia, spotted hyenas remain common, but the status of most other large predators on the park checklist – lion, leopard, cheetah, striped hyena and African wild dog – is at best uncertain.

Whatever its limitations when it comes to game viewing, Awash National Park has to be regarded as one of Ethiopia's premier birding destinations. The park checklist of 460-plus species includes several dry-country specials with a limited distribution, including the endemic Ethiopian cliff swallow and yellow-throated serin, and near-endemic sombre rock chat. Raptors are well represented, since many species breed in the gorge and on the volcano's slopes, and the park is also good for plains dwellers such as the localised Arabian bustard and African swallow-tailed kite, and the colourful northern carmine bee-eater, red-and-yellow barbet and Abyssinian roller.

GETTING THERE AND AWAY

By road Self-drivers coming from Addis Ababa should follow the Adama Expressway to its end, then continue eastward along the main surfaced road towards Dire Dawa. Metehara straddles the main road about 88km past Adama, and it's another 30km from there to Awash Saba, passing the main park entrance gate and ticket office to the right about halfway between the two towns. Allow 3–4 hours for the drive, depending on traffic as you leave Addis Ababa.

No direct road transport runs between Addis Ababa and the park, so you'll probably need to change vehicles at Adama, from where regular minibuses run to/from Awash Saba via Metehara (*US$2.50; 1½–2½hrs*). Coming from Dire Dawa or Harar, any bus bound for Addis Ababa could drop you at Awash Saba or Metehara, though you'll probably need to pay full fare. Heading to Dire Dawa or Harar, passing buses will usually be full, so you may need to return to Adama and catch a bus there.

By rail The new electric rail service between Addis Ababa and Djibouti stops at both Metehara and Awash Saba. Trains from Addis Ababa depart at 08.00 on alternate days and the travel time should be around 3 hours.

WHERE TO STAY, EAT AND DRINK *Map, page 442, unless otherwise stated*
There is no accommodation actually within the national park proper, but several attractive options are scattered around its borders. These include two upmarket lodges, one on the western border overlooking the Awash Falls and the other on the northeast border on a ridge above the Filwoha Hot Springs. For travellers on a more limited budget, several good options are available in Awash Saba and Metehara, the small towns that flank the park to the east and west respectively. The defunct Kereyou Lodge, still shown on most maps of the park, shows no sign of reopening any time soon.

Upmarket

 Doho Lodge (10 rooms) 011 882 9361; m 0912 770965; e doholodge@gmail.com; w doholodge.com. Opened in Mar 2015, this younger sibling to Awash Falls Lodge, set on Afar communal land just outside the northeast park boundary, lies 22km northwest of Awash Saba along a rough dirt road. It has a stunning location on a low ridge overlooking a small reed-fringed lake set among the Filwoha Hot Springs, & the 2-storey dining area is perfectly positioned to catch the sunset. You can boat on the lake, bathe or shower in a pair of steamy artificial pools fed by the springs, or just enjoy the plentiful birdlife in the fringing vegetation. Mammals are thin on the ground, but you're bound to hear hyenas at night, while Hamadryas baboons frequently overnight on the nearby cliffs. The en-suite bungalows boast a similar rusticity to Awash Falls Lodge, but are much newer, & mosquitoes seem to be less of a nuisance. *US$80/110/130 B&B sgl/dbl/twin, US$180 family room. Rates drop slightly Apr–Jul.* **$$$$$**

Awash Falls Lodge (25 rooms) 011 653 0245; m 0912 770965, 0930 097690; e awashfallslodge@gmail.com; w awashfallslodge.net. Located 11km south of the park gate on the

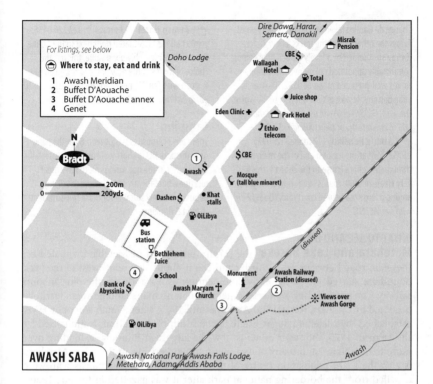

For listings, see below

🍽 **Where to stay, eat and drink**
1 Awash Meridian
2 Buffet D'Aouache
3 Buffet D'Aouache annex
4 Genet

AWASH SABA *Awash National Park, Awash Falls Lodge,*
Metehara, Adama, Addis Ababa

southwestern border of an adjacent conservation area, this attractively rustic lodge has a wonderful location facing the Awash Falls. The traditionally furnished en-suite stone, bamboo & thatch bungalows have plenty of character, but they are starting to look a bit rundown, & the mosquitoes can be ferocious, despite the screened windows & netted beds. A 2-storey restaurant & bar overlooking the falls serves a good variety of local & European dishes in the US$2.50–6 range. A variety of local treks & day trips can be organised, including to the hot springs & hyena caves, as well as overnight camping expeditions to Mt Fentalle. *From US$70/80/100/110 B&B sgl/dbl/twin/trpl, US$160–80 family room sleeping 4–5; all rooms US$20 cheaper May–Jul.* **$$$$$**

Budget

🏠 **Awash Meridian Hotel** [map, above] (54 rooms) ☎ 022 224 0051. This multistorey hotel, set in a large compound on the main road through Awash Saba, offers spacious 1st-class rooms with queen-size bed, netting, fan or AC, sat TV & en-suite hot shower, as well as 2nd-class rooms with TV, fan & en-suite cold shower, & similarly outfitted but

older & scruffier 3rd-class rooms. A good rooftop bar & courtyard restaurant are attached. Good value. *US$8/16/20 3rd-/2nd-/1st-class room.* **$$**

🏠 **Genet Hotel** [map, above] (27 rooms) m 0940 219717. Justifiably popular with tour operators, this 4-storey hotel on the main road through Awash Saba has the best rooms in town all with net, fridge, sat TV & en-suite hot shower. The restaurant is pretty good, too. Unfortunately it feels overpriced at the inflated *faranji* rate. *US$25/31 sgl/dbl with fan or US$32/37 sgl/dbl with AC; all rates B&B.* **$$$**

Shoestring

🏠 **Buffet D'Aouache** [map, above] (28 rooms) ☎ 022 224 0008, 011 550 9364. The oldest hostelry in Awash Saba, built by the French to service the Djibouti railway ('Aouache' being the French spelling of Awash), has been under Greek management for longer than anyone can remember. It's an unexpected gem at the price, all faded whitewashed colonial architecture draped in flowering creepers. The rundown but adequately comfortable rooms include the 'Head of State' Suite – reputedly where Haile Selassie &

451

13

Charles de Gaulle stayed in the hotel's glory days! Across the other side of the tracks a new 2-storey **annex** surrounded by a lovely garden houses more comfortably appointed dbl rooms. The restaurant serves well-prepared meals at US$2.50–4 on its wide balcony; service is slow but it's usually worth the wait. *US$3/5 dbl/twin using common shower, US$16 en-suite dbl or twin with fan.* **$–$$**

🏠 **Abune Pension** (17 rooms) m 0925 259321. Set at the eastern end of the main road through Metehara (close to the church), this has very clean en-suite rooms (cold shower only) set around a large manicured courtyard. *US$8/12 dbl with fan/AC.* **$$**

🏠 **Awash Hotel** (13 rooms) ☎ 022 226 0436; m 0912 013311. Situated right next to the Abune Pension & comparably good value, this has the choice of rooms in the new or old wing, all en suite & clean with fan, TV, net & private terrace. *US$8/10 dbl in old/new wing.* **$**

Camping
There are 2 campsites (*US$2/tent;* **$**) in the park, 1 near the park HQ (a short walk from the waterfall) & the other at the hot springs. Both have great locations, but lack any facilities worth talking about, & are only suitable for those self-sufficient in food & drinking water.

WHAT TO SEE AND DO
Metehara and Lake Beseka The scruffy little town of Metehara, situated on the main road between Addis Ababa and Harar about 3km southwest of the park boundary, started life in the early 20th century as a station on the old Djibouti railway. The surrounding area was something of a no man's land between territory occupied by the Afar, Kereyu and Amhara until 1965, when Dutch company HVA established the Metehara Sugar Estate to the south of the station. Nationalised by the Derg in 1975, the sugar estate is now the largest in Ethiopia, extending over more than 100km^2, and many of its 1,000-plus workers live in the town. Metehara is also the main population centre of the Kereyu Oromo, pastoralists who were expelled from the bordering national park after it was gazetted in the late 1960s, and whose striking traditional male hairstyle is cut short on the top but blossoms Afro-like on the sides. The town is only 7km south of Fentalle's crater and its night sky is occasionally lit with fireworks from the vents.

Metehara's main point of interest to travellers is Lake Beseka, a shallow body of saline water nestled in a depression between two fault-lines to the west of both the town and the national park. Located at the southern base of Fentalle, Bekele lies in a strange landscape of chunky black lava blocks deposited during recent eruptions, and it is fed entirely by subterranean hot springs associated with tectonic activity. For reasons that are unclear, Beseka has expanded greatly in recent decades, from around 3km^2 in the 1950s to around 45km^2 today. As a result, the main road that once crossed the lake via a causeway has been diverted about 1km north to skirt its shore, and it is feared that Metehara itself will be submerged within the next 20 years or so. In terms of scenery, the lake is quite a special spot, with the ragged edges of Fentalle looming to the north, and it also supports an interesting avifauna. A varied selection of water-associated birds includes a seasonal population of ferruginous duck and sporadic visits by the coast-dwelling western reef heron, while the surrounding rockscapes are prime territory for the near-endemic sombre rock chat, the rather similar blackstart, and several dry-country larks. The lake can easily be explored on foot from Metehara, either by following the old causeway immediately west of town, or walking along the shore. Try to visit in the early morning or late afternoon, when the exposed shore is relatively cool, and resist any temptation to freshen up in the lake, as crocodiles are reputedly present.

Aga Edu Hyena Cave Situated outside the national park on the southern slopes of Fentalle about 2km north of Lake Beseka, Aga Edu is a large lava fissure used as a den by a clan of at least 20, and possibly as many as 50, spotted hyenas. The cave is best visited between 18.00 and 19.00, when its inhabitants emerge to start their nocturnal foraging on the surrounding plains, often indulging in elaborate greeting and grooming rituals. To get there, follow the main road west to Addis Ababa for about 1km out of Metehara, then turn on to a motorable dirt track running north across the new railway track and follow it for about 2km to the tiny village of Aga Edu, where a community fee of US$10 per vehicle is levied. Travellers coming from Awash Falls Lodge will also need to pay US$10 for a scout to drive back through the park after dark.

Awash Falls Dramatic at any time of year but especially so during the rains, this frothing waterfall is formed by the Awash River as it tumbles over the black basaltic cliff at the head of the gorge that runs along the national park's southern boundary. The water cascades down in at least five different channels, separated by lushly forested islands, and there are several good viewpoints from the Awash Falls Lodge and its immediate surrounds. A short footpath leads to the base of the waterfall, where baboons come down to drink, crocodiles lurk in the shallows and monitor lizards crash clumsily through the undergrowth. The fringing woodland is good for birds. The park headquarters are situated above the waterfall and Beisa oryx and greater kudu are frequently seen around the staff buildings. The lodge overlooking the waterfall is a pleasant spot for a drink and (affordable) meal.

Southern Plains The main game-viewing loop through Awash National Park covers around 35km in total and runs south from the main entrance gate to Awash Falls before following a rough road running east to the abandoned Kereyou Lodge (the best place to scan the gorge for the as yet undescribed 'Ethiopian cliff swallow'), then cutting back north to the main gate via the Ilala Sala Plain. The most open part of the park, Ilala Sala is a good place to look for Beisa oryx and Soemmerring's gazelle, as well as the park's seven species of bustard, most notably the very localised and uncommon Arabian bustard. Other prominent dry-country birds include Abyssinian roller, the gorgeous northern carmine bee-eater (which breeds in sandbanks in the Awash Gorge) and various sandgrouse, larks, hornbills and waxbills. The circuit can normally be driven in any vehicle with reasonable clearance, though a 4x4 might be necessary after heavy rain, and should take around 3 hours, allowing for stops to look at game and at the waterfall and lodge, though it would justify a full day if you are birding.

Filwoha Hot Springs Situated on the park's northeast boundary, the Filwoha Hot Springs discharge around 50,000 litres of water per minute to feed a series of beautiful translucent blue pools surrounded by groves of tall doum palms. You can bathe in some of the pools, but test the water first as it is scaldingly hot when it first bubbles to the surface. Hamadryas baboon overnight in the cliffs above the springs and are frequently seen foraging in the vicinity by day. Other wildlife frequently seen around the springs includes warthog, greater kudu and lesser kudu. The springs can be reached along a rough 4x4-only 30km road running north from the main Harar road roughly opposite the main gate (allow 1 hour in either direction) or by following the 22km road running north from Awash Saba to Doho Lodge.

Mount Fentalle The northern skyline of Awash National Park is dominated by Mount Fentalle, a dormant volcano that rises more than 1,000m above the surrounding plains to a peak of 2,007m. The volcano's centrepiece is a magnificent and fully intact caldera whose 10km² floor lies around 350m below the narrow, jagged rim. The barren black lava flows to the west of Metehara were created by Fentalle's most recent major eruption, which probably occurred in the early 19th century, but the crater is pitted with steam vents which can sometimes be seen from the surrounding plains at night. The upper slopes of Fentalle are a favoured haunt of klipspringer and mountain reedbuck, while birders know it to be one of only two reliable sites for the endemic yellow-throated serin. A road runs most of the way to the crater rim, but it is in poor condition and you will most likely need to walk the last stretch – a steep 2-hour hike on exposed slopes, best done in the cool of the morning. To get to Fentalle, follow the Addis Ababa road west out of Metehara for about 8km, before turning on to a reasonable dirt road that heads northward across the Sobober Plains (in the direction of Aliyu Amba and Ankober, page 437). After 15km, turn east on to the rough 12km road to the crater rim, and follow it as far as possible before hiking the remainder.

Awash Saba The largest town in the vicinity of the national park, and the best equipped for budget travellers, Awash Saba stands on the lip of the Awash Gorge above the site where an iron bridge was built across the river by engineer Alfred Ilg during the late-19th-century reign of Emperor Menelik II. A station on the Djibouti railway was established there in 1917, and shortly thereafter it became the site of one of Ethiopia's first hotels (which evolved into the present-day Buffet D'Aouache; page 451) as well as the country's fourth post office. The town that mushroomed around the original railway station now houses a population estimated at 15,000, and a Monday market that attracts plenty of traditional Afar people from the surrounding plains. Otherwise, urban sightseeing is limited to a large church, a neat mosque, the disused railway station, and a nearby stone column memorial whose only apparent purpose is to provide a few goats with a sliver of afternoon shade.

By contrast, a viewpoint perhaps 300m southeast of the Buffet D'Aouache offers a magnificent view over the 150m-deep Awash River Gorge, the drama of which is accentuated by a row of low volcanic hills on the opposite side. For birders, there's some good raptor-scanning here – auger buzzard, vultures, kestrels and falcons – and a chance of seeing the elusive Ethiopian cliff swallow. The base of the gorge and bank of the Awash River can be reached along the same footpath that once serviced Alfred Ilg's iron bridge, and although the immediate environs have suffered from vigorous chomping by goats, there's some interesting-looking riverine woodland a kilometre or so back towards the park boundary. If you decide to hike down, be conscious that the gorge leads into the national park about 4km south of Awash Saba, and there's no telling what official attitudes would be were you to cross the line inadvertently.

Note that Awash Saba (Awash Seven) is often referred to as Awash, but we've used its full name here in order to avoid confusion with the town of Awash Arba (Awash Forty), which lies some 20km away on the Asaita road, not to mention the nearby river, gorge and national park.

Alledeghi Wildlife Reserve A rewarding goal for a day safari out of Awash, ideally with the earliest possible start, the underrated 1,830km² Alledeghi Wildlife Reserve (*entrance US$4.50 pp plus US$1/vehicle*) harbours Ethiopia's largest (and the world's most northerly) population of the endangered Grevy's zebra, estimated at around 150 individuals, and these are quite commonly seen from the limited road network. Small numbers of African wild ass, lion and cheetah are also reputedly present, but you are more likely to see Soemmerring's gazelle, Beisa oryx, gerenuk,

Hamadryas baboon and warthog. A good selection of dry-country birds includes Arabian bustard, Liechtenstein's sandgrouse, northern carmine bee-eater, golden-breasted starling and white-headed sparrow weaver. Also known as Halaldeghe, Alledeghi is reputedly earmarked to be upgraded to a national park in the near future. Accessible in a private 4x4 only, it can be reached by following the Harar road out of Awash Saba for about 6km then turning left at the prominent junction for Semera and Djibouti, and continuing north past Awash Arba until you see the entrance gate to the right.

Bilen-Hertale Controlled Hunting Area Protecting around 1,000km² of semi-arid savannah verging the east bank of the Awash River as it flows north out of Awash National Park, this controlled hunting area is named after the Bilen Hot Springs and Hertale Crater Lake, both of which lie about 12km west of the main road to Semera. The more regularly visited of these, the scalding Bilen Hot Springs is one of the places where Wilfred Thesiger set up camp on his Awash expedition in the 1930s, and it flows into a reed-lined pool which is big enough to swim in, provided you don't mind sharing the water with drinking camels brought down by Afar herders. Further north, the 13km² Hertale Crater Lake, set in the base of a shallow caldera, is an important watering point both for wildlife and for local Afar herders. The controlled hunting area harbours a selection of mammals similar to Awash National Park, including Beisa oryx, lesser kudu, Salt's dik-dik, warthog and Hamadryas baboon, along with Grevy's zebra, gerenuk and naked mole-rat, and more than 400 bird species.

Bilen-Hertale can be visited in a private 4x4 only. The most convenient base for exploring the area is the rustic and eco-friendly but now rather rundown **Bilen Lodge** [map, page 445] (*15 rooms;* ☏ *011 550 8869;* m *0911 223003;* e *info@villageethiopiatour.com;* w *villageethiopiatour.com;* **$$$$$**), which was built under consultation with local Afar communities and offers cultural activities such as village visits and camel treks with local Afar herders. To get there, follow the Harar road east of Awash Saba for about 6km, then turn left at the prominent junction for Semera, and continue for 50km until you see Bilen Lodge signposted to your left. To get to Lake Hertale, you need to follow the Semera road north for another 75km to the small town of Meteka, then turn left on to a side road that branches west at Meteka. After 20km, this arrives at Hertale, where you are bound to see Afar herders watering their camels and cattle, along with a varied selection of waterbirds. Meteka also marks the southern end of the Meteka Wetlands, a marshy stretch of the Awash floodplain that offers excellent birding all year round, but is most rewarding in the European winter when it forms part of a flyway used by hundreds of thousands of Palaearctic migrants.

AWASH TO HARAR AND DIRE DAWA BY ROAD

This is a drive of two distinct parts. Immediately east of Awash Saba, a bridge crosses the Awash River, giving way to a bleakly monotonous cover of dry acacia scrub where parties of colourfully dressed Oromo women appear from nowhere in an excited gossipy clatter, the odd camel or donkey wanders blithely along the road verge, and you may see the occasional Salt's dik-dik make a startled dash into the scrub. The second stage of the trip climbs from Chiro into the cool, moist Chercher Mountains, which provide a literal breath of fresh air after the hot, dusty plains, as well as fantastic views across densely cultivated fields and patches of juniper, eucalyptus and euphorbia woodland to row after row of verdant peaks.

ASEBOT SELASSIE Set on the peak of Debre Asebot (2,539m), this ancient monastery houses several ancient Ge'ez manuscripts describing the miracles performed by its founder Abuna Samuel. It can be reached along a rough 15km track that branches north towards the prominent mountain opposite the junction for Asebot town about 65km from Awash Saba and 12km before Mieso.

CHIRO About 100km east of Awash Saba, Chiro, formerly known as Asbe Teferi, was earmarked for great things in the early 1930s, when it was made capital of the model province of Chercher as part of a modernisation drive initiated by Emperor Haile Selassie. Today it supports a population of almost 60,000 and is rescued from visual forgettability by an attractive setting in the Chercher and Arba Gugu foothills, and the presence of a few balconied two-storey legacies of the Italian occupation. There's plenty of public transport heading out in all directions from Chiro, but if you're in need of a bed for the night there is no shortage of accommodation. Current pick, set in a green compound on the Harar side of town, is the **Agape Hotel** (*12 rooms;* \025 551 0818; **$$**), which charges US$10 for a small but neat en-suite bungalow with ¾ bed, TV and net, and also has an above-average restaurant. The **Burka Hotel** (*37 rooms;* \025 551 0208; **$$**) and **Kebesh International Lodge** (*18 rooms;* \025 551 0935; **$$**) also have decent en-suite rooms for around the same price.

KUNI MUKTAR MOUNTAIN NYALA SANCTUARY This small sanctuary flanking the village of Kuni 15km southeast of Chiro was set aside in 1989 to protect a vulnerable population of endemic mountain nyala resident on the forested slopes of the Jallo and Muktar, both of which rise to an altitude of above 3,000m. It is currently estimated to protect between 80 and 200 mountain nyala, one of the largest confirmed populations outside of the Bale Mountains. These endangered antelope are most easily located in the early morning or late afternoon, but it might well take 2 hours to find them. Also present are Menelik's bushbuck, reedbuck, spotted hyena and warthog, along with forest-associated avian endemics such as Abyssinian catbird.

Kuni Muktar is easily visited as a day trip out of Chiro, ideally with an early start. Follow the Dire Dawa road for 8km to Arbereketi, then turn right on to the Mechara road (which was being widened in preparation for asphalting in 2018) and continue for 7km to Kuni. Plenty of minibuses run between Chiro and Kuni. Once there, it is easy enough to find someone to help you locate the mountain nyalas; a recommended guide is Bayu (**m** 0936 775207). There is no accommodation in Kuni, but camping in the forest can be arranged through Bayu.

DINDIN FOREST AND ACHARE-AYNAGE CAVES Another important refuge for the mountain nyala, the little-studied but extensive Dindin Forest is an Afromontane assemblage set on the steep eastern slopes of Mount Arba Gugu, which rises to an elevation of 3,574m near the small town of Mechara, 100km southwest of Chiro. About 6km from Mechara, Achare-Aynage is Ethiopia's second most extensive caves network (after Sof Omar), with at least 16 entrances identified and more than 7km of passages surveyed by scientific expeditions over 2004–07 (for more details, visit **w** scholarcommons.usf.edu, search 'Mechara'). The 100km road to Mechara, which branches southwest from the Harar road at Arbereketi, 8km out of Chiro, used to be quite rough and slow going, but it should be partially or fully surfaced by the time you read this, rendering these once obscure sites considerably more accessible than in the past.

CHELENKO Flanking the Harar road about 115km east of Chiro, the small town of Chelenko was the site of the future Emperor Menelik's defeat of Emir Abdullah of Harar on 6 January 1887, an engagement that led directly to the annexation of Harar to Shewa and eventually to Ethiopia. The rout is still remembered with some bitterness locally, and in 2015 the town became the site of the Chelenko Martyrs Memorial, a striking red and white structure, centred on a statue of a white horseman and dedicated to the many Oromo, Harari and Somali soldiers who died in vain trying to protect Harar's autonomy. Perhaps not coincidentally, Chelenko has been a repeat flashpoint in recent anti-government demonstrations – it was close to here that two Selam buses were burned by an angry mob in 2016, while another protest led to the massacre of at least 15 civilians by security forces in December 2017.

KULUBI Some 30km west of the T-junction where the roads to Harar and Dire Dawa split, the small town of Kulubi enjoys a renown disproportionate to its size thanks to the church of Kulubi Gebriel, which stands on a hilltop 2.5km from the town centre. In 1896, Ras Makonnen, father of Haile Selassie, stopped at what was then a rather modest shrine to St Gebriel outside Kulubi to pray for assistance in the looming military confrontation with Italy. Ethiopia duly defeated Italy at Adwa, and when Ras Makonnen returned to Harar he ordered a magnificent church to be built at Kulubi in honour of the inspirational saint.

Aesthetically, it's debatable whether the domed sandstone church built by Ras Makonnen is of much inherent interest to anybody other than students of modern Ethiopian architecture. But, rather oddly given its relative modernity in a country liberally dotted with ancient churches of mysterious origin, Kulubi Gebriel has become the target of a fantastic biannual pilgrimage, one regarded by Ethiopian Christians as equivalent to the Islamic call to Mecca. On 26 July and 28 December, the days dedicated to St Gebriel, more than 100,000 Ethiopians from all over the country descend on the church, a festive occasion with few peers anywhere in Ethiopia. Aside from being a wonderful cultural spectacle, the pilgrimage can disrupt normal public transport patterns in the area for a few days, and bus seats are booked up weeks in advance.

DIRE DAWA

Ethiopia's second-largest city, Dire Dawa, a name derived from an Oromo phrase meaning 'plain of medicine', has a rather improbable location flanking a *wadi* (normally dry watercourse) carved by the Dachata River on the relatively dry plains at the northeastern base of the Chercher Mountains. The Dachata divides the city centre into two distinct parts, connected by a bridge in the north and by two seasonal causeways further south. Northwest of the watercourse, the gracious French-designed colonial-style quarter of Kezira comprises a neat grid of avenues, flanked by shady trees and staid European-style buildings, emanating from the central square in front of the old railway station. By contrast, Megaala, to the southeast of the riverine arc, has the more compact and organic feel typical of old Islamic towns, with all alleys apparently leading to the colourful bustle of its two vast markets. Overall, Dire Dawa lacks for compelling sightseeing by comparison with nearby Harar, and it draws mixed reactions from travellers. Some dismiss the city as hot, sticky and lacking in charm, while others wax elegiac about the French-bequeathed sense of urban order that permeates the bough-shaded avenues – a perception gap we suspect to be largely attributable to seasonality, with the year-round humidity most likely to be accentuated by searing temperatures over May to August.

HISTORY Dire Dawa is a modern city, but the surrounding area has a long history of human habitation, evidenced by the presence of several prehistoric rock art sites that date back more than 5,000 years. In medieval times, Harla, now a small village straddling the Harar road some 15km south of Dire Dawa, was the capital of a mysterious Somali-affiliated trade empire whose main port was Zeila, close to the present-day border of Somaliland and Djibouti. Not a great deal is known about the nature of the Harla Empire, but its inhabitants evidently converted to Islam during or before the 14th century, and were probably responsible for building the venerated 15th-century Abeyaziz Mosque at Hulul Mojo. In 1822, French Catholics established a mission at Awale, 20km southeast of Dire Dawa. In 1897, Dire Dawa, then known as Addis Harar (New Harar), was earmarked as the site of a major railway station on the soon-to-be-built Franco–Ethiopian line between Addis Ababa and Djibouti in 1897. Urban development started in 1902, when the first train rolled into the station. Because of its strategic location, the upstart town soon came to outrank Harar in commercial and industrial significance, though even as recently as 1970 it supported a significantly smaller population. In the post-Derg era, Dire Dawa experienced a fresh economic boom as a result of the secession of Eritrea, which left Ethiopia without a seaport. Its economic importance was further bolstered by the subsequent closure of the border with Eritrea, which left Djibouti and Berbera (Somaliland) as the only reliable ports serving Ethiopia. In the federal carve-up of 1995, Dire Dawa was one of only two Ethiopian towns accorded the status of a chartered city (the other being Addis Ababa), Since then, population has grown from 150,000 to an estimated 650,000.

GETTING THERE AND AWAY
By air Dire Dawa is the main air gateway to Harar. Ethiopian Airlines operates several flights to and from Addis Ababa daily, some of which continue to Jijiga. The modern airport lies about 2km north of the city centre. A charter taxi costs around US$5, but cheaper shared taxis are also available.

By rail A new electric railway service connects Addis Ababa to Djibouti via Dire Dawa, running in opposite directions on alternate days. In either direction, trains are scheduled to pass through Dire Dawa at around 13.00, and they leave not from the disused central railway station, but from a custom-built station at Melka Jebdu 10km to the northwest. For further details, see page 101.

By road Assuming that the superior Selam, Ethio and Sky buses resume service at some point during the lifespan of this edition, they used to charge around US$15 for the 10-hour trip to Addis Ababa, and departed from Dire Dawa in the main square in front of the old railway station. Other cheaper and less reliable bus services still cover this route, while regular minibuses run back and forth between Dire Dawa and Harar (US$1; 1½hrs) throughout the day, leaving from the main bus station, which lies a few hundred metres east of the Harar road behind a Coca-Cola factory.

 WHERE TO STAY Although it lacks for any genuinely upmarket accommodation, Dire Dawa is served by a fabulous selection of superior budget hotels, most of which offer significantly better value than their counterparts in Harar and Jijiga.

Moderate
 Samrat Hotel [459 B4] (58 rooms) 025 113 0600; e samrathoteldire@gmail.com; w samrathoteldire.com. The most upmarket

option in Dire Dawa is this centrally located Indian-owned hotel, whose comfortable & modern en-suite rooms come with AC, fan, large flatscreen TV & hot water. Rates include free airport pick-up.

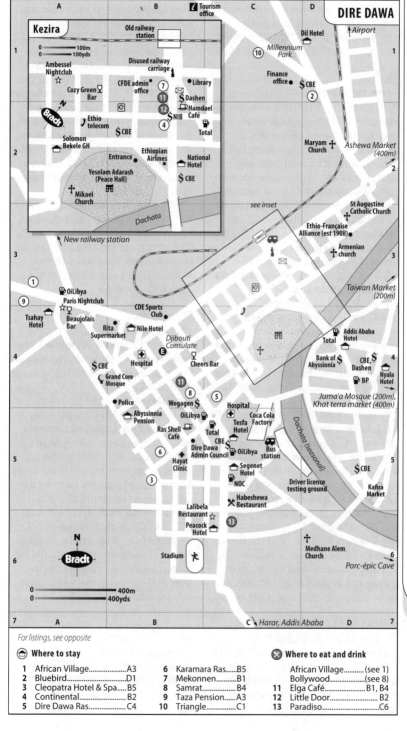

DIRE DAWA

Kezira

0 ———— 100m
0 ———— 100yds

Old railway station

Disused railway carriage

Ambessel Nightclub ☆

Cozy Green Bar

CFDE admin office

Library

Dashen

Hamdael Café

Ethio telecom

NIB

CBE

Total

Solomon Bekele GH

Entrance

Ethiopian Airlines

National Hotel

Yeselam Adarash (Peace Hall)

CBE

Mikael Church

Dachata

New railway station

ℹ Tourism office

Dil Hotel

↑ Airport

Millennium Park

Finance office

CBE

Maryam Church

Ashewa Market (400m)

see inset

St Augustine Catholic Church

Ethio-Française Alliance (est 1908)

Armenian church

Taiwan Market (200m)

OiLibya
Paris Nightclub ☆

Tsahay Hotel

Beaujolais Bar

Rita Supermarket

CDE Sports Club

Nile Hotel

Djibouti Consulate

Addis Ababa Hotel

Total

CBE
Dashen

BP

Nyala Hotel

CBE

Hospital

Cheers Bar

Bank of Abyssinia

Grand Core Mosque

Police

Wegegen

Hospital

Juma'a Mosque (200m),
Khat terra market (400m)

Abyssinia Pension

OiLibya

Ras Shell Café

Total

CBE

Tesfa Hotel

Coca Cola Factory

Dire Dawa Admin Council

OiLibya

Bus station

Hayat Clinic

Segenet Hotel

NOC

Habeshewa Restaurant

Driver licence testing ground

CBE

Kafira Market

Lalibela Restaurant ☆

Peacock Hotel

Stadium

Medhane Alem Church

Porc-épic Cave

N Bradt

0 ———— 400m
0 ———— 400yds

↓ Harar, Addis Ababa

For listings, see opposite

🏠 Where to stay

1 African Village.................A3
2 Bluebird...........................D1
3 Cleopatra Hotel & Spa.....B5
4 Continental......................B2
5 Dire Dawa Ras.................C4
6 Karamara Ras...................B5
7 Mekonnen........................B1
8 Samrat..............................B4
9 Taza Pension....................A3
10 Triangle............................C1

✖ Where to eat and drink

African Village...........(see 1)
Bollywood..................(see 8)
11 Elga Café...............B1, B4
12 Little Door.....................B2
13 Paradiso..........................C6

Other facilities include a good Indian restaurant, large, clean swimming pool, fitness centre, beauty salon & business centre. *US$39/51 standard sgl/dbl, suites from US$45/57 sgl/dbl; all rates B&B.* **$$$$**

Budget

☀ ⌂ African Village [459 A3] (16 rooms) \025 112 6006; **m** 0915 321333; **e** info@african-village.com; **w** african-village.com. Hidden on a side street northwest of the city centre, this peaceful Swiss-owned oasis feels like the kind of popular travellers' haunt you find all over southern Africa, with the marked exception of its strict prohibition on alcohol & unmarried couples sharing a room. The comfortable though compact en-suite *tukuls* have modern interiors, TV, fan & hot shower. Some rooms have a small kitchen area with fridge, others a private balcony. Amenities include an excellent restaurant. Superb value. *US$16/18/24 sgl/dbl/twins, suites from US$22.* **$$**

⌂ Cleopatra Hotel & Spa [459 B5] (22 rooms) \025 211 0303; **m** 0950 179602; **e** info@cleopatrahotelandspa.com; **w** cleopatrahotelandspa.com. This smart new central medium-rise has large, clean, comfortable rooms with king-size bed, fridge, flatscreen TV, writing desk & modern bathroom. Common areas are rather bland, but it's good value. *US$20/28 B&B dbl/twin.* **$$**

⌂ Triangle Hotel [459 C1] (122 rooms) \025 112 2193. This misleadingly named rectangular concrete block is the pick of a cluster of mid-range hotels situated near Millennium Park about 1km north of the city centre. The spacious en-suite rooms are a bit fuddy-duddy, but come with AC, sat TV, queen-size bed & hot water. There's also a decent restaurant, a bar & a swimming pool. *From US$20/28 B&B dbl/twin.* **$$**

⌂ Dire Dawa Ras Hotel [459 C4] (79 rooms) \025 111 3255; **e** ddrashotel1@gmail.com. This venerable former government high-rise, set in a pleasantly leafy garden in the heart of the city centre, has benefited from recent privatisation

& renovations, though it can't quite shake off its institutional 1970s feel. The agreeable en-suite rooms all come with AC & sat TV. Amenities include a ground-floor restaurant & a decidedly murky swimming pool. *From US$28 B&B dbl.* **$$$**

⌂ Bluebird Hotel [459 D1] (44 rooms) \025 113 0219/20; **m** 0915 731298. This well-established & sensibly priced hotel lies alongside the airport road 500m north of the city centre. Rooms are very clean & come with AC, sat TV & modern bathroom, while some also have a fridge & in-room safe. Other amenities include a good restaurant, a lobby bar with oversize leather couches, & Wi-Fi throughout. *US$16 dbl or twin.* **$$**

⌂ Karamara Ras Hotel [459 B5] (43 rooms) \025 111 3392; **e** info@karamararashotel.com. This former government hotel (also known as Ras 2) has plenty of character, a nice garden, a central location & recently renovated en-suite rooms with AC, fan, sat TV & hot water. *US$16/20 dbl in old/new bldg, US$26 suite.* **$$**

Shoestring

⌂ Taza Pension [459 A3] (18 rooms) \025 411 0134; **m** 0943 003939. This superior 3-storey pension opposite the African Village has spacious tiled en-suite rooms with fan, sat TV & hot shower. *US$12 dbl.* **$$**

⌂ Mekonnen Hotel [459 B1] (7 rooms) \025 111 3378; **m** 0943 623515. This long-serving favourite has plenty of character & a convenient location on the central square facing the old railway station. The rooms are a bit tired, but come with fan, net, TV, cold shower & in some cases a balcony. A decent restaurant is attached. Good value at the rock-bottom rates but often full. *US$4 dbl.* **$**

⌂ Continental Hotel [459 B2] (10 rooms) \025 111 1546. One could make too much of the fact that Evelyn Waugh stayed at this central hotel in its long-departed 1930s heyday. The leafy courtyard has a lot more going for it than the rather dingy rooms, which do at least have fans and en-suite showers. *US$6 dbl.* **$**

✕ WHERE TO EAT AND DRINK
Moderate to expensive

✕ Bollywood Restaurant [459 B4] \025 113 0600; ⊕ lunch & dinner daily. Situated on the ground floor of the Samrat Hotel, this authentic Indian restaurant serves good curry & tandoor dishes, as well as having a Chinese selection for

variety. You can eat indoors or around the hotel swimming pool. It's not the cheapest, but most dishes are on the right side of US$5.

✕ African Village [459 A3] \025 112 6006; ⊕ b/fast, lunch & dinner daily. Dire Dawa's best Western-style eatery is the stylishly rustic restaurant at the African Village. It has indoor or garden seating & serves a varied menu of salads, soups, steaks, pizzas, pastas, burgers & fish. No alcohol. *Mains US$3–4.*

✘ **Paradiso Restaurant** [459 C6] ☎025 111 3780; ⏰ 08.00–22.00 daily. This excellent restaurant, set in an atmospheric old house along the Harar road, serves a selection of Italian & Ethiopian dishes, including top-notch lasagne, along with steaks, cutlets & various roast meats. *Mains US$3–4.*

Cheap to moderate

✘ **Little Door** [459 B2] This great little local eatery close to the old railway station serves a variety of inexpensive local dishes, including excellent *ful*, for b/fast & lunch.

⊡ **Elga Café** [459 B1 & B4] There are 2 branches of this excellent café, 1 around the corner from the Mekonnen Hotel, the other next door to the Samrat Hotel. Both serve spicy mini-pizzas, various sweet treats, juices & coffee. The Samrat branch serves wine & beer.

NIGHTLIFE

☆ **Lalibela Restaurant** [459 C6] m 0915 731091; ⏰ 20.00–late. In addition to good Ethiopian fare, this traditional restaurant off the Harar road is one of the few places in town to serve *tej* (as well as the usual bottled beers), & there's excellent live music & dancing most nights.

♀ **Mekonnen Hotel** (Page 460) Draped with lush bougainvillea, the bar at this super-central hotel serves beer, coffee, pastries & snacks, & is a pleasant place to hang out or indulge in some people-watching.

♀ **Beaujolais Bar** [459 A4] Shady by day, cosy by night, this pretty garden bar close to African Village stocks a good selection of local & imported wines as well as the usual bottled beers & spirits. It also plays a varied selection of music at reasonable volume on speakers with unusual clarity.

OTHER PRACTICALITIES

Swimming pool The swimming pools at the central Samrat Hotel makes for an attractive refuge in the afternoon heat. It charges around US$2 to non-residents.

Tourist information The Department of Tourism [459 B1] (⏰ *07.30–noon & 14.00–17.30 Mon–Fri*) has an unsignposted office about 200m northwest of Millennium Park and can arrange optional guides for Porc-épic, Laga Oda and other local sites of interest. Before visiting Porc-épic or Laga Oda, you must also stop in to pay the entrance fee at the Finance Office of the Department of Trade and Investment [459 C1] (⏰ *07.30–noon & 14.00–17.30 Mon–Fri*), next to the Bluebird Hotel. Cameras are strictly forbidden in the latter building, even if they are tucked deep in your bag, a ruling that seems somewhat risible in an age where half the department's employees probably carry a smartphone with photographic capabilities.

WHAT TO SEE AND DO

Around town Though lacking in must-see landmarks, Dire Dawa is an agreeable town to explore on foot. The central feature of the old European quarter of Kezira is the old French-built railway station [459 B1], which will be of some interest to students of colonial architecture. The abandoned carriages and other paraphernalia in the adjacent railway yard will doubtless amuse railway buffs who're prepared to go through the tedious process of being granted permission by the Francophone officials at the Chemin de Fer Djibouto-Éthiopien (CFDE) office opposite, then paying a US$4 fee and waiting for a receipt. Otherwise, Kezira is a follow-your-nose kind of place, with minor gems such as the disused Armenian church and many old French and Greek mansions tucked away behind the leafy pavements. The city's most distinguished old building is the Yeselam Adarash (Peace Hall) [459 B2], a grand multistorey imperial residence built in the 1930s for Haile Selassie on the site of a more modest house built by Emperor Menelik II in the first decade of the 20th

13

century. The palace has been closed for years, and the building is difficult to see from outside the gates, but has been earmarked for future development as a local history museum. Millennium Park [459 C1], on the airport road about 1km north of the city centre, is decorated with replicas of the rock art at the nearby Porc-épic and Laga Oda caves.

Southeast of Dachata *wadi*, the narrow streets and cobbled lanes of Megaala are lined with pastel-painted houses and positively exude a sense of tight community. Megaala is home to most of the city's larger mosques and markets, the latter usually busiest in the morning when they are often attended by rural Oromo and Afar in traditional garb. Named after the coffee for which this part of Ethiopia is renowned, Kafira [459 D5] is the city's oldest and most colourful market, set behind a handsome Arabian-style arched façade on the north bank of the *wadi* about 700m south of the bridge. The larger covered market nicknamed 'Taiwan' [459 D3] is the place to buy electronic and other imported goods. A few hundred metres to its north, on the east bank of the *wadi*, Ashewa Market [459 D2] is known as the place to buy secondhand clothes, and it also hosts a livestock market spilling out on to the sandy riverbed. Finally, 700m east of the bridge past the Juma'a Mosque, the *khat terra* [459 D4] is a small market where eastern Ethiopia's most enthusiastically imbibed leaf is sold 24/7 by several vendors.

Porc-épic Cave [map, page 445] Discovered in 1929 by Pierre Teilhard de Chardin and Henri de Monfreid, and named after the porcupines that dwelt there at the time, Porc-épic (*entrance US$2.50, payable at the tourism office*) overlooks the Dachata *wadi* about 3km southeast of the city centre. Excavations undertaken in 1974 indicate that it was regularly used as a seasonal hunting encampment from 70,000 to 15,000 years ago, and the walls are adorned with around 60 faded schematic rock art paintings of humans and animals thought to be at least 5,000 years old. They aren't the finest examples of the genre, but the site is accessible on foot from town, though you must first visit the tourist office building to obtain a permit and pay the fee of US$2.50. To get there, follow the road running southeast out of town through Addis Katema until you reach a large southward bend in the Dachata *wadi*. Cross the riverbed, then follow the path to the prominent 140m-high cliff known as Gerad Erar. The cave is near the top of the cliff.

Laga Oda and Hulul Mojo [map, page 445] Also known as Legoda, the celebrated Laga Oda Rock Art Site (*entrance US$2.50, payable at the tourism office in Dire Dawa*) comprises a 60m-long limestone shelter that lies 22km southwest of Dire Dawa as the crow flies. The shelter was originally decorated with around 800 individual paintings, thought to be at least 5,000 years old (for more information, see *Rock Paintings of Laga Oda* by Pavel Cervicek, **w** jstor.org/stable/40341510). Tragically, there's not much to see today: most of the paintings were damaged a few years back by vandals who sprayed them with water in order to take better photographs, then in 2017 the face that held the few surviving paintings collapsed face down. A further deterrent to visiting is that this road runs through an area where anti-government feeling among the local Oromo is particularly high. If you're still game, then follow the Harar road out of Dire Dawa for 5km until you see the road to Laga Oda signposted to your right. After 24km, the road passes through Hulu Mojo, where the ruins of Abeyaziz Mosque, built in the 15th century by the Harla people, can be found close to a solitary small stele of unknown origin. It's another 7km, followed by a 10–20-minute walk, to Laga Oda.

Harla Also known as Harala, this small town straddling the asphalt Harar road 15km south of Dire Dawa is thought to have been the capital of the Harla Empire, which dominated trade between the Ethiopian interior and the Somali port of Zeila between the 12th and early 16th centuries. Little is known about the Harla people. According to local folklore, they were a race of giants, and immensely strong, but this legend can probably be attributed to the long narrow graves they left scattered around the eastern highlands. It is also uncertain what happened to the empire, though it seems likely its inhabitants converted to Islam under Somali influence, and were partly ancestral to the (phonetically similar) Harari people who have dominated the region since the 16th century. Several substantial relics of the old capital can be seen in Harla, including a ruined stone mosque, the wall of a stone well supported by a tangled ficus tree, and a few graves. Recently, two 11th-century Chinese coins were discovered at the site, suggesting trade links to the Far East that stretch back at least 1,000 years. No less intriguing is a tiny but beautifully engraved stone lunar calendar discovered and carried around by the semi-official caretaker, Ali Mussa, who will happily show interested visitors around for a negotiable fee (around US$4–8 seems fair). Regular minibuses run back and forth between Dire Dawa and Harla, taking less than 30 minutes.

HARAR

The spiritual heart of Ethiopia's Islamic community, the walled citadel of Harar is considered by some to be the fourth-holiest Islamic city after Mecca, Medina and Jerusalem. It is also an exceptionally pleasant city to visit: lively, welcoming and relaxed, yet possessing a cultural integrity and aura of lived-in antiquity that make it the most traditionalist of Ethiopia's larger towns. Boasting a moderate highland climate, Harar lies at the centre of a fertile agricultural area, one renowned for its high-quality coffee and *khat*. But its focal point is Harar Jugol, the 48ha walled city, a UNESCO World Heritage Site whose innumerable winding alleys lead past 83 private and public mosques (the world's largest such concentration) and the 102 *qubi* (shrines or tombs of important holy men) alluded to in the nickname Gey Ada (City of Saints).

Considering the prominent role played by Harar in past Muslim–Christian–Oromo conflicts, the modern town possesses a refreshing mood of religious and cultural tolerance. Indeed, while Harar Jugol is deeply Islamic in character, the newer part of town, which runs west along the main road to Addis Ababa, is predominantly Orthodox Christian, and the frizzy-headed traditionalist Oromo are also much in evidence, particularly in the market areas. What's more, for a city of such devout pedigree, Harar has an undercurrent that is more than a little – dare I say it – hedonistic. The compulsive chewing of *khat* dominates every aspect of public life and, to paraphrase the sentiments of one Muslim resident, you really do need something liquid to chill you out after a good chew. Any preconceptions about fundamentalist Harar can be washed down at the bars which, I suspect, come close to matching public mosques one for one within the old city walls. All in all, Harar is the sort of easy-going, cosmopolitan town where you could settle in for a week and do nothing more exerting than just soak up the atmosphere.

HISTORY Harar's early days are shrouded in legend. The city's foundation is often attributed to Emir Abu Bekr Muhammad of the Walashma dynasty, who abandoned their established capital at Dakar in favour of Harar in 1520. But while Abu Bekr's move was instrumental in pushing the city to prominence, Harar is certainly much older than this. The town is mentioned in an early 14th-century manuscript, and its oldest three mosques reputedly date from the 10th century. One tradition is that Harar was originally a Christian city and went by a different name until its patron saint, Sheikh Abadir Gey, led a group of 43 Arabian migrants here in the 10th century. According to this tradition, it is Sheikh Abadir who renamed the city Harar and organised its first Islamic administrative system. Others claim that Harar became Islamic as early as the 7th century, when it was settled by an Arabic community led by a contemporary and follower of the Prophet Muhammad called Sheikh Hussein. Yet another legend relating to the origin of Harar is that when Muhammad ascended to heaven, he saw the hill on which it stands as a shining light, and an angel told him it was the Mountain of Saints.

Harar rose to significance in an atmosphere of turmoil and bloodshed. Within five years of settling in Harar, Abu Bekr Muhammad was killed by the popular but highly militant imam **Ahmed Gragn**, who installed Umar Din, another member of the Walashma dynasty, as a puppet emir. Gragn then ordered his followers to stop paying tribute to Emperor Lebna Dengal following the latter's pillaging of the Islamic region of Hubut. In 1529, Lebna Dengal sent a punitive military expedition to Harar, but it was soundly defeated by Gragn's army. Inspired by this victory, Gragn then used Harar as the launchpad for a succession of bloody and destructive raids on the Christian empire. Gragn was killed in battle in 1543, but his jihad continued under the direction of his widow, Bati Del Wambara, and nephew Emir Nur Ibn al-Wazir. In 1559, the imperial army marched once more on Harar, and was once more defeated – indeed, Emperor Galawdewos was killed in the raid and his head paraded around town on a stake.

The long years of war took their economic toll. Following the defeat of Galawdewos, the jihad was more or less abandoned as the city faced a new threat in the form of the pagan Oromo who had taken occupation of much of southern Ethiopia during the long years of Muslim–Christian war. During the early 1560s, Emir Nur erected the tall protective walls that have enclosed Old Harar ever since. After Nur's death in 1567, however, Harar became increasingly vulnerable to attacks by the Oromo under two ineffective emirs in succession. In 1575, the emir was evicted by Mansur Muhammad, who abandoned Harar in favour of a new capital at the oasis of Awsa in the Danakil Desert. For almost a century, Harar was politically subordinate to Awsa.

Harar's resurrection began in 1647, when Emir Ali ibn Daud took control of the city and formed an autonomous ruling dynasty. Despite frequent fighting with the

RICHARD BURTON IN HARAR

The early European explorers of the African interior were, as a rule, prone to describing their 'discoveries' in somewhat hyperbolic terms. Perhaps the most noteworthy exception to this rule is the acerbic and unflattering description of Harar by Richard Burton, who, in 1855, became the first European to visit the most holy of Ethiopia's Islamic cities. Burton was not impressed, as the following edited extracts from his book *First Footsteps in Africa* make clear:

An irregular wall, lately repaired, but ignorant of cannon, is pierced with five large gates, and supported by oval towers of artless construction. The only large building is the Jami or Cathedral, a long barn of poverty-stricken appearance, with broken down gates and two whitewashed minarets of truncated conoid shape. The streets are narrow lanes, up hill and down dale, strewed with gigantic rubbish heaps, upon which repose packs of mangy one-eyed dogs. There are no establishments for learning, no endowments, as generally in the east, and apparently no encouragement to students: books also are rare and costly.

The Somali say of the city that it is a paradise inhabited by asses: certainly the exterior of the people is highly unprepossessing. Among the men, I did not see a handsome face: their features are coarse and debauched; many of them squint, others have lost an eye by smallpox, and they are disfigured by scrofula and other diseases.

The government of Harar is the Amir. These petty princes have a habit of killing and imprisoning all those who are suspected of aspiring to the throne. The Amir Ahmed succeeded his father about three years ago. His rule is severe if not just. Ahmed's principal occupations are spying on his many stalwart cousins, indulging in vain fears of the English, the Turks and the Hajj Sharmarkay, and amassing treasure by commerce and escheats.

He judges civil and religious causes in person. The punishments, when money forms no part of them, are mostly according to Koranic code. The murderer is placed in the market street, blindfolded, and bound hand and foot: the nearest of kin to the deceased then strikes his neck with a sharp and heavy butcher's knife, and the corpse is given over to the relations for Muslim burial. When a citizen draws dagger upon another or commits any petty offence, he is bastinadoed in a peculiar manner: two men ply their horsewhips upon his back and breast, and the prince, in whose presence the punishment is carried out, gives order to stop. Theft is punished by amputation of the hand.

Harar is essentially a commercial town: its citizens live, like those of Zayla, by systematically defrauding the Galla Badawin, and the Amir has made it a penal offence to buy by weight and scale. The citizens seem to have a more than Asiatic apathy, even in pursuit of gain. When we entered, a caravan was set out for Zayla on the morrow, after ten days, hardly half of its number had mustered.

Harar is still, as of old, the great 'halfway house' for slaves from Zangaro, Gurage and the Galla tribes. Abyssinians and Amharas, the most valued, have become rare since the King of Shewa prohibited the exportation. Women vary in value from 100 to 400 Ashfaris, boys from 9 to 150: the worst are kept for domestic purposes, the best are driven by the Western Arabs or the subjects of the Imam of Muskat, in exchange for rice and dates. I need scarcely say that commerce would thrive on the decline of slavery: whilst the Falateas or manrazzias are allowed to continue, it is vain to expect industry in the land.

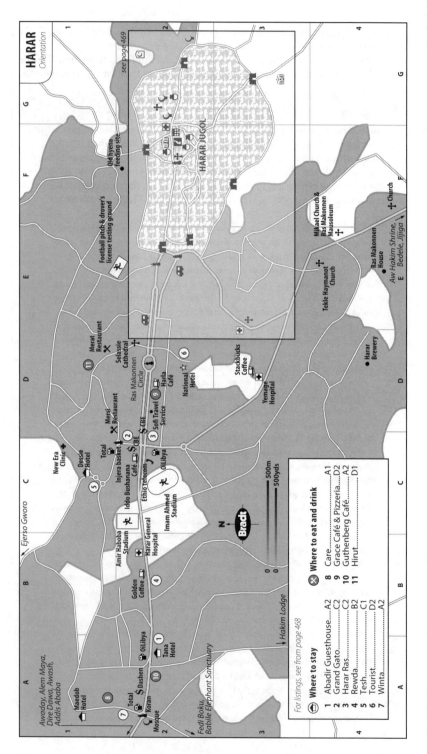

see page 469

HARAR JUGOL

Mikael Church &
Ras Makonnen
Mausoleum

Ras Makonnen
House

Aw Hakim Shrine,
Bedele, Jijiga

Church

Tekle Haymanot
Church

Harar
Brewery

Yemage
Hospital

Stacbucks
Coffee

National
Hotel

Hania
Café

Ras Makonnen
Circle

Selassie
Cathedral

Merat
Restaurant

Football pitch & drover's
license testing ground

Old hyena
feeding site

Mersi
Restaurant

Sofi Travel
Service

CBE

CBE

Ethio telecom

Oilibya

Total

New Era
Clinic

Dessie
Hotel

Injira basket

Iddo Bushanana
Café

Imam Ahmed
Stadium

Amir Haboba
Stadium

Harar General
Hospital

Golden
Coffee

Ejerso Gworo

Awaday, Alem Maya,
Dire Dawa, Awash,
Addis Ababa

Maedob
Hotel

Total

Koran
Mosque

Dashen

Oilibya

Tana
Hotel

Fedi Boku,
Babile Elephant Sanctuary

Hakim Lodge

Bradt

N

500m
500yds

For listings, see from page 468

Where to stay

1	Abadir Guesthouse	A2
2	Grand Gato	C2
3	Harar Ras	C2
4	Rewda	B2
5	Tesh	C1
6	Tourist	D2
7	Winta	A2

Where to eat and drink

8	Care	A1
9	Grace Café & Pizzeria	D2
10	Guthenberg Café	A2
11	Hirut	D1

Oromo, the walled city grew in stature over the next century to become the region's most populous and important trade centre, issuing its own currency and known by repute throughout the Islamic world. Only Muslims, however, were allowed to enter the city walls, and as a result its location was the source of more rumour than substance in the Christian world. The first European to visit Harar was British explorer **Richard Burton**, who spent ten anxious days in what he referred to as 'the forbidden city' in 1855, unsure of whether he was the emir's guest or prisoner (see box, page 465). Another famous 19th-century visitor was French poet **Arthur Rimbaud**, who abandoned writing aged 19 and then, after seven footloose years in Europe, moved to Harar in 1880, where he set up as a trader and was based until his death in 1891.

In the late 19th century, Harar was regarded as the most important trading centre in Ethiopia. This also made it a desirable acquisition for external powers, and the city's 200-plus years of autonomous rule came to an end when it was captured by Egypt in 1875. The Egyptian occupation collapsed in 1885, but two years later the city was captured by the King of Shewa, the future Emperor Menelik II, following his victory over Emir Abdullah at Chelenko in 1887. Menelik warded off the danger of renewed religious sectarianism by including several members of the emir's family in his new administration, which he headed with a Christian governor, Ras Makonnen – the father of the future Emperor Haile Selassie. Harar's commercial role has been secondary to that of Dire Dawa since the Djibouti railway opened in 1902. Nevertheless, it was still the third-largest town in Ethiopia as recently as 1968, and it remained the political capital of Hararge province throughout the Haile Selassie and Derg eras. Following the reshuffle of administrative regions in 1995, Harar retained its role as capital of the 334km^2 Harari Region, which is by far the smallest of Ethiopia's nine federal regions. Today it supports a population of at least 150,000, making it one of the 20 largest cities in the country.

GETTING THERE AND AWAY
By air Ethiopian Airlines operates daily return flights from Addis Ababa to Dire Dawa and Jijiga, but there are no direct flights to Harar. Most people fly in to Dire Dawa and arrange a transfer or catch a minibus from there to Harar. Ethiopian Airlines is represented in Harar by Sofi Travel Service (\ *025 666 4422;* m *0911 029602*) on the south side of the main street between the Harar Ras Hotel and Cozi Pizzeria.

By road Assuming that Sky, Selam and Ethio **buses** resume daily services between Addis Ababa and Harar (*US$15.50; around 10hrs*), the terminus [469 A1] for these coaches is on the north side of the main road to Addis Ababa, between Harar Gate and Ras Makonnen Circle. Alternatively, catch a bus or train to Dire Dawa, which is connected to Harar by a good 50km asphalt road traversed by a regular stream of **minibuses** taking about 1 hour in either direction. There is also plenty of transport along the recently surfaced road between Harar and Jijiga. The bus and minibus station [469 B2] is outside the city walls, more or less opposite Shewa Gate.

ORIENTATION Harar can be divided into three distinct parts. In the southeast, the old Islamic walled town of Harar Jugol, roughly oblong in shape and extending over 48ha, comprises a compact maze of narrow alleys lined with traditional Harari houses, mosques, Islamic shrines and other venerable buildings. Extending along the Dire Dawa road west of Harar Jugol as far as the Harar Ras Hotel, the main commercial centre, or what might be termed the old new town, is a predominantly

13

Christian zone centred on Ras Makonnen Circle and incorporating several imposing and/or timeworn buildings dating from the first half of the 20th century. Following the Dire Dawa road west of the Harar Ras Hotel is a newer quarter, much of which consists of post-Derg developments to accommodate the city's rapid population growth over the past quarter-century.

Five ancient gates punctuate the 3.5km circumference of the old town's walls, but the first point of entry for most visitors is the newer **Harar (or Duke's) Gate** [469 C1], a motor-friendly addition dating from the era of Haile Selassie. Harar Gate faces west and connects the old town to the new town, effectively forming the eastern terminus of the main road west to Dire Dawa and Addis Ababa. The only other direct passage between the old and new towns is **Shewa Gate** [469 C2] (known in Harari as Asmaddin Beri), which adjoins the old Christian Market opposite the main bus station. The other four gates, running in anticlockwise order from Shewa Gate, are Buda Gate (Bedri Beri in Harari) [469 D3], Sanga Gate (Sukutat Beri) [469 F3], Erer Gate (Argob Beri) [469 G2] and Fallana Gate (Assum Beri) [469 E1].

The most important landmark within the old walled city, at least for orientation purposes, is the open central square called Feres Megala [469 D2]. The main motorable road through the old walled town runs east from Harar Gate to Erer Gate via Feres Megala. Most of the shops and bars set within the old town walls lie alongside or very close to this main road, as do several important historical landmarks. A third motorable road runs southeast from Feres Megala to Sanga Gate via Gidir Megala (Grand Market) and a fourth, much shorter, runs north from the square to Fallana Gate. Strung between these main thoroughfares is a web of atmospheric pedestrian-only cobbled alleys which are confusing to navigate at first, though the city is too small for you to go far without encountering a main road or obvious landmark.

WHERE TO STAY Harar has the poorest hotel selection of any of Ethiopia's main urban tourist centres. There are a couple of adequate budget options and a selection of simple but characterful cultural guesthouses dotted around the old town, but quality moderate and upmarket lodgings are few and far between.

Upmarket

Grand Gato Hotel [466 C2] (21 rooms, more under construction) 025 466 0775; e info@ grandgato.com; w grandgato.com. This work-in-progress opposite the landmark Harar Ras is undoubtedly the town's smartest hotel, but it's debatable whether the large carpeted en-suite rooms with AC, flatscreen TV & hot shower do enough to justify the inflated rates. The restaurant & other common areas look decidedly unfinished & uninviting. *US$60/80/120 dbl/twin/suite B&B.* **$$$$**

Moderate

Wonderland Hotel [469 B1] (75 rooms) 025 466 1111/2222; . This modern new high-rise has a great location outside Harar Gate & is widely recognised as the pick of Harar's slim mid-range pickings. Clean brightly painted rooms come with flatscreen TV, fridge, safe, seating & hot

shower. The ground-floor restaurant is nothing to write home about. *From US$20/32 dbl/twin.* **$$**

Harar Ras Hotel [466 C2] (38 rooms) 025 666 0027; m 0930 179947. Flanking the Dire Dawa road 1km west of Harar Gate, this refurbished former government hotel has pleasant en-suite rooms with parquet or wood laminate floors, hot shower & sat TV. A decent indoor restaurant & shady terrace café with Wi-Fi serve draught beer & a good selection of pizzas, sandwiches & local dishes in the US$3–5 range. *US$20/32/40 sgl/dbl/suite.* **$$$**

Winta Hotel [466 A2] (12 rooms) m 0915 740050; e hilinawondimu@gmail.com; . Standing more than 2km from the old town, this attentively owner-managed hotel has spacious rooms with hot shower, TV & furniture that's colourful to a fault. The ground-floor restaurant is good. *From US$27 dbl.* **$$$**

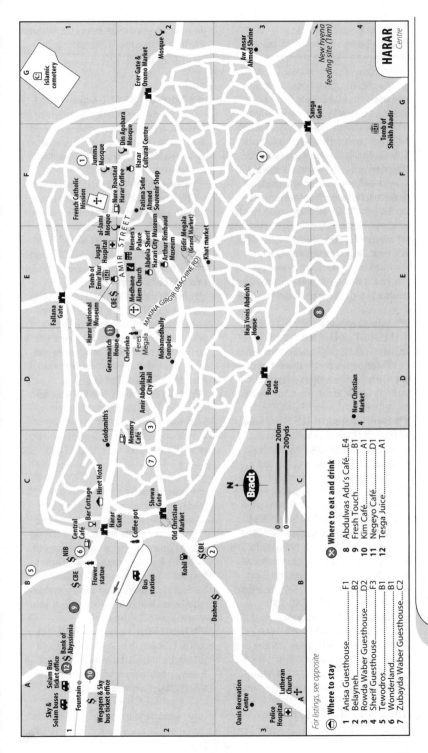

HARAR
Centre

Islamic cemetery

New hyena feeding site (1km)

Erer Gate & Oromo Market
Mosque
Din Agobara Mosque
Jumma Mosque
French Catholic Mission
Nure Roasted Harar Coffee
Harar Cultural Centre
al-Jami Mosque
AMIR STREET
Tomb of Emir Nur
Jugal Hospital
Menen's Palace
Fatima Sefir Ahmed Souvenir Shop
Harar National Museum
CBE
Medhane Alem Church
Abdela Sherif Harari City Museum
Arthur Rimbaud Museum
Gidir Megala (Grand Market)
Khat market
MAKINA GIRGIR (MACHINE RD)
Sanga Gate
Aw Ansar Ahmed Shrine
Tomb of Sheikh Abadir

Fallana Gate
Gerazmatch House
Chelenko
Feres Megala
Mohamedhally Complex
Haji Yonis Abdosh's House

Goldsmith's
Amir Abdullahi City Hall
Memory Café
Buda Gate
New Christian Market

Hiret Hotel
Bar Cottage
Central Café
NIB
CBE
Shewa Gate
Old Christian Market
Harar Gate
Coffee pot
CBE
Kobil

Sky & Selam buses
Selam Bus ticket office
Bank of Abyssinia
Fountain
Wegagen & Sky bus ticket office
Flower statue
Bus station
Dashen

Oasis Recreation Centre
Police Hospital
Lutheran Church

N
Bradt

0   200m
0   200yds

For listings, see opposite

Where to stay

1	Anisa Guesthouse........................F1
2	Belayneh.....................................B2
3	Rowda Waber Guesthouse.......D2
4	Sherif Guesthouse....................F3
5	Tewodros...................................B1
6	Wonderland...............................B1
7	Zubayda Waber Guesthouse....C2

Where to eat and drink

8	Abdulwas Adu's Café...E4
9	Fresh Touch...............B1
10	Kim Café....................A1
11	Negeyo Café..............D1
12	Tesga Juice................A1

Cultural guesthouses

Slotting in between the moderate & budget categories, our favourite accommodation in Harar comprises a quartet of broadly similar family-owned & -managed small guesthouses sited within the old walled city. Three of the guesthouses are set in traditional Harari homes & have beautifully decorated sitting rooms with rich carpets lining the floors & colourful baskets & plates adorning the whitewashed walls. The 4th was purpose built in traditional style in 2017. All are clean & cosy, with simply furnished but comfortable bedrooms. The phone numbers supplied below might not always connect you to somebody who speaks English, but email bookings can be directed to Hailu Gashaw (e *hailu_harar@yahoo.com*). None of these guesthouses is signposted, so you must either arrange a pick-up from the bus station or be prepared to wander around a bit & ask directions in order to find them.

🏠 **Anisa Guesthouse** [469 F1] (3 rooms) m 0915 330011, 0913 072931. This is the most basic of the cultural guesthouses, but also perhaps the friendliest, with a quiet location in the northeast part of Harar Jugol about 100m northeast of the French Catholic Mission. There is just 1 quite cramped common shower. *US$16 dbl B&B.* **$$**

🏠 **Sherif Guesthouse** [469 F3] (4 rooms) ☎025 666 2017; e abdelasherif@yahoo.com. Upping the ante somewhat is this brand-new guesthouse built uphill of Sanga Gate by the namesake founder of the well-established Abdela Sherif Harari City Museum. All rooms are en suite & furnished in traditional style, & there's plenty of parking space. *US$20/24 B&B dbl/twin.* **$$$**

🏠 **Rowda Waber Guesthouse** [469 D2] (4 rooms) ☎025 666 2211; m 0915 756439. The most consistently praised of the cultural guesthouses lies on a blind alley running north from Zagah Uda about 200m east of Shewa Gate. The b/fast is excellent. *US$16/32 dbl/twin B&B.* **$$**

🏠 **Zubayda Waber Guesthouse** [469 C2] (5 rooms) ☎025 666 4692; m 0910 284329. Situated on Zagah Uda 150m east of Shewa Gate, this was the first of the cultural guesthouses to be established, & it mostly gets great feedback, though the owners seem to rub some people up

the wrong way. Most rooms are en suite with nets, with the pick being the old honeymoon suite. *US$20/32 sgl/dbl B&B.* **$$$**

Budget

🏠 **Tesh Hotel** [466 C1] (14 rooms) m 0919 420577. It could be more central, but otherwise this clean, new hotel 1.5km northwest of the old town looks to be the pick in its range. Spacious en-suite rooms have solid beds, wall-mounted TV & hot shower. *US$12 dbl.* **$$**

🏠 **Belayneh Hotel** [469 B2] (22 rooms) ☎025 666 2030; m 0913 282716. This stalwart 4-storey hotel has a convenient location outside Shewa Gate & opposite the bus station. The compact en-suite rooms with hot shower, private balcony & TV are OK, but those facing the bus station can be noisy at night. There's an uninspiring rooftop restaurant. Fair value. *US$12/16/18 dbl/twin/trpl.* **$$**

🏠 **Rewda Hotel** [466 B2] (41 rooms) ☎025 666 9777; m 0915 321175; e harar_rewda@gmail.com. Pleasant, modern & sensibly priced hotel whose en-suite tiled rooms have hot water & sat TV. Ask for a room facing away from the road. A decent ground-floor restaurant & terrace café is attached. *US$14/20 dbl/twin.* **$$**

🏠 **Abadir Guesthouse** [466 A2] (46 rooms) m 0937 554763; e abadirguest@gmail.com. Situated on the Dire Dawa road 2km west of Harar Gate, this adequate option has large, clean en-suite rooms with reliable hot water. *US$13/15 sgl/dbl.* **$$**

Shoestring

🏠 **Tewodros Hotel** [469 B1] (20 rooms) ☎025 666 0217. This backpackers' favourite has a quiet location outside Harar Gate in an area frequented by hyenas after dark. The older ground-floor rooms sharing a common shower are rather unappealing, but the 1st-floor en-suite rooms with hot water & fresh bedding are great value, & those on the right-hand side as you enter overlook a field where hyenas might be seen from 21.30 onwards. *US$6 sgl with common shower, US$10 en-suite dbl.* **$**

🏠 **Tourist Hotel** [466 D2] (20 rooms) ☎025 666 0824. Set in an interesting but rundown old building, this stalwart cheapie remains the pick of a few very basic guesthouses clustered a block south of Ras Makonnen Circle. *US$8 en-suite dbl.* **$**

✖ **WHERE TO EAT AND DRINK** In addition to the restaurants listed below, the terrace café at the **Harar Ras** is a pleasant place for a meal, snack or drink, and very good value.

✖ Hirut Restaurant [466 D1] ☎025 666 0419; ⊕ 11.00–late daily. Tucked away on a back road 400m north of Ras Makonnen Circle, the top local eatery in Harar is renowned for its special *tibs* & roast chicken, but it also serves good local vegetarian dishes & a selection of salads, pastas & burgers. The traditional décor adds to the atmosphere, as does an aural backdrop of canned Ethiopian music. You can eat indoors or on the terrace. *Mains US$2–3*.

✖ Abdulwas Adu's Café [469 E4] m 0913 364862; ⊕ 08.00–21.00 daily. Backing up to the outer city wall between Buda & Sanga gates, & offering views towards Mt Hakim, this pretty garden restaurant is the ideal place to take a break between explorations of the old town. Local specialities such as camel meat *tibs*, roast goat or *injera* with Somali-style *hulbat* (a type of broth) are mostly in the US$2–3 range. It also serves local *sebazeyub* cookies & fresh juice, but no alcohol. Hyenas often walk past after dark.

✖ Fresh Touch [469 B1] m 0915 740109; ⊕ 08.00–22.00 daily. Recently relocated to a site 100m west of Harar Gate, this well-established favourite has smart indoor & outdoor seating, Wi-Fi, & an open kitchen preparing a lengthy menu of pizzas, stir-fries, grills, salads, burgers, sandwiches & Ethiopian dishes. *Mains US$3–6*.

✖ Care Restaurant [466 A1] ⊕ 06.00–22.00 daily. This bustling local eatery opposite the Winta Hotel serves the best *shekla tibs* in Harar (beef or goat) at US$2.50/250g, as well as a great platter of fasting food for US$1. Cheap draught is also available.

✖ Grace Café & Pizzeria [466 D2] ☎025 666 0476. This aptly named restaurant with indoor & terrace seating serves a good selection of pizzas & burgers. *Mains US$2–4*.

☕ Guthenberg Café [466 A2] ⊕ 06.30– 21.00 daily. This smart & unusually stylish new spot a few hundred metres west of the Abadir Hotel might be a little out of the way, but the pastries & coffee are excellent, & it also serves pizzas fresh from a special oven & other mains, mostly at around US$3.

☕ Kim Café [469 A1] ⊕ 07.00–22.00 daily. This purple café 400m west of Harar Gate is the pick of the pastry shops in the town centre, serving fresh fruit juice, pastries & ice cream.

☕ Tesga Juice [469 A1] The best juices in Harar are prepared at this 1st-floor place opposite Kim Café.

☕ Negeyo Café [469 D1] Located in the ground floor of a historic building on the north side of Feres Megala, this popular local coffee shop & eatery serves excellent b/fasts for little more than US$1.

NIGHTLIFE Harar is well endowed with bars, several of which lie within the walled city. The **Bar Cottage** [469 C1], with its organic banana-leaf walls, is almost as cosy as the name suggests. Outside the walled city, the rowdy bar at the **Tourist Hotel** plays a mixture of reggae and Ethiopian music, and hosts live music on some nights. More reliable for live music is the facing **National Hotel** [466 D2], where a traditional band usually cranks into action at 21.00.

SHOPPING Serious shoppers can test out their haggling skills with the fabric sellers at the **Makina Girgir** [469 E2], known locally as the *cigari* market, and then watch as one of the male tailors whips up a traditional Harari dress (a long kaftan with matching scarf) in a matter of minutes. The caffeine-addicted won't want to miss **Nure Roasted Harar Coffee** [469 F2] (⊕ *08.00–noon & 14.00–18.00 Mon–Sat*), located in the heart of the walled city, where for around US$4 you can pick up a 0.5kg bag of roasted coffee beans. **Fatima Sefir Ahmed Souvenir Shop** [469 F2] (⊕ *08.00–18.00 daily*), hidden on a side street just south of the main road in the walled city, has been recommended for handicrafts.

OTHER PRACTICALITIES

Swimming The only public facility in Harar, so far as we can ascertain, is the clean 30m swimming pool at the Oasis Recreation Centre [469 A3], which also has a café, children's playground and large-screen TV used to show football matches. Pool usage costs US$2.

Tourist information The tourist information office [469 E2] (⊕ *09.00–noon & 14.00–17.00 Mon–Fri*) is in the government building opposite the Harar National Museum. Gian Paulo Chiari's *Guide to Harar and Surroundings* (Arada Books, 2015) covers all sites in and around town in considerable depth, and can be bought at bookshops in Addis Ababa or through the publisher (w *aradabooks.com*).

Guides Harar is one city in Ethiopia where a good guide is crucial, as you may miss out on many of the best sites without their assistance. An official guide can be arranged through most of the hotels, or through the Harar Cultural Centre or tourist office; the going rate, with some room for negotiation out of season, is around US$15/20 per party for a half/full day. Guides recommended by readers in the past include Hailu Gashaw (m *0933 220319;* e *hailu_harar@yahoo.com*), Abdul Ahmed Mohammed (m *0915 740864, 0923 971490;* e *abadertourguide@ gmail.com*), Tewodros Belay Gebru (m *0913 543212, 0915 127828;* e *teddyharar@ gmail.com*), Lishan Katema (m *0913 451876, 0915 740249;* e *lishank876@gmail. com*), Tsegahun Admassu (m *0920 833295;* e *tseg56@yahoo.com*), Fasil Tilahun (m *0937 845759;* e *fasiltilahun37@gmail.com*) and Biniyam Woldesemayat (m *0913 448811;* e *biniym.weld@yahoo.com*), all of whom speak excellent English and are very professional. The young 'guides' who hang around Feres Megala accosting any passing *faranji* – or *faranjo* as they say locally – with an optimistic 'Remember me?' are generally lacking in knowledge and often irritatingly banal.

WHAT TO SEE AND DO
Harar Jugol Home to 82 mosques, 102 shrines, 5,500 houses and an estimated population of 22,000, the old Islamic citadel of Harar Jugol is enclosed by a 5m-high stone wall that effectively defined the full extent of the city until as recently as the Italian occupation. The wall was built in the 1560s by Emir Nur and hasn't changed shape significantly since then, though several renovations have taken place over the years. The town can be entered via any of the five traditional gates, or the newer Harar Gate, an addition dating to the Haile Selassie era. Travellers based in the new town or arriving by bus typically enter the walled city via the westerly Harar or Shewa gates, neither of which has an impact comparable to arriving at the southerly Buda Gate, from where a labyrinth of cobbled alleys flanked by traditional whitewashed stone houses winds uphill towards the central Feres Megala and Gidir Megala.

A guide (see above) is recommended for your first foray into Harar Jugol but, once you have your bearings, it's more fun perhaps to wander around on your own. The landmarks described below could be visited in roughly the prescribed sequence by entering the town at Harar or Shewa Gate, walking downhill to the central Feres Megala, then following Makina Girgir, with diversions to the Abdela Sherif and Arthur Rimbaud museums, to the main market, Gidir Megala. From the market, head north back to Amir Street and follow it eastward to Erer Gate, optionally stopping at the various landmarks that flank the road, and diverting north to the French Catholic Mission. Alternatively, just follow your nose – the old town, with its labyrinth of alleys and rich sense of community, is far more than the sum of its landmarks, and every turn reveals new points of interest.

Feres Megala [469 D2] The obvious place to start any walking tour of Harar, Feres Megala (literally 'Horse Market') is the largest open space in Harar Jugol, centred on a curious monument commemorating Menelik II's victory over the Emir of Harar at Chelenko in 1887. As its name suggests, it used to be a livestock market, but these days it might more aptly be titled Bajaji Megala. The square is lined with interesting old buildings. The hotel between the police station and the corner of the road to the Fallana Gate was formerly Gerazmatch House, built by the Egyptians during the occupation of 1875–85 and used as a warehouse by Arthur Rimbaud during the first year of his stay in Harar. On the east side of the square, the Church of Medhane Alem, built in 1890 on the site of a mosque constructed 15 years earlier by the unpopular Egyptian occupiers, had been described by Sylvia Pankhurst as 'a charming example of Ethiopian ecclesiastical architecture of the Menelik period'. A large *khat* market lies on the square's southern verge.

Gidir Megala and Makina Girgir [469 E2] The narrow alley leading southeast from Feres Megala is called Makina Girgir (Machine Road), in reference to the sewing machines of the (exclusively male) street tailors who work there. In addition to providing access to the Abdela Sherif and Arthur Rimbaud museums (see below), this alley leads downhill to the Gidir Megala (Grand Market), also sometimes referred to as the Islamic Market to distinguish it from its Christian counterpart outside the city walls. Despite being dominated by a rather monolithic Italian-era building, it is one of the liveliest urban markets in Ethiopia, particularly on Saturdays and in the afternoons, when it and the surrounding craft shops are a good place to buy curios. On the east side of the market, the whitewashed tomb of Sheikh Said Ali Hamdogn, an early leader of Harar, stands above a subterranean water source that can reputedly meet the needs of the whole town in time of drought. Immediately north of this stands the former Egyptian Bank.

Abdela Sherif Harari City Museum [469 E2] (✆ *025 666 2017;* e *abdelasherif@ yahoo.com;* w *everythingharar.com;* ⊕ *09.00–12.30 & 14.00–17.00 daily; entrance US$2, photography US$1*) This superb private museum 100m north of Makina Girgir is well worth a visit, more so perhaps than any of its official rivals. Among the many treasures on display are some of the 300-plus old Harari manuscripts collected by its curator and namesake Abdela Sherif, a collection of old coins minted in Harar during its 18th- and 19th-century heydays, as well as traditional costumes and household artefacts, firearms and musical instruments, along with eyebrow-raising incongruities such as carved giraffes of the type sold at curio stalls in Kenya and Tanzania. For music enthusiasts, the museum also houses an archive of more than 600 traditional recordings made in and around Harar since the 1940s, several of which can be heard on the museum's well-presented website.

The museum is also housed in one of Harar's best-known buildings, a beautiful and rather Indian-looking two-storey wide-balconied mansion often referred to locally as the Palace of Ras Makonnen, the father of Emperor Haile Selassie. Said by some to date from the late 1890s and by others from 1910, this house is reputedly where the future emperor spent much of his childhood, though other more reliable sources suggest that it was built by Ras Makonnen for his ally Menelik II (who, as it transpired, never had occasion to visit Harar after its construction). Partially gutted during the Italian occupation, the palace was restored as a museum and library in the early 1970s and formally opened by Haile Selassie, but this venture didn't survive the Derg and, when the first edition of this guidebook was researched in 1994, it was occupied by a traditional herbal practitioner who claimed to cure anything from gastritis to cancer.

Arthur Rimbaud Museum [469 E2] (⊕ *08.00–12.30 & 14.00–17.00 daily; entrance US$2, photography permitted*) Also 100m north of Makina Girgir, along an alley running parallel to that for the Abdela Sherif Museum, stands another vaguely oriental two-storey building, one often claimed locally to have been dwelt in by the retired poet during his final years in Harar. Architecturally, the building is most notable for its fine interior and frescoed ceiling, which locals say was painted by the poet, and it also offers great views over the town. So far as we can ascertain, however, it was constructed by an Indian merchant in 1908, a full 17 years after Rimbaud's untimely death. Despite this, it's conceivable that Rimbaud did once live in an older house on the same site, but more likely the association stems from the house having once featured in a movie about the poet's life.

Restored with the help of the Italian and French embassies and various other organisations, Rimbaud's House now functions as a museum. The ground-floor displays, dedicated to the poet, are arguably of marginal interest, with the exception of a couple of photographs taken during his stay in Harar. Far more compelling is the first-floor collection of turn-of-the-20th-century photographs of Harar. Providing a fascinating perspective on the modern development of the town, this collection disproves any talk of an unchanging Harar. The plain, one-storey, flat-roofed mud dwellings of the period bear less resemblance to anything seen here today than they do to houses found in some parts of the West African Sahel, or for that matter to the Argobba houses at nearby Koromi (page 478). Likewise, the traditional 'ball' hairstyles and plain robes worn by the women of Harar a century ago have now all but vanished in favour of more generic Ethiopian braided hairstyles and bright, colourful dresses. Also of interest are photographs of Medhane Alem Church while it was under construction, and Erer and Fallana gates before they crumbled away. Excellent stuff – all the better if you're fortunate enough to be led around by the articulate and erudite curator!

Amir Street Several points of interest lie along or off this road connecting Feres Megala to Erer Gate. Starting in the west, the **Harar National Museum** [469 E1] (⊕ *09.00–noon & 14.00–17.00 daily; entrance US$2*) isn't on a par with the Abdela Sherif Museum, but its potluck collection of traditional Harari, Oromo and Somali artefacts just about justifies the small entrance fee. A few doors up is the domed **tomb of Emir Nur** [469 E1], the 16th-century ruler credited with constructing the walls that still enclose Harar Jugol to this day. According to local tradition, the nearby al-Jami Mosque was founded in 1216, and the present-day building incorporates one minaret dating to the 1760s, but otherwise it is architecturally undistinguished and looks no more than 50 years old.

A block north of Amir Street, just past the mosque, is the still active **French Catholic Mission** [469 F1] established in 1857 by André Jarosseau, who would later go on to tutor Ras Tefari (the future emperor Haile Selassie) and various other prominent young Harar residents. Assuming you can find somebody to open it, the mission church, built in 1913 by Indian architects, has some beautiful paintings inside. Back on Amir Street, the **Harar Cultural Centre** [469 F2] (⊕ *08.00–12.30 daily & 14.00– 17.00 Mon–Sat; entrance US$2*) further out towards Erer Gate is worth visiting for its complete replica of a traditional city house (see box, page 475), furnished with hundreds of antique household objects donated by old Harari families.

Erer Gate [469 G2] Situated at the eastern end of Amir Street, Erer Gate was the main point of entry to Harar Jugol in the pre-motorised era, and it is where Richard Burton entered the city in 1855. Erer Gate is the site of a colourful Oromo *khat* market, and it is also the closest gate to the site used by the hyena men (page 476). Outside and a few hundred metres north of the Erer Gate, there stands an interesting Muslim cemetery comprising hundreds of graves, each of which is decorated by a unique and often very colourful painting. One reader comments:

A feature of Harar Jugol is its traditional *gey gars* (city houses), about 100 of which still survive more or less intact, including one said to have been built for Emir Yusuf in the 18th century. As viewed from the outside, these Harari houses are unremarkable rectangular blocks occasionally enlivened by an old carved door. But the interior design is unique to the town. The open-plan ground floor is dominated by a carpet-draped raised area where all social activity (ie: chewing *khat*) takes place. The walls are decorated with small niches and dangling items of crockery, including the famed Harar baskets, some of which are hundreds of years old. Above the main door are grilles from which carpets are hung to indicate there is a daughter of marriageable age in the family. When the carpets come down, newlyweds in Harar take residence in a tiny corner cell, where they spend their first week of wedlock in cramped, isolated revelry, all they might need being passed to them by relatives through a small service window.

'This place is really amazing during sunsets and sunrises. We spent time there every evening just sitting in silence, listening to the prayers coming from the mosques and feeling this extraordinary spiritual atmosphere.'

Outside Harar Jugol Although most sites of interest are concentrated within the city walls, a few landmarks outside it merit a look. About 200m south of Sanga Gate, the tomb of Sheikh Abadir, the religious leader who reputedly introduced Islam to Harar, is a recognised substitute for the pilgrimage to Mecca for Islamic Ethiopians who can't afford international travel. The new Christian Market, located 500m southeast of the Belayneh Hotel, is usually bustling with Oromo vendors who've come in from the villages for the day. In the new town, the Italian-built Amir Abdullahi City Hall, a block away from the Harar Gate, is a rather impressive example of colonial architecture, while the bronze Ras Makonnen statue on the eponymous circle was cast by renowned local artist Afewerk Tekle. Further out of town, about 5km along the Jijiga road and easily reached by *bajaj*, the church and cemetery at Deker offer a good view over the walled city (best for photography in the afternoon).

Mikael Church and surrounds [466 E4] A cluster of buildings associated with Ras Tefari (the future Emperor Haile Selassie) and his father, Ras Makonnen, stands about 1km south of the old town on the wooded foot slopes of Mount Hakim. Most conspicuous among these, verging the north side of the Jijiga road, is **Mikael Church**, which is claimed locally to have been founded in 1886 (in which case it would predate Menelik II's capture of Harar). An attractive square sandstone construction, the present church most likely dates to the early reign of Haile Selassie. It has four arched doors and a protruding circular apse on each side, as well as a wrap-around balcony shaded by an ornate wooden roof.

Tucked away in an overgrown garden behind the church, the **Ras Makonnen Mausoleum** is an oddly neglected, partially ruined domed outhouse constructed in 1906 as a temporary burial place for Ras Makonnen. Between 1920 and the late 1940s, interrupted by the Italian occupation, Haile Selassie constructed a much grander memorial to his father in the form of the **Tekle Haymanot Church** (also known as **Ras Makonnen Memorial**), a tall, narrow domed cruciform building that rather resembles Lalibela's Bet Giyorgis in relative dimensions, and stands on the opposite side of the Jijiga road to Mikael Church. According to one local legend, however, the local priests disobeyed orders to relocate the emperor's father's coffin to Tekle Haymanot, and the wide crack in the floor of the mausoleum was created by the angry spirit of Ras Makonnen when he decided to escape to the sarcophagus in the permanent memorial.

About 200m uphill of Tekle Haymanot, forking left at the only Y-junction, stands the three-storey **Ras Makonnen House**, a striking building whose rickety wooden exterior staircase leads to the a wrap-around first-floor balcony. The house was built by Ras Makonnen in the late 1890s and it is where the future Haile Selassie spent much of his childhood prior to it being donated to the Bank of Abyssinia in 1906 and serving as the British Embassy over 1910–36. It is now a very decrepit-looking private residence.

Hyena men of Harar One of Harar's most enduringly popular attractions is its renowned 'hyena men', who make their living by feeding wild hyenas after dusk on the outskirts of Harar Jugol, thereby providing proof that Ethiopians are capable of

HYENA FEEDING AND ASHURA

In 1990, Ahmed Zekaria of the Institute of Ethiopian Studies wrote an essay indicating that the practice of feeding hyenas may be loosely rooted in a much older annual ceremony called Ashura, which takes place in Harar on the eve of 10 Muharran (which will be 10 September in 2019, 29 August in 2020 and 18 August in 2021). According to the tradition related by Zekaria, the festival dates back to a famine many centuries ago, which forced the wild hyenas in the hills around Harar to attack livestock and even people. The people of Harar decided to feed the hyenas porridge to stave off their hunger, and after the famine ended they renewed their pact annually by leaving out a bowl of porridge covered in rich butter near Abobker shrine during the Ashura Festival. It is said that the hyenas' reaction to the porridge is a portent for the year ahead. If they eat more than half of the porridge, then the year ahead will be bountiful, but if they refuse to eat, or they eat the lot, then famine or pestilence is predicted. The practice of feeding meat to the hyenas on a daily basis is obviously quite a leap from an annual feeding ceremony involving porridge, but the Ashura Festival does indicate that the performance of the modern hyena man is rooted in a more ancient custom.

As something of a footnote to the above, Paul Clammer writes:

Ashura commemorates the death of Hussein, grandson of the prophet Muhammad, at the Battle of Kerbala in AD680. This battle created an ongoing schism between the two strands of Islam – those who thought the successor to Muhammad should be elected and those who favoured the hereditary claims of Hussein. The former won the battle and went on to form the majority Sunni branch of Islam, while the losers now form the numerically smaller Shia branch, which commemorates the martyrdom of Hussein at the Ashura Festival. All well and good, but Ethiopia's Muslims are exclusively Sunni and thus don't recognise Ashura, which means that whatever link exists between Ashura and the feeding of hyenas in Harar must be obscure and interesting indeed.

More legends regarding the hyenas of Harar are recounted on the informative blog w hararhyenas.wordpress.com.

perversity far beyond the call of duty. A highlight of any visit to Harar, even to those who have seen wild hyenas in less contrived proximity, this atmospheric spectacle usually starts at around 18.30, when the hyena man starts calling his familiars by name. After 10 minutes or so, the animals appear from the shadows, timidly at first, but they soon become bolder and start taking bones passed to them by human hand or mouth. Visitors are invited to feed the hyenas directly, too, before eventually the stock of bones runs out, and these spectral creatures slink back to whence they came.

Exactly how and when the bizarre practice of feeding the hyenas arose is an open question. One story is that it started during the great famine of the 1890s (see box, opposite), and it is certainly the case that the people of Harar have long believed hyenas to perform an important role in clearing the town of the *jinn* (invisible evil spirits) that occasionally possess one of the townsfolk. According to this legend, hyenas are the only creatures that can see the *jinn*, and they routinely attack them and swallow them alive, emitting their characteristic whoop as the evil spirit perishes. But while the nightly feeding of hyenas in Harar may well be rooted in such ancient folklore and customs, most sources indicate it's a modern phenomenon, probably initiated in the 1950s at Aw Ansar Ahmed Shrine, just outside Erer Gate, by a man called Dozo, who has reputedly had seven successors.

As a result of urban expansion, the main hyena-feeding [469 G4] site recently relocated from Aw Ansar Ahmed Shrine to a more remote location near a garbage dump about 2km further outside Erer Gate. This is too far out of town to be a realistic nocturnal goal on foot, certainly not to anybody who has seen a hyena's jaw in close-up action, so you will need to arrange it as a motorised trip with a guide (with the added bonus that the car headlights allow for better viewing in the dark) or rent a *bajaj* (expect to pay around US$6). A second hyena-feeding place, on a patch of open ground in front of the Christian slaughterhouse, is only 200m outside of Fallana Gate, so more realistic on foot, but these days it is generally less productive than the main site. Either way, the fee is US$4 per person, inclusive of photography.

Further afield

Awaday khat market Situated along the Dire Dawa road some 10km from Harar, the small town of Awaday is renowned as the site of the country's largest *khat* market. Copious amounts of eastern Ethiopia's finest are sold here for distribution to Somaliland, Addis Ababa and elsewhere, and the surrounding area lends itself to a particularly highly regarded variety of the leaf. The market is a fascinating place to visit; it operates daily, but tends to be busiest in the morning. There is plenty of direct transport from Harar to Awaday, and any vehicle heading to or from Dire Dawa can drop you there.

Lake Alem Maya Flanking the north side of the Dire Dawa road near the eponymous small town 16km from Harar, Lake Alem Maya (also spelt Haramaya) is the most southerly and accessible of a chain of freshwater bodies that also includes lakes Adele, Hora Jutu and Finkile. When full, the lake often supports concentrations of greater and lesser flamingo, as well as large numbers of white pelican, avocet, black-tailed godwit and up to 10,000 red-knobbed coots. Until recent years, the lake was at its best during the European winter, when a profusion of migrant waterfowl and waders boosted the resident birds. Since the late 1990s, however, Alemaya has tended to drain completely during the dry season, the start of which more or less coincides with the arrival of Palaearctic migrants to east Africa. There is direct transport from Harar to Alem Maya, and any vehicle heading to or from Dire Dawa can drop you there.

Ejerso Gworo Situated high in the mountains some 25km northeast of Harar as the crow flies, the village of Ejerso Gworo is best known as the birthplace of Ras Tefari on 23 July 1892. The site was chosen deliberately by Ras Makonnen and his wife Yeshimebet, the parents of the future Emperor Haile Selassie, because they had been unfortunate with the births of their previous children, and Ejerso Gworo complied with an ancient Ethiopian belief that the chance of a problematic birth decreases at a high altitude. There is no shrine at Ejerso Gworo to commemorate the birth of Haile Selassie, but the emperor did construct a church dedicated to Kidane Mihret there. En route to Ejerso Gworo, the road from Harar passes through Kombolcha (not to be confused with its namesake near Dessie), a somewhat larger town known for its bustling daily *khat* market.

In a private vehicle, Ejerso Gworo can easily be visited as a day trip out of Harar – expect the drive to take up to 90 minutes in either direction. There is no shortage of public transport covering the 18km road between Harar and Kombolcha, but transport on to Ejerso Gworo is rather more erratic. There are several basic hotels in Kombolcha, and at least one in Ejerso Gworo, should the need arise.

Koromi [map, page 445] One of the oldest settlements in this part of Ethiopia, the village of Koromi quite possibly predates nearby Harar. Legend asserts that it was founded by a North African holy man named Emir Abu Bakr, who led his followers to Ethiopia via Yemen and Somalia in around 1130. Known locally as the Argobba (which translates more or less as 'Arrivals'), the refugees settled briefly at Deker, 5km from present-day Harar along the Jijiga road, but eventually moved further south to what is now Koromi. According to this legend, the antecedents of the Harari people later migrated to the area from the vicinity of present-day Awash National Park and forged a good relationship with the Argobba, with whom they founded the city of Harar.

Today, the Argobba inhabit much of the hilly country immediately southeast of Harar, where they use sophisticated methods of terracing to grow cash crops such as coffee and *khat*. They share a common religion with their Harari neighbours, and speak the same language, albeit with sufficient variation in accent for any local to know the difference. Strongly traditional, with a general appearance similar to that of the Oromo, the Argobba are renowned for the beauty of their women, who certainly tend to be a striking apparition as they stroll through the countryside adorned by colourful robes, beaded jewellery and braided hair. They are also known for their 'double-faced' clothing, which can be worn either way around – the colourful side is reserved for weddings and other festive occasions, the black side for funerals.

Boasting an imperious clifftop setting chosen for its defensibility, Koromi is a labyrinthine conglomeration of a few dozen tightly packed stone houses, most of which are many hundreds of years old. The interiors are similar to the traditional homesteads of Harar, with the main difference being that they are neither plastered nor painted, while the rectangular stone exteriors, reminiscent of some Tigrayan houses, collectively evoke what Harar must have looked like in Burton's day. The views from Koromi are stunning, stretching for miles across the plains to the distinctive tabletop of Mount Gendebure in the vicinity of Kombolcha.

Koromi lies about 15km southeast of Harar by road and is accessible only by private vehicle or *bajaj*, or on foot. The most direct route entails branching south from the asphalt road to Jijiga at Deker, about 4km out of central Harar. The feeder road from Deker is currently in poor repair, however, so most drivers now prefer to continue on the asphalt for another 5km, then branch south at Haware. If you use the road from Deker, it is worth after 2.5km visiting the Aw Sofi shrine, burial place of its namesake saint, who is one of the most respected Muslim saints associated with the region's medieval conversion to Islam. After another 6km, the road from Deker passes Hajifaj, a tiny settlement named after an 18th-century holy man whose tomb stands in Harar. Hajifaj is the site of an important local market every Monday and Friday, when there may be some public transport there from Deker. Koromi lies 4km past Hajifaj, passing a striking balancing rock formation immediately to your right about three-quarters of the way there. No formal facilities for tourism exist at Koromi, so it is advisable to take a guide from Harar to ensure that all goes smoothly.

Mount Kundudo [map, page 445] Situated 20km northeast of Harar as the crow flies (but double that distance by road), Mount Kundudo is a striking 2,900m-tall basalt-capped limestone mountain whose beautiful tabletop, incised with a distinctive W-shape on the right, was extolled by Burton when he followed its base en route to Harar in 1855. Situated in Gursum *woreda*, the mountain offers a wealth of natural and archaeological attractions, and is the centrepiece of a proposed conservation area being lobbied for by Italian ecologist and professor Marco Viganó (w *etio.webs. com*). Points of interest include the spectacular Immis Falls, several old Islamic shrines among which is a tall stone tower dedicated to Sheikh Adem, and one of only three feral horse populations in Africa. An expedition led by Viganó discovered a beautiful limestone cave system in the mountains, as well as several superb rock art sites, details of which will not be disclosed until measures are in place to prevent them from being despoiled in the manner of the Laga Oda paintings. Unfortunately, Gursum stands at the epicentre of the violent Somali–Oromo clashes that took place around Harar in 2017, and recent attempts to develop the area for tourism have been stalled by security concerns that make it unsafe for travel.

Assuming the situation stabilises during the lifespan of this edition, Gursum can be explored from the *woreda* capital, Fugnan Bira, a reasonably substantial town set at an elevation of around 2,000m at the base of Mount Kundudo. In a private vehicle, the best way to get to Fugnan Bira is via Babile on the Jijiga road. On public transport, a few direct buses run between Harar and Fugnan Bira, but they tend to be very slow so you are better making your way to Babile and changing vehicles there. You can also drive or hitch up to the plateau via the Bedada Pass, which is where the feral horses live.

Babile livestock market Straddling the asphalt road to Jijiga about 30km east of Harar, the small town of Babile (population 20,000) shares its name with a popular brand of bottled sparkling water sourced from a nearby natural spring but bottled at a factory in Harar. Babile is best known today for the massive livestock market (*entrance US$2*) held on its northern outskirts every Monday and Thursday. Probably the most impressive Ethiopian market of its type after Bati, it is split across two large stone stockades, one reserved for camels and the other for cattle, sheep and goats. It usually gets into full swing at around 08.30 and camel trading activity tends to wind down after 10.30, but other livestock is sold until the late afternoon. Babile also hosts a busy general market on Saturdays. Plenty of minibuses travel back and forth between Harar and Babile, typically taking around 45 minutes, and it is also easy enough to find public transport on to Jijiga. The livestock market is quite difficult to find, but anyone can point the way – ask for *gamela gebeya* (camel market). A few basic hotels can be found in Babile should you want to spend the night there.

Valley of Marvels Some 5–10km east of Babile, the Jijiga road traverses the so-called Valley of Marvels, a desolate landscape of red earth, low acacia scrub, forbidding succulents and tall chimney-like termite mounds punctuated by gravity-defying balancing rock formations such as Dakata, which appears to be just one puff away from collapse. Inhabited by colourful Oromo pastoralists, the Dakata area also hosts a fair bit of wildlife, most visibly warthog and Hamadryas baboon, but various antelope and the occasional lion and hyena are also seen. The dry-country birdlife is terrific. Sadly, however, much of the natural vegetation has been cut down to make charcoal in recent years, and replaced by invasive cacti and other alien species. Coming from Harar, it is easy enough to get to the Valley of Marvels and back in a day using public transport to Jijiga. Dakata Rock lies close to the Jijiga road 7km past Babile, near the village of Dakata (marked by a few stalls).

Babile Elephant Sanctuary With thanks to Yirmed Demeke and Hailu Gashaw
[map, page 445] (*Entrance US$4 pp*) The arid country to the south of Harar supports an isolated elephant population afforded protection in the 6,982km² Babile Elephant Sanctuary, also known as the Harar Wildlife Sanctuary, which is bordered by the Gobelle River south of Harar and the Fafen River southwest of Jijiga. Some authorities assign the elephants of Babile to a unique race, *Loxodonta africana orleansi*, but further molecular and morphological analysis is required to determine the validity of this taxonomic distinction. Either way, following their probable extinction in Somalia, this is the last extant elephant population to occur in the eastern Horn of Africa, and must thus be regarded as a high conservation priority. The sanctuary also provides refuge to the black-maned Abyssinian lion, cheetah, various antelope including greater and lesser kudu, the striking Hamadryas baboon, and a spectacular selection of dry-country birds, including the endemic Salvadori's serin.

Despite the establishment of the sanctuary in 1962, the range of this isolated elephant population is thought to have shrunk by about 65% in the last 20 years. Furthermore, the elephant population has decreased from an estimated 300 in the 1970s to perhaps 200 today, and its vulnerability is underscored by the loss of at least 44 individuals to poachers over the course of 2012 and 2013. The elephants move seasonally between the Erer and Gobelle river valleys, but also sometimes venture up to 15km outside the sanctuary, particularly to the western ridge of the Gobelle Valley and the Upper Erer Valley.

The best time of year to seek out the elephants is the late rainy season, between June and September, when they are concentrated in the Upper Erer Valley to the southeast of Harar. There are two motorable tracks to this area, the more useful of which branches south from the Harar–Jijiga road at Bisidimo, 25km out of Harar, then continues for 30km to the sanctuary entrance, from where it is another 20km to the area where elephants are most often seen. It can take up to 90 minutes to hike from here into the valley, but the walk is not difficult because there is no gorge. The thick vegetation and high level of human encroachment means that the elephants tend to lurk in the densest thickets in the heat of the day, when they can be difficult to locate – and are prone to aggressive behaviour when surprised.

The elephants can also be sought between mid-November and early March, when they congregate in Upper Gobelle Gorge near Fedis District. To get there from Harar town, take the Fedis road southward from the Total filling station west of the town centre. After about 24km, the road passes through the small town of Fedis Boku, from where you need to continue driving for another 6–22km, depending on where the elephants are currently hanging out. If you are fortunate, you might find a herd resting under the ficus sycamore trees on the close rim of the gorge. If not, you will need to trek to the valley floor. This is a steep hike that requires a fair level of agility and takes about 30 minutes in either direction, ideally before 11.00 or after 16.00, when the animals are most active. It may well take several hours to locate any elephants.

You need a private vehicle to get to either site. This can be arranged through any guide in Harar and the cost usually works out at US$100 per party for a saloon car or (essential in the rainy season) US$150 for a 4x4. An armed scout (*US$8 per party*) is mandatory and can be picked up when you reach the sanctuary. There is no accommodation in the reserve, but it can easily be visited as a day trip out of Harar, though your chance of seeing the elephants is highest in the evening and early morning when they are most mobile (and it is also less likely you will startle them by stumbling on them at close quarters). Wear thick trousers and closed shoes for hiking in the bush. Note that this area experiences occasional outbreaks of banditry, and it is currently more potentially volatile than normal due to local Somali–Oromo tensions, so ask about current safety conditions in Harar before heading out.

JIJIGA

The capital of Somali Federal Region, Jijiga (also known as Jigjiga), 105km east of Harar, has existed by that name at least since 1842, when explorer W C Barker mentioned it as a stopover along the caravan route between Zeila and Harar. In 1893, when Captain Swayne passed through, it comprised a stockaded fort with a garrison of 25 men next to a group of wells. Today, it is one of the country's fastest-growing towns, with a rash of new high-rises recently built or under construction, newly surfaced trunk roads that don't quite succeed in taming the dust below, and a population now thought to be approaching the 200,000 mark. Jijiga is the closest Ethiopian town to the unrecognised state of Somaliland (still officially part of Somalia, despite having functioned as an independent state since 1991), has close trade links with its capital, Hargeisa, and is most usually visited only by travellers bound for the border post at Tog Wajaale, 75km to the east.

Unless you're heading on to Somaliland, or just desperate to see something of Ethiopia's most eastern federal region, Jijiga doesn't have a lot going for it. Despite its antiquity and status as regional capital, the ubiquitous presence of *khat*, and the vividly colourful *abaya* cloths worn by the women, the town has a less perceptible Somali feel than might be expected or hoped for. Things liven up slightly when you are confronted by Jijiga's focal point: a chaotically sprawling market of interest not so much for any traditional goods, but rather for the vast array of secondhand and electronic goods that have fallen off the back of Somaliland. Even so, the best thing about Jijiga is arguably the drive there from Harar via the spectacular Valley of Marvels (page 479).

GETTING THERE AND AWAY Ethiopian Airlines flies to Jijiga daily from Addis Ababa via Dire Dawa. The airport is 10km out of town and a shared taxi costs around US$5–7.50. The only realistic overland approach to Jijiga from within Ethiopia, the recently surfaced road from Harar, now takes up to 90 minutes in a private vehicle, while shared minibuses cost US$2 and take 2–3 hours. Minibuses from Jijiga to Tog Wajaale, the border town with Somaliland, also leave every 30 minutes or so. The main bus station in Jijiga lies about 1km along the road towards Tog Wajaale, and is connected to the town centre by regular *bajaji* and minibuses.

🏠 **WHERE TO STAY** *Map, page 482*

Accommodation in Jijiga is generally quite basic and uniformly overpriced, presumably because it caters mainly to an NGO market. The better places also tend to fill up early.

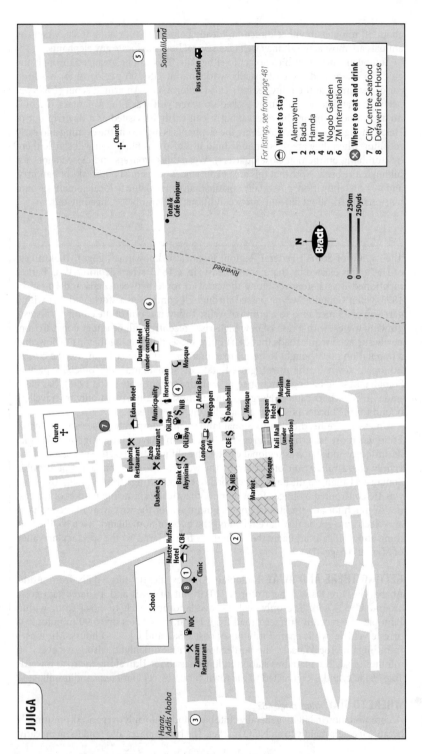

JIJIGA

Harar, Addis Ababa →

School

Church ✝

Church ✝

Somaliland →

Bus station

Total & Café Bonjour

Riverbed

Bracht

N

0 — 250m
0 — 250yds

Zamzam Restaurant ✕

NOC

Clinic ✚

Master Hurfane Hotel

$ CBE

Dashen $

Euphoria Restaurant ✕

Azeb Restaurant ✕

Bank of Abyssinia $

Edam Hotel

Municipality

OiLibya

OiLibya $

NIB $

London Café

Wegagen $

Africa Bar

Horseman

Mosque

Duule Hotel (under construction)

CBE $

Dahabshiil $

Mosque

NIB $

Market

Mosque

Kali Mall (under construction)

Deegaan Hotel

Muslim shrine

① ② ③ ④ ⑤ ⑥ ⑦ ⑧

For listings, see from page 481

🏠 **Where to stay**
1 Alemayehu
2 Bada
3 Hamda
4 MI
5 Nogob Garden
6 ZM International

✕ **Where to eat and drink**
7 City Centre Seafood
8 Defaveri Beer House

482

Moderate

⌂ ZM International Hotel (25 rooms)
📞 025 775 2926; **m** 0911 358642, 0946 700404; **e** info@zminternationalhotel.com; **w** zminternationalhotel.com. Easily the smartest hotel in Jijiga, the central ZM has comfortable & spacious rooms with wooden floors, net, fan & flatscreen TV. The ground-floor restaurant is about as funky as it gets in Jijiga, with bright fittings, whirling fans & a long, varied menu of grills, local dishes & pizzas in the US$4–10 range. It's one of the few restaurants that also serves alcohol. *US$48/60/72 B&B sgl/db/trpl.* **$$$$**

Budget

⌂ MI Hotel (27 rooms) 📞 025 278 2161. Situated in the bright blue 5-storey Haji Mohamed Building near the main roundabout, the en-suite rooms here are arranged around a skylit central courtyard & reached via a glass-sided lift. Rooms are spacious, clean & have good amenities – flatscreen TV, writing desk, fridge, hot shower – but the overall affect is a bit overbearing. Still, good value by Jijiga's standards. *From US$21 for a standard dbl or twin to US$36 for a VIP with king-size bed.* **$$$**

⌂ Hamda Hotel (32 rooms) 📞 025 775 4678. This popular budget hotel on the Harar side of town comes with a good 1st-floor restaurant serving Ethiopian & Western dishes for around US$3, as well as garden seating & a pastry shop. The clean rooms are quite spacious & most come with TV. *US$16/24 B&B sgl/dbl.* **$$$**

⌂ Nogob Garden Hotel (38 rooms) 📞 025 775 3837; **m** 0921 606032. This slightly surreal approximation of an upmarket hotel, set in small but presumably saliva-free gardens more or less opposite the bus station, has rundown en-suite rooms with sat TV & hot water, & a ground-floor restaurant serving typical Ethiopian fare. *US$16/24 B&B sgl/dbl.* **$$$**

Shoestring

⌂ Alemayehu Hotel (14 rooms) 📞 025 775 2814. Set around a large courtyard, the clean en-suite rooms at this well-priced hotel all come with TV. *US$12/18 dbl with cold/hot water.* **$$**

⌂ Bada Hotel (36 rooms) 📞 025 775 2841. Large but tired-looking en-suite rooms with TV, hot water & 24hr water supply. *US$12/16 sgl/dbl.* **$$**

✕ WHERE TO EAT AND DRINK *Map, opposite*

There are acceptable restaurants at the several hotels, with the ZM International Hotel being the pick for quality and the Hamda offering the best value for money.

✕ City Centre Seafood Restaurant **m** 0915 442222; ⊕ 08.00–21.00. This new restaurant has an English-speaking owner, comfortable seating & specialises in fish fresh from Berbera (Somaliland) served grilled or fried with rice & salad at US$6/ plate. No alcohol.

✕ Defaveri Beer House Alcohol isn't served widely in Jijiga, but this pleasant drinking hole on the west side of town has inexpensive St George on tap.

MORE FROM BRADT

For more on travel in Somaliland, why not check out Bradt's *Somaliland*? Visit **w** bradtguides.com/shop for a 10% discount on all our titles.

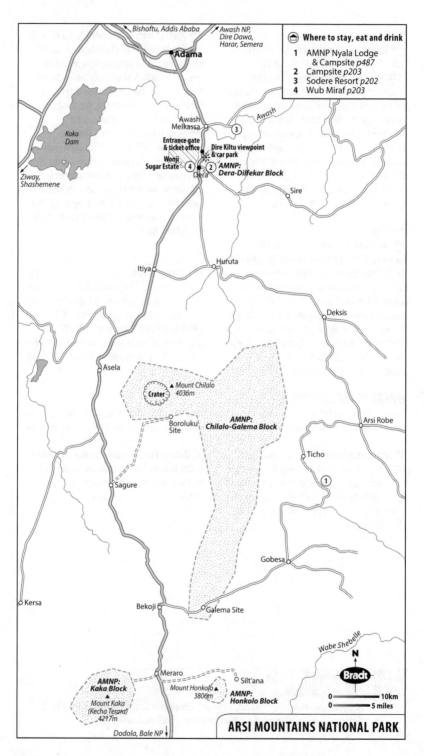

1 AMNP Nyala Lodge
  & Campsite *p487*
2 Campsite *p203*
3 Sodere Resort *p202*
4 Wub Miraf *p203*

ARSI MOUNTAINS NATIONAL PARK

Bale and the Southeast

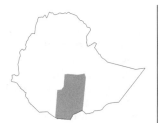

The main travel focus in the southeast is Bale Mountains National Park, which protects Ethiopia's second-highest mountain range along with an alluring cross section of endemic wildlife, including Ethiopian wolf, mountain nyala, Menelik's bushbuck, giant mole-rat and 16 bird species whose range is confined to Ethiopia/Eritrea. A wonderful trekking, wildlife and birding destination, Bale is also quite easily explored by car, and it is now the site of the country's premier ecolodge, set in the magical Harenna Forest at the southern base of the main massif. The other main natural attraction of the southeast is the remote road that runs south from Bale National Park to Yabello via Negele Borena, a route that is of particular interest to birdwatchers for offering the opportunity to see a host of dry-country specials along with highly localised endemics such as Ruspoli's turaco, Liben lark and Stresemann's bush crow. For those whose interest leans more towards culture and history, highlights of this thinly populated region include the ancient rock engravings and megalithic sites around Dilla, and the Borena singing wells in the vicinity of the Kenyan border south of Yabello.

There are two main approach roads to the Bale Mountains from the northwest and, unlike a few years back, both are now surfaced and in good condition. Coming directly from Addis Ababa, the shorter, quicker and less congested route involves driving east along the new Adama Expressway all the way to Adama, then heading south from Adama to the junction town of Dodola, passing en route through Arsi Zone, where the highland towns of Asela and Bekoji are potential springboards for a diversion to the new and little-visited Arsi Mountains National Park. If you use this route, it is about 370km/6 hours from Addis Ababa to the Bale Mountains park headquarters at Dinsho, 400km/6½ hours to Bale Robe, 410km/7 hours to Goba and 475km/10 hours to Bale Mountain Lodge. The alternative route, via Shashemene, is about 40km longer, and tends to be less relaxed due to the higher volume of traffic, but it is more popular with travellers because it ties in better with visits to the Rift Valley lakes and most other destinations in the south. Either way, the two routes converge at the small town of Dodola, which serves as the base for treks into the Adaba-Dodola Integrated Forest Management Project, a well-organised initiative that effectively forms a northwestern extension of the area protected by Bale Mountains National Park.

ARSI ZONE

An area of breezy, fertile highlands capped by two separate massifs topping the 4,000m mark, Arsi Zone has in the past been associated more with its agricultural bounty – not to mention the production of a quite astonishing number of Olympian runners – than it has with tourism. And while the zonal capital, Asela, used once to be a common stopover en route to the Bale Mountains, few would bother breaking there for more than a quick snack or coffee now that the road from Addis Ababa to Goba is surfaced in its entirety. This, hopefully, is set to change, however, following the recent establishment of the 931km² Arsi Mountains National Park, which comprises four discrete blocks, two of which incorporate extensive tracts of Afroalpine vegetation inhabited by endemics such as Ethiopian wolf, mountain nyala and Menelik's bushbuck, and are most easily accessed out of Asela or the more southerly town of Bekoji.

ASELA Best known perhaps as the birthplace of Olympic gold medallist Haile Gebrselassie, the zonal capital, Asela, stands at an altitude of 2,400m among orderly green fields of millet, maize, barley and rapeseed overlooked by Mount Chilalo 15km to the southeast. Should you need to stay over, there is no shortage of decent budget accommodation, including several hotels built by Olympic runners who hail from the region. The pick is the **Derartu Tulu Hotel** (*27 rooms;* ☏*022 331 2828; from US$18 en-suite dbl with sat TV;* **$$**), whose eponymous owner became the first black African woman to win an Olympic gold medal at Barcelona 1992. A cheaper and equally comfortable alternative, the recently built **Bezawork Hotel** (*19 rooms;* ☏*022 238 0317; US$12 en-suite dbl with hot shower;* **$$**) is situated opposite the Derartu Tulu on the road behind the Soljam Hotel. Both have a good and reasonably priced restaurant and bar.

BEKOJI Some 56km south of Asela, Bekoji lies at an altitude of 2,800m in an area of evocative frosty moorland where the local Oromo horsemen, swathed in warm shawls and blankets, are rather reminiscent in appearance of the Basotho of Lesotho. Unassuming though it might look, this small town and its immediate environs lay claim to being the birthplace of a rash of top long-distance runners, including Olympic medallists Derartu Tulu, Fatuma Bale Robe, Tirunesh Dibala and Kenenisa Bekele. Your best overnight options, both situated a few hundred metres north of the town centre along the Asela road, are the **Bale Hotel** (*15 en-suite rooms; US$7.50/11 sgl/dbl;* **$$**) and the **Wabe Hotel** (m *0911 866530; US$12 for a large carpeted en-suite dbl with king-size bed;* **$$**).

ARSI MOUNTAINS NATIONAL PARK (☏*022 333 0085;* m *0911 055342;* e *arsimtsnp@ gmail.com;* ⊕ *06.00–18.00 daily; entrance US$3.50 pp & US$1/car, mandatory scout fee US$8/party*) Established in 2011, the scenic and biodiverse Arsi Mountains National Park (AMNP) comprises four discrete sectors, three of which lie in the vicinity of Asela or Bekoji. By far the largest and most biodiverse sector, serving as the watershed for more than 50 streams and rivers, is the 792km² Chilalo-Galema Block, which protects Mount Chilalo, an extinct volcano with a 6km-wide crater and maximum elevation of 4,036m, and the narrow 55km-long Galema range running to its southeast. Further south, the 104km² Kaka Block protects the eponymous peak, which rises to 4,217m to the southwest of Bekoji, making it the fourth-highest massif in Ethiopia and nudging it into the top ten for all of Africa. To the southeast of Bekoji, the 22km² Honkolo Block is somewhat lower, rising to an elevation of 3,806m, and was incorporated into the park at the insistence of representatives of the local community. Chilalo-Galema and Kaka both support significant tracts of Afroalpine vegetation and associated wildlife, including an estimated 400-plus mountain nyala (the largest population outside Bale Mountains National Park), 100 Menelik's bushbuck and 50 Ethiopian wolves, as well as Bohor reedbuck, warthog, Anubis baboon, grey duiker, klipspringer, porcupine and even leopard. Birdlife seems to be poorly documented but one might expect the Afroalpine forest and moorlands to host most species associated with the same habitats in Bale.

There are several access points to AMNP, and wildlife viewing is generally best in the early morning and late afternoon. Best for tracking the Ethiopian wolf on foot is Boroluku Site, which is on the western slopes of the Chilalo-Galema Block, and is reached by driving south from Asela towards Bekoji for 22km, then turning left on to a dirt road and continuing east for another 25km. Mountain nyala are most conspicuous at Galema Site, which lies about 7km along a well-maintained dirt road connecting Bekoji to the small town of Gobesa, and runs through the park's Afroalpine zone for about 8km. The springboard for the Kaka and Honkolo Blocks is the village of Meraro, which straddles the asphalt road to Dodola about 15km south of Bekoji. From Meraro, drive west for 10km to reach the highest motorable point on Kaka, from where it takes a couple of hours on foot or horseback to reach the summit, a very scenic hike that comes with a near certainty of seeing mountain nyala, Menelik's bushbuck and other antelope, but you'd be fortunate indeed to spot a wolf, with fewer than ten thought to survive. Honkolo, which is of less ecological importance than the other blocks, but still supports good numbers of reedbuck and warthog, is easily explored on foot from the village of Silt'ana, which lies at its eastern base along a 20km wide road running east from the Dodola road 2km south of Meraro. The only one of these blocks accessible on public transport is Honkolo (regular minibuses run between Bekoji and Silt'ana), but Galema could be reached from Bekoji by *bajaj*.

Covered separately in this book (page 203), the smallest and most remote of Arsi Mountains National Park's four sectors is Dera-Dilfekar, a relatively low-lying sanctuary situated 50km north of Asela, known for its dense populations of greater and lesser kudu. Logistically, Dera-Dilfekar is best treated as a day excursion from nearby Adama or even Addis Ababa. Nevertheless, travellers heading to Chilalo-Galema, Kaka or Honkolo should be aware that the ticket office at Dera-Dilfekar is the only place where entrance and other park fees can be paid. This isn't a serious inconvenience coming from Addis Ababa via Adama, but it would require a significant backtrack were you to approach the park from Dodola, Bale, Shashemene or elsewhere in the south. The ticket office at Dera-Dilfekar will also arrange for you to pick up an armed scout, either at the park administrative office in Asela (housed in a multistorey building 50m north of the landmark Derartu Tulu Hotel), at Galema scout post or in Meraro.

The only accommodation serving the highlands sectors is **AMNP Nyala Lodge and Campsite** [map, page 484] (m *0911 613016;* f; *US$22/28 sgl/dbl B&B or US$12 camping;* **$$$**), which lies 7km south of the village of Ticho near the eastern border of the Chilalo-Galema Block and the source of the Wabe Shebelle River. Bookings must be made in advance and the management can provide full directions, but the easiest way to get there coming from Addis Ababa or Asela is to branch east at Bekoji on to the same road that traverses Galema Site, continuing for about 30km through Gobesa, then head north for around 30km in the direction of Ticho. An alternative route runs north from Asela via Huruta to Arsi Robe, from where it is about 23km southwest to Ticho then another 7km south along the Bekoji road to Nyala Lodge.

DODOLA AND THE ADABA-DODOLA IFMP

Set at an elevation of 2,400m a few kilometres east of the junction of the roads from Asela and Shashemene, the small town of Dodola lies in a large flat and fertile land, a rare region of Ethiopia where tractors and other agricultural machines are intensively used. It is also home to the Adaba-Dodola Integrated Forest

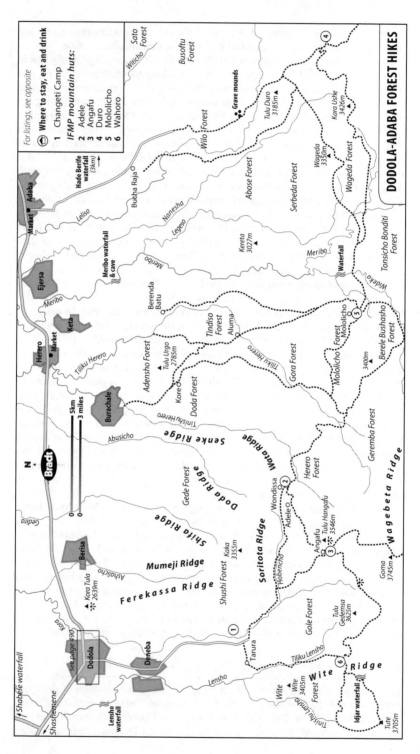

DODOLA-ADABA FOREST HIKES

For listings, see opposite

Where to stay, eat and drink

IFMP mountain huts:
1 Adele
2 Angafu
3 Duro
4 Mololicho
5 Wahoro
1 Changeti Camp

Sato
Wititcho Forest

Busoftu Forest

Grave mounds

Tulu Duro 3185m▲

Kara Ushe 3426m▲

Wageda 3350m▲

Wageda Forest

Tonsicho Bonditi Forest

Wilo Forest

Abose Forest

Serbeda Forest

Hade Berife waterfall (3km)→

Butcha Raja

Adaba
Market

Leliso

Nanesha

Legeso

Kereta 3027m▲

Meribo

Waterfall

Wideko

Meribo waterfall & cave

Meribo

Ejersa

Meribo

Herero
Market

Berenda Batu

Tindiso Forest

Aluma

Tiliku Herero

Gora Forest

Mololicho Forest

Berele Bushasho Forest

3400m

Keta
Market

Tiliku Herero

Adensho Forest

Tulu Urgo 2785m▲

Kore

Doda Forest

Tinishu Herero

Burachale

Abusicho

Senke Ridge

Wara Ridge

Herero Forest

Geremba Forest

Wagebeta Ridge

Gedira

Doda Ridge

Gede Forest

Shifa Ridge

Wondissa

Adele O

Hobencho

Angafu

Tulu Hangatu 3546m▲

Goma 3745m▲

N

Bradt

5km
3 miles
0   0

Berisa

Ashalicho

Mumeji Ridge

Ferekassa Ridge

Kora Tula 2639m

Shushi Forest

Kaka 3355m▲

Soritota Ridge

Tarura

Gole Forest

Tulu Gedemsa 3625m▲

Kora

Dodola
see page 490

Deneba

Lensho

Wite

Wite 3405m▲

Wite Forest

Tiliku Lensho

Tinishu Lensho

Idjar waterfall

Tute 3705m▲

Ridge

Shabele waterfall

Shashenene

Lensho waterfall

Management Project (IFMP) implemented by German aid organisation GTZ to help conserve the area's remaining Afromontane forest by creating employment and generating community earnings from tourism. This is a well-organised set-up that operates an elaborate network of mountain huts, tented camps and walking trails to the south of the main road running east to Adaba, where it offers affordable hiking and horseback trekking in a scenic area that incorporates about 500km² of natural forest and Afroalpine moorland, as well as plenty of endemic birds and other wildlife. The mountains covered by the trails are effectively a northwestern extension of the Bale Mountains, and there are plans to link these trails and huts with new huts in the national park's Web Valley.

FLORA AND FAUNA The dominant tree types in the forest zone of the IFMP are the African juniper, the coniferous *Podocarpus falcatus* and the fragrant *Hagenia abyssinica*. Many of these trees are giants over 500 years old. Above 3,200m, forest gives way to open moorland of St John's wort and heather (*Erica*), dotted with giant Angafu thistle shrubs with ball-shaped red flowers and giant lobelias. The juniper and hagenia forests protect a similar composition of birds to that found at Dinsho. Among the more visible species are wattled ibis, Rouget's rail, black-winged lovebird, yellow-fronted parrot, banded barbet, Abyssinian woodpecker, Abyssinian longclaw, Abyssinian catbird, white-backed black tit, Ethiopian oriole, white-cheeked turaco, black kite, augur buzzard and lammergeier. The most visible large mammals are vervet and guereza monkeys, but Ethiopian wolf, mountain nyala and Menelik's bushbuck inhabit the mountains and, although they are not as common as in Bale, they are sometimes seen by trekkers.

GETTING THERE AND AWAY In a private vehicle, Dodola lies about 4–5 hours' drive from Addis Ababa via Asela. Using public transport from the capital, it is easiest to take the Selam Bus to Goba and hop off at Dodola, even though this means paying full fare. Alternatively, catch a bus from Addis Ababa to Shashemene, and change vehicles there. Several buses or minibuses daily run back and forth between Dodola and Shashemene (*up to 1½hrs*), Asela (*2hrs*) and Bale Robe via Dinsho (*2½hrs*).

WHERE TO STAY, EAT AND DRINK
Dodola Town Map, page 490
Bale Mountain Motel (15 rooms) \022 660 0016; m 0912 944942. Set in wooded gardens a few doors up from the Guides Association, this hotel has long been a popular place to overnight before or after a hike into the IFMP. It is starting to look a little rundown, but the rooms are clean enough & it remains the best choice in town. The restaurant has a limited selection of Ethiopian & Western dishes in the US$2–3 range, as well as beers, soft drinks & coffee. *US$6 twin using common shower, US$7.50/12 sgl/dbl occupancy en suite with a ¾ bed & hot shower.* **$–$$**

Bisrat Pension (12 rooms) \022 666 1203. Also situated close to the Guides Association, this unsignposted pension has clean rooms with a ¾ bed & common showers (*US$4*) or with en-suite toilet & shower (*US$8*). **$**

Nasiba Musa (11 rooms) \022 890 2144; m 0913 382815. Exactly opposite the Rose Hotel, this inconspicuous 1st-floor guesthouse has 6 en-suite dbl rooms for US$6, 2 twins for the same price & 3 rooms with common shower at US$4. **$**

✕ Rose Hotel \022 666 0520. Located at the eastern end of town, this courtyard restaurant with umbrella-shaded tables serves a decent range of local meals & drinks. *Mains cost around US$3.*

Adaba-Dodola IFMP Map, page 488
Å Changeti Camp (10 beds) \022 666 0700; e baletrek@gmail.com; **f**. If you are here for trekking, the IFMP's tented camp at Changeti may be preferable to any hotel in town. It is only a 30min drive from Dodola, then 20mins more by foot or horse. Without a vehicle, you must start your trek by 14.00 for this to be an option. As with

14

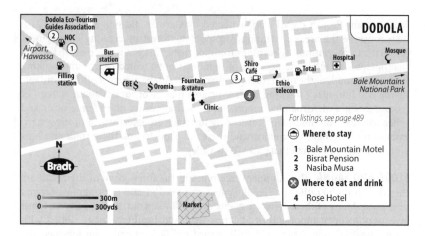

For listings, see page 489

Where to stay
1 Bale Mountain Motel
2 Bisrat Pension
3 Nasiba Musa

Where to eat and drink
4 Rose Hotel

the other IFMP camps, you must bring all your own food. *Camping US$3 pp.* **$**

🏠 **IFMP mountain huts** 📞 022 666 0700; e baletrek@gmail.com; 📧. The IFMP operates 5 simple but fully equipped mountain huts. Running from west to east, these are **Wahoro** (3,300m), **Angafu** (3,460m), **Adele** (3,300m), **Mololicho** (3,080m) & **Duro** (3,350m). Each comprises a hut with a communal eating area and 2 4-bed dorms, & includes facilities such as sheets, sleeping bags, blankets, towels, flip-flops, stoves, basic kitchenware, crockery, cutlery & kerosene lamps.

An outside annex has a toilet & shower. A cook can be arranged at the Eco-Tourism Guides Association in Dodola, or you can cook for yourself. Either way, you need to provide all your own supplies, which are best bought in Addis Ababa if at all possible, but, failing that, your guide will show you where to buy provisions locally. Clean water from springs or mountain streams is available, & water filters are in place at all huts. The camp keepers usually sell soft drinks, beers, wines & local spirits. *US$4 pp dorm bed, US$3 pp camping.* **$**

TOURIST INFORMATION AND GUIDES Situated on the west side of Dodola close to the Bale Mountain Hotel, the **Dodola Eco-Tourism Guides Association** (📞 *022 666 0700;* m *0913 348375;* e *baletrek@gmail.com;* 📧; ⊕ *08.30–17.00 daily*) effectively serves as the booking and tourist information office for the Adaba-Dodola IFMP. It is also where you pay all fees associated with a hike to the area. These are a US$4 entrance fee per person per visit, and a US$4 hut fee per person per night inclusive of bedding. A shower costs an additional US$0.50 and a fee of US$20 is due to the mandatory guide for up to four people (larger groups take a second guide). There's also an optional daily fee of US$20 per party for a cook, and a daily fee of US$5 per horse and US$5 per handler for those who want to explore on horseback. Except during the peak seasons of Christmas and Easter, booking isn't required – indeed, should you arrive early enough, you may be able to start your trek that same day.

HIKING AND TREKKING No prior riding experience is necessary to trek on horseback, but do check the horse you are allocated for saddle sores, and refuse any injured or bleeding animal. Hiking is also permitted, but ascending to an altitude of 3,500m can be tiring for those unacclimatised to high altitudes. Either way, a guide is mandatory. The best time to trek or hike is the dry season, between November and May. Afternoon showers are an almost daily occurrence during July and August, but it is possible to do all your hiking or trekking in the morning, and the wet conditions are compensated for by the lush vegetation and abundant wild flowers. A hat and sunblock are essential at all times of year, as is warm clothing and solid footwear.

The IFMP's trail circuit connects the permanent tented camp and five simple but fully equipped mountain huts described opposite. Six days are required to cover the full circuit, with approximate horseback times being 2 hours from Dodola to Changeti, 3 hours from Changeti to Wahoro, 5 hours from Wahoro to Angafu, 1 hour from Angafu to Adele, 4 hours from Adele to Mololicho, 6 hours from Mololicho to Duro, and 3½ hours from Duro to the eastern trail head. Depending on your level of fitness, hiking generally takes about 50% longer. It is possible to cut a day from the circuit by trekking directly between Angafu and Mololicho. The Guides Association in Dodola will be able to advise on a suitable itinerary, depending on your available time and interests.

Several shorter variations are possible, since the first three huts all stand within 4 hours of the western trail head, Mololicho lies about 3 hours from a central trail head near Herero village, and Duro lies about 3½ hours from the eastern trail head. With three nights to spare, you could loop between the three western huts; with one or two nights you could visit any one hut as a round trip. With an early start, it is even possible to visit Wahoro as a day trip. The trek from Wahoro to Angafu is nothing short of epic, while Duro is possibly the most beautiful hut for a one-night stay, offering great views of Bale's Harenna Forest. Angafu and Adele lie in the area where you are most likely to encounter wildlife. The Berenda Ridge, which can be hiked to as a day trip from Duro, is noted for its bamboo forest and as a good place for mountain nyala and Ethiopian wolf.

For those with limited time, the attractive Lensho Waterfall, about 30 minutes on foot from Dodola, forms a good goal for a guided day walk.

BALE MOUNTAINS AND SURROUNDS

The most extensive and tallest range in southern Ethiopia, the Bale Mountains rise eastward from the Rift Valley and northwest of the arid Somali Region to an altitude of 4,377m at Tullo Deemtu, Ethiopia's second-highest peak. Although heavily settled in parts, the mountains and their immediate environs incorporate around 6,000km^2 of contiguous wilderness, much of which is covered in indigenous montane and medium-altitude forest. The regional centrepiece is the 2,200km^2 Bale Mountains National Park (BMNP), which protects the range's upper slopes, including the 250km^2 Sanetti Plateau, which stands above 4,000m and supports the world's largest tract of Afroalpine moorland. Offering some superb hiking and trekking possibilities, BMNP is also surprisingly easy to explore in a vehicle, with the Sanetti Plateau being traversed by the highest all-weather road in Africa (built by the Derg to provide an emergency access route to the south). The main attractions of the park are its wild alpine scenery and exceptionally diverse fauna, which includes the world's largest population of the endangered Ethiopian wolf and mountain nyala, and the unique Bale monkey. BMNP also offers some of the finest birdwatching in Ethiopia.

GEOLOGY The Bale Massif comprises a vast lava plateau studded with half a dozen volcanic cones that rise to altitudes of greater than 4,200m. Despite being volcanic in origin, it predates the formation of the nearby Rift Valley, comprising trachytic, basaltic and other igneous rocks formed between 35 and 20 million years ago. Since then, the upper slopes have been moulded and the old volcanic peaks flattened during the course of two long periods of glacial activity, the most recent peaking around 13,000 years ago when the ice caps extended over a total of 180km^2. Some of the peaks still supported glacial activity as recently as 2,000 years ago, and they

14

still receive occasional snowfall, most often in the dry season between November and February. The national park is the most important watershed in southern Ethiopia, with an estimated 12 million people being dependent on the 40-plus rivers that rise on its upper slopes, or many lowland springs fed by subterranean water that originates here. Much of the water that flows eastward from Bale empties into the mighty Juba or Wabe Shebelle rivers before or after they cross the border into Somalia. Bale Mountains Park was established in 1970 and nominated for UNESCO's list of tentative World Heritage Sites in 2008.

HISTORY The Bale Mountains are named after a once powerful Muslim state that was founded in the area in the 11th century, conquered by Christian Emperor Amda Tsion in the early 14th century, and reverted to Muslim rule under Ahmed Gragn in the mid 16th century. The original Muslim state was renowned for producing high-quality cotton cloth, and also enjoyed a strong trade relationship with the Red Sea port of Zeila, in present-day Somaliland 500km to the northeast. It was also the base of 13th-century Arabian missionary Sheikh Hussein, a rather mysterious figure who is widely regarded to be the most important medieval proselytiser of Islam in the southern Ethiopian interior, and whose shrine in the lowlands about 100km northeast of the massif ranks among the country's most important Islamic pilgrimage sites. In 1942, the name of the former Muslim state was revived with the creation of Bale Province, which was centred on the eponymous mountains and governed from the town of Gobe prior to being split between the federal regions of Oromia and Somali in the administrative reshuffle of 1995.

FLORA AND FAUNA Bale protects a highly diverse flora. More than 1,300 species of flowering plant have been collected in BMNP, including 160 Ethiopian endemic species and 23 that are unique to the park. The dominant habitat type is Afroalpine moorland, which covers most of the northern slopes above 3,500m, including the Sanetti Plateau and Upper Web River Valley. In the far north, around the park headquarters at Dinsho, elevations of between 2,500m and 3,300m tend to support large tracts of juniper-hagenia woodland, while the Gaysay area, as passed through by the main road from Addis Ababa, is dominated by montane grassland. The slopes south of the Harenna Escarpment support the full spectrum of moist forest types: beautiful *Erica* forest at 3,800–3,400m, dense bamboo forest at 3,400–3,000m, and three altitudinal bands of evergreen Afromontane forest between the 3,000m and 1,700m contours. The moorland, as well as the open vegetation below the forest zone, is characterised by wonderful wild-flower displays, particularly between August and November. One of the most common and distinctive plants throughout the Bale region is the red-hot poker, an aloe-like shrub of the endemic African genus *Kniphofia*, identified by its spear-shaped orange, red and yellow flowers.

The Bale Mountains were one of the last parts of Africa to attract zoological exploration. The mountain nyala, for instance, remained unknown to science until 1908, despite its considerable bulk, fearless disposition and relative abundance in suitable habitats, and even then the type specimen collected by Ivor Buxton was shot in the mountains of Arsi rather than Bale. The earliest recorded visitor to the Sanetti Plateau was German naturalist Carl van Erlanger, who traversed it in 1899 and discovered the giant mole-rat in the process. Bizarrely, no further expedition to the upper slopes of Bale was documented between then and the late 1950s, when Finnish geographer Helmer Smels made several visits to the area, discovering – among other things – that the mountains hosted a previously unsuspected population of the rare Ethiopian wolf. It was British naturalist Leslie Brown who, upon visiting the mountains in 1963, first recognised that Bale might actually be the wolf's main stronghold, and it was he who proposed that the area be set aside as a national park. Only in 1974 did James Malcolm collect the first wolf census data to confirm Brown's suspicion that Bale hosted a significantly larger population of this endangered canid than the Simiens.

The favoured habitat of the Ethiopian wolf, as well as that of the giant mole-rat, which forms its main prey, are high-altitude moorlands such as the Sanetti and Web Valley. The wolves also sometimes stray into the juniper woodland around Dinsho, but large mammals more characteristic of this habitat include the endemic mountain nyala and Menelik's bushbuck, as well as warthog and bohor reedbuck. Commonly seen mammals of the extensive Harenna Forest include guereza, olive baboon, Menelik's bushbuck, bushpig and giant forest hog. The Bale monkey, a vulnerable species associated with bamboo thickets, is endemic to suitable habitats in the Harenna Forest. Large predators such as lion, leopard and possibly African wild dog are still resident in the park but are seldom seen by visitors. Less conspicuously, at least five rodent and three shrew species are endemic to the Bale Massif, along with four species of frog and two chameleons.

The African Birding Club recently named BMNP the continent's fourth-best birding site, on account of the exceptional wealth of rare and localised species among the 310 recorded. It is undoubtedly the best place in Ethiopia for endemic birds, with six full national endemics recorded alongside 11 species shared only with Eritrea, and several others unique to the Horn of Africa. BMNP is also the only known locality for the Bale parisoma, a recently described race of brown parisoma that many experts regard to be a full species. A casual visitor could hope to spot most of these endemics over the course of a few hours apiece at Dinsho and on the Sanetti Plateau. Endemics aside, Bale is a good place to pick up several localised highland birds and migrant waterfowl and raptors, and it supports isolated breeding populations of several other noteworthy species.

TOURIST INFORMATION AND GUIDES The **Bale Mountain Guides Association** (☏ *022 119 0758*; ▯ *0913 958802*; e *mohammed.worko13@gmail.com*) is situated at the entrance gate to the park headquarters at Dinsho, and its office functions as a one-stop shop for the payment of park fees, for obtaining reliable up-to-date advice about routes and facilities in the park, and for making all guiding, hiking and trekking arrangements. The entrance fee (*US$4 pp/24hrs, plus US$1/vehicle*) cannot be dealt with elsewhere, so travellers heading on to Sanetti or Harenna by road must stop here to pay and obtain a receipt, or they will be refused entry at the checkpoint between Goba and Sanetti. A local guide is not essential for self-drive trips to Gaysay, Sanetti or the Harenna Forest, but is mandatory for all hiking and horseriding treks. The members of the Guides Association were all thoroughly trained by the Frankfurt Zoological Society, and the going rate for their services is US$12 per party for a walk around the park headquarters, US$16 for a full-day excursion, and US$20 per day for overnight excursions. Under no circumstances should you make local guide arrangements elsewhere, or you run a high risk of ending up being taken around the mountains by an unqualified chancer.

Two excellent and unusually well-written booklets published in 2013 are theoretically sold at the Guides Association. The 76-page *Bale Mountains National Park Traveller's Guide* provides a very useful introduction to every aspect of the park, backing up the background information with useful practical detail and some great photos. The 52-page *Bale Mountains National Park Birding Booklet* provides

14

detailed information about the birding opportunities in the park, as well as a few key sites further south, and includes a complete and well-annotated checklist.

FISHING PERMITS Three of the park's rivers, the Denka, Web and Shaya, were stocked with rainbow and brown trout from Kenya during the late 1960s, and they still offer excellent fly fishing in a stunning wilderness setting. Three-day fishing permits can be bought in Dinsho for US$15, and fishing guides can be arranged by calling m 0911 333902. Anglers must bring all their own equipment and the catch is limited to five fish per person per day, with a minimum length limit of 25cm.

ORIENTATION There are two main access points to BMNP. The first, following the main surfaced road from Addis Ababa/Shashemene towards Goba, is the park headquarters at Dinsho, 1.5km east of the village of the same name. All hikes and horseback treks deeper into the park must be arranged at the Guides Association office, which lies 100m south of the main road at the entrance to the headquarters, and it is the only place where travellers driving to Sanetti can pay their entrance fees. The short but usually fruitful walking trail at the headquarters is the best place to look for mountain nyala and several species of forest birds. Continuing east from Dinsho along the surfaced road, it's about 30km to Bale Robe, which is now the largest town in the region, and has the best facilities for budget travellers, and another 12km to the former provincial capital Goba, site of the best mid-range hotel in the region. The second access point to the park lies about 15km south of Goba, where an all-weather road passes through a manned park checkpoint before summiting the northern escarpment of the Sanetti Plateau at its northern edge. This road runs across the plateau for about 25km before starting the descent to the village of Rira and upmarket Bale Mountain Lodge in the Harenna Forest.

GETTING THERE AND AWAY

By air Ethiopian Airlines resumed twice-weekly flights between Addis Ababa and Goba Airport (which, rather confusingly, lies about 5km east of Bale Robe off the road to Sof Omar) in late 2014, but suspended the service again in early 2015 to allow the dirt airstrip to be resurfaced. There have been several subsequent delays in the resumption of commercial flights, but the latest from Ethiopian Airlines, shortly before this edition went to print, is that the new runway and tower are finished, and flights are scheduled to resume in September 2018. Check our website w bradtupdates.com/ethiopia for further news. A helicopter pad at Bale Mountain Lodge has been used a few times by small groups of people.

By road Goba lies about 410km from Addis Ababa via Asela and Dodola, a drive that takes up to 8 hours in a private vehicle, and 200km from Shashemene via Dodola, a 3-hour trip. Should you be heading to Dinsho or Bale Robe, the drive will be slightly shorter, but if you intend to cross the Sanetti Plateau to stay in Bale Mountain Lodge, allow another 2 hours. A few kilometres before the road reaches Dinsho, it bisects BMNP's Gaysay sector, where you may see mountain nyala and even catch a glimpse of an Ethiopian wolf pack.

The best bus service from Addis Ababa, assuming the service has resumed by the time you read this, is the daily Selam Bus to/from Goba (*8hrs*), which can drop travellers at Dinsho village, at the entrance to the park headquarters 1.5km further on, or at Bale Robe. By normal bus, the trip will take a couple of hours more and costs slightly less. The minibus between Shashemene and Bale Robe (*3–4hrs*) can also drop you at Dinsho or the park headquarters. Several vehicles head back and forth daily between Bale Robe (which has taken over from Goba as the main regional transport hub in recent years) and Dodola (*2hrs*), Dinsho (*30–45mins*) and Goba (*15–20mins*).

The only direct road route south of Goba is the 275km all-weather dirt road to Negele Borena via the Sanetti Plateau, Harenna Forest and Dolo Mena. This could be driven in one day at a push, provided you got an early start, but most travellers who head this way are birders, who would almost certainly want to break up the trip over two or more days. Using public transport, up to ten buses daily run between Goba and Dolo Mena (*4–5hrs*).

A little-used but very scenic two-day 450km back route, suited only to travellers with their own 4x4 and camping gear, connects Awash National Park to Bale Robe via the spectacular Wabe Shebelle Gorge. It starts at Bordele, on the Dire Dawa road 28km east of Awash Saba, then runs southeast for about 50km, crossing the Agemetu Valley to Gelemso, from where a left turn at the main T-junction continues to Mechara, set below a tall forested mountain another 40km or so to the southwest. About 65km past Mechara, the road reaches the first of three gorges associated with the Wabe Shebelle River Gorge, then switchbacks downhill for 1,000m along narrow winding roads before crossing a bridge over the river and ascending to Dire Sheikh Hussein. Campers can either pitch a tent in the gorge or in the compound of the Culture and Tourism office in Dire Sheikh Hussein. The next day you could use the direct 175km road southwest to Bale Robe via Gasera, or head on south for 165km to Sof Omar Caves before driving 100km west to Bale Robe. For more information about Dire Sheikh Hussein, Sof Omar and Gasera, see from page 503.

GETTING AROUND

By car The three key sites – Dinsho park headquarters, Sanetti Plateau and the Harenna Forest – are all easily accessed in a private vehicle, ideally 4x4, though this may not be strictly necessary in the dry season. The Dinsho park headquarters is also readily accessible by public transport, since it lies right alongside the main surfaced road between Addis Ababa/Shashemene and Bale Robe. It is also possible to traverse the Sanetti Plateau and experience the thrilling descent into the Harenna Forest cheaply using one of the regular buses between Goba and Dolo Mena, though you'd have to be very lucky to see an Ethiopian wolf from a bus, as the latter tend to travel at speed. Another affordable possibility is to catch a Dolo Mena bus as far as Sanetti Campsite or Rira in the Harenna Forest, and spend a night or two there, first paying all fees in Dinsho and, as far as Sanetti Campsite is concerned, picking up a guide and, if necessary, camping gear there. The mandatory guide is not required for a stop in Rira. If you do this, try to get the earliest bus out of Goba, and be prepared to pay full fare to Dolo Mena. Be warned, too, that when you want to leave Sanetti or Rira, most passing traffic will be full, and there is no guarantee you will find a seat. It is generally easier to find transport out of the park in the morning than it is in the afternoon.

Hiking and trekking Time, fitness and tolerance for high altitudes and chilly climates permitting, the best way to explore Bale Mountains National Park is on foot or horseback using any of the designated campsites. Hiking routes range from the short and undemanding 2–3-hour Dinsho walking trail at the park headquarters to a seven-day circular hike or trek out of Dinsho taking in the Web Valley and Sanetti Plateau, or three days by sticking to the Web Valley. All hikes and horseback treks must be arranged through the Bale Mountain Guides Association at Dinsho (page 493).

Mandatory costs for Bale hikes are currently fixed at US$4 entrance per person per 24 hours, US$2 per tent camping per night and US$20 per party per day for the guide. An optional cook costs US$20 per day, and you can also pay him to buy all food (budget on US$7.50 per person per day), which is a lot simpler than doing it yourself. Camping gear can be hired at a negotiable nightly rate of US$7.50–10 per two-person tent, US$4–5 per sleeping bag and US$2–3 per roll-mat. No human porters are available, but horses can be rented for porterage at US$6 per day per animal, plus US$10 for the handler. If you don't walk back to Dinsho, you'll have to pay extra days for the guide or cook to get themselves back (unless they return in the car with you), as well as the horses and handlers. There is no water at the campsites and the cold northerly wind at altitudes of around 4,000m means you'll need some very warm clothes, including a waterproof windbreaker and a beanie or balaclava. Guides, cooks and horse handlers all expect tips; the equivalent of one day's fee seems to be the norm.

The most popular five- to seven-day itinerary is as follows:

Day One Ascend from Dinsho (3,100m) south to Sodota Campsite (3,500m) via the lovely Web Valley, home to plenty of Ethiopian wolves, and Fincha Habera Waterfall (*22km; 5–6hrs*)

Day Two Continue climbing southward to Keyrensa Campsite (3,750m), a rocky area frequented by klipspringers and rock hyrax (*20km; 4–5hrs*)

Day Three Head southeast to Rafu Campsite (3,990m) via the Rafu Valley, making a short diversion to a spectacular lava flow (*21km inc diversion; 4½–6hrs*)

Day Four Cross the Sanetti Plateau eastward, skirting the northern base of Tullo Deemtu, to Garba Guracha Campsite (3,950m) overlooking the lovely tarn of the same name, which lies in prime Ethiopian wolf territory (*18km; 5–6hrs*)

Day Five Be collected by minibus at Garba Guracha by prior arrangement, or ascend Bale's highest peak Tullo Deemtu (4,377m) via the Crane Lakes as a round day hike, camping at Garba Guracha for a second night (*24km; 6–7hrs*)

Day Six: Be collected by minibus at Garba Guracha by prior arrangement, or start heading back northward, overnighting at Worgona Campsite (3,950m), with a possible diversion to the peak of Mount Batu (4,203m) in the morning (*18km; 4–5hrs*)

Day Seven Descend northward to Dinsho along the Denka River (*21km; 5–6hrs*)

🏠 **WHERE TO STAY, EAT AND DRINK** Accommodation in and around BMNP is quite scattered and covered in greater detail from page 498. Backpackers can base themselves at the Dinsho park headquarters in a lovely campsite. It is supplemented by a few basic budget hotels in nearby Dinsho village. The small towns of Bale Robe and Goba are also viable bases for exploring the park, especially if you have a vehicle. Bale Robe has the better selection of budget offerings, but the top mid-range option is the Wabe Shebelle Hotel in Goba. Elsewhere in the park, non-camping options boil down to the superb upmarket Bale Mountain Lodge and a very basic budget lodge in the Harenna Forest (page 502). Possible future developments include the construction of private upmarket lodges at Dinsho and on the Sanetti Plateau.

Until such long-standing plans to build a network of mountain huts between Dinsho, the Web Valley and the Sanetti Plateau come to fruition, the only option for hikers heading beyond Dinsho is to camp at one of several designated campsites. These campsites have no facilities, and you must bring all of your own camping

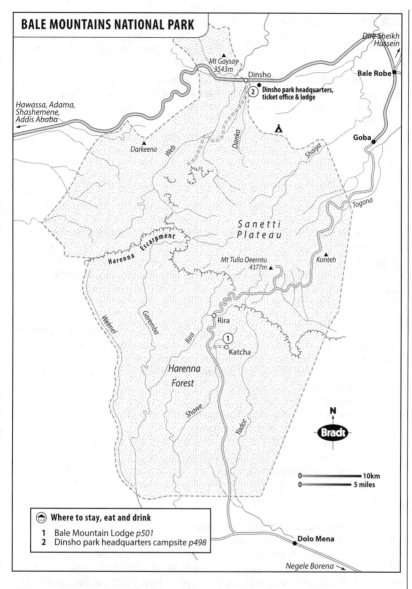

BALE MOUNTAINS NATIONAL PARK

Dire Sheikh Hussein

Mt Gaysay 3543m

Dinsho

Bale Robe

2 Dinsho park headquarters, ticket office & lodge

Hawassa, Adama, Shashemene, Addis Ababa

Darkeena

Web

Danka

Shaya

Goba

Togona

Sanetti Plateau

Harenna Escarpment

Mt Tullo Deemtu 4377m

Konteh

Welmel

Garemba

Rira

Rira

1 Katcha

Harenna Forest

Shawe

Yadot

N

Bradt

0   10km
0   5 miles

⊖ **Where to stay, eat and drink**

1   Bale Mountain Lodge *p501*
2   Dinsho park headquarters campsite *p498*

Dolo Mena

Negele Borena

equipment (which can be hired from the Guides Association) and food. Most of the campsites lack water too, so this needs to be carried with you. It is illegal to collect firewood within the park, but a stove or sustainable eucalyptus firewood can be arranged at the park entrance. There is a US$2 camping fee per tent.

If you plan to cross on foot directly from the Adaba-Dodola IFMP into the Bale Mountains National Park, one way or the other, arrangements should be made with either the **Dodola Eco-Tourism Guides Association** (page 490) in Dodola or the **Bale Mountain Guides Association** (page 493) in Dinsho. They will see that the necessary team of guides, eventually with horsemen and cooks, meet you on the other side of the crossing point close to the Duro IFMP mountain hut.

AROUND THE MOUNTAINS The following listings include the main sectors of the national park, as well as the towns of Bale Robe and Goba, and possible excursions to the Sof Omar Caves and Dire Sheikh Hussein in the lowlands east of Bale Robe.

Dinsho and the park headquarters The juniper-hagenia forest around the park headquarters and Dinsho Lodge, characterised by the herby aroma of fallen hagenia leaves, can be explored along the short but very rewarding Dinsho walking trail. This is a good place to look for the white-and-yellow bloom of *Rosa abyssinica*, Africa's only indigenous flowering rose. The light undergrowth allows for good game viewing. Dinsho supports Ethiopia's largest population of mountain nyala, and this exceptionally handsome antelope is abundant in the area – indeed, it's not unusual to come across four or five herds in the space of an hour. The superficially similar but much smaller and more solitary Menelik's bushbuck is common too, and you can also expect to see warthog, bohor reedbuck and possibly black-and-white colobus monkeys. Birdwatching around the headquarters is exceptional, although, as is often the case, you will probably see fewer birds in the forest proper than in fringe habitats, such as the broken woodland along the road between the entrance gate and the lodge. Common endemics and near-endemics include Abyssinian owl, black-winged lovebird, white-backed black tit, Abyssinian catbird, Abyssinian slaty flycatcher, thick-billed raven and white-collared pigeon, while other alluring forest birds include white-cheeked turaco, Abyssinian ground thrush, olive thrush and Cape eagle-owl.

The Ethiopian Wolf Conservation Programme's small **Natural History Museum** (w *ethiopianwolf.org*; ⊕ *08.00–17.00 Mon–Fri; entrance free*), 200m from Dinsho Lodge, displays a selection of tired-looking stuffed animals, including several endemics. At present, it is the only source of information on the natural history of Bale, with a focus on the endangered wolves and the programmes currently in effect to ensure their survival. It is hoped that it will eventually expand into a proper interpretation centre. In the meantime, the attached library is useful for researchers or anyone interested in Bale's flora and fauna.

The attractive montane village of Dinsho, recently uplifted by the arrival of electricity, straddles the Dodola–Bale Robe road 1.5km west of the park headquarters. It is distinguished only by its Tuesday market and the presence of a few basic but cheap hotels from where you could visit the park headquarters and explore its walking trail as a day trip.

 Where to stay, eat and drink Map, page 497

Dinsho Lodge Tucked away in the juniper forest at the park headquarters, this rustic old 1970s lodge was privatised some time back & closed in 2017 after years of decline. Prospects of it reopening in the near future are dim.

Mountain Nyala Pension (10 rooms) m 0912 007592. Comparatively new & situated in Dinsho village itself; rooms have en-suite toilet & shower. *US$8 sgl.* **$**

Dinsho campsite This basic campsite on a hill at the park headquarters offers panoramic views over Dinsho village & to several peaks. There is a long-drop toilet, but no available water on the spot. The hill is covered in heath-like vegetation & juniper forest, & there is plenty of wildlife to be seen. *US$2 per tent.* **$**

Balageru Restaurant m 0922 057428. Situated at the end of Dinsho town towards Bale Robe, this eatery specialises in meat dishes, *tibs* in particular (*US$3*). In addition to the usual Ethiopian fare, pasta & omelettes are also available for US$1.50.

Gaysay extension This northerly extension of Bale National Park protects the 3,543m Mount Gaysay, as well as some indigenous forest and an expanse of moist grassland that becomes quite marshy near the Gaysay River and Lake Bassasso. It is bisected for several kilometres by the Dodola road, starting about 3km west of Dinsho, making it highly accessible to travellers with limited time and without private transport. At least one Ethiopian wolf pack has a territory centred on the Gaysay extension, and it's a good place to view mountain nyala, Menelik's bushbuck and warthog. The spotted hyena is often seen in the early morning or at dusk, while serval can also be seen in the evenings. The marsh supports several bird species more normally associated with the Sanetti Plateau, most visibly Rouget's rail, which is very common here, and Abyssinian longclaw. Guided walks to Gaysay can be arranged at the park headquarters about an hour away on foot. It is also possible to hike to the top of Mount Gaysay.

Web River Valley Set at an elevation of roughly 3,500m some 10km southwest of Dinsho, the Web Valley supports a cover of low moorland similar in appearance to the Sanetti Plateau, albeit with a markedly different floral composition, dominated by herbaceous lady's mantle perennials of the genus *Alchemilla*. Abundant small rodents make the valley ideal territory for the Ethiopian wolf, several packs of which are resident and easily seen. A rough 11km track between Dinsho and the Web Valley takes about an hour to drive – 4x4 only – and involves crossing a natural rock bridge over the Denka River where rock hyrax are frequently observed. With an early start, it is possible to hike or trek to the Web Valley as a day trip out of Dinsho, stopping for a picnic lunch at the attractive Fincha Habera Waterfall. Most overnight hikes into Bale start with a hike through the Web Valley, overnighting at Sodota Campsite.

Sanetti Plateau The Sanetti Plateau (whose name derives from an Oromo phrase meaning 'place of strong winds' or more obtusely 'stunned cow', depending on whom you believe) is cited as the world's largest expanse of Afroalpine moorland, a montane habitat confined to altitudes of above 3,500m on East Africa's tallest mountains. Because such habitats are isolated from similar ones on other mountains, they tend to display a very high degree of endemism, and Sanetti is no exception. The plateau is renowned for supporting the world's most substantial population of Ethiopian wolf, while other characteristic mammals include golden jackal and klipspringer, neither of which is seen with great frequency, and smaller endemics such as Starck's hare and giant mole-rat. The plateau's dominant cover is clumped tussocks of subtly hued heathers interspersed with lichen-covered rocks, which give it a somewhat desolate and monotonous appearance when overcast, but accord it an ethereal beauty under blue skies, particularly in the soft light of early morning and late afternoon. A strange and striking plant unique to this and other Afroalpine habitats is the giant *Lobelia rynchopatelum*, which stands up to 6m tall, topped seasonally by a cluster of dark purple flowers, and whose corky bark and waxen leaves readily withstand extreme subzero temperatures.

The Sanetti Plateau can be driven to from Goba town in about 45 minutes. The road starts with a 1,300m hike in altitude, through tangled thickets and woodland where fields of red-hot poker point ever skywards. Look back, and the plains around Goba stretch to an indistinct horizon. For birders, forest patches along this road hold similar species to Dinsho, but are most notable as the best site for Bale parisoma, a small nondescript bird that can be quite unobtrusive and difficult to locate. Ascending above the forest zone, the alpine chat and endemic black-headed siskin are abundant, and moorland and chestnut-naped francolin often dart across the road. A few pairs of very confiding Rouget's rail are resident along the artificial

14

drainage stream that runs to the left of the road for about 1km. About 13km past Goba, the road levels out at around 4,000m, and you are surrounded by typical Afroalpine vegetation. Drive slowly, as the Ethiopian wolf is very common in this most northerly part of the plateau and often seen from the road, usually singly or in pairs sniffing out small rodents before they scurry to the safety of their burrows.

About halfway across the plateau the road skirts a series of crystal-clear tarns, where you can expect to see several endemic birds, as well as migrant waterfowl. At one or other of the tarns on the Sanetti Plateau, you can be confident of sighting the endemic blue-winged goose, wattled ibis and spot-breasted plover, as well as a representative of sub-Saharan Africa's only breeding population of ruddy shelduck and, in season, a number of migrant waterfowl. An isolated population of the localised wattled crane is present seasonally, and usually easy to observe when around. The variety of smaller birds is somewhat limited. Red-throated pipit, Thekla lark, Abyssinian longclaw and (seasonally) yellow wagtail are the common ground birds, while the lovely tacazze sunbird is often seen feeding on flowering aloes, and cinnamon bracken warbler is often seen in shrubby clumps of heather.

Raptors are very well represented on Sanetti. Commonest is the auger buzzard, sometimes seen in its localised melanistic phase. Kestrels and buzzards are quite conspicuous too: the rare saker falcon has been recorded three times on the plateau, though be aware that the more common lanner falcon here often has an unusually pale crown. Sanetti is a great place for large eagles. The tawny eagle is the most numerous of these, followed by the similar but darker steppe eagle. In 1993, it was discovered that Bale hosts what is presumably the only sub-Saharan breeding population of golden eagle, which is quite frequently seen. The otherwise uncommon imperial eagle is sometimes seen on the plateau during the northern winter. Sanetti also supports the only known sub-Saharan breeding population of the crow-like red-billed chough, which is usually seen foraging or flying low above the open vegetation.

In a private vehicle, a round trip to the plateau from Goba should take about 4 hours, depending on how long you choose to spend up there. You will also cross the plateau travelling between Goba and the new Bale Mountain Lodge. Travellers without a private vehicle can visit the plateau as part of a multi-day hike out of Dinsho, or on public transport between Goba and Dolo Mena.

Harenna Forest The second-largest forest in Ethiopia, Harenna comprises the entire southern half of BMNP and extends across large swathes of neighbouring community- and state-managed land to cover a total of more than 4,000km². Set on well-watered slopes descending southward from the Sanetti Plateau, it is a typical Afromontane cloudforest, denser and more overgrown than the juniper-hagenia woodland of the northern slopes, and it supports a far greater variety of trees. It also boasts very high levels of biodiversity and endemism, owing to its great altitudinal span and isolation from other similar habitats. Despite this, Harenna was practically unknown to science prior to 1983 when the Mengistu regime cut the all-weather road that connects Goba to Dolo Mena through the east side of BMNP.

Subsequent zoological expeditions have collected several previously undescribed amphibian and reptile species, including the tiny Harenna chameleon, and it is also the sole refuge of the bamboo-guzzling Bale monkey, but it seems likely that many other species await discovery. Surprisingly, the dense forest supports a relict population of dark-maned lions, which are seen with increasing frequency around Bale Mountain Lodge. The truly impressive giant forest hog – the world's largest swine species – is also seen with surprising regularity. Other large mammals resident in the forest include leopard, Anubis baboon, guereza monkey, bushbuck and bushpig, while the endangered African wild dog was seen as recently as 2011.

Harenna supports a wonderful variety of forest birds, with new records still coming in regularly as more birders explore the area. Endemics include white-backed black tit, Abyssinian catbird, Abyssinian woodpecker, Ethiopian oriole, yellow-fronted parrot and the taxonomically uncertain Bale parisoma and brown saw-wing swallow. It is the best place to see the tiny but very beautiful Abyssinian crimsonwing, while other conspicuous or desirable species include African cuckoo hawk, white-cheeked turaco, silvery-cheeked hornbill, brown-backed honeyguide, Abyssinian ground thrush, Abyssinian hill-babbler, Sharpe's starling, green-backed twinspot and yellow-bellied waxbill.

The main base for exploring Harenna is the small village of **Rira**, which lies 55km from Goba across the Sanetti Plateau. The last dramatic stretch of the road to Rira runs downhill from the southern end of the Sanetti Plateau, affording astounding views over the distant canopy, then switchbacks exhilaratingly through a beautiful Brothers Grimm forest of gnarled *Erica* trees laden with moss and swathed in old man's beard. There isn't much more to Rira than a small collection of mud huts set in a forest clearing, but it does now boast a small guesthouse, as well as lying only 8km north of Bale Mountain Lodge, which has done much to attract tourism to this once rather neglected part of the park since it opened in 2014.

Once at Rira, a short but lovely walking trail runs to a pair of pretty waterfalls tucked away in a bamboo-filled canyon west of the village. About 5km south of Rira in the direction of Bale Mountain Lodge, a curve in the road nicknamed Monkey Corner is a reliable site for the endemic Bale monkey, especially if you're prepared to walk a few hundred metres through the bamboo thickets immediately to its east. A more ambitious but very rewarding 3-hour round hike from Bale Mountain Lodge to the peak of Mount Gushuralle provides a good chance of seeing giant forest hog, various monkeys and a selection of forest birds. South of Bale Mountain Lodge, the road to Dolo Mena continues through the Harenna Forest for a further 40km or so, offering a good chance to see other forest wildlife, especially if you drive slowly in the early morning or later afternoon, and stop regularly to scan the forest for signs of life.

Where to stay, eat and drink

Bale Mountain Lodge [map, page 497] (11 rooms) m 0912 790802; e info@balemountainlodge.com; w balemountainlodge.com. Incontestably the best bush lodge anywhere in Ethiopia, this eco-friendly owner-managed gem, set at an altitude of 2,400m in the Harenna Forest 10km south of Rira, below a striking rocky prominence called Mt Gushuralle, has generated uniformly superlative feedback since it opened in 2014. The generous en-suite rooms are spaced around the property to ensure a sense of privacy & take advantage of the views, & all are attractively furnished using sustainable local materials & quality imported fittings. Three rooms have full disabled facilities. Electricity is sourced from a mini hydro-electric plant on a river running below the lodge, while drinking water is filtered from the source, & eco-friendly waste management policies include the recent installation of a small biogas plant. Knowledgeable guides are available to take visitors on a variety of activities ranging from hikes to a nearby waterfall or to the peak of Gushuralle (also nicknamed Elephant Mountain), to evening game drives, morning bird walks & day excursions to the Sanetti Plateau. The localised Bale monkey & awesome giant forest hog are frequently seen around the lodge, while a long list of avian specials regularly observed on morning bird walks includes African emerald cuckoo, Abyssinian catbird, Abyssinian hill-babbler & Abyssinian crimsonwing. Rates include 1 foot activity daily, excellent buffet meals & most drinks (tea, coffee, soft drinks, beer & house wine). *US$320 pp/night Oct–Apr & US$170 in other months.* **$$$$$**

Harenna Forest Hotel & Cultural Lodge (8 rooms) At the other end of the comfort scale, this locally run lodge in Rira offers basic, tired-looking & overpriced accommodation in traditional Sidama huts with ¾ beds. A small restaurant serves a few Ethiopian staples. Despite the steep price, it is worth considering as a budget base for exploring the Harenna Forest. *US$12/room.* **$**

Bale Robe Set at an altitude of 2,500m on the northeastern slopes of the Bale Massif, the bustling modern town of Bale Robe must be one of Ethiopia's fastest-growing settlements, barely recognisable today as the muddy eucalyptus-lined one-road backwater it was when the first edition of this guide was researched in 1994. It is of interest to tourists primarily as a potential base for exploring the nearby national park and more remote Sof Omar Caves and shrine to Sheikh Hussein, and offers the best range of budget accommodation in the area. Also of interest is the hectic Thursday market a block southeast of the bus station, as well as the **Bale Museum** (*022 665 1066;* ⊕ *08.00–17.00 Mon–Fri, assuming you can find someone to unlock it*) in the government buildings immediately north of the Bekele Molla Hotel.

Where to stay *Map, right*

Siko Mendo Hotel (30 rooms) *022 665 3060;* m *0910 981200.* The clean, modern en-suite rooms at this central new 3-storey hotel, a few hundred metres along the Sof Omar road, are currently the best in town. There's a 1st-floor vegetarian & alcohol-free restaurant serving Ethiopian & Western dishes, & a ground-floor café with good cakes, juice & coffee. A good bet overall. *US$15/25/30 B&B sgl/dbl/twin.* **$$–$$$**

Bekele Molla Hotel (24 rooms) *022 665 0065.* Clearly signposted on the Goba side of town between the bus station & main roundabout, this faded hotel remains a pretty attractive option, with large & airy en-suite rooms set around an overgrown grassy

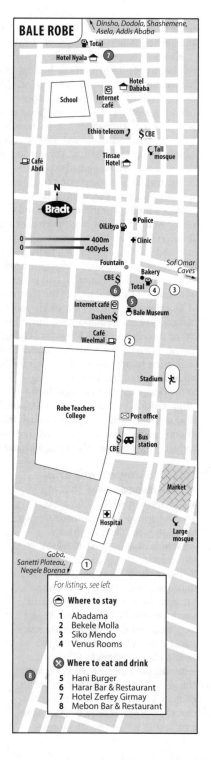

BALE ROBE

Dinsho, Dodola, Shashemene, Asela, Addis Ababa

Total
Hotel Nyala 7
Hotel Dababa
School | Internet café
Ethio telecom | $CBE
Café Abdi | Tinsae Hotel | Tall mosque
N
OiLibya | Police
0 400m
0 400yds
Fountain | Clinic
Sof Omar Caves
CBE $ | Bakery
6 | Total 4 | 3
Internet café | 5
Dashen $ | Bale Museum
Café Weelmal | 2
Stadium
Robe Teachers College
Post office
$ CBE | Bus station
Market
Hospital
Large mosque
Goba, Sanetti Plateau, Negele Borena | 1
8

For listings, see left

⌂ **Where to stay**
1 Abadama
2 Bekele Molla
3 Siko Mendo
4 Venus Rooms

✕ **Where to eat and drink**
5 Hani Burger
6 Harar Bar & Restaurant
7 Hotel Zerfey Girmay
8 Mebon Bar & Restaurant

compound. The restaurant serves adequate Ethiopian & Western dishes. *US$10/15/55 sgl/dbl/large presidential suite.* **$$**

 Abadama Hotel (23 rooms) 022 865 0260. Located south of the centre, this 2-storey hotel has clean but now rather rundown en-suite rooms with simple modern furnishings & hot shower. There's no restaurant, only a small café.

US$10/15 dbl/twin. **$–$$**

Venus Rooms (14 rooms) 022 665 2141. This tidy 1st-floor guesthouse is located opposite the flashy Café Parpili along a small side street that starts beside the Total petrol station on the road to the Siko Mendo Hotel. Despite its ambiguous name, it has decent en-suite rooms. *US$7.50 sgl with ¾ bed.* **$**

✕ Where to eat and drink *Map, opposite*

✕ **Hani Burger** This colourful café serves burgers, sandwiches & various Ethiopian staples, as well as *ful* or eggs for b/fast.

✕ **Harar Bar & Restaurant** Situated opposite Hani Burger, the place is a busy local eatery recommended for *tibs.*

✕ **Mebon Bar & Restaurant** On the road leading out of town towards Goba, this spectacular new garden restaurant serves quality dishes in the US$2–4 range. Toilets are unfortunately rustic.

♀ **Hotel Zerfey Girmay** Draught & bottled beer are served at this agreeable garden bar.

Goba
Separated from more northerly Bale Robe by a mere 10km of asphalt, Goba is a green, chilly, damp and rather subdued little town set at an altitude of 2,750m at the base of the main approach road to the Sanetti Plateau. Goba served as the capital of Bale Province from 1942 to 1995, but recent years have seen it supplanted by Bale Robe as Bale's main transport hub and population centre. Its main tourist asset is the out-of-town Wabe Shebelle Hotel, which offers excellent value for money in the mid-range category. A short distance along the road to Sanetti, the 2.5ha **Bale Beauty Nature Club** (m *0913 470100*; e *bbnclub@gmail.com*) is a community-run nature reserve centred on a tree nursery site that raises indigenous seedlings for local distribution.

🏠 Where to stay *Map, page 504*

🏠 **Goba Wabe Shebelle Hotel** (51 rooms) 022 661 0041. Set in large peaceful gardens about 1km back along the road to Bale Robe, this rather time-warped former government hotel is easily the nicest place to stay in Goba or Bale Robe, especially now that the once hyper-inflated *faranji* rates have been reduced to a more reasonable level. A busy restaurant/bar with Wi-Fi serves the usual Ethiopian fare supplemented by roasts, steak & pasta, in the US$2–4 range. The en-suite rooms are large & clean & have hot water & sat TV. *US$18/24 B&B dbl/twin (or US$60 for an immense salon).* **$$$**

Tweens Pension (10 rooms) Situated next to a CBE branch on the main roundabout, 2mins' walk from the bus station, this odd-looking place is the pick of a few otherwise dismal cheapies in Goba. *US$8 pp.* **$**

✕ Where to eat and drink *Map, page 504*

✕ **Harena Coffee Shop** m 0934 737373; e harenatradingplc@gmail.com; . Attractive & clean, this new popular tearoom-like café has a pleasant menu with sandwiches, pizza, pasta, burgers & salads in the US$1–4 range. A busy internet café is located on the 1st floor.

✕ **Nyala Pastry/Kiiya Juice** Situated side by side opposite the bus station, they serve freshly baked bread, cakes or coffee for the one, & a variety of good-looking fruit juices for the other.

Gasera
Situated 57km from Bale Robe by road, the small town of Gasera offers a magnificent viewpoint over the Wabe Shebelle Gorge, whose 1,000m-high cliffs support Ethiopia's most southerly population of Hamadryas baboon. To get there, follow the Dinsho road out of Bale Robe for 6km, then turn northward

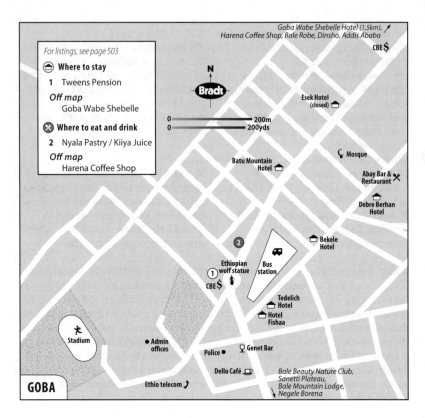

For listings, see page 503

Goba Wabe Shebelle Hotel (1.5km),
Harena Coffee Shop, Bale Robe, Dinsho, Addis Ababa

CBE $

Where to stay

1 Tweens Pension

Off map
Goba Wabe Shebelle

Where to eat and drink

2 Nyala Pastry / Kiiya Juice

Off map
Harena Coffee Shop

Esek Hotel
(closed)

Mosque

Batu Mountain
Hotel

Abay Bar &
Restaurant

Debre Berhan
Hotel

Bekele
Hotel

Ethiopian
wolf statue

Bus
station

CBE $

Tedelich
Hotel

Hotel
Fishaa

Stadium

Admin
offices

Police

Genet Bar

Dello Café

Bale Beauty Nature Club,
Sanetti Plateau,
Bale Mountain Lodge,
Negele Borena

Ethio telecom

GOBA

0 — 200m
0 — 200yds

N

on to a reasonable dirt road that leads through the small market town of Ali after another 10km. Turn right at the main intersection in Ali, and it's another 40km to Gasera.

Sof Omar Caves (*Negotiable entrance fee of US$20 levied by the caretaker*) This vast network of limestone caverns, reputedly the largest in Africa, lies at an elevation of 1,300m in the medium-altitude plains east of Bale Robe. It has been carved by the Web River, which descends from the Bale Highlands to the flat, arid plains that stretch towards the Somali border. Following the course of the clear aquamarine Web River underground for some 16km, the caves are reached through a vast portal that leads into the Chamber of Columns, a cathedral-like hall studded with limestone pillars that stand up to 20m high. A 1.7km trail leads from the entrance through several other chambers, taking about an hour to walk and crossing the river seven times. The caves are named after Sheikh Sof Omar, a 12th-century Muslim leader who used them as a refuge, and they remain an important site of pilgrimage for Ethiopian Muslims. Their religious significance can, however, be dated back further to the earliest animist religions of the area.

Sof Omar is regularly visited by birdwatchers because it is one of two sites where it's reasonably easy to see Salvadori's serin, a threatened and localised dry-country endemic with a bold yellow throat. The serin can be elusive, but the area holds several other good acacia-scrub species, notably orange-bellied parrot, blue-naped mousebird, Abyssinian scimitar-bill, sulphur-breasted bush-shrike, small grey flycatcher, brown-tailed chat, brown-tailed apalis, bristle-crowned and Fischer's starling, and Somali tit. Greater and lesser kudu are both common in the dry acacia scrub around Sof Omar, as is Salt's dik-dik.

Sof Omar lies about 100km from Bale Robe, a 2-hour drive in a private vehicle, along a good dirt road branching east at the town's main junction. Using public transport, you should have no problem finding transport as far as the small town of Goro, 58km east of Bale Robe. However, the only day when you can continue from Goro to Sof Omar on public transport is Saturday, the main market day. Best, therefore, would be to head out to Goro on Friday, spend the night at a basic hotel there, then catch the first transport to Sof Omar the next morning.

The area around Sof Omar is prone to occasional outbreaks of fighting between the local Oromo and Somali, so ask about security at the BMNP headquarters before heading out. During the rainy season you should also enquire about high water, which can render the caves impassable.

Dire Sheikh Hussein This village on the bank of the Wabe Shebelle River about 175km from Bale Robe is the site of the most important landmark in the northeast of Bale: a whitewashed dome shrine to Muslim proselytiser Sheikh Hussein ibn Malka, who is credited with converting the Bale Oromo. Undoubtedly a genuine historical figure, Sheikh Hussein is also shrouded in local legend, which claims that he was born in the 12th century, lived for 250 years, and spent the last 70 of them working miracles in the mosque later converted to become his shrine. The sheikh is still venerated by certain Muslim communities in Ethiopia, Somalia and Kenya, and his shrine is the target of two important pilgrimages, which attract thousands of chanting worshippers. These take place in June to commemorate the anniversary of the death of Sheikh Hussein, and in October to celebrate the birth of the Prophet Muhammad, the exact dates of which are determined by the lunar calendar. A direct 175km route to Dire Sheikh Hussein runs northeast from Bale Robe via Gasera, but it is also possible to use a longer (265km) route through Sof Omar Caves. There is no accommodation in Dire Sheikh Hussein, but you can camp in the compound of the Culture and Tourism office. From Dire Sheikh Hussein, it takes a full day to drive north to Awash National Park via the Wabe Shebelle Gorge (page 495). Ondřej Hanouse, a reader of the previous edition, writing in 2016, adds:

It is possible to get to Dire Sheikh Hussein on public transport. A bus runs to Dire from Jara. To Jara, you can get from Ginnir/Delo en route from Sof Omar (unpredictable), or directly from Bale Robe easily. The bus from Jara is very hard to predict. I waited for more than a day and in the end went with some guy on a motorbike instead. The buses are tied to the market days in Jara (Saturday, Tuesday) and Mechara, but it is not a 100%-safe rule. On the other hand, if the demand is high enough, there is even more than one bus. They start late afternoon from Jara and go through the night to arrive in Mechara in the morning and vice-versa. Price is around US$6, but you can also go on the back of a truck for the same price if you arrange it, which is definitely more adventurous and you get amazing freedom of looking around (the gorge is breathtaking even during a night without any moon). I have also seen one bus arrive to Dire from Jara only (not going further), but I have no clue how that runs.

In Dire itself, ask to be taken to the petrified praying chamber. It is in the side of one of the Wabe Shebelle cliffs, and it is a small grotto enclosed by petrified roots of ancient trees, covered in crystals. It is very small, but probably one of the most amazing things I have ever seen in my life.

Of interest primarily to dedicated birdwatchers, a rather remote route running south from the Harenna Forest to Yabello via Dolo Mena and Negele Borena offers the opportunity to tick off several localised endemics, notably the iconic Ruspoli's turaco, along with a number of species associated with the Somali border area. The first part of the route could also be used by backpackers as an alternative exit from the Harenna Forest, heading south as far as Negele Borena, then bussing back to Hawassa along a newly surfaced road through Adola. It is an area of considerable climatic and vegetational contrasts, with highland areas such as Harenna and Adola supporting large tracts of montane forest, while the arid lower-lying plains running east from Negele Borena and Yabello support a bleak cover of dry acacia scrub. On the whole, facilities are quite basic, though Negele Borena itself has a couple of decent budget hotels.

DOLO MENA After traversing the Sanetti Plateau and Harenna Forest, arriving in hot and dusty little Dolo Mena could hardly fail to be anticlimactic. Indeed, the tone of this small town takes some getting used to after a few days in the Bale Highlands: dusty acacia scrub replaces lush cultivated fields, camels throng a busy marketplace where locally grown *khat* and coffee beans are sold for distribution countrywide (Wednesday is the main market day), and their skimpily dressed Somali owners replace the blanketed horsemen of the highlands. A notable feature of the surrounding dry countryside is the localised succulent *Pyrenacantha malvifolia*, whose nickname 'monkey's chair' refers to its enormous caudex, a swollen water-storing tuber that has a diameter of up to 1.5m and sits above the ground like a spherical rock. Although Dolo Mena has little to hold travellers, and facilities are rather limited, southbound backpackers may well end up having to spend the night before they continue on to Negele Borena.

Getting there and away Dolo Mena lies less than 2 hours south of Bale Mountain Lodge in a private vehicle, a round trip undertaken by most keen birders staying at the lodge as it offers excellent access to the Harenna Forest. Using public transport, up to ten buses daily run between Goba and Dolo Mena (*US$2.75; 4–5hrs*) via Rira. Continuing south from Dolo Mena, there are direct buses to Negele Borena (*US$4; 6hrs*), but they operate on Wednesday and Sunday only. On other days, you would need to change vehicles at Bidire, but should still get through in a day with an early start.

🏠 Where to stay, eat and drink

🏠 **Hotel Bassufigaad** (10 rooms) ☎ 022 668 0053; m 0912 015960. Quite possibly the best thing to happen to Dolo Mena on the hotel front since the dawn of time, this new place around the corner from the market & bus station has a few rooms with a ¾ bed & en-suite cold showers. *US$4 sgl or dbl occupancy.* **$**

🏠 **Ganat Hotel** (12 rooms) m 0912 339290. About the best of Dolo Mena's older lodgings, this scruffy hotel opposite the Bassufigaad has basic rooms using common showers & a friendly English-speaking owner prepares simple but tasty local dishes. *US$3 dbl.* **$**

🏠 **Yenya Hotel** (10 rooms) m 0911 206421. This recent addition to the palette of local accommodation is situated 100m beyond the Ganat Hotel. The rooms have en-suite cold showers & common squat toilets. *US$6 sgl or dbl occupancy.* **$**

✖ **Family Siga Beit** Clearly visible at the entrance of Dolo Mena coming from the Harenna Forest, the restaurant serves good *tibs* and other Ethiopian dishes. *US$2–3.*

RUSPOLI'S TURACO

Perhaps the most eagerly sought of all Ethiopia's endemic birds is the green-and-scarlet turaco named after Prince Eugenio Ruspoli, the Italian explorer who collected the first specimen shortly before he was trampled to death by an elephant in a hunting accident in Somalia in December 1893. The specimen was taken to Europe and formally described in 1896, but the prince left no record of where it had been found, ensuring that its distribution and habitat remained an enigma to scientists until the early 1940s, when the first live specimen was recorded in the Arero Forest, 80km east of Yabello. Another 30 years would pass before a second population of the turaco was found at Genale. Several other sites have subsequently been discovered in the southeast of Ethiopia, and it is now thought to be commoner than was previously supposed. Today, this frugivore's known range extends over 12,000km², and the total population is thought to approach 10,000, since it is surprisingly habitat tolerant, and might be seen in any tall wooded area with fruiting trees. Nevertheless, it is vulnerable to deforestation, which appears to have led to an increase in hybridisation with the more widespread white-cheeked turaco, from which it can be distinguished by its floppy white crest. Still, the outlandish appearance of *Tauraco ruspolii*, combined with its unusual history and localised distribution, ensures that it still ranks as perhaps the most prized of Ethiopia's regularly observed endemic birds.

BIDIRE This relatively substantial town about 75km south of Dolo Mena is where southbound travellers will most likely need to change buses for Negele Borena. These run throughout the day, but in the unlikely event that you get stuck overnight, the Hotel Balbala opposite the CBE looks acceptable as these things go.

GENALE Perched on the south bank of the Genale River about 40km south of Bidire and 50km northeast of Negele Borena, this small town is renowned among birders as one of the most reliable sites to see the endemic Ruspoli's turaco. Unexpectedly, perhaps, the bird is seldom seen from the bridge over the perennial Genale River as it flows past town, but is commoner at two other nearby sites on the main road. These are the wide but normally dry riverbed spanned by a large bridge about 3km south of the Genale River, and a narrower watercourse crossed by a smaller bridge 14km north of the river. At both sites, the turaco is most likely to be observed in fruiting fig trees, and it is also occasionally seen in similar habitats between the two bridges. Informal local guides who know the turaco's habits might sometimes emerge at either site, but this cannot be relied upon. Other interesting species sometimes seen in the area include black sparrow-hawk, Narina trogon, Bruce's green pigeon and the highly localised white-winged dove and Juba weaver. There is no accommodation in Genale, but plenty of public transport runs back and forth from Negele Borena, making the bridge south of town a feasible goal for a day trip.

NEGELE BORENA Something of a throwback to Ethiopia as it was in the 1990s, Negele (often referred to as Negele Borena to avoid confusion with its namesake in Arsi) is a substantial town undermined by an aura of dusty impermanence reinforcing its long-standing status as a frontier town verging the arid badlands of the Somali Region. Its unique cultural blend of Oromo, Somali and Borena influences is personified by one of Ethiopia's most lively and absorbing markets, with activity peaking on Saturday, when camels and other livestock are sold. Negele isn't a town you'd go out of your way to visit, but it makes for a convenient stopover between the Bale Mountains and Yabello or Hawassa, as well as being a key overnight stop for birders seeking the localised Ruspoli's turaco and Liben lark.

History Founded in the early 20th century as the closest Ethiopian outpost to what was then the Juba Region of Italian Somaliland, Negele – rather ironically, given that its name literally means 'Peace' – has a long history of military engagement. It was the base from which Ras Desta Damtew launched an attack on the Italians at Dolo Odo in October 1935, and was razed three months later in a retaliatory bombardment led by General Graziani. In the 1960s, Negele served as the military base from which imperial troops attempted to quell the Bale Peasant Movement orchestrated out of Goba by Oromo leader Waqo Gutu. The Negele Rebellion of January 1974, wherein the NCOs and enlists of the Fourth Brigade arrested their commanding officers in protest against their terrible living conditions, then imprisoned a high-ranking investigator sent by the imperial government and forced him to eat and drink as they did, is now widely regarded to be the catalyst that led to the military overthrow of Haile Selassie in September that year. In August 1977, the Somali Army attempted to capture Negele, but was repelled by the local garrison. More recently, on the evening of 28 May 2008, the 17th anniversary of the overthrow of the Derg, a pair of bombs exploded a few minutes apart at two hotels in Negele, killing three people and injuring another five (the perpetrator has never been confirmed, though Somali jihadists claimed responsibility at the time).

Today, Negele Borena is the administrative capital of Guji Zone, which was created in 2002 from what was formerly the northern part of Borena Zone, and it supports a population of around 40,000.

Getting there and away Negele lies 590km southeast of Addis Ababa along a good surfaced road passing through Modjo, Shashemene, Hawassa, Adola (formerly Kebre Mengist) and Bitata. With a private car, you could drive through in a day at a push, and there is also one daily bus in either direction (*10hrs*), leaving at around 06.00. More useful perhaps to the average traveller leaving Negele Borena are the two daily buses to Hawassa (*5hrs*) and Shashemene (*5½hrs*), which also leave at around 06.00. If you miss these buses, minibuses for Adola leave throughout the day (*2hrs*), and it is easy enough to pick up transport to Hawassa from there.

Coming from the direction of Goba, a 275km road leads to Negele via Bale National Park, Dolo Mena, Bidire, Genale and Bitata (the latter being the junction with the main road to/from Adola and Hawassa). The road is unsurfaced for most of its length, the exception being the 20km of asphalt between Bitata and Negele. In a private vehicle, you could cover this route in a day, though this would be rather self-defeating were your objective to explore Bale National Park on the way. Using public transport, you'd most likely need to change vehicles and probably crash overnight at Dolo Mena, and would need to change vehicles again at Bidire, except on Wednesday and Sunday when direct buses run to Negele.

The rough and rutted 300km road directly connecting Negele to Yabello is unlikely to do any favours to anybody with a susceptible back, nor will it hold much of interest to the average traveller, but it is followed by almost all serious birdwatching tours through Ethiopia. With an early start, it can be covered in a day, but there is some basic accommodation in Arero, some 180km from Negele, should you want to break up the trip. It is worthwhile asking at the bus station for transport along this road, and

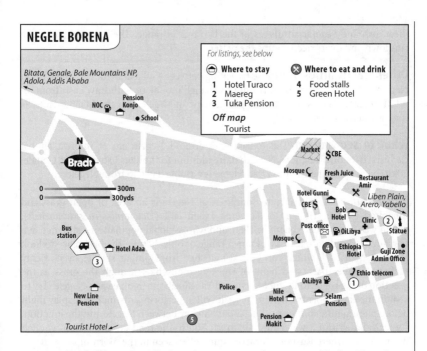

NEGELE BORENA

For listings, see below

🛏 **Where to stay**
1 Hotel Turaco
2 Maereg
3 Tuka Pension

Off map
Tourist

❌ **Where to eat and drink**
4 Food stalls
5 Green Hotel

Bitata, Genale, Bale Mountains NP, Adola, Addis Ababa

NOC
Pension Konjo
School
Bradt
0 ___ 300m
0 ___ 300yds
Bus station
Hotel Adaa
New Line Pension
Police
Tourist Hotel
Market
CBE
Mosque
Fresh Juice
Restaurant Amir
Hotel Gunni
CBE
Bob Hotel
Clinic
Statue
Post office
OiLibya
Mosque
Ethiopia Hotel
Guji Zone Admin Office
Ethio telecom
OiLibya
Nile Hotel
Selam Pension
Pension Makit
Liben Plain, Arero, Yabello

occasional pick-up trucks will also take passengers for a negotiable fee. These leave from the market at around 06.00, and the 300km ride takes a full day.

🛏 Where to stay *Map, above*
Budget
🛏 **Maereg Hotel** (32 rooms) ☎046 445 0108; m 0911 985059. This unsignposted 3-storey hotel on the roundabout opposite the Guji Zone Administration Office is easily the smartest in town, & the clean en-suite rooms come with nets & TV, but it's poor value at the inflated & inflexible *faranji* price, especially as the staff are unfriendly & speak no English, there's no restaurant or bar, & the billed hot water was unavailable on our latest inspection. *US$32/46 sgl/dbl.* **$$$**

🛏 **Hotel Turaco** (20 rooms) m 0911 373115, 0912 986324. The current 1st choice of most birding tours, this central 3-storey hotel, set in small green gardens, has acceptable en-suite rooms with net & hot water, though they are due a lick of paint. It also seems overpriced at the tourist

rate, especially as there's no restaurant, bar or Wi-Fi, but the staff are friendly & do speak a bit of English. *US$25 dbl, with some scope for negotiation.* **$$$**

Shoestring
🛏 **Tuka Pension** (8 rooms) m 0926 361319. The best-value lodge in Negele, this quiet & friendly pension close to the bus station has spotless, bright en-suite rooms with nets, sat TV & hot water. *US$6 dbl.* **$**

🛏 **Tourist Hotel** (11 rooms) m 0913 097888. Endowed with a large & pleasant garden, fair restaurant, shaded terraces, children's playground & a good view over the surrounding landscape, this is a good alternative to the Tuka pension. *US$6 for en-suite sgl room.* **$**

❌ Where to eat and drink *Map, above*
The row of food stalls two blocks west of the Ethiopia Hotel is well worth exploring – good *ful* and eggs in the morning, *shiro* and *injera* later in the day, and fresh coffee whenever the mood takes you.

The garden bar at the once-popular **Green Hotel** (☎046 445 0374) has a great atmosphere, and serves cheap draught beer along with a good selection of tasty meat, fish and vegetarian dishes in the US$1–2.50 range. The less said about the rundown and overpriced rooms the better.

Other practicalities For those travelling between Goba and Yabello, the CBE in Negele will be your one opportunity to change money or withdraw cash from an ATM. Internet access seems to be problematic in Negele, and the Maereg Hotel is the only place to offer Wi-Fi.

What to see and do The tourist sites around Negele are of interest almost exclusively to birdwatchers. Note that, in addition to the sites listed below, Genale, 50km back along the road to Dolo Mena, is a viable day trip from Negele.

Liben Plain The Liben Plain southeast of Negele is an area of open grassland inhabited by the critically endangered Liben lark (*Heteromirafra sidamoensis*), which was first collected here in 1968, and whose global population, estimated at a few hundred individuals, has a known range of only 30km^2. The best place to look for this small bird, which can be distinguished from similar species by its richly scalloped upper parts and habit of running mouselike through the grass, is the junction of the roads to Bogol Manyo and Yabello about 13km east of Negele. Try to visit in the early morning, when the males often perform a distinctive display flight before plummeting to the ground. About halfway between Negele and the junction, some 250m east of a watering hole to the south, the road crosses a well-wooded drainage line where Ruspoli's turaco is quite often seen in the morning.

Wadera This small town 60km from Negele along the road to Adola (Kebre Mengist) is the gateway to a highland area that still supports several large tracts of montane forest and most bird species associated with that habitat, including Narina trogon, yellow-fronted parrot and silvery-cheeked hornbill. It is also an excellent habitat for Ruspoli's turaco, which can be seen practically anywhere along the road between Wadera and Adola, but is particularly common in the wooded valley to the west of the road about 2.5km before you enter Wadera coming from the direction of Negele.

Abake Forest Sprawling across 25km^2 of highland slopes to the south of Adola (Kebre Mengist), this lush montane forest is home to guereza and grivet monkeys, as well as a wide variety of birds, including Ruspoli's turaco. The forest is also very accessible, since the 20km surfaced road between Adola and the mushrooming gold-mining settlement of Shikiso runs through it for several kilometres, and is traversed by regular minibuses. The least encroached-upon patch of forest starts about 1km past the Abake Forest Station in the direction of Shikiso.

YABELLO VIA MELKA GUDA AND ARERO Best driven over two days, the 300km dirt road connecting Negele to Yabello passes through a region of dry scrubby plains alleviated by a trio of excellent birding sites. The first of these, the Liben Plain, is covered above. The next, roughly 120km out of Negele, is the bridge across the Dawa River just past the small town of Melka Guda. This is a reliable place to pick up two species whose ranges are restricted to southeast Ethiopia and neighbouring Somalia: white-winged turtle dove and Juba weaver. Even if you miss these jackpots, a host of other good birds are common, notably black-bellied sunbird, golden pipit, Pringle's puffback, red-naped bush-shrike and bare-eyed thrush.

Another excellent place to stop, and possibly spend a night, is Arero, which lies about 60km past Melka Guda near to the most southerly forest in Ethiopia.

Local specials are headed by two endemics, the beautiful Ruspoli's turaco and rare Salvadori's seedeater, both of which are fairly common around there. More than 160 birds have been recorded in all, as has a fair variety of large mammals, notably bushbuck, bushpig and guereza monkey – even the occasional lion and leopard. Once through Arero, a wide variety of dry-country species includes the endemic Stresemann's bush crow and white-tailed swallow, along with black-capped social weaver, grey-headed silver-bill, Archer's grey-wing and little spotted woodpecker.

SOUTH TOWARDS MOYALE

The 500km road that runs south from Hawassa to the Kenyan border provides access to several worthwhile cultural, archaeological and ornithological attractions. The largest town through which it passes, and the first coming from the north, the relaxed agricultural hub of Dilla is known for its ancient rock engravings and medieval stelae fields. Further south, Yabello, set among low-lying acacia scrub populated by colourful Borena pastoralists and their cattle, is home to two of Ethiopia's most

STELAE OF SOUTHERN ETHIOPIA

An estimated 10,000 stelae (obelisks) are scattered across the south of Ethiopia, extending in a rough belt starting in Tiya (a UNESCO World Heritage Site) then running southeast to the vicinity of Negele Borena. Little concrete is known about the origin of these stelae or the societies that erected them. Local tradition attributes the erection of these so-called 'Gragn Stones' to 15th-century Muslim leader Ahmed Gragn, but the formative findings of archaeologist Roger Joussaume indicate that they are much older than this, having been erected over a 400-year period starting in the 9th century.

Two broad types of stele are recognised. The earlier style, dating from the 9th century onwards, comprises phallic stelae, whose cylindrical shape and incised rounded top leave little room for ambiguity about what they represent. The later anthropomorphic stelae, thought to date to the 12th century, typically have a more flattened shape and are engraved with symbolic human features, though many are cylindrical and were clearly modified from older phallic examples. Both types appear to have served as grave-markers, but while the bodies beneath the phallic stelae were generally buried in a foetal position, those below the anthropomorphic stelae were buried flat on their back.

Ethiopia's greatest concentration of stelae lies around Dilla, where 50 different sites have been identified in Gedeo Zone. Of the two largest, Tututi is comprised almost exclusively of phallic stelae, whereas Tutu Fela is dominated by the anthropomorphic type. Outside of Gedeo, the well-known stelae at Tiya and Silté, most likely erected at a later date than those further south, are flattened in the anthropomorphic style, but were carved with far greater sophistication and more abstract symbols.

It is not known to what extent these mysterious medieval grave-markers influenced the decorated tombstones still erected today by the Oromo, who are relatively recent arrivals to the area and might well have displaced the original stelae-erecting society. There are also some parallels between the stelae of Gedeo and the anthropomorphic wooden grave-markers of the Konso – who, interestingly, retain an oral tradition suggesting that they might have migrated to their present homeland from the eastern Rift Valley Escarpment around Dilla.

14

localised avian endemics, white-tailed swallow and Stresemann's bush crow, as well as being the junction for a regularly used route running west to Konso and South Omo. Popular excursions from Yabello include the Borena village of Dublock, known for its so-called singing wells, as well as the bizarre Lake Chew Bet, a small saline body of water set at the base of an immense volcanic crater. Finally, some 210km southeast of Yabello, via one of the loneliest roads in the country, the remote border town of Moyale is of interest only to travellers crossing to or from Kenya.

The Moyale road runs through one of the country's most important coffee-, vegetable- and fruit-growing areas, and provides access to an alternative and much-needed maritime outlet at Mombasa in Kenya. It is, therefore, difficult to understand why it is in such a terrible state of disrepair. Major roadworks, a constant feature for many years, only seem to make the situation worse. At present, it takes more than 3 hours to travel the 85km road from Hawassa to Dilla, and the conditions are not much improved beyond Dilla.

DILLA Bustling, breezy Dilla, the administrative capital of the SNNPR's Gedeo Zone, is an important centre of agriculture set amid the fertile green mountains of the eastern Rift Valley Escarpment. Renowned for producing high-quality coffee of the fêted Yirgacheffe varietal, the surrounding slopes are still covered in patches of indigenous forest interspersed with rustic homesteads and small *enset* plantations. It is also a thriving university town, thanks to the expansion of the original Dilla College of Teachers' Education, founded in 1996, to the massive Dilla University, which is split across three campuses and has a student population of more than 15,000. Dilla is a pleasant if unremarkable town, not unattractive from whichever direction you approach it, but for northbound travellers coming from the dusty badlands of the Ethiopia–Kenya border region it must – both literally and

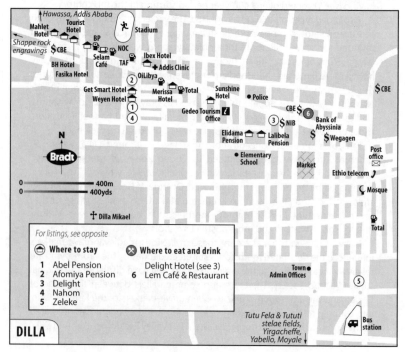

figuratively – come as a breath of fresh air. It is also a good place to break up the two-day trip between Addis Ababa and the border town of Moyale, and the best base from which to visit a number of important archaeological sites, including two major stelae fields and some fine prehistoric rock carvings.

Getting there and away Dilla lies 85km south of Hawassa along a severely deteriorating surfaced road with several sections now dominated by gravel, potholes and endless roadworks. Allow up to 3 hours in a private vehicle, slightly longer in one of the minibuses that run back and forth throughout the day. Alternatively, a few direct buses to/from Addis Ababa (*8–9hrs*) leave at 06.00 daily. Heading south, buses to Yabello (*5–6hrs*) and Moyale (*9–10hrs*) also leave at 06.00, or you could pick up a minibus to Yirgacheffe or Bule Hora (also known as Hagere Maryam) and travel in hops from there.

Where to stay *Map, opposite*

Moderate
🏠 **Delight Hotel** (36 rooms) 📞 046 331 2806/8; **e** delightinternationalhotel1@gmail. com; **w** delighthotelethiopia.com. This central multistorey hotel stands head & shoulders above everything else in Dilla. The smart, en-suite rooms come with sat TV, balcony & a modern bathroom with hot water, & there is also a good ground-floor restaurant & café, & Wi-Fi throughout. *US$20/36 B&B sgl/dbl*. **$$$**

Budget
🏠 **Afomiya Pension** (27 rooms) 📞 046 331 4444. Located at the west end of town, this comfortable hotel has fresh & clean en-suite rooms with tiled floors, net, sat TV & hot shower. Try for a room as far from the main road as possible. Rooms are set around a green courtyard & there's free Wi-Fi throughout. *US$12.50–15 en-suite dbl depending on size*. **$$**

Shoestring
🏠 **Nahom Hotel** (30 rooms) 📞 046 331 2841. This excellent cheapie, tucked away on a side road running south from the Afomiya, has decent en-suite rooms around a lovely shaded courtyard restaurant & bar. Showers are hot. *US$6/12 dbl with common/en-suite shower*. **$–$$**
🏠 **Abel Pension** (14 rooms) 📞 046 331 1902. The pick of a cluster of decent budget hotels on the side roads close to the Afomiya, this has clean, modern en-suite rooms with tiled floor, TV & hot water. *US$10 dbl*. **$**
🏠 **Zeleke Hotel** (20 rooms) 📞 046 331 2836; **m** 0911 728415. The closest hotel to the bus station, this long-serving establishment has adequate & well-priced en-suite rooms (cold showers only). Restaurant & bar attached. *US$5 en-suite dbl*. **$**

Where to eat and drink *Map, opposite*
The restaurant at the **Delight Hotel** is probably the best in Dilla, serving a good selection of Western and Ethiopian dishes in the US$3.50–5 range.

Situated on the main road opposite the CBE, the **Lem Café and Restaurant** is a gem, comprising a ground-floor café serving cakes, juices and coffee indoors or on a wide terrace, as well as a first-floor restaurant/bar whose bargain vegetarian lunch buffet (*US$2 per head*) is supplemented by a varied à la carte menu including fish cutlet, pizza, burgers and Ethiopian dishes for around US$2.50.

Tourist information and guides
ℹ️ **Gedeo Tourism Office** **m** 0916 170011; 🕐 08.30–12.30 & 13.30–17.30 Mon–Fri. The English-speaking staff at this office tucked away in a compound just south of the main road are a useful source of information about the stelae fields

in the surrounding area. Optional guides can be hired at US$10/day.
ℹ️ **Oromia District Office** **m** 0917 043893. Situated in the village of Guangua, about 7km south of Dilla, this is the authority in charge of the

rock engravings at Shappe, which (unlike Dilla) lies in Oromia Region rather than the SNNPR. An entrance fee of US$17.50/car to visit Shappe must be paid here, & the tourist officer may insist you also take him along as a guide for a negotiable fee of US$10–15.

What to see and do

Tutu Fela stelae field (*Entrance US$6*) This dense cluster of roughly 300 stelae lies within a small village encircled by natural forest and subsistence plantations of *enset* and coffee. Most of these megaliths are anthropomorphic, but several are (or were originally) phallic, hence the 'circumcision marks' near the top. Little excavation has taken place at Tutu Fela, but formative investigation has revealed numerous artefacts, ranging from iron and copper bracelets and beads to chisels and shards of pottery buried alongside the bodies in the graves below the engraved rocks.

Tutu Fela lies 20km from Dilla by road. To get there, head south towards Yabello, passing through Wonago after about 15km, then take the signposted dirt turn-off going up to the left after another 3km. Follow this for 2km until you reach a rough dirt track leading uphill to your left. You'll probably need to walk along this last track, which leads to the stelae after about 700m. Using public transport, any bus to Yirgacheffe can drop you at the junction 3km south of Wonago, from where it's a 30–40-minute walk to Tutu Fela.

Tututi stelae field (*Entrance US$6*) Only 5km southwest of Tutu Fela as the crow flies, this equally impressive but more dispersed megalithic site comprises around 1,200 (mostly phallic) stelae scattered in and around the village of Tututi. One stele here, measuring 7.55m from base to top but now collapsed, was probably the tallest ever erected in southern Ethiopia. Most of the other stelae at Tututi have toppled over: some have been incorporated into the bases of the local huts, or are used as seats or to sharpen knives, and one rather ignominiously props up a rustic latrine. Despite this, a few megaliths measuring up to 6m high still stand where they were erected more than 1,000 years ago.

The junction for Tututi is signposted to the right in the village of Chelba, 6.5km south of the junction for Tutu Fela. The first stele lies about 1.5km along this road, which gets very muddy after rains, sometimes rendering it impassable to vehicles. As with Tutu Fela, you could easily catch public transport to the junction, then walk to the stelae from Chelba, which takes about 20 minutes.

Shappe rock engravings (*Entrance US$17.50 per vehicle*) The best-known and most important of several prehistoric rock engravings in the vicinity of Dilla, situated about 8km from the town centre, Shappe (also known as Manchiti) comprises a partially collapsed frieze depicting some 70 cattle moving herd-like along a vertical face at the top of a narrow river gully. The individual figures at Shappe, ranging in length from 40cm to 70cm, are nearly identical in their highly stylised form, with unnaturally small heads, large decorated horns and grossly engorged udders. The art also has many affinities with similar sites in the vicinity of Harar and parts of Somaliland, while Roger Joussaume, the first Westerner to visit the site back in 1967, noted that the triangular objects that decorate the engraved horns resemble the buffalo-hair 'acorns' hung from the horns of the cattle of present-day Ethiopian pastoralists such as the Nuer and Dinka. Yet the identity of the society responsible for engraving these beautifully precise figures some 3,000–5,000 years ago remains a complete mystery, adding yet another layer to Ethiopia's enigmatically complex past.

In late 2000, local archaeologist Gizachew Abegaz discovered two lesser but still very intriguing engraving sites close to Shappe. Laga Harro, only 300m from

Shappe, is a small site that includes two engraved bovids, one apparently mounting the other, along with an anthropomorphic figure holding a spear and what appears to be a coffee pot, the only such engraving recorded in Ethiopia. About 8km from Shappe, Ejersa Gara Halo, a large horizontal panel set about 30m above the Ejersa River, includes six engraved cattle, as well as two anthropomorphic figures, one wearing what appears to be a penis sheath, the other seemingly jumping over a cow in a scene reminiscent of the bull-jumping ceremony still practised by the Hamar of South Omo today.

Before visiting Shappe and the associated sites, you are required to pay the entrance fee at the Oromia District Office in Guangua, 7km south of Dilla, and will also be expected to pick up a guide there. You then need to return to Dilla and follow the Hawassa road west from the town centre as far as the Mahlet Hotel. Here, instead of following the main road as it curves north towards Hawassa, continue west for 2km to the Education and Medical campus of Dilla University. The rock art site lies 6km southwest of this, but is difficult to find without a guide, which seems to be more or less mandatory anyway. Travellers without private transport can catch a minibus as far as the university, but they will have to walk the last 5–6km, and should carry plenty of drinking water.

YIRGACHEFFE The first town of substance on the Yabello road south of Dilla, Yirgacheffe (literally 'Cool Grass') not only is renowned for its high-quality coffee, but lends its name to one of Ethiopia's three premium bean varietals. You'd be unlikely to plan on spending a night there unless you're a coffee trader, but should you need to, the **Mahlet Hotel** (*12 rooms;* ☎*046 332 0030;* m *0926 242223;* **$$**) is far better value than anything in Dilla, charging US$17 for a smart spacious double with queen-size bed, net, sat TV and hot shower. If it's full, the **Lesiwon Hotel** (*30 rooms;* m *0916 510424;* **$**) to the left on the opposite side of the road is also pretty good value. You can drive the dreadful 40km between Dilla and Yirgacheffe in about 2 hours, and minibuses run back and forth all day.

BULE HORA The largest town between Dilla and Yabello, lying roughly halfway between them, Bule Hora was formerly known as Hagere Maryam, and is still shown by that name on many maps. It's a well-equipped but unremarkable town, and the last one that southbound travellers will pass through before descending to the dry Borena Plains, weaving past one last patch of juniper forest whose trees mostly share a distinctive wind-induced lean. If you need to overnight there, you're spoilt for choice, with the pick being the plush **Bule Hora Hotel** (*51 rooms;* ☎*046 443 0265;* **$$**), which charges US$16/21 for a smart spacious double/twin with queen-size bed, sat TV and hot shower, and also has a great terrace restaurant with meals in the US$2–3 range, draught beer and intermittent Wi-Fi. For a cheaper room, try the **Abara Pension** (*20 rooms;* m *0916 829968;* **$**), where neat, clean en-suite rooms with hot water cost US$8.

YABELLO The burgeoning administrative centre of Borena Zone, Yabello is also a route focus of growing significance, situated close to the junction of the main asphalt road between Addis Ababa and Moyale, a recently upgraded dirt road running west to Konso, and a rougher road running northeast to Negele Borena. Its location has made it a popular overnight stop on circular tours to South Omo, while the exclusive presence of two localised endemics in the immediate vicinity has made it a fixture on most dedicated ornithological trips through southern Ethiopia (see box, page 516). Several worthwhile attractions lie within day-tripping distance of

Yabello is an essential fixture on any birding itinerary through Ethiopia. The reason for this, quite simply, is that it lies at the heart of the territory inhabited by two of Africa's most range-restricted bird species. These are Stresemann's bush crow and the white-tailed swallow, respectively described in 1938 and 1942, and restricted to a radius of around 100km outside Yabello. Quite why these two birds occupy such a small territory is a mystery to ornithologists – the arid acacia scrub around Yabello is practically indistinguishable from that which covers much of southern Ethiopia and northern Kenya. Whatever the explanation, however, few self-respecting birders would visit Ethiopia and not come in search of these localised endemics, both of which are common within their restricted range.

Stresemann's bush crow is by far the more interesting of the two birds. Placed in the monospecific genus *Zavattariornis*, with its nearest genetic ally thought to be the European chough, this is a small, lightly built crow whose range extends into the Ethiopian Highlands. However, with its white head and belly, grey back, black wings, narrow pointed beak and bare blue face mask, Stresemann's bush crow bears little outward resemblance to any other corvid. Indeed, it is roughly the size of a roller, but holds itself more like a starling, and is usually seen in small flocks that hop along the ground like overgrown sparrow-weavers. Although little studied, this fascinating bird is totally unmistakable even at a distant glance, and easily seen along the main asphalt road around Yabello. A good place to look for the white-tailed swallow is the still-signposted junction for, and feeder road to, the all-but-defunct Borano (*sic*) Lodge on the Moyale road 7km south of Yabello.

Yabello's interest to birders is not limited to the two endemics. The road between Yabello and Negele is known for hosting several localised specials (page 506), while the acacia bush immediately around town, arid though it may be, supports a rich proliferation of colourful species more or less endemic to the dry scrub of northern Kenya and southern Ethiopia. Vulturine guinea fowl, golden-bellied starling, Abyssinian ground hornbill, white-headed buffalo-weaver, golden pipit, bare-faced go-away bird and the ubiquitous but aptly named superb starling are just a few of the more striking species you can expect to see in the area, along with a good selection of small raptors.

Yabello, notably the Borena singing wells at Dublock, the salt lake Chew Bet, and the vast but little-visited Yabello Wildlife Sanctuary. The town itself is not without a certain off-the-beaten-track charm, and it comes into its own on Saturday when its impressive market is attended by Borena pastoralists from miles around. It should be noted, however, that most of the relatively smart accommodation favoured by tour operators lies not in the characterful old town centre, but in the smaller and more utilitarian truck stop that has sprung up in recent years at the junction with the main Moyale road 5km to the east.

History Prior to the 20th century, Yabello was called Gadisa Obda (Shadow of Obda) in reference to the surrounding hills, known to the local Borena as Obda. The site of the present-day town, which boasts several good wells, hosted no permanent settlement back then, but it is where all Borena men of the Aba Gada, the most powerful age-set, would set up camp for the duration of the Ya'a ceremonial assembly (the name Yabello probably derives from Ya'a Balo, meaning 'Place of the Big Ya'a'). The modern town was founded shortly after 1897, the year in which the Borena region was conquered by Menelik II and annexed to Ethiopia. It served as administrative centre for Borena, but also as a military outpost to police long-standing conflicts between the Borena and their Guji and Gabra neighbours. Although Yabello served as an Italian military and air force base during the occupation, the town's first major growth spurt dates to the late 1940s and early 1950s, when it was settled by large numbers of migrants from Konso, an important livestock market was established, and a mission was founded there by Norwegian Lutherans. In recent years, long-standing tensions between the Borena and other pastoralist tribes, exacerbated by periods of crippling drought, have occasionally erupted into lethal violence. In 1992, an unknown number of Gabra were killed in a series of livestock raids, and the survivors had to be relocated by international aid agencies. In 2006, at least 100 people died in and around Yabello and Arero as a result of land clashes between the Borena and Guji, and thousands more fled from the environs of Yabello until things had settled down. Yabello has grown considerably in both size and importance since 2002, when Borena Zone was split into two, and it took over from Negele (now in Guji Zone) as the administrative capital of Borena. The population now stands at around 30,000.

Getting there and away Yabello's old town centre is situated 5km west of the Moyale road some 570km south of Addis Ababa, 290km south of Hawassa, 210km south of Dilla and 200km north of Moyale itself. The road is surfaced for most of its length, and you used to be able to get through from Addis Ababa in a day, but the stretch 'under repair' between Hawassa and Dilla, and beyond, makes that difficult these days. The drive to Moyale should take no longer than 4 hours. Heading west, the 125km drive to Konso now takes up to 3 hours, while the 270km road to Negele Borena takes a full day, allowing for stops at the main birding locations en route.

Public transport to Dilla or Moyale (*US$3*) is reasonably reliable. In addition to local minibuses between various small towns along these roads, a daily bus service connects Yabello and Dilla (*US$4*), taking around 6 hours in either direction. The daily bus between Dilla and Moyale stops in Yabello. It is generally easier to pick up public transport at the satellite junction town than it is in the old town centre.

Where to stay *Map, page 518*

A few years back, Yabello was serviced only by a handful of cheerless dirty dumps in the old town centre. Today, by contrast, at least a dozen relatively acceptable hotels are clustered at the Moyale–Yabello junction, all of a superior quality to anything in the old town. As a rule of thumb, you get better value the further north the hotel is from the junction. Arguably better than any of the hotels below are the Ahuzand Wabe pensions, which would be included in the listings at the local rate of US$10 for an en-suite double, but seem wildly overpriced at the *faranji* rate of around US$30!

Moderate

🏠 **Yabello Motel** (35 rooms) ☎046 446 0785; m 0911 725872. Located at the main junction next to the Total filling station, this hotel has something of a monopoly on the tour-group market, but the accommodation (all with net, TV & hot shower) is also possibly the most overpriced in all Ethiopia,

with *faranji* rates set at around 5 times higher than the market-driven local rates. Far better value is the garden bar & terrace restaurant, which serves a varied selection of Ethiopian & international dishes in the US$2–4 range. *US$40/55 dbl/twin in the rundown old wing, US$50/72 for a superior room in the new wing.* **$$$$**

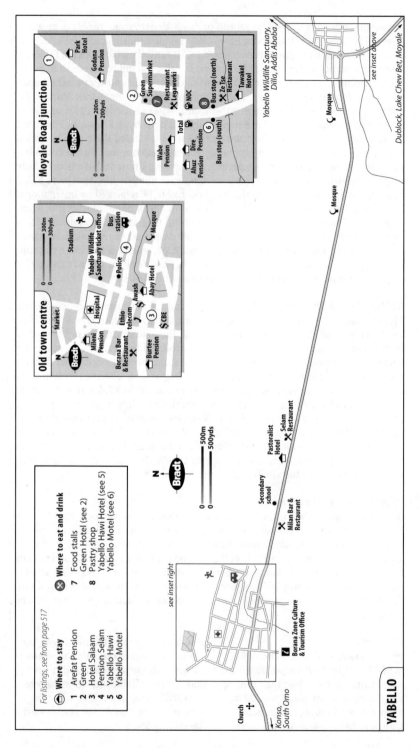

YABELLO

For listings, see from page 517

Where to stay
1 Arefat Pension
2 Green
3 Hotel Salaam
4 Pension Selam
5 Yabello Hawi
6 Yabello Motel

Where to eat and drink
7 Food stalls
   Green Hotel (see 2)
8 Pastry shop
   Yabello Hawi Hotel (see 5)
   Yabello Motel (see 6)

Moyale Road junction

Park Hotel
Godana Pension
Green Supermarket
Restaurant Legaworki
NOC
Bus stop (north)
Ze Tse Restaurant
Tawakel Hotel
Total
Wabe Pension
Dire Pension
Ahuz Pension
Bus stop (south)

N
Brad
0 200m
0 200yds

Old town centre

Stadium
Market
Hospital
Mileni Pension
Borana Bar & Restaurant
Burtee Pension
Ethio telecom
CBE
Awash
Abay Hotel
Police
Yabello Wildlife Sanctuary ticket office
Bus station
Mosque

N
Brad
0 300m
0 300yds

Church
Konso, South Omo

Secondary school
Milan Bar & Restaurant
Pastoralist Hotel
Selam Restaurant
Borana Zone Culture & Tourism Office

see inset right

N
Brad
0 500m
0 500yds

see inset above

Mosque
Mosque

Yabello Wildlife Sanctuary, Dilla, Addis Ababa
Dublock, Lake Chew Bet, Moyale

Budget

🏠 **Green Hotel** (15 rooms) m 0911 765784.
Probably the pick of the hotels lining the road
north of the junction, this has clean en-suite rooms
with writing desk, net, balcony & cold shower set
around a quiet green courtyard restaurant & bar.
US$10 dbl. **$**

🏠 **Arefat Pension** (20 rooms) m 0925
748374. Among the best-value options north of
the junction, this clean, new place offers the choice
of spacious en-suite rooms with writing desk,
wardrobe, TV & hot shower, or smaller rooms using
common showers. *US$4.50/8.50 dbl with common/
en-suite showers.* **$**

🏠 **Yabello Hawi Hotel** (23 rooms) ☎046 446
1114; m 0916 408056. Situated 100m north of
the main junction, this place offers a great variety
of clean rooms located around a large terrace. The
garden restaurant serves excellent *shekla tibs.*
Rates range from US$6 for a sgl with common
showers to US$20 for a large 1st-floor family room
with all amenities. **$–$$**

🏠 **Hotel Salaam** (25 rooms) ☎046 446 0039;
m 0913 430746. This 3-storey hotel on the main
road is easily the most commodious option in the
old town centre. The spacious en-suite rooms look
a little tired, but are reasonably priced & come
with TV & hot water. There's a ground-floor bar.
US$5 dbl. **$**

Shoestring

🏠 **Pension Selam** (10 rooms) ☎046 446
0056. Not to be confused with its near namesake
on the main road, this quiet, no-frills pension
has adequately clean rooms with ¾ bed using a
common shower. *US$3 sgl or dbl occupancy.* **$**

✖ Where to eat and drink *Map, opposite*

Most of the hotels around the junction serve food of some sort. The terrace
restaurant at the Yabello Motel is the pick, and no longer seems to have a differently
priced *faranji* menu, but the Yabello Hawi Hotel and Green Hotel are also worth a
try. A nameless pastry shop opposite the Yabello Motel serves cheap local meals, a
limited selection of cakes, and juice and coffee indoors or on the terrace. A row of
inexpensive food stalls lines the east side of the road north of the main junction.

What to see and do

Yabello Wildlife Sanctuary Extending over 2,500km² of thinly wooded semi-
arid acacia savannah northeast of Yabello town, this sanctuary was earmarked in
the 1960s to protect a small number of Swayne's hartebeest, which are now very
rare in the area. More likely to be seen are Burchell's zebra, Grant's gazelle and
Guenther's dik-dik, but the unique stretchy-necked gerenuk is also present, along
with greater and lesser kudu and a variety of small predators. Birding is exceptional,
with a good chance of sighting the endemic Stresemann's bush crow and the white-
tailed swallow, and more than 200 other dry-country species recorded, among
them ostrich, vulturine guinea fowl, Pringle's puffback, magpie starling, and black-
capped and grey-headed social weaver.

The signposted entrance to the sanctuary lies on the east side of the Dilla road
about 11km north of the junction for Yabello, but before visiting you need to pop
into the sanctuary office (☎046 446 0087; m 0916 178735), in the old town 5km
west of the junction, to pay entrance fees (*US$5 pp plus US$1–2 per car*) and pick
up a mandatory scout (*US$7.50/party/day*). This is also where you would need to
pay the US$2 camping fee to use the facility-free campsite about 1km east of the
signpost for the entrance gate.

Dublock singing wells Straddling the Moyale road 65km south of Yabello,
Dublock is an overgrown roadside renowned for the two so-called singing wells
set in a small evergreen grove no more than 500m to the east. The name 'singing
wells' refers to the Borena tradition of forming a chanting human chain to haul
buckets of water from the well to its lip, a communal activity that generally

14

THE BORENA

Perhaps the most rigid pastoralists of all southern Ethiopia's people, the Borena occupy a vast cross-border territory of arid land stretching from the escarpment north of Dilla south to the Uaso Ngiro River near the foot of Mount Kenya. Linguistically and ethnically, the Borena are essentially a southern branch of the Oromo, but their widespread adherence to a semi-nomadic lifestyle gives them more in common with other desert nomads of northern Kenya than with any modern Ethiopian ethnic groups.

Characteristically tall and lean, the Borena acquired a reputation as fearsome warriors among early European visitors, based on their regional supremacy at the time. In later years, as the Abyssinian highlanders made inroads into the northern part of their territory, many Borena families were forced to migrate southward, where they subsisted by cattle raiding and attacking agriculturist settlements in northern Kenya. Within Ethiopia, however, the Borena have a reputation as a peaceful and gracious people who hold strong taboos against unprovoked violence and raising one's voice in anger.

Staunchly traditional in both custom and dress, the Borena add a welcome splash of colour to the harsh, monotonous country they inhabit. The women, decorated similarly to some of the people of South Omo, drape colourful shawls and dresses from their shoulders, while the men walk around bare-chested with a sarong wrapped around their waist, and a spear or gun slung over their shoulder. In common with many other African pastoralists, Borena society is based on a rigid age-set system wherein males initiated into each age-based group, or *gada*, would move together through successive stages of life and responsibility. The Borena measure their wealth and worth in terms of the size of their herd. It is said that two Borena men will enquire about the state of each other's cattle long before they enquire about the health of wives, children and other such trivialities.

Drought and famine form a major threat to the traditional Borena lifestyle, regularly afflicting the region in years when it is denied its usual measly quota of precipitation. The most recent such drought occurred in 2011, resulting in the death of more than 250,000 Borena cattle, while crops grown to supplement the staple diet of milk and meat were completely destroyed. An unfortunate result of drought in Borena has often been increased tension with their Somali neighbours over water resources and grazing areas.

A remarkable feature of Borena culture is the 'singing well'. Many such wells are dotted around Borena territory, both in Ethiopia and in Kenya, each one supporting many thousands of cattle living for miles around. Water is retrieved from these wells communally, by a row of up to 50 men who sing and chant as they pass buckets from one to another – an inspiring sight. The most accessible singing well in Ethiopia lies immediately outside Dublock, on the main road between Yabello and Mega. This well can be visited in conjunction with the crater lake Chew Bet – a major source of the salt bars that have long formed an important export item in the Borena barter economy.

takes place only in the dry season, when herdsmen who live 2 hours distant will congregate around Dublock between around 09.00 and 14.00 to collect water for their livestock. Viewing the singing wells costs US$3 per person entrance, US$3 per vehicle and US$12 per party for a mandatory guide. On the way there, look out for wild animals such as Grant's gazelle, gerenuk, lesser kudu, Guenther's dik-dik and ground squirrels, which still persist here in low concentrations. For travellers dependent on public transport, it might be optimistic to stop off at Dublock unless you intend on staying the night, in which case the choice lies between two or three functional shoestring hotels unlikely ever to attract superlatives.

Lake Chew Bet Roughly 20km south of Dublock, a good gravel road heads eastward for 15km to the rim of the small crater lake known as Chew Bet (Salt House) in Amharic, and as El Sod (Place of Salt) by the Oromifa-speaking Borena. At once starkly beautiful and rather menacing, the inky-black lake, set at the base of a $2km^2$ crater with 200m-high walls, is an important regional centre of salt extraction, worked by the villagers on a 15 days on, 15 days off basis so as to keep levels sustainable. Unfortunately, your arrival at the crater rim is likely to be greeted by a swarm of hawkers, would-be guides and other hangers-on, as well as a few zealous members of the official **Chew Bet Guide Association**, who'll ask a village entrance fee of US$3 per person just to view the lake from the rim, and another US$3 for parking the car. Photography costs more, and anyone who's tempted to follow the steep footpath to the crater floor – advisable only in the cool of the early morning or late afternoon – will need to pay an extra US$12 per person for a mandatory guide to lead them there. For an additional US$18, the guide can even organise a staged photograph of someone diving into the water!

There's no accommodation in the village, but the raw salt is collected by regular pick-up trucks from Mega, which should make it easy enough for backpackers to get a lift to the lake – just make sure that the driver is willing to give you a lift back when his truck is full!

MEGA Bisected by the Moyale road 14km south of the junction for Chew Bet, Mega is the archetypal one-street town, nestled in a pretty valley that offers little in the way of sightseeing aside from the impressive hillside ruins of a Mussolini-era fort set alongside the main road 1km to the north. This stretch of the Moyale road passes through a rather unnatural-looking swathe of cropped grass that looks almost like a floodplain, but is presumably the result of a recent (in geological terms) fall of volcanic ash. For those seeking to break up the trip between Yabello and Moyale, Mega boasts a fair selection of shoestring accommodation, with the best option looking to be the Bathsheba Hotel (*10 rooms;* \ *046 448 0002; US$6 dbl with common shower;* **$**). Mega seems likely to start attracting the interest of birding tours, following a recent study suggesting that the black-fronted francolin, discovered there in 1930 but long thought to be a race of chestnut-naped francolin, should be classified as a full species. The francolin is known from five sites, all at altitudes of 1,480m or higher within a 25km radius of Mega, as detailed in a ten-page paper downloadable from **w** senckenberg.de (search 'black-fronted francolin').

MOYALE Lying 100km south of Mega, Moyale is in effect two different but economically interdependent towns that share a name but are divided by an international border. The Ethiopian town, supporting a population of around 25,000, is substantially the larger of the two and is better equipped when it comes to food, lodging and just about everything else. As with Yabello, Moyale is generally a peaceful and agreeable place, despite the endemic heat which peaks between January and March, but it is also prone to violent land disputes between local Borena and Somali communities. A clash of this sort resulted in 18 deaths over four days in July 2012, and tensions resurfaced in May 2017, when at least two people died.

14

Crossing through to Kenya, border formalities are relaxed, though the border does close from time to time so check the situation in advance. Visas for Kenya can be obtained on the spot (as they can these days at all Kenyan borders). Coming in the opposite direction, however, Ethiopian visas must be bought in advance or you are almost certain to be turned back and to have to return to Nairobi. As for finances, banks are located on both sides of the border, and outside banking hours it is easy enough to change hard currency into local cash with private traders. If you need to overnight on the Kenyan side of Moyale, the Hotel Sherif is about the best bet, though it really can't be recommended by comparison with what's available on the Ethiopian side, and water is often unavailable.

The 500km drive from Moyale and Isiolo, the gateway town to the Kenya Highlands, used to be among the most brutal road trips in East Africa but, following the completion of the surfaced Moyale–Marsabit–Isiolo highway in 2017, it can now be covered in one long, smooth day, whether in a private vehicle or using public transport. The completion of the surfaced road and increase in traffic also seems to have put paid to the periodic outbreaks of violent banditry that once characterised the region, but do check the current situation before you travel. It is still worth stopping halfway at the montane oasis of Marsabit, which has several budget hotels and lies adjacent to the forested Marsabit National Park, home to many elephants, antelopes and birds. An excellent campsite lies on the edge of town, close to the park entrance gate, and you can also camp at the little-used lodge which lies about 5km into the park on the edge of a stunning crater lake. From Isiolo, plenty of transport runs on to Nairobi along a blissfully surfaced road – buses take 5–6 hours, so you'll get through in a day.

Getting there and away Moyale lies about 700km from Addis Ababa, a trip that cannot realistically be done in fewer than two days, even with a private vehicle. Not allowing for stops, the drive from Yabello to Moyale shouldn't take longer than 3 hours in a private vehicle, but will take closer to 5 hours using the bus, which departs between 05.00 and 06.00 daily. If you want to head straight between Dilla and Moyale, there is at least one bus daily in either direction.

 Where to stay, eat and drink

Koket Borena Moyale Hotel (37 rooms) 046 444 1161. The best place in town, this hilltop lodge offers clean, neat en-suite accommodation in motel-style rooms or *tukuls* with hot water &

TV. Camping is also permitted & a good restaurant is attached. *US$12/24/32 sgl/twin/trpl. Camping US$5 pp.* **$$$**

15

The Southern Rift Valley Lakes

The stretch of the Rift Valley running south of Addis Ababa supports a string of seven beautiful lakes, all of which are reasonably accessible from the main asphalt road running south via the towns of Ziway, Shashemene and Sodo to Arba Minch. The most northerly of these lakes is Ziway, which is well worth a look for its birdlife and the possibility of exploring its ancient island monastery. Farther south, Lake Langano is a popular swimming and watersports resort, while nearby Abijatta and Shalla are protected in a national park renowned for its prolific birdlife, including seasonal flocks of tens of thousands of flamingos. South of Shashemene, the lushly vegetated shore of Lake Hawassa is another avian paradise, while the adjacent city of Hawassa is one of the most pleasant urban centres in Ethiopia and one of the very few to show clear evidence of town planning. Further south still, lakes Abaya and Chamo form the centrepiece of the scenic Nech Sar National Park, while the bordering town of Arba Minch is the road gateway to Konso and South Omo, as covered in the next chapter. Although the lakes and their birdlife are the main focal points of tourism in this part of Ethiopia, other attractions range from the Lephis Forest and Senkele Swayne's Hartebeest Sanctuary to the Rastafarian Quarter in Shashemene and the unique extended domed homesteads built by the Dorze people around Arba Minch.

ZIWAY

Spanning the main road through southern Ethiopia 160km from Addis Ababa, Ziway is a fast-growing town (population 50,000) whose profile has never been higher thanks to the nearby presence of a 475ha rose farm operated by Dutch company Sher Flowers and French-owned Castel Vineyard, which produced its first wines in 2014. The well-equipped town lies on the southwest shore of the largest and northernmost of Ethiopia's natural Rift Valley lakes, which extends over some 430km² and is also generally known as Ziway, though some locals refer to it by the Oromifa name of Dambal. Lying at an altitude of 1,636m and ringed by steep volcanic hills, the shallow lake is fed by two main perennial waterways, the Maki and Katar, and is drained at its southwestern tip by the Bulbula River, which flows into Lake Abijatta about 30km to the southwest.

Logistically, Ziway makes an ideal first stop heading south on a trip through the Rift Valley, thanks to its stupendous birdlife and the opportunity to take a boat out on the lake in search of hippos or to visit the historic island of Tullo Guddo. Central to the ecology of the lake is its abundant population of Nile tilapia, a flattish fish that can weigh up to 1.5kg and is an important prey item for larger waterbirds such as pelicans. The tilapia makes for fine eating: around 2,500 tonnes of fish are harvested annually, at a level said to be sustainable, and it forms the mainstay of most restaurant menus in town.

The single largest geographical feature on the African continent, the Great Rift Valley is also the only such feature anywhere on the planet that was visible to the first astronauts to reach the moon. The process of rifting started some 20 million years ago along a tectonic fault that stretches over 6,000km from the Red Sea to Mozambique's Zambezi Valley. The valley's gradual expansion has been accompanied by a large amount of volcanic activity, and its floor is studded with hundreds of eruption craters, many of which – most notably Erta Ale in Ethiopia and Ol Doinyo Lengai in Tanzania – are still highly active today. Africa's two highest peaks, Mount Kilimanjaro and Mount Kenya, are also volcanic products of the rifting process, even though they lie outside the Rift Valley. Millions of years from now, the Rift Valley will fill with ocean water, to split what is now Africa into two discrete land masses, much as happened millions of years ago when Madagascar was separated from the African mainland.

The Ethiopian portion of the Rift Valley runs from the Red Sea to Lake Turkana on the Kenyan border. In northern Ethiopia, it forms the Danakil Depression, an inaccessible and inhospitable desert that dips to an altitude of 116m below sea level, one of the lowest points on the earth's surface. South of the Danakil Depression, due east of Addis Ababa, the Rift narrows around Awash National Park to bisect the Ethiopian Highlands into the northwestern and southeastern massifs. In Ethiopia, as elsewhere along its length, the Rift Valley has formed an important barrier to animal movement and plant dispersal. For this reason, several animals are restricted to one or other side of the Rift, while populations of many animals that occur on both sides of the Great Rift, for instance Ethiopian wolves, form genetically distinct races.

The southern part of the Ethiopian Rift Valley is lower, warmer and drier than other densely populated parts of the country. Covered in acacia woodland and studded with lakes, it is also one of the few parts of Ethiopia that feels unequivocally African – in many respects the region is reminiscent of the Rift Valley lakes region of central Kenya. The six main lakes of the Ethiopian Rift formed during the last Ice Age, originally as two large lakes, one of which embraced what are now lakes Ziway, Abijatta, Shalla and Langano, the other lakes Abaya and Chamo. Although Ethiopia's Rift Valley is lower and hotter than the highlands, the lake region between Ziway and Arba Minch lies at a medium elevation of between 1,000m and 1,500m, and temperatures are rarely uncomfortably hot. Rainfall figures are lower than in the highlands, but the pattern is broadly similar, with one long rainy season generally starting in April and finishing in July or August.

South of Lake Chamo, the Rift Valley expands into the hot, barren scrublands of the Kenyan border region. The Rift here becomes less clearly defined, but it supports two further lakes, Chew Bahir and Turkana, both of which are practically inaccessible from the Ethiopian side (the vast bulk of Turkana's surface area lies in Kenya). The Kenyan border area is most notable for two of Ethiopia's most important national parks, Omo and Mago, which are among the most undeveloped game reserves in Africa, and noted not so much for their abundance of game (though most major plains animals are present) as for their wilderness atmosphere.

HISTORY According to tradition, refugee priests from Axum first settled in the Ziway area to escape the 9th-century purges of Queen Gudit. The priests carried the Ark of the Covenant with them for safekeeping, and stowed it away on Tullo Guddo Island for 70 years before it was considered safe to return it to Axum. This tradition is supported by the fact that the Zay people of the lake's islands speak a Tigrigna-like tongue quite distinct from the Oromifa spoken in the surrounding area, and also by the ancient Ge'ez manuscripts housed in the church on Tullo Guddo. Though it isn't entirely clear when the Zay arrived at the lake hinterland, it seems that they retreated to the islands in the wake of the war between Ahmed Gragn and the Christian empire, which opened the way for the Oromo to occupy most of the surrounding Rift Valley. During the 16th and 17th centuries, the Zay Christians led an isolated island-bound existence, entirely cut off from the main stream of Ethiopian Christianity. How the Zay survived these decades of isolation with their traditions intact is something of a mystery, one most probably explained by the fact that the Oromo were inept sailors and unable to build boats (indeed, the Oromo name for the Zay is Laki, which translates as 'rower', in reference to this distinguishing feature). As Christian–Muslim tensions eased, the islanders occasionally sailed to shore to trade, and became known to the Oromo as skilful weavers, but basically they remained an isolated community, dependent on their densely terraced cultivation and on the lake's abundant fish for survival. Rumours of their isolated brethren had always filtered through to the Christians of the highlands, where it was believed, correctly, that the churches on Ziway held a wealth of ancient *tabots* and illuminated religious manuscripts. It was only in 1886 that Emperor Menelik conquered the Ziway area and the liberated islanders were able to move back to the lakeshore. Today, just three of Ziway's islands are occupied, and most of the 5,000-odd Zay people living around the lake visit them for religious ceremonies only.

GETTING THERE AND AWAY Ziway lies 160km from Addis Ababa via Modjo. In a private vehicle, the fastest way to get there is probably to take the Adama Expressway as far as Modjo, then continue south along the main road for another 90km. Alternatively, the town is 180km from Addis Ababa via Tiya and Butajira, along surfaced roads that carry far less traffic than the stretch between Modjo and Ziway, and are generally regarded to be safer. Either way, depending on traffic, allow at least 3 hours in a private vehicle. Using public transport, regular minibuses connect Ziway to Modjo (*1½hrs*), Nazret (*2hrs*), Addis Ababa (*3–4hrs*), Shashemene (*1½hrs*) and Butajira (*1hr*). Minibuses to Butajira leave from the Butajira road about 150m west of Telecoms, but most other minibuses leave from the main bus station 200m further north.

🏠 **WHERE TO STAY** *Map, page 526*
Moderate

🏠 **Haile Resort** (52 rooms) 📞046 441 2828; m 0930 304040; e haileresortsziwaymkt@ gmail.com; w hailehotelsandresorts.com. This newly opened relative of its popular namesake in Hawassa isn't quite in the same premier division, but it's still far & away the best hotel in Ziway, set in large gardens running down to a stretch of lakeshore teeming with birdlife, & offering accommodation in modern tiled rooms with sat TV, nets, wood furniture & en-suite hot shower. Amenities include Wi-Fi, swimming pool, gym, sauna & one of the top restaurants in Ziway. *US$34/38/50 dbl/twin/suite w/days, rising by 15–20% over w/ends.* **$$$**

🏠 **Bethlehem Hotel** (32 rooms) 📞046 441 4104; e BethlehemHotelZewaye@yahoo.com. Situated close to the jetty, but lacking a lake view, this recently refurbished hotel has large, clean en-suite rooms with fridge, TV, Wi-Fi & hot shower,

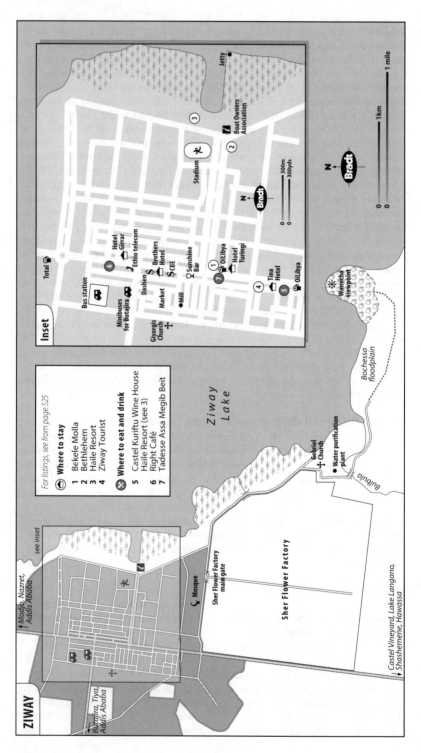

ZIWAY

↑ Butajira, Tiya,
Addis Ababa

↑ Modjo, Nazret,
Addis Ababa

see inset

Inset

Total ⛽

Bus station

Minibuses
for Butajira

Giyorgis
Church ✝

6 Hotel
Girrar

Ethio telecom ☎

Brothers
Hotel

Dashen $

Market

CBE $

Mill ●

Sunshine
Bar

Stadium 🏃

ℹ️

3

🏃

2

Boat Owners
Association

Jetty

7 Oillbya
Hotel
Turingi

1

4

5 Tina
Hotel

Oillbya

N

0   300m
0   300yds

Bradt

Ziway
Lake

For listings, see from page 525

🛏 **Where to stay**

1 Bekele Molla
2 Bethlehem
3 Haile Resort
4 Ziway Tourist

✕ **Where to eat and drink**

5 Castel Kuriftu Wine House
   Haile Resort (see 3)
6 Right Café
7 Tadesse Assa Megib Beit

ℹ️ 🏃

Sher Flower Factory

Sher Flower Factory
main gate

Mosque ☪

Water purification
plant ●

Gabriel ✝
Church

Bulbula

Bochessa
floodplain

Wanicha
viewpoint ✳

N

Bradt

0   1km
0   1 mile

↓ Castel Vineyard, Lake Langano,
Shashemene, Hawassa

526

as well as a very good restaurant serving mains for around US$4. *US$28 dbl or twin, US$36 deluxe.* **$$$**

Budget
🏠 **Bekele Molla Hotel** (25 rooms) ✆ 046 441 2571. This venerable & partially refurbished hotel is set in attractive & well-maintained flowering grounds immediately behind the OiLibya filling station. The 1-price-for-all policy means that the new rooms are very good value, coming as they do with net, TV, hot shower & private balcony, & the older & cheaper rooms with net but no TV are also

well priced for what you get. There is a pleasant restaurant & garden bar with decent inexpensive food & Wi-Fi. *US$8/14 old/new en-suite dbl.* **$$**

Shoestring
🏠 **Ziway Tourist Hotel** (36 rooms) m 0911 033842. Situated at the south end of the town centre, this once-popular hotel has seen better days, but the en-suite rooms with net, TV & shower are spacious enough & very reasonably priced. The shady garden restaurant serves excellent fish cutlet & other local dishes in the US$3–4 range. *US$6/11 old/new en-suite dbl.* **$–$$**

✗ WHERE TO EAT AND DRINK *Map, opposite*
In addition to the bespoke restaurants listed below, the lakeshore Haile Resort has a varied menu including pizzas, curries and grills in the US$5–6 range, and the municipality soon intends to open a local restaurant at the end of the jetty.

✗ **Tadesse Assa Megib Beit** m 0921 680397; ⏲ 09.00–21.00 daily. Situated on the main road opposite the Bekele Molla Hotel, this owner-managed restaurant is widely claimed to serve the best fish in Ziway, whether you like it whole grilled, or stewed in a spicy goulash or *wot* sauce, or filleted & fried as a cutlet. Beer is served. *Most mains are in the US$2–5 range.*

✗ **Castel Kuriftu Wine House** ✆ 046 441 2705; m 0916 320427; w kurifturesorts.com/castel-kuriftu; ⏲ 08.00–22.00 daily. Situated on the main road at the south end of the town centre, this fantastic stone, wood & thatch 2-storey construction, a joint venture between the Castel Winery & Kuriftu Resort, is easily one

of the most handsome restaurants in Ethiopia. It serves reasonably priced local wine by the glass or the bottle, as well as draught beer & the usual range of spirits, & the tempting menu includes marinated grilled fillet, a catch of the day (almost invariably tilapia), burgers & pizzas in the US$3–5 range. Unfortunately the food itself is a bit erratic & doesn't quite match the superb architecture & ambience.

🍺 **Right Café** m 0910 290224; ⏲ 07.30–21.00 daily. This shaded pavement café has a central location & serves everything from fresh juice & coffee to inexpensive burgers, doughnuts & other snacks.

TOURIST INFORMATION AND GUIDES
📋 **Boat Owners Association** [map, opposite] m 0927 340309; e ziwayboatservice@gmail.com; w rootsofethiopia.com; ⏲ 08.00–18.00 daily. Housed in a small building at the entrance to the jetty, this community-based organisation arranges a variety of boat tours to the islands on Lake Ziway. These include a 1½hr Bird Island & Hippo Tour, with an optional visit to Gelila Island costing

US$32.50/group for up to 4 people, a ½-day tour to Tullo Guddo (*US$66 for up to 4 people*), & a full-day trip combining Tullo Guddo with other points of interest (*US$85 for up to 4 people*). Rates are higher for larger groups. Proceeds are split between the guide, the boat owner & the association, but do not include church entrance fees (*US$2*) at Tullo Guddo.

WHAT TO SEE AND DO
Lakeshore birdwatching Although Ziway is less heralded in this respect than lakes Abijatta or Shalla, it still offers some of the best birdwatching in the Rift Valley, thanks to the large aggregations of water-associated species attracted to the reed-lined fringes by its thriving tilapia population. The best place to start is the jetty (*US$0.50 pp, payable at the Boat Owners Association office at the entrance*), close to the Haile

Resort, which serves as a raised marsh-fringed causeway teeming with birds, most visibly dozens and sometimes hundreds of the striking marabou stork and great white pelican. Look more closely over a couple of hours, however, and you might easily identify 50-plus species, including greater and lesser jacana, yellow-billed stork, black crake, lesser moorhen, black-tailed godwit, garganey and red-breasted pipit. The jetty is also a good spot for the localised black heron, whose unusual habit of fishing with its wings raised to form a canopy gives rise to its colloquial name of 'umbrella bird'.

Another great spot for (free) birdwatching is the Bochessa area on the southwest shore close to the outlet of the Bulbula River. This can be reached from the town centre by following the main road to Shashemene for about 1km, turning left at the signpost for the main entrance to the Sher Flower Factory, then continuing east (with the factory to your right) for about 1.5km until you reach the marshy lakeshore. From here, the road follows the shore for another 1.5km, then veers inland around Gebriel Church and a water purification plant for about 500m before crossing the river and following it for about 1km to its outlet. The plentiful birdlife along this road is more varied than at the jetty (but not so good for photography) and includes everything from colourful bee-eaters and weavers to the majestic African fish eagle and saddle-billed stork, plus various waterfowl, plovers, herons and cormorants. The endangered wattled crane is sometimes present in October and November. From the river outlet you could continue east across the open floodplain to Wamicha Viewpoint, a forested lakeside hill that offers lovely views over the lake, as well as an opportunity to see various woodland birds.

Hippo and Bird Island Tour Lake Ziway supports a healthy population of hippos, which are occasionally visible from the jetty but are more likely to be seen on the short boat excursion offered by the Boat Owners Association (page 527) for US$32.50 per group of four people, or by the Haile Resort (page 525) for US$10 per person. These tours also usually include a cruise around Bird Island, a year-round roost for the likes of African darter, white-breasted cormorant and sacred ibis, and you can ask also to get out at the island known as Galila (Amharigna for 'Galilee'), site of a small Ethiopian Orthodox Church.

Tullo Guddo Island The largest of Ziway's five islands comprises a steep-sided volcanic cone whose terraced slopes rise 250m above the lake surface to a 1,889m peak known as Tullo Guddo (Large Mountain) in Oromifa and Debre Tsion (Mount Zion) in Amharic. Situated about 15km east of Ziway town and clearly visible from it, the well-vegetated 6km² island is home to around 1,000 people, as well as to the monastery of Maryam Debre Tsion, established in AD842, or so legend has it, as a temporary sanctuary for the Ark of the Covenant. Originally built on the island's highest point, the church was relocated to the middle slopes in the 16th century, and then to its present site near the lakeshore in the 1990s. The remains of the two old churches can be seen by following a round 5km trail to the peak, or you can just walk directly to the new star-shaped church (*entrance US$2.50*), which is of little architectural interest but does include some well-executed modern paintings depicting biblical scenes – animals entering Noah's Ark two by two, and a truly poisonous-looking Eve tempting Adam with that fateful apple – seldom seen in older churches. The entrance fee includes access to a new museum, built in 2014 to house the monastery's famed collection of ancient Geez manuscripts, among them a 14th-century book containing vivid and beautiful illustrations of 19 popular saints. Many of these manuscripts were moved from mainland churches to the island for safekeeping during more turbulent times, as were more than 40 different *tabots*, which are now stowed away in a holy place that's off limits to casual visitors. The only way to visit the island and church is on a boat tour organised by the Boat Owners Association (page 527).

LAKES LANGANO, ABIJATTA AND SHALLA

Huddled together on the Rift Valley floor some 200km south of Addis Ababa, this trio of surprisingly divergent Rift Valley lakes is well established as a weekend retreat from Addis Ababa, but it also offers much to keen birdwatchers, walkers and other nature lovers. The main focal point for tourism is the freshwater Lake Langano, which is more developed for tourism than any other lake in the Ethiopian Rift Valley, boasting at least half a dozen beach resorts on its shores. Reputedly free of bilharzia, Langano and its resorts are a popular venue for swimming and a variety of watersports, and the more mainstream among them can take on a slightly manic sub-Club Med atmosphere over weekends, though the exclusive Sabana Lodge (page 531) and Africa Vacation Club (page 532) retain a pretty tranquil atmosphere at all times. A few of the more upmarket lakefront hotels have introduced a US$4 per person day entrance fee that entitles visitors to free drinks and food to that value. The fee is waived if you stay overnight.

In contrast to Langano, the more westerly lakes Abijatta and Shalla are the dominant features of the 887km² Abijatta-Shalla National Park (m *0912 152171;* e *abijattashallanp@yahoo.com; entrance US$4/24hrs, vehicle entrance US$1/car, mandatory scout US$6/party*), a fine birdwatching and hiking destination famed for its large flocks of flamingos, pelicans and waders.

GEOGRAPHY Some 40,000 years ago, Langano, Abijatta and Shalla were submerged below an inland sea whose surface stood more than 100m above the present-day level of the lakes. Sometimes referred to as Lake Galla, this vast freshwater body was fed by the rivers Awash and Modjo, and extended north via Lake Ziway to the vicinity of present-day Modjo town. It started to shrink about 20,000 years ago, owing to a drop in rainfall and a tectonic upheaval that caused the Awash and Modjo rivers to change their courses and divert eastward. Ziway became a separate lake around 4,000 years ago, while the three more southerly lakes divided perhaps 2,000 years ago. The only links between them today are the rivers Bulbula and Horakalo, which respectively flow out of Ziway and Langano to empty into Abijatta.

Despite their common origin and close proximity, the three southern lakes are very different in character. Langano, with a surface area of 305km² and depth of up to 45m, is a freshwater lake whose bilharzia-free waters look deceptively dirty due to a suspension of fine red-brown laterite particles carried down by various inlets that rise in the Arsi Highlands to the east. Only 5km to its west, the 175km² Abijatta is a shallow brackish pan, nowhere more than 14m deep, surrounded by tightly cropped grass flats exposed over the last couple of decades by a steady drop in water level that has caused its typical area to decrease by 30km². The more southerly Lake Shalla, separated from Abijatta by a hilly 3km-wide isthmus, is nestled within an immense volcanic caldera that collapsed 3.5 million years ago, and its surface is studded with a collection of small volcanically formed islands while its shore supports several fields of hot springs. Despite its relatively modest surface area of 330km², Shalla has been calculated to hold a greater volume of water than any other Ethiopian lake (including Tana, which covers an area almost ten times larger) owing to its mean depth of 86m and maximum depth of 257m. Shalla has no known outlet and acts as a sump for the surrounding lakes as a result of subterranean seepage.

15

FLORA AND FAUNA Open water accounts for around 60% of Abijatta-Shalla's area of 887km², and although much of the park's land has been settled and cultivated since the last years of the Derg, the remainder supports a cover of wooded savannah, as does the shore of nearby Langano. Trees and shrubs of the genus *Acacia* dominate, with at least five species present including the magnificent umbrella thorn *A. tortilis*, but there are also patches of fig and mahogany forest, notably on the eastern shore of Langano, while the shore of Abijatta comprises an open floodplain of saline deposits interspersed with stubbly grass. More than 75 mammal species have been recorded but many are now locally extinct, or very scarce, as a result of encroachment by cattle farmers and hunting. A few Grant's gazelle live in virtual captivity at the ostrich farm next to the main entrance gate, Anubis baboons are still quite common, and there may still be viable breeding populations of the likes of greater kudu, Abyssinian hare, black-backed jackal and spotted hyena.

By contrast, the birdlife at all three lakes is exceptionally varied, with more than 430 species recorded in Abijatta-Shalla, many of which can also be seen in the vicinity of Langano. Premier avian attractions are the flamingos that aggregate in their thousands in the shallows of Abijatta and the small crater lake Chitu, and the large flocks of pelican that are still commonly seen on the open water, even though most of them have now abandoned their former breeding ground on Shalla's practically inaccessible Pelican Island, an exodus attributable to the increased salinity and inhospitality to fish of Abijatta as its water level has dropped. The remaining acacia woodland around all three lakes supports a wide range of colourful and charismatic species associated with this habitat, while the open shores of Abijatta are exceptional for waders, particularly during the northern hemisphere winter.

GETTING THERE AND AWAY The three lakes lie about 200km from Addis Ababa, and are readily accessible from the main highway through the southern Rift Valley, travelling via Modjo (or Butajira) and Ziway. The highway actually bisects the small area of land separating Abijatta-Shalla National Park, whose eastern boundary runs along it, from Lake Langano. You'll know you are approaching the lakes when you cross the Bulbula River, then pass through the small town that shares its name, perhaps 25km south of Ziway. The many resorts on the western shore of Langano all lie 2–3km from the highway, and can be accessed via unsurfaced feeder roads signposted to the east between 8km and 20km south of Bulbula. The main Dole entrance gate to Abijatta-Shalla, which stands on the west side of the highway, is clearly signposted about 20km south of Bulbula opposite the turn-off for Simbo Beach Resort. To get to Hara Langano Eco Lodge on the east shore of Langano, follow the highway another 2km south of the park entrance gate, then turn on to a clearly signposted 16km dirt road to the left. Using public transport, any vehicle travelling between Ziway and Shashemene can drop you at the park entrance gate or at the junction for any of the resorts on the west shore of Langano, though you'll need to pay full fare to the next town. Hara Langano Eco Lodge is not accessible on public transport.

Lake Chitu and 10,000 Flamingos Lodge cannot be accessed directly from the main Dole entrance gate to Abijatta-Shalla. Instead, you need to travel about 45km south of Dole to Shashemene, then turn right on to the main road west to Sodo and Arba Minch. Precisely 21km out of Shashemene, turn right at Aware on to a reasonable dirt road that runs north to Chitu via the small market town of Sambute Shalla. A fair amount of public transport runs as far as Sambute Shalla, especially on the market day of Sunday, but you will need to walk or catch a *bajaj* the last 6km to the lake. Alternatively, the management of 10,000 Flamingos (page 532) can

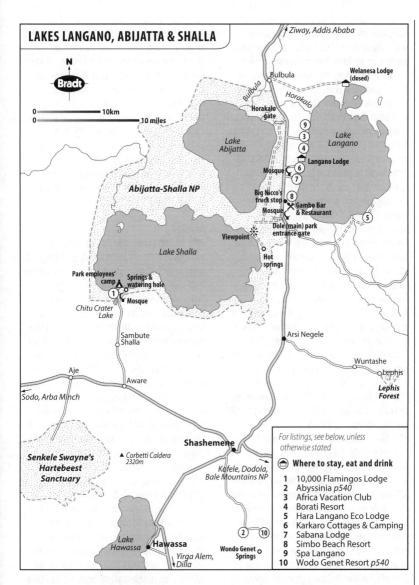

LAKES LANGANO, ABIJATTA & SHALLA

Ziway, Addis Ababa

Bulbula

Welanesa Lodge (closed)

Horakalo

Bulbula

Horakalo gate

Lake Abijatta

9
3
4

Lake Langano

Langano Lodge

Mosque

6
7

Abijatta-Shalla NP

Big Nicco's truck stop

8

Mosque

Gambo Bar & Restaurant

Dole (main) park entrance gate

5

Viewpoint

Hot springs

Lake Shalla

Park employees' camp

Springs & watering hole

1

Mosque

Chitu Crater Lake

Arsi Negele

Wuntashe

Lephis

Lephis Forest

Sambute Shalla

Aje

Aware

Sodo, Arba Minch

Senkele Swayne's Hartebeest Sanctuary

▲ Corbetti Caldera 2320m

Shashemene

Kofele, Dodola, Bale Mountains NP

Lake Hawassa

Hawassa

Wondo Genet Springs

2
10

Yirga Alem, Dilla

For listings, see below, unless otherwise stated

⊖ **Where to stay, eat and drink**

1 10,000 Flamingos Lodge
2 Abyssinia *p540*
3 Africa Vacation Club
4 Borati Resort
5 Hara Langano Eco Lodge
6 Karkaro Cottages & Camping
7 Sabana Lodge
8 Simbo Beach Resort
9 Spa Langano
10 Wodo Genet Resort *p540*

N 0 — 10km   0 — 10 miles

arrange taxi transfers from Shashemene, Bishoftu and Addis Ababa. There is no facility to collect entrance fees at Chitu, so they must be paid at the Dole entrance gate. However, the guards, if they show up, are known to be tolerant towards visitors coming from the directions of Sodo or Hawassa.

🏠 WHERE TO STAY, EAT AND DRINK *Map, above*

Upmarket

🏠 **Sabana Lodge** (25 rooms) 📞046 119 1181; e info@sabanalangano.com; w www. sabanalangano.com. The most stylish resort in the Langano area lies on the west shore about 3km

east of the main road, from which it is signposted roughly 15km past Bulbula. Approached by an attractive crushed red-lava driveway, it lies on a cliff overlooking the lake, with a footpath leading down to a swimming beach below. The A-frame bungalows, decorated in an earthy organic style that evokes an East African safari camp, have king-size bed, en-suite hot shower & private balcony. The glassed-in dining *tukul* serves excellent food & has a great view of the brown water below. The 6ha grounds still contain plenty of indigenous vegetation, & the birdlife is prolific. Activities include walking, kayaking & mountain biking, & a good spa is attached. *US$70/84/101 B&B sgl/dbl/trpl, with rates rising by around 20% over w/ends.* $$$$$

🏠 **Hara Langano Eco Lodge** (28 rooms) 📞 046 899 0537; m 0912 661009; e info@ haralangano.com; w haralangano.com. This recently rebranded retreat has an attractive natural setting on the east shore of Langano fringing a small swimming beach. It offers fishing rods for loan, while boat excursions cost around US$24–70/party depending on the size of the craft, & bird walks US$20/hr. All the en-suite bungalows come with hot water (🕐 *06.00–07.00 & 18.00–19.00 only*) & balcony. A good selection of meals, including vegetarian options, is served in a pleasant open-air dining room/bar, & the b/fast (included in the room rate) is excellent. We have had great feedback about the food, activities & friendly staff. *From US$65/105 w/days & US$105/135 w/ends sgl/dbl in a woodland lodge to US$125/175 w/days & US$180/245 w/ends sgl/dbl in a lakeside lodge.* $$$$$

🏠 **Africa Vacation Club** (38 rooms) 📞 046 119 1586; m 0116 639962; w africavacationclub. net. If you have deep pockets, this pricey new place is definitely worth the outlay. Ethiopia's first RCI-affiliated timeshare resort, but open to all comers, this family-oriented lodge offers accommodation in spacious 3-level *tukuls* – each with polished concrete floors, 2 bedrooms, 2 bathrooms, a fully equipped kitchen & a relaxed sitting room arranged in a circle that can accommodate up to 6 people. Facilities include a gleaming swimming pool, gift shop, breezy poolside bar & free Wi-Fi in public areas. The attached restaurant features Western & Ethiopian dishes, as well as freshly baked pizzas from a wood-fired oven. Plenty of activities are on offer including table tennis, kayaking, horseriding, beach soccer & volleyball. There is also a children's playground. *US$76 B&B dbl & US$146 per unit (sleeping up to 4), rising by around 25% over w/ends.* $$$$$

🏠 **Simbo Beach Resort** (74 rooms) m 0935 999097. The former Bekele Molla Hotel has a wonderful location on a sandy beach surrounded by acacia woodland & set below a tall cliff, only 3km from the main entrance to Abijatta-Shalla National Park. Accommodation is in clean but rather boringly decorated en-suite rooms with tiled floors, wooden furniture & hot shower. A brightly decorated restaurant with a beachfront terrace serves good Ethiopian & Western dishes, including pizza, in the US$3–6 range. Though popular with resident weekenders, it seems poor value at the inflated *faranji* prices. *From US$61/76 B&B sgl/dbl, with a 10% increase over w/ends.* $$$$$

Moderate

🏠 **10,000 Flamingos Lodge** (10 rooms) m 0946 959191; e 10000flamingoslodge@gmail. com; w 10000flamingoslodge.com. Opened in Oct 2015, the only lodge in Abijatta-Shalla National Park, constructed by the owners of Babogaya Lake Viewpoint in Bishoftu, has a remote but utterly fantastic location on the rim of Lake Chitu, which lies to the north of the Sodo road at Aware, 36km from Shashemene. The property offers wonderful views across the crater lake & its flamingo-lined shallows to an Oromo cattle-watering spot on the opposite side, as well as to the southern shore of Lake Shalla. Activities include walks within the national park, & the lodge may soon be bordered by a sanctuary for the endangered Nubian giraffe. Management can arrange taxi transfers from Shashemene, Bishoftu & Addis Ababa. No Wi-Fi. *US$55/65/90 B&B sgl/dbl/trpl.* $$$$

🏠 **Borati Resort** (12 rooms) m 0924 647979; e borati.resorts@gmail.com. The pick of the more affordable options, boasting a clifftop location on the west shore of Langano about 1km south of the Africa Vacation Club, this resort offers accommodation in sparsely furnished but attractive en-suite bungalows with hot water & a private balcony. You can walk down to the beach, which is also where the restaurant is located. No Wi-Fi. *Decent value at US$35 B&B sgl/dbl. Family room sleeping 5 US$84.* $$$$

🏠 **Spa Langano** (60 rooms) m 0911 938047. Signposted from the main road about 8km south of Bulbula, this government-run hotel, formerly the Wabe Shebelle & still often referred to by that name, has a vast & beautiful lakeshore location, but the grounds are littered with garbage, the atmosphere is gloomy & the en-suite accommodation is in a poor state of repair. *Poor value at US$37 B&B dbl. Family bungalow sleeping 6 US$110.* **$$$$**

Budget & camping

There are no budget options in the immediate vicinity of Langano or Abijatta-Shalla. Self-sufficient travellers in a private vehicle could camp in one of the facility-free campsites in Abijatta-Shalla for US$1.50 per tent (up to 4 people). Unless you have a tent, your best bet is to take a cheap room in Ziway or Arsi Negele, & to visit as a day trip.

⚔ Karkaro Cottages & Camping m 0911 683123; e willywarthog@msn.com; w karkarobeachcottages.com. The cottages at this attractive clifftop resort are aimed solely at long-stay renters (*min lease 1 month US$600*), but overlanders & campers with their own tent are welcome to drop by for a night or longer on the pleasant lakeside campground with toilet & shower. A small café serves b/fast for US$1.50 & pasta & fish dishes for around US$3–5. *Camping US$5/US$2.50 pp, adult/child, tent (3 person) & mattress rental US$7/night.* **$$**

WHAT TO SEE AND DO

Lake Langano The main attraction of Lake Langano, at least for most Addis Ababa weekenders, is that it is one of the few freshwater bodies in tropical Africa thought to be free of bilharzia, and thus safe for swimming. The probable absence of bilharzia from the lake is attributed to the same high mineral content responsible for the rusty-brown cast of its murky but clean water. Swimming aside, most of the resorts offer watersports at a price, while boat trips can be made to an island noted for its hot springs or in search of hippos and crocodiles. The lake and its acacia-lined shores support an excellent variety of bird species associated with aquatic and savannah habitats, while the lusher forest on the west shore near Hara Langano Eco Lodge also hosts a few forest specialists. Two previously undescribed birds, a cliff swallow and a serin with a white rump, were recently reported from the lake hinterland.

Lake Shalla Although Abijatta-Shalla is not the most impressive of national parks in terms of large wildlife, the stark Rift Valley scenery and rich avifauna make it alluring to hikers and birders. Walking is permitted, though it is advisable to take an armed guard for security, which can be arranged when you pay your fees at the Dole entrance gate. From the gate, a 12km round trip will allow you to visit a well-positioned viewpoint over the park's two lakes, and the impressive hot springs on the northeast shore of Lake Shalla. The water at the spring is so hot that local people use it to cook maize cobs, while the nearby pools, usually veiled in a cloud of steam, are popular with white-robed bathers. The surviving woodland around Lake Shalla is one of the best places in Ethiopia to see a good range of acacia-related species such as hornbills, starlings and sparrow-weavers.

Lake Abijatta Surrounded by a wide open floodplain due to its declining water level, Abijatta is a haven for algae-eating birds, in particular the mixed flocks of up to 300,000 greater and lesser flamingos that arrive in the shallows towards the end of the rainy season (September–October) and usually stick around for four months. During the European winter, the shallows and shore also support many thousands of migrant waders, including large flocks of avocet and occasional rarities such as Mongolian plover, Pacific golden plover, grey plover and red-necked phalarope, and the sky is a seething mass of darting European swallows. The eastern shore of Abijatta nudges to within 2km of the main highway, but the southeast corner of the lake is about 5km by foot or 4x4 from the Dole entrance gate, where all fees must be paid. Once at the lake, motorists can continue north along a track following the eastern shore for about 15km before exiting the park at the more northerly and usually unmanned Horakalo gate, which meets the main road immediately south of the bridge over the eponymous river.

Chitu Crater Lake Situated in Abijatta-Shalla National Park only 1.5km south of Lake Shalla, this picturesque, small (0.75km²) lake is nestled within a tuff explosion crater that formed some 10,000 years ago due to volcanic activity. The surface of the 20m-deep lake stands a full 80m below the crater rim, and its saline algae-rich shallows harbour a semi-resident flock of 10,000–20,000 flamingos. The Oromifa name Chitu translates as 'broken' in reference to a local tradition that the small lake was once connected with Shalla, which is true enough (both would have formed part of Lake Galla about 10,000 years ago), but the two would have been separate entities for thousands of years before the Oromo arrived in this part of the Rift Valley. Chitu was seldom visited by tourists, but this has changed since the 10,000 Flamingos Lodge opened on the crater rim in late 2015. Note that Chitu is accessed not from the main entrance to Abijatta-Shalla, but rather from Aware, on the main road running west from Shashemene towards Sodo.

LEPHIS FOREST

Set at an elevation of 2,150m on the Arsi Escarpment, the village of Lephis is the most accessible point along a tract of mostly indigenous forest that stretches for some 40km along the Rift Valley wall southeast of lakes Langano and Shalla. Developed for tourism a few years back by the Lephis Ecotourism Co-operative (LEC), the forest lies 25km from Arsi Negele, the most substantial town on the main road between Ziway and Shashemene, and within easy day-tripping distance of the likes of Langano and Hawassa. Quite a bit of wildlife still inhabits the forest, which can be explored on foot or horseback along three different guided trails. The most conspicuous mammal is the guereza monkey, several troops of which are likely to be seen on any of the trails, but Menelik's bushbuck and mountain nyala are also present. The rich forest avifauna includes the lovely white-cheeked turaco and vociferous silvery-cheeked hornbill, along with the more elusive Abyssinian ground thrush, Abyssinian catbird and Abyssinian woodpecker.

If you are in the vicinity of Lephis on Meskel or the Islamic holiday of Arafa, you might want to head to the village of Wuntashe, 5km back along the Arsi Negele road, to see the Lephis Gugs, an exciting biannual equestrian competition in which riders attempt to strike their opponent with a blunted stick.

Note that the LEC office was burned down during the unrest in 2016 and the organisation is no longer properly operational, but it is still possible to arrange tours with former LEC guide Hamid Tura (m 0928 828530), who is very knowledgeable, particularly about birds.

GETTING THERE AND AWAY The trail head lies about 25km from the main Shashemene road along a fair dirt road branching east from Arsi Negele immediately south of the Mami Hotel (two doors down from a branch of the CBE). Plenty of public transport connects Arsi Negele to Shashemene, Ziway and various other towns in the Rift Valley. Once in Arsi Negele, at least four buses travel to Lephis daily, taking around 90 minutes one-way, with traffic being heaviest on market days (Thursday and Sunday). If you want to go to Lephis and back using public transport in one day, it would be a good idea to overnight in Arsi Negele in order to catch the first bus out, which leaves at 06.30–07.00. The last bus back usually leaves at around 17.00 when hospital staff working in Lephis but living in Arsi Negele knock off for the day. You could also charter a *bajaj* from Arsi Negele to Lephis for around US$15–20 one-way.

WHERE TO STAY
Shoestring

🏠 **DH Café & Guest House** (24 rooms) m 0916 864317. One of several inexpensive hotels dotted around Arsi Negele, the DH Café can be seen on the main road above the Dashen Bank. The entrance, on the side road, has a large 'Kesumesitu' sign ('Reception' in Oromia) above the door. It has clean en-suite rooms with hot shower & TV. *From US$8 dbl.* **$**

🏠 **Fikir Restaurant** (34 rooms) m 0911 215953. This famed restaurant (see below) has recently put up a modern building holding a gym & sauna with clean en-suite rooms. *US$6/8 sgl/dbl.* **$**

Camping
There is an attractive campsite along the overnight Dungago Trail, & you may also be allowed to camp at site of the old LEC headquarters in Lephis village (*expect to pay around US$5 pp/night*). Both options are highly recommended to birdwatchers carrying camping gear, but the headquarters is also a useful fall-back for backpackers should they fail to find public transport back to Arsi Negele in the afternoon.

✕ WHERE TO EAT AND DRINK In Arsi Negele, the inexpensive Fikir Bar and Restaurant, which lies just off the west side of the Addis Ababa road some 300m north of the Dashen Bank, serves excellent fish cutlets and good fasting food. Camping at Lephis, you must either bring your food with you or arrange in advance for the guides to provide basic meals. A small restaurant close to the hospital in Lephis serves *shiro* and *injera* but not much else.

WHAT TO SEE AND DO Three guided trails are offered by the LEC each at a cost of US$15 for up to four people (including the guide and entrance fee, but excluding overnight camping). The most popular day walk is the Waterfall Trail, a 5km round hike on steepish slopes that takes around 2 hours, depending on how often you stop to look at monkeys and birds. The trail is named after a pretty 40m bridal-veil fall on the Lephis River as it tumbles over the escarpment into a rocky pool where you might well encounter the localised mountain wagtail and African black duck. The 10km Dongolo Trail goes deeper into the forest and can be walked in 4–6 hours as a day or overnight trail, camping at a site about halfway along the trail. Finally, the Birdwatching Trail is, as its name suggests, aimed at dedicated birders. The LEC can also arrange horseback excursions along the same routes at an additional charge of US$15 per person, ideally with a bit of advance notice.

SHASHEMENE

Shashemene is southern Ethiopia's most important travel crossroads, situated at the junction of the highway connecting Addis Ababa to Moyale and the more recently asphalted roads running eastward to Bale National Park via Dodola and southwest towards South Omo via Sodo and Arba Minch. In certain respects, it is the archetypal junction town: a mushrooming, amorphous and rather unprepossessing clutter of modern buildings whose fast-growing population includes a steady stream of migrants from the surrounding rural areas. Oddly enough, however, Shashemene's main claim to fame is a migrant community from outside Ethiopia, namely the 300-odd Rastafarian settlers from the Caribbean and elsewhere that live on the northern outskirts of town, on a tract of land donated to them by Haile Selassie I. Shashemene is also of interest for its proximity to the likes of the Lephis

Forest, Lake Chitu, Senkele Game Sanctuary and the hot springs at Wondo Genet. Unfortunately, given its strategic location, Shashemene is also the one town in Ethiopia that receives consistently negative reports from travellers, and while the hostility and crime issues that soured its reputation have abated in recent years, you should still assume that any self-professed teacher or civil servant who approaches you offering assistance is nothing of the sort. On the whole, unless you want to spend time in the Rastafarian Quarter, Shashemene makes for a less appealing overnight prospect than the nearby lakeside town of Hawassa or the resort at Wondo Genet.

HISTORY Shashemene has been an important regional marketplace for centuries. Its name probably derives from the Oromifa phrase *Saas Mana*, meaning 'House of Saas', after the founder of the Saasogo subgroup of the Hadiya people, who lived and was buried there. In the late 19th century it served as the base from which the imperial army of Menelik II conquered surrounding parts of what is now southern Ethiopia and annexed them to the empire. In May 1941, Shashemene suffered from heavy bombardment in one of the fiercest battles fought during the Allied campaign to liberate Ethiopia from its Italian occupiers. The municipality was founded in 1943 and a few years later Emperor Haile Selassie I donated around 200ha of private land north of the town centre as a gesture of thanks for all black people who had supported Ethiopia during the war. It was put under the auspices of an organisation called the Ethiopian World Federation, founded in 1937 in New York by Melaku E Bayen. The first Caribbean returnees settled there in 1955, and by the mid 1960s, newcomers were mainly Rastafarians from Jamaica. In 1974, the land grant was nationalised and many left the country. It was in the 1990s that Rastafarians resumed coming to Shashemene. Today this community numbers about 800 people of 20 citizenships. (For further background, get hold of Giulia Bonacci's *Exodus! Heirs and Pioneers, Rastafari Return to Ethiopia*, published by the University of the West Indies Press in 2015.)

More recently, Shashemene's strategic crossroads location in the fertile Rift Valley has ensured its rapid growth from a dusty junction settlement of around 5,000 people in the 1960s to its modern incarnation as a bustling modern town – to which Rastafarians contribute through various schools, services and activities – with a population approaching the 250,000 mark.

GETTING THERE AND AWAY Shashemene lies 250km from Addis Ababa along a good asphalt road via Modjo (or Butajira). Regular buses run back and forth between Shashemene and Addis Ababa throughout the day (*US$6; 5hrs*), the best being the more costly Sky Bus to Hawassa, 20km further south. There is also reasonably regular transport throughout the day to Ziway (*US$2; 1½hrs*), Sodo (*US$2.75; 2hrs*), Dodola (*US$1.50; 1hr*) and Dilla (*US$2; 2hrs*), while buses to destinations further afield, such as Arba Minch (*US$4.50; 4–5hrs*) or Goba (*US$4; 3–4hrs*), generally leave in the morning only. Minibuses to and from Hawassa leave every few minutes throughout the day, cost US$0.50, and take up to 30 minutes one-way. There are two bus stations in Shashemene. The old central station is the place to pick up transport to Hawassa, Ziway, Wondo Genet and Negele Borena. The new station on the southern bypass road, close to the junction for Bale, services Addis Ababa, Sodo, Arba Minch, Dodola, Goba, Dilla and Moyale.

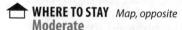

WHERE TO STAY *Map, opposite*

Moderate

Haile Hotel (52 rooms) ◊046 110 1007; m 0930 108484; e shashemene@haileresorts.

com; w haileresorts.com. This well-managed & central hotel has the best facilities in town, including a large inviting swimming pool, a sauna

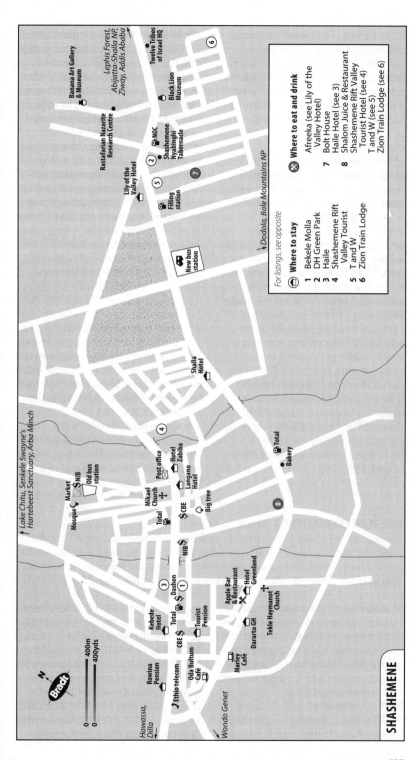

The Southern Rift Valley Lakes   SHASHEMENE

15

537

SHASHEMENE

Hawassa, Dilla

↑ *Lake Chitu, Senkele Swayne's Hartebeest Sanctuary, Arba Minch*

Wondo Genet

N

Bradt

400m
400yds

Rowina Pension

♫ Ethio telecom

Oda Bultum Café

Marley Café

Kebede Hotel

CBE $

NIB $

Total $

Dashen $

Tourist Pension

Darartu GH

Apple Bar & Restaurant

Hotel Greenland

Tekle Haymanot Church

Mosque ☾ Market

⛪ SNIB Old bus station

Mikael Church ✝

Total ⛽

$ CBE

Big tree

Post office ✉

Hotel Zabiba

Langano Hotel

Shalla Hotel

Total ⛽
Bakery

Filling station ⛽

Lily of the Valley Hotel

Shashemene Nyabinghi Tabernacle

NOC ⛽

Rastafarian Nazarite Research Centre

Banana Art Gallery & Museum

Black Lion Museum

Twelve Tribes of Israel HQ

Lephis Forest, Abijatta-Shalla NP, Ziway, Addis Ababa

↓ *Dodola, Bale Mountains NP*

New bus station

For listings, see opposite

🛏 **Where to stay**

1 Bekele Molla
2 DH Green Park
3 Haile
4 Shashemene Rift Valley Tourist
5 T and W
6 Zion Train Lodge

✕ **Where to eat and drink**

   Afreeka (see Lily of the Valley Hotel)
7 Bolt House
   Haile Hotel (see 3)
8 Shalom Juice & Restaurant
   Shashemene Rift Valley Tourist Hotel (see 4)
   T and W (see 5)
   Zion Train Lodge (see 6)

& gym, a great restaurant serving salads, pizza, grills, local food & fish in the US$3–6 range, a pastry shop, & Wi-Fi throughout. The compact but clean en-suite rooms are decorated in a modern style, & come with sat TV & hot water, & larger villas are also available. *Good value at US$30/35 B&B sgl/dbl, or US$37/42 for a villa.* **$$$**

Budget

🏠 **Zion Train Lodge** (6 rooms) m 0911 887681; e ziontrainlodge@hotmail.com; w www.ziontrainlodge.com. Run by a friendly French-speaking Rastafarian couple & located in the heart of the Rastafarian Quarter, this super-chilled lodge is an oasis of peace, greenery & good vibes. The rooms in the central building share a common shower, but are very comfortable & attractively decorated with hand-crafted bamboo furniture & traditional bedspreads. There are also Sidamo-style bamboo huts sleeping 2, & family *tukuls* sleeping 4 with 2 bedrooms & a private shower. The summer hut restaurant serves a healthy range of mostly vegetarian dishes including rice & vegetables, sandwiches, pizza, pasta, banana fritters, fresh fruit juice & milk drinks. Mains are typically US$4–6. Pick-ups from Addis Ababa can be arranged, as can day tours to Lephis Forest, Hawassa & Lake Ziway, at US$6.50/hr. *Camping US$6 pp, US$18 dbl using common shower, US$40/80 for 2-/4-person hut. Most credit cards accepted.* **$$$**

🏠 **DH Green Park Hotel** (32 rooms) 046 211 4142; m 0916 864317; e dhgreenparkhotel@ gmail.com. This new hotel, located east of the town centre at the large junction before the Lily of the Valley Hotel, has comfortable, clean & spacious rooms with wooden floors, sat TV & hot water. Prices at the time of the opening were extremely attractive. *US$12/16 dbl/twin.* **$$**

🏠 **Shashemene Rift Valley Tourist Hotel** (95 rooms) 046 110 5710; m 0910 058886. Situated alongside the old main road north of the town centre, this perennially popular hotel set in attractive green grounds has recently been upgraded to a smart 5-storey block. All rooms are en suite with hot water & sat TV. The so-called 2nd-level rooms appear to be a reasonable choice (*US$12/15 sgl/twin*). There's a good restaurant with a shady outdoor terrace & garden seating. *From US$9.75/19.25 dbl/twin.* **$$**

Shoestring

🏠 **Bekele Molla Hotel** (36 rooms) 046 110 3344. Situated along the main road opposite the Haile Hotel, this venerable & well-priced hotel has slightly timeworn but clean en-suite rooms with net, hot water & small private balcony facing the pretty garden. It often fills up early, so ring ahead to book. *From US$6.50 dbl.* **$**

🏠 **T and W Hotel** (5 rooms) m 0911 750426/091165. This rather discreet guesthouse opposite the Lily of the Valley Hotel has 5 rooms with common shower. It doubles up as a restaurant with Ethiopian dishes for less than US$3 & excellent fresh fruit juice for US$1. *US$6 sgl.* **$**

✖ WHERE TO EAT AND DRINK *Map, page 537*

The best eatery in the town centre is probably the restaurant at the Haile Hotel, while the food at the Zion Train Lodge stands out for health-conscious and vegetarian travellers. The garden restaurant and bar at the Shashemene Rift Valley Tourist Hotel, where monkeys can be numerous, has a pleasant green feel.

✖ **Shalom Juice & Restaurant** ⊕ 06.00– 21.00 daily. Offering the choice of shady pavement seating or a smart tiled interior, this excellent little place on the eastern bypass has a genuine pizza oven & a good selection of juices, & it also serves burgers, pasta dishes, salad & local fare, with most mains costing less than US$2.50.

✖ **Afreeka Restaurant** 10.00–22.00 daily; m 0974 425007; e afreekafinedining@gmail.com. Run by an efficient Rastafarian lady on the ground floor of the Lily of the Valley Hotel, the restaurant offers burgers, sandwiches, pasta & a few Jamaican dishes in the US$2–4 range.

✖ **Bolt House** m 0911 672830; ⊕ 10.00– 23.00 daily. For a taste of the Rastafarian way of life, you shouldn't miss this pleasant enclosed garden situated on a small street opposite the Lily of the Valley Hotel. Come to enjoy the music, the inexpensive fresh fruit juice, shakes & healthy Caribbean & Ethiopian food (*less than US$4*).

WHAT TO SEE AND DO Most places of interest within Shashemene lie in the Rastafarian Quarter, which is often referred to as Jamaica since most of the original settlers came from that island, though many residents from other parts of the world now object to the name. Annual celebrations are held by Rastafarians on 23 July and 2 November (respectively the birthday and anniversary of the coronation of Emperor Haile Selassie) and evening concerts are usually held in the headquarters of the Twelve Tribes of Israel, on the main road. Rural attractions within easy day-tripping distance of Shashemene include Wondo Genet (see below) and Senkele Swayne's Hartebeest Sanctuary (page 540), as well as Lephis Forest (page 534) and Chitu Crater Lake in the southwest of Abijatta-Shalla National Park (page 534).

Black Lion Museum (⏰ *09.00–17.00 Mon–Fri, but closed at time of writing*) This small museum on the main road through the Rastafarian Quarter is dedicated to the history of the first Jamaican settlers at Shashemene. It was closed in early 2015 following the death of the community leader who established it, and is very unlikely to reopen any time soon.

Shashemene Nyabinghi Tabernacle Located behind the NOC petrol station and still partially under construction, this circular structure is associated with Shashemene's Nyabinghi community, the founding order of Rastafari. It is named after a Ugandan queen and spiritual leader who incited a famous uprising against British colonialism. Regarded to be the strictest of Rastafarians, the Nyabinghi adhere to a policy of non-violence and vegetarianism, reflecting their belief that only Jah has the right to kill or destroy. They also claim that Haile Selassie I is still alive and well in their spiritual lives. The friendly and talkative caretaker is happy to give informal guided tours of the small site museum, where you can see a variety of interesting artefacts including a set of the famous Nyabinghi drums. The dress code requires women to be modestly dressed and with a head cover. No entrance fee is charged, but a donation is expected.

Banana Art Gallery and Museum (m *0911 104856;* ⏰ *07.00–19.00 daily; entrance US$2*) Situated about 500m north of the main road along a turn-off signposted opposite the Black Lion Museum, this place showcases the work of Ras Hailu, who originates from the Caribbean island of St Vincent but relocated to Ethiopia in 1994. Ras Hailu's speciality is beautiful collages made using nothing but differently shaded banana leaf cuttings. Artwork may be purchased at around US$20 per item, and the gallery also houses a museum of medals associated with the reign of emperors Menelik II and Haile Selassie I.

Wondo Genet [map, page 531] This popular hot springs resort lies among forested hills near the village of Wosha, 20km south of Shashemene. The nominal attraction is a swimming pool fed by the hot springs, which are said to have curative properties, and the boiling, bubbling vents where the hot water rises. But the area is also of great interest to hikers and nature lovers. Anubis baboon, guereza and grivet monkey can all be seen in the grounds of the hotel next to the springs, along with flocks of the comical silvery-cheeked hornbill and the beautiful white-cheeked turaco. The juniper-covered hills behind the hotel support a much greater variety of forest birds, including mountain buzzard, spotted creeper, Abyssinian woodpecker, Narina trogon, yellow-fronted parrot, banded barbet, double-toothed barbet, Ethiopian oriole, Ethiopian slaty flycatcher, tree pipit and black saw-wing. Also of interest, about 5km northwest of Wosha, swampy Lake Dabash supports a wide range of water and forest birds, and hippos, spotted hyenas and crocodiles are sometimes seen in the area. Wosha is a 30–40-minute drive from Shashemene, and regular minibuses cover the route for US$0.50 per person. From Wosha, a well-signposted 2.5km dirt road runs uphill to the hot springs and the hotel next to them. Outside the hotel, the well-organised Wondo Genet Ecotourism Guide Association (m *0928 768347;* e *wondogenetecoguides@gmail.com;* w *wondogenetecoguides.wordpress.com*) has a kiosk where you can arrange visits to the hot springs, guided bird walks, forest hikes and day trips to Lake Dabash for US$5–20 per group (up to four people).

⌂ *Where to stay, eat and drink* Map, page 531

⌂ **Wondo Genet Resort Hotel** (40 rooms) ☏ 046 119 0705; m 0911 089051. The former Wabe Shebelle Hotel, originally built as a private holiday residence for Emperor Haile Selassie, & still set in wooded grounds right next to the hot springs, has such a wonderful setting that it is tempting not to dwell too much on the time-warped 70s-style accommodation & restaurant, which could really do with some refurbishment. The en-suite rooms do all come with a hot shower & the restaurant offers spectacular sunset views over Lake Hawassa. Still, less than great value. *US$24/31 sgl/dbl.* **$$$**

⌂ **Abyssinia Hotel** (20 rooms) ☏ 046 114 0203. Also known as the Kedir Idris Hotel, this is the best of a few inexpensive options in Wosha, situated on the junction for the hot springs. The rooms are basic but clean. *US$7/9 sgl/dbl using common shower, US$12/16 sgl/dbl en suite.* **$$**

Senkele Swayne's Hartebeest Sanctuary [map, page 531] (*Entrance US$4.50 pp, plus US$1 per vehicle & US$10 per party for a mandatory scout*) This 58km² reserve in the hills west of Shashemene was created in 1976 to protect what was then the largest population of Swayne's hartebeest, an endangered Ethiopian endemic. The hartebeest population at Senkele stood at around 300, and it has fluctuated greatly since then due to periods of intensive poaching, but it probably stands at around 500 today, and sightings are practically guaranteed thanks to the reserve's small size and the open nature of the terrain. You're also all but certain to see the smaller oribi, while other residents of the light acacia woodland include greater kudu, waterbuck, warthog, Eurasian jackal and around 190 bird species.

Coming from Shashemene, follow the Arba Minch road west for 30km to the small town of Aje, then continue for another 5km until you see the turn-off to Senkele signposted to the left. From here, it'a 10km drive to the entrance gate. The reserve's road circuit is very limited, so walking is permitted, but access would be difficult without your own vehicle. There is no campsite or accommodation within the reserve, but a few basic hotels exist in Aje. However, in a private vehicle, it is easily visited as a day excursion from Shashemene, possibly in conjunction with the nearby Chitu Crater Lake (page 534), or en route to Arba Minch.

HAWASSA

Situated on the eastern shore of the eponymous lake only 25km south of Shashemene, the city of Hawassa doubles as a popular resort town and the capital of Ethiopia's most ethnically and linguistically diverse federal component, the Southern Nations, Nationalities and Peoples' Region (SNNPR). Hawassa is an unusually bright and modern city, with a compact, attractively laid-out centre and good amenities, making it a convenient and comfortable place to break up any journey between Addis Ababa and more southerly destinations. Its main attraction is undoubtedly the scenic Lake Hawassa, which extends over 90km² in an ancient volcanic caldera, making it the smallest lake in the Ethiopian Rift. Although it is quite shallow, with a maximum

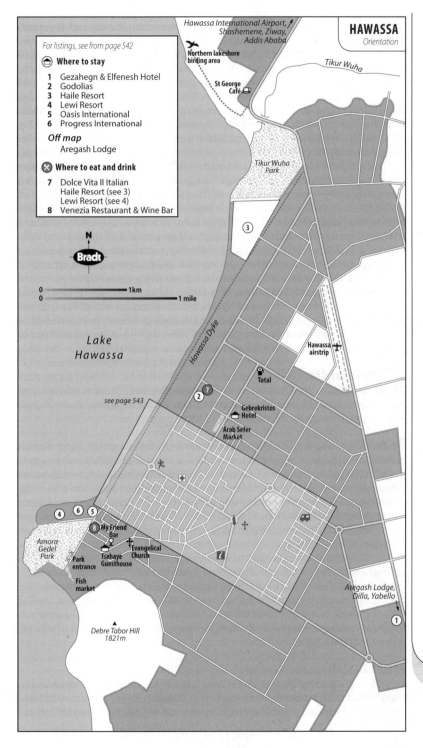

For listings, see from page 542

Where to stay

1 Gezahegn & Elfenesh Hotel
2 Godolias
3 Haile Resort
4 Lewi Resort
5 Oasis International
6 Progress International

Off map
   Aregash Lodge

Where to eat and drink

7 Dolce Vita II Italian
   Haile Resort (see 3)
   Lewi Resort (see 4)
8 Venezia Restaurant & Wine Bar

N

Bradt

0 ──────── 1km
0 ──────────── 1 mile

Lake
Hawassa

Hawassa International Airport,
Shashemene, Ziway,
Addis Ababa

Northern lakeshore
birding area

St George
Café

Tikur Wuha

Tikur Wuha
Park

Hawassa Dyke

③

Hawassa
airstrip

Total

② ⑦

see page 543

Gebrekristos
Hotel

Arab Sefer
Market

④ ⑥ ⑤

⑧ My Friend
   Bar

Amora
Gedel
Park

Park
entrance

Tsehaye
Guesthouse

Evangelical
Church

Fish
market

▲ *Debre Tabor Hill*
1821m

Aregash Lodge,
Dilla, Yabello

①

The Southern Rift Valley Lakes   HAWASSA

15

depth of 22m, and has no surface outlet, Hawassa is a freshwater lake and it supports a thriving fish population, as well as more than 70 species of aquatic bird. The lush lakeshore vegetation of dense sedge and scrub, shadowed by handsome old ficus trees, also supports plenty of monkeys and a rich variety of forest and woodland birds. Hippos are present, but generally only seen from a boat.

HISTORY Hawassa is the principal town of the Sidama, who speak a Cushitic language distantly affiliated to Oromifa. Oral tradition suggests that the Sidama have inhabited their present-day homeland, which stretches south from Hawassa to Dilla, at least since the 9th century AD. Prior to being conquered by Emperor Menelik II in the 1880s, Sidama comprised a loose coalition of smaller fiefdoms whose economy was based on agriculture and livestock. Back then, the fertile, well-watered eastern shore of Lake Hawassa was known as Ada'are, a Sidama word meeting 'Field of Cattle'. Hawassa itself is one of Ethiopia's youngest towns, founded by Haile Selassie in 1956 as a proposed industrial centre for the processing of agricultural products such as Sidama coffee, and to service the tourism potential of the adjacent lake. Originally called Awassa, the fledgling settlement was accorded municipal status in 1960, at which time it extended over less than 50ha and supported a population of around 2,000. The town's rise to modern prominence dates to 1978 when the Derg chose it to replace Yirga Alem as capital of Sidamo Province. In 1994, it was made capital of the newly created SNNPR, an amalgamation of Sidamo and four other Derg-era provinces. In 2009, the spelling Awassa was officially corrected to Hawassa, a Sidama word meaning 'big lake'. Hawassa is now the largest town in southern Ethiopia, with a population estimated at around 300,000.

GETTING THERE AND AWAY
By Air Ethiopian Airlines now flies at least once daily in either direction between Addis Ababa and the new Hawassa International Airport, which stands on the western lakeshore about 10km drive out of town.

By road Hawassa lies 275km south of Addis Ababa along the main asphalt highway to Moyale. The drive takes 4 5 hours in a private vehicle and slightly longer using public transport. The best service is the daily Sky Bus, which leaves Addis Ababa at 07.00, arrives at Hawassa 4 hours later, then starts the return trip at around noon. The ticket office and terminus are at the Alliance Business Centre on the east end of the main road (m *0934 395849*). More than a dozen cheaper but slower buses run back and forth to Addis Ababa daily, leaving Hawassa from the main bus station 500m southeast of the South Star International Hotel. This bus station also has regular departures to Shashemene (*30–45mins*), Ziway (*2hrs*), Sodo (*2½hrs*) and Dilla (*1½hrs*), and a couple of buses run daily to Arba Minch (*5hrs*). For transport to Goba and destinations in the southeast, head to Shashemene. For destinations along the Moyale road, such as Yabello, head to Dilla. On foot, the bus station is about 15 minutes from the main road and 30 minutes from the lakefront hotels, so you might want to catch one of the shared and chartered *bajaji* that queue up on the opposite side of the road.

 WHERE TO STAY *Map, opposite, unless otherwise stated*
Hawassa is graced by a vast selection of resorts and hotels catering to most tastes and budgets, and the listings below are of necessity selective. A very popular alternative to staying in Hawassa, particularly with tour groups headed south towards Yabello, is the rustically upmarket Aregash Lodge in Yirga Alem.

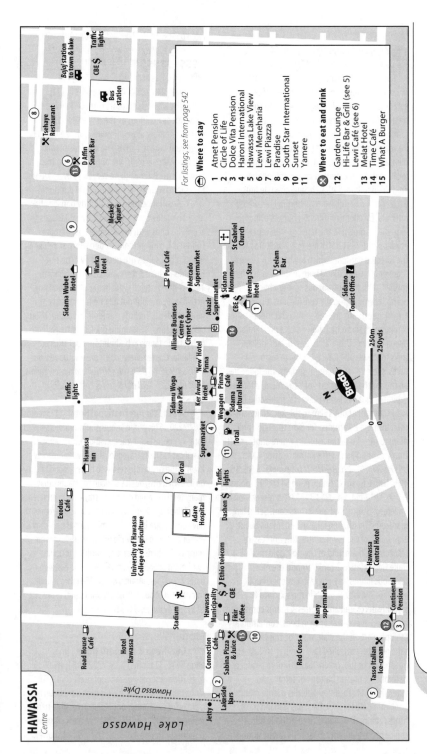

HAWASSA
Centre

Lake Hawassa

Hawassa Dyke

For listings, see from page 542

Where to stay
1. Atnet Pension
2. Circle of Life
3. Dolce Vita Pension
4. Haroni International
5. Hawassa Lake View
6. Lewi Meneharia
7. Lewi Piazza
8. Paradise
9. South Star International
10. Sunset
11. Yamere

Where to eat and drink
12. Garden Lounge
    Hi-Life Bar & Grill (see 5)
    Lewi Café (see 6)
13. Melat Hotel
14. Time Café
15. What A Burger

Jetty
Lakeside bars
Connection Café
Road House Café
Hotel Hawassa
Sabina Pizza & Juice
Fikir Coffee
Hawassa Municipality
CBE
Ethio telecom
University of Hawassa College of Agriculture
Stadium
Adare Hospital
Dashen
Total
Exodus Café
Hawassa Inn
Traffic lights
Sidamu Woga Hora Park
Ker Awud Hotel
New Hotel Pinna
Wegagen
Pinna Café
Sidama Cultural Hall
Supermarket
Total
Alliance Business Centre & Citynet Cyber
Abazir Supermarket
Sidama Wubet Hotel
Warka Hotel
Post Café
Mercado Supermarket
Meskel Square
D Affin Snack Bar
Tsehaye Restaurant
Bus station
Bajaj station to town & lake
CBE
Traffic lights
Sidamo Monument
Evening Star Hotel
CBE
St Gabriel Church
Selam Bar
Sidamo Tourist Office
Red Cross
Hany supermarket
Hawassa Central Hotel
Continental Pension
Tasso Italian Ice-cream

0 250m
0 250yds

The Southern Rift Valley Lakes HAWASSA

15

543

Upmarket

Aregash Lodge [map, page 541] (15 bungalows) ✆046 225 0575/1136; m 0912 639594; e info@aregashlodge.com; w aregashlodge.com. Situated on a coffee estate 45km south of Hawassa, Aregash Lodge, owned & managed by a Greek–Ethiopian family that started farming the plot more than 70 years ago, ranks among the country's most pleasant & best-run resorts. The rustic highland location is complemented by accommodation in en-suite bamboo-&-thatch Sidamo-style huts, each with 1 or 2 dbl rooms & brightly decorated interiors. Excellent continental buffets using fresh ingredients grown in the large on-site vegetable gardens cost US$12.50. Guests are welcome to visit the forested gardens, which are home to guereza & grivet monkeys, along with more than 100 bird species, with the outrageous silvery-cheeked hornbill being especially conspicuous. Upon arrival, guests are greeted with a traditional coffee ceremony that can be followed by a pre-dinner hyena viewing. Other activities include guided treks to the nearby forest & visits to historical caves, sacred sites & natural springs. The lodge lies on the southeast outskirts of Yirga Alem, a former capital of Sidamo. From Hawassa, follow the Dilla road south for about 35km to the Aposto junction, then turn left & continue for 8km through Yirga Alem to the end of the asphalt, where another left turn will bring you to the entrance after 400m. *US$70/80/105/120 B&B 1/2/3/4 people.* **$$$$$**

Haile Resort [map, page 541] (112 rooms) ✆046 220 8444; m 0963 313131; e reservation@haileresorts.com; w haileresorts.com. Set in large manicured fig-shaded lakeshore gardens about 2km north of the town centre, this impressive resort is the brainchild of Olympic gold medallist Haile Gebrselassie & ranks among the most luxurious lodges anywhere in Ethiopia. Public areas are swish & airy, while the spacious & stylishly decorated apts, suites & rooms come with hardwood queen-size or twin beds, contemporary Ethiopian art on the wall, state-of-the-art sat TV, safe, remote-controlled fan, minibar, free Wi-Fi, hot shower or tub, green-tea bathroom products, bathrobes & private balcony or terrace. An extensive list of facilities includes a large infinity pool, minigolf, lakeside bar, spa, walking track, fitness centre designed & used by Haile himself & a choice of 5 restaurants. Boat trips can be arranged.

From US$66/86 B&B dbl with garden/lake view, increasing slightly over w/ends, suites US$136. **$$$$–$$$$$**

Lewi Resort [map, page 541] (59 rooms) ✆046 221 4143; m 0916 313131; e info@lewihotelandresort.com; w lewiresort.com. Not as luxurious as the Haile Resort but correspondingly more affordable, the Lewi lies in large well-wooded lakeshore gardens teeming with monkeys & birds, yet only 1km from the town centre. It tends to be very busy over w/ends, but is much quieter & more tranquil during the week. Accommodation is in slightly garish split-level bungalows with steam showers, jacuzzis & circular beds with inbuilt speakers, or more subdued & conventional garden-view or deluxe rooms all en suite with nets, sat TV & balcony. Facilities include 3 restaurants, a piano bar, an 18th-century-styled wine bar & a fast-food hut. Activities, some but not all of which are free to hotel residents, include minigolf, mountain biking, steam & sauna, swimming pool, cinema (w/ends only), table tennis & badminton. Boat trips are available. *Garden-view rooms are very good value at US$39/55/65 B&B sgl/dbl/twin, lake view rooms start at US$85 B&B dbl & suites cost US$229.* **$$$$**

South Star International Hotel (113 rooms) ✆046 220 1616; e info@southstarinternationalhotel.com; w southstarinternationalhotel.com. Aimed mainly at business travellers, this new multistorey hotel in the city centre seems to be very good taken on its own terms, but it's difficult to imagine that many tourists would choose to stay here in preference to its lakeshore peers. The smart & spacious rooms all have queen-size bed, sat TV, minibar, safe, balcony & en-suite hot shower, while the larger deluxe rooms come with 2 beds & a jacuzzi. Facilities include a swimming pool on the 2nd floor, sauna & steam bath, 2 good restaurants, & free Wi-Fi throughout. *Fair value at US$69/99 sgl/dbl, with suites in the US$139–49 range.* **$$$$**

Moderate

Gezahegn & Elfenesh Hotel [map, page 541] (32 rooms) ✆046 212 5024; m 0935 377070; e reserve@gezahegnhotels.com; w gezahegnhotels.com. This high-end hotel has a pleasant swimming pool (also accessible to non-residents at US$3 or US$4 over w/ends) & sauna, & rooms with safe, balcony, DSTV & hot shower.

B&B US$48/58 standard sgl/dbl, US$68 deluxe dbl & US$130 suite; prices increase by US$10 Fri–Sun. **$$$$**

🏠 **Hawassa Lake View Hotel** (21 rooms) ☏046 220 8080; m 0916 828282; w hawassalakeviewhotel.com. This new boutique hotel close to the lakeshore has been widely praised for its comfortable accommodation & very reasonable rates. The spacious modern rooms all have contemporary furnishings, sat TV, Wi-Fi, en-suite hot shower & private balcony with a view over the lake (best from the top floors), while the ground floor houses the excellent Hi-Life Restaurant. *Good value, with rates starting at US$25 dbl (which, unlike most hotels in this category, excludes b/fast).* **$$$**

🏠 **Oasis International Hotel** [map, page 541] (38 rooms) ☏046 220 6452; m 0916 581490; e info@oasisinternationalhotel.com; w oasishotelhawassa.com. Located about 300m from the lake next to a patch of forest on the road out to the Lewi Resort, this bland modern 5-storey hotel is very businesslike in its approach & amenities, offering reasonably priced standard rooms with tiled floors, DSTV & hot-water shower, as well as deluxe rooms with king-size bed, & suites with fridge. *Decent value at B&B US$26/35 standard sgl/dbl, US$48 deluxe dbl, US$58 suite.* **$$$**

🏠 **Lewi Piazza Hotel** (39 rooms) ☏046 220 1654; e lewipiazza@gmail.com; w lewiresort.com. This more central & less upmarket older sister of the Lewi Resort is a blandly modern multistorey all-suite hotel with a good restaurant attached & Wi-Fi throughout. The sensibly priced & well-furnished suites all have king-size bed, sat TV, minibar & safe. A costlier standard suite also has a steam bath, while deluxe suites have private balcony, a 2-person jacuzzi tub & a massage chair. *B&B US$31/38/60 business/standard/deluxe suite.* **$$$**

🏠 **Godolias** [map, page 541] (46 rooms) m 0964 131984; e godoliashotel@gmail.com; w godoliashotel.com. Located just beside the Dolce Vita II restaurant, this brand-new hotel has very clean & comfortable rooms. *US$32/46/80 B&B dbl/twin/family.* **$$$**

Budget

✴ 🏠 **Progress International Hotel** [map, page 541] (24 rooms) m 0911 685003. This former government hotel has undergone several name changes since it was privatised a few years back, none of which has disguised the fact that the simple rooms, which come with net, hot shower & timeworn 1970s-style furnishings, are well due an overhaul. But the location on a particularly large & well-wooded stretch of lakeshore remains utterly delightful & arguably compensates for any other shortcomings. Indeed, the hotel gardens, with a small swimming pool, virtually function as a wildlife sanctuary: fish eagles nest in the fig trees, guereza & vervet monkeys & silvery-cheeked hornbills are regular visitors, woodland & waterbirds are everywhere, & even the odd hippo makes an appearance. An adequate restaurant overlooks the lake. *US$11/17/23 B&B sgl/twin/dbl.* **$$**

🏠 **Dolce Vita Pension** (10 rooms) ☏046 220 5050; m 0916 823159. Set in the leafy suburbs near the lake, the quiet, cosy & attractively decorated rooms at this affiliate to the eponymous Italian restaurant rank among the best value in town, coming as they do with sat TV, net, fan, fridge, small sitting area & en-suite hot shower. *US$18 dbl.* **$$**

🏠 **Lewi Meneharia Hotel** (40 rooms) ☏046 220 6310; e info@lewiresort.com; w lewiresort.com. One of several cheapies along the road to the bus station, this is the most downmarket of Hawassa's trio of Lewi hotels, but the en-suite rooms with TV, hot water & Wi-Fi are pretty good by any other standards, & very convenient for short stays. *US$12/16/22 sgl/dbl/twin.* **$$**

🏠 **Haroni International Hotel** (32 rooms) ☏046 220 0704; e hotelharoni@yahoo.com. The pick of a few similarly bland business hotels set along the main road through the town centre, the 5-storey Haroni stands out for its modern décor & good-value en-suite rooms with TV & hot shower. *US$20/25 B&B dbl/twin.* **$$–$$$**

🏠 **Yamere Hotel** (68 rooms) ☏046 220 0177/8. This long-serving hotel on the main street has an old wing offering clean & well-maintained en-suite rooms with hot shower & sat TV, & a new wing where larger rooms have fresh modern furnishings. An adequate restaurant is attached. *From US$12/20 dbl/twin.* **$$**

Shoestring

🏠 **Paradise Hotel** (34 rooms) ☏046 220 4368. This pleasant hotel in a quiet location close to the bus station offers fair value for money for a clean, tiled room with net & TV. The large patio area is a good place for a drink. *US$7/16 dbl with common/en-suite shower.* **$–$$**

🏠 **Sunset Hotel** (10 rooms) 📞046 220 6776. Clean-looking guesthouse with en-suite rooms. Located next to What A Burger towards the fish market. *US$8–10 depending on room size.* **$**

🏠 **Atnet Pension** (42 rooms) 📞046 220 1686. Select your room at this centrally situated guesthouse carefully, checking the running water

& avoiding proximity with the St Gabriel Church. *US$6–12 depending on room size.* **$–$$**

🏠 **Circle of Life** (12 rooms) m 0913 785191. This remarkable, small guesthouse-cum-garden is located near the extremity of the main jetty, where the lakeshore walk begins & from where boats can be hired. It is run by a militant Ethio–Irish Rastafarian couple. *US$6/10 sgl with common/en-suite shower.* **$**

✖ **WHERE TO EAT AND DRINK** *Map, page 543, unless otherwise stated*

In addition to the standalone restaurants listed below, the lakeshore eateries at the Haile and Lewi resorts are highly recommended, while cheap eats and drinks are available at the cluster of local bars and coffee shops running down to the main jetty.

Moderate to expensive

✖ **Hi-Life Bar & Grill** 📞046 221 1118; m 0930 108351; e contact@hi-life-hawassa. com; ⓕ; ⏰ 07.30–21.30 daily. Funky Ghanaian-influenced décor, superb fish dishes & kebabs, interrupted lake views & a well-stocked bar are the main selling points of this exceptional new restaurant spanning the ground floor & terrace of the Lake View Hotel. It also has a good selection of pizzas, burgers & Ethiopian fare, & an unusually imaginative b/fast selection including smoothies. *Very well priced at around US$3–6 for most mains.*

✖ **Venezia Restaurant & Wine Bar** [map, page 541] 📞046 220 0955; m 0916 513212; ⏰ 09.00–22.00 daily. This stylish 2-storey Italian restaurant, run by a very friendly Italian–Ethiopian couple, serves 15 types of pizza daily, as well as pasta dishes, grills & fresh fish with many of the hard-to-get ingredients imported direct from Italy. The chef prepares outstanding speciality dishes to order. A rooftop terrace bar serves wines from half a dozen countries. *Mains US$4–8.*

✖ **Dolce Vita II Italian Restaurant** [map, page 541] m 0916 823159; ⏰ 07.00–22.00 daily. Situated north of the town centre along the road to the Haile Resort, this popular restaurant serves some of the best Italian food in the country & features fresh pasta dishes, many with fish, along

with salads & good 'fasting food', & wood-fired pizzas in the evenings. *Mains US$3–5.*

Cheap to moderate

✖ **Melat Hotel** 📞046 212 0456; ⏰ 07.30–22.00 daily. The shady terrace restaurant at this small hotel near the bus station serves excellent fish, as well as various pasta & traditional dishes. *Most mains around US$3.*

✖ **Lewi Café** ⏰ 07.00–midnight daily. Part of the Lewi Meneharia Hotel, this popular garden restaurant is a pleasant place to chill out, with background Ethiopian music playing at a comfortable volume. It is known for its roast lamb, but pizza, pasta, fish & the usual Ethiopian dishes also feature on the long menu. *Mains US$3–4.*

✖ **Garden Lounge** ⏰ 09.00–midnight daily. Situated next to the original Dolce Vita, this funky garden bar serves a good selection of Ethiopian dishes, mostly for around US$3.

✖ **Time Café** 📞046 220 6331; ⏰ 07.00–21.00 daily. The outdoor terrace at this central Starbucks wannabe is a good spot to stop for coffee, smoothie or juices, or a quick snack of chips, pastries, burgers or sandwiches. *US$1–3.*

✖ **What A Burger** Awful name notwithstanding, this serves some of the tastiest & freshest burgers in town in a large garden near the main jetty. *US$2–3.*

WHAT TO SEE AND DO Hawassa offers limited urban sightseeing but the lakeshore is very rewarding for birdwatchers, and it also offers an opportunity to get close to guereza and grivet monkeys, or to take out a boat to look for hippos. In addition, most of the sites of interest listed under Shashemene – the likes of Wondo Genet, Senkele Swayne's Hartebeest Sanctuary and Lake Chitu – could almost as easily be visited as a day trip out of Hawassa.

Around town Notable landmarks are few and far between. The most prominent is the cylindrical Sidamo Monument, which towers above the main roundabout in front of St Gabriel Church like a giant rolled-up scroll, but in fact represents the leaf of the *enset* (false banana) plant, a mainstay of the local subsistence economy. The monument is also decorated with mosaics depicting scenes associated with Sidama history and tradition. On the main road 400m to the northwest, in front of the Sidama Cultural Hall, the **Sidamu Woga Hora Park** is a neat garden-like open space dotted with traditional statues. A few hundred metres north of the main road, the colourful Arab Sefer Market is a good place to buy locally made straw hats, mats and baskets, being particularly lively on the main market days of Monday and Thursday when it attracts villagers from all around the district.

Hawassa Dyke Built to prevent seasonal flooding, the lengthy dyke that follows the shore of Lake Hawassa, starting in front of the Hawassa Lake View Hotel and running north almost as far as the Haile Resort, doubles as a good walking trail, especially for birdwatchers. Fish eagle, silvery-cheeked hornbill, grey kestrel, several types of weaver, and the endemic black-winged lovebird, yellow-fronted parrot, banded barbet and Ethiopian oriole are common in patches bordering the dyke, while blue-headed coucal, Bruce's green pigeon and white-rumped babbler are regular in the marshy scrub. A variety of herons, storks, terns, plovers and waders might be seen in the water or along the shore, and there is perhaps no better place in East Africa to see the colourful and localised pygmy goose.

Amora Gedel Park [map, page 541] Also known as Guduma, this 26ha tract of riparian woodland to the south of the Lewi Resort once housed a recreational palace for Princess Tenagnework Tefari, the eldest daughter of Haile Selassie, but was set aside as a municipal park. For the time being it is of interest mainly for its plentiful monkeys and woodland birds – look out in particular for the endemic black-winged lovebird nesting in dead trees, as well as Bruce's green pigeon, double-toothed barbet and pearl-spotted owl. Tourists may be asked to pay an entrance fee of US$1 at the main gate, but it is unclear how legitimate this is.

Fish market [map, page 541] Hawassa's daily fish market (*asa gebeya*), set on a peninsula immediately south of the Amora Gedel Park, is a good place to see waterbirds such as pelicans and gulls, as well as getting close up to the ungainly marabou storks who are fed there with fish scraps provided by local boys. Catfish heads litter the ground, but there is a huge fig tree that provides some natural beauty. Inexpensive raw and cooked fish are available to eat. Based on our most recent visit, there no longer seems to be an entrance fee of US$1, or any obligation to take a guide, but it could be we just slipped through the net, so to speak!

Debre Tabor Hill [map, page 541] The isolated low mountain that rises to the immediate south of Hawassa was formerly known as Tilte, the Sidama name for a plate on which *injera* is served, on account of its flat circular top. It was renamed in 1958 when Haile Selassie came to inaugurate the recently founded town, and was struck by the hill's resemblance to Mount Tabor, which overlooks the Sea of Galilee in Israel. A relatively undemanding hike from the town centre or fish market leads to the peak, which offers wonderful views over Lake Hawassa and its hinterland. Note, however, that we received a report of at least two violent muggings on the hill in 2012, and were told locally that it is still risky to hike up unguided unless you leave all your valuables behind in your hotel room.

Boat trips The best way to see some of the hippos that inhabit Lake Hawassa is by boat, which can be arranged either through the Lewi Resort (*US$6 pp, min group size 7*) or through one of the private captains at the main jetty a couple of hundred metres west of the town centre (*negotiable but expect to pay around US$20 for a small group*). The boat trip usually lasts an hour or so and while hippo sightings aren't guaranteed, most people do at least get to see a few curious heads popping out of the water, along with charismatic waterbirds such as African fish eagle and great white pelican.

Tikur Wuha and the northeast lakeshore [map, page 541] Tikur Wuha (Black Water) is the name of the small river that flows into Lake Hawassa about 600m north of the Haile Resort, as well as the lushly vegetated but undeveloped 47ha park that divides the resort from the inlet, and the small township that has arisen on the western riverbank. The best access point to the northeast lakeshore around Tikur Wuha is the St George Café, a short distance north of the bridge across the river, where you can park a car (or hop off a *bajaj*) and walk a few hundred metres west to the lake. Hippos are sometimes seen from the shore there, and it is a good spot for the spectacular black-crowned crane and rather more inconspicuous lesser jacana. The marshy area overlooked by the bridge across the river is also a rewarding spot for birds, particularly African pygmy goose and for watching the occasional hippo family soaking in the river.

SODO

The substantial town of Sodo marks the crossroads of the main surfaced road between Shashemene and Arba Minch, the new asphalt road north to/from Addis Ababa via Hosanna, and a rougher unsurfaced road to Jimma in western Ethiopia. The capital of Wolayta Zone (and often referred to by that name), the town lies at a temperate altitude of around 2,000m on a green part of the Rift Valley Escarpment notable for its maize cultivation. Most travellers do no more than pass through Sodo en route to or from Arba Minch, and in all honesty the town has very little going for it aside from one small museum and the large market on the east side of the town centre, which is busiest on Saturdays. But surrounding parts of Wolayta are dotted with several under-publicised points of interest ranging from the eminently climbable Mount Damota to the twin waterfalls at Ajora off the Hosanna road. Sodo is also the springboard for visits to the little-known but surprisingly worthwhile Maze National Park, which supports an important population of the endemic Swayne's hartebeest and is also perhaps the last place in Ethiopia where wild lions are still seen with any regularity.

HISTORY Sodo is the principal town of the Omotic-speaking Wolayta, whose centralised kingdom, established in around 1250 by Kawo (King) Bitto, was an important regional power for almost 650 years. According to oral tradition, Bitto's successor Motolomi was the 'King of Damot' who was converted to Orthodox Christianity in around 1280 by Abuna Tekle Haymanot. Over subsequent centuries, Wolayta became an important centre of agriculture that maintained strong economic ties to the Solomonic Empire. In the aftermath of the 17th-century war between its Christian and Muslim neighbours, Wolayta underwent considerable territorial expansion under a succession of powerful kings, notably Kawo Sanna (1762–90), Amado (1822–48) and Gobe (1853–89). The fertile soils and bountiful agricultural produce of Wolayta made it highly desirable to Emperor Menelik II, who annexed it to Ethiopia in 1894 following a bloody campaign in which 118,000 Wolayta and 90,000 Shewan troops are said to have died before the kingdom's last ruler Kawo

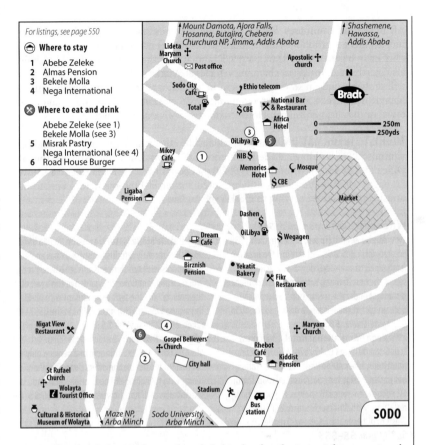

For listings, see page 550

🛏 **Where to stay**
1 Abebe Zeleke
2 Almas Pension
3 Bekele Molla
4 Nega International

❌ **Where to eat and drink**
Abebe Zeleke (see 1)
Bekele Molla (see 3)
5 Misrak Pastry
Nega International (see 4)
6 Road House Burger

↑ Mount Damota, Ajora Falls,
Hosanna, Butajira, Chebera
Churchura NP, Jimma, Addis Ababa

↑ Shashemene,
Hawassa,
Addis Ababa

Lideta
Maryam ✝
Church
✉ Post office

Apostolic ✝
church

Sodo City
Café

♪ Ethio telecom

Total

$ CBE

National Bar
❌ & Restaurant

Bradt

N

0 ———— 250m
0 ———— 250yds

Africa
Hotel

③

OiLibya 🖉   ⑤

Mikey
Café

①

NIB $

$ CBE

Memories
Hotel

☪ Mosque

Ligaba
Pension

Market

Dashen
$

OiLibya 🖉

$ Wegagen

Dream
Café

Birznish
Pension

● Yekatit
Bakery

❌ Fikr
Restaurant

Nigat View
Restaurant ❌

④

⑥

Gospel Believers'
✝ Church

City hall

Rhebot
Café

Kiddist
Pension

✝ Maryam
Church

②

St Rufael
Church
✝

ℹ Wolayta
Tourist Office

Stadium 🧍

🚌 Bus
station

SODO

Cultural & Historical
Museum of Wolayta

↓ Maze NP,
Arba Minch

Sodo University,
Arba Minch ↓

Tona conceded defeat. Sodo was founded shortly after the imperial conquest, only 8km west of Kawo Tona's destroyed capital at Dalbo, and it was granted municipal status in 1945. Perhaps out of respect for its long history, Wolayta was granted a high level of autonomy during the late imperial era, being ruled over by a succession of governors who answered directly to the emperor right up until the fall of Emperor Haile Selassie. Under the Derg, Wolayta was administered as part of Sidamo, then in 1995 it was incorporated into the North Omo Zone of the SNNPR. Wolayta experienced a major political crisis at the turn of the millennium, sparked by the central government's attempt to enforce an artificial composite Omotic language on the schools of Wolayta and elsewhere in North Omo. Following widespread rioting during which several civilians were killed in Sodo, the government abandoned this misguided plan in 2000, and went one step further by splitting Wolayta from the rest of North Omo as a discrete zone. Sodo became a university town in 2008 and it now supports a population approaching the 100,000 mark.

GETTING THERE AND AWAY Sodo can be reached from Addis Ababa along a good 310km asphalt road via Butajira and Hosanna, or a longer and busier 380km route through Modjo and Shashemene. Direct buses to/from Addis Ababa (*8hrs*) leave throughout the morning (last departure generally around 14.00), and generally use the former route. Minibuses to Hosanna (*1½hrs*), Arba Minch (*2½hrs*) and Shashemene or Hawassa (*2–4hrs*) generally run throughout daylight hours.

All buses and minibuses depart from the new bus station, which has a rather inconvenient location near the stadium at the south end of the town centre.

A daily bus to Jimma leaves at 09.00 and arrives the next morning. You could also bus through in stages, changing vehicles at Wukka and Tulcha. Either way, you will probably end up staying overnight in Tulcha, where accommodation options include the Engeda Hotel (*bar, restaurant; US$5 en-suite dbl;* $) on the road out of town, or the cheaper Kenean Hotel (*tukul-style rooms, great views;* $).

TOURIST INFORMATION Situated alongside the museum in the hilltop administrative buildings at the south end of the town centre, the Wolayta Tourist Office (\ *046 551 2863;* m *0913 170579;* e *info@visitwolayta.com*) stocks a handy 74-page tourist guide to this little-explored corner of Ethiopia, and seems to be unusually proactive in trying to market the region.

WHERE TO STAY *Map, page 549*

Abebe Zeleke Hotel (79 rooms) m 0930 505420, 0911 205525. Centrally located in large landscaped gardens, this new 6-storey hotel seems the best in town, with a pleasant outdoor restaurant under the tree in front. Suites include a steam bath & there is also a gym. *US$26/30/56 B&B sgl/dbl/suite.* **$$$**

Nega International Hotel (44 rooms) \ 046 180 0012; m 0919 707424. This functional multistorey block 400m west of the bus station has unremarkable but spacious tiled rooms with TV, fridge & en-suite hot shower. A ground-floor restaurant with Wi-Fi serves tasty Ethiopian & Western dishes in the US$3–4.50 range. *US$16/26 B&B sgl/twin.* **$$–$$$**

Bekele Molla Hotel (45 rooms) \ 046 551 2382. This recently refurbished stalwart has en-suite rooms with hot shower & private balcony set around a pleasant flowering garden in the heart of the town centre. The terrace restaurant with Wi-Fi has a varied menu, with most mains in the US$2–4 range. *US$12/20 sgl/dbl.* **$$**

Almas Pension (22 rooms) m 0930 505420, 0920 498090. This gem of a pension only 500m from the bus station offers clean en-suite rooms with tiled floor, dbl bed, ample cupboard space & powerful hot showers. *US$11.50 dbl.* **$$**

WHERE TO EAT AND DRINK *Map, page 549*

The best proper restaurants are probably those at the Abebe Zeleke Hotel, Nega International and Bekele Molla hotels. For lighter meals, **Road House Burger** (m *0911 069024;* ⊕ *07.30–21.00 daily*) close to Almas Pension has indoor and terrace seating, and serves great burgers and pizzas, as well as cakes, juices and coffees, while **Misrak Pastry** (m *0916 832495*) opposite the Bekele Molla is also excellent for pizzas, pastries, coffee and juice.

WHAT TO SEE AND DO
Cultural and Historical Museum of Wolayta (⊕ *08.00–12.30 & 13.30–17.30 Mon–Fri, entrance US$6*) Situated in the well-wooded zonal administrative compound at the southern end of town, this low-key museum is housed in a spectacular outsized replica of a traditional Wolayta hut, and displays a number of artefacts associated with King Tono and his defeat by Menelik II. Of particular interest are some examples of the large *marcuwa* coins used by the Wolayta in the 19th century, various traditional seats made of cane and *enset* leaves, clay pottery and some fantastic musical instruments, including a guitar-liked *dittaa* made from a giant leopard tortoise shell. Unfortunately, it is all displayed in a rather haphazard way, with no labels or interpretative material, which makes the entrance fee seem pretty steep, even though photography is permitted.

Mount Damota Also known as Damot, this important watershed is the tallest mountain in Wolayta, a dormant volcano whose peak rises to just below 3,000m to the immediate north of Sodo. Damota served for several centuries as the coronation and burial site for the Wolayta monarchy, and its slopes are studded with culturally significant forests and churches. A site of interest set at around 2,350m on its southwest slopes is the **Mochena Borago Cave** [map, page 444], a cathedral-sized rock shelter named after a long-dead prophet and tumbled over by a small but pretty waterfall. Palaeontological excavations show that Mochena Borago was inhabited by Stone Age hunter-gatherers from 55,000 until around 2,000 years ago, and items unearthed at the site include cooked grains, bones of livestock and wild animals eaten by the human inhabitants, 2,000-year-old ceramic figures, and an ancient clay oven. The cave can easily be reached by following the asphalt Hosanna road for 4km out of Sodo until you reach an inconspicuous signpost to the right. From there you can drive to within 200m of Mochena Borago along a steep but good 3km dirt road offering great views back to Sodo. A short footpath to the left, just before a church, leads to the cave itself.

Ajora Falls [map, page 444] The best-known scenic attraction in Wolayta, the Ajora Falls actually comprises two separate but parallel waterfalls, set perhaps 100m apart, and plunging 170m and 210m into a thickly wooded gorge formed by the Soke River, a tributary of the Omo. To get there, follow the surfaced Hosanna road north from Sodo for 28km to the small market town of Areka, then a few kilometres further north turn left on to a 25km dirt track running west to a viewpoint at the top of a steep cliff facing the waterfalls. A very steep and slippery footpath runs to the base of the gorge, and is used by locals, but be warned that stories abound of people falling to their death – even the sure-footed local livestock sometimes plunges off. At the top, an easy walk leads to the forest-fringed bank of the Ajacho River. There's a friendly traditional Wolayta village of beehive huts there too.

Maze National Park [map, page 444] (☏ 046 884 0411; m 0911 090759; e mazenationalpark@yahoo.com; entrance US$10 pp plus US$2/car, mandatory scout fee US$6/day or US$10 overnight) Proclaimed in 2005, the 220km² Maze National Park is centred on the Maze River, a tributary of the Omo that usually flows throughout the year but sometimes dries up at the end of the dry season. Less than 3 hours' drive from Sodo, it is one of Ethiopia's most underrated wildlife-viewing destinations, dominated by open savannah and grassland that reputedly supports around 800 Swayne's hartebeest, the largest extant population of this Ethiopian endemic, as well as an estimated 50 lions, which are regularly heard from the campsite and quite often seen on drives. Other conspicuous plains wildlife includes oribi, Defassa waterbuck, Bohor reedbuck, Anubis baboon and warthog, while the riparian forest around the campsite is home to plenty of guereza and grivet monkeys, and also offers a good chance of spotting the secretive bushbuck and greater kudu. The riparian forest at the campsite also supports some interesting birds, including broad-billed roller, grey-headed bush-shrike, silvery-cheeked hornbill, northern puffback and brown-throated wattle-eye. Despite being quite remote and seldom visited, the park forms a realistic goal for adventurous backpackers, since you can walk anywhere with a scout. For those with 4x4 transport, a circular 20km game-viewing track runs to the south of the main road, and a second 15km track runs north from close to the park headquarters to the campsite via the Zala River. More remote attractions include the geyser-like Bilbo Hot Springs on the Maze River in the far south of the park, and the Wenja Cave, a large natural shelter that can hold up to 300 people.

Getting there and away The park lies about 85km southwest of Sodo close to the small town of Murka. To get there in a private vehicle, follow the Arba Minch road south out of the town centre for 2km, then turn right just before the Total filling station, crossing a roundabout on the old main road after about 100m, and continue straight ahead for another 1.5km before turning left on to the Sawla road. It's around 80km from there to Murka, passing through the relatively substantial town of Selamber (literally 'Gate of Peace') about three-quarters of the way there. The park headquarters, where all fees must be paid, are prominently signposted on the right-hand side of the road about 1.5km past Murka. From the headquarters, it's another 10km drive west to the bridge across the Maze River. The 800m dirt track to the riverside campsite runs to the south a few hundred metres before the bridge.

Since walking with a scout is permitted, it is possible to visit Maze using public transport. Several buses daily run from Sodo to Sawla, a fairly large town that lies about 45km southwest of the national park. These cost US$4 and can drop travellers in Murka or at the park headquarters. Once you have paid your fees and arranged a scout, you can organise a *bajaj* to take you to the junction for the campsite and walk the last 800m there.

Where to stay, eat and drink If you have camping gear, by far the most attractive option is the lovely forested **campsite** on the east bank of the Maze River (*US$3/tent*; **$**). Facilities here are limited to a drop toilet (make sure your scout brings the keys) and water can be drawn from the river and boiled, but you would need to bring all other provisions with you. By day, the campsite is wonderful, with guereza monkeys staring down from the tall ficus trees, and a wealth of colourful birds calling and flying past. And it is truly magical after nightfall, with African scops owls peeping in the trees above a white noise of insects and frogs, and a good chance of hearing lions and hyenas.

Non-campers can stay at the very basic and inexpensive **Markos Hotel** (**$**), which stands next to the marketplace in Murka. Further afield, the two-storey **Tesfa Hotel** (**$**) in Selamber looks marginally better, and there are a few lodgings in Sawla, of which the **Geremo Hotel** (**$**) is probably the pick.

ARBA MINCH AND SURROUNDS

Founded as recently as 1960 to replace Chencha as the capital of the now defunct province of Gamo-Gofa, Arba Minch (literally 'Forty Springs') has since grown to be the largest town in Ethiopia's deep south, with a population of at least 100,000. Set at an elevation of 1,300m in the foothills of the Rift Valley Escarpment, it's a very scenic town, offering views to the east over lakes Chamo and Abaya and the lush groundwater forest fed by the eponymous springs, while its western backdrop is provided by mountains that rise close to 4,000m. Roughly 450km south of Addis Ababa by road, Arba Minch is significant to travellers both as the springboard for visits to the neighbouring Nech Sar National Park (which incorporates the above-mentioned lakes and springs) and as a convenient overnight stop en route to Konso and South Omo. The town is comprised of three discrete settlements. The oldest, but also the least interesting to travellers, is Limat (literally 'Development') north of the Kulfo River. Immediately south of the same river, downtown Sikela is the bustling commercial centre of Arba Minch, and the site of the main bus station, hospital and market. About 4km further south, uptown Shecha is a vaguely posher settlement dominated by government buildings, hotels and the homes of government employees. Until recently, Sikela and Shecha were quite distinct entities, but these days the asphalt road that connects them is lined with development, much of it associated with the University of Arba Minch (w *amu.edu.et*), a burgeoning institution founded in 1986 and now attended by around 15,000 students. The town also lies at the heart of a bountiful agricultural area, famed for its cotton, fruit and vegetable production, thanks largely to a modern irrigation scheme associated with the nearby lakes and rivers. Principal attractions in and around Arba Minch include Nech Sar National Park, which can be explored by road, by boat or on foot, and the highland village of Dorze, which is noted for its unusual traditional architecture.

GETTING THERE AND AWAY

By air Ethiopian Airlines operates daily flights between Addis Ababa and Arba Minch. The airport lies near the west shore of Lake Abaya about 4km from Sikela. A charter taxi in either direction should cost no more than US$5 and many hotels offer a shuttle service.

By road Arba Minch lies 450km from Addis Ababa along a good surfaced road via Hosanna (*7–8hrs in a private vehicle*), or 500km along an equally good but generally far busier and slower road via Shashemene. The two roads converge 120km from Arba Minch at Sodo. Direct buses between Addis Ababa and Arba Minch leave at 05.00 in either direction, and should be booked the afternoon before they depart. Direct buses to/from Shashemene or Hawassa also leave at 05.00. Alternatively, those who don't want such an early start can change vehicles at Sodo, which is now a major transport hub, with minibus connections to Arba Minch, Hosanna, Shashemene and Hawassa departing throughout the day in either direction, and to Addis Ababa until around 14.00.

Heading southwest from Arba Minch, the 360km road to Jinka via Karat-Konso and Weito is now surfaced almost in its entirety and can be driven in 5–6 hours in a private vehicle. Public transport in either direction leaves throughout the morning. More locally, at least seven buses run to Chencha via Dorze daily (*1½hrs*).

GETTING AROUND
Inexpensive minibuses and *bajaji* ply back and forth between Sikela and Shecha throughout the day.

WHERE TO STAY
Upmarket
Paradise Lodge [554 C5] (123 rooms) \046 881 3390, 011 833 3030; e info@paradiselodgeethiopia.com; w paradiselodgeethiopia.com. Far & away the best hotel in Arba Minch, if not anywhere in the deep south, the aptly named Paradise Lodge is set on a high bluff between Shecha & Sikela, & the sprawling green grounds offer a fabulous view over the lakes & forest of Nech Sar National Park. Accommodation is in well-built & beautifully decorated stone-&-thatch *tukuls* containing 4-poster bed with fitted net, writing desk, fridge, fan, sat TV, en-suite hot shower or tub & private balcony. Of the en-suite budget rooms 20 have the same facilities as the proper rooms, but are smaller & less attractively

decorated. An excellent restaurant, which makes the most of the view, has indoor & terrace seating, & serves a cosmopolitan selection of salads, sandwiches, fish, chicken, beef & Italian dishes, with most mains in the US$4–5.50 range. Other amenities include a lovely swimming pool area, 4x4 & boat trips into Nech Sar (*US$30/70 short/long*), Wi-Fi, spa services, beauty salon & free airport transfer. *US$63/73/75 B&B sgl/ dbl/twin, family rooms & suites US$80–250.* **$$$–$$$$**

Emerald Resort & Lodge [554 B6] (82 rooms) \046 881 1895; m 0911 203614, 0911 514192/3; e info@emeraldresortandlodge. com; w emeraldresortandlodge.com. Situated in large unkempt grounds on a rocky scarp 1km from Shecha, this lodge, formerly Swayne's Hotel,

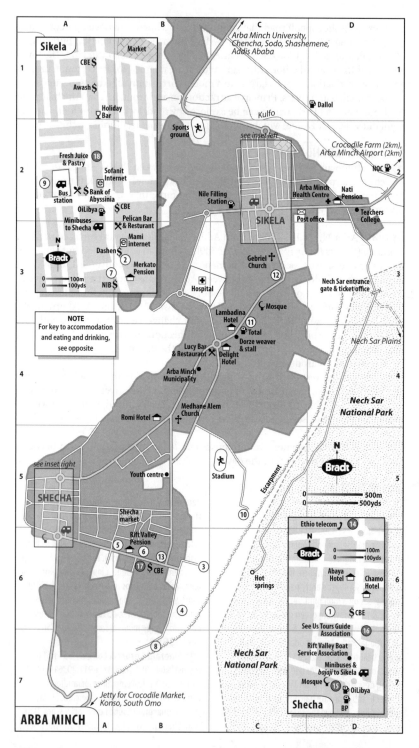

Sikela

Market

CBE $
Awash $
Holiday Bar

Sports ground

see inset left

Fresh Juice & Pastry (18)

Sofanit Internet

(9) Bus station
Bank of Abyssinia $

OiLibya
Minibuses to Shecha
Pelican Bar & Resturant

Mami internet

Dashen $ (2)

Merkato Pension

Bradt
0   100m
0   100yds

(7)

NIB $

NOTE
For key to accommodation and eating and drinking, see opposite

Arba Minch University, Chencha, Sodo, Shashemene, Addis Ababa

Kulfo

Dallol

Crocodile Farm (2km), Arba Minch Airport (2km)

NOC

Nile Filling Station

SIKELA

Arba Minch Health Centre
Nati Pension

Post office
Teachers College

Gebriel Church (12)

Nech Sar entrance gate & ticket office

Mosque

Lambadina Hotel (11)
Total
Dorze weaver & stall

Nech Sar Plains

Lucy Bar & Restaurant
Delight Hotel

Arba Minch Municipality

Nech Sar National Park

Medhane Alem Church

Romi Hotel

see inset right

SHECHA

Youth centre

Stadium

N
Bradt
0   500m
0   500yds

Escarpment

(10)

Shecha market

Rift Valley Pension
(5)   (6)
(17) $ CBE   (13)

(3)

Hot springs

(4)

(8)

Jetty for Crocodile Market, Konso, South Omo

ARBA MINCH

Ethio telecom (14)

N
Bradt
0   100m
0   100yds

Abaya Hotel
Chamo Hotel

(1) $ CBE

See Us Tours Guide Association (16)

Rift Valley Boat Service Association

Minibuses & *bajaji* to Sikela

Mosque (15)   OiLibya
BP

Shecha

Nech Sar National Park

affords a spectacular view over lakes Chamo & Abaya. The spacious en-suite bungalows are colourfully decorated in ethnic style & come with 2 dbl beds with nets, sat TV, stylish bathroom & private balcony (though only rooms 1–20 have lake views). The glassed-in restaurant has a very varied menu, with most dishes in the US$3–6.50 range. Amenities include a swimming pool & spa. Overall, though, it feels a bit neglected & service leaves something to be desired, making it poor value compared with the less expensive Paradise Lodge. *US$71/79 sgl/dbl occupancy.* **$$$$**

🛏 **Mora Heights Hotel** [554 B7] (24 rooms) ☎046 881 2158; m 0922 727395/6; e moraheightshotel@gmail.com; w moraheightshotel.com. Named after the Konso community houses that evidently inspired the architecture of its thatched bungalows, this new lodge close to the Emerald Hotel has spacious en-suite rooms with dbl or twin beds, netting, sat TV, hot shower & private balcony. The view is similar to the previous 2 lodges, or would be were it not obscured by wired fencing that we were told protects guests from Nech Sar's few remaining lions! The traditionally styled restaurant serves a fair selection of Western & local dishes in the US$2.50–4 range. As with the Emerald, it feels like poor value compared with the superior Paradise Lodge. *US$40/55 B&B sgl/dbl.* **$$$–$$$$**

Moderate

🛏 **Ezana Hotel Arba Minch** [554 B6] (36 rooms) ☎046 881 1201; m 0926 446270; e ezana40minch.hotel@gmail.com; w ezana-arbaminch-hotel.com. This bright pink 3-storey hotel lies in Shecha on the road out to the Bekele Molla. The comfortable en-suite rooms come with nets, sat TV, hot shower & Wi-Fi, & rates include a free airport transfer. A pleasant courtyard bar & restaurant serves draught beer & tasty *tibs*, *kitfo* or fish cutlet in the US$3–4 range. *Decent value at US$26/32/34 B&B sgl/dbl/twin.* **$$$**

🛏 **Bekele Molla Hotel** [554 B6] (32 rooms) ☎046 881 0046; m 0910 790598. Situated on the same scenic ridge as the neighbouring Emerald Hotel, the timeworn Bekele Molla is an affordable option for travellers seeking a great view over the lakes & acacia-studded gardens alive with birds & baboons. But the large en-suite rooms with hot water are in dire need of a makeover & seem poor value at the price. Decent & inexpensive meals are available in the moribund dining room or on a pretty terrace overlooking both lakes. *US$23/26 dbl/twin.* **$$$**

Budget

🛏 **Zebib Pension & Café** [554 B6] (33 rooms) ☎046 881 4788; m 0924 744242. This smart modern 2-storey pension on the Bekele Molla road has well-priced, attractively decorated & very comfortable en-suite rooms with queen-size bed, net, fridge, sat TV, Wi-Fi & hot water. The attached café, with indoor & outdoor seating, serves pasta, b/fast & Ethiopian fare for around US$2/plate, as well as pastries, juices & good coffee. *US$20/28 dbl/twin.* **$$$**

🛏 **Forty Springs Hotel** [554 B6] (21 rooms) ☎046 881 2138; m 0912 417288; e fortyspringshotel@gmail.com; w fortysprings. wordpress.com. Situated around the corner from Zebib Pension, this comfortable & well-managed 3-storey hotel is set in shady gardens rattling with weaver birds. The large, clean en-suite rooms are nothing special, but come with net, writing table, Wi-Fi, fridge & a powerful shower. The food is pretty good & well priced at US$3–4, & it also serves draught beer & fresh juices. The place has a strong South Omo connection: the manager is the sister of the owner of the Tourist Hotel in Turmi. *Decent value at US$16/20 dbl/ twin.* **$$–$$$**

15

🏠 **Arba Minch Tourist Hotel** [554 B3] (36 rooms) ✆046 881 2171; **m** 0924 704020. Situated close to the bus station in the heart of Sikela, this friendly place has comfortable & clean en-suite rooms with fridge, sat TV & hot water. An added attraction is the oasis-like garden restaurant & bar, which serves juices, cakes & draught beer along with an extensive selection of Western & Ethiopian dishes in the US$3–5 range. Located beyond this first garden is a more formal restaurant, & beyond this a large, usually crowded, back garden where local residents gather for drinks. *US$22.50/25/27 sgl/dbl/twin.* **$$$**

Shoestring

🏠 **Kairo Hotel** [554 A3] (35 rooms) ✆046 881 3407. Situated 100m south of the Tourist Hotel, on the opposite side of the road, this is one of numerous cheap dives in Sikela. *US$6 dbl using common shower, US$7/14 en-suite dbl with cold/hot water.* **$–$$**

🏠 **Mulu View** [554 A2] (34 rooms) **m** 0911 204488. Adjacent to the bus station in Sikela (so potentially noisy at night), the Mulu View is a newly built 3-storey cheapie with clean en-suite rooms & a small inner yard. *US$7/9/14 sgl/dbl/twin.* **$**

🏠 **Abyssinia Pension** [554 D6] (10 rooms) ✆046 881 0381. Set in a small wooded compound just off the main road through Shecha, this 1-price-for-all gem has clean en-suite rooms with TV & hot shower. *US$16 dbl.* **$$**

🏠 **Timret Pension** [554 C3] (14 rooms) ✆046 885 0125; **m** 0916 831011. Situated alongside the main road between Sikela & Shecha, this above-par cheapie has spacious, clean en-suite rooms with dbl bed, nets, table & hot shower. There's no restaurant & the nearby mosque might enforce an early wake-up. *US$10 dbl.* **$**

🏠 **Ramis Hotel** [554 C3] (34 rooms) ✆046 881 1798; **m** 0960 399099; **e** rameshotelarbaminch@ gmail.com. Heading up towards Shecha from Sikela you will soon find the brand-new Ramis Hotel on the left after the mosque & close to the Total filling station. The en-suite rooms represent excellent value. *US$10/12/16 sgl/dbl/family.* **$$**

✕ **WHERE TO EAT AND DRINK** The three clifftop hotels listed in the upmarket category all have restaurants with superb views and varied menus that aren't significantly pricier than most places in town. The Paradise Lodge is the best of the three, but less convenient than the Emerald Resort & Lodge or the cheaper Mora Heights Hotel for those staying in Shecha. The best place to eat in Sikela is probably the garden restaurant at the Arba Minch Tourist Hotel. The local speciality, served at all these restaurants and most of the places listed below, is *asa kutilet* (fish cutlet), which consists of a mound of fried battered tilapia and is usually served with a spicy green dip called *dataa*, a couple of crusty bread rolls and a plate of salad.

✕ **Roza Restaurant** [554 D7] **m** 0910 999611; ⏰ 08.00–22.00 daily. Something of a Shecha institution, this Italian–Ethiopian-owned restaurant serves delicious traditional wood-fired pizzas for around US$5 after 19.00.

✕ **Soma Restaurant** [554 D6] **m** 0911 737712; ⏰ 07.00–22.00 daily. This long-serving restaurant in Shecha used to be the place to try fish cutlet. It quite possibly still is, assuming you don't mind paying inflated *faranji* prices of US$5–9 for fish dishes (other dishes are cheaper).

✕ **Lemlem Beer Garden** [554 D5] Inexpensive draught beer & inexpensive local food, including fish cutlet, are on offer at this friendly garden bar in Shecha.

✕ **Zebib Café & Snack** [554 A2] ✆046 881 3676; ⏰ 06.30–20.00 daily. Not to be confused with its (equally good) namesake attached to the pension in Shecha, this 2-storey café in Sikala serves tasty sandwiches, burgers & pasta dishes for around US$1.50, as well as juices, coffee & pastries.

✕ **Wubit Restaurant** [554 B6] Located opposite the Forty Springs Hotel, Wubit serves inexpensive b/fasts including *ful* & yoghurt, plus vegetarian & fish mains for around US$2. Fresh fruit juices cost US$0.80.

TOURIST OPERATORS AND GUIDES The best places to arrange 4x4 and boat trips into Nech Sar are **Paradise Lodge** (page 553) and the **See Us Tour Guide Association**

[554 D7] (☎ *046 881 0117;* m *0912 119551, 0913 250641;* e *seeusarbaminch@yahoo. com;* w *seeusarbaminch.com;* ⏰ *08.30–12.30 &* *13.30–17.30 Mon–Sat*), which has its office on the main road through Shecha. Paradise Lodge offers full-day 4x4 trips into Nech Sar for US$170 per group (up to four people), as well as boat trips to Lake Chamo's Crocodile Market for US$38.50 per group (up to six people) and similar boat trips that carry on to the Nech Sar Plains for US$88 (up to six people). In all cases, the prices are exclusive of park fees, and travellers staying at other hotels are welcome to pop past and see whether they can join an existing group to share costs. Alternatively, See Us offers the same boat trips at almost identical prices, working in conjunction with the **Rift Valley Boat Service Association** (☎ *046 881 4080;* m *0911 726700*) on the opposite side of the same road.

WHAT TO SEE AND DO The main attraction in the immediate vicinity of Arba Minch is Nech Sar National Park, which incorporates the forest-fringed 40 springs for which the town is named, significant portions of lakes Chamo and Abaya, and the Nech Sar Plains to their east. Other points of interest are the Arba Minch Crocodile Farm a few kilometres out of town, and the distinctive homesteads built by the Dorze people who live in the highlands around the former provincial capital Chencha. The swimming pool at the Paradise Hotel is open to day visitors for a small fee.

Nech Sar National Park [map, page 558] (*Entrance US$4 pp/24hrs, plus US$1/ vehicle & US$2.50–20/party for an obligatory scout depending on the destination*) Spanning altitudes of 1,100–1,650m, the 514km^2 Nech Sar National Park (also known as Nechisar) protects a thrillingly beautiful landscape of mountains, lakes and forests immediately east of Arba Minch. Its most conspicuous features are the twin lakes Chamo and Abaya, which dominate the views from several hotels in Arba Minch. Abaya literally means 'Big Water' in the local tongue, and fittingly it is Ethiopia's second-largest lake, extending over 1,160km^2 and sometimes referred to as Kai Hayk (Red Lake) on account of its rusty hue, caused by a suspension of ferrous hydroxide. The southerly and more conventionally blue Lake Chamo, though smaller at 317km^2, hosts substantial hippo and crocodile populations, which can easily be visited by boat. Non-aquatic habitats include a dense groundwater forest bordering Arba Minch, the wide open grasslands of the more easterly Nech Sar (White Grass) Plains, and the knotted acacia scrub of the mountainous Egzer Dilday (Bridge of God) that divides the two lakes.

Nech Sar suffered years of neglect following the collapse of the Derg in 1991 when large tracts of land were settled by Guji Oromo pastoralists. By the end of the millennium, many of its large mammals – including elephant, buffalo, black rhinoceros, cheetah, African wild dog, Rothschild's giraffe, Grevy's zebra, Beisa oryx, eland, lesser kudu and gerenuk – had become extinct as a result of poaching and overgrazing. In 2004, a welcome attempt at revival was set in motion when the government signed a management contract with the African Parks Foundation (APF), a non-profit organisation that has played a significant role in rehabilitating similarly down-at-heel game reserves elsewhere in Africa. Sadly, the APF pulled out of the park in June 2008, citing their lack of confidence in its future sustainability due to non-compliance on the part of the Guji Oromo who graze their cattle on its plains.

The park officially supports 72 mammal species, but this checklist includes several species now known or thought to be extinct in the area, and some reports put the tally today as being as low as 40 species. Of these, the most conspicuous are Burchell's zebra, Grant's gazelle, Swayne's hartebeest, greater kudu, common bushbuck, hippopotamus, warthog, guereza, vervet monkey and Anubis baboon.

About half of the remaining mammals are bats, among them Africa's smallest species, the banana pipistrelle (*Neoromicia nanus*). By contrast, the avifauna is in excellent health, with around 275 species identified. The most rewarding habitats for birds are the forests and lakes, but it is the eastern plains that support the park's super-elusive star attraction: the Nechisar nightjar (*Caprimulgus solala*), first identified based on a single wing collected by a Cambridge zoological expedition in 1990, but not seen alive until as recently as 2009. Nech Sar is the only known Ethiopian locality for the white-tailed lark, and it protects an isolated population of white-fronted black chat.

Getting there and away The entrance gate and ticket office to Nech Sar lie 1km out of Arba Minch, and can be reached on foot or by car by following the airport road east from the main roundabout in Sikela, then turning right on to the side road more or less opposite the Nati Pension. It is permitted to walk to the entrance gate and then, with a scout, along the forested road to the hot springs. To go deeper into the park, you need a 4x4 (rentable from Paradise Lodge) and even then you may be unable to cross the rough track along the Bridge of God in the rains. The

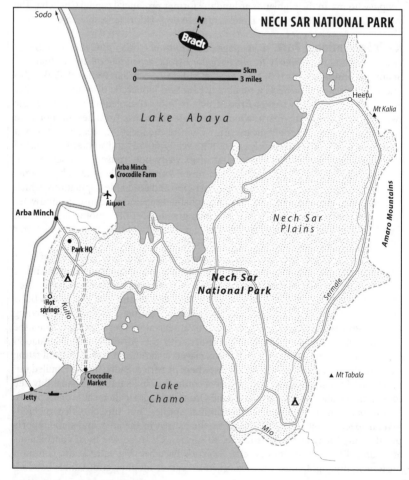

Crocodile Market is accessible by boat only, from a launching site on the west shore of Lake Chamo just off the Konso road, but before you head there, fees must still be paid at the ticket office.

Where to stay Most people visit Nech Sar as a day trip from Arba Minch. There are, however, four little-used campsites. The Forty Springs and Bridge of Kulfo campsites are both less than 5km from the headquarters on the forested banks of the Kulfo River, while Viewpoint is roughly 26km from the main gate and Viewpoint Hot Springs 35km. Camping costs US$2 per person. None of these sites has anything in the way of facilities, but if you're properly equipped they are blissfully peaceful and wonderfully sited for seeing forest animals.

Around the park

Arba Minch Hot Springs [map, opposite] The field of springs after which Arba Minch is named lies at the base of the cliff below Paradise Lodge. From the park entrance near Sikela, it can be reached on foot or by car along a well-maintained 3km dirt road. The springs aren't much to shout about, enclosed as they are by some ugly concrete buildings, but there is a small natural pool below them where swimming is permitted. Of greater interest is the lush groundwater forest, dominated by sycamore figs reaching up to 30m high, which lines the road out to the springs. Forest birds here are less prolific than might be expected, but do include the spectacular silvery-cheeked hornbill, while vervet monkey, guereza and Anubis baboons are common, and the odd dik-dik and bushbuck might be heard or seen crashing into the undergrowth. The obligatory scout to the springs costs US$2.50 per party.

Lake Chamo and the Crocodile Market [map, opposite] Often and rather misleadingly dubbed the Crocodile Market, the most popular attraction in Nech Sar is a stretch of reed-lined sand flats where large numbers of crocodiles often sun themselves gape-mouthed on the northeastern shore of Lake Chamo. The market is accessible by boat only, and while you'll no longer see the crocodiles in their hundreds, as some old photographs suggest to be the case, up to 20 individuals might gather there seasonally, and at any time of year you can expect to see several impressive specimens gliding menacingly below the water. No less of an attraction is the spectacular scenery, with both sides of the Rift Valley wall rearing up above the glassy surface of the lake, and the probability of seeing a few pods of hippos huddled up in the shallows. Conspicuous birds include African fish eagle, African marsh harrier, great white pelican, goliath heron, spur-winged plover, and much else besides. Boat trips can be arranged through the Paradise Lodge (page 553) or See Us Tour Guide Association (page 556), and leave from a launch about 10km south of Arba Minch, 1km off the surfaced road to Konso.

Nech Sar Plains [map, opposite] The best area for terrestrial game viewing is the open Nech Sar Plains, which lie to the east of the lakes. Burchell's zebra, with an estimated population of 300, is the commonest large mammal, but you should also see Grant's gazelle and, with a bit of luck, one of the 20-odd remaining Swayne's hartebeest. Coming by road from the entrance gate, the exhilarating but bumpy access road to the Nech Sar Plains crosses Egzer Dilday, and offers splendid views across Lake Chamo and its volcanically formed islands, as well as the possibility of seeing Guenther's dik-dik and greater kudu, along with acacia-associated birds such as rollers, sparrow-weavers and starlings. The area also seems to be particularly good for raptors. A popular alternative to driving is to go by boat, as an extension of a trip to the Crocodile

Market, then to hike on the plains for a few hours in the company of a scout. The Nech Sar Plains are also one of the best places in Ethiopia to see large grassland birds such as Abyssinian ground hornbill, secretary bird and various bustards, including the massive kori bustard. To stand any chance of seeing the legendary Nechisar nightjar, however, you would need to camp overnight on the plains.

Arba Minch Crocodile Farm [map, page 558] (⊕ 08.30–17.30 daily; guided tour US$10 pp) Situated 6km out of town near Lake Abaya, this rather overpriced government farm hosts several thousand crocodiles with an age range of one to six years. The crocodiles are hatched from eggs taken from the lake, but a number have been reintroduced to keep the natural population in balance. The farm consists of a dozen or so cages, each of which contains several hundred bored-looking crocodiles of a similar age. To get to the farm, follow the airport road out of Sikela for about 4km till you reach the clearly signposted turn-off. On the way you will cross a bridge over a river and later detour round the airport to your right. If you don't feel like the walk, vehicles heading towards the lakeside village of Lante will be able to drop you at the turn-off. The 2km of road between the turn-off and the farm passes through forest and thick scrub, excellent for birds and monkeys, and worth exploring in its own right even if you're not particularly interested in visiting the farm. The road continues past the farm for about 500m to a landing stage on the shore of Lake Abaya, where there is good birdwatching and a chance of seeing hippos and crocodiles in their natural state.

Dorze [map, page 444] Renowned for their remarkable beehive-on-steroids homesteads, the Dorze are a small Omotic-speaking ethnic group whose highland territory, only 30km² but established at least 500 years ago, lies 25km north of Arba Minch close to the small town of Chencha (which, incredibly, served as the capital of Gamo-Gofa Province until the 1960s). Set at an altitude of around 2,300–2,500m and reached by a scenic switchbacked road, Dorze is also known for its cold, misty weather and year-round moist climate, which makes it ideal for growing crops such as enset (false banana), tobacco and various tropical fruits. The main occupation, aside from subsistence farming, is cotton weaving. Indeed, the shama cloth produced and sold in Dorze – both plain white gabbi robes and brightly coloured scarf-like netalas – is regarded to be the finest in Ethiopia. Traditionally, every Dorze compound contains at least one cotton loom, which would be worked constantly by one or other member of the family, but these days much of the weaving takes place in co-operatives.

The main reason to visit the Dorze is their unique domed houses, which stand up to 6m tall (comparable to a two-storey building) and are constructed entirely from organic material. First, a bamboo scaffold is set in place, then a combination of grass and enset leaves is woven around it to create solid insulating walls and a roof. Most Dorze houses also have a low frontal extension, which looks a bit like a nose and is used as a reception area. The spacious interior of the huts is centred on a large fireplace, used for cooking and to generate heat, and different areas are set apart for sleeping and for smaller livestock. Although the Dorze speak an Omotic language, they are Orthodox Christians, and hold a long-standing taboo on any act of violence (such as hitting a child) taking place in the part of the hut reserved for animals, on the basis that Jesus was born in a manger. These enduring structures generally serve one married couple for a lifetime – should the base of the hut become infested by termites or rot, the entire structure can be lifted up and relocated to a close-by site.

The main concentration of traditional houses stands in and around the small town of Dorze, 8km before Chencha on the Arba Minch road. You can stop at any compound and ask to look around, but you will be expected to pay a fee of around US$5 to go inside or to take photographs. For a more organised introduction to the Dorze lifestyle, we would recommend the guided village tours offered by Mekonnen Lodge (see below) in Dorze Hayzo. These cost US$5 per person, take up to 90 minutes, and include visits to a couple of venerable Dorze homesteads, as well as a step-by-step guide to the production of *kocho*, a sour flatbread made from pulped and fermented *enset* paste, and a visit to the Besa Dorze Hayzo Weavers Co-operative next door. The best time to visit Dorze is Monday or Thursday, when a colourful market is held in the town centre about 1km south of Mekonnen Lodge. Also of interest is the impressive 30m-high Toro Waterfall, which can be reached from the village along a pretty 30-minute walking path – any local will be able to guide you. And if you are in the area at the right time, the Dorze celebration of Meskel (1 October) is reputedly very colourful.

Getting there and away The trip from Arba Minch to Dorze takes about 45 minutes in a private vehicle. Drive north out of Sikela along the surfaced Sodo road, crossing the bridge across the Kulfo River as you leave town, then after 11km turn left on to a dirt road that switchbacks uphill for 22km to Chencha. The junction for Dorze Eco-Lodge is on the right 11km along the road to Chencha, while Family Lodge stands on the left after another 1km, and the main village of Dorze is 1.5km further. Using public transport from Arba Minch, buses to Chencha can drop you at any of these points, provided you pay the full fare of US$1.25. At least half a dozen buses daily cover the route, with the busiest days being Tuesday and Saturday, when Chencha holds its main market. There might also be direct transport to Dorze on its market days, which are Monday and Thursday.

Where to stay, eat and drink

Dorze Eco-Lodge (10 rooms) m 0916 700538, 0928 829774; e tsehay@yahoo.com, info@dorzelodge.com; w dorzelodge.com. Set on a cliff edge offering a sweeping view back to Arba Minch & Lake Abaya, this fantastic lodge emulates a traditional compound, with accommodation provided in dome-shaped bamboo & *enset* leaf huts. New, similar stone-walled accommodations with en-suite bathrooms have recently been built. There's a large thatched-roof restaurant & lounge area serving a small menu of European/Ethiopian favourites (*b/fast costs US$4, lunch or dinner US$6*), as well as a bar located high up on a hilltop viewpoint overlooking the valley below. The friendly staff can arrange local guides & village walks, as well as hiking & horseriding treks. The only downside is there's no electricity, though a generator is on hand when needed. Coming on public transport, you can take a Chencha bus to the clearly signposted junction, but will need to walk the last rather steep 1km to the lodge. The older huts are no longer rented. *The new ones cost US$45 sgl or dbl & US$65 trpl.* **$$$**

Family Lodge (12 rooms) m 0916 465987. Situated on the west side of the main road between the junction for Dorze Eco-Lodge & Dorze market, this pleasant family-run lodge also offers Spartan accommodation in traditional huts using common showers, & tours to a nearby Dorze compound. A weaver works on-site, & cloth is available for sale. *Good value at US$8/16 B&B sgl/dbl, plus US$5 for lunch or dinner.* **$$**

Mekonnen Lodge (8 rooms) m 0916 709533. Situated 1km past Dorze market along the road to Chencha, this unsignposted lodge next to the Besa Dorze Hayzo Weavers Co-operative consists of a circle of traditional huts using common hot showers. Named after its friendly owner, it is set in a traditional family compound with a small central restaurant & bar, where you can order simple European dishes, as well as local fare. The lodge also offers excellent guided tours. *US$8 pp bed only, US$12 B&B.* **$$**

15

16

Konso and South Omo

Nothing else in Ethiopia prepares you for South Omo and Konso. Nor, for that matter, does much else in 21st-century Africa. Legend has it that many of the region's inhabitants were unaware that an entity such as Ethiopia existed until after the end of World War II. And while that assertion may be apocryphal, it is easy enough to believe when confronted by the extraordinary cultural integrity that characterises the inhabitants of the remote southwestern administrative zones of Debub Omo (South Omo) and Konso. Indeed, the descent from the green southern highlands though the craggier slopes of Konso on to the low-lying and thinly populated badlands of South Omo can feel like a journey not merely through space, but also through time, arriving at something as close as there is to an Africa untouched by outside influences. It seems facile to label South Omo a living museum but, in many respects, that is exactly what it is. Here, as many as two dozen different tribes, some numbering tens of thousands, others no more than 500, collectively represent all four of Africa's major linguistic groups, including the Omotic speakers, whose tongue is as endemic to South Omo as, say, the Ethiopian wolf is to the Abyssinian Highlands. The most renowned of the Omotic speakers, the Mursi, are best known for their practice of inserting large clay plates behind the lower lips of their women. Other important groups of South Omo include the Hamar, Karo and Aari, whose cultures and quirks of adornment – body scarring, body painting and the like – are treated more fully in text boxes scattered throughout this chapter. No less traditionalist, but far more urbanised, are the Konso, whose centuries-old hilltop villages, hemmed in by curvaceous stone walls, towered over by tall generation poles and dotted with eerie *waka* grave-markers, rank as perhaps the most beautiful traditional African settlements south of the Sahel.

TRAVEL PRACTICALITIES

Tourism in Konso and South Omo operates very differently from the rest of Ethiopia. Facilities, on the whole, tend to be more basic, and conditions are not so well suited to independent travel. Furthermore, unlike the rest of Ethiopia, the main focal point of tourism in Konso and South Omo is comprised not of historic sites, nor geographic landmarks, nor landscapes, nor wildlife, but of interacting, or attempting to interact, with rural cultures whose norms and mores are as far removed as can be from those of 21st-century Westerners. This cultural chasm generates plenty of scope for misunderstanding and tension between locals and tourists, often exacerbated by third-party factors, be it the ambiguous and sometimes downright exploitative role played by operators and guides from Addis Ababa, or the economic and political ramifications of modern developments such as the construction of dams higher up on the Omo River, or attempts to curb

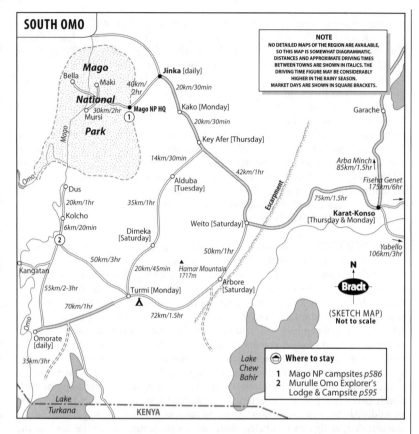

SOUTH OMO

NOTE
NO DETAILED MAPS OF THE REGION ARE AVAILABLE, SO THIS MAP IS SOMEWHAT DIAGRAMMATIC. DISTANCES AND APPROXIMATE DRIVING TIMES BETWEEN TOWNS ARE SHOWN IN ITALICS. THE DRIVING TIME FIGURE MAY BE CONSIDERABLY HIGHER IN THE RAINY SEASON. MARKET DAYS ARE SHOWN IN SQUARE BRACKETS.

Mago
Bella
Maki
National
Mursi
Park
Jinka [daily]
Mago NP HQ (1)
Kako [Monday]
Key Afer [Thursday]
Garache
Arba Minch 85km/1.5hr
Fiseha Genet 175km/6hr
Alduba [Tuesday]
Dus
Kolcho
Dimeka [Saturday]
Weito [Saturday]
Karat-Konso [Thursday & Monday]
Yabello 106km/3hr
Kangatan
Hamar Mountain 1717m
Turmi [Monday]
Arbore [Saturday]

40km/2hr
20km/30min
30km/2hr
20km/30min
14km/30min
42km/1hr
75km/1.5hr
35km/1hr
20km/1hr
6km/20min
50km/3hr
20km/45min
50km/1hr
55km/2-3hr
70km/1hr
72km/1.5hr

Escarpment

N
Bradt
(SKETCH MAP)
Not to scale

Omorate [daily]
35km/3hr

Lake Chew Bahir

⊖ **Where to stay**
1 Mago NP campsites *p586*
2 Murulle Omo Explorer's Lodge & Campsite *p595*

Lake Turkana
KENYA

settlement and subsistence hunting in protected areas such as Mago National Park. For all the above reasons, and more, it seems appropriate to include some general coverage of travel in Konso and South Omo before launching into the standard site-by-site coverage.

WHEN TO VISIT Unlike many other tourist areas in Ethiopia, travel in South Omo is limited by seasonal factors. C J Carr describes the region as 'highly unstable … in terms of precipitation and winds throughout the year, with great fluctuations often erratic in occurrence'. Travel along the new asphalt road to Jinka via Karat-Konso is fine throughout the year, but elsewhere the already poor roads often deteriorate during the rainy season, while the black cotton soil in Mago National Park can become treacherously sticky, bordering on impassable. And while precipitation is low – typically up to 400mm per annum – the unpredictable timing and quantity of rainfall regularly leads to local flooding or drought. Bearing this in mind, April and May, when the big rains usually fall, are best avoided. If the rains are early or late, or unusually heavy, March or June might be as bad. The rest of the year is normally fine, though the short rains, which generally fall in October, might put a temporary stop on travel.

INDEPENDENT TRAVEL Karat, the capital of Konso, is easily reached on public transport from Arba Minch, and several traditional Konso villages are within easy walking distance. By contrast, South Omo doesn't really lend itself to exploration on public transport. True, there are regular minibuses from Arba Minch and Karat-Konso to Jinka, the zonal administrative centre, and if you time things right, you could stop en route at the market at Weito or Key Afer. But most parts of Hamar Country are tricky to reach on public transport, as are Omorate and other sites along the Omo River, since the local trucks that occasionally ply these routes are forbidden from carrying *faranji* passengers. Mago National Park and associated Mursi villages are absolutely inaccessible on public transport, but could be visited by hiring a 4x4 in Jinka, ideally by putting together a small group to divide the cost. Be warned, however, that we regularly receive complaints about vehicles hired in Jinka, which are generally in poorer repair than anything you'd be offered in Addis Ababa. Several local agencies are said to organise motorbike tours and rental, and it's worthwhile enquiring with the local guides. Do check carefully the condition of the motorcycles available. In addition note that, at present, riding a motorbike in Mago National Park is forbidden.

ORGANISED TRIPS The normal way to explore the region covered by this chapter, and the easiest, is on a road safari out of Addis Ababa. A minimum of six days, but ideally longer, should be allocated for such a journey. If you don't want to join a large group tour, the best procedure is to arrange a bespoke tour with, or book a vehicle through, a recognised tour operator in Addis Ababa (page 89). Vehicle hire will generally work out at US$200–50 per day per party, inclusive of driver/guide, fuel and optional camping gear and cook, so the total cost per person will depend on group size and whether you opt to camp, use budget hotels or use smarter tourist lodges. The advantage of dealing with an acknowledged tour operator is that the vehicle will generally be in good shape, and the guide will have experience of the region, both of which are important considerations in remote and unpredictable South Omo. It is possible to arrange a private vehicle more cheaply upon arrival in Addis Ababa, with some hotels offering rates as low as US$150 per day, but be warned that, at this sort of price, there are no guarantees about the state of the vehicle or experience of the guide, and there will be little accountability should things go wrong.

Another option is an organised fly-in safari. This will generally be more costly than driving down, since you'll have to pay for a flight and the vehicle will need to drive from Addis Ababa to meet you, whether or not you are on board. The main advantage of flying down, aside from the added comfort, is that it cuts two days of travel either side off exploring South Omo. Indeed, now that Ethiopian Airlines flies four times a week to both Arba Minch and Jinka, you could fly into one of these towns, then travel one way by road through Konso and South Omo, and fly out from the other one. Renting the necessary car can be done in Addis, either through a tour operator or a hotel.

PLANNING AN ITINERARY Most tour operators specialised in South Omo can put together an itinerary for the region based on years of experience and knowledge of recent changes. Broadly, however, you would ideally want a minimum of six nights for a road trip out of Addis Ababa, allowing for one overnight stop in either direction, at last one night in Karat-Konso, and three nights split between Turmi and Jinka (the latter the best base for a day trip to a Mursi village). Eight nights would be better, and it would be easy to extend the trip further by adding more stops on the way to or from Addis Ababa. When you plan your itinerary, be cognisant that market days are generally the best time to visit any given town. The

At Timkat (Ethiopian Epiphany), thousands of worshippers gather at Fasilidas's Pool in Gondar to receive blessings pages 109 & 284

far left Hamar women tend to roll their hair in ochre and fat; the copper-coloured strands are known as *goscha*, and are a sign of health page 587

left Karo women often sport striking hairstyles page 595

far left Afar woman collecting water in Asaita page 370

left Mursi woman with lip plate. These are put in when the girls are around 16 years old, prior to marriage page 584

below A Hamar boy jumping the bulls to become a man in a ceremony at Turmi, South Omo Valley page 590

Hot on Africa

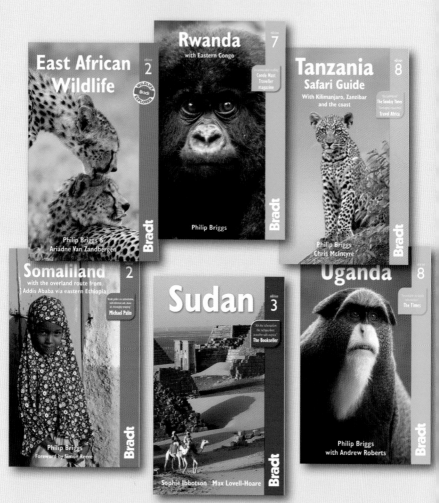

East African Wildlife
edition 2
Philip Briggs & Ariadne Van Zandbergen
Bradt

Rwanda
with Eastern Congo
edition 7
Philip Briggs
Bradt

Tanzania
Safari Guide
With Kilimanjaro, Zanzibar and the coast
edition 8
Philip Briggs
Chris McIntyre
Bradt

Somaliland
with the overland route from Addis Ababa via eastern Ethiopia
edition 2
Michael Palin
Philip Briggs
Foreword by Simon Reeve
Bradt

Sudan
edition 3
Sophie Ibbotson · Max Lovell-Hoare
Bradt

Uganda
edition 8
The Times
Philip Briggs
with Andrew Roberts
Bradt

Bradt
Pioneering guides to exceptional places

bradtguides.com/shop

GALAXY EXPRESS SERVICES
Tour & Travel
The Tour & Travel Specialist

IATA
ACCREDITED AGENT

GALAXY EXPRESS SERVICES PLC, established in 1991, is one of the best equipped tour operators in Ethiopia. We will plan your journeys and provide the very best service available, from car rental and air ticketing to customised tours, with efficient and responsive management, and a large fleet of new, well maintained vehicles manned by articulate, friendly, energetic and flexible veteran tour operators, multilingual guides and expert drivers. We plan trips which fit perfectly with your schedule and specific interests, at very competitive rates. Our goal is to deliver a fascinating Ethiopian experience to your total satisfaction.

TOUR OPERATIONS   CAR RENT

AIR TRAVEL SERVICES

Experience all the wonders of this marvellous destination with Galaxy Express Services, one of Ethiopia's foremost tour operators.

We offer a range of over 15 carefully designed package tours countrywide, focusing on nature, history, culture and wildlife, as well as surface transport around the country and individually tailored tours at very competitive prices.

Special Characteristics of Galaxy

❖ The only tour operator with branch offices in all of Ethiopia's four main northern historical sites – Bahir Dar, Gondar, Lalibela and Axum – where permanently stationed vehicles and professional guides are available at all times.

GALAXY EXPRESS SERVICES PLC.
TOUR OPERATION & AIR TICKETING
🏠 Yeha City Center 1st and 3rd Floor, in front of Addis Ababa Stadium.
✉ 8309, Addis Ababa, Ethiopia
📞 +251 115 51 03 55/51 05 61/51 79 64/51 76 46
📱 +251 911 200168 Fax: +251 115 511236
✉ galaxyexpress@ethionet.et
　 galaxyexpressservices1985@gmail.com
　 info@galaxyexpresstourethiopia.com
🌐 www.galaxyexpresstourethiopia.com

Grant Express Travel & Tours Services PLC (GETTS) is one of the best-equipped tour operators in Ethiopia with efficient and responsive management, and a large fleet of well-maintained vehicles manned by articulate, energetic and flexible, young multilingual guides.

P.O. Box 42662 – Addis Ababa – Ethiopia
Tel: 251 11 553 4678 / 4379
Mobile: 251 91 123 3289 Fax: 251 11 553 4395
gettsethiopia@gmail.com
www.gettsethiopia.com

best markets are probably the Saturday market at Dimeka, the Monday market at Turmi, the Tuesday market at Alduba and the Thursday market at Key Afer. Other market days are given under individual town entries, and on the map on page 563.

TOURIST AMENITIES The standard of accommodation in South Omo has improved greatly in recent years, at least when it comes to the upper end of the price scale. Adequate tourist lodges can now be found in Karat-Konso, Jinka and Turmi. Those on a tighter budget are less well catered for, though decent local hotels with en-suite rooms are available in Karat-Konso, Jinka, Turmi and Key Afer. By planning your travel with some care, you can avoid having to overnight in places such as Weito, Dimeka and perhaps Omorate, which provide unattractive accommodation only. An appealing budget option, assuming that you have a tent, is the agreeable campsites that can be found in Jinka, Mago National Park, Turmi, Key Afer, Arbore, Omorate and Murulle Lodge.

Culinary delights are few and far between in South Omo, though once again the options are far better than they were a few years back. Jinka has quite a few decent and affordable eateries, while budget travellers in Karat-Konso and Turmi can now also eat well and affordably not only at the established tourist lodges, but also at

PHOTOGRAPHY IN SOUTH OMO

Photography has come to dominate relations between travellers and the tribespeople of South Omo to such an extent that any less voyeuristic form of interaction seems to be all but impossible. As a result, you can assume that anybody you want to photograph individually will expect to be paid a small fee and, even in group situations such as markets, you might find that anyone who ends up in the frame or a general or group shot, or who thinks they have, will demand a payment too. The going rate varies from one person and one village to the next, but the birr equivalent of US$0.20 is now quite standard.

So far, nothing too contentious, but in many parts of South Omo it is customary not only for a photographic subject to ask a payment, but also to count every click of the shutter and to increment the fee accordingly. In addition, a mother carrying a baby will ask for a double payment. In other words, somebody who asks for US$0.20 might demand US$1 should you click the shutter five times, and US$2 if she has a child on her back! This can start to add up quickly, as well as creating an unpleasant and rather grasping atmosphere. If you really want to spend some time photographing one particular person, it's best to explain this and agree a higher rate in advance. Once the finances have been agreed, people are generally relaxed about being photographed, though even then it is also not uncommon for arguments to break out – these will usually be settled through good humour, and, if need be, giving in for what represents only a few cents.

The other obvious way around this area of contention is to pack away your camera, or at least reserve it for a few special occasions, and buy some postcards instead. Among other things, this approach will also allow you to engage more deeply with the people you meet and events you witness in South Omo. Even then, you may sometimes be approached by someone who demands to be photographed and to be paid for it. Such people sometimes become quite hostile if you don't accede to their demands, but generally the situation can be defused by humour.

quite a few guesthouses and eateries dotted around the towns. Elsewhere, you'll always find at least one local restaurant that serves the standard Ethiopian diet of *shiro* or *tibs*, occasionally supplemented by omelette or spaghetti.

If you are cooking for yourself, Jinka has a few decent supermarkets, but elsewhere the choice is limited. Water in South Omo is generally not safe to drink without purification, but the usual bottled water, soft drinks and beer are widely available, along with tea.

PERMITS AND FEES It is no longer required to carry any sort of permit to explore South Omo, though visitors to Omorate are expected to drop into the customs and immigration office and to produce their passport before they head into town. The Konso and Mursi villages charge visitors a customary fee, paid to the Guides Association in Karat-Konso and to the designated recipient in the Mursi villages. In other less touristic villages, you will certainly be approached to contribute to some kind of village fund and be offered the services of a guide, for a fee. These more-or-less legitimate fees must then be defined up front.

As a rule, visiting markets ought to be free and the authorities have issued instructions to the guides confirming this fact. Despite this, aspirant guides frequently latch on to unaccompanied travellers, sometimes even wielding an intimidating receipt book to bolster their credibility. Nevertheless, such services are generally optional and should be paid for only when accepted.

KARAT-KONSO

Karat, the administrative centre of Konso special *woreda*, is a low-rise medium-altitude junction town of 5,000 inhabitants situated on the banks of the seasonal Segen River 85km south of Arba Minch. Of logistical significance as the funnel through which must pass all road traffic into South Omo, Karat (sometimes spelt Karati) is also the urban focal point of the Konso Cultural Landscape, which was inscribed as a 55km² UNESCO World Heritage Site in 2011. Although Karat itself is architecturally undistinguished, it lies within easy day-tripping distance of a total of 11 UNESCO-registered Konso villages, atmospheric hilltop settlements whose upper stone terraces and fortified walls were first set in place up to 400 years ago. Despite its small size, Karat is equipped with several hotels, and it hosts a large traditional market, 2km along the Jinka road, every Monday and Thursday. Outsiders generally know the town as Konso rather than Karat, but we have referred to it as Karat-Konso below in order to preclude confusion with the Konso people and their eponymous territory.

HISTORY The Konso inhabit an isolated region of basaltic hills – essentially an extension of the southern highlands – set at altitudes of 1,500–2,000m, and flanked to the east by the semi-desert Borena lowlands and to the west by the equally harsh Lower Omo Valley. They have no strong tradition relating to their place of origin. Oral lore has it that the proto-Konso migrated to their present homeland from somewhere further east at least 750 years ago, when they displaced an agricultural people whom they refer to as the Waradaya and credit with constructing certain stone terraces and wells still in use today. The Konso speak an East Cushitic language, and have few apparent cultural links with the people of the surrounding lowlands or the Ethiopian Highlands, but although very independent minded, they have generally coexisted peacefully with neighbouring people, but less so with the central government. Trade has long formed an important part of the Konso

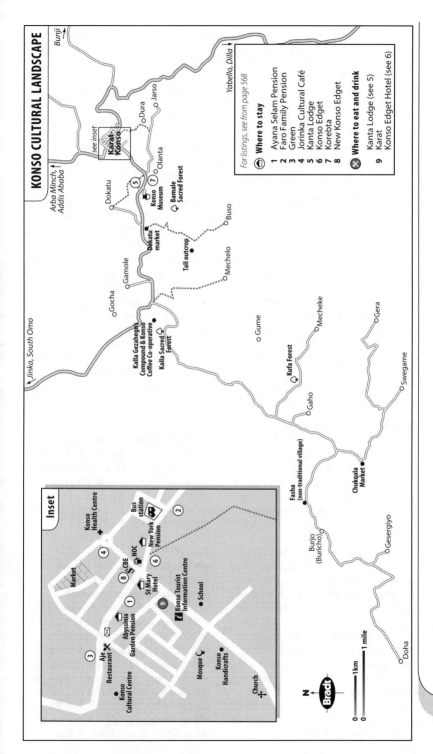

KONSO CULTURAL LANDSCAPE

Bunji

Arba Minch,
Addis Ababa

Jinka, South Omo

see inset

Karat-
Konso

Dokatu

Dura

Jarso

Olanta

Konso
Museum

Bamale
Sacred Forest

Buso

Dokatu
market

Tall outcrop

Mechelo

Gamole

Gocha

Kalla Gezahegn's
Compound & Konso
Coffee Co-operative

Kalla Sacred
Forest

Gume

Kufa Forest

Mecheke

Gera

Gaho

Swegame

Chukqala
Market

Fasha
(non-traditional village)

Burjo
(Buricho)

Gesergiyo

Doha

Yabello, Dilla

For listings, see from page 568

Where to stay

1 Ayana Selam Pension
2 Faro Family Pension
3 Green
4 Jorinka Cultural Café
5 Kanta Lodge
6 Konso Edget
7 Korebta
8 New Konso Edget

Where to eat and drink

Kanta Lodge (see 5)
9 Karat
Konso Edget Hotel (see 6)

Inset

Market

Konso
Health Centre

Bus
station

New York
Pension

NOC

CBE

St Mary
Hotel

Konso Tourist
Information Centre

School

Abyssinia
Garden Pension

Aje
Restaurant

Konso
Cultural Centre

Mosque

Konso
Handicrafts

Church

N

0   1km
0   1 mile

economy, thanks partly to its crossroads location on routes connecting northern Ethiopia, the Indian Ocean coast and the highlands of Kaffa to the west. Konso was annexed to Ethiopia in the 1890s after being conquered by the imperial army of Menelik II, who reputedly destroyed several settlements in the area and forced many people across the border into Kenya. The modern administrative centre of Karat-Konso was founded some time after this. Since 1995, Konso has enjoyed the status of a special *woreda* within the Southern Nations, Nationalities and Peoples' Region, which means it retains a higher degree of autonomy than normal *woredas*. The special *woreda* supports around 300,000 people and its governance and justice system are still tied closely to the traditional *kata* generation-grading system overseen by hereditary chiefs and elected committees of elders.

GETTING THERE AND AWAY The gateway town to South Omo, Karat-Konso lies at the junction of the new but not fully surfaced 85km road running south from Arba Minch, an unsurfaced 120km road running northwest from Yabello, and the 150km surfaced road running southeast from Jinka via Weito and Key Afer. It can also be accessed by a 175km dirt road from Fiseha Genet on the main road between Dilla and Yabello, but this is currently in very poor condition and not recommended. In a private vehicle, the drive to/from Arba Minch takes up to 2 hours, while it's about 3–4 hours to/from Yabello, and up to 3 hours to/from Jinka. Minibuses run back and forth to Arba Minch (*US$2.35*) and Jinka (*US$3.50*) from early morning until the late afternoon. On market days, Monday and Thursday, one bus in either direction connects Karat-Konso to Yabello (*US$5*); on other days there may be the occasional minibus or Isuzu truck, depending on demand, but this cannot be relied upon. If you are self-driving from Arba Minch, note that an excellent fish restaurant called **Chauffeur Asa Beit** can be found at Garache [map, page 563], some 45km south of Arba Minch or some 40km north of Karat-Konso.

🏠 **WHERE TO STAY** *Map, page 567*
Upmarket
🏠 **Kanta Lodge** (29 bungalows, 25 rooms) \046 773 0092, 011 618 2224–5; e hesstravelethiopia@ethionet.et; w hesstravelethiopia.com. Located 1.5km along the Jinka road, this hillside lodge operated by Hess Travel is comfortably the best place to stay in Karat-Konso. The spacious en-suite stone-&-thatch bungalows borrow from traditional Konso architecture, but have modern furnishings & fittings including hot water & private balcony. There are also cheaper rooms with less character but similar facilities in a block at the back. An above-average restaurant serves a varied selection of international & local dishes in the US$3–5 range. The vegetable, meat & poultry are said to come from the lodge's own farm. One can dine either indoors or on a pleasant stone terrace with views over the valley. Mosquito nets are available in all rooms, but it may be advisable to spray before you go to dinner. *US$45/64/84 B&B sgl/dbl/twin room, US$55/78/98 sgl/dbl/twin bungalow.* **$$$$**

🏠 **Korebta Hotel** (20 rooms) \046 773 0421; m 0911 210228, 0911 866864; e kklodge@karat. com. This new hotel & restaurant on the hill just opposite Kanta Lodge seems likely to attract a very similar clientele. The view over the surrounding landscape is great. *En-suite rooms are US$60/80/80 B&B sgl/dbl/twin.* **$$$$**

Budget
🏠 **New Konso Edget Hotel** (18 rooms) \046 773 0300; m 0930 069221, 0916 071504; e konsoedgethotel@gmail.com; w konsoedgethotel.com. Not to be confused with its older namesake on the opposite side of the main roundabout, this 3-storey hotel above the CBE is the standout budget lodge in Karat-Konso, offering comfortable & realistically priced accommodation in clean tiled rooms with en-suite hot shower. It also has free Wi-Fi & the town's best internet café. *US$18/20/23 sgl/dbl/twin.* **$$**

🏠 **Jorinka Cultural Café** (10 rooms, more under construction) m 0916 409471. This unsignposted new lodge, set in a big compound opposite the health centre, has large rooms with dbl bed, netting & en-suite undependable cold shower. Ask to be shown several rooms as a few have nightmarish bathrooms. *Fair value at US$12/15 sgl/dbl.* **$$**

🏠 **Green Hotel** (13 rooms) ☎046 773 0151; m 0913 880840. This quiet hotel on the Arba Minch road 500m northwest of the main roundabout has spacious but scruffy en-suite rooms with cold shower only. *Overpriced at US$12/16 sgl/dbl.* **$$**

Shoestring

🏠 **Faro Family Pension** (20 rooms) ☎046 773 0142; m 0948 055102. The pick of the cheapies, this friendly new lodge near the bus station has

clean rooms with a ¾ bed, net & en-suite cold shower, & common toilets. *Good value at US$4/6 sgl/dbl.* **$**

🏠 **Konso Edget Hotel** (29 rooms) ☎046 773 0300; m 0930 069221, 0916 071504; e konsoedgethotel@gmail.com, konsoedgethotel@yahoo.com. Set in a large compound on the main roundabout, the original Edget is popular with tour drivers & can get a bit noisy. The en-suite rooms are clean & bright with cold water only. A restaurant-cum-bar serves refrigerated drinks, fruit juice & decent local meals. Internet is available. *US$7/13 sgl/twin.* **$–$$**

🏠 **Ayana Selam Pension** (21 rooms) ☎046 773 0311; m 0927 104899. Acceptably clean rooms with a ¾ bed & use of common shower & toilet. *US$3/4 sgl/dbl occupancy.* **$**

✖ **WHERE TO EAT AND DRINK** *Map, page 567*
Kanta Lodge has the best food in town, as well a great setting, and it's not prohibitively expensive. Cheaper options include the café at the original Konso Edget Hotel, as well as the sometimes crowded Karat restaurant, beyond the St Mary Hotel, which serves excellent fried fish and other local dishes for less than US$1.

OTHER PRACTICALITIES The CBE on the main roundabout has an ATM and, for anybody heading to South Omo without stopping at Jinka, it will be the last opportunity to change or draw money. Note too that Konso – more specifically Kanta Lodge and the New Konso Edget Hotel – will also most likely be the last places with a semi-reliable internet or Wi-Fi connection. For curio hunters, Konso Handicrafts, just south of the tourist office, has a good selection of locally produced handicrafts, though it could be argued you are better off buying stuff directly from the women who line up outside most villages at the end of any given tour.

TOURIST INFORMATION AND GUIDES The **Konso Tourist Information Centre** (☎046 773 0395/6; e konsotourism@yahoo.com; ⏰ 07.00–17.00 *daily*), 250m south of the main roundabout, is a mandatory stop before exploring the Konso region further. This is where you must pay the daily village entrance fee of US$6 per person, which allows you to visit as many villages as you like, though some villages ask for an additional parking fee of US$2. It is also required that you pick up an official guide from the tourist office, at a cost of US$12 per party for half a day, or US$24 for a full day. The official guides based here are very knowledgeable and helpful, but will expect a fair tip. If you intend to visit the Konso Museum on the outskirts of town, or the chief's compound en route to Mecheke, the respective fees of US$1 and US$5 must also be paid here.

WHAT TO SEE AND DO
Konso Museum [map, page 567] (⏰ 08.00–17.00 *daily; entrance US$1 pp must be paid at the tourist centre, photography permitted*) Funded by the French government and opened in 2012, this hillside museum lies alongside the Jinka road 1.5km from Karat-Konso, more or less opposite Kanta Lodge. The main point of interest is a superb collection of *waka* grave-markers, most of which come from a cache that

The Konso rank among the most singular of African peoples. Mixed agriculturists, they make the most of the hard, rocky slopes that characterise their relatively dry and infertile homeland through a combination of extensive rock terracing, the use of animal dung as fertiliser, crop rotation and hard work. Their most important crop, sorghum, is harvested twice annually: after the short rains in June and July, and after the long rains in February and March. Sorghum is used to make a thick local beer, while the finely ground flour forms the base of the Konso staple *korkorfa* or *dama*, a sort of dough-ball cooked like a dumpling in a stew or soup. Other important crops include maize, beans and coffee. Oddly, the Konso shun coffee beans in favour of the leaves, which are sun-dried, then ground to a fine powder and mixed with sunflower seeds and various spices, to form an easily stored equivalent to instant coffee.

The most outwardly distinctive feature of Konso country is its aesthetically pleasing towns and villages, which bear an unexpectedly strong (and presumably coincidental) resemblance to the Dogon villages of Mali. Unusually for this part of Africa, the Konso traditionally live in congested centralised settlements, typically situated on the top of a hill and enclosed by stone walls measuring up to 2m high. These walled hilltop settlements usually have up to four entrance gates, and can be reached only via a few steep footpaths. In times past, this made the villages easily defensible, an important consideration for an isolated people whose territory was under constant threat of cattle raids and military attacks from the flanking lowlands.

Every village is governed by an elected committee of elders, known as a *kimaya*, as well as by the *apa timba* (father of the drum), whose role is to direct religious ceremonies, maintain oral traditions and administer justice. Both are supervised by the *pokalla*, a hereditary clan chief whose compound can be easily recognised because the roofs of all the buildings are topped with an ostrich shell rather than the more common pot. Traditionally, these governing classes are all from the high *etenta* caste of farmers and warriors. Lower-caste *xawda* families are forbidden from owning land and are charged with artisanal activities such as cotton weaving, tanning, pottery and metalwork. This caste distinction is no longer strictly maintained.

Within the defensive town walls, low stick-and-stone walls and leafy *Moringa stenopetelai* (*shiferaw*) trees enclose every individual compound to create a labyrinth of narrow, shady alleys. Each family compound typically consists of between three and five circular thatched stone huts, as well as an elevated granary or *kosa* used to store sorghum and maize, and a taller but smaller platform where freshly cooked food is stowed away too high for children to reach it. The compounds are entered via gateways, which are supported and covered by thick wooden struts, a defensive design that forces any aspirant attackers to crawl into the compound one by one.

Every village consists of a number of sub-communities, each of which is centred upon a *mora* or community house. This is a tall building with an open-sided ground floor supported by juniper trunks, and a sharply angled thatched roof covering a wooden ceiling. The ground floor serves as a shaded place where villagers – men, boys and girls, but not grown women – can relax, gossip, play and make important communal decisions. Customarily, all boys from the age of 12 upwards are required to sleep in the ceiling of the *mora* until they get married, and even married men are expected to spend part of the night there. This custom, though still enforced, derives from more beleaguered days when the older boys and men often needed to be mobilised quickly when a village was attacked. The *mora* also serves as a guesthouse for male visitors from other villages. Girls and women are not generally allowed to sleep in the *mora*, though these days some villages will make an exception for *faranji* tourists!

Konso society is structured around the *kata* generation-set, a system not dissimilar to the *gada* of the neighbouring Borena and Oromo, or that practised by the Maasai and Samburu of East Africa. Although the exact cycle differs from one village to the next, any given village will initiate a new generation – consisting of boys of between eight and 25 years old – every 18 years. Traditionally, young men who had not yet been initiated into a generation were usually permitted to marry, but any offspring that their wives produced would be killed at birth – a custom that is no longer practised. Should you happen to be in Konso country during December, January or September, this is when *kata* induction ceremonies take place, so it's worth asking about them locally. The highlight of the ceremony is the erection of an *olahita* (generation pole) in the village's ceremonial square, which usually stands alongside its oldest *mora*. These poles are always harvested from the *pokalla's* sacred forest, and make it easy to estimate the approximate age of any given village – just count the number of poles and multiply the total by 18! In the ceremonial square, you'll also usually see a large 'swearing stone', which people accused of a crime must swear upon to demonstrate their innocence.

The erection of poles and stones forms an important part of Konso ritual. In any village square, you'll see a number of so-called 'victory stones' standing to mark important events – generally victories over attempted raiders or conquerors – in the village's history. More famous are the Konso *waka*, carved wooden grave-markers that are often (and rather misleadingly) referred to as totems. Traditionally, a *waka* will be erected above the grave of any important Konso man or warrior, surrounded by smaller statues of his wives and defeated foes. The sombre facial features of the dead warrior are carved on to the *waka*, complete with enlarged and bucked teeth made from animal bones – creating a rather leery impression that is only reinforced by the impressively proportioned penis the deceased typically has clasped in his hand! Intriguingly, these grave-markers and victory stones have an obvious precursor in the stelae that mark medieval graves around modern-day Dilla, and oral tradition indicates that the proto-Konso migrated from about the right place at about the right time for there to be some link between these customs.

The practice of erecting engraved burial markers has largely disappeared in recent decades, and many of the finest remaining examples were recently collected by the regional tourist office before they could be damaged or sold to foreign collectors. They are now displayed in the Konso Museum, 1.5km out of Karat-Konso along the Jinka road. Although the Konso are animists by custom, the last 50 years have seen many youngsters convert to Protestant denominations. Traditional attire has also given way to the ubiquitous trousers or skirt and T-shirt. In most other senses, however, modern Konso society remains strikingly informed by, and in touch with, a unique and ancient cultural heritage.

was looted in the 1990s for the black market, only to be confiscated by border officials and stored away at the government office in Karat-Konso, in keeping with a local tradition that a fallen or displaced *waka* may not be re-erected at the grave it once marked. Other traditional artefacts and interesting photographs are displayed there, along with a wealth of interpretative material, making it well worth stopping in before you head out to the villages.

Konso Cultural Centre [map, page 567] (✆ 046 773 0419; ⊕ 09.00–12.30 & 14.00–17.30 daily; entrance free) Signposted on the left-hand side of the Arba Minch road 500m west of Karat-Konso's roundabout, this low-key cultural centre was established by an Italian corporation with the support of the European Union to provide a visual archive of the Konso people. A few photographic displays can be seen here, and it also has a good library, but funding dried up a while ago. The Konso Development Association recently announced that it will revive the venture.

Konso villages The main attraction in the vicinity of Karat-Konso is the 11 traditional villages integral to UNESCO's Konso Cultural Landscape World Heritage Site. These are all broadly similar in layout, as described in the box on page 570, and can be visited only on guided trips arranged through the Konso Tourist Information Centre in Karat-Konso, which is also where you pay your entrance and guide fees. Most visitors on organised tours are content to visit one or two individual villages, but the information centre can also arrange four- to five-day hikes through the Konso region, taking in several villages, as well as the hot springs at Doha and other traditional sites of interest. Travellers who arrive at Karat-Konso on public transport and are short on time can either stick to nearby villages such as Olanta, Dokatu and Gamole, or arrange 4x4 rental though the tourist office, which will cost around US$50 for half a day (sufficient time to visit at least two villages). Although the blanket fee covers entry to any village of your choice, and in theory photography, it is not acceptable to photograph individuals without paying them a few birr. Alternatively, you can usually arrange to photograph freely in any given family compound for a blanket fee in the ballpark of US$1–5, depending on group size. Brief descriptions of some of the most worthwhile villages follow, starting with those closest to Karat-Konso.

Olanta Practically bordering on Karat-Konso, Olanta is a much older village – a total of 36 generation poles dates it back some 650 years – which still functions as a self-contained traditional entity comprising 12 sub-communities and *mora* generation houses. It supports a population of around 4,500 in three concentric stone circles. There are more spectacular Konso villages, but Olanta's proximity to town and hassle-free atmosphere make it well worth a visit, particularly for those without private transport. To get there, follow the Jinka road about 1km past the tourist information office, until you reach the curve in the asphalt about 500m before Kanta Lodge. The outer wall of Olanta is about 100m south of the dirt road branching south from here.

Dokatu One of the oldest and largest villages in Konso, Dokatu has 43 generation poles, indicating an age of around 750 years, and 5,500 inhabitants, who live within or between its three concentric protective walls, and are divided into 16 communities, each with its own *mora*. Dokatu is particularly worth visiting on market days, Monday and Thursday, and is also known as the home of a renowned *waka* maker, but the children have a reputation for trailing behind tourists and becoming a nuisance. To get there, follow the Jinka road out of town for 1km past Kanta Lodge, until you see a large marketplace on your left. The walled hilltop village is visible to the right, a 600m walk northeast of the market.

Gamole Another large village that could be visited on foot from Karat-Konso, Gamole comprises 15 communities, each with their own *mora*, while the presence of 42 generation poles indicates it is almost as old as Dokatu. The village's highest and oldest circle is home to around 700 people, and includes the compound of a clan chief, while another 4,000-odd people live within the second and third circles, and a fourth circle is being constructed to contain several newly built compounds. Gamole is a very hassle-free village, and probably a better bet than Dokatu except on market days. Gamole lies about 5km from Karat-Konso by road. To get there, walk or catch a *bajaj* along the Jinka road for 1.8km past Dokatu market, then take a right turn, and you'll reach the outer wall after about 500m. If you feel like a tipple on the way out, ask around for Guyo's roadside *tej* bar.

Dura and Jarso These two smaller villages lie a few hundred metres apart only 1km southeast of Karat-Konso, west of the main road to Yabello. Dura is home to about 2,700 people split between 13 communities, each with its own *mora*, and has 27 generation poles, making it almost 500 years old. Jarso is similar in size and well known for its traditional weavers. Both see relatively few foreign visitors and have a peaceful hassle-free atmosphere. Dura can be reached from the main roundabout in Karat-Konso by following a 1km footpath that runs south from next to the old Konso Edget Hotel.

Buso This small but very scenic village lies 3.5km southwest of Karat-Konso as the crow flies, and can be reached on foot along a 2km path that runs south from Dokatu market on the Jinka road. The path runs past the sacred Bamale Forest to the left and an impressive rock outcrop to the right before arriving at the village, whose centrepiece is a small but uninhabited wooded hill. An unusual feature of Buso is a small field of angular, roughly hewn stone grave-markers situated close to the generation poles.

Mecheke The best known of the traditional Konso villages, Mecheke, set atop a tall hill some 13km from Karat-Konso, achieved its reputation because Angela Fisher did much of her exquisite Konso photography here. At least 400 years old, the town supports about 3,000 people split into ten sub-communities. In addition to the usual *mora* and generation poles, the village has four clusters of *waka* grave-markers, some estimated to be more than 150 years old. Mecheke is very used to tourists, which has its advantages – you're likely to be greeted by people playing the *kehaita* (a local musical instrument) and by weavers hoping to be photographed – but the youngsters here have also acquired a reputation for persistent low-key hassle. To reach Mecheke from Karat-Konso, follow the Jinka road for 5.5km, then turn left on to a dirt road at a signposted junction about 500m past the turn-off for Gamole. After another 5km, turn left on to a motorable track and follow it for 3km to a parking spot below the town walls. No public transport runs along this road.

Gesergiyo Although it's smaller and less characterful than the villages listed above, Gesergiyo is a popular goal with tour groups due to an adjacent formation of sand pinnacles whose vague resemblance to a row of skyscrapers led some local wag to christen it 'New York', a nickname that's stuck. Sculpted by occasional water flow in a normally dry gorge, it's a magnificent and very unusual phenomenon, since the pinnacles are made entirely of sand. Oral tradition has it that 'New York' is of supernatural origin. The story is that a local chief awoke one day to find his ceremonial drums had been stolen during the night. He enlisted the help of God, who swept away the earth from where the thieves had buried the drums, creating the sand formation in the process. It is said that the thieves, realising that God knows all, immediately confessed to their sins – their fate goes unrecorded! To this day, light-fingered Konso youngsters are taken to Gesergiyo as a reminder that God doesn't like thieves, and will see what they get up to. Gesergiyo lies 17km from Karat-Konso by road, and is easily visited in combination with Mecheke. Coming from Mecheke, drive back 3km to the last intersection, but instead of heading right towards Karat-Konso, turn left and continue for 6.5km, passing en route through Fasha, a not-so-traditional village known for its large Saturday market and century-old Ethiopian Orthodox church, reputedly the oldest such building in Konso territory.

Kalla Gezahegn's Compound and Konso Coffee Co-operative

Set in the juniper-dominated sacred Kalla Forest, the compound of Kalla (Chief) Gezahegn is a fascinating and atmospheric place, surrounded by several *waka* grave-markers signifying the final resting place of earlier chiefs and their wives, and with an interior cluttered with venerable chiefly artefacts ranging from beer vats to furniture. The paramount leader of the Kertita clan by descent and a city-based engineer by trade, the chief speaks good English and makes for a gracious and welcoming host, at least when he is around, and guided visits can be arranged with a guide from the Konso Tourist Information Centre at a charge of US$5 per person. The compound lies 7km west of Karat-Konso and can be reached by following the Jinka road out of town for 5.5km, then following the signposted Mecheke road south for 1.5km.

The title of Konso clan chief is strictly hereditary, and Gezahegn is 20th in a line that has lived in the same compound for about 500 years. The clan is an important patrilineal unit of Konso society – members of the same clan, for instance, are forbidden from marrying – and each of the nine clans is represented by its own elected local headman in any given Konso village. The paramount chief of any given clan acts as a spiritual guru, as well as in a judicial role; he and his immediate family live in total isolation, in order that he has no involvement in the day-to-day life of a community. The idea is that this will ensure his impartiality when settling intra-clan disputes and crimes, which are still often dealt with by the chief rather than national government. The Kertita lineage is one of only three of the original nine chieftaincies to survive into the present day.

It is customary in Konso for the death of a paramount clan chief to be denied after the event. An official embalmer tends (for which read mummifies) the chief, and word is given out that he is very ill. Only after nine years, nine months and nine days is it finally announced that the chief is dead, with full blame falling on the unfortunate embalmer, who is heavily fined for his predetermined failure. How and why this unusual custom arose is unknown. It has been suggested that a delayed announcement will allow time for a relative of the chief to remedy the problem should he have died without male issue. A more plausible explanation, given that it is tacitly realised that any chief being attended by an embalmer is unlikely to make a full recovery, is that the charade softens the blow of the departure of a popular and respected leader.

This custom was followed in 1990, when Gezahegn's grandfather, Kalla Koyote, died at an age of more than 100 years. The chief was duly embalmed and confined to his compound with influenza. This, however, was a difficult time in Konso, due to a severe local drought and the ongoing civil war, and it was felt that a living chief was better equipped to navigate any crises than a terminally ill one. Koyote's death was announced seven months after he had died, his embalmed body was buried in a ceremony that lasted for eight days, and his son Wolde Dawit was installed as chief. When Wolde Dawit passed away in 2004, his body was held in state for a relatively moderate nine days before it was buried and his son Gezahegn was installed as chief.

Situated very close to the clan chief's compound, the new Konso Coffee Co-operative, an initiative launched by Kalla Gezahegn and his brother Tariku, bills itself as the first fully tribal coffee co-operative in Ethiopia and provides a rare opportunity for tourists to witness green coffee bean production using the natural, dry method of processing the cherries. They may also rub shoulders with the Konso women who form part of the co-operative, and can even help them sort beans.

ALONG THE KONSO–JINKA ROAD

Now fully upgraded to asphalt, the 150km road between Karat-Konso and Jinka can be covered in about 2 hours in a private vehicle and usually takes an hour longer by minibus. The road is punctuated by the villages of Weito, Key Afer and Kako, which respectively lie about 70km west of Karat-Konso (at the junction of the old road to Turmi), 40km southeast of Jinka (close to the junction of the new and shorter road to Turmi) and halfway between Key Afer and Jinka. The three villages are of limited interest to tourists on six days of the week, but are well worth stopping at on their market days, which are Saturday in Weito, Thursday in Key Afer and Monday in Kako. For those without a private vehicle, it is easy enough to find transport between these villages and Jinka or Karat-Konso, and you could also think about overnighting in Weito or Key Afer the night before or after market day.

WEITO Situated at the junction of the Jinka and old Turmi roads 70km west of Karat-Konso and 5km past a bridge across the Weito River, this tiny Tsemai settlement is known for its busy Saturday market, also attended by Aari and Bana people. On other days, Weito has a rather dusty impermanent feel, with a lack of character suggesting it owes its existence entirely to its junction location. Indeed, the town's dominant feature is the **Weito Lodge** (m *0915 622357*), a large garden restaurant and hotel complex that attracts more passing truck traffic than it does colourful locals, and charges US$5 for a basic room with a ¾ bed using common showers or US$10 for an en-suite double, and also has food at jacked-up *faranji* prices.

KEY AFER The relatively large and cosmopolitan village of Key Afer is situated at a refreshing altitude of 1,800m about halfway along the surfaced road from Weito to Jinka, about 1km past the junction with the recently upgraded but not yet surfaced road south to Turmi via Dimeka. Key Afer is readily accessible on public transport, and well worth a stop on Thursdays, when it hosts a multi-cultural market – dominated by Aari, Bana and Hamar people – as colourful as any in the region. On non-market days, the town centre is relatively modern in feel, but the backstreets east of the market square are lined with traditional homes. An optional guide can be arranged through the Anomba Tour Guide Association, next to Sami Pension, and costs around US$10–15 per party.

SOUTH OMO: THE COMPLEXITIES

South Omo is often portrayed as some sort of cultural Garden of Eden. This notion is unduly romantic. The Mursi disfigure their adolescent girls monstrously. The ritualised whipping of women is integral to Hamar society. Regular outbreaks of intertribal fighting – usually provoked by cattle disputes – result in frequent murders. And such is the tenuous grip of conventional law-keeping that killers are seldom apprehended, but remain free to parade whatever mark of Cain is customary within their tribe. It's a rough neighbourhood. But still, there is much that is genuinely uplifting about the sheer tenacity that has allowed South Omo's incredible cultural and ethnolinguistic mosaic to survive into the 21st century largely intact. Romanticise it or condemn it, South Omo is what it is, and frankly it couldn't give a damn what outsiders think.

Nevertheless, the tribespeople of South Omo face numerous challenges as a result of increased globalisation, outside scrutiny and other agents of 21st-century social change. Controversy abounds. And it's a veritable playground for easily outraged zealots. Be it innocuities such as women going bare-breasted, or more consequential questions of misogynistic violence and intertribal killings, the anachronistic cultures of South Omo are riddled with beliefs and customs anathematic to human rights campaigners, or missionaries, or conservationists, or Ethiopian highlanders, or woman's rights advocates, or the national government, or ... well, the list goes on. Put simply, South Omo is just too far out of step with the rest of the modern world to remain as it is indefinitely.

The traditional South Omo economy, based around cattle herding and subsistence farming, is also under pressure. In part, this is an unavoidable consequence of population growth, which forces an ever-increasing number of people and livestock to subsist on the same finite tract of land, often at unsustainable levels. Externally imposed ventures such as the upriver Gibe III hydro-electric dam, inaugurated in December 2016, are also harbingers of change. According to the Ethiopian government, the construction of this immense dam will eliminate the occasionally destructive annual floods that blight South Omo, while the planned establishment of several sugarcane plantations downriver will grant a 'sustainable income and modern life' to the struggling pastoralists of South Omo. Others fear that the dam will have a devastating impact on more than half a million people, in both Ethiopia and Kenya, who depend on the Omo flood for their livelihoods and have no interest in forsaking their traditional ways to become plantation workers. Either way, whatever the rights and wrongs, for better or for worse, South Omo evidently stands on the cusp of massive economic change.

So ... where does tourism fit into all this? Well, tourism is pretty big business in South Omo these days, and it tends to be dominated by a two-way obsession with photography (page 565), which has undoubtedly led to interactions with tribespeople becoming more commercialised, sometimes to a degree that might become unpleasant. But does this really mean, as some concerned individuals assert, that tourism is hastening the demise of South Omo's traditional cultures? Probably not! As local tour guide Dehina Hunu points out: 'Ironically, tourism is protecting the tribes. Without it, all tribes from South Omo will disappear soon, because of the construction of the electricity dam ... Most of the tribes just don't realise it yet.' Certainly, it seems reasonable to assume that a tourist industry based on one-on-one encounters with the diverse ethnolinguistic groups of South Omo is more likely to reinforce tribal traditions than to undermine them.

When you visit South Omo and witness a Hamar bull-jumping ceremony, walk through a village market, or visit a traditional rural compound, what you are seeing, more than 99% of the time, is emphatically the real thing. Yes, the locals expect to be paid for photographs – and fair enough, too, when you put yourself in their position, and consider how irritating it might be to be descended upon day after day by yet another 4x4 full of insensitive camera-wielding *faranji* trying to sneak a few free photos. But this is where commercialisation begins and ends. Were you to stray unguided into a rural compound that doesn't routinely deal with tourists, odds are that its inhabitants would simply refuse to be photographed, rather than asking for money. Furthermore, it seems somewhat ironic for affluent gadget-laden visitors from materialistic Europe or North America to accuse the resilient and ascetic tribespeople of South Omo of being commercialised. Are our preconceptions of how 'primitive' tribespeople should interact with Western outsiders so rigid and culture-bound that any slight deviation blinds us from seeing things for what they are?

South Omo is riddled with such complexities and ambiguities. Many of these are highlighted in readers' letters and responses on our updates site (visit **w** bradtupdates.com/ethiopia and choose the 'South Omo' category), while a more objective overview of certain issues can be explored at David Turton's excellent site Mursi Online (**w** *mursi.org*). But to highlight one set of contradictions: most visitors to South Omo place a high priority on attending a Hamar bull-jumping ceremony, ideally one that is authentic rather than staged for tourists. Yet few would regard the vicious whipping of women that precedes an authentic bull-jump to be remotely acceptable in any other context. So if tourist dollars are helping keep alive the bull-jumping tradition, does that mean they are also sponsoring violence against women? On the other hand, if the bull-jumping ceremonies would continue irrespective of tourism, as seems probable, might the routine presence of Westerners not encourage the male whippers to tone down the violence and eventually phase it out all together? And is it not a little hypocritical for us outsiders to get all chin-strokey about the integrity of a traditional culture, and to become outraged when we sense any hint of commercialism there, yet to balk at those facets of the whole that are unacceptable to our moral system?

Perhaps pragmatism should rule. South Omo will change, with or without the tourist dollar. And issues surrounding tourism to the region are so complex, so easily politicised and so deeply intertwined with broader regional economic and social development, that it seems misguided for any but the most informed and impartial of outsiders to hold too many firm opinions. True, certain aspects of interaction between tribespeople and tourists can be jarring, specifically where photography is concerned. Ultimately, however, this is a rather superficial concern. And all things considered, tourism to South Omo, a few grey areas notwithstanding, is almost certainly doing more good than bad. So if you decide to visit South Omo, travel there with an open mind. Avoid single-issue politicising and rather aim to get your head around the whole complex picture. As one blunt reader recently put it: 'The people of South Omo are poor. Tourism is one way they can make some money. If you don't want to pay the fees, don't visit. And if you do visit, don't complain, just enjoy the experience.'

Where to stay, eat and drink

Sami Pension (5 rooms, more under construction) m 0930 069568. This agreeable lodge in the town centre has large modern en-suite rooms with dbl bed & running cold water. A bar is attached. *US$12 dbl*. **$$**

Nasa Hotel (12 rooms) m 0913 093093. Set in large green grounds practically opposite Sami Pension, this adequate lodge offers threadbare sgls with a ¾ bed & it also has the best eatery in town. *US$4/6 sgl without/with shower*. **$**

ALDUBA Situated alongside the Turmi road about 15km south of Key Afer, the small village of Alduba warrants a diversion on Tuesday, when the market attracts plenty of traditionally attired Hamar, Tsemai, Bana and Aari people.

KAKO Lying roughly halfway between Key Afer and Jinka, and sharing these towns' temperate highland climate, Kako is a small but attractive Aari village noted for its busy Monday market. For independent travellers, it would make for a straightforward day excursion out of Jinka. Basic rooms are available at a few places but none looks at all appealing, and there is plenty of public transport to and from Jinka.

JINKA

The administrative capital of South Omo Zone, Jinka is a modestly sized town perched at a relatively high, cool and damp altitude of 1,450m in a lush green valley run though by the perennial Neri River. Though not as isolated as it was a few years back, it has a rather quaint atmosphere that combines urban and rural attributes in equal proportion. Which of these comes to the fore will depend largely on whether you've cruised to Jinka on the asphalt road from Addis Ababa or Arba Minch, or bumped and skidded up from the sweltering dry plains that dominate the rest of South Omo. Straddling these two worlds, Jinka boasts amenities typical of small-town Ethiopia – filling stations, banks with ATMs, a clutch of acceptable hotels and restaurants – yet elements such as the grassy airstrip running through the town centre undermine any pretensions it might have to being much more than a small end-of-the-asphalt administrative centre in the back of beyond. Whatever else, Jinka is a likeable enough town, with a good museum, and a lively daily market most busy on Tuesdays and Saturdays, which attracts Aari and other rural traders from all over South Omo. It is also the best place for backpackers to rent a vehicle to see the Mursi or to visit Mago National Park.

HISTORY *With thanks to Dawit Teferi for access to his 200-page thesis* A History of Jinka
The region now known as South Omo Zone was incorporated into Ethiopia in 1894 under an imperial army led by Ras Wolde Giyorgis. From 1904, it was administered as a province named Bako after its capital town, perched at a lofty altitude of 2,300m in Aari territory 10km north of present-day Jinka. Bako had served as a military encampment under Ras Wolde Giyorgis in 1894, and Count Leonteff, the Russian co-administrator of Bako, praised it as a 'natural fortress [that] commanded all of the environs'. By 1910, the township supported 2,000 bamboo houses, as well as an Orthodox church dedicated to Kiddist Giyorgis (still in place today), a stone governor's residence, and a massive banquet hall. A road connecting Bako to an airstrip at present-day Jinka was constructed during the Italian occupation, but it had become impassable by the early 1950s. Indeed, by this time, the inaccessibility of Leonteff's 'natural fortress' was perceived to be a hindrance to economic development, leading to the short-lived relocation of the district capital to Hamar Koke, which stood in Hamar territory between present-day Turmi and Arbore, in 1954. The new site was abandoned three years later, mainly due to a scarcity of water.
In 1957, the district capital was returned to Aari territory. Instead of Bako, however, the governor chose the lower-lying Alga (an Amharic name meaning 'bed',

> ## THE AARI
>
> The most numerous ethnolinguistic group of South Omo is the Aari, who number around 320,000 according to recent estimates, and occupy a territory of around 2,500km² extending from Mago National Park to Jinka and Key Afer, and into the highlands further north. In common with the Hamar, the Aari speak an Omotic language, divided into nine mutually intelligible dialects associated with the nine traditional Aari states, each of which is presided over by a hereditary chief called a Babi. The highland-dwelling Aari around Jinka and their lowland counterparts have quite different economies, but both are mixed subsistence farmers who grow various grains and fruits (supplemented at higher altitudes by coffee and *enset*), keep livestock and produce excellent honey. In urban centres such as Jinka, most Aari people now mostly wear Western clothes. In more rural areas, you'll still see Aari women draped in the traditional *gori*, a dress made with *enset* and *koisha* leaves, and decorated around the waist and arms with colourful beads and bracelets. The Aari generally have a peaceful relationship with their neighbours, but conflict with the Mursi is not uncommon, and has often led to the latter being denied access to the markets at Jinka and Baka.

16

probably to show that the area was comfortable), which had some historic pedigree as the site of the region's oldest Orthodox church, established in the 1890s, and of an airstrip used during the Italian occupation. The relocation of the capital to Alga, or Jinka as it is known today, was probably made on impulse, after the governor landed a plane there in 1957 and realised the potential importance of air access in a region that still had no all-weather roads. Nevertheless, Alga proved to be an inspired choice thanks to its high rainfall, proximity to a perennial river and convenience as a market location. Within a couple of years, Bako had become overgrown and dilapidated as its residents flocked downhill to the new capital, which was soon entrenched as South Omo's largest settlement. Major landmarks back then included the grassy airstrip that still bisects the town centre, the governor's residence on the site of the present-day Yeshi Bar, and a health centre established alongside the airstrip in 1962.

It's unclear when Alga formally became known as Jinka. The two names were used interchangeably for several years, with Jinka gradually gaining favour over the course of the 1970s, though the northern part of town is still widely referred to as Alga (oddly, the provenance of the name Jinka is unknown to the local Aari, suggesting it was given to the locality before they settled there). By 1984, Jinka's urban population had grown to 5,000, and today it stands at around 30,000, some 90% of which comprises Amhara, Oromo and other outsiders. Pre-millennial Jinka remained very isolated from the rest of Ethiopia, but it recently acquired (theoretical) 24-hour electricity, and is now connected to Addis Ababa by a good surfaced road through Arba Minch and Konso. Recently opened a few kilometres south of town, a new international airport with a 2.5km surfaced runway has allowed for the resumption of scheduled flights from Addis Ababa, providing the region with a further potential economic boost.

GETTING THERE AND AWAY

By air Although the grassy airstrip around which Jinka was founded remains a prominent feature of the town centre, Ethiopian Airlines' four weekly flights (Tuesday, Wednesday, Friday and Sunday) land at the new airport a few kilometres south of town.

By road Jinka lies 150km from Karat-Konso along a surfaced road through Weito and Key Afer. Minibuses (US$3.50; 3–4hrs) run back and forth between the two throughout the day. There is also transport to Key Afer (US$0.50; 1hr) throughout the day, while direct buses to/from Arba Minch (US$4.75; 5–6hrs) usually leave between 06.00 and 10.00 only. A limited amount of transport to Dimeka, Turmi and Omorate can occasionally be found at the bus station, especially on market days (Monday, Tuesday, Thursday and Saturday).

 WHERE TO STAY *Map, opposite*

Upmarket

🏠 **Eco-Omo Safari Lodge** (16 safari tents, 4 bungalows) 046 775 1500, 011 861 2040 (Addis Ababa); e villaggioglobale@ethionet.et, info@eco-omo.com; w eco-omo.com. Fronting the Neri River on the western outskirts of Jinka, this pleasant Italian-owned lodge, set in a large compound frequented by guereza monkeys & plenty of birds, is the top option in the vicinity of Jinka. The en-suite safari tents have nets & hot shower & stand on wooden platforms leading out to a small balcony. There are also bungalows using common showers. The tents are cramped up in a tight row, which allows you to hear everything in the neighbouring tent, & we've also had complaints about the nocturnal noise from a nearby church. A stylish *tukul*-style restaurant with indoor & outdoor seating serves decent but quite pricey Italian-flavoured dishes in the US$4–9 range, & Wi-Fi is available 17.30–19.30 only. Trekking, horseriding &

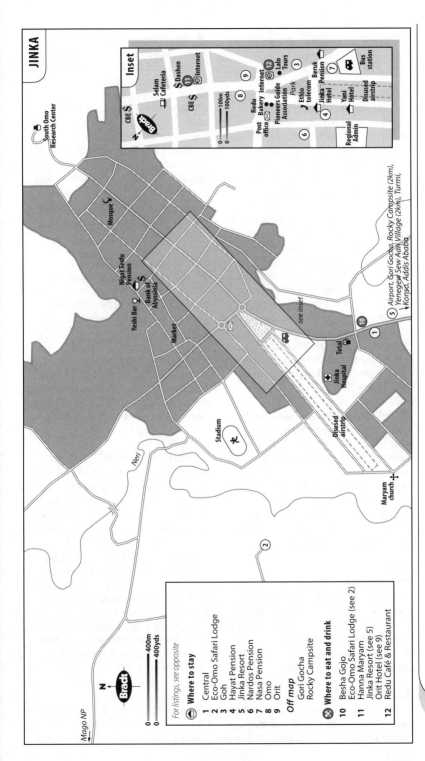

JINKA

Inset

South Omo
Research Center

Selam
Cafeteria

Dashen

Internet

CBE

CBE

Redu
Bakery Internet
Pioneers Guide
Association

Post
office

Ethio
telecom

Lalo
Tours

Park

Beruk
Pension

Jinka
Hotel

Yani
Hotel

Disused
airstrip

Bus
station

Regional
Admin

Mosque

Nigst Tesfu
Pension

Bank of
Abyssinia

Yeshi Bar

Market

Stadium

Neri

Mago NP

Jinka
Hospital

Total

Disused airstrip

Maryam
church

see inset

Airport, Gori Gocha, Rocky Campsite (2km),
Yenegew Sew Aari Village (2km), Turmi,
Konso, Addis Ababa

For listings, see opposite

Where to stay
1 Central
2 Eco-Omo Safari Lodge
3 Goh
4 Hayat Pension
5 Jinka Resort
6 Nardos Pension
7 Nasa Pension
8 Omo
9 Orit

Off map
Gori Gocha
Rocky Campsite

Where to eat and drink
10 Besha Gojo
Eco-Omo Safari Lodge (see 2)
11 Hanna Maryam
Jinka Resort (see 5)
Orit Hotel (see 9)
12 Redu Café & Restaurant

birdwatching trips can be arranged. *US$69/111 B&B en-suite sgl/dbl, US$34/58 sgl/twin using common shower.* **$$$$–$$$$$**

Moderate

🏠 **Nasa Pension** (20 rooms) 📞046 885 7469/85; **m** 0964 353535. Regarded by some operators to offer the best value in Jinka, this smart & well-run new 2-storey pension has tastefully decorated en-suite rooms with nets & balcony, & a convenient location opposite the old airstrip. You are well advised to avoid the rooms directly neighbouring the bus station where roaring motors & unwelcomed loud conversation will interfere with your sleep from 05.00. *US$18/23 dbl/twin.* **$$**

🏠 **Orit Hotel** (27 rooms) 📞046 775 0045; **m** 0930 069492; **e** orithotel@yahoo.com. Set in flowering mango-shaded gardens immediately east of the main intersection, this long-serving hotel has a smart 2-storey new wing whose en-suite rooms with hot water & TV are rated as the best in town by many operators. Shabbier but cheaper en-suite rooms are still available in the old wing. The popular restaurant has outdoor seating & a varied menu of local & Western dishes in the US$3–4 range. *US$17/30 dbl/twin (new wing), US$10 dbl (old wing).* **$$**

🏠 **Jinka Resort** (18 rooms) 📞046 775 0143; **m** 0923 470765. Set in attractive well-wooded grounds on the Karat-Konso road 600m south of the main intersection, this lodge looks great from the outside, but the tiled en-suite rooms with hot water are looking a little tired & seem quite functional at the rather steep *faranji* rates. A good restaurant is attached which serves steaks, goulash, chicken dishes & salads in the US$2–5 range, & it also does great juice. *US$30/32 sgl/dbl.* **$$$**

Budget

🏠 **Central Hotel** (19 rooms) 📞046 775 1699; **m** 0913 080553. Situated roughly opposite the Jinka Resort, this new 2-storey hotel, set back just far enough from the main road to reduce the noise factor, offers clean rooms with net & cold shower. As good value as you'll get in Jinka. *US$8/13 dbl with common/en-suite shower.* **$$**

🏠 **Hayat Pension** (12 rooms) **m** 0911 071194. This quiet & centrally located new pension has bright, clean, tiled en-suite rooms with a ¾ bed & cold en-suite shower. *Decent value at US$10 sgl or dbl occupancy.* **$$**

🏠 **Goh Hotel** (40 rooms) 📞046 775 0033; **m** 0916 855947. This agreeable, relatively modern & reasonably clean hotel is centred on a pleasant courtyard on the edge of the central airstrip. The en-suite rooms look a little weary considering the asking price, but the shoestring rooms using common shower are good value. The restaurant located in the adjoining property is reasonable. *US$18/23 en-suite sgl/dbl, or US$6 sgl using common shower.* **$–$$**

Shoestring

🏠 **Nardos Pension** (15 rooms) **m** 0937 712589. Set in central green grounds, this is the pick in this range, offering the choice of older rooms that use common showers, but have a net & balcony, or new en-suite rooms with TV. *US$10/16 dbl with common/en-suite shower.* **$$**

🏠 **Omo Hotel** (10 rooms) 📞056 775 1130/0067. Shabbier than the above, this central hotel, opposite the Orit, is a favourite haunt for truck drivers. Basic rooms with en-suite cold-water shower using a common toilet are loud. *US$10 dbl.* **$$**

Camping

⛺ **Rocky Campsite** **m** 0967 927135. This beautiful green site, 3km along the Karat-Konso road, has an attractive setting, common toilets & showers, 3 kitchen houses & a bar selling cold beers & soft drinks. You must bring your own food, but a cook is available if you don't feel like preparing it yourself. *US$4 pp & US$2 to rent a tent.* **$**

⛺ **Gori Gocha** **m** 0936 502791. Located on a green hillside offering a wonderful view over Jinka & the Neri Valley, this new campsite has no facilities other than a small site museum & bar that serves soft drinks & prepares meals to order. Getting there involves a steep & rough 5km uphill drive or hike from a junction on the Karat-Konso road immediately before the Rocky Campsite. Phone in advance. *US$10 pp.* **$$**

✕ WHERE TO EAT AND DRINK *Map, page 581*

The food at Eco-Omo Safari Lodge is very good but quite pricey, and it's well off the beaten track for anyone without transport. Of the centrally located hotels, Jinka Resort and Orit Hotel both serve a decent selection of well-priced Western and local dishes.

✖ Besha Gojo Restaurant ☎ 046 775 0568;
e besha.gojo@gmail.com; ⊕ 07.00–22.00 daily.
This friendly little restaurant is another top spot,
with dining either inside or at a small outdoor
eating area with covered bench tables. Western &
local dishes in the US$3–4 range include delicious
special *shiro* & a variety of soups & salads. The juice
is fresh & the beer ice cold. *US$2–3.*

✖ Redu Café & Restaurant ⊕ 07.00–22.00
daily. Located on the main roundabout with a
large, pleasant terrace, the Redu is the meeting
place in town. It serves fresh juice, cheap cakes &
sandwiches, plus pasta, fish & meat mains in the
US$2.50–3.75 range.

✖ Hanna Maryam ⊕ 07.00–22.00 daily.
Usually quite crowded, this popular eatery, 400m
from the roundabout after the Orit Hotel, serves
delicious & inexpensive Ethiopian foods of which
the *gomen besiga* (meat & cabbage) is a favourite.
Check you enter the correct door, as several
restaurants are located there side by side.

OTHER PRACTICALITIES Several banks with ATMs can be found along the main
road through Jinka. There are also a few internet cafés, though network availability
cannot be taken for granted. The well-stocked **Mercy Mini-Market** is the place to
head for should you be craving chocolate or other imported goods, and it's also a
good place to stock up with provisions for camping in more remote areas.

TOURIST INFORMATION AND GUIDES

ℹ Pioneers Guide Association [map, page
581] ☎ 046 775 1728; m 0916 856681; ⊕ 08.00–
17.00 daily. Situated on the west side of the main
roundabout, this semi-official association of 26
local guides also doubles as a tourist information
centre & car rental agency for visits to Mago
National Park & the nearby Mursi villages. Expect
to pay around US$150/day for a 4x4, inclusive of
driver & fuel, plus US$16–20/day for a guide.

Lalo Tours [map, page 581] m 0913 363077;
e lalotravel@gmail.com; f. Local tours, guiding
services & car rental can also be arranged through
this small company whose office is on the opposite
side of the roundabout.

Round Omo Valley Tour See Pioneers Guide
Association; or m 0985 516300; e firewtour@
gmail.com; f. New agency offering guided
motorbike trips through South Omo (*US$55/day*)
or self-drive motorbike rental (*US$50/day*).

WHAT TO SEE AND DO

South Omo Research Center [map, page 581] (☎ *046 775 0149;* m *0913 737228;*
e *sorc.ethiopia@gmail.com;* ⊕ *08.00–noon & 14.00–17.00 daily; entrance US$5,
photography permitted*) The one formal tourist attraction in Jinka is this German-
funded research centre, built on a hill overlooking the north end of the town centre
in the 1990s. The excellent anthropological museum provides a useful overview
of 16 different cultural groups associated with the South Omo region, and film
programmes and anthropological lectures can be set up for groups with advance
notice. Film offerings include ethnographic movies on the people of South Omo,
ie: *The Leap across the Cattle* by Ivo Strecker or *Two Girls Go Hunting* by Jean Lydall.
Souvenirs can be purchased at the museum gift shop, and the gardens offer an
attractive view over town.

Yenegew Sew Aari Village [map, page 581] (m *0932 715800; entrance US$8 pp
& guide fee US$12 for up to 10 people, US$16 up to 16 persons*) This enclave of semi-
traditional Aari culture lies off the Karat-Konso road about 3km from central Jinka.
Guided tours can be arranged through the Yenegew Sew Guides Association, which
is signposted at the entrance to the village on the right-hand side of the Karat-Konso
road, a few hundred metres past Rocky Campsite, opposite the construction and
industrial college. The tours include demonstrations of traditional Aari activities
such as pottery, ironworking and making *injera*, and photography is permitted.

Mago National Park [map, page 563] (**m** *0916 856427; entrance US$10 pp/day plus US$2 per car, mandatory scout fee US$6/day*) Established in 1979, the remote Mago National Park extends over an area of 2,162km² either side of the Mago River, which flows into the Omo on the southern boundary. Mago shares a 5km boundary with the more westerly and even more remote Omo National Park, and the two form a contiguous ecological unit with a total area of 6,230km², though crossing between the two directly is practically impossible due to the lack of a suitable bridge across the Omo River. The Omo-Mago ecosystem is potentially the closest thing in Ethiopia to the renowned savannah reserves of East Africa, a vast tract of sweaty, low-lying acacia woodland interspersed with small areas of open savannah, the pristine riparian forest that lines the Mago River, and the extensive Neri Swamp, rising sharply to the Rift Escarpment and the 2,528m-high Mount Mago in the north.

In practice, while Mago's extensive mammal checklist runs to 75-plus species, much of the larger wildlife has been depleted by decades of poaching and the likes of lion, buffalo, elephant, reticulated giraffe and Grevy's zebra are seldom seen these days. Defassa waterbuck appears to be the commonest large antelope, but gerenuk, tiang, bushbuck, Lelwel hartebeest, greater kudu, lesser kudu and the ubiquitous Guenther's dik-dik are also present. Primates are easily seen and include olive baboon, the savannah-dwelling patas and grivet monkeys, and the forest-associated guereza and DeBrazza's monkey – the latter an isolated population of a species typically associated with the West African rainforest. More than 300 bird species

THE MURSI

The most celebrated residents of South Omo are undoubtedly the Mursi, a distinctive group of pastoralists who number about 8,000, and whose roughly triangular territory is bounded by the Omo River to the south and west, and the Mago River to the east. The subject of several television documentaries and books, the Mursi are best known for one item of decoration, the *dhebi a tugoin* lip plates sported by the women. These plates are most often made of clay, and three main colour types (red-brown, black and white) are manufactured using different dyes during the firing process. Traditionally, the scarcer wooden lip plates, made only by men, are regarded to be more beautiful, particularly in the southern part of Mursi territory.

The wearing of lip plates is part of a voluntary initiatory process into womanhood. When a Mursi girl reaches her early or mid-teens, a slit is cut beneath her lower lip, creating a small hole between the lip and the tissue below. Over the next year, this gap is progressively stretched, forming a 'lip loop' large enough for a small circular clay or wooden plate, indented like a pulley, to be inserted between the lip and the mouth. As the lip stretches, so the plate is replaced with a larger one, a process that is repeated until eventually the gap is large enough to hold a plate with a diameter of up to 12cm (5 inches), and the woman can pull her distended lip loop over her head. Unusually for an initiation process, wearing a lip-plate is the choice of the individual girl, and many married Mursi women have never had their lips cut, a trend that seems to be increasing as a result of greater exposure to outsiders.

Several explanations have been put forward for the use of lip plates. It is often said that the larger the lip-plate a woman can wear, the greater her value when she is married, but this explanation ignores the fact that many marriages are arranged and bride prices decided before her lip is cut. An alternative and have been recorded, with typical dry-country specials boosted by more localised birds such as the Egyptian plover, Pel's fishing owl, black-rumped waxbill and dusky babbler. A more certain attraction than any wildlife – and the *raison d'être* for most tourist visits to the park – is the opportunity to visit and photograph the Mursi people encamped along the Mago River (see box, below). That said, while Mago is emphatically not suited to any first-time safari-goer hoping for a few quick snaps of lions and elephants, for those seeking a genuine bush experience – inclusive of rutted roads, primitive facilities, tsetse flies and mosquitoes – a few days camping along the Mago River might be just the ticket.

The main access point to Mago National Park is the headquarters, which lies in the north of the park about 40km southwest of Jinka. This is a rough and often steep dirt road that takes up to 2 hours to cover in the dry season, and might take twice as long, or become totally impassable, after heavy rain, which causes the black cotton soil to become very slippery. There is no public transport to the park, which means that the only option for independent travellers is to hire a 4x4 in Jinka, which will work out more cheaply if you can hook up with like-minded travellers to form a group. Be warned that vehicles hired in Jinka are generally in poorer repair than anything you'll be offered in Addis Ababa. For the time being, motorcycles are not allowed in the park. A few kilometres out of Jinka, the road passes what is effectively the park entrance gate. Here you must stop to pay the entrance fees listed on page 584, and pick up a mandatory armed scout. The park headquarters used to

probably false explanation, that the lip-plate makes a married Mursi woman unattractive to potential adulterers and slave raiders, does take on a grim ring of truth when you visit a village and realise that a lip-plate is far too heavy to be worn all the time, so that Mursi women spend most of their time wandering about with the distended lip hanging down limply as if in a monumental sulk. In reality, the original reason for adornment of lip plates is probably lost in the mists of time, and it is now simply a custom identified with many positive female attributes, ranging from strength and fertility, to loyalty to a husband, to an innate ability to rear good milk-bearing cattle.

The path to adulthood is no smoother for Mursi men. Traditionally, no Mursi man can marry unless he has won a ritual *thagine* fight, a brief but violent confrontation in which two contestants, painted in white chalk paste and wearing various protective and decorative adornments, pummel each other with heavy 2m-long donga poles. The pole is gripped firmly with both hands, the aim being to knock one's opponent to the ground with a hard blow to the body or head. The fights are refereed, and usually end when one opponent falls to the ground or retires hurt with broken or bruised fingers. In a clear victory, the winner will be carried away on the shoulders of other members of his age-set, then surrounded by unmarried girls of his mother's clan, who shade him protectively with a swathe of cotton cloth stretched between *donga* poles. A *thagine* is usually scheduled for a period when food is abundant, so that the participants are at their strongest and most likely to recover quickly from wounds.

Those seeking a more detailed introduction to Mursi history and culture, one beyond the scope of a countrywide guidebook, are advised to spend a couple of hours browsing the University of Oxford's comprehensive and thought-provoking website Mursi Online (w *mursi.org*).

be accessible from Murulle in the south, but the rough and frequently indiscernible 115km track that used to take 6 hours is now reputedly impassable.

If you want to overnight in the park, several very basic but equally beautiful campsites are tucked away in the fig forest lining the Mago River a few kilometres from the park headquarters (*US$3/tent*). Most people visit as a day trip out of Jinka, however, with the main point of the exercise being to visit one of three Mursi villages – Yilma, Marage and Hailoha – situated within the park about 80km from Jinka. Each of these villages charges an entrance fee of US$2.50 per car plus US$10 per person. A further fee of around US$0.20 per shutter click must be paid to any individual Mursi you want to photograph. Lip plates can be bought from the girls and women, should you fancy a souvenir.

HAMAR COUNTRY: DIMEKA, TURMI AND ARBORE

The Hamar women, with their characteristic high cheekbones, elaborate costumes of beads, cowries and leather, and thick copper necklaces, are among the most readily identifiable of the South Omo peoples (see box, page 587). The main towns of the Hamar are Dimeka and Turmi, both of which host colourful weekly markets (on Saturday and Monday respectively) and will reward anybody who settles into them for a few days. Turmi also boasts a good selection of accommodation at both extremes of the price and comfort range, making it a popular base for visits not only to traditional Hamar settlements, but also to the various ethnolinguistic groups that live alongside the Omo River. East of Turmi, the smaller town of Arbore, home to the people of the same name, verges on to Hamar Country and lies along a rough and tricky thoroughfare that entails crossing the unreliable sand bed of the Kaske River just east of Turmi. This little-used but very scenic back road connecting Turmi to Weito, offers the opportunity for a truly off-the-beaten-track diversion to the salty Lake Chew Bahir on the border with Kenya.

DIMEKA The principal town of Hamar Country, Dimeka straddles the main road from Jinka about 28km north of Turmi. More substantial and built-up than Turmi, it is correspondingly less traditional in overall mood, and only really worth a sightseeing stop or side trip on a Saturday or Tuesday, the main and subsidiary market days, when it is descended upon by traditionally attired Hamar villagers who walk there from miles around. The market also attracts a number of Bena agriculturists, who not only dress similarly to the Hamar but also share strong cultural affinities with them, and freely intermarry. The Dimeka Guides Association can arrange day hikes to traditional villages in the vicinity. Although the main road between Key Afer and Turmi passes through Dimeka, public transport from Jinka or elsewhere is limited to the above-mentioned market days. This situation may improve if plans to asphalt the road finally come to fruition. A few basic hotels are littered around Dimeka but they are all very grotty, with the Buska Bar and Tourist Hotel being marginally the pick if you are desperate. The best place to eat is the Abyssinia Hotel.

TURMI Tiny Turmi, with a population of little more than 1,000, is the main focal point of tourism not only in Hamar Country but also arguably in the whole of South Omo. It is also an important local route focus, situated at the junction of the main road running southwest from Key Afer to Omorate, as well as the less-used route running southeast from Weito via Arbore and a rougher road to Murulle on the banks of the Omo. Though not as traditional in feel as it was ten or 15 years ago, Turmi is still a good place for contact with rural Hamar, particularly on the main

The Hamar, who number about 70,000 and occupy a 5,000km² territory between the Omo River and Lake Chew Bahir, stand out as perhaps the archetypal people of South Omo. Not only do they speak one of the Omotic tongues unique to this small area of southern Ethiopia, but they also observe an elaborate and eclectic selection of body decorations that embraces the full gamut of Omo specialities, with the notable exception of lip plates.

Hamar women are particularly striking, adorned with thick plaits of ochre-coloured hair hanging down in a heavy fringe, cowhide skirts decorated with cowries, a dozen or more copper bracelets fixed tightly around their arms, and thick welts on their body created by cutting themselves and treating the wound with ash and charcoal. A distinctive item of female Hamar attire is the *kasha*, a thick goatskin, adorned with spectacular rows of cowries, that hangs apron-like from the neck to protect the woman's breasts against a malefic bad eye that would cause them to swell and allow blood to contaminate the milk. Married women also wear one or more thick copper necklaces, often with a circular wedge perhaps 10cm long projecting out of the front. The men, though also given to body scarring, are more plainly adorned except when they paint themselves with white chalk paste before a dance or ceremony. The clay hair buns fashioned on some men's heads indicate that they have killed a person or a dangerous animal within the last year.

In common with most other people of South Omo, the Hamar are semi-nomadic pastoralists by tradition, and the men take great pride in the size of their cattle herd. That said, in the 21st century, subsistence agriculture – of maize and sorghum in particular – plays a far greater role in feeding the average Hamar family than it might have done a century ago. The Hamar are closely allied to the Bena, whose territory lies to the north of theirs, and the two tribes speak a similar language and freely intermarry. By contrast, the Hamar tend to have antagonistic relationships with the Dasenech and Nyangatom, who occupy territory to the west.

The well-documented cultural links between ancient Egypt and highland Ethiopia may also extend to the Hamar and other people of South Omo. Professor Ivo Strecker, who has studied Hamar culture for three decades, and lived among them for long periods, notes that the environment and agro-pastoralist lifestyle of the Hamar are close to those of the early period of Egyptian civilisation. Furthermore, he has documented striking similarities between current-day utensils and decorations of the Hamar and identical items depicted on early Egyptian paintings, notably the *woko*, a type of hooked, forked herding stick, and the headrests used by Hamar men.

Although most visitors to South Omo visit a Hamar market at Turmi and Dimeka, it is also very rewarding to visit a smaller out-of-town Hamar community, which can be arranged through the tour guide association in either town. With their incredibly neat compounds constructed entirely from mud, wood and thatch, these small communities – which typically consist of a few extended families across perhaps 10–15 huts – are striking for their almost total lack of non-organic or Western artefacts. It might seem banal when put into words, but it is nevertheless rather sobering to encounter such simplicity and evident lack of material want, and to contrast it against our own restless need for distraction and accumulation of useless paraphernalia.

Konso and South Omo   HAMAR COUNTRY: DIMEKA, TURMI AND ARBORE

16

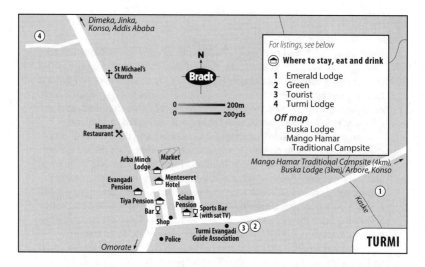

For listings, see below

Where to stay, eat and drink
1 Emerald Lodge
2 Green
3 Tourist
4 Turmi Lodge
Off map
  Buska Lodge
  Mango Hamar
    Traditional Campsite

Mango Hamar Traditional Campsite (4km),
Buska Lodge (3km), Arbore, Konso

TURMI

market day of Monday and the subsidiary market day of Thursday. Turmi is the established base from which to arrange a visit to a traditional Hamar compound or bull-jumping ceremony, and it is well placed for day trips to Omorate or the Omo River around Murulle.

Getting there and away Reaching Turmi is reasonably straightforward in a private vehicle. Indeed, if you are driving through South Omo you can scarcely avoid the place, since almost all roads lead to it. Public transport is non-existent except on market days (Monday and to a lesser extent Thursday), when you can more or less rely on a few vehicles coming through from Key Afer and Jinka.

Where to stay, eat and drink *Map, above*
A trio of not-quite-upmarket tourist lodges is scattered around Turmi. Lack of competition and the remote location means that these places, though perfectly acceptable taken on their own terms, all tend to feel quite basic, and thus rather poor value, by comparison with similarly priced accommodation elsewhere in Ethiopia. Unfortunately, there is not much in Turmi to bridge the quality gap between these tourist lodges and the half-dozen decidedly no-frills shoestring lodges that line the main road through the village, the one exception being the Mango Hamar Traditional Campsite, which at least has a beautiful out-of-town location on a forest-lined watercourse.

Upmarket

Buska Lodge (20 rooms) 011 156 7837/8; m 0911 618623; e info@buskalodge. com; w buskalodge.com; see ad, 5th colour section. The best lodge in South Omo sprawls along the lushly vegetated bank of the (normally dry) Kaske River 3km east of Turmi. The well-maintained green compound is spaciously laid out & features 120 plant species, as well as plenty of birds & monkeys. The spacious & well-ventilated stone-&-thatch bungalows all come with 1 large or

2 ¾ beds, en-suite hot shower & private balcony, & an additional 10 walk-in standing tents are also available. The friendly staff are well on top of things, & facilities include 2 *tukul*-style restaurants & a mini spa. *US$98/129/189 HB sgl/dbl/twin, US$23/33 sgl/dbl tent.* **$$$$$**

Emerald Lodge (36 rooms) 046 881 1895/2200; e info@emeraldresortandlodge. com; w emeraldresortandlodge.com. Set in large well-wooded grounds, this quiet & pleasant lodge, formerly known as Evangadi, lies about 1km from

588

Turmi in the same direction as Buska Lodge. The comfortable chalets all have tiled floors, 2 dbl beds with walk-in nets & en-suite hot shower. An open-sided thatched restaurant charges US$9 for a 3-course set menu. *US$65/84 B&B sgl/dbl negotiable.* **$$$$$**

🏠 **Turmi Lodge** (34 rooms) \011 663 1481; m 0911 697096; e splendoreth@yahoo.com. Situated a few hundred metres north of Turmi opposite St Michael's Church, this rather bland & functional camp comprises 4 long pink concrete blocks, each containing 6 spacious en-suite rooms with tiled floor, bamboo furniture, nets & modern bathroom with hot shower. The rooms are a long hike from the restaurant & bar, which serves buffets for around US$12 pp, as well as à la carte pizza, pasta & other Western dishes for around US$4. *US$65/75 B&B sgl/dbl.* **$$$$$**

Budget, shoestring & camping

🅰 **Mango Hamar Traditional Campsite** (3 rooms) This attractively situated community-run campsite lies 4km out of town in the lush & shady riparian fig woodland that flanks the bank of the normally dry Kaske River. The site is regularly visited by guereza monkeys & baboons, while plentiful forest birds include Bruce's green pigeon, black-headed oriole & grey-headed bush-shrike,

& the surrounding acacia scrub is a good place to seek out dry-country birds such as the gorgeous golden-bellied starling. Alongside the campsite is a water pump that produces potable water & attracts a steady stream of local Hamar villagers. Facilities include 2 toilets, 2 showers, a cooking hut, generator & fridge. Most people camp, but there are also 3 simple huts, each with dbl bed & netting but no bedding. *US$12 sgl/dbl room or US$6 camping per tent.* **$$**

🏠 **Tourist Hotel** (17 rooms) m 0912 417288. Situated about 500m east of Turmi's main road junction, this friendly spot with a helpful English-speaking manageress is one of the best cheapies in a town that's far stronger on quantity than quality when it comes to budget rooms. Older rooms are very basic but the new en-suite rooms have better amenities. An acceptable local restaurant serves great *shiro tegabino* & other local dishes in the US$2–4 range. *US$5/7.50 sgl/twin using common shower, US$18/22 en-suite sgl/dbl.* **$$**

🏠 **Green Hotel** (25 rooms) m 0926 350892. Located alongside the Tourist Hotel, this adequate cheapie has basic older rooms, as well as larger & nicer new rooms, all with proper screens on the windows. *US$6/8 dbl in old wing using common/en-suite shower, US$20 en-suite dbl in new wing.* **$$**

Tourist information and guides The Turmi Evangadi Guide Association (m *0910 818171, 0916 734915;* ⊕ *07.00–noon & 14.00–18.00 daily*), whose central office stands next to the Tourist Hotel, is the best place for independent travellers to arrange to visit any bull-jumping ceremony (see box, page 590) that might be taking place over the duration of their stay. To attend a ceremony, expect to pay US$10–15 per party for the guide, plus a non-fixed fee anywhere upwards of US$30. To access a more pristine Hamar village further afield, contact an English-speaking member of the Guides Association of Hamar Origin and Culture (m *0935 928887*).

THE ARBORE ROAD Flanking the eastern verges of Hamar Country, a 120km road runs northeast from Turmi to Weito. After crossing the bed of the generally dry but tricky Kaske River, it passes through an area of flat arid acacia scrub dominated by the austere Hamar Mountains, which rise to a height of 1,707m on the western horizon and were the site of a short-lived district capital called Hamar Koke in the mid 1950s. Today, the only urban punctuation en route is the relatively large but very rustic town of Arbore, which lies a few hundred metres east of the road some 70km northeast of Turmi, and incorporates only a handful of buildings that aren't constructed along traditional lines. The town is named for the Arbore people, who – in common with their linguistically and culturally affiliated Tsemai neighbours – migrated from Konso to their present homeland perhaps two centuries ago, and subsequently played an important role as trade middlemen between the Omo River and the Konso Highlands. The town of Arbore lies in an area where several tribal

HAMAR BULL JUMPING

The most important event in Hamar society is the bull-jumping ceremony, the culmination of a three-day-long initiation rite that might now be held at any time of year, but traditionally takes place after the biannual harvest, over late February to early April, or else July to September. The ceremony, also known as Ukule Bulla, is an essential rite of passage for any young man who wishes to marry the wife chosen for him by his parents, and to start building up his own family and cattle herd. It can be undertaken at any age from eight onwards, as decided by the young man and his immediate family, but late teens and early 20s is most normal.

There are several stages in the initiation process. Once a young man has announced to the community his intention to jump and the date, he is classified as an *ukule*, or donkey, and like a beast of burden he is expected to undertake any task demanded of him by his seniors. Having jumped successfully, he is classified as a *charkale*, who for the next eight days must hang out with other recent jumpers, face decorated with charcoal and butter, and is tasked with keeping the bulls calm at other jumping ceremonies. On the ninth day, he can wash off the charcoal and butter to join the ranks of the *maza* 'whippers', who are allowed to eat nothing but raw meat, milk and honey, and whose task it is to move from one ceremony to the next, whipping any of the jumper's female relatives who demand it. He will remain a *maza* until his family set a wedding date, usually after about two months, but often longer.

The day of the bull-jump begins with the initiate's female relatives getting drunk on sorghum until the *maza* arrive to whip them with thin, flexible rods. Although these beatings are ritualistic, and undertaken only at the request of the victim, there is great peer pressure on close female relatives of the initiate to demonstrate their loyalty and devotion by taunting the *maza* to hit them harder, resulting in huge bleeding gashes that eventually heal to leave horrific honorific scars. At the time of writing, the government is putting pressure on the Hamar to discontinue this brutal facet of the bull-jump, and the violence might be toned down when tourists are present, but one need only look at the backs of women recently returned from other ceremonies to recognise it still goes on when no outsiders are watching.

boundaries converge, and because the Arbore people routinely intermarry with other ethnic groups, it is also inhabited by a substantial number of Hamar and even Borena women – adding a cosmopolitan feel to the worthwhile Saturday market. There is no accommodation in Arbore, but the new **community campsite** charges US$5 per tent, plus an additional US$3 for a guard.

LAKE CHEW BAHIR The territory of the Arbore people runs as far south as little-visited Lake Chew Bahir, a vast but very shallow expanse of saline water and salt flats set at an altitude of 520m along the Kenyan border. Chew Bahir is a curious lake, noted for substantial fluctuations in water level and expanse. In the 1960s, for instance, it comprised 2,000km^2 of open water, parts of which were up to 8m deep, but for much of the rest of the last century the open water has amounted to a small rank swamp set in an otherwise dry salt pan. Since Chew Bahir has no outlet, and it lies in an area where evaporation outstrips rainfall fourfold, the key to its fluctuating water level is thought to be the level of Lake Chamo, which provides its main inflow via the Segen and Gelana Delai rivers.

It comes as no surprise to learn that this inhospitable sump, with water too saline to be drunk by man or beast, was perhaps the last African lake of comparable size

In the late afternoon, the initiate and *charkale* entourage gather together, and the latter paint their faces and bodies, while partially shaving the former's wild Afro hairstyle. The initiate is then rubbed with sand to cleanse his sins, smeared with cow dung to bolster his strength, and strapped with bark strips to ward off evil spirits. Finally, as the sun starts to sink, the castrated bulls (up to 30, though these days eight to ten is more common) are herded side by side into a row by the *charkale*, and the initiate, stark naked and sporting the remnants of a demented Afro, is expected to leap from the ground on to the spine of the first bull, then run over the rest of the bulls' backs, until he reaches the end of the row. He must then turn around and repeat the performance in the opposite direction, then again a third and fourth time before he has proved his worth to everybody's satisfaction. If he fails, he will have to wait a year and try again.

Much has been made about the authenticity and perceived devaluing of the bull-jumping ceremony in recent years, with many travellers complaining that it has now been reduced to a staged 'circus put on for the *faranji*'. There is some truth in this, especially if you visit the area out of initiation season, when staged ceremonies, in which local participants are often outnumbered by spectating tourists, frequently take place on the banks of the Little Kaske where it crosses the Arbore road about 3km out of Turmi. Equally, should you visit Hamar Country during the initiation season, when authentic ceremonies are held on an almost daily basis, you can be pretty confident of being taken to a more remote rural location to see the real thing. Either way, the bull-jumping tradition is undoubtedly very much alive, and the athleticism of the jumpers is quite awe-inspiring. As one reader recently wrote in response to the complaints:

> The Hamar people are cashing in on the tourists. It is normal. They have the right to do so. South Omo tourism is a big business these days; while it may seem 'circus-like', we cannot stop them from taking advantage of the tourist interest.

to remain unknown to Europeans. Indeed, the existence of Chew Bahir was little more than a rumour until April 1888, when Count Samuel Teleki arrived there fresh from having been the first European to set eyes on Lake Turkana. Teleki christened the lake in honour of Princess Stefanie, the consort of his Hungarian sponsor Prince Rudolf, but the older local name of Chew Bahir (literally 'Ocean of Salt') is preferred today.

Nominally protected within the vast Chew Bahir Wildlife Reserve, the lake and its hinterland of dry acacia woodland still support low volumes of ungulates such as Grevy's zebra, greater and lesser kudu, gerenuk and Grant's gazelle, as well as lion, spotted hyena and various small carnivores. More reliable is the birdlife in the permanent swamp that lies at the mouth of the Gelana Delai River, the closest part of the lake basin to Arbore. Lesser flamingos are usually present in concentrations ranging from a couple of thousand to hundreds of thousands, along with a variety of storks, waterfowl and waders. The surrounding acacia woodland is an important site for dry-country birds characteristic of the badlands that separate the highlands of central Kenya from those of southern Ethiopia: vulturine guinea fowl, Shelley's and golden-bellied starling, pink-breasted lark, scaly chatterer and grey-headed silver-bill are just a few of the more interesting species present.

16

Lake Chew Bahir can be reached in 3–4 hours from Arbore, bushwhacking along a very rough track that heads southeast from the Turmi road immediately south of town. The track is difficult to follow unless you know the way, and the lake's location on the sporadically sensitive Kenyan border makes it inadvisable to visit without an armed escort. This can sometimes be arranged at the police station in Arbore, though we recently heard from a birding group who were forbidden from travelling there altogether. You should also ensure that somebody in authority knows to send out a search party in the event of a breakdown or any other mishap – weeks may pass without a vehicle heading down this way! A full day must be allocated to the excursion – better still, take camping gear and spend the night at the lake – and it would be advisable to carry sufficient water and food to last a couple of days longer than you intend to spend there.

OMORATE AND THE OMO RIVER

Bizarrely, it is quite possible, and commonplace, to explore South Omo without ever actually seeing the large, powerful river for which the region is named. Indeed, the only two places where the Omo is reasonably accessible, at least to those with private vehicles, is the unkempt small end-of-the-road town of Omorate, accessed via a good 72km surfaced road running southwest from Turmi, and the more remote and rewarding cluster of villages around Kangatan, about 65km northwest of Turmi along a much rougher track. Two new bridges now span the Omo. The more northerly of these, at Kangatan, opened in February 2015, and a second bridge, at Omorate, has been operational since mid 2016. The extent to which these bridges will change tourist patterns in the region remains to be seen, considering the need to get written permission from the immigration authorities to use either of them.

OMORATE Still captioned on some maps by its occupation-era name of Kaleb, Omorate lies on the sweltering eastern bank of the Omo River about 50km north of where it empties into Lake Turkana. The archetypal tropical backwater, it is an unexpectedly large town, and not very traditional in mood except for the Dasenech women who go about bare-breasted. Omorate is imbued with a seedy, end-of-the-road atmosphere aggravated by temperatures that regularly soar above 40°C, and a suspension of fine clay dust and paucity of shade that make life pretty uncomfortable. Around the town lie the abandoned relics of an agricultural scheme that was initiated with North Korean funds under the Derg and faltered to a standstill soon afterwards. Improbably, Omorate, though it lies some distance from Kenya, also functions as a minor border town, with pick-up trucks from goodness-knows-where in Kenya regularly appearing on the opposite bank to unload mysterious parcels on to the local boats. In its favour, Omorate is a friendly enough place, and the Omo River, muddy though it may be, is really splendid and provides nigh irresistible, if not necessarily bilharzia-free, relief from the merciless heat. A few pleasant terraces overlooking the river can be found alongside the main road, but can be accessed only by walking through some nondescript coffee houses, the most famous of which is Enat Guada, 50m south of the Tourist Hotel. The river aside, the only reason tourists visit Omorate is to boat over to the Dasenech villages that stand on the opposite bank, an endeavour some visitors have described as frustrating and not worthwhile.

Getting there and away The 72km road from Turmi to Omorate – once nightmarish, but now entirely asphalted – passes through flat and relatively open savannah country inhabited by pairs of Guenther's dik-dik, the occasional gerenuk, and dazzlingly colourful and acrobatic flocks of white-throated and northern carmine bee-eaters. The only public transport to Omorate is a twice-weekly bus service from Jinka on Tuesday and Saturday. It is also to be assumed that the opening of the bridge will allow 4x4 access to Omorate from the Katesh side.

Paperwork Because Omorate lies so close to the border with Kenya, all visitors are required to stop at the immigration and customs office to show their passport or some other form of ID before crossing the river by boat to the Dasenech villages.

Where to stay, eat and drink

Dagmawi Hotel (6 rooms) m 0911 365903. This is about the newest & best of a half-dozen basic lodges in Omorate, & certainly the friendliest. Rooms are very basic & use a common cold shower. If it's full, several other lodges lie within 100m of it. *US$5 dbl.* **$$**

National Hotel (20 rooms) This long-serving hotel opposite the Dagmawi has basic rooms with common toilet & shower (*US$8*) &

serves reasonable Ethiopian food in the US$2–3 range. There's also a bar. **$$**

Masrecha Campsite m 0948 217766. Far nicer than any of the lodges is this shady riverside campsite, which has a few tents for hire if you don't have your own. The helpful owner can prepare basic fish & other meals, & there's a kiosk selling chilled beer on the premises. *US$5/tent.*

What to see and do

Dasenech villages Also known as the Galeb or Reshiat, the Dasenech range across a large territory west of the Omo River running south from Omorate to Lake Turkana. Local oral tradition, reinforced by that of the Turkana, recounts that the Dasenech migrated to their current homeland from a region called Nyupe, to the west of Turkana, after being forced out by the expansionist wars of the Turkana in the late 18th century. Like the Turkana, Samburu and Gabra of northern Kenya, the Dasenech were originally pure pastoralists, living an almost totally nomadic lifestyle. The abundant water frontage and fertile soil of their present territory has subsequently pushed them towards a more diverse subsistence economy, based around fishing and agriculture, as well as herding livestock. These nomadic roots

MURULLE AND THE MURLE

The origin of the name Murulle, pronounced with a rolling 'r', is enigmatic. Although Murulle has always been a place where wild and domesticated animals come to drink, thanks to the gentle decline of the riverbank, it has not supported a settlement, other than the modern lodge, in living memory. Yet the site is shown on several maps, often transliterated as Murle, dating right back to the one produced by Count Samuel Teleki based on his 1888 Turkana expedition. Stranger still, a Murle tribe does live in this part of Ethiopia, as mentioned in several accounts of European explorers, but to the west of the Omo River, near the Sudanese border. So the reason why the local Karo now refer to this part of the riverbank as Murulle, or Murle, is anybody's guess. It could be that some Murle people settled in the area at some point, or that it was the site of a fight between the Karo and Murle, or something similarly significant. Equally, given the inaccuracies that exist on most maps of South Omo, the name might simply stem from generations of cartographers having copied an error on the part of Teleki regarding the placement of the Murle territory!

are clearly seen today in the impermanent structures typical of Dasenech villages: small, flimsy domed huts strongly reminiscent of those built by other African desert pastoralists, from the Tuareg of the Sahara to the Nama of the Kalahari. One such village lies on the west bank of the Omo, practically opposite Omorate, and can be reached in a few minutes by utilising the flat-bottomed boat that serves as a ferry across the river. Taking a local guide from the Omorate Guide Association (m *0923 477058*), which doesn't so much have an office at the ferry jetty as lurks around it, is mandatory (*US$5 pp return for the boat, US$7.50 pp village entrance fee, US$15 per party for the guide, plus the usual additional US$0.20 per shutter click*).

The Guide Association can also organise a boat excursion to Lake Turkana at an extravagant cost of US$500–600 depending on the number of participants.

North Turkana About 15km from Omorate along the Turmi road, a very rough and little-used seasonal track runs south towards the small (around 50km²) northwest corner of Lake Turkana that lies in Ethiopian territory, as well as the Omo Delta, which empties into the lake on a northwestern peninsula after crossing into Kenya. This route should emphatically not be attempted except with a driver or local escort who already knows the way.

MURULLE, KANGATAN, AND KOLCHO Strung along a meandering but broadly west-flowing stretch of the Omo River about 50km upstream of Omorate and a similar distance northwest of Turmi, these three dot-on-a-map settlements are all of interest to tourists for different reasons. Murulle, though not a settlement in the conventional sense, is the site of an eponymous lodge that for many years ranked as South Omo's only upmarketish accommodation option, and still remains a more remote alternative to the cluster of lodges around Turmi. Kangatan, located on the opposite bank of the river 12km west of Murulle, is a little-visited traditional Nyangatom village set to assume greater logistical importance following the opening of a new bridge over the Omo there in February 2015, though this would depend upon greatly improving the state of the access roads to the area (page 592). Kolcho, about 6km north of Murulle by road, is renowned as the best place to see Karo body-painters at work.

Getting there and away The most direct route to Murulle, Kangatan or Kolcho entails turning on to a rough track that branches west from the Dimeka road about 6km north of Turmi, and following it northwest for around 2 hours. Murulle lies about 50km along this track and the 5km track to Kolcho branches to the right about 1km before the lodge. Heading to Kangatan, you need to branch left from the Murulle road after perhaps 40km, then continue west for another 20km. Another option coming from Omorate is the 55km very rough track that branches north from the Turmi road about 9km out of town, close to the airstrip. The latter passes through an area of dry red-earth savannah that supports fair amounts of wildlife. Guenther's dik-dik is common, and there is a good chance of seeing gerenuk, Grant's gazelle, tiang and bat-eared fox (the latter easily distinguished by its oversize ears and black 'bank robber' eye-mask). As for birds, colourful swooping bee-eaters do their best to steal the show, but look out too for raptors – we saw at least a dozen species including the handsome black-breasted snake eagle – and colourful red-and-yellow barbets performing their risible clockwork duets from the top of the prolific termite hills.

The track running north from Murulle to Mago National Park is no longer viable. It remains an open question what road links will be established west of the river following the opening of the new bridge.

Where to stay, eat and drink *Map, page 563*

🏠 **Murulle Omo Explorer's Lodge** (8 bungalows) 📞011 155 2128; e ervs@ethionet. et; w ethiopianriftvalleysafaris.com. Set in a shady riverine grove fringing the Omo River, this remote lodge offers decent accommodation in rather rundown en-suite bungalows with shady verandas. Originally built as a hunting camp to service the Murulle Hunting Concession, it now caters primarily to the ecotourism market, & plains wildlife, though hardly prolific, is far more visible than elsewhere in South Omo. In addition, guereza monkeys swing by the lodge on a daily basis, & birds are everywhere, notably the colourful & vociferous black-headed bush-shrike. Activities include game drives & guided nature walks, seasonal boat trips on the Omo River & traditional village visits. Accommodation *must* be pre-booked in Addis Ababa. *US$135/225 FB sgl/dbl.* **$$$$$**

🏕 **Murulle Campsite** The leafy campsite alongside the lodge & under the same management is by far the nicest place to camp in South Omo. Unlike the lodge, no advance booking is necessary, but it is important that campers are self-sufficient in terms of camping equipment (tents, mattresses, etc), as well as food & drinks, since the logistical difficulty of running a lodge in this remote corner of Ethiopia means it cannot serve meals or drinks to passing campers. *US$14 pp/night.* **$$**

What to see and do

Kangatan Kangatan is the most accessible habitation of the Nyangatom, a tribe of some 20,000 pastoralists who live to the west of the Omo River. They normally inhabit the land south of Omo National Park, but will move into the park's southern plains when water or grazing is scarce. The Nyangatom speak an Eastern Nilotic language, and their close affiliation with northern Kenya's Turkana people is evident in the tentacle-like tangle of leather necklaces and side-cropped hairstyles worn by the women. Like the Turkana, the Nyangatom are semi-nomadic hunters and cattle herders by custom, measuring their wealth by the size of their herd, though flood agriculture now plays an increasingly important role in their subsistence. They also share with the Turkana a reputation for aggression and ferocity in battle: even today, they are often involved in fatal altercations related to cattle raiding and intertribal rivalry with their Surma, Karo and Hamar neighbours.

Kangatan lies on the west bank of the Omo, perhaps 12km west of Murulle as the crow flies. The drive from Murulle takes 30–45 minutes, following the Omorate road south for about 10km, then turning right on to a track leading to a police compound on the eastern bank of the river facing Kangatan. You can now cross to Kangatan using the heavily guarded new bridge, though be warned that it may shut while the police who guard it are on their lunch break. A village visit costs around US$10 per party and you may still be expected to pay something to the redundant boatman who used to ferry tourists across the river.

Kolcho Murulle Lodge lies within the territory of the Karo, a tribe of around 1,500 Omotic speakers affiliated to the neighbouring Hamar. Pastoralists by tradition, the Karo lost their cattle herds to disease some years back, and they now subsist primarily by growing sorghum, maize and other crops along the river. In common with the Hamar, scarification plays an important role in Karo body decoration, and the men plaster their hair into tight buns after killing a human enemy or a dangerous animal. The hairstyle favoured by Karo women is rather striking: tightly cropped at the side, and tied into bulbous knots and dyed ochre on top, it makes them look as if they have rushed out of the bathroom without removing their shower cap. The Karo are best known, however, for the elaborate body painting they indulge in before important ceremonies. They dab their torsos with white chalk paint, reputedly in imitation of the plumage of a guinea fowl. Colourful face masks are painstakingly

16

prepared with a combination of pastes made by mixing water with chalk, charcoal, powdered yellow rock and iron ore. The best-known Karo settlement is Kolcho, a compact village of at most 50 simple huts set on a magnificent sand cliff overlooking a large sweep in the Omo River 6km from Murulle. You'd have to be unusually lucky to arrive when a genuine celebration is about to take place, but colourful dances can be arranged for around US$35 per party.

17

Southwest Ethiopia

Even the tamest western half of a country has a good chance of being dubbed its 'Wild West' by overenthusiastic marketers. But in the case of western Ethiopia, the epithet is thoroughly deserved. Not due to any surplus of gun-toting outlaws, but because the undulating jungle-swathed highlands west of Jimma and steamy tropical river scenes of Gambella retain a genuinely remote and untrammeled character, one that stands in bountiful contrast to the stark landscapes associated with the dry eastern borderlands. Indeed, this little-visited region, with its rich loamy soils and plentiful year-round rainfall nourishing an uninterrupted swathe of lush cultivation, dank natural forest and feral coffee, could easily deceive the unprepared visitor into thinking they had taken a wrong turn and ended up somewhere on the verdant slopes that characterise the Uganda–Congo border. Despite this natural abundance, the Wild West is difficult to recommend wholeheartedly to first-time visitors to Ethiopia. Beyond Jimma, travel conditions tend to be basic – dusty roads leading through long stretches of thinly inhabited countryside are traversed by unreliable public transportation, while hotels and restaurants, though plentiful, seldom satisfy beyond the most basic needs. Then again, as Ethiopia's northern and southern travel circuits become increasingly geared towards pricey package tourism, the under-publicised west will start to hold more allure for independent-minded travellers with plenty of time on their hands or a penchant for wilful off-the-beaten-track exploration.

THE WESTERN HIGHLANDS

The fertile highland region that stretches westward from the jagged Gibe River Gorge 150km outside Addis Ababa, encompassing the zones of Welega, Ilubabor and Kaffa, offers much to unhurried travellers looking for an alternative to the heavily trodden northern historical circuit. Its towns boast a refreshing social diversity: predominantly Oromo, but magnets for people of different ethnicities and religions from all over the country. On the street you'll hear as much conversation in Amharic as the native Oromifa, as well as splashes of local tribal languages, while religious affiliations amount to a three-way equilibrium of Muslims, Orthodox Christians and Protestants. Pristine highland rainforest covers much of the undulating countryside, while steep ravines cradle fast-flowing mountain streams, fed by the drenching seasonal rains of April to late September. Wild coffee was first cultivated in these forests (see box, page 599), and its domesticated cousin (*Coffea arabica*) is the mainstay of the agricultural rural economy. Indeed, the roads of the western highlands are lined with dust-covered coffee plantations, usually growing below a loose canopy of varied foliage and sprawling old ficus trees (the latter known locally as *odaa* and sacred to the Oromo). The dense forest cover of the western highlands also provides excellent opportunities for spotting monkeys and forest birds from the road.

JIMMA An important centre of coffee production and distribution, the modern market town of Jimma is comfortably the largest settlement in the western highlands, with an estimated population of 220,000. Many confuse the origins of the city's name with the Oromifa word for *khat* (not a bad guess actually, as the stimulant leaf is extremely popular in the area), but it actually derives from that of a much older kingdom whose former capital Jiren lies on the outskirts of the modern city. Jimma is visited by relatively few tourists and lacks any major attractions, but some interesting sightseeing is to be had around town, ranging from the small central museum and lively market area to the out-of-town Lake Boye, with its resident hippos, and the more remote but vastly underrated Chebera-Churchura National Park. Jimma also serves as a surprisingly comfortable springboard for journeys further west, boasting a decent selection of hotels with hot showers, as well as scattered Wi-Fi connections – amenities that are not to be taken for granted if you are setting off to the likes of West Omo, Gambella or Chebera-Churchura.

History Although Jimma served as the capital of an administrative region called Kaffa until 1994, it is – rather confusingly – situated to the northeast of the ancient kingdom of Kaffa, within the discrete kingdom of Jimma, which unlike Kaffa had its roots in the Oromo incursion of the 16th century and was predominantly Muslim rather than Christian. Blessed with richly fertile soils and noted for its fine coffee, Jimma served as an important centre of commerce at the convergence of several trade routes. By the 19th century, Jimma was the most powerful political entity in western Ethiopia, covering an area of 13,000km², and with an economy based on the sale and trade of coffee and other agricultural produce, precious metals, ivory and slaves captured in the far west. The market at Hirmata, the original name of Jimma, was the largest in western Ethiopia, attended by up to 30,000 people every Thursday.

The last autonomous ruler of Jimma was King Abba Jiffar, who ascended to the throne in 1878 and made his capital at Jiren, only 7km from the modern town of Jimma. Abba Jiffar took power at a time when the autonomy of kingdoms such as Jimma and Kaffa was severely threatened by the expansionist policies and military prowess of Shewa under the future Emperor Menelik II. Six years into his reign, Abba Jiffar, rather than resisting the inevitable, decided to throw his lot in with Shewa, and to pay tribute to Menelik.

After that, Jimma effectively became a semi-autonomous vassal state to Shewa, still under the rule of Abba Jiffar but overseen by a governor appointed by Menelik. Alexander Bulatovich, who travelled through western Ethiopia in 1897, described Jimma as one of the three 'richest and most industrial settlements' in the region and 'very densely populated'. Bulatovich also wrote that: 'The best iron items and cloth are fashioned there. Merchants from Jimma conduct trade with the southern regions and with Kaffa. All the residents of Jimma, as well as King Abba Jiffar, are Muhammadan.'

Jimma as we know it today is essentially a 20th-century creation, one that saw a great deal of development during the Italian occupation of the 1930s. Architectural elements from this period are especially visible in the old Italian stomping ground of Faranji Arada, which is still considered the social centre of town. As the capital of Kaffa Province, it had a brief renaissance under the 1980s socialist regime, serving as a popular leisure destination for party cadres and the Addis Ababa elite, who often visited not only for the beauty of the countryside, but also for its infamous prostitutes. In 1994, it was reconstituted as the head of the present-day Jimma Zone. Over subsequent decades, the government rather neglected Jimma in its push for modern development, preferring to direct funds to new federal capital and vacation hot spots such as Bahir Dar and Hawassa. Today the old city is getting

ETHIOPIAN COFFEE

Kaffa is generally regarded to be the region where the Arabica strain of coffee originated, and it is also where this plant was first cultivated. A popular legend, said variously to date to between the 3rd and 10th centuries, claims that a young herdsman named Kaldi first observed the stimulating properties of wild coffee. When his goats became hyperactive after eating the leaves and berries, Kaldi swallowed some of the berries himself, found that he too became abnormally excited, and ran to a nearby monastery to share his discovery. Initially, the monks didn't share the young goatherd's enthusiasm, but instead chastised him for bringing evil stimulants to their monastery and threw the offending berries into a fire. But then, seduced by the aromatic smell of the roasting berries, the monks decided to give them a go and found that they were unusually alert during their nocturnal prayers. Soon, it became accepted practice throughout Christian Ethiopia to chew coffee beans before lengthy prayer sessions, a custom that still persists in some parts of the country today. Later, it was discovered that the roasted berry could be ground to powder to produce a tasty and energising hot drink – one that still goes by a name derived from the Kaffa region in most places where it is drunk.

Thus goes the story, considered as good as fact and a point of pride for most Ethiopians. For those who like playing devil's advocate – and also don't plan on being invited for a cup of coffee again afterwards – it can be argued that there is little scientific or historical evidence backing up this strong local belief. The story of Kaldi the goatherd was not written down until nearly 800 years after it supposedly took place, hurting its credibility. Most historians cite evidence attributing the first consumption of the drink in its modern form to Yemeni monks around the 16th century, although there's no question that the beans were imported across Red Sea trade routes from Ethiopia. Coffee first arrived in Europe via Turkey in the 17th century, and it rapidly took off – more than 200 coffee shops reputedly traded in Venice alone by the early 18th century. Linguists attribute the word coffee's appearance in English in 1582 to a flow of alterations via the Dutch *koffie*, from the Turkish *kahve*, beginning at the Arabic phrase used to describe the stimulant drink, *qahhwat al-bun*, 'wine of the bean'. Despite a lack of consensus, the Ethiopians are no fools to be wary of Western accounts, which historically aren't the most ardent supporters of Afrocentric origins for anything.

A more infallible truth is that Ethiopia produces and consumes coffee in substantial quantities. Today, at nearly US$700 million, coffee exports account for 25–30% of Ethiopia's annual foreign revenue. Of Ethiopia's annual coffee crop of 6.5 million bags, 95% is still grown on subsistence farms and smallholdings, and about 40% remains to be consumed within this coffee-mad country. Furthermore, if it weren't for the shade-loving coffee plant (along with other forest products like honey and wild cardamom), the forests that still swathe the western highlands would most likely have been cut down for timber, charcoal and firewood, in the same way as they have in the heavily eroded plateaus of northern Ethiopia, which is more reliant on cultivating *tef*.

a long overdue facelift, causing a few headaches with roads being torn up and electricity and water shortages, but beginning to show progress and return slowly to former levels of prosperity.

17

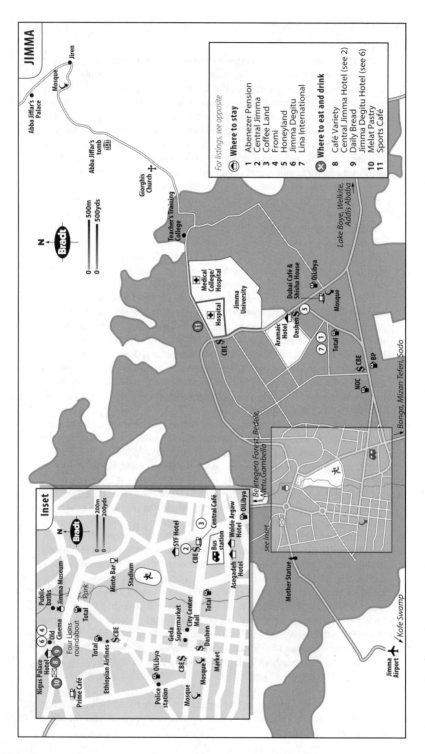

JIMMA

Along with every other town in its vicinity, Jimma has a strong argument for its claim to being the 'birthplace of coffee'. The bottom line is, if coffee in fact originated here, it was most likely spread throughout the fertile green hills of the Jimma, Kaffa, Ilubabor and Welega zones. Regardless of its exact point of origin, coffee is king in Jimma. Plantations cover much of the surrounding countryside, and a couple of plants can be found in most family compounds for home consumption. People drink cheap, tiny cups of it at street-side cafés from dawn to dusk, hotels and restaurants are named after it and the money from its sale and export is fuelling much of the construction boom visible around town.

Getting there and away

By air Ethiopian Airlines (☎ *047 111 7271*; e *jimtsm@ethiopianairlines.com*) flies between Addis Ababa and Jimma at least once a day. The airport lies about 3km from the town centre.

By road A daily coach service to and from Addis Ababa is operated by **Selam Bus** (*US$9; 6hrs; departs 05.00; tickets at the Central Jimma Hotel*) and **Sky Bus** (e *info@ skybusethiopia.com; Sky Bus is supposed to have an office at the Coffee Land Hotel, but better enquire at the bus station about travelling on their buses*). The bus station is opposite the Central Jimma. Be sure to book your tickets a couple of days in advance, and be aware that Selam Bus tickets cannot be reserved by phone – you must be present at the ticket office to buy a ticket, or have someone go for you. Otherwise, slower but cheaper local buses leave Addis Ababa from Merkato bus station at 06.00 daily. Buses to/from Nekemte and Metu leave at around 06.00 in either direction, and in both cases they stop for breakfast in Bedele between 10.00 and midday. A daily bus also runs east to Sodo, taking two days.

🏠 Where to stay   *Map, opposite*

Moderate

✳ 🏠 **Fromi Hotel** (21 rooms) ☎047 211 1111/2; e fromihoteljimma@gmail.com. The recently built Fromi represents a quantum leap for the better so far as comfort, cleanliness & appeal are concerned. From the shower to the fridge or the LCD TV, all appliances in the cute, smallish rooms are in perfect condition, & instead of sometimes heavy, unpleasant blankets, the beds have stylish Nordic-like thin duvets. The restaurant, with a few outdoor tables, is excellent & reasonably priced for all meals & drinks. *US$16/28/32 sgl/twin/suite.* **$$$**

🏠 **Jimma Degitu Hotel** (22 rooms) ☎047 211 0000/1; m 0913 208268. This privatised former government hotel is a fine place to stay, & is also known as an evening hot spot due to its multiple bars & new nightclub. A block of 12 luxury suites including a sofa-lined salon & jacuzzi/sauna are enticing after a long bus ride, while even the normal rooms are above average, with ample space & clean bathrooms. The older wing with cheap (*US$7*) smelly rooms isn't worth considering. Indoor & outdoor

restaurants offer a selection of local & Western dishes & great pizza (*US$2–4*). *US$12/20/32 sgl/ dbl/suite.* **$$**

🏠 **Honeyland Hotel** (59 rooms) m 0917 552061/16; e honeylandh@yahoo.com. This handsome business-class hotel is a little out of the way, but that may be a redeeming feature as the bus station neighbourhood is a light sleeper's worst nightmare. Rooms are clean & spacious with sat TV, reliable & fast Wi-Fi & en-suite hot shower. The 1st-floor rooms are near to the kitchen & restaurant so could get noisy. The large courtyard at the back is a peaceful & agreeably landscaped place to relax. *US$17/26/36 B&B sgl/dbl/suite.* **$$$**

Budget

🏠 **Coffee Land Hotel** (40 rooms) ☎047 111 9464; m 0911 206607. Conveniently located in front of the bus station, this 1-price-for-all hotel has spacious clean rooms with good Wi-Fi & sat TV, & it seems better all-round value than the similarly priced Central Jimma. The cramped restaurant/café has a limited menu, but if you're craving a burger by the pool, you can cross the road to eat, & come back to a significantly better room. *US$12/18 en-suite sgl/dbl.* **$$**

🏠 **Central Jimma Hotel** (154 rooms) 📞 047 211 1112; **m** 0930 106840; **e** info@centraljimmahotel.com; **w** centraljimmahotel.com. This ageing hotel remains popular with foreigners, mainly because of its restaurant & pool, but the rooms lag behind the competition when it comes to cleanliness & amenities. Try to get one of the much nicer rooms in the new building; rooms in the old block are notorious for insect problems. The Wi-Fi hasn't worked reliably in years. *US$10/12 sgl/dbl, US$24/60 dbl/suite new wing.* **$$**

Shoestring

🏠 **Lina International Hotel** (30 rooms) 📞 047 211 5000; **m** 0914 302917. Located at a distance from the city centre, close to the Honeyland Hotel, this family-run guesthouse doesn't quite live up to the 'international' billing, but it has a large choice of quiet rooms around a pleasant garden. The restaurant has a good reputation & the owner will arrange transport from & to town. *US$6/10 sgl cold/hot shower, then prices range US$10–20 depending on size of room & bed.* **$$**

🏠 **Abenezer Pension** (14 rooms) 📞 047 211 6486; **m** 0917 801327. Located a few hundred metres away from the Lina, this similar guesthouse has clean, basic en-suite rooms bordering a gravel yard. *US$10 sgl.* **$**

✗ Where to eat and drink   *Map, page 600*

The terrace restaurant at the **Central Jimma Hotel** is a reliable choice, featuring a full-size swimming pool and shady relaxed seating under a canopy of palms and trellised vines. The extensive menu offers both traditional and foreign dishes but the prices (*US$2.50–5*) are high for the quality. Pastries, juice and cakes are available too. A second restaurant/café on the street side of the hotel has a cheaper menu, presumably because it shares none of the tropical charm of the one out back.

The **Jimma Degitu Hotel** serves good Western and local meals for around US$2–4, and the patio is a relaxing place to try three types of local draught beer. Several juice and pastry shops and local restaurants line the main roads through the town centre. **Café Variety** on the ground level of the Nigus Palace Hotel deserves a special mention. **Melat Pastry** has good *ful*. For delicious, hot, freshly baked bread don't miss **Daily Bread** located next door to Café Variety. If you have transport or don't mind a 10-minute taxi ride, the **Sports Café**, opposite the university en route to Abba Jiffar's Palace, is popular with Jimma's expatriates and serves decent pizza and burgers.

For a break from the average Ethiopian or pseudo-Western fare try one of Jimma's Muslim restaurants, clearly marked by the crescent and star sign, many of which offer a delicious Middle Eastern-style roast lamb over a bed of basmati rice with a zesty red sauce known locally as *ruz haneed*.

Nightlife Across the car park from the Jimma Degitu Hotel, the air-conditioned **Club Teddy** is arguably the best nightclub outside Addis, and definitely the safest, touting a metal detector at the door, beefy bouncers and security cameras covering the action inside from all angles. The industrious owner insists the cameras are closely monitored by guards trained specifically to spot and intervene in violence and harassment that targets the club's female guests. Another perk for ladies wearing high heels is a supply of free-to-borrow flats for dancing.

What to see and do

Around town The only organised tourist attraction within the city centre is the **Jimma Museum** (📞 *047 111 5881;* ⊕ *08.30–noon & 13.30–15.00 daily; entrance US$1*), close to the Four Lions roundabout, where a selection of the personal effects of Abba Jiffar, the last independent king of Jimma, are housed alongside some worthwhile ethnographic displays relating to the Oromo and other local cultures. Also worth a look is the patch of riverine woodland behind the museum, the new home of the much improved **Jimma Library**. Its compound supports a resident troop of guereza monkeys, as well as the outlandish silvery-cheeked hornbill. At the other side of the city centre, the bustling **market** is worth a look, particularly if you are eager to buy some of the excellent local wood furniture and basketwork. Of interest to wealthier curio hunters (and evidence of Jimma's own relative wealth) are the numerous **jewellery shops** that line the main road, selling locally crafted, as well as imported, silver and gold products.

Abba Jiffar's Palace (⏱ *09.00–12.30 Mon–Fri, 14.00–17.30 daily; entrance US$1.25 pp inc guided tour*) Abba Jiffar was the charismatic, powerful – and exceptionally tall – king who ruled over Jimma from 1878 until his death in 1932. He is remembered today for his canny decision in 1884 to pay tribute to Menelik's then-expanding empire of Shewa in exchange for a degree of autonomy not conceded to fiefdoms that were co-opted into Shewa by force. The impressive palace, built by Abba Jiffar during the early years of his rule, still stands on a low hill at the former royal compound of Jiren, 8km from the city centre by road. Constructed at a cost of 400kg of gold and 65,000 Maria Theresa dollars – money gained largely through the ruler's active involvement in the slave trade – the palace is a fine example of an admittedly no more than diverting style of early colonial architecture. The largest of the four buildings in the palace compound, which served as the king's residence, spans two storeys, and its wide veranda and shady overhangs are reminiscent of early missionary buildings in parts of West Africa. The whitewashed interior, restored with partial funding from UNESCO, is somewhat austere at present, but it is expected that it will eventually be furnished with the authentic property of the king, currently on display at the Jimma Museum in town. The centrepiece of the building is a ground-floor auditorium enclosed by first-floor balconies (the inspiration perhaps for the similar public area of the Gojeb Minch Hotel in the city centre?), from where the king and his guests would watch musicians, gladiators and entertainers at play. Alongside the palace, the public mosque built by Abba Jiffar is still in active use today.

To reach the palace in a private vehicle, take the road to Jimma Hospital. Continue to Jiren, then turn left (north) along a dirt road that leads to the palace. Roughly 1.5km before reaching the palace, the tomb of Abba Jiffar lies on the left-hand side of the road. No public transport heads up to the palace: travellers without a vehicle can either catch a minibus or take a taxi to Jiren and walk the last 500m, or hire a bicycle from one of the stalls around the market.

Lake Boye This small marsh-fringed lake, situated no more than 200m south of the Addis Ababa road a few minutes' drive from Jimma, is a reliable and accessible spot to see hippos, and it also supports an interesting selection of water- and woodland birds. To reach Boye, follow the Addis Ababa road out of Jimma for about 8km. As you approach the turn-off, you'll notice a pine and eucalyptus plantation to your left, as well as two white signposts, one of which reads 'Bon Voyage'. Almost immediately after the second signpost, a rough dirt track leads through eucalyptus trees to within 50m of the lake. Lake Boye can easily be visited as a half-day trip from Jimma using public transport, or by hiring a taxi or bicycle.

The resident pod of hippos seems to favour the shallow western part of the lake, the end furthest from the main road – this can be reached by following a rough footpath alongside the eucalyptus trees for about 500m. The birdlife on the lake

17

and its marshy fringes includes the little grebe, white pelican, endemic blue-winged goose and wattled ibis, as well as a variety of herons, ducks and waders, of which painted snipe was our most notable sighting. Silvery-cheeked hornbills can be seen – and heard – in the patch of indigenous woodland on the far shore.

Kofe Swamp The perennial swamps that lie about 3km southwest of Jimma close to the airport are of some interest to birders, as are those at Kofe 4km further along the same road. These swamps are best known as a regular breeding site for the highly endangered and impressive wattled crane and the elusive red-chested flufftail. A good range of other water-associated bird species might be seen, particularly during the European winter, along with the endemic Abyssinian longclaw. No hippos are present, but small herds of Bohor reedbuck are sometimes encountered. As with the sites listed previously, Kofe can easily be visited as a day trip in a private vehicle, by bicycle or by taxi.

Beletegera Forest About 40km west of Jimma, this forest features densely packed pines and many subcanopy species. A few kilometres further on you will pass some of the tallest and spindliest eucalyptus trees in Ethiopia. Locals in the town of Shebe say you can find many species of monkeys and even lions there. A restriction on bringing locally made wood products back to Addis serves as a conservation effort.

Welkite and the Gibe River Gorge One of the largest settlements on the road between Jimma and Addis Ababa, Welkite is a busy transit town stopped at for breakfast or lunch by most buses covering this route. It is known for its *Gurage kitfo*, and hordes of street touts make a living by selling snacks and shining the shoes of the thousands of bus travellers who pass through every afternoon. The descent into the Gibe River Gorge, just after Welkite, follows a spectacular stretch of road with dense acacia woodland clinging to the hills and wild granite buttes in the distance. At the bottom of the gorge, the small village of Gibe (marked on some maps as Abelti) straddles the large river and stoic twin bridges. The 'real' Abelti, incidentally, lies on a tall mountain which you pass a bit further north – from here one of the more spectacular peaks can be summited on foot for a panoramic view of the gorge, well-earned after the breathtaking 2-hour round-trip scramble.

CHEBERA-CHURCHURA NATIONAL PARK (\047 227 0004; *entrance US$10 pp plus US$2/car, mandatory scout fee US$6/day or US$10 overnight*) Upgraded from a Controlled Hunting Area to a national park in 2005, Chebera-Churchura, named after the two villages that border it, extends across 1,215km² of undulating terrain on the western side of the Omo-Gibe Basin, about 120km south of Jimma by road. Boasting an altitudinal span of 700–2,450m, the park supports a wide variety of habitats, predominantly swampy jungle-like forest and lightly wooded savannah, and it is traversed by numerous streams and rivers, all of which eventually drain into the Omo. Slopes strewn with pockmarked black boulders are evidence of the area's volcanic past, as is a quartet of crater lakes (Bulo, Keribela, Shisha and Qako) and the numerous hot springs that litter the park. Chebera-Churchura is one of the last Ethiopian strongholds for the African elephant, supporting an estimated population of 500 according to the head scout, and it also supports substantial numbers of buffalo (thought by some experts to be a distinct 'dwarf' subspecies) and smaller relict populations of lion, leopard and various other large predators. Other mammals present include hippo, Defassa waterbuck, bushbuck, lesser

kudu, greater kudu, giant forest hog, bushpig, warthog, guereza, grivet monkey and Anubis baboon. The bird checklist currently stands at 270 species, including several forest specialists with a limited range in Ethiopia, and it seems likely to be added to as the park becomes better known (indeed, we noted a few species not included on the official checklist). Tourism development is in its infancy, but the park is reasonably accessible, whether in a private car or by public transport, and it offers much to keen walkers, birders and other nature lovers, most excitingly the opportunity to track elephant and buffalo on foot. Planned developments include the creation of a game-viewing road network linking the main entrance at Chebera to Churchura on the opposite side of the park, but for now it is only really suited to exploration on foot. Private investors are also sought to help develop higher-quality lodges and other facilities.

Getting there and away The park lies about 450km southwest of Addis Ababa via Jimma (where it would be advisable to overnight en route). From Jimma, follow the Sodo road south of town for about 80km of gravel road to Chida, where you need to fork to the right and continue for another 22km to Ameya along a newly asphalted stretch. Fork to the left at Ameya, then continue for 12km to the village of Chebera. The park entrance and main campsite lie just 1km out of Chebera, and the park headquarters, where you need to pay all fees and arrange a scout, is on the left-hand side of the road between them. Using **public transport**, plenty of passenger vehicles run back and forth between Jimma and Chida, and at least half a dozen connect Chida to Ameya. On market days (Tuesday, Friday and Sunday), you might well be able to pick up a lift between Ameya and Chebera (*US$1*), and a motorbike charter will cost only US$3.50 one-way. It's a 10–15-minute walk from Chebera to the campsite. The park can also be approached from Sodo, which lies 165km from Chida, though this will soon increase to around 225km due to a diversion around the Gibe III dam.

Where to stay, eat and drink A beautiful campsite has been carved into the riparian forest lining the Shoshuma River 1km from Chebera village. It has no facilities but you can wash in the river and it is well positioned for day hikes to look for elephants or visit the lakes. It is also theoretically possible to camp deeper in the park, for instance at the hot springs or on the crater rim above Lake Bulo, but the logistics of this are rather daunting owing to the poor roads. Either way, camping costs US$3 per tent, an overnight scout is mandatory, and the scouts can provide you with a tent by request. Campers would ideally bring their own food, but failing that a few local eateries in Chebera serve up tasty *tibs*, *shiro* and the local staple *siliso* (similar to cottage cheese and eaten with *injera*). Very basic groceries, soft drinks, tea and *tej* are also sold in the village.

A National Park guesthouse, located before the park, and comprising eight rooms with en-suite shower (*US$5 sgl*; **$**) is now open. In addition, basic accommodation is available at Ameya, only 12km from the park.

What to see and do
Around the campsite Guereza and grivet monkey appear to be resident in the riparian forest along the Shoshuma River, and the birding is superb. Among the more interesting species we noted here are silvery-cheeked hornbill, tambourine dove, blue-spotted dove, pygmy kingfisher, half-collared kingfisher, double-toothed barbet, blue-breasted bee-eater, yellow-billed, snowy-headed robin-chat, Abyssinian ground thrush, African thrush, white-rumped babbler, violet-backed

starling, mountain wagtail and spectacled weaver. The short walk back to the village overlooks a gorge carved by the Shoshuma River before it passes the campsite, and offers great views into the canopies of several large fig trees. A pleasant short walk from the campsite (to be undertaken only with a scout) leads 1.5km deeper into the park to a small set of hot springs surrounded by a clearing where Anubis baboon, bushbuck and more occasionally buffalo or elephant are sometimes seen. Check the fig branches above the springs for the pretty African green pigeon.

Maka Forest The most accessible of the park's several forests, Maka extends for about 10km^2 south of the Shoshuma River campsite. A swampy and unusually open-canopied patch of woodland, it is traversed by several streams, and feels more like a jungle than a forest. Maka is also the main haunt of a subpopulation of around 125 elephants, who are resident in the area for about 10 months of the year, but usually move deeper into the park over July and August. Despite the somewhat secretive nature of the forest-dwelling elephants, they are observed on a daily basis by the scouts that monitor them, and are almost certain to be seen (albeit fleetingly) by patient visitors who take a guided walk there in the morning (they tend to be more elusive in the afternoon). It's a truly exciting outing, with a vibe somewhat reminiscent of gorilla or chimp tracking, as you weave through the lush jungle trails on foot, listening out for the spine-chilling trumpeting calls that the scouts follow to locate their quarry. With luck, you will locate the elephants within an hour or two of setting out from the campsite. Other wildlife you're likely to see en route includes buffalo, bushpig and forest birds such as silvery-cheeked hornbill and white-cheeked turaco.

Deeper in the park At the time of writing, exploration of Chebera-Churchura is limited by the internal infrastructure, which amounts to one very rough 4x4-only road running for about 12km southwest from the campsite to the east bank of the Hadge River. It is permitted to walk on this road with a scout, with the main point of interest being the aforementioned hot springs, the cold water springs known as Nech Wuha (White Water) 5km from the campsite, and the twin waterfalls on the Bardo River about 3km further on. More ambitiously, 15km from the campsite, the pretty lily-covered Bulo Crater Lake is home to around 100 hippos, as well as lily associated birds such as African jacana and pygmy goose. With a 4x4, you could drive as far as the shallow Hadge River, then cross it on foot and continue walking for another hour or so to the lake, ascending the outer wall of the crater along a wide clear footpath trampled by hippos. Without a vehicle, it would be difficult to get to the lake and back in a day, but you could think about camping there overnight.

BONGA The administrative centre of Kaffa-Sheka Zone, Bonga lies around 100km to the southwest of Jimma, only 3km south of the main road to Mizan Tefari. It's an attractive enough town, sprawling along a high ridge that offers stirring views over the surrounding forested slopes, and also of some historical note, having served as the capital of the Kaffa Kingdom from the 16th to the late 19th century. As things stand, Bonga is seldom visited by tourists, but this looks set to change following the UNESCO designation of a vast area of the surrounding hillside as the Kafa Biosphere Reserve in 2011, and the recent opening of the country's first specialist coffee museum in the town centre.

History The medieval Kingdom of Kaffa, whose name is immortalised as the derivative of the words 'coffee' and 'café', lay to the southwest of Jimma in what is now the Kaffa-Sheka Zone of the Southern Nations, Nationalities and Peoples' Region.

The people of Kaffa are part of the Gibe ethnolinguistic group, and speak their own Kaficho language. A credible oral tradition states that Kaffa was founded in the late 14th century by the Minjo dynasty, and was originally ruled from a town called Shada, of which little is known except for its name. In the early 16th-century reign of King Bonkatato, the royal capital shifted to Bonga, which retained its importance into the 1880s, when Paul Soleillet, the first European visitor to Kaffa, regarded it to be the largest settlement in the region, and reported that a palace was still maintained there.

Kaffa, though it lay outside the Christian empire of the highlands, appears to have fallen under its sporadic influence. Oral traditions indicating that Emperor Sarsa Dengal's 16th-century expedition to western Ethiopia resulted in the limited introduction of Christianity to Kaffa are backed up by the presence of a monastery dating to around 1550 only 12km from Bonga town. Kaffa was too remote to be affected by the jihad of Ahmed Gragn, and it withstood the subsequent Oromo incursion into the western highlands by digging deep protective trenches around the major settlements. Kaffa remained an autonomous state from its inception until Emperor Menelik II conquered it in the late 19th century, and imprisoned its last king at Ankober.

Getting there and away There's plenty of public transport connecting Jimma to Bonga, a scenic 2–3-hour journey on a newly paved road.

Where to stay, eat and drink

Kaffa Development Association (KDA) Guesthouse (10 rooms) m 0924 660703, 0920 732146; e bonga.guesthouse@gmail. com; w kafa-biosphere.com/accommodation. This smart effort by local government to attract ecotourists to the under-utilised virgin forest of Kafa Biosphere Reserve comprises 2 separate guesthouses perched on a gated hillside overlooking the expansive wilderness below. Surrounded by manicured gardens & a seasonally green lawn, each modern abode is set up community-style with 5 bedrooms & 2 bathrooms. The master bedroom & bath in each are particularly lavish, & shared open sitting rooms are centred on cylindrical stone fireplaces that reach the full height of the vaulted ceilings. Food is made

to order on site. The comfort & privacy make it the pick of Bonga's hostelries. *US$18/24 sgl/twin.* **$$$**

Coffee Land Hotel (40 rooms) \ 047 331 0010; m 0912 709064. Situated alongside the feeder road from the main road between Jimma & Mizan Tefari, this pleasant hotel has pastel-painted rooms, all with tiled floor & nets. The restaurant serves delicious, well-priced Ethiopian & Western dishes. *From US$5 dbl using common cold shower, or US$14/20 en-suite sgl/dbl.* **$$**

Makira Hotel (44 rooms) \ 047 331 0647; m 0911 233024. This multistorey hotel near the Telecom tower has cheaper rooms than the Coffee Land, & a comparable restaurant. *US$5/10 sgl/dbl or twin.* **$**

What to see and do

Bonga International Coffee Museum Located on the road behind the KDA Guesthouse, this impressive-looking new museum has now finally opened after more than eight years in the making. The only coffee-specialised museum in the country, it focuses on the history of Kaffa's most famous crop, but also houses archaeological and historical artefacts uncovered in the zone, including the world's oldest coffee beans, which were discovered in Kumale Cave in the zone and date from the 3rd century AD.

Kafa Biosphere Reserve Sprawling for 7,600km² across the hills around Bonga, the UNESCO-sanctioned Kafa Biosphere Reserve (w *kafa-biosphere.com*) incorporates the former Bonga, Gesha and Gewata-Yeba forest reserves, which rank

In December/January 2017/18, we made a great overland trip, mostly with public transport, from Nekemte (where I was working) to Fort Portal (Uganda) following a little-used back route from Jimma to Jinka. From Jimma we first travelled to Bonga, where we stayed in the neat KDA Guesthouse, which is still going strong. After two nights in Bonga, the most adventurous part of our trip began. We identified a road between Bonga and Jinka, which I initially hadn't even found on Google Maps. This road can be partly done by public transport, but for the largest part needs to be done with personal 4x4 or by renting an Isuzu truck, like we did. The first stage can be done by public bus to a town called Ch'iri about 25km southwest of Bonga, which takes about 1 hour on a rough road. From there, another bus can be taken to a smaller town called Dishi, which is about 22km further south and another 1-hour drive. On a Sunday (the day that we travelled), this bus can bring people about 3km further south to the weekly market at Angela Goda.

In Dishi we rented an Isuzu truck for around US$150. First, we had to wait for about 3 hours at Angela Goda market, which meant that we had to travel partly in the evening unfortunately. Still, we left Angela Goda around 16.30 and travelled further south, from the highlands of Kaffa to the lowlands of South Omo. This is a rough road that is mostly travelled by government vehicles and a few investor farmers in cotton and sesame that can be found about 40km south of Dishi. From there it is not far to a very small settlement called Neda, where there is a police station from which we had to take a police officer, as there had been skirmishes further south around the Kuraz Sugar mill, a few weeks before, in which several people were killed in revenge killings. There was no escaping this and it cost us US$35 extra.

From Neda we travelled another 2½ hours, over very rough roads full of rocks and traversing a non-tourist savannah park, to the barracks of the Kuraz Sugar mill (not the actual sugar mill, which is 30km further south, and on the east side of the river), where we stayed for the night. The next morning, a ride of about 30 minutes over a paved road, crossing the Omo River, brought us to the town of Hana, capital of Salamago *woreda* in South Omo Zone. Hana is also the capital of the Bodi, the Omo tribe that is famous for their 'fattest man competition'; some tour operators even send groups here. From Hana, buses depart several times daily (at least two every morning) to Jinka, which is still a 3½-hour drive on a rough road with a serious climb at the end.

among the last remaining Ethiopian subtropical moist forests of any significant size. Recognised as a biodiversity hot spot, the reserve is home to more than 5,000 plant species and is also renowned for its abundance of sustainable non-timber forest products, including coffee, forest cardamom, forest pepper and honey. Relatively unexplored by outsiders, and managed by community-based committees, these closed-canopy forests also host large numbers of monkeys, a rich and largely undocumented avifauna, and numerous interesting natural features including hot springs and waterfalls. Popular day-hike destinations are **God's Bridge**, a stunning natural rock structure which forms a complete bridge and underlying cave over a mountain stream, and the **Mother Coffee Tree**, which is claimed to be the oldest living coffee tree. Guided walks ranging from a few hours to multi-day treks can be arranged through the Office of Culture and Tourism in Bonga (*047 331 0842*).

MIZAN TEFARI Whether you arrive there from Jimma in the east or Metu in the north, the road to the misty, half-finished highland town of Mizan Tefari (often abbreviated to Mizan) traverses one of the lushest of Ethiopian landscapes, climbing hill after verdant hill swathed in indigenous montane forest. Unlike the surrounding scenery, however, the town itself doesn't impress greatly. True enough, it's a friendly little place, set below an attractive backdrop of forested hills, but it is primarily of interest to travellers as a springboard for visits to the nearby Bebeka and Tepi coffee plantations, or the descent to the small Suri village of Kibish on the southwest frontier of the Omo Valley.

Getting there and away Most visitors to Mizan Tefari approach from the northeast via Jimma, a 250km road that passes through Bonga and Wushwush, the latter being home to the huge plantation that lends its name to Ethiopia's most popular brand of tea. The road is surfaced but in poor condition, and the drive still takes around 5 hours in a private vehicle, and up to 7 hours by bus. A worthwhile stop a few kilometres east of Wushwush, at least for aficionados of *tej*, is at Arat Silsa (literally '460', after a prominent signpost showing the distance from Addis Ababa in kilometres), where an isolated roadside shop sells a high-quality brew for less than US$0.50 per litre.

The rough 215km road from Metu to Mizan Tefari takes at least 6 hours in a private vehicle, and may be near impassable in the rainy season. If you have a capable vehicle, however, it's one of the most scenic routes in Ethiopia, twisting

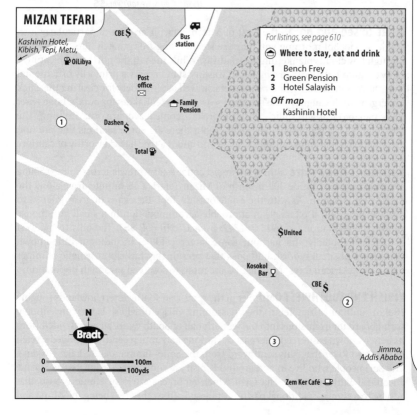

MIZAN TEFARI

Kashinin Hotel,
Kibish, Tepi, Metu,
OiLibya

CBE $

Bus station

Post office

Family Pension

Dashen $

Total

United $

Kosokol Bar

CBE $

Jimma,
Addis Ababa

Zem Ker Café

N

0 ——— 100m
0 ——— 100yds

For listings, see page 610

Where to stay, eat and drink
1 Bench Frey
2 Green Pension
3 Hotel Salayish
Off map
Kashinin Hotel

and diving through Afroalpine bamboo forest and thick misty jungle. On public transport it requires a full day, and you usually need to swap vehicles at Gore (25km south of Metu) and Tepi (50km before Mizan Tefari). Coming directly from Addis Ababa, there ought to be now daily Selam and Golden Bus services to Mizan Tefari. These take about 12 hours (page 141).

Where to stay, eat and drink   *Map, page 609*

Hotel Salayish (43 rooms) ☎047 335 0865; m 0917 551300. This recently renovated hotel is the clear pick in Mizan Tefari, but it often fills up quickly so call ahead. Rooms in the old wing are compact & clean with private balcony & hot shower, while those in the 3-storey new building are costlier, but more stylish & modern, & come with Wi-Fi. There are 2 restaurants attached, 1 traditional & 1 modern; the food is inexpensive, the bar is popular & the inner yard is a most pleasant place to have an evening drink & listen to an excellent choice of Ethiopian music. *US$23/35/67 B&B en-suite sgl/dbl or twin/suite (new wing), US$15 sgl with cold shower (old wing).* **$$$**

Kashinin Hotel m 0917 551910. A good alternative to the Salayish, this new hotel stands about 2.5km out of town close to the university campus. *Around US$30 dbl.* **$$$**

Green Pension (30 rooms) ☎047 335 0538. This clean & quiet hotel recently added a block of larger en-suite rooms above the neighbouring CBE bank. *US$4 sgl with common shower, US$7.50 en-suite dbl.* **$**

Bench Frey Hotel (58 rooms) m 0931 314947. The largest of Mizan's hotels has clean & realistically priced en-suite rooms with large beds & quite lacklustre bathrooms. The courtyard is filled with peculiar statues of naked people whose arms are raised to hold long-tossed-aside lanterns. *US$8/16 en-suite sgl/twin.* **$$**

What to see and do   To the west of Mizan Tefari is an area of particularly lush jungle. On a cool morning you may see steam rising from thatch huts as you pass through low clouds blanketing the roadway. While men in the north of the country carry a walking stick called a *dula*, out west most men carry a primarily ornamental spear horizontally across their shoulders, as well as a machete for clearing the thick undergrowth. If caught in the frequent seasonal torrential downpours, a huge *enset* (false banana) leaf will suffice as an umbrella – some leaves are over 3m long! The dirt road here is supposedly all-weather, but there are some sections that are not; extremely slippery mud can sneak up on you and is a true hazard worthy of caution.

Bebeka Coffee Estate   Ethiopia's largest coffee estate sprawls across some 6,500ha of lushly forested hillside 30km south of Mizan Tefari, a 45-minute drive along the road towards Kibish. As with the estate outside Tepi, Bebeka is of great interest to birdwatchers, and it offers clean affordable accommodation in a small guesthouse run by the plantation (m *0913 761742; from US$10 dbl;* **$$**). The hills to the west of Bebeka reputedly still harbour some larger wildlife, including a little-known population of small reddish buffaloes that presumably has closer genetic affinities to the West African forest race than to the more widespread savannah population.

KIBISH AND SOUTHWEST OMO   Set in the semi-arid southwestern lowlands roughly 180km south of Mizan Tefari, the unassuming village of Kibish is the conventional springboard for excursions into the western half of South Omo, an area divided from its better-known eastern counterpart by the long and until recently unbridged stretch of the Omo River that runs southward from the Sodo–Jimma road to Lake Turkana. The Suri people who live in and around Kibish are sometimes designated as Surma, an official Ethiopian umbrella term which embraces a trio of ethnic groups that adhere to a similar traditional pastoralist lifestyle (the other two being the Mursi and

If you think visiting the Mursi involves unpleasant money transactions to access their villages and be allowed to take pictures of still subjects, it is because you have not visited Kibish and the Suri. Here the whole range of human relations is made into a raw trading fair.

First you need to travel to the zone accompanied by an armed scout, whom you must pick up on the way at Dima and should cost you no more than US$12 a day. Then you have to pay an administrative tax of US$16 per person to be allowed to overnight in Kibish, and another US$4 to sleep in the most rustic hotel ever, unless you choose to camp in the proximity of the police station where you will be charged a few supplementary dollars. Thereafter you are supposed to call upon the services of a local guide and another armed local scout at a cost of another US$16 per person just to walk around the market and visit nearby villages where an additional entrance fee of US$6 is generally requested. Finally you will have to pay the equivalent of US$0.50 to every person you wish to photograph, twice the going amount in Hamar or Mursi country. If you have a Polaroid camera, handing out prints can help break the ice on a village visit.

You might be able to knock down a few dollars on some of these charges by resolute negotiations or by dismissing, rightfully, the local scout. But in all cases, you need to be very exact about what you expect: with generalised drunkenness increasing as the sun goes down, misunderstandings and unfulfilled promises can lead to street riots, here even more than elsewhere in Ethiopia, and the Suri participants are prompt to brandish the long fighting sticks for which their warriors are famous.

Despite this, Kibish does retain the harsh and authentic end-of-the-road feel of rural Africa. Elegant women who leave their left shoulder and breast uncovered, and submit themselves to a culture that requires women to wear large and spectacular lip plates and assorted earrings to conform to the indigenous ideal of feminine splendour, confront your Westerner's world-view. As does the recognition that these people inhabit a tough and exacting environment without running water, electricity, roads, motorised transportation, comfortable homes or any of the facilities that make our lives so easy.

You then wonder what keeps these wonderful people so energetic, so lively and fun, and so civilised within their own set of habits, customs and behaviours. And as you find your way through all the difficulties, you will thoroughly enjoy your time, sharing in a tavern a delicious bottle of 'yellow', the local honey wine that has here a flavour of cider, and trying to take part in their joyous way of life, with shouts and quarrels and the background music from the local inns. Ultimately, it is a far more authentic cultural encounter than anything you are likely to experience in a Mursi village. Just walking around, or sipping a soft drink on a stool in front of a local grocery, is a powerful experience.

Mekan) but is neither used nor liked by those to whom it is applied. That said, much like the Mursi (see box, page 584), the Suri are renowned for the lip plates worn by the women, and they participate in a rigid but egalitarian political system based around age-sets similar to those of the related Maasai of the Kenya–Tanzania border area.

Individual travellers seldom visit southwest Omo due to the paucity of public transport, but several specialist tour operators do offer 4x4 or hiking trips to the region. Kibish is the normal springboard for trips of this sort, but the village itself highlights the ugly side of cultural tourism, with its Suri residents affecting all manner of quirks associated with the region's other tribes to come across as a sort of South Omo one-stop shop.

There is no public transport to Kibish, and the drive from Mizan Tefari takes a good 5–6 hours in a private 4x4. The first semi-urban punctuation comes 30km south of Mizan Tefari in the form of Bebeka and its fantastically verdant coffee plantation. From there the road descends into more open savannah, studded with tall acacias and bands of riparian woodland that support rich birdlife. After 70km of this rough road and thinly inhabited countryside, the road emerges at Dima, a picturesque small market town that stands on the north bank of the Akabu River. Dima offers the choice of a few hotels, the best of which is the Hyat Pension, which offers budget rooms, local meals and cold drinks to passing travellers.

After crossing the Akabu, the road runs southeast for another 67km to Tulgit, a small traditional village centred on an American missionary outpost. A foreigner named John living here is said to accommodate guests in one of his houses, but he was absent the day we travelled there. It might be a good alternative to the lone rudimentary hotel in Kibish. On the way, you should see the occasional Suri cattle-herder wandering stark naked through the empty countryside, generally armed with a spear or gun as protection. It's another 15km to Kibish, a giddy descent that will probably take at least 45 minutes.

A relatively easy option for those without private transport is to visit the village of Tum, which is about 180km from Mizan Tefari on an unsurfaced road that runs south from the main road of Bonga 20km east of town. Tum hosts an important Saturday market that attracts many Suri from the outlying villages. To get there, you'll need to catch the early morning bus from Mizan Tefari on Friday, overnight at Tum's lone shoestring hotel, and eat at one of its dire restaurants. There is no charge to visit the market at Tum, but it would be wise to engage a local guide if offered. Be very discreet with your camera.

For a more ambitious multi-week trek in the area, try the Mizan Tefari-based guide Tizbt Sum Sum (m 0910 498048; e tizbtsuri@gmail.com; w sumsumphotoguide. weebly.com).

TEPI The small town of Tepi, 50km northwest of Mizan Tefari, is primarily of interest for the 6,000ha Tepi coffee estate on its immediate outskirts. The second-largest coffee estate in the country, it is of interest as much for the varied birdlife that rustles through the forest undergrowth (accessible by several walking trails that lead from the plantation guesthouse) as for the opportunity to investigate the production of western Ethiopia's finest export. The coffee served at the plantation is excellent, as might be expected. The plantation doesn't sell coffee beans, but they can be purchased at many shops in town for about US$3/kg. No fee is charged to tour the plantation, but you need permission from the Tepi council office in town.

Just past Tepi, on the road towards Gore, pockets of giant ferns abound. With a little imagination you might think you have been transported back to the Jurassic period, that is until a roadside group of baboons reminds you that you are firmly in the age of mammals. About 60km past Tepi the road forks and then forks again – not to worry, they all soon reconnect. You then ascend into the Highland Bamboo Conservation Area, the browner colour of the bamboo providing contrast to the many surrounding shades of green. About 87km north of Tepi you will come to the town of Masha, a good stop for lunch if you are heading to Gore and beyond.

Getting there and away Regular minibuses run back and forth along the rough but very scenic road between Mizan Tefari and Tepi. Bussing on to Gambella is less straightforward. Regular buses run as far as Masha, where the very small bus station indicates it is 'at the end of the line'. A few emphatically shoestring hotels are available in Masha, the pick being an anonymous new place signposted in Amharigna close to the bus station (*call the manager, Awol, at* m *0946 257487 for more info;* $), and the place to eat is Oldies Bar & Restaurant. Apparently there is a very nice waterfall and cave only 7km away. Occasional minibuses run along the rather poor dirt road to Gore. From Gore, minibuses regularly make the 3-hour descent to Gambella, but enquire beforehand where the buses leave from

Where to stay, eat and drink

Tepi Coffee Plantation Guesthouse
(29 rooms) 047 556 0062. The best place to stay in Tepi, this neat guesthouse with tiled en-suite chalets set in a large attractive park lies about 1km from the town centre. Traditional food & pasta are always available at its restaurant/bar, & Western dishes can be ordered in advance. *US$5 sgl with common shower/US$12 en-suite dbl or twin with TV in the new bldg.* $$

Genet Pension (35 rooms) 047 556 2145; m 0913 996606. Situated on the road

to Jimma about 200m past the turn-off to the coffee plantation, this pension has a choice of clean rooms with en-suite or common shower, in both cases with cold water only. *US$6/7 dbl with common/en-suite shower.* $

Tegist Hotel (26 rooms) 047 556 0227; m 0917 309673. The pick of the central lodges, though the tiled rooms with nets come with cold water only. *US$6/9.50 en-suite sgl/twin, US$4.50 common shower.* $–$$

METU The attractive capital of Ilubabor Zone, founded in 1913 at an altitude of 1,600m near the western escarpment of the Ethiopian Highlands, is of interest to travellers primarily as a springboard for the descent into the steamy tropical lowlands that flank the Baro River and the port of Gambella. Despite its well-wooded hilly surrounds, Metu is an unremarkable sort of place: a long and narrow highland town stretched out along a zigzagging 4km stretch of double-lane asphalt flanked by wide, welcoming sidewalks and several clusters of hotels, restaurants and shops. A recently inaugurated university 3km west of town has caused serious population pressure, adding to the existing water and electricity problems. The central market is lively and welcoming, or you could stretch your legs by taking a short walk or *bajaj* ride to the forest-fringed Sor River, which crosses the Bedele road some 2km northeast of the town centre (a good spot for monkeys and birds). Further afield, an excellent goal for a day trip is the impressive Sor Waterfall.

Getting there and away Coming from Mizan Tefari, a poorly maintained 220km seasonal dirt road runs northward to Metu via Tepi and Gore, a journey that should take up to 6 hours in a private vehicle and the best part of a full day by bus. A daily bus service along the newly tarred 170km road between Metu and Gambella leaves in either direction at around 06.00, and erratically every few hours after that. The journey takes around 4 hours.

Coming from Jimma or Nekemte, Metu lies about 115km from Bedele along an asphalted road in very poor condition. But this route provides some of the greenest scenery and traverses arguably the largest swathe of old-growth forest in Ethiopia, rivalled only by the stretch a little farther along the loop from Metu to Mizan. The drive between Bedele and Metu takes about 3 hours in a private vehicle or 4–5 hours by bus. Direct buses run between Jimma and Metu, but coming from Nekemte you will probably have to change buses at **Bedele**, a small dusty transit hub best known as the site of the Bedele Brewery, which is now owned by Heineken. If for some reason you need to spend the night in Bedele, the Hagere Selam Hotel (*43 rooms;* m *0917 551317;* **$$**) has a good ground-floor restaurant, en-suite rooms with TV and hot water for US$8/12 single/double, and single rooms with common shower at US$5. A recent alternative is the Central Pension (*24 rooms;* m *0911 712367; US$6/10 common shower/en suite;* **$**) opposite the Hagere Selam on the main roundabout, with slightly cleaner single rooms.

🏠 Where to stay   *Map, right*

The recent opening of a university has resulted in a real shortage of bedrooms in Metu. Local entrepreneurs have reacted to this by starting construction of perhaps a dozen new multistorey hotels in the town centre. So be sure to shop around when you look for accommodation because the recommended hotels below are likely to be superseded by newer options.

🏠 **Tinsae Hotel**   (33 rooms) m 0917 466062. The best hotel in downtown Metu was recently expanded with the addition of new deluxe rooms with queen-size bed, sturdy furnishings & en-suite hot bathtub. The restaurant & bar are popular, but the food isn't all that great. *US$4 with common shower, US$7.50/10/12.50 en-suite sgl/dbl/deluxe.* **$$**

🏠 **Horizon Pension**   (23 rooms) m 0917 806197. Located close to the Total petrol station on the way out of town towards Bedele, this private green compound is excellent for a peaceful night's sleep. Rooms are basic but clean, & there's a small restaurant/café with a limited menu, convenient for a quick b/fast. *US$5 with common shower, US$7.50 en suite.* **$**

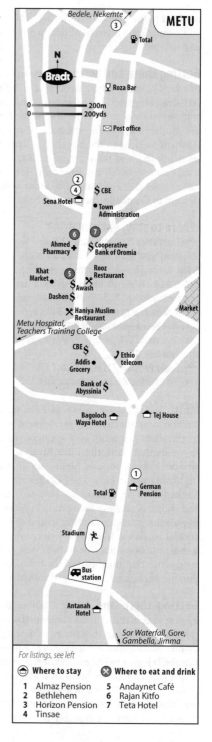

METU

Bedele, Nekemte
3
Total

N
Bradt
Roza Bar

0 ___ 200m
0 ___ 200yds

✉ Post office

2
4
Sena Hotel
$ CBE
● Town Administration

6   7
Ahmed Pharmacy
$ Cooperative Bank of Oromia

Khat Market
5
Rooz Restaurant
✗ Awash
Dashen $

✗ Haniya Muslim Restaurant

Metu Hospital, Teachers Training College

Market

CBE $
Addis ● Grocery
♪ Ethio telecom

Bank of Abyssinia $

Bagoloch Waya Hotel
Tej House

1
German Pension
Total

Stadium

Bus station

Antanah Hotel

Sor Waterfall, Gore, Gambella, Jimma

For listings, see left

⊖ **Where to stay**   ✗ **Where to eat and drink**
1 Almaz Pension   5 Andaynet Café
2 Bethlehem   6 Rajan Kitfo
3 Horizon Pension   7 Teta Hotel
4 Tinsae

Bethlehem Hotel (33 rooms) m 0961 501466. The rooms are comfortable enough, but loud at night & early morning, & with dodgy plumbing. Most Sun evenings a campfire on the patio in front is a popular gathering point. *US$8.50/16 en-suite depending on size of room & bed.* **$$**

Almaz Pension (12 rooms) m 0912 104692. If being close to the bus station is the first priority, this is the place to stay, as most of the better hotels & restaurants located downtown are a little far from the bus station for early morning departures. Almaz has simple & satisfactory bedrooms, just not in the best part of town. *US$5 with common shower, US$6.50 en suite.* **$**

✖ Where to eat and drink *Map, opposite*

For breakfast, **Andaynet Café** is the most popular spot in town with good *ful*, and *fatira* with honey. It is also the only place open at 05.30 for early departures. Lunch and dinner options are mostly local fare only. **Teta Hotel** and **Rajan Kitfo**, opposite each other on the main road, are good choices for Ethiopian meat and vegetarian dishes; the former is also a popular night-time dancing and drinking spot, while the latter boasts a clever downstairs, culturally themed dining room.

What to see and do

Sor Waterfall The main attraction in the vicinity of Metu is the Sor Waterfall, which is an impressive sight even in the dry season, plunging about 20m over a sheer rock amphitheatre surrounded by tall tree ferns and mist forest, and must be thoroughly spectacular after heavy rain. In the dry season, it is possible to walk to the bottom of the gorge and have a picnic or swim in the chilly pool at the waterfall's base.

To get there, follow the Gore road west out of Metu for 7km, then turn left at a sign (which ruins the suspense with a giant picture of the waterfall) to follow a rough and muddy track that passes the Gore water treatment plant after 7.5km and arrives at the village of Becho after another 5.5km. From the small village centre you can drive, but it's probably wiser to walk, following an even rougher 4km track, then an indistinct and slippery footpath through a patch of dense jungle alive with creepers, butterflies, baboons, guereza monkeys and birds – most visibly silvery-cheeked hornbill, Heuglin's robin-chat and Ethiopian oriole. More than likely you'll attract an entourage of enthusiastic children to lead you in the right direction, but if not, anybody will point you the right way – Bishaan Fincha'a is the local word for waterfall! After about 30 minutes of slipping and tripping through the forest, you'll hear the waterfall, the signal for a steep 10-minute descent – watch out for the vicious nettles – to a viewpoint near the top of a gorge.

The excursion is straightforward if you have a 4x4 vehicle, and you should be able to do the round trip in 3–4 hours. There is limited public transport from Metu to Becho in the form of 4x4 'taxis', but it all leaves in the morning and turns back almost immediately, so you'll have to either charter a vehicle or plan on staying in one of the very basic, US$2 rooms in Becho.

NEKEMTE Set at an altitude of around 2,100m some 200km west of Ambo, Nekemte is the principal town of the Welega Oromo, supporting a population of around 120,000. It was made the capital of the Welega Kingdom in the mid 19th century, during the reign of King Bekere Godana, and was conquered by Emperor Menelik in the 1880s. Prior to 1994 Nekemte, then known as Lekemti, served as capital of Welega Province. Today it is the administrative centre for the East Welega Zone of Oromia Region. It lies in a lushly forested and agriculturally productive area that also boasts considerable mineral wealth in the form of gold, platinum, copper, iron and lead. Nekemte itself is a leafy, pretty and busy small town whose primary roads are now all paved. Sites of interest include a museum and palace, as well as the out-of-town Didessa Wildlife Reserve.

Getting there and away The 320km drive from Addis Ababa to Nekemte via Ambo takes 5–6 hours in a private vehicle, not allowing for stops. Several direct buses cover the route daily of which the most comfortable belong to the Gada bus company and can be found at the main bus stations. These travel to Addis Ababa (*US$8*), Assosa (*US$8*) and Metu (*US$5*). Selam Bus also used to operate the route; services are currently suspended for political reasons, but may well resume in the future. The drive between Ambo and Nekemte passes through a well-watered highland area with panoramic views across the surrounding valleys and mountains, swathed in thick woodland and patches of forest west of Bako. A little-used but reasonably good 250km dirt road also connects Nekemte to Bure on the surfaced route between Addis Ababa and Bahir Dar. Using private transport, it is perfectly possible to travel between Nekemte and Bahir Dar in one (long) day using this road, but travellers dependent on public transport will probably need to break up the trip at Kosober, which straddles the road between Bure and Bahir Dar.

The road south to Bedele, and beyond to Metu and Gore, is currently under repair, with just the stretch from Nekemte to the Didessa sugar factory actually paved.

Where to stay, eat and drink *Map, opposite*

Dasalegn Hotel (30 rooms) \057 661 6162; e dessalegen.hotel@gmail.com. This smart 5-storey hotel near the roundabout offers a budget-friendly range of bright, clean rooms & a good restaurant & bar. The entrance is through a neat yard with delicately shaped boxwood, & outdoor tables & chairs situated on the side road to the left of the main building. *US$7 using common shower, US$12 en-suite dbl or twin.* **$–$$**

Benori Pension (24 rooms) \057 661 4096. This smart multistorey pension tucked off the main road about a block back from the Telecom office is a reasonable offering. The slick modern rooms come with tiled floor, en-suite hot shower, sat TV & free Wi-Fi. All it lacks is a restaurant. *US$12/17 dbl/twin inc b/fast.* **$$**

Farmland Hotel (30 rooms) \057 661 5150; e giginaof@gmail.com. This modern 5-storey hotel was the first in Nekemte to break into the semi-luxury class. The clean en-suite rooms are well finished & have a hot shower, Wi-Fi & sat TV. The ground-floor restaurant serves decent Western/Ethiopian dishes (*US$3–6*) & has an attractive neon-lit bar. Rooms with steam bath/sauna are available for an additional fee. *US$14.50/17.50/22.50/25 B&B sgl/dbl/queen/twin.* **$$**

Ijoo Hotel (43 rooms) \057 661 5761; m 0930 300150; e ijoohotel@gmail.com; w ijoohotel.com. Also in the higher-end price class, you get slightly less for your money here than at Farmland, but this newish 4-storey hotel is closer to the bus station. Clean, comfortable en-suite rooms come with Wi-Fi, sat TV & hot showers, & fridge in the more expensive ones. *From US$14/16/26 sgl/dbl/deluxe.* **$$**

Shalom International Hotel (32 rooms) \057 660 7070; m 0949 492424. What seems to be the latest entry in the higher-end accommodation options in Nekemte, the Shalom – 1km from the central roundabout on the Ambo road – includes a coffee shop, gym, sauna & a supermarket. A swimming pool is under construction. *US$16/26/sgl/dbl.* **$$**

What to see and do

Wollega Museum (⊕ 09.00–12.30 & 14.30–17.30 Tue–Sun; entrance US$2) Established in 1989, this ethnographic museum on the northern roundabout is definitely one of the best in the country. Visitors are greeted by the complete engine and propeller of an Italian fighter plane shot down nearby during the area's strong resistance to the occupation. Other displays include a vast collection of Oromo

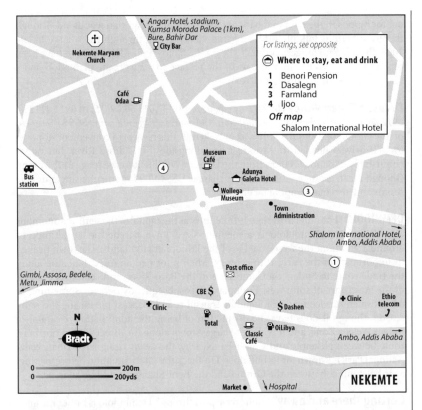

Angar Hotel, stadium,
Kumsa Moroda Palace (1km),
Bure, Bahir Dar
♀ City Bar

✝ Nekemte Maryam
Church

Café Odaa ▱

Bus station

Museum Café ▱

Adunya Galeta Hotel

④

Wollega Museum

③

Town Administration

Shalom International Hotel,
Ambo, Addis Ababa

Gimbi, Assosa, Bedele,
Metu, Jimma

Post office ✉

CBE $

①

② ＋Clinic

$ Dashen

＋Clinic

Ethio telecom ♪

＋Clinic

Total

Classic Café ▱

OiLibya

Ambo, Addis Ababa

N

Bradt

0 ——— 200m
0 ——— 200yds

Market ●   Hospital

NEKEMTE

For listings, see opposite

◐ **Where to stay, eat and drink**

1 Benori Pension
2 Dasalegn
3 Farmland
4 Ijoo
Off map
Shalom International Hotel

artefacts such as leatherware, basketwork, woodcarvings and musical instruments, as well as the first Bible translated into the local Oromo dialect. The guide speaks little English, but his imaginatively mimed demonstrations of how the various artefacts are made or used are almost as entertaining as the exhibits themselves. 'Seeining is beliving' [*sic*] says the flyer provided at the entrance of the museum …

Kumsa   Moroda   Palace (⊕   09.00–12.30   &   14.30–17.30   Tue–Sun; w *hambisfoundation.org; entrance US$2*) Located about 1km from Nekemte on the road towards Bure, this palace was built in the late 19th century by Moti Kumsa Moroda, the third and last king of Welega, shortly before or after his submission to Emperor Menelik and conversion to Christianity, whereupon he changed his name to Gebregziabher. It remained home to his descendants until they were forcibly relocated to Addis Ababa by the Derg. In addition to the main two-storey palace, which is noted for its authentic Oromo architectural style, another ten or so buildings dot the compound. The entrance fee includes a guided tour.

Didessa Wildlife Reserve [map, page 444] This 1,300km² reserve to the south of Nekemte protects a relatively pristine tract of medium-altitude deciduous woodland bisected by the Didessa River as it runs eastward from the main road towards Bedele. A watershed from which flow 15 streams and rivers, it is known to support 30 mammal species, including elephant, buffalo, hippo, bushbuck and guereza monkey, as well as a rich variety of birds. Access is restricted to the main Bedele road, which crosses the Didessa River some 65km south of Nekemte – look

17

out for hippos in the river and baboons and birds in the riparian woodland. Though there was serious talk of cutting a game-viewing road through the reserve in late 2005, this plan no longer appears to be on the table – indeed, it seems to have been replaced by the conversion of part of the reserve to a sugarcane plantation and a massive nearly finished sugar factory.

Didessa Green Valley Resort [map, page 444] (📞*011 663 9575;* m *0911 211258, 0912 795938;* e *wabekbonk@gmail.com, didessaresort@gmail.com;* **$$$$**) Situated on the Gimbi road about 55km west of Nekemte, this resort is a convenient stopover for self-drivers headed to Assosa. It lies alongside the Didessa River, but rather confusingly it is about 100km from the Didessa Wildlife Reserve (page 617) by road (though it can arrange visits there). It charges US$40/60 for en-suite single/double rooms and also has camping facilities.

DEMBIDOLO Founded in the late 19th century as the capital of the semi-autonomous Sayo Kingdom, Dembidolo is a medium-sized town perched at an altitude of around 1,700m on the western edge of the Ethiopian Highlands. The town peaked in importance in the early 20th century, when it formed an important stop along the trade route to Sudan via Gambella and the Baro River, and served as the seat of the governors of southwest Ethiopia. It has subsequently become something of a backwater, serviced by erratic public transport and inaccessible during the rainy season, though it does have the distinction of being the administrative capital of Kelem Welega Zone, and it is also the largest town along the direct 400km northern route between Nekemte and Gambella. Nearby, the newly designated **Dhati Walal National Park** is known for its buffaloes. Do check the safety situation before visiting, as tribal conflict between the Oromo and the Beni-Shangul could be an issue.

Getting there and away Public transport through Dembidolo is rather hit-and-miss. In theory, a bus to/from Nekemte leaves in either direction between 05.30 and 07.00 daily, costing US$6, and taking up to 15 hours, depending on the state of the road and the number of breakdowns. If this bus isn't running, you'll probably have to change vehicles at Gimbi, which lies 110km from Nekemte and 196km from Dembidolo. Heading to/from Gambella, 100km to the south, a minibus usually leaves Gambella at 06.00, reaching Dembidolo at midday or so, before turning around to get back to Gambella in the late afternoon, but this cannot be relied upon, especially after rain.

🏠 Where to stay, eat and drink

🏠**Dembidolo Hotel** (14 rooms) 📞057 555 2366. This new multistorey hotel is located near the Commercial Bank of Ethiopia on the road to the hospital. The clean en-suite rooms have hot water, & there's a good patisserie on the ground floor. *US$4.50–6 dbl, depending on the size & location of the room.* **$**

🏠**Birhan Hotel** (24 rooms) 📞057 555 0313. This long-serving lodge near the bus station has adequate rooms, as well as a friendly bar with sat TV. *US$4/5.50 dbl with common/private shower.* **$**

GAMBELLA REGION

The most westerly of Ethiopia's federal states, Gambella, named after its capital and principal town, is also officially the most thinly populated, extending over 29,783km² and supporting a population of 320,000. In historical, ethnic and climatic terms the region is something of an anomaly within Ethiopia, displaying stronger links to neighbouring South Sudan than to the highlands to its east. Geographically, this hot, humid, low-lying and swampy region is dominated by the sluggish Baro River and its various tributaries that flow across the South Sudanese border to form the backbone of the Blue Nile, which is navigable from Gambella all the way to its confluence with the White Nile at Khartoum.

The most accessible part of Gambella Region is its eponymous capital, an atmospheric and culturally rewarding seasonal river port that also offers some great low-key wildlife viewing. The region's most notable tourist attraction is Gambella National Park, which plays host to one of Africa's largest mammal migrations, when more than a million white-eared kob antelope cross there from South Sudan every spring, but it is a destination that can be reached only with considerable effort, as well as a reliable 4x4 and experienced driver. Sadly, however, while the region has plenty of unrealised tourism potential thanks to its combination of abundant wildlife and unique ethnic groups, its remote nature, coupled with a poor infrastructure epitomised by the lack of asphalt roads, make it a difficult target for time-pressed travellers. Indeed, this characterful region is a victim of a paradox that afflicts many burgeoning destinations: the authorities want tourists to show interest before investing significantly in the necessary infrastructure, while the tourists are staying away due to a lack of accessibility.

Note that unless you are planning to explore the national park, which is only accessible during the peak dry season (February to May), the most pleasant time to visit Gambella is during the rainy season (May to October), when the scenery is lush and green, and temperatures seldom hit the peaks of 40°C or more that are regularly recorded over February and March.

CULTURE AND HISTORY Five major ethnic groups populate Gambella Region. Of these, the Anuwak dominate in terms of the land they occupy, but the Nuer have the largest population. The Majong, Opo and Komo tribes are also scattered throughout the region in smaller numbers. The Anuwak speak a language closely related to that of the Luo in Kenya, and are fishermen and mixed agriculturists by tradition. Their elegantly enclosed homesteads give the region much of its character. The Nuer originated in Nilotic-speaking parts of South Sudan. Nuer men were once marked with six cuts across their forehead as a rite of passage. This practice has all but disappeared after falling out of favour with younger generations, as rumour has it that colonial powers who once occupied the port encouraged it as an easy method to tell the apparently similar tribes apart, but the lines persist as one of the many striking physical characteristics of the Nuer tribe.

The port of Gambella, whose name derives from the Anuwak word for the *Gardenia lutea* tree that grows widely in the vicinity, has a rather curious modern history. In the late 19th century Sudan fell under British rule, and the Baro, which is navigable as far as Khartoum, was seen by both Britain and Ethiopia as an excellent highway for exporting coffee and other produce from the fertile western highlands to Sudan and Egypt. The Ethiopian emperor granted Britain use of part of Ethiopia as a free port in 1902 and, after an unsuccessful attempt to establish a port elsewhere, Gambella was established in 1907. This tiny British territory, a few hundred hectares in size, was bounded by the Baro River to the south, the tributary which now bisects the town to the west, the patch of forest to the east of the modern town, and the small conical hill to its north. Gambella became a prosperous trade centre as ships from Khartoum sailed in regularly during the rainy season when the water was high, taking seven days downriver and 11 days upriver. The Italians captured Gambella in

1936, when the now-ruined fort near the Baro Gambella Hotel was built, but it was returned to Britain after a bloody battle in 1941. Gambella became part of Sudan in 1951, but it was reincorporated into Ethiopia five years later. The port ceased functioning under the Mengistu regime and it remains closed today.

Owing to complicated ethnic relations and a strategic location on Ethiopia's western frontier with South Sudan, Gambella has seen its fair share of conflict in recent decades. The good news is that the regular cross-border incursions orchestrated by the Sudan People's Liberation Army (SPLA) came to an abrupt end in July 2011, when the former rebels became the standing army of the newly independent Republic of South Sudan, thus ending a long civil war between northern and southern Sudan which some people perceive as a struggle of Christians in the south against Muslim oppression from the north.

The presidents of Sudan and South Sudan agreed then on trade, oil and security deals after days of talks in Ethiopia. But it unravelled into ethnic warfare in South Sudan less than two years later, when President Salva Kiir, a member of the majority Dinka group, turned on his former vice president, Riek Machar, a Nuer. Other tribes joined in, setting off a senseless war that has defied numerous agreements and ceasefires.

Beginning in 2017, famine has been declared in parts of South Sudan in what the UN describes as a manmade catastrophe caused by civil war and economic collapse. Tens of thousands of people have died in the conflict and more than two million have fled to neighbouring countries: Uganda is said to harbour more than one million Sudanese refugees, Ethiopia more than 400,000 and Kenya close to 100,000. In addition, almost two million people are internally displaced despite the presence of 17,000 UN peacekeepers in the country.

The rise in refugee numbers around Gambella has also caused the population of overseas aid workers to skyrocket, despite which there have been no recent reported problems involving foreigners in the region.

SECURITY Gambella is among the less stable parts of Ethiopia, and you are advised to check region-specific security warnings posted by the British Foreign and Commonwealth Office (w *https://www.gov.uk/foreign-travel-advice/ethiopia*) and other such institutions before you travel there. The past few years have witnessed sporadic attacks on large industrial farms by local pastoralists who were displaced from their ancestral grazing land to make way for them. The last reported attack of this type took place in the spring of 2014, and such incidents are generally restricted to remote corners of the region. There have also been isolated incidents of violence between militant members of Gambella's native tribes and the migrant highlanders seeking business opportunities in the economically untapped region. This tension has diminished since October 2012, when a bus shooting incident targeting highlanders resulted in a heavy-handed police crackdown on local militants.

One thing you can safely ignore is the unapologetically xenophobic warnings you occasionally hear in Addis Ababa and the western highlands with regard to the backwardness of Gambella's people and their uncivilised behaviour. Gambella could hardly be a friendlier town, and it takes no more than a few hours there to recognise the inaccuracy of such sentiments upon experiencing the town for the first time.

Indeed, its inhabitants typically exude an air of polite confidence when approaching foreigners, helped along by a surprisingly high proficiency in English, and greetings such as 'How's it going man?' or 'What's up brother?' are a welcome relief from the endless barrage of 'You You You!' or 'China!' often hurled at foreigners elsewhere in Ethiopia.

GAMBELLA Gambella is an oddity among Ethiopian towns, and a most appealing one. Lying at an altitude of 450m, the former British and Sudanese river port exudes an atmosphere of tropical languor, dictated by its lush riverine vegetation, its almost unbearable humidity, and by its remoteness from just about everywhere else. This powerful sense of place is underscored by the presence of the Baro River, whose brown waters roll lazily past town to create an almost absurdly accurate fulfilment of every Western archetype of a tropical African river port. Meanwhile, a plethora of white 4x4s, plastered with the logos of pretty much every NGO to be found in Ethiopia, are the most visible sign of the region's South Sudanese refugee population, which is now estimated at more than 200,000, most of them crowded in camps far out of sight but clearly not out of mind for the legion of foreign and local aid workers that currently call Gambella home.

Orientation Part of Gambella's charm lies in its spacious, amorphous layout, but this also makes it quite disorientating on first encounter. Coming from the east, you'll enter the town on an impressive double-lane concrete bridge which leads to a busy central roundabout circled endlessly by a fleet of *bajaji*. The road west from the roundabout leads to the recently relocated bus station and a few convenient clean but basic hotels and restaurants, ending abruptly after 500m and switching from asphalt to a dirt track running parallel to the swampland along the northern bank of the Baro. The road north off the roundabout immediately forks, with the right-hand lane going deeper into downtown Gambella and its bustling market area, while the left (rather straight) fork is the road to Dembidolo. Back at the roundabout, turning east brings you to a crumbling cement staircase on the right-hand side of the road after crossing a small bridge. This descends to a walking-only lane shaded by large fig trees which once was considered the town centre, and is now little more than a cool alley to escape the heat and attention of the main road, lined with a few noisy bars and outdoor cafés which quickly come to an end at the sandy northern shore of the Baro. A Nuer settlement of large and neat thatched huts can be found about 3km east of the roundabout, opposite the cisterns of the fuel depot, on the way to the National Park office. A large daily traditional village market also stands there as an interesting alternative to the more urban equivalent near the Waiza Pension.

Getting there and away Ethiopian Airlines flies in either direction between Addis Ababa and Gambella twice daily. The airport lies 15km out of town off a rough yet periodically maintained dirt road. Ethiopian Airlines has an office in town (\047 551 0099/2637). You can also buy your ticket online (if the internet is working) or by phone with telesales in Addis (if they answer the phone). As a last resort, try your luck by going out to the airport (*US$15 by taxi*). Assuming you have a ticket, the better hotels offer a free shuttle to the airport for the twice-daily flight to Addis.

Last-minute flight changes are commonplace, so visit the office the day before and/or morning of your return flight to get an updated departure time.

By road The most direct road route between Addis Ababa and Gambella is the northern one through Nekemte, and then Bedele and Metu. It is more than 700km long and now surfaced nearly all the way. Best to allow two days to get through in a private vehicle, overnighting in Nekemte. Using public transport, Golden Bus (m *0939 535353*) runs a direct daily coach service from Addis Ababa, taking 14 hours. A crowded public bus to Gambella leaves from the Merkato bus station in Addis Ababa first thing in the morning, overnighting in Bedele.

Gambella can also be approached from the northeast via Dembidolo but, due to security concerns and poor road conditions, public transportation is sparse.

Whether you are coming from Metu or Mizan Tefari, the turn-off to Gambella is at the small junction town of Gore. About 10km past Gore, the road passes through the enormous Gumaro tea plantation, with neatly manicured plants covering the fields into the distance. About 90 minutes out of Gore, the small highland village of Bure is a popular lunch stop for bus drivers. There isn't much to see at Bure today but Alexander Bulatovich, who passed through the village in 1897, mentioned that it lay at the junction of several trade routes and formed 'an important point of barter with tribes on this side of the Baro … and market for coffee'. Bulatovich described how people from the lowlands 'bring for sale elephant tusks and sometimes their livestock, and in exchange for that they buy ornaments, beads and cloth'. From Bure, between the 680km and 700km markers, you plummet more than 1km in altitude into the Baro Valley, a spectacular switchback drive on which every hairpin turn reveals a new perspective of the massive change in landscape between the Ethiopian Highlands and the marshy plains below. There's a corresponding temperature increase of 1°C per 150m downhill drop, making it a whopping 7°C hotter at the base, in an already warm climate.

The road flattens out and follows the course of the muddy Baro River for a while before an obligatory stop at a police checkpoint, where you'll be asked to present your passport and hand over your bags for a less than thorough search before crossing a bridge to enter the Gambella region. Approaching Gambella, the road passes through a thinly populated and primal savannah of acacia scrub and tall clumped grass. Both of these could use a trim as the thorny branches have overcome parts of the road, making it impossible to hang an elbow out of the window to cool off in the oppressive heat, as well as making your hair stand on end when the driver takes a high-speed corner straddling the dividing line while the view of the road ahead is completely obstructed by branches.

Buried somewhere among the vertical granite outcrops eerily protruding from the otherwise flat savannah is the unexpected location of a forgotten bit of American political history. On 7 August 1989, a twin propeller plane carrying US congressman Mickey Leland, a democrat from Texas, and 15 other passengers and crew slammed nose first into one of those peaks during bad weather, leaving no survivors. Reports of the lost plane, a flight from Addis Ababa to the Fugnido refugee camp on the Ethiopia–Sudan border, led to one of the largest American search and rescue missions ever conducted in the developing world. It took 18 aircraft two days to locate the wreckage in the remote area, with the closest site suitable to land a helicopter a trying 3-hour hike from where the plane went down.

Tourist information The Gambella Bureau of Culture and Tourism (⟍ *047 551 2351;* ⊕ *07.30–12.30 & 15.00–17.30 Mon–Fri*) is located in the same building as the excellent library, on the opposite side of the road before you reach the **UNHCR headquarters**. Here you can get information about visiting the national park, as well as surrounding villages including a nearby Anuwak settlement, lakes and waterfalls. The people at the **Gambella National Park office** (⟍*047 551 0912;* ⊕ *07.30–12.30 & 15.00–17.30 Mon–Fri*), located about 500m east of the main roundabout, are very knowledgeable and helpful when it comes to information about exploring outlying parts of Gambella Region. It's also here where you must pay your park fees.

⌂ **Where to stay** *Map, opposite*

⌂ **Grand Resort & Spa** (96 rooms) ⟍047 211 0000/1; m 0913 208268. This recently built 7-storey hotel stands about 100m north of the main roundabout on the right side of the road.

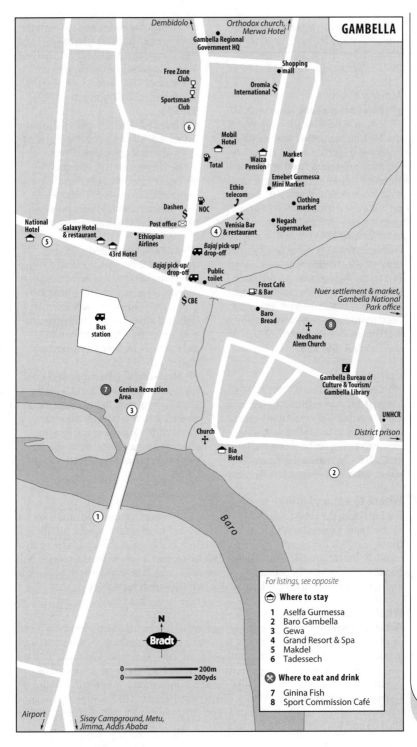

GAMBELLA

Dembidolo ↑
Orthodox church, ↑
Merwa Hotel

Gambella Regional
Government HQ

Shopping
mall

Free Zone
Club

Oromia
International $

Sportsman
Club

⑥

Mobil
Hotel

Market

Total

Waiza
Pension

Emebet Gurmessa
Mini Market

Ethio
telecom

Clothing
market

Dashen $
Post office ✉
NOC

④ Venisia Bar
& restaurant

Negash
Supermarket

National
Hotel

Galaxy Hotel
& restaurant

⑤

Ethiopian
Airlines

Bajaj pick-up/
drop-off

43rd Hotel

Bajaj pick-up/
drop-off

Public
toilet

$ CBE

Frost Café
& Bar

*Nuer settlement & market,
Gambella National
Park office*

Bus
station

Baro
Bread

Medhane
Alem Church

⑧

Gambella Bureau of
Culture & Tourism/
Gambella Library

⑦ Genina Recreation
Area

③

UNHCR

District prison

Church
✝

Bia
Hotel

②

①

Baro

N

Bradt

0 _____ 200m
0 _____ 200yds

Airport
↓

Sisay Campground, Metu,
↓ Jimma, Addis Ababa

For listings, see opposite

⌂ **Where to stay**

1 Aselfa Gurmessa
2 Baro Gambella
3 Gewa
4 Grand Resort & Spa
5 Makdel
6 Tadessech

✖ **Where to eat and drink**

7 Ginina Fish
8 Sport Commission Café

It has a business centre, restaurant, bar, terrace & garden, & offers a free shuttle service to the airport. All rooms have AC & large bathrooms. *US$40/55/70 sgl/twin/deluxe.* **$$$$**

Moderate

🏠 **Baro Gambella Hotel** (45 rooms) ☎ 047 551 0044; **m** 0931 540761; **e** tomyimer@gmail. com. This former government hotel, sometimes abbreviated to BGH Hotel, is set in a potentially very attractive but poorly maintained compound 1km east of the main roundabout after the bridge. It stands close to the north bank of the Baro River, but lacks a view of the water. The extra-large rooms in the new block used to be among the best in Gambella, & now feature AC, making them decent enough value for money. Even if you stay elsewhere, it is a nice place to hang out, with sat TV in the bar, plenty of monkeys & birds roaming the gardens, & an impressive capacity to keep a ready supply of cold beers & soft drinks in the face of regular power cuts & intense natural heat. *US$25 en-suite dbl in the old block, US$50 en-suite king-size with AC.* **$$–$$$**

Budget

🏠 **Gewa Hotel** (41 rooms) ☎ 047 151 1108. Located at the entrance of the Genina Recreation Area close to the bridge over the Baro River, this recently built hotel has comfortable standard rooms with a ceiling fan, hot shower, mosquito net & sat TV. A few more expensive rooms come with AC, but even in the hottest days, the ceiling

fans bring pleasant old-fashioned coolness to the rooms during daytime & can easily be turned off at night. The outdoor restaurant/bar serves excellent & reasonably priced food; the fish cutlets are recommended. *US$9 common shower, US$14/18 en-suite sgl/twin, US$18 sgl en-suite with AC.* **$$–$$$**

🏠 **Tadessech Hotel** (34 rooms) This yellow 2-storey hotel is located opposite the Total filling station on the road to Dembidolo. Dbl rooms all have cold-water en suites, with nets, TV & fan. The rooms are clean & neat around several courtyards, including a recently added outdoor bar & restaurant pleasantly shaded by trellised creeping vines. *US$8 sgl common shower, US$12 en-suite dbl.* **$$**

🏠 **Aselfa Gurmessa Hotel** (10 rooms) **m** 0911 205972. This small hotel down the hill on the left-hand side of the road immediately before the bridge as you enter Gambella is worth a try given its pretty riverside location & attractively landscaped setting. The freshly finished en-suite rooms are light & airy & come complete with tiled floor, sat TV, fan & net. A restaurant/bar is attached. *US$10 dbl.* **$$**

🏠 **Makdel Hotel** (18 rooms) **m** 0926 710245. This brand-new guesthouse located beside the National Hotel is a good choice for public transport travellers, being close to the entrance of the bus station. Behind the compound, the open marshland & forest leading to the riverside is a great spot for birdwatching. *US$10 en-suite sgl/ dbl.* **$$**

✕ Where to eat and drink *Map, page 623*

For breakfast, the hard-to-find café attached to the sport commission office, known as the **Sport Commission Café**, is well known for its excellent special *ful*. It's also the only choice for an early-morning departure as it's one of the few places open at 05.30. At lunchtime, the shady **Ginina Fish Restaurant** is sure to please, serving Nile perch, catfish or tilapia, depending on the day's catch. The fish is priced by the kilo and served either whole or filleted and mixed with fresh vegetables.

What to see and do

Around town Gambella's main attraction is its singular and absorbing sense of place. Specific points of interest include the isolated hilltop Orthodox church about 1km north of the town centre, and the cool and quiet Gambella Library, which comes as quite a surprise with its varied selection of English-language novels and classic literature. Strange though it may sound, it is worth visiting the Gambella Town and District Prison, 200m west of the UNHCR compound, as good handicrafts made on-site by the prisoners are available for sale. Cameras are not allowed and women must be 'suitably attired' (ie: no shorts!).

The town supports a surprising amount of wildlife, and its layout is such that just strolling around you can see plenty of birds and monkeys. It is worth devoting some time to the bridge over the Baro, although taking pictures of it from afar or from its railing is strictly prohibited. To the west of the bridge is a shady avenue that follows the river's course. During the rainy season this serves as the unofficial mango marketplace, where you can buy fresh fruit from immense piles on the ground while the same product may fall from one of the many trees overhead and land on your head. Just past this, the recreation area known as Ginina comprises a riverside cluster of outdoor coffee shops, as well as the Ginina Fish Restaurant, a great place to try the day's fresh catch, followed by a sweet coffee or tea, under the shade of the mango trees. The riverbank downriver of the bridge is also a regular haunt of the Egyptian plover, an eagerly sought bird with a very limited distribution in Ethiopia.

Local people wash and swim in the river without apparent concern, but every now and again somebody is taken by a crocodile, so it would definitely be chancy to leap into the water in areas not used by locals. The people of Gambella will still caution travellers with the sad story of Bill Olsen, the Peace Corps volunteer who took a holiday in Gambella in 1966, ignored local advice about a large crocodile known to live in a certain part of the river, and was never seen alive again. On the whole, better to stick to your hotel shower than to tempt a similar fate by leaping into the muddy Baro!

Sisay Campground (☎ *047 551 2047*; m *0917 804811*) If you have an urge to venture into the seemingly endless bush surrounding Gambella, but a trip to the park isn't possible, try this pristine campground, which lies on a bend in the river about 45 minutes out of town along the main road back to Bure, just before reaching a village called Bonga. A private venture developed in collaboration with the Gambella National Park team, this shady, well-manicured campsite has a beautiful isolated riverfront location, and the friendly owner is more than accommodating to a visitor's every want and need. A rope strung across the river and a handsome dugout canoe moored to the exposed roots of an old fig tree have been set up to ferry adventurous campers across the water to a heavily wooded private peninsula for exploring and spotting monkeys and birds. A single large tent is available to rent, as well as two small dirt-floored grass huts styled after local tribal shelters. Two vehicles are at your disposal to get back and forth from town and to transport supplies, as well as a couple of large cooler boxes to fill with any food/drinks you wish to purchase in town and bring out to the site. At your request – and expense – you can even arrange an evening campfire and whole sheep roast with the 24-hour guard and staff doing all the preparation and cooking. As the operation is brand new and hasn't seen any tourist traffic, it isn't quite clear if there is even a fee to camp, but all other services including transportation, food and equipment are priced at cost. Make arrangements well in advance through email at e traveltogambellateam@ gmail.com, or the contact numbers listed above.

GAMBELLA NATIONAL PARK [map, page 444] (*National Park office;* ☎ *047 551 0912; entrance US$4.50 pp/day, US$1/vehicle, US$12.50 for a guide, US$12.50 for a scout*) The country's largest protected area at 5,060km², the remote and little-known Gambella National Park also hosts Africa's second-largest antelope migration, which entails an estimated 1.2 million white-eared kob (a regional endemic) crossing from South Sudan into Ethiopia for around three months annually, usually arriving in March and departing in June. The park is also one of the last strongholds for the endangered Nubian giraffe, and it supports substantial numbers of buffalo, tiang, roan antelope, Nile lechwe, Lelwel hartebeest, olive baboon, patas monkey and guereza, along with seldom-seen relict populations of African elephant and lion (a recent helicopter survey counted only six of the latter). In addition, the park has been classified as a Level One Important Bird Area by BirdLife International, with 327 bird species recorded, many rare or endangered. Most notable perhaps is Ethiopia's only population of the elusive and weird-looking shoebill stork. Other interesting and unusual species include the country's only population of the localised Uelle paradise whydah, the lovely red-throated and little green bee-eaters, as well as black-faced firefinch, red-necked buzzard, Egyptian plover, African skimmer and several localised but drab cisticolas and other warblers.

Despite its impressive credentials as a top wildlife destination, Gambella National Park has been little more than a 'paper park' – marked off and labelled on a map, but with little or no conservation activity on the ground – since it was gazetted in 1973. Today, that looks set to change, as the park stands at a pivotal point in its more than 40-year existence. Fresh work undertaken by the park staff in collaboration with Addis Ababa University's Horn of Africa Research Centre over the past few years, together with a new partnership with African Parks Network, an international NGO which rehabilitates and maintains large parks all over the continent, means that this vast expanse of marshy savannah is finally getting the attention it deserves from conservation experts, who hope that this will in turn lead to more interest from tourists. For now, the park lacks any tourist infrastructure worth talking about (access roads are suited to 4x4s only, and accommodation options amount to DIY camping), but already offers much to tempt truly adventurous and suitably equipped travellers, and the potential for proper development is enormous.

Around the park According to the helpful warden, the best area for game viewing is Matara, which lies 185km west of Gambella town along a road running through the village of Inwany on the southern bank of the Baro. White-eared kob are likely to seen around Matara, while the nearby Duma wetlands are a good spot to search for the regionally endemic Nile lechwe. The distance from town and the poor condition of the road mean that you would need a reliable 4x4 to get there, and should plan on camping rough for at least one night. You'd also need to bring all your own food and drink, and arrange a game scout and possibly an armed guard through the National Park office. Expect to pay around US$150–200, including 4x4 hire, for a long day safari, depending on group size.

Less challenging would be to head south to the small towns of Abobo and Pifmwedo, which lie on the recently redrawn eastern boundary of the national park, 42km and 105km respectively from Gambella town. Although animals might be seen anywhere in this area (or, for that matter, nowhere), one worthwhile stop just a few kilometres from Abobo is at the Alwero Dam. Abobo has a few basic lodgings, and can be reached by public transport (currently only on Mondays and Fridays, when there is a convoy to tie in with the local market). Further south, Agenga can be reached in about 3 hours in a private 4x4 and has been earmarked as the site of the new national park headquarters, but is currently of limited interest in terms of wildlife-viewing possibilities. Also of interest is the very scenic Lake Tata, which lies off the road between Pifmwedo and Pachala. Occasional buses from Gambella to Gog via Abobo can drop you at the gravel junction to Lake Tata, from where it's less than an hour on foot to the shore. To visit the **Anuwak village** that lies alongside the lake you'll need to arrange a permit and guide at the tourist office in Gambella, as well as paying an entrance fee decided by the village leaders.

Another possibility would be to follow the new asphalt road that runs west, parallel to the Baro River skirting the northern border of the park, from Gambella to the South Sudanese border at Jikou. This takes you through an area inhabited by Anuwak fishermen and Nuer pastoralists whose lifestyles are virtually untouched by Western influences. This unspoiled atmosphere has been slightly eroded by the presence of two giant new refugee camps along the road. Each camp houses 50,000 people and has created its own mini town on the main road where entrepreneurial locals have set up makeshift shops fashioned from UNHCR tarpaulins. The traditional Gambella lifestyle could until recently be seen at the sprawling village of Itang, which stands on the northern bank of the Baro some 7km south of the Jikou road along a feeder road 50km from Gambella. These days, however, the village itself has lost much of its character (presumably due to the NGO dollar), but it does have a fine local fish restaurant! A more interesting option from Itang is to cross the river by dugout canoe and visit the more traditional village on the other side.

At least one bus connects Gambella and Itang daily, taking about 2 hours in either direction, and a couple of shops around the busy traditional market serve tea and basic food. There is little or no accommodation, so you would need to ask around for a bed in a local dwelling or make arrangements to camp at the police station. The area is rich in birds not easily seen elsewhere in Ethiopia, and there is some wildlife around (most visibly bushbuck, oribi and baboon). It is also potentially volatile, due to its location on the South Sudanese border, so do make enquiries before heading off – especially if you intend to continue onwards to the border village of Jikou.

Appendix 1

With thanks to Yared Belete of Grant Express Travel & Tours Services (GETTS)

LANGUAGE

Amharigna (pronounced Amharinya and more often known outside the country as Amharic) is a Semitic language that derives from Ge'ez, the language of the Axumites and the Ethiopian Orthodox Church to this day. Amharigna is the first language of the Amhara people who live in north-central Ethiopia. Along with English, Amharigna is still the official language of Ethiopia and is thus the language most often used between Ethiopians of different linguistic backgrounds, performing a similar role to that of Swahili in the rest of east Africa.

In practical terms, you will find that most Ethiopians who have been to high school speak passable, if idiosyncratic, English, though in many cases they get little opportunity to use it, and so are rather rusty. Except in Tigray and remote rural areas, almost everyone speaks some Amharigna, and – unless you stay exclusively in tourist hotels – you will find it difficult to get by without a few basic phrases. People are often very surprised and responsive if you can speak a few words of the language. If you spend a while in Tigray, and in Oromifa-speaking parts of southern Ethiopia (which includes the Rift Valley and most points east of it), it can be helpful to know a few words of the local tongue. In Tigray, the response to a tourist who can say even one Tigrigna phrase is less one of surprise than of total astonishment. It really is worth making the effort.

AMHARIGNA The section that follows is not meant to be a comprehensive introduction to Amharigna. A cheap and light grammar and mini dictionary, *Amharic for Foreigners* by Semere Woldegabir, is readily available in Addis Ababa and recommended to natural linguists who want to get to grips with the complex grammar and sentence construction of Amharigna, or the intricacies of pronunciation. My experience, however, suggests that most visitors will find this book more daunting than helpful and that the few basic phrases they need to know are buried beneath reams of detail that are of little use to somebody with no long-term interest in becoming fluent in the language. Better to carry Lonely Planet's *Amharic* phrasebook.

What follows is essentially the pidgin Amharigna I picked up over four months in the country. Most of this came not from books, which invariably confused me, but from English-speaking Ethiopians with a natural sympathy for the difficulties of learning a language from scratch. It could be argued that I should be getting a fluent Amharigna-speaker to write this. I would disagree: it is not difficult to get by in Amharigna, but only if you ignore its grammatical complications. I simply don't speak enough Amharigna to be able to complicate it, and what little I do speak was learnt the hard way. It is difficult to imagine that many tourists to Ethiopia will need more Amharigna than the simplified version that follows. If, after a couple of weeks, you exhaust what I learnt in four months, it only strengthens the case for keeping things simple.

But I do apologise to Amharigna speakers for any liberties that I might have taken with their language; my only excuse is that whatever errors might follow stood me in good stead during my time in Ethiopia; my only rejoinder is that you do some utterly bemusing things to my home language, and I would never let 'correctness' override the will to communicate.

It is worth noting that there is often no simple and correct English transcription of Amharigna words, as evidenced by such extremes of spelling as Woldio/Weldiya, Mekele/Maqale, Zikwala/Zouquela and even Addis Ababa/Adees Abeba. Generally, I have spelt Amharigna words as they sound to me. People who are unfamiliar with African languages should be aware that Amharigna, like most other African languages, is pronounced phonetically – the town name Bore is not pronounced like boar, but *Bor-ay*.

The magic word The one word that every visitor to Ethiopia should know is *ishee*. This is the sort of word that illustrates the gap between 'proper' grammar/dictionaries and the realities of being in a new country and trying to assimilate the language quickly. *Ishee*, more or less, means OK but (not unlike the English equivalent) it can be used in a variety of circumstances: as an alternative to the myriad ways of saying hello or goodbye, to signal agreement, to reassure people, etc. This is not just a foreigner's shortcut – *ishee* is the single most spoken word in Ethiopia, and I have often heard entire conversations that apparently consist of nothing more than two Ethiopians bouncing *ishees* backwards and forwards. Of course *ishee* is a colloquial word – but most people aren't out to take offence and they understand the problems facing foreigners who can't speak the local language; a foreigner smiling and saying the word *ishee* is as acceptable a signal of goodwill or friendliness as would be a foreigner smiling and saying 'OK' in Britain. Another useful catchphrase in some situations is *chigger yellem* – no problem. And, incidentally, 'OK' is also widely used in Ethiopia.

Greetings and farewells Useful all-purpose greetings are *tadias* and *tenayistillign*, which basically mean 'hello, how are you?' These are common greetings that can be used with anyone and on all occasions. In many parts of the country, the Arabic greeting *selam* (literally 'peace') is in common use. To ask how somebody is, ask *dehnaneh?* to a male and *dehnanesh?* to a female. The correct response, always, is *dehena*, pronounced more like '*dena*' or *dehnanegn* – I am well. There are tens of other greetings, depending on the time of day and the sex and number of people you are speaking to. There is little need for visitors to learn these greetings. If you want to anticipate them being used on you, all you need know is that they invariably start with the phrase *indemin-* and the correct response is invariably *dehena*. There are just as many ways of saying goodbye or farewell – *dehnahunu* or *chau* (adopted from and pronounced like the Italian *ciao*) is fine in most circumstances. Ethiopians often precede their *chau* with an *ishee*!

Some essentials The first barrier to be crossed when you travel in linguistically unfamiliar surroundings is to learn how to ask a few basic questions and to understand the answers. The answers first: *awo* means yes and *aydelem* means no. In casual use, these are often shortened to *aw* (pronounced like the 'ou' in our) and *ay* (pronounced like eye). Some Ethiopians replace their *aw* with a rather startling inhalation of breath.

In general travel-type queries, you'll often use and hear the words *aleh* (there is) and *yellem* (there is not). To find out if a place serves coffee (*buna*), you would ask *buna aleh?* The response should be *aleh* or *yellem*.

Once you have established that what you want is in the *aleh* state, you can ask for it by saying *ifelegalehu* (I want). More often, Ethiopians will just say what they want and how many – *and buna* (one coffee) or *hulet birra* (two beers). It is not customary to accompany your request with an *ibakih* or *ibakesh* (please, to a male and female respectively), but you should always say *ameseghinalehu* (thank you) when you get what you asked for. The response to thank you is *minimaydelem* (you're welcome).

629

If you don't want something – like, say, the green comb that a street hawker is thrusting in your face – then say *alfelagem* or simply shake your head. If this makes little impression, you can say *hid* (go) to children, or anyone who is obviously much younger than you, but you shouldn't really say something that overtly offish to an adult.

In Amharigna, the word *no* (pronounced like the English know) means something roughly equivalent to 'is'. In Amharigna conversations, Ethiopians often interject a *no* much as we might say 'true' or 'really'. Needless to say, this can cause a certain amount of confusion if you say 'no' to somebody who isn't familiar with English – they may well assume you are saying 'yes'.

The word for 'where' is *yet*, from which derive the questions *yetno?* (where is?), *wedetno?* (to where?) and *keyetno?* (from where?). The word for 'what' is *min*, which gives you *mindeno?* (what is it?), *lemin?* (why?), *minaleh?* (what is there?) and *indet?* (how?). *Meche?* means 'when?', which gives you *mecheno?* (when is it?); *man?* means 'who?'; and *sintno?* means 'how much?'.

Simple questions can be formed by prefixing the above phrases with a subject. Some examples:

Awtobus yemihedow?	Where is this bus going?
Migib minaleh?	What food is there?
Alga aleh?	Is there a room? (*alga* literally means 'bed')
Postabet yetno?	Where is the post office?
Wagaw sintno?	How much does it cost?
Sa'at sintno?	What (literally 'how much') is the time?
Simih mano?	What is your name? (male)
Simish mano?	What is your name? (female)
Hisap sintno?	How much is the bill?

Some useful Amharigna words

after/later	*behuwala*	come (male)	*na*
afternoon	*kesa'at behuwala*	correct	*lik*
again	*indegena*	cost	*waga*
and	*na*	(make a discount)	(*waga kenis*)
at	*be*	country (or region)	*ager*
bad	*metfo*	cow	*lam*
banana	*muz*	dirty	*koshasha*
beautiful	*konjo*	donkey	*ahiya*
bed	*alga*	egg	*inkulal*
beef	*yebere siga*	enough	*beki*
beer	*birra*	(enough!)	(*beka!*)
before	*befit*	Ethiopian	*Habesha* or *Ityopyawi*
bicycle	*bisikleet*	excuse (me)	*yikirta*
big	*tilik*	far	*ruk*
bus	*awtobus*	fast	*fetan*
but	*gin*	first	*andegna* or
car (or any motor	*mekeena*		*mejemerya*
vehicle)		fish	*asa*
cart	*gari*	food	*migib*
cent (or just money)	*santeem*	foreigner	*faranji*
chicken	*doro*	glass	*birchiko*
church	*bet kristyan*	go	*hid*
clean	*nitsuh*	good	*tiru*
coffee	*buna*	he	*issu*
cold	*kezkaza*	help	*irdugn*
come (female)	*ney*	here	*izih*

horse	*feres*	quickly	*tolo*
hospital	*hakim bet*	region	*bota*
hour	*sa'at*	restaurant	*migib bet*
house (or		river	*wenz*
building)	*bet*	road	*menged*
I	*ine*	room	*kifil*
in	*wust*	salt	*chew*
insect	*tebay*	sea	*bahir*
island	*desiet*	she	*iswa*
key	*kulf*	shop	*suk*
lake	*hayk*	short	*achir*
little	*tinish*	shower	*showa* or
luggage	*gwaz* or *shanta*		*metatebia bet*
me	*inay*	sleep	*inkilf*
meat	*siga*	slowly	*kes*
milk	*wotet*	small	*tinish*
money	*genzeb*	sorry	*aznallehu*
morning	*tiwat*	stop	*akum*
mountain	*terara*	sugar	*sukwar*
Mr	*Ato*	tall	*rejim*
Mrs	*Weyzero*	tea	*shai*
Miss	*Weyzerit*	thank you	formally,
much	*bizu*		*ameseghinalehu*, but
mutton	*yebeg siga*		*ishi* usually fine
near	*atageb* or *kirb*	there	*iza*
newspaper	*gazeta*	they	*innessu*
nice	*tiru*	ticket	*karnee* or *ticket*
night	*lelit*	today	*zare*
now	*ahun*	toilet	*shintabet*
of	*ye*	tomorrow	*nege*
or	*weyim*	very	*betam*
orange	*birtukan*	warm	*muk*
peace	*selam*	water	*wuha*
petrol	*benzeen*	yesterday	*tilant*
pig	*asama*	you (female)	*anchee*
problem	*chigger*	you (male)	*ante*

Numbers

1	*and*	20	*haya*
2	*hulet*	25	*haya amist* (*hamist*)
3	*sost*	30	*selasa*
4	*arat*	40	*arba*
5	*amist*	50	*hamsa*
6	*siddist*	60	*silsa*
7	*sabat*	70	*seba*
8	*simint*	80	*semagnya*
9	*zetegn*	90	*zetena*
10	*asir*	100	*meto*
11	*asra and*	200	*hulet meto*
12	*asra hulet*	1,000	*shee*
		1,000,000	*meelyon*

Days of the week

Sunday	*Ihud*	Thursday	*Hamus*
Monday	*Segno*	Friday	*Arb*
Tuesday	*Maksegno*	Saturday	*Kidame*
Wednesday	*Irob*		

Festivals

New Year	*Inkutatash*	Easter	*Fasika*
Christmas	*Gena*		

Time

See box, page 92.

TIGRIGNA Many people in Tigray speak no Amharigna, so a few words of the local language – which shares many words with Amharigna as the two are both derived from Ge'ez – might be useful:

bad	*himek*	milk	*tsaba*
banana	*mu-uz*	nice	*dehan*
beautiful	*gondjo*	no	*nanai*
black	*tselim*	No	*Yechone*
border	*dob*	OK	*hirai*
bus	*shishento*	rain	*zenab*
chicken	*dorho*	red	*kaje*
coffee	*buna*	room (in hotel)	*madakasi*
come (female)	*ne'e*	sick	*houmoum*
come (male)	*na'a*	tea	*shai*
egg	*unkulale*	thank you	*yekanyelay*
excuse me	*yikerta*	The coffee tastes good	*Oo-oum buna*
fine	*tsebuk*		
food	*migbi*	This way	*Uzi*
go	*kid*	today	*lomo anti*
good	*tsbuk*	toilet	*shintebet*
goodbye	*selamat* or *daahankun*	tomorrow	*naga*
hello	*selam*	water	*mai*
here	*hausi*	What is your name?	*Shimka men yoe?*
How are you? (female)	*Kemayla-hee?*	where?	*lave?*
		white	*tsada*
How are you? (male)	*Kemayla-ha?*	yes	*ouwa*
How much?	*Kendai?*	yesterday	*tsbah*
is there …?	*alo …?*		

Numbers

1	*hada*	6		*shidista*
2	*kilita*	7		*showata*
3	*salista*	8		*shimwunta*
4	*arbata*	9		*tishiata*
5	*hamishte*	10		*aseta*

OROMIFA Oromifa is the main language of southern Ethiopia, spoken throughout the Federal State of Oromia. Unlike Amharigna, it is transcribed using familiar Roman letters, though with little consistency in spelling. In theory, the consonants are doubled to denote a stress (with *manna*, for instance, you would stress the 'n') while doubled vowels denote that the sound of that vowel should be longer than a single vowel. In practice, the application of the doubled letter seems rather more arbitrary – one signpost in any given town might read 'hotela' (hotel), another 'hootteellaa', and others different variants thereof. There is no overwhelming need to speak any Oromifa – everybody in this area speaks some Amharigna – other than the delight that it will give Oromifa speakers to hear a *faranji* speak their language.

Some Oromifa words and phrases

again	*ammas, lammaffaa*	man	*dira*
bar	*manna buna*	market	*gabaaya/gabaa*
black	*guracha*	mineral water	*bishaan amo*
brown	*magala*	money	*qarshi*
bus	*awtobisii*	mosquito	*bookee busaa*
business	*daldala*	mother	*haadha*
buy	*bituu*	mountain	*tullu*
child	*muca*	no (I do not)	*wawu/laki*
church building	*mana kadhataa*	no problem	*rakkon hin jiru*
coffee	*buna*	now	*amma*
cost	*gati*	office	*wajira*
Did you understand?	*Isini galeeraa?*	please	*maaloo*
		police	*polisii*
Do you speak English?	*Afaan faranji ni beektaa?*	post office	*mana posta*
		quantity	*baay'ina*
drink	*dhugi*	red	*dima*
early	*dafee*	restaurant	*mana nyaataa*
eat	*nyaadhu*	road	*daandii, karaa*
enter	*deenaa*	room	*kutaa*
far	*fagoo*	shop	*sukii*
father	*abba*	sister	*obboleettii*
fire	*ibidda*	tea	*shaayii*
friend	*michu*	thank you	*galatoomi/ galatoomaa*
go	*deemuu*		
goodbye	*nagaan turi*	there	*achi*
green	*magarisa*	today	*har'a*
grey	*dalacha*	toilet	*mana fincaanii*
hello	*ashamaa/akkam/ attam*	tomorrow	*booru*
		traveller	*kara-adeemtuu*
here	*as*	village	*ganda*
hotel	*hoteela/ mana keessummaa*	water	*bishaan*
		We are visitors	*Nuyi duwwattoota*
house	*mana/manna*	What is your name?	*Maqaan kee eenyu?*
How are you?	*Attam jirta/jirtu?*	when	*yoom*
How much? (price)	*Mega?*	Where is it?	*Eessa?/Eessa dha?*
I am fine	*Nagaa/Fayyaa*	white	*adi*
lady	*gifti*	woman	*dubartii*
lake	*garba*	yellow	*kelloo*
late	*yeroo dabarsuu*	yes (I do)	*eeyyee*
light	*ibsaa*		

Days of the week

Sunday	*Dilbata*	Thursday	*Kamsa*
Monday	*Wiixata*	Friday	*Jimata*
Tuesday	*Kibxata*	Saturday	*Sanbata*
Wednesday	*Roobii*		

Numbers

1	*toko*	12	*kudha-lama*
2	*lama*	20	*digdama*
3	*sadi*	30	*sodoma*
4	*afur*	40	*afurtama*
5	*shan*	50	*shantama*
6	*jaha*	60	*jaatama*
7	*torba*	70	*torbatama*
8	*saddet*	80	*saddeettama*
9	*sagal*	90	*sagaltama*
10	*kudha*	100	*dhiba*
11	*kudha-tokko*	1,000	*kuma*

SPEAKING ENGLISH TO ETHIOPIANS As you learn to speak a bit of Amharigna, you will generally find your skill at communicating in the language is largely dependent on the imagination and empathy of the person you are speaking to. The moment some people realise you know a few words, they will speak to you as if you are fluent and make you feel thoroughly hopeless. Other people will take care to speak slowly and to stick to common words, and as a result you feel as if you're making real progress. The same principle applies in reverse and, as a result, many Ethiopians find it easier to communicate in English with native French- or Italian-speakers than they do with native English-speakers.

Communicating with Ethiopians is not just about learning Amharigna, but also about pitching your use of English to reflect Ethiopian idiosyncrasies of pronunciation, grammar and vocabulary. In other words, the English-language communication skills of any Ethiopian you meet will partly be dependent on *your* empathy and imagination.

The first and most obvious rule is to speak slowly and clearly. If you are not understood at first, don't simply repeat the same phrase but instead look for different, less complex ways of conveying the same idea.

A good way of getting a feel for pronunciation is to look at the English transcription of Amharigna words that were initially borrowed from English – *meelyon* (million), *giroseri* (grocery) or *keelometer* (kilometre). A common tendency is to make more emphatic vowel sounds. Another tendency, presumably because few Ethiopian words have consonants without a vowel in between, is to drop things like the 'r' in import (so it sounds like *impot*), or else to insert a vowel sound – often an 'ee' or 'i' – between consonants (I pointed one Ethiopian girl towards the market when she asked for a *pinipal*; it was only when she took out a pen and paper I realised it was a pen pal and not a pineapple she was after).

Remember, too, that there is always a tendency to use the grammatical phrasing of your home tongue when you speak a second language. For instance, an Ethiopian might ask you 'time how much?', which is a direct translation of *sa'at sintno?* They are more likely to understand *you* if you say 'time how much?' – or at least keep your question as straightforward as possible, for instance 'what is the time?' – than if you ask something more embroidered like 'do you happen to have the time on you?' Many English-speakers are inclined to fluff straightforward queries to strangers with apologetic phrasing like 'I'm terribly sorry' or 'could you tell me'. In an Ethiopian context, this sort of thing just obstructs communication.

You will find that certain common English words are readily understood by Ethiopians, while other equally common words draw a complete blank. The Amharigna word *bet* literally means 'house', but it is used to describe any building or even a room, so that a *postabet* is a post office, a *buna bet* is a coffee shop, and a *shintabet* is a toilet. You will thus find that Ethiopians often use the English word 'house' in a much looser context than we would. Another example of this is the phrase 'it is possible', which for some reason has caught on almost everywhere in Africa. 'It is possible to find a bus?' is more likely to be understood than 'do you know if there is a bus?' Likewise, 'is not possible' is a more commonly used phrase than 'it is impossible'.

This sort of thing occurs on an individual level as well as a general one. One Ethiopian friend used the word 'disturb' to cover every imaginable simile of the word. If a phrase like 'I am angry about this' or 'this is really noisy' didn't click, then 'I am much disturb over this' certainly would. Another middle-aged friend kept referring to a girl in her late teens as his parent – presumably he meant cousin. One young Ethiopian who befriended me kept talking about my family (he must have said 'I think you have good family' 50 times); it took me some time to realise that the family to which he was referring was in fact the hotel where I was staying. The point being not only to attune yourself to the nuances of English as it is spoken in Ethiopia, but also to pick up on the words favoured by individuals, and to try to stick to words you have heard them use.

Finally, you should be aware that when Ethiopians ask you to play with them, they only want to talk. This one has all sorts of potential for misunderstandings. I was thrown a little on my first night in Addis when a bar girl (local euphemism for prostitute) sat down at my table and suggested 'we play?' A woman travelling on her own might – understandably to us, but not to the enquirer – respond rather curtly to such a suggestion. This is because the Amharigna phrase used in the same situation – *techawot* (say something) – is the imperative of both *mechewawot* (talk) and *mechawot* (play)!

SOME ETHIOPIAN TRANSCRIPTIONS OF PLACE NAMES

Abiy Addi	አቢአዲ	Bati	ባቲ
Adadi	አዳዲ	Bedele	በደሌ
Adama/Nazret	አዳማ/ናዝሬት	Bilbilla	ቢልቢላ
Addis Ababa/Finfine	አዲስ አበባ/ፍንፍኔ	Bishoftu/Debre Zeyit	ቢሾፍቱ/ደብረዘይት
Addis Alem	አዲስ አለም	Butajira	ቡታጅራ
Adi Arkay	አዲ አርቃይ	Chencha	ጨንጫ
Adigrat	አዲግራት	Debark	ደባርቀ
Adwa	አድዋ	Debre Berhan	ደብረብርሃን
Akaki	አቃቂ	Debre Markos	ደብረማርቆስ
Alem Katema	አለም ከተማ	Debre Sina	ደብረሲና
Aliyu Amba	አልዩ አምባ	Debre Tabor	ደብረታቦር
Ambo	አምቦ	Dembidolo	ደምቢዶሎ
Ankober	አንኮበር	Dessie	ደሲ
Arba Minch	አርባ ምንጭ	Dilla	ዲላ
Arero	አረሮ	Dinsho	ዲንሾ
Arsi Negele	አርሲ ነገሌ	Dire Dawa	ድሬዳዋ
Asaita	አሳይታ	Djibouti	ጅቡቲ
Asela	አሰላ	Dodola	ዶዶላ
Atsbi	አጽቢ	Dola Mena	ዶሎመና
Awash	አዋሽ	Entoto	እንጦጦ
Axum	አክሱም	Fiche	ፍቼ
Babile	ባቢሌ	Gambella	ጋምቤላ
Bahir Dar	ባህር ዳር	Gefersa	ገፈርሳ

Goba	ጎባ	Negele	ነገሌ
Gondar	ጎንደር	Nekemte	ነቀምቴ
Gorgora	ጎርጎራ	Robe	ሮቢ
Harar	ሐረር	Sekota	ሰቆጣ
Hawassa	አዋሳ	Sela Dingay	ሰላድንጋይ
Hawzen	ሐውዜን	Senkele	ሰንቀሌ
Hayk	ሃይቅ	Shashemene	ሻሽመኔ
Hosanna	ሆሳእና	Shire Inda Selassie	ሽሬእንዳስላሴ
Jijiga	ጅጅጋ	Silté	ስልጤ
Jimma	ጅማ	Simien	ሰሜን
Jinka	ጅንካ	Sinkata	ሰንቃጣ
Karat/Konso	ካራት/ኮንሶ	Sodere	ሶደሬ
Kebre Mengist	ክብረመንግሥት	Sodo/Walaita	ሶዶ/ወላይታ
Kombolcha	ኮምቦልቻ	Sof Omar	ሶፍኡመር
Kosober/Injibara	ኮሶበር/እንጅብራ	Tarmabir	ጣርማበር
Lalibela	ላሊበላ	Tiya	ጢያ
Maichew	ማይጨው	Welkite	ወልቂጤ
Mega	ሜጋ	Woldia	ወልድያ
Mehal Meda	መሐል ሜዳ	Woliso	ወሊሶ
Mekele	መቀሌ	Wondo Genet	ወንዶገነት
Metehara	መተሐራ	Wukro	ውቅሮ
Metu	መቱ	Yabello	ያቤሎ
Mille	ሚሌ	Yeha	የሃ
Mizan Tefari	ሚዛን ተፈሪ	Zege	ዘጌ
Modjo	ሞጆ	Zikwala	ዝቋላ
Nechisar	ነጭሳር	Ziway	ዝዋይ
Negash	ነጋሽ		

Appendix 2

GENERAL GLOSSARY

Abba	Father (priest)
Abuna	The title of the metropolitan bishop, or head of the Ethiopian Orthodox Church
Amba	Hill or mountain with flat top, often the site of a monastery or church
Ambo	Fizzy bottled mineral water, named after the town from where it is sourced
Amharigna	Amharic, language of the Amhara people and national language of Ethiopia
Animist	Religion worshipping ancestors and/or animate objects (plants, animals)
Ato	Mister
Autobus (terra)	Bus (station)
Bet	Literally 'house', often used to denote a shop (eg: *buna bet* = coffee shop)
Beta Israel	Ethiopian group who practise an archaic form of Judaism
Bet Kristian	Church
Buna	Coffee
Coptic Church	Alexandria-based Church affiliated to but not synonymous with Ethiopian Orthodox Church
Derg	Military socialist dictatorship 1974–91
Endemic	Bird or mammal found only in one country
Enset	Type of plantain (false banana) grown widely in southern Ethiopia
Falasha	Derogatory term for the Beta Israel
Ful	Popular vegetarian breakfast dish, often very garlicky
Gabbi	Plain off-white cotton cloth worn toga-like by rural Ethiopian men, particularly in the north
Galla	Obsolete term for people now known as the Oromo
Gari	Horse-drawn cart used for carrying goods and passengers
Ge'ez	Archaic language, used in Ethiopian Church, root of Amharigna
Ghebbi	Palace or large house
Injera	Vast pancake made from fermented *tef*, the staple diet of Ethiopians
Itegue	Empress/Princess
Khat	Mildly narcotic leaf chewed in vast quantities in Muslim areas
Kidus	Saint
Kitfo	Local delicacy made with minced meat, often raw or very lightly cooked

Maize	Corn
Mana/Manna	Oromifa equivalent of Amharigna 'bet' (eg: *manna buna* = coffee house/shop)
Merkato	Market
Meskel	Cross; also the name of a religious ceremony and yellow flower
Monolithic church	Rock-hewn church standing free from the surrounding rock on all four sides
Monotheistic	One god; used to describe the Judaic faiths: Christianity, Islam and Judaism
Negus	King
Netela	Cotton cloth similar to *gabbi*, but with embroidered edge, worn by women
Nine Saints	5th–6th-century saints who were largely responsible for spread of Christianity beyond Axum
Oromifa	Language spoken by the Oromo people
Ras	Prince
Selassie	Trinity
Semi-monolithic church	Rock-hewn church standing free from the rock on three sides
Shai	Tea
Shama	White cloth worn toga-like by Ethiopian women
Shifta	Bandit
Stele (pl: stelae)	A standing stone or obelisk, usually marking a grave in Ethiopia
Tabot	Replica of the Ark of the Covenant that sanctifies an Ethiopian church
Tankwa	Papyrus boat
Tef	Grain endemic to the Ethiopian Highlands
Tej	Meadlike alcoholic drink made from honey or sugar
Tella	Thick low-alcohol 'beer' made from millet or barley
Tholoh	Tigrayan dish of barley balls dunked fondue-style in a spicy sauce
Tukul	Round thatched traditional house
Wat	Sauce, often spicy, eaten with *injera*
Waziro	Mrs

GLOSSARY OF KEY HISTORICAL AND LEGENDARY FIGURES IN ETHIOPIA

Following the Ethiopian custom, Ethiopian figures are listed by their name, not by their father's name. In the text, the titles 'Emperor' and 'King' are occasionally used interchangeably, in reference to particular heads of state.

Abadir Umar Arrida	13th-century sheikh regarded to be the holiest saint of Harar
Abba Jiffar II	Powerful late-19th-century ruler of Jimma
Abiy Ahmed	Prime Minister of Ethiopia who assumed office in April 2018
Abraha we Atsbeha	4th-century twin emperors of Axum who adopted these names after converting to Christianity
Afewerk Tekle	Ethiopia's leading post-World War II artist with noted works in St George Cathedral and Africa Hall in Addis Ababa
Afse, Abba	5th–6th century, one of the Nine Saints, founded church in Yeha
Ahmed Gragn	16th-century Muslim leader who waged jihad against Christian empire

Álvares, Francisco	16th-century Portuguese priest who spent a decade in Ethiopia, visiting Lalibela and other important sites
Aregawi, Abba	5th–6th century, one of the Nine Saints, founded Debre Damo Monastery
Arwe	Legendary serpent king of pre-Judaic cult of Axum area, killed by a royal ancestor of the Queen of Sheba
Aster Aweke	Popular modern Ethiopian female singer, now based in USA
Athanasius	4th-century Patriarch of Egyptian Coptic Church who baptised Frumentius and died a refugee in Ethiopia
Bani al-Hamuya	10th-century queen, led attack on Axum, often identified with Gudit, more likely from pagan Damot Empire
Basen	Important Axumite king, ruled at about the time of Christ
Bruce, James	18th-century Scottish explorer who travelled widely in Ethiopia, credited with finding source of Blue Nile (though he was in fact beaten there by Pedro Páez)
Burton, Sir Richard	19th-century explorer, first European to visit Harar
Cosmos Indicopleustes	Alexandrian merchant who visited Ethiopia in 6th century and wrote detailed account of trip
da Gama, Cristóvão	Leader of 16th-century Portuguese expedition to find Prester John, died in battle in Muslim war
de Covilhã, Pêro	Spanish Jesuit 'spy' sent by King John of Portugal to the Kingdom of Prester John during rule of Susenyos
Eleni	Influential wife of Zara Yaqob, whom she outlived by 50 years; regent during the early rule of Lebna Dengal
Ethiopic	Legendary great-grandson of Noah, said to have founded Ethiopia
Ezana	Pre-Christian name of Axumite emperor later known as Abraha, regarded to be greatest of Axumite rulers
Fasilidas	Emperor of Ethiopia 1632–67, son of Susenyos, restored Orthodox Church and civil order, founded Gondar
Frumentius	4th-century priest, converted Axumite rulers and became first Patriarch of Ethiopian Church
Ga'ewa	16th-century queen from Tigray who allied with Ahmed Gragn against the Christian empire and burned and destroyed many churches
Gadarat	2nd-century Axumite king credited with expanding the empire into modern Yemen
Galawdewos	Ethiopian emperor who defeated Ahmed Gragn in battle (with Portuguese assistance) in 1543
Garima, Abba	5th–6th century, one of the Nine Saints, founded eponymous monastery south of Adwa
Gebre Meskel	6th-century Axumite king, son of Kaleb, associated with foundation of several monasteries
Gebriel	Archangel Gabriel
Giyorgis	Ethiopian name for St George
Graziani, Rudolfo	Viceroy of Ethiopia during Italian occupation
Gudit	Legendarily militant 9th-century Beta Israeli queen, razed Axum and many churches in northern Ethiopia, also known as Yodit (Judith)
Habbuba, Emir	Legendary 10th-century founder of Harar
Haile Gebrselassie	Arguably Ethiopia's greatest track athlete, a two-times Olympic gold medallist and former world marathon record holder.

A2

Haile Selassie	Last Emperor of Ethiopia, murdered 1974
Hailemariam Desalegn	Prime Minister of Ethiopia 2012–18
Ilg, Alfred	Swiss adviser to Menelik II, played a major role in development of Ethiopia during Menelik's rule
Iskander	Emperor of Ethiopia 1478–94, ascended to throne aged eight, died in battle aged 24
Iyasu	Emperor of Ethiopia 1682–1706, strongest of Gonderine rulers
Iyasu V	Emperor of Ethiopia 1913–16, ousted in conspiracy led by Ras Tefari
Iyasus	Ethiopian name for Jesus, several variants of spelling in use
Iyasus Moa	Eminent monk trained at Debre Damo, founded Hayk Istafanos Monastery, helped 'restore' Solomonic rule
Jafar Taleb	6th–7th-century cousin and follower of Prophet Muhammad, founder of Islamic community in Ethiopia
Kaleb	6th-century Axumite king, successful military expansionist, built large palace outside modern Axum
Lalibela	12th-century emperor and saint, excavated the complex of churches in the town that is now named for him
Lebna Dengal	Emperor of Ethiopia 1508–40, name translates as 'Incense of the Virgin', died during war with Ahmed Gragn
Libanos, Abba	5th–6th century, one of the Nine Saints, eminent Monastery of Debre Libanos named for him
Lij Iyasu	see *Iyasu V*
Lucy	Name given to 3.5-million-year-old human skull found in Hadar in 1974
Makeda	Ethiopian name for Queen of Sheba
Maryam	Ethiopian name for Mary, mother of Jesus Christ
Meles Zenawi	Prime Minister of Ethiopia from 1991 until his death in 2012
Menelik I	Legendary Axumite king, credited by tradition with founding Axum in around 1000BC
Menelik II	Emperor of Ethiopia 1889–1913, defeated Italy at Battle of Adwa; co-founded Addis Ababa with wife Taitu
Mengistu Haile Maryam	Dictatorial leader of Ethiopia 1974–91
Mentewab	Queen Consort 1730–55 after death of husband Bakaffa, end of reign signalled end of Gonderine strength
Nakuta La'ab	Nephew and successor to Emperor Lalibela, founded eponymous monastery outside Lalibela town
Napier, Sir Robert	Led 1869 British military expedition that led to defeat and suicide of Tewodros II
Nur Ibn al-Wazir	Nephew and successor to Ahmed Gragn as leader of Harar, continued Gragn's jihad
Páez, Pedro	Spanish priest, first European to the Blue's Nile's source, converter of Susenyos to Catholicism, sparking a civil war and expulsion of Portuguese
Pantalewon, Abba	5th–6th century, one of the Nine Saints, founded eponymous monastery near modern Axum
Prester John	Legendary medieval figure, ruled rich Christian empire in Indies, possibly based on emperor of Ethiopia
Queen of Sheba	Legendary queen, claimed by Ethiopians as Axumite mother of Menelik I, more probably Yemeni
Remhai	3rd-century Axumite ruler associated with the largest stele (33m

	high) ever erected in ancient times
Ras Desta Damtew	Son-in-law of Haile Selassie, led unsuccessful military campaign against Italian invasion in 1936
Ras Makonnen	Nobleman appointed as governor of Harar by Menelik II, father of future Emperor Haile Selassie
Ras Mikael Ali	Powerful late-19th-century ruler of Wolo, ally of Menelik II, grandfather of Emperor Iyasu V
Ras Tefari	Pre-coronation name of Emperor Haile Selassie
Rimbaud, Arthur	Prodigal French poet who abandoned poetry aged 19 to end up dealing arms in Harar
Sahle Selassie	Expansionist ruler of Shewa 1813–47, paved way for grandson Menelik II's eventual rise to emperor
Salama, Abba	Pseudonymous with Frumentius
Solomon	King of Israel, legendarily said to have sired Menelik I
Susenyos	Early 17th-century emperor, converted by Portuguese Jesuits causing civil war, abdicated 1632
Taitu	Wife of Menelik II, co-founder of Addis Ababa
Tekle Haymanot	Priest who spread Christianity through Shewa in the 13th century, and founded Debre Libanos Monastery
Tekle Haymanot	10th-century emperor credited as founding Zagwe dynasty and effectively ending Axumite era
Tewodros II	Emperor of Ethiopia 1855–69, first emperor in a century to unify fiefdoms of various princes
Yakuno Amlak	13th-century emperor who founded (or restored) Solomonic dynasty
Yared	6th-century priest, patronised by King Gebre Meskel, credited with writing most Ethiopian church music
Yemrehanna Kristos	Medieval emperor, predecessor of Lalibela. Best known for the eponymous church he built near Bilbilla
Yodit	Synonymous with Gudit
Yohannes IV	Emperor of Ethiopia 1872–89, played a major role uniting Ethiopia
Zara Yaqob	15th-century emperor, founded several churches and monasteries, as well as the town of Debre Berhan
Zewditu	Empress of Ethiopia 1921–30, daughter of Menelik II

A2

Appendix 3

FURTHER INFORMATION

Books about Ethiopia aren't quite so thin on the ground as they were a few years back, though many interesting titles remain difficult to locate or are dauntingly expensive. Within Ethiopia, the best places to buy local-interest books are **BookWorld, Book Light** and the **Africans Bookshop** in Addis Ababa. The curio shop next to the ETC tourist office and shops in Bole Airport stock a good range too.

Few European or American bookshops stock much in the way of books about Ethiopia, but you can order most of the volumes listed below through online sellers such as amazon.com, amazon.co.uk or abebooks.co.uk (who are often also good sources of out-of-print books). The **Red Sea Press**, one of the most prolific publishers about Ethiopia and the Horn of Africa, has an online catalogue and ordering facilities at **w** africaworldpressbooks.com.

The definitive work on all things Ethiopian is the 6,000-page *Encyclopaedia Aethiopica*, compiled by the University of Hamburg's Hiob Ludolf Centre for Ethiopian Studies with the input of several hundred expert contributors, and published over five volumes between 2003 and 2014. Though the earlier volumes are starting to look a touch dated, and it employs a truly idiosyncratic transliteration system for Amharic names, this is the ultimate reference work for anybody with an enduring interest in Ethiopia, and can be ordered online at **w** www.harrassowitz-verlag.de.

BOOKS
General and coffee-table books

Batistoni, M and Chiari, P C *Old Tracks in the New Flower: A Historical Guide to Addis Ababa* Arada Books, 2004. This is a fascinating record of the early days of Ethiopia's capital, with illustrations and descriptions of about 100 of the most interesting old buildings scattered around the city.

Beckwith, C and Fisher, A *Africa Ark: People of the Horn* Harvill Press, 1990. Visually superlative and supplemented by informative text, this out-of-print book – ranging from South Omo to Tigray – remains one of the finest photographic documents about Africa ever produced.

Fitzgerald, Mary Anne and Marsden, Philip *Ethiopia: The Living Churches of an Ancient Kingdom* American University in Cairo Press, 2017. This beautifully photographed coffee-table book justifiably describes itself as 'the most comprehensive celebration yet published of the extraordinary Christian architectural and cultural heritage of Ethiopia'. Strong pictures are complemented by informative text.

Golzábez, J and Cebrián, D *Touching Ethiopia* Shama Books, 2004. This sumptuous 400-page tome can't quite decide whether it wants to be a coffee-table book or something more authoritative, but it succeeds remarkably well on both counts, and is particularly strong on the oft-neglected south, west and east.

Hancock, Graham *The Sign and the Seal* Heinemann, 1992. This lively account of the Ark of the Covenant's alleged arrival in Ethiopia is as popular with tourists as it is reviled by academics (the respected historical writer Paul Henze describes it as 'fiction masquerading as historical research'). It is, for all that, an entertaining work, one that captures the imagination and qualifies as almost essential reading.

Howard, Sarah *Culture Smart Ethiopia* Culture Smart, 2009. More useful to expatriates than casual visitors, this useful guide focuses on day-to-day customs and culture in modern Ethiopia.

Munro-Hay, Stuart *Ethiopia: The Unknown Land* I B Tauris, 2002. This authoritative site-by-site historical overview of Ethiopia's most popular antiquities is a superb companion to a more conventional travel guide for readers seeking more scholarly and detailed background information.

Munro-Hay, Stuart *The Quest for the Ark of the Covenant: The True Story of the Tablets of Moses* I B Tauris, 2005. A rebuff to the postulations in Hancock's *Sign and the Seal*, this provides a more scholarly assessment of the probable fate of the Ark – concluding, unsurprisingly, that it is almost certainly not (and never was) stashed away anywhere in Ethiopia.

Nomachi, Kazyoshi *Bless Ethiopia* Odyssey Publications, 1998. This photographically creative document of Ethiopia captures typical ecclesiastical scenes from unusual and striking angles. Highly recommended.

Pankhurst, Richard and Gerard, Denis *Ethiopia Photographed* Kegan Paul, 1997. This lovely and absorbing book is a must for old-photograph junkies, consisting of a wealth of photographs taken from 1867 to 1936, placed in context through accompanying text by Richard Pankhurst.

Pankhurst, Richard and Ingrams, Leila *Ethiopia Engraved* Kegan Paul, 1988. This book is a fascinating visual document of 17th- to 19th-century Ethiopia as seen through the engravings of contemporary European visitors.

Stranger, Yves *Ethiopia: Through Writers' Eyes* Eland Publishing, 2016. Excellent anthology of written descriptions of Ethiopia from ancient times to the 21st century.

van Dijk, Arjan and van Beurden, Jos *Ethiopia: Footsteps in Dust and Gold*, Stichting Kunstboak, 2014. Fabulous photo-oriented book dedicated to the various cultures of Ethiopia and placing them in both historical and contemporary context.

Williams, Frances M *Understanding Ethiopia* Springer Geoguides, 2016. Erudite and highly readable overview of the remarkable geological processes that shaped Ethiopia's diversity of modern landscapes, from the salt-crusted depths of the Danakil to the lofty peaks of the Simien.

Fiction

Gibb, Camilla *Sweetness in the Belly* Vintage, 2007. This provocative novel explores the issues of race and religion, looking beyond the Islamic stereotypes to follow the story of a young white British Muslim woman who struggles with cultural contradictions after moving to Harar in the 1970s and is then forced to flee back to the UK.

Mengiste, Maaza *Beneath the Lion's Gaze* Vintage, 2011. Set during the 1974 Ethiopian revolution, this beautifully written first novel by the American-based Ethiopian author is about drought, famine, civil war and one family's struggle to survive them all.

Verghese, Abraham *Cutting for Stone* Vintage, 2009. This fictional tale of medicine and miracles that moves from Addis Ababa to New York City and back again reads almost like a memoir – perhaps because its author is also a doctor.

Travel accounts

Álvares, Francisco *Prester John of the Indies: A True Relation of the Lands of Prester John* Cambridge: Published for the Hakluyt Society at the University Press, 1961. The oldest Ethiopian travelogue in existence, written by a Portuguese priest almost 500 years ago, remains a fascinating and often astonishingly insightful read, but it is out of print and very difficult to locate.

Buxton, David *Travels in Ethiopia* Praeger, 1967. Short but interesting document of Ethiopian travels in the immediate post-World War II era, has some interesting black-and-white photographs. Out of print but often available at a price at secondhand bookstalls in Addis Ababa.

Graham, John *Ethiopia off the Beaten Trail* Shama Books, 2001. John Graham was for several years the travel correspondent for the *Addis Tribune*, and this collection of informative and occasionally irreverent travel essays reflects his delight in exploring Ethiopia's less travelled corners, as well as capturing travel conditions there in the 1990s.

Henze, Paul *Ethiopian Journeys* Shama Books, 2001. Classic travel account of Ethiopia during the last years of the imperial era.

Kaplan, Robert *Surrender or Starve: Travels in Ethiopia, Sudan, Somalia and Eritrea* Vintage, 2003. This excellent and often rather chilling journalistic travelogue details the political factors that hugely exacerbated drought-related famines in the Horn of Africa during the 1980s.

Marsden, Philip *The Chains of Heaven: An Ethiopian Romance* HarperCollins, 2006. Marsden first visits a war-torn Ethiopia in 1982, then returns 12 years later to experience more of the country he fell in love with.

Murphy, Dervla *In Ethiopia with a Mule* John Murray, 1969. Recommended travelogue that describes an Ethiopia well away from any tourist trail.

Pakenham, Thomas *The Mountains of Rasselas* Seven Dials, 1999. This is a vivid and well-written account of the author's failed attempt to reach the remote Ethiopian mountain top where princes were imprisoned in the Gonderine period. Originally published in 1959, it was reissued in a glossy coffee-table format four decades later, complete with photographs taken in 1955 as well as more recent ones.

Rushby, Kevin *Eating the Flowers of Paradise* Flamingo, 1999. A fascinating book about the culture of *khat* consumption, half of which is set in Ethiopia, between Addis and Harar, before crossing the Red Sea from Djibouti to Yemen – as one reader notes, 'the book reads a lot better than *khat* tastes!'

Shah, Tahir *In Search of King Solomon's Mines* Arcade Publishing, 2003. Set mainly in Ethiopia, this compulsively readable and highly entertaining book follows the misadventures of a London based member of the Afghan aristocracy who is led on a wild goose chase by – of all things – a map, bought in a Jerusalem market, that purportedly shows the route to King Solomon's mines!

Thesiger, Wilfred *The Life of My Choice* HarperCollins, 1987. This includes childhood reminiscences of growing up in Abyssinia, Haile Selassie's coronation, the liberation campaign in 1941, treks in the south of the country, plus a vivid account of a six-month journey through the Danakil in 1933. Recommended, along with the same author's *Danakil Diaries*, particularly if you are heading into the eastern deserts.

Waugh, Evelyn *Remote People* Penguin, 1931. Witty travelogue detailing parts of Haile Selassie's coronation, plus travels in Djibouti and an account of the railway to Awash.

Waugh, Evelyn *When the Going Was Good* Penguin Modern Classics, 2012. One of several Waugh books that refer to his pre-occupation Abyssinian sojourn, this includes some interesting accounts of his travels there.

History and background

Bredin, Niles *The Pale Abyssinian* Flamingo, 2001. This highly readable biography of the explorer James Bruce is a good accompaniment to a trip in the north of the country.

Buxton, David *The Abyssinians* Thames & Hudson, 1970. This introduction to just about every aspect of Ethiopian history and culture is a bit dated, but well worth reading if you can locate a copy.

Getachew, Indrias *Beyond the Throne: The Enduring Legacy of Emperor Haile Selassie I* Shama Books, 2001. Edited by Richard Pankhurst, with a foreword by Harold Marcus, and endorsed by the royal family, this well-written and lavishly illustrated overview of Ethiopia's last emperor, with several never-seen-before photographs, is the first in a series of three related titles about Haile Selassie.

Gill, Peter *Famine and Foreigners: Ethiopia since Live Aid* Oxford University Press, 2010. The 1985 Ethiopian famine left an indelible imprint in the minds of people the world over. Gill, who wrote the definitive account of the disaster, *A Year in the Death of Africa*, returns to Ethiopia to investigate the real story of the last 25 years.

Henze, Paul *Layers of Time: A History of Ethiopia* Hurst, 2000. This approachable one-volume introductory history includes a useful overview of ancient and medieval Ethiopia, but is particularly good on modern history up to the fall of the Derg. Described by the noted Axumite historian Dr Stuart Munro-Hay as offering 'a well-balanced overview of Ethiopian history from the remotest past to modern times'.

Johanson, D and Wong, K *Lucy's Legacy: The Quest for Human Origins* Broadway Books, 2009. Coauthored by the palaeontologist who led the dig that unearthed the fossil 'Lucy', this is as up-to-date an overview as you'll find of that and subsequent hominid fossil discoveries in Ethiopia and nearby areas.

Kapuściński, Richard *The Emperor* Random House, 1983. This concise, impressionistic and strangely compelling account of the last days of Haile Selassie, transcribed from interviews with his servants and confidants, offers valuable insights into Ethiopia immediately before the 1974 revolution.

Lepage, Claude and Mercier, Jacques *Ethiopian Art: The Ancient Churches of Tigrai* Adpf, 2005. Boasting wonderful photographs, this book provides very detailed information about the key rock-hewn churches of Tigray.

Marcus, Harold *A History of Ethiopia* University of California Press, 2002. In this very readable general history, updated with new chapters in 2002, Marcus summarises all the initiate needs to know over a flowing and erudite 330 pages – a recommended starting point.

Marsden, Philip *The Barefoot Emperor: An Ethiopian Tragedy*, Harper Perennial 2008. This long-overdue biography of Tewodros II, the forward-looking emperor whose efforts to unify Ethiopia were halted by his suicide at Makdala in 1868, is written with a novelist's touch and is highly sympathetic to its tragic subject.

Mezlekia, Nega *Notes from the Hyena's Belly: An Ethiopian Boyhood* Picador, 2002. A fascinating account of a boy's life in Jijiga and the coming of the Derg, delving into local folklore, magic and customs.

Pakenham, Thomas *The Scramble for Africa* Jonathan Ball, 1991. One of the most crisp, unsentimental and informative books ever written about African history places Ethiopia's independence in a continental context. It was the winner of the W H Smith Literary Award, and is, in the words of Simon Roberts (*The Natal Witness*) 'Conrad's *Heart of Darkness* with the floodlights switched on'. Its Chapter 27 is as good an account as you'll find of the pivotal events in Ethiopia in around 1895–97.

Pankhurst, Richard *History of Ethiopian Towns from the Middle Ages to the Early 19th Century* Wiesbaden, 1982. The first in a two-volume series covering the origin and history of most large towns – and many small ones – in Ethiopia (the second deals with the mid 19th century onwards). An invaluable resource that deserves wider circulation.

Pankhurst, Richard *The Ethiopian Borderlands* Red Sea Press, 1997. This fascinating book provides a historical overview to those parts of Ethiopia that are generally ignored in mainstream texts.

Pankhurst, Richard *The Ethiopians (People of Africa)* Blackwell, 2001. This reissued title by the doyen of modern Ethiopian historical writing provides an excellent introduction to Ethiopia's varied cultures and social history.

Pearce, Jeff Prevail *The Inspiring Story of Ethiopia's Victory over Mussolini's Invasion, 1935–1941* Skyhorse, 2014. Lengthy but highly informative and readable history of the Italian invasion, the atrocities committed under it, and Ethiopia's eventual victory with the help of Allied troops.

Phillipson, David *The Monuments of Aksum* Addis Ababa University Press, 1997. Essentially an annotated translation of the original findings of the DAE Axum Expedition of 1906, this remains an excellent introduction to Axum's archaeological wealth, and also contains some great 20th-century photos.

Phillipson, David *Foundations of an African Civilisation: Aksum and the Northern Horn, 1000BC–AD1300* James Currey, 2014. Excellent, erudite and up-to-date overview of the rise of the pre-Axumite and Axumite civilisation and the eventual decline of the latter, with detailed chapters covering everything from its political and social structure to the emergence of the medieval Zagwe dynasty.

Plant, Ruth *Architecture of the Tigre* Ravens Education & Development Services, 1985. Out of print for several years, this remains the most detailed work on the remote rock-hewn churches of Tigray, and can be bought online through secondhand sellers.

Prunier, Gerard *Understanding Contemporary Ethiopia: Monarchy, Revolution and the Legacy of Meles Zenawi* Hurst & Co, 2015. The most up-to-date historical account of Ethiopia focuses on the post-Derg era, but places the recent political events it covers in a broader historical and cultural context.

Reader, John *Africa: A Biography of the Continent* Hamish Hamilton, 1997. This award-winning book, available as a Penguin paperback, provides a compulsively readable introduction to Africa's past, from the formation of the continent to post-independence politics – the ideal starting point for anybody seeking to place their Ethiopian experience in a broader African context.

Schofield, Louise *Eyesus Hintsa: An Ethiopian Journey through Landscape and Time* Scanplus, London, 2007. A small book that provides information about the Eyesus Hintsa rock-hewn church and conservation project.

Tibebu, Teshale *The Making of Modern Ethiopia 1896–1974* Red Sea Press, 1995. This book provides an excellent and original overview of modern Ethiopia and its ancient cultural roots, though coverage stops with the toppling of Haile Selassie in 1974. In a sense, it possibly provides a more meaningful and comprehensible introduction to Ethiopia than the straight general histories. Recommended.

Zewde, Bahru *A History of Modern Ethiopia 1855–1974* James Currey, 2001. Pitched at the general reader as much as the historian, this book is accurate, plainly written, affordable and generously illustrated, though a post-millennial update would be welcome. It is available in most bookshops in Addis Ababa for around US$5.

Health
Wilson-Howarth, Dr Jane and Ellis, Dr Matthew *Your Child Abroad: A Travel Health Guide (3rd Edition)* Bradt Travel Guides, 2014.

Art and music
Falceto, Francis *Abyssinie Swing: A Pictorial History of Modern Ethiopian Music* Shama Books, 2001. This monochrome document of the emergence of the (now almost forgotten) jazz-tinged music scene that blossomed in the dying years of the imperial era is utterly irresistible. The photographs, which span the years 1868 to 1973, are consistently evocative, while the text, though more concise than might be hoped for, is as authoritative as one would expect of a book compiled by the editor of the acclaimed *Ethiopiques* CD compilation series. All in all, it's an essential purchase for anybody with more than a passing interest in Ethiopia's rich musical heritage.

Gerster, Georg *Churches in Rock* Phaidon Press, 1970. Superb but long-out-of-print visual document of the Tigrayan rock churches, as well as lesser-known architectural gems such as Gayint Bethlehem, south of Lalibela.

Heldman, Marilyn *et al. African Zion: The Sacred Art of Ethiopia* Yale University Press, 1994. Expensive (£40) but beautiful, and written by leading scholars of Ethiopian and Byzantine art, this lavishly illustrated book covers the art of highland Ethiopia from the 4th to the 18th century.

Natural history For an excellent overview of Ethiopia's national parks and important natural entities, the 96-page *Glimpse at the Biodiversity Hotspots of Ethiopia* (Ethiopian Wildlife and Natural History Society, 2010) can be downloaded for free at **w** www.ewnhs. org.et/index.php/publications-downloads.

Mammals

Estes, Richard *The Safari Companion* Green Books (UK), Russell Friedman Books (SA), Chelsea Green (USA), 1999. This unconventional book might succinctly be described as a field guide to mammal behaviour. It's probably a bit esoteric for most one-off visitors to Africa, but a must for anybody with a serious interest in wildlife.

Kingdon, Jonathan *The Kingdon Field Guide to African Mammals* Bloomsbury, 2015. Now in its second edition, this is the most detailed, thorough and up to date of several titles covering the mammals of the region, transcending all expectations of a standard field guide, though at 600-plus pages, recommended only to those with a serious interest in mammal identification or natural history.

Last, Jill *Endemic Mammals of Ethiopia* Ethiopian Tourist Commission, 1982. This lightweight, slightly dated and very inexpensive booklet includes detailed descriptions of appearance and behaviour for Ethiopia's seven endemic mammal species and races. A worthwhile purchase!

Stuart, Chris *Photographic Guide to Mammals of Southern, Central and East Africa* Struik, 2014. This excellent mini-guide, compact enough to slip into a pocket, and also available for Kindle, is remarkably thorough within its inherent space restrictions, though Ethiopia's wildlife is less well covered than that of other, more popular, safari destinations.

Birds

Ash, J and Atkins, J *Birds of Ethiopia and Eritrea* Christopher Helm, 2009. Not a field guide but a more specialised hardcover bird atlas that maps the known distribution of a full 872 Ethiopian and Eritrean species across 132 grids, and provides more detailed background information than the field guide when it comes to individual species and to Ethiopian ornithology. Though not aimed at casual birders, it's an invaluable tool and source of data for regular visitors and residents. In addition, the highly detailed maps and text will be an invaluable research resource to anybody trying to maximise a birding itinerary in terms of ticking endemics and other localised species, as well as in assisting with the identification of tricky species.

Behrens, K, Barnes, K and Boix, C *Birding Ethiopia* Lynx, 2010. Another very useful addition to Ethiopian birding literature, this is an ideal complement to a field guide or bird atlas, coming across like a vastly extended and illustrated trip report – the perfect hands-on starting point for anybody planning a birding trip to Ethiopia.

Head, Vernon *The Search for the Rarest Bird in the World* Signal Books, 2015. An entertaining first-hand account of the 2012 expedition, led by Ian Sinclair, to see the first known living specimen of the Nechisar nightjar – until then, known only from a single wing collected 22 years earlier in Nech Sar National Park.

Redman, N, Stevenson, T and Fanshawe, J *Helm Field Guide to the Birds of the Horn of Africa* Christopher Helm, revised and expanded edition, 2016. As the only dedicated field guide to a vast region dominated by Ethiopia, but also including Eritrea, Djibouti, Somalia and Socotra, this is the one book that all birders to Ethiopia absolutely need. Every species recorded in the region is illustrated across 213 colour plates accompanied by detailed descriptions and distribution maps, and the overall standard is in line with the same publisher's superb *Birds of East Africa*.

Sinclair, I and Ryan, P *Birds of Africa South of the Sahara* Struik Publishers, 2003. The first and only field guide to this vast region covers all 2,100-plus species recorded there in 700-odd pages. The accurate illustrations are supported by reliable text and good distribution maps. Not as detailed as the field guide specific to the Horn of Africa, but it remains the second-choice field guide for Ethiopia.

Spottiswoode, C, Gabremichael, M and Francis, J *Where to Watch Birds in Ethiopia* Christopher Helm, 2010. An excellent complement to the same publisher's field guide and bird atlas, as listed above, this provides detailed coverage and GPS readings for 50 key birding sites, mostly in southern Ethiopia, along with photographs and descriptions of the country's 'top 50 species'. At 180-odd pages it is very portable, and it will be especially useful to birders travelling without a specialist local guide.

Tilahun, S, Edwards, S and Egziabher, T *Important Bird Areas of Ethiopia* Ethiopian Wildlife & Natural History Society, 1996. This detailed booklet provides a very detailed overview of Ethiopia's most important birding locales, and is of interest to ecologists and birders alike.

Vivero, Jose *The Endemic Birds of Ethiopia and Eritrea* Shama Books, 2001. This pocketbook provides the most detailed and up-to-date coverage yet of the 30-plus bird species endemic to Ethiopia and Eritrea, making it an excellent supplement to a standard field guide – though note that several recently recognised species, such as the Ethiopian cisticola, are excluded.

Literature

Jackman, Brian *Savannah Diaries* Bradt, 2014. A celebration of Africa's wild places and creatures, seen through the eyes of one of Africa's most distinguished observers.

Jackman, Brian, Scott, Jonathan and Scott, Angela *The Marsh Lions: The Story of an African Pride* Bradt, 2012. A wildlife classic, this is a compelling and fascinating account of the daily drama of life and death in Kenya's finest big-game country.

Kent, Princess Michael of *A Cheetah's Tale* Bradt, 2017. A wonderful story of a vanished Africa, of a girl growing up and of the incredible bond that can exist between humans and animals.

Scott, Jonathan and Scott, Angela *The Leopard's Tale* Bradt, 2013. A unique and moving portrait of Africa, and the most intimate record ever written about the secretive lives of leopards.

Other Africa guides For a full list of Bradt's Africa guides, see W bradtguides.com/shop.

Briggs, Philip *Northern Tanzania Safari Guide* (4th edition) Bradt Travel Guides, 2017

Briggs, Philip *Rwanda: with Virunga National Park and eastern Democratic Republic of Congo* (7th edition) Bradt Travel Guides, 2018

Briggs, Philip *Somaliland: with the overland route from Addis Ababa via Eastern Ethiopia* (2nd edition) Bradt Travel Guides, 2018

Briggs, Philip *Tanzania Safari Guide: with Kilimanjaro, Zanzibar and the coast* (8th edition) Bradt Travel Guides, 2017

Briggs, Philip *Uganda* (8th edition) Bradt Travel Guides, 2016

Ibbotson, Sophie and Max *Sudan* (3rd edition) Bradt Travel Guides, 2012

Lovell-Hoare, Sophie and Lovell-Hoare, Max *South Sudan* (1st edition) Bradt Travel Guides, 2013
McIntyre, Chris and McIntyre, Susie *Zanzibar* (9th edition) Bradt Travel Guides, 2017

Maps Most maps of Ethiopia are quite unreliable and out of date. The one genuine exception is listed below, but even this cannot be expected to reflect the rapid construction of new roads and upgrading of older ones. The best place to buy maps in the UK is Stanford's (**w** *stanfords. co.uk*). Maps can be ordered from amazon or **w** omnimap.com/catalog/int/ethiop.htm.

Äthiopien, Somalia, Eritrea & Dschibuti Reise Know-How Verlag (8th revised edition) 2015.
    Solid and regularly updated 1:1,800,000 road map printed on waterproof and tear-resistant paper.

WEBSITES
w **addisallaround.com** Up-to-date information about activities and events in Addis Ababa.
w **addismap.com** Useful online map of Addis Ababa, with some details of other parts of the country.
w **bestethiopia.com** Information about Ethiopian tourism.
w **bradtupdates.com/ethiopia** Reader-driven update site for this Bradt guide.
w **cyberethiopia.com** News, chat lines and useful links.
w **dancalia.it** Though mostly in Italian, this website is a superb source of information about the Danakil region.
w **ethioembassy.org.uk** Informative not only regarding pre-visit paperwork, but also current affairs. Online articles by the likes of Paul Henze.
w **ethiopia.travel** Website of the Ethiopian Tourist Organisation.
w **www.ethiopianairlines.com** Booking site for Ethiopian Airlines.
w **ethiopianhotelsguide.com** Ethiopian online hotel search and booking portal.
w **ethiopianrun.org** Details of the Great Ethiopian Run and Dasani Run.
w **ethiopians.com/Books_On_Ethiopia.htm** An excellent list of children's books about Ethiopia.
w **www.ewnhs.org.et** Ethiopian Wildlife and Natural History Society website.
w **goaddistours.com/food-tour** Food tours of Addis Ababa but also good recommendations of eateries, cafés and other such facilities.
w **www.mfa.gov.et** Ministry of Foreign Affairs website includes a full list of Ethiopian missions abroad and foreign missions in Ethiopia.
w **rootsofethiopia.com** A remarkable site with plenty of information on grass-roots tourism in Ethiopia.
w **safarilink.com** An impartial information resource that can be useful when planning African holidays.

Index

Page numbers in *italics* indicate maps.

INDEX OF ADVERTISERS